THE
ALL ENGLAND
LAW REPORTS
2002

Volume 3

Editor
CRAIG ROSE   Barrister

Butterworths
LexisNexis™

Members of the LexisNexis Group worldwide

United Kingdom	Butterworths Tolley, a Division of Reed Elsevier (UK) Ltd, Halsbury House, 35 Chancery Lane, LONDON, WC2A 1EL, and 4 Hill Street, EDINBURGH EH2 3JZ
Argentina	Abeledo Perrot, Jurisprudencia Argentina and Depalma, BUENOS AIRES
Australia	Butterworths, a Division of Reed International Books Australia Pty Ltd, CHATSWOOD, New South Wales
Austria	ARD Betriebsdienst and Verlag Orac, VIENNA
Canada	Butterworths Canada Ltd, MARKHAM, Ontario
Chile	Publitecsa and Conosur Ltda, SANTIAGO DE CHILE
Czech Republic	Orac sro, PRAGUE
France	Editions du Juris-Classeur SA, PARIS
Hong Kong	Butterworths Asia (Hong Kong), HONG KONG
Hungary	Hvg Orac, BUDAPEST
India	Butterworths India, NEW DELHI
Ireland	Butterworths (Ireland) Ltd, DUBLIN
Italy	Giuffré, MILAN
Malaysia	Malayan Law Journal Sdn Bhd, KUALA LUMPUR
New Zealand	LexisNexis Butterworths, WELLINGTON
Poland	Wydawnictwa Prawnicze PWN, WARSAW
Singapore	Butterworths Asia, SINGAPORE
South Africa	Butterworths Publishers (Pty) Ltd, DURBAN
Switzerland	Stämpfli Verlag AG, BERNE
USA	LexisNexis, DAYTON, Ohio

A CIP Catalogue record for this book is available from the British Library.

Printed and bound in Great Britain by William Clowes Ltd, Beccles and London

ISBN for the complete set of volumes: 0 406 85159 X
for this volume:

ISBN 0-406-95249-3

9 780406 952493

Visit Butterworths LexisNexis *direct* at www.butterworths.com

House of Lords

Court of Appeal

High Court of Justice

The Lord High Chancellor of Great Britain
The Lord Chief Justice of England
The President of the Family Division
The Vice-Chancellor
The Senior Presiding Judge for England and Wales
The puisne judges of the High Court

Chancery Division

The Lord High Chancellor of Great Britain
The Vice-Chancellor

Sir Francis Mursell Ferris
Sir John Edmund Frederic Lindsay
Sir Edward Christopher Evans-Lombe
Sir Robin Raphael Hayim Jacob
Sir William Anthony Blackburne
Sir Gavin Anthony Lightman
Sir Colin Percy Farquharson Rimer
Sir Hugh Ian Lang Laddie
Sir Timothy Andrew Wigram Lloyd

Sir David Edmund Neuberger
Sir Andrew Edward Wilson Park
Sir Nicholas Richard Pumfrey
Sir Michael Christopher Campbell Hart
Sir Lawrence Anthony Collins
Sir Nicholas John Patten
Sir Terrence Michael Elkan Barnet Etherton
Sir Peter Winston Smith

Queen's Bench Division

The Lord Chief Justice of England

Sir Patrick Neville Garland
Sir Michael John Turner
Sir Richard George Rougier
Sir Stuart Neil McKinnon
Sir Thomas Scott Gillespie Baker
Sir Douglas Dunlop Brown
Sir Michael Morland
Sir Roger John Buckley
Sir Anthony Brian Hidden
Sir John Michael Wright
Sir Peter John Cresswell
Sir Christopher John Holland
Sir Richard Herbert Curtis
Dame Janet Hilary Smith
Sir Anthony David Colman
Sir John Thayne Forbes
Sir Michael Alexander Geddes Sachs
Sir Stephen George Mitchell
Sir Rodger Bell
Sir Michael Guy Vicat Harrison

Sir William Marcus Gage
Sir Thomas Richard Atkin Morison
Sir Andrew David Collins
Sir Maurice Ralph Kay
Sir Anthony Hooper
Sir Alexander Neil Logie Butterfield
Sir George Michael Newman
Sir David Anthony Poole
Sir Martin James Moore-Bick
Sir Gordon Julian Hugh Langley
Sir Roger John Laugharne Thomas
Sir Robert Franklyn Nelson
Sir Roger Grenfell Toulson
Sir Michael John Astill
Sir Alan George Moses
Sir Timothy Edward Walker
Sir David Eady
Sir Jeremy Mirth Sullivan
Sir David Herbert Penry-Davey
Sir Stephen Price Richards

[continued on next page]

Queen's Bench Division *(continued)*

Sir David William Steel
Sir Charles Antony St John Gray
Sir Nicolas Dusan Bratza
Sir Michael John Burton
Sir Rupert Matthew Jackson
Dame Heather Carol Hallett
Sir Patrick Elias
Sir Richard John Pearson Aikens
Sir Stephen Robert Silber
Sir John Bernard Goldring
Sir Peter Francis Crane
Dame Anne Judith Rafferty
Sir Geoffery Douglas Grigson
Sir Richard John Hedley Gibbs
Sir Richard Henry Quixano Henriques
Sir Stephen Miles Tomlinson
Sir Andrew Charles Smith

Sir Stanley Jeffrey Burnton
Sir Patrick James Hunt
Sir Christopher John Pitchford
Sir Brian Henry Leveson
Sir Duncan Brian Walter Ouseley
Sir Richard George Bramwell McCombe
Sir Raymond Evan Jack
Sir Robert Michael Owen
Sir Colin Crichton Mackay
Sir John Edward Mitting
Sir David Roderick Evans
Sir Nigel Anthony Lamert Davis
Sir Peter Henry Gross
Sir Brian Richard Keith
Sir Jeremy Lionel Cooke
Sir Richard Alan Field
Sir Christopher John Pitchers

Family Division

The President of the Family Division

Sir Robert Lionel Johnson
Dame Joyanne Winifred Bracewell
Sir Jan Peter Singer
Sir Nicholas Allan Roy Wilson
Sir Nicholas Peter Rathbone Wall
Sir Andrew Tristram Hammett Kirkwood
Sir Hugh Peter Derwyn Bennett
Sir Edward James Holman
Dame Mary Claire Hogg

Sir Christopher John Sumner
Sir Anthony Philip Gilson Hughes
Sir Arthur William Hessin Charles
Sir David Roderick Lessiter Bodey
Dame Jill Margaret Black
Sir James Lawrence Munby
Sir Paul James Duke Coleridge
Sir Mark Hedley

Official Judgment Numbers
and
Paragraph References

Since 11 January 2001, official judgment numbers have been given to all judgments delivered in the House of Lords, Privy Council, both divisions of the Court of Appeal and the Administrative Court. All such judgments have fixed paragraph numbering, as do judgments delivered on or after 11 January 2001 in those parts of the High Court which did not then adopt the system of official judgment numbers (see Practice Note (judgments: neutral citation) [2001] 1 All ER 193 for the Court of Appeal and the High Court). On 14 January 2002 the system of judgment numbers was extended to all parts of the High Court (see Practice Direction (High Court judgments: neutral citation) [2002] 1 All ER 351). We have adopted the following practice in respect of judgments with official judgment numbers and official paragraph numbering:

- The official judgment number is inserted immediately beneath the case name;
- Official paragraph numbers are in bold in square brackets;
- Holding references in the headnotes, and any other cross-references, are to an official paragraph number, not to a page of the report;
- When such a judgment is subsequently cited in another report,

    (i) the official judgment number is inserted before the usual report citations in the case lists and on the first occasion when the case is cited in the text. Thereafter, only the report citations are given;

    (ii) All 'at' references are to the official paragraph number rather than to a page of a report, with the paragraph number in square brackets but not in bold;

    (iii) The 'at' reference is only given in conjunction with the first report cited; eg [2001] 4 All ER 159 at [16], [2001] AC 61. If an 'at' reference is included on the first occasion when the case is cited, it also appears alongside the official judgment number.

For the avoidance of doubt, these changes do not apply to reports of judgments delivered before 11 January 2001 or to the citation of such cases in other reports.

CITATION

These reports are cited thus:

[2002] 3 All ER

REFERENCES

These reports contain references to the following major works of legal reference described in the manner indicated below.

Halsbury's Laws of England

The reference 14 *Halsbury's Laws* (4th edn) para 185 refers to paragraph 185 on page 90 of volume 14 of the fourth edition of *Halsbury's Laws of England*.

The reference 15 *Halsbury's Laws* (4th edn reissue) para 355 refers to paragraph 355 on page 283 of reissue volume 15 of the fourth edition of *Halsbury's Laws of England*.

The reference 7(1) *Halsbury's Laws* (4th edn) (1996 reissue) para 9 refers to paragraph 9 on page 24 of the 1996 reissue of volume 7(1) of the fourth edition of *Halsbury's Laws of England*.

Halsbury's Statutes of England and Wales

The reference 26 *Halsbury's Statutes* (4th edn) 734 refers to page 734 of volume 26 of the fourth edition of *Halsbury's Statutes of England and Wales*.

The reference 40 *Halsbury's Statutes* (4th edn) (2001 reissue) 269 refers to page 269 of the 2001 reissue of volume 40 of the fourth edition of *Halsbury's Statutes of England and Wales*.

Halsbury's Statutory Instruments

The reference 14 *Halsbury's Statutory Instruments* (2001 issue) 201 refers to page 201 of the 2001 issue of volume 14 of the grey volumes series of *Halsbury's Statutory Instruments*.

Cases reported in volume 3

Digest of cases reported in volume 3

House of Lords petitions

This list, which covers the period 31 May 2002 to 4 September 2002, sets out all cases which have formed the subject of a report in the All England Law Reports in which an Appeal Committee of the House of Lords has, subsequent to the publication of that report, refused leave to appeal. Where the result of a petition for leave to appeal was known prior to the publication of the relevant report a note of that result appears at the end of the report.

Paragon Finance plc v Staunton [2002] 2 All ER 248. Leave to appeal refused 17 July 2002 (Lord Bingham of Cornhill, Lord Hope of Craighead and Lord Millett).

Lowe v Guise [2002] 3 All ER 454. Leave to appeal refused 18 July 2002 (Lord Nicholls of Birkenhead, Lord Hoffman and Lord Rodger of Earlsferry).

Rowe v Sanders (note) [2002] 2 All ER 800. Leave to appeal refused 23 July 2002 (Lord Slynn of Hadley, Lord Hoffman and Lord Millett).

R (on the application of Morgan Grenfell & Co Ltd) v Special Commissioner of Income Tax

c
[2002] UKHL 21

HOUSE OF LORDS

LORD NICHOLLS OF BIRKENHEAD, LORD HOFFMANN, LORD HOPE OF CRAIGHEAD, LORD
HOBHOUSE OF WOODBOROUGH AND LORD SCOTT OF FOSCOTE

10, 11, 15 APRIL, 16 MAY 2002

*Privilege – Legal professional privilege – Solicitor and client – Communications between
legal advisor and client – Inspector of taxes exercising statutory investigatory power to
investigate tax-related scheme – Whether provision entitling inspector to require
disclosure of material subject to legal professional privilege – Taxes Management Act
1970, s 20(1).*

The appellant taxpayer marketed a simple tax avoidance scheme to create chargeable
gains for clients who had available capital losses. Although the taxpayer had been
completely open about the way in which the scheme operated, an inspector of
taxes asked to see documents relating to the advice that the taxpayer had
obtained from leading counsel and solicitors about whether the scheme would
work. The taxpayer objected on the ground, inter alia, that the documents were
protected by legal professional privilege. A Special Commissioner gave his consent
to the issue by the inspector of a notice under s 20(1)[a] of the Taxes Management
Act 1970, which empowered the inspector to require a person, by such a notice,
to deliver to him such documents as were in that person's possession or power
and, in the inspector's opinion, contained or might contain information relevant
to any tax liability to which the person might be subject, or the amount of such
liability. The taxpayer applied for judicial review to quash the notice, contending,
inter alia, that the inspector was not entitled to require delivery of documents
subject to legal professional privilege. That contention was rejected by the
Divisional Court which dismissed the application. The Court of Appeal affirmed
that decision, and the taxpayer appealed to the House of Lords. In seeking to
uphold the decisions below, the Revenue contended that Parliament had
provided, in other provisions of the 1970 Act, a number of specific safeguards and
restrictions for the protection of the taxpayer, including an express preservation
of legal professional privilege for documents in the possession of a barrister,
advocate or legal advisor, and that accordingly no wider qualification of the
general words of s 20(1) had been intended.

---

a Section 20, so far as material, is set out at [3], below

Held – On its true construction, s 20(1) of the 1970 Act did not entitle an inspector
of taxes to require a taxpayer to deliver to him material that was subject to legal *a*
professional privilege. That privilege was a fundamental human right long
established in the common law. Although general words in a statute might
literally be capable of having some startling or unreasonable consequence, such
as overriding fundamental human rights, the courts would ordinarily construe
them as not having been intended to have that effect. An intention to override *b*
such rights had to be expressly stated or appear by necessary implication.
Section 20(1) contained no express reference to legal professional privilege, and
the provisions upon which the Revenue relied were not sufficient to create a
necessary implication that legal professional privilege was intended to be
excluded. It would have been irrational for Parliament to have preserved legal
professional privilege for documents in the hands of the lawyer but not for *c*
documents (which might well be copies or originals of the same documents) in
the hands of the taxpayer. Legal professional privilege was a single privilege for
the benefit of the client, whether the documents were in his hands or those of his
lawyer. Accordingly, the appeal would be allowed (see [1], [7]–[9], [22], [36],
[40]–[42], [46], [49], below). *d*

Price Waterhouse (a firm) v BCCI Holdings (Luxembourg) SA [1992] BCLC 583
overruled.

Dicta of Lord Denning MR and Diplock LJ in *Parry-Jones v Law Society*
[1968] 1 All ER 177 at 178, 180 and of Bingham LJ in *R v IRC, ex p Taylor (No 2)*
[1990] 2 All ER 409 at 413–414 disapproved.

Decision of the Court of Appeal [2002] 1 All ER 776 reversed. *e*

Notes

For communications subject to legal professional privilege, see 3(1) *Halsbury's
Laws* (4th edn reissue) para 526 and 44(1) *Halsbury's Laws* (4th edn reissue)
para 90, and for an inspector's power to require a taxpayer to produce documents *f*
in respect of his own tax liability, see 23 *Halsbury's Laws* (4th edn reissue)
para 1626.

For the Taxes Management Act 1970, s 20, see 42 *Halsbury's Statutes* (4th edn)
(1996 reissue) 178.

g

Cases referred to in opinions

AM & S Europe Ltd v EC Commission Case 155/79 [1983] 1 All ER 705, [1983] QB
878, [1983] 3 WLR 17, [1982] ECR 1575, ECJ.

B (a minor) v DPP [2000] 1 All ER 833, [2000] 2 AC 428, [2000] 2 WLR 452, HL.

Buttes Gas and Oil Co v Hammer (No 3), Occidental Petroleum Corp v Buttes Gas and *h*
Oil Co (No 2) [1980] 3 All ER 475, [1981] QB 223, [1980] 3 WLR 668, CA; *rvsd*
[1981] 3 All ER 616, [1982] AC 888, [1981] 3 WLR 787, HL.

Campbell v UK (1992) 15 EHRR 137, [1992] ECHR 13590/88, ECt HR.

Chantrey Martin & Co v Martin [1953] 2 All ER 691, [1953] 2 QB 286, [1953] 3 WLR
459, CA.

Foxley v UK (2000) 8 BHRC 571, [2000] ECHR 33274/96, ECt HR. *j*

Gomba Holdings UK Ltd v Minories Finance Ltd [1989] 1 All ER 261, [1988] 1 WLR
1231, CA.

IRC v West-Walker [1954] NZLR 191, NZ CA.

Parry-Jones v Law Society [1968] 1 All ER 177, [1969] 1 Ch 1, [1968] 2 WLR 397, CA;
affg [1967] 3 All ER 248, [1968] Ch 195, [1967] 3 WLR 1305.

a *Pepper (Inspector of Taxes) v Hart* [1993] 1 All ER 42, [1993] AC 593, [1992] 3 WLR 1032, HL.
Price Waterhouse (a firm) v BCCI Holdings (Luxembourg) SA [1992] BCLC 583.
R v Cox (1884) 14 QBD 153, [1881–5] All ER Rep 68, CCR.
R v Derby Magistrates' Court, ex p B [1995] 4 All ER 526, [1996] AC 487, [1995] 3 WLR 681, HL.
b *R v IRC, ex p Taylor (No 2)* [1990] 2 All ER 409, CA; *affg* [1989] 3 All ER 353, DC.
TC Coombs & Co (a firm) v IRC [1991] 3 All ER 623, [1991] 2 AC 283, [1991] 2 WLR 682, HL.
R v Secretary of State for the Home Dept, ex p Simms [1999] 3 All ER 400, [2000] 2 AC 115, [1999] 3 WLR 328, HL.
Rhondda's (Viscountess) Claim [1922] 2 AC 339, HL.
c *Stradling v Morgan* (1560) 1 Plowd 199, 75 ER 305.

Appeal

Morgan Grenfell & Co Ltd (MG) appealed with permission of the Appeal Committee of the House of Lords given on 25 July 2001 from the decision of the *d* Court of Appeal (Schiemann, Sedley LJJ and Blackburne J) on 2 March 2001 ([2001] EWCA Civ 329, [2002] 1 All ER 776, [2002] 2 WLR 255) dismissing an appeal from the decision of the Divisional Court (Buxton LJ and Penry-Davey J) on 8 November 2000 ([2001] 1 All ER 535, [2002] 2 WLR 255) dismissing its application for judicial review of (i) the issue of a written notice on 28 September 1999 by the second respondent, an inspector of taxes, in purported exercise of his *e* powers under s 20(1) of the Taxes Management Act 1970 requiring MG to disclose certain categories of documents which were covered by legal professional privilege; (ii) the decision of the first respondent Special Commissioner (Stephen Oliver QC) on 28 September 1999 giving consent under s 20(7) of the 1970 Act to the issue of the notice; and (iii) a written decision of the Special Commissioner *f* dated 16 April 1999 determining two preliminary issues in relation to the proposed issue of the notice. The facts are set out in the opinion of Lord Hoffmann.

David Pannick QC, Giles Goodfellow and *Javan Herberg* (instructed by *Slaughter and May*) for MG.
g *Timothy Brennan QC, Ingrid Simler* and *Diya Sen Gupta* (instructed by the *Solicitor of Inland Revenue*) for the Crown.

Their Lordships took time for consideration.

h 16 May 2002. The following opinions were delivered.

LORD NICHOLLS OF BIRKENHEAD.

[1] My Lords, I have had the advantage of reading in draft the speech of my noble and learned friend Lord Hoffmann. For the reasons he gives, with *j* which I agree, I would allow this appeal.

LORD HOFFMANN.

[2] My Lords, in the 1990s Morgan Grenfell (MG) marketed a simple tax-avoidance scheme to create chargeable gains for clients who had available capital losses. The gain arose out of a premium paid by MG for a long lease of property held by the client, which then took an underlease at a rack rent. The efficacy of

the scheme depended upon the client being able to deduct the rent and MG being able to deduct the premium as trading expenses. The client's position was uncontroversial but MG's was more problematic. MG contended that the long lease was a trading asset and that the premium was a payment on revenue account. The Inland Revenue disagreed. It said that the purchase of the lease fell outside the scope of MG's trading activities and that it was a capital asset. The premium was therefore a capital payment.

[3] The issue was debated between MG's tax advisors and the Revenue in the case of a scheme which had been sold to Tesco. There is no dispute that MG were completely open about the way the scheme operated. They did not conceal any relevant transactions. But the inspector asked to see documents relating to the advice which MG had obtained from leading counsel and solicitors about whether the scheme would work. MG objected on two grounds. First, that the documents were irrelevant. They would show no more than the opinions of the lawyers about the legal effect of transactions which had been fully disclosed. The second was that they were protected by legal professional privilege (LPP). The inspector invoked his power under s 20(1) of the Taxes Management Act 1970 (as substituted by s 57(1) of and Sch 6 to the Finance Act 1976 and amended by s 142 of the Finance Act 1989):

'Subject to this section, an inspector may by notice in writing require a person—(a) to deliver to him such documents as are in the person's possession or power and as (in the inspector's reasonable opinion) contain, or may contain, information relevant to—(i) any tax liability to which the person is or may be subject, or (ii) the amount of any such liability ...'

[4] On 28 September 1999 the inspector issued a notice under the section, demanding a wide range of documents relating to the advice MG had sought and received in connection with the Tesco transaction. MG issued judicial review proceedings to quash the notice on the grounds of ultra vires, contending, first, that the documents could not reasonably be thought to contain relevant information and secondly, that the 1970 Act upon its true construction did not entitle the inspector to require delivery of documents subject to LPP.

[5] The Divisional Court (Buxton LJ and Penry-Davey J) rejected both arguments and dismissed the application (see [2001] 1 All ER 535, [2002] 2 WLR 255). On the first point, the court accepted that the inspector could reasonably consider that the 'perception' of the transactions by MG and its advisors revealed by the documents might throw light on whether they formed part of MG's ordinary trading activities. On the second, they held that the general terms of s 20(1) ('such documents as are in the person's possession or power') could not be qualified to exclude documents subject to LPP.

[6] In the Court of Appeal (Schiemann, Sedley LJJ and Blackburne J ([2001] EWCA Civ 329, [2002] 1 All ER 776, [2002] 2 WLR 255)) MG did not pursue the first point and the Court of Appeal agreed with the Divisional Court on the second. It is solely on the construction of the 1970 Act that MG appeal to your Lordships' House.

[7] Two of the principles relevant to construction are not in dispute. First, LPP is a fundamental human right long established in the common law. It is a necessary corollary of the right of any person to obtain skilled advice about the law. Such advice cannot be effectively obtained unless the client is able to put all the facts before the advisor without fear that they may afterwards be disclosed and used to his prejudice. The cases establishing this principle are collected in

a the speech of Lord Taylor of Gosforth CJ in *R v Derby Magistrates' Court, ex p B* [1995] 4 All ER 526, [1996] AC 487. It has been held by the European Court of Human Rights to be part of the right of privacy guaranteed by art 8 of the European Convention for the Protection of Human Rights and Fundamental Freedoms (Rome, 4 November 1950, TS 71 (1953) Cmd 8969) (see *Campbell v UK* (1992) 15 EHRR 137; *Foxley v UK* (2000) 8 BHRC 571) and held by the Court of

b Justice of the European Communities to be a part of Community law (see *AM & S Europe Ltd v EC Commission* Case 155/79 [1983] 1 All ER 705, [1982] ECR 1575).

[8] Secondly, the courts will ordinarily construe general words in a statute, although literally capable of having some startling or unreasonable consequence, such as overriding fundamental human rights, as not having been intended to do so. An intention to override such rights must be expressly stated or appear by

c necessary implication. The speeches of Lord Steyn and myself in *R v Secretary of State for the Home Dept, ex p Simms* [1999] 3 All ER 400, [2000] 2 AC 115 contain some discussion of this principle and its constitutional justification in the context of human rights. But the wider principle itself is hardly new. It can be traced back at least to *Stradling v Morgan* (1560) 1 Plowd 199, 75 ER 305.

d [9] Section 20(1) contains no express reference to LPP and the question is therefore whether its exclusion must necessarily be implied. For this purpose it is necessary to examine s 20(1) in its context. It was first enacted as part of a group of sections dealing with the powers of tax authorities to obtain information, inserted into the 1970 Act by s 57(1) of and Sch 6 to the Finance Act 1976. These sections have since been amended and amplified on a number of occasions but

e the Revenue do not suggest that the amendments have changed the meaning which the relevant words in s 20(1) had in 1976. It is therefore sufficient to consider the 1976 provisions, the material part of which are for convenience reproduced as an appendix to these opinions.

[10] The argument for the Revenue is essentially that Parliament has provided

f a number of specific safeguards and restrictions for the protection of the taxpayer, including an express preservation of LPP for documents in the possession of a barrister, advocate or legal advisor. It therefore necessarily follows that no wider qualification of the general words of s 20(1) was intended.

[11] The first form of safeguard is some form of judicial or administrative control, graduated according to the intrusiveness of the power. Thus the

g inspector's power to require delivery of documents under s 20(1) or (3) requires the consent of a General or Special Commissioner (see sub-s (7)). Consent is not needed only if the Board of Inland Revenue itself makes the request under s 20(2). Likewise, only the Board may give a notice under s 20(1) or (3) to a barrister, advocate or solicitor (see s 20B(3)). Notices to tax accountants under s 20A(1)

h (see s 20A(3)) and searches under s 20C(1) require the consent or warrant (as the case may be) of 'the appropriate judicial authority', which in England means a circuit judge (see s 20D(1)(a)).

[12] The second restriction is the preservation or creation by s 20B(2) of a limited form of litigation privilege in tax appeals, analogous to that enjoyed by a

j party to civil or criminal proceedings. A notice by an inspector under s 20(1) or (3) cannot require the taxpayer to produce 'documents relating to the conduct of a pending appeal by [him]'. For some reason which seems to me unclear, this privilege does not protect the taxpayer when the notice has been given by the Board (see *R v IRC, ex p Taylor (No 2)* [1990] 2 All ER 409 at 413). It is in any case a litigation privilege which does not cover the same ground as (though it may overlap with) LPP. It applies to documents relating to the conduct of an appeal by, for example, a taxpayer in person, and not merely communications and documents relating to the obtaining of legal advice. On the other hand, it is confined the documents relating to a tax appeal, whereas LPP applies to legal advice whenever sought and for whatever purpose. The distinction between LPP and litigation privilege is succinctly stated by Lord Denning MR in *Buttes Gas and Oil Co v Hammer (No 3), Occidental Petroleum Corp v Buttes Gas and Oil Co (No 2)* [1980] 3 All ER 475 at 483–484, [1981] QB 223 at 243–244.

[13] The third restriction is that an inspector cannot give notices under s 20(1) or (3) or s 20A(1) to a barrister, advocate or solicitor. The decision to give such a notice must be taken at a higher administrative level, by the Board.

[14] Fourthly, by s 20B(9), a tax accountant (defined by s 20D(2) to include anyone who assists someone else in the preparation of his tax returns or accounts and so possibly including a lawyer) cannot be required by notice under s 20(3) to deliver 'documents which are his (the accountant's) property and originate as working papers of that relationship'.

[15] Fifthly, ss 20B(8) and 20C(3) deal specifically with LPP, but only in relation to documents in the possession of the lawyer. They cannot be required to be delivered by a notice under ss 20(3) or 20A(1) without the client's consent and they cannot be seized or removed under s 20C(1).

[16] In my opinion the first four safeguards or restrictions are concerned with questions so distinct from LPP that they provide no basis for any implication that it was intended to be excluded. The provisions for judicial or administrative control are intended to prevent abuse of the statutory powers. In the present case, for example, the Special Commissioner who consented to the notice under s 20(1) was required to be satisfied that 'in all the circumstances the inspector is justified in proceeding under this section' (see s 20(7)). That involves a judgment as to whether the inspector was acting reasonably. It requires the Special Commissioner to balance the public interest that the inspector should have information needed to make a correct assessment against the interests of the taxpayer in not having his privacy invaded further than necessary (compare *TC Coombs & Co (a firm) v IRC* [1991] 3 All ER 623, [1991] 2 AC 283). But LPP does not involve such a balancing of interests. It is absolute and is based not merely upon the general right to privacy but also upon the right of access to justice (see *R v Derby Magistrates' Court, ex p B* [1995] 4 All ER 526, [1996] AC 487).

[17] The second restriction by reference to litigation privilege also gives rise to no implication about LPP. It may well give rise to the implication that no litigation privilege was to exist other than in the circumstances specified in s 20B(2), as was held by the Court of Appeal in *R v IRC, ex p Taylor (No 2)* [1990] 2 All ER 409 at 413–414. But it has no bearing on LPP.

[18] The provision which requires that a notice to a barrister, advocate or solicitor should be given only by the Board does not in my opinion take the matter any further. It is entirely consistent with the preservation of LPP, which indeed is expressly preserved in such a case by s 20B(8).

[19] Finally, s 20B(9) is a curious provision which appears designed to protect the proprietary interest of the tax accountant in his working papers (compare *Chantrey Martin & Co v Martin* [1953] 2 All ER 691, [1953] 2 QB 286 and *Gomba Holdings UK Ltd v Minories Finance Ltd* [1989] 1 All ER 261, [1988] 1 WLR 1231). It has nothing to do with LPP.

[20] Although I appreciate that the Revenue rely upon the inference to be drawn from the cumulative effect of these various provisions, I do not consider that even cumulatively they come anywhere near giving rise to an implication

a that LPP was intended to be excluded. In my opinion, the Revenue stand or fall by the express references to LPP in ss 20B(8) and 20C(3). If these are consistent with the preservation of LPP for documents in the hands of the taxpayer, the other provisions are no more than makeweights.

[21] The argument for the Revenue on ss 20B(8) and 20C(3) is simple. If Parliament intended to preserve LPP in general, why did it specifically provide b for its preservation in respect of documents in the possession or power of a lawyer? The inescapable inference is said to be that LPP was not intended to be preserved for documents in the possession or power of the taxpayer. This was the view of the Divisional Court, the Court of Appeal and also Bingham LJ in *R v IRC, ex p Taylor (No 2)* [1990] 2 All ER 409 at 413–414.

[22] I see the force of this argument but I think that it has difficulties which c were not fully addressed either in the Court of Appeal or in *Ex p Taylor*. Why should Parliament want to preserve LPP for documents in the hands of the lawyer but not for documents (which may well be copies or originals of the same documents) in the hands of the taxpayer? The irrationality of such a scheme was commented upon by Advocate General Slynn in *AM & S Europe Ltd v EC* d *Commission* Case 155/79 [1983] 1 All ER 705 at 733, [1982] ECR 1575 at 1654–1655:

'If one considers the real purpose of the protection ... I can for my part see no justifiable distinction between such documents in the hands of the lawyer and in the hands of the client. If the lawyer has one copy and the client another, both should be protected. The request and the reply, if relating to e legal advice, are of the same nature. To tell the client that if he leaves his documents at his lawyer's office they will be protected but that, if he keeps them himself, they are not seems to me indefensible and likely to encourage, for example, the giving of oral advice if it is unfavourable advice, and the destruction or transfer to the lawyer's office of documents. It would be quite extraordinary that if the lawyer's documents were, by chance, left at the f client's premises, the day the inspector called, they must be produced, but that if the lawyer took his file away with him, they would not. In my opinion the rule covers communications between lawyer and client made for the purpose of obtaining or giving legal advice in whoever's hands they are and whether legal proceedings have begun or not. It covers also the contents of g that advice (given orally or in writing), in whatever form it is recorded, whether in a letter or in a summary or in a note or in minutes.'

[23] Mr Brennan QC, for the Inland Revenue, said that there was no real anomaly because the inspector could indirectly obtain documents in the possession of the lawyer by applying to the taxpayer. He would have to produce them on the h ground that, although in the lawyer's possession, he was entitled to them as against the lawyer and they were accordingly in his 'power'. The purpose of s 20B(8) was to prevent the lawyer from being placed in a situation in which he had a statutory duty which conflicted with his duty to his client. It eliminated conflict by providing that the duty to the client prevailed. If the Revenue wanted j the documents, they had to serve a notice on the client.

[24] I do not find this an adequate explanation. If Parliament had simply wanted to spare lawyers the difficulty of deciding which master to serve, it could just as easily have removed the problem by providing that documents in the hands of lawyers also had to be produced. Why should it have chosen to say that they could not be produced without the client's consent? If the client's consent is required when the documents are in the hands of the lawyer, why should it not

be required when they are in the hands of the client himself? It seems to me
strange to say that the lawyer could not produce the documents without the
client's consent, but leave it to be inferred that a client served with a notice under
s 20(1) would be obliged to give his consent. The documents in the hands of the
lawyer might be in the 'power' of the client but then again they might not. They
might be attendance notes or similar documents belonging to the lawyer. Or
he might have a lien over them for his fees. On any view, the Revenue's
entitlement to the documents would be subject to chance events in the way
Advocate General Slynn described.

[25] Despite these difficulties, one is bound to ask why Parliament should
have dealt expressly with documents in the hands of the lawyer but not with
those in the hands of the client. LPP is, after all, a single privilege, for the benefit
of the client, whether the documents are in his hands or that of his lawyer. When
the lawyer is served with a notice under ss 20(3) or 20A(1), he has no privilege of
his own but may, indeed must, assert that of his client.

[26] I think that the explanation may lie in *Parry-Jones v Law Society* [1968] 1 All ER
177, [1969] 1 Ch 1. The Law Society had a statutory power to make rules to
enforce compliance with the Solicitors' Accounts Rules and Solicitors' Trust
Accounts Rules and had made rules which entitled it for this purpose to require a
solicitor to produce documents relating to his practice (or any trust) of which he
was a solicitor trustee to an appointed investigator. Mr Parry-Jones objected to
such a request on the ground that some of the documents contained confidential
information relating to clients which could not be disclosed without their
consent. He issued a writ claiming an injunction to restrain the Law Society from
proceeding with its request. Buckley J ([1967] 3 All ER 248, [1968] Ch 195) struck
out the writ as disclosing no cause of action and his order was affirmed by the
Court of Appeal.

[27] Lord Denning MR dealt with the matter as follows:

'We all know that, as between solicitor and client, there are two privileges.
The first is the privilege relating to legal proceedings, commonly called legal
professional privilege. A solicitor must not produce or disclose in any legal
proceedings any of the communications between himself and his client
without the client's consent. The second privilege arises out of the
confidence subsisting between solicitor and client similar to the confidence
which applies between doctor and patient, banker and customer, accountant
and client, and the like. The law implies a term into the contract whereby a
professional man is to keep his client's affairs secret and not to disclose them
to anyone without just cause ... This particularly applies in the relationship
of solicitor and client. The solicitor is not to disclose his client's affairs to
anyone at all except under the most special and exceptional circumstances.
In reliance on these principles, the plaintiff says that the accountant sent by
the Law Society should not be allowed to see documents or information
relating to a client's affairs ... In my opinion the contract between solicitor
and client must be taken to contain this implication:—the solicitor must
obey the law, and, in particular, he must comply with the rules made under
the authority of statute for the conduct of the profession. If the rules require
him to disclose his client's affairs, then he must do so.' (See [1968] 1 All ER
177 at 178, [1969] 1 Ch 1 at 6–7.)

[28] Diplock LJ gave a judgment to similar effect:

a   'So far as the plaintiff's point as to privilege is concerned, privilege is irrelevant when one is not concerned with judicial or quasi-judicial proceedings because, strictly speaking, privilege refers to a right to withhold from a court, or a tribunal exercising judicial functions, material which would otherwise be admissible in evidence. What we are concerned with here is the contractual duty of confidence, generally implied though sometimes expressed, between

b   a solicitor and client. Such a duty exists not only between solicitor and client, but, for example, between banker and customer, doctor and patient, and accountant and client. Such a duty of confidence is subject to, and overridden by, the duty of any party to that contract to comply with the law of the land. If it is the duty of such a party to a contract, whether at common law or under statute, to disclose in defined circumstances confidential information,

c   then he must do so, and any express contract to the contrary would be illegal and void.' (See [1968] 1 All ER 177 at 180, [1969] 1 Ch 1 at 9.)

[29] Salmon LJ agreed.

[30] One could hardly imagine a stronger Court of Appeal, but I am bound to say that I have difficulty with the reasoning. It is not the case that LPP does no

d   more than entitle the client to require his lawyer to withhold privileged documents in judicial or quasi-judicial proceedings, leaving the question of whether he may disclose them on other occasions to the implied duty of confidence. The policy of LPP requires that the client should be secure in the knowledge that protected documents and information will not be disclosed at all.

e   The reasoning in *Parry-Jones'* case suggests that any statutory obligation to disclose documents will be construed as overriding the duty of confidence which constitutes the client's only protection. In the present proceedings, however, it is accepted that the client is protected by LPP and that this can be overridden only by primary legislation containing express words or necessary implication.

f   [31] It is unfortunate that the Court of Appeal was not referred to valuable judgments of the Supreme Court of New Zealand in *IRC v West-Walker* [1954] NZLR 191, which reached the opposite conclusion in the context of a statutory power to require the production of documents and information for the purposes of the administration of the taxing statutes. The New Zealand judges pointed out that LPP was not merely a rule of evidence but a substantive right founded on an

g   important public policy.

[32] This is not to say that on its facts *Parry-Jones'* case was wrongly decided. But I think that the true justification for the decision was not that Mr Parry-Jones' clients had no LPP, or that their LPP had been overridden by the Law Society's rules, but that the clients' LPP was not being infringed. The Law Society were

h   not entitled to use information disclosed by the solicitor for any purpose other than the investigation. Otherwise the confidentiality of the clients had to be maintained. In my opinion, this limited disclosure did not breach the clients' LPP or, to the extent that it technically did, was authorised by the Law Society's statutory powers. It does not seem to me to fall within the same principle as a case in which disclosure is sought for a use which involves the information being

j   made public or used against the person entitled to the privilege.

[33] In the light of *Parry-Jones'* case, it seems to me explicable that Parliament should wish to make it clear that even if the Court of Appeal was right in saying that the true basis for the client's right to prevent his lawyer from disclosing documents concerned with obtaining legal advice to the tax authorities (or any other non-judicial authorities) was a duty of confidence rather than LPP, no such disclosure could be required under ss 20(3) or 20A(1) without the client's consent.

No such provision was of course required in the case of documents in the hands
of the client himself, to which the duty of confidence was obviously irrelevant. *a*
Any protection to which such documents were entitled had to be based upon LPP
and, so far as it existed, would be subject to the principle that it could be removed
only by express language or necessary implication.

[34] Mr Brennan showed us the debates on the provisions which become
Sch 6 to the 1976 Act in Standing Committee E and on report in the House of *b*
Commons. He did not submit that they contained any material sufficiently
unambiguous to be admissible under the principle in *Pepper (Inspector of Taxes) v
Hart* [1993] 1 All ER 42, [1993] AC 593 but he produced them to show that the
question of LPP was brought to the attention of the House. So it was, but I find
no indication that the House was being told that the intention was to abolish or
restrict it. On the contrary, the Chief Secretary to the Treasury (Mr Joel Barnett), *c*
with the Solicitor-General (Mr Peter Archer QC) in attendance, said to the
Standing Committee (HC Official Report, SC E (Finance Bill), 10 June 1976,
col 686):

> 'I should make it quite clear—even without my hon. and learned Friend *d*
> sitting beside me—that the purpose of this part of the schedule is not to
> require privileged and confidential documents to be handed over to the
> Inland Revenue. That is certainly not the intention.'

[35] It is certainly true that some opposition amendments which were said to
be intended to ensure that LPP was preserved were not accepted by the *e*
government. But this was because they were thought (rightly or wrongly) either
to go beyond the scope of LPP at common law or to be unnecessary. The
Parliamentary material does not therefore assist in showing a clear intention to
override a fundamental human right.

[36] I therefore do not think that the provisions upon which the Revenue *f*
relies are sufficient to create a necessary implication that LPP was intended to be
excluded. This means that I respectfully think that the reasoning of Bingham LJ
in *R v IRC, ex p Taylor (No 2)* [1990] 2 All ER 409 at 413–414 was too broad. It
suggests that because Mr Taylor was the taxpayer, any documents subject to LPP
could have been demanded, whether the beneficiary of the LPP was the client or *g*
himself. In my opinion, Mr Taylor would have been entitled to refuse to produce
documents in respect of which he personally was entitled to LPP, such as legal
advice from counsel about his own tax affairs. But, as in *Parry-Jones v Law Society*
[1968] 1 All ER 177, [1969] 1 Ch 1, I do not suggest that the actual decision was
wrong. In the Divisional Court ([1989] 3 All ER 353) the Inland Revenue accepted *h*
that, as the information was sought under s 20(2) for the purpose of determining
Mr Taylor's own liability to tax, it could be used only for that purpose. It could
not, if subject to LPP, be used in connection with the tax liabilities of his clients.
Glidewell LJ (at 360) accepted this concession as correct and although he
suggested that the Revenue might make other use of a discovery that a particular
document existed, I am not sure that this is right. It is not necessary to decide the *j*
point, but I do not think that the Inland Revenue were entitled to use any
information supplied by Mr Taylor for another purpose. In consequence, I do
not think that the disclosure of the documents by Mr Taylor in confidence for the
limited purpose of determining his own tax liability infringed any LPP vested in
his clients. If I am wrong about this and technically it did, then I think that to that
extent the statute can be construed as having authorised it.

a [37] On the other hand, I respectfully think that the decision of Millett J on a similar point in *Price Waterhouse (a firm) v BCCI Holdings (Luxembourg) SA* [1992] BCLC 583 was wrong. The question was whether LPP could be overridden by a notice given by the Bank of England under s 39 of the Banking Act 1987 requiring production of documents which it 'may reasonably require for the performance of its functions under this Act' (s 39(3)). The Act contained no express language

b excluding LPP but s 39(13) provided that the section should not 'compel the production by a barrister, advocate or solicitor of a document containing a privileged communication made by him or to him in that capacity'. Millett J said (at 593) that sub-s (13) must be taken 'not only as making an exception to documents which may be required to be produced but also as marking the limits of that exception'. The judge remarked that it might seem strange that 'the Bank

c of England should be unable to compel the production of documents from the lawyer when it can compel their production from his client'. I agree. But I do not think that the judge's answer, namely that 'Parliament was not concerned to protect the interests of the client but those of the lawyer' is at all adequate. What are the interests of the lawyer? He has no interest in whether LPP is maintained

d or not. If the client chooses to divulge the information, there is nothing the lawyer can do about it. LPP is entirely in the interests of the client. For the reasons I have already given in connection with s 20(1) of the 1970 Act, I do not think that the existence of sub-s (13) was a sufficient ground for finding a necessary implication that LPP had been excluded.

e [38] The Revenue say that it is important for them to have access to the taxpayer's legal advice in those cases in which liability may turn upon the purpose with which he entered into a transaction or series of transactions. This is particularly true of some of the anti-avoidance provisions. But there are many situations in both civil and criminal law in which liability depends upon the state of mind with which something was done. Apart from the exceptional case in

f which it appears that the client obtained legal advice for the purpose of enabling himself better to commit a crime (see *R v Cox* (1884) 14 QBD 153, [1881–5] All ER Rep 68) this is not thought a sufficient reason for overriding LPP. The court must infer the purpose from the facts.

[39] It is of course open to Parliament, if it considers that the Revenue require

g such powers, to enact them in unambiguous terms. But there is also the Human Rights Act 1998 to be borne in mind. The appellants put forward an alternative submission that, if your Lordships agreed with the construction given to s 20(1) by the Court of Appeal, you should make a declaration that it was incompatible with the right to privacy under art 8 of the European Convention for the Protection of Human Rights and Fundamental Freedoms 1950 (as set out in Sch 1 to

h the Human Rights Act 1998). In the circumstances it is unnecessary for your Lordships to pronounce upon the point. It is however the case, as I have mentioned, that the European Court of Human Rights has said that LPP is a fundamental human right which can be invaded only in exceptional circumstances (see *Foxley v UK* (2000) 8 BHRC 571 at 581 (para 44)). Mr Brennan said that the

j public interest in the collection of the revenue could provide the necessary justification but I very much doubt whether this is right. Nor is it sufficient to say simply that the power is not used very often. That is no consolation to the person against whom it is used. If new legislation is passed, it will have to be seen whether it is limited to cases in which the interference with LPP can be shown to have a legitimate aim which is necessary in a democratic society.

[40] I would allow the appeal and quash the notice.

LORD HOPE OF CRAIGHEAD.

[41] My Lords, I have had the advantage of reading in draft the speech of my
noble and learned friends Lord Hoffmann and Lord Hobhouse of Woodborough.
I agree with them and for the reasons which they have given I too would allow
the appeal.

LORD HOBHOUSE OF WOODBOROUGH.

[42] My Lords, I agree that this appeal should be allowed. The question to be
decided falls within a very narrow compass and since this House is differing from
unanimous decisions of the courts below ([2001] 1 All ER 535, [2002] 2 WLR 255
(Divisional Court); [2001] EWCA Civ 329, [2002] 1 All ER 776, [2002] 2 WLR
255 (Court of Appeal)) I will shortly state in my own words my reasons for
agreeing with the opinion of my noble and learned friend Lord Hoffmann.

[43] The question is one of statutory construction. It is now accepted for the
purposes of this litigation that the documents in respect of which the right to
demand production remains in dispute contain or may contain information
relevant to a tax liability to which Morgan Grenfell may be liable or its amount
and that they are documents which are subject to legal professional privilege
(advice privilege) which has not been waived. It is likewise accepted that the
character of the privilege is that described in the speech of Lord Taylor of
Gosforth CJ in your Lordships' House in *R v Derby Magistrates' Court, ex p B* [1995]
4 All ER 526 at 541–542, [1996] AC 487 at 508: its character is absolute and—

> 'if a balancing exercise was ever required in the case of legal professional
> privilege, it was performed once and for all in the sixteenth century, and
> since then has applied across the board in every case, irrespective of the
> client's individual merits.'

At the least, some and, more probably, all of these premises would benefit from
further examination but they have not been the subject of argument on the
present appeal. The question of construction is therefore whether the statute
empowers the Revenue to require the delivery up to them of documents
notwithstanding that they are covered by legal professional privilege.

[44] The next step in the legal analysis is also not disputed and was expressly
adopted by the Court of Appeal. The principle of statutory construction is
succinctly stated in a quotation from the speech of Lord Hoffmann in *R v Secretary
of State for the Home Dept, ex p Simms* [1999] 3 All ER 400 at 412, [2000] 2 AC 115 at
131:

> 'Parliamentary sovereignty means that Parliament can, if it chooses,
> legislate contrary to fundamental principles of human rights ... The
> constraints upon its exercise by Parliament are ultimately political, not legal.
> But the principle of legality means that Parliament must squarely confront
> what it is doing and accept the political cost. Fundamental rights cannot be
> overridden by general or ambiguous words. This is because there is too
> great a risk that the full implications of their unqualified meaning may have
> passed unnoticed in the democratic process. In the absence of express
> language or necessary implication to the contrary, the courts therefore
> presume that even the most general words were intended to be subject to
> the basic rights of the individual. In this way the courts of the United
> Kingdom, though acknowledging the sovereignty of Parliament, apply
> principles of constitutionality little different from those which exist in

a   countries where the power of the legislature is expressly limited by a constitutional document.'

The context in which Lord Hoffmann was speaking was human rights but the principle of statutory construction is not new and has long been applied in relation to the question whether a statute is to be read as having overridden some basic tenet of the common law (see *Viscountess Rhondda's Claim* [1922] 2 AC 339 and *B (a minor) v DPP* [2000] 1 All ER 833, [2000] 2 AC 428). The protection given by the common law to those entitled to claim legal professional privilege is a basic tenet of the common law as has been reaffirmed by *B*'s case.

[45] It is accepted that the statute does not contain any express words that abrogate the taxpayer's common law right to rely upon legal professional privilege. The question therefore becomes whether there is a necessary implication to that effect. A necessary implication is not the same as a reasonable implication as was pointed out by Lord Hutton in *B*'s case [2000] 1 All ER 833 at 855, [2000] 2 AC 428 at 481. A *necessary* implication is one which necessarily follows from the express provisions of the statute construed in their context. It distinguishes between what it would have been sensible or reasonable for Parliament to have included or what Parliament would, if it had thought about it, probably have included and what it is clear that the express language of the statute shows that the statute must have included. A necessary implication is a matter of express language and logic not interpretation.

[46] In the present case the statutory language falls a long way short of meeting this criterion. The arguments advanced by the Revenue are fully discussed in the opinion of my noble and learned friend. I agree with his conclusion. At best from the point of view of the Revenue the legislation is equivocal. Left to myself I would incline to the view that the implication, if any, is that the legislature was intending to preserve the legal professional privilege of the taxpayer rather than abrogate it; otherwise, why preserve it in respect of documents in the hands of the advisor when the client has not consented to waive the privilege? Further, the argument that a general public interest in collecting revenue for the Executive suffices (in peace time) implicitly to override the basic right and public interest represented by legal professional privilege is contrary to the authorities and the principles which the Revenue accept that those authorities lay down.

[47] The present appeal thus falls to be decided applying the well-established principles of statutory construction to be found in English law. The appellants do not need the assistance of the Human Rights Act 1998 or the European Convention for the Protection of Human Rights and Fundamental Freedoms 1950. The judgments of the European Court of Human Rights in *Foxley v UK* (2000) 8 BHRC 571, and the Court of Justice of the European Communities in *AM & S Europe Ltd v EC Commission* Case 155/79 [1983] 1 All ER 705, [1982] ECR 1575 show a general recognition of the importance of legal professional privilege.

[48] There were cited to your Lordships decisions of the courts of other common law jurisdictions which have also arrived at conclusions very similar to those of your Lordships in this case. I do not wish to add anything to what my noble and learned friend has said in this connection nor to what he has said about the English authorities which will now have to be read with the judgment of this House. Attention has rightly been drawn by my noble and learned friend to what was said by Glidewell LJ in *R v IRC, ex p Taylor (No 2)* [1989] 3 All ER 353 at 360 concerning the implicit restriction upon the use which may be made of

documents which are obtained under a statutory power and its possible *a*
interaction with the question whether a client's privilege will be infringed by
requiring the disclosure of documents by the professional advisor. It is a general
principle that where a power is given for a particular purpose it is not permissible
to use that power for a collateral purpose.

LORD SCOTT OF FOSCOTE.   *b*

[49] My Lords, I have had the advantage of reading in draft the speech of my
noble and learned friend Lord Hoffmann. I agree with it, and for the reasons
which he has given I, too, would allow the appeal.

Appeal allowed.
c

Kate O'Hanlon   Barrister.

APPENDIX

'20. *Power to call for documents of taxpayer and others.*—(1) Subject to this *d*
section, an inspector may by notice in writing require a person to deliver to
him such documents as are in the person's possession or power and as (in the
inspector's reasonable opinion) contain, or may contain, information
relevant to any tax liability to which the person is or may be subject, or to the
amount of any such liability.

(2) Subject to this section, the Board may by notice in writing require a *e*
person to deliver, to a named officer of theirs, such documents as are in
the person's possession or power and as (in the Board's reasonable opinion)
contain, or may contain, information relevant to any tax liability to which he
is or may be subject, or to the amount of any such liability.

(3) Subject to this section, an inspector may, for the purpose of enquiring *f*
into the tax liability of any person ("the taxpayer"), by notice in writing
require any of the persons who in relation to the taxpayer are subject to this
subsection to deliver to the inspector or, if the person to whom the notice is
given so elects, to make available for inspection by a named officer of the
Board, such documents as are in his possession or power and as (in the
inspector's reasonable opinion) contain, or may contain, information *g*
relevant to any tax liability to which the taxpayer is or may be, or may have
been, subject, or to the amount of any such liability.

(4) The persons so subject are—(a) the taxpayer's spouse, and any son or
daughter of his; (b) in so far as the inspector's enquiries relate to liability of
the taxpayer in respect of income, profits or gains that were, or may have *h*
been, derived from—(i) any business (past or present) carried on by the
taxpayer or his spouse, or (ii) any business (past or present) with whose
management either of them was concerned at a material time, any person
who is carrying on a business, or was doing so at a material time, and any
company whether carrying on a business or not ... *j*

(7) Notices under this section are not to be given by an inspector unless
he is authorised by the Board for its purposes; and—(a) a notice is not to be
given by him except with the consent of a General or Special Commissioner;
and (b) the Commissioner is to give his consent only on being satisfied that
in all the circumstances the inspector is justified in proceeding under this
section ...

(9) To the extent specified in section 20B below, the above provisions are subject to the restrictions of that section.

20A. *Power to call for papers of tax accountant.*—(1) Where after the passing of the Finance Act 1976 a person—(a) is convicted of an offence in relation to tax (whenever committed) by or before any court in the United Kingdom; or (b) has awarded against him a penalty incurred by him (whether before or after the passing of that Act) under section 99 of this Act, and he has stood in relation to others as tax accountant, an inspector authorised by the Board for the purpose of this section may by notice in writing require the person to deliver to him such documents as are in his possession or power and as (in the inspector's reasonable opinion) contain information relevant to any tax liability to which any client of his is or has been, or may be or have been, subject, or to the amount of any such liability. For this purpose section 20(8) above applies, substituting "the client" for "the taxpayer" ...

(3) A notice is not to be given to any person under this section unless with the consent of the appropriate judicial authority; and that authority is to give his consent only on being satisfied that in all the circumstances the inspector is justified in so proceeding ...

(5) To the extent specified in section 20B below, the above provisions are subject to the restrictions of that section.

20B. *Restrictions on powers under ss. 20 and 20A.*—(1) Before a notice is given to a person by an inspector under section 20(1) or (3), or under section 20A, the person must have been given a reasonable opportunity to deliver (or, in the case of section 20(3), to deliver or make available) the documents in question; and the inspector must not apply for consent under section 20(7) or, as the case may be, section 20A(3), until the person has been given that opportunity.

(2) A notice under section 20(1) does not oblige a person to deliver documents relating to the conduct of any pending appeal by him; a notice under section 20(3) does not oblige a person to deliver or make available documents relating to the conduct of a pending appeal by the taxpayer; and a notice under section 20A does not oblige a person to deliver documents relating to the conduct of a pending appeal by the client. "Appeal" means appeal relating to tax.

(3) An inspector cannot under section 20(1) or (3), or under section 20A(1), give notice to a barrister, advocate or solicitor, but the notice must in any such case be given (if at all) by the Board; and accordingly in relation to a barrister, advocate or solicitor for references in section 20(3) and (4) and section 20A to the inspector there are substituted references to the Board ...

(8) A notice under section 20(3) or section 20A(1) does not oblige a barrister, advocate or a solicitor to deliver or make available, without his clients consent, any document with respect to which a claim to professional privilege could be maintained.

(9) A notice under section 20(3) does not, in the case of a person who (in the course of a business carried on by him) has stood in relation to another as tax accountant, oblige that person to deliver or make available documents which are his (the accountant's) property and originate as working papers of that relationship.

20C. *Entry with warrant to obtain documents.*—(1) If the appropriate judicial authority is satisfied on information on oath given by an officer of the Board that—(a) there is reasonable ground for suspecting that an offence involving

any form of fraud in connection with, or in relation to, tax has been
committed and that evidence of it is to be found on premises specified in the *a*
information; and (b) in applying under this section, the officer acts with the
approval of the Board given in relation to the particular case, the authority
may issue a warrant in writing authorising an officer of the Board to enter
the premises, if necessary by force, at any time within 14 days from the time
of issue of the warrant, and search them ...   *b*

(3) On entering the premises with a warrant under this section, the officer
may seize and remove any things whatsoever found there which he has
reasonable cause to believe may be required as evidence for the purposes of
proceedings in respect of such an offence as is mentioned in subsection (1)
above. But this does not authorise the seizure and removal of documents in
the possession of a barrister, advocate or solicitor with respect to which a *c*
claim to professional privilege could be maintained ...

20D. *Interpretation of ss 20 to 20C.*—(1) For the purposes of section 20A
and 20C above, "the appropriate judicial authority" is—(a) in England and
Wales, a Circuit judge; (b) in Scotland, a sheriff; and (c) in Northern Ireland,
a county court judge.   *d*

(2) For the purposes of sections 20 and 20A, a person stands in relation to
another as tax accountant at any time when he assists the other in the
preparation of returns or accounts to be made or delivered by the other for
any purpose of tax; and his clients are all those to whom he stands or has
stood in that relationship.'

a # Chellaram and another v Chellaram and others (No 2)
[2002] EWHC 632 (Ch)

b CHANCERY DIVISION

LAWRENCE COLLINS J

22, 25 FEBRUARY, 16 APRIL 2002

c *Practice – Service – Service by post – Service by first class post at individual's last known residence – Whether such service establishing jurisdiction over defendant not domiciled or present in England at time of service – CPR 6.5(6).*

Practice – Service out of the jurisdiction – Action for breach of express trust – Whether applicable law or domicile of trust to be determined for jurisdiction purposes as at date when court seised of proceedings or when cause of action arose – Civil Jurisdiction and
d *Judgments Act 1982, Sch 1, art 5(6) – CPR 6.20(11).*

The claimants were beneficiaries under two settlements. They brought proceedings in England for breach of trust against a number of defendants who, save in one case, were alleged to be either the trustees or former trustees of the settlements.
e The defendants contended that neither trust was still subsisting when the proceedings had been commenced; alternatively, that Bermudan law was the applicable law governing the trusts when the English court had become seised of the proceedings. The beneficiaries claimed that, at the time when their causes of action arose, English law was the applicable law of the trusts. None of the defendants was domiciled in England, but two were domiciled in other
f contracting states of the Brussels Convention on Jurisdiction and the Enforcement of Judgments in Civil and Commercial Matters 1968 (as set out in Sch 1 to the Civil Jurisdiction and Judgments Act 1982). Under art 5(6)[a] of the convention, a person domiciled in a contracting state could, in another contracting state, be sued as trustee of a trust created, inter alia, by a written instrument, in the courts of the contracting state in which the trust 'is' domiciled. Of the
g defendants domiciled in non-convention states, four were served outside the jurisdiction, with the permission of the court, pursuant to CPR 6.20(3)[b] and (11). Under r 6.20(3), permission could be given to serve a defendant outside the jurisdiction where the defendant was a necessary or proper party to a claim made against someone on whom the claim form had been or would be served (whether
h the service was in England or outside England, and whether it was within or without a convention country). Permission could be granted under r 6.20(11) if a claim were made for any remedy which might be obtained in proceedings to execute the trusts of a written instrument where 'the trusts ought to be executed according to English law', and the person on whom the claim form was to be
j served 'is' a trustee of the trusts. Another defendant, S, who was neither domiciled in a convention state nor present in England at the time of service, was purportedly served by first class post to the address at which he stayed on his very occasional visits to London. Under CPR Pt 6, a claim form could be served by

---

a   Article 5, so far as material, is set out at [28], below
b   Rule 6.20, so far as material, is set out [26], below

first class post, and for that purpose the place of service of an individual was, by
CPR 6.5(6)^c, his 'last known residence'. On applications by all but one of the
defendants to set aside the orders for permission to serve outside the jurisdiction,
or for declarations that service had not been properly effected or that the court
had no jurisdiction, issues arose, inter alia, as to (i) whether, as the beneficiaries
contended, the CPR had changed the rules of jurisdiction by allowing a
defendant, who was not domiciled or present in England, to be sued in England
by virtue of service on him at his last known residence; and (ii) whether, for the
jurisdictional purposes of CPR 6.20(11) and art 5(6) of the convention, the critical
date for determining the applicable law of a trust was, as the beneficiaries argued,
the date when the cause of action arose, or, as the defendants contended, the date
when the court became seised of the proceedings.

Held – (1) CPR Pt 6 had not changed the fundamental rule of English procedure
and jurisdiction that a defendant could be served with originating process
within the jurisdiction only if he were present in the jurisdiction at the time of
service or deemed service. Although Pt 6 contained general rules about service of
documents and did not only apply to service of a claim form, CPR 6.5 had not
swept away the general principle so far as it related to service of the claim form.
It followed in the instant case that S had not been validly served since he had not
been present in England at the time of service. In any event, the address to which
the claim form had been sent was used only occasionally by him on the rare
occasions when he visited London. In those circumstances, there was no
evidence that it ever was a 'residence' and it could not therefore be his 'last
known residence' within the meaning of CPR 6.5(6) (see [47], below).

(2) For the purposes of CPR 6.20(11) and art 5(6) of the convention, the
governing law or domicile of a trust was to be tested as at the date of the
proceedings rather than the date when the cause of action arose. As regards
r 6.20(11), the condition that 'the trusts ought to be executed according to English
law' had to be fulfilled, in the instant case, when permission to serve out was
sought, and it was not sufficient that English law applied to the trusts at the time
when the cause of action had arisen. That construction was supported by the
other condition that the defendant 'is' a trustee of the trusts. Similarly, in the case
of art 5(6), its application to a person sued as trustee of a trust which 'is' domiciled
in a contracting state supported the construction that the time of the proceedings
was the critical time. In the instant case, there was no basis for jurisdiction under
CPR 6.20(11) or art 5(6), and it followed that there was no basis for service of
additional necessary or proper parties under CPR 6.20(3). Accordingly, the orders
granting permission to serve outside the jurisdiction would be set aside, as would
service on those defendants who had been served or purportedly served, and the
court would declare that it had no jurisdiction to hear the claims (see [151], [163],
[164], [194], below)

Per curiam. No fair-minded and informed observer can conclude that there
will be a real possibility that a judge, whether a former barrister or solicitor, will
have the slightest inclination to act in breach of the judicial oath and favour a set
of chambers or firm of which he is a former member. In that context, there is no
reason to distinguish the situation of solicitors from that of barristers on the
ground that solicitors practise as partnerships while barristers share premises,

---

c   Rule 6.5, so far as material, is set out at [36], below

a staff, practice development (or marketing) and the expenses associated therewith, but not profits (see [197], below).

Notes

For the special jurisdiction in relation to trusts under the Brussels Convention, see 8(1) *Halsbury's Laws* (4th edn reissue) para 643, and for service by first class b post and service out of the jurisdiction with permission of the court, see 37 *Halsbury's Laws* (4th edn reissue) paras 320, 346.

For the Civil Jurisdiction and Judgments Act 1982, Sch 1, art 5, see 11 *Halsbury's Statutes* (4th edn) (2000 reissue) 1185.

Cases referred to in judgment

c *Ace Insurance SA-NV v Zurich Insurance Co* [2001] EWCA Civ 173, [2001] 1 All ER (Comm) 802.

Amin Rasheed Shipping Corp v Kuwait Insurance Co, The Al Wahab [1983] 2 All ER 884, [1984] AC 50, [1983] 3 WLR 241, HL.

Bank of Credit and Commerce International SA (in liq) and its former employees, Re d [2001] All ER (D) 41 (Dec).

Bank of Dubai Ltd v Abbas [1997] IL Pr 308, CA.

Barclays Bank of Swaziland Ltd v Hahn [1989] 2 All ER 398, [1989] 1 WLR 506, HL.

Cadogan Properties Ltd v Mount Eden Land Ltd [2000] IL Pr 722, CA.

Canada Trust Co v Stolzenberg (No 2) [2000] 4 All ER 481, [2002] 1 AC 1, [2000] 3 WLR 1376, HL.

e *Chellaram v Chellaram* [1985] 1 All ER 1043, [1985] Ch 409, [1985] 2 WLR 510.

Godwin v Swindon BC [2001] EWCA Civ 1478, [2001] 4 All ER 641, [2002] 1 WLR 997.

Hagen, The [1908] P 189, [1908–10] All ER Rep 21, CA.

Harrods (Buenos Aires) Ltd, Re [1991] 4 All ER 334, [1992] Ch 72, [1991] 3 WLR 397, CA.

Holder v Holder [1968] 1 All ER 665, [1968] Ch 353, [1968] 2 WLR 237, CA.

f *Iveagh v IRC* [1954] 1 All ER 609, [1954] Ch 364, [1954] 2 WLR 494.

Konamaneni v Rolls-Royce Industrial Power (India) Ltd [2002] 1 All ER 979, [2002] 1 WLR 1269.

Locabail (UK) Ltd v Bayfield Properties Ltd [2000] 1 All ER 65, [2000] QB 451, [2000] 2 WLR 870, CA.

Lubbe v Cape plc [2000] 4 All ER 268, [2000] 1 WLR 1545, HL.

g *Marlborough (Duke of) v A-G (No 1)* [1945] 1 All ER 165, [1945] Ch 78, CA.

Medicaments and Related Classes of Goods (No 2), Re [2001] ICR 564, [2001] 1 WLR 700, CA.

Mulox IBC Ltd v Geels Case C-125/92 [1993] ECR I-4075.

Official Solicitor v Stype Investments (Jersey) Ltd [1983] 1 All ER 629, [1983] 1 WLR 214.

h *Pauling's Settlement Trusts, Re, Younghusband v Coutts & Co* [1961] 3 All ER 713, [1962] 1 WLR 86; *affd in part* [1963] 3 All ER 1, [1964] Ch 303, [1963] 3 WLR 742, CA.

Porter v Magill, Weeks v Magill [2001] UKHL 67, [2002] 1 All ER 465, [2002] 2 WLR 37.

Rolph v Zolan [1993] 4 All ER 202, [1993] 1 WLR 1305, CA.

j *Royal Bank of Scotland plc v Etridge (No 2), Barclays Bank plc v Coleman, Bank of Scotland v Bennett, Kenyon-Brown v Desmond Banks & Co (a firm)* [2001] UKHL 44, [2001] 4 All ER 449, [2001] 3 WLR 1021.

Seaconsar Far East Ltd v Bank Markazi Jomhouri Islami Iran [1993] 4 All ER 456, [1994] 1 AC 438, [1993] 3 WLR 756, HL.

Spiliada Maritime Corp v Cansulex Ltd, The Spiliada [1986] 3 All ER 843, [1987] AC 460, [1986] 3 WLR 972, HL.

Taylor v Lawrence [2002] EWCA Civ 90, [2002] 2 All ER 353.
Winter v Winter [1894] 1 Ch 421.

Applications

The second to eighth defendants, Murli Tahilram Chellaram (Murli), Lal Lokumal Chellaram (Lal), Sham Lokumal Chellaram (Sham), Pishu Tahilram Chellaram (Pishu), Chellwood Holdings Ltd (Chellwood), Bermuda Trust Co Ltd (Bermuda Trust) and Mohan Shewakram Chellaram (Mohan), applied (i) for orders setting aside the orders of Master Bragge on 27 June 2001 giving the claimants, Vishal Harish Chellaram and Ashwin Harish Chellaram, permission to serve outside the jurisdiction on certain of the defendants the claim form in their action for breach of trust, or (ii) for declarations that service had not been properly effected or that the court had no jurisdiction. The first defendant, Lokumal Kishinchand Chellaram, had not been served, and took no part in the applications. The facts are set out in the judgment.

Patrick Lawrence (instructed by *Anderson's Litigation*) for the claimants.
Antony White QC (instructed by *Wedlake Bell*) for Murli and Pishu and (instructed by *Herbert Smith*) for Lal, Sham and Chellwood.
Colin Nasir of *Linklaters & Alliance* for Bermuda Trust.
James Pickering (instructed by *Singh Karran & Co*) for Mohan.

Cur adv vult

16 April 2002. The following judgment was delivered.

LAWRENCE COLLINS J.

(I) INTRODUCTION
[1] The Chellaram family is a well-known trading family, of which the claimants and all of the non-corporate defendants are members. The family is no stranger to litigation. There has already been litigation in Singapore, in London, in Bombay and in Bermuda which has some relevance to the background to, or the issues in, this case. The litigation in London resulted in the decision of Scott J (as he then was) in *Chellaram v Chellaram* [1985] 1 All ER 1043, [1985] Ch 409 in proceedings to which I shall refer as *Chellaram v Chellaram (No 1)*.

[2] These proceedings were brought by the claimants for relief in connection with what they claimed were breaches of trust in relation to four settlements, one made in 1943, one in 1946 and two in 1975. The claimants were beneficiaries under each of these trusts. The 1943 and 1946 trusts were established by their great-grandfather, and the assets of those trusts are buildings in Bombay. The claimants have alleged that their father's cousins and their uncle, the trustees, have been in breach of trust by letting the properties at a loss to persons connected with themselves and have failed to provide proper accounts.

[3] The 1975 trusts were established by their father and their uncle, and the trust assets consisted of shares representing part of the businesses run by their cousins outside India. The allegations relating to those trusts will be set out in detail later, but (at the risk of oversimplification) they are that their cousins, the trustees, diminished the value of the trust assets and later, as part of the settlement of *Chellaram v Chellaram (No 1)*, procured their sale at an undervalue to themselves or to companies controlled by them.

[4] All of the defendants are, or are alleged to be, outside the jurisdiction. Two
a of the defendants were purportedly served by the posting of the claim form and
particulars of claim to addresses in London, and the other defendants were the
subject of a series of orders made on 27 June 2001 giving permission to effect
service outside the jurisdiction (even though, on the claimants' case, permission
was not required in relation to two of the defendants).

b   [5] These are applications by the defendants (other than the first defendant,
who has not been served) to set aside the orders, or for declarations to the effect
that service has not been properly effected or that the court has no jurisdiction (or
for orders that if the court has jurisdiction, it should not be exercised). The case
raises a number of novel points on jurisdiction and choice of law in relation to
trusts, and an important point on postal service under the CPR.

c   [6] The claimants have discontinued the proceedings in so far as they relate to
the 1943 and 1946 settlements, but the settlements are relevant not only by way
of background, but also because the defendants claim that (a) orders for service
outside the jurisdiction in this action should be set aside because (among other
reasons) the claimants did not disclose the existence of proceedings in India which
d claimed an interest in property which was subject to the 1943 and 1946
settlements, and (b) the existence of those proceedings is one factor (among
others) tending to show that England is not the forum conveniens for the
proceedings in relation to the 1975 trusts.

(II) DRAMATIS PERSONAE

e   [7] The Chellaram trading enterprise was originally based in Bombay, India
and was started by Kishinchand Chellaram (Kishinchand), who died in 1951,
leaving three sons. There had been another son, Asandas, who effected a partition
of his share in the family property in 1932, and who does not play a part in the
story.

f   [8] A family tree (showing the male line of the relevant parts of the family) is
set out in an appendix to this judgment. Kishinchand's eldest son, Tahilram
Chellaram (Tahilram), died in 1943, leaving three sons, all of whom worked with
him in the business: Ram Chellaram (Ram), who died in 1987, and Murli
Chellaram (Murli), the second defendant, and Pishu Chellaram (Pishu), the fifth
defendant.

g   [9] His second son, Shewakram Chellaram (Shewakram), died in 1949, and he
and his wife Lachmibai Chellaram (Lachmibai), who died in 1997, had two sons,
Mohan Chellaram (Mohan), the eighth defendant, and Harish Chellaram (Harish),
who died in 1990. Harish was married to Radhika Chellaram (Radhika), who is
still alive, and they had two sons, Vishal Chellaram (Vishal) and Ashwin Chellaram
h (Ashwin), who are the claimants.

[10] His third son was Lokumal Chellaram (Lokumal), the first defendant, and
he and his wife Kamlabai Chellaram (Kamlabai) had two sons, Lal Chellaram
(Lal) and Sham Chellaram (Sham), the third and fourth defendants.

[11] According to the defendants, after the death of Kishinchand, the family
j business traded as three branches. The Lokumal Group is the business run and
owned by Lokumal, Lal and Sham. The Tahilram Group is the business run
and owned by Murli and Pishu (Ram having died in 1987). Murli is unable to
manage his own affairs, as a result of injuries sustained in an accident last year.
The Shewakram Group comprised, following the death of Shewakram, the assets
owned by or on behalf of Lachmibai (who died in 1997), Mohan, Harish (who
died in 1990), Radhika, and the claimants.

[12] According to the claimants, the original business eventually traded as two branches, the Lokumal Group and Tahilram Group, and not three. The Shewakram Group had interests in both the other two branches, and did not control any part of the original enterprise. Any businesses in which the Shewakram Group had an interest were controlled by either the Lokumal or Tahilram Group. Nothing turns for present purposes on this difference of emphasis.

[13] Chellwood Holdings Ltd (Chellwood), the sixth defendant, is a Gibraltar company in the Lokumal Group and is owned by Lal and Sham. In 1985 Chellwood purchased shares (representing interests in the Lokumal Group businesses) which were subject to the 1975 trusts.

[14] Bermuda Trust Co Ltd (Bermuda Trust), the seventh defendant, is a Bermudan company and the trustee arm of the Bank of Bermuda. It became a trustee of the 1975 trusts in 1985.

[15] Mr H G Advani (Mr Advani) was an advisor of very long standing (since the early 1930s) to Kishinchand and to the family. He was a senior lawyer, and was described in the *Chellaram v Chellaram (No 1)* proceedings as the doyen of the Bombay Bar. He was a trustee of three of the four trusts which are the subject matter of these proceedings, he advised on several of the important steps taken by the family, and drafted many of the documents, and acted as an arbitrator in valuing shares in the family businesses which the Shewakram Group sold to the other groups in 1985. He died in 1991.

(III) JURISDICTION

[16] The principal questions on the existence of jurisdiction (as distinct from discretion to exercise jurisdiction) which arise in this case are (a) whether Sham was properly served by post at an address in London which the claimants say was his last known residence; (b) whether any of the defendants is domiciled in England for jurisdictional purposes; (c) whether any of the defendants is domiciled in a state or territory to which the Brussels Convention on Jurisdiction and the Enforcement of Judgments in Civil and Commercial Matters 1968 (as set out in Sch 1 to the Civil Jurisdiction and Judgments Act 1982) (the 1968 convention) applies, and, if so, whether the court may assume jurisdiction under the provision in the 1968 convention relating to trusts; (d) which of the defendants are domiciled in countries or territories to which the 1968 convention does not apply, and whether the provisions in CPR 6.20 authorising service on necessary and proper parties, and on trustees, apply to them.

[17] The following countries are (or may be) relevant countries for the purposes of domicile or residence: (a) England, where Lal and Sham, the third and fourth defendants, are (or were) said to have residences to which the claim form and particulars of claim were sent by post in June 2001, and from where the claimants have suggested that Chellwood, the sixth defendant, is managed; (b) Hong Kong, where Lokumal, the first defendant, is domiciled, and where Sham, the fourth defendant, says he is resident; (c) India, where Murli and Pishu, the second and fifth defendants, are domiciled, and where Mohan, the eighth defendant, says he is domiciled; (d) Spain, where Lal says he is domiciled; (e) Gibraltar, where Chellwood is incorporated, and where the claimants say that Mohan, the eighth defendant, is domiciled; and (f) Bermuda, where Bermuda Trust, the seventh defendant, is incorporated.

[18] The 1968 convention is given effect by the 1982 Act. It applies to Spain as a contracting party. It also applies to Gibraltar as a result of the Civil Jurisdiction and Judgments Act 1982 (Gibraltar) Order, SI 1997/2602, made under the power

a in s 39 of the 1982 Act to make provision to regulate as between the United Kingdom and specified territories (including any colony) jurisdiction and the enforcement of judgments.

[19] Where the 1968 convention applies, a defendant who is domiciled in another state or territory to which it applies can only be sued in the United Kingdom by virtue of the rules set out in the convention (see arts 2 and 3 of the

b 1968 convention). As from 1 March 2002, the 1968 convention (and the parallel Lugano Convention) will, for most contracting states be replaced, as regards proceedings commenced from that date, by Council Regulation (EC) 44/2001 (on jurisdiction and the recognition and enforcement of judgments in civil and commercial matters) (OJ 2001 L12 p 1), but the relevant provisions of the Council Regulation are not materially different.

c [20] The English court can only have jurisdiction in relation to defendants domiciled outside countries or territories to which the 1968 convention (or the Lugano Convention) applies if (a) they submit to the jurisdiction (which none has); or (b) they have been validly served within the jurisdiction (as the claimants allege Sham has been); or (c) they fall within one of the heads of CPR 6.20

d pursuant to which permission to serve a defendant outside the jurisdiction may be obtained.

Domicile

[21] The effect of art 52 of the 1968 convention is that whether a party is domiciled in the United Kingdom depends on the law of the United Kingdom.

e For the purpose of proceedings in England, an individual will be domiciled in England if and only if (a) he is resident in England and (b) the nature and circumstances of his residence indicate that he has a substantial connection with England (see s 41(3) of the 1982 Act). If a party is not domiciled in the United Kingdom then, in order to determine whether that party is domiciled in another

f contracting state, the English court applies the law of that state (see art 52). Residence is not defined but means a settled or usual place of abode, which connotes some degree of permanence or continuity (see *Bank of Dubai Ltd v Abbas* [1997] IL Pr 308 at 311–312).

[22] The domicile of a company is its seat, and in order to determine the seat, the court applies its rules of private international law (see art 53). The relevant

g rules of private international law are enacted in s 42 of the 1982 Act. A foreign corporation will have its seat in England only if its central management and control is exercised in the United Kingdom, and that management and control is exercised in England or it has a place of business in England (see s 42(3) and (4)). It will have its seat in another state or territory to which the 1968 convention

h applies, if it is incorporated under the law of that state or territory and has its registered office there, or its central management and control is exercised there (unless the courts of that state or that territory would not regard it as having its seat there) (see s 42(6) and (7)).

[23] The domicile of the defendants is only in part common ground. Where

j it is not common ground, the onus is on the claimants to show a good arguable case if they wish to establish that a defendant is domiciled in a particular state or territory (see *Seaconsar Far East Ltd v Bank Markazi Jomhouri Islami Iran* [1993] 4 All ER 456, [1994] 1 AC 438; *Canada Trust Co v Stolzenberg (No 2)* [2000] 4 All ER 481 at 491, [2002] 1 AC 1 at 13). The standard is therefore more stringent than that of showing merely a serious issue to be tried, but less stringent than proof on the balance of probabilities.

[24] The position of the parties on domicile, and, where they differ, my findings are these. (a) It is accepted that Lokumal, the first defendant, is domiciled in Hong Kong. (b) It is accepted that Murli and Pishu, the second and fifth defendants, are domiciled in India. (c) Lal, the third defendant, is domiciled in Spain, where he has been resident for 15 years, and whose law regards him as domiciled there (see art 52 of the 1968 convention); Vishal, the first claimant, said that until evidence was served he considered that Lal was resident in London, and that the London address at which he was purportedly served was his usual residence, but the claimants now accept that he is domiciled in Spain. (d) Sham, the fourth defendant, is resident in Hong Kong, and the nature and circumstances of his residence establish that he is domiciled there. The claimants have asserted, but have not put forward any cogent evidence, that he is domiciled in England. He holds a United Kingdom passport, and he occasionally stays at a flat in St John's Wood which is owned by a family trust. But he has been a permanent resident of Hong Kong since 1984. From that time he has managed and run his business from Hong Kong where his principal activity is in shipping. All his children were brought up and received the major part of their education in Hong Kong. He spends approximately nine to ten months a year in Hong Kong and the remaining two to three months mostly on business in Asia. From December 1999 until the inception of these proceedings he was in London for a total of about five days on transit from the United States to Hong Kong. The evidence is clear in the sense that there is neither the requisite residence in, nor substantial connection with, England. (e) Chellwood, the sixth defendant, has its seat (and therefore its domicile) in Gibraltar, where it is incorporated and registered, and the claimants have not supported or pursued their assertion that it is run from England with any evidence. (f) It is accepted that Bermuda Trust, the seventh defendant, has its seat (and therefore its domicile) in Bermuda, where it is incorporated and registered. (g) Mohan, the eighth defendant, says that he is domiciled in India. The claimants say that he is resident and domiciled in Gibraltar. But the evidence on his behalf is that although he does visit Gibraltar for a few months each year, he has his residence in India, and visits Gibraltar only on a tourist visa. I am satisfied that the claimants have not shown a good arguable case that he is domiciled in Gibraltar, and I will proceed on the basis that he is a non-convention defendant.

Jurisdiction under CPR 6.20

[25] The claimants sought and obtained permission to serve Lokumal, Murli, Pishu and Bermuda Trust pursuant to CPR 6.20(3) and (11). Under CPR 6.20(3) permission may be given to serve a defendant outside the jurisdiction where the defendant is a necessary or proper party to a claim made against someone on whom the claim form has been or will be served (whether the service is in England or outside England, and whether it is within or without a 1968 convention country). This is of practical relevance where there is no independent head of jurisdiction against a defendant who is not domiciled in a 1968 convention country or territory, but other defendants can be served in England, or in non-convention or convention countries.

[26] Permission may be granted under CPR 6.20(11) to serve out of the jurisdiction if—

'a claim is made for any remedy which might be obtained in proceedings to execute the trusts of a written instrument where—(a) the trusts ought to

a   be executed according to English law; and (b) the person on whom the claim
     form is to be served is a trustee of the trusts.'

     [27] I should also mention (although they have not been relied on by any
     party) CPR 6.20(14) and (15) which provide for jurisdiction, in the case of claims
     in constructive trust and restitution, where the defendant's alleged liability arises
b   out of acts committed within the jurisdiction.

     Jurisdiction under the 1968 convention
     [28] So far as defendants who are domiciled in 1968 convention countries are
     concerned, art 6(1) (jurisdiction over additional parties by virtue of proceedings
     against defendant domiciled in the forum) has no application because it is not
c   now argued that any defendant is domiciled in England. The only head of
     jurisdiction on which the claimants rely is art 5(6), which provides:

         'A person domiciled in a Contracting State may, in another Contracting
         State, be sued ...
d   (6) as settlor, trustee or beneficiary of a trust created by the operation of a
         statute, or by a written instrument, or created orally and evidenced in writing,
         in the courts of the Contracting State in which the trust is domiciled ...'

     [29] The effect of art 53 of the 1968 convention is that in proceedings in
     England the domicile of a trust depends on the law of the United Kingdom. By
     s 45(3) of the 1982 Act, a trust is domiciled in England if and only if English law is
e   the system of law with which the trust has its closest and most real connection.

     Service
     [30] I will proceed on the basis that, except in the case of Sham, where the
     question of the validity of service has an important practical effect, it is not
f   necessary for present purposes to make any finding with regard to the validity of
     service, since (where service has not been validly effected) it can be effected again
     if the English court has jurisdiction. The claimants have purported to serve all the
     defendants, except Lokumal, the first defendant. They have accepted that their
     purported service in India on Murli, the second defendant, and Pishu, the fifth
     defendant, was invalid because personal service was not effected and because the
g   service was effected by persons without proper authority.

     (IV) THE ISSUES
     [31] The principal issues are these. The first is whether the CPR have effected
     a major change to the rules of jurisdiction, so that a defendant who is not
h   domiciled or present in England can now be sued here by virtue of service on him
     at his last known residence. That in turn depends on whether the effect of the
     decision of the House of Lords in *Barclays Bank of Swaziland Ltd v Hahn* [1989] 2
     All ER 398, [1989] 1 WLR 506 (that under the Rules of the Supreme Court service
     by post within the jurisdiction was only permissible if the defendant was in
j   England at the time the writ was served or deemed to be served) survives the
     introduction of the CPR.
     [32] The practical effect of this point is that Sham was not present in England
     when the claim form was sent by post to the address at which he stays when he
     is in London. If service is valid then the court would have jurisdiction over Sham,
     and the court could give permission for service on other non-convention defendants
     as necessary or proper parties under CPR 6.20(3). Since this point does not

depend on an appreciation of the facts of the case it will be dealt with in the next section. *a*

[33] The second set of issues also relates to the non-convention defendants. It includes the question of the applicability and interpretation of CPR 6.20(11) concerning claims in relation to trusts. It also raises the issues (a) whether the claimants can satisfy the court that England is the forum conveniens for the claims against those defendants; (b) whether the permission granted by Master Bragge to *b* serve these defendants outside the jurisdiction should be set aside for non-disclosure; and (c) whether the claimants have established a serious issue to be tried on the merits of their claim.

[34] The third set of issues relates to the question whether the 1968 convention defendants (Lal and Chellwood) can be sued under art 5(6) of the *c* 1968 convention.

[35] The applicability of CPR 6.20(11) and art 5(6) raises some novel and difficult questions. There are more than 800 pages of evidence on these applications, but there is not much dispute about the essential history. Where the parties differ, I will not of course make any findings, except to the extent that it is necessary, in particular, to decide whether the claimants have established a good *d* arguable case for jurisdiction and (for CPR 6.20 purposes) a serious issue to be tried on the merits. But because the jurisdictional issues cannot be fully appreciated without an understanding of the factual circumstances they will be dealt with in section (XIV), below.

e

(V) SERVICE UNDER CPR 6.5 AND THE DECISION IN BARCLAYS BANK OF SWAZILAND LTD v HAHN

[36] The effect of CPR Pt 6 is that a claim form may be served by (among other methods) first-class post, and for that purpose by CPR 6.5(6) the place of service of an individual is the 'usual or last known residence'. By CPR 6.7(1) a document served by first class post is deemed to be served the second day after it *f* was posted (excluding Saturday, Sundays and public holidays).

[37] The claim form and particulars of claim were sent by first class post under cover of a letter from the claimants' solicitors dated 7 June 2001, addressed to Sham at a flat in Imperial Court, Prince Albert Road, St John's Wood, London. Sham is resident in Hong Kong. The flat belongs to a family trust, and he and members *g* of his family stay in the property if and when they visit England. He was not at that address in June 2001.

[38] The deemed date of service was 11 June 2001 (because 9 and 10 June were a Saturday and Sunday). Sham was in Hong Kong until 9 June 2001 and in Bombay from 10–16 June 2001. *h*

[39] Lal was served in the same way at another flat in London, but no issue arises with regard to Lal in this regard, because he is domiciled in Spain, and the English court can only assert jurisdiction over him if it is authorised to do so by the 1968 convention.

[40] The defendants rely on *Barclays Bank of Swaziland Ltd v Hahn* [1989] 2 All ER *j* 398, [1989] 1 WLR 506 and Dicey and Morris *Conflict of Laws* (13th edn, 2000) p 294 (para 11-084), for the proposition that, for jurisdictional purposes, it is not necessary that the defendant be in England when the proceedings are issued, but he must be in England when they are served.

[41] The *Barclays Bank* case was a decision on the provision in RSC Ord 10, r 1(2) that—

a   'A writ for service on a defendant within the jurisdiction may, instead of being served personally on him, be served—(a) by sending a copy of the writ by ordinary first-class post to the defendant at his usual or last known address, or (b) if there is a letter box for that address, by inserting through the letter box a copy of the writ enclosed in a sealed envelope addressed to the defendant.'

b   The date of service was, unless the contrary was shown, deemed to be the seventh day after the date on which the copy was sent to the address (see RSC Ord 10, r 1(3)).

[42] In that case the defendant's wife rented a flat in England, and he and his wife spent no more than three months a year there. A copy of the writ was c   inserted through the letterbox about two hours before the defendant arrived in England. Having been warned that the envelope had been put through the letterbox, he did not go to the flat, and returned to Geneva the next day. The result of the deeming provisions was that the writ was deemed to be served a week later, when the defendant was still in Geneva. It was held that for the d   purposes of RSC Ord 10, r 1 the defendant had to be within the jurisdiction at the time of service of the writ, but that he was duly served on the day he arrived because the evidence was that the copy writ came to his knowledge when he was within the jurisdiction.

[43] Lord Brightman said:

e   '... I accept the appellant's proposition that the defendant must be within the jurisdiction at the time when the writ is served, and I do not find it possible to agree the Court of Appeal's approach. This approach would mean that a writ could validly be served under Ord 10 on a defendant who had once an address in England but had permanently left this country and settled elsewhere ... This appears to me to outflank Ord 11 (relating to f   service of process outside the jurisdiction) in every case where the defendant was formerly resident in this country and is capable of being contacted abroad within seven days. I feel no doubt that the words "within the jurisdiction" apply to the defendant, and not to the writ for service.' (See [1989] 2 All ER 398 at 402, [1989] 1 WLR 506 at 510–511.)

g   [44] The claimants say that the decision in the *Barclays Bank* case, being a decision under the Rules of the Supreme Court, has no application for the purposes of the CPR which are 'a new procedural code' (see CPR 1.1). They rely on the approach that new provisions in the CPR are not to be limited by practices and attitudes that attach to the former rules of court, and that even provisions h   plainly based on provisions formerly found in the Rules of the Supreme Court would not necessarily be interpreted and applied in accordance with the case law built up around those provisions.

[45] They say that there is no fundamental rule of procedure that a defendant outside the jurisdiction cannot be served within the jurisdiction, and rely on *Rolph v* j   *Zolan* [1993] 4 All ER 202, [1993] 1 WLR 1305, a case on the County Court Rules, which provided that a document could be served on a defendant 'by first class post to his last known residence'. In that case the county court summons was sent by post to the defendant at his address in England at a time when he (a former solicitor) had emigrated to Spain and started a new career as a guitarist and flamenco dancer. A friend of the defendant collected his mail and posted it on to Spain with the result that he received the summons. It was held by the

Court of Appeal, first, that the County Court Rules were not limited, as a matter of construction, to service only on a defendant who was within the jurisdiction. Secondly, the Court of Appeal rejected a submission to the effect that s 76 of the County Courts Act 1984 limited the application of the County Court Rules to defendants within the jurisdiction at the time of service. Section 76 provided that 'the general principles of practice in the High Court may be adopted and applied to proceedings in a county court'. The submission was rejected for two reasons: first, s 76 was primarily directed to extending the powers of the county court where the County Court Rules made no express provision, and not to curtailing its powers. Secondly, the interpretation of RSC Ord 10, r 1 in *Barclays Bank of Swaziland Ltd v Hahn* [1989] 2 All ER 398, [1989] 1 WLR 506 was a specific limitation and not a general principle of practice within the meaning of s 76: postal service was a matter of specific rules, and not a matter of general principles of practice.

[46] *Rolph's* case is a decision on the former County Court Rules. The new regime under the CPR does not require me to follow decisions on the previous rules. In my judgment the decision does not bind me to hold that CPR 6.5 applies to defendants who are outside the jurisdiction at the time of service, or that it has effected a major change in the principles applicable to jurisdiction over persons outside England.

[47] In my judgment there are two separate reasons why Sham has not been validly served. First, the claimants have not adduced any evidence which casts doubt on Sham's evidence that the address in St John's Wood is used only occasionally by him on the rare occasions when he visits London. In these circumstances there is no evidence that it ever was a 'residence' and it therefore cannot be his 'last known residence'. Secondly, it has always been, and remains, a fundamental rule of English procedure and jurisdiction that a defendant may be served with originating process within the jurisdiction only if he is present in the jurisdiction at the time of service, or deemed service. The *Barclays Bank* case is simply an illustration of this principle (as is another case, not cited in argument, *Cadogan Properties Ltd v Mount Eden Land Ltd* [2000] IL Pr 722, in which the Court of Appeal held that if the defendant is outside England, an order for substituted service in England could not be obtained unless permission to serve proceedings out of the jurisdiction had been obtained). CPR Pt 6 contains general rules about service of documents and does not only apply to service of a claim form (see *Godwin v Swindon BC* [2001] EWCA Civ 1478, [2001] 4 All ER 641, [2002] 1 WLR 997), but I do not consider that CPR 6.5 has swept away the general principle so far as it relates to service of the claim form.

(VI) THE FACTS: THE 1943 AND 1946 TRUSTS

The 1943 trust

[48] The 1943 trust was established by Kishinchand Chellaram in April 1943 for the benefit of the wives and male children of Shewakram and Lokumal. The funds were to be divided equally into two separate trust funds: (1) the Lachmibai trust fund, for the wife and male children of Shewakram; and (2) the Kamlabai trust fund, for the wife and male children of Lokumal.

[49] The net income of the respective trust funds was to be provided to the wife for the support, maintenance, education and advancement and otherwise for the benefit of her and her children born before the date of the creation of the trust (ie in the case of the Lachmibai trust fund, Mohan and Harish). Lachmibai

a had, during her lifetime, absolute discretion as to the use of the revenue derived from the trust assets of the Lachmibai trust fund. Upon the death of the survivor of Lachmibai and Shewakram, the trust fund would be held by the trusts such that that the male descendants of Shewakram would obtain on distribution an equal share of the trust assets depending on their respective father's share.

[50] The original trustees of the 1943 trust were Tahilram, Shewakram and
b Lokumal. After Tahilram and Shewakram died, Mr Advani and Murli were appointed trustees. After Mr Advani died, Lal and Sham also became trustees, by deed of appointment dated 5 January 1993. The present trustees are Lokumal, Murli, Lal and Sham.

[51] The present beneficiaries of the 1943 trust assets are: as to the Lachmibai trust fund (representing 50% of the whole): Mohan (25% of the whole), and the
c claimants (12.5% each of the whole); as to the Kamlabai trust fund: Kamlabai (50% of the whole) during her lifetime, thereafter Lokumal during his lifetime, and thereafter Sham and Lal (25% each of the whole).

[52] The trust monies were invested in real estate in Bombay, which is now called Central Building No 2, which was acquired in May 1943. The property is
d fully tenanted. There is also a Bombay bank account which is used for the administrative costs associated with the administration of Central Building No 2 and its tenancies.

The 1946 trust

e [53] The 1946 trust was established by Kishinchand Chellaram in July 1946. The trust was established for the benefit of Lachmibai and the male children of Shewakram. The net income of the trust fund was to be provided to Lachmibai during her lifetime or to Shewakram in the event that he survived her. Upon the death of the survivor of Lachmibai and Shewakram, the trust fund was to be held by the trustees to divide amongst the male children and all the male issue of the
f male line descending from Shewakram per stirpes in equal shares. Any male descendent had to attain the age of majority before receiving his share. Until that time, the trustees were required to provide the net income for the maintenance, upbringing, education and general welfare of the sons of Lachmibai and Shewakram.

g [54] The original trustees were Shewakram, Lokumal and Murli, and Lokumal and Murli are the surviving trustees. The present beneficiaries of the 1946 trust are: Mohan (50%) and the claimants (25% each).

[55] The trust monies were invested in property, a 30% share of a building in Bombay called Carmichael House. There is also a Bombay bank account which
h is used for the administrative costs associated with the administration of Carmichael House and its tenancies. There was also a trust part interest in another building on the site, Chellaram House, but that interest was, it would seem, disposed of some time ago.

Complaints concerning the 1943 and 1946 trusts
j
[56] The figures put before the court indicate that the rental income from the two properties is relatively modest: in the case of Central Building No 2, it barely breaks even, and in the case of Carmichael House the expenditure exceeds income by more than £1,000 p a. The defendants say that because the tenancies for the properties in the 1943 and 1946 trusts come under the Indian Rent Control Act (whereby tenants' occupation is protected and rental increases are limited to

nominal annual amounts) it is difficult to value the properties or the claimants'
interest in them.   *a*

[57] In 1998 the trustees of the 1943 trust requested the beneficiaries to pay a
contribution to the expenses of Central Building No 2 to make up a shortfall.
After Indian lawyers for the trustees sought approval from the beneficiaries to
distribute the trust assets, the claimants' London solicitors in early 2001 sought
inter alia full accounts for the 1943 and 1946 trusts for the period 'pre-1980' to the   *b*
date of their letter. In correspondence thereafter they took the position that
information supplied was not sufficient, and that their clients had no intention of
releasing the trustees from their obligations. The claimants then commenced
these proceedings, making the allegations which are set out in [124], below.

Governing law of the 1943 and 1946 trusts   *c*

[58] There can be no doubt that the 1943 and 1946 trusts, and their administration,
are governed by Indian law, and the claimants accept that the governing law is
that of India, and that the Indian courts can exercise jurisdiction over them. They
were created in India by an Indian settlor over Indian property with trustees who
were then resident in India, and were drafted by Indian lawyers, and are registered   *d*
in Bombay. They refer specifically to the Indian Income Tax Act for authorised
payments and the Indian Trusts Act 1882 for authorised investments. The only
assets are property in Bombay and the bank accounts used for their
administration. The administration of the trusts is dealt with in India under
powers of attorney granted by the trustees to directors of the Indian companies   *e*
of the Lokumal or Tahilram Groups.

[59] There is no case for any other governing law. The only foreign connection
is the residence of three of the trustees in the case of the 1943 trust (Lokumal and
Sham in Hong Kong and Lal in Spain) and of Lokumal in the case of the 1946
trust. Neither trust, nor its administration, has any connection with England.

                                                                           f

(VII) THE 1975 TRUSTS

[60] On 14 February 1975, two trusts were created by Harish (the father of the
claimants) and Mohan (the claimants' uncle) (the 1975 trusts and separately the
Harish trust and the Mohan trust). The 1975 trusts were drafted in Bombay by
Mr Advani.
                                                                           g

Background: Kaycee (Bermuda) Ltd and Chellsons (Bermuda) Ltd

[61] When Shewakram died in 1949, his interest in the Chellaram family
trading enterprises outside India was inherited by Lachmibai, his widow. Prior
to the death of Shewakram, the Chellaram family businesses were already being   *h*
conducted mainly by Lokumal and Murli. In about 1960, the Chellaram businesses
outside India became subsidiaries of a Bermudan holding company, Kaycee
(Bermuda) Ltd (Kaycee), with shareholdings of 36% for the Lokumal Group, 34%
for the Tahilram Group and 30% for the Shewakram group (which at that time
was effectively represented by Lachmibai, Shewakram's widow).

[62] In about 1973, the Lokumal Group and Tahilram Group decided to effect   *j*
a separation of their trading interests outside India from one another with
Lachmibai opting to retain her 30% interest in both groups. To implement this
separation the Lokumal Group was to control Kaycee as the holding company for
the Lokumal Group businesses and the Tahilram Group was to control another
Bermudan company, Chellsons (Bermuda) Ltd (Chellsons), as the holding company

a   for the Tahilram Group businesses. Lachmibai was to have a 15/51 interest in Kaycee and a 15/49 interest in Chellsons, ie 30% of the whole. The Lokumal Group (Lokumal, Lal and Sham) was to have 36/51 of Kaycee, and the Tahilram Group (Murli, Pishu and Ram) was to have 34/49 of Chellsons. The businesses to be allotted to each group were settled by an arbitration award made by Mr Hobart Moore in 1974.

b
The trusts

[63] According to the defendants, in about 1973 or 1974, Mr Advani advised Lachmibai, for Indian fiscal and exchange control reasons, to give one half of her 30% interest in Kaycee and Chellsons to each of her sons, Mohan and Harish, and c   require them to settle their shares in discretionary trusts with Lachmibai remaining as a named beneficiary in both those settlements. It seems that because Mohan and Harish were non-resident Indians (NRIs) the shares would not be subject to Indian tax or exchange control. Vishal's evidence is that the gift was an absolute one and quite separate from the creation of discretionary trusts, but nothing turns on this.

d
[64] The assets of the 1975 trusts established by Harish and Mohan were the shareholdings in Kaycee and Chellsons. Mohan and Harish were the respective settlors. The original trustees were Ram, and Mr K Rupchand and Mr G R Bharwani (who managed the Chellsons London company).

[65] The beneficiaries were in the case of the Harish Trust: Lachmibai, e   Mohan, Radhika, the claimants, the wife and any children of Mohan, children and remoter issue of the father and mother of the settlor (Shewakram and Lachmibai), and the spouses of the aforesaid and the spouses of any adopted child of the settlor. In the case of the Mohan Trust the beneficiaries were: Lachmibai, Harish, Radhika, the claimants, children and remoter issue of the father and f   mother of the settlor (Shewakram and Lachmibai), spouses of the beneficiaries listed above and the spouses of any adopted children of the settlor.

[66] The trust deeds provided that during the lifetime of the respective settlors, and in the event that the whole or part of the trust fund consisted of shares in Kaycee or Chellsons, the trustees would not without the written consent of the settlor dispose or deal with the shares. The vesting day was the g   period of 20 years or earlier when the claimants attained the age of majority or any day, which the trustees declared to be that day. What the beneficiaries obtained on the vesting day was at the absolute discretion of the trustees (cl 4(c)).

[67] Clause 15(a) of each of the trust deeds provided:

h
'Notwithstanding anything herein contained if it shall appear to the Trustees beneficial to the Trust Fund and in the interest of the Beneficiaries so to do the Trustees may at any time or times and from time to time by Deed declare that this Settlement shall from the date of such declaration or where any date therefor is specified therein from such date take effect in j   accordance with the Law of some other place in any part of the World and that the forum for the administration hereof shall thenceforth be the Courts of that place and as and from the date aforesaid the Laws of the Country named in such declaration shall be the Laws applicable to this Settlement and the Courts of that Country shall be the forum for the administration thereof but subject to power conferred by this Clause.'

a

Eskay 1 formed to hold Kaycee and Chellsons shares

[68] In October 1976, probably on the advice of Mr Advani, Eskay (Bermuda) Ltd (Eskay 1), a Bermudan company, was formed to hold those shares in Kaycee and Chellsons which were subject to the 1975 trusts. The shares in Eskay 1 were expressly held by Mohan, Harish and Conyers Dill & Pearman (the well-known *b* Bermuda law firm) for the trustees of the 1975 trusts.

Change in trustees and separation of Lokumal Group and Tahilram Group interests

[69] In 1981 the following events occurred. First, Mr Rupchand and Mr Bharwani retired as trustees of the 1975 trusts, the continuation as trustee of Ram was *c* confirmed and Sham, Lal, Murli and Mr Advani were appointed as new trustees of each of the 1975 trusts.

[70] Secondly, there was a restructuring of the interests of the 1975 trusts in the Chellaram businesses. Prior to the reconstruction the trustees of each of the 1975 trusts contained members of the Lokumal Group (Lal and Sham) and the *d* Tahilram Group (Ram and Murli), and the interest of the trusts in Kaycee (the Lokumal Group vehicle) and Chellsons (the Tahilram Group vehicle) was held through Eskay 1. According to the defendants, the Lokumal Group and Tahilram Group wished to complete the separation of their business interests by also separating their responsibility as trustees of the shares in Kaycee and Chellsons.

[71] In addition, according to the defendants (and not contradicted by the *e* claimants), at that time it was the practice to reinvest the profits of Kaycee and Chellsons in the businesses and accordingly neither Kaycee nor Chellsons declared dividends for distribution to members. Lachmibai wished to receive a dividend for the Shewakram family and, in order to ensure income for the trusts, which held their interests through Eskay 1, it was decided that a class of *f* preferential shares in Kaycee and Chellsons would be created to enable dividends to be paid so as to benefit only the trusts. As will appear, the claimants take a radically different view of the change.

Reconstruction of share capital of Kaycee and Chellsons

[72] The following steps were taken. First, the shares held by Eskay 1 in *g* Kaycee and Chellsons were converted into 'B' shares, and all the remaining shares (ie those held by the Lokumal Group and the Tahilram Group) in Kaycee and Chellsons were designated 'A' shares. The 'B' shares were given a minimum guaranteed and preferential dividend of 6% but had restricted voting rights. The minimum guarantee in respect of dividend did not affect the right of the 'B' *h* shareholders to receive dividends pari passu with the right to dividends payable in respect of the 'A' shares.

[73] The defendants say that the restriction on voting rights was a recognition of the fact that the holders were not interested, and had voluntarily not participated, in the management of the relevant companies. The voting restrictions *j* did not apply to certain important decisions of Kaycee or Chellsons, including any consideration of merger of the company with or into any other corporation; any sale of the company or any sale of a substantial portion of the company's assets; and the dissolution or winding up of the company.

[74] The claimants assert in the particulars of claim (as their parents did in *Chellaram v Chellaram (No 1)*) that this reconstruction diminished the value of the

a   assets of the 1975 trusts through the creation of 'B' shares, which were of less
value than the unconverted shares which they represented. But they do not say
why the 'B' shares were less valuable than the 'A' shares, and Vishal does not
answer the evidence of Sham that the 'A' and 'B' shares were treated equally in
the only transaction in which their value was relevant, to which I will turn in the
next section.

b

Kayshewak and Eskay 2 hold shares in Kaycee and Chellsons: trustees rearranged

[75] Second, Eskay 1 was replaced as the shareholder in Kaycee and Chellsons by
two new Bermudan companies, one of which was ultimately called Kayshewak Ltd
(Kayshewak), which held the trust interests in Kaycee and the other called Eskay
c   (Bermuda) Ltd (Eskay 2) (after Eskay 1 had been placed into liquidation), which
held the trust interests in Chellsons. All of the shares in Kayshewak and Eskay 2
were held (in the case of the Eskay 2 shares through a nominee company) for the
trustees of the 1975 trusts.

[76] Third, the trust assets were divided into two funds, an 'A' fund
comprising the Kayshewak shares; and a 'B' fund comprising the Eskay 2 shares.
d   The trustees were rearranged so that members of the Lokumal Group (Lokumal,
Lal and Sham) became trustees of the 'A' fund, ie Kayshewak shares, Kayshewak
being the company which held the shares in Kaycee, the Lokumal Group
company. Members of the Tahilram Group (Ram, Murli and Pishu) became
trustees of the 'B' fund Eskay 2 shares, Eskay 2 being the company which held the
e   shares in Chellsons, the Tahilram Group company. Mr Advani was a trustee of
both funds.

(IX) THE PROCEEDINGS IN SINGAPORE AND IN ENGLAND IN 1983/1985

[77] According to the claimants, in May or August (both dates are found in the
f   documents) 1983 the trustees of the 1975 trusts ceased making payments to
Harish and Radhika who had until then been receiving $250,000 pa from the
family interests. In August 1983 they were removed as directors of K Chellaram
& Sons (Far East) Pte Ltd, a Chellaram Singapore company, and allegations of
fraud were made against them in Singapore proceedings by Murli (who then had
overall responsibility for managing the business affairs of the Tahilram Group).

g   [78] In December 1983, Harish and Radhika and their sons, the claimants in
these proceedings (as minors), brought proceedings in the High Court in London
against the then trustees of the 1975 trusts (Lokumal, Murli, Lal, Sham, Pishu,
Ram, and Mr Advani) in *Chellaram v Chellaram (No 1)*. They sought inter alia
accounts in respect of both trusts from the dates of their creation, and an order
h   removing the defendants as trustees and appointment of new trustees in their
place.

[79] The complaints by the plaintiffs in *Chellaram v Chellaram (No 1)* were that
the trustees had failed to prepare and provide proper accounts of the trusts; the
effect of the conversion of the shares into class 'B' shares had diminished their
j   value, and the defendants had procured the conversion in breach of trust for their
own benefit; no reasonable trustee could properly have declined to exercise his
discretion to provide Radhika and Harish with an income equivalent to that
which had been cut off, and to produce such income; and the allegations of fraud
in the Singapore proceedings had caused such a breakdown of trust that it had
become impossible for the defendants to exercise their powers and discretions
vis-à-vis the plaintiffs in good faith.

[**80**] Each of the defendants entered appearances or instructed their solicitors
Norton, Rose, Botterill & Roche (Norton Rose) to accept service on their behalf.
The defendants then sought a stay of the proceedings on the ground that England
was not the forum conveniens.

[**81**] Scott J refused a stay (see *Chellaram v Chellaram* [1985] 1 All ER 1043,
[1985] Ch 409). He did not decide on the governing law of the trusts. He said that
he was originally strongly inclined to regard the law of India as the proper law of
the settlements, but he had become less certain. The beneficiaries were an Indian
family, and the trustees were all Indian in origin, and the settlements were drawn
up in Bombay, by an Indian practitioner, and the settlors were Indian in origin
and domiciled in India at the date of the settlement. Those factors pointed
strongly to the law of India being the proper law. But the trust property was
Bermudan, and the underlying assets, in the form of the operating companies,
were all situated outside India, and the purpose of the settlements was in part to
escape Indian taxation and Indian exchange control. But, most important, was
the identity of the three original trustees, two of whom were permanently
resident in England, and the third being the member of the family who in 1975
appeared to have the closest connection with England. The inference was
inescapable that the parties to the settlement contemplated that administration
would take place in London.

[**82**] Although India was a more convenient locality as far as the personal
circumstances of the parties and any witnesses were concerned, a stay was
refused principally on these grounds. There was some doubt whether the
Bombay court would have jurisdiction over the non-Indian defendants, even if
they submitted to its jurisdiction. It might take from seven to ten years to get a
hearing, and a minimum delay of seven years might expose the plaintiffs to
considerable hardship. It was common ground that the payments had ceased and
that the financial position of Harish and his family had correspondingly
worsened. A delay might represent a serious injustice. The commencement of
the action in England was not an exercise in forum shopping, since there was
always a strong connection between England and the settlements, and between
England and the Chellaram family. Administration of the settlements was
intended at the date of the settlements to take place in England. Such
administration as had taken place since the date of the settlement had taken place
in England, four of the defendants held British passports, and all the defendants
as well as the plaintiffs regularly spent time in England. Each of the defendants
was either served personally or voluntarily submitted to the jurisdiction by giving
instructions to Norton Rose to accept service.

(X) SETTLEMENT OF THE PROCEEDINGS AND THE SALE OF THE SHEWAKRAM TRUST
INTERESTS IN KAYCEE AND CHELLSONS TO THE LOKUMAL AND TAHILRAM GROUPS

Background

[**83**] In 1985 an agreement was reached whereby the Singapore and London
proceedings were discontinued, and which was intended to turn into cash the
interests of the beneficiaries of the 1975 trusts in Kaycee and Chellsons. According
to the defendants in these proceedings, relations within the family had reached the
point where each side wanted a clean break. The Lokumal Group and the
Tahilram Group wished to have absolute control and ownership of their businesses
and the Shewakram Group no longer wished to be tied into those businesses but
to be paid out their share.

a [84] The method by which this aim was achieved must be understood, according to the defendants, in the light of the tax advice the family had received. They say that it was understood by the trustees, following written advice from the accountants Moore, Stephens & Co (Moore, Stephens) to Norton Rose, that the decision in *Chellaram v Chellaram (No 1)* that the administration of the trust assets was conducted in the United Kingdom and that some of the trustees had

b English connections (Scott J having held that the trustees had English addresses and appeared to visit England regularly), led to a risk that the Inland Revenue would argue that all revenue flowing from Kayshewak and Eskay 2 to the 1975 trusts would be liable to United Kingdom tax. In any event, the cost of defending a lengthy inquiry by the Inland Revenue would be extremely expensive. The advice of the accountants in November 1984 was therefore that none of the

c trustees should be United Kingdom-resident, that the current trustees should resign and an independent, professional offshore trustee be appointed in the Channel Islands or Bermuda.

[85] The claimants allege that the appointment of Bermuda Trust was for the purpose of enabling breaches of trust to be effected by seeking to avoid the

d necessity for court approval in England under RSC Ord 80, r 10, but Vishal says nothing about the evidence that it was solely for tax reasons. RSC Ord 80, r 10 provided that no compromise of a monetary claim by an infant would, so far as it related to that claim, be valid without the approval of the court.

Heads of agreement and supplemental agreement: change of trustees and
e *agreement to sell shares*

[86] The following steps were then taken. First, on 29 March 1985 heads of agreement (negotiated mainly in Bombay and executed in Bombay, Hong Kong and Singapore) were agreed between (a) Harish and Radhika on behalf of themselves and the claimants (as minors), (b) Lokumal, Lal, and Sham, and

f (c) Murli, Pishu and Ram. It was agreed that all the trustees of the 1975 trusts would resign in favour of the Bank of Bermuda, who would act as trustee in respect of both of the 1975 trusts; the assets of the trusts would vest to the extent of one-third each in (a) Radhika and Harish and the claimants; (b) Lachmibai; and (c) Mohan. Radhika and Harish would then sell their shareholdings in Kayshewak to the Lokumal Group (Lokumal, Lal and Sham) and in Eskay 2 to the Tahilram

g Group (Murli, Pishu and Ram).

[87] The price of the shares to be sold was to be fixed by arbitrators, with Radhika and Harish appointing Mr M B Chanrai (a successful international businessman and the brother-in-law of Harish and Mohan) as their arbitrator, and the purchasers appointing Mr Advani as their arbitrator. They were to conduct

h two separate, final and binding arbitrations in respect of the Eskay 2 shares on the one hand and the Kayshewak shares on the other. It was also provided that because the arbitrations would be family arbitrations and the arbitrators had been known to all parties for a long time, the parties were to be barred from moving the court for their removal for misconduct; and that the parties might be heard,

j but were not entitled to legal or accountancy assistance at the hearings.

[88] The agreement was conditional on withdrawal of proceedings in England and Singapore, but the parties had the right to seek redress from the courts if the arbitration failed. Certain payments were to be made upon withdrawal of the litigation on account for the share sales. Part of the proceeds were to be used by Harish and Radhika to reduce their indebtedness to the Singapore company which had been the subject of the Singapore proceedings.

[89] Clause 18 provided:

a

'The parties expressly agree that only the courts of Bermuda shall have jurisdiction over this Agreement and agree to exclude the UK courts from any jurisdiction whatsoever over this Agreement directly or indirectly.'

[90] Second, on 31 May 1985 a deed supplemental to the heads of agreement *b* (the supplemental agreement) was entered into between Lachmibai, Harish, Radhika (on their own behalf and that of their children, the claimants), Mohan, Lokumal, Lal, Sham, Murli, Pishu, Ram and Mr Advani.

[91] They agreed to appoint the Bank of Bermuda as trustee in place of the family trustees, and Mohan, Harish and Radhika (both themselves and on behalf of their children) ('the beneficiaries') agreed not to challenge or impugn the *c* appointment. All rights against the family trustees that the beneficiaries might have had were given up as well as any rights to the Kayshewak and Eskay 2 shares once transferred to the relevant purchasers. In addition it was agreed that a letter of wishes would be presented to the new trustee which was scheduled to the deed. The effect of the letter of wishes was to indicate that the intention was to *d* make an early appointment to Harish and Radhika and their sons of two-thirds of the Mohan trust fund, with a later appointment of one-third of each of the trust funds to Lachmibai and one-third of the Harish trust fund to Mohan. The supplemental agreement was signed by the parties in Jersey, Singapore and Bombay in May 1985. Since the supplemental agreement was supplemental to the heads of agreement it was no doubt impliedly governed by the same choice *e* of law and choice of jurisdiction provisions.

[92] Third, on the same day Bermuda Trust was appointed under the powers in the 1975 trusts as a new trustee in place of the Chellaram family trustees. Mr Advani remained as trustee.

f

Choice of law and jurisdiction for 1975 trusts

[93] Fourth, on 31 May 1985, purportedly pursuant to cl 15 of the 1975 trust deeds, the Chellaram family trustees declared in relation to each of the 1975 trusts:

'I. This settlement shall continue to take effect in accordance with the *g* Hindu Family Law being the proper law of the Settlement. 2. Without prejudice to the provisions of paragraph (I) above the forum for the administration of the Settlement shall henceforth be Bermuda.'

[94] The claimants suggest that the declarations were ineffective because they *h* seem to bear a date of 10 June 1985, which is after the trustees resigned, but there is other evidence that execution took place on 31 May 1985. In any event, it is likely that this choice was not authorised by cl 15(a). Even if the reference to Hindu family law is to be taken as a choice of Indian law, cl 15(a) does not authorise the choice of different laws to govern the trust and its administration. *j*

[95] Later that year, in October/November 1985, Bermuda Trust and Mr Advani executed deeds in respect of each of the 1975 trusts declaring:

'The Settlement shall henceforth take effect in accordance with the laws of the said Islands of Bermuda [and] the Courts of the said Islands of Bermuda shall henceforth be the forum for the administration of the Settlement.'

a
[96] Only the deed relating to the Harish trust has been located, but I am satisfied for the purposes of this application by the contemporary correspondence that there were deeds for both trusts.

Appointment of shares

b
[97] Fifth, Bermuda Trust and Mr Advani as trustees of the Mohan and Harish Trusts made the following appointments: (a) under the Mohan trust, on 29 July 1985, 50,000 Kayshewak shares were appointed to Harish (25%), Radhika (25%) and the claimants (25% each); and on 18 November 1985, 25,000 Kayshewak shares were appointed to Lachmibai; and (b) under the Harish trust, on 18 November 1985, 50,000 Kayshewak shares were appointed to Mohan, and 25,000 Kayshewak shares were appointed to Lachmibai.

c
[98] The second 18 November 1985 deed appointed the same number of Eskay 2 shares in the same proportions, and I infer that this was so in the case of the other appointments also.

Arbitration

d
[99] The 'B' shares of Kaycee were the principal assets of Kayshewak. In November 1984 Moore, Stephens had arrived at a valuation range of between $17 and $21 as an approximate fair value (based on the accounts to 30 June 1983) for both the 'A' and 'B' shares of Kaycee, on the assumption that no distinction was to be drawn between the two classes of shares.

e
[100] Following a formal hearing in Jersey at the offices of Moore, Stephens, the arbitrators on 29 July 1985 valued the Kayshewak shares at $45 per share, which represented a valuation of the Kaycee shares at $25. The amount due to Radhika and Harish and their sons was therefore $2,250,000. The award recited that the arbitrators had determined the value and that the parties had agreed to the valuation and had requested the arbitrators to make the award by consent.

f
The Kayshewak award states: 'This Award shall be enforced either in the Courts of Jersey where it has been made or in Bermuda and in no other jurisdiction.' It was signed by all parties, including Harish and Radhika on behalf of the claimants.

[101] The Eskay 2 arbitration resulted in a valuation of £180,000. The consent award stated: 'The law of Bermuda shall apply to this award.'

g
[102] The defendants have put in detailed evidence to support their contention that the valuation of the Kayshewak and Eskay 2 shares was done on a proper basis. According to the defendants, the valuations by Moore, Stephens and the arbitrators were all made without any distinction being made between 'A' shares and 'B' shares of Kaycee and Chellsons. They say that at no time since the delivery of the awards in 1985 until these proceedings had Harish, Radhika

h
or the claimants complained about the values arrived at by the arbitrators; during the course of the valuation the arbitrators reviewed all relevant company files documents and records, and were also afforded the assistance of Moore, Stephens; the arbitrators also heard formal and informal representations from all parties, over a period of about two months. They relied on the computations and

j
statements prepared by Moore, Stephens and also sought independent verification of the values of real properties and vessels and various other important key assets.

[103] The defendants say that the price of £180,000 at which the Eskay 2 shares were valued was fair and generous because their value was directly dependent on the value of its shareholding in Chellsons, which in turn was dependent on the financial position of the Chellsons Group as a whole, which was very grave because the Central Bank of Nigeria had defaulted on bills payable to Chellsons

which were security for debts owed by Chellsons to banks and other lenders. The
defendants say that contemporary documents show that at the time when the *a*
valuation of the Eskay shares took place, the Chellsons Group was fighting for its
survival. The claimants have not contradicted this evidence.

[104] The claimants say that the arbitrators based their valuation on the
financial advice provided by accountants employed by the companies controlled
by the defendants who bought the shares. The particulars of claim do not put *b*
forward any positive case. It is simply said that the claimants do not accept the
valuations.

(XI) COMPLETION OF SALE AND TREATMENT OF PROCEEDS OF SALE AGREEMENT BY
CLAIMANTS' PARENTS: KAYSHEWAK AWARD SUPPLEMENTAL AGREEMENT

[105] By an agreement dated 7 August 1985 and signed in Jersey, called the *c*
Kayshewak Award Supplemental Agreement, Harish and Radhika agreed with
the purchasers of the Kayshewak shares (Lokumal, Lal, Sham and Chellwood)
that during the minority of their sons, the claimants, or unless the Bermuda court
should otherwise order, they would invest the proceeds of sale of the claimants'
share of the sale of the Kayshewak shares (50%) in investments authorised under *d*
the laws of Bermuda.

[106] They represented to the purchasers that they had agreed to sell the
shares of their sons on the same terms as all other selling shareholders in the belief
that the sale was on the best terms reasonably obtainable and 'in the best interests
and advantage' of their sons (as minors). They covenanted to procure that as and
when their sons came of age each of them would ratify and confirm the sale, and *e*
until such ratification they would keep the purchasers indemnified against any
claims by or on behalf of the claimants.

Completion of sale and receipt of proceeds

[107] Harish and Radhika instructed the new trustees of the 1975 trusts *f*
(Mr Advani and Bermuda Trust) to transfer the 50,000 shares in Kayshewak
which Harish and Radhika held for themselves and the claimants to Chellwood
as nominated purchaser. Harish and Radhika were subsequently paid the money
for those shares by Chellwood as set out below.

[108] The awards related only to the shares in which Harish and Radhika and
their sons had an interest. The remaining 100,000 Kayshewak shares in the hands *g*
of the 1975 trustees were transferred to Mohan and Lachmibai by a deed of
appointment executed in respect of both 1975 trusts on 18 November 1985, and
were sold to Chellwood for the same price as fixed in the consent award. I infer
that the Eskay 2 shares were treated in a similar manner when they (or perhaps
shares in a nominee company) were transferred to Murli, Pishu and Ram (or their *h*
company).

[109] Following execution of the deeds of appointment the Bank of Bermuda Ltd
wrote to the Gibraltar lawyers who had dealt with the appointment of Bank of
Bermuda earlier, Triay & Triay, on 2 December 1985 to say: 'These Deeds have
effectively terminated the Settlements, subject to completion of the transfers of *j*
ownership of the Kashewak and Eskay shares.'

[110] Harish and Radhika were paid the sums due to them and their sons for
the Kayshewak shares. Vishal accepted in an affidavit in the Indian proceedings
that Harish and Radhika had been paid in full. $1,125,000 represented the sum
due to the claimants. In respect of that sum, their parents received two amounts
of $375,000 on 7 August 1985 and on 14 October 1985. A third instalment of

a $375,000 was included in a payment on 20 October 1988 of $630,066·53 to the trustees of the Geneva Trust, which is referred to below. The $535,000 capital component of the final instalment paid by Chellwood was used to make the payments of $267,500 to each of the claimants in 1992 and 1995, when they signed the releases referred to below. There is no dispute about these payments.

[111] The Eskay 2 shares had been valued in the 1985 arbitration at £180,000.
b Not all of the price has been paid. £50,000 of the Eskay award was paid to the claimants' parents in 1986. It is said by on behalf of Murli and Pishu that other payments in satisfaction of the award were made by Ram. There is evidence from Murli's son, Suresh Murli Chellaram, that both claimants, after they had reached the age of majority, pressed Murli for payment of the balance of the sale price, which Murli had not paid because of the financial position of the Tahilram
c Group. Vishal does not deny that he asked for payment, although he says he did not 'press' for payment.

Geneva Trust and execution of releases

[112] There were proceedings in Bermuda by Lal and Sham against Harish
d and Radhika in connection with the final payments due to them for the benefit of the claimants in connection with the sale of the Kayshewak shares. There was no evidence before me on the nature of the action, but it was discontinued on condition that Radhika established a trust in Geneva over the then unpaid proceeds of sale due to the claimants from Chellwood for the Kayshewak shares. The trust fund was $630,000. The trustees were United Overseas Bank and Trust
e Co (Bahamas) Ltd and P N Bhagwati J. Bhagwati J was a former Chief Justice of India (and is now chairman of the United Nations Human Rights Committee), and he was involved in settling the terms of the trust. Harish was not a party to the trust deed, but on the date of its execution, 30 June 1988, he approved its terms in the form of a separate confirmation.

f [113] The trustees were to hold the trust fund as to half each for the claimants on their attaining 21. It was to be invested, prior to distribution, as permitted by the laws of Bermuda. The income of the trust prior to their attaining majority could be applied for their benefit, maintenance and advancement, such sums being payable to their parents or guardians upon receipt of an undertaking to use the funds as directed.

g [114] The deed provided that the trustees should not pay and distribute the trust fund to either of the claimants until each of them had executed a deed of release. If they did not execute a deed of release within 90 days of their attaining their majority, then the trust in their favour would determine and the fund would be held for Radhika and Harish to be applied solely to meet any liability under the
h indemnity in favour of Lokumal, Lal and Sham in the Kayshewak Award supplemental agreement. The release was to be in favour of Lokumal, Lal, Sham and Chellwood in respect of any matter arising out of *Chellaram v Chellaram (No 1)*, the Kayshewak consent award or the sale of shares pursuant thereto or otherwise howsoever arising during the minority of the releasor in any way touching or
j concerning any interest of the releasor in Kayshewak or the operation thereof or of any subsidiary or associate or the trusts affecting the same.

[115] Each of the claimants signed releases and were paid out part of their share of the Geneva Trust fund ($267,500 each) when they reached the age of 21 on 18 June 1992, in the case of Vishal, and 25 April 1995, in the case of Ashwin. The releases recited the *Chellaram v Chellaram (No 1)* proceedings, and also that the litigation had been settled by the submission to arbitration and the

Kayshewak consent award; that their interests in the proceeds of sale of the shares in Kayshewak was $562,500 each; that Lal and Sham had purchased the shares for Chellwood, and had paid $375,000 of that sum to Radhika and Harish as trustees for the claimants, and the balance had been paid to the trustees of the Geneva trust.

[116] Vishal says that if he had not signed within 90 days he would have received nothing, and he needed the money to go to university in England: but in the event he bought a property for his family and he needed the money for the Indian litigation dealt with in the next section.

(XII) INDIAN PROCEEDINGS

[117] In 1991 the claimants in these proceedings commenced proceedings in the High Court at Bombay against 18 members of the Chellaram family (including all of the individual defendants in these proceedings) and against seven Chellaram companies or partnerships.

[118] The proceedings were, according to Vishal, instituted on the claimants' behalf by their mother Radhika, after her mother-in-law Lachmibai had excluded the claimants from a family-owned property which they regarded as an ancestral home. In those proceedings it is alleged that the business of Kishinchand, and Lokumal, Tahilram, and Shewakram, was run as a joint Hindu Undivided Family (HUF), and that the HUF had worldwide concerns and firms, situated all over the world.

[119] Consequently it is claimed that, through their father Harish, they are entitled to a one-ninth share in the entire property and assets of the joint Hindu family properties of the HUF, or alternatively, if the Shewakram group had separated, for a declaration that they are jointly entitled to a one-third share in the Shewakram group of the Kishinchand HUF properties. The prayer seeks a declaration that the plaintiffs are jointly entitled to a one-ninth share of the property or properties belonging to the HUF, disclosed and undisclosed, with particulars of the disclosed properties in an exhibit, which includes Carmichael House and Central Building No 2.

[120] An interim order for disclosure of all properties and business assets in India was also sought, in which it was submitted by Vishal that it was obvious that all the businesses and properties, within India, held by the Kishinchand Chellaram family were all the joint Hindu family businesses and properties in which the claimants had an undivided share, right, title and interest.

[121] In one of his affidavits in support of the application (4 November 1996) Vishal submitted that the existence of an HUF in India and abroad was clearly established by inter alia the allegations in the statement of claim in *Chellaram v Chellaram (No 1)*, the 1985 heads of agreement, the supplemental agreement, the Kayshewak consent award, and the Eskay consent award. The affidavit concluded by submitting that although these agreements related to the joint businesses and properties outside India, it was obvious that all the businesses and properties in India were all subject to the joint Hindu family regime.

[122] Interim relief was refused by Rebello J on 19 August 1999. He noted that the heads of all the three families had chosen to deny the existence of an HUF. He said that the various trusts (without specifying which) created by which the plaintiffs had become beneficiaries negated the concept of an HUF, since if there was an HUF and if the plaintiffs were members of it, they could not be made beneficiaries in respect of the HUF property.

a [123] The claimants' position is that although the subject matter of the Indian proceedings includes properties in Bombay which are subject to the trusts, the proceedings do not relate to the trusts or their assets; and that the references to the worldwide assets of the HUF were purely historical, and that the proceedings related only to Indian assets, and that was why no foreign companies were joined as defendants.

b
(XIII) THE PRESENT PROCEEDINGS

[124] The allegations in the particulars of claim in relation to the 1943 trust and the 1946 trust (now discontinued) are as follows. (1) Lokumal, Murli, Lal and Sham have let the properties in Bombay to persons connected to themselves on terms which have resulted in the income being less (or allegedly less) than the c running costs of the properties, and have asked the claimants for a contribution to the losses being made. (2) No proper accounts have been provided despite requests being made by the claimants in 1998 and by their solicitors in January 2001, and the claimants have received no part of their interest in the capital or income of the trusts and seek the removal of the present trustees accordingly.

d [125] The relief claimed is that those defendants deliver accounts of the capital and income of the 1943 trust and 1946 trust from 14 February 1997 to date, and be removed as trustees of the settlements and be replaced by fit and proper persons.

[126] With regard to the 1975 trusts, the allegations are as follows. (1) Lokumal, e Murli, Lal, Sham and Pishu in breach of their duties as trustees procured the conversion of the shares owned by the trusts in Chellsons and Kaycee into 'B' shares, whose value immediately after their creation and since was less than that of the unconverted shares which they represented. (2) During August 1983 the trustees ceased to make payments from trust income in favour of Harish or Radhika, and since that date had made no payment to either claimant and f provided no trust accounts. (3) The 1985 heads of agreement and supplemental agreement, purportedly settling all the litigation in Singapore and England, were executed by the trustees and the claimants' parents, who had no authority to do so on behalf of the claimants who were then minors, and their execution comprised a breach of trust by the defendants because the intention and effect was to benefit the trustees and the claimants' parents at the expense of the g claimants. (4) In particular, the heads of agreement were in breach of trust because (a) they procured for the trustees (for no benefit to the beneficiaries) a release from the breaches of trust mentioned above in consideration (inter alia) of the claimants' parents being released from the separate claims against them in the Singapore actions; (b) they enabled the trustees to purchase trust property h and to do so not at its market value but according to the discretion of the arbitrators, one of whom was himself a trustee, Mr Advani, and the other was the husband of a sister of Mohan and Harish. (5) Accordingly the heads of agreement comprised an agreement which was void or voidable, and the claimants (who, it is alleged, only became aware of its terms during the year 2000) seek to avoid it. j (6) The purported appointment of Bermuda Trust as a trustee to act jointly with Mr Advani as continuing trustee of the 1975 trusts in May 1985 was for the purpose of enabling the breaches of trust, and was consequently void or voidable at the instance of the claimants, and in either event is ineffective to release the existing trustees. (7) The advance of the interests of Vishal and Ashwin to Harish and Radhika 'as bare trustees' by the deeds of appointment of 29 July 1985 was a breach of trust, and it caused the property appointed to pass out of the control of

the trustees. (8) The claimants do not accept the valuation of the 50,000 shares in Kayshewak at $2,250,000 or the valuation of the shares in Eskay 2 at £180,000, but *a* no part of the sale proceeds of either shareholding has been paid to either claimant, and that, save as mentioned, neither of the claimants had ratified or confirmed the sale or any part of any agreement comprised or reflected in the heads of agreement. But it is accepted that each of the claimants received $267,500 allegedly as part of the sale proceeds of the Kayshewak shares. (9) The *b* releases are not binding because neither claimant had any knowledge of the circumstances of the litigation, the arbitration or the sale of the shares when they executed the releases, or had any sight of the trust documents therein mentioned. (10) By a proposed amendment a claim that the releases were procured by the undue influence of Lokumal, Lal and Sham is abandoned. Instead, it is alleged that the releases are unenforceable because by the terms of the Geneva trust it *c* was provided that the moneys that remained due to the claimants as a result of the sale of the trust assets should only be released to them if they executed the release within 90 days of their coming of age; the trust deed was made to the knowledge of and at the instigation of Lokumal, Lal and Sham; no attempt was made to ascertain the value of the claim against the ex-trustees which it was *d* proposed that they should release; the moneys to be paid to them from the trust were moneys to which they were entitled in any event, whether as payment pursuant to the sale of trust assets if that transaction was binding on them, or as payment on account of their entitlement to compensation from the trustees in the event of the sale of the trust assets being set aside; in the circumstances it was unfair and inequitable for the execution of the releases to have been obtained by *e* the threatened withholding of money to which they were beneficially entitled.

[127] The relief claimed with regard to the 1975 trusts is that the first to fifth defendants deliver accounts of capital and income; that the releases signed in 1992 and 1995 be declared void or set aside; a declaration that the claimants are entitled to the entire capital and income of the trust fund of the Mohan Trust, and a *f* declaration that they are each entitled to 25% of the assets of Harish Trust; an order removing such of the first to seventh defendants as are trustees of the 1975 trusts and their replacement by some fit and proper persons, and all necessary and consequential vesting orders; an inquiry as to the amount of loss suffered by the trust estates and the beneficial interests of each claimant by reason of the reconstruction and conversion in 1981/1982, and the arbitration and share sales *g* of 1985; a declaration that the trusts are entitled to 75,000 shares in Eskay 2 and Kayshewak or the assets representing those shares, or alternatively an inquiry as to the assets of the trusts; a declaration that the first to fifth defendants remain liable as trustees to make good the losses and replenish the trust estates accordingly; alternatively an inquiry as to the amount of income and the size of *h* the trust estates to which the claimants should have become entitled since the company reconstruction in 1981/1982, and an order that the first to fifth defendants do account for the amount found due on the inquiry.

(XIV) JURISDICTION

j

General

[128] Since Sham and Lal were not validly served in England, the English court will only have jurisdiction in these proceedings in one of the following circumstances.

[129] First, as regards the defendants who are domiciled outside the states or territories to which the 1968 convention applies (Lokumal, Sham, Murli, Pishu,

a   Bermuda Trust and Mohan) the court may assume jurisdiction if either (a) the case comes within the trust provision of CPR 6.20(11); or (b) the defendant is a necessary or proper party under CPR 6.20(3) to proceedings against another defendant who is amenable to the jurisdiction either under CPR 6.20(11) or under the trust provision of art 5(6) of the 1968 convention.

[130] Second, as regards the defendants who are domiciled in a state or
b   territory to which the 1968 convention applies (Lal and Chellwood), the court has jurisdiction only if art 5(6) is applicable. Since there is no defendant who is domiciled in England, there is no basis for jurisdiction over additional parties under art 6(1).

[131] It has been well established for more than 100 years that a claimant cannot pursue causes of action against a foreign defendant under CPR 6.20 (and
c   its predecessor RSC Ord 11) which are not within the provisions for service out of the jurisdiction, even if the claimant has other claims which are within it (see cases in Dicey and Morris Conflict of Laws (13th edn, 2000) p 310 (para 11-129)). It is therefore not permissible to join with claims covered by CPR 6.20 claims which are not within any of the heads of jurisdiction. In my judgment the same
d   principle applies in the case of the 1968 convention.

[132] In cases to which CPR 6.20 applies, in addition the claimants must show, because the burden is on them, that England is clearly the appropriate forum (see Spiliada Maritime Corp v Cansulex Ltd, The Spiliada [1986] 3 All ER 843, [1987] AC 460), and the court will not give permission unless satisfied that England is the proper place in which to bring the claim (see CPR 6.21(2A)). Unless and until
e   there is a decision of the European Court or of the House of Lords to the contrary, where the English court has jurisdiction under the 1968 convention, the proceedings may be stayed in favour of the courts of a non-contracting state (see Re Harrods (Buenos Aires) Ltd [1991] 4 All ER 334, [1992] Ch 72, applied to defendants domiciled in other contracting states in Ace Insurance SA-NV v Zurich
f   Insurance Co [2001] EWCA Civ 173, [2001] 1 All ER (Comm) 802) if the defendant can show that there is another available forum, having competent jurisdiction, which is more suitable for the trial of the action, ie in which the case may be tried more suitably for the interests of all the parties and the ends of justice, unless the claimant can show that there are circumstances by reason of which justice requires that a stay should nevertheless not be granted (see, for example, Lubbe v
g   Cape plc [2000] 4 All ER 268 at 273–276, [2000] 1 WLR 1545 at 1553–1555).

[133] In the section on domicile ([23], above) I referred to the rule, applicable to both convention and non-convention cases, that the claimant must establish a good arguable case that the court has jurisdiction. In non-convention cases, the claimant must also establish a serious issue to be tried on the merits.

h   [134] But where the question of jurisdiction depends, not on some free-standing question such as domicile, but on elements which are linked to the elements of the claim, the claimant must equally establish that the requisite elements of jurisdiction exist. The question of the requisite standard of proof was addressed fully in the context of jurisdiction in contract cases under RSC Ord 11, r 1(1)(e) (now CPR 6.20(5)) by Lord Goff of Chieveley in Seaconsar Far East Ltd v Bank Markazi
j   Jomhouri Islami Iran [1993] 4 All ER 456 at 464–466, [1994] 1 AC 438 at 453–455. The effect of the decision is that where jurisdiction depends on several elements, for example that there was a contract, that it was broken, and that it was broken within the jurisdiction, then a good arguable case for each of those elements must be established.

[135] The good arguable case test was accepted as the appropriate test for domicile in the context of the 1968 convention in Canada Trust Co v Stolzenberg (No 2)

[2000] 4 All ER 481 at 491, [2002] 1 AC 1 at 13, and there is no reason to doubt that
it applies also to the more complex jurisdictional provisions of the 1968
convention (and has been so applied in several decisions in the Court of Appeal:
see Dicey and Morris pp 338–339 (para 11-225, n69)).

[136] Where jurisdiction depends on a question of law or construction, the
court will decide it rather than apply the good arguable case test (see cases in Dicey
and Morris p 309 (para 11-127, n34). That approach has consistently been applied
to cases where jurisdiction has depended on the applicable law of a contract for the
purposes of what is now CPR 6.20(5)(c). In such cases the court does not consider
whether the claimant has a good arguable case that the contract is governed by
English law, but rather whether the contract *is* governed by English law. Some
of the most important cases on the applicable law of a contract at common law
were decided under predecessors of this rule (see, for example, *Amin Rasheed
Shipping Corp v Kuwait Insurance Co, The Al Wahab* [1983] 2 All ER 884, [1984] AC
50) and I do not consider that anything in the *Seaconsar* case is intended to throw
doubt on their approach. Accordingly in a case such as this, if jurisdiction
depends on the identification of the applicable law, the claimant would have to
satisfy the court that the applicable law was English law, and the good arguable
case test would only have a role to play if there were a relevant factual issue (for
example, if an express choice of law were said to be ineffective on the facts of the
case).

Law applicable to trusts and jurisdiction
[137] Both CPR 6.20(11) and art 5(6) are in terms concerned with express
trusts. CPR 6.20(11) provides that a claim form may be served out of the
jurisdiction if—

> 'a claim is made for any remedy which might be obtained in proceedings
> to execute the trusts of a written instrument where—(a) the trusts ought to
> be executed according to English law; and (b) the person on whom the claim
> form is to be served is a trustee of the trusts.'

Article 5(6) provides:

> 'A person domiciled in a Contracting State may, in another Contracting
> State, be sued ...
> (6) ... as settlor, trustee or beneficiary of a trust created by the operation of a
> statute, or by a written instrument, or created orally and evidenced in writing,
> in the courts of the Contracting State in which the trust is domiciled ...'

[138] Accordingly, neither CPR 6.20(11) nor art 5(6) applies to constructive
trusts. CPR 6.20(14) makes special provision for constructive trusts, and it is clear
both from the text of art 5(6) and from the Schlosser Report on the 1978
Accession Convention (by which the United Kingdom acceded to the 1968
convention, and which introduced art 5(6)) (OJ 1979 C59 p 71 at 107 (para 117)),
that art 5(6) does not apply to constructive trusts.

[139] The effect of CPR 6.20(11) and art 5(6), as implemented in the United
Kingdom, is that the relevant connecting factor for the purposes of jurisdiction in
the case of CPR 6.20(11) is the law according to which 'the trusts ought to be
executed,' which must be English law, and in the case of art 5(6) (as implemented
by s 45(3) of the 1982 Act) is 'the system of law ... with which the trust has its
closest and most real connection', which must be English law.

a [140] CPR 6.20(11) applies only to claims against a person who 'is' a trustee of the trusts, and art 5(6) applies only to an action against a defendant 'as settlor, trustee or beneficiary of a trust'.

[141] Both CPR 6.20(11) (which had its origin in the nineteenth century) and art 5(6) (which originated in 1978) pre-date the Recognition of Trusts Act 1987, which implements the Convention on the Law Applicable to Trusts and on their

b Recognition (Hague, 1 July 1985; TS 14 (1992); Cm 1823) (the Hague Convention). Although the formulations differ, each is referring to the applicable law, and in each the starting point will be the Hague convention rules. I consider it likely that the wording of CPR 6.20(11) is apt to encompass claims which may depend on English law either as the law applicable to the trust itself or as the law governing its administration, while art 5(6) is probably limited to claims in relation to trusts

c governed by English law.

[142] The position prior to the 1987 Act, which is reflected in the judgment of Scott J in *Chellaram v Chellaram (No 1)*, was that in the absence of an express or implied choice a trust was governed by the system of law with which it had its closest and most real connection (see *Chellaram v Chellaram* [1985] 1 All ER 1043

d at 1051–1052, [1985] Ch 409 at 424–425; and cf *Duke of Marlborough v A-G (No 1)* [1945] 1 All ER 165 at 168, [1945] Ch 78 at 83 ('the law by reference to which the settlement was made and which was intended by the parties to govern their rights and liabilities'); *Iveagh v IRC* [1954] 1 All ER 609 at 612, [1954] Ch 364 at 370). In *Chellaram v Chellaram (No 1)* Scott J expressed the view that the rights and duties of the trustees were governed by the proper law of the settlement (and not by the

e law of the place of administration if different); and that if the court had personal jurisdiction over the trustees the inherent jurisdiction of the court to remove and appoint trustees was a matter of machinery for English law as the lex fori, and could be exercised regardless of the governing law of the trust or the law governing the administration of the trust (see [1985] 1 All ER 1043 at 1056–1057,

f [1985] Ch 409 at 481).

[143] Under art 6 of the Hague Convention:

'A trust shall be governed by the law chosen by the settlor. The choice must be express or be implied in the terms of the instrument creating or the writing evidencing the trust, interpreted, if necessary, in the light of the

g   circumstances of the case.'

[144] By art 7:

'Where no applicable law has been chosen, a trust shall be governed by the law with which it is most closely connected.

h   In ascertaining the law with which a trust is most closely connected reference shall be made in particular to—(a) the place of administration of the trust designated by the settlor; (b) the situs of the assets of the trust; (c) the place of residence or business of the trustee; (d) the objects of the trust and the places where they are to be fulfilled.'

j

[145] By art 8 the law specified by arts 6 or 7 is to govern the validity of the trust, its construction, its effects and the administration of the trust. In particular that law is to govern the appointment, resignation and removal of trustees; the relationships between the trustees and the beneficiaries including the personal liability of the trustees to the beneficiaries; the variation or termination of the trust; the distribution of the trust assets; and the duty of trustees to account for

their administration. By art 9 a severable aspect of the trust, particularly matters
of administration, may be governed by a different law.

[146] By art 10 the law applicable to the validity of the trust is to determine
whether that law or the law governing a severable aspect of the trust may be
replaced by another law. Under English law the governing law may be changed
with the concurrence of the beneficiaries (see *Duke of Marlborough v A-G (No 1)*
[1945] 1 All ER 165 at 169–70, [1945] Ch 78 at 85) and probably also by the exercise
of a power reserved in the trust instrument (see Dicey and Morris *The Conflict of
Laws* (13th edn, 2000) p 1094 (para 29-020); *Lewin on Trusts* (17th edn, 2000) p 293
(para 11-42)). But it is not changed merely by a change in circumstances such as
a change in the trusteeship (see *Duke of Marlborough's* case [1945] 1 All ER 165 at
169–170, [1945] Ch 78 at 85).

[147] By art 22 the Hague Convention applies to trusts regardless of the date
on which they were created, but, by s 1(5) of the 1987 Act, art 22 is not to be
construed as affecting the law to be applied in relation to anything done or
omitted before the Act came into force (on 1 August 1987: Recognition of Trusts
Act 1987 (Commencement) Order, SI 1987/1177).

The time for testing the applicable law for jurisdictional purposes

[148] One of the questions canvassed in this case is the critical date for
determining the applicable law for the jurisdictional purposes of CPR 6.20(11)
and art 5(6). The claimants argue for the date when the causes of action arose,
which they say was before the change to Bermuda law was made, with the
consequence (they argue) that English law applies as the law with the closest and
most real connection with the 1975 trusts, and accordingly gives the English
court jurisdiction under both CPR 6.20(11) and art 5(6).

[149] The defendants say that the critical date for determining whether
English law is the applicable law and whether the defendant 'is' a trustee
(CPR 6.20(11)) or whether the defendant is sued as a trustee of a trust which 'is'
domiciled in England (art 5(6)), is the date when the court is seised of the
proceedings. At that date, the defendants say that either there was no subsisting
trust, or if there was, it was governed by Bermuda law.

[150] In *Winter v Winter* [1894] 1 Ch 421 the then current version of what is
now CPR 6.20(11) provided that service was permissible out of the jurisdiction
where the action was for the—

'execution (as to property situate within the jurisdiction) of the trusts of
any written instrument, of which the person to be served is a trustee, which
ought to be executed according to the law of England ...'

The defendant was the sole trustee of a settlement executed in England. The
defendant had sold the consols comprised in the settlement and had left England,
and there was not at that time, nor had there at any time since been, any property
subject to the trusts of the settlement situate within the jurisdiction. The action
was for the administration of the trusts. Stirling J (at 423) held that service should
be set aside because the words 'as to property situate within the jurisdiction'
limited the generality of the rule and imposed a condition which had to be
fulfilled in order that service out of the jurisdiction might properly be allowed. It
referred to property which was actually situate within the jurisdiction, and not
simply property which ought to be, or if the trusts were duly executed would be,
so situate. Although the rule did not in terms define the periods at which the
property was to be situate within the jurisdiction, since the rule related to service,

a the relevant period was when leave to effect service was given. But in *Official Solicitor v Stype Investments (Jersey) Ltd* [1983] 1 All ER 629, [1983] 1 WLR 214 Whitford J said that but for *Winter's* case he would have taken the relevant date as the date on which the cause of action accrued rather than the date of the application for leave to serve out of the jurisdiction.

[151] In this case the question in relation to CPR 6.20(11) is whether the
b condition that 'the trusts ought to be executed according to English law' must be fulfilled when permission to serve out is sought, or whether it is sufficient that English law applied to the trusts at the time of the cause of action. I consider that the first construction is the correct one, and is supported by the other condition that the defendant 'is' a trustee of the trusts. So also in the case of art 5(6) its application to a person sued as a trustee of a trust which 'is' domiciled in a
c contracting state supports the construction that the time of the proceedings is the critical time.

[152] It is also supported not only by *Winter's* case but also by part of the reasoning which led the House of Lords to hold in *Canada Trust Co v Stolzenberg (No 2)* [2000] 4 All ER 481, [2002] 1 AC 1 that for the purposes of the Lugano
d Convention (and therefore also the 1968 convention) the date for determining whether a defendant was domiciled in the United Kingdom or in another contracting state was the date when the proceedings were instituted, and not when they were served. One of the factors which led Lord Steyn, in the leading speech, to that conclusion was the aim of the convention (citing *Mulox IBC Ltd v Geels* Case C-125/92 [1993] ECR I-4075 at 4103 (para 11)) to allow the plaintiff
e easily to foresee the court before which he may bring an action and the defendant reasonably to foresee the court before which he may be sued.

[153] Finally it is supported by the strict approach to interpretation of both CPR 6.20 and the 1968 convention. In the context of what is now CPR 6.20 it has been said on many occasions, applying *The Hagen* [1908] P 189, 201, [1908–10]
f All ER Rep 21, that where there is doubt as to the construction of any of its heads, the doubt should be resolved in favour of the foreigner (or, more strictly, against the exercise of extra-territorial jurisdiction). In the case of the 1968 convention the European Court has emphasised on several occasions that the exceptions to art 2, which gives primacy to the court of the domicile, are to be construed strictly (see cases cited at Dicey and Morris *Conflict of Laws* (13th edn, 2000) p 281
g (para 11–051)).

[154] I will, however, in case I am wrong on this point, also consider the question of the applicable law at the time when the cause of action is said to have arisen.

h *1943 and 1946 trusts*
[155] Neither CPR 6.20(11) nor art 5(6) can apply to the 1943 or 1946 trusts. It is common ground that they are governed by Indian law, and there is no possible basis for English jurisdiction.

j *1975 trusts*
[156] It is central to the claimants' case on the merits in relation at least to Lokumal, Lal and Sham that they can avoid the effect of the releases which they signed when they attained majority in 1992 and 1995 respectively. That is why the particulars of claim originally pleaded undue influence (and why the claimants now seek to plead that they were obtained unfairly and inequitably), and also sought an order that the releases be declared void or be set aside. The defendants

argued that the claimants' case on the releases was so weak that it did not raise a
serious issue to be tried, but in my judgment there is a more fundamental
objection to the claim for a declaration relating to the releases.

[157] There is no basis for an argument that the claims relating to the releases
fall within CPR 6.20(11) or art 5(6), and the court has no jurisdiction to deal with
them as independent claims for the reason given in [131], above. But the
claimants now say that they are really matters for reply to a defence of release,
and that it is not necessary for the releases to be pleaded as a part of their positive
case. I shall proceed on the basis that that submission is correct.

[158] So far as the 1975 trusts are concerned, on the construction of CPR 6.20(11)
which I have preferred, even if the trust subsists, the only person who 'is' a trustee
is Bermuda Trust, and the other non-convention defendants could only be served
under CPR 6.20(3) (which would make a difference because of the even more
special care which must be exercised before service is authorised under that
head). But the assets of the trusts have been distributed, and Bermuda Trust, the
sole trustee, acknowledged as long ago as 1985 that the trusts were at an end.

[159] This is a hurdle which could be overcome in theory if the claimants had
a good arguable case that the deeds of appointment were ineffective to transfer
the trust property. If there is a transfer of trust property in breach of trust for
which the trustees remain accountable, the trust relationship remains and the
fruits of the claim will be held on the same trusts. But it is noteworthy that the
claimants do not plead that the deeds of appointment were invalid, perhaps
because to do so might entail that the sums paid to Harish and Radhika and to the
claimants will become repayable.

[160] But, in any event, in the second choice of law in 1985 the trustees chose
Bermuda law and jurisdiction for the trusts, and therefore there is prima facie no
basis for a contention that the trusts ought to be executed according to English
law. The trustees had the power under cl 15(a) to select the applicable law, and
that choice is prima facie effective as a combined result of the common law and
arts 6(1) and 10 of the Hague Convention.

[161] There is no good arguable case for impugning the validity of the choice
of applicable law. There is no reason to believe that there was any reason for the
change other than to distance the trusts from United Kingdom tax law. There is
clear and contemporary evidence produced by the defendants that the change to
a Bermuda-based trustee and the choice of Bermuda law and jurisdiction in 1985
was tax-driven, to avoid an argument that United Kingdom tax law might apply
to the income from the Kaycee and Chellsons shares. Although it is alleged in the
particulars of claim that the appointment of Bermuda Trust was effected for the
purpose of enabling the breaches of trust, Vishal has not sought in any way to
contest the evidence on the reason for the appointment (or the choice of
Bermuda law). To do so he would have to show that the 1984 letter from Moore,
Stephens to Norton Rose recommending the change of trustee was bogus
window-dressing. It is not surprising that he has not sought to do so. But unless
he has something to say about the defendants' evidence about the change, I do
not see how the claimants can possibly establish a good arguable case that the
choice of Bermuda law is ineffective, and that therefore as at the date of the
proceedings the trusts ought to have been executed according to English law.

[162] In the case of the 1968 convention defendants (Lal and Chellwood),
art 5(6) applies only to a defendant who is sued 'as settlor, trustee or beneficiary'.
Chellwood is a defendant because it purchased the shares, but it is not a settlor,
trustee or beneficiary of the trusts. At most it might be a constructive trustee, but

a (as I have mentioned) art 5(6) does not apply to constructive trusts. Nor is Lal any longer a trustee, and, decisively (and for the same reasons as in relation to CPR 6.20(11)) the trusts are not domiciled in England, because they would not (if they still existed) have their closest and most real connection with English law. I do not doubt that in deciding whether it is English law with which the trusts have their closest connection, it is permissible to take into account the express choice of Bermuda law to negate that connection.

b

[163] Since there is no basis for jurisdiction under CPR 6.20(11) or art 5(6), there is no basis for service of additional necessary or proper parties under CPR 6.20(3).

[164] If I am wrong in my conclusion that the governing law or domicile of the trusts is to be tested as at the date of the proceedings rather than the date when *c* the cause of action arose, I would be faced with the same difficulty as Scott J in *Chellaram v Chellaram (No 1)*. For the reasons given in [136], above (although this was not the subject of argument), if this question arose in the present proceedings it would be for the claimants to show that English law was the applicable law, and I doubt whether there would be any factual issues such that the question would *d* fall to be decided on the good arguable case basis. The court would have to come to its own view. Since in these circumstances the question of jurisdiction would be linked with the actual alleged breaches of trust it is likely that the effect of s 1(5) of the Recognition of Trusts Act 1987 would be that the common law rules would prevail if they led to a result different from that under the Hague Convention.

[165] Scott J's initial view was that the trusts were governed by Indian law, but *e* he was left with doubts because the trust property was shares in Bermudan companies and the underlying assets were outside India; the purpose of the trusts was to escape Indian tax and exchange control and two of the three original trustees were in London. Accordingly he did not find it easy to see why, if the parties had intended Indian law to govern the trusts, they would have arranged *f* for an English administration. But he did not decide the question of the governing law.

[166] By art 7 of the Hague Convention, in the absence of a choice of the applicable law, a trust is governed by the law with which it is most closely connected. In ascertaining that law reference is to be made 'in particular' to (a) the place of administration designated by the settlor—no such place was *g* designated; (b) the situs of the assets of the trust—this was Bermuda if account only is taken of the shares in Kaycee and Chellsons which were settled, but many other countries (especially in Asia and Africa) if the underlying assets are taken into account; (c) the place of residence or business of the trustees—Mr Rupchand and Mr Bharwani were resident in London at the date of the settlements, and the *h* evidence of Ram's residence was inconclusive, although he then had substantial London connections; (d) the objects of the trust and the places where they were to be fulfilled—there was no one place to which these factors could point. In the light of the paucity of authority at common law, I doubt if there is any significant difference between the art 7 and the likely approach at common law.

j [167] Because the approach to this question was not the subject of argument (and, in view of my other holdings, further argument would serve little point) I will simply indicate that in my judgment it is likely that Indian law was the law with which the trusts were most closely connected. They were drafted in India by Indian lawyers for a family of Indian origin with strong Indian ties, but with international interests, and it is very doubtful that the fact that at least two of the trustees were in London, and that it was contemplated (but not required) that administration would (at least initially) take place in London would have made English law the law with the closest connection.   *a*

(XV) DISCRETION AND FORUM CONVENIENS

[168] It is for the claimants to show that England is 'the proper place in which to bring the claim' against the non-convention defendants (see CPR 6.21(2A)). Since the exercise of jurisdiction would involve bringing foreign parties to   *b* England: 'The effect is, not merely that the burden of proof rests on the plaintiff to persuade the court that England is the appropriate forum for the trial of the action, but that he has to show that this is clearly so' (see *Spiliada Maritime Corp v Cansulex Ltd, The Spiliada* [1986] 3 All ER 843 at 858, [1987] AC 460 at 481 per Lord Goff).

[169] I have to approach this question on the hypothesis that not only would   *c* the court have jurisdiction under CPR 6.20 against the non-convention defendants, but also that the court would have jurisdiction over Lal, in each case on the hypothesis that the trusts are governed by English law and, in the case of the non-convention defendants, that there are serious issues to be tried on the merits of the case.   *d*

[170] This is a case in which the claimants cannot show that England would clearly be an appropriate forum. On the above hypotheses, the only connections with England would be (a) the trusts would be governed by English law; (b) the settlement in 1985 related (in part) to English proceedings; and (c) the individual defendants have access to homes in England when they visit. But the governing law is not a weighty factor when there is no reason to suppose that the law   *e* applicable in the competing jurisdiction is any different. The heads of agreement in 1985 were expressly governed by Bermuda law, the supplemental agreement was, no doubt, impliedly governed by the same law, and the consent awards were governed by Bermuda law. The fact that the individual defendants can travel to England is a very minor factor, compared with the fact that, apart from Lal, they   *f* are all based in India (as is Radhika, who is bound to be a party on the indemnities which she gave in the Kayshewak award supplemental agreement if the proceedings continue) and Hong Kong, and that the claimants are in Singapore.

[171] Against that, there are proceedings in India against all of the individual defendants. It is clear that the application for interim relief in those proceedings was limited to property in India. There is evidence from the defendants that the   *g* proceedings as a whole relate to property worldwide. The pleadings and Vishal's affidavit in those proceedings support that view, and it is difficult to see how the claim to a HUF could be limited to Indian property, although such a claim would be inconsistent with the claims made in these proceedings. But even if the Indian proceedings do not raise the same issues as these proceedings, or even deal with   *h* the same property as the 1975 trusts, it is plain that the determination of the Indian proceedings will require an investigation of the way in which the Chellaram family dealt with their assets both in India and outside. The offer by the claimants to discontinue the Indian proceedings if the English court assumes jurisdiction over this action is purely tactical in nature.   *j*

[172] India is an available forum. The evidence for the defendants from their Indian lawyer, Mr Malkani, is that the claim in the present Indian proceedings could be amended to include claims in relation to the 1975 trusts. It may be true, as Vishal asserts, that that would not be an easy task, because the trust claims are incompatible with the claim that an HUF exists, but it is the claimants' problem if they are making inconsistent claims. Even if it could not be amended, the court

would have jurisdiction in fresh proceedings. Jurisdiction in Bombay is governed by the Letters Patent (Bombay), which grants jurisdiction if the cause of action arose within the local limits of the court, or if the defendant was resident or carried on business or worked for gain there. Mr Malkani's opinion is that all of the individual defendants have the requisite connection with Bombay and could be sued there as having addresses or businesses there. He also confirms that Chellwood and Bermuda Trust could effectively submit to the jurisdiction of the Bombay court. Scott J in *Chellaram v Chellaram (No 1)* ([1985] 1 All ER 1043 at 1059, [1985] Ch 409 at 435) expressed some doubt as to whether a defendant could submit to the jurisdiction of the Bombay High Court, but in *Konamaneni v Rolls-Royce Industrial Power (India) Ltd* [2002] 1 All ER 979, [2002] 1 WLR 1269 fuller evidence in relation to proceedings in Hyderabad persuaded me that submission was possible and Mr Malkani relies on the decisions of the Indian Supreme Court to which I referred when accepting evidence to that effect. Mr Malkani also says that they could be added as defendants with the permission of the court, but he does not give authority for that view. An undertaking has already been given by Lal and Sham on their own behalf and on behalf of Chellwood, and the court can take this into account in considering whether there is an alternative forum (see *Lubbe v Cape plc* [2000] 4 All ER 268 at 272–277, [2000] 1 WLR 1545 at 1552–1556).

[173] The following factors point to India as the forum conveniens. First, there are already proceedings pending there which raise the issue of the property rights in the Chellaram family, and an Indian court is far better equipped to understand the intricacies of these family relationships. If there were proceedings in England, the same matters would be ventilated in two jurisdictions. Second, several of the most important witnesses are in India: Murli, Pishu and Mohan (although there may be doubts about the ability of Murli and Mohan to give effective evidence); Radhika (who, as I have said, would no doubt be joined as a party by Lokumal, Lal, Sham and Chellwood on the indemnities which she gave); Mr Chanrai and his assistant (concerning the consent awards, Mr Advani having died in 1991); and former Chief Justice Bhagwati (concerning the Geneva Trust and the releases).

[174] Lokumal and Sham are in Hong Kong, and the claimants are in Singapore. Lal has not, of course, suggested that it would be inconvenient for him to attend. The only important witnesses who would not be compellable in India are the lawyers involved in the 1985 settlement, Macfarlanes and Norton Rose. But it is not realistic to suppose that they would not attend if asked to by their clients, and privilege, unless waived, would prevent them being compelled by any other party to give evidence. The partner in Moore, Stephens who dealt with the matter has since died, and the representatives of Bermuda Trust and of United Overseas Bank would be only marginally relevant witnesses.

[175] I do not consider that any assistance in this exercise is to be derived from *Chellaram v Chellaram (No 1)*. In that case the defendants had been served in England or had submitted to the English jurisdiction, and the decision was based on stay principles, where the burden is on the defendant to show that there is another more appropriate forum. The following factors were held to be relevant: (1) there was doubt whether the Bombay court would have jurisdiction over non-Indian parties; (2) delay in Indian proceedings might expose the plaintiffs to considerable hardship; (3) India would be more convenient so far as witnesses were concerned, but the geographic factor was not of great importance; (4) it was not a case of forum shopping because administration was intended to take place

in London; (5) it was not a case of lis alibi pendens; (6) all defendants had either
been served in England or had instructed solicitors to accept service on their
behalf.

[176] I have already dealt with the point on the jurisdiction of the Indian court.
This may not be a case of lis alibi pendens in the sense that the same issues are
before the Indian courts, but it is a case in which there are proceedings in India to
which all of the individual defendants are parties and which will cover much of
the same ground.

[177] On delay Scott J ([1985] All ER 1043 at 1059, [1985] Ch 409 at 435) said
that, in view of the fact that Harish and Radhika had had no payments since 1983,
a delay of seven to ten years might represent a serious injustice to them. This is
not a case of an application for a stay of proceedings, and in *Konamaneni's* case
[2002] 1 All ER 979 at [59], [176], I expressed the view that in cases of service out
of the jurisdiction delay in the foreign court would only be a factor if it were so
great that the foreign court could not be regarded as an available forum. I also
said that it was well known that problems of delay in Indian proceedings have
lessened in recent years. The evidence in the present proceedings suggests that
any delay would be a maximum of four to five years and that it may be possible
to obtain an expedited hearing because of the age of some of the parties. This is
not a case where the claimants are being kept out of their money. They and their
parents have received all the money to which they were prima facie entitled, and
these are proceedings in substance to set aside a settlement 16 years before the
proceedings were instituted, and nine years after Vishal, and six years after
Ashwin, became entitled to bring them. In this case delay in the Indian
proceedings is not a factor which can make England the clearly appropriate
forum.

[178] On the hypothesis that the court would not exercise jurisdiction, not
only because the claimants had not shown that England was the clearly
appropriate forum, but also because India was the appropriate forum, and that
the proceedings would continue against the non-convention defendants in India,
then there would be an overwhelming case for a stay of proceedings against Lal
if (contrary to my view) the English court had jurisdiction over him under
art 5(6).

[179] I should add two points on the forum conveniens aspect. First, there is
little to be said for Bermuda as an alternative forum, and even Bermuda Trust did
not press for it. Second, Vishal said in his witness statement that former Chief
Justice Bhagwati had apparently condoned breaches of trust and had filed
evidence in support of the defendants, and accordingly Vishal had 'a real and
justifiable fear that we will not be able to achieve justice in India'. Vishal's
advisors should not have allowed this unworthy suggestion to be made, and it has
now been abandoned.

(XVI) SERIOUS ISSUE TO BE TRIED
[180] On the view which I have taken on the jurisdiction and forum conveniens
issues, the question of the strength of the claim in relation to CPR 6.20 does not arise,
and I will therefore deal with it shortly. There can be little doubt that the claimants'
case is, on the evidence adduced so far, a very weak one.

[181] There are two basic complaints. The first (which was also the subject of
Chellaram v Chellaram (No 1)) is that the 1981 reconstruction was a breach of trust
because the conversion of the trust shares in Kaycee and Chellsons to 'B' shares was
procured for the benefit of Lokumal, Lal, Sham, Murli and Pishu and diminished the

a value of the trust estate. But the claimants have not answered the evidence that the reason for the reconstruction was to ensure an income flow for Lachmibai and that the 'A' and 'B' shares were treated equally in the 1985 valuations.

[182] The second complaint is that the 1985 settlement and its implementation was a breach of trust because it involved self-dealing by the trustees (through the indirect sale of the trust assets to them or their companies) and its intention and
b effect was to benefit the trustees and Harish and Radhika at the expense of the claimants. But there is unanswered evidence that there was no prejudice to the claimants because the shares were properly valued, and (as regards the Kayshewak shares) the claimants executed deeds of release on attaining their majority, and directly received part of the proceeds of sale, and (as regards the Eskay 2 shares) pressed for payment direct to themselves.
c [183] The purchase of trust property by a trustee is not void. It is voidable within a reasonable time at the instance of a beneficiary (see *Holder v Holder* [1968] 1 All ER 665 at 677–678, [1968] Ch 353 at 398). These proceedings were commenced some nine years after Vishal attained his majority and six years after Ashwin did so.

[184] For the reasons I have given, the validity of the deeds of release could arise
d in English proceedings only in reply to the defendants' reliance on them, since there is no basis of jurisdiction for a positive claim. The claimants asserted in the particulars of claim that the deeds of release were not binding for two reasons.

[185] The first was that neither claimant had any knowledge of the circumstances of the litigation, the arbitration or the sale of shares when they executed the releases, or had any sight of the trust documents mentioned therein. That
e contention had been preceded by a statement that the claimants only became aware of the terms of the heads of agreement in the year 2000. These pleas are demonstrably untrue. The recitals to the deeds of release referred in terms to the previous litigation, the settlement, the arbitration and the sale of shares, and in his 1996 affidavit in the Indian proceedings Vishal himself gave a full account of
f *Chellaram v Chellaram (No 1)* and of the settlement in 1985 and exhibited the statement of claim (which set out the terms of the trusts fully), the heads of agreement, the supplemental agreement and the awards. When he was confronted with this material in the evidence for the defendants, all he could say was this:

g   'Although I had previously been aware of the existence of the 1975 trusts and 1985 agreement, it was only in 2000 that I gained sufficient information and understanding to make decisions about my own position in relation to these disputes. It is in that context that the word "aware" is used in para 38 in the particulars of claim settled by counsel.'

h [186] The second contention was that the releases were procured by the undue influence of Lokumal, Lal and Sham. It was said that the claimants lacked any independent legal advice and were ignorant of the nature of the breaches of trust which they were purportedly releasing. This contention has been abandoned. It was bound to fail. By the time the releases were executed litigation was already
j being pursued on the claimants' behalf in India by legal advisors who had responsibilities to them. Even if it were arguable (which I do not consider it is) that there was then the requisite relationship of trustee and beneficiary, it could not be said that the Lokumal defendants had taken an advantage which was only explicable on the basis that there had been undue influence (see *Royal Bank of Scotland plc v Etridge (No 2), Barclays Bank plc v Coleman, Bank of Scotland v Bennett, Kenyon-Brown v Desmond Banks & Co (a firm)* [2001] UKHL 44 at [32], [2001] 4 All ER

449 at [32], [2001] 3 WLR 1021). The burden would therefore have been on the
claimants to show actual undue influence. Bhagwati J, who was a trustee of the
Geneva Trust appointed by the claimants' mother, gave evidence that there was
no undue influence, and it has not been contradicted.

[187] That contention has been replaced by another contention, that the
releases were ineffective because it was 'unfair and inequitable' for their
execution to have been obtained by the threatened withholding of money (under
the terms of the Geneva Trust) to which they were entitled. Although the court
can consider all the circumstances with a view to seeing whether it is fair and
equitable that a beneficiary who has acquiesced in, or given his concurrence to, a
breach of trust should be able to turn round and sue the trustees (see *Re Pauling's
Settlement Trusts, Younghusband v Coutts & Co* [1961] 3 All ER 713, [1962] 1 WLR
86; affirmed in part by the Court of Appeal [1963] 3 All ER 1, [1964] Ch 303) that
inquiry is concerned with the requisite degree of knowledge. There is no
principle of the law of contract or trusts which makes a release ineffective simply
because it is unfair. This is not a case where the releases could be said to have
been wrung from the claimants by 'distress or terror' (see *Lewin on Trusts* (17th
edn, 2000) p 1219 (para 39-74)).

[188] In my judgment the weakness of the claim is such that I would have held
that for the purposes of service out of the jurisdiction under CPR 6.20 there
would not have been a serious issue to be tried on the merits for much of the
claim, and if there had been jurisdiction under art 5(6) the case would have been
ripe for an application to strike much of it out. Some qualification is necessary
because I have not heard full argument on the extent to which the claim in
respect of the Eskay 2 shares, where there was no release, and where the evidence
on acquiescence and concurrence is not so powerful, falls to be treated in the
same way as the claim in relation to the Kayshewak shares.

(XVII) NON-DISCLOSURE

[189] This issue, like the other subsidiary issues, would only have arisen if the
court had jurisdiction, and if England had been shown by the claimants to be the
forum conveniens. On the without notice application for permission to serve out
the duty of the applicant is to make full and fair disclosure of all the material facts,
and I set out the relevant principles in *Konamaneni v Rolls-Royce Industrial Power
(India) Ltd* [2002] 1 All ER 979, [2002] 1 WLR 1269.

[190] The witness statement in support of the application was defective in
many respects, but in at least two ways it plainly failed to make full and fair
disclosure, and exhibited particulars of claim which in one important and
material respect were untrue and misleading. The existence of overlapping
proceedings between the same parties in other jurisdictions is always a highly
material factor on an application for permission to serve out. There was no
mention of the Indian proceedings, in which all of the individual defendants in
this action were also defendants. The English proceedings at the time of the
application concerned not only the 1975 trusts but also the 1943 and 1946 trusts.
There can be no doubt that the Indian proceedings commenced ten years before,
and still continuing, concerned the title to the property comprised in the
complaints of breach of trust in the English proceedings even if it was not so clear
that the 1975 trust assets were also comprised in the Indian claim. The failure to
refer to the Indian proceedings was a material non-disclosure, because it was
relevant to forum and also to the merits of the claim (since the claims in the
Indian action were inconsistent with the claims in these proceedings).

a [191] The second point is that the account in the witness statement of *Chellaram v Chellaram (No 1)* is misleading. It says that the court had already accepted jurisdiction and held that England was the proper place for the dispute regarding the 1975 trusts, without disclosing that (a) in that case all the defendants had been personally served in England or instructed solicitors to accept service on their behalf; (b) except as regards the reconstruction in 1981, there were no *b* similar issues; (c) the principles applied by Scott J were not those applicable in a case of permission to serve out of the jurisdiction.

[192] Finally, the witness statement referred to and relied on, in support of the application, the particulars of claim. I have already set out the evidence showing that the statement in the particulars of claim that the claimants only became aware of the terms of the heads of agreement in the year 2000 was demonstrably *c* false and designed to give the impression that the proceedings for equitable relief had been brought promptly.

[193] In my view these would have been sufficiently serious failures to justify setting aside the orders.

d (XVIII) CONCLUSION
[194] The orders of Master Bragge will be set aside, as will service on those defendants who have been served, or purportedly served, and I will make a declaration that the court has no jurisdiction to hear the claims.

(XIX) POSTSCRIPT: THE POSITION OF HERBERT SMITH
e [195] Lal, Sham and Chellwood are represented by Herbert Smith, and the partner responsible is Ms Anna Pertoldi. Herbert Smith is a large firm of solicitors in the City of London, with more than 150 partners, of whom more than 50 specialise in litigation. I was a partner in that firm from 1971 until the end of September 2000 (when I was appointed to the High Court bench), and Ms Pertoldi worked in the same group as I did between 1988 and 1999 (both before and after *f* she became a partner), and worked with me on several cases. The claimants made an application that I should disqualify myself, but withdrew the application on the morning of the hearing. It would have been another case (the others being *Locabail (UK) Ltd v Bayfield Properties Ltd* [2000] 1 All ER 65, [2000] QB 451 and *Re Bank of Credit and Commerce International SA (in liq) and its former employees* *g* [2001] All ER (D) 41 (Dec)) in which parties raised the question whether I should have heard, or should hear, matters which have been assigned to me, on the ground that I was, or had been, a partner in the firm of Herbert Smith.

[196] In *Taylor v Lawrence* [2002] EWCA Civ 90 at [60], [2002] 2 All ER 353 at [60] the Court of Appeal concluded that the appropriate test for potential bias was the test in *Re Medicaments and Related Classes of Goods (No 2)* [2001] ICR 564, [2001] *h* 1 WLR 700 as modified by Lord Hope of Craighead in *Porter v Magill, Weeks v Magill* [2001] UKHL 67 at [102], [2002] 1 All ER 465 at [102], [2002] 2 WLR 37:

> 'The court must first ascertain all the circumstances which have a bearing on the suggestion that the judge was biased. It must then ask whether those
j > circumstances would lead a fair-minded and informed observer to conclude that there was a real possibility ... that the tribunal was biased.'

[197] The judgment in *Taylor's* case emphasises that in this country it is an everyday occurrence that barristers appear before judges who were former members of their chambers, and who will therefore be likely to have worked very closely with them. The judgment does not deal in this respect with the position of solicitors, but there is no reason to believe that different considerations apply,

and, indeed, every reason to the contrary. There is no reason to distinguish the
situation of solicitors on the ground that solicitors practise as partnerships while   *a*
barristers share premises, staff, practice development (or marketing) and the
expenses associated therewith, but not profits. No fair-minded and informed
observer could conclude that there would be a real possibility that a judge,
whether a former barrister or solicitor, would have the slightest inclination to act
in breach of the judicial oath and favour a set of chambers or firm of which the   *b*
judge was a former member.

Order accordingly.

Celia Fox   Barrister.

APPENDIX

Chellaram Family tree: Lokumal, Tahilram and Shewakram branches male line

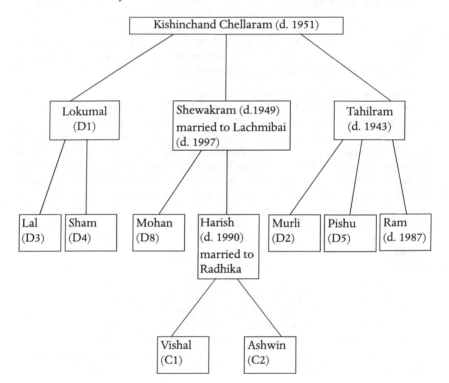

a R (on the application of Fuller and others) v Chief Constable of Dorset Police

[2001] EWHC Admin 1057

b QUEEN'S BENCH DIVISION (ADMINISTRATIVE COURT)

STANLEY BURNTON J

8, 9 NOVEMBER, 12 DECEMBER 2001

Police – Powers – Power to remove trespassers on land – Direction requiring trespassers
c *to leave land – Local authority requiring travellers to leave its land in two days – Police*
immediately giving statutory direction requiring travellers to leave site in two days –
Whether direction requiring trespassers to leave land valid if not giving trespassers
opportunity to comply with occupier's request to leave – Whether direction for
trespassers to leave land valid if requiring them to leave at future time – Criminal Justice
d *and Public Order Act 1994, s 61.*

In July 2001 a group of travellers encamped without authorisation at a rubbish tip
site which fell within the responsibility of two local authorities—the borough
council, which owned the site, and the county council. After various site visits
and discussions, the authorities made it clear that the site, which by then
e contained some 13 'live-in' vehicles, would be tolerated until the end of August,
subject to good behaviour. However, following an incident in which two police
officers were allegedly forcibly detained by travellers at the site, the police proposed
the issuing of a direction under s 61[a] of the Criminal Justice and Public Order Act
1994, requiring the travellers to leave the site. Under s 61(1), the senior police
f officer present at the site could make such a direction if he reasonably believed
that two or more persons were trespassing on land and were present there with
the common purpose of residing there for a period, that reasonable steps had
been taken by or on behalf of the occupier to ask them to leave and (a) that any
of those persons had caused damage to the land or to property on that land or had
used threatening, abusive or insulting words or behaviour towards the occupier,
g a member of his family or an employee or agent of his, or, (b) that those persons
had between them six or more vehicles on the land. Section 61(4)(a) provided
that a person committed a criminal offence if, knowing that a direction under
sub-s (1) had been given which applied to him, he failed to leave the land 'as soon
as reasonably practicable'. The local authorities agreed with the police's proposal
h to issue a s 61 direction. As a result, on 29 August the borough council gave the
travellers written notice that they were trespassers and required them to leave on
31 August. A police inspector then gave a direction, purportedly under s 61 of the
1994 Act, requiring the travellers to leave the site by 31 August. Four of the
travellers—three mothers with young children and a pregnant woman—brought
j proceedings against the police, seeking, inter alia, a declaration that no valid
direction had been given under s 61. Issues arose as to (i) whether the power to
make a direction under s 61 could only be lawfully exercised after the trespassers
had failed to comply with the occupier's request for them to leave, and
(ii) whether s 61 permitted a valid direction to be given to leave at a future time.

---

a   Section 61, so far as material, is set out at [40], below

Held – (1) On the true construction of s 61 of the 1994 Act, a direction could only *a* be given under that section after the trespassers had failed to comply with the occupier's request to leave. Section 61 was to be construed narrowly as it created a criminal offence, and Parliament should not be taken to have intended to introduce the possibility of criminal sanctions in respect of trespassers who had complied with requests to leave. Whereas s 61(1)(a) applied to persons who had been guilty of criminal or other misconduct, s 61(1)(b) applied to persons who *b* might have been perfectly well-behaved. Parliament was unlikely to have intended to bring the criminal law to bear on such trespassers who had not refused to leave when asked. On that basis, it was implicit in s 61 that trespassers had to have failed to comply with steps taken by the occupier to ask them to leave before the power to give a direction could lawfully be exercised. In the instant case, therefore, the s 61 direction was not lawful or valid since the travellers had *c* not been given an opportunity, before it was given, to comply with the borough council's request on 29 August that they leave by 31 August (see [42], [43], [46], [48], [83], below).

(2) On its true construction, s 61 of the 1994 Act did not permit the giving of a direction to trespassers to leave at a future time. The natural reading of s 61(1), *d* read together with sub-s (4), was that a direction was an order for the trespassers to leave with their vehicles immediately rather than at a future time. The words 'as soon as reasonably practicable' in s 61(4) meant 'as soon as reasonably practicable after the giving of a direction'. If a direction could be given to quit at some time sufficiently in the future, it would be inappropriate to provide for an offence of failing to leave as soon as reasonably practicable before the expiration *e* of the time permitted by the direction: the offence would be a failure to leave by the time specified in the direction. Indeed, it would be quite wrong to render criminal a failure to leave as soon as reasonably practicable before the expiration of the time permitted by the direction. It followed in the instant case that the s 61 direction was also invalidated in that it was not a direction to the travellers to *f* leave immediately or as soon as reasonably practicable, but rather a direction to leave in two days' time (see [47], [84], below).

Per curiam. (1) Section 61 of the 1994 Act is compatible with the European Convention for the Protection of Human Rights and Fundamental Freedoms 1950 (as set out in Sch 1 to the Human Rights Act 1998). The right to a fair trial under art 6[b] is not engaged by a law making it a criminal offence to fail to comply *g* with a direction by a police officer to leave certain land. The fact that the procedure under s 61 is effective without the local authority having to give trespassers a previous opportunity to be heard before a court does not mean that that section is incompatible with art 6. A person who challenges his arrest or prosecution does so before a court, and that process will comply with art 6. Nor *h* is there any infringement of the right to peaceful enjoyment of possessions under art 1[c] of the First Protocol to the convention. As regards a traveller's right to respect for his private and family life and for his home under art 8[d] of the

---

b   Article 6, so far as material, provides: '1. In the determination of his civil rights and obligations or *j* of any criminal charge against him, everyone is entitled to a fair and public hearing within a reasonable time by an independent and impartial tribunal established by law ...'

c   Article 1, so far as material, provides: 'Every natural or legal person is entitled to peaceful enjoyment of his possessions. No one shall be deprived of his possessions except in the public interest and subject to the conditions provided for by law and by the general principles of international law.

     The preceding provisions shall not, however, in any way impair the right of a State to enforce such laws as it deems necessary to control the use of property in accordance with the general interest ...'

a   convention, a measure that prevents him from residing in his vehicle on
identified land may infringe that right, but it does not necessarily do so.
Interference with art 8 rights may be justified on the grounds referred to in
art 8(2), and the unlawfulness of the establishment of an encampment is a
relevant and significant factor in determining whether its removal is so justified.
Moreover, in considering the right of travellers to respect for their private and
b   family life, the nature of that life must be borne in mind. The degree of
interference, if there is such, with their family life will be significantly attenuated
as compared with persons who have a stationary lifestyle (see [54], [57], [59], [60],
[63], [66], [74], [75], below).

(2) Although a local authority must consider the convention rights of
trespassers living on their land and their human needs generally when deciding
c   whether or not to enforce its right to possession of that land, the police, as a law
enforcement authority, are in a different position. They do not have the
responsibilities of social service or housing authorities, or the means of carrying
out the welfare inquiries that may be required of those authorities. While the
police must not act in breach of convention rights, they are entitled to assume, in
d   the absence of material to the contrary, that a local authority seeking their
assistance is not acting in breach of human rights. Proceedings against the police
challenging a s 61 direction, given to enforce an authority's decision to seek
possession of its land, are not a proxy means of challenging the substantive
decision of the local authority (see [67]–[69], below).

e   **Notes**
For statutory powers to remove trespassers on land, see 45(2) *Halsbury's Laws* (4th
edn reissue) para 522.

For the Criminal Justice and Public Order Act 1994, s 61, see 12 *Halsbury's
Statutes* (4th edn) (1997 reissue) 1430.

f   **Cases referred to in judgment**
Chapman v UK (2001) 10 BHRC 48, ECt HR.
Gillow v UK (1986) 11 EHRR 335, [1986] ECHR 9063/80, ECt HR.
James v UK (1986) 8 EHRR 123, [1986] ECHR 8793/79, ECt HR.
Pepper (Inspector of Taxes) v Hart [1993] 1 All ER 42, [1993] AC 593, [1992] 3 WLR
g   1032, HL.
R v A [2001] UKHL 25, [2001] 3 All ER 1, [2002] 1 AC 45, [2001] 2 WLR 1546.
R v Concannon [2001] EWCA Crim 2607, [2002] Crim LR 213.
R v Hillingdon London BC, ex p McDonagh [1999] LGR 459.
R v Hillingdon London BC, ex p Ward [2001] EWHC Admin 91, [2001] LGR 457.
h   *R v Lambert* [2001] UKHL 37, [2001] 3 All ER 577, [2001] 3 WLR 206.
R v Lincolnshire CC and Wealden DC, ex p Atkinson (1996) 8 Admin LR 529.
R v Wolverhampton Metropolitan BC, ex p Dunne (1996) 29 HLR 745, DC.
SK v UK (App no 19599/92, unreported), E Com HR.
South Bucks DC v Porter, Chichester DC v Searle, Wrexham County BC v Berry,
j   *Hertsmere BC v Harty* [2001] EWCA Civ 1549, [2002] 1 All ER 425, [2002] 1 WLR
1359.

---

d   Article 8, so far as material, provides: '1. Everyone has the right to respect for his private and family
life, his home …
2. There shall be no interference by a public authority with the exercise of this right except such as
is in accordance with the law and is necessary in a democratic society … for the prevention of
disorder or crime … or for the protection of the rights and freedoms of others.'

Application for judicial review

By application dated 30 August 2001 the claimants, Josette Fuller, Amanda Wright, *a*
Tina Tarr and Julie Booth, sought against the defendant, the Chief Constable of
Dorset Police, judicial review of a direction given by an inspector of the force on
29 August 2001 under s 61 of the Criminal Justice and Public Order Act 1994
requiring them to leave on 31 August 2001 an unauthorised encampment on land
owned by Weymouth and Portland Borough Council. The Secretary of State for *b*
the Home Department participated in the proceedings as an interested party.
The facts are set out in the judgment.

Catrin Lewis (instructed by *Christopher Johnson*, Community Law Partnership,
　Birmingham) for the claimants.
Andrew Fraser-Urquhart (instructed by *Kathy Rice*) for the chief constable. *c*
Nathalie Lieven (instructed by the *Treasury Solicitor*) for the Secretary of State.

Cur adv vult

12 December 2001. The following judgment was delivered. *d*

STANLEY BURNTON J.

Introduction

[1] Section 61 of the Criminal Justice and Public Order Act 1994 is one of the
provisions of that Act creating special procedures for the eviction of trespassers *e*
from land. Apart from the supplementary powers conferred by s 62, the others
are ss 77–79. Although the headings to those sections are in general terms, the
provisions appear to be aimed at gipsies and travellers: persons with an
unconventional nomadic lifestyle, living in caravans or trailers, moving from
time to time in their vehicles from place to place, and sometimes encamping on *f*
open land without the permission of the landowner. These provisions do not
apply to buildings other than, in the case of s 61, agricultural buildings and
scheduled monuments; they make specific provision for the trespassers' vehicles,
and they apply to trespassers who reside or intend to reside on the land in
question. They create unusual powers, backed by criminal sanctions.

[2] In these proceedings the claimants raise questions of general importance *g*
concerning: (1) the effect of s 61 of the 1994 Act; (2) whether s 61 is compatible
with rights conferred by the European Convention for the Protection of Human
Rights and Fundamental Freedoms 1950 (as set out in Sch 1 to the Human Rights
Act 1998); (3) if s 61 is compatible, the duties of police officers when
implementing their powers under that provision in relation to the needs and *h*
welfare of those sought to be evicted.

The facts: (a) the public authorities

[3] On 11 July 2001 a group of travellers arrived at Lodmoor rubbish tip site,
Weymouth, Dorset (the site) and encamped there. The local authorities for the *j*
site are Weymouth and Portland Borough Council, to whom the land belongs,
and Dorset County Council.

[4] Both local authorities had in place policies and procedures relating to
unauthorised traveller encampments. The borough council had adopted the
same approach as the county council, and as a result was able to use the county's
gipsy and traveller liaison service. The service includes a liaison officer who has

a developed good relationships with gipsies and travellers, who has the necessary skills and experience to carry out welfare inquiries. At the times material to these proceedings, she was Ms Nia Bailey. The borough council had also adopted a draft protocol for the management of unauthorised encampments, and suggested toleration criteria. The county council's policy was reflected in a draft statement of gipsy and traveller policy. That document pointed out that the county council

b had no official sites for new travellers in Dorset or any official transit sites or temporary stopping places. It stated:

> 'Instead, the County Council has for several years implemented a policy of sensitive management which is consistent with the government's good practice guidelines.'

c It also stated:

> 'Decisions on managing unauthorised encampments will be informed by an assessment of the specific health, education and welfare needs of the Travellers and their children. The education needs of children are an important consideration and will be taken into account in deciding whether
d encampments should be tolerated until half term of the end of term.'

[5] The local authorities soon became aware of the Lodmoor encampment, and on 13 July 2001 Ms Bailey visited the site. She handed out copies of a document containing the borough council's toleration criteria. In relation to behaviour, the document states: '... intimidatory behaviour, if substantiated, following
e complaint will not be tolerated.'

[6] The document envisages that the written agreement of trespassers to their leaving the site may be obtained. No such agreement was obtained in this case.

[7] She visited the site again on 16 July. She completed assessment forms, recording that there were then 13 'live-in' vehicles on the site, with 20 adults and
f 4 pre-school age children. There was then no record of a pregnant woman among them.

[8] On 17 July 2001, a meeting was held between officers of the two local authorities to consider their response to the encampment. Liaison with Dorset Police had already taken place, and it had been agreed that the police would
g support a period of toleration of the encampment at the site. At the meeting of 17 July 2001, the local authorities agreed to seek to negotiate a leaving date for the travellers, by which they would move on. The information available at the meeting was that the travellers might be willing to leave by the end of August 2001. The consensus at the meeting was that the encampment would be tolerated for a short period, subject to the good behaviour of the occupants. The recommendation
h of Mr Ayre, the officer of the county council responsible for the implementation of gipsy travellers policy, to the borough council was that, in the light of the preliminary human needs assessment, they should tolerate the encampment until the end of August 2001. Mr Ayre advised that it was inappropriate to evict the travellers immediately because the encampment was not causing any particular
j nuisance and he considered it necessary for detailed welfare checks on them to be undertaken. It had already been noticed that a pregnant woman was living at the site. According to Mr Ayre's witness statement, his staff and those of the borough council made it clear that, subject to good behaviour, the encampment would be tolerated until the end of August. That date was an important date for the borough council, because a contract for the production of compost on the site was due to start in September (although later its start was postponed).

[9] On 23 July 2001, Melanie Earnshaw, a solicitor employed by the borough council, and Mike Evans, of the county council's gipsy and traveller liaison service, visited the site and spoke to a group of the travellers. They discussed the end of August as the agreed leaving date, which seemed to be generally acceptable. More travellers had joined the group, and Ms Earnshaw asked for needs audit forms to be completed and told those present of the importance of informing the local authorities of their welfare needs. Ms Earnshaw had heard that there was a pregnant lady among the group and asked about her. She was told that she had left.

[10] Ms Bailey visited the site again on 13 August 2001. She informed a group of the travellers that there would be a possible alternative site for them at the end of August at White Horse Hill, Came Down in Dorset, about two miles from Weymouth town centre, and within reach of the educational and medical facilities accessible from the site. The travellers stated that they wanted to stay in Weymouth town centre. In his third witness statement, Mr Johnson, the claimants' solicitor, states that the claimants were unwilling to move to White Horse Hill because of an incident of arson to a travellers' bus that had taken place there.

[11] However, on 14 August 2001 what was regarded by the police as a serious incident took place at the encampment. It involved two police officers, who were forcibly detained at the site by travellers. According to the officers involved, the main gates had been chained against them, preventing them from leaving. They were abused, suffered minor assaults and their vehicle was damaged, and had only been able to negotiate their release by agreeing that the land belonged to the travellers and that they would not return. The police evidence is that the officers found the incident traumatic and had been fearful for their safety.

[12] As a result of that incident, a meeting was held on 21 August between representatives of the local authorities, including Mr Ayre, and Insp Gillott of Dorset Police. They were disturbed by the incident of 14 August, the more so because Mr Ayre was aware of a similar incident when a dog handler employed by West Dorset District Council had been held captive by a group of travellers, some of whom might be at Lodmoor. Mr Ayre was concerned for the safety of his staff. He felt that behaviour such as that on 14 August required effective sanction. In addition, there was concern that the encampment had almost doubled in size.

[13] Inspector Gillott stated that the police proposed issuing a s 61 direction. The representatives of the local authorities agreed with that course of action. Mr Ayre informed Insp Gillott of the results of the local authorities' welfare inquiries, which had been undertaken on visits on 13 July and 7 and 13 August 2001, namely that there were a pregnant woman and a number of children on the site, and that arrangements had been made for the maternity care of the pregnant woman. He also informed him about mechanical problems with some of the travellers' vehicles. Inspector Gillott was satisfied that the travellers' welfare considerations had been sufficiently taken into account.

[14] In the result it was decided to give the travellers 48 hours' notice to vacate the site. Some of those at the meeting were concerned for the safety of the enforcement officer of the local authorities when he attended the site to post notices that the toleration criteria had been breached by the incident of 14 August and requiring the travellers to quit the site. In consequence, it was agreed to abandon a previous plan to serve notices to quit on 25 August 2001, and instead to post the notices at the same time as the giving of the s 61 direction. In this way the local authorities and the police would avoid two separate attendances at the site, the first for the giving of notices to quit by the enforcement officer, and the

a second subsequently for the giving of the s 61 notice. It should be noted, however, that the gipsy liaison officer of the county council disagreed. The minutes report her as saying:

> *b* 'Nia felt that the Council Officers would be safe because the Travellers are aware that the Notices are to be posted at the end of the month as she had warned them of this happening. In the time Nia has been at Dorset County Council, nothing has ever happened to Officers posting notices on large encampments.'

[15] The minutes of the meeting make no mention of the pregnant woman at the site or the children. However, according to the witness statement of *c* Richard Burgess, director of environmental services for the borough council, they were discussed and the conclusion reached that there was no evidence that the proposed action would be detrimental to the well-being of the pregnant woman, and that any action should be taken before the beginning of the school term to avoid detriment to the children's education.

d [16] There was a gipsy encampment adjacent to the travellers'. It was excluded from the proposed action under s 61 of the 1994 Act, because the police were satisfied that they had not been involved in the incident of 14 August.

[17] On 28 August, Ms Earnshaw returned from leave. She was informed of what had occurred and the action that had been agreed. She asked whether *e* further welfare inquiries had been made since July. She was told that they had, that there was a pregnant woman and young children on the site, but that because of the breach of the toleration criteria, reports of criminal and intimidatory behaviour and excessive fouling in the vicinity of the site, it was considered appropriate to require the travellers' immediate removal.

f [18] As a result of the meeting of 21 August, 'Operation Veil' was planned and carried out on Wednesday 29 August 2001. By then there were about 30 travellers' vehicles at the site, most of them inhabited. Mr Brock, the enforcement officer of the borough council, and Inspector Gillott approached several vehicles and spoke to the occupants. Mr Brock informed them that the borough council as owner of the land was treating the travellers as trespassers. A written notice *g* was given, informing those on the land that they were trespassers and requiring them to leave by 10.00 am on 31 August 2001, 'failing which appropriate proceedings will be taken to secure and enforce your removal', and stating:

> *h* 'You should be aware that Weymouth and Portland Borough Council will if necessary support the Police in exercising their powers under Section 61 of the Criminal Justice and Public Order Act 1994.'

[19] Inspector Gillott followed by giving a direction, purportedly under s 61 of the 1994 Act, and handed out written notices containing the direction. Other officers also handed out the written notices and placed them on vehicles. The *j* direction required the travellers on the site to leave it by 31 August 2001. According to the police, there was considerable hostility on the part of the travellers and shouting and screaming. Three travellers were arrested in relation to the incident of 14 August. Two cannabis plants were seized, and a traveller arrested for its possession. Public order trained officers in protective equipment were in attendance, and were brought forward to deter violence. In the event, the operation passed with hostility from the travellers but without violence.

The facts: (b) the claimants

[20] The first claimant, Mrs Josette Fuller, is aged 28 and has one son, aged four. She arrived at the site at the end of July or the beginning of August 2001. She has a caravan but no towing vehicle, and relies on other people to give her a tow. She has been travelling for some six years. She lived in a narrowboat for a year and came back on the road in June 2001. She suffers from epilepsy. By the end of August 2001, she had arranged for her son to start school in the area in September. According to Ms Bailey, she offered herself as a point of contact for the mothers on the site and for Julie Booth.

[21] Ms Amanda Wright has two children, aged six and two-and-a-half respectively. The older child had been at a school until February 2000, when he had to leave as a result of evictions. She was concerned that his schooling should continue. By the end of August 2001, she had obtained a flat, but according to the claimants' evidence she had not been able to move into it because she needed to obtain furniture for it.

[22] Ms Tina Tarr has three-year-old twins, whom she was trying to get into a local nursery. She stated that she wanted a period of stability for that purpose. By the end of August 2001, she had been on the site about a month.

[23] Ms Julie Booth had moved onto the site at about the beginning of August 2001. At the end of August 2001 she was a few days over nine months pregnant. She is the pregnant woman referred to by officers of the local authorities as mentioned above. She had had difficulty in obtaining a midwife and doctor. According to Ms Bailey, she discussed the arrangements for Ms Booth's confinement with her on two occasions during August. On the first occasion, Ms Bailey reminded her that all of the travellers were expected to leave by the end of August. She asked her whether she had any family or friends with whom she could stay. She said she had not. Ms Bailey asked her if she wanted her to inquire about temporary accommodation for her. Ms Booth replied that her life was on the road, that she wished to remain on the road, and ideally would have a 'home birth' in her vehicle. Mrs Fuller told Ms Bailey of Ms Booth's difficulties in finding a midwife, and Ms Bailey arranged a visit by a midwife to Ms Booth at the site. Ms Booth was booked into Dorchester Hospital for the birth. According to Ms Booth, at the end of August her vehicle needed repairs.

[24] The claimants' evidence as to the incident of 14 August 2001 conflicts with that of the police. According to Mrs Fuller, it was 'mainly' small children who surrounded the police car, and it was children who had locked the gate. She points out that ultimately no one was charged in relation to that incident. Ms Wright too thinks that it was a child who locked the gate, and that the incident was shorter than suggested by the police.

[25] I do not have to make a finding as to whose version of the incident of 14 August is true. I none the less cannot help but contrast the detail of the statements of the two police officers involved with the vagueness of the claimants' statements. In addition, the police reaction to the incident was curious indeed if it simply involved a number of children.

[26] The claimants' evidence is that the travellers kept to the toleration criteria. They do not admit in terms that the travellers received copies of the document setting out the toleration criteria, but that evidence seems to imply that they must have done so.

[27] None of the claimants admits having agreed to leave the site at the end of August. Equally, notwithstanding the evidence served on behalf of the defendant, they did not deny knowing that an agreement to vacate the site at the end of

a August had been made. Mrs Fuller's evidence, set out in the second witness statement of her solicitor Mr Johnson, is as follows:

> 'She herself made no direct agreement to leave by the end of August 2001 and she believes that some of the people who might have come to that agreement are no longer on the site and certainly did not consult her.'

b Mr Johnson's statement of the evidence of Ms Tarr is: 'She did not enter into any agreement herself to leave by the end of August 2001.' As to Ms Wright, he states: 'She did not enter into any direct agreement to leave by the end of August 2001.' Mr Johnson says nothing about Ms Booth's agreement to or knowledge of the departure date of 31 August 2001. In that connection I refer to *c* the evidence of Ms Bailey summarised in [23], above.

[28] I have to say that I consider the parts of Mr Johnson's second witness statement referred to in the previous paragraph of my judgment to be carefully drafted and apparently evasive. He does not explain what he means, in the cases of Mrs Fuller and Ms Wright, by a 'direct agreement'. There is no denial of an *d* agreement having been made by some of the travellers on the site, and if one was made it must surely have been discussed among them. In view of the above statements, the absence of any denial of knowledge of such an agreement, and the obvious probabilities, I can only conclude that all of the claimants were aware that the local authorities had requested that the site be vacated by the end of *e* August 2001, and that some travellers at least had agreed to go.

[29] I arrived at this conclusion without reference to the newspaper article in the Dorset Echo of 30 August 2001, headlined 'Travellers ask for more time to leave site'. The photograph accompanying the article, showing police in riot gear entering the site on 29 August, was exhibited to Mr Johnson's second witness *f* statement, as evidence of the police's overreaction to the incident of 14 August and to the needs of the moment. In consequence, the defendant showed me the complete text of the article. It included the following:

> 'Josett (sic), a 28-year-old mum, said: "We have been in regular contact with the gypsy liaison people from Dorset County Council and it was agreed *g* that we could stay until the end of August. We have filled in self-assessment forms and they are aware that some of us are not ready to leave just yet because there are things we need to do like fix our vehicles ... (The police) arrested our mechanic who fixes vehicles and without him we cannot do a lot ... If we were given more time to prepare ourselves we would be happy. *h* We have always intended to leave because we know there is work for us in other parts of the country." Russ, 29, who lives with his pregnant partner Julie, 20, said: "We just need a couple more days and then we will go ..." Julie added: "I'm due to give birth any day now and I would prefer to stay here at least until after the weekend."'

j Josette Fuller was 'a 28-year-old mum', and Julie Booth was, as mentioned above, due to give birth any day. However, Mrs Fuller states that she was misquoted by the journalist in question, and did not say that she had agreed to leave the site by the end of August.

[30] The article also contained statements by travellers accusing the police of being unnecessarily heavy-handed when carrying out 'Operation Veil'.

The commencement of these proceedings

[31] On 29 August 2001, the claimants' solicitors sent a letter to the police demanding the withdrawal of the s 61 notice and a reply by 5 pm that day. The letter referred to the duties of local authorities, and to the judgment of Sedley J in *R v Lincolnshire CC and Wealden DC, ex p Atkinson* [1996] 8 Admin LR 529 and to the DETR/Home Office's *Managing Unauthorised Camping: A Good Practice Guide* (October 1998), and questioned whether the local authority had carried out their necessary inquiry process. No letter was sent to either local authority.

[32] Dorset Police replied the same day, stating:

'... the presence of this group of travellers has been the subject of ongoing dialogue, involving local and county authority agencies and the police. The County Council Gypsy and Traveller Liaison Officer has been fully involved. We are satisfied that the actions taken today are compliant with current legislation and that it was appropriate to serve the S 61 notices.'

The letter also referred to 'the occurrence of a serious criminal offence at the site', which was a reference to the incident of 14 August 2001.

[33] These proceedings were commenced on 30 August 2001. The claimants claim: (1) a declaration that no valid direction under s 61 of the 1994 Act was given; (2) an order quashing the defendant's decision to issue the direction; (3) a declaration that the provisions of s 61 are incompatible with the convention.

[34] Neither local authority was made a defendant or named as an interested party. The borough council, as landowner, was obviously an interested party, and it is difficult to see why they were not named as such, unless the claimants' solicitors were unaware of the ownership of the site. In any event, however, given the suggestion that the local authorities had not carried out adequate inquiries of the travellers, they should have been named as interested parties. Doubtless it was for this reason that Maurice Kay J, on 3 September 2001, when granting permission to apply for judicial review and a stay, ordered that the local authority (presumably the borough council) be served within seven days.

[35] The claimants' evidence did not refer to the fact that some of the travellers on the site had agreed to leave at the end of August, or any discussions with the gipsy and traveller liaison officer to that effect. Nor did their evidence give any indication as to the length of time the claimants wished to remain on the site. In my judgment those were relevant facts that should have been put before the court.

Events since the commencement of proceedings

[36] After the end of August Mrs Fuller managed to get her son into a nearby school. At the date of the hearing before me, on 8 and 9 November 2001, her position was that she wanted to remain in the Weymouth area for the sake of her son's education. Amanda Wright's older son entered a local school. Ms Tarr's twins were found places in a nursery, where she wanted them to remain until Christmas. Ms Booth had a baby boy in September. Mr Johnson's second witness statement, dated 1 November 2001, said nothing about Ms Wright's flat or her need for furniture, and did not say where she was living at that date. The lacuna in the evidence was filled by Ms Bailey's witness statement of 8 November 2001, which stated that Ms Wright had received grants for furniture and that she had been told that Ms Wright would shortly move into the flat, and confirmed by Mr Johnson's third witness statement of the same date.

a [**37**] In response to my questions, I was told that the claimants seek a further period of toleration, until after Christmas 2001. However, their position had not been communicated to the local authorities. All of the claimants are concerned that, if their proceedings are unsuccessful, they would be evicted from the site at short notice.

b *Section 61 and the 1998 Act*

[**38**] In order to decide whether a statutory provision is compatible with the convention, it is first necessary to construe it. However, its construction may be affected by s 3 of the 1998 Act, and as the decisions of the House of Lords in *R v A* [2001] UKHL 25, [2001] 3 All ER 1, [2002] 1 AC 45 and in *R v Lambert* [2001] UKHL 37, [2001] 3 All ER 577, [2001] 3 WLR 206 demonstrate, the effect of that section
c may be drastic. Only in extremis will a statutory provision be construed to be incompatible.

[**39**] In the present case, I propose first to construe s 61 of the 1994 Act without reference to s 3 of the 1998 Act; I shall then consider whether it is necessary to have recourse to s 3; I shall then be able to reach a conclusion on the issue of
d compatibility.

[**40**] Sections 61 and 62 of the 1994 Act, so far as is relevant, are as follows:

'**61.** *Power to remove trespassers on land.*—(1) If the senior police officer present at the scene reasonably believes that two or more persons are trespassing on land and are present there with the common purpose of
e residing there for any period, that reasonable steps have been taken by or on behalf of the occupier to ask them to leave and—(a) that any of those persons has caused damage to the land or to property on the land or used threatening, abusive or insulting words or behaviour towards the occupier, a member of his family or an employee or agent of his, or (b) that those
f persons have between them six or more vehicles on the land, he may direct those persons, or any of them, to leave the land and to remove any vehicles or other property they have with them on the land.

(2) Where the persons in question are reasonably believed by the senior police officer to be persons who were not originally trespassers but have become trespassers on the land, the officer must reasonably believe that the
g other conditions specified in subsection (1) are satisfied after those persons became trespassers before he can exercise the power conferred by that subsection.

(3) A direction under subsection (1) above, if not communicated to the persons referred to in subsection (1) by the police officer giving the direction,
h may be communicated to them by any constable at the scene.

(4) If a person knowing that a direction under subsection (1) above has been given which applies to him—(a) fails to leave the land as soon as reasonably practicable, or (b) having left again enters the land as a trespasser within the period of three months beginning with the day on which the
j direction was given, he commits an offence and is liable on summary conviction to imprisonment for a term not exceeding three months or a fine not exceeding level 4 on the standard scale, or both.

(5) A constable in uniform who reasonably suspects that a person is committing an offence under this section may arrest him without a warrant.

(6) In proceedings for an offence under this section it is a defence for the accused to show—(a) that he was not trespassing on the land, or (b) that he

had a reasonable excuse for failing to leave the land as soon as reasonably *a* practicable or, as the case may be, for again entering the land as a trespasser ...

(9) In this section ... "land" does not include—(a) buildings other than—(i) agricultural buildings within the meaning of, in England and Wales, paragraphs 3 to 8 of Schedule 5 to the Local Government Finance Act 1988 ... (ii) scheduled monuments within the meaning of the Ancient Monuments and Archaeological Areas Act 1979; (b) land forming part *b* of—(i) a highway unless it is a footpath, bridleway or byway open to all traffic within the meaning of Part III of the Wildlife and Countryside Act 1981, is a restricted byway within the meaning of Part II of the Countryside and Rights of Way Act 2000 or is a cycle track under the Highways Act 1980 or the Cycle Tracks Act 1984 ... "occupier" (and in subsection (8) "the other occupier") means—(a) in England and Wales, the person entitled to *c* possession of the land by virtue of an estate or interest held by him; and ... "property", in relation to damage to property on land, means—(a) in England and Wales, property within the meaning of section 10(1) of the Criminal Damage Act 1971; and ... "damage" includes the deposit of any substance capable of polluting the land; "trespass" means, in the application *d* of this section—(a) in England and Wales, subject to the extensions effected by subsection (7) above, trespass as against the occupier of the land; (b) in Scotland, entering, or as the case may be remaining on, land without lawful authority and without the occupier's consent; and "trespassing" and "trespasser" shall be construed accordingly; "vehicle" includes—(a) any vehicle, whether or not it is in a fit state for use on roads, and includes any *e* chassis or body, with or without wheels, appearing to have formed part of such a vehicle, and any load carried by, and anything attached to, such a vehicle; and (b) a caravan as defined in section 29(1) of the Caravan Sites and Control of Development Act 1960; and a person may be regarded for the purposes of this section as having a purpose of residing in a place *f* notwithstanding that he has a home elsewhere.

62. *Supplementary powers of seizure.*—(1) If a direction has been given under section 61 and a constable reasonably suspects that any person to whom the direction applies has, without reasonable excuse—(a) failed to remove any vehicle on the land which appears to the constable to belong to him or to be in his possession or under his control; or (b) entered the land as *g* a trespasser with a vehicle within the period of three months beginning with the day on which the direction was given, the constable may seize and remove that vehicle.

(2) In this section, "trespasser" and "vehicle" have the same meaning as in section 61.' *h*

[41] It is also necessary to consider s 67(1), (4), (7) and (8) of the 1994 Act:

'(1) Any vehicles which have been seized and removed by a constable under section 62(1) or 64(4) may be retained in accordance with regulations made by the Secretary of State under subsection (3) below ... *j*

(4) Any authority shall be entitled to recover from a person from whom a vehicle has been seized such charges as may be prescribed in respect of the removal, retention, disposal and destruction of the vehicle by the authority ...

(7) Any authority having custody of vehicles under regulations under subsection (3) above shall be entitled to retain custody until any charges under subsection (4) are paid.

a

(8) The power to make regulations under subsection (3) above shall be exercisable by statutory instrument which shall be subject to annulment in pursuance of a resolution of either House of Parliament.'

[42] In construing s 61 of the 1994 Act on the basis of common law principles, it is necessary to bear in mind that because it creates a criminal offence it is to be narrowly construed. Indeed, it creates a draconian procedure. I accept the

b claimants' point that travellers are likely to comply with a direction under s 61 through fear of arrest and the forcible removal and detention of their vehicles although they may have an arguable justification for remaining on the land. Section 61 must, I think, be all the more narrowly construed for that reason.

[43] The claimants submitted, with my encouragement, that s 61(1) assumes

c that the steps taken by the occupier to ask the trespassers to leave have been ineffective: ie they have refused to leave. Whereas s 61(1)(a) applies to persons who have already been guilty of criminal or other misconduct, s 61(1)(b) applies to persons who may have been perfectly well-behaved. It seems to me that Parliament was unlikely to have intended to bring the criminal law to bear on such trespassers who had not refused to leave when asked. On this basis, s 61(1)

d is to be read as impliedly requiring that the trespassers have not complied with the occupier's request that they leave as a condition of the making of a direction by the police under the section.

[44] Having considered her position overnight, Miss Lieven, on behalf of the Secretary of State, accepted that s 61 is to be so construed. She referred me to an

e extract from Hansard, but she did not submit that it complied with the requirements laid down in *Pepper (Inspector of Taxes) v Hart* [1993] 1 All ER 42, [1993] AC 593. Mr Fraser-Urquhart, on behalf of Dorset Police, submitted that there was no such implied restriction on the making of a direction under s 61. He submitted that the words are clear, and that the implication of a requirement into

f a statute is inappropriate. He also submitted that s 61 permitted a valid direction to be given to leave at a future time.

[45] I appreciate that in the present case, given the local authorities' and the police fears of violence at the site, the requirement of a refusal or failure to comply with the borough council's request that the travellers leave the site would have led to a duplication of visits to the site by public authorities with additional

g cost, diversion of resources and risk of violence. However, there was in the event no violence (although one does not know whether that was by reason of the overwhelming police presence or because the apprehensions of violence were exaggerated). In addition, Mr Johnson's evidence as to the rarity of travellers refusing to leave land when faced with a direction under s 61 may be significant.

h [46] It is clear that legislative implication is not necessarily illegitimate (see the examples cited in *Bennion on Statutory Interpretation* (2nd edn, 1992) pp 363–369). It is difficult to see why s 61 of the 1994 Act should require the occupier to take steps to ask the trespassers to leave if their compliance with that request is irrelevant to the power to give a direction. In my judgment, it is implicit in s 61

j that the trespassers must have failed to comply with the steps taken by the occupier to ask them to leave before the power to give a direction can lawfully be exercised. I do not think that Parliament should be taken to have intended to introduce the possibility of criminal sanctions to trespassers who comply with requests to leave.

[47] The second point on the construction of s 61 relates to the terms of a direction that may be given under it. The natural reading of s 61(1), read together

with sub-s (4), is that a direction is an order to the trespassers to leave with their
vehicles immediately (ie as soon as reasonably practicable), rather than at a
future time. In my judgment, the words in sub-s (4) 'as soon as reasonably
practicable' mean 'as soon as reasonably practicable after the giving of a direction'.
If a direction may be given to quit at some time sufficiently in the future, say two
days after the giving of the direction, it would be inappropriate to provide for an
offence of failing to leave as soon as reasonably practical: the offence would be a
failure to leave by the time specified in the direction. Indeed, it would be quite
wrong to render criminal a failure to leave as soon as reasonably practicable
before the expiration of the time permitted by the direction. This interpretation
of sub-s (4)(a) is to some extent supported by the reference to 'the day on which
the direction was given' in para (b): one would expect both paragraphs of the
subsection to be referring to the same starting time.

[48] This interpretation of the requirements of s 61 as to the content of a
direction is consistent with my conclusion that a direction may only be given
after the trespassers have failed to comply with the occupier's request that they
leave. If the trespassers have failed to comply with the occupier's request, there
is no reason for a direction not to take immediate effect. The occupier may ask
the trespassers to leave by some future date. If they do so, no question of a s 61
direction arises. If they fail to do so, their departure may be enforced under s 61,
in which event they must leave as soon as reasonably practicable.

[49] It is worth mentioning that this conclusion is consistent with the *Good
Practice Guide*:

> 'Reasonable steps to get Gypsies or Travellers to leave must always be
> taken by the occupier of the land (including a local authority) *before* the police
> can initiate action under section 61.' (My emphasis.)

[50] Having construed s 61 of the 1994 Act, I turn to consider the question of
its compatibility with the convention.

[51] The claimants contend that the use of s 61 involves breaches of arts 3, 6,
and 8 of the convention and art 1 of the First Protocol. The defendant disputes
that there was any infringement of any convention rights in this case, and the
Secretary of State disputes that there is any incompatibility between s 61 and any
convention rights.

[52] Section 61 confers a power on the police. They have a discretion whether
to make a direction or not. If they make a direction, they may apply it to some,
and not necessarily all, of the persons whom they believe to be trespassers on the
land in question. The police, as a public authority, are under a duty to act
compatibly with convention rights. It would be unlawful for the police to give a
direction if the result of doing so were to infringe convention rights. Furthermore,
s 61(6)(b) creates a defence for the accused to show that he had a reasonable
excuse for failing to leave the land as soon as practicable, and I accept
Mr Fraser-Urquhart's submission that the defence includes an infringement of
convention rights. In these circumstances, the question for me to determine is
not whether s 61 is capable of being used so as to infringe convention rights, but
whether a direction under s 61 necessarily infringes such rights.

Article 3 of the convention
[53] Article 3 prohibits torture and inhuman or degrading treatment or
punishment. A direction under s 61 of the 1994 Act, if complied with, involves
none of these things. If it is not complied with, a person is liable to arrest and his

a vehicle may be seized, and he may be prosecuted. Arrest is not of itself inhuman or degrading treatment, and it is not punishment. (That is not to say that brutality during arrest could not be within art 3: but if so that is by reason of the brutality, not the arrest as such.) The seizure and removal of a vehicle belonging to a person is not the subject of art 3: it may fall within art 1 of the First Protocol, which I consider below. Prosecution, as such is not the subject of art 3: it falls

b within art 6 of the convention. Neither imprisonment nor a fine, which may result from a successful prosecution, is inhuman or degrading treatment. Article 3 is not engaged.

Article 6 of the convention

c [54] Article 6, headed 'Right to a fair trial' is concerned with procedure, not with substantive law (see *R v Concannon* [2001] EWCA Crim 2607, [2002] Crim LR 213, and the decision of the Commission in *SK v UK* (App no 19599/92, unreported). Article 6 would not be infringed if Parliament introduced legislation making all trespass a criminal offence. A law making it a criminal offence to fail to comply with a direction by a police officer to leave certain land does not, in my

d judgment, engage art 6.

[55] No argument was addressed to me as to whether, in the light of *R v Lambert* [2001] 3 All ER 577, [2001] 3 WLR 206, s 61(6) of the 1994 Act should be interpreted as imposing merely an evidential burden on the accused or a persuasive burden, and I express no concluded view on that question. It is

e possible to interpret s 61(4) of the 1994 Act as creating a criminal offence only in relation to persons who are trespassers. My provisional view is that s 61(6) should be interpreted as imposing an evidential burden only. This is particularly appropriate in the case of s 61(6)(a). If s 61(6) is interpreted as creating an evidential burden only, the argument for incompatibility is further weakened.

f [56] The charges that may be levied for the removal, retention, disposal or destruction of vehicles, under s 67 of the 1994 Act, are not a penalty: they must be reasonable charges for the matters mentioned, and may be avoided by due removal of the vehicle pursuant to a direction under s 61, and, if a vehicle is removed by the police, the charges may be minimised by prompt collection of the vehicle. In addition, in my judgment, they are not payable as a result of the

g determination by the police of a criminal charge within the meaning of art 6. Section 67 creates a civil debt, and the lawfulness of any charge made under or pursuant to it, as well as the seizure and detention of any vehicle, may be challenged in a court of law. It was not argued before me that s 62 of the 1994 Act on its true construction is confined to the seizure and removal of vehicles of

h trespassers, and again I express no concluded view on this question, save that in my judgment it is possible so to construe it if it were necessary to do so to render it compatible with the convention.

[57] It follows that the fact that the procedure under s 61 is effective without the local authority having to give trespassers a previous opportunity to be heard before a court does not mean that s 61 is incompatible with art 6. A person who

j challenges his arrest or prosecution will do so before a court, and that process will comply with art 6.

Article 8 of the convention

[58] There are two aspects of art 8 that require consideration: the right to respect for private and family life and the right to respect for one's home.

[59] As the recent judgment of the Court of Appeal in *South Bucks DC v Porter,*
Chichester DC v Searle, Wrexham County BC v Berry, Hertsmere BC v Harty [2001]   *a*
EWCA Civ 1549, [2002] 1 All ER 425, [2002] 1 WLR 1359 shows, a measure that
prevents a gipsy, and equally a traveller, from residing in his vehicle on identified
land may infringe art 8 rights. But it will not necessarily do so. Interference with
art 8 rights may be justified on the grounds referred to in art 8(2). Interference
with an art 8 right by a public authority must satisfy the tests of necessity and   *b*
proportionality. The *South Bucks* case concerned the exercise by the court of its
power to grant injunctions in aid of planning controls under s 187B of the Town
and Country Planning Act 1990. Simon Brown LJ said:

'[2] The appellants in each case are gipsies, living in mobile homes on land
which they occupy in breach of planning control. In all four cases the court   *c*
granted injunctive relief requiring them (whether immediately or otherwise)
to move off site. At the heart of these appeals lies art 8 of the [convention].
It is not disputed that such removals constitute an interference with the
gipsies' right to respect for their private life, family life and home within the
meaning of art 8(1). But nor is it in dispute that the interference is "in
accordance with the law" and is pursued "for the protection of the rights ...   *d*
of others" within the meaning of art 8(2), namely through the preservation
of the environment.
[3] The question ultimately arising in these cases is, therefore, whether
the interference is "necessary in a democratic society", ie whether it answers
to a "pressing social need" and in particular is proportionate to the legitimate   *e*
aim pursued. That, however, as all parties agree, is not in these cases a
question for us ...'

[60] It follows that the exercise of the power conferred by s 61 of the 1994 Act
will not necessarily infringe art 8 rights of the occupiers of the land they are
required to vacate.   *f*

Article 1 of the First Protocol
[61] It seems to me to be questionable whether a landowner who compels a
trespasser to remove his possessions from his land interferes with the peaceful
enjoyment by the trespasser of his possessions within the meaning of art 1 of the   *g*
First Protocol: the trespasser is free to enjoy his possessions elsewhere.
[62] Be that as it may, the second paragraph of this article preserves the right
of a state to enforce such laws as it deems necessary to control the use of property
in accordance with the general interest. The decision of the European Court of
Human Rights in *James v UK* (1986) 8 EHRR 123 shows that permanent deprivation   *h*
of ownership of property may be justified under art 1 of the First Protocol; far less
is required to justify the temporary interference with possession involved in the
forcible removal of a vehicle from land when the owner of that vehicle has no
right for it to be on the land. In *James'* case, the court said (at 142 (para 46)):

'Furthermore, the notion of "public interest" is necessarily extensive. In   *j*
particular, as the Commission noted, the decision to enact laws expropriating
property will commonly involve consideration of political, economic and
social issues on which opinions within a democratic society may reasonably
differ widely. The Court, finding it natural that the margin of appreciation
available to the legislature in implementing social and economic policies
should be a wide one, will respect the legislature's judgment as to what is "in

a the public interest" unless that judgment be manifestly without reasonable foundation.'

[63] I see no reason why this statement does not apply to ss 61 and 62 of the 1994 Act. Parliament did deem it necessary in the general interest to create a summary procedure for the removal of the vehicles of persons reasonably *b* thought to be trespassers on land within the meaning of s 61 who fail to quit the land when requested by the occupier and fail to comply with a police direction under that section. I have no material before me to justify a conclusion that there is manifestly no reasonable foundation for the enactment of ss 61 and 62. It follows that ss 61 and 62 do not involve the infringement of art 1 of the First Protocol.

c [64] In these circumstances it is unnecessary for me to consider the application of s 3 of the 1998 Act to ss 61 and 62 of the 1994 Act.

[65] The argument in the present case was concluded before the judgment of the Court of Appeal in the *South Bucks* case. That case concerned the power of the court to grant an injunction under s 187B of the 1990 Act to restrain breaches *d* by gipsies of planning restrictions. It does not seem to have been argued on behalf of the appellants in those cases that s 187B is incompatible with convention rights: the argument was whether the grant of injunctions under that section resulted in an infringement of the appellants' rights under art 8 on the facts of each individual case. The grant of an injunction of course carries with it the threat of contempt proceedings for its breach and possible imprisonment for *e* contempt. I find it difficult to see how s 61 of the 1994 Act, which is aimed at trespassers, could be incompatible with convention rights if s 187B of the 1990 Act, which extends (but is not confined) to a person's use of his own land, is not.

[66] I conclude that ss 61 and 62 of the 1994 Act are compatible with convention rights.

f
The position of the police
[67] Mr Fraser-Urquhart sought to rely on the decision of Carnwath J in *R v Hillingdon London BC, ex p McDonagh* [1999] LGR 459, a decision that curiously (given the identity of the defendant) was not cited to me in *R v Hillingdon London BC, ex p Ward* [2001] EWHC Admin 91, [2001] LGR 457. In *McDonagh's* *g* case, Carnwath J held that a local authority was under no obligation to make inquiries to carry out investigations of the kind referred to in the *Good Practice Guide*, relevant to their obligations under homelessness, children's, education and social services legislation, when seeking possession of a caravan site owned by it from a traveller unlawfully on the site. I do not think it possible to distinguish that *h* case from the present on the ground that in that case the local authority was proceeding by way of county court proceedings rather than under ss 61 or 77 of the 1994 Act. If a local authority's failure to make such investigations is not a ground for judicial review of its decision to seek possession, it cannot be relevant in the county court proceedings either. However, as far as I can see, the decision *j* of the Divisonal Court in *R v Wolverhampton Metropolitan BC, ex p Dunne & Rafferty* (1996) 29 HLR 745 was in turn not cited to Carnwath J. Even assuming that *McDonagh's* case was correctly decided, it has been overtaken by the enactment of the 1998 Act. On the basis of the 1998 Act, the Court of Appeal in the *South Bucks* case departed from previous decisions in which it had been held that the court was bound to grant an injunction under the 1990 Act without reference to the needs of gipsies. The same applies to the position of local

authorities seeking possession of their land from gipsies and travellers. In my *a*
judgment, a local authority must consider the convention rights of trespassers
living on their land and their human needs generally when deciding whether or
not to enforce its right to possession of that land.

[68] However, the police are not in the same position as a local authority. The
police are a law enforcement authority. They do not have the responsibilities of
social service or housing or education authorities, or the means of carrying out *b*
the welfare inquiries that may be required of those authorities. The police must
not act in breach of convention rights; but in the absence of information to the
contrary they are entitled to assume that a local authority seeking their assistance
is not acting in breach of human rights.

[69] In the present case, the decision to require the travellers to vacate the site
was made by the borough council whose land it was. No proceedings have been *c*
brought to challenge that decision. I accept Mr Fraser-Urquhart's submission
that in these circumstances I must treat that decision as lawful and valid.
Proceedings against the police challenging a s 61 direction given to enforce a local
authority's decision to seek possession of its land are not a proxy means of
challenging the substantive decision of the local authority. *d*

[70] It follows that the present proceedings properly relate to the means
chosen to enforce the borough council's decision rather than the decision itself.
The decision of the police whether to give a direction is very much an operational
one. In my judgment, in circumstances such as the present, unless they have
information to the contrary, they are entitled to assume that the local authority's
decision has been lawfully made, that all necessary welfare inquiries have been *e*
made, and that there is no reason why eviction should not be enforced.

[71] It follows from my above conclusions that the only convention right
engaged when the decision was made to evict the travellers from the site was that
under art 8: the right to respect for private and family life and one's home.

[72] The function of the court in the present context is a review function. It *f*
differs from the function of the court on an application by a local authority for an
injunction under s 187B of the 1990 Act, when the court is exercising an original
jurisdiction (see the judgment of Simon Brown LJ in the *South Bucks* case [2002]
1 All ER 425 at [35]). The decision by the police to make a direction under s 61 of
the 1994 Act is subject to the usual tests for judicial review on human rights and *g*
other grounds.

[73] I can dispose of the right to respect for the claimants' home summarily.
The concept of home in art 8 involves a degree of continuity (see *Gillow v UK*
(1986) 11 EHRR 335). That is absent in the present case. The travellers had
arrived only in July and knew from an early stage that their presence would be *h*
tolerated only until the end of August.

[74] In *Chapman v UK* (2001) 10 BHRC 48 at 72 (para 102), the European Court
of Human Rights stated, in a passage I cited in *Ex p Ward* [2001] LGR 457 at 464:

'When considering whether a requirement that the individual leave his or
her home is proportionate to the legitimate aim pursued, it is highly relevant *j*
whether or not the home was established unlawfully. If the home was
lawfully established, this factor would self-evidently be something which
would weigh against the legitimacy of requiring the individual to move.
Conversely, if the establishment of a home in a particular place was
unlawful, the position of the individual objecting to an order to move is less
strong. The court will be slow to grant protection to those who, in conscious

a defiance of the prohibitions of the law, establish a home on an environmentally protected site. For the court to do otherwise would be to encourage illegal action to the detriment of the protection of the environmental rights of other people in the community.'

b In my view, the principle there set out is applicable to the right to respect for family life under art 8, as well as to the right to respect for one's home, and apart from the penultimate sentence is applicable in the present case. The unlawfulness of the establishment of an encampment is a relevant and significant factor in determining whether its removal is justified under art 8(2).

[75] In considering the right of the claimants to respect for their private and family life, one must bear in mind the nature of that life. It is a transient life,
c involving travel from time to time from encampment to encampment. They do not have or intend to create the long-term connections with an area, its people and its institutions of persons with a conventional, geographically more fixed, lifestyle. Their children will necessarily move from school to school, assuming that there are vacancies at schools in the vicinity of their encampments. The
d degree of interference, if there is such, with their family life will be significantly attenuated as compared with persons who have a stationary lifestyle.

[76] Any eviction from an encampment may involve some interference with family life, and I see no distinction between s 61 of the 1994 Act and civil procedures in this regard.

[77] Article 8 rights are qualified by the matters referred to in art 8(2). A lawful
e direction under s 61 is by definition in accordance with the law. A justification for interference with an art 8 right must be 'necessary in a democratic society' in the interests specified. A democratic society should be tolerant of the unconventional way of life of minorities. Conversely, however, minorities with unconventional ways of life should be sensitive to the needs and values of the conventional majority.
f The removal of trespassers from land, when that land is privately owned, is justified as necessary for the protection of the rights and freedoms of others. Where the land belongs to a public authority, it may not be an 'other'. However, in the present case, the eviction of the travellers was necessary in the interests of the economic well-being of the country, in that the borough council wished to have a contract for the conversion of compost carried out there. In addition,
g there was concern for public safety, following and caused by the incident of 14 August 2001 and the growing size of the encampment. For the reason mentioned in [25], above, I should if necessary have accepted the police account of that incident. That incident, as described by the police, would have justified the making of a direction under s 61 in order to enforce the borough council's
h right to possession of the site.

[78] Three factors weaken the case of the claimants for the protection of their art 8 rights: the temporary nature of their encampment, the illegality of its establishment and continuation, and the period of toleration that was to expire at the end of August 2001, as they had known for some considerable time before
j 31 August. In these circumstances, I would hold that the eviction of the travellers was justified under art 8(2). Interference with the school and nursery attendance of the children on the site was inevitable, and while I have sympathy with the families concerned, I bear in mind that the attendance of the children at their schools and nursery must have been arranged after the local authorities had made it clear that they wanted the site vacated at the end of August; and that disruption of the travellers' children's education is inherent in their way of life.

[79] In the present case, there was liaison and a sharing of information between the police and the local authorities. At the meeting held between the police and the local authorities, there was nothing to indicate that it was inappropriate for the local authority to obtain possession of the site at the end of August 2001. On the information before them, the police were entitled to proceed on the basis that the decision of the local authorities to obtain possession of the site was lawful. There was nothing to indicate that, if the travellers refused to leave the site, a s 61 direction would be inappropriate. The incident of 14 August, on the basis of the police statements, justified proceeding by way of s 61. In my judgment, the police were reasonably satisfied that it was lawful and appropriate to give a direction under s 61.

[80] It may be that, had it been necessary to make a direction on 31 August, they would have found that Ms Booth should not be required to move; but that contingency did not occur. If her or her baby's health were at risk if she were evicted on 31 August, the police should have excepted her from the direction as soon as they became aware of her condition. In any event, a refusal on her part to leave in such circumstances would not be a criminal offence, since she would have had a reasonable excuse for failing to leave; and a constable would not be entitled to arrest her, or to remove her vehicle under s 62 of the 1994 Act, for the same reason.

[81] I add that if the local authorities had been made parties to these proceedings, and judicial review sought of their decision to obtain vacant possession of the site, I should have wanted to investigate further the position of Julie Booth as at the end of August. I appreciate that the evidence is that at the meeting of 21 August there was an assurance that her maternity needs were catered for. However, I have no specific evidence other than that a booking had been made for her at Dorchester Hospital. On the evidence before me, I am not clear that, if she had been forced to leave the site, she could have gone to Dorchester Hospital for the birth, and I see no pressing need for her to quit the site before the birth. However, Ms Booth's situation should not have resulted in the retention of the encampment as a whole.

Conclusions

[82] Section 61 of the 1994 Act is compatible with the convention.

[83] The travellers on the site were not given an opportunity to comply with the borough council's request on 29 August 2001 that they leave by 31 August before the direction was given under s 61. For the reasons given above, the direction was premature. It was not a lawful or valid direction under that section.

[84] The direction was also invalidated in that it was not a direction to the travellers to leave immediately or as soon as reasonably practicable, but a direction to leave in two days' time, ie on 31 August 2001.

[85] If, on 31 August 2001, the travellers had failed to leave the site, in my judgment a direction under s 61 would have been lawful. It is however questionable whether it should have extended to Julie Booth.

Other matters

[86] As I indicated above, if it is sought to challenge the decision of a local authority to obtain possession of land belonging to it, it is necessary to make the authority a defendant in the judicial review proceedings. An application for judicial review against the police is liable to relate solely to the procedure

a proposed to obtain possession rather than the substantive issue whether the local authority lawfully decided to obtain possession of its own land.

[87] Although I did not hear argument on the question of interim relief in cases such as the present, two matters are worth stating. First, if an application for interim relief is made in a case such as the present, the claimants should in their evidence state for what period of time they seek to remain on the site in
b question and why. If interim relief is granted, it should not in general extend beyond that period.

[88] Secondly, where interim relief is sought on the basis of the personal needs of some only of the travellers on a site, such as those with young children or who are ill or in an advanced stage of pregnancy, the court should consider whether, if interim relief is given, it should extend to all those on the site. The claimants'
c evidence should if possible inform the court of the numbers of persons and vehicles on the site and give some information about other persons on the site.

[89] I shall hear counsel on the terms of the order to be made in the light of my above judgment.

Order accordingly.

Alexander Horne   Barrister.

Vellino v Chief Constable of Greater Manchester

[2001] EWCA Civ 1249

COURT OF APPEAL, CIVIL DIVISION

SCHIEMANN, SEDLEY LJJ AND SIR MURRAY STUART-SMITH

20, 21 JUNE, 31 JULY 2001

Police – Negligence – Duty to take care – Person in custody – Escape – Whether police having duty of care to prevent person suffering injury in foreseeable attempt to escape from police custody.

The claimant lived in a second floor flat, where he was frequently arrested. Often, when the police came to arrest the claimant, he would seek to evade arrest by jumping from the windows of his flat to the ground floor below. His propensity for escaping by that method was very well known to the police. In September 1994 the claimant was arrested at the flat. Almost immediately afterwards, he jumped from a window of the flat and injured himself, fracturing his skull, and suffering severe brain damage and tetraplegia. He commenced proceedings for negligence against the defendant chief constable, claiming that the latter was vicariously liable for the acts of two police officers whom he alleged had stood idly by as he was making his escape. The judge dismissed the claim, holding that the police had not owed the claimant a duty of care. On his appeal, the claimant contended that the police had been under a duty to prevent him sustaining foreseeable injury whilst foreseeably attempting to escape from custody. The issue arose whether the circumstances gave rise to the operation of the principle ex turpi causa non oritur actio, and, if so, whether that precluded the existence of the duty of care contended for by the claimant.

Held – (Sedley LJ dissenting) Escaping from custody was a sufficiently serious criminal offence to attract the operation of the ex turpi causa principle, and in those circumstances the police did not owe an arrested person a duty to take care that he was not injured in a foreseeable attempt to escape police custody. There was an overlap between the considerations going to the question whether there was a duty and those which attended the defence of ex turpi causa. In the circumstances of the instant case, it was not unjust to deny the claimant a right to damages, and accordingly the appeal would be dismissed (see [7]–[9], [28], [35]–[37], [62], [71], below).

Notes

For the the test for determining notional duty of care and for wrongdoers, see 33 *Halsbury's Laws* (4th edn reissue) paras 604, 608.

Cases referred to in judgments

Burrows v Rhodes [1899] 1 QB 816, [1895–9] All ER Rep 117, DC.

Cakebread v Hopping Bros (Whetstone) Ltd [1947] 1 All ER 389, [1947] KB 641, CA.

Caparo Industries plc v Dickman [1990] 1 All ER 568, [1990] 2 AC 605, [1990] 2 WLR 358, HL.

Clunis v Camden and Islington Health Authority [1998] 3 All ER 180, [1998] QB 978, [1998] 2 WLR 902, CA.

Colburn v Patmore (1834) 1 Cr M & R 73, 149 ER 999.

a   *Cross v Kirkby* (2000) Times, 5 April, [2000] CA Transcript 321.
     Hall v Hebert [1993] 2 SCR 159, Can SC.
     Holman v Johnson (1775) 1 Cowp 341, [1775–1802] All ER Rep 98, 98 ER 1120.
     Kirkham v Chief Constable of the Greater Manchester Police [1990] 3 All ER 246, [1990]
         2 QB 283, [1990] 2 WLR 987, CA.
     Lane v Holloway [1967] 3 All ER 129, [1968] 1 QB 379, [1967] 3 WLR 1003, CA.
b   *National Coal Board v England* [1954] 1 All ER 546, [1954] AC 403, [1954] 2 WLR
         400, HL.
     Pitts v Hunt [1990] 3 All ER 344, [1991] 1 QB 24, [1990] 3 WLR 542, CA.
     Reeves v Metropolitan Police Comr [1999] 3 All ER 897, [2000] 1 AC 360, [1999] 3 WLR
         363, HL.
     Revill v Newbery [1996] 1 All ER 291, [1996] QB 567, [1996] 2 WLR 239, CA.
c   *Sacco v Chief Constable of South Wales Constabulary* [1998] CA Transcript 1382.
     Saunders v Edwards [1987] 2 All ER 651, [1987] 1 WLR 1116, CA.
     Scott v Brown Dearing McNab & Co [1892] 2 QB 724, [1891–4] All ER Rep 654.
     Shelley v Paddock [1980] 1 All ER 1009, [1980] QB 348, [1980] 2 WLR 647, CA.
     Stapley v Gypsum Mines Ltd [1953] 2 All ER 478, [1953] AC 663, [1953] 3 WLR 279, HL.
d   *Stovin v Wise (Norfolk CC, third party)* [1996] 3 All ER 801, [1996] AC 923, [1996]
         3 WLR 388, HL.
     Thackwell v Barclays Bank plc [1986] 1 All ER 676.
     Tinsley v Milligan [1993] 3 All ER 65, [1994] 1 AC 340, [1993] 3 WLR 126, HL.

Cases also cited or referred to in skeleton arguments

e   *Butler (or Black) v Fife Coal Co Ltd* [1912] AC 149, HL.
     Capital and Counties plc v Hampshire CC [1997] 2 All ER 865, [1997] QB 1004, CA.
     Costello v Chief Constable of Northumbria [1999] 1 All ER 550, CA.
     *Darker (as personal representative of Docker, deceased) v Chief Constable of the West
         Midlands Police* [2000] 4 All ER 193, [2001] 1 AC 435, HL.
f   *Derbyshire CC v Times Newspapers Ltd* [1992] 3 All ER 65, [1992] QB 770, CA; *affd*
         [1993] 1 All ER 1011, [1993] AC 534, HL.
     DPP v Jones [1999] 2 All ER 257, [1999] 2 AC 240, HL.
     Elguzouli-Daf v Comr of Police of the Metropolis [1995] 1 All ER 833, [1995] QB 335, CA.
     Hague v Deputy Governor of Parkhurst Prison, Weldon v Home Office [1991] 3 All ER 733,
         [1992] 1 AC 58, [1991] 3 WLR 388, HL.
g   *Hillen and Pettigrew v ICI (Alkali) Ltd* [1936] AC 65, [1935] All ER Rep 555, HL.
     Jebson v Ministry of Defence [2000] PIQR P201, CA.
     Kent v Griffiths [2000] 2 All ER 474, [2001] 1 QB 36, CA.
     Langley v Dray [1998] PIQR P314, CA.
     McFarlane v Tayside Health Board [1999] 4 All ER 961, [2000] 2 AC 59, HL.
h   *Mullaney v Chief Constable of West Midlands Police* [2001] EWCA Civ 700, [2001] All ER
         (D) 191 (May).
     Osman v UK (1998) 5 BHRC 293, ECt HR.
     Webb v Chief Constable of Merseyside Police [2000] 1 All ER 209, [2000] QB 427, CA.
     White v Chief Constable of the South Yorkshire Police [1999] 1 All ER 1, [1999] 2 AC
         455, HL.
j   *Z v UK* [2001] 2 FCR 246, ECt HR.

Appeal

By action dated 11 April 2001 the claimant, Carlo Vellino, appealed from the decision of Elias J on 26 June 2000 dismissing his proceedings for negligence against the defendant, the Chief Constable of Greater Manchester. The facts are set out in the judgment of Schiemann LJ.

David Stockdale QC and *Hugh Davies* (instructed by *Davies & Co*, Stockport) for the
claimant.   a
Andrew Edis QC and *David Mercer* (instructed by *Weightmans*, Liverpool) for the
defendant.

Cur adv vult

31 July 2001. The following judgments were delivered.   b

SCHIEMANN LJ.
[1] The issue in this case is whether the police owe to an arrested person a duty
to take care that he is not injured in a foreseeable attempt by him to escape from
police custody. Elias J concluded that the police owed no such duty. He found   c
against the claimant on liability and the claimant appeals to this court.
[2] The judge started his careful judgment as follows.

'The claimant, Carlo Vellino, was something of a folk hero in his local
community. He was frequently in trouble with the police and had a string
of convictions for such offences as burglary and theft, drugs and motoring   d
offences, occasional violence, and also for failing on numerous occasions to
appear at court or surrender to bail. Given that record, he was inevitably
very well known to the police. He lived at 159 Grange Avenue, which was
a flat on the second floor, together with his girlfriend, Tracy Peel, and two
children, the younger of whom was his own child. The claimant was
frequently arrested at his flat but often, when the police came to arrest him,   e
he would seek to evade arrest by jumping from the windows of his flat to the
ground floor below. This was obviously a foolhardy and potentially highly
dangerous activity. Generally it seems that he would descend by lowering
himself from a balcony which adjoined the kitchen in the flat and, once by
hanging from the balcony. He would drop to the ground below.   f
Exceptionally it seems that he had even been known to jump from the
second floor window without having the benefit of first being able to reduce
the risk by hanging from the balcony. It is plain from the evidence that I have
heard that his propensity for escaping by this method was very well known
both to neighbours and friends within the community, and to the local
police. On the evening of 17 September 1994 at about 10.30 pm the claimant   g
was arrested pursuant to a warrant issued by the magistrates at Stockport
on 12 September 1994 for failure to appear in court on that day. Almost
immediately thereafter the claimant jumped from a second floor bedroom
window of the flat, which was adjacent to the kitchen, and suffered an
extremely tragic accident. Amongst other injuries, the claimant fractured his   h
skull, suffered severe brain damage and tetraplegia. He is now totally
dependent upon others for all his needs. He alleges that the defendant, who
is the Chief Constable of Greater Manchester, is vicariously liable for
negligent acts of certain police officers, namely Constable Illidge and
Proudlove who, it is said, stood idly by as he was making his escape and let   j
him jump from the flat to the ground below.'

[3] It seems that at about 9.30 pm Sgt Roberts was informed that the claimant
was wanted on a warrant. He resolved to attempt to arrest him the following
morning. At 10.20 pm a complaint was received by the police about a noisy party
being held at the claimant's flat. Sergeant Roberts went there with other officers.
When Sgt Roberts saw the situation in the flat and saw the claimant he resolved

a to arrest him then and there. Two officers took hold of the claimant who struggled and they arrested him. Someone else at the party then punched Sgt Roberts who let go of the claimant and tried to defend himself. However the other officer, PC Illidge, retained hold of the claimant. This was in a sitting room. Opposite the sitting room was a bedroom.

[4] The evidence as to what happened thereafter was conflicting and the judge b had little confidence in any of it. However he found that in due course the claimant leaped out of a window in a bedroom. Both PC Illidge and PC Proudlove were at that time in the bedroom.

[5] The judge said:

c 'I am satisfied on the evidence that I have heard that the two officers were in the room with the claimant when he jumped from the window. PC Proudlove in his evidence accepted that were he in the room, which he strongly denied, then he clearly would have been able to prevent the claimant from jumping from the window. This is plainly right. I can only infer, therefore, that they did permit the claimant to leap from the window d for whatever reason, with the tragic consequences that ensued. Accordingly, in my judgment, if there is a duty of care on these policemen to prevent this kind of injury occurring to the claimant, then there is a breach of that duty by their failure to stop him from taking action which was so obviously and inherently dangerous to him.'

e [6] The judge held that it was foreseeable that the claimant would suffer physical injury in the circumstances of the present case and that the police knew that the claimant had a tendency to jump from a window in a manner which inevitably risked serious injury.

[7] The judge said this in relation to the legal issues:

f 'Analytically there are two different questions, was there a duty of care and, if so, is the defendant prevented from recovering damages by the application of the principle ex turpi causa non oritur actio. In fact, however, in my judgment the two questions interrelate, but I will begin by considering them independently. There is no doubt that the police owe a duty of care to g an arrested person. They must take reasonable care to ensure that he does not suffer physical injury as a consequence of their own acts, such as if they are driving carelessly or the acts of a third party, but the question here is whether they owed any duty to protect him from himself, in circumstances where the conduct of the claimant involves the commission of a criminal h offence at common law, i e whether they must take reasonable care to ensure he does not injure himself, as a consequence of his own deliberate decision to escape from custody.'

[8] After considering Caparo Industries plc v Dickman [1990] 1 All ER 568 at 573, 583, [1990] 2 AC 605 at 617, 633, Stovin v Wise (Norfolk CC, third party) [1996] 3 All ER j 801 at 808, [1996] AC 923 at 932 and Reeves v Metropolitan Police Comr [1999] 3 All ER 897, [2000] 1 AC 360, the judge concluded that the mere fact that the claimant suffered injury as a result of his own deliberate act did not automatically inhibit the imposition of a duty of care on the police. He concluded that the considerations which determine whether it is fair just and reasonable to impose a duty of care were essentially the same as those which determine whether the ex turpi causa defence is applicable.

[9] He then considered *Clunis v Camden and Islington Health Authority* [1998] 3 All ER 180, [1998] QB 978, *Kirkham v Chief Constable of the Greater Manchester Police* [1990] 3 All ER 246, [1990] 2 QB 283, and *Sacco v Chief Constable of South Wales Constabulary* [1998] CA Transcript 1382 and came to the conclusion that the existing authorities strongly support the view that escaping from custody was a sufficiently serious criminal offence to attract the operation of the ex turpi causa principle and that in those circumstances the police owed to an arrested person no duty to take care that he was not injured in a foreseeable attempt by him to escape from police custody. He accepted that the police were under a public law duty not negligently to permit a person to escape from custody but held that this was not a duty owed to the escaper.

[10] The defence had however also pleaded contributory negligence on the part of the claimant. The judge held that if, contrary to his view, the police were under a duty owed to the claimant to take care that he did not hurt himself while trying to escape and if, contrary to his view, the principle of ex turpi causa could not avail the police, then the police were in breach of such a duty but he assessed the claimant as being two-thirds to blame for his own misfortune.

[11] A number of submissions which appeared in the skeleton argument for the claimant were not persisted in. The most important was a submission that the conduct of the officers went beyond negligent omission and amounted to active encouragement of the claimant to take life-threatening risks. The judge's findings do not justify the former assertion and there is no appeal against them. Nothing in this judgment is intended to contain any expression of view as to what rights a claimant might have in such circumstances. I record that the submissions based on an alleged breach of the claimant's rights under art 2 of the European Convention on Human Rights and Fundamental Freedoms 1950 (as set out in Sch 1 to the Human Rights Act 1998) were not pursued.

[12] The essence of the claimant's case was that the officers were under a duty not negligently to let him escape. They were in clear breach of that duty. What followed was foreseeable. While the claimant accepted that he was two thirds to blame for what had happened, the judge had found that the officers were one third to blame. The claimant had suffered horrendous injuries and it was disproportionate to absolve the officers entirely in circumstances where their conduct had been in breach of their duty and where they had been negligent. In this context the following cases were drawn to our attention: *Burrows v Rhodes* [1899] 1 QB 816 at 822, [1895–9] All ER Rep 117 at 121, *Lane v Holloway* [1967] 3 All ER 129 at 131, 133, [1968] 1 QB 379 at 386, 389, *Shelley v Paddock* [1980] 1 All ER 1009 at 1012, [1980] QB 348 at 357, *Saunders v Edwards* [1987] 2 All ER 651 at 660, 664, [1987] 1 WLR 1116 at 1127, 1132–1133, *Revill v Newbery* [1996] 1 All ER 291, [1996] QB 567 and *Cross v Kirkby* (2000) Times, 5 April, [2000] CA Transcript 321.

[13] It is common ground that under our law two persons can stand aside and watch a third jump to his death: there is no legal duty to rescue. Not all legal systems adopt that as their approach but for better or for worse that is the established position in English law. It is common ground that, prior to uttering the words 'I arrest you', the police owed him no duty to prevent him hurting himself while trying to escape.

[14] How then is the position of the police in the present case to be distinguished from that of the ordinary citizen? The submission is that by arresting the claimant they notionally took him into their care and owed him a duty of care. The claimant relies on *Reeves's* case. There the claimant committed suicide whilst in a cell in a police station. It was accepted in the House of Lords that the police were in breach of their duty of care to the prisoner, a known suicide risk.

a [15] For my part I am content to assume, without so deciding, that when a police officer arrests a citizen the police officer puts himself in a relationship with that prisoner which can involve the police officer in having some duties for the breach of which the prisoner can sue. But in every case one has to identify the particular duty which it is that has allegedly been broken.

[16] For instance if the officer detains the citizen then I would accept that he
b must take reasonable care that the citizen is not injured by lack of water. The officer might, if the roof showed signs of collapsing, be under a duty to take or let the citizen out of the flat where he was arrested. The fact that the citizen would never have been detained had he not previously committed a crime would not prevent an action from succeeding. The reasoning behind that approach is that by the fact of detention the man is prevented from getting his own water or escaping
c danger. It is not the arrest which gives rise to the duty of care to the man. It is his detention. That is also why there is a duty to try and prevent known suicide risks in prison from committing suicide.

[17] However, where a man breaks away from the arresting officer the position is manifestly different. By so doing the man commits a crime and he is no longer
d in the immediate power of the officer.

[18] Mr Stockdale QC who appeared for the claimant had a difficult case and had some difficulty in formulating his propositions as to the nature of the duty of care which was allegedly broken.

[19] To suggest that the police owe a criminal the duty to prevent the criminal from escaping, and that the criminal who hurts himself while escaping can sue the
e police for the breach of that duty, seems to me self-evidently absurd. No policy reason has been suggested for the law adopting such a course. Mr Stockdale expressly disavowed this way of putting his case.

[20] I understood him to submit that the police are under a duty owed to the claimant to prevent him from sustaining foreseeable injury whilst foreseeably attempting to escape from custody. This with respect seems to me equally untenable:
f it would require the police to hold him in the loosest of grasps so that there was no danger of him wrenching his shoulder as he struggled to break free. Again no policy reason has been suggested for declaring this to be the law.

[21] Moreover, even this formulation does not cover the present case. The claimant injured himself after he had escaped from custody, if by that one means
g containment by the police in some physical sense rather some jurisprudential concept.

[22] The difficulties which Mr Stockdale had in formulating the duty of care would only be intensified if his concepts were expressed in terms of the criminal's rights. In contexts such as this the police duties to the criminal give rise to
h correlative rights in the criminal. It would be difficult without making oneself sound foolish to formulate a right in the criminal against the police not to be exposed to danger whilst escaping which is perhaps why Mr Stockdale did not try.

[23] Similarly in the context of prisoners there is in my judgment no right in a prisoner who hurts himself while leaping from a high boundary wall to be compensated on the basis that it is foreseeable that prisoners will try and escape and
j that if they leap off high walls they may well hurt themselves.

[24] *National Coal Board v England* [1954] 1 All ER 546, [1954] AC 403 shows that there can be circumstances where a claimant who is committing a criminal act none the less has a remedy against a defendant who is also committing a criminal act. In that case the House of Lords ruled that a claim by the injured claimant should succeed notwithstanding the fact that he and a fellow employee, acting in concert, had knowingly broken regulations under the Coal Mines Act 1911

designed to prevent workmen coupling up explosives. It proceeds from the
principle that the purpose of Parliament in passing the relevant Act was to provide
a remedy in circumstances such as those before the House. That case has been
followed in a number of Factories Act cases. However in my judgment it is of no
present assistance. No statutory provision to the effect that an escaping criminal
who hurts himself in the very attempt of escape has a remedy against the police
who negligently let him escape has been drawn to our attention.

[25] The judge cited a passage from a judgment of mine in *Sacco's* case with
which Thorpe LJ agreed which still represents my opinion:

> 'There is, we are told, no case in which it has been established that a person
> in this situation is entitled to recover damages from the police. We are being
> asked to create a precedent to that effect. I see no reason why we should do
> so, but there is a number of reasons for my reluctance to give this plaintiff any
> relief. First, he seems to me to be guilty of his own misfortune. He did
> something which he knew or must be taken to have known was dangerous.
> In so far as his appreciation of the dangers involved was lessened by his intake
> of alcohol that was also his own fault. Second, he was engaged in a criminal
> act, namely attempting to escape from lawful custody. As a matter of legal
> policy, I see no reason to permit a man to recover damages against the police
> if he hurts himself as part of that illegal enterprise. The basis of such recovery
> must be either an allegation of a breach of duty owed to him not to let him
> escape, or of a duty owed to him to take care that he does not hurt himself if
> he tries to escape. I see no reason to create such a duty owed to him. It is
> common ground the policy of the law is not to permit one criminal to recover
> damages from a fellow criminal who fails to take care of him whilst they are
> both engaged in a criminal enterprise. The reason for that rule is not the law's
> tenderness towards the criminal defendant, but the law's unwillingness to
> afford a criminal plaintiff a remedy in such circumstances. I see no reason why
> that unwillingness should be any less because a defendant is a policeman and
> not engaged in any crime.'

[26] I am prepared to assume for the purposes of the present case that the police
negligence in letting the claimant leap out of the window was such as to amount
to a crime although, in fairness to the officers, I must make clear that I am making
no finding to that effect and, so far as I know, no court has. That assumption
however does not in my judgment have the effect of strengthening the claimant's
case. If the police were not at the moment of arrest under a duty owed to the
claimant to take care that he did not hurt himself whilst escaping then I fail to see
how it can be said that the police had such a duty thrust on them at the moment he
broke free.

[27] Finally, I point out that, if we were to accept the submissions of
Mr Stockdale, it would lead to the oddest results. Suppose that with the claimant
there had been another man who thought that the police were after him for some
crime. The police come in and arrest the claimant first. The other man rightly
thinks he is about to be arrested. It is foreseeable, as it often must be, that those
who think they are about to be arrested will make a run for it. Both the claimant
and the other man leap out the window. The police just stand by and gaze instead
of blocking the physical progress of either and without going on to arrest the other
man. The claimant and the other man suffer injuries. Mr Stockdale accepts that
the other man would have no remedy but asserts that the claimant has. That result
would surely be indefensible.

[28] At the conclusion of the argument I was of the view that the appeal must fail essentially for the reasons given by the judge. He pointed out that there is an overlap between the considerations which go to the question 'is there a duty?' and those which attend the defence of ex turpi causa. I agree. He based his decision on absence of duty rather than on that defence. So would I.

[29] Nevertheless, we reserved judgment because of the imminent publication of the Law Commission's consultation paper on *The Illegality Defence in Tort* (2001) (Law Com no 160). It draws attention to some cases to which no reference was made in argument and to various unsatisfactory features of some of the reasoning in relation to the ex turpi causa defence in some of the cases although it expressly states that it considers the outcome in the cases was correct—para 4.87.

[30] There is nothing in the paper to suggest that in a case such as the present the law as it currently stands in this court entitles the claimant to succeed or that this court can or that the House of Lords or Parliament should, reform the law so as to enable someone in the present claimant's position to succeed.

[31] Since preparing the above I have read Sedley LJ's judgment in draft. He considers that arresting officers owe a prisoner a duty not to afford both a temptation to escape and an opportunity of doing so when there is a known risk that the prisoner will do himself real harm. He considers that this duty was breached in this case.

[32] Such a duty would be most attractively pronounced in a case where the arresting officer had provided the prisoner with a car known by the officer to be life-threateningly defective. I do not find it necessary to pronounce on such a case in the present case.

[33] In the present case the judge made no finding that the officers had done anything positive to facilitate the escape by the claimant. Indeed that had not been alleged. All the officers were found to have done is that they stood idly by whilst the claimant made his escape through the window when they could, and should in pursuit of their duty as constables, have prevented him from making his escape.

[34] I have also read Sir Murray Stuart-Smith's judgment in draft. I gratefully accept what he says concerning the *National Coal Board* case.

[35] In the present circumstances I do not find it unjust to deny the claimant a right to damages. As I observed in *Sacco*'s case in a passage cited by the Law Commission at para 2.45:

> 'Whether one expresses the refusal of a remedy as being based on absence of causation, absence of duty in these circumstances, absence of a breach of a wider duty, or as being based upon the application of a wider principle that a plaintiff as a matter of policy is denied recovery on tort when his own wrongdoing is so much part of the claim that it can not be overlooked, or because the plaintiff had voluntarily assumed the risk of it, is perhaps a matter of jurisprudential predilection on the part of the judge.'

[36] Like Elias J I would find that in the present case that the officers did not owe the claimant any duty to bar his progress through the window.

[37] I would therefore dismiss this appeal.

SEDLEY LJ.

[38] It is worth recalling, first of all, how the argument from turpitude entered this case. The claimant, who had no memory of the event, alleged on the basis of what was able to be pieced together that the officers who had him in their custody, knowing of his practice of jumping or dropping from a height to avoid

arrest, stood by and let him do it when it was plain that he might injure himself. *a*
It was only as a fallback that the defendant pleaded that if that were the case his
action was barred because escape was a crime. The real defences were that he
had wrested himself from the grip of the arresting constables and was the sole
author of his own injury, and that he was owed no duty of care by them. But Elias J
concluded that in principle a duty of care was owed to an arrested person, and
that the self-exculpating account given by the two arresting officers was untrue. *b*
That left open the question what had happened in the bedroom. With nobody
on whose word he could rely, the soundest inference the judge could draw was
that the officers had permitted the claimant to jump. He had found earlier in his
judgment that they knew of his propensity to do so. As Schiemann LJ points out,
the finding falls short of active encouragement. The action was dismissed because
the judge, rightly treating the existence of a duty of care in the circumstances he *c*
had established as coextensive with the turpitude doctrine, held that the latter
barred the claim. His clear findings, however, make it possible to disaggregate
the two things for the purposes of this appeal.

[39] So the claimant was guilty of the crime of escape from lawful custody and
the officers were guilty of the crime of permitting a prisoner to escape. When *d*
therefore the defendant fell back on the turpitude doctrine he was relying on a
finding which implicated his own officers in a crime which—as Elias J went on
contingently to find—was a partial cause of the claimant's injuries. In this court
neither side has sought to disturb the apportionment of liability, had the judge
found it to exist, as resting one-third on the police and two-thirds on the claimant. *e*

[40] At the conclusion of the argument it appeared to me that on these facts
this appeal had to fail, essentially for the reasons given by Sir Murray Stuart-Smith
in his judgment. (I will indicate later in this judgment why I would respectfully
differ in any event from some of Schiemann LJ's reasoning.) Putting it baldly, it
appeared to be the law that if the claimant was engaged in criminal or immoral
conduct (turpis means literally ugly and figuratively shameful) his claim is barred *f*
even if the defendant was also engaged in such conduct. But our decision has
coincided with the publication of the Law Commission's consultation paper on
The Illegality Defence in Tort (2001) (Law Com no 160); and even in the short
interval between our reserving judgment and the publication of the working
paper, my own research had led me to doubt whether we had had all the help we *g*
needed on the law. Now that we have the benefit of the Law Commission's
research and, at the court's invitation, of counsel's further written submissions,
I have reached the conclusion that this appeal ought to be allowed and that the
claimant should have judgment for the one-third of his damages to which the trial
judge considered his own contributory conduct reduced his entitlement. *h*

[41] It is well settled that the court will refuse its aid to a claimant who, for
example, sues on a contract tainted by fraud, at least where the defendant too was
implicated in the fraud. Here it is readily apparent that if it were to adjudicate the
court would be compounding the litigants' misconduct and permitting one of
them to profit by his own wrongdoing. Where the dishonesty is unilateral, it is *j*
in general only the dishonest party who will be prevented from suing, and for a
similar reason. Applied to tort actions, the principle has been recently applied in
undiluted and undifferentiated form in the recent decisions of this court in *Pitts v
Hunt* [1990] 3 All ER 344, [1991] 1 QB 24 and *Sacco v Chief Constable of South Wales
Constabulary* [1998] CA Transcript 1382. In the latter case Beldam LJ, who had
also given the principal judgment in the former case, cited the rule in its early
form as stated by Lord Mansfield CJ in *Holman v Johnson* (1775) 1 Cowp 341 at 342,

a [1775–1802] All ER Rep 98 at 99: 'No court will lend its aid to a man who founds his cause of action upon an immoral or illegal act.'

[42] He added Lord Lyndhurst CB's holding in *Colburn v Patmore* (1834) 1 Cr M & R 73 at 83, 149 ER 999 at 1003, that a person who is declared by law to be guilty of a crime cannot be allowed to recover damages against another person who has participated in its commission. *Sacco's* case itself concerned a claimant who had

b jumped from a moving police van in which he was being conveyed in custody to the police station, and who accordingly lost his claim.

[43] While these three propositions appear in the present state of the law of tort to be parts of a single doctrine by which the court declines jurisdiction once it has found the claim to be tainted with illegality, reflection shows that they are not necessarily so. Even where the only illegal act is that of the claimant, it is a

c question of legal policy whether he should fail because (as was the case in *Sacco's* case) he is the author of his own misfortune or because (as held by Lord Mansfield CJ and reiterated in *Sacco's* case) his act was criminal, or whether he should necessarily fail at all. In most cases the doctrine of voluntary acceptance of risk will prevent a criminal from suing a fellow offender for, say, injuries negligently

d inflicted on him in the course of a robbery. But it cannot, as Andrew Edis QC for the defendant accepts, cover the case of a criminal who is wantonly shot, whether by armed police or by a fellow criminal, albeit while committing a crime.

[44] But why not? Because, it is argued, the cause of action will be assault rather than negligence. But that is not a relevant distinction in the turpitude doctrine: it applies across the board. The reason has to be that the tort is either

e unrelated or is out of proportion to the criminality. I do not accept the submission of Mr Edis that this reasoning applies only to offences so minor as to be on the fringe of true criminality. We know that, at least where the tort is trespass to the person, it may apply to claimants who are committing quite serious crimes.

[45] If this is right, the suicide cases such as *Reeves v Metropolitan Police Comr*

f [1999] 3 All ER 897, [2000] 1 AC 360 have a bearing despite the fact they are predicated on suicide no longer being a crime. (The criminality of suicide, at least as a secular offence, was no more than a legal fiction necessary to give a foundation to the crimes of attempting and abetting suicide.) They establish that the state owes a duty of care to those whom, against their will, it takes into its custody. Of course a ubiquitous duty of care does not imply a uniform standard

g of care. The standard is heavily affected in general by the circumstances and in particular by the custodians' knowledge or ignorance of the detainee's tendencies to self-harm.

[46] Arrest is different from prolonged detention in degree, but not in kind. The sometimes unbearable pressure of isolation which detention in custody can

h create is not present in the moments following a lawful arrest, and the appropriate standard of care is accordingly quite different. But this is not to say that the only duty owed by arresting officers is to the public, nor that the standard of care is so low that the duty cannot in practice be breached. The present case, on the judge's uncontested contingent finding, is a good example. And suppose for a moment that the facts in *Sacco's* case had been that the van had set off with

j the rear doors open and the drunk claimant seated by them without a firm police hold on him. There is no obvious reason why there should not have been a breach of the duty of care owed to him whether he fell out *or* jumped out, since in his drunken state either will have been foreseeable. A large share of the blame would have rested on him, drunk or not, if he had jumped, but little or none if he had fallen out. Given the ability of the law for over half a century to apportion blame, I see little substantial justice in such circumstances in sacrificing a judicial apportionment of responsibility on the altar of a doctrinaire refusal to adjudicate. There is no residual or underlying injustice in apportionment: indeed where it is *a* the claimant who has effectively put the defendant in breach of duty, his contributory fault may extinguish his claim entirely.

[47] The approach I have described was taken by the majority of the Court of Appeal (Evans and Millett LJJ) in *Revill v Newbery* [1996] 1 All ER 291, [1996] QB 567, in which an award of damages to a burglar who was shot by the occupier was *b* upheld. Evans LJ considered that to deny the claimant compensation for an assault which went beyond self-defence was a different thing from denying him the fruits of his crime and was akin to outlawing him. Millett LJ took the view that in such a case there was simply no room for the turpitude doctrine. It was only Neill LJ who, albeit concurring in the result, based himself on the Occupiers Liability Act 1984; but he too started from a common law position which *c* excluded the turpitude doctrine. In my respectful view the Law Commission is wrong in paras 2.49–2.52 to allocate this decision to the head of statutory techniques for limiting the doctrine: it is a common law case, and one which seems to me difficult to reconcile with the reasoning of the majority (Dillon and Beldam LJJ; Balcombe LJ took a different and pragmatic line) in *Pitts v Hunt*, the *d* progenitor of *Sacco's* case.

[48] Equally significantly, in the field of what one can call ordinary personal injury litigation the turpitude doctrine has been consciously eliminated by the courts on policy grounds. In road accident cases, for example, it is common enough to find that the injured claimant has contributed to the accident by speeding or driving with faulty brakes; but I know of no decision that such a *e* claimant cannot sue another driver who has negligently caused his injuries. Nor can I see any justice in so deciding when the criminal law is there to deal with his criminality and the power to apportion damages will deal with his own contribution to his injuries.

[49] It is only since the conclusion of oral argument that we have had *f* submissions on the decision of the House of Lords in *National Coal Board v England* [1954] 1 All ER 546, [1954] AC 403. There the employer sought to use the turpitude doctrine to answer the claim of a miner who had been injured in a premature detonation but who was himself (as the House went on to hold) one-quarter to blame for his injury because in breach of regulations—a criminal act—he had coupled the cable to the detonator himself instead of leaving it to the *g* shotfirer. Lord Porter said:

'My Lords, save in one case, I cannot find that such a plea has ever been put forward in circumstances similar to these as excusing common law negligence. If it were sound it would be a defence to many actions in which it was not *h* raised and might also be a defence to many claims for compensation. Conceivably it may be a defence in certain cases between the parties participes criminis, but the argument that it may be a defence between the two persons involved does not support a conclusion that a third party whose servant is one of two involved in disobeying a regulation, and so participating in a criminal offence, is thereby excused from liability.' (See *j* [1954] 1 All ER 546 at 552, [1954] AC 403 at 418.)

[50] He cited with approval what had been said by Cohen LJ in *Cakebread v Hopping Bros (Whetstone) Ltd* [1947] 1 All ER 389 at 395, [1947] KB 641 at 654:

'The maxim *ex turpi causa* is based on public policy, and it seems t me plain that on the facts of this case public policy, far from requiring that this action *a*   shall be dismissed, requires that it shall be entertained and decided on its merits.'

[51] 'Like him', Lord Porter went on:

b   'I cannot believe that a breach of a statutory obligation drafted to ensure the adoption of a careful method of working is a "turpis causa" within the meaning of the rule. Indeed, the adage itself is generally applied to a question of contract, and I am by no means prepared to concede where concession is not required that it applies also to the case of a tort. This view is, in my opinion, in conformity with the Law Reform (Contributory Negligence) Act, 1945, which, after enacting, in s 1(1), that a claim shall not *c*   be defeated by reason of the fault of one person where the damage is partly caused by the fault of another, then goes on, in s 4, to define "fault" as meaning "negligence, breach of statutory duty or other act or omission."' (See [1954] 1 All ER 546 at 552, [1954] AC 403 at 419.)

d   [52] He went on to point out that if turpitude was a complete answer in personal injury cases, the House would have had of its own motion to dismiss the action in the then recent case of *Stapley v Gypsum Mines Ltd* [1953] 2 All ER 478, [1953] AC 663.

[53] Lord Oaksey and Lord Tucker agreed, without elaboration, that the turpitude doctrine had no application to a case such as the one before the House. *e*   But Lord Reid ([1954] 1 All ER 546 at 555, [1954] AC 403 at 424) highlighting the words 'his claim shall not be defeated', held that in tort actions the 1945 Act had shut out the turpitude doctrine in favour of apportionment. Pointing out that the 1945 Act covers all forms of fault, viz 'negligence, breach of statutory duty or other act or omission which gives rise to a liability in tort', and that almost all *f*   breaches of statutory duty are crimes, he said:

'Reading the appropriate part of this definition back into s 1 makes it provide that where a person suffers damage as the result partly of his own breach of statutory duty which would, apart from this Act, give rise to the defence of contributory negligence his claim shall not be defeated ... *g*   whatever the former position may have been, it is now clear that the appellants cannot rely on this defence [viz turpitude].'

[54] Lord Asquith ([1954] 1 All ER 546 at 557–558, [1954] AC 403 at 428) agreed with both Lord Reid and Lord Porter. The decision is thus arguably binding *h*   authority not simply for the proposition that the maxim does not apply in industrial accident cases (a proposition which, if I may say so, lacks a discernible rationale) but for Lord Reid's view that the 1945 Act has eliminated the turpitude defence in tort. Even if not, it certainly establishes that the criminality of an act which has contributed to the claimant's own loss does not without more bar the claim. If, alternatively, it establishes—as Schiemann LJ considers it does—that a *j*   claimant who is committing a criminal act nonetheless has a remedy against a defendant who is also committing a criminal act, then that is precisely the present case. In either event I do not consider that we are bound by the recent cases in which this court, apparently without having had its attention drawn to the *National Coal Board* case, has held that criminality, at least if it is serious, bars a tort claim without more. The legal reality has become what Bingham LJ described in *Saunders v Edwards* [1987] 2 All ER 651 at 665–666, [1987] 1 WLR 1116 at 1134:

'Where issues of illegality are raised, the courts have ... to steer a
middle course between two unacceptable positions. On the one hand it
is unacceptable that any court of law should aid or lend its authority to a
party seeking to pursue or enforce an object or agreement which the law
prohibits. On the other hand, it is unacceptable that the court should, on
the first indication of unlawfulness affecting any aspect of a transaction,
draw up its skirts and refuse all assistance to the plaintiff, no matter how
serious his loss or how disproportionate his loss to the unlawfulness of
his conduct.'

[55] If so, what test should fill the space? The authorities are in my view not
reconcilable: in their present state, as the Law Commission says (para 1.5), 'it is
difficult to predict an outcome or to explain the outcome in terms of the apparent
rationale of the illegality defence'. It is clear that since the passage of the 1945 Act
the power to apportion liability between claimant and defendant in tort actions
of all kinds has afforded a far more appropriate tool for doing justice than the
blunt instrument of turpitude. In many cases, classically where both parties have
been involved in a single criminal enterprise, the outcome would be the same.
But the present case is unusual in that the offences committed by claimant and
defendant, while causally connected, were not joint. The claimant's offence was
able to be committed only because the constables' had been committed first.
This, it seems to me, while not in terms what the House of Lords in the *National
Coal Board* case had in mind, is also not what Lord Mansfield CJ and Lord
Lyndhurst had in mind. Nor is it the same situation as in *Sacco*'s case, where the
sole causative act was the claimant's own. Albeit escape cases are a long way
from the suicide cases, the logic of the law cannot properly differ. Of course one
can postulate untenable cases, as Schiemann LJ does in [19], [22]–[23], above; but
parody is not the same as paradigm. In respectful disagreement with him I
consider that arresting officers owe a prisoner a duty not to afford both a
temptation to escape and an opportunity of doing so when there is a known risk
that the prisoner will do himself real harm, even if much of the blame for hurting
himself will ultimately come to rest on the prisoner himself. That duty was
breached in this case, and I do not believe that a legal system which shuts its eyes
to such things is doing justice, especially—but not only—where the officers'
neglect is also a crime. To deny the claimant redress in such a situation because
of his own offending is both to make him an outlaw and to reward the
misconduct of his captors. To apportion responsibility, as Elias J would have
done had he not considered his path to be blocked by doctrine, is in my view to
do justice.

[56] While I respectfully accept that the exegesis of the present state of the law
set out in the concluding passage of Sir Murray Stuart-Smith's judgment is the
nearest one can come to a consistent account of it, for the reasons I have
given I do not think that the authorities are consistent or, therefore, that it is an
analysis that we are bound to adopt. The approach suggested in the preceding
paragraph is not only open to us on existing authority but corresponds with the
two most helpful pointers noted in the Law Commission's paper (which, again in
respectful disagreement with Schiemann LJ, seems to me to point to a real need
for clarification and reform of the law in this field). One is the search for a
consistent and defensible principle to be found in *Hall v Hebert* [1993] 2 SCR 159
where McLachlin J (at 179–180), writing for the majority of the Canadian
Supreme Court, spoke of—

a   '... a need in the law of tort for a principle which permits judges to deny recovery to a plaintiff on the ground that to do so would undermine the integrity of the justice system. The power is a limited one. Its use is justified where allowing the plaintiff's claim would introduce inconsistency into the fabric of the law, either by permitting the plaintiff to profit from an illegal or wrongful act, or to evade a penalty prescribed by criminal law. Its use is not

b   justified where the plaintiff's claim is merely for compensation for personal injuries sustained as a consequence of the negligence of the defendant.'

[57] (It will be observed that this corresponds with the distinction drawn by Evans LJ in *Revill's* case.) The other pointer is what Bingham LJ went on to say in the passage I quoted earlier from *Saunders v Edwards* [1987] 1 All ER 651 at 666,

c   [1987] 1 WLR 1116 at 1134:

'... on the whole the courts have tended to adopt a pragmatic approach to these problems, seeking where possible to see that genuine wrongs are righted so long as the court does not thereby promote or countenance a nefarious object or bargain which it is bound to condemn. Where the

d   plaintiff's action in truth arises directly ex turpi causa, he is likely to fail ... Where the plaintiff has suffered a genuine wrong, to which the allegedly unlawful conduct is incidental, he is likely to succeed ...'

[58] These two approaches run comfortably in parallel. Adopting them, as I consider we are free to do, they do not in my judgment point to the barring of

e   the court's door to this claimant, who is seeking not to profit by his own wrong but to be compensated to such extent as is appropriate for the defendant's wrong. They point to a fair apportionment of blame between his captors, who illegally gave him the opportunity to jump from a dangerous height when it was predictable that he would do so, and the claimant himself, who recklessly and illegally took advantage of the opportunity and was in the judge's view twice as

f   much to blame for his dreadful injuries as his captors.

[59] I mentioned at the start of this judgment the potential disaggregation of the duty of care from the turpitude doctrine. If one is driven, as Elias J considered he was, to dismiss the claim, it does not matter whether it is because there is no duty of care or no cause of action or no jurisdiction. This corresponds, I think,

g   with Schiemann LJ's reasoning both in *Sacco's* case and in the present case. But once turpitude is understood, as I believe the modern common law understands it, not as an indiscriminate barrier to unworthy claimants but as a large-mesh filter for criminality in claims, the difference becomes critical. Once through it, as I consider this claim is entitled to go, the next and discrete questions are whether there was a duty of care; if there was, what standard of care it imported

h   in the situation facing the court; whether in the light of the standard the duty was broken; and whether, if it was, the claimant is nevertheless partly or wholly responsible for his own loss. The judge's and my own answers to these, set out above, entitle the claimant to an appropriate fraction of his damages.

[60] The House of Lords in *Tinsley v Milligan* [1993] 3 All ER 65, [1994] 1 AC

j   340 rejected the 'public conscience' test articulated by Hutchison J in *Thackwell v Barclays Bank plc* [1986] 1 All ER 676 as a filter on claims with a criminal dimension. We are not now required, in other words, to look over our shoulders at what we fear the press will make of our decisions in this already difficult field. The public conscience, an elusive thing, as often as not turns out to be an echo chamber inhabited by journalists and public moralists. To allow judicial policy to be dictated by it would be as inappropriate as to let judges dictate editorial policy.

It is not difficult, for example, to visualise how some sections of the media would choose to report a decision along the lines which I have proposed. The Law Commission's scholarly and constructive working paper has so far been reported under the headline 'Law paves way for thugs to sue victims' (Daily Express, 30 June 2001) and has earned the Law Commission the soubriquet 'Enemy of the people' (Sunday Times, 1 July 2001). In a free society such comment is perfectly permissible and its influence on public opinion no doubt considerably greater than that of a judgment or a Law Commission paper. The public may one day have to decide through the democratic process whether it wants the law to legitimise the use of firearms against intruders in a society which at present has a gun homicide rate 150 times lower than the United States. But to expect a judiciary to modify its decisions as to what the law and justice require because of what it fears the media would make of them is to ask for the surrender of judicial independence. The 'fair, just and reasonable' test is now the established judicial control on ground-breaking in tort. If the law were ever to revert to an exogenous test, it should be one which gauges the response of people who actually know what the court's reasoning is; and no court which has confidence in its own reasoning should be worried about that.

[61] For the reasons I have given I would allow this appeal, remit the case for the assessment of damages and direct the entry of judgment for the claimant for one-third of the sum assessed.

SIR MURRAY STUART-SMITH.

[62] I agree that this appeal should be dismissed for the reasons given by Schiemann LJ. I will also state my own reasons since we are not all in agreement. It is common ground that if the facts are such that the maxim ex turpi causa non oritur actio is applicable, it does not matter whether the correct legal analysis is that the defendants owed no duty of care, because the third limb of the test in *Caparo Industries plc v Dickman* [1990] 1 All ER 568, [1990] 2 AC 605, namely that it is just fair and reasonable to impose a duty of care, is not satisfied, or that the maxim affords a free standing reason for holding that the cause of action does not arise or cannot be pursued. The question in this appeal therefore is whether the judge was correct in holding that the maxim did apply.

[63] There are many statements of the principle to be found in the reports. In *Pitts v Hunt* [1990] 3 All ER 344 at 351, [1991] 1 QB 24 at 41 Beldam LJ said, after reviewing the authorities:

'I have quoted at some length the considerations which have led courts to refuse on grounds of public policy to permit a person to enforce a claim to indemnity for they illustrate to my mind how the courts have adjusted the application of the maxim to changing social conditions and in particular to the policy underlying the Road Traffic Acts. They establish, I believe, that it is the conduct of the person seeking to base his claim on an unlawful act which is determinative of the application of the maxim.'

[64] In *Sacco v Chief Constable of South Wales Constabulary* [1998] CA Transcript 1382, a case where the claimant sustained injury when he escaped from police custody by jumping from the police van, Beldam LJ said (at p 10):

'Finally, I would reject Mr Rees's submission that the decision of this court in *Reeves v Metropolitan Police Comr* [1999] 3 All ER 897, [2000] 1 AC 360 renders the judge's conclusion on public policy untenable. The actions of the a   deceased in that case were not unlawful, nor were they criminal. In *Scott v Brown Dearing McNab & Co* [1892] 2 QB 724 at 728, [1891–4] All ER Rep 654 at 657, Lindley LJ said of the maxim ex turpi causa non oritur actio: "This old and well-known legal maxim is founded in good sense, and expresses a clear and well-recognised legal principle, which is not confined to indictable offences. No Court ought to enforce an illegal contract or allow itself to be

b   made the instrument of enforcing obligations alleged to arise out of a contract or transaction which is illegal, if the illegality is duly brought to the notice of the Court, and if the person invoking the aid of the Court is himself implicated in the illegality. It matters not whether the defendant has pleaded the illegality or whether he has not. If the evidence adduced by the plaintiff proves the illegality the Court ought not to assist him." The rule was stated

c   by Lord Mansfield CJ in *Holman v Johnson* (1775) 1 Cowp 341 at 342, [1775–1802] All ER Rep 98 at 99 to be a rule of public policy that: "No court will lend its aid to a man who founds his cause of action upon an immoral or illegal act." There are many other statements to the same effect. I point for example to the observations of Lord Lyndhurst CB in *Colburn v Patmore*

d   (1834) 1 Cr M & R 73 at 83, 149 ER 999 at 1003 where he said that a person who is declared by law to be guilty of a crime cannot be allowed to recover damages against another who has participated in its commission. I can see no reason, for my part, why a defendant, who is not participating in a crime, should be in a less favourable position.'

e   [65] And Schiemann LJ, giving the second of three grounds upon which the claim failed, said:

'Second, he was engaged in a criminal act, namely attempting to escape from lawful custody. As a matter of legal policy, I see no reason to permit a man to recover damages against the police if he hurts himself as part of that

f   illegal enterprise. The basis of such recovery must be either an allegation of a breach of a duty owed to him not to let him escape, or of a duty owed to him to take care that he does not hurt himself if he tries to escape. I see no reason to create such duties owed to him. It is common ground that the policy of the law is not to permit one criminal to recover damages from a fellow criminal who fails to take care of him whilst they are both engaged on

g   a criminal enterprise. The reason for that rule is not the law's tenderness towards the criminal defendant, but the law's unwillingness to afford a criminal plaintiff a remedy in such circumstances. I see no reason why that unwillingness should be any the less because the defendant is a policeman and not engaged in any crime.'

h   [66] In *Tinsley v Milligan* [1993] 3 All ER 65 at 79–80, [1994] 1 AC 340 at 361 Lord Goff of Chieveley, in the part of his speech agreed by Lord Browne-Wilkinson ([1993] 3 All ER 65 at 84, [1994] 1 AC 340 at 369) reaffirmed the principle and decisively rejected the public conscience test which had originated in the judgment of Hutchison J in *Thackwell v Barclays Bank plc* [1986] 1 All ER 676 and

j   approved by Nicholls LJ in the Court of Appeal in *Tinsley's* case.
    [67] In *Cross v Kirkby* (2000) Times, 5 April, [2000] CA Transcript 321 Judge LJ said (at para 103):

'In my judgment, where the claimant is behaving unlawfully, or criminally, on the occasion when his cause of action in tort arises, his claim is not liable to be defeated ex turpi causa unless it is also established that the facts which give rise to it are inextricably linked with his criminal conduct. I have deliberately expressed myself in language which goes well beyond questions of causation in the general sense.'

[68] Since the conclusion of the oral argument, the court has invited further submission on *National Coal Board v England* [1954] 1 All ER 546, [1954] AC 403. There are many industrial injury cases which are based on breach of statutory duty on the part of the defendant and where the defendant relies on breach of statutory duty by the claimant as amounting to contributory negligence. A breach of statutory duty can only give rise to liability in tort, if the statutory duty is imposed for the benefit of a class of persons, the claimant falls within that class and it is apparent that the criminal sanction is not intended to be the sole remedy. Most, if not all, safety and health legislation falls within that compass, and gives rise to liability in tort for its breach and can be relied upon as 'fault' within the definition contained in s 4 of the Law Reform (Contributory Negligence) Act 1945. That section does not refer to crime, but to 'breach of statutory duty ... which gives rise to liability in tort'. The crime of escape does not give rise to any liability in tort. Nor is it a statutory offence. Neither is it an 'act which gives rise to liability in tort'.

[69] In my judgment the 1945 Act has no bearing on the present case. There is nothing inconsistent with the *National Coal Board* case in the judge's decision. In that case their Lordships may have doubted whether the maxim ex turpi causa had any application in tort. Many decisions of this court since hold that it does.

[70] From these authorities I derive the following propositions. (1) The operation of the principle arises where the claimant's claim is founded upon his own criminal or immoral act. The facts which give rise to the claim must be inextricably linked with the criminal activity. It is not sufficient if the criminal activity merely gives occasion for tortious conduct of the defendant. (2) The principle is one of public policy; it is not for the benefit of the defendant. Since if the principle applies, the cause of action does not arise, the defendant's conduct is irrelevant. There is no question of proportionality between the conduct of the claimant and defendant. (3) In the case of criminal conduct this has to be sufficiently serious to merit the application of the principle. Generally speaking a crime punishable with imprisonment could be expected to qualify. If the offence is criminal, but relatively trivial, it is in any event difficult to see how it could be integral to the claim. (4) The 1945 Act is not applicable where the claimant's action amounts to a common law crime which does not give rise to liability in tort.

[71] Applying these principles it is common ground that the claimant has to rely on his criminal conduct in escaping lawful custody to found his claim. It is integral to the claim. The crime of escape is a serious one; it is a common law offence for which the penalty is at large. It is almost invariably punished by a sentence of imprisonment, although the length of the sentence is usually measured in months rather than years. In my judgment it is plainly a sufficiently serious offence for the purpose of the application of the maxim. I would have reached this conclusion in any event; but it accords with the judgments of the Court of Appeal in *Sacco*'s case.

Appeal dismissed. Permission to appeal refused.

Kate O'Hanlon   Barrister.

30 April 2002. The Appeal Committee of the House of Lords refused permission to appeal.

a

Practice Statement

CHANCERY DIVISION
SIR ANDREW MORRITT V-C
15 APRIL 2002

b

Company – Administration order – Reports on court file – Right to inspect reports – Restriction order – Circumstances in which order may be made – Insolvency Rules 1986, rr 2.2, 7.31(5).

c
SIR ANDREW MORRITT V-C gave the following direction at the sitting of the court.

1. This practice statement is supplemental to that of Nicholls V-C dated 17 January 1994 (see *Practice Note (insolvency: administration orders: independent report)* [1994] 1 All ER 324, [1994] 1 WLR 160). It concerns the different forms of order ('restriction order') the court may make in exercise of the powers conferred by r 7.31(5) of the
d Insolvency Rules 1986, SI 1986/1925, to restrict the right to inspect any report on the court file made in support of an application for the administration order under r 2.2.

2. Whether or not a restriction order should be made will depend on the facts of each case and, in particular, whether the report refers to confidential information the disclosure of which would or might make the purposes for which the
e administration order is being sought, or for which it has been made, more difficult to achieve. For instance a restriction order may be justified where the report contains information about the perceived market for any assets of the company which it is anticipated may be sold in the administration or the period during which it is anticipated that the trading of the company will be continued
f by any administrator and the prospects for such trading.

3. Applicants for a restriction order should bear in mind that a report made under r 2.2 is part of the evidence in support of a petition for an administration order which is to be placed on the court's file to which creditors or contributories have a right of access conferred by r 7.31(1), (2) and (4). It follows that applicants will be expected to show good reasons why the whole or any part of the report
g should be withheld from inspection.

4. Applicants should consider the possibility that the interests of the administration would be adequately protected if the court were to order that the report, or parts of the report, be not open to inspection, but that a copy of the report redacted as regards sensitive names, figures or other passages be filed as well, which would
h be open to inspection. With that in mind, if authors of such a report envisage that matters on which they need to report, or which they need to annex to their report, may be sensitive, they should consider whether to deal with those matters in a separate appendix or annex which can readily be redacted. Applicants should also consider whether an order preventing inspection of all or any part of a report without permission should be made only for a limited time or for a time subject to periodic review by the court.

Celia Fox Barrister.

Practice Statement   *a*

CHANCERY DIVISION
SIR ANDREW MORRITT V-C
15 APRIL 2002

Practice – Companies Court – Schemes of arrangement – Creditor issues – Applicant's *b*
responsibilities – Companies Act 1985, s 425.

SIR ANDREW MORRITT V-C gave the following direction at the sitting of the court.

1. This practice statement replaces the *Practice Note* [1934] WN 142 issued by
Eve J. It is directed to the practice to be followed on applications pursuant to s 425
of the Companies Act 1985 seeking the sanction of the court to a scheme of   *c*
arrangement between a company and its creditors. A change in practice is required
to avoid, if possible, the waste of costs and court time illustrated in *Re Hawk
Insurance Co Ltd* [2001] 2 BCLC 480. The purpose is to enable issues concerning the
composition of classes of creditor and the summoning of meetings to be identified
and if appropriate resolved early in the proceedings. To achieve these objects the
following practice should be observed.   *d*

2. It is the responsibility of the applicant to determine whether more than one
meeting of creditors is required by a scheme and if so to ensure that those meetings
are properly constituted by class of creditor so that each meeting consists of
creditors whose rights against the company are not so dissimilar as to make it
impossible for them to consult together with a view to their common interest.   *e*

3. The present practice whereby the applicant may bring an application before
either the judge or the registrar will continue but applications in respect of substantial
schemes will be listed before a judge. In appropriate cases applications brought before
the registrar should be adjourned to a judge. Where possible the judge before whom
the application is first brought on should retain carriage of the scheme throughout.

4. It is the responsibility of the applicant by evidence in support of the   *f*
application or otherwise to draw to the attention of the court as soon as possible
any issue which may arise as to the constitution of meetings of creditors or which
otherwise affect the conduct of those meetings (creditor issues). For this purpose
unless there are good reasons for not doing so the applicant should take all steps
reasonably open to it to notify any person affected by the scheme that it is being   *g*
promoted, the purpose which the scheme is designed to achieve, the meetings of
creditors which the applicant considers will be required and their composition.

5. In considering whether or not to order meetings of creditors (a meetings
order) the court will consider whether more than one meeting of creditors is
required and if so what is the appropriate composition of those meetings.

6. Where a creditor issue has been drawn to the attention of the court it will   *h*
also consider whether to give directions for the resolution of that issue including
if necessary directions for the postponement of meetings of creditors until that
resolution has been achieved.

7. Directions for the resolution of creditor issues may include orders giving
anyone affected by a meetings order a limited time in which to apply to vary   *j*
or discharge that order with the creditors meetings to take place in default of any
such application within the time prescribed. While creditors who consider that they
have been unfairly treated will still be able to appear and raise objections on the
hearing of the petition to sanction the scheme, the court will expect them to show
good reason why they did not raise a creditor issue at an earlier stage.

Celia Fox   Barrister.

a

R (on the application of Burkett and another) v Hammersmith and Fulham London Borough Council

[2002] UKHL 23

b

HOUSE OF LORDS

LORD SLYNN OF HADLEY, LORD STEYN, LORD HOPE OF CRAIGHEAD, LORD MILLETT AND LORD PHILLIPS OF WORTH MATRAVERS MR

4, 5 MARCH, 23 MAY 2002

c

House of Lords – Appeal from Court of Appeal, Civil Division – Jurisdiction – Judicial review – Court of Appeal granting permission to appeal against refusal of permission to apply for judicial review but dismissing appeal – Whether House of Lords having jurisdiction to hear appeal from Court of Appeal's decision dismissing appeal.

d

Judicial review – Application for judicial review – Application for permission to apply for judicial review – Requirement that application be made within three months 'from the date when grounds for the application first arose' – Whether three-month time limit for challenging grant of planning permission running from actual grant of permission or from preliminary resolution authorising conditional grant of permission –

e *RSC Ord 53, r 4(1) – CPR 54.5(1).*

In September 1999 the planning committee of the defendant local planning authority passed a resolution (the resolution), authorising one of the authority's officers to grant outline permission for a large development, subject to two conditions precedent. Nearly seven months later, in April 2000, the claimant, who lived adjacent to the site

f of the proposed development, submitted an application for permission to apply for judicial review of the resolution. Under RSC Ord 53, r 4(1)[a]—later replaced by a provision to similar effect in CPR 54.5(1)[b]—such an application had to be made within three months 'from the date when grounds for the application first arose' (the time limit provision). In May 2000, before the High Court gave its decision on the claimant's application, the developer fulfilled the final condition precedent, and the

g authority granted outline permission. At a subsequent hearing, the court accepted that the claimant's grounds for judicial review were arguable, but refused permission to apply because of delay, holding that the grounds for the application had arisen when the authority had passed the resolution, not when planning permission had actually been granted. The claimant applied to the Court of Appeal for permission to

h appeal. It granted permission, but dismissed the appeal itself, holding that the resolution had been specified as the decision to be challenged and that, while nothing in the resolution had been irrevocable until planning permission had actually been granted, the time limit provision required an objector to strike at the earliest reasonable moment at a process which, if the objection were sound, would otherwise

j end in an unlawful grant of planning permission. On the claimant's appeal to the House of Lords, a preliminary issue arose as to whether the House had jurisdiction to hear an appeal from a decision of the Court of Appeal dismissing an appeal from a refusal to give permission to apply for judicial review.

---

a   Rule 4(1) is set out at [17], below
b   Rule 54.5(1) is set out at [17], below

Held – (1) Where the Court of Appeal had granted permission to appeal from a
refusal to give permission to apply for judicial review, and had then heard the
appeal but dismissed it, the House of Lords had jurisdiction to hear an appeal
from the dismissal of the appeal. There was nothing in statute or case law that
provided any support for a view to the contrary, and it was wholly unacceptable
that the House should not have jurisdiction to hear such an appeal. Moreover, it
had never been suggested that appeals to the Court of Appeal against the refusal
by the High Court of permission to apply for judicial review were caught by the
rule that, whenever a power was given to a court or tribunal by legislation to
grant or refuse permission to appeal, the decision of that authority was, from the
very nature of the thing, final and conclusive. It followed that the House did have
jurisdiction to hear the appeal in the instant case (see [7], [11], [13], [14], [55], [57],
[58], [67], [68], below); dictum of Lord Diplock in *Re Poh* [1983] 1 All ER 287 at 288
disapproved; *Lane v Esdaile* [1891] AC 210 distinguished.

(2) In respect of a challenge to the grant of planning permission, the
three-month time limit for bringing judicial review proceedings ran from the date
when planning permission had actually been granted, not from the date of an
earlier resolution. Although the court had jurisdiction to entertain an application
by a citizen for judicial review in respect of a resolution before or after its adoption,
he was not required to apply for such relief on pain of losing his right to judicial
review of the actual grant of planning permission that affected his rights. Such a
view was supported by various policy considerations. The time limit provision
could deprive a citizen of the right to challenge an undoubted abuse of power, and
such a challenge might involve not only individual rights but also community
interests. That weighed in favour of a clear and straightforward interpretation that
would yield a readily ascertainable starting date. Further, legal policy favoured
simplicity and certainty rather than complexity and uncertainty. Finally, the
preparation of a judicial review application, particularly in a town planning matter,
was a burdensome task. It was therefore unreasonable to subject a judicial review
applicant to the uncertainty of a retrospective decision by a judge as to the date of
the triggering of the time limit under the rules of court. It followed in the instant
case that time began to run from the grant of planning permission in May 2000, not
from the resolution in September 1999. Although the application for judicial
review had been directed against the resolution, that was not an insuperable
obstacle. In public law the emphasis should be on substance rather than form, and
there was no reason why a suitable amendment could not be granted to cure any
procedural difficulty. Accordingly, the appeal would be allowed (see [5], [8], [31],
[42], [44]–[46], [50], [51], [54], [55], [67], [68], below); *R v Secretary of State for Trade
and Industry, ex p Greenpeace Ltd* [1998] Env LR 415 disapproved.

Notes

For the time limit for bringing proceedings for judicial review and for appeals
against a refusal to grant permission to apply, see 1(1) *Halsbury's Laws* (4th edn)
(2001 reissue) paras 70, 168.

Cases referred to in opinions

Berkeley v Secretary of State for the Environment [2000] 3 All ER 897, [2001] 2 AC 603,
    [2000] 3 WLR 420, HL.
Bett Properties Ltd v Scottish Ministers 2001 SLT 1131, Ct of Sess.
Brown v Hamilton DC 1983 SC (HL) 1.
Clark v University of Linconshire and Humberside [2000] 3 All ER 752, [2000] 1 WLR
    1988, CA.

a   *Housing of the Working Classes Act 1890, Re, ex p Stevenson* [1892] 1 QB 609, CA.

Kemper Reinsurance Co v Minister of Finance [2000] 1 AC 1, [1998] 3 WLR 630, PC.

Lane v Esdaile [1891] AC 210, HL

O'Reilly v Mackman [1982] 3 All ER 1124, [1983] 2 AC 237, [1982] 3 WLR 1096, HL.

Poh, Re [1983] 1 All ER 287, [1983] 1 WLR 2, HL.

R v Ceredigion CC, ex p McKeown [1998] 2 PLR 1.

b   *R v Dairy Produce Quota Tribunal for England and Wales, ex p Caswell* [1990] 2 All ER 434, [1990] 2 AC 738, [1990] 2 WLR 1320, CA.

R v Rochdale MBC, ex p B, C, and K [2000] Ed CR 117.

R v Secretary of State for Trade and Industry, ex p Eastaway [2001] 1 All ER 27, [2000] 1 WLR 2222, HL.

c   *R v Secretary of State for Trade and Industry, ex p Greenpeace Ltd* [1998] Env LR 415.

R v Secretary of State for Trade and Industry, ex p Greenpeace Ltd [2000] Env LR 221.

R v West Oxfordshire DC, ex p CH Pearce Homes Ltd (1986) 26 RVR 156.

Singh v Secretary of State for the Home Dept 2000 SLT 533, Ct of Sess.

Sunday Times v UK (1979) 2 EHRR 245, ECt HR.

d   *Swan v Secretary of State for Scotland* 1998 SC 479, Ct of Sess.

Uprichard v Fife Council [2001] Env LR 122.

West v Secretary of State for Scotland 1992 SC 385, Ct of Sess.

World Wildlife Fund (WWF) v Autonome Provinz Bozen Case C-435/97 [2000] 1 CMLR 149, ECJ.

e
Appeal

The claimant, Sonia Burkett, appealed with permission of the Appeal Committee of the House of Lords given on 23 July 2001 from the decision of the Court of Appeal (Ward, Sedley and Jonathan Parker LJJ) on 13 December 2000 ([2001] 3 PLR 1) dismissing an appeal brought by her and her late husband, Robert
f Burkett, from the order of Richards J on 29 June 2000 refusing their renewed application for permission to apply for judicial review of a resolution of the planning committee of the defendant local authority, Hammersmith and Fulham London Borough Council, on 15 September 1999 authorising the director of the environment department to grant outline planning permission to the interested party, St George (West London) Ltd (the developer), for the mixed use development
g of land at Imperial Wharf, Imperial Road, London SW6, subject to conditions. The facts are set out in the opinion of Lord Steyn.

Robert McCracken, Richard Harwood and Angela Ward (instructed by Richard Buxton, Cambridge) for Mrs Burkett.
h Timothy Straker QC and Andrew Tabachnik (instructed by Andrew Berisford) for the local authority.

Robin Purchas QC and Joanna Clayton (instructed by Masons) for the developer.

Their Lordships took time for consideration.
j

23 May 2002. The following opinions were delivered.

LORD SLYNN OF HADLEY.

[1] My Lords, this appeal raises an important question in the context of planning law. The facts and the issues are set out in the speech of my noble and learned friend Lord Steyn to which I gratefully refer.

[2] In summary, a committee of the local planning authority decided on 15 September 1999 that planning permission should be granted for a large-scale development in Fulham subject to certain conditions being fulfilled. On 6 April 2000 the appellant, Mrs Burkett, applied for leave to move for judicial review of that decision. On 12 May 2000 planning permission was actually granted.

[3] At that time RSC Ord 53, r 4(1) provided that an application for leave to apply for judicial review should be made 'promptly and in any event within three months from the date when grounds for the application first arose'. If the relevant date was 15 September 1999 the application was clearly out of time. Richards J and the Court of Appeal ([2001] 3 PLR 1) refused permission on the ground that the application was out of time.

[4] It is clear that if the challenge is to the resolution (as it may be) time runs from that date, but the question on the present appeal is whether, if the application is amended to challenge the grant of planning permission rather than the resolution, time runs from 15 September 1999 or 12 May 2000.

[5] In my opinion, for the reasons given by Lord Steyn, where there is a challenge to the grant itself, time runs from the date of the grant and not from the date of the resolution. It seems to me clear that because someone fails to challenge in time a resolution conditionally authorising the grant of planning permission, that failure does not prevent a challenge to the grant itself if brought in time, ie from the date when the planning permission is granted. I realise that this may cause some difficulties in practice, both for local authorities and for developers, but for the grant not to be capable of challenge, because the resolution has not been challenged in time, seems to me wrongly to restrict the right of the citizen to protect his interests. The relevant legislative provisions do not compel such a result nor do principles of administrative law prevent a challenge to the grant even if the grounds relied on are broadly the same as those which if brought in time would have been relied on to challenge the resolution.

[6] The question whether an obligation to apply 'promptly' is sufficient to satisfy European Community law or convention rights as to certainty does not arise in this case and I do not comment on it.

[7] As to the preliminary objection to the House's jurisdiction, this case is plainly distinguishable from Re Poh [1983] 1 All ER 287, [1983] 1 WLR 2 since the Court of Appeal here gave leave to appeal from the judge and heard the appeal. It is wholly unacceptable that the House should not have jurisdiction to hear such an appeal. I consider in any event that the dictum in Re Poh which is relied on for the contrary result should be laid to rest.

[8] I would accordingly allow the appeal and remit the substantive question to the High Court for decision.

LORD STEYN.

[9] My Lords, this appeal raises important questions of law in regard to delay in launching judicial review proceedings. The context is town planning. The proposal concerns a large development at Imperial Wharf, Fulham, London. The appellant is Mrs Burkett who lives in a ground floor maisonette adjoining the site. She believes that the development will have an adverse effect on her quality of life and the health of her family. The respondent is the London Borough of Hammersmith and Fulham (the local authority). St George (West London) Ltd is the developer and is joined in the proceedings as an interested party (the developer). It will be necessary to explain the circumstances of the case in some detail. There is, however, an anterior legal question to be considered.

(I) Jurisdiction

a

[10] The issue arises in this way. Mrs Burkett and her late husband applied for judicial review. The matter came before Richards J. He refused permission on the grounds of delay. The Court of Appeal granted permission to the applicants to appeal from the decision of Richards J. After a full inter partes hearing the Court of Appeal ([2001] 3 PLR 1) refused permission to seek judicial review on

b grounds of delay and dismissed the appeal. The Court of Appeal refused leave to appeal to the House of Lords. An Appeal Committee granted leave to appeal.

[11] Relying on the decision of the House of Lords in *Re Poh* [1983] 1 All ER 287, [1983] 1 WLR 2 counsel for the local authority submitted that the House does not have jurisdiction to hear an appeal from a decision by the Court of Appeal refusing permission to seek judicial review. In *Re Poh* the judge had

c refused leave to apply for judicial review. The applicant appealed ex parte by originating motion to the Court of Appeal who refused leave. The applicant sought leave to appeal to the House. The House ruled that there was no jurisdiction to grant leave. Giving the brief reasons of the House Lord Diplock observed ([1983] 1 All ER 287 at 288, [1983] 1 WLR 2 at 3):

d

> 'Their Lordships are not concerned with the procedure whereby this application moved from the Divisional Court to the Court of Appeal, because the question we have to consider is whether this House has jurisdiction to entertain the application. Counsel instructed by the Treasury Solicitor has taken the preliminary point that the House has no jurisdiction
>
> e under the Appellate Jurisdiction Act 1876 to entertain an appeal from refusal of leave to apply for judicial review under RSC Ord 53. He relies upon the construction of s 3 of the 1876 Act, which was approved by this House in *Lane v Esdaile* [1891] AC 210 ...'

Three points need to be noted about this statement. First, *Lane v Esdaile* is only

f authority for the general proposition that whenever a power is given to a court or tribunal by legislation to grant or refuse leave to appeal, the decision of that authority is, from the very nature of the thing, final and conclusive (see *Re Housing of the Working Classes Act 1890, ex p Stevenson* [1892] 1 QB 609). Secondly, Lord Diplock extended this rule to an appeal from a refusal of leave to apply for judicial review. Thirdly, Lord Diplock gave no reasons for this

g extension of the principle in *Lane's* case.

[12] The decision in *Poh's* case has proved troublesome. In *Kemper Reinsurance Co v Minister of Finance* [2000] 1 AC 1, [1998] 3 WLR 630 the Privy Council cast doubt on the reasoning in *Poh's* case. Lord Hoffmann observed that a renewed application to the Court of Appeal under RSC Ord 59, r 14(3) is a true appeal with

h a procedure adapted to its ex parte nature. Referring to *Poh's* case, Lord Hoffmann stated ([2000] 1 AC 1 at 18, [1998] 3 WLR 630 at 642):

> 'It would not be right for their Lordships to make any comment upon this decision in its application to appeals from the English Court of Appeal to the House of Lords. But the judgment expressly disclaimed any expression of
>
> j view upon the nature of "the procedure whereby this appeal moved from the Divisional Court to the Court of Appeal". The decision is therefore not inconsistent with their Lordships' opinion that the application to the Court of Appeal is a true appeal, not excluded by the principle in *Lane v. Esdaile*. Their Lordships accept that this conclusion makes it difficult to identify the reasoning by which the House of Lords decided that the principle applied to a further appeal to the House of Lords ...'

In *R v Secretary of State for Trade and Industry, ex p Eastaway* [2001] 1 All ER 27, [2000] 1 WLR 2222 the House considered *Re Poh* [1983] 1 All ER 287, [1983] 1 WLR 2, but did not have to rule on its status. *Ex p Eastaway* is only authority for the proposition that when the Court of Appeal has refused permission to appeal in the face of a first instance refusal of permission to seek judicial review the House has no jurisdiction to give leave to appeal (see [2001] 1 All ER 27 at 32–33, [2000] 1 WLR 2222 at 2228).

[13] Counsel for the local authority submitted that the decision in *Re Poh*, read with the observation that '[their] Lordships are not concerned with the procedure whereby this application moved from the Divisional Court to the Court of Appeal', appears to deprive the House of jurisdiction to entertain the present appeal. A material difference, however, is that in the present case the Court of Appeal granted leave to appeal and heard the appeal. It would be extraordinary if in such a case the House had no jurisdiction. Nothing in statute law or in *Lane v Esdaile* provides any support for such a view. Moreover, as Lord Hoffmann pointed out in *Kemper Reinsurance Co v Minister of Finance* [2000] 1 AC 1 at 18, [1998] 3 WLR 630 at 642, it has never been suggested either before or after the decision in *Re Poh* that appeals to the Court of Appeal against refusal by the High Court of leave to apply for judicial review are caught by the rule in *Lane's* case. In my view the conclusion is inescapable that Lord Diplock's ex tempore observation was not correct. It follows that the House has jurisdiction to grant leave to appeal against a refusal by the Court of Appeal of permission to apply for judicial review.

[14] The jurisdictional objection to the hearing of the appeal must be rejected.

(II) The legal background

[15] In order to make the case intelligible it is necessary to set out some of the legal background to the planning application. Environmental assessment pursuant to Council Directive (EEC) 85/337 (on the assessment of the effects of certain public and private projects on the environment) (OJ 1985 L175 p 40) (as amended by Council Directive (EEC) 97/11) (OJ 1997 L73 p 5) is a fundamental instrument of European Community policy. The preambles of the directive include the following:

'Whereas ... the best environmental policy consists in preventing the creation of pollution or nuisances at source, rather than subsequently trying to counteract their effects; whereas they affirm the need to take effects on the environment into account at the earliest possible stage in all technical planning and decision-making processes; whereas to that end they provide for the implementation of procedures to evaluate such effects ... Whereas development consent for public and private projects which are likely to have significant effects on the environment should be granted only after prior assessment of the likely significant effects of these projects has been carried out; whereas this assessment must be conducted on the basis of the appropriate information supplied by the developer, which may be supplemented by the authorities and by the people who may be concerned by the project in question ...'

Article 2 provides:

'1. Member States shall adopt all measures necessary to ensure that, before consent is given, projects likely to have significant effects on the environment by virtue *inter alia*, of their nature, size or location are made subject to a a   requirement for development consent and an assessment with regard to their effect.'

Article 5 provides:

'3. The information to be provided by the developer in accordance with paragraph 1 shall include at least:

b   —a description of the project comprising information on the site, design and size of the project,

—a description of the measures envisaged in order to avoid, reduce and, if possible, remedy significant adverse effects ...'

The directive creates rights for individuals enforceable in the courts (see *World* c *Wildlife Fund (WWF) v Autonome Provinz Bozen* Case C-435/97 [2000] 1 CMLR 149 at 177–178 (paras 69–71); *Berkeley v Secretary of State for the Environment* [2000] 3 All ER 897, [2001] 2 AC 603). There is an obligation on national courts to ensure that individual rights are fully and effectively protected (see *Berkeley*'s case [2000] 3 All ER 897 at 900, [2001] 2 AC 603 at 608 per Lord Bingham of Cornhill and [2000] 3 All d   ER 897 at 909, [2001] 2 AC 603 at 618). The directive seeks to redress to some extent the imbalance in resources between promoters of major developments and those concerned, on behalf of individual or community interests, about the environmental effects of such projects.

[16]   It is unnecessary to describe the familiar planning regime enshrined in the Town and Country Planning Act 1990. For present purposes it is sufficient to e   point out that there is a general prohibition on the grant of planning permission without consideration of environmental information (see reg 4 of the Town and Country Planning (Assessment of Environmental Effects) Regulations 1988, SI 1988/1199).

[17]   Persons aggrieved by planning decisions may seek permission to apply for judicial review. Rules of court govern the making of judicial review applications. f   For present purposes provisions dealing with delay are directly relevant. At the relevant time RSC Ord 53, r 4(1), was in force. It provided:

'An application for leave to apply for judicial review shall be made promptly and in any event within three months from the date when grounds for the application first arose unless the Court considers that there is good g   reason for extending the period within which the application shall be made.'

It has now been replaced by CPR 54.5(1). It provides in respect of applications for judicial review: 'The claim form must be filed—(a) promptly; and (b) in any event not later than 3 months after the grounds to make the claim first arose.'

h   [18]   It is also necessary to draw attention to s 31(6) of the Supreme Court Act 1981. It provides:

'Where the High Court considers that there has been undue delay in making an application for judicial review, the court may refuse to grant— (a) leave for the making of the application; or (b) any relief sought on the j   application, if it considers that the granting of the relief sought would be likely to cause substantial hardship to, or substantially prejudice the rights of, any person or would be detrimental to good administration.'

The differences between the rules of court and s 31(6) are analysed in Craig *Administrative Law* (4th edn, 1999) pp 791–793. Pertinent to the present context is the fact that s 31(6) contains no date from which time runs and accordingly no specific time limit. It is, however, a useful reserve power in some cases, such as

where an application made well within the three-month period would cause
immense practical difficulties. An illustration is *R v Rochdale MBC, ex p B, C, and K*   a
[2000] Ed CR 117. Having referred to s 31(6), Mr David Pannick QC (sitting as a
deputy judge of the High Court) stated (at 120):

> 'In my judgment, it is absolutely essential that, if parents are to bring
> judicial review proceedings in relation to the allocation of places at
> secondary school for their children, the matter is heard and determined by   b
> court, absent very exceptional circumstances, before the school term starts.
> This is for obvious reasons relating to the interests of the child concerned,
> the interests of the school, the interests of the other children at the affected
> school and, of course, the teachers at that school.'

The good sense of this approach is manifest.   c

[19] Finally, for the sake of completeness, I refer to the statement by Wade
and Forsyth *Administrative Law* (8th edn, 2000) p 688 that the most active
remedies of administrative law—declaration, injunction, certiorari, prohibition,
mandamus—are discretionary and the court may therefore withhold them if it
thinks fit. On the other hand, as the same authors point out, '[t]he true scope for   d
discretion is in the law of remedies, where it operates within narrow and
recognised limits ...'

(III) *The planning application*

[20] Imperial Wharf is a site comprising some 32 acres. It had formerly been
used by British Gas for operational purposes, and parts of the site had been let out   e
for industrial use. On 26 February 1998 the developer applied to the local
authority for outline planning permission for—

> 'A mixed use development comprising 1,803 residential units (1,303 private
> flats and 500 affordable dwellings in the form of flats and houses), an hotel,
> class A1 retail, class A3 restaurant, Class D community uses, health and   f
> fitness club, Class B1 offices, public open space and riverside walk, together
> with associated car parking, landscaping and access roads.'

It is one of the largest current development sites in London. The application for
outline planning permission proposed that design, external appearance and
landscaping of the whole development were to be reserved for later determination.   g
The proposed scheme was not in accordance with the development plan. On
16 March 1998 the local authority asked the developer to submit an environmental
statement with the planning application. On 27 May 1998 the developer submitted
a document described as an environmental statement.

[21] The agreed statement of facts and issues explains the potential impact of   h
the development on Mrs Burkett and her daughter. Mrs Burkett lives with her
asthmatic daughter. Their home and garden are immediately adjacent to the site.
Her husband died after the Court of Appeal decision. He had been a chronic
diabetic with a liver disorder and had been housebound for much of the time.
Works have regularly caused dust to cover all the surfaces in the maisonette. A
particular concern has been the effect of the development on the health of the   j
family. In 1999, at a tenants' association meeting, Mr and Mrs Burkett were
advised that they could not remove the paving blocks from their garden and
replace them with lawn because of problems of contamination. This was
apparently due to previous contamination of the land. On 30 July 1999
Mrs Burkett's solicitors, Richard Buxton, then assisting a pressure group on a pro
bono basis, wrote to the local authority warning that the environmental

a   statement was inadequate and that it would be unlawful to approve the planning application. This letter was drawn to the attention of the relevant committee when it came to consider the planning application.

[22] On 15 September 1999 the local authority's planning and traffic management committee considered the application. The committee resolved to refer the application to the Secretary of State as a departure from the development plan. It
b   further resolved to authorise the director of the environment department of the local authority to grant outline permission subject to (i) completion of a satisfactory agreement enforceable pursuant to s 106 of the 1990 Act and (ii) there being no contrary direction on behalf of the Secretary of State from the Government Office for London. On 5 October 1999 the Government Office for
c   London imposed a direction pursuant to art 14 of the Town and Country Planning (General Development Procedure) Order 1995, SI 1995 / 419 prohibiting the grant of permission. On 24 February 2000 the Government Office for London decided not to call in the application and lifted the prohibition under art 14. On 28 March 2000 Richard Buxton wrote to the local authority expressing concerns about the inadequacies of the environmental statement and inviting reconsideration
d   by the local authority. On 29 March 2000 the local authority replied asking for further particulars of the claimed inadequacies.

(IV) *The judicial review application*

[23] On 6 April 2000 Mr and Mrs Burkett submitted an application for permission
e   to apply for judicial review. Form 86A identified the decision to be challenged as the resolution of 15 September 1999. It described the substantive relief sought as '[a]n order for certiorari to quash the above resolution'. It will be observed that the application was made more than six months after the resolution of 15 September 1999. On 17 April 2000 Richard Buxton sent a copy of the application for judicial review to the local authority again inviting them to reconsider the resolution for
f   the grant of planning permission. On 19 April 2000 the local authority told the Crown Office that it might wish to make representations both on delay and on the substantive grounds of challenge. The local authority told the developer of the application. On 25 April 2000 Richard Buxton reminded the local authority that it had a complete copy of the application for permission to apply for judicial review. In early May 2000 the developer and the local authority lodged
g   representations with the court.

(V) *Grant of planning permission*

[24] On 12 May 2000 the local authority and the developer completed an
h   agreement under s 106 of the 1990 Act in respect of the developer's planning obligations. Acting on the authority of the resolution of 15 September 1999 the director of the environment department of the local authority granted outline planning permission on the same day.

(VI) *The decision at first instance and in the Court of Appeal*
j   [25] On 18 May 2000 Newman J refused permission to apply for judicial review on the papers in respect of both delay and merits. On 29 June 2000 Richards J accepted, after reading what he described as detailed skeleton arguments from the local authority and the developer, but without hearing oral arguments from them, that the grounds for judicial review were, on the merits, arguable but refused permission on the grounds of delay. In an unreported judgment Richards J addressed the critical question as follows:

'When did grounds for the application first arise? [Counsel for the applicants] submits that it was reasonable to wait until the Secretary of State's decision not to call the application in. Alternatively, he would, if necessary, contend that the relevant date is the date when planning permission was actually granted. In my judgment, however, the relevant date was the date when the [local authority] passed its resolution to grant outline planning permission. That was the operative decision. That—not some later event—is what is challenged in the Form 86A. The fact that there were still a number of contingencies before the formal grant of planning permission does not mean that grounds for the application arose only at some later date. The existence of those contingencies is a matter to be considered in relation to the discretion to extend time, if there was a failure to apply promptly. It does not, in my view, lead to the conclusion that time did not begin to run at the date of the resolution.'

In the circumstances, and particularly in the absence of a clear warning by the applicants to the local authority, the judge refused to extend time.

[26] On 20 November 2000 the Court of Appeal granted permission to appeal and heard the appeal. The Court of Appeal did not examine the merits of the substantive issues. It concentrated on the issue of delay. Counsel for the applicants had argued that the final grant of planning permission is the single event from which all rights and obligations flow and it is therefore the date from which time runs against the citizen. In the judgment of the court (Ward, Sedley and Jonathan Parker LJJ), given on 13 December, this argument is dismissed on the following ground ([2001] 3 PLR 1 at 4 (para 8)):

'The applicants' argument, as [counsel for the local authority] amply demonstrated, faces two initial hurdles. One is that their Form 86A, lodged on 6 April 2000, specifies the resolution of 15 September 1999 as the decision to be challenged. The other is that, on the face of it, it is right to do so, since Ord 53 r 4(1) of the Rules of the Supreme Court, which were then in force, in terms required an application for leave to be "made promptly and in any event within three months from the date when grounds for the application first arose". Since the impugned environmental impact statement was as necessary to the resolution as to any subsequent steps, the logic of measuring time from the resolution seems inescapable.'

Acknowledging (at 5 (para 10)) 'that nothing in a resolution is irrevocable until planning permission is actually granted' the Court of Appeal observed (at 5 (para 11)):

'We do not doubt the legal accuracy of any of this, but it fails, in our judgment, to disturb the proposition that where the same objection affects the initial resolution as will affect the eventual grant of permission, it is as a simple matter of language at the date of the resolution that the objection, and therefore the grounds for the application first arise. We do not accept [counsel for the applicants'] submission that to give effect to this construction of Ord 53 r 4(1), any more than to its successor provision in Part 54 of the Civil Procedure Rules, would disrupt the statutory environmental impact regime. What it does is require an objector to strike, at the earliest reasonable moment, at a process that, if the objection is sound, will otherwise end in an unlawful grant of planning permission. By doing so, it supports the objectives of [Council Directive (85/337/EEC)] and the [1988] regulations, and attempts to keep disruption to a minimum.'

a On this basis the Court of Appeal concluded that the judge's refusal to extend time was a decision open to him. The Court of Appeal dismissed the appeal and refused leave to appeal to the House of Lords.

[27] On 23 July 2001 an Appeal Committee of the House of Lords granted leave to appeal.

b (VII) *The principal issues*

[28] For the purposes of the appeal to the House it must be assumed—as Richards J and the Court of Appeal had done—that Mrs Burkett has an arguable case on the substantive merits of her judicial review application. The only issues on this appeal relate to the matters of delay.

c [29] Richards J and the Court of Appeal held that the three-months' time limit for seeking judicial review ran from the date of the resolution of 15 September 1999 and not from the date of the decision not to call in the planning application on 24 February 2000 or the decision to grant planning permission on 12 May 2000. The local authority and developer submit that the decisions below were correct as a matter of domestic law and are unaffected by European law.
d Mrs Burkett's primary contention is that the time limit of three months only ran against her from the date of the actual grant of planning permission. Alternatively, she contends that time only runs from the time that the Secretary of State decided not to call in the application. She relies in the first place on the proper construction of the rules of court as a matter of domestic law. But she also
e prays in aid the European principles of legal certainty and effective enforcement of Community law in support of her contention.

[30] It will be convenient first to consider the principal issue of the interpretation of the rules of court under domestic law. In my view oral argument convincingly showed that the real choice is between holding that under RSC Ord 53, r 4(1), the grounds for the application first arose on (a) the
f date of the resolution or (b) the date of the actual grant of planning permission, the latter being the first date by which rights and obligations were created. The date when the Secretary of State decided not to call in the application has little to commend it as the operative date. So far as finality is relevant, that date left the planning decision in suspense. I will therefore concentrate on what I regard as
g the real choice before the House.

(VIII) *A procedural point*

[31] Richards J and the Court of Appeal regarded it as a serious obstacle that the application for judicial review was directed against the resolution of 15 September
h 1999. That was the case because the application had been made before the grant of permission. If this is an insuperable obstacle, the important points of law involved in this appeal would have to await decision in another case. In my view this difficulty can be overcome. In public law the emphasis should be on substance rather than form. If the correct construction of the rules is that in respect of a challenge to planning permission time only runs from the date of the
j grant of permission, it would be unjust to dismiss the appeal on this ground. Counsel for Mrs Burkett put forward a suitable amendment directed to the grant of permission on 12 May 2000. In my view there is no reason why such an amendment, and any other consequential amendments, cannot be granted. In this way any procedural difficulty can be cured. It is therefore possible to put this technical point to one side and to concentrate on the legal issues before the House.

(IX) The status of the resolution

[32] The resolution of 15 September 1999 gave authority to a designated council official to grant planning permission subject to (i) there being no call in decision by the Secretary of State and (ii) completion of a satisfactory agreement enforceable pursuant to s 106 of the 1990 Act. There were therefore two conditions precedent to a binding planning permission coming into existence. It is common ground that the resolution by itself created no legal rights. Only upon the fulfilment of both conditions precedent, and the grant of planning permission, did rights and obligations as between the local authority, the developer and affected individuals come into existence. Until all these things had happened the resolution was revocable not by the designated official but by the local authority itself.

[33] The first condition precedent was fulfilled on 24 February 2000 when the Secretary of State decided not to call in the application. The second condition was fulfilled on 12 May 2000 when the s 106 agreement was concluded. Only on that date was it possible to grant planning permission giving rise to rights and obligations. It is this second condition which requires some further explanation.

[34] The resolution of 15 September 1999 was adopted by the committee against the background of a supplementary agenda which informed members:

> 'Critical to the assessment of this application is the proposed 106 agreement which needs to be understood as part of the overall proposal. Without this proposal this proposal would be wholly unacceptable.'

The proposal for which members of the committee voted on 15 September 1999 was therefore inchoate. It would be wrong to assume that the negotiation and conclusion of the agreement of the s 106 agreement was a formality. It was only completed eight months after the initial resolution, and three months after the Secretary of State's decision not to call in the application. It was a complex agreement running to about 190 pages. Some of the provisions were apparently in planning terms of major importance. While the House has not examined the agreement, counsel for Mrs Burkett pointed out that it included provisions regarding highway improvements, work on a roundabout nearby, the provision of 60 units of housing for a social landlord, and other material provisions. I did not understand this to be a matter of dispute.

[35] The position is therefore that until 12 May 2000 it was uncertain whether the resolution of 15 September 1999 would be implemented.

(X) The interpretation and application of the rules of court

[36] I have already drawn attention to the provisions of s 31(6) of the 1981 Act. Nobody has suggested that the outcome of the appeal in the present case can be affected by s 31(6). The debate has centred on the correct interpretation and application of the rules of court. That is how I will approach the matter. There is no material difference between the provisions of RSC Ord 53, r 4(1) and CPR 54.5(1). I will address the language of the former.

[37] The case was decided by the Court of Appeal not on the ground of a lack of promptitude in making the judicial review application but on the ground that more than three months had elapsed after the resolution of 15 September 1999. Whether that is the correct date depends on the interpretation and application of the words 'from the date when grounds for the application first arose'. If in respect of a challenge to the actual grant of permission time runs (to use convenient shorthand for the statutory words) from the date of the resolution, the decisions below were correct. On the other hand, if in respect of a challenge to the actual grant of permission time runs from the date of the grant, the

a decisions below were wrong. This is the critical issue. In considering this question one must bear in mind that RSC Ord 53, r 4(1) (and for that matter CPR 54.5(1)) are not specifically targeted at town planning applications. These provisions apply across the spectrum of judicial review applications. Making due allowance for the special features of town planning applications, an interpretation is to be preferred which is capable of applying to the generality of cases.

b [38] Leaving to one side for the moment the application of Ord 53, r 4(1) on the running of time against a judicial review applicant, it can readily be accepted that for substantive judicial review purposes the decision challenged does not have to be absolutely final. In a context where there is a statutory procedure involving preliminary decisions leading to a final decision affecting legal rights, *c* judicial review may lie against a preliminary decision not affecting legal rights. Town planning provides a classic case of this flexibility. Thus it is in principle possible to apply for judicial review in respect of a resolution to grant outline permission and for prohibition even in advance of it (see generally Wade & Forsyth *Administrative Law* (8th edn, 2000) p 600; Craig *Administrative Law* (4th edn, 1999) pp 724–725; Fordham *Judicial Review Handbook* (3rd edn, 2001) *d* pp 102–103 (para 4.8.2)). It is clear therefore that if Mrs Burkett had acted in time, she could have challenged the resolution. These propositions do not, however, solve the concrete problem before the House which is whether in respect of a challenge to a final planning decision time runs under Ord 53, r 4(1) from the date of the resolution or from the date of the grant of planning permission. It does not *e* follow from the fact that if Mrs Burkett had acted in time and challenged the resolution that she could not have waited until planning permission was granted and then challenged the grant.

[39] As a matter of language it is possible to say in respect of a challenge to an alleged unlawful aspect of the grant of planning permission that 'grounds for the *f* application first arose' when the decision was made. The ground for challenging the resolution is that it is a decision to do an unlawful act in the future; the ground for challenging the actual grant is that an unlawful act has taken place. And the fact that the element of unlawfulness was already foreseeable at earlier stages in the planning process does not detract from this natural and obvious meaning. The context supports this interpretation. Until the actual grant of planning *g* permission the resolution has no legal effect. It is unlawful for the developer to commence any works in reliance on the resolution. And a developer expends money on the project before planning permission is granted at his own risk. The resolution may come to nothing because of a change of circumstances. It may fall to the ground because of conditions which are not fulfilled. It may lapse *h* because negotiations for the conclusion of a s 106 agreement break down. After the resolution is adopted the local authority may come under a duty to reconsider its decision if flaws are brought to its attention (see *R v West Oxfordshire DC, ex p CH Pearce Homes Ltd* (1986) 26 RVR 156). Moreover, it is not in doubt that a local authority may in its discretion revoke an outline resolution. In the search for the *j* best contextual interpretation these factors tend to suggest that the date of the resolution does not trigger the three-month time limit in respect of a challenge to the actual grant of planning permission.

[40] The contrary argument is that it is disruptive of good administration for a citizen to delay his application until the actual grant of planning permission. This is the view which Richards J and the Court of Appeal adopted. It was also a view forcefully expressed by Laws J in the Divisional Court in *R v Secretary of State*

for Trade and Industry, ex p Greenpeace Ltd [1998] Env LR 415. In the context of a
challenge to the award of North Sea licences he said (at 424):   *a*

> '... a judicial review applicant must move against the substantive act or
> decision which is the real basis of his complaint. If, after that act has been
> done, he takes no steps but merely waits until something consequential and
> dependent upon it takes place and then challenges that, he runs the risk of   *b*
> being put out of court for being too late.'

This observation was cited with approval by Richards J and the Court of Appeal
adopted this reasoning. It is necessary to point out, however, that the judge in
Ex p Greenpeace based his decision not only on the rules of court but also on
broader considerations of his view of the function of the court in upholding the   *c*
rule of law (see [1998] Env LR 415 at 422).

[41] The decision in *Ex p Greenpeace* was subsequently followed in a number
of lower court decisions. There were also decisions to a contrary effect and there
are cases where the court treated time as running from the date of the actual
grant of planning permission without any examination of the issue. There is
some discussion of such cases in two articles: Jones and Phillpot 'When He Who   *d*
Hesitates is Lost: Judicial Review of Planning Permissions' [2000] JPL 564 and
Roots and Walton 'Promptness and Delay in Judicial Review—An Update on the
Continuing Saga' [2001] JPL 1360. These cases involve judgments on applications
for permission to apply for judicial review. Such cases are generally not regarded
as authoritative (see *Clark v University of Linconshire and Humberside* [2000] 3 All ER   *e*
752 at 761–762, [2000] 1 WLR 1988 at 1998–1999, per Lord Woolf MR). For my
part the earlier decisions, other than the important judgment of Laws J in *Ex p
Greenpeace*, can be regarded as overtaken by the Court of Appeal decision in the
present case. It is therefore on the reasoning in *Ex p Greenpeace* and in the Court
of Appeal judgment that I must concentrate.

[42] The core of the reasoning of the Court of Appeal is that—   *f*

> 'the impugned environmental impact statement was as necessary to the
> resolution as to any subsequent steps [and] the logic of measuring time from
> the resolution seems inescapable.' (See [2001] 3 PLR 1 at 4 (para 8).)

In my view there is no such inevitable march of legal logic. In law the resolution   *g*
is not a juristic act giving rise to rights and obligations. It is not inevitable that it
will ripen into an actual grant of planning permission. In these circumstances it
would be curious if, when the actual grant of planning permission is challenged,
a court could insist by retrospective judgment that the applicant ought to have
moved earlier for judicial review against a preliminary decision 'which is the real   *h*
basis of his complaint' (see *R v Secretary of State for Trade and Industry, ex p
Greenpeace Ltd* [1998] Env LR 415 at 424). Moreover, an application to declare a
resolution unlawful might arguably be premature and be objected to on this
ground. And in strict law it could be dismissed. The Court of Appeal was alive
to this difficulty and observed that 'an arguably premature application can often
be stayed or adjourned to await events'. This is hardly a satisfactory explanation   *j*
for placing a burden on a citizen to apply for relief in respect of a resolution which
is still devoid of legal effect. For my part the substantive position is straightforward.
The court has jurisdiction to entertain an application by a citizen for judicial
review in respect of a resolution before or after its adoption. But it is a jump in
legal logic to say that he must apply for such relief in respect of the resolution on
pain of losing his right to judicial review of the actual grant of planning

a permission which does affect his rights. Such a view would also be in tension with the established principle that judicial review is a remedy of last resort.

[43] At this stage it is necessary to return to the point that the rule of court applies across the board to judicial review applications. If a decision-maker indicates that, subject to hearing further representations, he is provisionally minded to make a decision adverse to a citizen, is it to be said that time runs
b against the citizen from the moment of the provisional expression of view? That would plainly not be sensible and would involve waste of time and money. Let me give a more concrete example. A licensing authority expresses a provisional view that a licence should be cancelled but indicates a willingness to hear further argument. The citizen contends that the proposed decision would be unlawful.
c Surely, a court might as a matter of discretion take the view that it would be premature to apply for judicial review as soon as the provisional decision is announced. And it would certainly be contrary to principle to require the citizen to take such premature legal action. In my view the time limit under the rules of court would not run from the date of such preliminary decisions in respect of a challenge of the actual decision. If that is so, one is entitled to ask: what is the
d qualitative difference in town planning? There is, after all, nothing to indicate that, in regard to RSC Ord 53, r 4(1), town planning is an island on its own.

[44] In *Ex p Greenpeace* and in the Court of Appeal in the present case the view was taken that the selection of the date of the resolution as the appropriate date would facilitate good administration. There are two sides to this proposition. It
e contemplates time running against a citizen before his rights are affected, thereby potentially involving a loss of a right to challenge what may perhaps be an abuse of power which in the interests of good administration should be exposed. Undoubtedly, there is a need for public bodies to have certainty as to the legal validity of their actions. That is the rationale of Ord 53, r 4(1). On the other hand, it is far from clear that the selection of the actual grant of planning permission as
f the critical date would disadvantage developers and local authorities. In their careful article 'When He Who Hesitates is Lost: Judicial Review of Planning Permissions' [2000] JPL 564 at 588, Jones and Phillpot argue:

g   'There would be a greater incentive for both the planning authority and the developer to move to ensure that the formal grant of planning permission is issued more speedily. This could be of advantage to developers wishing to progress the development of the site. From a public policy point of view it is important that speedy progress is made to issue the formal planning permissions for appropriate development.'

h For my part the arguments in favour of time running from the date of resolution in the present case have been given undue weight by the Court of Appeal. In any event, there are a number of countervailing policy considerations to be considered.

[45] First, the context is a rule of court which by operation of a time limit may
j deprive a citizen of the right to challenge an undoubted abuse of power. And such a challenge may involve not only individual rights but also community interests, as in environmental cases. This is a contextual matter relevant to the interpretation of the rule of court. It weighs in favour of a clear and straightforward interpretation which will yield a readily ascertainable starting date. Entrusting judges with a broad discretionary task of retrospectively assessing when the complaint could first reasonably have been made (as a prelude

to deciding whether the application is time-barred) is antithetical to the context of a time limit barring judicial review.

[46] Secondly, legal policy favours simplicity and certainty rather than complexity and uncertainty. In the interpretation of legislation this factor is a commonplace consideration. In choosing between competing constructions a court may presume, in the absence of contrary indications, that the legislature intended to legislate for a certain and predictable regime. Much will depend on the context. In procedural legislation, primary or subordinate, it must be a primary factor in the interpretative process, notably where the application of the procedural regime may result in the loss of fundamental rights to challenge an unlawful exercise of power. The citizen must know where he stands. And so must the local authority and the developer. For my part this approach is so firmly anchored in domestic law that it is unnecessary, in this case, to seek to reinforce it by reference to the European principle of legal certainty.

[47] Unfortunately, the judgment in *R v Secretary of State for Trade and Industry, ex p Greenpeace Ltd* [1998] Env LR 415 and the judgment of the Court of Appeal, although carefully reasoned, do not produce certainty. On the contrary, the proposition in *Ex p Greenpeace* (at 424), 'that a judicial review applicant must move against the substantive act or decision which is the real basis of his complaint', leaves the moment at which time starts to run uncertain. This is illustrated by the way in which Laws J in a lengthy judgment proceeded retrospectively to assess the various dates by which the applicants could have applied for judicial review. In a case note published on *Ex p Greenpeace*, 'All Litigants are Not Equal: Delay and the Public Interest Litigant' [1998] JR 8, Dr Forsyth (co-author of the standard textbook) commented (at 10):

'This obligation resting upon applicants to apply for judicial review as soon as the real basis of their complaint had been identified is onerous and uncertain. It may be pointed out that notwithstanding that he had the luxury of being able to view each event in its proper context as revealed by subsequent events, the judge found it difficult to decide what the precise date was. How much more difficult must it be for the applicant who lacks this perspective and to whom the significance of each event is obscure to judge when the real basis of their complaint has come to the fore? In truth, the basis of a complaint is often constructed *ex post facto*, but the judgment ignores this reality.'

Laws J saw it as a matter of the court imposing 'a strict discipline in proceedings before it' and administering justice 'case by case'. The difficulty with this approach is, however, that it does not provide the relative certainty in respect of the operation of the time limit under Ord 53, r 4(1), which a citizen might be entitled to expect.

[48] While I must avoid distraction from the main point, it is of passing interest that the sequel to *Ex p Greenpeace* as decided by Laws J was a decision by Maurice Kay J in the same ongoing dispute in which a rather different approach on a number of public law points prevailed (see *R v Secretary of State for Trade and Industry, ex p Greenpeace Ltd* [2000] Env LR 221).

[49] There is appended to Mrs Burkett's printed case a list of dates which on the Court of Appeal judgment may be held to be the operative dates even where the challenge is to the grant of planning permission. For my part I would not necessarily be willing to accept the realism of all the suggested dates. But on the reasoning of the Court of Appeal and the arguments of the respondents dates

a earlier than the resolution (eg a recommendation to the planning committee) may in future have to be treated as operative dates. Indeed, on the rationale of the Court of Appeal judgment, and the argument for the respondents, time could start to run when a planning authority, before the adoption of any resolution, accepted a deficient environmental statement and placed it on the register pursuant to reg 14(2) of the 1988 regulations. Almost certainly there will be other

b potential dates even where the challenge is to the final decisions. Not surprisingly, the practice in the Divisional Court has been inconsistent. There has been criticism in professional journals of the failure of the Court of Appeal in the present case to bring a measure of certainty to this corner of the law (see Edwards and Martin 'Time Gentleman, Please' (2001) 103 EG 128; comment on the Court

c of Appeal decision by Edwards [2001] JPL 775 at 785–786; Roots and Walton 'Promptness and Delay in Judicial Review—An Update on the Continuing Saga' [2001] JPL 1360; compare also the earlier article of Jones and Phillpot 'When He Who Hesitates is Lost: Judicial Review of Planning Permissions' [2000] JPL 564). At present there now appears to be a confusing number of different potential starting points. They involve the court retrospectively assessing when it was

d reasonable for an individual to apply for judicial review. The lack of certainty is a recipe for sterile procedural disputes and unjust results. By contrast if the better interpretation is that time only runs under Ord 53, r 4(1), from the grant of permission the procedural regime will be certain and everybody will know where they stand.

e [**50**] Thirdly, the preparation of a judicial review application, particularly in a town planning matter, is a burdensome task. There is a duty of full and frank disclosure on the applicant (see *The Supreme Court Practice 1999*, 1, 916, para 53/14/57). The applicant must present to the court a detailed statement of his grounds, his evidence, his supporting documents in a paginated and indexed

f bundle, a list of essential reading with relevant passages sidelined, and his legislative sources in a paginated indexed bundle. This is a heavy burden on individuals and, where legal aid is sought, the Legal Services Commission. The CPR and the Practice Direction—Judicial Review, supplementing Pt 54, contain similar provisions; see also the Pre-Action Protocol for Judicial Review. An applicant is at risk of having to pay substantial costs which may, for example,

g result in the loss of his home. These considerations reinforce the view that it is unreasonable to require an applicant to apply for judicial review when the resolution may never take effect. They further reinforce the view that it is unfair to subject a judicial review applicant to the uncertainty of a retrospective decision by a judge as to the date of the triggering of the time limit under the rules of court.

h [**51**] For all these reasons I am satisfied that the words 'from the date when the grounds for the application first arose' refer to the date when the planning permission was granted. In the case before the House time did not run therefore from the resolution of 15 September 1999 but only from the grant of planning permission on 12 May 2000. It follows that in my view the decisions of Richards J

j and the Court of Appeal were not correct.

(XI) *The European law issues*

[**52**] Given the conclusion I have reached it is unnecessary in this case to consider the arguments on European law. And there is no need for a reference to the Court of Justice of the European Communities pursuant to art 234 of the EC Treaty.

(XII) *Promptitude*

[53] This case has not turned on the obligation of a judicial review applicant to act *a* 'promptly' under the rules. In these circumstances I confine my observations on this aspect to two brief matters. First, from observations of Laws J in *R v Ceredigion CC, ex p McKeown* [1998] 2 PLR 1 the inference has sometimes been drawn that the three-months' limit has by judicial decision been replaced by a 'six weeks' rule'. This is a misconception. The legislative three-months limit cannot be contracted by a *b* judicial policy decision. Secondly, there is at the very least doubt whether the obligation to apply 'promptly' is sufficiently certain to comply with European Community law and the European Convention for the Protection of Human Rights and Fundamental Freedoms 1950 (as set out in Sch 1 to the Human Rights Act 1998). It is a matter for consideration whether the requirement of promptitude, read with the three-months' limit, is not productive of unnecessary uncertainty and practical *c* difficulty. Moreover, Craig *Administrative Law* (4th edn, 1999) p 794 has pointed out:

'The short time limits may, in a paradoxical sense, increase the amount of litigation against the administration. An individual who believes that the public body has acted ultra vires now has the strongest incentive to seek a *judicial resolution* of the matter immediately, as opposed to attempting a *negotiated* *d* *solution*, quite simply because if the individual forbears from suing he or she may be deemed not to have applied promptly or within the three month time limit'

And in regard to truly urgent cases the court would in any event in its ultimate discretion or under s 31(6) of the 1981 Act be able to refuse relief where it is appropriate to do so (see Craig *Administrative Law* p 794). The burden in such *e* cases to act quickly would always be on the applicant (see Jones and Phillpot 'He Who Hesitates is Lost: Judicial Review of Planning Permissions' [2000] JPL 564 at 589).

(XIII) *Disposal*   *f*

[54] For these reasons, as well as the reasons given by my noble and learned friend Lord Slynn of Hadley, I would allow the appeal and remit the matter for decision by the High Court on the substantive issues.

LORD HOPE OF CRAIGHEAD.

[55] My Lords, I have had the advantage of reading in draft the speech of my *g* noble and learned friend Lord Steyn. Subject only to some observations which I should like to add to what he has said on the questions of jurisdiction and promptitude, I agree with it. I too would allow the appeal.

Jurisdiction   *h*

[56] In my opinion the principle upon which the decision of this House in *Lane v Esdaile* [1891] AC 210 proceeded was correctly identified by Lord Esher MR in *Re Housing of the Working Classes Act 1890, ex p Stevenson* [1892] 1 QB 609 at 611 when he said:

'I am, on principle and on consideration of the authorities that have been *j* cited, prepared to lay down the proposition that, wherever power is given to a legal authority to grant or refuse leave to appeal, the decision of that authority is, from the very nature of the thing, final and conclusive and without appeal, unless an appeal from it is expressly given. So, if the decision in this case is to be taken to be that of the judge at chambers, he is the legal authority to decide the matter, and his decision is final; if it is to be taken to be that of the High

a
Court, then they are the legal authority entrusted with the responsibility of deciding whether there shall be leave to appeal, and their decision is final. In either case there is no appeal to this court. What was said in the case of *Lane* v. *Esdaile* [1891] AC 210 supports the view that I am taking.'

[57] There is no doubt that this rule was extended in *Re Poh* [1983] 1 All ER
b 287, [1983] 1 WLR 2 when it was applied to an appeal from a refusal of leave to apply for judicial review. I also think that Lord Diplock's observation ([1983] 1 All ER 287 at 288, [1983] 1 WLR 2 at 3) that this House is not concerned with the procedure by which the application in question moved to the Court of Appeal is difficult to reconcile with what was said in *Ex p Stevenson*. The fact that the Court of Appeal granted permission to the applicants to appeal from the decision
c of Richards J shows that the decision of the judge to refuse permission was not treated as final and conclusive and without appeal in that court.

[58] For these reasons I do not think that there is any sound basis for holding that, where the Court of Appeal has granted leave to appeal against a refusal of permission to apply for judicial review and then heard the appeal, this House has no jurisdiction
d to entertain a further appeal against a refusal of permission by the Court of Appeal.

Promptitude

[59] I share my noble and learned friend's doubt as to whether the provision in CPR 54.5(1) that the claim form must be filed 'promptly' is sufficiently certain
e to comply with the right to a fair hearing within a reasonable time in art 6(1) of the European Convention for the Protection of Human Rights and Fundamental Freedoms 1950 (as set out in Sch 1 to the Human Rights Act 1998) and, in that respect, also with European Community law. But, as his point may have some implications for the law and practice of judicial review in Scotland and as the current state of the law and practice in Scotland might be of some interest if r 54.5(1)
f were to be reformulated, I should like to add these comments.

[60] The principle of legality, which covers not only statute but also unwritten law, requires that any law or rule which restricts convention rights must be formulated with sufficient clarity to enable the citizen to regulate his conduct (see *Sunday Times v UK* (1979) 2 EHRR 245 at 270–271 (paras 47, 49)). He must be able,
g if need be with appropriate advice, to foresee, to a degree that is reasonable in the circumstances, the consequences which a given action may entail. The problem is that the word 'promptly' is imprecise and the rule makes no reference to any criteria by reference to which the question whether that test is satisfied is to be judged.

[61] As Lord Clyde and Dennis Edwards point out in their *Judicial Review*
h (2000) p 430 (para 13.14), there is no specific time-limit for the making of an application for judicial review in Scotland nor is it thought that there is any need for one. The explanation for the absence of a specific statutory time limit is to be found in the history of the supervisory jurisdiction of the Court of Session which preceded the introduction of a new procedure for judicial review by r 260B of the Rules of the Court of Session 1965, SI 1965/321. A full account of it is set out in the opinion of the
j court in *West v Secretary of State for Scotland* 1992 SC 385 at 393–401. It had long been recognised that the Court of Session had jurisdiction to control any excess or abuse of power or a failure to act by an inferior body or tribunal. But this jurisdiction was of little use in practice, as it took so long under the existing procedure to obtain a decision from the court. What was needed, as Lord Fraser of Tullybelton pointed out in *Brown v Hamilton DC* 1983 SC (HL) 1 at 49, was a reform of the procedure for obtaining judicial review of decisions by public bodies which would provide

litigants in Scotland with ready access to the court for the obtaining of the appropriate remedies.

[62] The reforms introduced by r 260B of the 1965 rules are now to be found in Ch 58 of the Rules of the Court of Session 1994, 1994/1443. They were essentially procedural in nature. It was not the intention to narrow the supervisory jurisdiction from what it had previously been. One aspect of that jurisdiction was that it had never been subject to any specific statutory time limit. A research study was carried out into the operation in practice of judicial review of administrative action in Scotland by staff at the School of Law at the University of Glasgow. They concluded that there was no case for the introduction of a strict time limit within which a petition must be brought (see 'Judicial Review Research' 1996 SLT (News) 164–165). Rule 58.3 of the 1994 rules, which provides for the making of applications for judicial review, says nothing about the time within which such applications must be made.

[63] The principal protection against undue delay in applying for judicial review in Scotland is not to be found therefore in any statutory provision but in the common law concepts of delay, acquiescence and personal bar (see Clyde and Edwards *Judicial Review* pp 433–434 (para 13.20)). The important point to note for present purposes is that there is no Scottish authority which supports the proposition that mere delay (or, to follow the language of CPR 54.5(1), a mere failure to apply 'promptly') will do. It has never been held that mere delay is sufficient to bar proceedings for judicial review in the absence of circumstances pointing to acquiescence or prejudice (see *Singh v Secretary of State for the Home Dept* 2000 SLT 533 at 536 per Lord Nimmo Smith; *Uprichard v Fife Council* [2001] Env LR 122 at 134 per Lord Bonomy; *Bett Properties Ltd v Scottish Ministers* 2001 SLT 1131 at 1136–1137, per Lord Macfadyen, although (at 1137) he reserved his opinion on this point. As Lord Nimmo Smith said in *Singh's* case (at 536), none of the cases in Scotland provide support for a plea of unreasonable delay, separate and distinct from a plea of mora, taciturnity and acquiescence, in answer to an application for judicial review.

[64] On the other hand it has repeatedly been acknowledged that applications in such cases should be brought as speedily as possible. Ample support for this approach is to be found in the well-known observations of Lord Diplock in *O'Reilly v Mackman* [1982] 3 All ER 1124 at 1131, [1983] 2 AC 237 at 280–281 to the effect that the public interest in good administration requires that public authorities and third parties should not be kept in suspense for any longer period than is absolutely necessary in fairness to the person affected by the decision; see also *R v Dairy Produce Quota Tribunal for England and Wales, ex p Caswell* [1989] 3 All ER 205, [1990] 2 AC 738. But decisions as to whether a petition should be dismissed on the ground of delay are made in the light of the circumstances in which time was allowed to pass. As Lord President Rodger put it in *Swan v Secretary of State for Scotland* 1998 SC 479 at 487:

'It is, of course, the case that judicial review proceedings ought normally to be raised promptly and it is also undeniable that the petitioners let some months pass without starting these proceedings. None the less, in considering whether the delay was such that the petitioners should not be allowed to proceed, we take into account the situation in which time was allowed to pass.'

[65] In *Ex p Caswell* [1990] 2 All ER 434 at 441, [1990] 2 AC 738 at 749–750 Lord Goff of Chieveley said that he did not think that it would be wise to attempt to formulate any precise definition or description of what constitutes detriment to good administration. As he pointed out, the interest in good administration lies

a essentially in a regular flow of consistent decisions and in citizens knowing where they stand and how they can order their affairs. Matters of particular importance, apart from the length of time itself, would be the extent of the effect of the relevant decision and the impact which would be felt if it were to be reopened. These observations, which were made in the context of an application to extend the period under RSC Ord 53, r 4(1), are consistent with the Scottish approach to

b the question whether the application should be allowed to proceed. The question whether the delay amounts to acquiescence or would give rise to prejudice such as to bar the remedy is inevitably one of fact and degree.

[66] There is clearly much force in the point which my noble and learned friend makes that the obligation to apply 'promptly' is, without more, too uncertain to satisfy the requirements of convention law. But in my opinion the

c factors which are relevant to a plea of mora, acquiescence and taciturnity in Scottish practice provide an appropriate context for the taking of decisions on this point. They provide a sufficiently clear and workable rule for the avoidance of undue delay in the bringing of these applications, as experience of the operation of judicial review in Scotland has shown. I do not think that it would be

d incompatible with his convention rights for an applicant who must be taken to have acquiesced in the decision which he seeks to bring under review, or whose delay has been such that another interested party may be prejudiced, to be told that his application cannot proceed because he has delayed too long in bringing it.

LORD MILLETT.

e [67] My Lords, I have had the advantage of reading in draft the speeches of my noble and learned friends, Lord Slynn of Hadley and Lord Steyn. For the reasons they give I too would allow the appeal.

LORD PHILLIPS OF WORTH MATRAVERS MR.

f [68] My Lords, I have had the advantage of reading in draft the speeches of my noble and learned friends, Lord Slynn of Hadley and Lord Steyn. For the reasons they give I too would allow the appeal.

Appeal allowed.

Dilys Tausz   Barrister

Lindsay v Customs and Excise Comrs   a

[2002] EWCA Civ 267

COURT OF APPEAL, CIVIL DIVISION

LORD PHILLIPS OF WORTH MATRAVERS MR, JUDGE AND CARNWATH LJJ

19, 20 FEBRUARY 2002   b

Customs and excise – Forfeiture – Vehicle used for carriage of thing liable to forfeiture – Customs and Excise Commissioners refusing to restore respondent's vehicle pursuant to policy on forfeiture of vehicles used for smuggling – Policy not taking into account value of forfeited vehicle and not distinguishing commercial smuggling from c *importation for social distribution – Whether policy lawful – Human Rights Act 1998, Sch 1, Pt II, art 1.*

Tribunal – Value Added Tax and Duties Tribunal – Jurisdiction – Review officer dismissing respondent's appeal against refusal to restore forfeited vehicle – Tribunal allowing respondent's appeal and ordering restoration of vehicle or payment of d *compensation in lieu – Whether tribunal having jurisdiction to make such an order – Finance Act 1994, s 16(4).*

The respondent purchased a new car for about £12,000. Four months later, as he was about to drive his car onto the shuttle train in Calais to return to England   e after a shopping expedition, he was stopped by a British customs officer in the control zone. The officer found that he was carrying a substantial quantity of cigarettes and tobacco in his car. The respondent said that he had purchased some of the goods for members of his family with money provided by them. The officer told him that he should have paid duty on the goods (assessed at   f approximately £3,500), and purported to forfeit both the goods and the respondent's car pursuant to statutory powers. The respondent subsequently asked the Customs and Excise Commissioners to review the seizure of his vehicle, but they declined to restore it to him. That decision was affirmed by the review officer who referred, inter alia, to the policy of the commissioners to forfeit, and not to restore, privately-owned vehicles that had been used for the   g improper importation of excise goods, even on the first occasion when they had been so used. The commissioners' policy did not suggest that any regard should be paid to the value of the car; nor did it suggest, save in one exceptional case, that it was relevant to consider whether the goods were being imported to be distributed between family and friends or whether the importation was pursuant   h to a commercial venture under which the goods were to be sold at a profit. On appeal to the Value Added Tax and Duties Tribunal, the respondent relied on his right to the peaceful enjoyment of possessions under art 1[a] of the First Protocol to the European Convention for the Protection of Human Rights and Fundamental Freedoms 1950 (as set out in Sch 1 to the Human Rights Act 1998). The tribunal held that the commissioners' policy did not achieve the fair balance between   j individual rights and the public interest required to justify interference with that right since it prevented the reviewing officer from giving any real consideration to the question of proportionality; that the difference between the value of the respondent's car and the amount of the duty payable was disproportionate; that

---

a   Article 1 is set out at [41], below

a   the reviewing officer should have taken that into account; and that the deprivation of the vehicle had caused the respondent to suffer undue hardship. Accordingly, the tribunal allowed the appeal and ordered the commissioners to restore the vehicle to the respondent or pay him compensation in lieu. That order was purportedly made under s 16(4)[b] of the Finance Act 1994 which, inter alia, empowered the tribunal to direct that the decision appealed against would cease

b   to have effect. The commissioners appealed. Since the case raised issues of principle that arose in hundreds of similar cases, permission was given to appeal direct to the Court of Appeal.

Held – Although the commissioners' policy could not have been condemned if it had been confined to those who were using their cars for commercial smuggling,

c   ie smuggling goods in order to sell them at a profit, it was flawed because it failed to draw a distinction between the commercial smuggler and the driver importing goods for social distribution to family or friends in circumstances where there was no attempt to make a profit. Even in such a case, the scale of importation, or other circumstances, might be such as to justify forfeiture of the car. Where,

d   however, the importation was not for the purpose of making a profit, the principle of proportionality required that each case should be considered on its particular facts, including the scale of importation, whether it was a 'first offence', whether there was an attempt at concealment or dissimulation, the value of the vehicle and the degree of hardship that would be caused by forfeiture. In the instant case, the review officer had appeared to have correctly understood the

e   policy as rendering irrelevant the truth of the respondent's story, the value of his car and the effect of the deprivation upon him. It followed that the tribunal had correctly decided that the review officer's decision could not stand since she had failed to have regard to all material considerations. However, the tribunal had no jurisdiction under s 16(4) of the 1994 Act to order the restoration of the respondent's

f   vehicle or the payment of compensation in lieu. In making that order, the tribunal had done more than direct that the review officer's decision cease to have effect. It had purported to reverse it, and had thereby exceeded its jurisdiction. The appropriate order was for the commissioners to conduct a further review of the review officer's decision in the light of the decisions of the tribunal and the court. Save to that extent, the appeal would be dismissed (see [63], [64], [66], [67], [69],

g   [71], [74], below).

Allgemeine Gold-und Silberscheideanschalt v United Kingdom (1986) 9 EHRR 1 and *Air Canada v UK* (1995) 20 EHRR 150 considered.

Notes

h   For the right to property, see 8(2) *Halsbury's Laws* (4th edn reissue) para 165, and for the forfeiture of vehicles used for the carriage of a thing liable for forfeiture and for the powers of the Value Added Tax and Duties Tribunal on appeal, see 12(2) *Halsbury's Laws* (4th edn reissue) paras 1154, 1244.

For the Finance Act 1994, s 16, see 13 *Halsbury's Statutes* (4th edn) (2000 reissue) 438.

For the Human Rights Act 1998, Sch 1, Pt II, art 1, see 7 *Halsbury's Statutes*
j   (4th edn) (1999 reissue) 525.

Cases referred to in judgments

Air Canada v UK (1995) 20 EHRR 150, ECt HR.
Allgemeine Gold-und Silberscheideanschalt v United Kingdom (1986) 9 EHRR 1, ECt HR.

---

b   Section 16(4) is set out at [10], below

Customs and Excise Comrs v JH Corbitt (Numismatists) Ltd [1980] 2 All ER 72, [1981]   *a*
    AC 22, [1980] 2 WLR 653, HL.
Dereczenik v Customs and Excise Comrs (7 June 2001, unreported).
Goldsmith v Customs and Excise Comrs [2001] EWHC Admin 285, [2001] 1 WLR 1673.
Hopping v Customs and Excise Comrs (9 October 2001, unreported).
Lithgow v UK (1986) 8 EHRR 329, [1986] ECHR 9006/80, ECt HR.
Louloudakis v Demosio Case C-262/99 (2001) ECR I-5547.   *b*
R v Customs and Excise Comrs, ex parte EMU Tabac SARL (Imperial Tobacco intervening)
    Case C-296/95, [1998] All ER (EC) 402, [1998] QB 791, [1998] 3 WLR 298, [1998]
    ECR I-1605.
Sporrong & Lönnroth v Sweden (1982) 5 EHRR 35, [1982] ECHR 7151/75, ECt HR.

Cases also cited or referred to in skeleton arguments   *c*
Associtated Provincial Picture Houses Ltd v Wednesbury Corp [1947] 2 All ER 680,
    [1948] 1 KB 233, CA.
Aston Cantlow and Wilmcote with Billesley Parochial Church Council v Wallbank
    [2001] EWCA Civ 713, [2001] 3 All ER 393, [2001] 3 WLR 1323.
Bowd v Customs and Excise Comrs [1995] V & DR 212.   *d*
British Oxygen Co Ltd v Minister of Technology [1970] 3 All ER 165, [1971] AC 610,
    [1970] 3 WLR 488, HL.
Commission of the European Communities v Greece Case C-210/91 [1992] ECR I-6735.
*De Freitas v Permanent Secretary of Ministry of Agriculture, Fisheries, Lands and
    Housing* [1999] 1 AC 69, [1998] 3 WLR 675, PC.
Garage Molenheide BVBA v Belgium Joined case C-286/94, C-340/95, C-401/95,   *e*
    C-47/96 [1998] All ER (EC) 61, [1997] ECR I-7281.
Hauer v Land Rheinland-Pfalz Case 44/79 [1979] ECR 3727.
Jose Teodoro de Andrade v Director da Alfândega de Leixões Case C-213/99 (2000) ECR
    I-11083.
Luisi and Carbone v Ministero del Tesoro Joined cases 286/82, 26/83 [1984] ECR 377.   *f*
Messrs Schoonbroodt and Transports AM Schoonbroodt Belgium Case C-247/97 [1998]
    ECR I-8095.
P v S Case C-13/94 [1996] All ER (EC) 397, [1996] ECR I-2143.
R (on the application of Professional Contractors Group) v IRC [2001] EWCA Civ 1945,
    [2001] All ER (D) 356 (Dec).
R v A [2001] UKHL 25, [2001] 3 All ER 1, [2002] 1 AC 45, [2001] 2 WLR 1546.   *g*
*R v International Stock Exchange of the United Kingdom and the Republic of Ireland Ltd,
    ex p Eastside Cheese Co* (1998) 47 BMLR 1.
Trinity Mirror plc v Customs and Excise Comrs [2001] EWCA Civ 65, [2001] All ER
    (D) 178 (Jan).
Wasa Liv Omsesidigt v Sweden App No 13013/87 (1988) 58 DR 163, ECom HR.   *h*
Watson and Belmann, Re Case 118/75 [1976] ECR 1185.
Whiting v Customs and Excise Comrs (4 July 2001, unreported).

Appeal
The Customs and Excise Commissioners appealed with permission of the   *j*
Value Added Tax and Duties Tribunal (Rodney P Huggins, chairman) granted
on 3 December 2001 from its decision on 1 November 2001 allowing an appeal
by the respondent, John Richard Lindsay, from the decision of a Customs and
Excise Review Officer (Diane Florence) on 22 December 2000 confirming the
decision of the commissioners on 4 October 2000 refusing to restore to the
respondent a motor vehicle that had been forfeited by a customs officer on 23 July

a 2000 on the grounds that it was carrying goods that were liable to forfeiture. The facts are set out in the judgment of Lord Phillips of Worth Matravers MR.

Hugh McKay and *Nicola Shaw* (instructed by the *Solicitor for Customs and Excise*) for the commissioners.

b *Philip Baker* and *Claire Simpson* (instructed by *Woodcraft and Wright*, Ilford) for Mr Lindsay.

The following judgments were delivered.

LORD PHILLIPS OF WORTH MATRAVERS MR.

c

INTRODUCTION

[1] In March 2000 Mr Lindsay, the respondent, bought himself a beautiful new car. It was a millennium special edition of a Ford Focus, coloured yellow. He paid about £12,000 for it, a discount of £3,000 on the showroom price, granted to

d him because his father had worked for Ford. On 23 July 2000 he was about to drive onto the shuttle in Calais to return to England after an early morning shopping expedition. When he entered the 'control zone' he was stopped by a British Customs officer. She found that he was carrying a substantial quantity of cigarettes and tobacco. He said that he had purchased some of this for members of his family with money provided by them. She then said that he should have

e paid duty on the goods. She purported to forfeit both the dutiable goods and Mr Lindsay's car, in which those goods were being carried.

[2] Mr Lindsay challenged the Customs' right to forfeit his car, following a procedure which I shall describe in due course. His challenge was successful. On 1 November 2001 the Value Added Tax and Duties Tribunal (the tribunal) ruled

f that the decision to deprive him of his car was disproportionate and would cause him undue hardship. His car should be restored to him or he should be paid compensation in lieu.

[3] This case raises issues of principle which arise in hundreds of similar cases which are 'in the pipeline'. For this reason permission has been given by the single judge to the Commissioners for Customs and Excise (the commissioners) to

g appeal against the tribunal's decision direct to the Court of Appeal. The appeal has been given an expedited listing. This course was rendered possible because the tribunal indorsed its decision with a certificate that the decision involved a point of law relating wholly or mainly to the construction of an enactment, a statutory instrument and the Community treaties and Community instruments

h which had been fully argued before it and fully considered by it: see the Value Added Tax Tribunals Appeals Order 1986, SI 1986/2288, art 2(b).

THE STATUTORY FRAMEWORK

[4] The commissioners have a considerable armoury which they can bring to

j bear against those who bring excise goods into this country without paying duty on them. Criminal proceedings can be brought pursuant to s 170 of the Customs and Excise Management Act 1979. Under that section the commissioners have to establish that the defendant fraudulently intended to evade the payment of duty. Their policy is, however, only to bring a criminal prosecution in the most serious cases. Their normal course is to rely, by way of sanction, upon statutory powers of forfeiture and condemnation, which do not involve a finding that a criminal

offence has been committed. That is the course that they adopted in the present
case.

[5] The statutory scheme, which covers both substance and procedure, is
complex. The best place to start is with the Excise Duties (Personal Reliefs) Order
1992, SI 1992/3155 as amended by the Excise Duties (Personal Reliefs) Amendment
Order 1999, SI 1999/1617 and the Channel Tunnel (Alcoholic Liquor and
Tobacco Products) Order 2000, SI 2000/426 (the 1992 order), which deals with
the circumstances in which relief from liability to pay duty is, and is not, available.

[6] The 1992 order applies to goods subject to excise duty (excise goods) which
are imported into the United Kingdom. It includes provisions which deal
specifically with 'shuttle train goods'. These are goods brought into the 'control
zone' at Calais by a passenger who is about to embark in the shuttle train (the
shuttle) for passage from France to England. Such goods are treated as having
been imported into the United Kingdom for the purpose of the regulations. This
case is concerned with such goods, and accordingly I shall extract from the 1992
order the relevant provisions that relate to them. These are as follows:

'**Interpretation**

2.—(1) In this Order—"Community traveller" means a person who makes
a journey between a member State and the United Kingdom ... or a person
who is about to embark or has embarked on a shuttle train in France for a
journey to the United Kingdom ... "cross-border shopping" means the
obtaining of excise goods duty and tax paid in the Economic Community
provided that payment has not been, and will not be, reimbursed, refunded
or otherwise dispensed with ... "own use" includes use as a personal gift
provided that if the person making the gift receives in consequence any
money or money's worth (including any reimbursement of expenses incurred
in connection with obtaining the goods in question) his use shall not be
regarded as own use for the purpose of this Order ...

Relief from duty of excise – cross-border shopping

3. Subject to the provisions of this Order a Community traveller entering
a control zone or the United Kingdom shall be relieved from payment of any
duty of excise on excise goods which he has obtained for his own use in the
course of cross-border shopping and which he has transported.

Relief from duty of excise – conditions – shuttle train goods

3A.—(1) In relation to shuttle train goods, this article shall have effect for
the purpose of determining whether relief has been treated as having been
afforded under article 3 above.

(2) No relief shall be treated as having been afforded if the goods are held
for a commercial purpose.

(3) Where the shuttle train goods exceed any of the quantities shown in
the Schedule to this Order the Commissioners may require the person
holding the goods to satisfy them that the goods are not held for a
commercial purpose.

(4) In determining whether or not any person holds shuttle train goods for
a commercial purpose regard shall be taken of the factors listed in
sub-paragraphs (a) to (j) of article 5(2) below.

(5) If the person holding the goods is required so to do but fails to satisfy
the Commissioners that he does not hold them for a commercial purpose, it
shall be presumed that the goods are held for a commercial purpose.

a

(6) Where the person holding the goods so fails to satisfy the Commissioners that he does not hold them for a commercial purpose, for the purpose of any proceedings instituted in accordance with paragraph 8 of Schedule 3 to the Customs and Excise Management Act 1979 or any appeal under section 16 of the Finance Act 1994, his failure shall cause the goods to be treated as "goods held for a commercial purpose"...'

b

The factors listed in art 5(2) are the following:

'(a) his reasons for having possession or control of those goods; (b) whether or not he is a revenue trader; (c) his conduct in relation to those goods and, for the purposes of this sub-paragraph, conduct includes his intentions at any

c

time in relation to those goods; (d) the location of those goods; (e) the mode of transport used to convey those goods; (f) any document or other information whatsoever relating to those goods; (g) the nature of those goods including the nature and condition of any package or container; (h) the quantity of those goods; (i) whether he has personally financed the purchase of those

d

goods; and (j) any other circumstance which appears to be relevant.'

[7] Finally, the Schedule referred to in art 3A provides:

'Tobacco products

(a) 800 cigarettes; (b) 400 cigarillos (that is to say cigars weighing not more

e

than 3 grammes each); (c) 200 cigars; (d) 1 kilogramme of tobacco products other than in a form mentioned in paragraph (a), (b) or (c) above;

Alcoholic beverages

(e) 10 litres of spirits; (f) 20 litres of intermediate products (that is to say products defined as intermediate products in Article 17(1) of the Council

f

Directive 92/83/EEC); (g) 90 litres of wines (but only 60 litres may be sparkling wines); (h) 110 litres of beer.'

[8] I now turn to the statutory provisions which lay down the consequences of importing excise goods without paying duty. Section 49 of the 1979 Act provides that goods that are imported without payment of duty chargeable on

g

them are subject to forfeiture. Section 141 provides, so far as material, that where anything becomes liable to forfeiture, any vehicle which has been used for its carriage also becomes liable to forfeiture. Section 152 provides, so far as material, that the commissioners may, as they see fit, restore, subject to such conditions as they think proper, anything forfeited or seized under the 1979 Act.

h

[9] Finally, I turn to the provisions that deal with procedure. Under Sch 3 to the Act, if the Customs' right to forfeit is challenged, the Customs have to take out condemnation proceedings in the magistrates' court. Although he initially made such a challenge, Mr Lindsay subsequently withdrew this. Instead he has pursued a challenge, not of the commissioners' statutory powers, but of the

j

manner in which they exercised those powers. The avenue that he pursued was open to him by virtue of certain provisions of the Finance Act 1994. Sections 14–16 of the 1994 Act, when read together with Sch 5 to that Act, provide for a two-tier system of review and appeal of decisions which include that taken to forfeit Mr Lindsay's car. The first stage was to seek a review of the decision from a Customs and Excise Review Officer, a Mrs Diane Florence. By letter dated 22 November 2000 she confirmed the decision.

[10] Mr Lindsay appealed from Mrs Florence's decision to the tribunal. Under Sch 5 to the 1994 Act a decision whether or not to forfeit a vehicle is deemed to be a decision 'as to an ancillary matter'. Section 16(4) of the 1994 Act provides:

'In relation to any decision as to an ancillary matter, or any decision on the review of such a decision, the powers of an appeal tribunal on an appeal under this section shall be confined to a power, where the tribunal are satisfied that the Commissioners or other person making that decision could not reasonably have arrived at it, to do one or more of the following, that is to say—(a) to direct that the decision, so far as it remains in force, is to cease to have effect from such time as the tribunal may direct; (b) to require the Commissioners to conduct, in accordance with the directions of the tribunal, a further review of the original decision; and (c) in the case of a decision which has already been acted on or taken effect and cannot be remedied by a further review, to declare the decision to have been unreasonable and to give directions to the Commissioners as to the steps to be taken for securing that repetitions of the unreasonableness do not occur when comparable circumstances arise in future.'

'GOODS HELD FOR A COMMERCIAL PURPOSE'

[11] The documentary evidence in this case suggested to me that there was a degree of confusion as to what was meant by 'goods held for a commercial purpose' in the 1992 order. When I explored this with Mr Hugh McKay, who appeared for the commissioners, it became apparent that this was indeed the case. The order is intended to give effect to the provisions of Council Directive (EEC) 92/12 (on the general arrangements for products subject to excise duty and on the holding, movement and monitoring of such products) (OJ 1992 L76 p 1) (the directive) and the confusion stems from that directive.

[12] The directive deals with the incidence of excise duty within the internal market. Article 6 provides that 'excise duty shall become chargeable at the time of release for consumption'. Article 7 of the directive provides that, where products released for consumption in one member state are being held 'for commercial purposes' in another member state, excise duty shall be levied in the latter member state.

[13] Article 8 provides: 'As regards products acquired by private individuals for their own use and transported by them, the principle governing the internal market lays down that excise duty shall be charged in the Member State in which they are acquired.'

[14] Article 9 provides:

'1. Without prejudice to Articles 6, 7 and 8, excise duty shall become chargeable where products for consumption in a Member State are held for commercial purpose in another Member State.

In this case, the duty shall be due in the Member State in whose territory the products are and shall become chargeable to the holder of the products.

2. To establish that the products referred to in Article 8 are intended for commercial purposes, Member States must take account, *inter alia*, of the following:
—the commercial status of the holder of the products and his reasons for holding them,
—the place where the products are located or, if appropriate, the mode of transport used,

a
—any document relating to the products,
—the nature of the products,
—the quantity of the products.
For the purposes of applying the content of the fifth indent of the first subparagraph, Member States may lay down guide levels, solely as a form of evidence. These guide levels may not be lower than:

b
    (a) *Tobacco products*

cigarettes	800 items
cigarillos (cigars weighing not more than 3g each)	400 items
cigars	200 items
smoking tobacco	1,0 kg;

c
    (b) *Alcoholic beverages*

spirit drinks	10 l
intermediate products	20 l
wines (including a maximum of	
60 l of sparkling wines)	90 l
beers	110 l.'

d
[15] Thus the directive makes express provision for products acquired by private individuals for their own use and for products which are held for a commercial purpose. The directive does not expressly provide for the case of the private individual who buys goods on behalf of others but not in circumstances which would naturally be described as being 'for a commercial purpose'. An

e
example is the holidaymaker who purchases some cigarettes for and at the request of a relative who has provided him with the purchase money.

[16] Mr Baker submitted that, under the directive, such a situation would be deemed to be one where the goods were held 'for a commercial purpose'. He further submitted that the same was true of the references to holding goods 'for

f
a commercial purpose' in the 1992 order. His submission was that holding goods 'for a commercial purpose' was the precise antithesis of holding goods 'for one's own use'. Thus, any person with excise goods in his car would either be holding them for his own use or holding them for a commercial purpose. So far as Mr Lindsay was concerned, if he had bought cigarettes for members of his family, he was holding them 'for a commercial purpose' even though he was not going

g
to make any profit from the transaction.

[17] Mr McKay may be right about the directive, although the only authority that bears on the point to which we were referred lends no support to his thesis (see *R v Customs and Excise Comrs, ex parte EMU Tabac SARL (Imperial Tobacco intervening)* Case C-296/95, [1998] All ER (EC) 402, [1998] QB 791, [1998] ECR

h
I-1605). So far as the 1992 order is concerned, I cannot accept that a holidaymaker who is bringing back some cigarettes for his sister, in anticipation that she will reimburse him the purchase price, can properly be said to be holding the cigarettes 'for a commercial purpose'. The holidaymaker will be liable to pay duty on the cigarettes by reason of the provisions of the Tobacco Products Duty Act 1979. He will not be entitled to relief because he has not obtained the

j
cigarettes for his own use. It does violence to the English language, however, to say that he is holding the goods 'for a commercial purpose'.

[18] At various stages of the story with which we are concerned, there has been confusion as to whether Mr Lindsay was deprived of duty relief because he was not holding the cigarettes and tobacco for his own use, or because he was holding them 'for a commercial purpose'. This confusion was unfortunate. As

I shall explain, I consider that there is a very significant distinction between a man
who is bringing cigarettes into England to distribute to members of his family   *a*
against reimbursement, and a man who is bringing cigarettes into England in
order to sell them at a profit. At no time does anyone appear to have thought it
material to consider into which category Mr Lindsay fell.

THE COMMISSIONERS' POLICY   *b*
   [19] Customs Officer Robert Pennington, who is employed in the commissioners'
law enforcement directorship, gave evidence to the tribunal of the commissioners'
policy in relation to the forfeiture of vehicles:

   '55. The [commissioner's] policies are designed to penalise those who
   make a living from selling alcohol and tobacco without payment of duty, not   *c*
   the honest Community travellers. In 1993 when the single market was
   introduced the revenue eroded on smuggled excise goods brought into the
   United Kingdom was in the region of £30 to £40m. By the year 2000 this had
   escalated to £3·8b from tobacco smuggling alone. To try and keep abreast of
   this increasing problem more robust methods of dealing with the seizure and
   reclamation of vehicles used to smuggle excise goods into the United   *d*
   Kingdom were initially brought into force in 1998. Then the general practice
   was that, if an individual had excise goods seized for the first time, the vehicle
   could only be restored after the payment of a sum of £250 or a sum
   equivalent to 50% of the duty due on the goods seized as liable to forfeiture
   whichever was the greater.
      56. Despite this tougher policy being applied, the use of vehicles in excise   *e*
   smuggling continued in an upward trend and to outline this, in 1998, a total
   of 3,163 vehicles were seized containing excise goods with a revenue value
   of £142m and in 1999 there were 5,200 vehicles seized containing excise
   goods to the value of £348m.
      57. The United Kingdom government introduced its current policy on   *f*
   13 July 2000 after the Paymaster General had, on 22 March 2000, reaffirmed
   the government's commitment to ensure that smugglers face the toughest
   possible sanctions and penalties available. Now vehicles are seized and not
   restored on the first attempt they are detected being used in smuggling. This
   policy applies to all types of motor cars and light commercial vehicles except
   those which are genuinely rented. Only exceptional circumstances can   *g*
   justify a departure from the policy. An example was a motor car adapted for
   and used by a disabled driver.'

   [20] Mr Pennington added that individual applications for restoration were
considered on their own merits and officers bore in mind the need for   *h*
proportionality.
   [21] We asked to see the document in which the policy was originally
promulgated. It was in the form of a circular letter (a DCL) dated 13 July 2000 to
various Customs officers, including review officers. I shall read a few extracts
from this document:
                                                                                        j
   '1. The Government's intention to tackle tobacco smuggling announced
   on 22 March by the Paymaster General included not only a £209 million
   investment in Customs but also a commitment to ensure that those caught
   would face the most severe penalties and sanctions available.
      2. One of the most direct ways to strike at the smugglers' activities is by
   seizing the vehicles they use to smuggle in their contraband. As the Paymaster

a General has said, we are determined to ensure that this sanction is as tough as it can be. The more effective this sanction is, the more we will hit the smugglers in the pocket and reduce the profitability of their illegal trade.

3. We are now in the process of applying the toughest possible sanctions in terms of our vehicle seizure policy. We are tackling the different components involved - e g privately owned cars and light goods vehicles,
b hire or lease vehicles and commercial tractors & trailers - in separate, but coherent, bite-size chunks ...

6. This revised policy sends out a strong message about vehicles to all those involved in smuggling: there are no second chances - if you use it, you will lose it. This policy is aimed at those who are profiting from smuggling or who are deliberately flouting the law. We would expect discretion to be
c applied where it is a case of the infrequent honest traveller who is genuinely unaware of the conditions of the Personal Reliefs order and has made modest purchases on behalf of family who have not travelled ...

Revised Policy - 'No Second Chances'

8. With immediate effect, our headline policy will be that any car or light
d goods vehicle (other than rented) used for smuggling or for transporting smuggled or diverted excise goods within the UK will be seized and not restored. Restoration will be very much the exception, not the rule, irrespective of whether it is the first time the smuggler has been caught. This policy is to be applied vigorously both at the ports and at all inland locations where it can
e be proved that a vehicle was used to transport goods which are liable to seizure ...

11. Occasions which merit on the spot restoration will be very rare and by their nature unpredictable. Therefore, this DCL does not attempt to explore every possible scenario when restoration on the spot might be applicable. It leaves that decision to officers on the ground, with the advice of their senior
f officers where appropriate, who have the necessary expertise and experience. However, in general, the decision to restore should be because:

*it would be entirely disproportionate to refuse to restore the vehicle (one example could be on a first time 'technical' offence where a minimal amount of tobacco has been bought back for a relatives consumption with payment
g at cost)

*it would be seen as inhumane not to restore.

12. It is important for seizing officers to bear in mind the issues of proportionality and human rights (ECHR) when considering whether restoration is appropriate. It is not intended that restoration will be an
h option in any other circumstances.'

THE PRIMARY FACTS

[22] The following primary facts were found by the tribunal:

'26. [Mr Lindsay] is a night lorry driver who works at nights on weekdays
j solely in Great Britain. He lives at his parents' home in Dagenham, Essex and has a girlfriend who lives elsewhere. They have two children aged six and three and his girlfriend is pregnant. He supports his young family. He has four sisters and one brother. The four sisters are all married and live in their own homes ...

29. In the year 2000 on 13 May, 27 May, 11 June and 9 July, [Mr Lindsay] made journeys in his vehicle from Cheriton to Coquelles and thence into

France and Belgium to purchase cigarettes, tobacco and alcohol ... The last *a* two occasions were Sunday trips and [Mr Lindsay] used the early bird service of the Channel tunnel shuttle train leaving Cheriton at approximately 5.30 am and arriving back at Coquelles between 9.15 am and 9.30 am. The summer time in France and Belgium is one hour ahead of the United Kingdom.

30. On Sunday 23 July 2000 [Mr Lindsay], accompanied by his father, *b* drove his vehicle from Dagenham to catch the same early bird service as before from Cheriton at about 5.30 am. As on the previous occasions, the sole purpose of the visit was to buy excise goods whose retail price in Belgium and France is considerably less than in the United Kingdom because of the United Kingdom excise duties. They drove to a town in Belgium called Adinkerke, just across the border with France where they purchased *c* the cigarettes and tobacco. The cost was £2,107 and they paid in cash. The cost of the cigarettes and tobacco included Belgian excise duty.

31. They then returned to France and stopped at a store near Calais to purchase the alcohol ... [Mr Lindsay] and his father went through French Customs and were stopped at 8.55 am by British Customs officers at the *d* juxtaposed immigration control at Coquelles.

32. [Mr Lindsay] and his father were interviewed by Customs officer, Laura Bloomfield. She was told that they had been to France that morning to a cash and carry supermarket off junction 19 on the motorway system. They were returning to Dagenham where they lived when they were stopped. [Mr Lindsay] was asked what he had bought and he replied "booze, *e* cigarettes and tobacco". The back of the car and the unlocked boot were examined and found to contain goods which consisted of: (i) two boxes of Benson & Hedges cigarettes (totalling 15,300 with a revenue value of £2,026·62); (ii) one box of Superkings cigarettes (totalling 3,200 with a revenue value of £418·56); (iii) one box of Golden Virginia hand-rolling *f* tobacco; and (iv) one box of Old Holborn hand-rolling tobacco (weighing together 10 kg with a revenue value of £951), (v) there were also loose cartons of Silk Cut cigarettes and a few cases of beer and bottles of spirits ...

33. [Mr Lindsay] and his father were asked who were the owners of the goods. [Mr Lindsay] replied that the goods belonged to both of them. When asked whether all of them were intended for the two of them, [Mr Lindsay] *g* replied that some of them were for other family members who had already paid some money for cigarettes.'

THE SEIZURE

[23] What has been described as a 'civil caution' was given by Officer *h* Bloomfield in the following terms:

'You have in your possession excise goods in excess of the guidance levels, which for tobacco is one kilogram, cigarettes is 800. Relief from payment of UK excise duty is afforded subject to the condition that these goods are not imported or held or used for a commercial purpose. I require you to satisfy *j* me that these goods have not been imported for a commercial use. If you fail to do so, then these goods will be seized as being liable to forfeiture. However, at this point you are not under arrest and you are both free to leave these controls.'

[24] Both Mr Lindsay and his father indicated that they understood the caution, but made no further comment and were asked no further questions.

a
[25] The excise goods and vehicle were then seized by the commissioners.
[26] This is the first example of the confusion that I referred to earlier in relation to the test for entitlement to relief. Mr Lindsay had already stated that some of the cigarettes were for members of his family, who had paid for them. That was enough to establish that he was not entitled to relief in respect of them. The statement in the caution, that if Mr Lindsay failed to satisfy Officer Bloomfield

b that the goods had not been imported for commercial use they would be seized, was not appropriate when she already had information justifying seizure. Had it been the commissioners' policy to draw a distinction between (1) importation for family or friends against reimbursement and (2) importation for sale at a profit then it would have been appropriate to explore whether to accept Mr Lindsay's explanation that the former was the position. This was not, however, the case.

c It should be noted, that the reason for seizure that Officer Bloomfield recorded in her notebook was that the levels of excise goods brought in were above the guidance level and that Mr Lindsay had received payment for these from members of his family.

d [27] Subsequently, additional information was provided by or on behalf of Mr Lindsay as to the circumstances in which he had purchased the cigarettes and tobacco. He, his father and mother were heavy smokers. He and his father smoked hand-made cigarettes from Old Holborn and Golden Virginia tobacco. He would smoke up to 50 of these a day. In addition they would smoke manufactured cigarettes on social occasions. Other members of his family were

e also heavy smokers. Nine-hundred pounds of the money used to buy the cigarettes and tobacco had been provided by his sister Jane and her husband, his brother Steve and his girlfriend and his sisters, Clare and Jackie. A quantity of the cigarettes acquired were for their use.

[28] This account does not appear to have been challenged. The tribunal observed, 'the reason for the trip is not in dispute—to purchase cheap cigarettes,

f tobacco and alcohol for themselves and other members of their immediate family'. Had it been considered material whether the purchase had been for members of the family or for commercial re-sale, I consider that it would have been surprising if the former had been accepted without question. Mr Lindsay had made four previous trips on the shuttle to purchase cigarettes, tobacco and alcohol in the previous three months. He had stated that he had only purchased

g 400 cigarettes on each occasion, but the tribunal does not appear to have accepted this part of his evidence. The cigarettes and tobacco in Mr Lindsay's car on 23 July would have kept him and his immediate family going for many months, however hard they puffed. It seems to me that, had the issue been raised, the tribunal could properly have concluded that Mr Lindsay was using his vehicle for

h commercial smuggling.

THE FIRST RECONSIDERATION
[29] On 2 August 2000 Mr Lindsay's solicitors wrote to the commissioners challenging their seizure of his vehicle on the ground that they had wrongly found that there was a commercial purpose behind the importation of the goods.

j I have not seen their letter, but I suspect that this may have evidenced further confusion as to the test for entitlement to relief from duty. This letter led to the initiation of the condemnation proceedings, which were subsequently withdrawn. At that point Mr Lindsay asked to have the seizure of his vehicle reviewed.

[30] The commissioners declined to offer the vehicle for restoration to Mr Lindsay. The reasons for not doing so were set out in a letter dated 4 October

2000 from Officer Skues. He explained that the commissioners' efforts were
directed towards deterring and detecting fraud, failure to pay duty that was due, *a*
irregularities and encouraging compliance with procedures established to control
movements of excise goods. Against this background: (i) the appellant had
tobacco and cigarettes many times in excess of the guidance levels; (ii) he had
received payment for the goods imported on behalf of persons not travelling;
(iii) he had declined to stay and answer questions and therefore failed to satisfy *b*
the officers as to his entitlement.

[31] I interpose to comment that the third reason evidenced a misunderstanding
of the true position.

THE REVIEW

[32] Mr Lindsay then appealed against this decision to the review officer, *c*
Mrs Florence, by letter of 16 October 2000. He made a number of points in that
letter, including the fact that he was paying for his vehicle through a finance
company and a bank loan. He did not mention the value of the vehicle.

[33] In her decision letter of 22 November, rejecting this appeal, Mrs Florence
stated, in the course of outlining the facts: *d*

'The Officer explained to you that due to the quantity of excise goods you
were importing you were required to satisfy her that the excise goods were
for your own use and not some other (commercial) purpose. She told you
that if you failed to so the goods would be liable to forfeiture.'

e

[34] Later, when explaining why there was no entitlement to duty relief, she
said:

'Relief from the payment of any excise duty afforded under the 1992 Order
is only if the goods are for own use and that the individual has transported
them. This is not the case here. You had entered into a commercial *f*
transaction with your family to purchase excise goods on their behalf. They
are deemed not to be for "own use" under the legal definition quoted earlier,
therefore there is no relief from the payment of excise duty on these goods
and this rendered them liable to forfeiture.'

[35] Here again there is confusion between purchase for family members and *g*
purchase for a commercial purpose.

[36] In refusing to reverse the commissioners' decision, Mrs Florence said this:

'Restoration Policy
    With effect from 14 July 2000 the Commissioners' policy regarding *h*
privately owned vehicles used for the improper importation of excise goods
is that they will not be restored, even on the first occasion they are so used.
That policy applied at the time of the seizure of the vehicle. A car may
however, be restored to a third party where it has been stolen and the matter
was reported at the time ... Relief from the payment of any excise duty *j*
afforded under the 1992 Order is only if the goods are for own use and that
the individual has transported them. This is not the case here. You had
entered into a commercial transaction with your family to purchase excise
goods on their behalf. They are deemed not to be for "own use" under the
legal definition quoted earlier, therefore there is no relief from the payment
of excise duty on these goods and this rendered them liable to forfeiture.'

THE TRIBUNAL'S DECISION

a   [37] In his notice of appeal to the tribunal, Mr Lindsay, through his solicitor, Mr Woodcraft, referred for the first time to the value of his vehicle. He advanced the following contentions:

'7. The seizure of Mr Lindsay's car was a penalty out of all proportion to the question or amount of tobacco involved. The car was new and worth

b   approximately £15,000. Mr Lindsay having purchased the car with a finance agreement with Ford Credit in the sum of approximately £12,000.

8. The amount of tobacco in question amounted to £2,107. Even if the duty on that was the same amount again, since the tobacco has been seized by Customs and Excise and its restoration is not being sought by Mr Lindsay,

c   Mr Lindsay has already effectively incurred a substantial penalty equal to the duty which would have been paid. For the car to be seized on top of that is oppressive and disproportionate to the matter concerned. Seizing a car of this value exceeds even the amount of the fine which would ordinarily be payable in a criminal matter.'

d   [38] The tribunal, chaired by Mr Rodney Huggins, heard oral evidence from Mr Lindsay, supported by his mother, and from the various Customs officers involved in the procedure. The tribunal produced a reasoned decision twenty pages in length. The argument advanced on behalf of Mr Lindsay included the contention that 'the forfeited goods were intended for the private use of the appellant and members of his immediate family and there was no commercial

e   element'. In relation to this submission, the tribunal held (at para 69):

'Except for [Mr Lindsay's] mother, the others had given [Mr Lindsay] some £900 for their cigarettes. The total cost of the cigarettes and tobacco acquired in Adinkerke, Belgium was £2,107 and therefore approximately 43·8% of the total goods were bought with money provided by others and

f   this quantity was not for "own use" of [Mr Lindsay] and his father. We consider these words "own use" do not include other members of the family who pay in advance for tobacco brought back for their use. [Mr Lindsay's] mother does not come within this category because her cigarettes were a gift from [Mr Lindsay] and his father. We also find that this arrangement with

g   other members of the family made the transaction 'commercial' since they were benefiting financially from the transaction in that the excise goods were cheaper than in the United Kingdom. [Mr Lindsay] and his father were effectively agents for other members of the family in this enterprise.'

[39] While the first part of this paragraph was plainly correct, the same cannot

h   be said of the penultimate sentence. The fact that the other members of the family were benefiting financially from the transaction because the goods were cheaper than in the United Kingdom did not make the transaction 'commercial' within the normal meaning of that word. Were it otherwise, Mr Lindsay's purchase for his own use could also have been said to be 'commercial'. This is a

j   further example of the scope for confusion about the appropriate test.

[40] However, the principal issue before the tribunal, was whether the commissioners' decision not to restore Mr Lindsay's car to him was one that they 'could not reasonably have arrived at'—within the meaning of those words in s 16(4) of the 1994 Act. Since the coming into force of the Human Rights Act 1998, there can be no doubt that if the commissioners are to arrive reasonably at a decision, their decision must comply with the European Convention for the

Protection of Human Rights and Fundamental Freedoms 1950 (as set out in Sch 1 to the Human Rights Act 1998). Quite apart from this, the commissioners will not arrive reasonably at a decision if they take into account irrelevant matters, or fail to take into account all relevant matters (see *Customs and Excise Comrs v JH Corbitt (Numismatists) Ltd* [1980] 2 All ER 72 at 80, [1981] AC 22 at 60, per Lord Lane). It was argued before the tribunal that the commissioners' decision fell at both hurdles. It violated the convention in that it involved depriving Mr Lindsay of his rights under art 1 of the First Protocol to the convention to the peaceful enjoyment of his possessions in circumstances which were disproportionately harsh. By the same token, because of the policy which was applied, the decision ignored the relationship that the value of the car bore to the duty that should have been paid, although this was a highly relevant matter.

[41] Article 1 of the First Protocol provides:

'Every natural or legal person is entitled to the peaceful enjoyment of his possessions. No one shall be deprived of his possessions except in the public interest and subject to the conditions provided for by law and by the general principles of international law.

The preceding provisions shall not, however, in any way impair the right of a State to enforce such laws as it deems necessary to control the use of property in accordance with the general interest or to secure the payment of taxes or other contributions or penalties.'

[42] In the course of referring to a previous decision of the tribunal in the case of *Dereczenik v Customs and Excise Comrs* (7 June 2001, unreported) the tribunal cited the following passage from the judgment of the Strasbourg court in *Air Canada v UK* (1995) 20 EHRR 150 at 173 (para 36):

'According to the Court's well-established case law, the second paragraph of Article 1 must be construed in the light of the principle laid down in the Article's first sentence. Consequently, an interference must achieve a "fair balance" between the demands of the general interest of the community and the requirements of the protection of the individual's fundamental rights. The concern to achieve this balance is reflected in the structure of Article 1 as whole, including the second paragraph: there must therefore be a reasonable relationship of proportionality between the means employed and the aim pursued.'

[43] The tribunal applied this test and found that, on the facts of this case, it was not satisfied. The essence of their reasoning appears in the following passages:

'82. ... We accept the evidence of Customs Officer Florence that the policy was hardened considerably and no consideration is given to the value of the motor vehicle seized in relation to the value of the duty sought to be avoided. The tribunal accepts that the [commissioners] have the right to exercise a policy with regard to such seizure, but it must achieve the "fair balance" referred to in the *Air Canada* case. In our judgment the current policy does not achieve the fair balance since it excludes the reviewing officer from giving any real consideration to proportionality which, as has been demonstrated in this decision, is a fundamental concept of European law ...

84. In this appeal, under the present policy, the reviewing officer considering restoration of a vehicle is excluded by the commissioners' policy

a
from giving full consideration to all relevant matters when deciding whether or not to restore the vehicle to its owner subject to conditions or otherwise. The evidence of Mrs Florence on this point is quite clear. Her discretion under s 152 of [the 1979 Act] is fettered by the policy ...

85. The commissioners are entitled to formulate a policy, but where that policy restrains a discretion conferred by statute, that policy is at first sight unreasonable.

b

86. The tribunal finds that the value of the vehicle at time of seizure was at least £10,500. The reasons for that are that the new cost was just under £12,000 and Glass's guide for a year-old Ford Focus was £8,500. This car was four months'old and only had 5,000 miles on the clock. The excise duty assessed on the forfeited goods was approximately £3,500. These values are disproportionate and this factor should have been taken into account by the reviewing officer. She should not have ignored it.

c

87. [Mr Lindsay] is a lorry driver with a partner and small family of two children to support. He also has to pay hire purchase instalments on his motor car with most of the loan of £6,000 outstanding at the date of seizure. We find that by being deprived of his vehicle he suffers undue hardship.'

d

[44] Accordingly the tribunal allowed the appeal. There is a dispute as to whether the terms in which they did so fell within their jurisdiction, so it is necessary to recite those terms verbatim:

e

'Exercising its power under s 16(4) of the Finance Act 1994 the tribunal directs that the seized vehicle is to be restored to [Mr Lindsay]. In the event of the vehicle having been disposed of, or having deteriorated whilst in the custody of customs, then the tribunal has given guidance in para 86 of this decision as to the value pertaining at the date of the seizure which the commissioners shall take into account when compensating the appellant. If the parties are unable to agree the amount of compensation then either party is at liberty to apply to the tribunal for a direction in this respect.'

f

THE ISSUES BEFORE US

[45] I have expressed some reservation about Mr Lindsay's evidence that the goods in his car were destined only for himself and his close family. That evidence has, however, been accepted and it is not for this court to review the tribunal's findings of fact. The major issue before this court is one of principle. It is whether the current policy of the commissioners so fetters their discretion when reviewing decisions taken to forfeit vehicles of those who evade duty on cigarettes, tobacco and alcohol as to prevent them from considering proportionality and thus to render their decisions unlawful.

g

h

THE COMMISSIONERS' CONTENTIONS

[46] The commissioners challenge the jurisdiction of the tribunal to direct the commissioners to return Mr Lindsay's car to him, or to pay compensation in lieu. That challenge is, however, subsidiary to their challenge to the finding that their policy is unlawful. That finding is, so they submit, at odds with the decision of the President of the VAT and Duties Tribunals, Mr Stephen Oliver QC, in the case of *Hopping v Customs and Excise Comrs* (9 October 2001, unreported). The commissioners' submissions are largely founded on that decision and, in particular, on the following passages:

j

'26. ... So is application of the "use it and lose it" policy proportionate? In the words of the *Air Canada* decision ((1995) 20 EHRR 150) the question is whether the policy and the decision as to its application in the present circumstances represents a reasonable relationship for the proportionality between the means employed and the aim pursued.

27. We start with the aim pursued. We see this as a legitimate aim for the reasons already given. The aim is found in the summary of [the policy officer's] evidence. The policy is designed to check the increase in smuggling and the loss of revenues and the damage to the business of local traders.

28. On the other side of the balance is the means employed. Seizure and the refusal to restore the vehicle are, on first impression, direct violations of the owner's fundamental right of peaceful enjoyment of this vehicle. The result is capable of being arbitrary to the point of extravagant. The financial loss resulting from the refusal to restore an expensive car could many times exceed the loss of revenue sought from the smuggling operation. A less invasive way of dealing with the seized car might be to offer to release it on payment of a prescribed amount. Those are negative features which on their face tell against the commissioners' policy being a proportionate reaction. But there are other factors which tend to balance up the "means employed" by the commissioners with the aim pursued. The first of these is that the actual means employed, i e seizure and refusal to restore, is a suitable way of preventing smuggling. Take away the vehicle and it can no longer be used for bootlegging. When a vehicle has been used every ten days to make short round trips to Calais and back it is realistic that that vehicle should be removed from circulation as a means of bootlegging. Second, to refuse to restore is even-handed. It is a course of action that is blind to the value of the vehicle and to the financial means of the owner. In other words it treats all bootleggers alike. This tends to outweigh the other, less invasive, course open to the commissioners of offering to return the vehicle on payment of a monetary amount. Third, the owner who makes a bootlegging trip to France and whose vehicle is taken will know the score before he embarks on his smuggling operations. In a real sense he ventures his vehicle as one of the stakes of his dishonest enterprise. He foregoes his claim to any unqualified fundamental right of peaceful enjoyment of the vehicle before he sets off on his trip. Fourthly, so long as the seizure and refusal to restore the vehicle does not cause physical suffering or result in excessive inconvenience to defenceless third parties, its impact will be directed at the owner.

29. Every case will have to be dealt with on its own facts. But in principle we do not see a lack of balance when the factors set out above are brought into the reckoning. Where the owner is the driver he will know that he risks losing the vehicle when he sets out to bootleg. He takes the risk and loses when he is caught.'

[47] Mr McKay submitted that the principles set out in this passage were correct. He emphasised that the current policy was one which had been reached incrementally and only after less stringent policies had failed. The amount of revenue being lost was cogent justification for the policy. The tribunal's criticism of the failure to have regard to the value of the vehicle was misplaced. That was a factor which the policy could properly disregard.

MR LINDSAY'S CONTENTIONS

[48] On behalf of Mr Lindsay, Mr Philip Baker has added an extra string to the bow that was deployed before the tribunal. There it was Mr Lindsay's case that the commissioners' policy precluded the application of proportionality that was an essential if the requirements of the convention were to be observed. Before us Mr Baker has broadened his attack on that policy by contending that it also precludes the application of the doctrine of proportionality that forms an essential element of European Community law.

[49] Mr Baker submitted that the principle expounded by the Strasbourg court in the *Air Canada* case was only the starting point. To say that a balance had to be struck between the interests of the community and the rights of the individual did not go far enough. It was necessary to consider whether the deprivation of the individual's property was fair to the individual. The Strasbourg jurisprudence showed that the individual should not be subjected to an excessive burden (see *Lithgow v UK* (1986) 8 EHRR 329 at 371–382 (para 120)). It was impossible to apply the appropriate test of proportionality without having regard to, among other matters, the value of the vehicle seized. The review officer had failed to do so because she was fettered by the commissioners' policy.

[50] Mr Baker was critical of the decision in *Hopping v Customs and Excise Comrs* (9 October 2001, unreported). In particular, he submitted that it was not 'even-handed' to disregard the value of the vehicle and the financial means of the owner. Both had to be taken into account if the effect of the penalty was not to be arbitrary and potentially unfair.

[51] Turning to European Community law, Mr Baker submitted that here also the principle of proportionality had to be observed. Where penalties were imposed for the unlawful importation of goods, they must not be disproportionate (see *Louloudakis v Demosio* Case C-262/99 (2001) ECR I-5547 at paras 63–69).

THE APPLICABLE PRINCIPLES

Human rights

[52] The commissioners' policy involves the deprivation of people's possessions. Under art 1 of the First Protocol to the convention such deprivation will only be justified if it is in the public interest. More specifically, the deprivation can be justified if it is 'to secure the payment of taxes or other contributions or penalties'. The action taken must, however, strike a fair balance between the rights of the individual and the public interest. There must be a reasonable relationship of proportionality between the means employed and the aim pursued (*Sporrong & Lönnroth v Sweden* (1982) 5 EHRR 35 at 50–51 (para 61), [1982] ECHR 7151/7535; *Air Canada* as cited in [49], above). I would accept Mr Baker's submission that one must consider the individual case to ensure that the penalty imposed is fair. However strong the public interest, it cannot justify subjecting an individual to an interference with his fundamental rights that is unconscionable.

European Community law

[53] It does not seem to me that the doctrine of proportionality that is a well-established feature of European Community law has anything significant to add to that which has been developed in the Strasbourg jurisprudence. There is, however, a passage in *Louloudakis's* case, which is helpful in the present context in that it is of general application. I quote from para 67:

'Subject to those observations, it must be borne in mind that, in the absence of harmonisation of the Community legislation in the field of the penalties applicable where conditions laid down by arrangements under such legislation are not observed, the Member States are empowered to choose the penalties which seem appropriate to them. They must, however, exercise that power in accordance with Community law and its general principles, and consequently with the principle of proportionality.'

[54] There are then references to Strasbourg authority. The judgment continues:

'The administrative measures or penalties must not go beyond what is strictly necessary for the objectives pursued and a penalty must not be so disproportionate to the gravity of the infringement that it becomes an obstacle to the freedoms enshrined in the treaty.'

CONCLUSIONS

[55] Broadly speaking, the aim of the commissioners' policy is the prevention of the evasion of excise duty that is imposed in accordance with European Community law. That is a legitimate aim under art 1 of the First Protocol to the convention. The issue is whether the policy is liable to result in the imposition of a penalty in the individual case that is disproportionate having regard to that legitimate aim. More specifically, did it have that effect in the case of Mr Lindsay?

[56] Mr McKay argued that the policy paid due regard to the principle of proportionality. When considering whether to restore a forfeited vehicle, the review officer would always give due consideration to the representations made by the owner. The demands of proportionality would be borne in mind.

[57] It is true that the DCL referred to making a decision to restore when it would be 'entirely disproportionate to refuse to restore' and required seizing officers to 'bear in mind the issues of proportionality and human rights'. The general tenor of the letter made it plain, however, that restoration should only be ordered in exceptional circumstances, and this message was reinforced by the example given of such circumstances—'a first time "technical offence" where a minimal amount of tobacco has been brought back for a relative's consumption with payment at cost'. The policy did not suggest that any regard should be paid to the value of the car. More significantly, in my view, it did not suggest that, save in the exceptional case referred to above, it was relevant to consider whether the goods were being imported to be distributed between family and friends or whether the importation was pursuant to a commercial venture under which the goods were to be sold at a profit.

[58] In this context it is appropriate to refer to the comments of the Strasbourg court in *Allgemeine Gold-und Silberscheideanschalt v United Kingdom* (1986) 9 EHRR 1 at 14 (para 54):

'It is first to be observed that although there is a trend in the practice of the Contracting States that the behaviour of the owner of the goods and in particular the use of due care on his part should be taken into account in deciding whether or not to restore smuggled goods—assuming that the goods are not dangerous—different standards are applied and no common practice can be said to exist. For forfeiture to be justified under the terms of the second paragraph of Article 1, it is enough that the explicit requirements of this paragraph are met and that the State has struck a fair balance between the interests of the State and those of the individual. The striking of a fair balance depends on many factors and the behaviour of the owner of the a property, including the degree of fault or care which he has displayed, is one element of the entirety of circumstances which should be taken into account.'

[59] In that case the court held that the forfeiture by the Customs of 140 Krugerrands, which had been smuggled into the country in breach of import b restrictions, did not violate art 1 of the First Protocol.

[60] In considering the commissioners' policy it is appropriate to bear in mind the scale of the evil against which it is directed. Mr Baker referred us to a report by the Comptroller and Auditor General released a week ago which includes details of measures taken by the Customs to combat fraud. This records a large number of options available against tobacco smuggling, only one of which is c 'increased emphasis on asset confiscation to remove the economic rewards of smuggling'. Yet the target over a five-year period is no more than to reduce the proportion of the United Kingdom market that is represented by smuggled cigarettes from 21% to no more than 18%. The statistics referred to by Mr Pennington demonstrate that the average revenue value of goods in vehicles d seized exceeds £50,000. The trade that is carried on in smuggled cigarettes is massive.

[61] It is also relevant to bear in mind that the free movement of persons within the internal market, albeit that this is subject to the requirement for shuttle travellers to drive through the control zone, greatly facilitates the illicit importation of excise goods into the United Kingdom. When reckoning up the e risk, the potential smuggler will have regard not merely to the consequences of apprehension but to the likelihood that this will occur.

[62] Finally it is right to bear in mind that notice is given to travellers that they are only entitled to bring back excise goods duty free if they are for their own use and that smuggling can lead to the forfeiture of their vessels. Anyone who uses f his car for smuggling is likely to be taking a calculated risk.

[63] Having regard to these considerations, I would not have been prepared to condemn the commissioners' policy had it been one that was applied to those who were using their cars for commercial smuggling, giving that phrase the meaning that it naturally bears of smuggling goods in order to sell them at a profit. Those who deliberately use their cars to further fraudulent commercial g ventures in the knowledge that if they are caught their cars will be rendered liable to forfeiture cannot reasonably be heard to complain if they lose those vehicles. Nor does it seem to me that, in such circumstances, the value of the car used need be taken into consideration. Those circumstances will normally take the case beyond the threshold where that factor can carry significant weight in the h balance. Cases of exceptional hardship must always, of course, be given due consideration.

[64] The commissioners' policy does not, however, draw a distinction between the commercial smuggler and the driver importing goods for social distribution to family or friends in circumstances where there is no attempt to j make a profit. Of course even in such a case the scale of importation, or other circumstances, may be such as to justify forfeiture of the car. But where the importation is not for the purpose of making a profit, I consider that the principle of proportionality requires that each case should be considered on its particular facts, which will include the scale of importation, whether it is a 'first offence', whether there was an attempt at concealment or dissimulation, the value of the vehicle and the degree of hardship that will be caused by forfeiture. There is open

to the commissioners a wide range of lesser sanctions that will enable them to impose a sanction that is proportionate where forfeiture of the vehicle is not justified.

[65] I do not think that it would be impractical to distinguish between the truly commercial smuggler and others. The current regulations shift the burden to the driver of showing that he does not hold the goods 'for commercial purposes' when these exceed the quantity in the Schedule. In a case such as the present, the driver importing for family or friends should be in a position to demonstrate that that is the case if called upon to do so (see *Goldsmith v Customs and Excise Comrs* [2001] EWHC Admin 285 at [24], [2001] 1 WLR 1673, per Lord Woolf CJ).

[66] Unfortunately, in the present case and, I suspect, in others, the Customs officers have drawn no distinction between the true commercial smuggler and the driver importing goods for family and friends. Because of the confusion to which I referred at the outset, the cars of both have been treated as subject to almost automatic forfeiture. Review Officer Florence appears to have understood that the commissioners' policy rendered it irrelevant whether or not Mr Lindsay's story was true and equally irrelevant the value of his car and the effect that its deprivation would have on him. I believe that she correctly interpreted the policy.

[67] For these reasons, I consider that the tribunal was correct to decide that Mrs Florence's decision could not stand because she had failed, when reaching it, to have regard to all material considerations. To that extent the commissioners' appeal must be dismissed. It remains to consider whether the terms of the relief directed by the tribunal fell within their jurisdiction.

JURISDICTION

[68] The tribunal directed that Mr Lindsay's vehicle should be restored to him and that, if this were not possible, the commissioners should pay him compensation. In so doing they purported to be exercising jurisdiction conferred by s 16(4) of the 1994 Act. That subsection expressly spells out the powers of the tribunal in the circumstances of this case. They include the power to direct that the decision appealed against ceased to have effect and to require the commissioners to conduct a further review of the original decision in accordance with the directions of the tribunal. Mr Baker sought to persuade us that that was all that the tribunal had done. The decision appealed against was that the vehicle should not be restored. If that decision ceased to have effect, it followed, inevitably, that the vehicle would have to be restored and the tribunal had done no more than give this direction.

[69] I do not agree. The tribunal have done more than direct that Mrs Florence's decision ceased to have effect. They have purported to reverse it. That is something that they had no jurisdiction to do. To make this plain it is only necessary to contrast sub-s (4) of s 16 with sub-s (5), which provides:

'In relation to other decisions, the powers of an appeal tribunal on appeal under this section shall also include power to quash or vary any decision and power to substitute their own decision for any decision quashed on appeal.'

[70] I consider that the appropriate order is that the commissioners conduct a further review of Review Officer Florence's decision in the light of the decision of the tribunal and this judgment. I consider that the appropriate order is that the

a   commissioners conduct a further review of Review Officer Florence's decision in the light of the decision of the tribunal and this judgment.

JUDGE LJ.

[71] I agree with the judgment of Lord Phillips of Worth Matravers MR on the issues of principle and their application to this appeal. My brief observations are b   by way of emphasis only. There is usually a marked distinction between those who smuggle alcohol, cigarettes and tobacco for profit and those who, without profit, smuggle amounts in excess of the permitted limits for their personal use and occasional distribution to family members and close friends. The vehicles used by those whose activity falls into either category are liable to be seized.

[72] Given the extent of the damage caused to the public interest, it is, in my c   judgment, acceptable and proportionate that, subject to exceptional individual considerations, whatever they are worth, the vehicles of those who smuggle for profit, even for a small profit, should be seized as a matter of policy. However, the equal application of the same stringent policy to those who are not importing for profit fails adequately to recognise the distinction between them and those d   who are trading in smuggled goods. Accordingly the policy is flawed.

[73] In my judgment, the question whether the power to seize the vehicle of a non-profit making smuggler should be exercised is fact-dependent, requiring a realistic assessment of all the circumstances of the individual case, including the alternative sanctions available to the commissioners, rather than the virtually automatic imposition of a burdensome and, at times, oppressive prescribed e   penalty.

CARNWATH LJ.

[74] I agree with the judgment of Lord Phillips of Worth Matravers MR on both issues.

Appeal dismissed save in relation to jurisdiction issue. Permission to appeal refused.

Kate O'Hanlon   Barrister.

Re Railtrack plc (in railway administration) Winsor v Bloom and others

[2002] EWHC 1027 (Ch)

CHANCERY DIVISION

SIR ANDREW MORRITT V-C

8, 9, 21 MAY 2002

Company – Administration order – Effect – Requirement of leave to commence proceedings against company – Railway administration order – Application to Rail Regulator for directions requiring company owning track to enter into access contract with other company to use track – Whether commencement and continuation of procedure for seeking such directions requiring leave of court or consent of special railway administrators – Insolvency Act 1986, s 11(3)(d) – Railways Act 1993, s 17, Sch 6, para 2(b).

Under the Railways Act 1993, the railtrack in Great Britain was vested in R plc. Section 17ᵃ of the 1993 Act empowered the Rail Regulator, on application by any person, to direct R plc to enter into an access contract granting permission to the applicant to use the track for the purpose of operating trains. In October 2001 a railway administration order was made in respect of R plc. Under that order, the defendants were appointed special railway administrators. Subsequently, a freight train operator made an application to the Regulator pursuant to s 17. The administrators objected to a number of the terms in the proposed access contract, and contended that the s 17 application was subject to s 11(3)(d)ᵇ of the Insolvency Act 1986. Under that provision, 'no other proceedings' could be brought against a company or its property, without the consent of the administrator or the leave of the court, during the period for which an administration order was in force. By virtue of para 2(b)ᶜ of Sch 6 to the 1993 Act, the reference to 'proceedings' in s 11(3)(d) of the 1986 Act was to include a reference to any proceedings under or for the purposes of s 55 of the 1993 Act (the making of orders by the Regulator to secure compliance with a condition or requirement in a licence, franchise or closure) or s 57A of that Act (the making of penalties for contravening a condition or requirement of a licence). In subsequent proceedings, the Regulator sought a declaration that s 11(3)(d) of the 1986 Act did not cover determinations by him of applications made under s 17 of the 1993 Act.

Held – On the true construction of s 11(3)(d) of the 1986 Act, as modified by para 2(b) of Sch 6 to the 1993 Act, the consent of the special railway administrators or the leave of the court was required for the commencement and continuation of the process by which a direction was obtained under s 17 of the 1993 Act. Such a conclusion was consistent both with the nature and purpose of a railway administration, namely the transfer of the undertaking as a going concern to some

---

a   Section 17, so far as material, provides: '(1) The Regulator may, on the application of any person, give directions to a facility owner requiring him to enter into an access contract with the applicant ... '

b   Section 11(3) is set out at [3], below

c   Paragraph 2(b) is set out at [17], below

a   other company so as to ensure that the relevant activities could be properly carried on, and with the functions and responsibilities of the special railway administrators, who were the principal agents for achieving that purpose as officers of the court. It was also consistent with the nature of the procedure under s 17 of the 1993 Act. That procedure could result in a direction that had an important impact on the management of the affairs, business and property of the

b   company in railway administration, which was entrusted to the special railway administrators. Furthermore, the procedure down to the making of an order under ss 55 and 57A of the 1993 Act was not dissimilar to that prescribed by s 17. If the procedure prescribed by ss 55 and 57A were to be treated as proceedings for the purpose of s 11(3) of the 1986 Act as modified, there could be no rational basis for concluding that Parliament had intended the s 17 procedure to be treated

c   differently. Accordingly, a declaration would be granted that s 11(3) of the 1986 Act did cover determinations by the Regulator of applications made under s 17 of the 1993 Act (see [22], [39], [41], [42], [44]–[46], below).

   Bristol Airport plc v Powdrill [1990] 2 All ER 493 and *Re Rhondda Waste Disposal Ltd* [2001] Ch 57 considered.

d   **Notes**

   For the prohibition on bringing proceedings against a company in administration without the consent of the administrators or the leave of the court and for the meaning and effect of a railway administration order, see respectively 7(3) *Halsbury's Laws* (4th edn reissue) para 2091 and 39(1) *Halsbury's Laws* (4th edn

e   reissue) para 289.

   For the Insolvency Act 1986, s 11, see 4 *Halsbury's Statutes* (4th edn) (1998 reissue) 746.

   For the Railways Act 1993, s 17, Sch 6, para 2, see 36 *Halsbury's Statutes* (4th edn) (1994 reissue) 637, 839.

f   **Cases referred to in judgment**

   Air Ecosse Ltd v Civil Aviation Authority 1987 SC 285, Ct of Sess.
   Atlantic Computers Systems plc, Re [1992] 1 All ER 476, [1992] Ch 505, [1992] 2 WLR 367, CA.
   Bristol Airport plc v Powdrill [1990] 2 All ER 493, [1990] Ch 744, [1990] 2 WLR 1362, CA.

g   *Carr v British International Helicopters Ltd (in administration)* [1994] 2 BCLC 474, EAT.
   Rhondda Waste Disposal Ltd, Re [2001] Ch 57, [2000] 3 WLR 1304, CA.
   Straume (A) (UK) Ltd v Bradlor Developments Ltd [2000] BCC 333.

   Cases also cited or referred to in skeleton arguments

   A-G v Guardian Newspapers Ltd (No 2) [1988] 3 All ER 545, [1990] 1 AC 109, Ch D,
h   CA and HL.
   Argosam Finance Co Ltd v Oxby (Inspector of Taxes) [1964] 3 All ER 561, [1965] Ch 390, CA.
   Australian Consolidated Press Ltd v Uren [1967] 3 All ER 523, [1969] 1 AC 590, PC.
   Barnato (decd), Re, Joel v Sanges [1949] 1 All ER 515, [1949] Ch 258, CA.
j   *Biosource Technologies Inc v Axis Genetics plc (in administration)* [2000] 1 BCLC 286.
   Colquhoun v Brooks (1888) 21 QBD 52, CA; *affd* (1889) 14 App Cas 493, [1886–90] All ER Rep 1063, HL.
   Dean v Wiesengrund [1955] 2 All ER 432, [1955] 2 QB 120, CA.
   Glasgow Navigation Co v Iron Ore Co [1910] AC 293, HL.
   National Electric Theatres Ltd v Hudgell [1939] 1 All ER 567, [1939] Ch 553.
   Quazi v Quazi [1979] 3 All ER 897, [1980] AC 744, HL.

Claim

By proceedings commenced by Pt 8 claim form on 26 April 2002 by the claimant, Thomas Winsor, in his capacity as the Rail Regulator, against the defendants, Alan Robert Bloom, Christopher John Wilkinson Hill, William Scott Martin and Michael David Rollings, the joint special railway administrators of Railtrack plc (in railway administration), the Regulator sought a declaration that s 11(3) of the Insolvency Act 1986, as it applied to companies in railway administration by virtue of s 59(3) of, and Sch 6 to, the Railways Act 1993, did not cover determinations by the Regulator of applications made under s 17 of the 1993 Act. The facts are set out in the judgment.

Phillip Sales and *Ben Hooper* (instructed by the *Treasury Solicitor*) for the Rail Regulator.
Gabriel Moss QC and *Stephen Atherton* (instructed by *Slaughter and May*) for the special railway administrators.

Cur adv vult

21 May 2002. The following judgment was delivered.

SIR ANDREW MORRITT V-C.

Introduction

[1] On 7 October 2001 a railway administration order, as defined in s 59 of the Railways Act 1993, was made in respect of Railtrack plc (Railtrack). The defendants are the special railway administrators appointed thereunder. So long as the railway administration order is in force s 11(3) of the Insolvency Act 1986, as modified by the 1993 Act, precludes the commencement or continuation of certain proceedings without the consent of the special railway administrators or the leave of the court.

[2] The claimant is the Rail Regulator. As such he has the functions and powers and is subject to the duties prescribed by the 1993 Act. By s 17 he is entitled, subject to following the prescribed procedure, to direct Railtrack to enter into an access contract granting permission to the other party to use the track for the purpose of operating trains. If such a direction is made it is enforceable by injunction pursuant to s 144 of the 1993 Act. It is common ground that proceedings against Railtrack under s 144 come within s 11(3) of the 1986 Act as modified. The question for my determination is whether the earlier proceedings under s 17 do too.

[3] The answer depends on the true construction of s 11(3) as modified, in particular the words 'no other proceedings ... against the company or its property' in para (d). The subsection provides (the modifications required by the 1993 Act being shown in bold):

'(3) During the period for which an administration order is in force—
(a) no resolution may be passed or order made for the winding up of the company; (b) no administrative receiver of the company may be appointed; (c) no other steps may be taken to enforce any security over the company's property, or to repossess goods in the company's possession under any hire-purchase agreement, except with the consent of the administrator or the leave of the court and subject (where the court gives leave) to such terms as the court may impose; and (d) no other proceedings (**reference to which**

a   shall include a reference to any proceedings under or for the purposes of
sections 55 or 57A of the Railways Act 1993) and no execution or other
legal process may be commenced or continued, and no distress may be
levied, against the company or its property except with the consent of the
administrator or the leave of the court and subject (where the court gives
leave) to such terms as aforesaid.'

b
[4] To put the subsection into its proper context and to explain the arguments
it is necessary to describe the 1993 Act in a good deal more detail.

The Railways Act 1993
[5] The 1993 Act was the means whereby the nationalised railway network
c   was privatised. It was substantially amended by the Transport Act 2000. Except
where otherwise stated I shall refer to the amended version. Part II dealt with the
reorganisation of the railways. In accordance with its provisions the railtrack
throughout England, Wales and Scotland became vested in Railtrack. The
railtrack, trains, stations and light maintenance depots are described as 'railway
d   assets'. The operator of any such asset requires either a licence or an exemption
for which ss 6–16 provide. Obviously the operator of a train will also need the
permission of the owners to its use of the track, stations and light maintenance
depots. Those items are 'railway facilities'; s 83(1). Sections 17–22 deal with
access contracts whereby the applicant obtains the permission of the owner to his
use of that railway facility.
e   [6] Section 17(1) empowers the Rail Regulator, on the application of any
person, to give directions to a facility owner, such as Railtrack, requiring him to
enter into an access contract granting the applicant permission, but not a lease, to
use the track, station or maintenance depot as the case may be for the purpose of
operating trains. The procedure by which such a direction is sought and obtained
f   is laid down in Sch 4.
[7] Schedule 4 specifies what details the application must contain (para 2). On
receipt of the application the Rail Regulator is required to send a copy of it to the
facility owner and invite his representations and, subsequently, to send a copy of
those representations to the applicant and ask for his response (para 3). By para 4
the Rail Regulator is required to do the same with regard to interested persons,
g   as ascertained from the facility owner, being those third parties whose consent
would be required to the conclusion of an access contract in the form sought. In
practice the Rail Regulator often holds an oral hearing as well. Paragraph 5
requires the decision to be sent to the applicant, facility owner and interested
party and to contain any necessary directions. Such directions may include an
h   award of compensation to an interested party. The direction is binding on the
person to whom it is given (para 6(1)), though the facility owner may be absolved
from compliance if the applicant fails to enter into the access contract (para 5(4)).
[8] Sections 23–54 deal with franchising of passenger services, passenger
transport authorities and executives, closures and ancillary matters. None of them
j   is directly material to the question I have to decide, but it is to be noted that
provision is made in those sections too for directions to be given for the enforcement
of duties by the Secretary of State, see for example ss 24(6) and 34(17).
[9] Sections 55–58 deal with enforcement by the Rail Regulator or the Strategic
Rail Authority of conditions or requirements contained in a licence, franchise or
closure. Sections 55 and 57A are directly relevant as they are specifically referred to
in s 11(3)(d) of the 1986 Act as modified by the 1993 Act and quoted in [3], above.

[10] Section 55 authorises the Rail Regulator to make orders to secure compliance with a condition or requirement contained in a licence, franchise or closure; it does not apply to an access contract made pursuant to s 17. Such orders may be provisional or final. Section 56 sets out the procedure to be followed in the case of a final order or the confirmation of a provisional order. Due notice must be given to the licensee, an opportunity to make representations must be afforded to him and the Rail Regulator must consider those representations. Any order made must be served and publicised as required by that section. A person aggrieved by any order, final or provisional, may apply to the court under s 57 within 42 days of service of the order on him. Section 57 enables the court to quash the order if the making or confirmation of it was not within the powers conferred by s 55 or the applicant had been substantially prejudiced by a failure to observe the procedural requirements of s 56. Subject to that jurisdiction the validity of a final or provisional order cannot be questioned in any legal proceedings whatever. The order creates a duty owed to anyone who might be affected by its contravention and is, ultimately, enforceable by injunction (s 57(4) and (7)).

[11] Sections 57A–57F contain substantially similar provisions relating to penalties for contravening a condition or requirement of a licence. In such a case the jurisdiction of the court to quash the penalty is wider. In addition to the two grounds comparable to those provided for by s 57 the court may also intervene on limited grounds of unreasonableness (s 57F(1)(c)). A penalty is recoverable by the Strategic Rail Authority with interest under s 17 of the Judgments Act 1838.

[12] Section 144 also deals with enforcement. So far as relevant it provides:

'(1) It shall be the duty of any person to whom a direction is given under this Act to comply with and give effect to that direction ...

(2) Without prejudice to any right which any person may have to bring civil proceedings in respect of any contravention or apprehended contravention of any direction given under this Act, compliance with any such direction shall be enforceable by civil proceedings, by the person by whom the direction was given, for an injunction or interdict or for any other appropriate relief.

(3) Any power conferred by this Act to give a direction shall, unless the context otherwise requires, include power to vary or revoke the direction.'

It is plain that s 144 applies to a direction given under s 17. But there are many other provisions in the Act under which directions may be given which are also subsequently enforceable under s 144. I have already referred to ss 24(6) and 34(17). Other provisions for directions are to be found in ss 72(4) and 73(4).

[13] Sections 59–65 deal with railway administration orders and make provisions to deal with an insolvent railway company. But before referring to them it is convenient to consider the position of the Rail Regulator. The office was created by s 1. The general duties of the Rail Regulator are set out in s 4. He is required by sub-s (1) to exercise his functions under Pt I in the manner which he considers best calculated—

'(za) to facilitate the furtherance by the Authority of any strategies which it has formulated with respect to its purposes; (a) to protect the interests of users of railway services; (b) to promote the use of the railway network in Great Britain for the carriage of passengers and goods, and the development of that railway network, to the greatest extent that he considers economically practicable; (ba) to contribute to the development of an a integrated system of transport of passengers and goods; (bb) to contribute to the achievement of sustainable development; (c) to promote efficiency and economy on the part of persons providing railway services; (d) to promote competition in the provision of railway services for the benefit of users of railway services; (e) to promote measures designed to facilitate the making by passengers of journeys which involve use of the services of more than one

b passenger service operator; (f) to impose on the operators of railway services the minimum restrictions which are consistent with the performance of his functions under this Part; (g) to enable persons providing railway services to plan the future of their business with a reasonable degree of assurance.'

[14] I should also refer to s 4(5)(b) which requires the Rail Regulator in the
c exercise of his functions—

'to act in a manner which he considers will not render it unduly difficult for persons who are holders of network licences to finance any activities or proposed activities of theirs in relation to which the Regulator has functions under or by virtue of this Part ...'

d
[15] It is not disputed that these provisions, in particular s 17, apply as well after as before a railway administration order is made. The question is whether or not the railway administration order imposes additional requirements so that the consent of the special railway administrators or the leave of the court is required not only to the enforcement of a direction made under s 17 but also to
e the commencement and continuation of the process by which such a direction is obtained.

[16] Section 59 provides for what are called 'railway administration orders' to be made in respect of protected railway companies, as defined. Subsection (2) provides that the purposes of a railway administration order are:

f '... (a) the transfer to another company, or (as respects different parts of its undertaking) to two or more different companies, as a going concern, of so much of the company's undertaking as it is necessary to transfer in order to ensure that the relevant activities may be properly carried on; and (b) the carrying on of those relevant activities pending the making of the transfer.'

g
Relevant activities are defined by s 59(6)(b) as the carriage of passengers or the management of a network, station or maintenance depot. Section 59(3) applies Sch 6, which contains modifications to Pt II of the 1986 Act, to a railway administration order. Provision for modified forms of company administration have also been made in other contexts, for example in the Water Industry Act
h 1991.

[17] By para 1 of Sch 6 to the 1993 Act, ss 11–23 and 27 of the 1986 Act apply with the modifications specified in other paragraphs in the Schedule. There are many modifications. By para 2(b), in s 11 of the 1986 Act 'the reference in subsection (3)(d) to proceedings shall include a reference to any proceedings
j under or for the purposes of section 55 or 57A of this Act'. I have reproduced s 11(3)(d) as modified in [3], above. Paragraph 6 provides that the duty of the administrator as provided by s 17 of the 1986 Act shall be 'to manage the affairs, business and property of the company in accordance with proposals, as for the time being revised under section 23'. Paragraph 9 amends s 23 of the 1986 Act so as to provide for the proposals to be submitted to amongst others the Rail Regulator. Section 27 of the 1986 Act is amended so as to entitle the Secretary of

State to apply to the court if he considers that the special railway administrators
are exercising their powers or proposing to do so in a manner which will not best
ensure the achievement of the purposes of the railway administration order (see
para 10 of Sch 6 to the 1993 Act).

[18] Section 60 of the 1993 Act provides for railway administration orders to
be made on the petition of the Secretary of State or, with his consent, of the
Strategic Rail Authority if, amongst other grounds, the company is or is likely to
be unable to pay its debts. Section 61 provides that petitions to wind up a
protected railway company are to be served on the Secretary of State or the
Strategic Rail Authority to enable them to consider whether to apply for a railway
administration order instead. Section 62 precludes a voluntary winding up of a
protected railway company otherwise than with the leave of the court, due notice
having been given to the Secretary of State or Strategic Rail Authority for the like
purpose. Sections 63 and 64 authorise the Secretary of State to provide financial
assistance to a company in railway administration by way of loan or guarantee.

The facts

[19] On 28 February 1994 Railtrack was incorporated as a wholly owned
subsidiary of Railtrack Group plc. As I have already recorded the railtrack
network throughout England, Wales and Scotland was and is vested in Railtrack.
Accordingly any train operator would need to have access contracts with
Railtrack. Many have been granted without opposition from Railtrack or the
special railway administrators.

[20] As I have already recorded a railway administration order in respect of
Railtrack was made on the petition of the Secretary of State under s 60 on 7 October
2001 on the ground that Railtrack was or was likely to be unable to pay its debts.
An order was made by Ferris J on 21 December 2001 extending the time within
which the special railway administrators were required to produce the statement
of their proposals for achieving the purposes of the order required by s 23 of the
1986 Act as modified by the 1993 Act. Such proposals were produced on 2 April
2002. They record the position in the railway administration and the steps taken
to achieve the statutory purpose set out in s 59(2).

[21] English Welsh and Scottish Railway Ltd (EWS) is a substantial freight
train operator. On 7 February 2002 EWS applied to the Rail Regulator pursuant
to s 17 of the 1993 Act for an access contract with Railtrack to replace that due to
expire on 31 May 2002. The application was duly served on Railtrack and
representations were sent by the special railway administrators to the Rail
Regulator in March 2002. The special railway administrators objected to a
number of the terms in the proposed access contract on the grounds that such
terms would inhibit the achievement of the purpose of the railway administration
order. In that connection, and for the first time, they contended that s 11(3) of
the 1986 Act as modified applied to the application made by EWS pursuant to
s 17. On 26 March 2002 EWS instituted proceedings seeking a declaration that
s 11(3) as modified was not so applicable.

[22] By 25 April 2002 the special railway administrators and EWS had
composed their differences and so informed the Rail Regulator. The Rail
Regulator was concerned to have the question of law as to the applicability of
s 11(3) as modified to the s 17 procedure determined and himself commenced the
proceedings now before me on 26 April 2002. The special railway administrators
contended that such proceedings were hypothetical and not such as the court
should entertain. I rejected that submission in a judgment I gave on 8 May. The

a special railway administrators disclaimed any intention to appeal from that decision and I proceeded to hear the claim of the Rail Regulator on its merits. The relief sought by the Rail Regulator is a declaration that—

b 'Section 11(3) of the Insolvency Act 1986, as it applies to companies in railway administration by virtue of s 59(3) and Sch 6 to the Railways Act 1993, does not cover determinations by the Rail Regulator of applications made under s 17 of the 1993 Act.'

The case for the Rail Regulator

[23] The Rail Regulator emphasises that s 4 requires him to discharge his functions under s 17, amongst other provisions in Pt I of the 1993 Act, in accordance c with the various public interests s 4 identifies. He points out that he is amenable to judicial review. He submits that the process provided for by s 17 is essentially regulatory and quite unlike an arbitration or other resolution of a private dispute.

[24] The Rail Regulator relies on the decisions of the Court of Appeal in *Bristol Airport plc v Powdrill* [1990] 2 All ER 493, [1990] Ch 744 and *Re Rhondda Waste Disposal Ltd* [2001] Ch 57, [2000] 3 WLR 1304 and of the Court of Session in *Air d Ecosse Ltd v Civil Aviation Authority* 1987 SC 285 as generally supportive of his contentions that the phrase 'other proceedings' in s 11(3)(d) of the 1986 Act as modified does not comprehend the s 17 procedure.

[25] The Rail Regulator also relies on the terms of para 2(b) of Sch 6 to the 1993 Act whereby express references to ss 55 and 57A of that Act were introduced e into s 11(3)(d) in its application to railway administrations. He submits that those words are apt to apply s 11(3) to the ss 55 and 57A procedures but to no others. He contends that such express inclusion presupposes that other regulatory procedures are not included. He accepts that s 11(3) does apply to any application under s 144 to enforce a direction made after the s 17 procedure has been completed but contends that that is the consequence of such procedure being in f court.

The case for the special railway administrators

[26] The special railway administrators challenge all these contentions. They point out that the fact that the Rail Regulator has to act in the public interest and in a regulatory capacity is no ground for excluding the s 17 procedure from the g ambit of s 11(3) when criminal proceedings are comprehended (see *Re Rhondda Waste Disposal Ltd*) and two regulatory procedures, those provided by ss 55 and 57A, are expressly included.

[27] The special railway administrators submit that the cases relied on by the Rail Regulator either do not support his case, are inapplicable to the circumstances h of this case or, to be pursued in higher courts if necessary, are wrong. They contend that the modification required by Sch 6, para 2(b) by its use of the words 'shall include' supports their case by recognising that the phrase 'other proceedings ... against the company or its property' is in its context wide enough to comprehend regulatory procedures other than those expressly mentioned.

j
Conclusion

[28] I propose to start with the decisions to which both parties referred for such assistance as they may provide. I accept, of course, that the decisions of the Court of Appeal are binding on me and that of the Court of Session is at least highly persuasive. However this case does not concern s 11(3) of the 1986 Act but to some provisions of it incorporated by reference into the 1993 Act and there

subject to substantial modification. Both the context and the words used are
different. It is not to be assumed that the phrase 'other proceedings' bears the
same meaning in the 1993 Act as it does in the 1986 Act.

[29] In *Bristol Airport plc v Powdrill* [1990] 2 All ER 493, [1990] Ch 744 an
administration order had been made in respect of a charter airline. Thereafter
aircraft of which it was the lessee and operator were detained under s 88 of the
Civil Aviation Act 1982 at Bristol and Birmingham airports for failure to pay
airport dues. The issues were whether leave to detain was required under s 11(3)
of the 1986 Act and if so whether it should be granted. Harman J concluded that
leave was required because the exercise of the rights of detention amounted
either to 'other proceedings' or levying a distress within para (d) of s 11(3) or a
step taken to enforce a security within para (c). The Court of Appeal concluded
that the exercise of a right of detention was within para (c) but was not a distress
or 'other proceedings' within para (d).

[30] After setting out the facts, the terms of s 88 of the 1982 Act, the features
of an administration and the issues, Browne-Wilkinson V-C considered the
proper approach to the construction of the 1986 Act. He said:

'The judge was very much influenced in his construction by the manifest
statutory purpose of Pt II of the Act. I agree with this approach. The
provisions of Pt II themselves, coupled with the mischief identified in the
Cork Report, show that the statutory purpose is to install an administrator,
as an officer of the court, to carry on the business of the company as a going
concern with a view to achieving one or other of the statutory objectives
mentioned in s 8(3). It is of the essence of administration under Pt II of the
1986 Act that the business will continue to be carried on by the
administrator. Such continuation of the business by the administrator
requires that there should be available to him the right to use the property of
the company, free from interference by creditors and others during the
usually short period during which such administration continues. Hence the
restrictions on the rights of creditors and others introduced by ss 10 and 11
of the 1986 Act. In my judgment in construing Pt II of the Act it is legitimate
and necessary to bear in mind the statutory objective with a view to
ensuring, if the words permit, that the administrator has the powers
necessary to carry out the statutory objectives, including the power to use
the company's property.' (See [1990] 2 All ER 493 at 501, [1990] Ch 744 at
758–759.)

In my view that principle is equally applicable to a consideration of the true
construction of the provisions of the 1993 Act setting up the system for railway
administration orders.

[31] Browne-Wilkinson V-C considered the meaning of the phrase 'other
proceedings' in s 11(3)(d) of the 1986 Act. He said:

'In my judgment the natural meaning of the words "no other proceedings
… may be commenced or continued" is that the proceedings in question are
either legal proceedings or quasi-legal proceedings such as arbitration. It is
true that the word "proceedings" can, in certain contexts, refer to actions
other than legal proceedings, eg proceedings of a meeting … Further, the
reference to the "commencement" and "continuation" of proceedings indicates
that what Parliament had in mind was legal proceedings. The use of the
word 'proceedings' in the plural together with the words 'commence' and

a 'continue' are far more appropriate to legal proceedings (which are normally so described) than to the doing of some act of a more general nature. Again, it is clear that the draftsman when he wished to refer to some activity other than "proceedings" was well aware of the word "steps" which he used in s 11(3)(c). The judge took the view that the words "other proceedings" covered "every sort of step against the company, its contracts or its property,

b which may be taken and the intention of Parliament by s 11 is to prevent all such, without the leave of the court or the consent of the administrators." In my judgment, however anxious one may be not to thwart the statutory purpose of an administration, the judge's formulation must be too wide. If the word "proceedings" has this wide meaning, all the other detailed prohibitions in s 11(3) would be unnecessary. Moreover such a construction

c would introduce great uncertainty as to what constituted commencement or continuation of proceedings ... In my judgment, the judge's view would produce an undesirable uncertainty which, in view of my construction of s 11(3)(c), it is unnecessary to introduce into the Act.' (See [1990] 2 All ER 493 at 506–507, [1990] Ch 744 at 765–766.)

d The question is whether those considerations are equally applicable in the different context of the 1993 Act.

[32] In *Re Rhondda Waste Disposal Ltd* [2001] Ch 57, [2000] 3 WLR 1304 the Court of Appeal was concerned with the question whether the prosecution of a company in administration for failure to comply with the conditions attached to

e its waste disposal licence required the consent of the administrators or the court under s 11(3) of the 1986 Act. The judge concluded that such consent was required because a prosecution was 'other proceedings' and refused to give it. The prosecutor appealed. The Court of Appeal agreed with the judge.

[33] Scott Baker J, with whom Henry and Robert Walker LJJ agreed, concluded

f that the phrase 'other proceedings' did include a criminal prosecution. He said ([2001] Ch 57 at 67–68, [2000] 3 WLR 1304 at 1314 (para 27)):

'Having concluded that ejusdem generis has no place in the construction of these sections I turn to the natural meaning of the words. It seems to me that they have a plain and clear meaning. The words: "No other proceedings

g and no execution or other legal process may be commenced or continued ... against the company or its property" cover on their face all judicial and quasi judicial proceedings. There is no qualification to "other proceedings". The sections do not say "no other civil proceedings"; nor is there any reference to excluding any particular category of proceedings, e g criminal proceedings. The words used are entirely apt, submits Mr Davies for the company, to

h include all judicial proceedings. There are other sections in the 1986 Act that specify offences by a company, e g section 30. It is to be inferred that the draftsman intended that proceedings for such offences should fall under the umbrella of "other proceedings" in sections 10 and 11, otherwise they would have been expressly excluded.'

j [34] In the light of those principles it has been decided that proceedings before an industrial tribunal (*Carr v British International Helicopters Ltd* (*in administration*) [1994] 2 BCLC 474) and the adjudication procedure provided for by s 108 of the Housing Grants, Construction and Regeneration Act 1996 (*A Straume (UK) Ltd v Bradlor Developments Ltd* [2000] BCC 333) require consent under s 11(3) to their commencement or continuation against a company in administration.

[35] Considerable reliance was placed by the Rail Regulator on the decision of the Court of Session in *Air Ecosse Ltd v Civil Aviation Authority* 1987 SC 285. In that case Air Ecosse had a licence from the Civil Aviation Authority (CAA) for a route in Scotland. One of its competitors applied to the CAA for its revocation and the grant of a new licence to itself. An administration order was then made against Air Ecosse. As no consent to the continuation of the revocation proceedings had been obtained Air Ecosse sought an injunction to prevent the CAA from considering the matter. An injunction was refused by both the Lord Ordinary and, on appeal, by the Court of Session.

[35] The Court of Session based its decision on two grounds. The first was that to fall within the phrase 'other proceedings' they must be brought by a creditor. It is common ground that that is not the law of England as demonstrated by the decision of the Court of Appeal in *Re Rhondda Waste Disposal Ltd*. The second ground was that it could not have been the intention of Parliament that the regulatory powers of the CAA should be limited by an unconnected Insolvency Act. Thus, Lord McDonald said (1987 SC 285 at 302):

> 'I also take the view that it is unlikely that Parliament would intend to limit the powers which it has conferred upon the CAA by the terms of an insolvency statute. It must be assumed that the CAA will exercise these powers strictly in accordance with their statutory remit and in a judicial fashion. I find it difficult to envisage what benefit will accrue to members of the public who make use of air transport if leave of the court has to be obtained before the CAA can consider an application for the revocation of a licence held by an operator company which is subject to an administration order. It may be of importance to the survival of the company or to the advantageous disposal of its undertaking that its licence should not be revoked. It may also be, as suggested by the reclaimers, that some procedure can be devised within the administration process whereby leave of the court can quickly be granted or refused. These are not, however, matters which fall within the general objectives of the CAA under sec. 4 of the 1982 Act, to which their activities must be directed.'

Similarly Lord Robertson (at 299) considered that—

> 'in view of the public duty aspect of the CAA's functions in relation to the licences I do not think the CAA's hearings in relation to the revocation of the licences and and granting of licences to BA—albeit relating to the same routes—can be said properly to be "proceedings against the company or its property" within the meaning of sec. 11(3)(d). They are hearings in relation to the discharging of the CAA's public duty as laid on them in the 1982 Act. The CAA's duty in relation to these matters is as set out in secs. 4, 65 and 66 of the 1982 Act: it may be that the petitioners' ability to carry out their duties under the licences is in question at such hearings, but it is not the only question thereat, and I am not convinced that the hearings can be said to be "proceedings against the company or its property" within the meaning of sec. 11(3)(d). They are not in the strict legal sense proceedings against the company at all.'

Lord Ross expressed the same opinion (at 295–296) where he said:

> 'There is a further reason for preferring the construction for which the respondents contended. If the petitioners' argument were well-founded, and

a   the hearing before the first respondents was to be covered by sec. 11(3)(d) the result would be that the first respondents would be unable to consider the revocation of the petitioners' air transport licence unless the administrator consented to their doing so or the court granted leave for the first respondents to entertain the application. In my opinion, this would constitute a serious infringement of the first respondents' powers conferred upon them
b   by Parliament, and if it were the intention of Parliament so to restrict the first respondents' powers I would have expected that to be the subject of express provision. Moreover, if the contention for the petitioners were well-founded, the result would be that where licences of various kinds were held by a company and an administration order relating to that company had been made, a licensing authority would be disabled from dealing with or revoking
c   the licence without the consent of the administrator or the leave of the court. That would be a surprising result, and I am not persuaded that it is what Parliament intended. I cannot detect in any of the provisions of the Act of 1986 relating to administration orders any indication that licences held by a company in relation to which an administration order has been made should
d   be immune from control by the licensing authority.'

[37] The views expressed by the members of the Court of Session were in the context that there was no mention in the relevant part of the 1982 Act to the process of administration under the 1986 Act. Nor was there any reference in s 11(3) of the 1986 Act to regulatory proceedings under the 1982 Act. Whilst the
e   views of the members of the Court of Session are entitled to the greatest respect, the context of the 1993 Act, ss 59–65 and Sch 6, in particular para 2(b), are so different that I do not think the decision or reasoning of the Court of Session will bear the weight the Rail Regulator seeks to put upon them.

[38] In the light of all these considerations the proper starting point must be
f   the purpose of the railway administration procedure for which the 1993 Act provides. The procedure is plainly the legislative preference for dealing with an insolvent protected railway company, hence the provisions of ss 61 and 62 seeking to inhibit both a compulsory and a voluntary winding up until the Secretary of State has had an opportunity to place the company in question into railway administration. Likewise financial assistance from the public purse is
g   only available under ss 63 and 64 where the company is subject to a railway administration order.

[39] The purpose of such an administration is the transfer of the undertaking as a going concern to some other company so as to ensure that the relevant activities, namely the carriage of passengers or the management of a network,
h   station or maintenance depot may be properly carried on. The principal agents for achieving that purpose are the special railway administrators as officers of the court. As Nicholls LJ observed in *Re Atlantic Computers Systems plc* [1992] 1 All ER 476 at 490, [1992] Ch 505 at 529:

j   'An administrator is an officer of the court. He can be expected to make his decision speedily, so far as he can do so. He may be able at least to make an interim decision, such as agreeing to pay the current rents for the time being. The administrator should also make his decision responsibly. His power to give or withhold consent was not intended to be used as a bargaining counter in a negotiation in which the administrator has regard only to the interests of the unsecured creditors.'

[40] Both the Secretary of State and the Rail Regulator are in a position to
contribute to the special railway administrators' proposals for achieving the
statutory purpose because copies must be sent to them pursuant to s 23 as modified.
Only the Secretary of State is entitled to apply to the court for an order under s 27
of the 1986 Act as modified if he considers that the conduct or proposals of the
special railway administrators will not best achieve that purpose.

[41] The conclusion I draw from these considerations is that it would be   *b*
entirely consistent with the nature and purpose of a railway administration and
with the functions and responsibilities of the special railway administrators if the
consent of the special railway administrators or the leave of the court is required
for procedures prescribed by the 1993 Act which may affect the company or its
property. The 1993 Act provides for procedures in addition to those specifically
mentioned in the modification of s 11(3)(d) of the 1986 Act. Whether or not such   *c*
procedures can be described as regulatory they are certainly similar to legal or
quasi-legal or -judicial proceedings.

[42] Section 17 prescribes the process by which a person wishing to operate
trains obtains the necessary permission to use the facilities needed for that purpose,
be they railtrack, stations or maintenance depots. The procedure is one which is   *d*
susceptible both of commencement and continuation; it has some similarities
with ordinary civil proceedings or arbitrations, though there are also differences.
It may result in a direction which has an important impact on the management
of the affairs, business and property of the company in railway administration
which, by s 17 of the 1986 Act as modified, is entrusted to the special railway
administrators. Indeed such a direction could frustrate the achievement of the   *e*
statutory purpose. Accordingly, even though the Rail Regulator is subject to the
duties imposed by s 4 and to judicial review and notwithstanding that some
element of the procedure may be properly described as regulatory the nature of
the s 17 procedure is entirely consistent with the need to obtain the consent of the
special railway administrators or the leave of the court for its commencement or   *f*
continuation.

[43] It was submitted on behalf of the Rail Regulator that it was sufficient
protection of the functions and duties of the special railway administrators if the
process of enforcement prescribed by s 144 of the 1993 Act could, as he accepted,
only be instituted with the consent of the special railway administrators or the court.
In my view the protection for the statutory purpose afforded by the application   *g*
of s 11(3) as modified only to proceedings under s 144 would be insufficient. First,
the s 17 procedure may give rise to substantial expenditure in time and money
which is best avoided. Second, its conclusion gives rise to an obligation. It is true
that the Rail Regulator may subsequently revoke the direction under s 144(3) but
a successful applicant may already have invoked the obligation imposed on the   *h*
facility owner by Sch 4, para 6(1) in other contexts than enforcement proceedings
under s 144. There is nothing unusual in a requirement for consent under
s 11(3) at more than one stage. For example, it commonly happens that consent
is sought and given to commencing negligence proceedings so that the claimant
may obtain the benefit of the company's insurance cover but then refused if it is   *j*
sought to enforce the resulting judgment against the company's assets.

[44] Given that it would be consistent with both the purpose of a railway
administration and the nature of the s 17 procedure that consent should be
required under s 11(3) as modified it is necessary also to consider the words used.
Schedule 6, para 2(b) of the 1993 Act requires the words 'other proceedings' to
'include a reference to any proceedings under or for the purposes of' ss 55 and 57A.

a   Those sections provide for orders to be made at the conclusion of out of court procedures which may well lead on to court proceedings properly so called. It is clear that the procedure down to the making of the order is not dissimilar to that prescribed by s 17. The word 'include' may recognise that others of the same type are already included, as the special railway administrators submit, or it may presuppose that they are not, as the Rail Regulator maintains.

b   [45] I prefer the first alternative. If the procedure prescribed by ss 55 and 57A leading up to the making of the orders of the Rail Regulator are to be treated as proceedings for the purposes of s 11(3) as modified I can see no rational basis for concluding that Parliament intended the s 17 procedure to be treated differently. Both prescribe a procedure which ends in a legal obligation. Both are subsequently enforceable by court proceedings which require separate consent under s 11(3).

c   If 'other proceedings ... against the company or its property' in s 11(3)(d) as modified does not include all proceedings analogous to those under or for the purposes of ss 55 and 57A then what is it which brings in the enforcement procedure provided for in s 144? The answer must lie in the generality of the words 'other proceedings', but if the generality brings in s 144 I see no reason

d   why, in the context of the 1993 Act as a whole, it should exclude s 17.

[46] In conclusion I consider that the nature of both a railway administration and a s 17 application and the words used all indicate that Parliament intended the words 'other proceedings ... against the company or its property' in s 11(3)(d) of the 1986 Act as modified to comprehend the s 17 procedure. It follows that I reject the claim of the Rail Regulator. Subject to any further argument on the

e   form of my order, I consider that I should make a declaration in the form sought but omitting the word 'not'.

Order accordingly. Permission to appeal granted.

Celia Fox   Barrister.

BEC Pension Trustee Ltd v Sheppeck   a
[2002] EWHC 101 (Ch)

CHANCERY DIVISION

ETHERTON J

19, 20 DECEMBER 2001, 30 JANUARY 2002   b

Pension – Pension scheme – Surplus fund – Industry-wide pension scheme for non-associated employers – Scheme divided into sections with each section representing different employer or group of employers – Whether each section of scheme constituting separate 'qualifying scheme' for purposes of satisfying preconditions on distribution of surplus to employer – Whether new requirement on giving of notice applying to scheme governed by previous statutory regime – Pension Schemes Act 1993, ss 1, 102(2), 108 – Pensions Act 1995, s 76(3)(d) – Pensions Act 1995 (Commencement No 10) Order 1997, art 6.   c

The claimant was the trustee of a centralised 'industry-wide' pension scheme for   d
non-associated employers in the construction industry. The scheme was divided
into different sections, with each section representing a different employer or
group of employers. On 5 April 1997 the formal winding up of the scheme
commenced. Several sections of the scheme had a surplus of assets over liabilities,
but others were in deficit. In respect of the sections with sufficiently substantial   e
surplus assets, the trustee proposed to provide for annual increases for pensions
in that section at a rate known as 5% LPI; to use half of the remaining surpluses
to fund additional improvements for the section's members; and to pay the other
half to the section's employer. Under s 108[a] of the Pension Schemes Act 1993, no
payment could be made out of the resources of a 'qualifying scheme' to an
employer of persons in the description or category of employment to which the   f
scheme related until such time as provision had been made by the scheme for
every pension under it to be increased as mentioned in s 102(2)(b)[b] of the Act.
The amount mentioned in that provision was 5% LPI. On 6 April 1997, the day
after the commencement of the winding up, s 108 of the 1993 Act was replaced
by a new statutory regime contained in the Pensions Act 1995. Section 76[c] of that
Act established new preconditions on the exercise of a power to distribute assets   g
to the employer on winding-up, including a requirement for the giving of notice
to members of the scheme, in accordance with prescribed requirements, of a
proposal to exercise the power. The new regime was subject to transitional
provisions contained in the Pensions Act 1995 (Commencement No 10) Order
1997, the order which brought into force the provision that repealed s 108 of the   h
1993 Act. For the purposes of any distribution of excess assets to the employer in
relation to a scheme which began to be wound up before 6 April 1996, art 6(b)[d]
of the 1997 order provided that s 108 of the 1993 Act 'shall continue' to have effect
as if the order had not come into force. On an application by the trustee for
guidance, the court was required to determine whether each section of the   j
scheme constituted a separate 'qualifying scheme' for the purposes of s 108 of the

a   Section 108 is set out at [19], below
b   Section 102(2) is set out at [34], below
c   Section 76, so far as material, is set out at [25], below
d   Article 6, so far as material, is set out at [22], below

a 1993 Act, so that the requirement for a 5% LPI increase before the distribution of surplus to an employer had to be met only in respect of members of that employer's section, or whether the precondition on payment of surplus to an employer could be met only if there were 5% LPI increases for all members throughout the entire scheme, including members in those sections which were in deficit. That issue turned on whether each section constituted an 'occupational pension scheme' as defined in s 1[e] of the 1993 Act and a 'qualifying scheme' within the meaning of s 102(2) of the Act. A further issue arose as to whether the notice provisions under s 76(3)(d) of the 1995 Act had to be satisfied in relation to the trustee's proposals, notwithstanding that s 108 of the 1993 Act, which contained no similar notice provisions, continued to apply to the winding up of the scheme.

b

c

Held – (1) On the true construction of s 108 of the 1993 Act, and the related definitions of the expressions 'qualifying scheme' in s 102(2) and 'occupational pension scheme' in s 1 of the Act, each section of the scheme constituted a 'qualifying scheme' within the meaning of s 108. Such a construction gave effect to the policy underpinning s 108, namely to ensure that there was a fair balance between the employer's and members' interests in surplus assets. In the case of a sectionalised industry-wide scheme, in which some sections were in surplus and others in deficit, a conclusion to the contrary would compel the trustee to apply assets for the benefit of members of other sections, even if those members had never had any connection of any kind with the employer of the transferring section and his employees, whose contributions had created the surplus. That was a bizarre and capricious consequence, and it was impossible to discern any rational policy justification for it. In contrast, the correct interpretation was consistent with and gave effect to the purpose and context of s 108 without unduly offending the actual language used in the section and related definitions (see [60], [61], [64], below).

d

e

f   (2) On the true construction of art 6 of the 1997 order, s 76 of the 1995 Act, including the notice provisions in sub-s (3)(d), did not apply to the scheme. The 1995 Act brought into operation a wholly different statutory regime in relation to the payment of surplus assets to an employer. The intuitive reaction to art 6, which provided that s 108 of the 1993 Act was to continue to apply in relation to certain schemes, was that the new regime was not intended to apply to such schemes unless, and then only to the extent that, it had been made clear that the two statutory regimes were to run alongside and to be supplemental to one another (see [70], [76], [82], below); *Harwood-Smart v Caws* [2000] PLR 101 followed.

g

h

Notes

For the distribution of excess assets on the winding up of a scheme, see 44(2) *Halsbury's Laws* (4th edn reissue) para 851.

For the Pension Schemes Act 1993, s 1, see 33 *Halsbury's Statutes* (4th edn) (2001 reissue) 588. Sections 102 and 108 of the 1993 Act have been repealed by the Pensions Act 1995, ss 122, 177, Sch 3, paras 22, 25, Sch 7, Pt I.

j

For the Pensions Act 1995, s 76, see 33 *Halsbury's Statutes* (4th edn) (2001 reissue) 891.

---

e   Section 1, so far as material, is set out [36], below

Cases referred to in judgment

Fry v IRC [1958] 3 All ER 90, [1959] Ch 86, [1958] 3 WLR 381, CA.   *a*
Hanlon v Law Society [1980] 2 All ER 199, [1981] AC 124, [1980] 2 WLR 756, HL.
Harwood-Smart v Caws [2000] PLR 101.
Melville v IRC [2000] STC 628; *affd* [2001] EWCA Civ 1247, [2001] STC 1271, [2002]
 1 WLR 407.
Thrells Ltd (in liq) v Lomas [1993] 2 All ER 546, [1993] 1 WLR 456.   *b*

Cases also cited or referred to in skeleton arguments

Courage Group's Pension Schemes, Re, Ryan v Imperial Brewing and Leisure Ltd [1987]
 1 All ER 528, [1987] 1 WLR 495.
Swansea City and County v Johnson [1999] 1 All ER 863, [1999] Ch 189.
Westminster City Council v Haywood [1997] 2 All ER 84, [1998] Ch 377, CA.   *c*

Claim

The claimant, BEC Pension Trustee Ltd (the Trustee), sought, pursuant to CPR Pt 8,
the guidance of the court on the application to the BEC Pension Scheme of s 108
of the Pension Schemes Act 1993, s 76 of the Pensions Act 1995 and the Occupational   *d*
Pension Schemes (Payment to Employers) Regulations 1996. The proceedings
were contested in a representative capacity by the defendant, Arthur George
Sheppeck, a member of the scheme. The facts are set out in the judgment.

Paul Newman (instructed by *Slaughter and May*) for the Trustee.
Caroline Furze (instructed by *Mayer Brown Rowe & Maw*) for the defendant.   *e*

Cur adv vult

30 January 2002. The following judgment was delivered.

ETHERTON J.   *f*

Introduction

[1] In these proceedings, commenced under CPR Pt 8, BEC Pension Trustee Ltd
(the Trustee), which is the trustee of the BEC Pension Scheme (the Scheme),
seeks guidance from the court on the application to the Scheme of s 108 of the   *g*
Pension Schemes Act 1993, s 76 of the Pensions Act 1995 and the Occupational
Pension Schemes (Payments to Employers) Regulations 1996, SI 1996/2156.

[2] Those provisions impose restrictions on the distribution of assets out of an
occupational pension scheme to an employer of scheme members.

The Scheme   *h*

[3] The Scheme was established by a trust deed dated 1 December 1973. It is
now governed by a definitive amending deed and rules dated 1 August 1985, as
amended (the deed).

[4] The Scheme is what is known as a centralised 'industry-wide' scheme.
Such schemes are divided into sections, each section with an employer involved   *j*
in the particular industry in question, but with no other necessary association
between the employers. In the present case, the participating employers are all
connected with the construction industry.

[5] In the *Occupational Pension Schemes Practice Notes* on the approval of
occupational pension schemes, issued by the Inland Revenue (2001 version) (IR 12
(2001)), two categories of centralised pension schemes, which contain provisions

a enabling more than one employer to participate, are described. The material parts of the notes are as follows:

'**Introduction**

21.1 A scheme's documentation may contain provisions enabling more than one employer to participate. Where more than one employer participates

b the scheme is regarded as a centralised scheme. Each employer participating in the scheme must be under an obligation to observe the rules of the scheme. This condition is usually met by the employer being a party to the documents governing the scheme or undertaking the necessary obligations by a separate document. Centralised schemes fall into 2 very different categories and different requirements need to be satisfied if they are to be approved. The 2 categories

c are: (a) schemes established to provide benefits solely for employees of *associated employers* and/or for employees of employers who are associated through a *permanent community of interest*, and (b) schemes established to provide benefits for the employees of any employer, whether or not those employers are associated.

d 21.2 The rationale for centralised schemes is that they are able to provide a degree of expertise and lower administrative costs which would not be possible if each employer were to establish its own scheme.

Associated Employers ...

21.4 A centralised scheme for *associated employers* may provide benefits for an employee (including a *controlling director*) by reference to his or her *final*

e *remuneration* from an aggregate service for the participating employers irrespective of moves from one to another as though they comprise one employer ... A centralised scheme for or including employers associated through a *permanent community of interest* may, in relation to employees of those employers, also provide benefits on this basis except for *controlling*

f *directors* where benefit provision in respect of service and *final remuneration* with such employers must be calculated separately ...

Non-Associated Employers

21.10 Many existing centralised schemes for non-associated employers fall within the category of "industry-wide" schemes which are usually sponsored

g by a professional or trade association and available only to employers in a particular industry. Other schemes are established on a commercial basis (e.g. by a life office) and are open for any employer to participate.

21.11 Schemes in either category can be approved with the minimum of restriction if they are established as simplified defined contribution schemes

h which comply with the requirements of Part 22 for automatic approval.

21.12 The Inland Revenue are also prepared to approve centralised schemes for non-associated employers which take the more conventional form where benefits, rather than just contributions, are limited. In general such schemes should follow simple straightforward lines to ease the

j problems of administration which can flow from the separation of the employer and the *administrator*. The quality of administration is very pertinent to the approval of such a scheme ...

21.15 Normally the basis of funding will be that each employer provides benefits only for its own employees, but the Inland Revenue will be prepared to consider the use of controlled funding where the employers accept that, taking one year with another, substantial cross subsidies will not occur.'

[6] As I have said, the Scheme is a centralised scheme for non-associated employers, within para 21.10 of IR 12 (2001), the only association between the employers being that they carry on business in the construction industry. The Scheme is divided into sections, each section representing a different employer or group of employers. The Scheme has 116 sections.

[7] The following provisions of the deed are material to the issues which the court is asked to determine in these proceedings.

[8] Rule 1 of the general rules of the Scheme defines the following expressions as having the following meanings:

'**"Confederation"** means the BUILDING EMPLOYERS CONFEDERATION or any successor for the time being thereof ...

"Contributing Employer" means in relation to a person employed by all or any of the Contributing Employers that one or more of the Contributing Employers by which that person is employed and in relation to a person formerly employed by all or any of the Contributing Employers that one or more of the Contributing Employers by which such person was last employed.

"Contributing Employers" means the Confederation and any Body connected with the Confederation which has agreed to participate in the Scheme in accordance with the provisions of the Trust Deed and Rules.'

'**"Body connected with the Confederation"** means any person or corporation which shall fall within either of the following classes:—
Class A—Companies firms and individual employers who are members of the Confederation and are engaged in the carrying out of building operations or of operations ancillary thereto and also companies which are subsidiaries within the meaning of Section 154 of the Companies Act 1948 of any such company as aforesaid whether such company is itself a member of the Confederation or not and which are themselves so engaged.
Class B—Associations societies organisations incorporated bodies or firms (not being within Class A) formed for or whose principal objects include purposes connected with the Building Industry or for the benefit of persons engaged or employed in the Building Industry ...'

[9] The following clauses in the deed are material:

'Separate accounts for separate sections of the Scheme

15A.(1) The Trust Company shall keep in relation to each Contributing Employer a separate account recording: (a) Amounts contributed by that Contributing Employer to the Scheme and the amounts contributed by each Member to the Scheme while employed by the Contributing Employer. (b) The benefits paid to date to and in respect of each such Member. (c) Any amounts transferred into or out of the Scheme in respect of any such Members or persons claiming through any such Members. (d) The expenses or levies to be borne out of the Trust Assets in respect of any such Members or persons claiming through or by reference to them. (e) The investment income, gains and losses to be allocated to such account on such basis as the Trust Company may from time to time determine. (f) Such other adjustments in respect of such account as the Trust Company determines to be appropriate.

Section Balances

(2) The amount determined by the Trust Company as at any date to be the balance on the account prepared under Clause 15A(1) by the Trust Company in relation to a Contributing Employer is referred to in this Clause 15A as a "Contributing Employer's Section Balance" ...

Entry of Contributing Employers

31.(1) THE Trust Company shall enter into a deed with the Confederation or with any Body connected with the Confederation binding itself to comply with and to observe the provisions of this Deed and the Rules and it shall thereby become a Contributing Employer as from a date to be specified in such deed but not so that there shall be granted to the Confederation or Body connected with the Confederation as a Contributing Employer any right privilege or power reserved to the Confederation by this Deed and PROVIDED THAT the participation in the Scheme of any Body connected with the Confederation will not prejudice Revenue Approval ...

Events giving rise to determination of the Scheme

36.(1) SUBJECT to sub-clause (2) the Scheme shall be determined and the Trust Assets shall be wound up upon the happening of either of the following events (whichever shall first occur) ... (b) if the Confederation gives the Trust Company six months' (or such shorter period as the Trust Company and the Confederation may agree) notice in writing of its intention to terminate the Scheme ...

Trust Company's powers on the determination of the Scheme

(2) Upon the happening of either of the events referred to in paragraphs (a) and (b) of sub-clause (1) the Trust Company shall have all or any of the following powers:—(a) subject to Clause 37(1B) (Crystallisation of order of priority on winding-up) to postpone the determination of the Scheme and during the period of such postponement to continue the Scheme as a paid-up arrangement with frozen benefits in which event no further person shall be admitted to membership of the Scheme no further contributions shall be payable to the Trust Assets and no further benefits shall accrue under the Rules ... (f) to determine that the Scheme shall begin to be wound up at any time after the Trust Company has acted under (a) above ...

Application of Section Balances

37.(1A) The provisions of Clause 37(2) shall apply separately subject to Clause 37(1B) (Crystallisation of order of priority on winding up) in relation

to each Section Balance (as that expression is defined in Clause 15(A)(2)) and
the Contributing Employer or the Group of Contributing Employers (as that
expression is defined in Clause 15(A)(3)) to which that Section Balance
relates and that part of:

• Part 1 of the Trust Assets [AVC assets], together with

• that part of Part 2 of the Trust Assets [other, ie non-AVC assets]
determined by the Trust Company to be equal in value to that Section
Balance.'

[10] Clause 37(2)(A) (dealing with part 1 assets) and cl 37(2)(B) (dealing with
part 2 assets) set out the order of priority of the application of assets on winding
up. Clause 37(2)(B)(h) confers power on the Trustee, in its entire discretion, after
consultation with the Scheme's actuary and with the relevant contributing
employers, to augment certain benefits payable under the Scheme, subject to
Inland Revenue limits.

[11] Clause 37(2)(B)(i) provides that, last in the order of priority of distribution
of assets on winding up, any unexpended balance shall be applied as follows:

'(i) NINTH: (i) in paying any balance unexpended to the Contributing
Employers in such proportions as, subject to compliance with Section 108 of
the Pension Schemes Act 1993, to the extent applicable, the Trust Company
shall determine having regard to any special requirements of the Commissioners
of Inland Revenue.'

[12] The Scheme was terminated with effect from 30 June 1992, pursuant to a
notice given to the Trustee under cl 36(1)(b) of the deed. From that date, the
Scheme ceased to admit new members, the benefits of existing members ceased
to accrue, and the normal contributions of employers and members ceased to be
payable.

[13] Pursuant to its power to do so under cl 36(2)(a) of the deed, the Trustee
resolved to postpone the determination of the Scheme, and, during the period of
that postponement, to continue the Scheme as a paid-up arrangement.

[14] The winding up of the Scheme formally commenced on 5 April 1997.

[15] The principal asset of the Scheme was an insurance policy with Legal &
General.

[16] The following appears from the latest actuarial valuation report of the
Scheme, as at 31 December 1999. Eighty-four of the sections have a surplus of
assets over liabilities calculated on the 'annuity basis', that is to say, on the
assumption that all the benefits of the Scheme have to be secured by the purchase
of annuities. Those surpluses ranged, as at the valuation date, from over £1,700
to £1·99m. One section was, at the valuation date, exactly in balance on the
annuity basis. Thirty-one of the sections were, as at the valuation date, in deficit
on the annuity basis. The amount of the deficit ranged from £700 to nearly
£1·2m.

[17] In respect of each section of the Scheme with sufficiently substantial
surplus assets, the Trustee wishes and has proposed in principle to: (i) provide for
annual increases to pensions in that section when they come into payment, at the
rate of 5% or the percentage increase in the retail price index for the relevant year,
whichever is the lesser (5% LPI); (ii) use half of the remaining surplus to fund
additional benefit improvements for the section's members; and (iii) pay the
other half of the remaining surplus (less the appropriate tax) to the section's
employer.

Section 108 of the 1993 Act

a

[**18**] Clause 37(2)(B)(i) expressly requires compliance with s 108 of the 1993 Act, prior to the payment of any balance of surplus assets to contributing employers.

[**19**] Section 108 provides as follows:

b

'(1) No payment shall be made out of the resources of a qualifying scheme which is constituted by trust deed to or for a person who is or has been the employer of persons in the description or category of employment to which the scheme relates until such time as provision has been made by the scheme for every pension which commences or has commenced under it to be increased as mentioned in section 102(2)(b).

c

(2) Nothing in subsection (1) applies in relation to payments made to or for a person by virtue of his or any other person's membership of the scheme in question.'

[**20**] The amount mentioned in s 102(2)(b) of the 1993 Act is 5% LPI.

[**21**] The principal provisions of the 1995 Act came into force on 6 April 1997, which was the day after the formal commencement of the winding up of the

d Scheme. By virtue of art 2(3) of the Pensions Act 1995 (Commencement No 10) Order 1997, SI 1997/664, s 177 of the 1995 Act, which repealed s 108 of the 1993 Act, came into force on 6 April 1997. Subject to transitional provisions in art 6 of the 1997 order, s 108 of the 1993 Act was replaced, as from that date, with a new regime concerning the payment of surplus in an occupational pensions scheme to an employer, which is principally contained in ss 37, 76 and 77 of the 1995 Act.

e

[**22**] Article 6 of the 1997 order, which contains the transitional provisions concerning the application of s 108 of the 1993 Act after 6 April 1997, provided, so far as is relevant, as follows:

f

'For the purposes of … (b) any distribution of excess assets to the employer in relation to a scheme which begins to be wound up before the principal appointed day, section 108 of the 1993 Act (no payments to employers from non-complying schemes) shall continue to have effect as if this Order had not come into force.'

The 'principal appointed day' was 6 April 1997. As I have said, the formal commencement of the winding up of the Scheme began immediately before that

g date.

The first issue

[**23**] As I have said, the Trustee intends, in principle, that, in relation to each section of the Scheme with sufficient surplus, there should be a distribution to the

h section's employer, after providing for 5% LPI increases to pensions and additional benefits for the section's members. The first issue, which has arisen (the first issue), is whether, in order to comply with s 108 of the 1993 Act, it is a precondition of any payment of surplus to an employer that there should be 5% LPI increases in pensions in respect only of members of that employer's section,

j or whether it is necessary for there to be 5% LPI increases for all members throughout the entire Scheme, including members in those sections which are in deficit. There are, in fact, insufficient assets in the Scheme as a whole to fund such increases across the entire Scheme.

[**24**] The Trustee proposes to give any existing employer the opportunity to set up a new pension scheme, and transfer the surplus from the employer's section to the new scheme. Where, however, the employer chooses not to take

up that opportunity or cannot do so, for example, where the employer no longer
exists, the first issue will arise.

[25] As I have said, s 76 of the 1995 Act came into operation on 6 April 1997,
as did the 1996 regulations. Section 76 provides, so far as material, as follows:

'**76.** *Excess assets on winding up.*—(1) This section applies to a trust scheme
in any circumstances if—(a) it is an exempt approved scheme, within the
meaning given by section 592(1) of the Taxes Act 1988, (b) the scheme is
being wound up, and (c) in those circumstances power is conferred on the
employer or the trustees to distribute assets to the employer on a winding
up.

(2) The power referred to in subsection (1)(c) cannot be exercised unless
the requirements of subsections (3) and (in prescribed circumstances) (4),
and any prescribed requirements, are satisfied.

(3) The requirements of this subsection are that—(a) the liabilities of the
scheme have been fully discharged, (b) where there is any power under
the scheme, after the discharge of those liabilities, to distribute assets to any
person other than the employer, the power has been exercised or a decision
has been made not to exercise it, (c) the annual rates of the pensions under
the scheme which commence or have commenced are increased by the
appropriate percentage, and (d) notice has been given in accordance with
prescribed requirements to the members of the scheme of the proposal to
exercise the power.'

[26] Regulation 12 of the 1996 regulations expressly provides that, for the
purposes of complying with the statutory preconditions for any distribution of
excess assets to an employer on winding up an 'industry-wide' scheme, in
accordance with s 76 of the 1995 Act, each section of such a scheme is to be
considered separately and distinct from other sections of the scheme. Accordingly,
the first issue does not arise in relation to the winding up of any such scheme
which takes place after 5 April 1997.

The second issue

[27] The second issue arises as a result of the interrelationship between s 108
of the 1993 Act, s 76 of the 1995 Act, and the 1996 regulations.

[28] The prescribed notice 'requirements' specified in s 76(3)(d) of the 1995
Act are contained in reg 7 of the 1996 regulations. The second issue, which has
arisen (the second issue), is whether those notice provisions must be satisfied in
relation to the Trustee's proposals, notwithstanding that s 108 of the 1993 Act,
which contains no similar notice provisions, continues to apply to the winding up
of the Scheme.

The parties and their representative capacities

[29] Master Moncaster made an order on 5 July 2001 appointing the Trustee
to represent all those employers of the sections of the Scheme which are
sufficiently in surplus to give rise to a potential payment to the employer
pursuant to the Trustee's declared intention, and also those members of the
Scheme who would benefit from the argument that s 108 applies to each section
of the Scheme independently of other sections. Master Moncaster also ordered
that Mr Arthur Sheppeck, the defendant, who is a member of one of the sections
of the Scheme which is in surplus, should represent all other employers and
members of the Scheme.

a [30] Although the trustee of a trust fund commonly takes a neutral position in proceedings for the interpretation of the trust's documents, joining representative beneficiaries to argue the opposing contentions, Master Moncaster was invited to make, and did make, the representation order in relation to the Trustee in the present case, in the interests of efficiency and the saving of costs, bearing in mind particularly the substantial deficit in many sections of the Scheme.

b [31] As to the second issue, it was agreed between the parties that the Trustee would put forward arguments in support of the contention that s 76 of the 1995 Act does not apply to the winding up of the Scheme, and the defendant would argue the contrary.

[32] Before me, Mr Paul Newman has appeared for the Trustee, and Miss Caroline Furze has appeared for the defendant.

c

Submissions on the first issue

[33] Mr Newman's primary argument is that, applying the statutory definition of 'qualifying scheme' in the 1993 Act, each section of the Scheme is a separate 'qualifying scheme' for the purposes of s 108 of the 1993 Act.

d [34] Section 102(2) of the 1993 Act defined 'qualifying scheme' as follows:

'This Chapter applies to any occupational pension scheme—(a) which is neither a public service pension scheme nor a money purchase scheme; and (b) the rules of which do not require the annual rate of every pension to be increased each year by at least the appropriate percentage of that rate; and in this Chapter such a scheme is referred to as a "qualifying scheme".'

e

[35] The Scheme satisfies the requirements of (a) and (b) of s 102(2), and so is a 'qualifying scheme' if it is an 'occupational pension scheme'.

[36] The expression 'occupational pension scheme' is defined as follows in s 1 of the 1993 Act:

f

'... "occupational pension scheme" means any scheme or arrangement which is comprised in one or more instruments or agreements and which has, or is capable of having, effect in relation to one or more descriptions or categories of employments so as to provide benefits, in the form of pensions or otherwise, payable on termination of service, or on death or retirement, to or in respect of earners with qualifying service in an employment of any such description or category ...'

g

[37] Mr Newman submitted that, on a literal and fair reading of that definition of 'occupational pension scheme', each section of the Scheme satisfies the statutory definition.

h

[38] Mr Newman concedes that the Scheme as a whole also satisfies the statutory definitions of 'qualifying scheme' and 'occupational pension scheme' in the 1993 Act. He submitted, however, that, applying normal rules of statutory interpretation, each section of the Scheme should be treated as a 'qualifying scheme' for the purposes of s 108 of the 1993 Act. In this connection, he cited and relied upon the following statement of Romer LJ in *Fry v IRC* [1958] 3 All ER 90 at 94, [1959] Ch 86 at 105:

j

'It seems to us that on the language of [the section] neither the view of [the defendants] nor that of the plaintiff can be said to be obviously wrong. The court then, when faced with two possible constructions of legislative language, is entitled to look to the results of adopting each of the alternatives respectively in its quest for the true intention of Parliament.'   *a*

[39] Mr Newman submitted that the defendant's interpretation of s 108 produces consequences which are absurd and impractical. He pointed out, for example, that, pursuant to the Inland Revenue's requirements for the approval of 'industry-wide' schemes, such schemes normally preclude any cross-subsidies   *b* between sections: see para 21.15 of IR 12 (2001), which I have set out earlier in this judgment at [5], above, and which reproduces the identical language in para 21.15 of the 1991 version of IR 12. Accordingly, if, as in the case of the Scheme, some sections of a sectionalised industry-wide scheme are in deficit, s 108 could not, on the defendant's interpretation, be satisfied unless the scheme's provisions were changed, either pursuant to a power of amendment contained in the trust   *c* deed or pursuant to an application to the court under s 57 of the Trustee Act 1925. Mr Newman submitted that any such amendment, however, would or might imperil Inland Revenue approval. He further submitted that, if such steps were not taken, then excess assets might simply be held indefinitely by the trustees: for example, if the trustee did not have a unilateral power to augment benefits, or if   *d* the amount of surplus available for increasing benefits would take benefits above Inland Revenue limits.

[40] In any event, he submitted, even if the trustee of a sectionalised, industry-wide scheme was empowered, whether by the scheme's provisions or s 108 itself, to apply assets in one section for the benefit of members in another section, which is in deficit, there would be practical difficulties in determining   *e* how the surplus is to be applied in order to enable a payment to the employer under s 108. The various possibilities postulated by Mr Newman were that s 108 expressly or implicitly requires the full shortfall of any section in deficit to be funded, with 5% LPI increases on top; or alternatively, 5% LPI increases should be applied on the benefits which should have been provided, if there had been no   *f* deficit; or alternatively, 5% LPI increases should be made to the benefits actually provided by the section in question.

[41] Mr Newman submitted that none of those alternative possible consequences of the defendant's interpretation of s 108 of the 1993 Act gives effect to any discernible or sensible policy. He submitted that the manifest policy objective of s 108 is to achieve a fair balance between the employer and the members in the division of   *g* any surplus assets. That objective would not be achieved by compelling the employer of one section to apply assets for the benefit of members of other sections, if such members do not have and may never have had any employment or industrial or business connection with him. In short, the effect of the defendant's interpretation, Mr Newman submitted, unduly penalises the employer of a   *h* section, for no apparent policy purpose. Indeed, the defendant's construction of s 108 runs counter to the consistent policy, reflected in IR 12 (2001), that there should be no cross-subsidy between different sections of an industry-wide scheme.

[42] By way of an alternative argument, should Mr Newman fail in his submission that each section of the Scheme falls within the definition of   *j* 'occupational pension scheme' in s 1 of the 1993 Act, Mr Newman relies upon the opening words in s 1, 'unless the context otherwise requires'. He submitted that, by reason of the absurd and impractical consequences of the defendant's interpretation of s 108 of the 1993 Act, and by virtue of the manifest policy considerations behind s 108, the context requires that the Trustee's interpretation of s 108, in relation to the Scheme, be accepted.

a [43] Mr Newman pointed out that the interpretation of s 108, for which the Trustee contends, accords with the understanding of the relevant regulatory authorities, that is to say, the Occupational Pensions Board and its successor, the Occupational Pensions Regulatory Authority (OPRA), and also the Inland Revenue. A letter from the Department of Social Security to Slaughter and May dated 26 October 1998 explains that this is why it is not considered necessary or appropriate to amend the legislation.

b [44] Miss Furze's starting position was that, on its face, s 108 applies to the Scheme as a whole. It satisfies the definition of 'qualifying scheme' in s 102(2) and, in particular, the definition of 'occupational scheme' in s 1 of the 1993 Act. She also emphasised the express reference in s 108 to 'every pension', which, she submitted, must mean every pension payable in every section.

c [45] Moreover, she submitted, it is extremely difficult fairly to view the Scheme as comprising separate and distinct schemes for each section. She emphasised, in this context, and elsewhere in her submissions, that there is no express prohibition in the Scheme against the application of the assets in one section for the benefit of members in another section; and also that it was inevitable, as the Scheme's provisions themselves reflect, to maintain divisions between the sections in financial and accounting terms. She graphically described the sections as 'leaky membranes', rather than watertight compartments. Indeed, it is not in dispute that assets of the various sections were in fact pooled for investment purposes.

d [46] Miss Furze also relied upon various statutory provisions which, she submitted, showed that Parliament certainly had in mind that a sectionalised scheme might be treated as a single scheme. She drew my attention, for example, to s 153(5)(a) of the 1993 Act, which expressly provides for the making of regulations to modify various sections of the 1993 Act, but not including s 108, in their application 'to any occupational pension scheme which applies to earners in employments under different employers'.

f [47] Such regulations were made in relation to s 144 of the 1993 Act, which provides, in the circumstances there specified, that where a scheme is in deficit, the amount of the deficit is to be treated as a debt due from the employer to the trustees of the scheme. The Occupational Pension Schemes (Deficiency on Winding Up etc) Regulations 1994, SI 1994/895, modified s 144 in relation to a sectionalised industry-wide scheme. Regulation 3 of the 1994 regulations provides, so far as material, as follows:

'Scheme which applies to more than one employer

3. In the application of section 144 of the Act to a scheme which applies to earners in employments under different employers and in respect of which there are members in pensionable service under the scheme—(a) that section is modified by adding, after subsection (1), the following subsections—

"(1A) The amount of the debt due from each employer shall be such amount as, in the opinion of the actuary referred to in regulation 2(3) of the Occupational Pension Schemes (Deficiency on Winding up etc.) Regulations 1994, bears the same proportion to the deficiency under the scheme as the amount of the scheme's liabilities attributable to employment with that employer (including liabilities in respect of any transfer credits allowed under the scheme in connection with employment with that employer) bears to the total amount of the scheme's liabilities.

(1B) Where a scheme which applies to earners in employments under different employers is divided into two or more sections and the provisions

of the scheme are such that—(a) different sections of the scheme apply to
different employers, (b) contributions payable to the scheme by an
employer, or by an earner in employment under that employer, are
allocated to that employer's section, and (c) a specified part or proportion
of the assets of the scheme is attributable to each section and cannot be
used for the purposes of any other such section, each section of the scheme
shall be treated as a separate scheme for the purposes of this section."'

[48] Miss Furze also referred, in this context, to the definition of 'occupational
pension scheme' in s 176 of the 1995 Act, which gives the expression the same
meaning as in s 1 of the 1993 Act. She pointed out, and Mr Newman agreed, that
there are several instances in the 1995 Act in which the draftsman, in referring to
an occupational pension scheme, is plainly referring to the entire scheme. Where
it is intended that such statutory provisions in the 1995 Act are to be modified in
relation to a sectionalised scheme, in order that separate sections of such a
scheme are to be treated as separate schemes, regulations have been made
specifically for that purpose. She emphasised that, in relation to ss 37, 76 and 77
of the 1995 Act, which, as I have said, replace s 108 of the 1993 Act, precisely such
modification was made in the 1996 regulations. Regulation 12 of those regulations
is in the following terms:

'**Schemes with more than one employer**
    12.—(1) Where a scheme in relation to which there is more than one
employer is divided into two or more sections and the provisions of the
scheme are such that—(a) different sections of the scheme apply to different
employers or groups of employers (whether or not more than one section
applies to any particular employer or groups including any particular
employer); (b) contributions payable to the scheme by an employer, or by a
member in employment under that employer, are allocated to that employer's
section (or, if more than one section applies to the employer, the section
which is appropriate in respect of the employment in question); and (c) a
specified part or proportion of the assets of the scheme is attributable to each
section and cannot be used for the purposes of any other section, sections 37,
76 and 77 of the 1995 Act and these Regulations shall apply as if each section
of the scheme were a separate scheme.'

She submitted that, Parliament's recognition, in the very context of the successor
provisions to s 108 of the 1993 Act, that the expression 'occupational pension
scheme' includes a sectionalised scheme, and that express provision by statutory
instrument is required if the separate sections of such a scheme are to be treated
as separate schemes, is a compelling reason for saying s 108 applies to such a
scheme as a whole and, further, that s 108 does not provide a sufficient 'context'
for giving the expression 'occupational pension scheme' any other meaning than
its statutory definition in s 1 of the 1993 Act.

[49] Miss Furze relied upon the following passage in the speech of Lord Lowry
in *Hanlon v Law Society* [1980] 2 All ER 199 at 218, [1981] AC 124 at 193–194, as
authority that the 1994 regulations and the 1996 regulations may be relied upon
as an aid to the interpretation of the expression 'occupational pension scheme' in
the 1993 and 1995 Acts:

'A study of the cases and of the leading textbooks (Craies on Statute Law
(7th Edn, 1971, p 158), Maxwell on the Interpretation of Statutes (12th Edn,
1969, pp 74–75), 36 Halsbury's Laws (3rd Edn) para 606, p 401) appears to me

a
to warrant the formulation of the following propositions. (1) Subordinate legislation may be used in order to construe the parent Act, but only where power is given to amend the Act by regulations or where the meaning of the Act is ambiguous. (2) Regulations made under the Act provide a parliamentary or administrative contemporanea expositio of the Act but do not decide or control its meaning: to allow this would be to substitute the rule-making

b
authority for the judges as interpreter and would disregard the possibility that the regulation relied on was misconceived or ultra vires. (3) Regulations which are consistent with a certain interpretation of the Act tend to confirm that interpretation. (4) Where the Act provides a framework built on by contemporaneously prepared regulations, the latter may be a reliable guide to the meaning of the former. (5) The regulations are a clear guide, and may

c
be decisive, when they are made in pursuance of a power to modify the Act, particularly if they come into operation on the same day as the Act which they modify. (6) Clear guidance may also be obtained from regulations which are to have effect as if enacted in the parent Act.'

d
Miss Furze submitted that the principles in (1), (3) and (5) in that passage apply in the present case.

[50] Miss Furze submitted that the words 'unless the context otherwise requires' at the beginning of s 1 of the 1993 Act, which includes the definition of 'occupational pension scheme', do not permit a construction of s 108 of the 1993 Act under which each section of the Scheme would constitute a separate

e
qualifying scheme.

[51] Miss Furze submitted that, so far as concerns the application in the present case of those words 'unless the context otherwise requires', the test is whether the statutory context of s 108 compels the adoption of a different meaning to the statutory definition of 'occupational pension scheme' in s 1. She

f
relies upon the following statement by Lightman J in *Melville v IRC* [2000] STC 628 at 634–635 (para 16):

'It is accordingly incumbent on the commissioners at the second stage to establish (in the language of s 272) that the context requires some other conclusion. I have been referred to no authority which considers the

g
meaning of the formula in s 272 "except when the context otherwise requires", but the term "requires" connotes a degree of necessity. The contra-indication stipulated for must (as it seems to me) be clearer and stronger than that stipulated for in the formula adopted in the 1925 legislation "unless the contrary intention appears". It is not sufficient that on balance the context affords indicia or pointers in one direction or favours one

h
construction to another, let alone that one construction would be preferred to the other in the absence of the interpretation clause. The statutory interpretation must be adopted unless the context compels the adoption of another.'

j
That approach of Lightman J was approved by the Court of Appeal ([2001] EWCA Civ 1247 at [32], [2001] STC 1271 at [32], [2002] 1 WLR 407).

[52] Miss Furze submitted that, far from the context of s 108 compelling the adoption of a different meaning of the expression 'occupational pension scheme' from the express statutory definition in s 1 of the 1993 Act, as regards sectionalised industry-wide schemes, the legislative history concerning s 108 reinforced the conclusion that Parliament intended, in s 108, to refer to the entire

scheme, whether or not the scheme was a sectionalised one. I have already
mentioned Miss Furze's emphasis, in this context, on the successor provisions to
s 108, namely ss 37, 76 and 77 of the 1995 Act and the 1996 regulations. Turning
to the statutory precursor of s 108, she relied upon s 11(1) of the Social Security
Act 1990, which inserted in the Social Security Pensions Act 1975 provisions
similar to those subsequently contained in ss 102(2) and 108 of the 1993 Act. The
definition of 'occupational pension scheme', for that purpose, was contained in
s 66(1) of the 1975 Act. That definition was identical to the definition in s 1 of the
1993 Act, save that there was no overriding qualification, as is found in s 1, 'unless
the context otherwise requires'. This conclusively shows, Miss Furze submitted,
that the Trustee's interpretation of s 108 of the 1993 Act cannot be supported by
the words 'unless the context otherwise requires' in s 1 of the 1993 Act, since
there is no reason whatever to suppose that s 108 was intended to have any
different meaning and effect than the predecessor provisions in the 1975 Act, as
amended by the 1990 Act.

[53] Miss Furze rigorously opposed the notion, advanced by Mr Newman,
that the defendant's interpretation of s 108 produces results which are absurd or
impractical. She submitted, as I have said, that there is no express prohibition in
the deed on the application of assets of one section for the benefit of another
section, and that it was impossible, or at least very difficult, in practice, to prevent
an intermingling of assets and cross-subsidy between the sections of the Scheme.
She rejected Mr Newman's proposition that s 108 might never, in practice, be
satisfied in the case of a sectionalised industry-wide scheme, in which some
sections were in deficit and some in surplus, because they would not have any
express provision for cross-subsidy and, if they were amended to include such
provisions, the Scheme would be in serious danger of losing Inland Revenue
approval.

[54] Miss Furze's stance in relation to these points was, briefly, as follows. She
submitted that s 108 itself directly empowered the granting of 5% LPI increases
throughout a scheme, whether or not any express provision was also contained
in the scheme itself. In that connection, she relied upon the decision and
reasoning of Nicholls V-C in *Thrells Ltd (in liq) v Lomas* [1993] 2 All ER 546, [1993]
1 WLR 456. In that case Nicholls V-C was concerned with, among other things,
the application to an occupational pension scheme of s 11 of the 1990 Act, which,
as I have already said, inserted in the 1975 Act provisions similar to those in s 108.
He found that the scheme's rules did not confer any power to confer 5% LPI
increases, but held that increases should be made such as to enable s 11 of the
1990 Act to operate. The following passage is particularly relevant:

> 'The trustee should administer and wind up the scheme accordingly. For
> the avoidance of doubt I add that the trustee's power to apply scheme funds
> in satisfying the payment condition [LPI increases] derives from a combination
> of the statute and the liquidator's claim to the surplus. Section 11(3) of the
> 1990 Act precludes the liquidator, who is claiming payment, from objecting
> to this application of funds to which otherwise he would be entitled.' (See
> [1993] 2 All ER 546 at 558, [1993] 1 WLR 456 at 470.)

[55] Further, she pointed out that, in the present case, the Scheme does, in
fact, contain a power of amendment, which would enable the Scheme's
provisions to be amended so as to permit any payments or increases in benefit
necessary under s 108 as a precondition of the distribution of surplus to the
employer. In the case of other schemes, where there is no suitable power of

a amendment, application could be made to the court for the relevant powers to be granted pursuant to s 57 of the 1925 Act.

[56] So far as concerns the position of the Inland Revenue, and infringement of the principle in para 21.15 of IR 12 (2001), she submitted that Mr Newman had overstated the rigour with which the Inland Revenue adhered to the principle of no cross-subsidy between sections of a sectionalised industry-wide scheme. She

b pointed out that para 21.15 of IR 12 (2001) does not state that principle in absolute terms. Further, as an illustration of the flexibility of the Inland Revenue, she relied upon the fact that, in the case of the Scheme itself, the Inland Revenue had acceded to a request by the Trustee that the assets in certain sections of the Scheme be available to fund general expenses of the winding up. She also submitted that the Inland Revenue would be most unlikely to pursue a policy

c which produced a conflict with the requirements of Parliament in s 108 of the 1993 Act. Finally, she submitted that Inland Revenue practice could not alter the true meaning of s 108 or override its provisions.

[57] Miss Furze submitted that, even if, contrary to her other submissions, it was not possible, in the case of any particular sectionalised scheme, to satisfy the

d preconditions, under s 108, of a distribution of assets to an employer on a winding up, the assets would not be 'frozen'. They could be used to augment benefits. In any event, she said, there were other situations in which surplus assets could not be returned to an employer, including, for example, a case in which the trust deed and rules contained no power, or alternatively an express prohibition, on the return of assets to the employer.

e [58] She submitted that Parliament did not consider there to be any problem with the operation of s 11(3) of the 1990 Act or s 108 of the 1993 Act, since Parliament re-enacted in s 108 the corresponding provisions of s 11(3), and, moreover, no regulations were ever made to modify the operation of s 108 in relation to sectionalised schemes, even though s 153(1) of the 1993 Act conferred

f power to amend the definition of 'qualifying scheme' in s 102 of that Act.

[59] Finally she submitted, if there was any practical problem with the application of s 108 to sectionalised schemes, then Parliament, by casting s 108 as a prohibition, deliberately threw on the employer the risk of any such problem.

Decision on the first issue

g [60] In my judgment, on the proper construction of s 108 of the 1993 Act, and the related definitions of the expressions 'qualifying scheme' in s 102(2) and 'occupational pension scheme' in s 1 of the 1993 Act, each section of the Scheme constitutes a 'qualifying scheme' within s 108.

[61] Such a construction gives effect to the policy lying behind s 108, whereas

h the construction for which the defendant, in his representative capacity, was obliged to contend is consistent with no discernible rational policy and would, as Mr Newman submitted, produce absurd results. Miss Furze, when pressed by me, stated that the policy behind s 108 was the grant of 5% LPI increases to members of a scheme, prior to the distribution of any surplus benefits to an

j employer. That, it seems to me, states the effect of s 108, but is not an adequate statement of the policy considerations that lie behind it. Mr Newman contended, and I accept, that the policy underlying s 108 is to ensure that there is a fair balance between the employer's and members' interests in surplus assets. In the case of a sectionalised industry-wide scheme, in which some sections are in surplus and others are in deficit, the effect of the defendant's construction would be to compel the trustee to apply assets for the benefit of members of other sections, even if those members had never had any connection of any kind with the employer of the transferring section and his employees, whose contributions had created the surplus. That is, on any footing, a bizarre and capricious consequence. It is impossible to discern any rational policy justification for it.

[62] Further, as Mr Newman said, the defendant's interpretation would produce a situation in which the surplus in one section would have to be applied, for the benefit of the members of a section in deficit, in one or other of three possible ways, namely (1) increasing the benefits of members of the underfunded section to the level they would have been if they had been fully-funded and paying 5% LPI on top; or (2) paying 5% LPI on such benefits as there would have been if the section had been fully-funded; or (3) funding 5% LPI of the actual benefits provided in the section in deficit. Miss Furze conceded that those were the three applicable alternatives. She accepted that the first two were unlikely to have been intended. The difficulty with the third, it seems to me, is that s 108 of the 1993 Act plainly proceeds on the assumption, which is entirely logical, that LPI increases would only be granted where benefits have been fully-funded and a surplus exists. The third alternative, however, would leave the underfunded benefits of members in the section in deficit, but provide for a 5% LPI increase on them. This, again, is a bizarre and capricious result.

[63] The Trustee's interpretation of s 108 does not, however, give rise to any such bizarre, absurd or capricious consequences. It gives effect to the policy underlying s 108. I agree with Mr Newman that the construction of s 108, for which the Trustee contends, is achieved either by the application of the express definition of 'occupational pension scheme' in s 1 of the 1993 Act, or alternatively by giving that expression a special meaning in the context of the application of s 108 to a sectionalised industry-wide scheme. I agree with Mr Newman that the statutory definition of 'occupational pension scheme' in s 1 of the 1993 Act is sufficiently broad to encompass each section of the Scheme individually. Miss Furze, as I have said, emphasised that the sections of the Scheme were not watertight compartments in financial or accounting terms, and pointed out that the assets had been pooled for investment purposes. That, however, does not undermine the fact the terms of the Scheme were designed to achieve a compartmentalisation of each section for financial and accounting purposes through the provisions of rules 15A and 37(1A) of the Scheme.

[64] The Trustee's interpretation of s 108 is not precluded, in my judgment, by s 153(5)(a) of the 1993 Act or the 1994 regulations, or the provisions of the 1995 Act and regulations made under that Act, including, for example, the 1996 regulations, which make specific provision for each section of a sectionalised scheme to be treated as a separate scheme in certain cases. Each statutory provision must be interpreted in the light of all relevant circumstances, including its purpose and its context. As I have said, the defendant's interpretation is consistent with neither the purpose nor the context of s 108. On the other hand, the Trustee's interpretation is consistent with and gives effect to the purpose and context of s 108 without unduly offending the actual language used in the section and related definitions.

[65] Nor, it seems to me, do the provisions of the 1975 Act and the 1990 Act assist. As I have said, I accept Mr Newman's primary submission that the statutory definition of the expression 'occupational pension scheme', which is identical in both the 1975 Act and in the 1993 Act, is sufficiently wide to embrace each individual section of the Scheme, as well as the Scheme as a whole. Furthermore, contrary to the submission of Miss Furze, I see no reason why the

a addition of the words 'unless the context otherwise requires' in s 1 of the 1993 Act should not be applicable in the context of the application of s 108 to sectionalised industry-wide schemes merely because those words did not appear in the definition of 'occupational pension scheme' in the 1975 Act. To my mind, the legislative history, including the fact that s 108 re-enacted s 11(3) of the 1990 Act and that no regulations were ever made modifying s 108 in relation to sectionalised
b industry-wide schemes, is a neutral indicator of the correct interpretation of s 108 and its statutory precursor. That legislative history could, equally well, be said to support the Trustee's contentions.

[66] In the light of my reasoning above, it is not necessary to take into account Mr Newman's further submission, in support of the Trustee's interpretation of s 108, that the policy of the Inland Revenue, in relation to cross-subsidies in a
c sectionalised scheme, embodied in para 21.15 of IR 12 (2001), is inconsistent with the defendant's interpretation. Miss Furze is undoubtedly correct in her submission that the Inland Revenue's policy cannot alter the clear meaning and effect of a statutory provision, nor override it. The Inland Revenue's policy is, it seems to me, material only in the following respects. It supports the conclusion, which is
d in any event apparent from the provisions of s 153(5)(a) of the 1993 Act and the 1994 regulations, that Parliament was aware of the existence of industry-wide sectionalised pension schemes when it enacted the 1993 Act. It also supports the conclusion that a sensible policy is to prevent, rather than encourage, the use of surplus assets in an occupational pension scheme, created by the contributions of one set of employers and employees, being used to benefit wholly unrelated
e employers and employees. Sections 603 and 611(3) and Sch 22 to the Income and Corporation Taxes Act 1988, which concern the need to reduce excess surplus in a pension scheme in certain circumstances in order to avoid adverse fiscal consequences and which enable the Inland Revenue to treat as separate schemes, for this purpose, individual sections of a sectionalised scheme, may be said,
f broadly speaking, to proceed upon the same hypothesis.

[67] Nor is it necessary for me to reach a conclusion on Mr Newman's submission that a consequence of the interpretation of the defendant would be, in many cases, to freeze the distribution of surplus assets for no one's benefit, or, alternatively, to imperil Inland Revenue approval. I will, however, make the
g following observations. First, notwithstanding the judgment and conclusions of Nicholls V-C in *Thrells Ltd (in liq) v Lomas* [1993] 2 All ER 546, [1993] 1 WLR 456, that case does not seem to me to be clear authority for the proposition that s 108 of the 1993 Act confers directly on the trustee of a sectionalised scheme power to transfer assets to other sections of the scheme, where no such power is contained in the scheme's provisions. While I agree with Miss Furze that such a proposition
h appears to be implicit in the decision in the case, the point is not clearly addressed by Nicholls V-C, and it does not appear to have been argued before him, and, critically, the only persons who would be disadvantaged by such an interpretation of s 108 were not separately represented before him. Second, since s 108 applied throughout the existence of any scheme (and not just on winding up), the
j defendant's construction of s 108 would appear to drive a coach and horses through the Inland Revenue's policy in para 21.15 of IR 12 (2001). Third, it does not seem to me to advance the merits of the defendant's interpretation that another situation in which surplus assets may be frozen, and cannot be returned to the employer, is where the provisions of a scheme expressly prohibit both the improvement of benefits beyond Inland Revenue limits and the return of assets to the employer. That situation does not seem to me to bear rationally or

helpfully on a situation where there is an express power to return surplus assets to the employer.

The second issue

[68] The 1997 order, as I have said, brought into force on 6 April 1997 s 76 of the 1995 Act and also the provision in the 1995 Act which repealed s 108 of the 1993 Act. Article 6 of the 1997 order provided, however, that:

'For the purposes of ... any distribution of excess assets to the employer in relation to a scheme which begins to be wound up before the principal appointed day, section 108 of the 1993 Act ... shall continue to have effect as if [the] Order had not come into force.'

[69] As I have also said, the 1996 regulations, which provide for the service on members of two sets of notices in connection with proposals to distribute excess assets to the employer, in accordance with s 76(3)(d) of the 1995 Act, also came into force on 6 April 1997.

[70] Mr Newman, on behalf of the Trustee, submitted that, in the case of a scheme which began to be wound up before 6 April 1997 and, accordingly, to which s 108 continues to apply, all the provisions of s 76 of the 1995 Act, including the notice provision in s 76(3)(d), are impliedly excluded and do not apply.

[71] Mr Newman relied, in support of his submission, on the difference between art 6 of the 1997 order, which provides that s 108 shall continue to apply to schemes which began to be wound up before 'the principal appointed day', and the wording of art 11 of the 1997 order, which provides that ss 73 and 74 of the 1995 Act (which concern preferential liabilities on winding up and discharge of liabilities by insurance) do not apply to any scheme which has begun to be wound up before that date. He submitted that the reason for that difference in wording between arts 6 and 11 of the 1997 order is that the former relates to a section of the 1995 Act which is intended to replace a section of the 1993 Act, whereas the latter relates to sections of the 1995 Act which are not to be found in any previous legislation. Accordingly, the thrust of art 11 is necessarily and clearly negative. He submitted that support can be found for that approach and distinction in the decision of Rimer J in *Harwood-Smart v Caws* [2000] PLR 101, particularly at 115–116:

'50 [Counsel for the defendant] submits that the provisions of para 6 of the Commencement Order are consistent with his contention that s77 of the 1995 [Act] applies to schemes which were already in winding up prior to 6 April 1997. He says that s108 of the 1993 Act and its replacement, s76 of the 1995 Act, are only dealing with cases in which there is a power to pay surplus to employers. By contrast, s77 of the 1995 Act is dealing with a different situation, one in which there is a prohibition on payments to employers and which is not dealt with in the 1993 Act. [Counsel for the defendant] therefore submits that there is no reason for not construing s 77 as applying to a winding up which commenced prior to 6 April 1997. To do so does not involve any conflict or inconsistency with the type of situation to which s 108 is directed.

51 I recognise the force of that argument and, although I do not find the statutory intentions of article 6 to be very clearly expressed, I accept it. I accept therefore that, as s77 itself appears to say, it applies to schemes which were already in winding up at the time the section came into force.'

a [72] Mr Newman pointed out that the Trustee's interpretation of the 1997 order reflects the understanding and approach of OPRA and the Inland Revenue.

[73] Miss Furze, for the defendant, submitted that there is nothing in art 6 of the 1997 order which precludes the application of s 76 of the 1995 Act to schemes which began to be wound up before 6 April 1997. Her submission, in other words, is that s 108 of the 1993 Act and s 76 of the 1995 Act subsist side by side in

b relation to such schemes, and both sets of statutory provisions must be complied with in respect of such schemes.

[74] Miss Furze submitted that support for this interpretation is given by s 76(1)(b) of the 1993 Act which provides that s 76 applies to a trust scheme in any circumstances if 'the scheme *is being* wound up' (Miss Furze's emphasis).

c [75] Miss Furze also relied, in support of her interpretation, on the decision of Rimer J in *Harwood-Smart*'s case. She relied upon the result of his decision, namely that s 77 of the 1995 Act, which prohibits payment of surplus to employers of certain schemes without first complying with the stringent requirements of that section, including the augmentation of all benefits to Inland Revenue limits, subsists alongside s 108 of the 1993 Act in relation to schemes

d which began to be wound up before 6 April 1997. She drew attention to the fact that the headings to both ss 76 and 77 of the 1995 Act refer expressly to 'excess assets' on or after winding up. Miss Furze also relied upon the provisions of reg 15 of the 1996 regulations. She submitted that the transitional provisions set out in that regulation are very limited, and do not support any case that s 76 does not apply to schemes which, pursuant to art 6 of the 1997 order, continue to be

e governed by s 108.

[76] In my judgment, the Trustee's approach to the second issue is to be preferred. The 1995 Act brought into operation a wholly different statutory regime in relation to the payment of surplus assets to an employer. The new regime is primarily contained in ss 37, 76 and 77 of the 1995 Act. The intuitive reaction to

f art 6 of the 1997 order, which provides that s 108 shall continue to apply in relation to certain schemes, is that the new regime is not intended to apply to such schemes unless, and then only to the extent that, it has been made clear that the two statutory regimes are to run alongside and be supplemental to one another.

[77] That intuitive approach is supported by the reasoning of Rimer J in *Harwood-Smart*'s case. It seems to me that he was, implicitly or explicitly, there

g accepting that the effect of art 6 of the 1997 order is that s 76 of the 1995 Act is excluded where, pursuant to the terms of that article, s 108 continues to apply.

[78] Further, the interpretation for which the defendant contends, produces an unusual result. Section 108 of the 1993 Act applies to every occupational pension scheme which is a 'qualifying scheme'. On the other hand, s 76 of the

h 1995 Act only applies to exempt approved schemes, within s 592(1) of the 1988 Act. Both ss 108 and 76, however, require LPI increases to pensions prior to any distribution of assets to the employer. It follows, on the defendant's interpretation, that there was no need to provide that s 108 should continue to apply to exempt approved schemes since, in relation to such schemes, the restriction in s 108 was

j carried over to s 76. One would have expected, if Parliament intended so to provide, that art 6 of the 1997 order would have been worded so as to stipulate that s 108 of the 1993 Act would continue to apply to those schemes, already in winding up, which are not exempt approved schemes.

[79] Furthermore, reg 15 of the 1996 regulations is, in my judgment, more supportive of the Trustee's interpretation than the defendant's. Those regulations contain the notice provisions specified in s 76(1), (3)(d) of the 1995 Act.

Regulation 15 provides that, in the case of distribution of any excess assets to the employer, in relation to a scheme which began to be wound up before 6 April 1997, certain earlier regulations specified in reg 15(1) 'shall continue to have effect, as if these Regulations had not been made and sections 108 and 136 [of the 1993 Act] had not been repealed' (see reg 15(2)). That wording is consistent with the exclusion of the s 76 regime in its entirety, and specifically in relation to the notice provisions in s 76(3)(d), in a case in which the winding up of a scheme began before 6 April 1997.

[80] I do not consider that the phrase 'is being wound up' in s 76(1)(b) of the 1995 Act, or the heading to that section and to s 77, are cogent reasons to come to a different conclusion. So far as concerns the wording of s 76(1)(b), the relevant and critical provisions are the transitional provisions in the 1997 order and in the 1996 regulations rather than the wording of s 76 itself. The wording of s 76(1)(b) is perfectly capable of being read as applying only to schemes which began to be wound up after the coming into effect of s 76. Indeed, as Mr Newman observed, the identical phrase 'is being wound up' appears in s 74 of the 1995 Act, but the 1997 order made clear that s 74 does not apply to schemes which began to be wound up before s 74 came into operation.

[81] So far as concerns the heading to ss 76 and 77 of the 1995 Act, Miss Furze relied upon the reference in both of them to 'excess assets' and sought, on the basis of that identity of words, to transfer to s 76 Rimer J's treatment of s 77 in *Harwood-Smart*'s case. I have already commented, however, that, in my judgment, the reasoning of Rimer J is more consistent with the interpretation advanced on behalf of the Trustee than that advanced on behalf of the defendant.

[82] Accordingly, I conclude that, on the proper interpretation of art 6 of the 1997 order, s 76, including, in particular, the notice provisions in s 76(3)(d), do not apply to the scheme.

Orders

[83] I shall hear counsel as to the form of any declaratory or other relief to be contained in the order.

Order accordingly.

Celia Fox　Barrister.

a

Farrand v Lazarus and others
[2002] EWHC 226 Admin

QUEEN'S BENCH DIVISION (DIVISIONAL COURT)

SIMON BROWN LJ AND GOLDRING J

b   8 FEBRUARY 2002

Trade description – False trade description – Application in course of trade or business – Disclaimer of false trade description – Secondhand car – Dealers attaching disclaimer to car stating that mileage reading was incorrect – Dealers knowing true mileage of car but not disclosing it – Whether dealer having obligation to disclose true mileage of car if knowing that odometer materially understating mileage – Trade Descriptions Act 1968, s 1(1)(b).

c

The defendants were partners in a secondhand car business. All vehicles offered for sale by them displayed a standard disclaimer notice in the immediate vicinity of the odometer. The disclaimer, which was in common usage throughout the motor trade industry, stated that the defendants did not guarantee the accuracy of the recorded mileage, and that to the best of their knowledge and belief the reading was incorrect. Two of the cars on offer for sale had been purchased by the defendants at auction with warranted mileages in excess of 100,000 miles. However, their odometers only had five figures, and they therefore understated the actual mileages by 100,000 miles. The defendants were charged, inter alia, with four offences of offering to supply and supplying goods to which a false description had been applied contrary to s 1(1)(b)[a] of the Trade Descriptions Act 1968. They were convicted in the magistrates' court. On their appeal, the Crown Court held that anyone seeing the disclaimer would have understood that the mileage on the odometer was incorrect and that, while it would be good practice for a dealer to make known to a customer the true mileage of a vehicle if he knew it to be different from that shown on the odometer, the law did not require him to do so. Accordingly, the appeal was allowed, and the prosecution appealed by way of case stated.

d

e

f

g   **Held** – Where a dealer knew the true mileage of a motor vehicle and that it was materially understated by the vehicle's odometer, the law required him to disclose the true mileage to a prospective customer. Although, in the ordinary way, dealers were under no positive duty to disclose the defects and disadvantages of their wares, they were required to volunteer the truth, in so far as they knew it, with regard to inaccurate mileage readings. In the instant case, the disclaimer seriously understated the fact that the defendants knew perfectly well not only that the reading was incorrect, but that it was grossly and potentially misleadingly so. Moreover, the proforma nature of the disclaimer and the fact that it was common to all cars sold at the defendants' garage depreciated its impact. It could hardly have been further from the sort of emphatic contradiction of the message sent by the odometer that was required to neutralise its effect. Only exposure to the known fact and extent of the falsity of the registered mileage would achieve that. Accordingly, the appeal would be allowed (see [17]–[21], [28]–[31], below).

h

j

R v Southwood [1987] 3 All ER 556 applied.

---

a   Section 1 is set out at [1], below

Notes

For the prohibition of false trade descriptions and for disclaimers, see 41 *a* *Halsbury's Laws* (4th edn reissue) paras 466, 471.

For the Trade Descriptions Act 1968, s 1, see 39 *Halsbury's Statutes* (4th edn) (1995 reissue) 32.

Cases referred to in judgments   *b*
Corfield v Starr [1981] RTR 380, DC.
Newman v Hackney LBC [1982] RTR 296, DC.
Norman v Bennett [1974] 3 All ER 351, [1974] 1 WLR 1229, DC.
R v Hammertons Cars Ltd [1976] 3 All ER 758, [1976] 1 WLR 1243, CA.
R v Southwood [1987] 3 All ER 556, [1987] 1 WLR 1361, CA.
Southend BC v White (1991) 156 JP 463, DC.   *c*

Cases also cited or referred to in skeleton arguments
R v Bull [1997] RTR 123, CA.
Bury MBC v Real [1993] COD 375, DC.

d

Case stated

The prosecution appealed by way of case stated from the decision of the Crown Court at Coventry (Judge Nicholls sitting with two justices) on 15 March 2001 allowing an appeal by the respondents, Frank Arthur Lazarus, Lyndy Lazarus and Cordelia Lazarus-Keene, from their conviction at Coventry Magistrates' Court on 28 May 1999 of, inter alia, four offences of offering to supply and supplying goods *e* to which a false description had been applied contrary to s 1(1)(b) of the Trade Descriptions Act 1968. The questions for the opinion of the High Court are set out at [15], below. The facts are set out in the judgment of Simon Brown LJ.

David Travers (instructed by *Christopher Hinde*, Coventry) for the prosecution.   *f*
Stephen Spence (instructed by *Neil Davidson*, Peterborough) for the third respondent.
The first and second respondents did not appear and were not represented.

SIMON BROWN LJ.

[1] This is a prosecutor's appeal by way of case stated from the order of the Crown Court at Coventry (Judge Nicholls and two justices) on 15 March 2001 *g* allowing the respondents' appeal against their conviction by a deputy stipendiary magistrate sitting in the Coventry Magistrates' Court on 28 May 1999, of a number of offences under s 1 of the Trade Descriptions Act 1968. Section 1 provides:

'(1) Any person who, in the course of a trade or business,—(a) applies a false trade description to any goods; or (b) supplies or offers to supply any *h* goods to which a false trade description is applied; shall, subject to the provisions of this Act, be guilty of an offence.'

[2] Before identifying the particular offences here in question, it is convenient first to set out the facts of the case which, indeed, were never in dispute. The three respondents were at all material times partners in a secondhand car *j* business known as Andrews Garage.

[3] The prosecution arose out of their purchase and subsequent offer for sale of two particular cars, respectively a Ford Fiesta, G802 RAL and a Ford Escort, M441 YTU. The respondents purchased the Fiesta at auction on 12 February 1993 with a warranted mileage of 151,105 miles and subsequently resold it to

a different customers on three occasions; the car being returned to them each time. The respondents purchased the Escort at auction on 22 August 1997 with a warranted mileage of 115,679 miles.

[4] The odometers on each car have only five figures and thus it was that on purchase the Fiesta displayed a mileage of 51,105 miles, the Escort 15,679 miles. On 29 October 1997 trading standards officers inspected the garage and saw the
b two cars on offer for sale on the forecourt. The mileage readings on their respective odometers were, at that date, the Fiesta 75,844 miles, the Escort 15,889 miles.

[5] On each car in the immediate vicinity of the odometer was affixed a sticker reading:

'Code of Practice for the Motor Industry
c 1. We do not Guarantee the Accuracy of the Recorded mileage.
2. To the best of our knowledge and belief the reading is correct/incorrect.'

(On each vehicle the word 'correct' was deleted.)

[6] A similarly-worded disclaimer was affixed to every car in the garage. That form of disclaimer was (and we understand remains) in common use throughout
d the motor trade, having been produced by the Motor Agents Association (now called the Retail Motor Institute). The code of practice was written in consultation with the Office of Fair Trading. Part 3.8 of the code of practice reads:

'Reasonable steps will be taken to verify the recorded mileage of a used car and dealers will use their best endeavours to obtain a signed statement from
e the previous owner as to the car's mileage. Dealers should pass on any known facts about an odometer reading to a prospective customer.'

[7] Posters were visible within the garage which bore general disclaimers as to the mileages of vehicles on the premises.
f [8] On 21 May 1997 the appellant trading standards officer had sent to the respondents a card entitled 'Trade Descriptions Act 1968 Mileages of Used Motor Vehicles', which included the following paragraphs:

'What is the importance of a mileometer reading?
A mileometer reading is a trade description. It will be regarded as an
g accurate indication of the distant travelled by the vehicle, unless positive and effective steps are taken to ensure that customers are informed that it is meaningless and not to be relied upon ...

What is a disclaimer notice?
A disclaimer notice is one which expressly disclaims or contradicts the
h mileometer reading. The wording and size is important and it should be placed on the speedometer so it is as bold, precise, and compelling as the mileometer reading itself. It must effectively bring home to any prospective customer the fact that the reading may not be true and should not be relied upon as indicating the true distance travelled by the vehicle ... A disclaimer
j notice is no protection to any trader who has altered a mileometer reading, replaced an odometer, or knows a higher mileage has been travelled ...

What if a mileage is found or known to be untrue?
If this is the case and the true mileage is known, a similarly effective notice should be placed alongside the mileometer reading indicating it is incorrect and stating the true mileage.'

[9] The leaflet then went on to say, as was plainly the case, that it was 'not an authoritative document on the law'.

[10] On 18 March 1998, some few months, therefore, after the trading standards officer's visit, a customer at the garage, Victoria MacManus, saw the Fiesta for sale on the forecourt and on 20 March she bought it. It was supplied to her with a used vehicle proposal form stating the vehicle's mileage as 75,879 miles. For reasons which I shall shortly indicate, it is unnecessary to set out the facts found with regard to that proposal form.

[11] On those facts 12 informations had originally been laid against each of the respondents. The magistrate dismissed two and found the rest proved: five were allegations of applying a false trade description to goods contrary to s 1(1)(a) of the 1968 Act, five were allegations variously of offering to supply and supplying goods to which a false trade description was applied contrary to s 1(1)(b) of that Act.

[12] The Crown Court allowed the respondent's appeal in respect of all ten offences. The present appeal is directed to four only, namely four of the five offences charged under s 1(1)(b). These four are as follows:

'(A) on the 29th October 1997 offering to supply a Ford Fiesta ... to which a false trade description was applied by means of an odometer reading of 75,844 when the car had travelled in excess of that mileage.

(B) on the 18th March [1998] a like offence offering to supply the [Fiesta] to one Victoria MacManus.

(C) on the 20th March 1998 a similar offence in respect of supplying [the Fiesta] to one Victoria MacManus.

(D) on the 29th October 1997 offering to supply a Ford Escort motor car ... to which a false trade description was applied by means of an odometer reading of 15,889 when the car had travelled in excess of that mileage.'

[13] The fifth offence under s 1(1)(b) related to the proposal form which had been supplied with the Fiesta, but that particular case turned entirely on its own special facts and very sensibly Mr Travers, for the appellant authority, has chosen not to appeal about that. As will readily be appreciated, the four offences with regard to which this appeal *is* now pursued all stand or fall together and they raise an issue of no small importance in this area of the law.

[14] The Crown Court expressed its conclusions with regard to these four offences in para 8 of the case stated as follows:

'We were of the opinion that:

8.1 Anyone seeing the disclaimer would understand that the mileage on the odometer was incorrect.

8.2 While it would be good practice for a dealer to make known to a customer the true mileage of a vehicle if he knew it to be different from that shown on the odometer that is not a requirement in law. The law prohibits the supply of goods to which a false trade description is applied but does not require a trader to give additional information.

8.3 While it may constitute a civil wrong the 1968 Act does not go so far as to require a dealer who says he is applying the code of practice for the motor industry to give further information.

8.4 This was an effective disclaimer in all cases except that [with regard to the proposal form] and no one could be misled by being told the odometer reading was incorrect.'

a   [15] The questions posed for the decision of this court are as follows:

'I Whether the traders when told the mileage travelled by the cars in question exceeded the mileage shown on the odometer by 100,000 miles had effectively disclaimed the odometer readings?

II Whether the reading on the odometer had been disclaimed by the use of a sticker alongside the odometer bearing the words:

b   "Code of Practice for the Motor Industry

1. We do not Guarantee the Accuracy of the Recorded Mileage.

2. To the best of our knowledge and belief the read is correct/incorrect."

(With the word "correct" struck through)

(a) in any event and

c   (b) in particular [having regard to pt 3.8 of the code of practice].'

[16] The many authorities helpfully put before us, and which we had an opportunity to consider before this short hearing began, amply establish two propositions. First, that although a false odometer reading on its face constitutes a false trade description, its effect can, in certain cases, be neutralised by a

d   sufficient disclaimer notice (see particularly *Norman v Bennett* [1974] 3 All ER 351, [1974] 1 WLR 1229 and *R v Hammertons Cars Ltd* [1976] 3 All ER 758, [1976] 1 WLR 1243). Second, that no disclaimer notice can be effective in cases under s 1(1)(a) of the Act, cases that is where the dealer has himself, for whatever reason, either altered the odometer (see particularly *Corfield v Starr* [1981] RTR 380, *Newman v Hackney LBC* [1982] RTR 296 and *R v Southwood* [1987] 3 All ER 556, [1987] 1 WLR

e   1361) or replaced it (see *Southend BC v White* (1991) 156 JP 463). Any defence in those s 1(1)(a) cases can only arise under s 24 of the Act, the due diligence provision.

[17] The present case seems to me to fall somewhere between those two extremes. The question it raises is this: what is the position of the dealer who

f   does not himself alter or replace the odometer, but who knows the vehicle's true mileage and knows that the odometer materially understates it? To neutralise the description by a sufficient disclaimer, must he disclose the true mileage, as the appellant authority's advice leaflet and the industry's code of practice suggest, or is that rather to be regarded merely as 'good practice' and not 'a requirement in law' as the Crown Court concluded in para 8.2 of its conclusions? That is the

g   issue of principle which arises here.

[18] More narrowly, of course, the issue arising on the particular facts of the instant case is this: was it sufficient for these respondents to place alongside the odometers of these two cars, which from the vendor's warranties obtained at auction they knew to have been 'round the clock', their standard disclaimer

h   stating merely that the recorded mileage was not guaranteed and 'to the best of our knowledge and believe ... is incorrect'?

[19] In whichever form one poses the question, to my mind there is only one answer to it and that, with respect, is not the answer given by the Crown Court.

[20] If one starts with the particular facts of this case and asks simply the

j   question suggested by *Norman*'s case [1974] 3 All ER 351, [1974] 1 WLR 1229, the case which first adumbrated the doctrine of disclaimer, was this particular disclaimer 'as bold, precise and compelling as the trade description itself?' The answer must surely be No.

[21] To suggest merely that the reading on these odometers was incorrect to the best of the respondents' knowledge and belief seriously understated the fact that they knew perfectly well not only that the reading was incorrect, but that it

was grossly and potentially misleadingly so. The proforma nature of the disclaimer, moreover, and the fact that it is common to all cars sold at the respondents' garage again tend to depreciate its impact. Indeed, it could hardly be further from the sort of emphatic contradiction of the message sent by the odometer that to my mind was required to neutralise its effect. In my judgment, only disclosure of the known fact and extent of the falsity of the registered mileage figures would have achieved that here.

[22], [23] This approach, moreover, accords with what seems to me the most authoritative of the decisions before us with regard to the application of s 1(1) to odometers, *R v Southwood* [1987] 3 All ER 556, [1987] 1 WLR 1361. There Lord Lane CJ, having reviewed all the leading cases in the field, said this:

'Thus the defendant who by making inquiries discovers the falsity of a reading would no doubt be able to protect himself by frankly disclosing the result of his enquiries in such way that any purchaser would be in the same state of knowledge as the dealer himself.' (See [1987] 3 All ER 556 at 564, [1987] 1 WLR 1361 at 1370.)

[24] Then a little later he said:

'If someone buys a car with a false reading already registered on the instrument the falsity of which comes to his knowledge, his protection against a charge under s 1(1)(b) will then be a suitable and candid intimation to the customer of the falsity, thereby bringing himself within s 24(1).' (See [1987] 3 All ER 556 at 564–565, [1987] 1 WLR 1361 at 1371.)

[25] I recognise, of course, that that case was concerned more particularly with the s 24 defence, but the requirement for such frank disclosure should have no less application when it comes to assessing the sufficiency of a disclaimer. If, moreover, the dealer's duty to take that sort of positive and specific corrective action arose as it was held to arise in *Southend BC v White* (1991) 156 JP 463, where the dealer had had no alternative but to fit a new dashboard displaying inevitably a false odometer reading, I find it difficult to see why any lesser duty should exist in the circumstances of the present case. Whether the defence in these circumstances is properly to be regarded as one arising under s 24 or (as, for the purposes of this appeal I am assuming) by way of a disclaimer negativing the prima facie false description, in my judgment, it fails here.

[26] I should mention briefly one particular concern expressed by Mr Spence in the course of his helpful submissions on behalf of the third respondent (the other two not being represented although, of course, the position of all three is identical) namely that were the dealer in such a case to represent that the car had, in fact, travelled 100,000 miles more than shown by its odometer, that itself might be alleged to be a false description, since the warranty which the dealer himself originally received might have been false, even perhaps to the extent that the vehicle had travelled *twice* around the clock.

[27] That, to my mind, is an unconvincing objection to the approach recommended by the appellant's leaflet and by the trade code, and which I believe to represent not merely good practice but the law, namely that the dealer should tell his customers what he knows. Were the dealer to indicate in a case such as this that the vehicle has travelled to his knowledge not less than 100,000 miles beyond its displayed mileage, I cannot suppose that he would be at risk of criminal prosecution.

a [28] I recognise, of course, that in the ordinary way dealers are under no positive duty to disclose the defects and disadvantages of their wares. Generally, they are entitled to be economical with the truth, although not, of course, to lie. With regard to inaccurate mileage readings, however, that, in my judgment, is not the law. In this limited respect they are required to volunteer the truth in so far as they know it.

b [29] It follows that I, for my part, would answer the questions posed by the case stated in the negative and would allow this appeal.

[30] Mr Travers told the court at the outset that his client's concern was to establish the principle involved in this appeal. These offences occurred some considerable time ago and understandably, and as I think rightly, Mr Travers has not invited us to remit the matter for further consideration by the Crown Court.

c

GOLDRING J.

[31] I agree.

d *Appeal allowed. Leave to appeal refused, but court certifying that a point of law of general public importance was involved in its decision, namely 'Whether a motor trader, knowing or having reasonable grounds for believing that the mileage travelled by a vehicle substantially exceeds that shown on the odometer, has effectively disclaimed the odometer reading merely by stating that it is incorrect, without revealing the truth as he knows it.'*

Dilys Tausz   Barrister.

Aoun v Bahri and another   *a*

[2002] EWHC 29 (Comm)

QUEEN'S BENCH DIVISION (COMMERCIAL COURT)

MOORE-BICK J   *b*

15, 26 NOVEMBER 2001, 6 FEBRUARY 2002

Costs – Security for costs – Jurisdiction – Jurisdiction to order security where claimant having changed address since commencement of claim 'with a view to evading the consequences of the litigation' – Jurisdiction to order security where claimant having *c* *'taken steps in relation to his assets that would make it more difficult to enforce an order for costs against him' – Whether jurisdiction in respect of change of address confined to change of address given on claim form – Whether 'consequences of the litigation' confined to order for payment of defendant's costs at end of litigation – Whether provision dealing with steps taken by claimant in relation to his assets concerned with his motivation – CPR 25.13(2)(d),(g).* *d*

The claimant was an Australian national of Lebanese origin and owned a house in Australia. In February 2000 the claimant, who was then resident in Athens and had no connections with the United Kingdom, brought proceedings in England against two former business associates. A few weeks after bringing proceedings, *e* he moved from the address given on the claim form, but continued to reside with his family in Athens at two other addresses. In October 2000 the solicitors acting for one of the defendants asked the claimant's then solicitors to agree in principle to provide security for costs. During the latter part of 2000, the claimant's wife and family returned to Australia, but in December the claimant moved with his family to England. The claimant eventually sold his house in Australia. He *f* intended to put about a quarter of the proceeds into a new house that he was buying in London and to use the balance for the purposes of his business. After not receiving any proposals as regards security for their costs, the defendants applied for orders for security. They contended, inter alia, that the claimant had moved to England rather than Australia in order to avoid having to give security *g* for costs, and that accordingly the court could order him to provide such security on the ground that he had changed his address since the commencement of the claim 'with a view to evading the consequences of the litigation' within the meaning of CPR 25.13(2)(d)[a]. They also relied on r 25.13(2)(g) which gave the court jurisdiction to make an order for security where a claimant had 'taken *h* steps in relation to his assets that would make it difficult to enforce an order for costs against him'. On the application, issues arose, inter alia, as to (i) whether para (2)(d) was concerned only with a change of address from that given in the claim form rather than any subsequent change of address; (ii) whether 'the consequences of the litigation' in para (2)(d) were confined to an order for the *j*

---

a   Rule 25.13, so far as material, provides: '(1) The court may make an order for security for costs under rule 25.12 if—(a) it is satisfied, having regard to all the circumstances of the case, that it is just to make such an order; and (b) (i) one or more of the conditions in paragraph (2) applies ...
(2) The conditions are ... (d) the claimant has changed his address since the claim was commenced with a view to evading the consequences of the litigation; ... (g) the claimant has taken steps in relation to his assets that would make it difficult to enforce an order for costs against him.'

a payment of a defendant's costs at the end of proceedings; and (iii) whether para (2)(g), like para (2)(d), was concerned with the claimant's motivation.

Held – (1) On its true construction, CPR 25.13(2)(d) was not concerned only with a change of address from that given on the claim form, and 'the consequences of the litigation' were not confined to an order for the payment by the claimant of the
b defendant's costs at the end of the proceedings. Sub-paragraph (2)(d) was aimed at the claimant who sought to go to ground to avoid his obligations, and it was therefore quite possible for the mischief at which it was aimed to arise on a second or subsequent change of address. As regards 'the consequences of the litigation', the bringing of proceedings in England gave rise to various consequences for the claimant, including, depending on the circumstances of the
c case, the possibility of being ordered to provide security for the defendant's costs. A claimant who changed his address during the course of the action with a view to avoiding any of the ordinary consequences of the litigation invited inquiry into whether he was likely to honour a liability for costs. It was, therefore, consistent with the purpose of the rules for the court to have the power in such cases to
d consider whether, as a matter of discretion, an order for security should be made. In the instant case, however, the court was satisfied on the evidence that the claimant's decision to take up residence in England was motivated by personal and family considerations rather than a desire to avoid giving security for costs. It followed that the claimant did not fall within r 25.13(2)(d) (see [18], [19], [23], [24], below).
e (2) On its true construction, CPR 25.13(2)(g) was not concerned with the claimant's motivation, though that might be relevant to the exercise of the court's discretion, but with the effect of steps that he had taken in relation to his assets. The contrast between the wording of sub-para (g) and that of sub-para (d) was marked, and there was no basis for construing sub-para (g) as if it read 'with
f a view to making it difficult to enforce an order for costs against him'. In the instant case, the claimant's sale of his Australian house was a step in relation to his assets that would make it difficult to enforce an order for costs against him, and that was sufficient to give the court jurisdiction under para (2)(g) to make an order for security for costs. In the circumstances of the case, it was just to make such an order in favour of both defendants (see [25], [26], [29], [45], below).
g

Notes

For conditions to be satisfied in respect of an order for security for costs, see 37 *Halsbury's Laws* (4th edn reissue) para 835.

h **Cases referred to in judgment**

AP (UK) Ltd v West Midlands Fire and Civil Defence Authority [2001] EWCA Civ 1917, [2001] All ER (D) 252 (Nov).
Chandler v Brown [2001] CP Rep 103.
De Beer v Kanaar & Co (a firm) [2001] EWCA Civ 1318, [2002] CLC 114.
j *Shah v Barnet London BC* [1983] 1 All ER 226, [1983] 2 AC 309, [1983] 2 WLR 16, HL.

Cases also cited or referred to in skeleton arguments

Akinde v Secretary of State for the Home Dept [1993] Imm AR 512, CA.
Al-Zahrany v Secretary of State for the Home Dept [1995] Imm AR 510, CA.
Alexander v Immigration Appeal Tribunal [1982] 1 All ER 763, [1982] 1 WLR 1076, HL.
Giles v Rhind [2001] 2 BCLC 582.

Hossain v Immigration Officer, Heathrow [1990] Imm AR 520, EAT.
IRC v Lysaght [1928] AC 234, [1928] All ER Rep 575, HL.
Johnson v Gore Wood & Co (a firm) [2001] 1 All ER 481, [2001] 2 WLR 72, HL.
Khawaja v Secretary of State for the Home Dept [1983] 1 All ER 765, [1984] 1 AC 74, HL.
Knight v Ponsonby [1925] 1 KB 545, CA.
Levene v IRC [1928] AC 217, [1928] All ER Rep 746, HL.
Leyvand v Barasch [2000] 11 LS Gaz R 37.
Macrae v Macrae [1949] 2 All ER 34, [1949] P 397, CA.
Parkinson v Myer Wolf & Manley [1985] CA Transcript 1088.
Patel v Immigration Appeal Tribunal [1983] Imm AR 76, CA.
R v Immigration Appeal Tribunal, ex p Shaikh [1981] 3 All ER 29, [1981] 1 WLR 1107.
R v Immigration Officer, ex p Chan [1992] 2 All ER 738, [1992] 1 WLR 541, CA.
R v Secretary of State for the Home Dept, ex p Arjumand [1983] Imm AR 123.
R v Secretary of State for the Home Dept, ex p Patel [1986] Imm AR 515, CA.
R v Secretary of State for the Home Dept, ex p Saffu-Mensah [1991] Imm AR 43; *affd*
    sub nom *Saffu-Mensah v Secretary of State for the Home Dept* [1992] Imm AR 185,
    CA.

Applications for security for costs

By applications issued respectively on 5 and 20 April 2001, the defendants, Hassan
Bahri and Costas Angelou, applied for orders under CPR 25.12 requiring the
claimant, Mohamad Ali Aoun, to provide security for their costs of proceedings
for breach of contract, breach of fiduciary duty and fraud brought against them
by Mr Aoun. The facts are set out in the judgment.

Graham Dunning QC and *Stephen Houseman* (instructed by *Constant & Constant*) for
    Mr Bahri.
Huw Davies (instructed by *Barlow Lyde & Gilbert*) for Mr Angelou.
Nigel Jacobs (instructed by *Jeffrey Green Russell*) for Mr Aoun.

Cur adv vult

6 April 2002. The following judgment was delivered.

MOORE-BICK J.
    [1] This is an unusual application for security for costs. The claimant, Mr Aoun,
is a businessman who for some years has been involved in various commercial
enterprises mainly related to the operation of vessels carrying liquefied petroleum
gas. Until some time in 1999 these enterprises were carried on in conjunction
with the defendants, Mr Bahri and Mr Angelou. At some point during that year,
however, the parties' relationship collapsed and Mr Aoun has now brought these
proceedings against his former business associates to recover very substantial
sums by way of damages for breach of contract, breach of fiduciary duty and
fraud. It is quite clear that the breakdown of their relationship has given rise to a
considerable degree of animosity between the parties.
    [2] Mr Aoun was born in Lebanon and is a Lebanese citizen. However,
following his marriage in 1987 he and his wife went to live in Australia. He
acquired Australian nationality the same year. Until recently he owned a house
in Australia, but over the past few years he has lived in various countries
including Dubai, Greece and latterly the United Kingdom.

a [3] The present action was begun on 3 February 2000, but it is not the only litigation that has been commenced between these parties. In May 2000 Mr Angelou began proceedings in the First Court of Piraeus against Mr Aoun which led to the filing by Mr Aoun on 14 June 2000 of a pleading in which he gave his address as Beirut, Lebanon. On 13 October 2000 Mr Bahri's solicitors, Constant & Constant, wrote to Mr Aoun's then solicitors, Clyde & Co, seeking

b their agreement in principle to provide security for costs. Clyde & Co responded by saying that Mr Aoun lived in Athens, not Beirut, but that they would take his instructions. Despite two reminders, no proposals were forthcoming and so Constant & Constant issued their application on 5 April this year. A similar application was issued by Barlow Lyde & Gilbert on behalf of Mr Angelou on 20 April.

c [4] The defendants submit that the court has jurisdiction under CPR 25.13(2) to order Mr Aoun to provide security for costs on the following grounds: (a) that he is ordinarily resident outside the jurisdiction and is not a person against whom a claim can be enforced under the Brussels or Lugano Conventions (r 25.13(2)(a)); (b) that he has changed his address since the claim was commenced with a view to evading the consequences of the litigation (r 25.13(2)(d)); (c) that he gave an

d incorrect address in the claim form (r 25.13(2)(e)); and (d) that he has taken steps in relation to his assets that would make it more difficult to enforce an order for costs against him (r 25.13(2)(g)).

[5] The question of Mr Aoun's ordinary place of residence assumed a particular prominence in this application and the evidence relating to it developed significantly in the course of preparation for, and even during the course of, the

e hearing. It was principally because of the apparently unsatisfactory way in which Mr Aoun had dealt with this issue that when the matter came before me in July I took the unusual step of directing that he should attend the hearing of the application to enable him to be cross-examined. It is fair to say, however, that he did not resist the application; indeed, he seemed very willing to make himself

f available for that purpose.

[6] Mr Aoun did attend the hearing and was cross-examined at some length. His evidence assisted me in a number of respects, both in relation to the question of his ordinary place of residence and in relation to other issues. For reasons that will become apparent in due course, it became clear in the course of argument that Mr Aoun's ordinary place of residence is a matter of some sensitivity and

g I therefore propose to return to it after I have considered the other heads of jurisdiction on which the defendants rely.

Incorrect address given in the claim form

[7] It is convenient to begin with the defendants' contention that the address

h given for Mr Aoun in the claim form, 112 Agiou Nikolaou Street, Glyfada, Athens, was incorrect. Mr Dunning QC (whose submissions on this issue were adopted by Mr Davies) submitted that Mr Aoun's evidence concerning his address in Athens at and around the time of the issue of the claim form was wholly unsatisfactory and that in the absence of any more reliable evidence I should find

j that he had left the address in Agiou Nikolaou Street during January 2000 as his first witness statement implied.

[8] In that first witness statement Mr Aoun gave a brief account of where he had lived between his marriage in 1987 and the present time. He said that he had lived in Australia until 1992 when he moved to Geneva. After living there for about a year he moved to Dubai where he remained for a few more years. He eventually moved with his family to Athens in August 1999. He said that from

then on he had lived in Greece until he and his family moved to London in early *a*
December 2000.

[9] Mr Aoun originally said that he had moved into a house here in London on
2 December, the date on which the tenancy agreement had been signed. It
subsequently became clear from an examination of his passport, however, that he
did not enter the United Kingdom until 7 December 2000. This was one of the
discrepancies in his evidence that Mr Dunning relied on, but I am unable to attach *b*
a great deal of importance to it. I accept Mr Aoun's explanation that when he
made that statement he checked the date of the tenancy agreement to see when
he obtained possession of the house, but did not also check with his passport the
date on which he actually entered the country. It may be said that he was less
careful in giving his evidence than he should have been, but nothing turns on the
precise date and I can see no reason why Mr Aoun should have wished to pretend *c*
that he moved in on 2 December rather than 7 December.

[10] In a witness statement made at the end of June in response to Mr Aoun's
evidence Mr Dickinson of Constant & Constant took issue with much of what
Mr Aoun had said about his place of residence in the period between 1997 and
1999. He pointed out, among other things, that Mr Aoun had been in Athens on *d*
several occasions prior to 1999 and that in 1997 he had given an address in Beirut
to the Lebanese police rather than an address in Dubai. I do not attach any
importance to the fact that his passport shows that he was in Greece on various
occasions before 1999. His statement that he entered Greece for the first time in
1999 (another apparent discrepancy relied on by Mr Dunning) was made in the
context of dealing with his permanent residence, not relatively brief visits for *e*
business or other reasons. It is quite clear that for many years Mr Aoun has
travelled a very great deal on business, both to Greece and to many other
countries.

[11] In a second witness statement Mr Aoun responded to Mr Dickinson by
giving the various addresses at which he said he had resided in Greece from *f*
February 1999. These included the address at 112 Agiou Nikolaou Street, Athens,
where he said he had lived between 1 March and about May 1999 and an address
at Zaimei Street, Athens, where he said he had lived from about May 1999 to
April 2000. Finally, he said he had lived at another address in Athens, 1 Fillinon
Street, between June and December 2000.

[12] If what Mr Aoun said in that witness statement were true, it would follow *g*
that he was not living at 112 Agiou Nikolaou Street when the claim form was
issued on 3 February 2000. However, in a statement made on the first morning
of the hearing he sought to correct what he said had been a mistake by his
solicitors, saying that he had lived at 112 Agiou Nikolaou Street between
December 1999 and 28 February 2000. He said that from 1 March 2000 to October *h*
or November 2000 he had an apartment at Zaimei Street and from June to
December 2000 he had taken a house on Fillion (sic) Street for his family.

[13] As Mr Dunning pointed out, this degree of uncertainty on the part of
Mr Aoun as to his address of two years ago is surprising and does tend to cast
some doubt on his veracity. However, I think that one can now see that
something did indeed go wrong when his evidence was compiled. Mr Aoun had *j*
exhibited to his first statement rent receipts relating to two apartments at 112 Agiou
Nikolaou Street, one on the second floor and one on the third floor. He had put
these forward as 'a copy of a letter from the landlord' showing that when he left
the property all outstanding amounts had been paid. The receipts are both dated
8 December 1999 and record the payment of rent for the second floor apartment
and the third floor apartment for the period up to 3 January 2000. They can

a scarcely be described as 'a letter from the landlord', so I am inclined to accept Mr Aoun's explanation that at least in this respect there was a mistake. In those circumstances I am unable to accept Mr Dunning's submission that these documents, when taken together with his statement, are reliable evidence that Mr Aoun left that address on 3 January.

b [14] Mr Aoun exhibited to his second statement an agreement terminating a lease on the second floor apartment at 112 Agiou Nikolaou Street. It is dated 8 February 2000 and recites the fact that he and a Mr Tzoutzourakis had entered into a lease of the second floor apartment on 3 December 1999 and declares that Mr Aoun thereby terminated the lease and returned the keys. The agreement describes the apartment as 'already evacuated'. Mr Aoun had said nothing about the occupation of these two separate apartments in any of his statements,

c including his fourth statement made just before the hearing began, but he did give the impression that he and his family had moved out of their apartment in Agiou Nikolaou Street at short notice because of his fear of Mr Bahri. Indeed, on many occasions during his evidence he emphasised that he and his family had been continually harassed by Mr Bahri while they were living at different

d addresses in Athens.

[15] In cross-examination, however, Mr Aoun gave an account of his occupation of the apartments at Agiou Nikolaou Street which differed in at least one important respect from what he had said previously. He said that he and his family had originally occupied the second floor apartment and his parents the third floor apartment, but that he had moved into the third floor apartment when

e his parents moved out to emigrate to Australia. However, Mr Aoun's evidence of when his parents had gone to Australia was very vague. At an earlier point in his evidence he had said they had left Greece 'very late in 2000', but that clearly would not fit with the evidence of the agreement terminating the lease and he started to bring the date of their departure back to May or even April that year.

f However, even that was two or three months after the date of the termination agreement. He did not provide a satisfactory explanation for any of these obvious discrepancies.

[16] Mr Dunning submitted that in this matter, as in many others, Mr Aoun was caught up in his own lies. I would agree that Mr Aoun is not a witness whose evidence, at least in relation to this matter, can be relied on with any great degree

g of confidence, though I think that is due as much to his willingness to make ill-considered statements as to any desire to mislead. Mr Dunning also pointed out that by his own admission Mr Aoun had not wanted his address to become known to Mr Bahri and that he knew that the claim form would be served on both defendants soon after it had been issued. All that is quite true, but the fact

h remains that the documents do tend to support the conclusion that Mr Aoun rented both apartments at Agiou Nikolaou Street at least until early February 2000 and that he gave one up at about that time. I think that it is more likely than not that he did occupy one or other of them during that period. I am less inclined to accept that he occupied the third floor flat until the end of that month, but that

j is another matter. For these reasons, despite the fact that the evidence is not wholly satisfactory, I am not persuaded that the address given in the claim form was incorrect at the time it was issued.

Change of address since the commencement of the action with a view to evading the consequences of the litigation

[17] It is common ground that Mr Aoun has changed his address on more than one occasion since the commencement of the action. The only question is

whether he has done so with a view to evading the consequences of the litigation. *a*
His first change of address occurred when he moved from 112 Agiou Nikolaou
Street, but it has not been suggested that that was prompted by anything to do
with the present action.

[18] It might be thought that CPR 25.13(2)(d) is only concerned with a change
of address from that given in the claim form, but it is not expressly limited in that
way and I can see no reason to construe it as if it were. Paragraph (2) as a whole *b*
is concerned only with establishing the court's jurisdiction to order security for
costs; the decision whether to order security in any given case is a matter of the
court's discretion and will depend on the particular circumstances of the case.
The court can in any event only make such an order if it is satisfied that it is just
to do so (see CPR 25.13(1)). In these circumstances I think Mr Dunning is right *c*
in submitting that para (2) should generally be given a broader rather than a
narrower construction. Apart from that, however, para (2)(d) is aimed at the
claimant who seeks to go to ground to avoid his obligations and it is quite
possible, therefore, for the mischief at which para (2)(d) is aimed to arise on a
second or subsequent change of address.

[19] For similar reasons I also accept Mr Dunning's submission that the *d*
expression 'the consequences of the litigation' should not be construed as being
confined to an order for the payment by the claimant of the defendant's costs at
the end of the proceedings. Bringing proceedings in this country gives rise to
various consequences for a claimant, one of which, depending on the circumstances
of the case, is that he may be ordered to provide security for the defendant's costs. *e*
This is simply one of the many incidents of litigating in this country under the
existing rules of court. A claimant who changes his address during the course of
the action with a view to avoiding any of the ordinary consequences of the
litigation invites inquiry into whether he is likely to honour a liability for costs if
he is unsuccessful at the end of the day. It is consistent with the purpose of the
rules, therefore, for the court to have the power in such cases to consider *f*
whether, as a matter of discretion, an order for security should be made.

[20] Towards the end of 2000 Mr Aoun left Greece and moved with his family
to this country. Mr Dunning submitted that one, indeed the primary, reason for
his doing so was his desire to avoid providing security for the defendants' costs of
these proceedings. But even if that was not the dominant motive, the provisions *g*
of para (2)(d) were satisfied if it was a material factor behind his decision.

[21] The first request for security for costs was made in October 2000, some
two months before Mr Aoun left Greece. Mr Dunning pointed out, quite correctly,
that Mr Aoun had no previous connections with this country, whether in the
form of a right of abode, a previous period of residence, existing family ties or *h*
current business interests. On the contrary, all his connections were with Greece,
the Middle East (in particular Lebanon and Dubai) and Australia.

[22] Mr Aoun explained in cross-examination his motives for coming to live in
this country and for bringing his family here. They included a desire to live in a
safe and congenial environment and to bring up his children in an English-speaking *j*
society. He accepted that those particular objectives could have been achieved
by moving back to Australia, but he said that he wished to remain in Europe in
order to be able to build up his business interests without having to overcome the
difficulties posed by a substantial time difference and in order to be able to give
his personal attention to the present proceedings. For these reasons this country,
and in particular London, was for him an obvious choice.

[23] Having heard Mr Aoun give evidence on these matters I am satisfied that his decision to take up residence with his family in this country was motivated by personal and family considerations rather than a desire to avoid giving security for costs. Despite all the unsatisfactory aspects of Mr Aoun's evidence about his address in Greece at any given time, it seems reasonably clear that he was living in Athens in the autumn of 2000, although his wife and children returned to Australia at some time during the latter part of the year. I have no reason to think that before the defendants made their request for security in October 2000 Mr Aoun himself was aware of the court's jurisdiction to order a claimant to provide security for a defendant's costs. When that request was made his solicitors said they would take his instructions and no doubt they did so. It is likely that in the course of doing so they outlined the terms of CPR 25.13 in so far as they might relate to him and that they gave him a broad explanation of the circumstances in which the court might be expected to make an order of that kind. Mr Jacobs submitted that since Greece is a Brussels Convention country, Mr Aoun, as his solicitors must have been aware, was no better off coming to London than he would have been staying in Athens. That may be so, but moving to Australia would be a different matter altogether. Mr Aoun said in evidence that his wife and children had returned to Australia towards the end of 2000 and had lived with her brother for a time because their own house had been let, but he did not say that they had left Greece in a hurry or that they had gone to Australia as a temporary measure because they had nowhere else to go. In this connection Mr Dunning drew my attention to a document filed on Mr Aoun's behalf in Greek proceedings on 6 December 2000 in which it was stated that his family resided with him permanently in Australia.

[24] I think it is certainly possible that, having moved his family back to Australia with the intention of joining them there, Mr Aoun decided, on receiving advice from his solicitors about the court's jurisdiction to order security for costs, to move to this country rather than Australia. However, there is very little positive evidence to support that conclusion and in the end I do not consider that the evidence justifies drawing that inference. Accordingly, I am not satisfied that Mr Aoun falls within para (2)(d).

Taking steps in relation to his assets that would make it difficult to enforce an order for costs against him

[25] Mr Dunning submitted that, unlike sub-para (d), sub-para (g) of CPR 25.13(2) is worded objectively. It is not concerned with the claimant's motivation, though that may be relevant to the exercise of the court's discretion, but with the effect of steps he has taken in relation to his assets. This is a question of construction that was touched on by Park J in *Chandler v Brown* [2001] CP Rep 103 but left open for decision on another occasion.

[26] In my view Mr Dunning's submission is correct. The contrast between the wording of sub-para (g) and that of sub-para (d) is marked and I can see no basis for construing sub-para (g) as if it read 'with a view to making it difficult to enforce an order for costs against him'. If that had been the intention of those who drafted the rules they could very easily have said so. Nor is there any need to construe the provision in that way in order to limit its impact on claimants given the fact that the court can in any case order security only if it is satisfied that it is just to do so.

[27] In the present case there is little evidence as to the extent or nature of Mr Aoun's realisable assets other than the house in Australia. Certainly there is

no evidence that he has any significant assets in this country which might readily *a*
be made available to satisfy a liability for costs. He says that he has an indirect
interest in an office building in Greece and in a number of liquid petroleum gas
carriers, but in each case the property in question is owned by a private overseas
company with bearer shares. Leaving aside any question of mortgages or other
prior interests in the property itself, Mr Aoun is not the majority shareholder in
any of these companies and his shares would not represent assets readily available *b*
to satisfy a liability for costs. The company through which he now does business
is half owned by his brother-in-law. It is incorporated in the British Virgin Islands
and does not appear to own any substantial assets.

[28] The only step taken by Mr Aoun in relation to his assets on which the
defendants can rely is the recent sale of his house in Australia. The sale price was
the equivalent of about £400,000. A freehold property (provided it is unencumbered) *c*
is clearly an asset against which a judgment for costs could be enforced and that
remains the case even though the property is situated abroad, though the ease
with which that can be done will no doubt depend on the country in which it is
situated. Enforcement against property in Australia should not pose undue
difficulties. The only question, therefore, is whether the sale of that property has *d*
made it difficult to enforce an order for costs against him. In this context it should
be borne in mind that if this litigation does not reach a premature conclusion, the
costs are likely to be very substantial indeed and that Mr Aoun does not appear
to have other assets readily available to satisfy any order for costs that might be
made against him. In these circumstances any step in relation to that asset which
makes it difficult to enforce an order for costs against it will, on the evidence *e*
currently available, make it difficult to enforce an order for costs against
Mr Aoun.

[29] Mr Aoun says that he intends to put about a quarter of the proceeds of the
sale of his Australian house into a new house he is buying in London and to use
the balance for the purposes of his business. In these circumstances I have no *f*
doubt that the sale of his Australian property has had a significant effect on the
ease with which an eventual judgment for costs could be enforced against him.
Converting that asset into cash makes it readily disposable, but that by itself is not
enough since it might represent nothing more than a step on the way to
converting it into other assets of equal value. For example, if the whole of the
sale price were reinvested in a new house in this country, it would be easier to *g*
enforce an order for costs against him than it was before. The same would
probably be true if his intention were to reinvest the sale proceeds in ordinary
securities. In the present case, however, the realisation of the Australian property
is the first step towards making use of it to provide capital for his business
ventures. There is nothing in the evidence to suggest that the bulk of the *h*
proceeds of sale will remain available in one form or another to satisfy an order
for costs. In my judgment Mr Aoun's sale of the Australian house is, therefore, a
step in relation to his assets that would make it difficult to enforce an order for
costs against him. This is sufficient to give the court jurisdiction to make an order
for security for costs. *j*

Mr Aoun's ordinary place of residence

[30] In further witness statements made at the end of June this year
Mr Dickinson of Constant & Constant and Mr Wise of Barlow Lyde & Gilbert
raised for the first time the question of Mr Aoun's permission to stay in this
country, pointing out that neither he nor any member of his family has British

a citizenship. The introduction of this question, and Mr Aoun's response to it, have been mainly responsible for the expansion of the issues well beyond the bounds of what might normally be expected on an application of the present kind.

[31] Mr Aoun entered this country as a visitor in December 2000 with permission to remain for up to six months. He was subject to no restrictions other than a prohibition against taking up employment or having recourse to

b public funds. Since then he has travelled abroad on various occasions and each time he has returned he has been granted a fresh entry permit in the same terms.

[32] It was common ground that the test for 'ordinary residence' in this country is whether the person concerned is habitually and normally resident here, apart from temporary or occasional absences of long or short duration (see Shah v Barnet London BC [1983] 1 All ER 226, [1983] 2 AC 309). By 'habitually

c resident' is meant residence adopted voluntarily and for settled purposes (see [1983] 1 All ER 226 at 234, [1983] AC 309 at 342 per Lord Scarman). Mr Aoun has been living in this country with his wife and family since December 2000, he is in the course of buying a house here, his children are at school here and his youngest child was born here. There is no doubt that he is living here voluntarily and

d I have no doubt that he would like to continue living here for the foreseeable future. I think it is clear that he has adopted this country as his place of residence for settled purposes, at any rate for the time being, and he has put in train an application for permission to reside here in order to establish a business. I have no doubt that he is at the moment ordinarily resident here.

[33] However, Mr Davies (whose argument on this issue was adopted by

e Mr Dunning) submitted that Mr Aoun cannot be regarded as ordinarily resident for the purposes of CPR 25.13(a) because he is not here lawfully. In support of his argument he relied on another passage in the speech of Lord Scarman in Shah's case [1983] 1 All ER 226 at 235, [1983] 2 AC at 343–344 where he said:

f   '... I unhesitatingly subscribe to the view that "ordinarily resident" refers
        to a man's abode in a particular place or country which he has adopted
        voluntarily and for settled purposes as part of the regular order of his life for
        the time being, whether of short or of long duration. There is, of course, one
        important exception. If a man's presence in a particular place or country is
        unlawful, eg in breach of the immigration laws, he cannot rely on his unlawful

g   residence as constituting ordinary residence ...'

[34] Mr Davies submitted that although Mr Aoun has permission to remain in this country as a visitor, he obtained that permission by misleading the immigration authorities when he entered the country. He also submitted that by reason of his business activities in this country Mr Aoun is in breach of the conditions attaching

h to his permission to enter and remain here.

[35] These are serious allegations which depend in part on findings as to what took place when Mr Aoun presented himself at immigration control on last entering this country. They raise issues which in my view are not really suitable to be determined on an application for security for costs, and even though in this

j case Mr Aoun has given evidence and so has had an opportunity to respond to the points made against him, I do not think that there has been an opportunity to investigate the matter fully. It would be particularly unfortunate if I were to express any view about Mr Aoun's immigration status on the basis of incomplete evidence that might have an effect, one way or the other, on his application for a residence permit. That is a matter best left to the Home Office to be determined on its merits in the ordinary way. I do not in any way criticise the defendants for raising this question. However, since I have already reached the conclusion that I have jurisdiction to make an order for security for costs under CPR 25.13(2)(g), it has become unnecessary to decide it and in all the circumstances I think it preferable not to do so.

Discretion

[36] Mr Dunning submitted that there are at least three grounds on which it would be appropriate for the court to make a substantial order for security for costs in this case: the shortage of assets readily available to meet an order for costs; Mr Aoun's lack of any substantial connection with this jurisdiction; and the nature of his response to this application in general and the unsatisfactory and contradictory nature of his evidence in opposition to it in particular. To these he added the limited prospects of success at trial, although he accepted that that is a factor which the court can properly take into account only in clear cases.

[37] Although the court's discretion in CPR 25.13(1) is quite general, the terms of CPR 25.13(2) itself provide some indication of the circumstances which are likely to be relevant to its exercise in the case of a personal litigant. Broadly speaking, these are that there are grounds for thinking that the claimant's assets may be located in a jurisdiction where they are not readily amenable to execution or that the claimant himself may take steps to avoid his liability. In this context Mr Dunning drew my attention to the decision of the Court of Appeal in *De Beer v Kanaar & Co (a firm)* [2001] EWCA Civ 1318, [2002] CLC 114 in which the court relied on doubts about the claimant's probity, on the difficulties in enforcing an order for costs over assets abroad and on the ease with which those assets could be moved or otherwise disposed of.

[38] I do not propose to analyse Mr Aoun's evidence at length, but, as I have already indicated, I accept Mr Dunning's submission that it was shot through with inconsistencies and discrepancies. Many of these seem to me to reflect an exceptionally casual attitude to giving evidence rather than a deliberate intention to mislead; others are less easily explained. None the less, I think that there are more solid grounds in favour of making an order in this case. I have already commented on the nature and extent of Mr Aoun's assets and on the manner in which he proposes to deal with them. Apart from the proceeds of his Australian property they are not in a form which makes them readily available to meet an award of costs. Although Mr Aoun has offered to ensure that shares that he holds are retained by his solicitors pending the outcome of the action, they do not represent assets which the defendants could easily realise, as I have already explained.

[39] As far as the proceeds of the Australian property are concerned, there are no strong grounds for thinking that Mr Aoun would deliberately place these beyond the reach of the defendants, but he has expressed an intention to invest most of them in his business ventures. As far as one can tell, therefore, they will no longer be available to meet a liability of this kind and there is no reason to think that they will in fact generate other assets which might take their place. I do not think it is enough, therefore, for Mr Jacobs to say that Mr Aoun is bringing his assets into this country. One is entitled to see what is the likely outcome of the steps he has already taken in relation to those assets.

[40] Mr Aoun says that he intends to invest part of the sale proceeds in a new house which he is currently buying in this country and it has been suggested that that property, which he says is mainly to be financed by an unsecured loan from his brother-in-law, would itself provide sufficient security for any liability to the

a defendants. I am unable to accept that. Even if the new house were to be conveyed into Mr Aoun's name alone without any encumbrances, it would be difficult to ensure that it remained available for satisfying an order for costs without formal steps being taken to preserve the defendants' position. In any event, in the case of an asset of this kind it is generally preferable to require the claimant to provide security in the form of a bank guarantee or similar instrument
b which can be supported by a charge on the property (see *AP (UK) Ltd v West Midlands Fire and Civil Defence Authority* [2001] EWCA Civ 1917, [2001] All ER (D) 252 (Nov)). If the claimant is unable to provide a commercial guarantee against the security of the property, it is unlikely that the court will require the defendant to accept security in the form of a charge, though it may do so in an appropriate case. There is nothing, however, to suggest that that would be appropriate in the
c present case.

[41] Mr Dunning made two further submissions based on the nature of the claim being made by Mr Aoun in these proceedings. The primary way in which Mr Aoun puts his case is as a claim for damages for fraud and breach of fiduciary duty in relation to the management and operation of a number of vessels which
d the parties had agreed to operate as a joint venture. He seeks to recover by way of damages the diminution in value of his beneficial interest in the various companies through which the joint venture was conducted. Recently, however, Mr Aoun has indicated that he will seek to amend his particulars of claim to allege in the alternative that there was a partnership between himself and the two defendants. The underlying facts on which he relies are the same, however, and
e it is clear that if this litigation is fought to judgment it will prove burdensome and very expensive because the parties' business arrangements encompassed nine vessels, each separately owned, and a further eight companies.

[42] Mr Dunning submitted that, however it is formulated, Mr Aoun's claim is manifestly weak. He submitted, therefore, that this is one of those cases in
f which the court can take into account the merits of the claimant's case as a factor going to the exercise of its discretion. He also submitted that an additional reason for ordering security for costs in the present case is to prevent Mr Aoun from making expansive allegations against the defendants that can only be countered at great expense.

[43] I can well understand why Mr Dunning makes those submissions, but
g this is clearly a complex case. On an application of this kind the court does not need to, nor should it in my view, embark on any assessment of the merits. As far as Mr Dunning's second point is concerned, it is true that the allegations of fraud and breach of fiduciary duty are not pleaded as fully as they might be, but the pleadings were settled by highly-respected counsel and I see no grounds for
h thinking that there was inadequate material to support them. I do not think it appropriate, therefore, to take either of these matters into account in reaching a decision.

[44] What seems to me to be most important in this case is the fact that Mr Aoun is pursuing very substantial litigation against these two defendants who
j will inevitably be put to a great deal of expense in meeting his allegations. Although he is currently settled in this country, he has few assets here of a fixed nature and he has, moreover, shown that he is eminently capable of making a home for himself and his family in different parts of the world when circumstances make it desirable to do so. In my view there are solid grounds for thinking that if he is unsuccessful in this litigation and is ordered to pay the defendants' costs it will be difficult to enforce such an order against him.

Although it appears to be accepted that he is indirectly interested in the ships
which he operated with the defendants as a shareholder of the owning
companies, the extent of his interest is disputed and the value of the equity in the
ships is uncertain. His offer to deposit his shares in the owning companies is
therefore of limited value. He has said that he is also willing to deposit with his
solicitors his shares in a company which owns an office building in Athens, but
again there is the difficulty that Mr Aoun is not the majority shareholder in the
company and there is no reason to think that it would be easy for the defendants
to enforce an order for costs against the assets themselves. The fact is that if any
of these shares have any realisable commercial value, it would be more
appropriate for Mr Aoun to use them as counter-security for a bank guarantee in
favour of the defendants.

[45] Mr Aoun has said that he is unable to put up substantial security, but that
assertion does not sit happily with the suggestion that his shares in the various
companies to which I have referred should be sufficient security for the
defendants. Nor is it supported by any detailed description of his assets or his
sources of finance. Moreover, it is clear from other evidence before the court that
apart from his commercial interests he has been able to obtain a substantial
amount of support from his wife's family. On the material before me I am unable
to find that an order for security would have the effect of stifling his claim. In
these circumstances I am satisfied that it would be just to make an order for
security in favour of both defendants.

[46] Mr Bahri seeks security in the sum of £315,000 and Mr Angelou in the
sum of over £270,000, in each case in respect of the period up to and including the
exchange of witness statements. These are very large sums by any standards.
I accept that they reflect the nature and magnitude of the litigation, but I think
that allowance must be made for the likelihood of a reduction on a detailed
assessment and for the possibility that this case may settle at an early stage. I think
it also right to ensure that the total amount of security ordered is not so great as
to be oppressive. I shall therefore hear counsel further on the amount and form
in which security should be provided.

Order accordingly.

Martyn Gurr   Barrister.

Sharif and others v Garrett & Co (a firm)

[2001] EWCA Civ 1269

COURT OF APPEAL, CIVIL DIVISION

SIMON BROWN, CHADWICK AND TUCKEY LJJ

21, 31 JULY 2001

Solicitor – Negligence – Damages – Action struck out for want of prosecution – Assessment of damages against solicitors where action struck out because delay on their part had rendered impossible fair trial of action – Approach to be adopted.

In February 1985 part of the claimants' warehouse was destroyed by fire. The insurance arranged by brokers to cover the risk did not pay, and so the claimants retained the defendant firm of solicitors to sue the brokers. In April 1992 the claim against the brokers was struck out for want of prosecution, the judge holding that it was not fair for the action to proceed because it was impossible to investigate, inter alia, the availability of alternative insurance cover and the ability of the brokers to obtain it. The claimants then brought proceedings against the solicitors. Liability was admitted and it was agreed that, if their claim against the brokers had succeeded, the claimants would have recovered losses resulting from the fire of at least £842,000 plus interest. At the assessment of damages in November 1999, the claimants called no evidence. The judge allowed the solicitors to call the broker who had been responsible for the placement and an insurance expert. The latter gave evidence that the claimants' risk was uninsurable with the conventional market, although he accepted that there were other insurance markets outside the United Kingdom in which the brokers might have sought to place the risk, but which they had not tapped. The claimants contended that the court ought to find that cover might have been secured in an unspecified overseas market, but the judge rejected that contention on the basis that the claimants had called no evidence in support of it. Accordingly, he held that the only losses that the claimants were entitled to recover were the premium paid for the insurance and the costs paid to the solicitors plus interest, some £23,000 in total. On the claimants' appeal, the Court of Appeal considered the correct approach to the assessment of damages for loss of a claim where that claim had been struck out on the grounds that a fair trial of the issues was no longer possible as a result of delay by the claimants' solicitors. The solicitors contended that, if there were evidence that helped the judge to determine whether the claimant had lost a chance and to assess its value, he should hear it even if, in effect, that involved trying the issue in the original action, and that it would not be just to solicitors to assume the issue against them in the face of available evidence to the contrary.

Held – (1) Where a claim had been struck out on the grounds that a fair trial of the issue or issues was no longer possible as a result of delay by the claimants' solicitors, and the claimant subsequently brought a claim for negligence against the solicitors in respect of the lost claim, the judge, in assessing the claimant's prospects of success in the original claim, had to start with the conclusion, reached by the judge on the striking out application, that no fair trial had been possible. He could not, and therefore should not, attempt to try the issue or issues himself, particularly on the evidence of the defendant in the original proceedings. That did not mean that those issues had to be assumed against the solicitor since the legal burden remained on the claimant to show that he would have succeeded on them. However, such a result might be produced in practice by the application of two settled principles, namely (i) that the evidential burden lay on the solicitors to show that the litigation had been of no value to their client, so that he had lost nothing by their negligence in causing it to be struck out, and (ii) that, if and in so far as the court might have greater difficulty in discerning the strength of the claimant's original claim than it would have had at the time of the original action, such difficulty should not count against him, but rather against his negligent solicitors. In such a case, the claimant would normally be expected to be able to show that he had had real and substantial prospects of success. The judge then had to evaluate those prospects by making a realistic assessment of the claimant's prospects of success if the original litigation had been fought out. If he were asked to hear evidence that the other side would have called in the first action, or expert evidence of the kind called in the instant case, he could agree to do so, but he should not feel bound to do so if he were of the opinion that he could otherwise make a fair evaluation. If he did hear such evidence, it would simply be for the purpose of enabling him to form a better broad view of the merits of the claim (see [18], [21], [22], [36], [45], below); *Mount v Barker Austin (a firm)* [1998] PNLR 493 considered.

(2) In the instant case, the judge's approach had not been correct. The claimants' evidential difficulty was the very reason why their claims had been struck out in the first place. It should not have been held against them seven-and-a-half-years later. The judge could not and should not have attempted to try the issue of whether alternative insurance cover would have been available. Although there were obvious difficulties with the case against the brokers, they did not justify the conclusion that the prospects of success were negligible. The judge should have held that the claimants had had a real and substantial claim against the brokers on the basis that, but for their negligence, they would have obtained alternative cover. Accordingly, the appeal would be allowed, and, taking into account their prospects of success and other factors, the claimants would be awarded £250,000 damages on the basis that that would have been the value of their claim if it had come to trial in July 1989 (see [27]–[29], [34]–[36], [41], [42], [44], [45], below).

Notes

For damages for loss of an opportunity, see 12(1) *Halsbury's Laws* (4th edn reissue) paras 962–968.

Cases referred to in judgments

Allied Maples Group Ltd v Simmons & Simmons (a firm) [1995] 4 All ER 907, [1995] 1 WLR 1602, CA.

Armory v Delamirie (1722) 1 Stra 505, [1558–1774] All ER Rep 121, 93 ER 664.

Harrison v Bloom Camillin (a firm) [2000] Lloyd's Rep PN 89.

Kitchen v Royal Air Forces Association [1958] 2 All ER 241, [1958] 1 WLR 563, CA.

Mount v Barker Austin (a firm) [1998] PNLR 493, CA.

Cases also cited or referred to in skeleton arguments

Buckley v National Union of General and Municipal Workers [1967] 3 All ER 767.

a *Kenning v Eve Construction Ltd* [1989] 1 WLR 1189.
    Oksuzoglu v Kay [1998] 2 All ER 361, CA.
    Sainsbury (J) plc v Broadway Malyan [1999] PNLR 286.
    Swale Storage & Distribution Services Ltd v Sittingbourne Paper Co Ltd (1998) 95(34)
        LSG 32, CA.
    Yardley v Coombes (1963) 107 Sol Jo 575.

b
Appeal
The appellants, Mohammed Sharif, Mohammed Ghafoor and Mohammed Arshad Sharif, trading as M Sharif Cash and Carry (a firm), appealed with permission of the Court of Appeal granted on 28 September 2000 from the decision of Judge Perrett QC in the Birmingham District Registry (Mercantile List) on 27 January 2000 that they were entitled to damages of only £23,000 plus interest in their proceedings for negligence against the respondent firm of solicitors, Garrett & Co. The facts are set out in the judgment of Tuckey LJ.

c

Christopher Gardner QC and *Paul Emerson* (instructed by *Shakespeares*, Birmingham)
d   for the appellants.
Robert Moxon-Browne QC and *Francis Bacon* (instructed by *Beachcroft Wansbroughs*,
    Bristol) for the solicitors.

Cur adv vult

e 31 July 2001. The following judgments were delivered.

TUCKEY LJ (giving the first judgment at the invitation of Simon Brown LJ).

Introduction
    [1] In February 1985 part of the appellants' cash and carry warehouse in
f Birmingham was destroyed by fire. The insurance arranged by brokers (PBL) to cover this risk did not pay and so the appellants retained the respondent solicitors to sue PBL. The claim against PBL was struck out for want of prosecution in 1992 and these proceedings against the solicitors followed. Liability was admitted and it was agreed that if the appellants' claim against PBL had succeeded they would have recovered losses resulting from the fire of at least £842,000 plus interest.
g However, on the assessment of damages Judge Perrett QC held that the only losses they were entitled to recover were the premium paid for the insurance (about £12,000) and the costs paid to the solicitors (about £11,000) plus interest. The appellants appeal with the permission of this court saying the judge was wrong to conclude that their prospects of recovering their uninsured losses from
h PBL were negligible. They say their prospects were good and the judge should have awarded them substantial damages for loss of a chance.

The insurance
    [2] In view of the judge's unchallenged finding that the appellants would have
j established negligence against PBL, it is not necessary to relate the insurance history at great length. However, the appellants had a poor claims record. Between 1977 and February 1983 they were insured by the Phoenix who paid a flood claim of £14,000 in 1977 (in respect of other premises), a flood claim of £37,000 in May 1982 and a fire claim of £1·3m in August 1982. In February 1983 the Phoenix declined to renew cover for the cash and carry warehouse without saying why. The appellants then obtained cover from INA for 12 months but INA

declined to renew, apparently as a result of information they had received from
the Phoenix, which they refused to divulge. At this stage PBL were approached *a*
to try and arrange cover and purported to have done so for 12 months from 23
March 1984 through a company or firm called MGM whom, it was claimed, held
binding authorities from a number of major insurance companies. In fact MGM
had no such authority and in October 1984 they informed PBL that the risk had
been transferred to a company called St Eustatius. This company was registered *b*
in the Dutch Antilles. The appellants were simply advised by PBL in November
1984 that the cover should be placed elsewhere as soon as possible.

[3] The judge found that the appellants—

> 'were misled from the date of supposed inception of the MGM policy into
> believing that they were viably insured against the perils in respect of which *c*
> they had paid a premium. No prudent insurance broker should have assumed
> in those circumstances that cover had been successfully effected; still less
> should a prudent insurance broker have been cajoled into assuming that
> cover was transferred to St Eustatius ... I find therefore that had the action
> come to trial the claimant would have succeeded in establishing that PBL *d*
> were negligent in allowing the claimants to suppose and in themselves
> believing that there had at any time been viable and/or continuing insurance
> cover against the perils paid for by the claimants for the period in which the
> fire occurred.'

[4] PBL's documents show that between November 1984 and the date of the *e*
fire they approached a firm of Lloyd's brokers in London and two insurance
companies and a broker (Stewart Wrightson) in Birmingham who were unable
to place or declined to accept the risk.

The proceedings against PBL   *f*

[5] The solicitors were retained soon after the fire. As well as PBL, St Eustatius,
MGM and their principal were defendants to the proceedings which were started
in March 1986. By this time St Eustatius had refused to pay the fire claim on the
ground, among others, that the appellants had failed to disclose the 1977 flood
claim. They had also contended that cover was limited to £750,000.

[6] The statement of claim settled by counsel alleged that St Eustatius were *g*
liable for the full value of the claim and that the 1977 flood claim was not material.
The claim was put against PBL in the alternative on the basis that, if the 1977
flood claim was material, it had not been disclosed on the proposal form on PBL's
advice and that they had failed to inform the appellants that their cover was
limited. It was alleged that if the appellants had been informed that their cover *h*
was limited to £750,000, they would have obtained additional or alternative
cover.

[7] Soon after the proceedings were issued St Eustatius went into liquidation
and it became clear that they and the other defendants, apart from PBL, were not
worth suing.   *j*

[8] By 16 April 1987 the solicitors were reporting to the appellants' loss
adjusters as follows: 'After several conferences with counsel and our insurance
expert, we take the view that there are reasonable prospects of success ...' This
is the only record of their having expressed any view about the merits of the
claim. It is common ground that at no stage did they advise the appellants that
their claim was hopeless or likely to fail. Indeed from this time right up to the

a time when the claim was struck out they were saying to the appellants that they thought that PBL's solicitors were likely to make an offer of settlement.

[9] Following the conferences referred to in the letter to the adjusters, counsel drafted an amended statement of claim which was served in July 1987 so, as he said, 'to re-cast the claim in order to make (PBL) the primary target'. To this end he deleted the allegations relating to the St Eustatius cover and PBL's responsibility b for its avoidance and/or limitation and alleged that PBL were negligent in much the same way as the judge found. The consequences of this negligence were pleaded as follows:

c 'By reason of the ... breaches ... The Plaintiffs at all material times until the said fire believed themselves to be insured. In the circumstances they took such normal precautions as a prudent insured should take as follows ... Had they realised they were not insured they would have taken the extreme precautions that they have taken since the fire (which are set out below) and would have avoided the damage they suffered ...'

In the advice which accompanied the draft amendment, counsel noted (as was d the fact) that the claim was now very different and that its success depended upon the court accepting the expert's view that PBL had been negligent. He continued:

'Causation is also a crucial question. Of course an insured is required to take all reasonable precautions. Might a man not take extreme precautions if he knows that he is not insured which he might not take if he thought he e was insured? ... If the expert is adamant that the client would be expected to take the same precautions whether he was insured or not, it would be difficult if not impossible to establish liability.'

[10] It is clear from the documents that the expert was not prepared to alter his views on this point. What is not clear is why counsel did not at this stage plead f that if the appellants had been told that they were not insured, they would have obtained other cover or other cover on terms. This was a question which had been considered by the expert and which counsel specifically dealt with when he later advised in 1989. He described one of PBL's real defences as:

g 'Plaintiffs have suffered no damage ... since their claims record was so poor that they would not have obtained other insurance anyway and (PBL's) strenuous efforts in about November and December 1984 ... were unavailing.'

He continued:

h 'This is a substantial defence and one which I find very troubling. The Plaintiffs could lose on this point and, as a result, be landed with all the costs of the action. There appear to be two possible answers to it. Our expert suggests that [PBL] should have selected their most likely, friendly (i.e. supportive) insurer and asked what improvements in security would enable the risk as thus improved to be acceptable despite the claims record. The j documents disclosed by [PBL] indicate that this was not done. What likelihood was there in the circumstances that such a ... course might have proved successful? This is of course a matter of speculation. What is our expert's view as to this? If he feels that there was a reasonable chance and can back up his opinion with examples, the client would, at the very least, be entitled to damages for loss of that chance through the breach of contract and negligence of [PBL]. The value of such a chance would be assessed as a

percentage of the total recoverable damage suffered. As the claim is very
substantial the damages recovered under such head would also be substantial.   *a*
It is essential that the expert is consulted as to this as soon as possible. If,
having seen the efforts made by [PBL] he comes to the conclusion that there
was no chance of placing the insurance anywhere else, we would have to fall
back on the second of our two answers.'
                                                                                  b
That was a reference to the point which had been pleaded to the effect that if they
had known they were uninsured the appellants would have taken extreme
precautions to prevent fire.

[11] The expert's reply to these questions came in a supplementary report
dated August 1989. He said:
                                                                                  c
'I am asked whether another insurer would have accepted the risk if
improvements were made. All such risks are capable of being insured
subject to two matters. First, the moral hazard. Insurers must be convinced
that clients ran their business efficiently, that their integrity was beyond
reproach and that they were likely to co-operate over whatever stipulations   *d*
as to security were made following surveys. Second, the claims history.
Some proposers are clearly accident prone. The incidence of claims may
appear such that only some inherent fault, not necessarily negligence exists
in a client's make-up ... A prudent and experienced broker may well be able
to extract such answers from his client as to convince first himself and then
underwriters that no element of moral hazard or inherent propensity to   *e*
accident is involved. His duty is then to put pressure on their most friendly
insurer to carry out thorough fire, flood and burglary surveys of the premises
on a no commitment basis. If necessary offering a co-insurance clause. Not
50% as here, but a sufficiently significant proportion—perhaps 25%—as to
satisfy the insurers that the client was as involved, pro rata to the depths of   *f*
the respective pockets ...'

He added: 'The broker should have tried. What the Plaintiff lost is a chance.' In
his earlier report he pointed out that the appellants were in the worst of all
possible situations—believing they were insured when, effectively, they were not.

[12] I should say in relation to moral hazard that in 1985 the solicitors saw the   *g*
appellants' accountant who had had a meeting in 1984 with the loss adjusters who
had acted for the Phoenix in the claims against them. They had told him they
were satisfied as to the circumstances of all the claims otherwise payment would
not have been made and there was no reason to believe that the appellants were
in any way implicated in the fire or other claims which had been made. It is also   *h*
the case that the appellants had other insurances which had been renewed
without difficulty. Their problems were confined to the cash and carry warehouse
and its contents.

[13] To return to the history. From the end of 1989 the action effectively went
to sleep due to the inaction of the solicitors despite the appellants' repeated   *j*
attempts to spur them on. Although he had asked for a large amount of further
information in his 1989 advice, no further advice was sought from counsel and
very little of the further information he had asked for was obtained before PBL
applied to strike the claim out at the end of 1991.

[14] This application was heard by Tucker J on 2 April 1992. The note of that
part of his judgment dealing with prejudice says:

a   'First witness memories have faded. In that regard the plaintiffs' counsel submitted that this was a complex commercial case based on documents. I disagree. It is clear that witness evidence is required, for example to deal with the question of security arrangements, the availability of alternative insurance cover and the ability of [PBL] to obtain such cover. In my view it would be impossible to investigate such matters now.'

b   There was no appeal from this decision.

The assessment

[15] The hearing of the assessment took place in November 1999—15 years after PBL were alleged to have been negligent. It was agreed that the documents
c   relating to the insurance and the proceedings against PBL could be relied on as evidence of their contents. The appellants called no evidence. Despite objection from the appellants the judge allowed the solicitors to call Mr McGreevy, the PBL broker responsible for this placement, and Mr Gray, an insurance expert. Mr McGreevy's evidence was directed primarily to saying that PBL had not been
d   negligent. The judge summarised Mr Gray's evidence as follows:

'In 1982 this risk was uninsurable with the conventional market ... His opinion was confirmed by the exhaustive efforts made by PBL which failed to elicit a single quotation. He said in evidence that if Stewart Wrightson (a very large firm of brokers with a lot of muscle) could not place the business,
e   no one could. He agreed that there were other, non-United Kingdom insurance markets in which it might have been sought to place the risk and that PBL had not tapped such markets.'

[16] The judge then records counsel for the appellants' submission that the
f   court—

'ought to find that although the United Kingdom conventional market was unwilling to provide cover, even at an enhanced premium, cover might yet have been secured in some other overseas but otherwise unspecified market.'

g   He continued:

'I wish I could accept his submission but the claimants called no evidence in support of that contention and it is the experience of this court, as exemplified in this case with insurers based abroad who are not licensed to
h   underwrite business in the United Kingdom, that secondary or tertiary markets, even if they are persuaded to accept the business, are notoriously fickle when claim time comes. So, in the absence of any evidence to the contrary, I regrettably conclude that in any market worth the premium or even a greatly enhanced premium the claimants were uninsurable.'

j   [17] The judge had earlier rejected the way in which the case had been pleaded against PBL in the amended statement of claim. He said that as no positive evidence had been called about the extent or spread of the fire and what might have happened if the fire brigade had attended earlier, he was unable to conclude that extreme precautions would have prevented or limited the consequences of the fire.

The law

[18] There is no dispute between the parties about the law which applies to the assessment of damages in a case such as this. The applicable principles were admirably summarised by Simon Brown LJ in *Mount v Barker Austin (a firm)* [1998] PNLR 493 at 510–511 as follows:

'1. The legal burden lies on the plaintiff to prove that in losing the opportunity to pursue his claim (or defence to counter-claim) he has lost something of value *i.e.* that his claim (or defence) had a real and substantial rather than merely a negligible prospect of success ... 2. The evidential burden lies on the defendants to show that despite their having acted for the plaintiff in the litigation and charged for their services, that litigation was of no value to their client, so that he lost nothing by their negligence in causing it to be struck out. Plainly the burden is heavier in a case where the solicitors have failed to advise their client of the hopelessness of his position ... If, of course, the solicitors *have* advised their client with regard to the merits of his claim (or defence) such advice is likely to be highly relevant. 3. If and insofar as the court may now have greater difficulty in discerning the strength of the plaintiff's original claim (or defence) than it would have had at the time of the original action, such difficulty should not count against him, but rather against his negligent solicitors. It is quite likely that the delay would have caused such difficulty and quite possible, indeed, that that is why the original action was struck out in the first place. That, however, is not inevitable: it will not be the case in particular (a) where the original claim (or defence) turned on questions of law or the interpretation of documents, or (b) where the only possible prejudice from the delay can have been to the other side's case. 4. If and when the court decides that the plaintiff's chances in the original action were more than merely negligible it will then have to evaluate them. That requires the court to make a realistic assessment of what would have been the plaintiff's prospects of success had the original litigation been fought out. Generally speaking one would expect the court to tend towards a generous assessment given that it was the defendants' negligence which lost the plaintiff the opportunity of succeeding in full or fuller measure.'

[19] These principles are largely taken from the leading cases of *Kitchen v Royal Air Forces Association* [1958] 2 All ER 241, [1958] 1 WLR 563 and *Allied Maples Group Ltd v Simmons and Simmons (a firm)* [1995] 4 All ER 907, [1995] 1 WLR 1602 and have been applied in a number of cases to which we were referred. But there is no authority which gives any guidance as to how the court should approach its task in a case where the original claim has been struck out because a fair trial of the issue or issues in question was no longer possible as a result of delay by the claimant's solicitors. We have been asked to give guidance because we are told that such cases are typical of those made against solicitors.

[20] Mr Moxon-Browne QC, for the solicitors, says that the task which the judge has to perform when striking out is different from the assessment which the judge has to make when considering whether the claimant has lost a chance and, if so, what it is worth. If there is evidence to help him with this difficult task, he should hear it even if this does in effect involve trying the issue. It would not be just to solicitors to assume the issue against them in the face of available evidence to the contrary.

a

[21] Although on a strike out the judge may not have to investigate whether or not an issue or issues can still be fairly tried in great detail, I think his conclusion that no such trial is possible must be the starting point for the judge who later has to make an assessment of the claimant's prospects of success. He cannot and therefore should not attempt to try the issue or issues himself, particularly on the evidence of the negligent solicitor's former clients' opponent in the original

b

proceedings. In a case like the present where the legal burden is on the claimant to show that he would have succeeded on the issue or issues in question, I do not go so far as to say that they must be assumed against the solicitor, but the application of the second and third principles in *Mount's* case may in practice produce this result. So, in such a case one would normally expect the claimant to be able to show that he had real and substantial prospects of success. This will

c

not produce unjust results; what would be unjust is for the judge to try an issue which has already been held to be untriable because of the solicitor's negligent delay.

[22] The judge then has to evaluate those prospects applying the fourth principle in *Mount's* case. This is a difficult task but no more difficult than many

d

others involved in the assessment of damages where the court has to predict the unknown. Here, the judge is having to put a value on the claim. This is not a science, but is a task which lawyers are used to performing. The judge will obviously need to consider all the relevant material which was available up to the time when the original claim was struck out, including documents disclosed and witness statements exchanged by the other side. If he is asked to hear the

e

evidence which the other side would have called, or expert evidence of the kind called in this case, he may agree to do so but I do not think he should feel bound to do so if he thinks he can otherwise make a fair evaluation. If he does hear such evidence, it would simply be for the purpose of enabling him to form a better broad view of the merits of the claim.

f

The appeal

[23] The main point on the appeal is whether the judge properly applied the *Mount* principles in reaching the conclusions which he did. But before considering this, I think it is convenient to deal with the point taken in the respondent's notice which is that by the amendment to their statement of claim in July 1987 the

g

appellants abandoned any case that if they had been properly advised by PBL they would have obtained alternative insurance. So, it is submitted, the judge should not have considered this question at all.

[24] I have set out the history of the proceedings in some detail in order to deal with this point. From that history it seems to me quite clear that it was never

h

intended to abandon this allegation. It should have been made in the amended statement of claim, but if the case had been properly conducted by the solicitors I have no doubt that the pleadings would have been amended to make the necessary allegations before trial. Both parties were preparing for trial on the basis that this would have been one of the main issues. The judge does not deal

j

with this point in his judgment, but I have no doubt that he was right to proceed on the basis that it was, or would have been, the appellants' case that if they had been properly advised by PBL, alternative insurance would have been obtained.

[25] So I return to the main point of the appeal. Mr Gardner for the appellants accepts that the judge did set out the *Mount* principles in his judgment. But, he submits, when he came to make the crucial findings to which I have referred, the judge failed to apply them. He effectively tried the issues of insurability and

extreme precautions himself on the evidence which was called at the hearing and drew adverse inferences against the claimants for their failure to call evidence. Mr Moxon-Browne, on the other hand, submits that the solicitors discharged the heavy burden on them of showing that neither of the ways in which causation was put had any real prospect of success. On the issue of insurability, he relies on the appellants' poor claims record, PBL's unsuccessful efforts to obtain alternative cover for them, the evidence of Mr Gray which was to much the same effect as a report from another expert obtained on behalf of PBL and the views of the appellants' own counsel and expert in the original proceedings to which I have referred.

[26] The starting point for any consideration of the appellants' prospects of success on the issue of insurability ought to have been Tucker J's finding that it was not fair for the action to proceed against PBL because it was impossible to investigate, among other things, the availability of alternative insurance cover and the ability of PBL to obtain it. If that was the position in 1992, seven-and-a-half years later the task would have been even more difficult. The point is underlined by the fact that in 1984 Mr Gray had only been in the industry for two years and so had to seek the views of others as to the state of the market at that time for the purpose of giving evidence.

[27] Nevertheless, in the passage dealing with insurability which I have quoted, the judge appears to have overlooked what I have just said. He refers to the fact that 'the claimants called no evidence in support of their contention' and 'in the absence of evidence to the contrary'. I do not think this was the right approach. The appellant's evidential difficulty was the very reason why their claims had been struck out in the first place. It should not have been held against them seven-and-a-half years later. The judge could not and should not have attempted to try that issue.

[28] There were obvious difficulties with the case against PBL, but I do not think they justified the judge's conclusion that the prospects of success were negligible. PBL's documented attempts to obtain alternative cover were not impressive. There were obviously markets which had not been approached. The presumption that foreign insurers do not provide effective cover is entirely unjustified. The suggestions made by the appellants' expert of cover being provided subject to improved security measures and/or risk sharing by the insured (co-insurance) were viable alternatives which could have been pursued. If PBL had felt themselves unable to take any of these steps they could and should have said so. The real problem which they created was that the appellants believed they were insured when they were not.

[29] For these reasons I think the judge should have held that the appellants had a real and substantial claim against PBL on the basis that, but for PBL's negligence, they would have obtained alternative cover. This makes it unnecessary to consider the alternative way in which the appellants put their case except as part of the overall assessment of the appellants' prospects. But here again it seems to me that the judge placed an unjustified evidential burden on the appellants. Despite this, however, there were formidable difficulties about putting the case in this way. The most obvious one arose from what the appellants' expert was saying. His point was that whether or not someone is insured should not make any difference to the precautions he takes to avoid loss. Put another way, an insured is required to act in the same way as a prudent uninsured. It follows that an insurer or, as here, an insurance broker, cannot be expected to foresee that someone who thinks he is insured would take different precautions if he knew he

a was uninsured. For this reason I think the judge was right to conclude that the appellants' prospects of succeeding in this alternative way of putting their case were negligible.

b [30] So, how should the appellants' prospects of success be rated having regard to the fourth principle in *Mount v Barker Austin (a firm)* [1998] PNLR 493 and the broad view of the merits which the judge was required to take? The parties took up extreme positions. Mr Gardner submitted that the full value of the claim should only be reduced by 10% to reflect what he called the risks of litigation. Mr Moxon-Browne submitted that its value should be measured by the payment into court of £26,000 which PBL made and which he suggests the appellants were tempted to take.

c [31] I do not think either party's stance is realistic. Although the judge found that the appellants would have established negligence, the claim was not entirely straightforward because PBL (apparently in common with other brokers in the market at the time) were the victims of fraud by those behind MGM. The causation argument, as I have said, posed obvious difficulties. As their counsel said in 1989, the appellants could well have lost on this point. This must be

d reflected in a substantial way in any assessment of their prospects. Other factors which would have affected the amount which the appellants recovered are that at the outset they would almost certainly have had to pay a much larger premium to obtain cover and would probably have had to pay for expensive security measures and take a share of say 25% of the risk as a condition of obtaining it. They were also likely to incur legal costs in pursuing the claim against PBL. Of

e course, if they had been successful they would have recovered most but by no means all of those costs, but if they had failed the exposure was substantial.

[32] In short, there was a substantial risk that the appellants would lose altogether and if they won they were most unlikely to recover the full value of their claim.

f [33] As I have said, the appellants' losses as a result of the fire were agreed to be at least £842,000. Interest to mid-1989 added about 65% to whatever the claim was worth. The judge records the appellants' contention that their losses were understated by about £150,000 because they had been unable fully to reinstate the building and its fixtures and fittings to their pre-fire condition through impecuniosity caused by PBL's negligence. The judge did not decide whether they were right

g about this and we are not in a position to do so although I think it should be taken into account in the broad assessment which has to be made.

[34] Taking account of the appellants' prospects of success and the other factors to which I have referred, I would award the appellants £250,000 on the basis that this is what their claim (including interest) was worth if it had come to

h trial in July 1989. That means that they are entitled to interest on this amount for 12 years. This award will be in substitution for the amount awarded by the judge so my assessment has taken account of the fact that the appellants did pay premium and costs of about £23,000 which they have not got back.

[35] For these reasons I would allow this appeal and substitute an order which

j reflects what I have said for the order made by the judge.

CHADWICK LJ.

[36] I have had the advantage of reading, in draft, the judgments of the other two members of the court. I agree with those judgments and wish only to emphasise the particular feature of this case. The judge fell into the error of seeking to try the very issue which Tucker J had held, some seven years earlier, could not be the

subject of a fair trial. This was a course which, in the interests of a due
administration of justice, the judge ought to have been astute to avoid.   *a*

SIMON BROWN LJ.

[37] This is a claim for damages against solicitors for loss of the opportunity to
litigate (or settle) an earlier claim for damages against insurance brokers. The full
facts of the case are described in Tuckey LJ's judgment and I need not repeat   *b*
them.

[38] In stating the principles generally applicable to this class of case, I indicated
in *Mount v Barker Austin (a firm)* [1998] PNLR 493 at 510, 511 a two-stage approach.
First, the court has to decide whether the claimant has lost something of value or
whether on the contrary his prospects of success in the original action were
negligible. Secondly, assuming the claimant surmounts this initial handle, the   *c*
court must then 'make a realistic assessment of what would have been the
plaintiff's prospects of success had the original litigation been fought out'.

[39] With regard to the first stage, the evidential burden rests on the negligent
solicitors: they, after all, in the great majority of these cases will have been
charging the claimant for their services and failing to advise him that in reality his   *d*
claim was worthless so that he would be better off simply discontinuing it. The
claimant, therefore, should be given the benefit of any doubts as to whether or
not his original claim was doomed to inevitable failure. With regard to the
second stage, the *Armory v Delamirie* (1722) 1 Stra 505, [1558–1774] All ER Rep 121
principle comes into play in the sense that the court will tend to assess the   *e*
claimant's prospects generously given that it was the defendant's negligence
which has lost him the chance of succeeding in full or fuller measure.

[40] The particular question raised by this appeal concerns the extent to which
it is appropriate for the court hearing the loss of opportunity claim (a) to entertain
primary factual evidence and (b) to reach clear conclusions whether of fact or of
law. The question arises here in the context of the original claim having been   *f*
struck out in April 1992 for want of prosecution on the ground that the witnesses'
memories had faded and 'it would be impossible to investigate such matters [as
the availability of alternative insurance cover] now'.

[41] The judge below seems to have tried this claim for all the world as if he
were seised of the original action against the insurance brokers. Not only did he   *g*
hear live evidence from the brokers—called, somewhat unattractively, by the
defendant solicitors—but he treated the lack of oral evidence from the claimants
in precisely the same way as if he had been deciding the original action. This is
perhaps best exemplified by a passage in the judgment with regard to whether or
not the claimants had disclosed to their brokers the full extent of their claims
history (a point no longer relied on by the defendants but of relevance for   *h*
illustrative purposes):

> '... loath as I am to invoke the burden of proof in the circumstances of this
> unhappy case, I can find no facts upon which to favour, on the balance of
> probabilities, the claimants' version of events, which was put to Mr McGreevy   *j*
> [the broker] in cross-examination but which was never attested to by the
> claimants in evidence. Had the action come to trial, the trial judge is likely
> to have heard evidence from Shahid [the claimants' witness] upon the
> non-disclosure point: there would have been no reason, in that notional trial,
> for the reluctance to resort to oral evidence which was demonstrated by the
> claimants in the trial of these proceedings. I have pondered whether I could

a in any way be justified in concluding that there was "a chance", if not a probability, of Shahid's evidence having been preferred to that of Mr McGreevy at the notional trial, but, not having heard Shahid's evidence on the point in these proceedings, I am in no position to evaluate whether that chance was negligible or more substantial than that.'

b [42] That I would regard as an impermissible approach. If it were correct, then logically, assuming that disclosure was the determinative issue, the claimants would have lost the case irrespective of why Shahid was not called—even, therefore, had he died. It seems to me that such claims should not fail merely because, often through the passage of time, the judge hearing the second action is unable to determine whether the chance of success in the first
c action had been 'negligible or more substantial than that'. Most obviously this must be so in a case like the present where the original action was struck out for the very reason that it was no longer possible to try it fairly.

[43] In his valuable judgment in *Harrison v Bloom Camillin (a firm)* [2000] Lloyd's Rep PN 89 at 99, Neuberger J said:

d   'First, in some loss of a chance cases the court may think it right to view the prospects on a fairly "broad brush" basis; in other cases it may be correct to look at the prospects in far greater detail. In my view, the present case falls in the latter category. Secondly, at least in the present case, I believe that the court should be comparatively prepared to come to a clear conclusion on the
e   likely outcome on at least some of the matters which would have been in issue in the action. My reasons for these two conclusions are as follows. First, the evidence and arguments in relation to the various issues which would have arisen in the action have been substantially more extensive than in most loss of a chance cases. Secondly, the difference in time between the notional hearing of the action and the hearing of these proceedings is not
f   very substantial (less than three years). Thirdly, so far as the merits are relevant (as to which see the fourth proposition of Simon Brown LJ in *Mount*) most of the delay (any delay before November 1992 and any delay after July 1995) was attributable more to the claimants rather than to the defendants (who were responsible for the delay between November 1992 and July 1995).
g   On the other hand, it would be wrong to be too ready to make firm findings as to what the court would have decided in the action on at least some of the issues which have been debated. First, it may be wrong in principle to do so because an issue might well be arguable either way even if I have a view on it. Secondly, the oral and documentary evidence available to me is, I am
h   satisfied, less than would have been available in the action. On witnesses, I did not hear from some witnesses who I believe would have been called in the action. Also, a further [two-and-three-quarter years], while not substantial, is a significant period during which memories can be expected to weaken. Some of the documentation which would have been available in the action but was not available to me could be crucial.'

j [44] Whilst it is unsurprising that on the very different facts of that case the court was indeed prepared to 'look at the prospects in far greater detail' and 'to come to a clear conclusion on the likely outcome on at least some of the matters which would have been in issue in the [original] action', to my mind wholly different considerations apply here. The delay here was far longer than there. It was entirely attributable to the defendants rather than the claimants. And by

1992 it had already made the original action untriable. In these circumstances I
agree with Tuckey LJ that the judge below could not and should not have
attempted seven-and-a-half years later to try (and purport to reach a clear
conclusion on) the issue as to whether alternative insurance cover would have
been available (on any terms) to the claimants 15 years earlier.

[45] I agree too with the rest of Tuckey LJ's judgment as to the proper
approach to bring to bear upon this claim and with the result which he proposes.
The appeal is accordingly allowed and judgment will be entered for the claimants
in the substantially larger sum indicated.

Appeal allowed.

Dilys Tausz   Barrister.

a

Kuwait Airways Corp v Iraqi Airways Co (No 3)

[2002] UKHL 19

b

HOUSE OF LORDS

LORD NICHOLLS OF BIRKENHEAD, LORD STEYN, LORD HOFFMANN, LORD HOPE OF CRAIGHEAD AND LORD SCOTT OF FOSCOTE

15–17, 21–24, 28, 29 JANUARY, 16 MAY 2002

c *Conflict of laws – Foreign law – Recognition – Foreign law flagrantly breaching international law – Whether English court entitled to refuse recognition of foreign law on grounds of breach of international law – Whether non-recognition extending to both limbs of rule of double actionability in tort.*

d *Tort – Wrongful interference with goods – Conversion – Denial of rights of ownership – Whether deprivation of owner for purposes of conversion requiring defendant to take goods from owner's possession.*

Tort – Wrongful interference with goods – Causation – 'But for' test – Application of 'but for' test in cases of successive conversion – Proper approach.

e In August 1990, in flagrant and subsequently admitted breach of international law, Iraq invaded and purported to annex Kuwait. During the invasion, Iraqi forces seized ten aircraft belonging to the claimant, the Kuwaiti state airline, and took them to Iraq. In September, as part of its attempt to extinguish the existence of Kuwait as a separate state, the Iraqi government adopted a resolution (the resolution) dissolving the claimant and transferring its property to the defendant, *f* the Iraqi state-owned airline. On the day that the resolution became effective, the defendant's board passed resolutions implementing it. The defendant later applied for certificates of airworthiness for the aircraft, painted some of them in its livery and used one on internal commercial flights. In January 1991 the claimant brought proceedings in England against the defendant for conversion of *g* the aircraft. Shortly afterwards, during the military action by coalition forces against Iraq, six of the aircraft (the Iran six) were evacuated by the defendant to Iran on the orders of the Iraqi government. In July and August 1992, after the liberation of Kuwait, those aircraft were flown back to Kuwait, but the claimant had to pay Iran a substantial amount for the cost of keeping, sheltering and maintaining them. It sought to recover that sum as damages in its action against *h* the defendant, together, inter alia, with several other heads of loss in relation to the Iran six. In order to succeed in its action, the claimant had to show that the proceedings satisfied the double actionability rule, ie it had to show that the defendant's acts would have been tortious if performed in England and were also civilly actionable under the law of the country where they had in fact occurred, namely Iraq. On a trial of certain issues relating to liability, the judge *j* held that the defendant had wrongfully interfered with the claimant's aircraft. However, on a subsequent trial of issues relating to causation, remoteness and quantum, another judge held that the claimant would have suffered the losses claimed even if the defendant had not wrongfully interfered with the aircraft, and accordingly he dismissed the action. The Court of Appeal reversed that decision in respect of the Iran six, and held that the claimant was entitled in principle to *a* recover in respect of the sum paid to Iran and all but one of the other heads of loss relating to those aircraft. On its appeal to the House of Lords, the defendant contended that, by virtue of the resolution, the claimant had not been the owner of the aircraft when the defendant had performed the acts complained of; that a breach of international law could not be a ground for the English court to refuse to recognise a foreign decree as contrary to public policy since the acts of a foreign *b* sovereign state were non-justiciable; and that accordingly the claim could not satisfy either limb of the double actionability rule. Alternatively, the defendant contended that its actions could not constitute conversion since, inter alia, they did not amount to a deprivation of the use and possession of the claimant's goods. The defendant further contended that the Iran six would have been flown to Iran even if they had not been incorporated into its fleet, and that accordingly the *c* claims in respect of those aircraft failed on a simple 'but for' test of causation.

Held – (Lord Scott dissenting) The appeal would be dismissed for the following reasons—

(1) It was legitimate, in appropriate circumstances, for an English court to *d* have regard to the content of international law in deciding whether to recognise a foreign law, and the 'non-justiciable' principle did not require the court to shut its eyes to a breach of an established principle of international law committed by one state against another when the breach was plain and acknowledged. In the instant case, the breach of international law was so fundamental that, as a matter of public policy, the English court would decline to recognise the resolution as *e* effectual to divest the claimant of its title to the aircraft. Moreover, both limbs of the double actionability rule fell to be applied on the footing that the resolution was to be disregarded. Accordingly, the resolution did not bar the claimant's action (see [25]–[29], [31], [113], [114], [117], [118], [124], [125], [140], [146], [148], [149], [168], below); *Buttes Gas and Oil Co v Hammer (Nos 2 and 3)* [1981] 3 All ER *f* 616 explained and distinguished; *Chaplin v Boys* [1969] 2 All ER 1085 and *Oppenheimer v Cattermole (Inspector of Taxes)* [1975] 1 All ER 538 considered.

(2) For the purposes of the tort of conversion, 'depriving' was not to be understood as meaning that the wrongdoer actually had to take the goods himself from the possession of the owner. Rather, an owner was equally deprived of *g* possession when he was excluded from possession, or possession was withheld from him by the wrongdoer. Whether the owner was excluded from possession could sometimes depend upon whether the wrongdoer exercised dominion over the goods. Similarly, mere unauthorised retention of another's goods was not conversion of them. Detention had to be adverse to the owner, excluding him from the goods. It had to be accompanied by an intention to keep them. In the *h* instant case, the defendant had intended to keep the aircraft as its own and had treated them as its own. It followed that the defendant had wrongfully interfered with the aircraft, and its acts would therefore have been tortious if done in England (see [40]–[44], [119], [120], [124], [125], [169], below).

(3) In applying the 'but for' test in cases of successive conversion, it was *j* necessary to bear in mind that each person in a series of conversions wrongfully excluded the owner from possession of his goods. The wrongful acts of a previous possessor did not diminish the claimant's claim in respect of the wrongful acts of a later possessor. The test called for a comparison between the owner's position if he had retained his goods and his position having been deprived of them by the

a defendant. Loss that the owner would have suffered even if he had retained the goods was not loss caused by the conversion. However, where unforeseen circumstances prevented the wrongdoer from returning the goods, the loss flowing from those unforeseen circumstances should be borne by the wrongdoer, not by the innocent owner of the goods. In the instant case, the claimant would not have suffered any of the heads of loss that it was claiming if it had not been

b unlawfully deprived of its goods by the defendant. If it had retained possession of the Iran six, the aircraft would not have been evacuated to Iran. As regards the individual heads of loss, the Court of Appeal's decision had been correct in each case (see [82], [83], [85], [92]–[95], [105], [123]–[125], [130], [169], [170], below).

Per curiam. Where a person has converted another's goods in good faith, reasonable foreseeability is the test for liability for consequential loss, but a

c person who has knowingly converted another's good will be liable for consequential loss flowing directly and naturally from the breach (see [103], [104], [125], [169], below).

Decision of the Court of Appeal [2001] 1 All ER (Comm) 557 affirmed.

d ## Notes

For refusal to recognise a foreign law on grounds of public policy and the double actionability rule, see 8(1) *Halsbury's Laws* (4th edn reissue) paras 849, 894, and for the essence of conversion and consequential damage, see 45(2) *Halsbury's Laws* (4th edn reissue) paras 548, 630.

e ## Cases referred to in opinions

A-G v Blake (Jonathan Cape Ltd, third party) [2000] 4 All ER 385, [2001] 1 AC 268, [2000] 3 WLR 625, HL.

Barnett v Chelsea and Kensington Hospital Management Committee [1968] 1 All ER 1068, [1969] 1 QB 428, [1968] 2 WLR 422.

f *BBMB Finance (Hong Kong) Ltd v Eda Holdings Ltd* [1991] 2 All ER 129, [1990] 1 WLR 409, PC.

Blathwayt v Lord Cawley [1975] 3 All ER 625, [1976] AC 397, [1975] 3 WLR 684, HL.

Bonnington Castings Ltd v Wardlaw [1956] 1 All ER 615, [1956] AC 613, [1956] 2 WLR 707, HL.

g *Brandeis Goldschmidt & Co Ltd v Western Transport Ltd* [1982] 1 All ER 28, [1981] QB 864, [1981] 3 WLR 181, CA.

Breavington v Godleman (1988) 169 CLR 41, Aust HC.

Butler v Egg and Egg Pulp Marketing Board (1966) 114 CLR 185, Aust HC.

Buttes Gas and Oil Co v Hammer (Nos 2 and 3) [1981] 3 All ER 616, [1982] AC 888,

h [1981] 3 WLR 787, HL.

Cambridge Water Co v Eastern Counties Leather plc [1994] 1 All ER 53, [1994] 2 AC 264, [1994] 2 WLR 53, HL.

Carr v Fracis Times & Co [1902] AC 176, HL.

Chaplin v Boys [1969] 2 All ER 1085, [1971] AC 356, [1969] 3 WLR 322, HL.

j *Chellaram v Chellaram* [1985] 1 All ER 1043, [1985] Ch 409, [1985] 2 WLR 510.

Cooper v Chitty (1756) 1 Burr 20, 97 ER 166.

Corcoran v Corcoran [1974] VR 164, Vic SC.

Dobree v Napier (1836) 2 Bing NC 781, 132 ER 301.

Empresa Exportadora de Azucar v Industria Azucarera Nacional SA, The Playa Larga and Marble Islands [1983] 2 Lloyd's Rep 171, CA.

Empress Car Co (Abertillery) Ltd v National Rivers Authority [1998] 1 All ER 481, *a*
[1999] 2 AC 22, [1998] 2 WLR 350, HL.
Ewing v Orr Ewing (1883) 9 App Cas 34, HL.
Fouldes v Willoughby (1841) 8 M & W 540, 151 ER 1153.
Fuld (dec'd) (No 3), In the estate of, Hartley v Fuld [1965] 3 All ER 776, [1968] P 675,
[1966] 2 WLR 717.
Halley, The (1868) LR 2 PC 193, 16 ER 514, PC.   *b*
Helbert Wagg & Co Ltd, Re, Re Prudential Assurance Co [1956] 1 All ER 129, [1956]
1 Ch 323, [1956] 2 WLR 183.
Hiort v London and North Western Rly (1879) 4 Ex D 188, CA.
Hollins v Fowler (1875) LR 7 HL 757, [1874–80] All ER Rep 118, HL; *affg* sub nom
Fowler v Hollins (1872) LR 7 QB 616, Ex Ch.   *c*
IBL Ltd v Coussens [1991] 2 All ER 133, CA.
John Pfeiffer Pty Ltd v Rogerson [2000] HCA 36, Aust HC.
Kuwait Airways Corp v Iraqi Airways Co [1995] 3 All ER 694, [1995] 1 WLR 1147, HL.
Kuwait Airways Corp v Iraqi Airways Co (No 2) [2001] 1 WLR 429, HL.
Lipkin Gorman (a firm) v Karpnale Ltd [1992] 4 All ER 512, [1991] 2 AC 548, [1991]
3 WLR 10, HL.   *d*
Loucks v Standard Oil Co of New York (1918) 120 NE 198, NY Ct of Apps.
Machado v Fontes [1897] 2 QB 231, CA.
Marfani & Co Ltd v Midland Bank Ltd [1968] 2 All ER 573, [1968] 1 WLR 956, CA.
McGhee v National Coal Board [1972] 3 All ER 1008, [1973] 1 WLR 1, HL.
Nicaragua v United States of America [1986] ICJ Reports 14, 98–100, Int Ct of Just.   *e*
Oppenheimer v Cattermole (Inspector of Taxes) [1975] 1 All ER 538, [1976] AC 249,
[1975] 2 WLR 347, HL.
*Overseas Tankship (UK) Ltd v Morts Dock and Engineering Co Ltd, The Wagon Mound
(No 1)* [1961] 1 All ER 404, [1961] AC 388, [1961] 2 WLR 126, PC.
Overseas Tankship (UK) Ltd v The Miller Steamship Co Pty, The Wagon Mound (No 2) *f*
[1966] 2 All ER 709, [1967] 1 AC 617, [1966] 3 WLR 498, PC.
Phillips v Eyre (1870) LR 6 QB 1, Ex Ch; *affg* (1869) LR 4 QB 225.
R v Lesley (1860) Bell 220, 169 ER 1236.
Red Sea Insurance Ltd v Bouygues SA [1994] 3 All ER 749, [1995] 1 AC 190, [1994]
3 WLR 926, PC.
Reeves v Comr of Police of the Metropolis [1999] 3 All ER 897, [2000] 1 AC 360, [1999] *g*
3 WLR 363, HL.
Rylands v Fletcher (1868) LR 3 HL 330, [1861–73] All ER Rep 1, HL.
Saleslease Ltd v Davis [1999] 1 WLR 1664, CA.
Seymour v Scott (1862) 1 H & C 219, Ex Ch.
Smith New Court Securities Ltd v Scrimgeour Vickers (Asset Management) Ltd [1996] *h*
4 All ER 796, [1997] AC 254, [1996] 2 WLR 1051, HL.
Solloway v McLaughlin, McLaughlin v Solloway [1937] 4 All ER 328, [1938] AC 247, PC.
*South Australia Asset Management Corp v York Montague Ltd, United Bank of
Kuwait plc v Prudential Property Services Ltd, Nykredit Mortgage Bank plc v Edward
Erdman Group Ltd* [1996] 3 All ER 365, [1997] AC 191, [1996] 3 WLR 87, HL.   *j*
Stansbie v Troman [1948] 1 All ER 599, [1948] 2 KB 48, CA.
Warren v Warren [1972] Qd R 386, Qld SC.
Wickham Holdings Ltd v Brooke House Motors Ltd [1967] 1 All ER 117, [1967] 1 WLR
295, CA.
Williams v Peel River Land and Mineral Co Ltd (1886) 55 LT 689, CA.

Appeal and cross-appeal

a
The defendant, Iraqi Airways Co (IAC), appealed with permission of the Appeal Committee of the House of Lords given on 1 May 2001 from that part of the order of the Court of Appeal (Henry, Brooke and Rix LJJ) on 21 December 2000, giving effect to its decision on 10 November 2000 ([2001] 1 All ER (Comm) 557, [2001] 3 WLR 1117), whereby it (i) dismissed IAC's appeal from the decision of

b Mance J on 30 July 1998 ([1999] CLC 31) in which he held that IAC had wrongfully interfered with ten aircraft owned by the claimant, Kuwait Airways Corp (KAC), and (ii) allowed in part an appeal by KAC from the order of Aikens J on 7 April 2000 ([2000] 2 All ER (Comm) 360) dismissing its proceedings against IAC on the ground that it had not suffered any recoverable damage in respect of any of the aircraft. KAC cross-appealed with permission of the Appeal

c Committee of the House of Lords given on 1 May 2001 from that part of the Court of Appeal's order affirming the decision of Aikens J in respect of four of the aircraft and one head of loss relating to the other six aircraft. The facts are set out in the opinion of Lord Nicholls of Birkenhead.

d *David Donaldson QC* and *Stephen Nathan QC* (instructed by *Landau & Scanlan*) for IAC.
Geoffrey Vos QC, Christopher Greenwood QC, Joe Smouha and *Samuel Wordsworth* (instructed by *Howard Kennedy*) for KAC.

Their Lordships took time for consideration.

e
16 May 2002. The following opinions were delivered.

LORD NICHOLLS OF BIRKENHEAD.

[1] My Lords, on 2 August 1990 military forces of Iraq forcibly invaded and
f occupied Kuwait. They completed the occupation in the space of two or three days. The Revolutionary Command Council of Iraq (RCC) then adopted resolutions proclaiming the sovereignty of Iraq over Kuwait and its annexation to Iraq. Kuwait was designated a 'governate' within Iraq.

[2] When the Iraqi forces took over the airport at Kuwait they seized ten commercial aircraft belonging to Kuwait Airways Corp (KAC): two Boeing 767s,
g three A300 Airbuses, and five A310 Airbuses. They lost no time in removing these aircraft to Iraq. By 9 August nine of the aircraft had been flown back to Basra, in Iraq. The tenth aircraft, undergoing repair at the time of the invasion, was flown direct to Baghdad a fortnight later. On 9 September the RCC adopted a resolution dissolving KAC and transferring all its property worldwide, including
h the ten aircraft, to the state-owned Iraqi Airways Co (IAC). This resolution, Resolution 369, came into force upon publication in the official gazette on 17 September. On the same day IAC's board passed resolutions implementing RCC Resolution 369.

[3] On 11 January 1991 KAC commenced these proceedings against the
j Republic of Iraq and IAC, claiming the return of its ten aircraft or payment of their value, and damages. The aircraft were valued by KAC at $US630m. The damages claimed at the trial exceeded $US800m.

[4] The UN Security Council's deadline for Iraq's withdrawal from Kuwait expired at midnight on 15 January 1991. Military action by coalition air forces began 24 hours later. The airfield at Mosul, in the north of Iraq, suffered several

attacks from the air. In late January and early February 1991 four of the ten *a* aircraft seized from KAC, moved to Mosul for safety reasons, were destroyed by coalition bombing. The aircraft destroyed were the two Boeing 767s and two A300 Airbuses. In these proceedings these four aircraft have become known as 'the Mosul Four'. The other six aircraft, known as 'the Iran Six', were evacuated by IAC to Iran at much the same time. Following negotiations with the government of Iran these six aircraft were flown back eventually to Kuwait in *b* July and August 1992. KAC later paid Iran a substantial amount, $US 20m, for the cost of keeping, sheltering and maintaining them.

The proceedings

[5] The proceedings have had a lengthy procedural history, including an earlier appeal to your Lordships' House: see *Kuwait Airways Corp v Iraqi Airways Co* *c* [1995] 3 All ER 694, [1995] 1 WLR 1147. On that occasion the House was concerned with challenges to the jurisdiction of the English court. The House decided, on 24 July 1995, that the writ had been effectively served on IAC but not on the state of Iraq. The House also decided that IAC could not claim state immunity regarding the acts of which KAC was complaining, in so far as they were done *d* after RCC Resolution 369 came into force. IAC's retention and use of the aircraft as its own did not constitute acts done in the exercise of sovereign immunity. KAC then continued the proceedings against IAC alone.

[6] The trial of the action was split between issues relating to liability and those relating to damages. Certain issues relating to liability were tried by *e* Mance J. On these issues KAC achieved a large measure of success. Mance J held that IAC had wrongfully interfered with KAC's ten aircraft: see [1999] CLC 31. Issues relating to causation, remoteness and amount of damages were tried by Aikens J. He held that KAC had failed to establish it had suffered any recoverable damage in respect of any of the aircraft. KAC would have suffered the losses claimed even if IAC had not wrongfully interfered with the aircraft. He dismissed *f* the action: see [2000] 2 All ER (Comm) 360.

[7] Both parties appealed. IAC appealed against the rulings of Mance J on liability, and KAC appealed against the conclusions of Aikens J on damages and his dismissal of the action. The judgment of the Court of Appeal, comprising Henry, Brooke and Rix LJJ, was given in November 2000: see [2001] 1 All ER *g* (Comm) 557, [2001] 3 WLR 1117. KAC was partly successful. Its claims in respect of the Mosul Four still failed but, save in one respect, its claims regarding the Iran Six succeeded.

[8] IAC then appealed against this decision to your Lordships' House. IAC submits that the action should be dismissed in its entirety. Aikens J's decision was correct, and should be restored. KAC cross-appealed. KAC contends that its *h* claims regarding the Mosul Four were wrongly dismissed by both courts below. KAC also contends it should succeed on the head of damages on which it failed in the Court of Appeal.

[9] A further procedural matter should be noted. In May 2000 KAC petitioned the House to vary its order of 24 July 1995. The variation sought was that IAC *j* should not benefit from sovereign immunity for the period 9 August 1990 to 16 September 1990. The ground of the petition was that, in respect of its activities in this period, IAC had obtained the judgment of the House by fraud. Evidence of IAC witnesses was perjured. On 27 July 2000 the House dismissed the petition: *Kuwait Airways Corp v Iraqi Airways Co (No 2)* [2001] 1 WLR 429. The appropriate

a   procedure was for KAC to commence a fresh action. On 16 October 2000 KAC started new proceedings. This new action (the perjury action) is due to be tried shortly.

[10] A notable feature of the present proceedings is that this is a claim in tort for damages in respect of events having no connection with this country. The acts of which complaint is made took place in Iraq. Nor do the parties themselves *b*   have any connection with England. Both IAC and KAC had places of business in London, but that is of no real significance. As international airlines, no doubt they had branch offices in several countries.

[11] At an early stage in the proceedings IAC raised an 'inconvenient forum' objection to the jurisdiction of the English court. The basis of the objection was that the United Nations Organisation had established a compensation commission *c*   for the purpose of considering claims against Iraq for damage and loss caused by its invasion of Kuwait. Evans J rejected this objection, and his decision was not the subject of an appeal. At a later stage IAC raised a further forum non conveniens objection but subsequently abandoned this. Thus it came about that the English court accepted jurisdiction to decide the issues raised in the *d*   proceedings.

[12] Given that the alleged wrongs were committed in Iraq, and given also the absence of any particular connection with any other country, it is to be expected that when adjudicating upon KAC's claims an English court would apply the law of Iraq. As English law now stands, that would be so. The general rule is that the *e*   law to be used for determining issues relating to tort is the law of the country in which the events constituting the tort occurred: see ss 9(1) and 11(1) of the Private International Law (Miscellaneous Provisions) Act 1995. But the events of which complaint is made by KAC occurred long before this statute was enacted. Accordingly, as was common ground between the parties, in the present proceedings the court has to apply the so-called double actionability rule, as *f*   generally understood since the decision of the House in *Chaplin v Boys* [1969] 2 All ER 1085, [1971] AC 356. The rule is that, in order to be actionable here, the acts done abroad must satisfy both limbs of a dual test. The acts must be such that, if done in England, they would be tortious. Additionally, the acts must be civilly actionable under the law of the country where they occurred.

g   [13] KAC immediately comes up against an obvious difficulty. In order to satisfy the double actionability test KAC must show it was the owner of the aircraft when IAC did the acts of which KAC is complaining. But, on the face of things, that was not so. By September 1990 the aircraft had been seized by the government of Iraq and moved from Kuwait to Iraq. Under Iraqi law, RCC Resolution 369 was effective to divest KAC of its ownership of the aircraft and *h*   vest title in IAC. Under Iraqi law the subsequent repeal of this decree did not retrospectively give KAC a title it did not otherwise have during the relevant period. Under English conflict of laws principles the transfer of title to tangible movable property normally depends on the lex situs: the law of the country where the movable was situated at the time of the transfer. Likewise, governmental *j*   acts affecting proprietary rights will be recognised by an English court as valid if they would be recognised as valid by the law of the country where the property was situated when the law takes effect. Here, that was Iraq.

[14] KAC does not dispute these propositions. Nor does KAC contend that the lex situs of the aircraft was the law of Kuwait as the place where, presumably, the aircraft were registered. KAC's response is that in the present case, as a

matter of overriding public policy, an English court will altogether disregard a
RCC Resolution 369. An English court will not regard this decree of Iraqi law as
effective to divest KAC of its title to the ten aircraft.

RCC Resolution 369 and English public policy

[15] Conflict of laws jurisprudence is concerned essentially with the just
disposal of proceedings having a foreign element. The jurisprudence is founded b
on the recognition that in proceedings having connections with more than one
country an issue brought before a court in one country may be more
appropriately decided by reference to the laws of another country even though
those laws are different from the law of the forum court. The laws of the other
country may have adopted solutions, or even basic principles, rejected by the law
of the forum country. These differences do not in themselves furnish reason why c
the forum court should decline to apply the foreign law. On the contrary, the
existence of differences is the very reason why it may be appropriate for the
forum court to have recourse to the foreign law. If the laws of all countries were
uniform there would be no 'conflict' of laws.

[16] This, overwhelmingly, is the normal position. But, as noted by Scarman J d
in *In the estate of Fuld (dec'd) (No 3), Hartley v Fuld* [1965] 3 All ER 776 at 781, [1968]
P 675 at 698, blind adherence to foreign law can never be required of an English
court. Exceptionally and rarely, a provision of foreign law will be disregarded when
it would lead to a result wholly alien to fundamental requirements of justice as
administered by an English court. A result of this character would not be acceptable e
to an English court. In the conventional phraseology, such a result would be
contrary to public policy. Then the court will decline to enforce or recognise the
foreign decree to whatever extent is required in the circumstances.

[17] This public policy principle eludes more precise definition. Its flavour is
captured by the much repeated words of Judge Cardozo that the court will
exclude the foreign decree only when it 'would violate some fundamental principle f
of justice, some prevalent conception of good morals, some deep-rooted tradition
of the common weal': see *Loucks v Standard Oil Co of New York* (1918) 120 NE 198
at 202.

[18] Despite its lack of precision, this exception to the normal rule is well
established in English law. This imprecision, even vagueness, does not invalidate g
the principle. Indeed, a similar principle is a common feature of all systems of
conflicts of laws. The leading example in this country, always cited in this context,
is the 1941 decree of the National Socialist government of Germany depriving
Jewish émigrés of their German nationality and, consequentially, leading to the
confiscation of their property. Surely Lord Cross of Chelsea was indubitably right h
when he said that a racially discriminatory and confiscatory law of this sort was
so grave an infringement of human rights that the courts of this country ought to
refuse to recognise it as a law at all: *Oppenheimer v Cattermole (Inspector of Taxes)*
[1975] 1 All ER 538 at 566–567, [1976] AC 249 at 277–278. When deciding an issue
by reference to foreign law, the courts of this country must have a residual
power, to be exercised exceptionally and with the greatest circumspection, to j
disregard a provision in the foreign law when to do otherwise would affront basic
principles of justice and fairness which the courts seek to apply in the
administration of justice in this country. Gross infringements of human rights are
one instance, and an important instance, of such a provision. But the principle
cannot be confined to one particular category of unacceptable laws. That would

be neither sensible nor logical. Laws may be fundamentally unacceptable for *a* reasons other than human rights violations.

[19] The question raised in the present proceedings is whether Resolution 369 of the RCC is of this character. This decree was one of the RCC resolutions issued with a view to giving effect to the integration of Kuwait into Iraq following the invasion. It was part and parcel of the Iraqi seizure of Kuwait and its assets and *b* the assimilation of these assets into the political, social and economic structure of Iraq.

[20] That this seizure and assimilation were flagrant violations of rules of international law of fundamental importance is plain beyond argument. International reaction to the invasion was swift. On the first day of the invasion, 2 August 1990, the UN Security Council condemned the invasion as a breach of the peace and *c* demanded immediate Iraqi withdrawal (Resolution 660). On 6 August the Security Council determined that Iraq had usurped the authority of the legitimate government of Kuwait. All member states were to take specified measures to restore the authority of the legitimate government of Kuwait. The council called upon all states to take appropriate measures to protect assets of the legitimate *d* government of Kuwait and its agencies, and not to recognise any regime set up by the occupying power (Resolution 661). On 9 August the Security Council decided that the annexation of Kuwait by Iraq had no legal validity and was null and void. The council called upon all states not to recognise this annexation, and to refrain from any action which might be interpreted as an indirect recognition of the annexation (Resolution 662). Later resolutions of the Security Council *e* included Resolution 674 (29 October 1990) which condemned the seizure by Iraq of public and private property in Kuwait and reminded Iraq of its liability under international law for loss and damage caused to Kuwaiti nationals and institutions. On 29 November 1990 the council authorised military action against Iraq (Resolution 678).

f [21] In the event no state recognised Iraq's annexation of Kuwait or its authority in Kuwait. On 2 March 1991 the UN Security Council laid down conditions for a ceasefire. The conditions included demands that Iraq should rescind its purported annexation of Iraq, accept in principle its liability under international law for any loss or damage caused to Kuwait and its nationals and corporations, and begin to return all Kuwaiti property immediately (Resolution 686). *g* On 5 March 1991 Iraq accepted these obligations and repealed Resolution 369 of the RCC.

[22] The effect of these Security Council decisions, as a matter of international law, is clear. Iraq and Kuwait are both members of the United Nations. Article 2(4) of the United Nations Charter provides that in their international *h* relations all members shall refrain from the use of force against the territorial integrity of any state. This is also a principle of customary international law binding on states independently of the provisions of the Charter: see the International Court of Justice in *Nicaragua v United States of America* [1986] ICJ Reports 14, 98–100, at paras 187–188.

j [23] Further, art 25 of the United Nations Charter provides that the members of the United Nations agree to accept and carry out the decisions of the Security Council in accordance with the Charter. Chapter VII of the Charter empowers the Security Council to determine that there exists a breach of the peace. When the council has made such a determination, as happened in the present case on the very day of the invasion, the council may decide upon measures to restore

international peace and security. These measures include both military and
non-military measures. Decisions of the Security Council taken under these
Ch VII powers are legally binding upon all members of the United Nations: see
the opinion of the International Court of Justice concerning *Legal Consequences for
States of the Continued Presence of South Africa in Namibia* [1971] ICJ Reports 16,
53–56, paras 115–125. The Security Council resolutions mentioned above were
decisions taken under Ch VII.

[24] On behalf of IAC Mr Donaldson submitted that the public policy
exception to the recognition of provisions of foreign law is limited to
infringements of human rights. The allegation in the present action is breach of
international law by Iraq. But breach of international law by a state is not, and
should not be, a ground for refusing to recognise a foreign decree. An English
court will not sit in judgment on the sovereign acts of a foreign government or
state. It will not adjudicate upon the legality, validity or acceptability of such acts,
either under domestic law or international law. For a court to do so would offend
against the principle that the courts will not adjudicate upon the transactions of
foreign sovereign states. This principle is not discretionary. It is inherent in the
very nature of the judicial process: see *Buttes Gas and Oil Co v Hammer (Nos 2 and 3)*
[1981] 3 All ER 616 at 629, [1982] AC 888 at 932. KAC's argument, this submission
by IAC continued, invites the court to determine whether the invasion of
Kuwait by Iraq, followed by the removal of the ten aircraft from Kuwait to Iraq
and their transfer to IAC, was unlawful under international law. The courts
below were wrong to accede to this invitation.

[25] My Lords, this submission seeks to press the non-justiciability principle
too far. Undoubtedly there may be cases, of which the *Buttes* case is an illustration,
where the issues are such that the court has, in the words of Lord Wilberforce,
'no judicial or manageable standards by which to judge [the] issues'—

'the court would be in a judicial no man's land: the court would be asked
to review transactions in which four foreign states were involved, which
they had brought to a precarious settlement, after diplomacy and the use of
force, and to say that at least part of these were "unlawful" under
international law.' (See [1981] 3 All ER 616 at 633, [1982] AC 888 at 938.)

This was Lord Wilberforce's conclusion regarding the important inter-state and
other issues arising in that case: see his summary ([1981] 3 All ER 616 at 632–633,
[1982] AC 888 at 937).

[26] This is not to say an English court is disabled from ever taking cognisance
of international law or from ever considering whether a violation of international
law has occurred. In appropriate circumstances it is legitimate for an English
court to have regard to the content of international law in deciding whether to
recognise a foreign law. Lord Wilberforce himself accepted this in the *Buttes* case
([1981] 3 All ER 616 at 629, [1982] AC 888 at 931). Nor does the 'non-justiciable'
principle mean that the judiciary must shut their eyes to a breach of an
established principle of international law committed by one state against another
when the breach is plain and, indeed, acknowledged. In such a case the
adjudication problems confronting the English court in the *Buttes* litigation do
not arise. The standard being applied by the court is clear and manageable, and
the outcome not in doubt. That is the present case.

[27] Against this background I return to the question whether as a matter of
public policy an English court ought to decline to recognise RCC Resolution 369

a as effectual to divest KAC of its title to its aircraft. Mance J and the Court of Appeal said that an English court should so decline. I agree with them.

[28] The acceptability of a provision of foreign law must be judged by contemporary standards. Lord Wilberforce, in a different context, noted that conceptions of public policy should move with the times: see *Blathwayt v Lord Cawley* [1975] 3 All ER 625 at 636, [1976] AC 397 at 426. In *Oppenheimer v*
b *Cattermole (Inspector of Taxes)* [1975] 1 All ER 538 at 567, [1976] AC 249 at 278, Lord Cross said that the courts of this country should give effect to clearly established rules of international law. This is increasingly true today. As nations become ever more interdependent, the need to recognise and adhere to standards of conduct set by international law becomes ever more important. RCC Resolution 369 was not simply a governmental expropriation of property within
c its territory. Having forcibly invaded Kuwait, seized its assets, and taken KAC's aircraft from Kuwait to its own territory, Iraq adopted this decree as part of its attempt to extinguish every vestige of Kuwait's existence as a separate state. An expropriatory decree made in these circumstances and for this purpose is simply not acceptable today.

d [29] I have already noted that Iraq's invasion of Kuwait and seizure of its assets were a gross violation of established rules of international law of fundamental importance. A breach of international law of this seriousness is a matter of deep concern to the worldwide community of nations. This is evidenced by the urgency with which the UN Security Council considered this incident and by its successive resolutions. Such a fundamental breach of international law can
e properly cause the courts of this country to say that, like the confiscatory decree of the Nazi government of Germany in 1941, a law depriving those whose property has been plundered of the ownership of their property in favour of the aggressor's own citizens will not be enforced or recognised in proceedings in this country. Enforcement or recognition of this law would be manifestly contrary to
f the public policy of English law. For good measure, enforcement or recognition would also be contrary to this country's obligations under the UN Charter. Further, it would sit uneasily with the almost universal condemnation of Iraq's behaviour and with the military action, in which this country participated, taken against Iraq to compel its withdrawal from Kuwait. International law, for its part, recognises that a national court may properly decline to give effect to legislative
g and other acts of foreign states which are in violation of international law: see the discussion in *Oppenheim's International Law* (9th edn, 1992) vol 1, pp 371–376, para 113.

Iraqi law of usurpation and RCC Resolution 369

h [30] IAC had another string to its bow. It advanced a further argument based on RCC Resolution 369. Even if this decree is disregarded in considering the first limb of the double actionability rule (tortious if done in England), it would not be right to disregard it when applying the second limb (civilly actionable under the foreign law). In considering whether the impugned acts would have been civilly actionable in Iraq, one must examine how an Iraqi court would have been
j required to rule on KAC's claim in autumn 1990. An Iraqi court would have had regard to the entirety of Iraqi law, including RCC Resolution 369. KAC's claim for misappropriation (usurpation) of the ten aircraft would have failed. When applying the second limb of the rule the foreign law must be taken as it is. An English court should not treat as civilly actionable under Iraqi law a state of affairs which, in fact, would not have been so actionable. An English court should not,

by excision of part of the foreign law, treat as existing under foreign law a cause of action which the foreign law did not actually recognise at the time.

[31] I cannot accept this argument. For reasons already given, in these proceedings an English court will not regard RCC Resolution 369 as effective to transfer ownership of the ten aircraft from KAC to IAC. In the eyes of an English court KAC remained the owner. The double actionability rule, in both its limbs, falls to be applied on this footing. If an English court were to proceed otherwise the court would be giving effect to the unacceptable RCC Resolution 369. The court would be recognising that, in deciding KAC's claims against IAC, properly brought in an English court, Resolution 369 was effective to divest KAC of its title to the aircraft. Given the public policy objection to recognising the purported effect of this decree, that would be a bizarre conclusion.

[32] I must elaborate a little more. Stated more fully, IAC's argument invokes two different aspects of the law of Iraq: (1) as the lex situs, governing the effectiveness of the transfer of ownership by RCC Resolution 369; and also (2) as the lex loci delicti, governing the impugned conduct of IAC in Iraq. IAC seeks to apply Iraqi law as the lex situs under (1) as a ground for excluding any liability which would otherwise exist in accordance with Iraqi law as the lex loci delicti under (2). I am not attracted by this reasoning. Given that the lex situs under (1) is not acceptable to an English court in these proceedings, the just result is to apply the lex loci delicti under (2) on the footing that Iraqi law as the lex situs under (1) is to be disregarded.

[33] There is sufficient flexibility in the double actionability rule for the court to take this course. The double actionability rule is one of the principles applied by an English court in seeking to arrive at a just result when the claims involve a foreign element. When approving this rule in *Chaplin v Boys* the majority of the House observed that this was a 'general' rule which would 'normally' apply to foreign torts. The rule should be interpreted flexibly, 'so as to leave some latitude in cases where it would be against public policy to admit or to exclude claims': see [1969] 2 All ER 1085 at 1092, 1104, [1971] AC 356 at 378, 391–392 per Lord Hodson and Lord Wilberforce respectively. The existence and width of this flexibility were affirmed by the Privy Council in *Red Sea Insurance Ltd v Bouygues SA* [1994] 3 All ER 749, [1995] 1 AC 190. Adapting the language of Lord Hodson in *Chaplin v Boys*, in the present case it would be contrary to public policy to permit application of the repugnant Iraqi law as the lex situs under (1) to exclude claims KAC would otherwise have against IAC in accordance with Iraqi law as the lex loci delicti under (2). I add that the position would be the same if these proceedings had been governed by the current law, set out in the Private International Law (Miscellaneous Provisions) Act 1995: see ss 11(1) and 14(3)(a)(i).

[34] The House was not referred to any decision where this point has arisen in proceedings relating to a tort committed abroad. But the conclusion I have reached accords with the established position regarding claims in contract. The effect of disregarding a provision of foreign law as manifestly contrary to public policy may be to render enforceable in England a contract which is not enforceable by its proper law: see, for example, *Empresa Exportadora de Azucar v Industria Azucarera Nacional SA, The Playa Larga and Marble Islands* [1983] 2 Lloyd's Rep 171 at 190.

[35] Nor can I accept IAC's suggested distinction between a claim for delivery up and a claim for damages for wrongful interference in Iraq. According to this submission, an English court would have compelled IAC to hand over the aircraft

a had they been flown to Heathrow airport, but the court will not award damages for their wrongful misappropriation in Iraq. I do not think this suggestion really makes sense. The vice which causes an English court to disapply Resolution 369 is apt to have a like consequence in the adjudication of both these claims.

[36] This approach can hardly be unjust to IAC. IAC was fully aware of how its possession of the ten KAC aircraft came about. Effectively, the government of *b* Iraq had stolen the aircraft from Kuwait. IAC took the risk that its title might not be recognised outside Iraq. It may be that in practice IAC had no option but to proceed as it did and accept possession of these aircraft thrust upon it by the government of Iraq. That may be so. The government of Iraq, very probably, would not have tolerated the return of the aircraft by IAC to KAC. That is not an issue now before the House. On the earlier appeal the House decided this feature *c* does not mean that the acts done by IAC after RCC Resolution 369 came into force were acts done by IAC 'in the exercise of sovereign authority' within s 14(2)(a) of the State Immunity Act 1978. Accordingly these acts do not qualify IAC for immunity from the jurisdiction of the English court.

d *Double actionability: conversion*

[37] I turn, then, to apply the double actionability rule on the footing that the transfer of title purportedly made by RCC Resolution 369 is to be disregarded. IAC submitted that its acts would not have been tortious if done in this country. The relevant tort is conversion. But, so it was submitted, the acts done by IAC post-17 September 1990 did not constitute conversion. IAC did not *take* the *e* aircraft. The aircraft had already been taken from KAC by the government of Iraq in the exercise of sovereign authority, before the crucial date of 17 September 1990. IAC did not *dispose* of the aircraft. KAC does not rely upon the removal of the Iran Six from Baghdad to Iran, which occurred after the issue of the writ on 11 January 1991, as an act of conversion. Nor is this a case of wrongfully *keeping* *f* the aircraft. IAC had possession of the aircraft, but mere unauthorised possession or detention is not an act of conversion. Demand and refusal to deliver up are required, as under the old tort of detinue, which did not occur here. Anyway, such a demand would have been unreal: KAC could not have required delivery other than in Iraq and that would have been impossible.

g [38] Nor, it was submitted, do the acts done by IAC after 17 September 1990 suffice, even if they constituted a denial of KAC's title. Denial of title is not of itself conversion: see s 11(3) of the Torts (Interference with Goods) Act 1977. To constitute conversion there must be a concomitant deprivation of use and possession. In support of this submission Mr Donaldson fastened upon a statement in *Clerk and Lindsell on Torts* (17th edn, 1995) p 636, para 13-12: '... conversion is an *h* act of deliberate dealing with a chattel in a manner inconsistent with another's right *whereby that other is deprived of the use and possession of it.*' (My emphasis.) A similar passage appears in *Salmond and Heuston on the Law of Torts* (21st edn, 1996) pp 97–98. In the present case, it was said, none of the acts of IAC deprived KAC of use or possession of the aircraft. Some of IAC's acts were entirely abstract, such as *j* applying for certificates of airworthiness. Even the physical acts, such as repainting or flying the aircraft, had no impact on KAC's possession.

[39] In my view this line of argument was misconceived. I need not repeat the journey through the textbooks and authorities on which your Lordships were taken. Conversion of goods can occur in so many different circumstances that framing a precise definition of universal application is well nigh impossible. In

general, the basic features of the tort are threefold. First, the defendant's conduct was inconsistent with the rights of the owner (or other person entitled to possession). Second, the conduct was deliberate, not accidental. Third, the conduct was so extensive an encroachment on the rights of the owner as to exclude him from use and possession of the goods. The contrast is with lesser acts of interference. If these cause damage they may give rise to claims for trespass or in negligence, but they do not constitute conversion.

[40] The judicially-approved description of the tort in *Clerk and Lindsell* encapsulates, in different language, these basic ingredients. The flaw in IAC's argument lies in its failure to appreciate what is meant in this context by 'depriving' the owner of possession. This is not to be understood as meaning that the wrongdoer must himself actually take the goods from the possession of the owner. This will often be the case, but not always. It is not so in a case of successive conversions. For the purposes of this tort an owner is equally deprived of possession when he is excluded from possession, or possession is withheld from him by the wrongdoer.

[41] Whether the owner is excluded from possession may sometimes depend upon whether the wrongdoer exercised dominion over the goods. Then the intention with which acts were done may be material. The ferryman who turned the plaintiff's horses off the Birkenhead to Liverpool ferry was guilty of conversion if he intended to exercise dominion over them, but not otherwise: see *Fouldes v Willoughby* (1841) 8 M & W 540.

[42] Similarly, mere unauthorised retention of another's goods is not conversion of them. Mere possession of another's goods without title is not necessarily inconsistent with the rights of the owner. To constitute conversion detention must be adverse to the owner, excluding him from the goods. It must be accompanied by an intention to keep the goods. Whether the existence of this intention can properly be inferred depends on the circumstances of the case. A demand and refusal to deliver up the goods are the usual way of proving an intention to keep goods adverse to the owner, but this is not the only way.

[43] Here, on and after 17 September 1990 IAC was in possession and control of the ten aircraft. This possession was adverse to KAC. IAC believed the aircraft were now its property, just as much as the other aircraft in its fleet, and it acted accordingly. It intended to keep the goods as its own. It treated them as its own. It made such use of them as it could in the prevailing circumstances, although this was very limited because of the hostilities. In so conducting itself IAC was asserting rights inconsistent with KAC's rights as owner. This assertion was evidenced in several ways. In particular, in September 1990 the board of IAC passed a resolution to the effect that all aircraft belonging to the (dissolved) KAC should be registered in the name of IAC and that a number of ancillary steps should be taken in relation to the aircraft. In respect of nine aircraft IAC then applied to the Iraqi Directorate of Air Safety for certificates of airworthiness and re-registration in IAC's name. IAC effected insurance cover in respect of five aircraft, and a further four after the issue of the writ. Six of the aircraft were overpainted in IAC's livery. IAC used one aircraft on internal commercial flights between Baghdad and Basra and for training flights. The two Boeing 767s were flown from Basra to Mosul in mid-November 1990.

[44] Mance J concluded that in these circumstances IAC had wrongfully interfered with all ten aircraft. In the Court of Appeal Brooke LJ said:

'The board resolution makes it completely clear that as soon as RCC Resolution 369 came into effect IAC resolved to treat these ten aircraft as their own and to exercise dominion over them in denial of KAC's rights, and this continuing usurpation and conversion of KAC's aircraft subsisted right up to the issue of the writ in this action by which KAC demanded the return of all these aircraft.' (See [2001] 1 All ER (Comm) 557 at 579, [2001] 3 WLR 1117 at 1146 (para 74).)

I agree. IAC's acts would have been tortious if done in this country.

Double actionability: usurpation

[45] I turn now to consider whether IAC's acts were civilly actionable in Iraq. Again, this is on the footing that RCC Resolution 369 was ineffective to divest KAC of its title. Articles 192–201 of the Iraqi Civil Code provide remedies for the civil wrong of usurpation, or misappropriation. The code contains no definition of usurpation. Mance J held that under Iraqi law a usurper need not actually take the asset from the possession or control of its owner. Property can be usurped by keeping. Whether keeping amounts to usurpation depends on a combination of factors, including whether the alleged usurper has conducted himself in a manner showing that he was 'keeping' the asset as his own.

[46] The Court of Appeal upheld this finding of Iraqi law. The Court of Appeal also decided that Mance J was entitled to hold that, ignoring RCC Resolution 369, as a matter of Iraqi law IAC had wrongfully usurped KAC's aircraft by acting as it did: see [2001] 3 WLR 1117 at 1223–1224 (paras 399–402). These conclusions were not challenged in your Lordships' House.

The Mosul Four

[47] Thus far I have concluded that the conduct of which KAC complains meets the requirements of the double actionability rule. The conduct would have been tortious if done in this country and was civilly actionable as usurpation in Iraq. I turn next to the question of damages. To be recoverable in these proceedings the heads of damage claimed by KAC must also meet the requirements of both limbs of the double actionability rule. This was common ground between the parties.

[48] It is at this stage that, on the application of Iraqi law, KAC's claims regarding the Mosul Four failed in the courts below. Iraqi law, as found by Mance J, does not recognise a head of loss consisting of the value of the goods at the time of the wrongful usurpation. What is required is some further loss, such as the destruction by bombing at Mosul. Moreover, if the property usurped is physically lost or damaged, as happened in the case of the Mosul Four, the owner must show that this loss or damage would not have occurred but for the usurpation (the so-called 'but for' test). The burden of proof is on the owner unless the usurper was acting in bad faith. Admittedly that is not the present case. IAC acted in the belief that RCC Resolution 369 gave it a good title. This also was common ground. (In this regard, and to this extent, the existence of this decree will be recognised by an English court. This is not giving effect to Resolution 369. This is doing no more than accepting the existence of this decree as the explanation for IAC's state of mind.)

[49] In your Lordships' House KAC acknowledged that its claim for the value of the Mosul Four depends on satisfying the Iraqi law 'but for' test. Likewise, all

other claims for financial loss consequent upon the destruction of the Mosul Four depend on satisfying this test.

[50] Aikens J observed that, in applying this test and making findings on how the Mosul Four, and indeed all ten aircraft, would have been positioned before and during the hostilities 'but for' the usurpation of IAC, he was having to speculate on a grand scale. But this, he said, was an exercise he had to perform. After carefully considering the evidence he concluded that, in the absence of usurpation by IAC and the incorporation of the ten KAC aircraft into IAC's fleet, the disposition of the ten aircraft would have been exactly the same as it was in fact. Without the usurpation of IAC the Iraqi authorities would still have parked the Mosul Four at Mosul and made no attempt to move them afterwards. These four aircraft would still have been destroyed by the coalition bombing. Accordingly, KAC's claims regarding the Mosul Four wholly failed.

[51] The Court of Appeal rejected KAC's challenge to this conclusion. KAC could not discharge the burden of disproving the judge's factual conclusions. On one matter the Court of Appeal did disturb the findings of Aikens J regarding the whereabouts of the Mosul Four. The judge found that on 17 September 1990, when RCC Resolution 369 came into force, the two Boeing 767s and one of the A300 Airbuses (AHF) were at Basra. The other A300 Airbus (AHG) was already at Mosul. The two Boeing 767s and Airbus AHF were flown from Basra to Mosul on 17 November 1990. Differing from the judge, the Court of Appeal held that the A300 Airbus AHF was flown from Tekrit to Mosul at the end of August 1990 and not, as the judge had found, from Basra to Mosul on 17 November 1990. This difference of view did not affect the overall outcome.

[52] In your Lordships' House KAC mounted a sustained challenge to the Court of Appeal's decision. The primary ground advanced by Mr Vos was that the Court of Appeal misunderstood and misapplied the Iraqi law 'but for' requirement. This requirement, it was submitted, does not mean that the court should consider whether the same result might have been caused by another wrongful activity by someone else. Still less does it enable IAC to advance a case that, absent IAC's acts of conversion, the aircraft would still have been distributed as they were because the government of Iraq would still have delegated to IAC the task of looking after them. Rather this requirement means only that the court should consider what would have happened if the usurper had not committed the wrong. The proper comparison is between what actually happened to the Mosul Four and what would have happened to them if IAC had acted lawfully. Had IAC acted lawfully it would not have moved the aircraft to Mosul. They would have remained at Basra airport. Basra airport was not damaged by coalition bombing. KAC further submitted, in the alternative, that to discharge the onus of proof imposed upon it by the Iraqi law 'but for' requirement, all it had to do was to prove there was a substantial chance the Iraqi government would have treated KAC's aircraft differently. It was not necessary for KAC to prove this would have been so.

[53] I need not elaborate further on these arguments, none of which was advanced in the courts below. They all suffer from the same fatal defect. Each of them raises a question of Iraqi law, but none of them was put to the expert witnesses on Iraqi law. Iraqi law is a matter of evidence. The House cannot entertain an argument dependent on an interpretation of Iraqi law on which the expert witnesses had no opportunity to comment.

[54] KAC also challenged the Court of Appeal's factual conclusions. In one respect the challenge is well founded. This relates to the one factual point on

which the Court of Appeal disagreed with Aikens J, concerning the whereabouts of A300 Airbus AHF. On this point I found KAC's submissions, set out in its written case, compelling. In my view the Court of Appeal fell into error on this point. This does not affect the outcome of these appeals. In all other respects I have been unable to see, in the considerable amount of detailed material put before the House, any ground of substance on which the Court of Appeal can be said to have misdirected itself in any significant regard. Nor is the overall conclusion of Aikens J and the Court of Appeal so inherently improbable that something must have gone awry in their reasoning.

[55] KAC also sought to attack the reliability of the evidence given by IAC witnesses, praying in aid the contents of documents of which discovery was made belatedly, after the trial in front of Aikens J had finished. This is not a matter to which, at this stage, the House can attach any weight. The apparent discrepancies between the witnesses' evidence and these documents, and the reasons for these discrepancies, are matters par excellence which can only be investigated satisfactorily by examination and cross-examination in the course of oral evidence. If the perjury action comes to trial, no doubt this investigation will take place.

[56] As I see it, save for the one point I have mentioned regarding the movements of A300 Airbus AHF, no basis has been established for this House to disturb the factual conclusions of the Court of Appeal, substantially concurrent as they are with those of the judge.

[57] It follows that KAC's appeal against the dismissal of its claims regarding the Mosul Four must fail. On the facts in this case KAC has not been able to surmount the hurdle of the Iraqi law 'but for' test.

The Iran Six

[58] The Iraqi law 'but for' test applies only to a head of loss involving or arising from *physical* loss or damage. This principle of Iraqi law does not apply to claims regarding the Iran Six, because the Iran Six were recovered, largely undamaged, by KAC. The test under Iraqi law for these claims is whether the loss resulted 'naturally' from the usurpation. The parties were agreed that this test is no more stringent than the requirements of the English law of conversion. Accordingly, when considering the recoverable heads of damage regarding the Iran Six, Iraqi law can be put aside. A head of loss recoverable under English law will also be recoverable under Iraqi law and the requirements of the double actionability rule will thus be met as regards both laws.

[59] In one respect Aikens J and the Court of Appeal expressed divergent views on the English law of conversion. The judge held that a threshold 'but for' test applies in English law when measuring the damages recoverable in cases of wrongful interference with goods. Accordingly, KAC's claims in respect of the Iran Six failed. This was because, as he found, the Iran Six would have been flown to Iran even if they had not been incorporated into the IAC fleet.

[60] The Court of Appeal reached a different conclusion on the requirements of the English law of conversion. Brooke LJ rejected the 'but for' test as a test of universal application ([2001] 1 All ER (Comm) 557 at 623–624, [2001] 3 WLR 1117 at 1256–1257 (paras 520–522)). Rather, the rule is that in addition to whatever figure may be attributed to the value of the converted goods, the claimant is prima facie entitled to recover all losses flowing naturally and directly from the defendant's acts of conversion, provided they are not too remote.

[61] Applying this test, the Court of Appeal held that in principle the following claims made by KAC in respect of the Iran Six succeeded: the amount paid to the Iranian government for the return of the Iran Six ($US20m); the cost of repairing the Iran Six ($US11m); loss of profits ($US66m); the cost of hiring substitute aircraft capacity for carrying cargo ($US46m); and the cost of hiring substitute aircraft capacity for carrying passengers ($US99m). The court entered judgment for KAC for $US20m and otherwise remitted the claims to the High Court for assessment. The amounts claimed for loss of profits and cost of substitute aircraft capacity include claims in respect of the Mosul Four. To that extent the figures need adjustment in any event. The Court of Appeal rejected KAC's claim for finance costs associated with its purchase of new aircraft ($US290m). All the amounts claimed are more precisely stated, and their composition elaborated, in the judgment of Aikens J: see [2000] 2 All ER (Comm) 360 at 378–379 (para 37).

[62] On these appeals KAC seeks to uphold the views of the Court of Appeal, save that it seeks to reverse that court's rejection of its claim for finance costs. IAC, for its part, seeks to uphold the views of Aikens J. In challenging the views of the Court of Appeal, IAC submitted there must be a causal nexus between the acts relied upon as constituting the tort of conversion and the loss being claimed. Here there was no such nexus, for the reason given by Aikens J. The damage suffered by KAC failed the 'but for' test.

The Iran Six: causation and the 'but for' test in the tort of conversion

[63] This submission, and the divergent views of the judge and the Court of Appeal, make it necessary to consider the role of the 'but for' test in the assessment of damages in the tort of conversion. I start by going back to first principles regarding the measure of damages in this tort. In days past, when forms of action and pleading technicalities reigned supreme, awards of damages for trover and detinue may have been made in accordance with set formulae. Those days have long gone. As long ago as 1879 Thesiger LJ, in *Hiort v London and North Western Rly* (1879) 4 Ex D 188 at 199, observed that the action of trover had been surrounded by technicalities which might in some instances have worked injustice. He continued:

'I think, however, of late the tendency of the courts has been to treat this action with more common sense than it had been previously treated. Just as in other actions of tort it is held that a person to whom a wrong has been done can only recover the damages which flow from the wrong; so in an action of trover it is the tendency of the courts to apply the same rule.'

In that case the Court of Appeal awarded the plaintiffs nominal damages of one shilling in respect of the defendants' conversion of 60 quarters of oats worth £79. The goods would have been equally lost to the plaintiffs if, instead of being misdelivered, they had been retained and properly delivered by the railway company under the subsequent lawful orders given by the plaintiffs.

[64] Similarly, in *Williams v Peel River Land and Mineral Co Ltd* (1886) 55 LT 689 at 692–693, Bowen LJ, whose judgments are invariably instructive, was scathingly dismissive of the idea that substantial damages should be awarded in an action for wrongful detention of goods when there has been no substantial loss. He said:

'You do not give damages in an action for detention in poenam; it is not a paternal correction inflicted by the court, but simply compensation for the *a* loss ... I cannot think that the law could really lay down anything so ridiculous as that a man should be compensated whether he suffered damages or not.'

[65] This approach has been adopted by the Court of Appeal on several occasions. In 1966 it was applied in *Wickham Holdings Ltd v Brooke House Motors Ltd* [1967] 1 All ER 117 at 120, [1967] 1 WLR 295 at 299–300. In refusing to
b award damages measured by reference to the value of the Rover car converted by the garage dealer, Lord Denning MR said that the plaintiff finance company was 'only entitled to what it has lost by the wrongful act of the defendants'. Again, in *Brandeis Goldschmidt & Co Ltd v Western Transport Ltd* [1982] 1 All ER 28 at 31–32, [1981] QB 864 at 870, failing evidence of loss resulting from the wrongful
c detention of copper, the court awarded only nominal damages. Having acquired the copper for use as a raw material in its business, the fall in the market value of the copper occasioned the plaintiff no loss. Brandon LJ could not see why there should be any universally applicable rule for assessing damages for wrongful detention of goods: 'Damages in tort are awarded by way of monetary compensation for a loss or losses which a plaintiff has actually sustained'. This
d view was echoed by the Court of Appeal in *IBL Ltd v Coussens* [1991] 2 All ER 133 at 139 and 142.

[66] A similar approach has been adopted by the High Court of Australia, in *Butler v Egg and Egg Pulp Marketing Board* (1966) 114 CLR 185. Damages for the eggs converted by the producer were assessed, not on their value at the time of
e the conversion, but upon the actual loss sustained by the defendant, namely, the profit the board would have made on a resale of the eggs.

[67] I have no hesitation in preferring and adopting this view of the present state of the law. The aim of the law, in respect of the wrongful interference with goods, is to provide a just remedy. Despite its proprietary base, this tort does not stand apart and command awards of damages measured by some special and
f artificial standard of its own. The fundamental object of an award of damages in respect of this tort, as with all wrongs, is to award just compensation for loss suffered. Normally (prima facie) the measure of damages is the market value of the goods at the time the defendant expropriated them. This is the general rule, because generally this measure represents the amount of the basic loss suffered by the plaintiff owner. He has been dispossessed of his goods by the defendant.
g Depending on the circumstances some other measure, yielding a higher or lower amount, may be appropriate. The plaintiff may have suffered additional damage consequential on the loss of his goods. Or the goods may have been returned.

[68] This approach accords with the conclusion of the Law Reform Committee in its *Eighteenth Report on Conversion and Detinue* (Cmnd 4774 (1971))
h that the general rule as respects the measure of damages for wrongful interference should be that the plaintiff is entitled to recover the loss he has suffered. The committee considered this conclusion was 'right in principle', and added, in para 91:

j 'In many cases the value of the chattel itself will either represent this loss or form an important element in its calculation; but consideration of the value of the chattel should not be allowed to obscure the principle that what the plaintiff is entitled to recover is his true loss.'

This committee had a distinguished membership including, among others, Lord Pearson and Lord Diplock.

[69] How, then, does one identify a plaintiff's 'true loss' in cases of tort? This question has generated a vast amount of legal literature. I take as my starting point the commonly accepted approach that the extent of a defendant's liability for the plaintiff's loss calls for a twofold inquiry: whether the wrongful conduct causally contributed to the loss and, if it did, what is the extent of the loss for which the defendant ought to be held liable. The first of these inquiries, widely undertaken as a simple 'but for' test, is predominantly a factual inquiry. The application of this test in cases of conversion is the matter now under consideration. I shall return to this in a moment.

[70] The second inquiry, although this is not always openly acknowledged by the courts, involves a value judgment ('*ought* to be held liable'). Written large, the second inquiry concerns the extent of the loss for which the defendant ought fairly or reasonably or justly to be held liable (the epithets are interchangeable). To adapt the language of Jane Stapleton in her article 'Unpacking "Causation"' in Cane and Gardner *Relating to Responsibility* (2001) p 168, the inquiry is whether the plaintiff's harm or loss should be within the scope of the defendant's liability, given the reasons why the law has recognised the cause of action in question. The law has to set a limit to the causally connected losses for which a defendant is to be held responsible. In the ordinary language of lawyers, losses outside the limit may bear one of several labels. They may be described as too remote because the wrongful conduct was not a substantial or proximate cause, or because the loss was the product of an intervening cause. The defendant's responsibility may be excluded because the plaintiff failed to mitigate his loss. Familiar principles, such as foreseeability, assist in promoting some consistency of general approach. These are guidelines, some more helpful than others, but they are never more than this.

[71] In most cases, how far the responsibility of the defendant ought fairly to extend evokes an immediate intuitive response. This is informed common sense by another name. Usually, there is no difficulty in selecting, from the sequence of events leading to the plaintiff's loss, the happening which should be regarded as the cause of the loss for the purpose of allocating responsibility. In other cases, when the outcome of the second inquiry is not obvious, it is of crucial importance to identify the purpose of the relevant cause of action and the nature and scope of the defendant's obligation in the particular circumstances. What was the ambit of the defendant's duty? In respect of what risks or damage does the law seek to afford protection by means of the particular tort? Recent decisions of this House have highlighted the point. When evaluating the extent of the losses for which a negligent valuer should be responsible the scope of the valuer's duty must first be identified: see *South Australia Asset Management Corp v York Montague Ltd, United Bank of Kuwait plc v Prudential Property Services Ltd, Nykredit Mortgage Bank plc v Edward Erdman Group Ltd* [1996] 3 All ER 365, [1997] AC 191. In *Reeves v Comr of Police of the Metropolis* [1999] 3 All ER 897, [2000] 1 AC 360 the free, deliberate and informed act of a human being, there committing suicide, did not negative responsibility to his dependants when the defendant's duty was to guard against that very act.

[72] The need to have in mind the purpose of the relevant cause of action is not confined to the second, evaluative stage of the twofold inquiry. It may also arise at the earlier stage of the 'but for' test, to which I now return. This guideline principle is concerned to identify and exclude losses lacking a causal connection with the wrongful conduct. Expressed in its simplest form, the principle poses

the question whether the plaintiff would have suffered the loss without ('but for')
the defendant's wrongdoing. If he would not, the wrongful conduct was *a*
cause of the loss. If the loss would have arisen even without the defendant's
wrongdoing, normally it does not give rise to legal liability. In *Barnett v Chelsea
and Kensington Hospital Management Committee* [1968] 1 All ER 1068, [1969] 1 QB
428 the night watchman's death did not pass this test. He would have died from
arsenic poisoning even if the hospital casualty department had treated him
properly. Of course, even if the plaintiff's loss passes this exclusionary threshold
test, it by no means follows that the defendant should be legally responsible for
the loss.

[73] This threshold 'but for' test is based on the presence or absence of one
particular type of causal connection: whether the wrongful conduct was a
necessary condition of the occurrence of the harm or loss. In *Barnett's* case the
hospital's negligence was not a necessary element in the conditions which led to
the watchman's death. He would have died anyway. In very many cases this test
operates satisfactorily, but it is not always a reliable guide. Academic writers have
drawn attention to its limitations: see, for example, the late Professor Fleming's
The Law of Torts (9th edn, 1998) pp 222–230, and Markesinis and Deacon *Tort Law*
(4th edn, 1999) pp 178–191. Torts cover a wide field and may be committed in an
infinite variety of situations. Even the sophisticated variants of the 'but for' test
cannot be expected to set out a formula whose mechanical application will
provide infallible threshold guidance on causal connection for every tort in every
circumstance. In particular, the 'but for' test can be over-exclusionary.

[74] This may occur where more than one wrongdoer is involved. The classic
example is where two persons independently search for the source of a gas leak
with the aid of lighted candles. According to the simple 'but for' test, neither
would be liable for damage caused by the resultant explosion. In this type of case,
involving multiple wrongdoers, the court may treat wrongful conduct as having
sufficient causal connection with the loss for the purpose of attracting
responsibility even though the simple 'but for' test is not satisfied. In so deciding
the court is primarily making a value judgment on responsibility. In making this
judgment the court will have regard to the purpose sought to be achieved by the
relevant tort, as applied to the particular circumstances.

[75] One situation where the courts have had to grapple with the multiple
wrongdoers' conundrum concerns how far the liability of one wrongdoer should
be diminished by loss flowing from the conduct of another wrongdoer. This has
arisen particularly in the context of personal injuries, where the plaintiff was first
injured by one wrongdoer and later by another, and in the context of a ship
suffering successive collisions at sea. Another situation is where the defendant's
wrongful act caused damage to the plaintiff, but even if he had acted lawfully the
same or similar damage would have been produced by the wrongful act of
someone else.

[76] Elements of both these situations are present in the instant case. The
government of Iraq had already seized KAC's aircraft before IAC wrongfully
converted them. And even if IAC had not converted them in autumn 1990,
presumably the government of Iraq or some other emanation of the state would
have wrongfully retained possession of the aircraft.

[77] I turn therefore to consider the purpose sought to be achieved by the tort
of conversion. Conversion is the principal means whereby English law protects
the ownership of goods. Misappropriation of another's goods constitutes conversion.

Committing this tort gives rise to an obligation to pay damages. Payment of damages may have proprietary consequences. Payment of damages assessed on the footing that the plaintiff is being compensated for the whole of his interest in the goods extinguishes his title: see s 5 of the Torts (Interference with Goods) Act 1977. Further, when the defendant is in possession of the plaintiff's goods, the remedies available to the plaintiff include a court order that the goods be delivered up: see s 3.

[78] Consistently with its purpose of providing a remedy for the misappropriation of goods, liability is strict. As Diplock LJ said in *Marfani & Co Ltd v Midland Bank Ltd* [1968] 2 All ER 573 at 577–578, [1968] 1 WLR 956 at 970–971, one's duty to one's neighbour is to refrain from doing any voluntary act in relation to his goods which is a usurpation of his property or possessory rights in them. Whether the defendant still has the goods or their proceeds matters not. Nor does it matter whether the defendant was a thief or acted in the genuine and reasonable belief the goods were his. Cleasby B's aphorism, uttered in 1872 in *Fowler v Hollins* (1872) LR 7 QB 616 at 639, still represents the law: 'persons deal with the property in chattels or exercise acts of ownership over them at their peril'. This, he observed, was regarded as a salutary rule for the protection of property.

[79] Some aspects of this rule have attracted criticism. Vindication of a plaintiff's proprietary interests requires that, in general, all those who convert his goods should be accountable for *benefits* they receive. They must make restitution to the extent they are unjustly enriched. The goods are his, and he is entitled to reclaim them and any benefits others have derived from them. Liability in this regard should be strict, subject to defences available to restitutionary claims such as change of position: see *Lipkin Gorman (a firm) v Karpnale Ltd* [1992] 4 All ER 512, [1991] 2 AC 548. Additionally, those who act dishonestly should be liable to make good any *losses* caused by their wrongful conduct. Whether those who act innocently should also be liable to make good the plaintiff's losses is a different matter. A radical re-appraisal of the tort of conversion along these lines was not pursued on these appeals. So I shall say nothing more about it.

[80] The existing principle of strict liability as described above is deeply ingrained in the common law. It has survived at least since the days of Lord Mansfield in *Cooper v Chitty* (1756) 1 Burr 20, 97 ER 166. The hardship it may cause to those who deal innocently with a person in possession of goods has long been recognised. Blackburn J noted this in the leading case of *Hollins v Fowler* (1875) LR 7 HL 757 at 764, [1874–80] All ER Rep 118 at 122. The hardship arises especially for innocent persons who no longer have the goods. There has been some statutory amelioration of the principle, in the Factors Acts and elsewhere, but in general the principle endures.

[81] Consistently with this principle, every person through whose hands goods pass in a series of conversions is himself guilty of conversion and liable to the owner for the loss caused by his misappropriation of the owner's goods. His liability is not diminished by reason, for instance, of his having acquired the goods from a thief as distinct from the owner himself. In such a case, it may be said, looking at the successive conversions overall, the owner is no worse off as a result of the acts of the person who acquired the goods from the thief. Such a person has not 'caused' the owner any additional loss.

[82] In one sense this is undoubtedly correct. The owner had already lost his goods. But that is really nothing to the point for the purposes of assessing damages for conversion. By definition, each person in a series of conversions

wrongfully excludes the owner from possession of his goods. This is the basis on
which each is liable to the owner. That is the nature of the tort of conversion.
The wrongful acts of a previous possessor do not therefore diminish the plaintiff's
claim in respect of the wrongful acts of a later possessor. Nor, for a different reason,
is it anything to the point that, absent the defendant's conversion, someone else
would wrongfully have converted the goods. The likelihood that, had the
defendant not wronged the plaintiff, somebody would have done so is no reason
for diminishing the defendant's liability and responsibility for the loss he brought
upon the plaintiff.

[83] Where, then, does this leave the simple 'but for' test in cases of successive
conversion? I suggest that, if the test is to be applied at all, the answer lies in
keeping in mind, as I have said, that each person in a series of conversions
wrongfully excludes the owner from possession of his goods. The exclusionary
threshold test is to be applied on this footing. Thus the test calls for consideration
of whether the plaintiff would have suffered the loss in question had he retained
his goods and not been unlawfully deprived of them by the defendant. The test
calls for a comparison between the owner's position had he retained his goods
and his position having been deprived of his goods by the defendant. Loss which
the owner would have suffered even if he had retained the goods is not loss
'caused' by the conversion. The defendant is not liable for such loss.

[84] The Court of Appeal decision in *Hiort v London and North Western Rly*
(1879) 4 Ex D 188, mentioned above, can be analysed in this way. Hiort would
equally have received no payment for his goods if, instead of misdelivering the
goods, the railway company had delivered them in accordance with his
instructions. *Hiort*'s case was not a case of successive conversions. But the like
comparison can equally be made in such a case.

[85] For these reasons I consider KAC's claims in respect of the Iran Six do not
fail at the threshold stage. Had KAC not been unlawfully deprived of its goods
by IAC, KAC would not have suffered any of the heads of loss it is now claiming.
Had KAC retained possession of the Iran Six, the aircraft would not have been
evacuated to Iran.

[86] Furthermore, contrary to IAC's submission, it would not be right to
award damages by reference to the (insignificant) losses caused to KAC by the
individual acts evidencing conversion, such as overpainting and using one aircraft
for commercial flights. The wrongful conduct lay in unlawfully depriving KAC
of its aircraft.

The Iran Six: 'user damages'

[87] I have noted that the fundamental object of an award of damages for
conversion is to award just compensation for loss suffered. Sometimes, when the
goods or their equivalent are returned, the owner suffers no financial loss. But
the wrongdoer may well have benefited from his temporary use of the owner's
goods. It would not be right that he should be able to keep this benefit. The court
may order him to pay damages assessed by reference to the value of the benefit
he derived from his wrongdoing. I considered this principle in *A-G v Blake*
(*Jonathan Cape Ltd, third party*) [2000] 4 All ER 385 at 391–394, [2001] 1 AC 268 at
278–280. In an appropriate case the court may award damages on this 'user
principle' in addition to compensation for loss suffered. For instance, if the goods
are returned damaged, the court may award damages assessed by reference to the
benefit obtained by the wrongdoer as well as the cost of repair.

[88] Recognition that damages may be awarded on this principle may assist in making some awards of damages in conversion cases more coherent. For example, I respectfully think this is the preferable basis for the award of damages in *Solloway v McLaughlin, McLaughlin v Solloway* [1937] 4 All ER 328, [1938] AC 247 in respect of Solloway's misappropriation of the 14,000 shares deposited with him by McLaughlin. McLaughlin suffered no financial loss from the misappropriation, because equivalent shares were returned to McLaughlin when he closed his account. But Solloway profited by the fall in the value of the shares by selling them when they were deposited with him and repurchasing them at the lower market price obtaining when McLaughlin closed his account.

[89] A similar observation may be made regarding the outcome in *BBMB Finance (Hong Kong) Ltd v Eda Holdings Ltd* [1991] 2 All ER 129, [1990] 1 WLR 409. The owner recovered all his shares or their equivalent. The wrongdoer's misuse of the shares caused the owner no financial loss. But, on the face of the transactions (the facts relating to the unpresented cheque are obscure), the defendant benefited by selling the owner's shares at a high price and replacing them with shares bought at a lower price.

[90] In the present case no claim for an award of 'user damages' has ever been pleaded or formally formulated. Mr Vos sought to advance such a claim before your Lordships' House regarding the Iran Six. I consider it is much too late in these protracted proceedings for KAC now to advance this new claim for the first time.

The Iran Six: intervening acts, and the costs of recovery and repair

[91] The Iran Six were sent to Iran on the orders of the government of Iraq. They were impounded there by the government of Iran until their eventual return.

[92] These facts do not excuse IAC from liability for the adverse financial consequences of the detention of the aircraft in Iran. A person who misappropriates another's goods does so at his own risk. That is the nature of the wrong. He takes upon himself the risk of being unable to return the goods to their rightful owner. It matters not that he may be prevented from returning the goods due to unforeseen circumstances beyond his control. The reason for his non-return of the goods, or his delay in returning the goods, is neither here nor there so far as his liability to the owner is concerned. If the goods are eventually returned, thereby diminishing the financial loss suffered by the owner, this must be taken into account. But the wrongdoer's liability ought fairly to extend to compensating the owner for the loss he sustains by virtue of his temporary loss of his goods, regardless of the impact any unforeseen circumstances may have had on the wrongdoer. The loss flowing from the unforeseen circumstances should be borne by the wrongdoer, not the innocent owner of the goods. Additionally, provided the amount is not out of proportion to the value of the goods, the wrongdoer ought to reimburse the owner for any money spent on recovering the goods or carrying out necessary repairs.

[93] Here, after much negotiation, in July 1992 the Iranian government notified the Kuwaiti government of its willingness to release the Iran Six. The aircraft were flown back to Kuwait in July and August 1992 on the understanding that payment would be agreed subsequently. In March 1994 KAC agreed to pay $US20m to the government of Iran for the costs and expenses of keeping, sheltering and maintaining the Iran Six. The payment was made in four tranches

a
and was completed by the end of September 1994. Had the Iranian government insisted on this payment being made before releasing the aircraft, there could be no room for doubt that KAC was fairly entitled to recover this expenditure from IAC. It was the cost incurred by KAC in regaining its aircraft. I do not think the precise sequence of events which occurred, with the aircraft released before the amount payable was agreed or the payment was made, alters the position.

b
If KAC had not adhered to the arrangements made at the time of the release it would have placed itself in an impossible position for the future, if only in terms of overflying and landing rights in relation to Iran.

[94] Nor is there any room for doubt that, in principle, IAC is responsible for the reasonable costs incurred by KAC in overhauling and repairing the aircraft when they were returned.

c

The Iran Six: consequential losses

[95] KAC was an operating airline. The ten aircraft seized in the invasion were the major part of its fleet. When the hostilities ended KAC found itself without most of its aircraft It was eminently to be expected that until the missing aircraft
d
were replaced, KAC would need to hire substitute aircraft capacity, both for passengers and cargo. Furthermore, it was eminently to be expected that until substitute capacity was obtained KAC would suffer losses of business and might suffer loss of profits. I see no reason to question that IAC's liability to KAC ought to extend to meeting the reasonable costs of chartering substitute aircraft and
e
making good any loss of profits.

[96] The other head of consequential loss claimed by KAC comprises finance costs associated with buying replacement aircraft. This claim is more difficult. The basis of this claim is as follows. Faced with the destruction of the Mosul Four and the detention of the Iran Six, KAC decided to buy new rather than
f
secondhand replacements. As Kuwait's flag carrier, KAC customarily bought new aircraft rather than used aircraft. In the normal course KAC replaced its aircraft on a 15-year cycle. Its practice was to accumulate funds needed to buy replacement aircraft over this 15-year cycle. Since KAC's aircraft were seized broadly in the middle of their 15-year life cycles, KAC had to borrow money to buy replacement aircraft between 1991 and 1995. KAC calculated that the
g
additional cost of replacing the ten aircraft in the middle rather than at the end of their 15-year cycles was about $US290m. KAC gives credit for the sale prices obtained for the Iran Six and for the scrap value of the Mosul Four.

[97] Had the matter rested there KAC's claim might have been supportable, due allowance being made for the betterment resulting from the early
h
replacement of the fleet. But there is more to the story. The new aircraft bought by KAC were not mere replacements for the ten aircraft misappropriated by IAC. Having lost most of its fleet, KAC used the occasion to carry out a fundamental reappraisal of its aircraft requirements in the light of changing market conditions. These requirements dictated that the composition of KAC's fleet should be
j
significantly different from its existing fleet. Different aircraft, with different specifications, were called for. Accordingly, in the early 1990s KAC did not seek to restore the airline to the position which would have existed if the Mosul Four had survived intact and the Iran Six had not become temporarily unavailable. KAC did not set out to replace the aircraft it had lost with the same models, or the closest available. It did not just buy new for old. The ten aircraft seized included

five Airbus A310-200s. New aircraft of this model were still available for purchase from Airbus, but KAC chose to buy different aircraft.

[98] This was not an unreasonable course for KAC to take. Indeed, it would have made no commercial sense for KAC to replace the ten aircraft without regard to its current and anticipated aircraft requirements. KAC was forced to review its aircraft requirements, and it seized the opportunity to make significant changes in the composition of its fleet. This may well have been a commercially wise decision. But I do not think it would be right to saddle IAC with the finance costs associated with this substantial restructuring of KAC's fleet. In agreement with the Court of Appeal and with the view expressed by Aikens J on this point, although not for precisely the same reasons, I would not allow this head of claim.

[99] The parties presented to the House extensive written and oral arguments on whether the test for liability for consequential loss in cases of conversion is reasonable foreseeability as distinct from whether the loss arises naturally and directly from the wrong. By consequential loss I mean loss beyond that represented by the value of the goods. The route I have followed in reaching my conclusions on KAC's claims under this head makes it strictly unnecessary to express any opinion on this point. Nevertheless, in the absence of clear authority, I ought to state my view briefly.

[100] Expressed in terms of the traditional guideline principles, the choice is between confining liability for consequential loss to damage which is 'foreseeable', as distinct from damage flowing 'directly and naturally' from the wrongful conduct. In practice, these two tests usually yield the same result. Where they do not, the foreseeability test is likely to be the more restrictive. The prevalent view is that the more restrictive test of foreseeability is applicable to the torts of negligence, nuisance and *Rylands v Fletcher* (1868) LR 3 HL 330, [1861–73] All ER Rep 1: see the two *Wagon Mound* cases (*Overseas Tankship (UK) Ltd v Morts Dock and Engineering Co Ltd, The Wagon Mound (No 1)* [1961] 1 All ER 404, [1961] AC 388 and *Overseas Tankship (UK) Ltd v The Miller Steamship Co Pty, The Wagon Mound (No 2)* [1966] 2 All ER 709, [1967] 1 AC 617) and *Cambridge Water Co v Eastern Counties Leather plc* [1994] 1 All ER 53, [1994] 2 AC 264. The Court of Appeal recently applied this test to the tort of conversion, apparently without any contrary argument, in *Saleslease Ltd v Davis* [1999] 1 WLR 1664, although the members of the court differed in the application of the principle to the facts of the case.

[101] In contrast, the less restrictive test is applicable in deceit. The more culpable the defendant the wider the area of loss for which he can fairly be held responsible: see the discussion by my noble and learned friend Lord Steyn in *Smith New Court Securities Ltd v Scrimgeour Vickers (Asset Management) Ltd* [1996] 4 All ER 796 at 790–795, [1997] AC 254 at 279–285.

[102] This bifurcation causes difficulty with the tort of conversion. Dishonesty is not an essential ingredient of this wrong. The defendant may be a thief, or he may have acted wholly innocently. Both are strictly liable. But it seems to me inappropriate they should be treated alike when determining their liability for consequential loss. Parliament, indeed, has recognised that for some purposes different considerations should apply to persons who steal goods, or knowingly receive stolen goods, and persons who can show they bought the goods in good faith. In respect of the tort of conversion the Limitation Act 1980 prescribes different limitation provisions for these two types of cases: see ss 3 and 4.

a [103] I have already mentioned that, as the law now stands, the tort of conversion may cause hardship for innocent persons. This suggests that foreseeability, as the more restrictive test, is appropriate for those who act in good faith. Liability remains strict, but liability for consequential loss is confined to types of damage which can be expected to arise from the wrongful conduct. You deal with goods at the risk of discovering later that, unbeknown to you, you

b have not acquired a good title. That is the strict common law principle. The risk is that, should you not have acquired title, you will be liable to the owner for the losses he can expect to have suffered as a result of your misappropriation of his goods. That seems the preferable approach, in the case of a person who can prove he acted in the genuine belief the goods were his. A person in possession of goods knows where and how he acquired them. It is up to him to establish he

c was innocent of any knowing wrongdoing. This is the approach Parliament has taken in s 4 of the 1980 Act.

[104] Persons who knowingly convert another's goods stand differently. Such persons are acting dishonestly. I can see no good reason why the remoteness test of 'directly and naturally' applied in cases of deceit should not apply in cases of

d conversion where the defendant acted dishonestly.

[105] I would dismiss both appeals, and pay tribute to the meticulous care and thoroughness of Mance J, Aikens J and the Court of Appeal in their treatment of the factual and legal complexities in these proceedings.

e **LORD STEYN.**

[106] My Lords, the subject matter of this action was ten commercial passenger aircraft belonging to Kuwait Airways Corp (KAC) which were at Kuwait International Airport on 2 August 1990 when Iraq invaded Kuwait. Iraq completed its occupation of Kuwait within three days and proclaimed the integration of Kuwait into Iraq. Iraq systematically set about plundering the assets

f of Kuwait. On 9 September 1990 the government of Iraq (called the Revolutionary Command Council) promulgated Resolution 369. It read as follows:

'I. (1) That the Kuwait Airways Corporation be dissolved and all its fixed and liquid assets, rights and liabilities be transferred to the Iraqi Airways Co, who will register all assets in accordance with domestic and international

g laws. (2) All assets belonging to Kuwait Airways are to be transferred to the Iraqi Airways Co, as soon as this resolution comes into effect.

II. All activities of Kuwait Airways offices abroad must cease and all their assets are to be transferred to the Iraqi Airways Co, in accordance with clause I of this resolution.

h III. The board of Iraqi Airways is to conduct a complete survey of all Kuwait Airways personnel and determine the level of the workforce in the light of current needs and central directives.

IV. All withdrawal authorisations granted to Kuwait Airways employees are cancelled from the date this resolution comes into effect …'

j On 17 September 1990 Resolution 369 came into effect. On the same day Iraq Airways Co (IAC) implemented Resolution 369. Previously, and on various dates in August 1990, IAC pilots had flown the ten aircraft to Iraq. At the time of the promulgation and coming into effect of Resolution 369 the ten aircraft were in Iraq.

[107] The international response to Iraq's flagrant breach of international law was prompt and comprehensive. On 2 August 1990 the United Nations Security Council adopted Resolution 660 which condemned the invasion of Kuwait as a breach of international peace and security. This was followed by a series of supplementary Security Council resolutions which decreed that the annexation of Kuwait was null and void; called on member states to give no recognition directly or indirectly to any aspect of the annexation; and required all states to impose sanctions on Iraq. These measures were duly taken under Ch VII of the United Nations Charter.

[108] On 17 January 1991, coalition forces began air strikes in Iraq and Kuwait. By 28 February 1991 the Gulf War had been won and Iraq defeated. On 28 February 1991, the coalition forces suspended their offensive. This was followed on 2 March 1991 by UN Security Council Resolution 686 which noted that the coalition offensive had been suspended; required Iraq immediately to rescind its actions purporting to annex Kuwait; required it to accept liability under international law and called upon Iraq to return all property seized by it. On 3 March 1991, Iraq agreed to comply with Resolution 686. Iraq withdrew from Kuwait. On 5 March 1991, Iraq promulgated Resolution 55 which abrogated all Iraqi Resolutions enacted from 2 August 1990 relating to Kuwait, including Resolution 369. This resolution took effect in Iraqi law on 18 March 1991.

[109] The fate of the KAC aircraft was as follows. The four KAC aircraft at Mosul (the 'Mosul Four') were destroyed by coalition bombing at Mosul airport in late January and early February 1991. The other six aircraft were flown to Iran between 15 January and 4 February 1991. These aircraft (the 'Iran Six') were not returned to KAC by the government of Iran until July to August 1992 and then only in return for an eventual payment by Kuwait to Iran of $US 20m for storage, sheltering and maintenance costs.

[110] KAC brought an action in the Commercial Court against IAC for conversion of the ten aircraft. IAC, a state-controlled enterprise, raised the defence of state immunity. In 1995 the House of Lords held that IAC was entitled to state immunity in relation to the removal of the aircraft from Kuwait to Iraq, which were exercises of governmental power by Iraq. But the House of Lords held that IAC was not entitled to immunity in relation to the retention and use of the aircraft from 16 September 1990, immediately before Resolution 369 came into force. It was held that no sovereign immunity attached to IAC's subsequent conduct in treating the aircraft as belonging to them: *Kuwait Airways Corp v Iraqi Airways Co* [1995] 3 All ER 694, [1995] 1 WLR 1147. The action proceeded. It is unnecessary to dwell on the forensic history. I must, however, record my admiration of the massive and excellent judgments of Mance J, Aikens J and the Court of Appeal. They enable the House to put to one side the minutiae of the case and to concentrate on the essentials. The shape of the case before the House appears from the following part of the executive summary of the effect of the judgment of the Court of Appeal ([2001] 1 All ER (Comm) 557 at 562, [2001] 2 WLR 1117 at 1127–1128):

'1. By this judgment of the court, the Court of Appeal upheld the judgment of Mance J ([1999] CLC 31). In particular, it ruled that an English court was entitled to decline to recognise Resolution 369 of the Revolutionary Command Council of Iraq. It held that ... the resolution was extra-territorial in its effect; and that it would be contrary to English public policy to grant

a
recognition to a resolution which was in breach of clearly established principles of international law ...

2. The court also upheld that part of the judgment of Aikens J ([2000] 2 All ER (Comm) 360) in which he found that KAC could not recover damages in respect of the loss of the Mosul Four ... The court upheld the ruling on the facts and upheld his decision on the law because, as required by Iraqi law,

b
KAC was not able to show that the physical damage to the aircraft would not have occurred but for the usurpation ...

3. The court allowed KAC's appeal against that part of the judgment of Aikens J in which he held that KAC was not entitled to recover loss flowing naturally and directly from IAC's wrongful usurpation and conversion of the Iran Six. Although it upheld his findings of fact in all material respects, it held

c
that he was wrong to apply a 'but for' test as a matter of English law, and that in relation to usurped and converted goods which had not been physically lost or damaged there was no material distinction between the Iraqi law of usurpation and the English law of conversion, which is a tort of strict liability ...

d
4. The action will therefore be remitted to the Commercial Court for an assessment of the damages flowing naturally and directly from the wrongful usurpation and conversion of the Iran Six.'

The status of Resolution 369

[111] Two questions arise. The first is whether the recognition of Resolution
e
369 would be contrary to English public policy. The second arises in this way. KAC's claim must satisfy the so-called double actionability rule, viz it must be sustainable both under the Iraqi law of usurpation and under the English law of conversion: see *Chaplin v Boys* [1969] 2 All ER 1085, [1971] AC 356. The double actionability point has been formulated as follows: for the purpose of
f
determining whether the acts of IAC were actionable under Iraqi law, must regard be had to the totality of Iraqi law, including Resolution 369, or can that resolution be treated as excised from the corpus of Iraqi law for this purpose if it is contrary to English public policy? The Court of Appeal held that recognition of Resolution 369 would be contrary to English public policy and must be wholly disregarded. The grounds of its decision on public policy were twofold. First, the
g
Court of Appeal refused to give effect to it because of its extraterritorial and exorbitant scope. Secondly, the Court of Appeal held that recognition of the resolution would be contrary to English public policy because it breached established principles of international law.

[112] The first reason is not a very secure foothold for the decision.
h
Undoubtedly, an English court would be right to refuse to give effect to the resolution in relation to KAC's property outside Iraq, e g in KAC's London office. But why should the resolution have no effect on the aircraft which were on Iraqi soil at the relevant time? After all, it is well established that courts must not sit in judgment on the acts of a foreign government within its own territory. The
j
Court of Appeal explained:

'Resolution 369 opens with the provision for KAC's dissolution. It is in that context that all its rights and liabilities, and all its assets, are to be transferred to IAC. If, however, the provision for KAC's dissolution is ineffective for recognition in this forum, it is hard to see why a limited transfer of such assets as happened to be situate in Iraq at the relevant time should be

recognised. Moreover, there is no separate provision for transfer of KAC's
assets located in Iraq. It is not therefore as though the application of a blue
pencil rule to extraterritorial assets could save a provision dealing with assets
within Iraq.' (See [2001] 3 WLR 1117 at 1216 (para 369).)

For my part this is not a satisfactory reason. Notionally, and by applying a blue
pencil, it was entirely possible to sever the extraterritorial effect of the resolution
from its territorial effect within Iraq. I would, therefore, not accept this part of
the reasoning of the Court of Appeal.

[113] The second ground for the Court of Appeal's decision on Resolution
369, although not directly supported by any earlier precedent, is much stronger.
It invoked public policy as a justification for not applying otherwise applicable
principles of private international law. The foundation of it is that the annexation
of Kuwait, and Resolution 369, was a flagrant breach of international law. If any
proof was required, the Security Council resolutions establish this fact beyond
doubt. In any event, the Iraqi state unequivocally accepted that in annexing
Kuwait and passing Resolution 369 it had acted in breach of international law.
This is the context against which IAC argued, relying on *Buttes Gas and Oil Co v
Hammer (Nos 2 and 3)* [1981] 3 All ER 616, [1982] AC 888, that 'the issues' are not
justiciable. Counsel for IAC relied on what he described as an absolute rule in the
Buttes case that courts in England will not adjudicate upon acts done abroad by
virtue of sovereign authority ([1981] 3 All ER 616 at 629, [1982] AC 888 at 932 per
Lord Wilberforce). For my part this is too austere and unworkable an
interpretation of the *Buttes* case. There were rival claims by rulers to part of the
continental shelf and there was a dispute about the motives of a foreign ruler
([1981] 3 All ER 616 at 632–633, [1982] AC 888 at 937). Lord Wilberforce found
that there were 'no judicial or manageable standards by which to judge these
issues' and 'the court would be in a judicial no-man's land'. He added: 'it is not
to be assumed that these matters have now passed into history, so that they now
can be examined with safe detachment' ([1981] 3 All ER 616 at 633, [1982] AC 888
at 938). The *Buttes* case was an unusual case decided on a striking-out application
and without the benefit of a Foreign Office certificate. But reading Lord
Wilberforce's judgment as a whole I have no doubt that counsel for IAC is wrong
in seeking to derive from it the categorical rule put forward. In any event, in the
present case there is no difficulty in adjudicating on Iraq's gross breaches of
international law. There is no relevant issue: Iraq accepted the illegality of the
annexation and of Resolution 369. In agreement with the Court of Appeal I
would reject the argument based on non-justiciability.

[114] That brings me to the next step in the reasoning of the Court of Appeal,
viz that because the annexation of Kuwait and Resolution 369 constituted a
breach of international law it would be contrary to English public policy to
recognise Resolution 369. The conception of public policy is, and should be,
narrower and more limited in private international law than in internal law:
Cheshire and North's Private International Law (13th edn, 1999) p 123. Local values
ought not lightly to be elevated into public policy on the transnational level. But,
rightly, the Court of Appeal found support in *Oppenheimer v Cattermole (Inspector
of Taxes)* [1975] 1 All ER 538, [1976] AC 249. In that case the House of Lords
considered a Nazi law which discriminated against Jews. The flavour of the decision
appears from the following passage in the judgment of Lord Cross of Chelsea, with

a whom Lords Hailsham of St Marylebone LC, Hodson, Pearson and Salmon agreed:

> 'But I think—as Upjohn J thought (see *Re Helbert Wagg & Co Ltd* ([1956] Ch 323 at 334))—that it is part of the public policy of this country that our courts should give effect to clearly established rules of international law. Of course on some points it may be by no means clear what the rule of international
> *b* law is. Whether, for example, legislation of a particular type is contrary to international law because it is "confiscatory" is a question on which there may well be wide differences of opinion between Communist and capitalist countries. But what we are concerned with here is legislation which takes away without compensation from a section of the citizen body singled out
> *c* on racial grounds all their property on which the state passing the legislation can lay its hands and, in addition, deprives them of their citizenship. To my mind a law of this sort constitutes so grave an infringement of human rights that the courts of this country ought to refuse to recognise it as a law at all.' (See [1975] 1 All ER 538 at 567, [1976] AC 249 at 278.)

d It is true, of course, that the present case does not involve human rights. That is how counsel for IAC sought to confine the public policy exception stated in *Oppenheimer's* case. I would reject this argument. It is true that the Court of Appeal broke new ground. It was the first decision to hold that the acts of a foreign state within its territory may be refused recognition because they are contrary to public international law. On the other hand, the Court of Appeal built
e on *Oppenheimer's* case which was permeated, as the Court of Appeal observed, by considerations of the public international law. In my view the Court of Appeal was right to extend the public policy exception beyond human rights violations to flagrant breaches of public international law. It does not follow, however, that every breach of international law will trigger the public policy
f exception. The present case is, however, a paradigm of the public policy exception. If the statutory enactment of the exception in s 14(3) of Private International Law (Miscellaneous Provisions) Act 1995 had been engaged it would have been a classic case for the application of that provision. Marching logic to its ultimate unreality, counsel for IAC submitted that the United Nations Charter and Security Council resolutions are not incorporated into our law and must be
g disregarded. Displaying a commendable internationalism the Court of Appeal observed ([2001] 3 WLR 1117 at 1218 (para 378)):

> '... the very matters which are before the court, and which KAC seek to rely on for the purpose of showing that Resolution 369 should not be
> *h* recognised, have already been determined, if not by an international court, at any rate by an international forum, of which nearly all the nations of the world are members, and whose decisions are binding on all those nations, including the United Kingdom and Iraq.'

I would endorse this observation. I would add a few observations. Not only has
j the United Nations Charter been adhered to by virtually all states, that is 189 states, but even the few remaining non-members have acquiesced in the principles of the charter: *Restatement of the Law Third, The Foreign Relations Law of the United States* (1986) vol 1, p 27, para 102, comment (h). It is generally accepted that the principles of the United Nations Charter prohibiting the use of force have the character of jus cogens, ie is part of peremptory public international law,

permitting no derogation: see *Restatement*, p 28, para 102, comment (k). Security
Council resolutions under Ch VII of the charter, and therefore the resolutions in   *a*
question here, were binding in law on all members including the United
Kingdom and Iraq. And, under art 2(6) of the United Nations Charter, the
resolutions called on the few non-members of the United Nations to abide by
the resolutions, and they at least acquiesced. There was a universal consensus on the
illegality of Iraq's aggression. Moreover, in the light of the letter of Sir Franklin   *b*
Berman, the legal advisor of the Foreign and Commonwealth Office, of
7 November 1997, describing the United Kingdom's consistent position as to the
binding effect of the Security Council resolutions, it would have been contrary to
the international obligations of the United Kingdom were its courts to adopt an
approach contrary to its obligations under the United Nations Charter and under
the relevant Security Council resolutions. It follows that it would be contrary to   *c*
domestic public policy to give effect to Resolution 369 in any way.

[115] This conclusion on English public policy does not reflect an insular
approach. Our domestic public policy on the status of Resolution 319 does not
stand alone. In recent years, particularly as a result of French scholarship, principles
of international public policy (l'ordre public veritablement international) have   *d*
been developed in relation to subjects such as traffic in drugs, traffic in weapons,
terrorism, and so forth: see a magisterial paper by Professor Pierre Lalive,
'Transnational (or Truly International) Public Policy and International Arbitration,
ICCA' in Sanders (ed) *Comparative Arbitration Practice and Public Policy in
Arbitration* (1986) p 257, pp 284–286; Fouchard, Gaillard and Goldman *International
Commercial Arbitration* (1999) p 953 et seq; Redfern and Hunter *Law and Practice of*   *e*
International Commercial Arbitration (3rd edn, 1999) p 152, para 3-27; Craig, Park
and Paulsson *International Chamber of Commerce Arbitration* (3rd edn, 2000) pp 338–
346, para 17.04. Similarly, there may be an international public policy requiring
states to respect fundamental human rights: *Restatement*, vol 2, pp 152 et seq,
para 701. The public policy condemning Iraq's flagrant breaches of public   *f*
international law is yet another illustration of such a truly international
public policy in action. This international dimension reinforces the view of the
Court of the Appeal.

[116] There is no scope for treating Resolution 369 as only in part contrary to
public policy. The nature and width of the public policy engaged here, based on   *g*
flagrant breaches of international law, strikes at the root of the Iraqi annexation
policy and the entirety of Resolution 369. There is no basis for severance of any
part of it. It follows that IAC's argument on Resolution 369 for the purpose of
invoking the act of state doctrine, in respect of what was done on Iraqi soil, must
be rejected.

[117] It is now necessary to turn to the consequences of this conclusion for the   *h*
double actionability point. The court is obliged, in the words of Lord Cross of
Chelsea, in *Oppenheimer's* case [1975] 1 All ER 538 at 567, [1976] AC 249 at 278, 'to
refuse to recognise it as a law at all'. It may not recognise Resolution 369 for any
purpose. One might have thought that it follows inexorably that IAC's argument
based on Resolution 369 must fail. Counsel for IAC accepted that this would   *j*
necessarily be so in any action for delivery up of the aircraft in an English court if
maintainable here. But he argued that it is different where KAC must establish
an actionable usurpation under Iraqi law. He argued that in constructing a tort
under Iraqi law the plaintiff must necessarily take account of the whole corpus of
Iraqi law which must include Resolution 369. In such a case, he argued, an

a English court cannot excise part of Iraqi law in deciding whether a tort has been committed under Iraqi law. Plausibly as the argument was dressed up it ought not to succeed. Postulate, for example, an action in tort in the English courts for recovering loss caused by negligent mistatements which are prima face actionable under the applicable foreign law and under English law. The defendant relies on the underlying contract which excludes all liability for negligent statements. The

b contract is valid under the law of the country where it was made: it is not contrary to the public policy of that country. But the contract is contrary to English public policy. Once an English court concludes, in accordance with the stringent test applicable in respect of transnational transactions to which I referred in [114], above, that recognition of the contract would be contrary to English public policy, it follows in my view that the defendant would not be entitled to rely on

c the exception clause in defence to the tort claim. To permit to do so would be an affront to English public policy. The answer to the argument of IAC is that an acceptance of it would run counter to clear public policy. To accept it would seriously erode the public policy here engaged. The general position is straightforward. An English court may not give direct or indirect recognition to Resolution 369 for

d any purpose whatever. An English court may not recognise any Iraqi decree or act which would directly or indirectly enable Iraq or Iraqi enterprises to retain the spoils or fruits of the illegal invasion.

[118] In considering whether KAC has established a sustainable usurpation under Iraqi law, the court must wholly disregard Resolution 369. It cannot in any way be set up by IAC as a defence in whole or part to a usurpation claim by KAC

e under Iraqi law.

Conversion

[119] Despite elaborate citation of authority, I am satisfied that the essential feature of the tort of conversion, and of usurpation under Iraqi law, is the denial

f by the defendant of the possessory interest or title of the plaintiff in the goods: see Todd *The Law of Torts in New Zealand* (3rd edn, 2001) para 11.3 for an illuminating discussion. When a defendant manifests an assertion of rights or dominion over the goods which is inconsistent with the rights of the plaintiff he converts the goods to his own use. I am therefore in agreement with the legal analysis of the Court of Appeal.

g [120] It is unnecessary to review yet again the battleground of the trial so carefully described by the Court of Appeal. On the facts, I agree with the Court of Appeal that it was correct to conclude that IAC embarked on a policy of incorporating the ten aircraft belonging to KAC into their fleet. It was realistic to consider the cumulative effect of the evidence concerning all ten aircraft rather

h than to concentrate on the conduct in respect of each aircraft separately. It matters not exactly how far the policy was implemented in respect of particular aircraft. The overall picture left no doubt in my mind that IAC had planned and initiated a process of incorporating the ten aircraft in their fleet.

j *The Mosul Four*

[121] KAC had to show, in accordance with Iraqi law, that physical damage to the aircraft would not have occurred but for the usurpation. In the light of the undisputed findings of fact of Aikens J, the issue before the Court of Appeal largely turned on what were the correct inferences. Despite detailed argument to the contrary, I have been left unpersuaded that the Court of Appeal erred in

concluding that KAC failed to discharge this burden. On the contrary, I incline to
the view the conclusion of the Court of Appeal was correct.   *a*

[122] Given this conclusion no other issues on the Mosul Four arise for
decision. Specifically, I express no view on the valuation issues.

The Iran Six

[123] In my view the Court of Appeal made a correct decision when it allowed *b*
KAC's appeal against the decision of Aikens J on the Iran Six.

Disposal

[124] For the reasons given by my noble and learned friends Lord Nicholls of
Birkenhead and Lord Hope of Craighead, as well as the reasons I have given, I
would dismiss the appeals of IAC and KAC.   *c*

LORD HOFFMANN.

[125] My Lords, I have had the advantage of reading in draft the speech of my
noble and learned friend Lord Nicholls of Birkenhead. I agree with it and add a
few remarks only on the causal requirements of an action in conversion.   *d*

[126] Mr Donaldson's submission amounted to saying that it was a general rule
of liability in tort that the tortious act must have been at least a *necessary* condition
of the damage. That might not be enough but was a threshold requirement. It
follows that the plaintiff must always fail if he cannot prove on the balance of
probabilities that the damage would not have happened anyway. In the present *e*
case, KAC could not show that but for the tortious acts of IAC they would not
have been kept out of possession of their aeroplanes. The Iraqi government
would have retained them or given them to some other state institution.

[127] My Lords, it would be an irrational system of tort liability which did not
insist upon there being *some* causal connection between the tortious act and the
damage. But causal connections can be of widely differing kinds. Sometimes the *f*
act may have been a necessary condition but followed by a voluntary human act
or exceptional natural event (novus actus interveniens). Such a causal connection
is usually insufficient to found liability in negligence. But in the case of certain
kinds of duty, even in negligence, it will be enough. It may be sufficient to show
that the act was a necessary condition, even if the subsequent voluntary act of a *g*
third party (*Stansbie v Troman* [1948] 1 All ER 599, [1948] 2 KB 48) or the plaintiff
himself (*Reeves v Comr of Police of the Metropolis* [1999] 3 All ER 897, [2000] 1 AC
360) was also a necessary condition. And the same may be true when liability is
strict: see *Empress Car Co (Abertillery) Ltd v National Rivers Authority* [1998] 1 All ER
481, [1999] 2 AC 22. Sometimes the act cannot be shown to have been even a *h*
necessary condition but only to have added substantially to the probability that
the damage would be suffered. But in some situations even this limited causal
connection will suffice: see *Bonnington Castings Ltd v Wardlaw* [1956] 1 All ER 615,
[1956] AC 613; *McGhee v National Coal Board* [1972] 3 All ER 1008, [1973] 1 WLR 1.

[128] There is therefore no uniform causal requirement for liability in tort.
Instead, there are varying causal requirements, depending upon the basis and *j*
purpose of liability. One cannot separate questions of liability from questions of
causation. They are inextricably connected. One is never simply liable; one is
always liable *for* something and the rules which determine what one is liable for
are as much part of the substantive law as the rules which determine which acts
give rise to liability. It is often said that causation is a question of fact. So it is, but

a so is the question of liability. Liability involves applying the rules which determine whether an act is tortious to the facts of the case. Likewise, the question of causation is decided by applying the rules which lay down the causal requirements for that form of liability to the facts of the case.

[129] In the case of conversion, the causal requirements follow from the nature of the tort. The tort exists to protect proprietary or possessory rights in property; it

b is committed by an act inconsistent with those rights and it is a tort of strict liability. So conversion is 'a taking with the intent of exercising over the chattel an ownership inconsistent with the real owner's right of possession': *Fouldes v Willoughby* (1841) 8 M & W 540 at 550, 151 ER 1153 at 1157 per Rolfe B. And the person who takes is treated as being under a continuing strict duty to restore the chattel to its owner. It follows, first, that it is irrelevant that if IAC had not

c taken possession of the aircraft, someone else would have done so. Secondly, it is irrelevant that, having taken possession, IAC would have been prevented from restoring the aircraft (even if it had wished to do so) by circumstances beyond its control: the orders of the Iraqi government and their detention in Iran. The liability is strict. Thus the causal questions are answered by reference to the

d nature of the liability.

[130] When one comes to consequential loss, the causal requirements are different. The primary purpose of conversion is to protect the proprietary or possessory interest in the chattel. Thus the cost of putting the aircraft into repair or paying a ransom for their recovery from Iran is part of the damage or expenditure incurred in mitigation of the damage to the proprietary interest. But

e when one comes to real consequential losses, such as the cost of hiring substitute aircraft, the cost of financing the purchase of new ones and loss of profit, there is no reason why causal requirements which are considered fair in other cases of consequential loss flowing from wrongful acts should not also be applied. For the reasons given by Lord Nicholls of Birkenhead, I would agree that these

f requirements are in principle satisfied in respect of the hire of substitute aircraft and the loss of profits, but that although the failure of IAC to restore the aircraft was a necessary condition of the decision to buy a new fleet, that decision was a voluntary act which on conventional principles made the causal connection with IAC's tortious conduct insufficient.

g **LORD HOPE OF CRAIGHEAD.**

[131] My Lords, the facts of this case have been fully narrated by my noble and learned friend Lord Nicholls of Birkenhead, and I gratefully adopt his narrative.

h [132] The decision of this House in *Kuwait Airways Corp v Iraqi Airways Co* [1995] 3 All ER 694, [1995] 1 WLR 1147 provides the background to the issues of law with which we are concerned. As Lord Goff of Chieveley explained ([1995] 3 All ER 694 at 711, [1995] 1 WLR 1147 at 1163) in that case, the taking of the aircraft belonging to Kuwait Airways Corp (KAC) and their removal from Kuwait Airport to Iraq constituted an exercise of governmental power by the state of

j Iraq. The participation of Iraqi Airways Co (IAC) in that action, by supplying engineers and pilots who performed the task of preparing the aircraft for flying and then flying them from Kuwait to Iraq in August 1990, was not just a job of work. On the contrary, IAC was closely involved with the state of Iraq in the last stage of an enterprise which entailed both the seizure of the aircraft and their removal to Iraq to be used for such purposes as the government of Iraq should direct. The House held that in so doing it was acting in the exercise of sovereign authority. But the situation changed after Revolutionary Command Council (RCC) Resolution 369 came into effect on 17 September 1990. As from that date IAC's retention and use of the aircraft as its own were acts done not in the exercise of sovereign authority but in consequence of the vesting or purported vesting of the aircraft in it by legislative decree.

[133] The House left open for further consideration the question whether the issues arising from the acts of IAC of which KAC complains are justiciable in the English courts. As Lord Goff explained ([1995] 3 All ER 694 at 713, [1995] 1 WLR 1147 at 1165) it was not possible at that stage to ascertain with any precision what, on the facts of the case, were the issues raised by KAC's claim against IAC and IAC's defence to that claim. Now these issues are out in the open following the trial of the issues relating to liability by Mance J, on which he gave judgment on 29 July 1998: [1999] CLC 31. The situation which has been revealed by the evidence about the activities of IAC and the Iraqi government is not perhaps as clear-cut as the majority of their Lordships believed it to be when they held that IAC was not acting in the exercise of sovereign immunity after RCC Resolution 369 came into effect. But it is common ground that the focus of attention has now shifted entirely to questions about the effect of the resolution on the remedy which KAC seeks to obtain under domestic law in the English courts.

[134] These questions, which form the subject matter of the first chapter of IAC's appeal, can best be grouped under two main headings which, in their logical order, are as follows: (1) is the effectiveness of Resolution 369 as a legislative act vesting title in the aircraft in IAC justiciable in the English courts; (2) if it is, and Resolution 369 is held to offend against English public policy, does it nevertheless have to be recognised as vesting title to the aircraft in IAC for the purposes of the principle of double actionability? I agree with all that my noble and learned friend Lord Nicholls of Birkenhead has said in answer to these questions. But I should like to add these observations.

Justiciability

[135] Important questions of principle are raised by the highly unusual facts of this case. There is no doubt as to the general effect of the rule which is known as the act of state rule. It applies to the legislative or other governmental acts of a recognised foreign state or government within the limits of its own territory. The English courts will not adjudicate upon, or call into question, any such acts. They may be pleaded and relied upon by way of defence in this jurisdiction without being subjected to that kind of judicial scrutiny. The rule gives effect to a policy of 'judicial restraint or abstention': see *Buttes Gas and Oil Co v Hammer (Nos 2 and 3)* [1981] 3 All ER 616 at 628–630, [1982] AC 888 at 931–934 per Lord Wilberforce. As the title to moveable property is determined by the lex situs, a transfer of property effected by or under foreign legislation in the country where the property is situated will, as a general rule, be treated as effective by English law for all relevant purposes.

[136] It would clearly be possible for a 'blue pencil' approach to be taken to Resolution 369, by reading it down so that it applied only to the property of KAC that was situated at the time of the resolution within its own territory. The normal rule is that legislative action applied to property within the territorial jurisdiction will be internationally recognised, despite the fact that it has been combined with action which is unenforceable extraterritorially. If this approach

a is adopted, that part of Resolution 369 which vested title in the aircraft in IAC will
provide IAC with a complete defence to this action. Its legality in international
law will not be justiciable in these proceedings.

[137] IAC accepts, however, that the normal rule is subject to an exception on
grounds of public policy. The proposition which it accepts is that the exception
applies if the foreign legislation constitutes so grave an infringement of human
b rights that the courts of this country ought to refuse to recognise the legislation
as a law at all: *Oppenheimer v Cattermole (Inspector of Taxes)* [1975] 1 All ER 538 at
567, [1976] AC 249 at 278 per Lord Cross of Chelsea. The proposition which it
disputes is that the public policy exception extends to breaches of international
law. IAC's argument is presented as one of principle. Arguments directed to
breaches of international law are non-justiciable. The public policy exception
c must be tightly restricted. The only exception that has been judicially recognised
is the human rights exception. As that exception is not invoked in this case, it has
a complete defence to these proceedings under the act of state rule.

[138] It is clear that very narrow limits must be placed on any exception to the
act of state rule. As Lord Cross recognised in *Oppenheimer's* case [1975] 1 All ER
d 538 at 566–567, [1976] AC 249 at 277–278, a judge should be slow to refuse to give
effect to the legislation of a foreign state in any sphere in which, according to
accepted principles of international law, the foreign state has jurisdiction. Among
these accepted principles is that which is founded on the comity of nations. This
principle normally requires our courts to recognise the jurisdiction of the foreign
e state over all assets situated within its own territories: see [1975] 1 All ER 538 at
571, [1976] AC 249 at 282 per Lord Salmon. A judge should be slow to depart
from these principles. He may have an inadequate understanding of the
circumstances in which the legislation was passed. His refusal to recognise it may
be embarrassing to the executive, whose function is so far as possible to maintain
f friendly relations with foreign states.

[139] But it does not follow, as Mr Donaldson QC for IAC has asserted, that the
public policy exception can be applied only where there is a grave infringement of
human rights. This was the conclusion that was reached on the facts which were
before the House in *Oppenheimer's* case. But Lord Cross based that conclusion on a
wider point of principle. This too is founded upon the public policy of this country.
g It is that our courts should give effect to clearly established principles of international
law. He cited with approval Upjohn J's dictum to this effect in *Re Helbert Wagg &*
Co Ltd, Re Prudential Assurance Co [1956] 1 Ch 323 at 334. As Upjohn J put it ([1956]
1 All ER 129 at 140, [1956] 1 Ch 323 at 349) the true limits of the principle are to be
found in considerations of public policy as understood in the courts. I think that
h Mr Donaldson sought to achieve a rigidity which is absent from these observations
when he said that, whatever norm one finds that has been abused, it cannot be
applied in our law if it is a manifestation of international law and does not fall
within the recognised exception relating to human rights.

[140] As I see it, the essence of the public policy exception is that it is not so
j constrained. The golden rule is that care must be taken not to expand its
application beyond the true limits of the principle. These limits demand that,
where there is any room for doubt, judicial restraint must be exercised. But
restraint is what is needed, not abstention. And there is no need for restraint on
grounds of public policy where it is plain beyond dispute that a clearly established
norm of international law has been violated.

[141] The facts which bear on this issue are quite straightforward. The United Nations Charter and the Security Council resolutions which were adopted in response to the invasion of Kuwait provide the context. The aims of the charter as set forth in the preamble seek to ensure that armed force is not used save in the common interest, and that conditions are established under which justice and respect for the obligations arising from treaties and other sources of international law can be maintained. Membership of the United Nations carries with it the obligation to accept and carry out the decisions of the Security Council, on which members have conferred the primary responsibility for the maintenance of peace and security: Ch V, arts 24, 25.

[142] Among the resolutions which were adopted by the Security Council after the Iraqi invasion were Resolution 660 on 2 August 1990 which condemned the invasion and demanded that Iraq withdraw from Kuwait immediately and unconditionally, Resolution 661 on 6 August 1990 which called upon all states not to recognise any regime set up by the occupying power, and Resolution 662 on 9 August 1990 which decided that Iraq's annexation of Kuwait under any form and whatever pretext had no legal validity and was considered null and void. Resolution 662 also called upon all states 'not to recognise that annexation, and to refrain from any action or dealing that might be interpreted as an indirect recognition of the annexation'.

[143] The removal of the aircraft from Kuwait took place on 6–8 August 1990 when nine KAC aircraft were flown from Kuwait to Basra, and 22 August 1990 when the remaining aircraft was flown to Baghdad. These acts were plainly in breach of the Security Council resolutions. So too was RCC Resolution 369, which purported to vest in IAC all the fixed and liquid assets of KAC including all assets of Kuwait Airways offices abroad. Moreover, Resolution 369, which was designed to cement that act by depriving KAC permanently of all its assets wherever situated, was of an exorbitant character. Standing the Security Council resolutions, which as a member of the United Nations Iraq (on 5 March 1991 when RCC Resolution 55 was passed) was later to recognise, these were breaches of international law.

[144] It is not disputed that our courts are entitled on grounds of public policy to decline to give effect to clearly established breaches of international law when considering rights in or to property which is located in England. A state lacks international jurisdiction to take property outside its territory, so acts of that kind are necessarily ineffective: Dr FA Mann *Further Studies in International Law* (1990) p 175. There could be no question of Resolution 369 being regarded as effective in the English courts as a transfer to IAC under the lex situs of any of KAC's rights in any property that happened to be situated in this country. IAC could not rely on the act of state doctrine if England was the country of the lex situs at the time when the breaches of international law were committed. But why should effect not also be given here to international law where to do so can be justified on grounds of public policy?

[145] In my search for an answer this question I would take as my guide the observations of Lord Wilberforce in *Blathwayt v Lord Cawley* [1975] 3 All ER 625 at 636, [1976] AC 397 at 426. He said that conceptions of public policy should move with the times and that widely-accepted treaties and statutes may point in the direction in which such conceptions, as applied by the courts, ought to move. It would seem therefore to be contrary to principle for our courts to give legal effect to legislative and other acts of foreign states which are in violation of

a international law as declared under the Charter of the United Nations: see Mann p 176; *Oppenheim's International Law* (9th edn, 1992) vol 1, p 376. The Security Council has played a key role in recent months, following the events of 11 September 2001, by imposing obligations on all states to suppress terrorist financing and deny terrorists safe havens in which to operate. It is now clear, if it was not before, that the judiciary cannot close their eyes to the need for a *b* concerted, international response to these threats to the rule of law in a democratic society. Their primary role must always be to uphold human rights and civil liberties. But the maintenance of the rule of law is also an important social interest.

[146] Security Council Resolution 662 called upon all states to refrain from any action which might be interpreted as an indirect recognition of the *c* annexation. There is no doubt that the responsibility for answering this call lies in the first instance with the executive arm of government. But, in seeking which direction to take in such matters where decisions must be taken on grounds of public policy, the judges should try to work in harmony with the executive. Furthermore, as the Court of Appeal observed, there is nothing precarious or *d* delicate, and nothing subject to diplomacy, which judicial adjudication might threaten in this case ([2001] 3 WLR 1117 at 1207 (para 334)). The taking of KAC's property in breach of Iraq's obligations under the Charter of the United Nations was a clear example of an international wrong to which legal effect should not be given.

e [147] There could be no embarrassment to diplomatic relations in our taking this view. In his letter of 7 November 1997, which was written in response to a request by Longmore J on 24 October 1997, Sir Franklin Berman, then legal advisor to the Foreign and Commonwealth Office, informed the court that the conduct of Her Majesty's Government in the United Kingdom has been strictly in conformity with the requirements of the resolutions and all other pertinent *f* decisions of the Security Council relating to the Iraqi invasion and occupation of Kuwait. Nor can it be said that the court needs to defer to the act of the foreign state because it has an inadequate understanding of the circumstances in which Resolution 369 was passed. The arguments for giving effect to international law as declared by the resolutions of the Security Council could hardly be more *g* compelling.

[148] For these reasons I would hold that a legislative act by a foreign state which is in flagrant breach of clearly established rules of international law ought not to be recognised by the courts of this country as forming part of the lex situs of that state. This was the conclusion that Dr FA Mann advocated in his article *h* 'International Delinquencies before Municipal Courts' (1954) 70 LQR 181; see also his *Further Studies in International Law*, pp 177–183. At p 202 of the article he said:

'1. When the conflict rule of the forum refers the court to a foreign law (lex *j* causae), the court will not apply the latter if and in so far as it expresses or results from an international delinquency ...

5. The question whether an international delinquency has been committed is to be answered according to the generally accepted principles of international law, but a municipal court will not answer it affirmatively except where both the law and the facts are clearly established.'

[149] I would endorse everything that is said in that passage, and I would apply
it to this case. Respect for the act of state doctrine and the care that must be taken
not to undermine it do not preclude this approach. The facts are clear, and the
declarations by the Security Council were universal and unequivocal. If the court
may have regard to grave infringements of human rights law on grounds of
public policy, it ought not to decline to take account of the principles of
international law when the act amounts—as I would hold that it clearly does in
this case—to a flagrant breach of these principles. As Upjohn J indicated in *Re Helbert
Wagg & Co Ltd, Re Prudential Assurance Co* [1956] 1 All ER 129 at 140, [1956] 1 Ch
323 at 349, public policy is determined by the conceptions of law, justice and
morality as understood in the courts. I would hold that the effectiveness of
Resolution 369 as vesting title in IAC to KAC's aircraft is justiciable in these
proceedings, and that such a flagrant international wrong should be deemed to
be so grave a matter that it would be contrary to the public policy of this country
to give effect to it.

Double actionability

[150] The acts with which this case is concerned took place before the coming
into force of the Private International Law (Miscellaneous Provisions) Act 1995.
Section 10 of that Act abolished the common law rule which required
actionability under both the law of the forum and the law of the place where the
events constituting an alleged tort or delict took place for the purpose of determining
whether or not the tort or delict was actionable. So the question which arises
under this heading must be determined under the common law.

[151] The argument for IAC is that, irrespective of the view taken of
Resolution 369 under the act of state rule, KAC's claim under conversion must
fail under the common law rule of double actionability because this rule requires
that Iraqi law must be applied to the question whether the acts of IAC would have
been actionable in that country. It is said that, in reaching its decision on this
question in the autumn of 1990, an Iraqi court would have had to have had regard
to the entire corpus of Iraqi law including that part of Resolution 369 which
vested the aircraft in IAC. On this view, the Iraqi court would have been bound
to hold that IAC was not liable for its alleged acts of usurpation. In response to
this argument KAC seek to rely on an exception to the double actionability rule
which allowed the law of a single country only to be applied for the purpose of
determining the issue, or one of the issues, arising in the case. This rule too was
abolished by s 10 of the 1995 Act, but we are concerned here with the common
law rules as they stood before the Act came into force.

[152] The common law on this point was examined by Lord Slynn of Hadley
in *Red Sea Insurance Ltd v Bouygues SA* [1994] 3 All ER 749, [1995] 1 AC 190. The
central issue in that case was whether a defendant could rely solely on the lex loci
delicti to establish liability in tort when the lex fori did not recognise such liability.
The board held that, while the general rule of English law with regard to foreign
torts as explained in *Phillips v Eyre* (1870) LR 6 QB 1 required the conduct to be
both actionable as a tort according to English law if it had been committed in
England and actionable in civil proceedings according to the law of the country
where the act was done, a plaintiff could rely exceptionally, in an appropriate
case, exclusively on the lex loci delicti even if under the lex fori his claim would
not be actionable.

a   [153] The ratio of that decision was that there was a need for some flexibility in the application of the rule, as the majority of this House in *Chaplin v Boys* [1969] 2 All ER 1085, [1971] AC 356 recognised ([1969] 2 All ER 1085 at 1104, 1093, 1116, [1971] AC 356 at 391–392, 378, 406 per Lord Wilberforce, Lord Hodson and Lord Pearson respectively). The present case raises the same question, but it is the other way round. Here the acts complained of would have been actionable under

b   English law, the lex fori, if committed in this country. But it is said that they were not actionable in Iraq under the lex loci delicti because the effect of Resolution 369 was to vest the aircraft in IAC.

  [154] As Lord Slynn said in the *Red Sea Insurance Ltd* case [1994] 3 All ER 749 at 753–754, [1995] 1 AC 190 at 197, the question has a long history and has led to considerable discussion in the decisions of the common law courts and in

c   academic writings. After a detailed and careful review of all this material he summed the matter up in this way ([1994] 3 All ER 749 at 761–762, [1995] 1 AC 190 at 206):

d   'Their Lordships, having considered all of these opinions, recognise the conflict which exists between, on the one hand, the desirability of a rule which is certain and clear on the basis of which people can act and lawyers advise and, on the other, the desirability of the courts having the power to avoid injustice by introducing an element of flexibility into the rule. They do not consider that the rejection of the doctrine of the proper law of the tort as part of English law is inconsistent with a measure of flexibility being

e   introduced into the rules. They consider that the majority in *Chaplin v Boys* recognised the need for such flexibility. They accept that the law of England recognises that a particular issue between the parties to litigation may be governed by the law of the country which, with respect to that issue, has the most significant relationship with the occurrence and with the parties. They

f   agree with the statement of Lord Wilberforce ... as to the extent and application of the exception. They accept, as he did, that the exception will not be successfully invoked in every case or even, probably, in many cases and that "The general rule must apply unless clear and satisfying grounds are shown why it should be departed from and what solution, derived from what other rule, should be preferred" (see [1969] 2 All ER 1085 at 1104, [1971]

g   AC 356 at 391).'

  [155] The fact that the question raised in this case is the other way round from that in the *Red Sea Insurance* case is not in itself an obstacle to the same approach being applied here. This can be seen from the two Australian intranational tort

h   cases which were mentioned by Lord Slynn in the course of his judgment. In *Warren v Warren* [1972] Qd R 386 the plaintiff was injured in a car accident while on a temporary visit to New South Wales, where she had no right of action in tort against her husband. She began her action in Queensland, where she was ordinarily resident and domiciled, where such a right of action did exist. The

j   defendant's application to set aside the writ was dismissed. Matthews J held that there was a degree of flexibility in the rule which admitted of exception where clear and satisfactory grounds were shown why it should be departed from and that, on the facts of that case, it was right to apply the law of the forum even if the acts were not actionable by the law of the locus delicti. A decision to the same effect on similar facts was reached in *Corcoran v Corcoran* [1974] VR 164.

[156] In *John Pfeiffer Pty Ltd v Rogerson* [2000] HCA 36 the High Court of Australia held that these and other decisions to the like effect did not properly take account of the fact of federal jurisdiction or the nature of the Australian federation, and that the double actionability rule should be discarded with regard to claims brought in an Australian court in respect of a civil wrong arising out of acts or omissions that occurred wholly within one or more of the law areas of the Commonwealth of Australia. The rule now is that the lex loci delicti is to be applied by courts in Australia as the law governing all questions of substance to be determined in a proceeding arising from an intranational tort: joint judgment (para 102). But the double actionability rule survives in the case of a tort committed outside Australia, as the High Court expressly limited its discussion to the issues arising in intranational and not international torts. So the pre-*Rogerson* cases are still of interest where issues arise under the common law of this country as to whether the rule can be displaced in favour of the law of one country only for the purpose of determining liability for an alleged tort or delict.

[157] The point which requires further examination here is whether the basis in principle for recognising a degree of flexibility in the application of the rule can be applied to the circumstances of this case. It appears from Lord Wilberforce's discussion of this point in *Chaplin v Boys* [1969] 2 All ER 1085 at 1104, [1971] AC 356 at 391–392 that the situation which he had in mind was one where to apply the relevant foreign rule would not serve the interests which it was designed to meet. This was likely to be so particularly in cases where the parties had come together for different purposes for different pre-existing relationships and from the background of different legal systems. The solution which he favoured was one which enabled the foreign rule to be displaced in favour of the law of the place which had the most substantial connection with the circumstances of the case.

[158] In *Breavington v Godleman* (1988) 169 CLR 41 the High Court of Australia was far from unanimous in its support for what Deane J described (at 127) as 'a largely instinctive flexible exception'. But Toohey J was in favour of it, provided that it was appreciated that it did not confer an unfettered judicial discretion enabling the rule to be applied in a way that was purely arbitrary. He expressed his understanding of the exception in this way (at 163):

> 'It is only in special circumstances where, after examination of the policy underlying the law which may be applied and the interests of the parties to be affected, it is clear that the lex loci delicti has no real connection with the proceedings, that the exception can be invoked, enabling a plaintiff to recover damages available in the lex fori but not available in the lex loci delicti. Such a requirement should do much to alleviate any fears that unacceptable uncertainty will be introduced into this area of the law.'

[159] Nevertheless, if the scope for flexibility is as limited as Toohey J indicated it is in this passage, the facts of this case would seem to prohibit its application. It cannot be said that the lex loci delicti has no real connection with these proceedings, as one of the parties to the action has its principal place of business in Iraq where the alleged acts of conversion took place. Nor can it be said, to adopt the test indicated by Lord Slynn in the *Red Sea Insurance* case [1994] 3 All ER 749 at 761–762, [1995] 1 AC 190 at 206, that English law is the system of law which has the most significant relationship with the occurrence and with the parties. The argument in favour of excluding that part of Iraqi law under which it would have been held by an Iraqi court that the title to the aircraft was vested

a in IAC at the time when the alleged acts of conversion were committed is directed solely to the fact that Resolution 369, upon which that part of Iraqi law would have been founded, was in breach of international law. The question is whether there is sufficient flexibility in the double actionability rule to enable this aspect of the lex loci delicti to be excluded and the question of IAC's title to the aircraft to be decided exclusively by the lex fori.

b [160] The Court of Appeal, agreeing with Mance J, held that the answer to this question was provided by the argument that to give effect to Resolution 369 would offend against English public policy. It held that, once public policy requires not only that a foreign law or act should not be recognised to the extent that it purports to act extraterritorially but that it should not be recognised at all, then it is impossible to have regard to it for any purpose: [2001] 3 WLR 1117 at *c* 1222 (paras 391–392). This proposition was restated (at 1223 (para 394)) in these terms:

> 'Where, however, the foreign act of state plea fails, whether because the act of state purports to legislate extraterritorially or because the English court refuses to recognise the foreign law even though acting territorially,
d the foreign law ceases to be of relevance whether as lex situs or as lex loci delicti.'

[161] I think that this approach has much to commend it. The question of title is normally determined by the lex situs. In this case the question of title has to be addressed to determine whether under the lex loci delicti the alleged tort is *e* actionable. Although the double actionability issue is concerned with the lex loci delicti, the question of title is referred under that law to the lex situs. So the underlying issue as to whether the title conferred on IAC by the lex situs should be recognised in this country is the same, whatever the context. But I think that there are two further problems which need to be addressed.

f [162] The first problem arises from the fact that counsel for KAC accepted that Resolution 369 is not wholly irrelevant to application of the lex loci delicti to this case. It was conceded before Mance J that, as IAC acted in the belief that the resolution gave it a good title to the aircraft, the burden of proof that the loss or damage would not have occurred but for the usurpation falls on KAC. So it is not accurate to say that it is impossible to have regard to the effect of Resolution 369 *g* for any purpose whatever in these proceedings. It cannot be treated as if it did not exist. It is accepted that it forms part of the factual background.

[163] That having been said, I think that a clear distinction can be drawn between questions of fact, such as the state of mind of IAC, and questions of law, such as whether IAC had a good title to the aircraft. It would be wholly unrealistic *h* to ignore Resolution 369 and its contextual importance as a matter of history. But its effect in law raises a different issue, and it is to that issue only that the public policy objection relates. Moreover the flexible approach to the double actionability rule which permits the lex loci delicti to be disapplied does not insist on its disapplication across the board. It permits an approach which allows all the issues *j* to be determined according to the lex loci delicti other than the one which gives rise to the objection.

[164] The second problem raises a more fundamental point. It goes to the heart of the much discussed question as to scope of the exception which permits flexibility. As Lord Wilberforce said in *Chaplin v Boys* [1969] 2 All ER 1085 at 1104, [1971] AC 356 at 391, the general rule must apply unless clear and

satisfying grounds are shown why it should be departed from. Unless a rigorous approach to this question is adopted, the application of the exception is at risk of giving rise to much uncertainty and to the criticism alluded to in the Australian cases that it has become instinctive and arbitrary. This requirement is preserved by s 12 of the 1995 Act. It provides that the general rule in s 11 that the applicable law is the law of the country in which the events constituting the tort or delict in question occur may be displaced in favour of the law of another country, but it permits this only if 'it is substantially more appropriate' for the law of the other country to be applied.

[165] An objection to the law of a country other than the forum may be founded on grounds of public policy. This fact is recognised by s 14(3)(a)(i) of the 1995 Act, which provides that nothing in Pt III of the Act authorises the application of the law of a country outside the forum as the applicable law for determining issues arising in any claim in so far as to do so would conflict with principles of public policy. But I do not think that it is enough, in the circumstances of this case, simply to assert that the law of the country where the events occurred conflicts with public policy in this country. It all depends on the context and the nature of the objection on grounds of public policy.

[166] There is nothing in this case which connects the laws of this country with the events constituting the alleged tort, other than the fact that this is the country where the proceedings were brought. As my noble and learned friend Lord Scott of Foscote has observed, this is an action in tort that has nothing whatever to do with England. So I would have no difficulty in holding that, in a case of this kind, a principle of English public policy which was purely domestic or parochial in character would not provide clear and satisfying grounds for disapplying the primary rule which favours the lex loci delicti.

[167] But the public policy objection which is raised in this case is plainly not of that character. It is based on the Charter of the United Nations and the resolutions which were made under it. It is founded on a principle of public policy which places Resolution 369 firmly into its international context. There is a clear point of contact between this part of the lex loci delicti and the breaches of international law to which our courts are entitled to decline to give effect on grounds of public policy.

[168] It is not just that recognition by our courts of this part of the lex loci delicti might be interpreted as an indirect recognition of the annexation, contrary to UN Security Council Resolution 662. The whole basis upon which RCC Resolution 369 proceeded was the subject of universal international condemnation. It was one of a series of acts which were performed in clear breach of international law. I would hold therefore that, as the public policy objection is truly international in character, there is a sound basis in principle for severing this part of the lex loci delicti and disregarding entirely any legal effects which would be given under Iraqi law to the resolution which purported to vest the title to KAC's aircraft in IAC.

Other issues

[169] I respectfully agree with what my noble and learned friend Lord Nicholls of Birkenhead has said on all the remaining issues raised in the appeal by IAC. I agree, for the reasons which he has given, that the conduct of which KAC complains meets the requirements of the double actionability rule. I also agree with what he has said about the issues raised in the appeal by KAC regarding the

a Mosul Four and the Iran Six. I wish in particular to associate myself with what he has said about the tests for liability for consequential loss beyond that represented by the value of the goods in cases of conversion, and the distinction which he has drawn in that regard between those who have acted in good faith and those who have acted dishonestly.

b *Conclusion*

[170] For the reasons given by my noble and learned friends Lord Nicholls and Lord Steyn, and for these further reasons, I would dismiss these appeals.

LORD SCOTT OF FOSCOTE.

c [171] My Lords, the facts relevant to this appeal and cross-appeal have been set out comprehensively in the judgments of Mance J and Aikens J in the High Court and in the judgment of the Court of Appeal delivered by Brooke LJ. Facts of particular importance have been highlighted in the opinions of my noble and learned friends Lord Nicholls of Birkenhead, Lord Steyn and Lord Hope of Craighead, which I have had the opportunity of reading in draft. These opinions

d identify the issues before the House and, if I may respectfully say so, express with clarity their conclusions, broadly concurring, on these issues. To my regret there is one point, which I believe to be important, and another, less important, on which I have the misfortune to disagree.

[172] The main point, in summary, is this. I am unable to accept that the double actionability rule is satisfied. It is common ground that the conduct of

e IAC for which KAC are seeking a tortious remedy would not in fact have been actionable under Iraqi law. Under Revolutionary Command Council (RCC) Resolution 369, a part of Iraqi law at the relevant time, IAC's conduct was lawful. The disapprobation of Resolution 369, strongly expressed in the opinions of my noble and learned friends and from which I do not in the least dissent, does not

f in my opinion, for reasons that I will try to explain, justify treating as tortious under Iraqi law conduct that was in fact lawful under Iraqi law.

The factual background

[173] There are two aspects of the factual background which are, in my

g opinion, of critical importance.

[174] KAC's action for conversion of its aircraft is an action in tort. But it is an action in tort which has nothing whatever to do with England save that England has made itself available as the forum for the litigation. The conduct that constituted the conversion complained of was conduct that took place wholly in Iraq. Other acts relevant to KAC's cause of action, eg the initial removal of the

h aircraft from Kuwait to Iraq, their detention in Iran, the payment by KAC to Iran of the $US 20m, took place in Kuwait or in Iran. None took place in England. The defendant, IAC, is an Iraqi corporation. It is a state-owned corporation. Its directors are Iraqi. The claimant, KAC, is a Kuwaiti state-owned corporation with Kuwaiti directors. Each of the aircraft was registered in Kuwait. England

j was, I repeat, no more than the forum for the litigation. The cause of action sued on was, therefore, in no sense an English tort. It was, as a matter of description, an Iraqi tort.

[175] Second, over the whole of the period relevant to this litigation, Iraq was, and for that matter still is, under the control of a dictatorial regime. IAC, although a state-owned corporation, possessed under Iraqi law independent corporate

personality but had no alternative in relation to the KAC aircraft than to
comply with Resolution 369. At no stage, whether before or after 17 September
1990, when Resolution 369 came into effect, would it have been possible for IAC
to have returned the aircraft to KAC. The removal of the Iran Six aircraft to Iran
could not have been carried out otherwise than in accordance with directions
from some arm of the Iraqi government, probably the military, and pursuant to
arrangements made at governmental level between Iraq and Iran. This is the
factual background against which IAC's liability in conversion must be assessed.

Double actionability

[176] English case law has for a long time skirted around the question whether
the concept of the proper law of a tort should play a part, and if so what part, in
English private international law. The legislature, by enacting Pt III of the Private
International Law (Miscellaneous Provisions) Act 1995, and in particular ss 11 and 12,
has accepted and adopted that concept. But Pt III came into effect on 1 May 1996
(see Private International Law (Miscellaneous Provisions) Act 1995 (Commencement)
Order 1996, SI 1996/995) and does not have retrospective effect. It is English
common law rules of private international law that must be applied to the
question that arises in the present case.

[177] A foreign action in personam, by which I mean an action in personam
that derives its existence from some foreign system of law, can be sued on in
England provided that the writ or other originating process can be served on the
defendant (see *Dicey and Morris on the Conflicts of Laws* (12th edn, 1993) vol 1,
p 270, rule 22). So, an action on a foreign contract governed by some foreign law
can be sued on in England. Actions of this sort are commonplace in the
Commercial Court. Less common but quite possible is an action by a beneficiary
under a foreign trust seeking some form of in personam relief against the foreign
trustees (*Ewing v Orr Ewing* (1883) 9 App Cas 34 and *Chellaram v Chellaram* [1985]
1 All ER 1043, [1985] Ch 409). These trust actions, too, can be brought in England
provided the trustees can be served, and subject always to forum non conveniens
arguments. In none of these examples of in personam actions sued on in England
does English law require that the matter complained of, breach of contract or
breach of trust as the case may be, be actionable under English law as well as
actionable under the applicable foreign law. But, of course, unless the matter
complained of were actionable under the applicable foreign law there would be
no action to sue on in England. A cause of action would not have come into
existence.

[178] This simple approach has not been adopted in tort cases. Where the
cause of action has resulted from allegedly tortious conduct in a foreign country,
it is not clear from the English case law whether the cause of action is to be
regarded as an English tort, a condition of actionability of which is that it be
actionable also under the law of the foreign country, or as a foreign tort for which
a remedy will not be given in England unless the conduct, if done in England,
would have been actionable under English law.

[179] In many of the decided cases, there is to be found a substantial factual
connection with England. Language that appears to treat the case as falling within
the former category is, therefore, not surprising.

[180] In *The Halley* (1868) LR 2 PC 193, 16 ER 514 a British ship had been
involved in a collision in Belgian waters. The collision was due to the negligence
of the pilot whom the shipowners had been compelled by Belgian law to employ.

a Under English law they would not have been vicariously liable for his negligence. Under Belgian law they were liable. Selwyn LJ, giving the judgment of the board, appears to have treated the cause of action sued on as a Belgian cause of action. He said 'the liability of the appellants, and the right of the respondents to recover damages from them, as the owners of the *Halley*, if such liability or right exists in the present case, must be the creature of the Belgian law' (see (1868) LR 2 PC 193

b at 202, 16 ER 514 at 276). He then posed the question—

> 'whether an English Court of Justice is bound to apply and enforce that law in a case, when, according to its own principles, no wrong has been committed by the defendants, and no right of action against them exists.'

c He answered his question in the negative:

> '... the English Court admits the proof of the Foreign law ... as one of the facts upon which the existence of the tort, or the right to damages, may depend, and it then applies and enforces its own law so far as it is applicable to the case thus established; but it is ... alike contrary to principle and authority to hold, that an English Court of Justice will enforce a Foreign
d Municipal law, and will give a remedy in the shape of damages in respect of an act which, according to its own principles, imposes no liability on the person from whom the damages are claimed.' (See (1868) LR 2 PC 193 at 203–204, 16 ER 514 at 277.)

e **[181]** The language of the passage first cited seems to place the case firmly in the second of the two categories to which I have referred. The cause of action was a Belgian cause of action but it could not be sued on in England if, under English law, no liability on the defendant would result from the conduct complained of. But the third of the cited passages seems to treat the cause of action as an English tort and as falling in the first of the two categories.

f **[182]** In *Phillips v Eyre* (1869) LR 4 QB 225 and (1870) LR 6 QB 1 the plaintiff's cause of action was treated as a Jamaican tort. There was a defence available to the defendant under Jamaican law, so the plaintiff could not succeed in his action in England. The facts of the case are too well known to need lengthy repetition. The defendant, while Governor of Jamaica, had imprisoned the plaintiff and subjected him to a number of serious assaults. The plaintiff brought an action in
g England for false imprisonment and assault. The defendant pleaded that an after-the-event Act of Indemnity, relieving him of liability for the tort, had been passed by the Jamaican legislature. The issue was whether this plea was good. Both the Court of Queen's Bench and, on a writ of error, the Exchequer Chamber held that it was.

h **[183]** The judgment of Queen's Bench was delivered by Cockburn CJ. He tested his conclusion by supposing that the Act of Indemnity had preceded the acts which had given rise to the action. He said ((1869) LR 4 QB 225 at 239):

> 'We cannot doubt that in such a case no right of action would arise here. It appears to us clear that where by the law of another country an act
j complained of is lawful, such act, though it would have been wrongful by our law if committed here, cannot be made the ground of an action in an English court.'

The judgment in Exchequer Chamber given by Willes J ((1870) LR 6 QB 1 at 28) was to the same effect:

'A right of action, whether it arise from contract governed by the law of the place or wrong, is equally the creature of the law of the place and subordinate thereto ... [T]he civil liability arising out of a wrong derives its birth from the law of the place, and its character is determined by that law.'

These passages treat the plaintiff's cause of action as a Jamaican cause of action. The Act of Indemnity, a part of Jamaican law, barred the action; so there was no cause of action on which the plaintiff could sue in England. The Act of Indemnity had been enacted after the events of which the plaintiff complained had taken place. So the Act had divested the plaintiff of a pre-existing cause of action. But Willes J's analysis of what the situation would have been if the Act of Indemnity had preceded the false imprisonment and the assaults is instructive. In that event no cause of action could have come into existence. He refers to tortious civil liability as deriving its 'birth' from the law of the place where the tort was committed. This analysis is important. Every tortious cause of action must derive its existence, its birth, from some system of law. In *Phillips v Eyre* that system of law was Jamaican law. To much the same effect are dicta in some of the older cases that were cited in *Phillips v Eyre* (see *R v Lesley* (1860) Bell CC 220 and *Dobree v Napier* (1836) 2 Bing NC 781, 132 ER 301 cited at (1869) LR 4 QB 225 at 240–241).

[184] *Carr v Fracis Times & Co* [1902] AC 176 was, like the present, a conversion case. British goods on board a British ship had been seized in Muscat waters by a British subject acting under the authority of a proclamation issued by the Sultan of Muscat. An action for conversion of the goods was brought in England against the British subject who had seized them. The trial judge entered judgment for the defendant but the Court of Appeal reversed the decision. This House, approving and following *Phillips v Eyre*, allowed the appeal. Lord Halsbury LC, in the course of argument, put to the counsel for the respondent 'the case of a black before the Emancipation Act bringing an action in this country because his liberty had been restrained in Jamaica' (at 178). Counsel accepted that no such action would lie. Lord Halsbury LC posed the question 'Why' and answered it (at 179):

'Because the thing done, though contrary to our English law, was, according to the law of Jamaica at that time, a lawful act, and therefore no complaint in respect of the supposed tort committed in Jamaica could have been made a subject of action in this country.'

Lord Halsbury LC made it clear (at 189) that the declaration of the Sultan of Muscat that had authorised the seizure of the goods was determinative of the legality of the seizure under Muscat law:

'[The Sultan] has authorised it and declared authoritatively that it was a perfectly lawful act according to the law of Muscat, and I am of opinion that no English tribunal is capable of going behind that declaration and saying that the Sultan of Muscat was wrong in his exposition of his own law ... [I]t appears to me that any other decision would be open to very serious questions of policy if, in every case where the lord of a country has declared what the law of his own country is, it were open to an English tribunal to enter into the question and to determine, as against him, what was the law of his country.'

a
[185] *Carr's* case, like *Phillips v Eyre*, treated the cause of action sued on in England as a foreign cause of action. Where a foreign cause of action is concerned the double actionability rule never comes into play unless the cause of action is actionable under the foreign law.

[186] In *Machado v Fontes* [1897] 2 QB 231 an action for libel was brought in England in respect of a pamphlet published in Brazil. The defendant filed a
b defence denying the libel but later applied for leave to amend his defence by adding a plea that publication of the pamphlet did not give rise to any civil liability for damages under Brazilian law. The Court of Appeal held that the plea was bad. The publication of the libellous pamphlet was a criminal offence in Brazil and, accordingly, unjustifiable under Brazilian law. That was enough to sustain the civil action for damages in England. The libel did not need to be actionable in a
c civil suit in Brazil. In so finding the Court of Appeal was treating the case as falling within the first of the two categories to which I referred, that is to say, as an English tort with a condition of actionability in England dependent on the foreign law. The decision of the Court of Appeal was, however, overruled by a majority in this House in *Chaplin v Boys* [1969] 2 All ER 1085, [1971] AC 356.

d   [187] In *Chaplin v Boys* the cause of action sued on was, save that the car accident which gave rise to the action took place in Malta, in all respects an English tort. Both plaintiff and defendant were British subjects serving in the British armed forces and, although normally resident in England, were stationed temporarily in Malta. The car accident in Malta had been caused by the defendant's
e negligence. The plaintiff sued in England for damages. The issue was whether general damages, for pain and suffering, loss of amenities etc, which were available under the law of England but not under the law of Malta, could be awarded. The trial judge applied English law to the issue, the Court of Appeal affirmed his decision and this House dismissed the appeal. In doing so the members of the Appellate Committee expressed, in somewhat differing terms,
f views about the double actionability rule. A majority of their Lordships concluded that *Machado v Fontes* had been wrongly decided. The double actionability rule required, they held, that the allegedly tortious act be actionable in civil proceedings under the law of the foreign country where the act had been done. But the rule, they thought, was not an inflexible one. Both Lord Hodson and
g Lord Wilberforce advocated the use of flexibility in applying the rule: see [1969] 2 All ER 1085 at 1091, 1104, [1971] AC 356 at 377, 391–392. The flexibility they had in mind, however, was a flexibility that would enable the court to apply English law, the lex fori, rather than the lex loci delicti to a discrete issue in a case where the only significant connection between the action and the foreign country was that the allegedly tortious act on which the action was based had taken place
h in the foreign country. It may be that they would, if the 'only significant connection' criterion were satisfied, have allowed the lex fori rather than the lex loci delicti to be applied to the case as a whole: nb Lord Hodson's approving reference ([1969] 2 All ER 1085 at 1091, [1971] AC 356 at 377) to the dictum of Wightman J in *Seymour v Scott* (1862) 1 H & C 219 at 235 and Lord Wilberforce's
j remarks ([1969] 2 All ER 1085 at 1104, [1971] AC 356 at 391–392).

[188] There was nothing, however, in either Lord Hodson's speech or Lord Wilberforce's speech, or in the other *Chaplin v Boys* speeches, which suggested that, in a case where the only connection with England was that the action had been brought in England, the advocated flexibility could enable the court to waive the requirement that the allegedly tortious act be such as to give rise to civil

actionability under the law of the country where the act was done, still less where a
that country was in every significant respect the country of the tort.

[189] In *Red Sea Insurance Ltd v Bouygues SA* [1994] 3 All ER 749, [1995] 1 AC
190 my noble and learned friend Lord Slynn of Hadley, giving the judgment of
the Privy Council, held that, conceptually at least, the flexibility advocated in
Chaplin v Boys might justify the exclusive application of the lex loci delicti, so that
a tortious remedy might be allowed notwithstanding that the lex fori would not b
have allowed any remedy. Lord Slynn accepted that the doctrine of the proper
law of the tort had not become part of English law but he did not regard the
introduction of flexibility into the double actionability rule as inconsistent with
the rejection of that doctrine. He said:

'[Their Lordships] accept that the law of England recognises that a c
particular issue between the parties to litigation may be governed by the law
of the country which, with respect to that issue, has the most significant
relationship with the occurrence and with the parties.' (See [1994] 3 All ER
749 at 762, [1995] 1 AC 190 at 206.)

Chaplin v Boys had concerned merely a discrete issue to which, it was held, the lex d
fori could be applied to the exclusion of the lex loci delicti. In the *Red Sea Insurance*
case it was the whole case to which, conceptually, Lord Slynn held the lex loci
delicti could be applied to the exclusion of the lex fori. The same criterion,
however, 'the most significant relationship with the occurrence and with the
parties', would be applicable. For my part I can discern no difference between e
this approach and a 'proper law of the tort' approach.

[190] However, the flexibility advocated in *Chaplin v Boys* and accepted and
extended by Lord Slynn in the *Red Sea Insurance* case cannot, in my opinion, assist
KAC in the present case. What is proposed here is not that the law of the country
with the most significant relationship etc should be applied but that the law of
that country should be disapplied. It is Iraq with which KAC's case against IAC f
has the most significant relationship. It is an Iraqi tort that KAC is prosecuting,
not an English tort. The flexibility advocated in *Chaplin v Boys* and the *Red Sea
Insurance* case cannot, in my opinion, possibly justify treating this action for
conversion of the KAC aircraft as if it were a tort governed by English law, or
justify the waiving of the requirement of civil actionability under Iraqi law. g

[191] The justification for waiving the requirement of civil actionability under
Iraqi law has been based on what are said to be the requirements of international
law and of English public policy. The international law imperatives produced by
the United Nations Security Council response to Iraq's invasion of Kuwait,
described in the opinions of my noble and learned friends, require that the courts h
of this country give no recognition to Resolution 369. It is argued that since,
absent Resolution 369, title to the aircraft would have remained vested in KAC,
the question of IAC's liability for conversion under Iraqi law should be examined
and answered on the footing that KAC remained owners of the aircraft and that
Resolution 369 did not form part of the corpus of Iraqi law. It is argued that
obedience to the various United Nations Security Council resolutions and, in j
particular, Resolution 662, requires no less. As to public policy, it is argued that,
having regard to the flagrant breach of international law that Iraq's invasion of
Kuwait undoubtedly constituted, it would be contrary to public policy if any
recognition were to be given to Iraq's confiscation of the KAC aircraft or to
Resolution 369.

a

[192] I am in respectful agreement with much of the premiss on which these international law and public policy arguments are based. I agree that English courts ought not to recognise Iraq's confiscation of the aircraft nor the dissolution of KAC nor the purported vesting of the aircraft in IAC. If any of the aircraft had found their way to England, or to any other United Nations member state prepared to comply with United Nations Security Council Resolution 662, KAC could have successfully asserted title to the aircraft. I agree that in the eyes of the courts of this country, KAC remained the owners of the aircraft.

b

[193] The present action, however, is not an action in rem to recover property, whether the aircraft or the proceeds of sale of the aircraft, which belongs to KAC. The action is an action in personam for tort. Willes J in *Phillips v Eyre* referred to the law of the place from which the 'wrong derives its birth' (see (1870) LR 6 QB 1 at 28). From what system of law does KAC's action for conversion derive its birth? Certainly not from English law. It can only be the law of Iraq. The law of Iraq at the relevant time included Resolution 369. It is an unquestionable fact that under the law of Iraq at the relevant time IAC's conduct in relation to the aircraft was lawful and did not give rise to any civil liability. A cause of action in personam under Iraqi law did not come into existence.

c

d

[194] This conclusion does not depend on the vesting of the aircraft in IAC under Resolution 369. If Resolution 369 had never been passed but, instead, there had been an enactment in Iraq excluding any civil or criminal liability arising out of any dealings in Iraq with Kuwait's assets, the conclusion would be the same. In that event, too, a cause of action against IAC for conversion of the KAC aircraft could not have come into existence under the law of Iraq.

e

[195] The public policy argument is no better. Reliance was placed on *Oppenheimer v Cattermole (Inspector of Taxes)* [1975] 1 All ER 538, [1976] AC 249, in which a Nazi law which discriminated against Jews had to be considered. Lord Cross of Chelsea said ([1975] 1 All ER 538 at 567, [1976] AC 249 at 278): 'To my mind a law of this sort constitutes so grave an infringement of human rights that the courts of this country ought to refuse to recognise it as a law at all.' The issue in *Oppenheimer's* case was whether the appellant was entitled under United Kingdom fiscal legislation to double taxation relief. He claimed relief on the ground that he had dual nationality, British and German. One of the Revenue's arguments was that because he had been deprived of his German nationality under the discriminatory legislation in question, he was not entitled to the double taxation relief. In the event, despite the odious nature of the discriminatory legislation, the House agreed with the Revenue that for other reasons Mr Oppenheimer was not a German national at the relevant time and so was not entitled to double-taxation relief. In my opinion, *Oppenheimer's* case, far from assisting KAC, identifies the flaw in the public policy objections that KAC is taking. Lord Cross, at an earlier passage in his speech than that cited, postulated discriminatory legislation by Ruritania under which the property of a Ruritanian citizen who had been convicted of treason was forfeited and he was deprived of his Ruritanian citizenship. Lord Cross continued:

f

g

h

j

'Our courts would certainly refuse to entertain an action by the Ruritanian state to obtain possession of the traitor's property here; but I can see no sufficient reason why we should continue to regard him as a Ruritanian citizen for the purpose of deciding whether or not he was entitled to property here, his right to which depended on his being or not being a

Ruritanian citizen at some point of time.' (See [1975] 1 All ER 538 at 566, [1976] AC 249 at 276.)

It is implicit in Lord Cross' example that although the courts of this country may refuse to give effect to odious or barbarous foreign legislation, the existence of the legislation may nevertheless have to be recognised as a fact. So here.

[196] In his opinion at [117], above, my noble and learned friend Lord Steyn has postulated the case of an action in tort brought in England for recovery of loss caused by negligent misstatement inducing a contract. He postulates a negligent misstatement that would prima facie be actionable under the law of the foreign country where it was made and would also be actionable in England. But the contract contains a clause excluding all liability for negligent misstatement. The contract is valid under the law of the foreign country, presumably its proper law, but for some reason or other it would be contrary to English public policy to enforce it or to recognise it. Is the defendant entitled, in an action in England on the tort claim, to rely on the exclusion clause in the contract? The answer given by my noble and learned friend is No. He says that to permit the defendant to do so would be an affront to English public policy. But since the contract is valid under the law of the foreign country, its proper law, the exclusion clause would be binding on both parties under the law of the foreign country. That being so, the question whether the tort action could succeed if brought in England would require the court to decide whether England or the foreign country was the country with the most significant relationship with the circumstances of the case and with the parties: see the *Red Sea Insurance* case. In effect, the court would have to decide whether the tortious cause of action sued on was one which could derive its existence from English law or whether the relationship with England was so slight that the cause of action could only be derived from the foreign law. In the latter case there would be no cause of action on which the plaintiff could sue in England. The 'affront to English public policy' said to be constituted by the refusal of the foreign law to recognise the existence of the tortious cause of action cannot, in my opinion, be a sufficient condition for the creation by English law of a cause of action out of facts with no significant relationship to England.

[197] My noble and learned friend's point that it would be an affront to English public policy not to recognise the tort claim in England could apply equally well to contract claims. Suppose a contract between two citizens of a foreign country made in the foreign country and the proper law of which is the law of the foreign country. One party commits, or is alleged to have committed, a breach of the contract. There is then an event in the foreign country that purports to bar the action for breach of contract. The event might be a discriminatory and odious piece of legislation. It might be a release which the would-be claimant has been procured to sign by means which by English standards would be repugnant and unacceptable. None the less, under the law of the foreign country, the proper law of the contract, the event has had the result that the claimant has no cause of action for the alleged breach of contract. Would English law permit the contractual cause of action to succeed notwithstanding that under the proper law of the contract the action would fail? The question is indistinguishable from that posed by my noble and learned friend. It could not, in my opinion, be argued that English law would create an in personam contractual cause of action that was incompatible with the proper law of the contract. Why should there be any difference where the cause of action is a tortious one and the only connection with England is that England

a is the forum for the action? The 'affront' to English public policy would be the same.

[198] This brings me back to my fundamental objection to the application of the double actionability rule proposed by my noble and learned friends. It cannot, in my opinion, be English law that is the system of law from which KAC's cause of action derives its existence. The only connection between the conversion and England is that England is the forum of the suit. It is not a function ever
b claimed for English law to provide tortious causes of action to citizens of foreign countries who are injured by acts in those countries committed by other citizens of foreign countries. Nor should it be. *Phillips v Eyre* and *Carr v Fracis Times & Co* [1902] AC 176 constitute high authority that a foreign tort not actionable in the foreign country in question cannot be sued on in England. On the facts of this
c case there is, in my opinion, neither principle nor authority that justifies English law in providing KAC with a cause of action in conversion against IAC. I would, therefore, allow IAC's appeal and dismiss KAC's appeal on this ground.

The Mosul Four

d [199] On the footing that KAC's action can surmount the double actionability hurdle, I respectfully agree with the reasons given by my noble and learned friend Lord Nicholls of Birkenhead for dismissing KAC's appeal regarding the Mosul Four.

e *The Iran Six*

[200] On the footing that KAC succeed on the double actionability issue, the House must decide the issues relating to the damages KAC is entitled to recover from IAC. The six aircraft were all eventually recovered by KAC but KAC is claiming various heads of consequential loss.

f [201] The first essential, in my opinion, is to identify the wrongful acts or omissions from which the losses in question are said to flow. There were a number of individual acts of IAC, e g re-registration of the aircraft in IAC's name, repainting the aircraft in IAC livery, use of one of the aircraft for commercial flights within Iraq, that were relied on by KAC as acts of conversion. However, the conversion or usurpation that was proved against IAC was essentially the
g incorporation of the aircraft into IAC's fleet. The individual acts were simply indicative of that process: see [2001] 1 All ER (Comm) 557 at 579, [2001] 3 WLR 1117 at 1146 (para 73) per Brooke LJ in the Court of Appeal. But IAC's incorporation of the aircraft into its fleet was, on the facts of this case, a conversion/usurpation of a very peculiar sort. It was not a misappropriation of
h the aircraft from KAC. The aircraft had already been misappropriated by the state of Iraq. That usurpation was protected from civil action by state immunity. This House so held. Nor is it possible to contend that IAC's incorporation of the aircraft into its fleet deprived KAC of them. If IAC had not incorporated them into its fleet, KAC would still not have recovered them. Moreover, it was not within the power of IAC to restore the aircraft to KAC. Lord Nicholls in his
j opinion has analysed the position that arises where there is a series of conversions with each person in the series wrongfully excluding the owner from possession of his goods. Each successive converter is liable to the true owner. Each has, consciously or unconsciously, withheld the goods from the true owner. This analysis does not seem to me to work in the present case. True it is that IAC was

treating KAC's aircraft as its own but IAC was not in any meaningful sense depriving KAC of the aircraft.

[202] Accordingly, in my opinion, the approach to the damages issue should be one which holds IAC responsible for damage to the aircraft caused by IAC's retention of them but which does not hold IAC responsible for loss suffered by KAC through being deprived of the aircraft. The latter loss was, on the facts of this case, not caused by IAC's acts of usurpation but would have been suffered anyway.

The removal of the Iran Six to Iran and the payment of $US 20m

[203] The removal of these six aircraft to Iran was, as Lord Nicholls has observed, done on the orders of the Iraqi government. It was not, on the facts, something for which IAC were responsible. Nor, in my opinion, was their removal to Iran a likely or foreseeable result of the incorporation of the aircraft into the IAC fleet. A fortiori, their continued detention in Iran after hostilities had ceased and Iran's extraction of $US 20m as the price of their release cannot, in my opinion, be described as consequences flowing naturally or directly from IAC's incorporation of the aircraft into its fleet.

[204] These conclusions do not, I think, depend upon any controversial opinion as to the rule of remoteness of damage in conversion cases. They depend upon the limited nature of the conversion/usurpation for which IAC can be held responsible and the absence of any sufficient causal connection between that usurpation and the end result for which damages are sought.

Conclusion on damages

[205] If, therefore, contrary to any opinion, KAC has a cause of action for conversion, I would, in relation to the Iran Six, confine KAC's claim to the deterioration suffered by the aircraft while they were being retained by IAC as part of its fleet. I would allow IAC's appeal and dismiss KAC's cross-appeal accordingly.

Appeal and cross-appeal dismissed.

Celia Fox   Barrister.

Huck v Robson

[2002] EWCA Civ 398

COURT OF APPEAL, CIVIL DIVISION
SCHIEMANN, TUCKEY AND JONATHAN PARKER LJJ
1, 21 MARCH 2002

Costs – Order for costs – Indemnity costs – Power to award indemnity costs where defendant failing to beat claimant's Pt 36 offer – Whether offer of settlement by claimant before commencement of proceedings capable of being a Pt 36 offer – CPR 36.2(4), 36.10, 36.21.

The claimant was injured when her car collided with a car driven by the defendant. Before proceedings were issued, the defendant's insurers offered to compromise the liability issue on the basis of a 50:50 split. That offer was rejected by the claimant who subsequently, but again before the commencement of proceedings, made an offer to settle the dispute on the basis that the defendant was 95% liable. The claimant's offer was stated to be open for 21 days and was described as a Pt 36 offer. The defendant's insurers failed to accept the offer, and proceedings were subsequently commenced. At trial, the judge held that the defendant was solely responsible for the accident. The claimant then asked the judge to award her costs on an indemnity basis for the period subsequent to the last day on which the offer could have been accepted. Where a defendant had been held liable for more than the proposals contained in a claimant's Pt 36 offer, CPR 36.21[a] required the court to award the claimant costs on that basis unless it considered it unjust to do so. The judge held that it was nonsensical for a case to be decided on a 95% to 5% split, that the claimant's offer had been derisory, that it was inevitable that the defendant would reject it and that in those circumstances it would be unjust to award indemnity costs. The claimant appealed, contending that the judge had erred in his application of r 36.21. Relying on r 36.2(4)[b], which provided that a Pt 36 offer 'may be made at any time after proceedings have started', the defendant contended that the claimant's offer had not been a Pt 36 offer at all since it had been made before proceedings had commenced, and that accordingly r 36.21 did not apply. Instead, he contended that the offer was merely a matter that the court would take into account in exercising its discretion on costs. He relied on r 36.10[c] which provided that, if a person made an offer to settle before proceedings began which complied with the provisions of that rule, the court would take that offer into account when making any order as to costs. Rule 36.10(2) provided that such an offer had to be expressed to be open for at least 21 days after the date on which it had been made and otherwise had to comply with Pt 36.

Held – Where an offer had been made before the commencement of litigation which complied with the requirements of CPR 36.10, the court would take that offer into account as a Pt 36 offer, and accordingly r 36.21 would apply to it. Such

---

a   Rule 36.21 is set out at [21], below
b   Rule 36.2, so far as material, is set out at [16], below
c   Rule 36.10, so far as material, is set out at [18], below

a conclusion was consistent with the purpose of r 36.10, namely to enable a party to make an offer that complied with CPR Pt 36, and had all the consequences of a Pt 36 offer, before the commencement of proceedings. The philosophy underlying Pt 36 was the need to provide encouragement to litigants or prospective litigants to resolve their disputes by agreement. So far as claimants were concerned, that philosophy was reflected in the provisions of r 36.21 which provided incentives in the form of awards of interest and indemnity costs. The need for an incentive to encourage a claimant to make an offer of settlement before the commencement of proceedings was at least as great, if not greater, than the need for an incentive to compromise proceedings that were already on foot. It followed in the instant case that the judge had been correct to proceed on the basis that the offer was one to which r 36.21 applied. However (Jonathan Parker LJ dissenting), he had approached the exercise of his discretion on the wrong basis since he had been unduly influenced by the probable fact that no judge, if the case had come to trial, would have decided that liability should be split 95% to 5%. That conclusion, although correct, was irrelevant. While there could be circumstances where the claimant would not be awarded his costs on an indemnity basis, notwithstanding that he had recovered in full after making a Pt 36 offer for marginally less, in a case such as the instant one the court was not required to measure the offer against the likely outcome. In such litigation, a claimant with a strong case would often be prepared to accept a discount from the full value of the claim to reflect the uncertainties of litigation. Such offers were not usually based on the likely apportionment of liability but merely reflected the reality that most claimants preferred certainty to the ordeal of a trial and uncertainty about its outcome. If such a discount were offered and rejected, there was nothing unjust in allowing the claimant to receive the incentives to which she was entitled under the CPR. Accordingly, the appeal would be allowed (see [51]–[57], [63], [68]–[71], [75], [78], [80]–[85], below).

Notes

For the time when a Pt 36 offer is made, the requirement for the court to take into account an offer to settle made before the commencement of proceedings and the costs consequences where a claimant does better than his Pt 36 offer, see 37 *Halsbury's Laws* (4th edn reissue) paras 813, 815, 826.

Cases referred to in judgments

Ford v GKR Construction Ltd [2000] 1 All ER 802, [2000] 1 WLR 1397, CA.
McPhilemy v Times Newspapers Ltd (No 2) [2001] EWCA Civ 933, [2001] 4 All ER 861, [2002] 1 WLR 934.
Petrotrade Inc v Texaco Ltd [2001] 4 All ER 853, [2002] 1 WLR 947, CA.
Kiam v MGN Ltd (No 2) [2002] EWCA Civ 66, [2002] 2 All ER 242.

Appeal

The claimant, Rosalind Huck, appealed with permission of Mantell LJ granted on 2 October 2001 from the decision of Deputy Circuit Judge Townend QC, in the Carlisle County Court on 30 July 2001, refusing to award on an indemnity basis the costs of her successful action against the defendant, Tony Robson. The facts are set out in the judgment of Jonathan Parker LJ.

a　William Braithwaite QC and William Waldron (instructed by Bleasdale & Co, Whitehaven) for Mrs Huck.
Nicholas Bacon (instructed by Keoghs, Bolton) for Mr Robson.

Cur adv vult

b　21 March 2002. The following judgments were delivered.

JONATHAN PARKER LJ (giving the first judgment at the invitation of Schiemann LJ).

[1] This is an appeal by Mrs Rosalind Huck, the claimant in the action, against an order for costs made on 30 July 2001 by Deputy Circuit Judge Townend QC, *c*　sitting at the County Court at Carlisle. The order for costs followed the hearing of the issue of liability for a road traffic accident. The hearing resulted in a finding by the judge that the defendant in the action, Mr Tony Robson, was 100% liable for the accident. By his order, the judge ordered Mr Robson to pay Mrs Huck's costs of the claim and of Mr Robson's counterclaim, on the standard basis.

d　[2] Permission to appeal was granted by Mantell LJ at an oral hearing, on the ground that the appeal raises a point of some general importance under CPR Pt 36 as to the award of indemnity costs in favour of a claimant who has obtained a judgment which is more advantageous to him than the proposals contained in an earlier offer made by him in accordance with CPR Pt 36.

[3] It is Mrs Huck's case that, pursuant to CPR 36.21, the judge ought to have *e*　ordered Mr Robson to pay her costs on an indemnity basis, with interest at an enhanced rate, as from 27 October 2000, ie as from the expiry of 21 days after she had made an offer in accordance with CPR Pt 36. By that offer, Mrs Huck proposed a compromise of the liability issue on the basis that Mr Robson was 95% liable for the accident—a proposal which Mr Robson rejected. He had *f*　previously proposed a 50/50 split on liability, and he maintained that proposal.

[4] The background to the appeal is, in summary, as follows.

[5] In the action, Mrs Huck claims damages for personal injuries sustained in the accident, which occurred on 16 April 1999 on a narrow lane in Cumbria between two cars travelling in opposite directions. Her case is that she saw Mr Robson's car approaching and pulled over onto her nearside to allow it to *g*　pass, and that Mr Robson braked but lost control of his car, which skidded into hers. Her case is that her car was stationary at the moment of impact. Mr Robson's pleaded case, on the other hand, was that the lane was at that point too narrow for two cars to pass, and that the two cars skidded into each other. He specifically denied that Mrs Huck's car was stationary at the time of the *h*　collision.

[6] By letter dated 18 August 1999 from AXA Direct (Mr Robson's insurers) to Bleasdale & Co (Mrs Huck's solicitors), AXA Direct offered to compromise the liability issue on the basis of a 50/50 split. The material part of the letter, which was an open letter, reads as follows:

j　　'We have considered the locus report prepared by your engineer but we do not feel that this contains any conclusive evidence that supports either party in this accident. The photographs confirm that this was a very narrow road and the road surface was not in a good condition. Our insured advises us that he met your client's vehicle on a particularly bad bend in the road where it was too narrow to pass and both cars skidded before colliding with each

other. These comments are supported in the Police report where the Police
comment that both vehicles travelled around the bend colliding on their
off-side and the vehicles braked but skidded on the mud on the road. There
is no evidence that supports the fact that either party attempted to avoid this
collision more than the other and we feel that the matter should be settled
on a 50/50 liability split.'

[7] Mrs Huck's response to this offer is not in evidence, but it is clear from
subsequent correspondence that she rejected it.

[8] By letter dated 12 September 1999, this time headed 'Without prejudice',
AXA Direct maintained the offer.

[9] The next letter in our bundle is a letter from Bleasdale & Co to AXA Direct
dated 18 September 2000 (that is to say, a year or so later). The letter, which is
headed 'Part 36 offer', reads as follows:

'We refer to the above matter and are instructed to put forward our
Client's proposal in respect of liability only. We can confirm that our Client
will accept a 95/5% split on liability. This proposal will remain open for a
period of 21 days after which it can only be accepted with leave of the court
or with the consent of all other parties.'

[10] It appears that that letter may not have evoked a response, because on 6
October 2000 Bleasdale & Co wrote again to AXA Direct in identical terms. By
letter dated 15 October 2000 AXA Direct responded as follows (so far as material):
'We maintain our offer to settle on a 50/50 liability split and reaffirm this as a Part
36 offer on liability.'

[11] Proceedings were commenced on 7 November 2000, and the hearing on
liability took place on 26 July 2001.

[12] The judge began his judgment by commending Mr Robson for his
honesty, observing how refreshing it was to come across a completely honest
witness. He continued:

'Mr Robson in his evidence accepts that he was at fault but he believed, he
said, it was not entirely his fault. He was asked why he criticised the other
driver and he said: "I can't answer that question". He also said he could not
say if the other driver had skidded at the time he was skidding. He also said
he did not know if the other car was stationary at the time of impact. He
would have been guessing had he done so. He did say, of course, that at the
time he saw the other car it was moving towards him. That was the
impression I got, of course, from Mrs Huck's evidence. She would not have
stopped had the other car not been moving towards her. But the overall
cause of this accident, in my judgment, is the fact that Mr Robson was going
a bit too fast for this road at this place and he unfortunately met mud on the
road, otherwise he might have been able to stop, I do not know. It is very
difficult with the geography which has been presented to me. But it seems
to me that a combination of those factors, his going somewhat too fast and
the mud on the road, caused this impact. Mrs Huck's driving cannot be
criticised, it seems to me. In those circumstances, there must be judgment
for the claimant in 100% terms, I suppose is how one puts it, when the issue
is as to liability.'

a
[13] Mr William Waldron (appearing for Mrs Huck) then addressed the judge on the question of costs. He drew the judge's attention to Bleasdale & Co's letter dated 6 October 2000, and continued:

> '... in those circumstances, because the [defendant] has been held liable for more than the offer and the judgment is more advantageous to the claimant [than the offer], your Honour may order costs for the claimant on the
b
> indemnity basis from 27 October. I invite your Honour to do that.'

[14] In the result, as indicated earlier, the judge declined to accept that invitation, and awarded Mrs Huck her costs on the standard basis.

[15] However, before I examine the judge's reasons for so doing, as they appear from the discussion between the judge and Mr Waldron, it is convenient
c
to set out at this point the relevant provisions of the CPR.

[16] I start with CPR Pt 36, the relevant provisions of which are as follows:

> '36.1(1) This Part contains rules about—(a) offers to settle and payments into court; and (b) the consequences where an offer to settle or payment into court is made in accordance with this Part.
d
> (2) Nothing in this Part prevents a party making an offer to settle in whatever way he chooses, but if that offer is not made in accordance with this Part, it will only have the consequences specified in this Part if the court so orders ...
>
> 36.2(1) An offer made in accordance with the requirements of this Part is
e
> called—(a) if made by way of payment into court, "a Part 36 payment"; (b) otherwise "a Part 36 offer"...
>
> (2) The party who makes an offer is the "offeror".
>
> (3) The party to whom an offer is made is the "offeree".
>
> (4) A Part 36 offer or a Part 36 payment—(a) may be made at any time after proceedings have started; and (b) may be made in appeal proceedings ...'
f
[17] Rules 36.3 and 4 deal with offers by a defendant to settle a claim which is wholly or partly a money claim. They are not material for present purposes. Nor are r 36.5 (form and content of a Pt 36 offer), r 36.6 (notice of a Pt 36 payment), r 36.7 (offer to settle a claim for provisional damages), r 36.8 (time when a Pt 36 offer or a Pt 36 payment is made and accepted), or r 36.9 (clarification of a Part 36
g
offer or a Part 36 payment notice).

[18] CPR 36.10 provides as follows (so far as material):

> '(1) If a person makes an offer to settle before proceedings are begun which complies with the provisions of this rule, the court will take that offer into account when making any order as to costs.
h
> (2) The offer must—(a) be expressed to be open for at least 21 days after the date it was made ... and (c) otherwise comply with this Part.'

[19] I need not, I think, read rr 36.11–36.19 inclusive.

[20] CPR 36.20 deals with the costs consequences where a claimant fails to
j
better a defendant's Pt 36 offer or a Pt 36 payment. It provides as follows:

> '(1) This rule applies where at trial a claimant—(a) fails to better a Part 36 payment; or (b) fails to obtain a judgment which is more advantageous than a defendant's Part 36 offer.
>
> (2) Unless it considers it unjust to do so, the court will order the claimant to pay any costs incurred by the defendant after the latest date on which the

payment or offer could have been accepted without needing the permission of the court.'   *a*

[21] Rule 36.21 deals with the costs consequences where the claimant betters his own Pt 36 offer. I must read the whole of the rule.

'(1) This rule applies where at trial—(a) a defendant is held liable for more; or (b) the judgment against a defendant is more advantageous to the *b* claimant, than the proposals contained in a claimant's Part 36 offer.

(2) The court may order interest on the whole or part of any sum of money (excluding interest) awarded to the claimant at a rate not exceeding 10% above base rate for some or all of the period starting with the latest date on which the defendant could have accepted the offer without needing the *c* permission of the court.

(3) The court may also order that the claimant is entitled to—(a) his costs on the indemnity basis from the latest date when the defendant could have accepted the offer without needing the permission of the court; and (b) interest on those costs at a rate not exceeding 10% above base rate.

(4) Where this rule applies, the court will make the orders referred to in *d* paragraphs (2) and (3) unless it considers it unjust to do so. (Rule 36.12 sets out the latest date when the defendant could have accepted the offer)

(5) In considering whether it would be unjust to make the orders referred to in paragraphs (2) and (3) above, the court will take into account all the circumstances of the case including—(a) the terms of any Part 36 offer; (b) *e* the stage in the proceedings when any Part 36 offer or Part 36 payment was made; (c) the information available to the parties at the time when the Part 36 offer or Part 36 payment was made; and (d) the conduct of the parties with regard to the giving or refusing to give information for the purposes of enabling the offer or payment into court to be made or evaluated.

(6) Where the court awards interest under this rule and also awards *f* interest on the same sum and for the same period under any other power, the total interest may not exceed 10% above base rate.'

[22] I turn next to CPR Pt 44, which deals with costs. Rule 44.3 deals with the court's discretion in relation to costs, and the circumstances to be taken into account when exercising that discretion. I refer to this rule because Mr Nicholas *g* Bacon, who appears for Mr Robson, submits, among other things, that the offer in question was not a Pt 36 offer since it was made before the commencement of proceedings, and that the effect of r 36.10 is that it is to be taken into account by the court in exercising its discretion as to costs.

[23] The relevant provisions of Pt 44 are as follows: *h*

'44.3(1) The court has discretion as to—(a) whether costs are payable by one party to another; (b) the amount of those costs; and (c) when they are to be paid.

(2) If the court decides to make an order about costs—(a) the general rule is that the unsuccessful party will be ordered to pay the costs of the successful *j* party; but (b) the court may make a different order …

(4) In deciding what order (if any) to make about costs, the court must have regard to all the circumstances, including—(a) the conduct of all the parties; (b) whether a party has succeeded on part of his case, even if he has not been wholly successful; and (c) any payment into court or admissible

a   offer to settle made by a party which is drawn to the court's attention
     (whether or not made in accordance with Part 36) ...
         (5) The conduct of the parties includes—(a) conduct before, as well as
     during, the proceedings and in particular the extent to which the parties
     followed any relevant pre-action protocol; (b) whether it was reasonable for
     a party to raise, pursue or contest a particular allegation or issue; (c) the
b   manner in which a party has pursued or defended his case or a particular
     allegation or issue; and (d) whether a claimant who has succeeded in his
     claim, in whole or in part, exaggerated his claim ...
         44.4 (1) Where the court is to assess the amounts of costs (whether by
     summary or detailed assessment) it will assess those costs—(a) on the
     standard basis; or (b) on the indemnity basis, but the court will not in either
c   case allow costs which have been unreasonably incurred or are unreasonable
     in amount ...
         (2) Where the amount of costs is to be assessed on the standard basis, the
     court will—(a) only allow costs which are proportionate to the matters in
     issue; and (b) resolve any doubt which it may have as to whether costs were
d   reasonably incurred or reasonable and proportionate in amount in favour of
     the paying party ...
         (3) Where the amount of costs is to be assessed on the indemnity basis,
     the court will resolve any doubt which it may have as to whether costs were
     reasonably incurred or were reasonable in amount in favour of the receiving
e   party.
         (4) Where—(a) the court makes an order about costs without indicating
     the basis on which the costs are to be assessed; or (b) the court makes an
     order for costs to be assessed on a basis other than the standard basis or the
     indemnity basis, the costs will be assessed on the standard basis ...
f   44.5 (1) The court is to have regard to all the circumstances in deciding
     whether costs were—(a) if it is assessing costs on the standard basis—(i)
     proportionately and reasonably incurred; or (ii) were proportionate and
     reasonable in amount, or (b) if it is assessing costs on the indemnity basis—(i)
     unreasonably incurred; or (ii) unreasonable in amount ...
         (3) The court must also have regard to—(a) the conduct of all the parties,
g   including in particular—(i) conduct before, as well as during, the proceedings;
     and (ii) the efforts made, if any, before and during the proceedings in order
     to try to resolve the dispute; (b) the amount or value of any money or
     property involved; (c) the importance of the matter to all the parties; (d) the
     particular complexity of the matter or the difficulty or novelty of the
h   questions raised; (e) the skill, effort, specialised knowledge and responsibility
     involved; (f) the time spent on the case; and (g) the place where and the
     circumstances in which work or any part of it was done.'

     [24] I can now return to the discussion about costs which followed delivery of
     the judge's judgment, and to Mr Waldron's invitation to the judge to award
j   Mrs Huck her costs on an indemnity basis as from 27 October 2000. The judge's
     immediate response, referring to Mrs Huck's offer to split liability 95/5 in her
     favour, was that the offer 'was not an offer of anything', and that it was 'derisory'
     and 'meaningless'. 'It is nothing', he said.
     [25] When Mr Waldron said that he had heard of offers by a claimant to accept
     a compromise on liability of the basis of 99·9% liability by the defendant and 0·1%

by the claimant, the judge commented that an 80:20 split might be realistic, and
that he had even known of cases being resolved on the basis of a 90:10 split, but
that he had never heard of a case being resolved at 95:5, and that he would regard
such a result as 'nonsensical'. Mr Waldron then submitted that by virtue of
r 36.21, to which he referred the judge, the court was bound to award indemnity
costs unless it would be unjust to do so. The judge responded that he considered
that it would be unjust so to order. The judge then inquired as to the approximate
value of the claim. Mr Waldron suggested (without committing himself) that it
might be worth between £17,500 and £40,000. The judge then said:

> 'In my judgment 95% on the kind of value that we are talking about here
> was no kind of offer and it seems to me inevitable that the defendant would
> reject it. In those circumstances, in my judgment it would be unjust to award
> indemnity costs even though I have found that the claimant succeeds in the
> proportion of 100%.'

[26] Mr Waldron then said: 'For my own purposes and understanding, is it
your Honour's judgment, as I understand it to be … that the injustice is that the
offer was derisory and meaningless?'

[27] To which the judge replied: 'It was derisory, yes.'

[28] The judge accordingly went on to award Mrs Huck her costs on the
standard basis.

[29] By her grounds of appeal, Mrs Huck contends firstly that the judge failed
to appreciate that the application of r 36.21 depends solely upon whether the
judgment against Mr Robson on the issue of liability was more advantageous to
her than her offer of a 95:5 split, as in the event it was. Secondly, she contends
that the judge failed to give sufficient weight to para (4) of the rule, which
provides that the court will order costs on an indemnity basis 'unless it considers
it unjust to do so', and that Mr Robson's view of the offer was not a relevant
consideration. Thirdly, she contends that in concluding that it would be unjust
to order costs on an indemnity basis, the judge failed to have regard to the various
matters set out in para (5) of the rule. Fourthly, she contends that the judge's
decision to award costs on the standard basis was wrong, and that his reasoning
was flawed and led him to make a decision so perverse as to indicate that he must
have fallen into error.

[30] Although Mr Waldron did not expressly invite the judge to award interest
on the indemnity costs, pursuant to para (3)(b) of r 36.21, section 5 of Mrs Huck's
appellant's notice includes a claim for such interest.

[31] By a respondent's notice, Mr Robson raises the contention that the offer
in question was not a Pt 36 offer; that it is merely a matter which the court will
take into account in exercising its discretion as to costs, and that accordingly the
judge was not obliged by paras (3) and (4) of r 36.21 to award costs on an
indemnity basis.

[32] Mr Bill Braithwaite QC (who leads Mr Waldron on this appeal) submits
that the offer is a Pt 36 offer, or at least is to be treated as if it were. He submits
that the true effect of r 36.10 is that it is to be taken into account by the court *under*
Pt 36, and that r 36.21 accordingly applies to it.

[33] Turning to the application of r 36.21 itself, Mr Braithwaite submits that
the only precondition for the application of r 36.21 to the offer in question is
that Mrs Huck should have bettered that offer (which indisputably occurred,
since Mr Robson was held to be 100% liable). Accordingly, indemnity costs

a should be awarded as from 27 October 2000, with interest from that date, *unless it would be unjust so to order* (see paras (3) and (4) of the rule). That, he submits, is the only issue.

[34] On that issue, Mr Braithwaite criticises the judge for not having referred expressly to each of the four factors listed in r 36.21(5)—the only one of such factors to which he referred expressly being the terms of the offer. Mr Braithwaite

b submits that the fact that the judge failed to do so indicates that he did not have the relevant factors sufficiently in mind.

[35] In any event, submits Mr Braithwaite, there was no basis for the conclusion that it would be unjust to make the costs order sought.

[36] He reminds us, by reference to the decisions of this court in *Petrotrade Inc v*
c *Texaco Ltd* [2001] 4 All ER 853, [2002] 1 WLR 947 and *McPhilemy v Times Newspapers Ltd (No 2)* [2001] EWCA Civ 933, [2001] 4 All ER 861, [2002] 1 WLR 934, that an order for indemnity costs under r 36.21 does not imply any disapproval of the defendant's conduct, still less does it carry any element of stigma; nor is it intended to be punitive. He submits that a claimant who betters his own Pt 36 offer, by however small a margin, is prima facie entitled to
d indemnity costs under the rule, and that there are no grounds in the instant case for depriving Mrs Huck of that prima facie entitlement.

[37] Mr Braithwaite submits that the judge was in error in approaching the question whether it would be unjust to award Mrs Huck indemnity costs by asking himself whether there was a possibility of the court making a finding of contributory fault by her of less than 10%. Mr Braithwaite accepts that such a
e finding would not have been appropriate in the circumstances of the instant case, but he submits that Mrs Huck's offer is to be regarded not as an assessment of the likelihood of a particular outcome if the issue of liability went to trial but rather as an assessment by her of the risk she would be running if it did so. She was, he asserts, confident of her case that her car was stationary at the moment of impact,
f and in the event that confidence was resoundingly justified. The fact that her offer reflected that degree of confidence ought not, he submits, to serve to deprive her of the indemnity costs to which she would otherwise be entitled under the rule.

[38] As to the judge's inquiry about the estimated value of the claim,
g Mr Braithwaite submits that the value of the claim is not a material factor. A 5% discount on even a small claim cannot be described as nominal.

[39] Turning to the four factors listed in para (5) of the rule, Mr Braithwaite submits (as to (a), the terms of the offer) that the offer gave Mr Robson the opportunity to resolve the issue of liability with the benefit of a 5% discount; (as to (b), 'the stage in the proceedings when [the offer] ... was made') that the offer
h was made in advance of the commencement of proceedings and would, if accepted, have avoided the need for any trial on liability; (as to (c), the information available to the parties at the time when the offer was made) that the information available to the parties in October 2000 was identical to that which was available at trial; and (as to (d), the conduct of the parties) that Mrs Huck's conduct cannot
j be criticised, whereas Mr Robson's defence that Mrs Huck was 50% to blame for the accident (a defence which he had maintained throughout) effectively collapsed at trial on the admissions to which the judge referred at the start of his judgment.

[40] Mr Braithwaite further submits that the judge was in error in attaching what appeared to be significant weight upon his own evaluation of the

reasonableness of Mr Robson in rejecting the offer, whereas the only relevant
question was whether Mrs Huck had bettered her own offer; that the judge
effectively penalised Mrs Huck for assessing her prospects of success in the action
as extremely good; that the implication of the judge's reasoning was that a
claimant with a strong claim would always have to concede at least a 10%
reduction before he could take advantage of the provisions of r 36.21; and that the
judge failed to take account of the fact that had Mr Robson conceded before the
hearing that he did not know whether or not Mrs Huck's car was stationary when
the accident occurred a trial of the liability issue might have been avoided
altogether.

[41] In support of the respondent's notice, Mr Bacon (for Mr Robson) submits
that the offer contained in the letter dated 6 October 2000 was not a Pt 36 offer at
all, since it was made before proceedings were commenced. In support of this
submission he relies on para (4)(a) of r 36.2, which provides that a Pt 36 offer 'may
be made at any time after proceedings have started'. Mr Bacon submits that the
offer in question was an 'offer to settle before proceedings are begun', of a kind
which the court will 'take into account' under r 36.10. Mr Bacon submits that
'take into account', in that context, means that the court will take it into account
in exercising its discretion as to costs, but that r 36.21 does not apply to it.

[42] It follows, submits Mr Bacon, that Mrs Huck's grounds of appeal are
misconceived in so far as they are premised on the existence of a Pt 36 offer.
Rather, the judge was exercising a general discretion, and there are no grounds
on which his exercise of that discretion can be challenged in an appellate court.

[43] If and in so far as (contrary to his primary submission) the offer in
question was a Pt 36 offer, or falls to be treated as such, Mr Bacon submits that it
is apparent from the transcript of the discussion concerning costs which followed
delivery of his judgment that the judge appreciated that the condition for the
application of r 36.21 was that Mrs Huck should have bettered her own offer, and
that in the event that condition had been fulfilled, and that the judge then went
on (correctly, on this basis) to consider whether in the circumstances of the
instant case it would be unjust to award indemnity costs.

[44] Mr Bacon warns us against concluding from the judge's references to
admissions made by Mr Bacon in the course of his oral evidence that Mr Bacon
had run the action up to trial on the issue of liability by persisting in a defence
which he knew to be false. Mr Bacon submits that it is clear from the judge's
references to Mr Bacon's honesty as a witness that the judge did not take that
view; on the contrary, the judge was plainly satisfied that Mr Bacon honestly
believed that he was not solely to blame for the accident.

[45] Mr Bacon submits that in the circumstances of the instant case a finding
of contributory fault on the part of Mrs Huck of less than 10% was not a realistic
possibility, and that in consequence the judge was fully entitled to regard
Mrs Huck's offer as being one which Mr Robson would inevitably reject.

[46] Mr Bacon submits that, in order to qualify as a Pt 36 offer, the offer must
represent a genuine and realistic attempt to dispose of the dispute by agreement,
and that the court is entitled to conclude that an offer by a claimant which the
defendant will inevitably refuse does not meet that requirement.

[47] In support of this submission, Mr Bacon relies on the fact that one of the
matters to which the court will have regard in considering whether it would be
unjust to award indemnity costs under r 36.21 is the terms of the offer itself (see
para (5)(a) of the rule). This was, he submits, the crucial factor in the instant case,

a as the judge made abundantly clear. He submits that the fact that the judge did not make specific reference to each of the matters listed in para (5) of the rule does not in any way vitiate his decision. In concluding that it would be unjust to award indemnity costs, the judge no doubt had all those factors in mind.

[48] Accordingly, submits Mr Bacon, even if (contrary to his primary submission) the offer was one to which r 36.21 applied, the judge's decision that it would by

b unjust to award indemnity costs is not a decision with which this court should interfere.

[49] Before turning to the issues, I should record that I accept Mr Bacon's submission that this court should not proceed on the basis that (in effect) Mr Robson maintained a defence on liability which he knew to be false, only to capitulate at the hearing. I agree with Mr Bacon that had the judge taken that

c view, far from commending Mr Robson for his honesty he would have expressed himself very differently and might well have come to a different conclusion on the crucial question whether it would be unjust to award Mrs Huck indemnity costs. We have not seen the transcript of Mr Robson's evidence and are accordingly in no position to form our own view, but the judge's comments

d are entirely consistent with Mr Robson having frankly admitted, under pressure of cross-examination, that he could not say for sure that Mrs Huck's car was still moving at the moment of impact, although he believed that to be the case. In the circumstances, this court should not in my judgment draw any inferences adverse to Mr Robson from the admissions which the judge records him as having made in the course of his evidence beyond the plain fact that those admissions were

e fatal to his case that both parties were equally to blame.

[50] I turn, then, to the issue raised by the respondent's notice; that is to say, the issue whether the offer is one to which r 36.21 applies.

[51] The issue turns on the true meaning and effect of r 36.10, and in particular of the words 'the court will take that offer into account' (see r 36.10(1)). In my

f judgment the purpose and effect of r 36.10 is to enable a party to make an offer which complies with CPR Pt 36, and which has all the consequences of a CPR Pt 36 offer, before proceedings are commenced. As Lord Woolf MR said in *Ford v GKR Construction Ltd* [2000] 1 All ER 802 at 810, [2000] 1 WLR 1397 at 1403: 'Under the CPR it is possible for the parties to make offers to settle before litigation commences.'

g [52] Later he said:

> 'If the process of making Pt 36 offers before the commencement of litigation is to work in the way which the CPR intend, the parties must be provided with the information which they require in order to assess whether
h to make an offer or whether to accept that offer. Where offers are not accepted, the CPR make provision as to what are to be the cost consequences ... of not accepting an offer which, when judged in the light of the litigation, should have been accepted.' (See [2000] 1 All ER 802 at 810, [2000] 1 WLR 1397 at 1403.)

j [53] Read in context, the words 'the court will take that offer into account' in r 36.10 mean, in my judgment, that where an offer has been made before the commencement of litigation which complies with the requirements of the rule (which in turn requires that the offer comply with the remainder of Pt 36) the court will take that offer into account *as a Pt 36 offer*, and accordingly that where the offer has been made prior to the commencement of proceedings by the

prospective claimant rr 36.20 or 36.21 (as the case may be) will apply to it. I reject
Mr Bacon's submission that r 36.21 means no more than that the court will take
such an offer into account when exercising its discretion as to costs. In the first
place, such a provision would be otiose since r 44.3 provides that in exercising its
discretion as to costs the court will have regard to (among other things) the
conduct of the parties before the commencement of the proceedings (see
r 44.3(4)(a) and (5)(a)), and, more importantly in the present context: 'any ...
admissible offer to settle made by a party which is drawn to the court's attention
(whether or not made in accordance with Part 36)' (see r 44.3(4)(c)).

[54] In the second place, the specific requirements of r 36.10(2) (viz that the
offer be expressed to be open for at least 21 days, that (if made by a prospective
defendant) it includes an offer to pay the prospective claimant's costs up to the
expiry of the 21 days, and that it otherwise complies with Pt 36) limit the category
of pre-litigation offers which the court will 'take into account' to those which are
equivalent to Pt 36 offers made after the commencement of proceedings.

[55] In any event, I can see no logical reason why costs consequences which
follow from an offer which fulfils the requirements of Pt 36 and which is made
after the commencement of proceedings should not equally follow from an offer
which also fulfils those requirements but which is made before proceedings are
commenced. Indeed, I can see very good reasons why the consequences should
be the same. The philosophy underlying Pt 36 is the need to provide
encouragement to litigants or prospective litigants to resolve their disputes by
agreement. So far as claimants are concerned, paras (2) and (3) of r 36.21 reflect
that philosophy by providing incentives in the form of awards of interest and
indemnity costs. In the context of the instant action, the relevant incentive is
provided by para (3) (indemnity costs). Absent some such incentive under the
CPR, there would be no reason for a claimant to make a Pt 36 offer. As Simon
Brown LJ said in *Kiam v MGN Ltd (No 2)* [2002] EWCA Civ 66 at [8], [2002] 2 All ER
242 at [8]:

> 'If the claimant thought that, even if he were to make and then beat an
> offer, he was going to get no more than his costs on the standard basis, why
> would he make it? It would afford him no advantage at all. He would do
> better simply to claim at large and recover his costs whatever measure of
> success he gained. His position is, in short, quite different from that of the
> defendant who plainly has every incentive to make a settlement offer,
> generally by way of payment into court, irrespective of the basis on which
> any costs order will be made.'

[56] The need for an incentive to encourage a claimant to make an offer of
settlement before proceedings are commenced is at least as great as the need to
make one where proceedings are already on foot. Indeed, one would have
thought that the need for an incentive to make offers of settlement which might
avoid proceedings altogether would be regarded as, if anything, greater than the
need for an incentive to compromise proceedings which are already on foot.

[57] Accordingly the judge was right, in my judgment, to proceed on the basis
that the offer made in the instant case was one to which r 36.21 applied.

[58] I turn, then, to the question whether the judge's decision that it would be
unjust to award Mrs Huck her costs on an indemnity basis is one with which this
court should interfere.

a [59] I turn first to Mr Braithwaite's criticism of the manner in which the judge expressed his decision on costs, in that in reaching that decision the judge did not expressly refer to the matters listed in para (5) of the rule as being factors which the court will take into account in considering that question; the only factor to which he made express reference being the terms of the offer itself.

[60] In my judgment it is not obligatory for a judge, when giving his decision
b on the question whether it would be unjust to award indemnity costs under r 36.21, to make express reference to each of the four factors listed in para (5) of the rule: nor did Mr Braithwaite go so far as to suggest that it was. At the same time, it may well be a counsel of prudence for a judge to do so, if only to forestall the argument that because he did not expressly refer to a particular factor, he cannot have had that factor in mind.

c [61] I turn, therefore, to Mr Braithwaite's challenge to the substance of the judge's decision on costs.

[62] True it is that once a claimant has bettered his own offer, even though he may have done so by the narrowest of margins, then r 36.21 will apply. But, as Mr Braithwaite rightly accepts, it does not follow that indemnity costs will
d necessarily be ordered. In every case where the rule applies, the question for the court is whether it would be unjust to make such an order. In this sense, a claimant who has bettered his Pt 36 offer has a prima facie entitlement to indemnity costs.

[63] At the same time, it is in my judgment implicit in r 36.21 that, consistently with the philosophy underlying Pt 36 (to which I have already referred), in order
e to qualify for the incentives provided by paras (2) and (3) of the rule, a claimant's Pt 36 offer must represent at the very least a genuine and realistic attempt by the claimant to resolve the dispute by agreement. Such an offer is to be contrasted with one which creates no real opportunity for settlement but is merely a tactical step designed to secure the benefit of the incentives. That is not to say that the
f offer must be one which it would be unreasonable for the defendant to refuse; that would be too strict a test, and would introduce considerations of punishment and moral condemnation which (on the authority of *Petrotrade Inc v Texaco Ltd* [2001] 4 All ER 853, [2002] 1 WLR 947 and *McPhilemy v Times Newspapers Ltd (No 2)* [2001] 4 All ER 861, [2002] 1 WLR 934) are irrelevant in the context of para (3) of r 36.21. Indeed, the terms of the offer may reflect a degree of optimism and
g confidence on the part of the claimant/offeror. Provided only that the offer represents a genuine and realistic offer to resolve the dispute by agreement, it is for the claimant to decide at what level to pitch his offer. In some cases, an offer which allows only a small discount from 100% success on the claim may be a genuine and realistic offer; in other cases, it may not. It is for the judge in every
h case to consider whether, in the circumstances of that particular case, and taking into account the factors listed in para (5) of r 36.21, it would be unjust to make the order sought.

[64] As Chadwick LJ said in *McPhilemy's* case [2001] 4 All ER 861 at [7]:

'There is no doubt that the question whether or not it was unjust to make
j orders under paras (2) and (3) of r 36.21 was a question for the judge to determine in the exercise of his discretion ... If the judge took into account the matters which he ought to have taken into account, and left out of account matters which he ought not to have taken into account, it would be wrong in principle for this court to interfere with his decision. It could only do so if satisfied that the decision was so perverse that the judge must have

fallen into error. This court must respect the judge's exercise of the
discretion which has been entrusted to him. The court must resist the
temptation to substitute its own view for that of the judge unless satisfied
that his discretion has been exercised on a basis which is wrong in law; or that
the conclusion which he has reached is so plainly wrong that his exercise of
the discretion entrusted to him must be regarded as flawed.'

[65] In the instant case, it is plain from the comments which he made during
Mr Waldron's submissions on costs that the judge considered that the offered
discount of 5% was, in truth, illusory and that that was the basis for his conclusion
(p 7) that it was inevitable that the offer would be rejected. As I read the
transcript, that conclusion founded his decision that it would be unjust to treat
the offer as entitling Mrs Huck to indemnity costs under para (3) of the rule. In
particular, I do not understand the judge to have reached that decision on the
basis that in a personal injury case the court will never apportion liability more
precisely than in multiples of 10%: had he taken that view, he would plainly have
been wrong. Rather, his comments about findings of 5% contributory fault were,
as I read them, made in the particular context of the instant case, where he
regarded it as plain that there was no real possibility of any outcome on liability
other than either 100% or 50%.

[66] Given Mr Robson's pleaded defence that both parties were equally to
blame, and given the earlier offer by Mr Robson's insurers of a 50:50 split on
liability, the judge was, in my judgment, entitled to regard the offer as being one
which Mr Robson would inevitably reject and on that basis to conclude, in the
exercise of his discretion, that it would in the circumstances be unjust to order
indemnity costs.

[67] I would accordingly dismiss this appeal.

TUCKEY LJ.

[68] Like Schiemann LJ I agree with the first 62 paragraphs of Jonathan
Parker LJ's judgment and that the crucial question which the judge had to answer
was whether it was unjust to award the claimant indemnity costs despite the fact
that she had 'beaten' her CPR Pt 36 offer.

[69] I think it is clear that the judge deprived the claimant of indemnity costs
simply because liability would never have been apportioned 95:5. Jonathan
Parker LJ says that this was within the judge's discretion because such an offer did
not create any real opportunity for settlement in a case where there was no real
possibility of any outcome other than 50:50 or an outright win for the claimant
(see [63], [65], above). Schiemann LJ says that the fact that no judge would
apportion liability 95:5 is irrelevant. A defendant can choose not to accept such
an offer but if the claimant beats it there is nothing unjust in awarding indemnity
costs.

[70] I think Schiemann LJ is right about this. I do not think that the court is
required to measure the offer against the likely outcome in a case such as this. In
this type of litigation a claimant with a strong case will often be prepared to
accept a discount from the full value of the claim to reflect the uncertainties of
litigation. Such offers are not usually based on the likely apportionment of liability
but merely reflect the reality that most claimants prefer certainty to the ordeal of
a trial and uncertainty about its outcome. If such a discount is offered and
rejected there is nothing unjust in allowing the claimant to receive the incentives

a to which he or she is entitled under the rules. On the contrary, I would say that this is a just result.

[71] I would however add that if it was self-evident that the offer made was merely a tactical step designed to secure the benefit of the incentives provided by the rule (eg an offer to settle for 99·9% of the full value of the claim) I would agree with Jonathan Parker LJ that the judge would have a discretion to refuse
b indemnity costs. But that cannot be said of the offer made in this case, which I think did provide the defendant with a real opportunity for settlement even though it did not represent any possible apportionment of liability. I would therefore allow this appeal.

SCHIEMANN LJ.
c
[72] There are policy reasons which lead some jurisdictions in general to deny a successful claimant all costs, and other jurisdictions including our own in general to deny successful claimants some of their costs—the difference between the standard and the indemnity bases of taxation in particular.

[73] The general policy stance traditionally adopted in this country is that a
d claimant who obtains all he asks for should be awarded his costs on a basis which does not amount to full recovery. There is a case for having a general policy stance that such a claimant should be awarded his costs on the indemnity basis. However, that has not been the traditional stance adopted in this country. Nor is it the stance adopted by the CPR.

e [74] There is no express provision in CPR Pt 44 as to the relevant factors which a court is to bear in mind in exercising its discretion as to whether to award costs on the standard or the indemnity basis. Nevertheless, when construed in the light of the overriding objective—see in particular CPR 1.1 (2)(c)—and the default position prescribed by CPR 44.4, the general presumption must be that costs will be awarded on the standard basis.

f [75] I have nothing to add to what Parker LJ has said in the first 62 paragraphs of his judgment.

[76] In particular I agree that a claimant who has bettered his Pt 36 offer has a prima facie entitlement to indemnity costs. The general presumption that a successful claimant only receives costs on the standard basis is displaced by
g r 36.21(4).

[77] The crucial question to be addressed by the judge in the present case was that posed in r 36.21(4): will it be *unjust* to award the claimant his costs on an indemnity basis? It is important to bear in mind that this is the way the question is phrased. The question is not: will it be unjust *not* to award the claimant his costs on an indemnity basis?
h
[78] The judge addressed this question in the passages quoted by Jonathan Parker LJ in [24]–[27], above. The judge identifies the following consideration as the circumstance which drove him to the view that to award the claimant costs on the indemnity basis would be *unjust*, namely, the fact that it was inevitable that the defendant would reject the offer made by the claimant. I do not accept that this
j is a relevant, still less a conclusive, factor in deciding whether the award of costs to the claimant on the indemnity basis would be *unjust*.

[79] It is not clear whether the judge arrived at his view in the light of (1) his impression of the defendant formed at the trial or (2) what he understood to be the claimant's understanding at the time he made the offer of the likely reaction of the defendant or (3) what a reasonable defendant to a road traffic accident would

do when faced with an offer by the claimant to settle the question of liability on the basis of a proportion 95:5 or (4) what a reasonable defendant would have done *a* if he had been the driver of the defendant's car at the time of the crash and had been subsequently faced with this Pt 36 offer or (5) a view that it was inevitable that if the case were fought the judge would not apportion liability 95:5.

[80] As to (1), this seems to me irrelevant to the question whether it is just to deprive a claimant of the indemnity costs to which he is prima facie entitled. The *b* answer to that question should not depend on the forensic fortitude of a particular defendant. As to (2), we were not told of any relevant evidence on this point. But in any event I consider it irrelevant. Again, the answer to the question whether it is just to deprive a claimant of his indemnity costs should not depend on the claimant's understanding of the defendant's forensic fortitude. As to (3), again this seems to me irrelevant. Rule 36.21(5) tells the judge to take into *c* account all the circumstances of the case. There is no suggestion that other traffic accidents are relevant. As to (4), I do not categorise the defendant's reaction in the present case as unreasonable. Nor would he have been behaving unreasonably if he had accepted the claimant's Pt 36 offer. I however see nothing unjust in awarding a claimant his indemnity costs in circumstances where the defendant *d* chooses not to accept an offer to settle for less than that to which the claimant is entitled. If it was consideration (5) which motivated the judge then in my judgment he fell into error. I accept that it was all but inevitable that no judge would apportion liability 95:5 but this seems to me an irrelevant consideration.

[81] Nevertheless, I accept, like my Lords, that circumstances can exist where, notwithstanding that a claimant has recovered in full after making a Pt 36 offer *e* for marginally less, he will not be awarded costs on the indemnity basis. I do not consider that Pt 36 was intended to produce a situation in which a claimant was automatically entitled to costs on the indemnity basis provided only that he made an offer pursuant to r 36.10 in an amount marginally less than the claim.

[82] The judge had a discretion. Unlike Parker LJ but like Tuckey LJ I consider *f* that in the present case the judge approached the exercise of his discretion on a wrong basis. The judge was unduly influenced by the probable fact that no judge, if the case came to trial, would decide that liability should be split 95:5. I regard this conclusion, although correct, as irrelevant. We are therefore entitled to exercise this discretion afresh.

[83] Like Tuckey LJ, I do not consider it just in the circumstances of the present *g* case to deprive the claimant of costs on the indemnity basis. Justice in the individual case is what r 36.21(5) bids us to take into account; not justice in general as between claimants and defendants or views as to social policy in general.

[84] I would therefore allow the appeal and order that the claimant's costs be assessed on the indemnity basis. *h*

[85] That being the conclusion of the majority, this appeal will be allowed and the decision of the judge will be set aside.

Appeal allowed.

James Brooks   Barrister.

a
Cooke v Secretary of State for Social Security

[2001] EWCA Civ 734

b COURT OF APPEAL, CIVIL DIVISION

CLARKE, HALE LJJ AND BUTTERFIELD J

25 APRIL 2001

Court of Appeal – Permission to appeal – Application for permission to appeal –
c Application for permission to appeal from decision of social security commissioner –
Approach to be adopted by Court of Appeal in determining whether appeal has real
prospect of success – Access to Justice Act 1999, s 55(1).

On an application to the Court of Appeal for permission to appeal from a decision
d of a social security commissioner, made on an appeal from a tribunal, the court
should take a robust attitude when determining whether the proposed appeal
will have a real prospect of success. Although such an appeal falls outside s 55(1)[a]
of the Access to Justice Act 1999, which permits a second-tier appeal from a
decision of the High Court or a county court only where the Court of Appeal
considers that the appeal will raise an important point of principle or practice, or
e there is some other compelling reason for that court to hear it, many of the
reasons underlying that provision apply with equal force in such circumstances.
It is a highly specialised field of law, and there is an independent two-tier appellate
structure. While it is important that such appeal structures have a link to the
ordinary court system, the ordinary courts should approach such cases with an
f appropriate degree of caution. It is quite probable that, on a technical issue of
understanding and applying the complex social security legislation, the
commissioner will have got it right, and the Court of Appeal should take an
appropriately modest view, especially when it has heard only one side of the
argument, of the likelihood of the commissioner having erred (see [14]–[17], [20],
[21], below).

g   Per curiam. The point is also relevant to other similar appeal structures, e g the
employment tribunals and the Employment Appeal Tribunal, the adjudicators
and the Immigration Appeal Tribunal, the leasehold valuation tribunals and the
Lands Tribunal. However, there are significant differences between the social
security appeal system and those that may affect matters. Some are private law
h tribunal systems rather than government and citizen or applicant systems, and
other considerations may arise (see [18], [20], [21], below).

Notes

For second appeals from appeals in county courts and the High Court and for
j appeals from social security commissioners, see respectively 37 *Halsbury's Laws*
(4th edn reissue) para 1521 and 44(2) *Halsbury's Laws* (4th edn reissue) para 365.

    For the Access to Justice Act 1999, s 55, see 11 *Halsbury's Statutes* (4th edn) (2000
reissue) 1523.

---

a   Section 55(1) is set out at [14], below

Case referred to in judgments

R v Social Security Comr, ex p Chamberlain [2000] TLR 586.

Appeal

The claimant, Alwyn Cooke, appealed with permission of the Court of Appeal from the decision of Deputy Social Security Commissioner Hereward on 26 May 2000 dismissing her appeal from the decision of the Wigan Disability Appeal Tribunal on 12 April 1999 dismissing her appeal from the decision of an adjudication officer on 24 July 1998 granting an application by the defendant, the Secretary of State for Social Security, for a review of a decision on 9 October 1996 awarding her for life the higher rate mobility and care components of disability living allowance. The facts are set out in the judgment of Hale LJ.

Rajeev Thacker (instructed by *Stephensons*, Wigan) for the claimant.
David Forsdick (instructed by *the Solicitor for the Department of Social Security*) for the Secretary of State.

HALE LJ (giving the first judgment at the invitation of Clarke LJ).

[1] This is a claimant's appeal against the decision of Deputy Social Security Commissioner Hereward dated 26 May 2000. She dismissed the claimant's appeal from the decision of the Wigan Disability Appeal Tribunal made on 12 April 1999. Permission to appeal to this court was refused by Social Security Commissioner Rowland on 31 August 2000. On 4 December 2000 I adjourned the application for an oral hearing with both parties to attend, and the appeal to follow if permission was granted. Among my reasons for doing so was that the question arises as to whether an application such as this, from a second and highly expert judicial tier of appeal, should be regarded as akin to a second-tier appeal from the High Court or a county court and thus, although not technically within s 55(1) of the Access to Justice Act 1999, subject to a similar threshold test. We have today granted permission to appeal, in part to enable us to express a view on that question.

[2] The history of the case is this. The claimant, Ms Cooke, suffers from low back pain. She had a laminectomy twice in 1986. She also suffers from arthritis and fibromyalgia. She had a total right knee replacement in 1992 and she suffers from depression and a skin condition. She first claimed disability living allowance in February 1993. This was disallowed. On appeal, however, the higher rate mobility component was awarded until February 1995. This was later renewed until 9 February 1997. The highest rate care component was awarded on review until that same date. On 22 August 1996 she applied for the renewal of both awards. She filled in a claim pack and a report was later obtained from her general practitioner. No other assessment was made at that time. On 9 October 1996 both awards were extended for life with effect from 9 February 1997.

[3] However, she was visited by a visiting officer on 23 April 1998. The visiting officer filled in the questionnaire on her behalf. The officer found a discrepancy between what had previously been on record and what was observed during the visit. As a result the claimant was examined by Dr Spielmann. His report is dated 1 July 1998. This records her own account of her relevant symptoms, his own clinical findings and his opinion. His main conclusion was that 'the clinical findings do not support the extent of the disability claimed'. He did, however,

a state that there had been no change in the circumstances over the last 12 months, that is since 1 July 1997.

[4] Hence the Secretary of State made an application to an adjudication officer for a review or correction of the earlier decision. This application was based on a relevant change of circumstances within the meaning of s 30(2)(b) of the Social Security Administration Act 1992 because of 'a reduction in mobility and care
b needs as shown in recent medical evidence'. The adjudication officer's decision on 24 July 1998 was that there had been a relevant change of circumstances since the last decision. Her mobility and care needs had been reduced. Initially disability living allowance was withdrawn altogether as from 1 July 1998, but the claimant applied for a review within three months as provided for under s 30(1) of the 1992 Act and the adjudication officer decided that she was entitled to the
c care component at the lowest rate, but not to any mobility component.

[5] She appealed to the disability appeal tribunal. She produced evidence from her general practitioner and from her consultant rheumatologist, Dr Jones. The tribunal upheld the adjudication officer's decision. On the mobility component they found:

d
'There are conflicts in Ms Cooke's own evidence over the years. For example in a renewal claim submitted in August 1996 Ms Cooke stated that she gets severe discomfort as soon as she starts walking. In contrast in the disability living allowance questionnaire completed by her on 23 April 1998 she states that she cannot walk far, she is in pain all the time and could walk
e perhaps 50–60 yards in ten minutes before the onset of severe discomfort.'

They conclude:

'Because of the inconsistencies in the distances stated by Ms Cooke between 1996 and 1999 the tribunal is satisfied, on the balance of
f probabilities, that she can walk at least 50 yards before the onset of severe discomfort brought on by pain in her back and left knee. We reached this conclusion because it is based on the evidence of the examining medical practitioner [Dr Spielmann] and Dr Jones. Their findings in this respect are in the opinion of the tribunal entirely consistent. Furthermore, taking account of Dr Spielmann's findings, we consider, on the balance of probabilities,
g that at the date of the adjudication officer's review decision she should have been able to walk a further 50 yards before having to halt again because of the onset of severe discomfort.'

That being so they concluded that she did not then qualify for the higher rate of
h mobility component. They went on to consider whether she qualified for the lower rate and found that she did not.

[6] As far as the care component was concerned, they stated:

'We believe that Ms Cooke both in the questionnaire and in her evidence to the tribunal, was overstating her care needs. We do not doubt for one
j moment that she suffers pain because of her condition and noted that Dr Jones states that she is at the severe end of the pain spectrum. Nonetheless, taking account of Dr Spielmann's clinical findings, which the tribunal accept, we do not consider that her grip with either hand is as impaired as is suggested by Ms Cooke. Nor, for the same reason, do we consider that Ms Cooke is having the amount of difficulty getting up and

downstairs most of the time as she maintains and as is stated by Dr Jones in his letter.'

They earlier found that because of her physical disabilities as at 15 September 1998—

'Ms Cooke reasonably required assistance from another person in connection with her bodily functions of bathing (getting into and out of the bath—once per day) and washing parts of her body difficult to reach (once or twice a day). She also reasonably required assistance with dressing (one/two times a day because of problems with buttons).'

They did not, however, find that she needed assistance with her toilet needs:

'In the 1996 renewal claim pack Ms Cooke stated that she needed help getting to and using the toilet two or three times per night taking 10–15 minutes each time. On the basis of that statement she was found to have night care needs at the time of renewal of her care award of 1996. In contrast in the 1998 disability living allowance questionnaire Ms Cooke made no reference to needing assistance in using the toilet but stated that she needed assistance getting to the toilet on one or two occasions per night, taking about ten minutes each time. In view of this difference between the 1996 claimed night needs and the 1998 claimed night needs we prefer, on the balance of probabilities, to accept the findings of Dr Spielmann to the effect that Ms Cooke does not require assistance getting out of the bed by day or by night and getting to the toilet at night. In these circumstances and in the absence of any other stated night care needs we are satisfied that Ms Cooke does not require from another person prolonged or repeated attention in connection with her bodily functions at night.'

Therefore she did not qualify for the higher rate care component.

[7] Their conclusion was this:

'In our opinion there was sufficient evidence (including in particular the examining medical practitioner's report) before the adjudication officer on 24 July 1998 to suggest that there had been a relevant change of circumstances since the decision dated 9 October 1996. The relevant change of circumstances was that as at 24 July 1998 the evidence available to the adjudication officer suggested that Ms Cooke's mobility needs were not sufficient to justify an award of the higher rate mobility component and that her care needs were only sufficient to justify an award of the lowest rate care component from the same date.'

The deputy social security commissioner upheld the tribunal's decision. The relevant part, for this purpose, of her decision explained that the medical report provided 'evidence that the circumstances were not as they had previously been accepted to be'.

[8] The main argument on this appeal, both before the social security commissioner and here, is a simple one. It is not enough to show that the disability appeal tribunal would come to a different conclusion from the earlier adjudication officer. The adjudication officer only has jurisdiction to review a case after three months under s 30(2) of the 1992 Act in defined circumstances.

a   The only relevant ones that might have been employed in this case are those in paras (a) and (b) of that subsection:

> '(a) the adjudication officer is satisfied that the decision was given in ignorance of, or was based on a mistake as to, some material fact; or (b) there has been any relevant change of circumstances since the decision was given ...'

b

It is common ground between the parties in this case that it is well established in social security law that the threshold to establish the jurisdiction to review is low. However, it is also common ground that it is not enough to show, either a mistake within the meaning of para (a), or a change in circumstances within the meaning of para (b), that a later doctor forms a different opinion from the one

c   formed earlier. It still has to be shown either that there has been a change or that there has been a mistake.

[9] This was established in the decision of Lightman J in the case of *R v Social Security Comr, ex p Chamberlain* [2000] TLR 586, approving the approach of Social Security Commissioner Mesher in case no CIB 3899/97. The commissioner

d   refers to 'the well established principle that the existence of a medical opinion which differs from some previous opinion does not in itself constitute a relevant change of circumstances'. He goes on to state:

> 'Where the operative decision that a claimant is incapable of work was given following an actual all work test assessment, the mere existence of a

e   > subsequent report from an examining medical officer or of a subsequent unfavourable all work test assessment does not itself amount to a relevant change of circumstances or indicate that the operative decision was given under a mistake as to a material fact. That would be to confuse the outcome of a review with the establishment of grounds for carrying out a review.'

f   Mr Commissioner Mesher was there preferring the submissions on behalf of the claimant. He went on to say:

> 'I accept that as a matter of practice an appeal tribunal may start ... by asking whether it has been shown to its satisfaction that the all work test is not satisfied at the date of the adjudication officer's assessment. However,

g   > in considering whether that has been shown, the appeal tribunal must consider and give proper weight to the evidence on which the previous decision was based.'

He then goes on to give examples of differences that there might be and

h   concludes: 'Then the principle ... comes into play that the expression of a new medical opinion is not itself a relevant change of circumstances, but may be evidence of an actual change of circumstances or a mistake of fact.' That much is common ground.

[10] In *Ex p Chamberlain* there was nothing to suggest either a mistake or a change. There were simply two different assessments on the same set of facts.

j   In this case, however, there was evidence, from the discrepancies in the claimant's own statements and the later doctor's report, to suggest either a mistake or a change. The Secretary of State might have applied to the adjudication officer for a review on two alternative bases. He did not do so. As the deputy social security commissioner pointed out, it was charitable to the claimant to assume that there had been a change rather than a mistake because then no question of repayment or pursuing the issue of whether there had been a deliberate inaccuracy in 1996 arose. The tribunal therefore approached this as a change of circumstances case.

[11] Mr Thacker on behalf of the claimant criticises the tribunal for not following the two-stage process through properly. It did not first ask whether there were grounds for review and then ask whether the claimant was now entitled. It did not expressly compare the circumstances as they existed in 1996 with those as they existed in 1998. He points out that they did not disagree with Dr Spielmann's report that her condition had been unchanged since 1 July 1997, that is, a year before his examination. That, he points out, does not leave long for a change to have taken place since October 1996 when the adjudication officer made his earlier decision.

[12] However, it is clear from the extracts which I have quoted that the tribunal did compare what the claimant herself had said about her condition in 1996 with what they found the facts to be in 1998 on the basis of what she had said to the visiting officer and to Dr Spielmann and Dr Spielmann's own opinion. There were two crucial points. Firstly, on the mobility component the claimant must be virtually unable to walk. It is an accepted benchmark of that ability to be able to walk for 50 yards. In 1996 she had said that she experienced severe discomfort as soon as she started walking. In 1998 she had said that on good days she could walk to the end of the road. The tribunal found that she could walk for 50 yards and then a further 50 yards after a rest. Secondly, for the higher-rate care component the claimant must need prolonged or repeated attention at night. In 1996 she had said that she needed help getting to and using the lavatory. In 1998 she had given somewhat confusing answers to Dr Spielmann but the first had been: 'I can get to the toilet and can use it by myself.' The tribunal found that she did not need help day or night. The tribunal were not invited, and were not prepared uninvited, to hold that she had been mistaken or untruthful in what she had said in 1996. That being so, on the basis of those differences they were bound to conclude that there had been a change. That was a finding of fact which could not be challenged on appeal.

[13] There was also no error of law. This was different from the well-established principles endorsed in *Ex p Chamberlain*. As Social Security Commissioner Rowland said when refusing permission to appeal to this court:

> 'The deputy commissioner referred to a medical report which provides evidence that circumstances are not as they had previously been accepted to be which is not the same as a report which merely offered a different opinion on the basis of the circumstances.'

There was therefore in my view no error of law in this case. In my judgment, therefore, this appeal must fail.

[14] However, that leaves the question of the criterion for the grant of permission to appeal in such cases. Section 55(1) of the Access to Justice Act 1999 provides as follows:

> 'Where an appeal is made to a county court or the High Court in relation to any matter, and on hearing the appeal the court makes a decision in relation to that matter, no appeal may be made to the Court of Appeal from that decision unless the Court of Appeal considers that—(a) the appeal would raise an important point of principle or practice, or (b) there is some other compelling reason for the Court of Appeal to hear it.'

a That criterion is clearly intended to be a somewhat different test from the usual criterion for the grant of permission to appeal, which is whether the appeal would have a real prospect of success, or there is some other compelling reason for the Court of Appeal to entertain it. Now is not the time to debate the precise differences between those two tests. It is clear from the words of the section that it does not apply to the appeal in this case. But many of the reasons underlying

b that provision apply with equal force in these circumstances, and indeed some might think them stronger.

[15] Firstly, this is a highly specialised area of law which many lawyers—nindeed, I would suspect most lawyers—rarely encounter in practice. Secondly, there is an independent two-tier appellate structure. (Indeed, under the system

c as it was when this case was decided the adjudication officer himself had a degree of independence from the Secretary of State.) After the initial decision there is a fresh hearing before a specialist tribunal which is chaired by a lawyer and has an appropriate balance of experience and expertise amongst its members. After that there is an appeal on a point of law to a highly expert and specialised legally-qualified body, the social security commissioners. Thirdly, it is essential that that

d tribunal structure is sufficiently expert to be able to take an independent and robust view, particularly in cases where the government agency has gone wrong. It must be in a position to see through what the relevant sponsoring department is saying when it is arguing the case.

[16] It is also important that such appeal structures have a link to the ordinary

e court system, to maintain both their independence of government and the sponsoring department and their fidelity to the relevant general principles of law. But the ordinary courts should approach such cases with an appropriate degree of caution. It is quite probable that on a technical issue of understanding and applying the complex legislation the social security commissioner will have got it

f right. The commissioners will know how that particular issue fits into the broader picture of social security principles as a whole. They will be less likely to introduce distortion into those principles. They may be better placed, where it is appropriate, to apply those principles in a purposive construction of the legislation in question. They will also know the realities of tribunal life. All of this should be taken into account by an appellate court when considering

g whether an appeal will have a real prospect of success.

[17] In my view the Court of Appeal should take an appropriately modest view, especially when it has heard only one side of the argument, of how likely it is that the commissioner will have got it wrong. Obviously, however, that will differ according to the nature of the problem presented and the arguments in

h issue. In my view this case is a good example. The principle which was advanced on paper in support of the appeal is common ground between the parties. On examination of all the relevant material, which is now before us and was not before, it becomes plain that the tribunal and the commissioner did not err in law. One reason for that was the sensible and considerate approach of the Secretary of

j State and the adjudication officer in advancing the case for review. It would not be in the overall interests of this claimant or any other for this court to take a line which encouraged the Secretary of State to argue the alternative ground for review when there was no need to do so. Hence, I agree with Mr Forsdick for the Secretary of State that, although s 55 does not apply, a robust attitude to the prospect of success criterion ought to be adopted in these cases.

[18] The point is also relevant for other similar appeal structures, such as those
of the employment tribunals and Employment Appeal Tribunal, those of the
adjudicators and Immigration Appeal Tribunal, those of the leasehold valuation
tribunals and the Lands Tribunal. However, there are significant differences
between this system and those which may affect matters. Some of these are
private law tribunal systems, rather than government and citizen or applicant
systems, and there may be other considerations which we have not had the
opportunity of looking at in this case. I would therefore confine my views on this
last point to this particular tribunal structure, while expecting that similar
arguments may be appropriate if they arise elsewhere.

[19] For all those reasons I would dismiss the appeal.

BUTTERFIELD J.

[20] I agree.

CLARKE LJ.

[21] I also agree.

Appeal dismissed.

Gillian Crew   Barrister.

a
Newham London Borough Council v Skingle and another
[2002] EWHC 1013 (Ch)

b
CHANCERY DIVISION
JACOB J
14, 23 MAY 2002.

c
Pension – Pension scheme – Local government pensions – Non-contractual overtime – Regulations providing that 'non-contractual overtime' not constituting remuneration for purposes of calculating retirement pension – Meaning of 'non-contractual overtime' – Local Government Pension Scheme Regulations 1995, reg C2(2)(a).

d The respondent pensioner had been an employee of the appellant local authority. Like many other local government employees, the pensioner had worked overtime in addition to normal hours. His contract of employment had set out an agreed rate for overtime, but had not provided that either the authority or the pensioner could insist upon any overtime working. The pensioner's retirement pension was related to his 'remuneration' as defined in Pt C of the Local Government Pension Scheme Regulations 1995. Regulation C2(2)(a)[a] provided that 'remuneration', as defined in para (1), did not include payments for 'non-
e contractual overtime'. There was a similar exclusion, in para (2)(c), for any payment made to an employee in consideration of loss of holidays. On a complaint by the pensioner to the Pensions Ombudsman, the latter found that the pensioner had not been contractually bound to work overtime, but held that his overtime payments did not constitute payment for 'non-contractual
f overtime' within the meaning of para (2)(a) since the contract had provided for a rate of pay if overtime were worked. The Ombudsman therefore concluded that any overtime was contractual, that accordingly payments for such overtime fell within the general definition of 'remuneration' in para (1) and that they were therefore to be taken into account for the purposes of calculating the pensioner's retirement benefits. The local authority appealed to the High Court.
g

Held – On the true construction of reg C2(2)(a) of the 1995 regulations, 'non-contractual overtime' meant overtime not called for by the contract, i e voluntary overtime. The mere provision in the contract of a rate of pay if optional overtime were worked did not make the overtime contractual. The word
h 'overtime' indicated time spent working beyond the basic hours provided by the contract, but did not mean time spent working at some other employment— it was work on the job that was being referred to. If payment for all work on the job (normal hours plus all overtime, voluntary or not) counted as 'remuneration', the exclusion would be meaningless. Some payment for work
j done on the job was clearly to be excluded, and that could only be payment for work done on the job which was not required by the contract, namely voluntary overtime. That view was confirmed by the exclusion in para (2)(c). If an employee worked for part of his holiday entitlement and was paid, he was

---

a   Regulation C2, so far as material, is set out at [4], below

in effect doing much the same thing as overtime during a working week. It hardly
seemed rational that voluntary overtime should be included, but similar voluntary
work during holidays excluded. Accordingly, the Ombudsman had erred in his
construction of the regulations, and the appeal would be allowed (see [9], [10], [12],
[21], below).

Notes
For the local government pension scheme, see 29(1) *Halsbury's Laws* (4th edn
reissue) paras 362–363.

The Local Government Pension Scheme Regulations 1995 have been replaced by
the Local Government Pension Scheme Regulations 1997. For the 1997 regulations,
see 14 *Halsbury's Statutory Instruments* (2001 issue) 622.

Appeal
Newham London Borough Council (the borough) appealed from a determination
of the second respondent, the Pensions Ombudsman, on 30 January 2002 that
overtime payments made by the borough to the first respondent, Gary Skingle,
were to be taken into account in calculating his retirement benefits. The
Ombudsman took no part in the appeal. The facts are set out in the judgment.

Jacques Algazy (instructed by *Amanda Kelly*) for the borough.
Nicholas Randall (instructed by *Thompson Solicitors*) for Mr Skingle.

Cur adv vult

23 May 2002. The following judgment was delivered.

JACOB J.
[1] This is an appeal by the London Borough of Newham (the borough) from
a determination of the Pensions Ombudsman of 30 January 2002. He found in
favour of the pensioner, Mr Skingle, the first respondent. There were earlier
proceedings between the parties concerned with the issue with which I am
concerned, including an appeal to the Secretary of State for the Environment,
Transport and the Regions. In these, Mr Skingle was unsuccessful. He accordingly
took the matter to the Pensions Ombudsman, claiming maladministration
arising from an error of law. I am only indirectly concerned with those earlier
proceedings. Because a question of law arises, appeal lies to the court (s 151(4) of
the Pension Schemes Act 1993).

[2] The point at issue is short but important. It is important because it has
application to a wide range of local government employees and, possibly, also to
other public service employees.

[3] Mr Skingle is now retired. His pension depends upon his final earnings.
Like many other local government employees, he worked not only normal hours
but overtime. Does his final salary for the purposes of computing his pension
include his overtime earnings? If it does he will have a larger pension than if
his overtime earnings in his last year of work do not count. Many employees
work overtime. Hence the general importance.

The legislation to be construed

a

[4] The relevant regulations are the Local Government Pension Scheme Regulations 1995, SI 1995/1019. Although these have been replaced by the Local Government Pension Scheme Regulations 1997, SI 1997/1612, there is no relevant or material difference between the two sets of regulations. Mr Skingle's pension is related to his 'remuneration'. This is defined in Pt C of the regulations as follows:

b

> 'C2.—(1) Subject to paragraphs (2) and (3) and Schedule C5 (limitations on contributions and benefits), in these regulations 'remuneration', in relation to an employee, means the total of: (a) all the salary, wages, fees and other payments paid to him for his own use in respect of his employment, and (b) the money value of any benefits provided for him by reason of his employment, and any other payment or benefit specified in his contract of employment as a pensionable emolument.'

c

The regulations then go on to provide exceptions to this basic definition:

> '(2) "Remuneration" does not include—(a) payments for non-contractual overtime; (b) any travelling or subsistence allowance or any other allowance paid to an employee in respect of expenses incurred in relation to the employment; (c) any payment made to an employee in consideration of loss of holidays; (d) any payment accepted by an employee in lieu of notice to terminate his contract of employment; (e) any payment made to an employee as an inducement not to terminate his employment before the payment is made; (f) subject to paragraph 7 of Schedule C2, the money value to the employee of the provision of a motor vehicle or any payment accepted by him in lieu of such provision ...'

d

e

[5] This case is concerned with the meaning of exception (a)—what does 'non-contractual overtime' mean? Were Mr Skingle's overtime earnings 'payments for non-contractual overtime'?

f

[6] I proceed initially on the same premise as did the Ombudsman, namely that Mr Skingle's contract of employment provided for a basic salary for a basic working week (of 36 hours). The contract also set forth an agreed rate for overtime. But it did not provide that either the authority or Mr Skingle could insist upon any overtime working. There was no compulsory overtime.

g

[7] The Ombudsman put his conclusion this way:

> 'There was nothing to stop him [working] overtime (and being paid for it), but he was in no sense contractually bound to [do so] himself. My understanding that he was entitled to be paid for such overtime work is based on the reference to such payments being made not at his usual rate of pay but at the abated caretakers rate. That he was not bound to undertake such work himself does not mean that the remuneration he received was non-contractual. On the contrary it seems to me that there were specific contractual arrangements for such payments. I agree with Newham, however, that there was no obligation on Mr Skingle to undertake such work. It is not clear to me what payments for overtime working could fall within a definition of "non-contractual overtime" and I suspect there is a need to amend the regulations either to provide some definition of the term or to replace the wording with some other term. It may be possible to amend the regulations to accord with what Newham tells me is the accepted

h

j

practice in local government. For the moment, however, I need to interpret
the regulations as presently enacted and it is clear to me that the payments
made to Mr Skingle should not be regarded as being payment for non-
contractual overtime but should be regarded as part of remuneration within
the definition of reg C2(1) and thus to be taken into account for the purposes
of calculating his retirement benefits.'

[8] So the Ombudsman's reasoning ran: the contract provided for the rate of
pay if overtime was worked. Hence any overtime was contractual. It was not
outside the contract.

[9] The borough say that is wrong: 'non-contractual overtime' means overtime
not called for by the contract—non-compulsory, that is voluntary, overtime is
what is meant. The mere provision in the contract of employment for a rate of
pay if optional overtime is worked does not make the overtime 'contractual'.
Despite Mr Randall's attractively-presented argument, I have concluded that the
borough are right. Here are my reasons.

[10] Focus first on the word 'overtime'. This indicates time spent working
beyond the basic hours provided by the contract. But it does not mean time spent
working at some other employment—it is work on the job that is being referred to.
Now if payment for all work on the job (normal hours plus all overtime, voluntary
or not) counts as the 'remuneration', the exclusion is meaningless. That cannot
be right. Some payment for work on the job is clearly to be excluded—and that
can only be payment for work done on the job which is not required by the
contract—namely voluntary overtime.

[11] Mr Randall felt the force of this, as did the Ombudsman. The latter could
not find any meaning to 'non-contractual overtime' ('it is not clear to me what
payments for overtime could fall within [the definition]'). Mr Randall suggested
ex gratia payments for voluntary additional hours not recognised officially as
overtime. That is too loose a concept—an ex gratia payment is just a gift and
would not fall within the basic definition of remuneration at all. Remuneration
is 'payments ... in respect of employment'.

[12] I am confirmed in this view by a second order argument. This is based on
exclusion (c)—payment for loss of holidays. If an employee works for part of his
holiday entitlement and gets paid, he is in effect doing much the same thing as
overtime during a working week. It hardly seems rational that voluntary overtime
should be included, but similar voluntary work during holidays excluded.
Originally it was Mr Randall who prayed this provision in his aid. He said:
'look, payment for work done in lost holiday time is excluded specifically, the
same could have been done for voluntary overtime but it was not.' When the
provision was turned against him he suggested instead that it was aimed at
something altogether different—payments for lost holidays that were never
taken at all, as for instance may happen when an employee leaves without
having taken his full holiday entitlement. But the provision is not so limited—it
covers both payments in lieu of holidays and payments for working during
holidays.

[13] Mr Randall raised several other points which I should mention briefly.
He submitted that the provision, being an exception, should be construed
narrowly. Whilst this is a principle of interpretation of European legislation, I am
not aware that it is a principle for the construction of our domestic legislation.
Besides, even if one applies the principle one must give the exception some

a   sensible meaning. As I have said, none can be found if 'non-contractual overtime' covers both compulsory and voluntary overtime.

[14] Next he submitted that the alternative argument did violence to the actual language, that it amounted to substitution of the word 'compulsory' for the word 'contractual'. That at first appealed to me, but on reflection I think it appealed because of the way Mr Randall put it. If one reads 'contractual' as

b   'called for by the contract' there is no such violence.

[15] Mr Randall also submitted that the borough's construction made no sense in the real workplace. There, he said, many workers in practice do overtime and are happy to do so. It makes no difference whether they are required to do so or not. Many workers indeed do overtime not just for more money but

c   because they want to see their jobs done properly. From his evidence Mr Skingle, as a good public servant, fell in that class. Why in practice should one sort of overtime be included, but another not? The answer is that is what the exception does—it differentiates between contractual and non-contractual overtime.

[16] Finally I should mention arguments based on administrative convenience.

d   If one does the calculation simply on an employee's basic pay the sums are easy. But if one has to consider whether a particular piece of overtime was required by the contract there might be difficulties. It is easy to envisage a contract under which some overtime may be voluntary and some compulsory. In practice there could be difficulties in knowing which was which when one came to look at the actual position. Furthermore, if not all overtime was included, an unscrupulous

e   employer who could require an employee to do overtime under the contract, might deliberately refrain from doing so in an employee's last year so as reduce the pension. In the end I think the arguments cut both ways—they are equally valid whichever construction is adopted. I get no help from them.

[17] I conclude that the Ombudsman fell into error of law in construing the

f   regulations. That brings me to Mr Randall's alternative argument which he raises by way of a respondent's notice. He says that in any event Mr Skingle's overtime was worked pursuant to a contractual obligation, that it was 'contractual overtime'.

[18] Mr Skingle was employed as a site supervisor (in common parlance, caretaker) at a community school. The Pensions Ombudsman held that Mr Skingle's contract included terms contained in two documents headed 'Site Supervisor—

g   Purpose of Job' and 'Job Specification'. He made no such finding in relation to a third document headed 'Site Supervisors' Agreement'. It is not open to me on appeal to hold that this document in fact also formed part of the contract. Mr Randall did not actually contend otherwise though he took me to it.

[19] Neither of the two documents say Mr Skingle had to work overtime

h   when called upon by the employer. Nor did a third document, called the 'purple book', which also contained terms of his employment. The 'Site Supervisor— Purpose of Job' document says nothing about hours of work. The 'Job Specification' merely says (at para 8) that the employee is to 'manage and operate systems of staff cover for lettings and other out-of-hours usage of the premises'. It adds a

j   note: 'the duties of this post may involve working outside normal hours, including weekends and bank holidays, as necessary' but that does not necessarily mean extra hours rather than unusual hours. The 'purple book' again has nothing about overtime, merely saying that the employer should discourage working outside usual hours and that 'where such working arrangements are unavoidable, the officer shall be entitled to the appropriate allowances'.

[20] Mr Randall suggests that despite these contractual terms, the borough
could require Mr Skingle to work overtime, and if he refused that would be a
breach of his contract. In practice the position was that lettings out of hours had
to be manned and it was Mr Skingle's job to arrange cover. Often he could not
find anyone and did the job himself. But I can see no basis upon which he could
have been compelled to do that—even if no other employee could be found.

[21] Accordingly I think the Ombudsman was right in his construction of the
contract, though for the reasons I have given earlier on, the appeal is allowed.

Appeal allowed.

Neneh Munu   Barrister.

R (on the application of Mullen) v Secretary of State for the Home Department

[2002] EWHC 230 (Admin)

QUEEN'S BENCH DIVISION (DIVISIONAL COURT)

SIMON BROWN LJ AND SCOTT BAKER J

13, 21 FEBRUARY 2002

Compensation – Crime – Scheme – Statutory and ex gratia schemes compensating persons whose convictions had been quashed on appeal out of time or who had been wrongly convicted – Whether compensation under statutory scheme payable only to those ultimately proved innocent – Whether Secretary of State's determination incompatible with claimant's right to fair hearing – Whether Secretary of State entitled to depart from policy on ex gratia scheme – Criminal Justice Act 1988, s 133 – Human Rights Act 1998, Sch 1, Pt I, art 6.

In 1989 the British authorities procured the unlawful deportation from Zimbabwe of the claimant, the alleged quartermaster of an IRA unit in London. He was arrested on arrival in England, and in 1990 was sentenced to 30 years' imprisonment after being convicted of conspiracy to cause explosions likely to endanger life or cause serious injury to property. In 1998 he was given leave to appeal against his conviction out of time. The appeal proceeded on the basis that the claimant had been properly convicted if it had been fair to try him. It was allowed on the grounds that the conduct of the authorities had constituted an abuse of process which, if it had come to light at the time, would have justified the court staying the prosecution in the exercise of its discretion, and that in those circumstances the claimant's conviction was unsafe. Following his release, the claimant applied to the Secretary of State for compensation under s 133[a] of the Criminal Justice Act 1988, the provision that gave effect to the United Kingdom's treaty obligations under the International Covenant on Civil and Political Rights (the covenant). Section 133(1) required the Secretary of State to pay compensation to a person whose conviction had been quashed on an appeal out of time on the ground that a 'new or newly discovered fact' showed 'beyond reasonable doubt' that there had been a 'miscarriage of justice', while s 133(3) provided that the Secretary of State was to determine whether there was a right to such compensation. He concluded that the claimant had no such right, and also refused an alternative application for compensation under an ex gratia scheme. That scheme was based on a written statement by the Secretary of State in 1985 (the policy) which had indicated that he would be prepared to pay compensation to a person who had spent time in custody following a wrongful conviction or charge where, inter alia, that had resulted from serious default on the part of a member of a police force or some other public authority. Although the Secretary of State accepted that the claimant's case fell within the policy, he concluded that it would be an affront to justice to make a payment. The claimant applied for judicial review, contending (i) that the quashing of his conviction because of the newly discovered fact as to the unlawfulness of his deportation showed beyond reasonable doubt that there had been a 'miscarriage of justice' within the meaning of s 133(1); (ii)

---

a   Section 133, so far as material, is set out at [5], below

that s 133(3) was incompatible with the claimant's right to a fair hearing 'by an independent and impartial tribunal' under art 6[b] of the European Convention for the Protection of Human Rights and Fundamental Freedoms 1950 (as set out in Sch 1 to the Human Rights Act 1998); and (iii) that the Secretary of State had not been entitled to depart from the policy or, alternatively, that it had been irrational for him to do so in the circumstances of the case.

Held – (1) On the true construction of s 133 of the 1988 Act, a 'miscarriage of justice' meant the wrongful conviction of an innocent accused, and accordingly compensation went only to those ultimately proved innocent, not to all those whose convictions had been adjudged unsafe. Such a conclusion was consistent with the covenant which only obliged states to compensate those ultimately found to be innocent. Moreover, s 133(1) could readily be seen not to give a right to compensation to all appellants whose out of time appeals had ultimately succeeded on the basis of some 'new or newly discovered fact', but only to those who had been shown 'beyond reasonable doubt' to have suffered a miscarriage of justice. That could only refer to those proved innocent. In the instant case, it had been shown beyond reasonable doubt that there had been an abuse of process in bringing the claimant to trial, but that 'newly discovered fact' did not itself show beyond reasonable doubt that there had been a miscarriage of justice. The quashing of the claimant's conviction had been a vindication of the rule of law, not the righting of a mistaken verdict. Accordingly, the first ground of challenge failed (see [19], [25], [26], [39]–[41], below).

(2) Although the Secretary of State was not 'an independent and impartial tribunal' when determining, under s 133(3) of the 1988 Act, an application for compensation, his decision was subject to the court's supervisory jurisdiction, and that jurisdiction was sufficient in the instant case to comply with art 6(1) of the convention. The Secretary of State's decision had turned entirely upon his understanding of s 133. If he were wrong, his decision could be challenged and corrected by judicial review, and there was no question of the supervisory jurisdiction providing an insufficient power of review in such circumstances. It followed that the second ground of challenge also failed. As regards the third ground, it was impossible to suggest that the Secretary of State could never in any circumstances depart from his stated policy with regard to the payment of ex gratia compensation. Nor was the departure from the policy in the instant case irrational or unfair. The claimant was not to be treated as if he were entirely innocent. Accordingly, the Secretary of State had been entitled to refuse him an ex gratia payment, and the application would therefore be dismissed (see [28], [29], [32]–[34], [36], [37], [42], below).

Notes

For independent and impartial tribunal in the context of the right to a fair hearing, see 8(2) *Halsbury's Laws* (4th edn reissue) para 140, and for compensation for miscarriages of justice and ex gratia payments to persons wrongly charged or convicted, see 11(2) *Halsbury's Laws* (4th edn reissue) paras 1521, 1523.

For the Criminal Justice Act 1988, s 133, see 12 *Halsbury's Statutes* (4th edn) (1997 reissue) 1078.

For the Human Rights Act 1998, Sch 1, Pt I, art 6, see 7 *Halsbury's Statutes* (4th edn) (1999 reissue) 523.

---

b   Article 6, so far as material, is set out at [6], below

Cases referred to in judgments

Bennett v Horseferry Road Magistrates' Court [1993] 3 All ER 138, sub nom *R v Horseferry Road Magistrates' Court, ex p Bennett* [1994] 1 AC 42, [1993] 3 WLR 90, HL.

Bryan v UK (1995) 21 EHRR 342, [1995] ECHR 19178/91, ECt HR.

McCann v UK (1996) 21 EHRR 97, [1995] ECHR 18984/91, ECt HR.

R (on the application of Wilkinson) v Broadmoor Special Hospital Authority [2001] EWCA Civ 1545, [2002] 1 WLR 419.

R v Latif, R v Shahzad [1996] 1 All ER 353, [1996] 1 WLR 104, HL.

R v MacDonald, R v Atherley, R v Bristol [1998] Crim LR 808, CA.

R v Mullen [2000] QB 520, [1999] 3 WLR 777, CA.

R v North and East Devon Health Authority, ex p Coughlan (Secretary of State for Health intervening) [2000] 3 All ER 850, [2001] QB 213, [2000] 2 WLR 622, CA.

R v Secretary of State for the Home Dept, ex p Bateman (1995) 7 Admin LR 175, CA.

Application for judicial review

The claimant, Nicholas Mullen, applied for judicial review of the decision of the defendant, the Secretary of State for the Home Department, on 6 March 2000, confirmed on 15 March 2001, refusing him compensation under s 133 of the Criminal Justice Act 1988 or an ex gratia payment under the Secretary of State's policy, announced on 29 November 1985, on the making of such payments to persons wrongly charged or convicted. The facts are set out in the judgment of Simon Brown LJ.

Campaspe Lloyd-Jacob (instructed by *Christian Fisher*) for the claimant.

Philip Sales and *Hugo Keith* (instructed by the *Treasury Solicitor*) for the Secretary of State.

Cur adv vult

21 February 2002. The following judgments were delivered.

SIMON BROWN LJ.

Introduction

[1] On 8 June 1990 at the Central Criminal Court the claimant was convicted of conspiracy to cause explosions likely to endanger life or cause serious injury to property and was sentenced to 30 years' imprisonment. He was alleged to have acted as quartermaster for an active IRA unit in London. He had been arrested in Zimbabwe on 6 February 1989, immediately put on a plane to England and arrested on arrival at Gatwick the following day.

[2] Leave to appeal against conviction out of time was granted on 19 January 1998. On 4 February 1999, after the claimant had been in prison for ten years, the Court of Appeal allowed his appeal. His deportation from Zimbabwe to the United Kingdom, in which the British authorities had been involved, represented a 'blatant and extremely serious failure to adhere to the rule of law' and involved a clear abuse of process. The claimant's conviction was accordingly to be regarded as 'unsafe' notwithstanding that there was 'no challenge to the propriety of the outcome of the trial itself'. The Court of Appeal's judgment is reported: *R v Mullen* [2000] QB 520, [1999] 3 WLR 777.

[3] Following the claimant's release, his solicitors applied on his behalf for compensation pursuant to s 133 of the Criminal Justice Act 1988 or, failing that,

under the ex gratia scheme based on the Secretary of State's written statement of
29 November 1985. By letter dated 6 March 2000, finally confirmed on 15 March
2001, the Secretary of State refused to pay compensation on either basis.

[4] Before the court now is the claimant's challenge to both limbs of that
decision. In addition, he seeks a declaration that s 133 is incompatible with art 6
of the European Convention for the Protection of Human Rights and Fundamental
Freedoms 1950 (as set out in Sch 1 to the Human Rights Act 1998) (the European
Convention on Human Rights).

[5] Section 133 of the 1988 Act, so far as presently material, provides:

'(1) Subject to subsection (2) below, when a person has been convicted of
a criminal offence and when subsequently his conviction has been reversed
or he has been pardoned on the ground that a new or newly discovered
fact shows beyond reasonable doubt that there has been a miscarriage of
justice, the Secretary of State shall pay compensation for the miscarriage of justice
to the person who has suffered punishment as a result of such conviction
… unless the non-disclosure of the unknown fact was wholly or partly
attributable to the person convicted.
(2) No payment of compensation under this section shall be made unless
an application for such compensation has been made to the Secretary of
State.
(3) The question whether there is a right to compensation under this
section shall be determined by the Secretary of State.
(4) If the Secretary of State determines that there is a right to such
compensation, the amount of the compensation shall be assessed by an
assessor appointed by the Secretary of State.
[I need not read sub-s (4A), inserted by the Criminal Appeal Act 1995,
which specifies certain matters to which the assessor must have regard in
assessing compensation.]
(5) In this section "reversed" shall be construed as referring to a conviction
having been quashed—(a) on an appeal out of time …'

[6] Two issues arise out of these provisions: first, on the proper construction
and application of s 133(1) was the quashing of this claimant's conviction because
of the newly discovered fact as to the unlawfulness of his deportation to stand
trial a quashing 'on the ground that [this] fact show[ed] beyond reasonable doubt
that there has been a miscarriage of justice'? Secondly, is the requirement in
art 6(1) of the European Convention on Human Rights that 'in the determination
of his civil rights and obligations … everyone is entitled to a fair and public hearing
… by an independent and impartial tribunal established by law' breached by the
stipulation under s 133(3) that a claimant's right to compensation 'shall be
determined by the Secretary of State'?

[7] A third issue arises out of the claim for an ex gratia payment. The 1985
statement indicates two broad categories of case in which the Secretary of State
is prepared to pay ex gratia compensation to a person who has spent time in
custody 'following a wrongful conviction or charge'. These are first, where this
'has resulted from serious default on the part of a member of a police force or of
some other public authority'; secondly, where there are other exceptional
circumstances, in particular the emergence at trial or on appeal within time of
facts which 'completely exonerate the accused person'.

[8] The Secretary of State accepted that this claimant's case falls within the first
of those two categories but, having regard to its exceptional circumstances, in

a particular the fact that the claimant was 'properly convicted', he thought it right to depart from his usual policy and decided not to make an ex gratia payment. He concluded that to do so would be 'an affront to justice'. Was the Secretary of State entitled to depart from his policy in this way? That is the third issue which arises on this application.

[9] With that brief introduction let me turn now to the first and principal issue
b arising: do the circumstances of this case give rise to a statutory right to compensation under s 133 of the 1988 Act? I shall discuss this issue under the heading 'miscarriage of justice'.

Miscarriage of justice

[10] In considering the rival arguments under this head it is essential to bear in
c mind the precise basis upon which the claimant's appeal came to be allowed. As already indicated, this was not because the court had any doubts as to the correctness of the jury's verdict, but rather because it regarded the trial as one which ought not to have taken place at all. Let me quote the relevant passages from the judgment. First, as to the facts:

d 'In summary, therefore, the British authorities initiated and subsequently assisted in and procured the deportation of the defendant, by unlawful means, in circumstances in which there were specific extradition facilities between this country and Zimbabwe. In so acting they were not only encouraging unlawful conduct in Zimbabwe, but they were also acting in
e breach of public international law.' (See [2000] QB 520 at 535, [1999] 3 WLR 777 at 789.)

[11] Next, as to the propriety of the conviction:

'No challenge is sought to be made to the conduct of the trial itself and the appeal has proceeded on the basis that, if it was fair to try him, the defendant
f was properly convicted.' (See [2000] QB 520 at 524, [1999] 3 WLR 777 at 779.)

'... the defendant, as he now concedes, was properly convicted ...' (See [2000] QB 520 at 534, [1999] 3 WLR 777 at 788.)

Although the claimant has subsequently disputed making any concession to that
g effect, the plain fact is that no argument was ever advanced that he was not in fact guilty of the offence charged against him: '... there is no criticism of the trial judge or jury, and no challenge to the propriety of the outcome of the trial itself ...' (see [2000] QB 520 at 540, [1999] 3 WLR 777 at 794).

[12] As to abuse of process, the basis upon which the court allowed the appeal,
h the following passages in the judgment are important:

'This court recognises the immense degree of public revulsion which has, quite properly, attached to the activities of those who have assisted and furthered the violent operations of the I.R.A. and other terrorist organisations. In the discretionary exercise, great weight must therefore be attached to the
j nature of the offence involved in this case. Against that, however, the conduct of the security services and police in procuring the unlawful deportation of the defendant in the manner which has been described represents, in the view of this court, a blatant and extremely serious failure to adhere to the rule of law with regard to the production of a defendant for prosecution in the English courts. The need to discourage such conduct on the part of those who are responsible for criminal prosecutions is a matter of public policy to

which, as appears from [*Bennett v Horseferry Road Magistrates' Court* [1993] 2 All ER 138, sub nom *R v Horseferry Road Magistrates' Court, ex p Bennett* [1994] 1 AC 42 and *R v Latif, R v Shahzad* [1996] 1 All ER 353, [1996] 1 WLR 104], very considerable weight must be attached.' (See [2000] QB 520 at 535–536, [1999] 3 WLR 777 at 789.)

[13] The reference there to the 'discretionary exercise' was a reference back to *R v Latif, R v Shahzad* [1996] 1 All ER 353 at 361, [1996] 1 WLR 104 at 112–113 where Lord Steyn said:

'… it is for the judge in the exercise of his discretion to decide whether there has been an abuse of process, which amounts to an affront to the public conscience and requires the criminal proceedings to be stayed (see [*Bennett's* case]). *Bennett* was a case where a stay was appropriate because a defendant had been forcibly abducted and brought to this country to face trial in disregard of extradition laws. The speeches in *Bennett* conclusively establish that proceedings may be stayed in the exercise of the judge's discretion not only where a fair trial is impossible, but also where it would be contrary to the public interest in the integrity of the criminal justice system that a trial should take place … the judge must weigh in the balance the public interest in ensuring that those who are charged with grave crimes should be tried and the competing public interest in not conveying the impression that the court will adopt the approach that the end justifies any means.'

[14] I return now to the court's judgment in *R v Mullen*:

'… certainty of guilt cannot displace the essential feature of this kind of abuse of process, namely the degradation of the lawful administration of justice.' (See [2000] QB 520 at 534, [1999] 3 WLR 777 at 788.)

'… the discretion has to be exercised on the basis that, but for the unlawful manner of his deportation, he would not have been in this country to be prosecuted when he was, and there was a real prospect that he would never have been brought to this country at all … we have no doubt that the discretionary balance comes down decisively against the prosecution of this offence. This trial was preceded by an abuse of process which, had it come to light at the time, as it would have done had the prosecution made proper voluntary disclosure, would properly have justified the proceedings then being stayed. Inasmuch as that discretionary exercise now falls to be carried out by this court, we conclude that, by reason of this abuse of process, the prosecution and therefore the conviction of the defendant were unlawful.' (See [2000] QB 520 at 536, [1999] 3 WLR 777 at 790.)

[15] The important point of principle established in *R v Mullen* was, of course, that the meaning of 'unsafe' in s 2 of the Criminal Appeal Act 1968 (as amended by s 2 of the Criminal Appeal Act 1995) was broad enough to permit the quashing of a conviction on the sole ground that it followed upon an abuse of process prior to trial.

[16] Those being the circumstances in which the claimant's conviction came to be quashed, his case on the present application, skilfully and resolutely advanced by Miss Lloyd-Jacob, can now be summarised as follows: the claimant's conviction was no less a miscarriage of justice because it was consequent upon a trial which ought not to have taken place at all than had he been rightly tried but wrongly convicted. That this is so, indeed, Miss Lloyd-Jacob submits, is apparent

a from other passages in the court's judgment in *R v Mullen*. Before s 2 of the 1968 Act was amended, it included the proviso that an appeal might be dismissed if no miscarriage of justice had actually occurred. The court summarised ([2000] QB 520 at 533, [1999] 3 WLR 777 at 787) the views expressed by Sir John Smith QC in an article 'The Criminal Appeal Act 1995: (1) Appeals Against Conviction' [1995] Crim LR 920 to the effect that the 1995 Act had had no substantive effect

b and the ultimate question of whether there has been a miscarriage of justice is the same as whether the conviction is unsafe: 'The effect of the amendment is simply to concentrate the mind on the real issue in every appeal from the outset.'

[17] The court returned to the point and concluded:

c '... in our judgment, for a conviction to be safe, it must be lawful; and if it results from a trial which should never have taken place, it can hardly be regarded as safe. Indeed, the *Oxford English Dictionary* gives the legal meaning of "unsafe" as "likely to constitute a miscarriage of justice". Sir John Smith's article does not deal with "unsafe" in relation to abuse ... But, for the reasons which we have given, we agree with his 1995 conclusion that "unsafe" bears a broad meaning and one which is apt to embrace abuse of

d process of the *Bennett* or any other kind.' (See [2000] QB 520 at 540, [1999] 3 WLR 777 at 793–794.)

[18] Whilst, therefore, as the Secretary of State points out, the Court of Appeal in *R v Mullen* was not required directly to decide whether the claimant's conviction constituted a miscarriage of justice but rather, under the law as it now

e stands, whether it was 'unsafe', inferentially they appear to have concluded that it *was* a miscarriage. This being so, the argument runs, there can be no sound reason for ascribing a different meaning to the expression 'miscarriage of justice' where it appears in s 133(1) of the 1988 Act. Such a conclusion is suggested also by the decision of the Court of Appeal in *R v Secretary of State for the Home Dept,*

f *ex p Bateman* (1995) 7 Admin LR 175. Bateman had been convicted of various offences of conspiracy. On appeal out of time his conviction was quashed because certain statements had been wrongly admitted in evidence at trial. These were statements from important New Zealand witnesses whom he had wanted called and cross-examined. Although his claim for compensation under s 133 failed, it failed only because the wrongful admission of evidence was held not to be 'a new

g or newly discovered fact'. Bingham MR in the course of his judgment said (at 182):

'He is entitled to be treated, for all purposes, as if he had never been convicted. Nor do I wish to suggest that Mr Bateman is not the victim of what the man in the street would regard as a miscarriage of justice. He has

h been imprisoned for three-and-a-half years when he should not have been convicted or imprisoned at all ... The man in the street would regard that as a miscarriage of justice and so would I.'

[19] The Secretary of State's contrary argument is in two parts. First, it is submitted that s 133 was enacted to give effect to the United Kingdom's treaty

j obligations undertaken upon ratification of the International Covenant on Civil and Political Rights (New York, 16 December 1966; TS 6 (1977); Cmnd 6702) and accordingly the term 'miscarriage of justice' in s 133 bears the same meaning as in art 14(6) of that covenant rather than whatever meaning it may bear in our domestic legal system. Under the covenant states are only obliged to compensate those ultimately found to be innocent. Secondly, and consistently with that approach, s 133(1) can readily be seen not to give a right to compensation to all

appellants whose out of time appeals ultimately succeed on the basis of some
'new or newly discovered fact', but only to those who are shown 'beyond
reasonable doubt' to have suffered a miscarriage of justice. This, therefore, can
only refer to those proved innocent. Let me consider each limb of the argument
in turn.

[20] Article 14(6) of the covenant reads:

'When a person has by a final decision been convicted of a criminal offence
and when subsequently his conviction has been reversed or he has been
pardoned on the ground that a new or newly discovered fact shows
conclusively that there has been a miscarriage of justice, the person who has
suffered punishment as a result of such conviction shall be compensated
according to law, unless it is proved that the non-disclosure of the unknown
fact in time is wholly or partly attributable to him.'

[21] In giving effect to this obligation, Parliament omitted from s 133(1) the
phrase 'by a final decision', reflecting it instead in the definition of 'reversed' in
s 133(5) by referring there to 'an appeal out of time'; and substituted for the word
'conclusively' in art 14(6) the hallowed expression 'beyond reasonable doubt'.
The right to compensation thus arises only when each of four conditions is
satisfied: (i) the conviction is quashed on an appeal out of time (not, therefore, when
a timeous appeal succeeds, nor, of course, on an acquittal at trial); (ii) the appeal
succeeds on the ground of a new or newly discovered fact; (iii) the appellant was
in no way responsible for the previous non-disclosure of that fact; and (iv) that
fact shows beyond reasonable doubt that there has been a miscarriage of justice.

[22] Otherwise s 133 faithfully and accurately gives effect to the United
Kingdom's international law obligation under art 14(6) of the covenant. That
being so, submits Mr Sales, the court should have regard to art 3 of the Seventh
Protocol to the European Convention on Human Rights (which precisely reproduces
the language of art 14(6)) and, more particularly, to the explanatory report
relating to that protocol which, with regard to art 3, states at para 25: '... the
intention is that States would be obliged to compensate persons only in clear
cases of miscarriage of justice, in the sense that there would be acknowledgement
that the person concerned was clearly innocent.'

[23] True it is that the United Kingdom has never ratified that protocol.
Nevertheless, submits Mr Sales, the explanatory report is a legitimate aid to the
construction of an international obligation expressed in these terms. Article 31 of
the Vienna Convention on the Law of Treaties (Vienna, 23 May 1969; TS 58
(1980); Cmnd 7964) requires that a treaty be interpreted in accordance with the
ordinary meaning to be given to its terms in their context, that context being
recognised to include any travaux préparatoires. The explanatory report constitutes
such a document; a committee of experts were there proposing a text identical to
art 14(6) of the covenant by way of a protocol to the European Convention on
Human Rights and were providing an authoritative commentary upon its
application. The document is analogous to that of a Law Commission report
leading to domestic legislation.

[24] Turning to the second limb of the argument, the Secretary of State submits
that in any event this is the natural meaning of the expression 'miscarriage of
justice' used in this context. It simply makes no sense to talk in terms of an abuse
of process (consisting of the claimant's illegal deportation to stand trial) showing
beyond reasonable doubt that there has been a miscarriage of justice. As the
authorities (including *R v Mullen* itself) show, where, as here, there has been an

a abuse of process, there is a discretionary balance to be struck by the court as to whether the proceedings should be stayed (if the question arises at trial) or the conviction quashed (if the question arises on appeal) as 'an affront to the public conscience' (as Lord Steyn put it in *R v Latif*) or 'an affront to justice' (as Auld LJ put it in *R v MacDonald, R v Atherley, R v Bristol* [1998] Crim LR 808 also cited in *R v Mullen*). That balance is not struck 'beyond reasonable doubt': the use of that *b* expression of itself implies that the appellant must be shown to have been erroneously convicted rather than subject to an unlawful process.

[25] In my judgment the Secretary of State's argument is unanswerable. What was shown beyond reasonable doubt here was that there had been an abuse of process in bringing the claimant to trial. That was the 'newly discovered fact'. But that fact did not itself show beyond reasonable doubt that there had been a *c* miscarriage of justice. All that it showed was that the court needed to conduct a 'discretionary exercise' to decide in effect which of two important public interests should prevail: the public interest in trying, convicting and punishing the guilty or that in discouraging breaches of the rule of law and preserving the integrity of the criminal justice system. It preferred the latter. True, it had 'no doubt' that *d* the balance came down 'decisively' in the claimant's favour. But that was by no means to find that he was innocent, still less that he was plainly so. Rather it was a judgment that the lawful administration of justice would be affronted by his remaining convicted and imprisoned.

[26] In short, a miscarriage of justice in the context of s 133 means, in my judgment, the wrongful conviction of an innocent accused. Compensation goes *e* only to those ultimately proved innocent, not to all those whose convictions are adjudged unsafe. The quashing of the claimant's conviction in this case was a vindication of the rule of law, not the righting of a mistaken verdict. Although, as prosecuting counsel in *R v Mullen* submitted and the Court of Appeal held ([2000] QB 520 at 533, [1999] 3 WLR 777 at 787), the word unsafe 'can refer to a *f* miscarriage of justice in the round, including such abuse of process as would have prevented proceedings', that is not the sense in which the expression miscarriage of justice is used in s 133. The Court of Appeal in *R v Secretary of State for the Home Dept, ex p Bateman* (1995) 7 Admin LR 175 (of which I was a member) was simply not required to address the point now arising: both appeals there failed on other grounds. Bingham MR's dictum quoted in [18], above, cannot carry the day. This *g* principal ground of challenge must in my judgment fail.

[27] The second and third issues I can deal with altogether more briefly.

Article 6

[28] That the Secretary of State is not 'an independent and impartial tribunal' *h* when determining under s 133(3) an application for compensation made under s 133(2) is plain and indisputable. His decision is, however, as this and other cases show, subject to the court's supervisory jurisdiction. Is this jurisdiction sufficient to comply with art 6(1)of the European Convention on Human Rights? That question, the Strasbourg jurisprudence establishes, falls to be answered on the *j* facts of the particular case in which it arises—see, for example, the European Court of Human Rights' judgment in *Bryan v UK* (1995) 21 EHRR 342 at 360 (para 45). As the court there said, in assessing the sufficiency of the review, one must have regard amongst other things to 'the content of the dispute, including the desired and actual grounds of appeal'.

[29] The dispute in the present case is simply one of law: what is the true construction of s 133(1)? What in this context is the meaning of the expression

'miscarriage of justice'? All the relevant facts of the case were decided on the criminal appeal. In applying the statute the Secretary of State had no facts to find and no judgment to make. His decision turned entirely upon his understanding of the section, and as to this he was either right or wrong. If he was wrong, his decision could be challenged and corrected by judicial review. There can be no question of the supervisory jurisdiction providing an insufficient power of review in a case like the present.

[30] As Scott Baker J pointed out in argument, however, one can well envisage s 133 claims in which the Secretary of State may have to reach his own factual judgment—if, for example, the prosecution were to concede the appeal and the Court of Appeal itself, therefore, did not to need to adjudicate upon the circumstances of the case. Were the Secretary of State in those circumstances to refuse compensation and a challenge to ensue, the question raised today could theoretically arise again. To my mind, however, the problem realistically would not be one of the compatibility of s 133(3) with art 6 but rather as to the intensity of review appropriate on such a judicial review application. As the recent Court of Appeal decision in R (on the application of Wilkinson) v Broadmoor Special Hospital Authority [2001] EWCA Civ 1545, [2002] 1 WLR 419 amply demonstrates, the court on judicial review can and will if necessary assess any relevant facts for itself even to the extent of ordering the attendance of witnesses for cross-examination.

Ex gratia compensation

[31] Miss Lloyd-Jacob advances two submissions with regard to the Secretary of State's refusal to make an ex gratia payment despite his acknowledging that the case falls within one of the categories in which such payments are ordinarily made. Her first and wider submission is that where, as here, the Secretary of State has announced his policy and thus created a general expectation that he will follow it, it is necessarily unfair and impermissible for him to depart from it in any circumstances. Her second and narrower contention is that it was irrational of the Secretary of State to refuse payment here.

[32] The first argument is to my mind impossible. There are, of course, cases in which substantive legitimate expectations have been built up where nowadays public authorities will be required to honour their statements of policy or intention. All this is exhaustively and authoritatively discussed by the Court of Appeal in R v North and East Devon Health Authority, ex p Coughlan (Secretary of State for Health intervening) [2000] 3 All ER 850 at 868–880, [2001] QB 213 at 238–251 (paras 51–82 inclusive). As, however, is there made plain, the question for the court is ultimately one of reasonableness and fairness. Would a departure from policy represent an abuse of power? That is a question to be asked in the circumstances of the particular case. It cannot in my judgment be suggested that the Secretary of State can never in any circumstances depart from his stated policy with regard to the payment of ex gratia compensation. He should, of course, give the person concerned an opportunity to say why in his particular case the policy should be applied rather than disapplied. But no problem of that sort arises here. The opportunity was given and taken. The Secretary of State was simply not persuaded.

[33] What, then, of the claimant's narrower contention that it was irrational and unfair for the Secretary of State to depart from his stated policy in the particular circumstances of this case? Miss Lloyd-Jacob's argument in this regard centres upon the particular reason given by the Secretary of State for departing from his usual policy here, namely on the ground that it would be 'an affront to

a justice' to compensate the claimant financially for the abuse of process. This, she submits, is quite inconsistent with the Court of Appeal's judgment by which, it will be remembered, the claimant's conviction was itself quashed as 'an affront to justice'. Powerful though at first blush the argument appears, in my judgment it is not on analysis sustainable. True it is that, but for the abuse of process in which police officers and other representatives of public authority were involved,

b this claimant might never have stood trial. True, too, his time in custody was greatly extended by the Crown's failure to make proper disclosure of the documents which ultimately established that abuse of process. But it is surely one thing to hold that it is in those circumstances an affront to justice that the claimant should remain convicted and imprisoned; quite another to say that justice requires him also to be compensated for his years in custody.

c [34] For my part I see no inconsistency between the Court of Appeal's quashing of the claimant's conviction as an affront to justice and the Secretary of State's refusal to compensate him by reference to the same principle. What price should be paid to vindicate the rule of law and the integrity of the criminal justice system? The Court of Appeal thought that these interests required the

d claimant's appeal to be allowed: his conviction had been secured at too high a price. But by no means does it follow that the claimant should also be financially compensated for his loss of liberty.

[35] In this connection Mr Sales draws our attention to *McCann v UK* (1996) 21 EHRR 97, the 'death on the rock' case. The European Court of Human Rights, there, despite by a narrow majority finding art 2 of the European Convention on

e Human Rights to have been breached, nevertheless dismissed the applicants' claim for financial compensation. As stated at 178 (para 219): '… having regard to the fact that the three terrorist suspects who were killed had been intending to plant a bomb in Gibraltar, the Court does not consider it appropriate to make an award under this head.'

f [36] The wrongdoing in the present case, just as in *McCann v UK*, was not all on one side. The claimant is not entitled to be treated for all the world as if he was entirely innocent. In my judgment the Secretary of State was entitled to refuse him an ex gratia payment.

[37] I would dismiss this application.

g **SCOTT BAKER J.**

[38] Not everyone who is wrongly convicted is entitled to compensation; nor indeed, in the ordinary course of events, are those who are remanded in custody and subsequently acquitted. However, Parliament has provided in s 133 of the Criminal Justice Act 1988 the narrowly defined circumstances in which

h statutory compensation is to be paid. Additionally, the Secretary of State spelt out in 1985 two categories of case where the state would ordinarily pay ex gratia compensation.

[39] The first question for the Secretary of State, which was one of law, was whether the claimant qualified for compensation under the statute. It was and

j is a pure question of construction. In my judgment, for the reasons given by Simon Brown LJ, he reached the correct answer that the claimant did not qualify.

[40] This is not a conclusion that should occasion any surprise bearing in mind there has never been any challenge to the integrity of the claimant's trial as such. He was properly convicted on the evidence. The conviction was set aside because of the circumstances in which he was bought into the country to be tried.

[41] Like Simon Brown LJ I found the argument of Mr Sales as to the true meaning of 'miscarriage of justice' in s 133 compelling. There was no miscarriage of justice in the sense in which the expression is used in that section. Accordingly the claimant does not qualify for compensation under the statute.

[42] Whether or not the claimant was to be paid compensation under the ex gratia scheme was a matter for the Secretary of State's judgment. True, the claimant qualified under the first category but there is no rule of law that required him to authorise payment in this case.

Application dismissed. Permission to appeal refused.

Dilys Tausz   Barrister.

a # Fairchild v Glenhaven Funeral Services Ltd and others

Fox v Spousal (Midlands) Ltd

b ## Matthews v Associated Portland Cement Manufacturers (1978) Ltd and others

[2002] UKHL 22

c HOUSE OF LORDS

LORD BINGHAM OF CORNHILL, LORD NICHOLLS OF BIRKENHEAD, LORD HOFFMANN, LORD HUTTON AND LORD RODGER OF EARLSFERRY

22 APRIL, 7–9, 16 MAY, 20 JUNE 2002

d *Negligence – Causation – Breach of duty causing or materially contributing to damage – Causal connection between breach of duty and damage – Employee developing mesothelioma after being exposed to asbestos dust by successive employers in breach of duty – Employee unable to establish that either employer or both of them responsible for mesothelioma on 'but for' test of causation – Whether employee precluded from recovering*
e *damages for mesothelioma against any employer when employed by successive employers during period of exposure to asbestos.*

In three appeals to the House of Lords, claims were brought against employers by, or on behalf of the estates of, former employees. In each case, the employee
f had been employed at different times and for differing periods by more than one employer; both employers had been subject to a duty to take reasonable care or to take all practicable measures to prevent the employee from inhaling asbestos dust because of the known risk that such dust, if inhaled, might cause a mesothelioma; both employers had breached that duty in relation to the employee during the periods of his employment by each of them with the result
g that, during both periods, the employee had inhaled excessive quantities of asbestos dust; the employee had been found to be suffering from a mesothelioma; and any cause of the employee's mesothelioma other than the inhalation of asbestos dust at work could be effectively discounted. The question arose whether, in those circumstances, the employee was entitled to recover damages
h against either employer or both of them, even though, because of the current limits of scientific knowledge, he was unable to prove on the balance of probabilities that his mesothelioma was the result of inhaling asbestos dust during his employment by one or other or both of his employers. The Court of Appeal answered that question in the negative, holding, on the basis of the conventional 'but for' test of tortious liability, that the employee had failed to
j prove against either employer that his mesothelioma would not have occurred but for the breach of duty by that employer, and had similarly failed to prove against both of them that it would probably not have occurred but for the breach of duty by both of them together. The claims were therefore dismissed. On appeal, their Lordships were required to determine whether, in the special circumstances of such a case, a modified approach to proof of causation was required by principle, authority or policy.

Held – An employee was entitled to recover damages against both employers in the circumstances set out above. That conclusion was consistent with principle, and also with authority, properly understood. The overall object of the law of tort law was to define cases in which the law could justly hold one party liable to compensate another, and it would be contrary to principle to insist on the application of a rule that appeared to yield unfair results. Moreover, authority established that, in certain special circumstances, the court could depart from the usual 'but for' test of causal connection and treat a lesser degree of causal connection as sufficient, namely that the defendant's breach of duty had materially contributed to causing the claimant's disease by materially increasing the risk of the disease being contracted. In the circumstances of the instant cases, it would be just, and in accordance with common sense, to treat the conduct of both employers, in exposing the employee to a risk to which he should not have been exposed, as making a material contribution to the employee contracting a condition against which it was the duty of both employers to protect him. Any injustice that might be involved in imposing liability on a duty-breaking employer in such circumstances was heavily outweighed by the injustice of denying redress to the victim. Policy considerations therefore weighed in favour of allowing the employee to recover against both employers, and that conclusion followed even if one of them was not before the court. Although it had not been suggested that the employee's entitlement against either employer should be for any sum less than the full compensation to which he was entitled, either employer could seek contribution against the other or against any other employer liable in respect of the same damage in the ordinary way. Accordingly, the appeals would be allowed (see [9], [13], [21], [33]–[36], [40]–[44], [47], [63], [74], [108], [116], [119], [126], [143], [154], [155], [169], [171], below).

McGhee v National Coal Board [1972] 3 All ER 1008 explained and applied.

Dictum of Lord Bridge in *Wilsher v Essex Area Health Authority* [1986] 3 All ER 801 at 881–882 disapproved.

Notes

For causation, see 12(1) *Halsbury's Laws* (4th edn reissue) paras 854, 855.

Cases referred to in opinions

B v Bayer Nederland BV (9 October 1992, NJ 1994, 535), Hoge Raad.
Baker v Willoughby [1969] 3 All ER 1528, [1970] AC 467, [1970] 2 WLR 50, HL.
Baldwin (EM) & Son Pty Ltd v Plane (1999) Aust Torts Reports 81-499, NSW CA.
Bendix Mintex Pty Ltd v Barnes (1997) 42 NSWLR 307, NSW CA.
Benmax v Austin Motor Co Ltd [1955] 1 All ER 326, [1955] AC 370, [1955] 2 WLR 418, HL.
Birkholtz v RJ Gilbertson Pty Ltd (1985) 38 SASR 121, S Aust SC.
Blatch v Archer (1774) 1 Cowp 63, 98 ER 969.
Bonnington Castings Ltd v Wardlaw [1956] 1 All ER 615, [1956] AC 613, [1956] 2 WLR 707, HL; *affg* 1955 SC 320, Ct of Sess.
Caparo Industries plc v Dickman [1990] 1 All ER 568, [1990] 2 AC 605, [1990] 2 WLR 358, HL.
Caswell v Powell Duffryn Associated Collieries Ltd [1939] 3 All ER 722, [1940] AC 152, HL.
Chappel v Hart (1998) 195 CLR 232, Aust HC.
Cook v Lewis [1951] SCR 830, Can SC.
Craig v Glasgow Corp 1919 SC(HL) 1.
Donoghue (or M' Alister) v Stevenson [1932] AC 562, [1932] All ER Rep 1, HL.

a *Empress Car Co (Abertillery) Ltd v National Rivers Authority* [1998] 1 All ER 481,
   [1999] 2 AC 22, [1998] 2 WLR 350, HL.
   Fitzgerald v Lane [1987] 2 All ER 455, [1987] QB 781, [1987] 2 All ER 455, CA; *affd*
   [1988] 2 All ER 961, [1989] AC 328, [1988] 3 WLR 356, HL.
   Gardiner v Motherwell Machinery and Scrap Co Ltd [1961] 3 All ER 831, [1961] 1 WLR
   1424, HL; *affg* 1961 SC(HL) 1.

b *Haag v Marshall* (1989) 61 DLR (4th) 371, BC CA.
   Hadley v Baxendale (1854) 9 Exch 341, [1843–60] All ER Rep 461, 156 ER 145.
   Hotson v East Berkshire Area Health Authority [1987] 2 All ER 909, [1987] AC 750,
   [1987] 3 WLR 232, HL.
   Kay v Ayrshire and Arran Health Board [1987] 2 All ER 417, HL.

c *Kuwait Airways Corp v Iraqi Airways Co (No 3)* [2002] UKHL 19, [2002] 3 All ER 209,
   [2002] 2 WLR 1353.
   Litzinger v Kintzler (Cass civ 2e, 5 June 1957, D 1957 Jur 493), French Cour de
   Cassation.
   M'Kew v Holland & Hannen & Cubitts (Scotland) Ltd 1970 SC(HL) 20.
   March v E & M H Stramare Pty Ltd (1991) 171 CLR 506, Aust HC.

d *McGhee v National Coal Board* [1972] 3 All ER 1008, [1973] 1 WLR 1, HL; *rvsg* 1973
   SC(HL) 37.
   Naxakis v Western General Hospital (1999) 197 CLR 269, Aust HC.
   Nicholson v Atlas Steel Foundry & Engineering Co Ltd [1957] 1 All ER 776, [1957]
   1 WLR 613, HL.

e *Oliver v Miles* (1926) 50 ALR 357, Miss SC.
   Quinn v Cameron & Robertson Ltd [1957] 1 All ER 760, [1958] AC 9, [1957] 2 WLR
   692, HL.
   Rahman v Arearose Ltd [2001] QB 351, [2000] 3 WLR 1184, CA.
   Reeves v Metropolitan Police Comr [1999] 3 All ER 897, [2000] 1 AC 360, [1999] 3 WLR
   363, HL.

f *Rutherford v Owens-Illinois Inc* (1997) 67 Cal Rptr 2d 16, Cal SC.
   Senior v Ward (1859) 1 E & E 385, 120 ER 954.
   Sentilles v Inter-Caribbean Shipping Corp (1959) 361 US 107, US SC.
   Sindell v Abbott Laboratories (1980) 26 Cal 3d 588, Cal SC.
   Snell v Farrell (1990) 72 DLR (4th) 289, Can SC.

g *Summers v Tice* (1948) 199 P 2d 1, Cal SC.
   Vyner v Waldenberg Bros Ltd [1945] 2 All ER 547, [1946] KB 50, CA.
   Wakelin v London and South Western Rly Co (1886) 12 App Cas 41, HL.
   Wallaby Grip (BAE) Pty Ltd v Macleay Area Health Service (1998) 17 NSWCCR 355,
   NSW CA.

h *White v Chief Constable of the South Yorkshire Police* [1999] 1 All ER 1, [1999] 2 AC
   455, [1998] 3 WLR 1509, HL.
   Wilsher v Essex Area Health Authority [1988] 1 All ER 871, [1988] AC 1074, [1988]
   2 WLR 557, HL; *rvsg* [1986] 3 All ER 801, [1987] QB 730, [1986] 3 WLR 425, CA.

Appeals

j

Fairchild v Glenhaven Funeral Services Ltd and ors

The claimant, Judith Fairchild (suing as widow and administratrix of the estate of
Arthur Eric Fairchild, deceased), appealed with permission of the Appeal
Committee of the House of Lords given on 7 February 2002 from the decision the
Court of Appeal (Brooke, Latham and Kay LJJ) on 11 December 2001 ([2001]
EWCA Civ 1881, [2002] 1 WLR 1052) dismissing her appeal from the decision of

Curtis J on 1 February 2001 dismissing her action for damages against, inter alia,
the second defendant, Waddingtons plc. Permission to appeal was refused in ~a~
respect of the Court of Appeal's dismissal of Mrs Fairchild's appeal from the
dismissal of her action against the third defendant, Leeds City Council. Proceedings
against the first defendant, Glenhaven Funeral Services Ltd, had been
discontinued by a consent order on 19 July 2000. The Association of British
Insurers was given permission to intervene on the appeal solely for the purpose ~b~
of making submissions that the claim had already been settled. The facts are set
out in the opinion of Lord Bingham of Cornhill.

Fox v Spousal (Midlands) Ltd

The claimant, Doreen Fox (suing as widow and administratrix of the estate of
Thomas Fox, deceased), appealed with permission of the Appeal Committee of ~c~
the House of Lords given on 30 January 2002 from the decision of the Court of
Appeal (Brooke, Latham and Kay LJJ) on 11 December 2001 ([2001] EWCA Civ
1881, [2002] 1 WLR 1052) dismissing her appeal from the decision of Judge
Mackay sitting as a judge of the High Court in Liverpool on 27 March 2001
dismissing her claim for damages against the defendant, Spousal (Midlands) Ltd. ~d~
The Association of British Insurers was given permission to intervene on the
appeal solely for the purpose of making submissions that the claim had already
been settled. The facts are set out in the opinion of Lord Bingham of Cornhill.

Matthews v Associated Portland Cement Manufacturers (1978) Ltd and anor

The claimant, Edwin Matthews, appealed with permission of the Appeal ~e~
Committee of the House of Lords given on 30 January 2002 from the decision of
the Court of Appeal (Brooke, Latham and Kay LJJ) on 11 December 2001 ([2001]
EWCA Civ 1881, [2002] 1 WLR 1052) allowing an appeal by the defendants,
Associated Portland Cement Manufacturers (1978) Ltd and British Uralite plc,
from the decision of Mitting J in the High Court in Manchester on 11 July 2001 ~f~
giving judgment for Mr Matthews in the sum of £155,000 in his claim for damages
for personal injury against the defendants. The Association of British Insurers
was given permission to intervene on the appeal solely for the purpose of making
submissions that the claim had already been settled. The facts are set out in the
opinion of Lord Bingham of Cornhill.
~g~

Brian Langstaff QC and *Andrew Hogarth* (instructed by *OH Parsons & Partners*) for
    Mrs Fairchild.
Stephen Stewart QC and *Michael Rawlinson* (instructed by *Halliwell Landau,*
    Manchester) for Waddingtons.
Sir Sydney Kentridge QC, David Allan QC and *Matthew Phillips* (instructed by *John* ~h~
    Pickering & Partners, Manchester, with *Field Fisher Waterhouse* acting as their
    London agents) for Mrs Fox and Mr Matthews.
Nigel Wilkinson QC and *William Vandyck* (instructed by *Head of Legal Department,*
    AMP (UK) Services Ltd) for Spousal.
Stephen Stewart QC, Michael Rawlinson and *Sarah Spear* (instructed by *Berrymans*
    Lace Mawer) for the defendants in the Matthews appeal. ~j~
Lord Brennan QC (instructed by *Beachcroft Wansbroughs*) for the intervenor.

Their Lordships took time for consideration.

16 May 2002. Lord Bingham of Cornhill announced that the appeals would be
allowed for reasons to be given later.

a 20 June 2002. The following opinions were delivered.

LORD BINGHAM OF CORNHILL.

[1] My Lords, on 16 May 2002 it was announced that these three appeals would be allowed. I now give my reasons for reaching that decision.

[2] The essential question underlying the appeals may be accurately expressed

b in this way. If (1) C was employed at different times and for differing periods by both A and B, and (2) A and B were both subject to a duty to take reasonable care or to take all practicable measures to prevent C inhaling asbestos dust because of the known risk that asbestos dust (if inhaled) might cause a mesothelioma, and (3) both A and B were in breach of that duty in relation to C during the periods of C's employment by each of them with the result that during both periods C

c inhaled excessive quantities of asbestos dust, and (4) C is found to be suffering from a mesothelioma, and (5) any cause of C's mesothelioma other than the inhalation of asbestos dust at work can be effectively discounted, but (6) C cannot (because of the current limits of human science) prove, on the balance of probabilities, that his mesothelioma was the result of his inhaling asbestos dust

d during his employment by A or during his employment by B or during his employment by A and B taken together, is C entitled to recover damages against either A or B or against both A and B? To this question (not formulated in these terms) the Court of Appeal (Brooke, Latham and Kay LJJ), in a reserved judgment of the court ([2001] EWCA Civ 1881, [2002] 1 WLR 1052), gave a negative answer. It did so because, applying the conventional 'but for' test of tortious

e liability, it could not be held that C had proved against A that his mesothelioma would probably not have occurred but for the breach of duty by A, nor against B that his mesothelioma would probably not have occurred but for the breach of duty by B, nor against A and B that his mesothelioma would probably not have occurred but for the breach of duty by both A and B together. So C failed against

f both A and B. The crucial issue on appeal is whether, in the special circumstances of such a case, principle, authority or policy requires or justifies a modified approach to proof of causation.

[3] It is common ground that in each of the three cases under appeal conditions numbered (1) to (5) above effectively obtained. During his working life the late Mr Fairchild worked for an employer (whose successor was wrongly

g identified as the first-named defendant) who carried out sub-contract work for the Leeds City Council in the early 1960s and may have built packing cases for the transportation of industrial ovens lined with asbestos. He also worked for a builder, in whose employment he cut asbestos sheeting both to repair various roofs and while renovating a factory for Waddingtons plc. In the course of his

h work Mr Fairchild inhaled substantial quantities of asbestos dust containing asbestos fibre which caused him to suffer a mesothelioma of the pleura, from which he died on 18 September 1996 at the age of 60. Waddingtons plc accepted at trial that it had exposed Mr Fairchild to the inhalation of asbestos fibres by a breach of the duty owed to him under s 63 of the Factories Act 1961.

j (Waddingtons plc was not an employer, but nothing turns on this distinction with the other cases.) It thereby admitted that he had been exposed to a substantial quantity of dust or had been exposed to dust to such an extent as was likely to be injurious to him. After the death of Mr Fairchild his widow brought this action, originally against three defendants (not including the builder). She discontinued proceedings against the first-named defendant, and on 1 February 2001 Curtis J dismissed her claim against Waddingtons plc and the Leeds City Council. The Court of Appeal dismissed her appeal against that decision in the

judgment already referred to, finding it unnecessary (because of its decision on
causation) to reach a final decision on all aspects of her common law claim against
the Leeds City Council. She challenges that causation decision on appeal to the
House.

[4] The late Mr Fox was employed as a lagger by Spousal (Midlands) Ltd (then
known by a different name) for one-and-a-half to two years between about 1953
and 1955. In the course of this employment he worked at various different
premises. Typical lagging work involved the removal of old lagging, the mixing
of lagging paste, the cutting of lagging sections and the sweeping up of dust and
debris. Asbestos materials were used on a daily basis. The activities of laggers
generated high levels of dust containing asbestos. In these circumstances Mr Fox
was exposed to large amounts of asbestos dust, often for many hours each day.
He was described by a witness as being covered in dust from head to foot. No
measures were taken to protect him from such exposure. From 1955–1989 he
worked as a docker/holdsman in the Liverpool Docks. Until the late 1960s or
early 1970s asbestos fibre was imported into Liverpool Docks in sacks. Mr Fox
told his wife that he was regularly involved in moving asbestos cargo and that
asbestos was regularly released into his breathing area. The work of handling
asbestos cargoes would have exposed Mr Fox to substantial amounts of dust and
it is unlikely that any measures would have been taken to protect him from such
exposure. But there is no evidence of when and for how long and how frequently
Mr Fox handled cargoes containing asbestos, nor of what cargoes he handled, nor
of the identity of his employers when he was engaged in handling asbestos.
Spousal do not dispute that they were in breach of duty in exposing Mr Fox to
substantial amounts of asbestos dust in the course of his employment by them.
In 1995 he developed symptoms of mesothelioma and he died on 24 April 1996 at
the age of 63. It is accepted that his condition was caused by exposure to asbestos
dust. After his death his widow brought these proceedings against Spousal. Her
claim was dismissed by Judge Mackay, sitting as a judge of the Queen's Bench
Division in Liverpool on 27 March 2001. Her appeal against that decision was
dismissed by the Court of Appeal in the judgment already referred to. She
challenges that decision on appeal to the House.

[5] Mr Matthews was employed by Associated Portland Cement
Manufacturers (1978) Ltd from 1973–1981 at their factory in Strood, Kent. He
was exposed to asbestos during the last four years of this employment when
working as a boilerman. Each day he spent some time (up to about an hour) in
the boilerhouse where the boiler and ancillary pipework were lagged with
asbestos material. On a number of occasions (adding up to about two days in all)
he was in close proximity to men removing lagging from pipes, and such work
created large amounts of asbestos dust. On a daily basis he was exposed to dust
and debris from the lagging. He walked across pipework disturbing the lagging.
He regularly swept the floor in the boilerhouse, stirring up asbestos dust and
debris. No effective measures were taken to protect him from exposure to
asbestos dust. For five to six weeks in January and February 1973 Mr Matthews
was employed by British Uralite plc at their factory in Higham, Kent, where the
company manufactured pipes from asbestos material, and Mr Matthews worked
on this process. Large amounts of dust containing asbestos fibres were created
by the manufacturing process and such dust permeated the atmosphere of the
factory. During each working day Mr Matthews had prolonged and substantial
exposure to asbestos dust. No measures were taken to protect him against such
exposure. Between 1965 and 1967 Mr Matthews was employed by Maidstone
Sack and Metal and was again exposed to significant quantities of asbestos dust.

For 12 months of this period he operated a scrap metal press and some of the items fed into the press had asbestos linings. For about two weeks he worked in a boilerhouse in Chatham Dockyard dismantling a boiler and pipework, during which time he spent a day removing asbestos lagging from the boiler and pipes, which was dusty work. Maidstone Sack and Metal can no longer be sued. Mr Matthews consulted his doctor complaining of chest pain in March 1999. In February 2000 a diagnosis of mesothelioma was made. His condition has continued to deteriorate, and his life expectancy is now measured in months. Associated Portland Cement and British Uralite admit that Mr Matthews' mesothelioma was caused by exposure to asbestos dust, and that each of them exposed Mr Matthews to asbestos dust in breach of duty. Mr Matthews issued proceedings against both these companies in April 2001. On 11 July 2001 Mitting J gave judgment in his favour against both defendants and awarded damages. The defendants appealed against that decision, and the Court of Appeal allowed their appeal and set aside the award in Mr Matthews' favour. He has appealed against that decision. It should be recorded that, before the hearing of his appeal in the House, the defendants agreed to pay Mr Matthews the sum awarded by the judge with interest and costs, without prejudice to the issues in the appeal.

[6] It has been recognised for very many years, at any rate since the 'Report on Effects of Asbestos Dust on the Lungs and Dust Suppression in the Asbestos Industry' by Merewether and Price in 1930 and the making of the Asbestos Industry Regulations 1931, SR & O 1931/1140, that it is injurious to inhale significant quantities of asbestos dust. At first, attention was focused on the risk of contracting asbestosis and other pulmonary diseases. It is a characteristic of asbestosis that the disease, once initiated, will be influenced by the total amount of dust thereafter inhaled. Thus in the case of asbestosis the following situation may arise. C may contract asbestosis as a result of exposure to asbestos dust while employed by A, but without such exposure involving any breach of duty by A. C may then work for B, and again inhale quantities of asbestos dust which will have the effect of aggravating his asbestosis. If this later exposure does involve a breach of duty by B, C will have no claim against A but will have a claim against B. B will not escape liability by contending that his breach of duty is not shown to have had any causative effect.

[7] From about the 1960s, it became widely known that exposure to asbestos dust and fibres could give rise not only to asbestosis and other pulmonary diseases, but also to the risk of developing a mesothelioma. This is a malignant tumour, usually of the pleura, sometimes of the peritoneum. In the absence of occupational exposure to asbestos dust it is a very rare tumour indeed, afflicting no more than about one person in a million per year. But the incidence of the tumour among those occupationally exposed to asbestos dust is about 1,000 times greater than in the general population, and there are some 1,500 cases reported annually. It is a condition which may be latent for many years, usually for 30–40 years or more; development of the condition may take as short a period as ten years, but it is thought that that is the period which elapses between the mutation of the first cell and the manifestation of symptoms of the condition. It is invariably fatal, and death usually occurs within one to two years of the condition being diagnosed. The mechanism by which a normal mesothelial cell is transformed into a mesothelioma cell is not known. It is believed by the best medical opinion to involve a multi-stage process, in which six or seven genetic changes occur in a normal cell to render it malignant. Asbestos acts in at least one of those stages and may (but this is uncertain) act in more than one. It is not known what level of exposure to asbestos dust and fibre can be tolerated without

significant risk of developing a mesothelioma, but it is known that those living in
urban environments (although without occupational exposure) inhale large
numbers of asbestos fibres without developing a mesothelioma. It is accepted
that the risk of developing a mesothelioma increases in proportion to the quantity
of asbestos dust and fibres inhaled: the greater the quantity of dust and fibre
inhaled, the greater the risk. But the condition may be caused by a single fibre,
or a few fibres, or many fibres: medical opinion holds none of these possibilities
to be more probable than any other, and the condition once caused is not
aggravated by further exposure. So if C is employed successively by A and B and
is exposed to asbestos dust and fibres during each employment and develops a
mesothelioma, the very strong probability is that this will have been caused by
inhalation of asbestos dust containing fibres. But C could have inhaled a single
fibre giving rise to his condition during employment by A, in which case his
exposure by B will have had no effect on his condition; or he could have inhaled
a single fibre giving rise to his condition during his employment by B, in which
case his exposure by A will have had no effect on his condition; or he could have
inhaled fibres during his employment by A and B which together gave rise to his
condition; but medical science cannot support the suggestion that any of these
possibilities is to be regarded as more probable than any other. There is no way
of identifying, even on a balance of probabilities, the source of the fibre or fibres
which initiated the genetic process which culminated in the malignant tumour.
It is on this rock of uncertainty, reflecting the point to which medical science has
so far advanced, that the three claims were rejected by the Court of Appeal and
by two of the three trial judges.

Principle

[8] In a personal injury action based on negligence or breach of statutory duty
the claimant seeks to establish a breach by the defendant of a duty owed to the
claimant, which has caused him damage. For the purposes of analysis, and for the
purpose of pleading, proving and resolving the claim, lawyers find it convenient
to break the claim into its constituent elements: the duty, the breach, the damage
and the causal connection between the breach and the damage. In the generality
of personal injury actions, it is of course true that the claimant is required to
discharge the burden of showing that the breach of which he complains caused
the damage for which he claims and to do so by showing that but for the breach
he would not have suffered the damage.

[9] The issue in these appeals does not concern the general validity and
applicability of that requirement, which is not in question, but is whether in
special circumstances such as those in these cases there should be any variation
or relaxation of it. The overall object of tort law is to define cases in which the
law may justly hold one party liable to compensate another. Are these such
cases? A and B owed C a duty to protect C against a risk of a particular and very
serious kind. They failed to perform that duty. As a result the risk eventuated
and C suffered the very harm against which it was the duty of A and B to protect
him. Had there been only one tortfeasor, C would have been entitled to recover,
but because the duty owed to him was broken by two tortfeasors and not only
one, he is held to be entitled to recover against neither, because of his inability to
prove what is scientifically unprovable. If the mechanical application of generally
accepted rules leads to such a result, there must be room to question the
appropriateness of such an approach in such a case.

[10] In *March v E & M H Stramare Pty Ltd* (1991) 171 CLR 506 at 508, Mason CJ,
sitting in the High Court of Australia, did not 'accept that the "but for" (causa sine

a   qua non) test ever was or now should become the exclusive test of causation in
negligence cases' and (at 516) he added:

> 'The "but for" test gives rise to a well-known difficulty in cases where there
> are two or more acts or events which would each be sufficient to bring about
> the plaintiff's injury. The application of the test "gives the result, contrary to
> common sense, that neither is a cause": *Winfield and Jolowicz on Tort*, 13th ed
b   (1989), p. 134. In truth, the application of the test proves to be either
> inadequate or troublesome in various situations in which there are multiple
> acts or events leading to the plaintiff's injury: see, e.g., *Chapman v. Hearse,
> Baker v Willoughby* ([1969] 3 All ER 1528, [1970] AC 467); *McGhee v. National
> Coal Board* ([1972] 3 All ER 1008, [1973] 1 WLR 1); *M'Kew* (see *M'Kew v
c   Holland & Hannen & Cubitts (Scotland) Ltd* 1970 SC(HL) 20) (to which I shall
> shortly refer in some detail). The cases demonstrate the lesson of
> experience, namely, that the test, applied as an exclusive criterion of
> causation, yields unacceptable results and that the results which it yields
> must be tempered by the making of value judgments and the infusion of
> policy considerations.'
d

[11] In *Snell v Farrell* (1990) 72 DLR (4th) 289 at 294, Sopinka J, delivering the
judgment of the Supreme Court of Canada, said:

> 'The traditional approach to causation has come under attack in a number
> of cases in which there is concern that due to the complexities of proof, the
e   probable victim of tortious conduct will be deprived of relief. This concern
> is strongest in circumstances in which, on the basis of some percentage of
> statistical probability, the plaintiff is the likely victim of the combined
> tortious conduct of a number of defendants, but cannot prove causation
> against a specific defendant or defendants on the basis of particularized
> evidence in accordance with traditional principles. The challenge to the
f   traditional approach has manifested itself in cases dealing with non-traumatic
> injuries such as man-made diseases resulting from the widespread diffusion
> of chemical products, including product liability cases in which a product
> which can cause injury is widely manufactured and marketed by a large
> number of corporations.'

g   McLachlin J, extra-judicially ('Negligence Law—Proving the Connection', in Mullany
and Linden *Torts Tomorrow, A Tribute to John Fleming* LBC Information Services
1998, p 16), has voiced a similar concern:

> 'Tort law is about compensating those who are wrongfully injured. But
h   even more fundamentally, it is about recognising and righting wrongful
> conduct by one person or a group of persons that harms others. If tort law
> becomes incapable of recognising important wrongs, and hence incapable of
> righting them, victims will be left with a sense of grievance and the public
> will be left with a feeling that justice is not what it should be. Some perceive
> that this may be occurring due to our rules of causation. In recent years, a
j   conflation of factors have caused lawyers, scholars and courts to question
> anew whether the way tort law has traditionally defined the necessary
> relationship between tortious acts and injuries is the right way to define it, or
> at least the *only* way. This questioning has happened in the United States and
> in England and has surfaced in Australia. And it is happening in Canada.
> Why is this happening? Why are courts now asking questions that for
> decades, indeed centuries, did not pose themselves, or if they did, were of no

great urgency? I would suggest that it is because too often the traditional "but-for", all-or-nothing, test denies recovery where our instinctive sense of justice—of what is the right result for the situation—tells us the victim should obtain some compensation.'

[12] My noble and learned friend Lord Hoffmann has, on more than one occasion, discouraged a mechanical approach to the issue of causation. In *Empress Car Co (Abertillery) Ltd v National Rivers Authority* [1998] 1 All ER 481 at 487, [1999] 2 AC 22 at 29, he said:

'The first point to emphasise is that commonsense answers to questions of causation will differ according to the purpose for which the question is asked. Questions of causation often arise for the purpose of attributing responsibility to someone, for example, so as to blame him for something which has happened or to make him guilty of an offence or liable in damages. In such cases, the answer will depend upon the rule by which responsibility is being attributed.'

More recently, in *Kuwait Airways Corp v Iraqi Airways Co (No 3)* [2002] UKHL 19 at [128], [2002] 3 All ER 209 at [128], he said:

'There is therefore no uniform causal requirement for liability in tort. Instead, there are varying causal requirements, depending upon the basis and purpose of liability. One cannot separate questions of liability from questions of causation. They are inextricably connected. One is never simply liable; one is always liable *for* something and the rules which determine what one is liable for are as much part of the substantive law as the rules which determine which acts give rise to liability.'

Laws LJ was reflecting this approach when he said in *Rahman v Arearose Ltd* [2001] QB 351 at 367–368, [2000] 3 WLR 1184 at 1199–1200:

'So in all these cases the real question is, what is the damage for which the defendant under consideration should be held *responsible*. The nature of his duty (here, the common law duty of care) is relevant; causation, certainly, will be relevant—but it will fall to be viewed, and in truth can only be understood, in light of the answer to the question: from what kind of harm was it the defendant's duty to guard the claimant ... Novus actus interveniens, the eggshell skull, and (in the case of multiple torts) the concept of concurrent tortfeasors are all no more and no less than tools or mechanisms which the law has developed to articulate in practice the extent of any liable defendant's responsibility for the loss and damage which the claimant has suffered.'

[13] I do not therefore consider that the House is acting contrary to principle in reviewing the applicability of the conventional test of causation to cases such as the present. Indeed, it would seem to me contrary to principle to insist on application of a rule which appeared, if it did, to yield unfair results. And I think it salutary to bear in mind Lord Mansfield's aphorism in *Blatch v Archer* (1774) 1 Cowp 63 at 65, 98 ER 969 at 970 quoted with approval by the Supreme Court of Canada in *Snell v Farrell*:

'It is certainly a maxim that all evidence is to be weighed according to the proof which it was in the power of one side to have produced, and in the power of the other to have contradicted.'

Authority

a

[14] In *Bonnington Castings Ltd v Wardlaw* [1956] 1 All ER 615, [1956] AC 613, the pursuer contracted pneumoconiosis as a result of inhaling silica dust. The dust came from two sources, a pneumatic hammer and swing grinders, both in the dressing shop where he worked. The dust emanating from the pneumatic hammer involved no breach of duty by the employer, but that from the swing

b grinders did. In a claim against his employer he succeeded before the Lord Ordinary, Lord Wheatley, and by a majority in the First Division of the Court of Session, the Lord President (Lord Clyde) dissenting. The issue on appeal was whether the employer's admitted breach of duty in relation to the swing grinders had caused the pursuer's disease. In his leading opinion, Lord Reid ([1956] 1 All ER 615 at 618, [1956] AC 613 at 620) made plain that 'the employee must, in all

c cases, prove his case by the ordinary standard of proof in civil actions; he must make it appear at least that, on a balance of probabilities, the breach of duty caused, or materially contributed to, his injury'. He pointed out ([1956] 1 All ER 615 at 618, [1956] AC 613 at 621) that pneumoconiosis is caused by a gradual accumulation in the lungs of minute particles of silica inhaled over a period of

d years, and he regarded the real question as 'whether the dust from the swing grinders materially contributed to the disease' ([1956] 1 All ER 615 at 618, [1956] AC 613 at 621). He considered that any contribution which was not de minimis must be material. The evidence showed that even if more dust came from the pneumatic hammer than from the swing grinders, there was enough dust from the grinders to make a substantial contribution towards the pursuer's disease

e ([1956] 1 All ER 615 at 619, [1956] AC 613 at 622). The pursuer was accordingly entitled to succeed. With these conclusions, Viscount Simonds, Lord Tucker, Lord Keith of Avonholm and Lord Somervell of Harrow agreed, Lord Keith ([1956] 1 All ER 615 at 622, [1956] AC 613 at 626) laying stress on the nature of pneumoconiosis as a disease of gradual incidence and on the cumulative effect of

f inhalation of dust from the grinders over a period, which might be small in proportion but substantial in total quantity. The case differs from the present in two obvious respects. First, the pursuer had only one relevant employer, who was not legally liable for producing some of the dust which the pursuer inhaled but was potentially liable for the balance. Secondly, pneumoconiosis is, like asbestosis, a condition which is aggravated by the inhalation of increased

g quantities of dust so that, even if the 'innocent' dust had been the first and major cause of the condition, the 'guilty' dust, if in significant quantities, could properly be said to have made it worse.

[15] *Nicholson v Atlas Steel Foundry and Engineering Co Ltd* [1957] 1 All ER 776, [1957] 1 WLR 613 was factually a variant of *Wardlaw*'s case. The claim was made

h by the widow and children of Mr Nicholson, who had worked in the dressing shop of the defenders' steel foundry, had inhaled dust containing minute siliceous particles while doing so, had contracted pneumoconiosis and had died. The complaints made in the action related not to the creation of dust in the dressing shop but to the defenders' failure to provide adequate ventilation to extract the dust. It was common ground that the deceased must inevitably have inhaled a

j quantity, even a large quantity, of noxious particles about which he could have no cause of complaint, and the only question was whether, in addition to those particles, he was, owing to the fault of the defenders in failing to provide adequate ventilation, bound to have inhaled a number of other particles which made a material contribution to his illness ([1957] 1 All ER 776 at 777–778, [1957] 1 WLR 613 at 616). The Lord Ordinary found for the family, but his decision was reversed by the First Division. In the House the argument centred on the

statutory duty to provide proper ventilation imposed by s 4(1) of the Factories
Act 1937, and Viscount Simonds said:

'... if the statute prescribes a proper system of ventilation by the circulation
of fresh air so as to render harmless so far as practicable all fumes, dust and
other impurities that may be injurious to health generated in the course of
work carried on in the factory, and if it is proved that there is no system, or
only an inadequate system, of ventilation, it requires little further to establish
a causal link between that default and the illness due to noxious dust of a
person employed in the shop. Something is required as was held in
Wardlaw's case. I was a party to that decision and would not in any way
resile from it. But it must not be pressed too far. In the present case there
was, in my opinion, ample evidence to support the appellants' case.' (See
[1957] 1 All ER 776 at 779, [1957] 1 WLR 613 at 618.)

Since the family could not complain of the production of dust, and the deceased
had been forced to inhale some noxious particles without having any legal
complaint, it was doubly incumbent on the employer to safeguard him against
any additional risk ([1957] 1 All ER 776 at 778, [1957] 1 WLR 613 at 616). Viscount
Simonds' conclusion was clearly expressed:

'... for it appears to me that [the evidence] clearly established that dust
containing dangerous particles of silica was emitted into the air by the
operation of pneumatic hammers on the castings, that this dust hung about
in concentrated form longer than it would have if there had been better
ventilation, and that improved roof ventilators were practicable and would
have effectively improved the conditions. It follows that, owing to the
default of the respondents, the deceased was exposed to a greater degree of
risk than he should have been, and, though it is impossible even
approximately to quantify the particles which he must in any event have
inhaled and those which he inhaled but need not have, I cannot regard the
excess as something so negligible that the maxim "de minimis" is applicable.
Accordingly, following the decision in *Wardlaw*'s case, I must hold the
respondents liable.' (See [1957] 1 All ER 776 at 781, [1957] 1 WLR 613 at
619–620.)

Lord Oaksey and Lord Morton of Henryton agreed. Lord Cohen agreed and said:

'Pneumoconiosis is a progressive disease. The longer a workman is
exposed to an intense cloud the graver must be the risk of infection. In the
present case, it is clearly established by the evidence that, at any rate down
to 1949, the tool with which the deceased was working on dirty castings
created a thick cloud of dust which must have necessarily included siliceous
particles to an extent which cannot be classed as "de minimis". The
respondents are, admittedly, not to blame for the generation of this cloud,
but any failure to provide proper ventilation must, I think, lengthen the
period during which the cloud remains intense. It seems to me to follow that
the respondents' failure to provide adequate ventilation must increase the
risk to which the workmen are exposed. Reading the evidence as a whole, I
think it establishes that (to use the language of LORD REID in *Wardlaw*'s case
([1956] 1 All ER 615 at 618, [1956] AC 613 at 620)) "on a balance of
probabilities, the breach of duty caused, or materially contributed to", the
injury.' (See [1957] 1 All ER 776 at 782, [1957] 1 WLR 613 at 622.)

a Lord Keith of Avonholm ([1957] 1 All ER 776 at 787, [1957] 1 WLR 613 at 627) regarded it as common sense that better ventilation would have appreciably diminished the dust which was in the air for the deceased to inhale and accordingly concluded that his death from pneumoconiosis should be ascribed at least partially to the fault of the defenders. Again the case involved a single employer: but the dust, although 'innocent' when first produced became, in
b effect, 'guilty' because of the employer's conduct in allowing it to remain in the air for an excessive period. It is noteworthy that two members of the House (Viscount Simonds and Lord Cohen) attached significance to the exposure of the deceased to an increased risk.

[16] *Gardiner v Motherwell Machinery and Scrap Co Ltd* [1961] 3 All ER 831, [1961] 1 WLR 1424, another Scottish case, concerned a pursuer who had worked
c for the defenders for a period of some three months, demolishing buildings, and had contracted dermatitis. In an action against the defenders he claimed that they should have provided him with washing facilities but had failed to do so and that their failure had caused him to suffer from dermatitis. This contention was upheld by the Lord Ordinary (Lord Kilbrandon) who awarded him damages. The
d defenders did not on appeal challenge the finding of breach but contended that the pursuer had failed to prove any connection between his disease and the work which he had been doing. The First Division accepted this argument and found for the defenders, a decision against which the pursuer appealed. In his leading opinion in the House, Lord Reid considered at some length the conflict of medical evidence at the trial and its treatment by the First Division, and expressed
e his conclusion:

> 'In my opinion, when a man who has not previously suffered from a disease contracts that disease after being subjected to conditions likely to cause it, and when he shows that it starts in a way typical of disease caused by such conditions, he establishes a prima facie presumption that his disease
f was caused by those conditions. I think that the facts proved in this case do establish such a presumption. That presumption could be displaced in many ways. The respondents sought to show, first, that it is negatived by the subsequent course of the disease and, secondly, by suggesting tinea pedis as an equally probable cause of its origin. I have found the case difficult but, on the evidence as it stands, I have come to the opinion that they have failed on
g both points. If the appellant's disease and consequent loss should be attributed to the work which he was doing in the respondents' service, it was not argued that they were not liable.' (See [1961] 3 All ER 831 at 832–833, [1961] 1 WLR 1424 at 1429.)

h Lord Cohen and Lord Guest agreed, as did Lord Hodson although with some initial hesitation. Lord Guest ([1961] 3 All ER 831 at 833, [1961] 1 WLR 1424 at 1431) described the question as a pure question of fact whether on the balance of probabilities the dermatitis had arisen from the pursuer's employment. The House would seem to have regarded the pursuer as establishing a prime facie case
j which the defenders had failed to displace.

[17] In the course of the present appeals much argument was directed to the decision of the House in *McGhee's* case. The earlier stages of that case are reported at 1973 SC(HL) 37 and are important in understanding what the House decided. Mr McGhee had been employed by the National Coal Board for about 15 years, almost always working in pipe kilns. For some four-and-a-half days he then worked at a brick kiln, giving up because of a dermatitic condition which

had by then developed. The work inside the kiln was very hot and very dusty. The heat made men sweat profusely and the operation of the fan caused them to be covered in dust and grit. The pursuer contended that his dermatitis had been caused by his period of working in the brick kiln, short though it had been. The employers contended that his work had not caused the dermatitis and that it was non-occupational in origin. There was at the trial a conflict of medical evidence but the Lord Ordinary (Lord Kissen) held that the pursuer had contracted the dermatitis in the course of his work at the brick kiln and as a result of his exposure to dust and ashes when working there (at 39). Counsel for the pursuer accepted at trial that he could not establish a breach of statutory duty nor a breach of common law duty based on a failure to ventilate, but relied on two alleged breaches by the employers: of a duty to take care that the kiln had cooled sufficiently before men went in to work in it and of a duty to take reasonable care to provide adequate showers to enable men to remove dust from their bodies. The Lord Ordinary rejected the first of these complaints on a number of grounds, including the lack of proof that the breach of duty, even if established, had caused or materially contributed to the dermatitis: it was not enough that a reduction of heat would have lessened the risk (at 41). The Lord Ordinary concluded (at 42) that the employers were at fault in failing to provide showers but found against the pursuer on the basis of evidence given by two expert dermatologists, Dr Hannay and Dr Ferguson, called by the pursuer and the employers respectively. He said (at 42–43):

> 'As I have maintained earlier, the pursuer, in order to succeed, must also establish, on a balance of probabilities, that this fault on the part of the defenders "caused or materially contributed to his injury", that is to his contracting dermatitis. Dr Hannay's evidence was that he could not say that the provision of showers would probably have prevented the disease. He said that it would have reduced the risk materially but he would not go further than that. Dr Ferguson said that washing reduces the risk. Pursuer's counsel maintained that a material increase in the risk of contracting a disease was the same as a material contribution to contracting the disease and that Dr Hannay established this by his evidence. I think that defenders' counsel was correct when he said that the distinction drawn by Dr Hannay was correct and that an increase in risk did not necessarily mean a material contribution to the contracting of the disease. The two concepts are entirely different. A material increase in risk may refer only to possibilities and may not make a possibility into a probability. It may strengthen the possibility but that cannot mean that in all such cases the possibility has become a probability. What the pursuer has to show is that, as he avers, he would not have contracted the disease but for the defenders' breach of duty. He has to show that this was probable and the degrees of risk have no relevance unless they make the contraction of the disease more probable than not contracting the disease. He cannot succeed if the only inference from the evidence is that lack of shower baths is a possibility as a cause of his having contracted the disease and the provision of shower baths would have increased the possibility but not made it a probability. That is the only inference which I can draw from Dr Hannay's evidence and that was the best evidence for the pursuer. Causal connection between fault and the contraction of the disease has not been established.'

a [18] The pursuer appealed to the First Division against the dismissal of his claim. The medical evidence given at the trial was reviewed in detail, and in particular an exchange between cross-examining counsel and Dr Hannay (at 43–44, 47, 50):

b 'Q. Do I understand you to say you are not in a position to say that the provision of showers would probably have prevented his contracting this skin trouble?
A. No one could say that that would prevent that man developing the condition. It would be likely to reduce the chances.'

c In answer to further questions the doctor repeated his opinion that he could only say that the provision of showers would have reduced the chances of the pursuer contracting dermatitis and that that was as far as he was able to go. In the course of his judgment the Lord President, Lord Clyde, considered the pneumoconiosis cases and expressed his conclusion (at 44):

d 'But in contrast to the pneumoconiosis cases, the present case is essentially concerned with proof of the causal connection between the fault alleged (i.e. inadequate washing facilities) and the development of dermatitis. Even if the pursuer had established (as he did not) that the absence of washing facilities increased the risk of the pursuer getting dermatitis, that would clearly not prove that the absence of these facilities caused the disease, nor indeed
e would it go any distance towards proving it. For risk of dermatitis and causation of dermatitis are two quite separate matters.'

Lord Migdale was of the same opinion (at 47–48):

f 'Counsel for the pursuer contended that as it was now accepted that the failure to provide a shower was a breach of the duty which the defenders owed to the pursuer to take reasonable steps for his well-being, the doctors' evidence that it would have materially reduced the risk of dermatitis is enough to link the failure with the injury. Counsel for the defenders, on the other hand, contended that the test of causal connection between the breach and the injury is whether the provision of a shower would, on a balance of
g probabilities, have prevented the dermatitis. The Lord Ordinary says an increase in risk does not mean a material contribution to the contracting of the disease. A material increase in risk may refer only to possibilities and it does not make a possibility into a probability. "What the pursuer has to show is that, as he avers, he would not have contracted the disease but for
h the breach of duty". He has to show this on a balance of probabilities. In my opinion this is correct. Unless the pursuer can point to evidence that shows that a shower would more probably have avoided the disease than not, he cannot succeed and I do not find that evidence in this case.'

j Lord Johnston (at 50) was more hesitant, but in view of the other opinions did not feel inclined to take the view that the evidence was sufficient to allow him to hold that the test of the balance of probability had been satisfied.

[19] On appeal to the House counsel for the pursuer faced the problem, as he had at trial and in the First Division, that his own evidence precluded a finding that the absence of a shower had probably caused the pursuer's dermatitis. Mr Davidson QC accordingly relied on the evidence that provision of a shower would have materially reduced the risk to contend that he had made out a prima

facie case. The contrary argument for the employers was advanced by Mr James
Mackay QC, as reported (at 51):

> 'It was accepted that [the provision of washing facilities] would have been
> a reasonable precaution, but it did not follow that this would have eliminated
> the risk. The employee might have developed dermatitis in any event. If the
> precaution would not have prevented the disease, the appellant was not
> entitled to damages. In the case of pneumoconiosis the inhalation of
> dangerous dust inevitably created a basis for the disease by accumulation,
> whereas in the case of dermatitis a particle of grit would cause the disease
> only if there were an abrasion which opened up the layer below the horny
> outer layer of the skin. In the case of pneumoconiosis all the particles could
> be blamed. It was not so in the case of dermatitis. The mere fact that shower
> baths would have reduced the chances of the contraction of the disease did
> not mean that what was probable would thereby have been rendered
> improbable.'

Thus the issue, as presented to the House, was whether the pursuer could
succeed despite his inability to show that he would probably not have suffered
dermatitis but for the defenders' failure to provide the showers which they
should have provided.

[20] In the House, opinions were given by all five members of the Appellate
Committee which heard the appeal and the appeal was allowed ([1972] 3 All ER
1008, [1973] 1 WLR 1). Lord Reid, giving the first opinion, described the pursuer's
complaint based on the failure to provide shower facilities as raising 'a difficult
question of law' ([1972] 3 All ER 1008 at 1009, [1973] 1 WLR 1 at 3). He pointed
out that the breach of duty in relation to showers was admitted, and it was
admitted that the disease was attributable to the work which the pursuer had
performed in the brick kiln, but it was contended that the pursuer had not proved
that the defenders' failure to carry out the admitted duty had caused the onset of
the disease ([1972] 3 All ER 1010, [1973] 1 WLR 1 at 3). Lord Reid's understanding
of the evidence, and his view of the proper approach to it, appear from the
following passage of his opinion ([1972] 3 All ER 1008 at 1010–1011, [1973] 1 WLR
1 at 4–5):

> 'In the present case the evidence does not shew—perhaps no one
> knows—just how dermatitis of this type begins. It suggests to me that there
> are two possible ways. It may be that an accumulation of minor abrasions of
> the horny layer of skin is a necessary precondition for the onset of the
> disease. Or it may be that the disease starts at one particular abrasion and
> then spreads, so that multiplication of abrasions merely increases the
> number of places where the disease can start and in that way increases the
> risk of its occurrence. I am inclined to think that the evidence points to the
> former view. But in a field were so little appears to be known with certainty
> I could not say that that is proved. If it were then this case would be
> indistinguishable from *Wardlaw*'s case. But I think that in cases like this we
> must take a broader view of causation. The medical evidence is to the effect
> that the fact that the man had to cycle home caked with grime and sweat
> added materially to the risk that this disease might develop. It does not and
> could not explain just why that is so. But experience shews that it is so.
> Plainly that must be because what happens while the man remains
> unwashed can have a causative effect, although just how the cause operates
> is uncertain. I cannot accept the view expressed in the Inner House that once

the man left the brick kiln he left behind the causes which made him liable to develop dermatitis. That seems to me quite inconsistent with a proper interpretation of the medical evidence. Nor can I accept the distinction drawn by the Lord Ordinary between materially increasing the risk that the disease will occur and making a material contribution to its occurrence. There may be some logical ground for such a distinction where our knowledge of all the material factors is complete. But it has often been said that the legal concept of causation is not based on logic or philosophy. It is based on the practical way in which the ordinary man's mind works in the every-day affairs of life. From a broad and practical viewpoint I can see no substantial difference between saying that what the respondents did materially increased the risk of injury to the appellant and saying that what the respondents did made a material contribution to his injury.'

Lord Wilberforce acknowledged the need for the pursuer to establish both a breach of duty and a causal connection between the default and the disease complained of ([1972] 3 All ER 1008 at 1011, [1973] 1 WLR 1 at 5), and also the difficulties of proof which the pursuer faced ([1972] 3 All ER 1008 at 1012, [1973] 1 WLR 1 at 5–6):

'[The pursuer's medical expert] could not do more than say that the failure to provide showers materially increased the chance, or risk, that dermatitis might set in.'

Lord Wilberforce accepted that merely to show that a breach of duty led to an increase of risk was not enough to enable a pursuer to succeed, but continued ([1972] 3 All ER 1008 at 1012, [1973] 1 WLR 1 at 6):

'But the question remains whether a pursuer must necessarily fail if, after he has shown a breach of duty, involving an increase of risk of disease, he cannot positively prove that this increase of risk caused or materially contributed to the disease while his employers cannot positively prove the contrary. In this intermediate case there is an appearance of logic in the view that the pursuer, on whom the onus lies, should fail—a logic which dictated the judgments below. The question is whether we should be satisfied in factual situations like the present, with this logical approach. In my opinion, there are further considerations of importance. First, it is a sound principle that where a person has, by breach of duty of care, created a risk, and injury occurs within the area of that risk, the loss should be borne by him unless he shows that it had some other cause. Secondly, from the evidential point of view, one may ask, why should a man who is able to show that his employer should have taken certain precautions, because without them there is a risk, or an added risk, of injury or disease, and who in fact sustains exactly that injury or disease, have to assume the burden of proving more: namely, that it was the addition to the risk, caused by the breach of duty, which caused or materially contributed to the injury? In many cases of which the present is typical, this is impossible to prove, just because honest medical opinion cannot segregate the causes of an illness between compound causes. And if one asks which of the parties, the workman or the employers should suffer from this inherent evidential difficulty, the answer as a matter in policy or justice should be that it is the creator of the risk who, ex hypothesi, must be taken to have foreseen the possibility of damage, who should bear its consequences.'

Having referred to *Wardlaw's* and *Nicholson's* cases Lord Wilberforce concluded:

a

'The present factual situation has its differences: the default here consisted not in adding a material quantity to the accumulation of injurious particles but by failure to take a step which materially increased the risk that the dust already present would cause injury. And I must say that, at least in the present case, to bridge the evidential gap by inference seems to me something of a fiction, since it was precisely this inference which the medical b expert declined to make. But I find in the cases quoted an analogy which suggests the conclusion that, in the absence of proof that the culpable condition had, in the result, no effect, the employers should be liable for an injury, squarely within the risk which they created and that they, not the pursuer, should suffer the consequence of the impossibility, foreseeably c inherent in the nature of his injury, of segregating the precise consequence of their default.' (See [1972] 3 All ER 1008 at 1013, [1973] 1 WLR 1 at 7.)

Lord Simon of Glaisdale ([1972] 3 All ER 1008 at 1014, [1973] 1 WLR 1 at 8) considered that *Wardlaw's* and *Nicholson's* cases established a rule—

'that where an injury is caused by two (or more) factors operating d cumulatively, one (or more) of which factors is a breach of duty and one (or more) is not so, in such a way that it is impossible to ascertain the proportion in which the factors were effective in producing the injury or which factor was decisive, the law does not require a pursuer or plaintiff to prove the impossible, but holds that he is entitled to damages for the injury if he proves e on a balance of probabilities that the breach or breaches of duty contributed substantially to causing the injury. If such factors so operate cumulatively, it is, in my judgment, immaterial whether they do so concurrently or successively.'

Lord Simon then continued: f

'The question, then, is whether on the evidence the appellant brought himself within this rule. In my view, a failure to take steps which would bring about a material reduction of the risk involves, in this type of case, a substantial contribution to the injury. In this type of case a stark distinction between breach of duty and causation is unreal. If the provision of shower g baths was (as the evidence showed) a precaution which any reasonable employer in the respondents' position would take, it means that such employer should have foreseen that failure to take the precaution would, more probably than not, substantially contribute towards injury; this is sufficient prima facie evidence.'

h

Lord Simon regarded 'material reduction of the risk' and 'substantial contribution to the injury' as mirror concepts. Any other conclusion would mean that the defenders were under a legal duty which they could, on the present state of medical knowledge, ignore (see [1972] 3 All ER 1008 at 1015, [1973] 1 WLR 1 at 9). Lord Kilbrandon appears to have adopted a more orthodox approach to j tortious liability. He said:

'When you find it proved (a) that the defenders knew that to take the precaution reduces the risk, chance, possibility or probability of the contracting of a disease, (b) that the precaution has not been taken, and (c) that the disease has supervened, it is difficult to see how those defenders can demand more by way of proof of the probability that the failure caused a   or contributed to the physical breakdown … In the present case, the appellant's body was vulnerable, while he was bicycling home, to the dirt which had been deposited on it during his working hours. It would not have been if he had had a shower. If showers had been provided he would have used them. It is admittedly more probable that disease will be contracted if a shower is not taken. In these circumstances I cannot accept the argument

b   that nevertheless it is not more probable than not that, if the duty to provide a shower had been neglected, he would not have contracted the disease. The appellant has, after all, only to satisfy the court of a probability, not to demonstrate an irrefragable chain of causation, which in a case of dermatitis, in the present state of medical knowledge, he could probably never do.' (See [1972] 3 All ER 1008 at 1016, [1973] 1 WLR 1 at 10.)

c
In Lord Salmon's opinion the question before the House was whether the pursuer's dermatitis was proved to have been caused or materially contributed to by the defenders' negligence ([1972] 3 All ER 1008 at 1016, [1973] 1 WLR 1 at 11). He rejected the view, expressed by the Lord President (see [18], above) that to increase the risk of injury was not, in the circumstances of this case, to cause the

d   injury. In such a case he regarded it as unrealistic and contrary to ordinary common sense to hold that the negligence which materially increased the risk of injury did not materially contribute to causing it ([1972] 3 All ER 1008 at 1017, [1973] 1 WLR 1 at 11–12). He observed:

e   'I think that the approach by the courts below confuses the balance of probability test with the nature of causation. Moreover, it would mean that in the present state of medical knowledge and in circumstances such as these (which are by no means uncommon) an employer would be permitted by the law to disregard with impunity his duty to take reasonable care for the safety of his employees.' (See [1972] 3 All ER 1008 at 1018, [1973] 1 WLR 1 at 12.)

f   Lord Salmon's conclusion was expressed in these terms:

'In the circumstances of the present case, the possibility of a distinction existing between (a) having materially increased the risk of contracting the disease, and (b) having materially contributed to causing the disease may no doubt be a fruitful source of interesting academic discussions between

g   students of philosophy. Such a distinction is, however, far too unreal to be recognised by the common law.' (See [1972] 3 All ER 1008 at 1018, [1973] 1 WLR 1 at 12–13.)

[21] This detailed review of *McGhee*'s case permits certain conclusions to be

h   drawn. First, the House was deciding a question of law. Lord Reid expressly said so ([1972] 3 All ER 1008 at 1009, [1973] 1 WLR 1 at 3). The other opinions, save perhaps that of Lord Kilbrandon, cannot be read as decisions of fact or as orthodox applications of settled law. Secondly, the question of law was whether, on the facts of the case as found, a pursuer who could not show that the defender's breach had probably caused the damage of which he complained

j   could nonetheless succeed. Thirdly, it was not open to the House to draw a factual inference that the breach probably had caused the damage: such an inference was expressly contradicted by the medical experts on both sides; and once that evidence had been given the crux of the argument before the Lord Ordinary and the First Division and the House was whether, since the pursuer could not prove that the breach had probably made a material contribution to his contracting dermatitis, it was enough to show that the breach had increased the risk of his contracting it. Fourthly, it was expressly held by three members of the House ([1972] 3 All ER 1008 at 1011, 1014, 1018, [1973] 1 WLR 1 at 5, 8, 12–13 per Lord Reid, Lord Simon and Lord Salmon respectively) that in the circumstances no distinction was to be drawn between making a material contribution to causing the disease and materially increasing the risk of the pursuer contracting it. Thus the proposition expressly rejected by the Lord Ordinary, the Lord President and Lord Migdale was expressly accepted by a majority of the House and must be taken to represent the ratio of the decision, closely tied though it was to the special facts on which it was based. Fifthly, recognising that the pursuer faced an insuperable problem of proof if the orthodox test of causation was applied, but regarding the case as one in which justice demanded a remedy for the pursuer, a majority of the House adapted the orthodox test to meet the particular case. The authority is of obvious importance in the present appeal since the medical evidence left open the possibility, as Lord Reid pointed out ([1972] 3 All ER 1008 at 1010, [1973] 1 WLR 1 at 4) that the pursuer's dermatitis could have begun with a single abrasion, which might have been caused when he was cycling home, but might equally have been caused when he was working in the brick kiln; in the latter event, the failure to provide showers would have made no difference. In *McGhee's* case, however, unlike the present appeals, the case was not complicated by the existence of additional or alternative wrongdoers.

[22] In *Wilsher v Essex Area Health Authority* [1988] 1 All ER 871, [1988] AC 1074 a problem of causation arose in a different context. A prematurely-born baby was the subject of certain medical procedures, in the course of which a breach of duty occurred. The baby suffered a condition (abbreviated as RLF) of a kind which that breach of duty could have caused, and the breach of duty increased the risk of his suffering it. But there were a number of other factors which might have caused the injury. In the Court of Appeal ([1986] 3 All ER 801 at 829, [1987] QB 730 at 771–772) Mustill LJ concluded a detailed review of *McGhee's* case by making this statement of principle:

'If it is an established fact that conduct of a particular kind creates a risk that injury will be caused to another or increases an existing risk that injury will ensue, and if the two parties stand in such a relationship that the one party owes a duty not to conduct himself in that way, and if the other party does suffer injury of the kind to which the risk related, then the first party is taken to have caused the injury by his breach of duty, even though the existence and extent of the contribution made by the breach cannot be ascertained.'

Omitted from this statement is any reference to condition (5) in the composite question formulated in [2], above at the outset of this opinion. It was on this omission that Browne-Wilkinson V-C founded his dissenting opinion:

'To apply the principle in *McGhee v National Coal Board* [1972] 3 All ER 1008, [1973] 1 WLR 1 to the present case would constitute an extension of that principle. In *McGhee* there was no doubt that the pursuer's dermatitis was physically caused by brick dust the only question was whether the continued presence of such brick dust on the pursuer's skin after the time when he should have been provided with a shower caused or materially contributed to the dermatitis which he contracted. There was only one possible agent which could have caused the dermatitis, viz brick dust, and there was no doubt that the dermatitis from which he suffered was caused by that brick dust. In the present case the question is different. There are a number of different agents which could have caused the RLF. Excess oxygen was one a of them. The defendants failed to take reasonable precautions to prevent one of the possible causative agents (eg excess oxygen) from causing RLF. But no one can tell in this case whether excess oxygen did or did not cause or contribute to the RLF suffered by the plaintiff. The plaintiff's RLF may have been caused by some completely different agent or agents, eg hypercarbia, intraventricular haemorrhage, apnoea or patent ductus arteriosus. In addition

b to oxygen, each of those conditions has been implicated as a possible cause of RLF. This baby suffered from each of those conditions at various times in the first two months of his life. There is no satisfactory evidence that excess oxygen is more likely than any of those other four candidates to have caused RLF in this baby. To my mind, the occurrence of RLF following a failure to take a necessary precaution to prevent excess oxygen causing RLF provides

c no evidence and raises no presumption that it was excess oxygen rather than one or more of the four other possible agents which caused or contributed to RLF in this case. The position, to my mind, is wholly different from that in *McGhee*, where there was only one candidate (brick dust) which could have caused the dermatitis, and the failure to take a precaution against brick

d dust causing dermatitis was followed by dermatitis caused by brick dust. In such a case, I can see the common sense, if not the logic, of holding that, in the absence of any other evidence, the failure to take the precaution caused or contributed to the dermatitis. To the extent that certain members of the House of Lords decided the question on inferences from evidence or presumptions, I do not consider that the present case falls within their

e reasoning. A failure to take preventive measures against one out of five possible causes is no evidence as to which of those five caused the injury.' (See [1986] 3 All ER 801 at 834–835, [1987] QB 730 at 779.)

f On the defendants' appeal to the House, this passage in the Vice-Chancellor's judgment was expressly approved by Lord Bridge of Harwich, who gave the only opinion, with which Lord Fraser of Tullybelton, Lord Lowry, Lord Griffiths and Lord Ackner concurred, and the appeal was allowed ([1988] 1 All ER 871 at 881–883, [1988] AC 1074 at 1090–1092). It is plain, in my respectful opinion, that the House was right to allow the defendants' appeal in *Wilsher's* case, for the reasons which the Vice-Chancellor had given and which the House approved. It

g is one thing to treat an increase of risk as equivalent to the making of a material contribution where a single noxious agent is involved, but quite another where any one of a number of noxious agents may equally probably have caused the damage. The decision of the Court of Appeal did indeed involve an extension of the *McGhee* principle, as Mustill LJ recognised ([1986] 3 All ER 801 at 829, [1987]

h QB 730 at 771–772). Lord Bridge was also, as I respectfully think, right to describe the observations of Lord Wilberforce on reversal of the burden of proof (see [20], above) as expressing a 'minority opinion' ([1988] 1 All ER 871 at 879, [1988] AC 1074 at 1087), if Lord Wilberforce was suggesting more than that the proof of an increased risk can found a prima facie case which casts an evidential burden on

j the defendant. But much difficulty is caused by the following passage in Lord Bridge's opinion in which, having cited the opinions of all members of the House in *McGhee's* case, he said:

'The conclusion I draw from these passages is that *McGhee v National Coal Board* laid down no new principle of law whatever. On the contrary, it affirmed the principle that the onus of proving causation lies on the pursuer or plaintiff. Adopting a robust and pragmatic approach to the undisputed

primary facts of the case, the majority concluded that it was a legitimate
inference of fact that the defenders' negligence had materially contributed to
the pursuer's injury.   The decision, in my opinion, is of no greater
significance than that and the attempt to extract from it some esoteric
principle which in some way modifies, as a matter of law, the nature of the
burden of proof of causation which a plaintiff or pursuer must discharge once
he has established a relevant breach of duty is a fruitless one.' (See [1988] 1
All ER 871 at 881–882, [1988] AC 1074 at 1090.)

This is a passage to which the Court of Appeal ([2002] 1 WLR 1052 at [103]) very
properly gave weight, and in argument on these appeals counsel for the
respondents strongly relied on it as authority for their major contention that a
claimant can only succeed if he proves on the balance of probabilities that the
default of the particular defendant had caused the damage of which he complains.
As is apparent from the conclusions expressed in [21], above, I cannot for my part
accept this passage in Lord Bridge's opinion as accurately reflecting the effect of
what the House, or a majority of the House, decided in *McGhee's* case, which
remains sound authority.   I am bound to conclude that this passage should no
longer be treated as authoritative.

The wider jurisprudence

[23] The problem of attributing legal responsibility where a victim has
suffered a legal wrong but cannot show which of several possible candidates (all
in breach of duty) is the culprit who has caused him harm is one that has vexed
jurists in many parts of the world for many years.   As my noble and learned friend
Lord Rodger of Earlsferry shows (see [157]–[160], below) it engaged the attention
of classical Roman jurists.   It is indeed a universal problem calling for some
consideration by the House, however superficially, of the response to it in other
jurisdictions.

[24] Professor Christian von Bar (*The Common European Law of Torts* (2000),
vol 2, pp 441–443) has written:

'The phenomenon of double causation is thus an insufficient argument
against the but—for test.   It is merely peripheral.   Of greater importance are the
many cases in which, although one cannot speak of a scientifically ascertainable
or explicable "cause" and "effect", courts have awarded compensation on the
basis of fault and probability.   German law on medical negligence provides
the example of the reduced burden of proof of causation in cases of grave
treatment errors.   Recent environmental legislation has reacted to the
problem of scientifically uncertain causal relationships in a similar manner.
The reversal of the burden of proof regarding causation is no more than a
reduction of the probability required for attribution.   A further development
has arisen in the Netherlands regarding liability for medicines in the context
of DES liability.   The Hoge Raad's solution, on the basis of Art 6.99BW, of
holding jointly liable to cancer sufferers the manufacturers of all those
carcinogenic medicines available at the time when the victims' mothers had
taken those substances is clearly unjustifiable under the *conditio sine qua non*
rule.   If the issue is seen to be whether the victim or the person posing the risk
is better positioned to bear that risk, the solution is more comprehensible.'

In similar vein, Professor Walter van Gerven (van Gerven, Lever and Larouche *Cases,
Materials and Text on National, Supranational and International Tort Law* (2000) p 441),
surveying the tort law of, in particular, Germany, France and Britain, wrote:

'In many cases, it will be possible for the victim to show that he or she has suffered injury, that it has been caused by someone who must have been at fault, but the author of that fault will not be identifiable. The best that the victim will be able to achieve is to define a class of persons of which the actual tortfeasor must be a member. Strictly speaking, however, the basic *conditio sine qua non* test will not be met, since it cannot be said of any member of the class that the injury would not have happened "but for" his or her conduct, given that in fact any other member could have caused the injury. Nonetheless, all the legal systems studied here have acknowledged that it would be patently unfair to deny recovery to the victim for that reason.'

At p 461, after reference to *McGhee*'s case and *Wilsher*'s case, van Gerven added:

'*McGhee* had put English law on the same path as German law, albeit with a different and arguably stronger rationale (negligent creation of risk instead of impossibility for the plaintiff to prove causation). Furthermore, it must be noted that some French legal writers are advocating that French law moves away from *perte d'une chance* towards a reversal of the burden of proof on the basis of the negligent creation of risk. It is unfortunate that the House of Lords retreated from *McGhee* at a time when laws were converging. In the end, the sole relief for the plaintiff under English law is that it suffices for the purposes of causation to show that the conduct of the defendant made a material contribution to the injury, even if it was not its sole cause.'

He concluded (at p 465):

'In certain cases, the plaintiff can show that he or she suffered injury, that it was caused by some person and that the other conditions of liability are otherwise fulfilled but for the fact that the actual tortfeasor cannot be identified among the members of a class of persons. In these cases, the strict application of the "but for" test would result in the claim of the plaintiff being dismissed, but all systems under study here make an exception to the rules of causation to provide the plaintiff with compensation.'

[**25**] In Germany cases of this kind have been held to be covered by the second sentence (to which emphasis has been added) of BGB (Bürgerliches Gesetzbuch) para 830.1 which provides:

'If several persons have caused damage by an unlawful act committed in common each is responsible for the damage. *The same rule applies if it cannot be discovered which of several participants has caused the damage by his act.*'

Of this provision, Markesinis and Unberath *The German Law of Torts* (4th edn, 2002) p 900 states:

'Paragraph 830.1, second sentence, applies the same rule to a different situation where several persons participate in a course of conduct which, though not unlawful in itself, is potentially dangerous to others. The difference between this and the previous situation lies in the fact that whereas in the former case of joint tortfeasors the loss is caused by several persons acting in consort, in the latter case only one person has caused the loss but it is difficult if not impossible to say which one has done so. (The classic illustration is that of the huntsmen who discharge their guns simultaneously and the pellets from one unidentifiable gun hit an innocent

passer-by.) In this case, as well, para 830 BGB adopts the same rule and
makes all the participants liable to the victim for the full extent of damage.'

It is evident that this approach has been applied in Germany in a number of
different situations: see Palandt *Bürgerliches Gesetzbuch* (61st edn, 2002) para 830.
Thus cases decided on this basis have included personal injury caused by several
individuals throwing stones in a fight; personal injury of a pedestrian who passes
a construction site operated by different companies; personal injury by a New
Year's Eve rocket launched by a group of individuals who were all firing rockets;
liability of several hunters for the personal injury of a passer-by; liability of a
houseowner for the personal injury of a pedestrian who walks on a dangerous
path and is hurt on the borderline between the houseowner's land and an
unfinished street owned by the local authority; and personal injury of a patient
after various interrelated operations conducted by different doctors. The extent
to which this approach to causation may be subject to certain restrictive
conditions appears to be a matter of some uncertainty; see *van Gerven*, p 446.

[26] The BGB is not alone in expressly recognising the problem of the
indeterminate defendant. Article 926 of the Greek Civil Code, entitled 'Damage
caused by several persons' provides:

'If damage has occurred as a result of the joint action of several persons, or
if several persons are concurrently responsible for the same damage, they are
all jointly and severally implicated. The same applies if several persons have
acted simultaneously or in succession and it is not possible to determine
which person's act caused the damage.'

The second sentence of this provision would appear to cover the contingency
under consideration, although the contrary has been asserted: *Unification of Tort
Law: Causation* (2000) p 77. A somewhat similar provision is to be found in the
Austrian Civil Code:

'1302 In such a case, if the injury is inadvertent, and it is possible to
determine the portions thereof, each person is responsible only for the
injuries caused by his mistake. If, however, the injury was intentional, or if
the portions of the individuals in the injury cannot be determined, all are
liable for one and one for all; however, the individual who has paid damages
is granted the right to claim reimbursement from the others.'

A similar provision is also found in the Netherlands Civil Code (art 6.99 BW: see
[29], below).

[27] The problem of attribution has repeatedly arisen in the context of
shooting incidents, described by Professor Markesinis as 'The classic illustration'
in the passage quoted in [25], above. In *Litzinger v Kintzler* (Cass civ 2e, 5 June
1957, D 1957 Jur 493), where a group of huntsmen fired a salvo to mark the end
of a deer hunt and the plaintiff was shot, the French Cour de Cassation held the
whole group liable since 'the whole group created a risk through its negligent
conduct, and the injury to the plaintiff constituted a realisation of that risk' (see
van Gerven, at pp 442–444). It appears that this reasoning (depending on a broad
view of acting in concert) has been reaffirmed in later cases (ibid). In Spain, a
provision of the Hunting Act 1970 provides that 'In the case of hunting with
weapons, if the author of the personal injury is not known, all members of the
hunting party shall be jointly and severally liable'. This is not a problem which is
confined to Europe. In *Summers v Tice* (1948) 199 P 2d 1 each of two defendants
at or about the same time shot at a quail and in doing so fired towards the plaintiff

a who was struck by shot. The Supreme Court of California referred (at 3) to earlier authority and said:

'These cases speak of the action of defendants as being in concert as the ground of decision, yet it would seem they are straining that concept and the more reasonable basis appears in *Oliver v. Miles* ((1926) 50 ALR 357), supra.

b There two persons were hunting together. Both shot at some partridges and in so doing shot across the highway injuring plaintiff who was travelling on it. The court stated they were acting in concert and thus both were liable. The court then stated ..."We think that ... each is liable for the resulting injury to the boy, although no one can say definitely who actually shot him. *To hold otherwise would be to exonerate both from liability, although each was*

c *negligent, and the injury resulted from such negligence."* [Emphasis added].'

The conclusion of the court was expressed (at 4, 5 (paras 5 and 7)):

'When we consider the relative position of the parties and the results that would flow if plaintiff was required to pin the injury on one of the defendants only, a requirement that the burden of proof on that subject be shifted to

d defendants becomes manifest. They are both wrong-doers—both negligent toward plaintiff. They brought about a situation where the negligence of one of them injured the plaintiff, hence it should rest with them each to absolve himself if he can ... We have seen that for the reasons of policy discussed herein, the case is based upon the legal proposition that, under the

e circumstances here presented, each defendant is liable for the whole damage whether they are deemed to be acting in concert or independently.'

The *Summers* alternative liability theory was incorporated in the Restatement Second of Torts, s 433B, subdivision (3) pp 441–447, which provides:

f 'Where the conduct of two or more actors is tortious, and it is proved that harm has been caused to the plaintiff by only one of them, but there is uncertainty as to which one has caused it, the burden is upon each such actor to prove that he has not caused the harm.'

The Supreme Court of Canada confronted this situation in *Cook v Lewis* [1951]

g SCR 830, in which Cartwright J, with whom a majority agreed, said (at 842):

'I do not think it necessary to decide whether all that was said in *Summers v Tice* should be accepted as stating the law of British Columbia, but I am of opinion, for the reasons given in that case, that if under the circumstances of the case at bar the jury, having decided that the plaintiff was shot by either Cook or Akenhead, found themselves unable to decide which of the two

h shot him because in their opinion both shot negligently in his direction, both defendants should have been found liable.'

[28] In a Norwegian case (see Nils Nygaard *Injury/Damage and Responsibility* (2000) pp 342–343) F was a passenger on a motor scooter and was injured in an

j accident caused either by a cable stretched across the street by a construction company or by the motor scooter falling onto him or as a result of collision with a truck, or by any combination of these factors. In giving judgment (RG 1969 p 285 at 293) the Norwegian court said:

'As stated in the beforementioned conclusions made by experts, they could not conclude whether the situation that resulted in crushed bones in F's left hip region, was a result of falling on the cobble stones in the street or from

the truck's front tyre, that ended up on top of F's left hip region. It is possible
that the injuries were partially a result of the fall and being hit by the truck.
We cannot say anything definite about this. The court finds that it cannot
conclude whether it is the fall or being hit by the truck or a combination of
both these factors that caused the injury. After a collective evaluation of the
whole event the court finds that A (construction company), the scooter and
the truck each have a part in F getting injured and each of them must
naturally be seen as adequate cause of injury.'

This decision bears a strong resemblance to that reached by the English Court of
Appeal in *Fitzgerald v Lane* [1987] 2 All ER 455, [1987] QB 781, decided after the
decision of the Court of Appeal in *Wilsher's* case but before the decision of the
House of Lords.

[29] Increasingly in recent years, the problem of attribution has arisen in more
complicated factual situations. *Sindell v Abbott Laboratories* (1980) 26 Cal 3d 588
was a class action for personal injuries said to have resulted from pre-natal
exposure to the anti-miscarriage drug diethylstilbestrol (DES) which had been
manufactured by one of a potentially large number of defendants. The plaintiff
could not identify which particular defendant had manufactured the drug
responsible for her injuries. However, her complaint alleged that the defendants
were jointly and individually negligent in that they had manufactured, marketed
and promoted DES as a safe drug to prevent miscarriage without adequate
testing or warning of its dangerous side effects; that they had collaborated in their
marketing methods, promotion and testing of the drug; that they had relied on
each others' test results; that they had adhered to an industry-wide safety
standard; and that they had produced the drug from a common and mutually
agreed generic formula. The court distinguished *Summers's* case on the basis that
in that case all the parties who were or could have been responsible for the harm
to the plaintiff were joined as defendants, whereas in *Sindell's* case there were
approximately 200 drug companies which had made DES, any of which might
have manufactured the injury-producing drug. The court held that it would be
unfair, in such circumstances, to require each defendant to exonerate itself.
Further, it said that there might be a substantial likelihood that none of the five
defendants joined in the action had made the DES which caused the injury, and
that the offending producer, not named, would escape liability. The court
surmounted this problem by adapting the *Summers* rule so as to apportion liability
on the basis of the defendant's market share (see (1980) 26 Cal 3d 588 at 593–595,
602–603, 604–605 and 612–613). A very similar case concerning the same drug
arose in the Netherlands in *B v Bayer Nederland BV* (9 October 1992, NJ 1994, 535)
which turned on art 6.99 BW. That provision is in these terms:

'Where the damage may have resulted from two or more events for each
of which a different person is liable, and where it has been determined that
the damage has arisen from at least one of these events, the obligation to
repair the damage rests upon each of these persons, unless he proves that the
damage is not the result of the event for which he himself is liable.'

In para 3.7.1 of its judgment the Hoge Raad held:

'The facts of the present case fall under that provision, on the assumption
that it can be proved that [i] each of the firms which put DES in circulation
in the relevant period was at fault in so doing and could thus be held liable,
[ii] the total injury of each victim could have been caused by any of these

"events"—i.e. putting DES in circulation—and [iii] the injury occurred
because of at least one of these "events" ... [art 6.99BW] aims to remove the
unfairness arising from the fact that the victim must bear his or her own
damage because he or she cannot prove whose action caused his or her
harm. The victims in the present case are faced with such an evidentiary
difficulty ...'

In para 3.7.5 of its judgment the court said:

'It is sufficient for each DES daughter to establish ... in relation to each of
the pharmaceutical companies: (i) that the pharmaceutical company in
question put DES in circulation during the relevant period and can therefore
be found liable because it committed a fault; (ii) that another or several other
producers—regardless of whether they are parties to the proceedings or
not—also put DES in circulation during the relevant period and can
therefore also be found liable because it (they) committed a fault; and
(iii) that she suffered injury that resulted from the use of DES, but that it is
no longer possible to determine from which producer the DES originated."
In principle the burden of proof on these issues rests on the DES daughter
concerned.'

See *van Gerven*, pp 447–448.

[30] Cases decided in the High Court of Australia do not disclose a clear ratio
on which the appellants were able to rely before the House, although they drew
attention to dicta which were helpful to them. For example, in *Chappel v Hart*
(1998) 195 CLR 232 at 244 (para 27) McHugh J said, in a passage reminiscent of
McGhee's case, although without referring to that case:

'Before the defendant will be held responsible for the plaintiff's injury, the
plaintiff must prove that the defendant's conduct materially contributed to
the plaintiff suffering that injury. In the absence of a statute or undertaking
to the contrary, therefore, it would seem logical to hold a person causally
liable for a wrongful act or omission only when it increases the risk of injury
to another person. If a wrongful act or omission results in an increased risk
of injury to the plaintiff and that risk eventuates, the defendant's conduct has
materially contributed to the injury that the plaintiff suffers whether or not
other factors also contributed to that injury occurring. If, however, the
defendant's conduct does not increase the risk of injury to the plaintiff, the
defendant cannot be said to have materially contributed to the injury
suffered by the plaintiff. That being so, whether the claim is in contract or
tort, the fact that the risk eventuated at a particular time or place by reason
of the conduct of the defendant does not itself materially contribute to the
plaintiff's injury unless the fact of that particular time or place increased the
risk of the injury occurring.'

In that case McHugh J dissented on the facts but in *Naxakis v Western General
Hospital* (1999) 197 CLR 269 both Gaudron J (at 279 (para 31)) and Callinan J
(at 312 (para 127)) quoted what he had said with approval. In Canada, Sopinka J,
speaking for the Supreme Court in *Snell v Farrell* (1990) 72 DLR (4th) 289 at 299
said:

'I have examined the alternatives arising out of the *McGhee* case. They
were that the plaintiff simply prove that the defendant created a risk that the
injury which occurred would occur. Or, what amounts to the same thing,

that the defendant has the burden of disproving causation. If I were
convinced that defendants who have a substantial connection to the injury
were escaping liability because plaintiffs cannot prove causation under
currently applied principles, I would not hesitate to adopt one of these
alternatives. In my opinion, however, properly applied, the principles
relating to causation are adequate to the task. Adoption of either of the
proposed alternatives would have the effect of compensating plaintiffs
where a substantial connection between the injury and the defendant's
conduct is absent. Reversing the burden of proof may be justified where two
defendants negligently fire in the direction of the plaintiff and then by their
tortious conduct destroy the means of proof at his disposal. In such a case it
is clear that the injury was not caused by neutral conduct. It is quite a
different matter to compensate a plaintiff by reversing the burden of proof
for an injury that may very well be due to factors unconnected to the
defendant and not the fault of anyone.'

Sopinka J suggested (at 328) that dissatisfaction with the traditional approach to
causation stemmed to a large extent from its too rigid application by the courts
in many cases, and that causation need not be determined by scientific precision.
Despite this judgment the Manitoba Court of Appeal, in *Webster v Chapman* (1997)
155 DLR (4th) 82 held, relying on *McGhee*'s case, that no distinction should be
made in that case between materially increasing the risk of damage and materially
contributing to the damage.

[31] There is a small but important body of authority on the problem of
attribution in mesothelioma cases where the plaintiff has been exposed to
asbestos during employment by more than one employer. *Bendix Mintex Pty Ltd
v Barnes* (1997) 42 NSWLR 307 was such a case. A majority of the Court of Appeal
of New South Wales held against the plaintiff on the causation issue, relying on
Wilsher's case among much other authority. Stein JA dissented, citing with
approval the following passage from the judgment of King CJ in *Birkholtz v RJ
Gilbertson Pty Ltd* (1985) 38 SASR 121 at 130:

'... the law's view of causation is less concerned with logical and
philosophical considerations than with the need to produce a just result to
the parties involved. Where a defendant is under a legal duty to take
precautions to protect the plaintiff from the risk of contracting disease, and,
by omitting those precautions he substantially increases the risk of the
plaintiff contracting that disease, the law treats that increase in risk as a
sufficient basis, in the absence of evidence showing how the infection
occurred, for an inference that the omission of the precautions materially
contributed to the contracting of the disease. Justice requires such an
approach to the problem of causation and it is the approach which was taken
by the House of Lords in *McGhee v National Coal Board*.'

The majority decision in the *Bendix* case was followed in *Wallaby Grip (BAE) Pty
Ltd v Macleay Area Health Service* (1998) 17 NSWCCR 355. A different result was
reached in *EM Baldwin & Son Pty Ltd v Plane* (1999) Aust Torts Reports 81–499, but
on different medical evidence. A different view of the law was also expressed in
Rutherford v Owens-Illinois Inc (1997) 67 Cal Rptr 2d 16. In a judgment with which
the Chief Justice and all save one member of the Supreme Court of California
concurred, Baxter J observed (at 19):

a   'Proof of causation in such cases will always present inherent practical difficulties, given the long latency period of asbestos-related disease, and the occupational settings that commonly exposed the worker to multiple forms and brands of asbestos products with varying degrees of toxicity. In general, however, no insuperable barriers prevent an asbestos-related cancer plaintiff from demonstrating that exposure to the defendant's asbestos products was,

b   in reasonable medical probability, a substantial factor in causing or contributing to his risk of developing cancer. We conclude that plaintiffs are required to prove no more than this. In particular, they need *not* prove with medical exactitude that fibers from a particular defendant's asbestos-containing products were those, or among those, that actually began the cellular process of malignancy.'

c   Baxter J reviewed earlier cases such as *Summers*'s case and *Sindell*'s case and specifically addressed the factual possibility that a mesothelioma may be caused by inhalation of a single fibre, acknowledging (at 30–31) that the single fibre theory raised an apparently unanswerable question 'which particular fibre or fibres actually caused the cancer to begin forming[?]'. He observed (at 31) that

d   plaintiffs could not be expected to prove the scientifically unknown details of carcinogenesis or trace the unknowable path of a given asbestos fibre. For reasons given very clearly but at some length Baxter J rejected a burden-shifting approach to cases of this kind. The judgment concluded (at 36):

e   'In the context of a cause of action for asbestos-related latent injuries, the plaintiff must first establish some threshold *exposure* to the defendant's defective asbestos-containing products, *and* must further establish in reasonable medical probability that a particular exposure or series of exposures was a "legal cause" of his injury, i.e., a *substantial factor* in bringing about the injury. In an asbestos-related cancer case, the plaintiff need *not*

f   prove that fibers from the defendant's product were the ones, or among the ones, that actually began the process of malignant cellular growth. Instead, the plaintiff may meet the burden of proving that exposure to defendant's product was a substantial factor causing the illness by showing that in reasonable medical probability it was a substantial factor contributing to the plaintiff's or decedent's risk of developing cancer.'

g   The dissent of Mosk J related solely to the court's decision on shifting of the burden: he considered (at 38) that the decision of the majority would deprive numerous plaintiffs suffering from latent diseases caused by exposure to asbestos in the workplace from recovering full compensation.

h   [32] This survey shows, as would be expected, that though the problem underlying cases such as the present is universal the response to it is not. Hence the plethora of decisions given in different factual contexts. Hence also the intensity of academic discussion, exemplified by the articles of the late Professor Fleming ('Probabilistic Causation in Tort Law' 68 Canadian Bar Review, No 4, December 1989, 661) and Professor Robertson ('The Common Sense of Cause in

j   Fact' (1996–1997) 75 Tex L Rev 1765). In some jurisdictions, it appears, the plaintiff would fail altogether on causation grounds, as the Court of Appeal held that the present appellants did. Italy, South Africa and Switzerland may be examples (see *Unification of Tort Law: Causation* (2000) pp 90, 102 and 120). But it appears that in most of the jurisdictions considered the problem of attribution would not, on facts such as those of the present cases, be a fatal objection to a plaintiff's claim. Whether by treating an increase in risk as equivalent to a material

contribution, or by putting a burden on the defendant, or by enlarging the
ordinary approach to acting in concert, or on more general grounds influenced
by policy considerations, most jurisdictions would, it seems, afford a remedy to
the plaintiff. Development of the law in this country cannot of course depend on
a head-count of decisions and codes adopted in other countries around the world,
often against a background of different rules and traditions. The law must be
developed coherently, in accordance with principle, so as to serve, even-handedly,
the ends of justice. If, however, a decision is given in this country which offends
one's basic sense of justice, and if consideration of international sources suggests
that a different and more acceptable decision would be given in most other
jurisdictions, whatever their legal tradition, this must prompt anxious review of
the decision in question. In a shrinking world (in which the employees of
asbestos companies may work for those companies in any one or more of several
countries) there must be some virtue in uniformity of outcome whatever the
diversity of approach in reaching that outcome.

Policy

[33] The present appeals raise an obvious and inescapable clash of policy
considerations. On the one hand are the considerations powerfully put by the
Court of Appeal ([2002] 1 WLR 1052 at [103]) which considered the claimants'
argument to be not only illogical but—

> 'also susceptible of unjust results. It may impose liability for the whole of
> an insidious disease on an employer with whom the claimant was employed
> for quite a short time in a long working life, when the claimant is wholly
> unable to prove on the balance of probabilities that that period of
> employment had any causative relationship with the inception of the
> disease. This is far too weighty an edifice to build on the slender foundations
> of *McGhee v National Coal Board*, and Lord Bridge has told us in *Wilsher v Essex
> Area Health Authority* that *McGhee* established no new principle of law at all.
> If we were to accede to the claimants' arguments, we would be distorting the
> law to accommodate the exigencies of a very hard case. We would be
> yielding to a contention that all those who have suffered injury after being
> exposed to a risk of that injury from which someone else should have
> protected them should be able to recover compensation even when they are
> quite unable to prove who was the culprit. In a quite different context Lord
> Steyn has recently said in [*White v Chief Constable of the South Yorkshire Police*
> [1999] 1 All ER 1 at 30, [1999] 2 AC 455 at 491] that our tort system sometimes
> results in imperfect justice, but it is the best the common law can do.'

The Court of Appeal had in mind that in each of the cases (*Wardlaw's, Nicholson's,
Gardiner's* and *McGhee's* cases) discussed in [14]–[21], above there was only one
employer involved. Thus there was a risk that the defendant might be held liable
for acts for which he should not be held legally liable but no risk that he would be
held liable for damage which (whether legally liable or not) he had not caused.
The crux of cases such as the present, if the appellants' argument is upheld, is that
an employer may be held liable for damage he has not caused. The risk is the
greater where all the employers potentially liable are not before the court. This
is so on the facts of each of the three appeals before the House, and is always likely
to be so given the long latency of this condition and the likelihood that some
employers potentially liable will have gone out of business or disappeared during
that period. It can properly be said to be unjust to impose liability on a party who
has not been shown, even on a balance of probabilities, to have caused the

a damage complained of. On the other hand, there is a strong policy argument in favour of compensating those who have suffered grave harm, at the expense of their employers who owed them a duty to protect them against that very harm and failed to do so, when the harm can only have been caused by breach of that duty and when science does not permit the victim accurately to attribute, as between several employers, the precise responsibility for the harm he has

b suffered. I am of opinion that such injustice as may be involved in imposing liability on a duty-breaking employer in these circumstances is heavily outweighed by the injustice of denying redress to a victim. Were the law otherwise, an employer exposing his employee to asbestos dust could obtain complete immunity against mesothelioma (but not asbestosis) claims by employing only those who had previously been exposed to excessive quantities

c of asbestos dust. Such a result would reflect no credit on the law. It seems to me, as it did to Lord Wilberforce in McGhee's case [1972] 3 All ER 1008 at 1013, [1973] 1 WLR 1 at 7, that—

d 'the employers should be liable for an injury, squarely within the risk which they created and that they, not the pursuer, should suffer the consequence of the impossibility, foreseeably inherent in the nature of his injury, of segregating the precise consequence of their default.'

Conclusion

[34] To the question posed in [2], above, I would answer that where
e conditions (1)–(6) are satisfied C is entitled to recover against both A and B. That conclusion is in my opinion consistent with principle, and also with authority (properly understood). Where those conditions are satisfied, it seems to me just and in accordance with common sense to treat the conduct of A and B in exposing C to a risk to which he should not have been exposed as making a material
f contribution to the contracting by C of a condition against which it was the duty of A and B to protect him. I consider that this conclusion is fortified by the wider jurisprudence reviewed above. Policy considerations weigh in favour of such a conclusion. It is a conclusion which follows even if either A or B is not before the court. It was not suggested in argument that C's entitlement against either A or B should be for any sum less than the full compensation to which C is entitled,
g although A and B could of course seek contribution against each other or any other employer liable in respect of the same damage in the ordinary way. No argument on apportionment was addressed to the House. I would in conclusion emphasise that my opinion is directed to cases in which each of the conditions specified in (1)–(6) of [2], above is satisfied and to no other case. It would be
h unrealistic to suppose that the principle here affirmed will not over time be the subject of incremental and analogical development. Cases seeking to develop the principle must be decided when and as they arise. For the present, I think it unwise to decide more than is necessary to resolve these three appeals which, for all the foregoing reasons, I concluded should be allowed.

j [35] For reasons given above, I cannot accept the view (considered in the opinion of my noble and learned friend Lord Hutton) that the decision in McGhee's case was based on the drawing of a factual inference. Nor, in my opinion, was the decision based on the drawing of a legal inference. Whether, in certain limited and specific circumstances, a legal inference is drawn or a different legal approach is taken to the proof of causation, may not make very much practical difference. But Lord Wilberforce, in one of the passages of his opinion in McGhee's case quoted in [20], above, wisely deprecated resort to fictions and it

seems to me preferable, in the interests of transparency, that the courts' response
to the special problem presented by cases such as these should be stated explicitly.
I prefer to recognise that the ordinary approach to proof of causation is varied
than to resort to the drawing of legal inferences inconsistent with the proven
facts.

LORD NICHOLLS OF BIRKENHEAD.

[36] My Lords, I have no hesitation in agreeing with all your Lordships that
these appeals should be allowed. Any other outcome would be deeply offensive
to instinctive notions of what justice requires and fairness demands. The real
difficulty lies is elucidating in sufficiently specific terms the principle being applied
in reaching this conclusion. To be acceptable the law must be coherent. It must
be principled. The basis on which one case, or one type of case, is distinguished
from another should be transparent and capable of identification. When a
decision departs from principles normally applied, the basis for doing so must be
rational and justifiable if the decision is to avoid the reproach that hard cases
make bad law. I turn therefore to consider the departure from the normal, and
the basis of that departure, in the present appeals.

[37] In the normal way, in order to recover damages for negligence, a plaintiff
must prove that but for the defendant's wrongful conduct he would not have
sustained the harm or loss in question. He must establish at least this degree of
causal connection between his damage and the defendant's conduct before the
defendant will be held responsible for the damage.

[38] Exceptionally this is not so. In some circumstances a lesser degree of
causal connection may suffice. This sometimes occurs where the damage flowed
from one or other of two alternative causes. Take the well-known example
where two hunters, acting independently of each other, fire their guns carelessly
in a wood, and a pellet from one of the guns injures an innocent passer-by. No
one knows, and the plaintiff is unable to prove, from which gun the pellet came.
Should the law of negligence leave the plaintiff remediless, and allow both
hunters to go away scot-free, even though one of them must have fired the
injurious pellet?

[39] Not surprisingly, the courts have declined to reach such an unjust
decision: see *Summers v Tice* (1948) 199 P 2d 1, a decision of the Supreme Court of
California, and *Cook v Lewis* [1951] SCR 830, a decision of the Supreme Court
of Canada. As between the plaintiff and the two hunters, the evidential difficulty
arising from the impossibility of identifying the gun which fired the crucial pellet
should redound upon the negligent hunters, not the blameless plaintiff. The
unattractive consequence, that one of the hunters will be held liable for an injury
he did not in fact inflict, is outweighed by the even less attractive alternative, that
the innocent plaintiff should receive no recompense even though one of the
negligent hunters injured him. It is this balance ('outweighed by') which justifies
a relaxation in the standard of causation required. Insistence on the normal
standard of causation would work an injustice. Hunting in a careless manner and
thereby creating a risk of injury to others, followed by injury to another person,
is regarded by the law as sufficient causal connection in the circumstances to
found responsibility.

[40] This balancing exercise involves a value judgment. This is not at variance
with basic principles in this area of the law. The extent to which the law requires
a defendant to assume responsibility for loss following upon his wrongful
conduct always involves a value judgment. The law habitually *limits* the extent
of the damage for which a defendant is held responsible, even when the damage

a passes the threshold 'but for' test. The converse is also true. On occasions the threshold 'but for' test of causal connection may be over-exclusionary. Where justice so requires, the threshold itself may be lowered. In this way the scope of a defendant's liability may be *extended*. The circumstances where this is appropriate will be exceptional, because of the adverse consequences which the lowering of the threshold will have for a defendant. He will be held responsible

b for a loss the plaintiff might have suffered even if the defendant had not been involved at all. To impose liability on a defendant in such circumstances normally runs counter to ordinary perceptions of responsibility. Normally this is unacceptable. But there are circumstances, of which the two hunters' case is an example, where this unattractiveness is outweighed by leaving the plaintiff without a remedy.

c [41] The present appeals are another example of such circumstances, where good policy reasons exist for departing from the usual threshold 'but for' test of causal connection. Inhalation of asbestos dust carries a risk of mesothelioma. That is one of the very risks from which an employer's duty of care is intended to protect employees. Tragically, each claimant acquired this fatal disease from

d wrongful exposure to asbestos dust in the course of his employment. A former employee's inability to identify which particular period of wrongful exposure brought about the onset of his disease ought not, in all justice, to preclude recovery of compensation.

[42] So long as it was not insignificant, each employer's wrongful exposure of its employee to asbestos dust and, hence, to the risk of contracting mesothelioma,

e should be regarded by the law as a sufficient degree of causal connection. This is sufficient to justify requiring the employer to assume responsibility for causing or materially contributing to the onset of the mesothelioma when, in the present state of medical knowledge, no more exact causal connection is ever capable of being established. Given the present state of medical science, this outcome may

f cast responsibility on a defendant whose exposure of a claimant to the risk of contracting the disease had in fact no causative effect. But the unattractiveness of casting the net of responsibility as widely as this is far outweighed by the unattractiveness of the alternative outcome.

[43] I need hardly add that considerable restraint is called for in any relaxation of the threshold 'but for' test of causal connection. The principle applied on these

g appeals is emphatically not intended to lead to such a relaxation whenever a plaintiff has difficulty, perhaps understandable difficulty, in discharging the burden of proof resting on him. Unless closely confined in its application this principle could become a source of injustice to defendants. There must be good reason for departing from the normal threshold 'but for' test. The reason must

h be sufficiently weighty to justify depriving the defendant of the protection this test normally and rightly affords him, and it must be plain and obvious that this is so. Policy questions will loom large when a court has to decide whether the difficulties of proof confronting the plaintiff justify taking this exceptional course. It is impossible to be more specific.

j [44] I should comment briefly on the much discussed case of *McGhee v National Coal Board* [1972] 3 All ER 1008, [1973] 1 WLR 1. As I understand it, the decision of your Lordships' House is an example of the application of the approach discussed above. In the circumstances of that case the House departed from the usual threshold 'but for' test of causal connection and treated a lesser degree of causal connection as sufficient. The novelty in the decision lay in the adoption of this approach in this country and, further, in the type of claim to which this approach was applied: there, as with the present appeals, the field of industrial

disease. Given the medical evidence in *McGhee*'s case, it was not open to the
House, however robustly inclined, to draw an inference that the employer's
negligence had in fact caused or materially contributed to the onset of the
dermatitis in the sense that, but for that negligence, the dermatitis would not
have occurred. Instead, a less stringent causal connection was regarded as
sufficient. It was enough that the employer had materially increased the risk of
harm to the employee: see [1972] 3 All ER 1008 at 1011, 1013, 1014, 1018, [1973]
1 WLR 1 at 5, 7, 8, 12–13 per Lord Reid, Lord Wilberforce, Lord Simon of Glaisdale
('failure to take steps which would bring about a material reduction of the risk')
and Lord Salmon, respectively.

[45] In an area of the law already afflicted with linguistic ambiguity I myself
would not describe this process of legal reasoning as a 'legal inference' or an
'inference of causation'. This phraseology tends to obscure the fact that when
applying the principle described above the court is not, by a process of inference,
concluding that the ordinary 'but for' standard of causation is satisfied. Instead,
the court is applying a different and less stringent test. It were best if this were
recognised openly.

LORD HOFFMANN.

[46] My Lords, In one of the three appeals before your Lordships, the
appellant Mr Matthews is suffering from a cancer (mesothelioma) caused by
exposure to asbestos. Between 1973 and 1981 he was exposed to substantial
quantities of asbestos dust in the course of successive employments by the two
respondents, Associated Portland Cement and British Uralite. It is accepted that
both employers were in breach of duty—the link between asbestos and cancer
was well known by the mid-1960s—and that both exposures contributed
substantially to the risk that he would contract the disease. But the precise
mechanism by which asbestos causes cancer is unknown. It may be caused by the
mutation of a single cell caused by a single asbestos fibre. At any rate, it is
impossible to say that it was more likely to have been caused by the exposure to
asbestos during employment with the one respondent rather than the other. And
on that ground the Court of Appeal ([2001] EWCA Civ 1881, [2002] 1 WLR 1052)
has held that Mr Matthews' claim must fail. It was said to be a rule of law that in
order to succeed against either respondent, he must prove that, but for its breach
of duty, he would not have contracted the disease. It applied the same rule to the
other two appeals before your Lordships, which raise a similar point.

[47] My Lords, in my opinion the rule applied by the Court of Appeal is not a
correct statement of the causal connection between breach of duty and damage
which the law requires in a case such as this. I think it is sufficient, both on
principle and authority, that the breach of duty contributed substantially to the
risk that the claimant would contract the disease.

[48] I shall first consider the question in principle. It is axiomatic that the law
will not impose liability to pay compensation for damage unless there is a
relevant causal connection between the damage and the defendant's tort, breach
of contract or statutory duty. But what amounts to a relevant causal connection?

[49] Everyone agrees that there is no scientific or philosophical touchstone for
determining the relevant causal connection in any particular case. The relevance
of a causal connection depends upon the purpose of the inquiry. In the present
case, the House is required to say what should be the relevant causal connection
for breach of a duty to protect an employee against the risk of contracting (among
other things) mesothelioma by exposure to asbestos.

[50] It is frequently said that causation is a question of fact or a matter of common sense. Both of these propositions are true but they need to be analysed with some care in order to avoid confusion.

[51] First, in what sense is causation a question of fact? In order to describe something as a question of fact, it is necessary to be able to identify the question. For example, whether someone was negligent or not is a question of fact. What is the question? It is whether he failed to take reasonable care to avoid such damage as a reasonable man would have foreseen might result from his conduct. That question is formulated by the law. It is the law which says that failure to take reasonable care gives rise to liability. And the question is then answered by applying the standard of conduct prescribed by the law to the facts.

[52] The same is true of causation. The question of fact is whether the causal requirements which the law lays down for that particular liability have been satisfied. But those requirements exist by virtue of rules of law. Before one can answer the question of fact, one must first formulate the question. This involves deciding what, in the circumstances of the particular case, the law's requirements are. Unless one pays attention to the need to determine this preliminary question, the proposition that causation is a question of fact may be misleading. It may suggest that one somehow knows instinctively what the question is or that the question is always the same. As we shall see, this is not the case. The causal requirements for liability often vary, sometimes quite subtly, from case to case. And since the causal requirements for liability are always a matter of law, these variations represent legal differences, driven by the recognition that the just solution to different kinds of case may require different causal requirement rules.

[53] Then there is the role of common sense. Of course the causal requirements for liability are normally framed in accordance with common sense. But there is sometimes a tendency to appeal to common sense in order to avoid having to explain one's reasons. It suggests that causal requirements are a matter of incommunicable judicial instinct. I do not think that this is right. It should be possible to give reasons why one form of causal relationship will do in one situation but not in another.

[54] In my opinion, the essential point is that the causal requirements are just as much part of the legal conditions for liability as the rules which prescribe the kind of conduct which attracts liability or the rules which limit the scope of that liability. If I may repeat what I have said on another occasion, one is never simply liable, one is always liable *for* something—to make compensation for damage, the nature and extent of which is delimited by the law. The rules which delimit what one is liable for may consist of causal requirements or may be rules unrelated to causation, such as the foreseebility requirements in the rule in *Hadley v Baxendale* (1854) 9 Exch 341, [1843–60] All ER Rep 461. But in either case they are rules of law, part and parcel of the conditions of liability. Once it is appreciated that the rules laying down causal requirements are not autonomous expressions of some form of logic or judicial instinct but creatures of the law, part of the conditions of liability, it is possible to explain their content on the grounds of fairness and justice in exactly the same way as the other conditions of liability.

[55] In the law of negligence, for example, it has long been recognised that the imposition of a duty of care in respect of particular conduct depends upon whether it is just and reasonable to impose it. Over vast areas of conduct one can generalise about the circumstances in which it will be considered just and reasonable to impose a duty of care: that is a consequence of *Donoghue (or M' Alister) v Stevenson* [1932] AC 562, [1932] All ER Rep 1. But there are still situations in which Lord Atkin's generalisation cannot fairly be applied and in which it is necessary to

return to the underlying principle and inquire whether it would be just and reasonable to impose liability and what its nature and extent should be: see *Caparo Industries plc v Dickman* [1990] 1 All ER 568, [1990] 2 AC 605.

[56] The same is true of causation. The concepts of fairness, justice and reason underlie the rules which state the causal requirements of liability for a particular form of conduct (or non-causal limits on that liability) just as much as they underlie the rules which determine that conduct to be tortious. And the two are inextricably linked together: the purpose of the causal requirement rules is to produce a just result by delimiting the scope of liability in a way which relates to the reasons why liability for the conduct in question exists in the first place.

[57] Across most grounds of liability, whether in tort, contract or by statute, it is possible to generalise about causal requirements. These generalisations are explored in detail by Hart and Honoré *Causation in the Law* (2nd edn, 1985). They represent what in ordinary life would normally be regarded as the reasonable limits for attributing blame or responsibility for harm: for example, that the defendant's conduct was a necessary condition for the occurrence of the harm (the 'but for' test), that it was not caused by the informed and voluntary act of another responsible human being and so on. To that extent, these causal requirements are based upon common sense. But, as Hart and Honoré also point out, there are situations in which these generalisations would fail to give effect to the reasons why it was thought just and reasonable to impose liability. For example, if it is thought just and reasonable to impose a duty to take care to protect someone against harm caused by the informed and voluntary act of another responsible human being, it would be absurd to retain a causal requirement that the harm should not have been so caused. An extreme case of this kind was *Reeves v Metropolitan Police Comr* [1999] 3 All ER 897, [2000] 1 AC 360, in which the defendant accepted that in the circumstances of the case, he owed a duty to take reasonable care to prevent a responsible human being from causing injury to himself. Your Lordships decided that in those circumstances it would be contradictory to hold that the causal requirements of the tort excluded liability for harm so caused. Thus the causal requirements are always adapted to conform to the grounds upon which liability is imposed. Again, it may be said that this is no more than common sense. But it is capable of rational explanation.

[58] The same link between the grounds of liability and the causal requirements can be seen in cases of statutory liability. Sometimes the causal requirements are expressly stated; if not, the courts will construe the statute as requiring the causal connection which best gives effect to its policy. In *Empress Car Co (Abertillery) Ltd v National Rivers Authority* [1998] 1 All ER 481, [1999] 2 AC 22 this House decided that the causal requirements of a statutory duty not to 'cause ... polluting matter ... to enter any controlled waters' did not exclude liability in cases in which the immediate cause of the pollution was the deliberate act of a responsible third party. It based this conclusion on the policy of the statute to impose a strict liability for the protection of the environment.

[59] My Lords, even the much derided 'last opportunity rule' which was applied in cases of contributory negligence before the Law Reform (Contributory Negligence) Act 1945 was in my opinion a perfectly rational attempt by the courts to fashion the causal requirements of the tort of negligence so as best to achieve a just and fair result in a situation in which the law insisted that any contributory negligence was a complete bar to recovery. To say that it was illogical or inelegant seems to me neither here nor there. If it is recognised that the causal requirements are a matter of law and that the last opportunity rule was a development of the common law to mitigate the rigour of the contributory

a   negligence rule, there was nothing illogical about it. As for inelegance, it was the best which could be done in the circumstances.

[60] The problem in this appeal is to formulate a just and fair rule. Clearly the rule must be based upon principle. However deserving the claimants may be, your Lordships are not exercising a discretion to adapt causal requirements to the individual case. That does not mean, however, that it must be a principle so b   broad that it takes no account of significant differences which affect whether it is fair and just to impose liability.

[61] What are the significant features of the present case? First, we are dealing with a duty specifically intended to protect employees against being unnecessarily exposed to the risk of (among other things) a particular disease. Secondly, the duty c   is one intended to create a civil right to compensation for injury relevantly connected with its breach. Thirdly, it is established that the greater the exposure to asbestos, the greater the risk of contracting that disease. Fourthly, except in the case in which there has been only one significant exposure to asbestos, medical science cannot prove whose asbestos is more likely than not to have produced the cell mutation which caused the disease. Fifthly, the employee has contracted the d   disease against which he should have been protected.

[62] In these circumstances, a rule requiring proof of a link between the defendant's asbestos and the claimant's disease would, with the arbitrary exception of single-employer cases, empty the duty of content. If liability depends upon proof that the conduct of the defendant was a necessary condition of the e   injury, it cannot effectively exist. It is however open to your Lordships to formulate a different causal requirement in this class of case. The Court of Appeal was in my opinion wrong to say that in the absence of a proven link between the defendant's asbestos and the disease, there was no 'causative relationship' whatever between the defendant's conduct and the disease. It depends entirely upon the level at which the causal relationship is described. To f   say, for example, that the cause of Mr Matthews' cancer was his significant exposure to asbestos during two employments over a period of eight years, without being able to identify the day upon which he inhaled the fatal fibre, is a meaningful causal statement. The medical evidence shows that it is the only kind of causal statement about the disease which, in the present state of knowledge, a g   scientist would regard as possible. There is no a priori reason, no rule of logic, which prevents the law from treating it as sufficient to satisfy the causal requirements of the law of negligence. The question is whether your Lordships think such a rule would be just and reasonable and whether the class of cases to which it applies can be sufficiently clearly defined.

h   [63] So the question of principle is this: in cases which exhibit the five features I have mentioned, which rule would be more in accordance with justice and the policy of common law and statute to protect employees against the risk of contracting asbestos-related diseases? One which makes an employer in breach of his duty liable for the claimant's injury because he created a significant risk to his health, despite the fact that the physical cause of the injury *may* have been j   created by someone else? Or a rule which means that unless he was subjected to risk by the breach of duty of a single employer, the employee can never have a remedy? My Lords, as between the employer in breach of duty and the employee who has lost his life in consequence of a period of exposure to risk to which that employer has contributed, I think it would be both inconsistent with the policy of the law imposing the duty and morally wrong for your Lordships to impose causal requirements which exclude liability.

[64] My Lords, I turn from principle to authority. The case which most *a*
closely resembles the present is *McGhee v National Coal Board* [1972] 3 All ER 1008,
[1973] 1 WLR 1, which my noble and learned friend Lord Bingham of Cornhill
has analysed in some detail. There too, the employer was under a duty (to
provide washing facilities) specifically intended to protect employees against
being unnecessarily exposed to the risk of (among other things) a particular
disease, namely dermatitis. Secondly, the duty was one intended to create a civil *b*
right to compensation for injury relevantly connected with its breach. Thirdly, it
was established that the longer the workman exerted himself while particles of
dust adhered to his skin, the greater was the risk of his contracting dermatitis.
Fourthly, the mechanism by which dust caused the disease was unknown, so that
medical science was unable to prove whether the particular dust abrasions which
caused the dermatitis were more likely than not to have occurred before or after *c*
the dust would have been removed if washing facilities had been provided. All
that could be said was that the absence of facilities added materially to the risk
that he would contract the disease. Fifthly, the employee contracted the disease
against which he should have been protected.

[65] My Lords, in these circumstances, which in my opinion reproduce the *d*
essential features of the present case, the House decided that materially
increasing the risk that the disease would occur was sufficient to satisfy the causal
requirements for liability. It is true that Lord Wilberforce spoke of reversing the
burden of proof and imposing liability unless the employer could prove that
washing would have made no difference. But I respectfully think that it is *e*
artificial to treat the employer as having a burden of proof in a case in which ex
hypothesi the state of medical knowledge is such that the burden cannot be
discharged. There are also passages in the speeches which suggest that materially
increasing the risk of disease is being treated as equivalent to materially
contributing to the injury—making the illness worse than it would otherwise
have been. But this, as Lord Wilberforce pointed out ([1972] 3 All ER 1008 at *f*
1013, [1973] 1 WLR 1 at 7), is precisely what the doctors did not say. They refused
to say that it was more likely than not that the absence of washing facilities had
had any effect at all. So when some members of the House said that in the
circumstances there was no distinction between materially increasing the risk of
disease and materially contributing to the disease, what I think they meant was *g*
that, in the particular circumstances, a breach of duty which materially increased
the risk should be treated *as if* it had materially contributed to the disease. I
would respecfully prefer not resort to legal fictions and to say that the House
treated a material increase in risk as sufficient in the circumstances to satisfy the
causal requirements for liability. That this was the effect of the decision seems to *h*
me inescapable.

[66] The grounds upon which the House was willing to formulate a special
causal requirements rule in *McGhee's* case seem to me equally applicable in this
case. So Lord Wilberforce said:

'... if one asks which of the parties, the workman or the employers, should *j*
suffer from this inherent evidential difficulty [i.e. the absence of knowledge
of the mechanism by which dust caused the disease], the answer as a matter
of policy or justice should be that it is the creator of the risk who, ex
hypothesi, must be taken to have foreseen the possibility of damage, who
should bear its consequences.' (See [1972] 3 All ER 1008 at 1012, [1973] 1 WLR
1 at 6.)

a   Lord Simon of Glaisdale said:

'To hold otherwise would mean that the respondents were under a legal duty which they could, in the present state of medical knowledge, with impunity ignore.' (See [1972] 3 All ER 1008 at 1015, [1973] 1 WLR 1 at 9.)

Lord Salmon said:
b
'... it would mean that in the present state of medical knowledge and in circumstances such as these (which are by no means uncommon) an employer would be permitted by the law to disregard with impunity his duty to take reasonable care for the safety of his employees.' (See [1972] 3 All ER 1008 at 1018, [1973] 1 WLR 1 at 12.)

c
[67] I therefore regard *McGhee's* case as a powerful support for saying that when the five factors I have mentioned are present, the law should treat a material increase in risk as sufficient to satisfy the causal requirements for liability. The only difficulty lies in the way *McGhee's* case was explained in *Wilsher v Essex Area Health Authority* [1988] 1 All ER 871, [1988] AC 1074. The latter was
d   not a case in which the five factors were present. It was an action for clinical negligence in which it was alleged that giving a premature baby excessive oxygen had caused retrolental fibroplasia, resulting in blindness. The evidence was that the fibroplasia could have been caused in a number of different ways including excessive oxygen but the judge had made no finding that the oxygen was more
e   likely than not to have been the cause. The Court of Appeal ([1986] 3 All ER 801, [1987] QB 730) held that the health authority was nevertheless liable because even if the excessive oxygen could not be shown to have caused the injury, it materially increased the risk of the injury happening.

[68] The Court of Appeal reached this conclusion by treating the causal requirement rule applied in *McGhee's* case as being of general application. Mustill LJ
f   said:

'If it is an established fact that conduct of a particular kind creates a risk that injury will be caused to another or increases an existing risk that injury will ensue, and if the two parties stand in such a relationship that the one party owes a duty not to conduct himself in that way, and if the other party does
g   suffer injury of the kind to which the risk related, then the first party is taken to have caused the injury by his breach of duty, even though the existence and extent of the contribution made by the breach cannot be ascertained.' (See [1986] 3 All ER 801 at 829, [1987] QB 730 at 771–772.)

h   [69] The House of Lords, in a speech by Lord Bridge of Harwich with which all other noble Lords concurred, rejected this broad principle. I would respectfully agree. The principle in *McGhee's* case is far narrower and I have tried to indicate what its limits are likely to be. It is true that actions for clinical negligence notoriously give rise to difficult questions of causation. But it cannot possibly be said that the duty to take reasonable care in treating patients would be virtually
j   drained of content unless the creation of a material risk of injury were accepted as sufficient to satisfy the causal requirements for liability. And the political and economic arguments involved in the massive increase in the liability of the National Health Service which would have been a consequence of the broad rule favoured by the Court of Appeal in *Wilsher's* case are far more complicated than the reasons given by Lord Wilberforce for imposing liability upon an employer who has failed to take simple precautions.

[70] I therefore think that *Wilsher*'s case was correctly decided. The appellants have not made any submission to the contrary. But the grounds upon which *McGhee*'s case was distinguished are unsatisfactory. Lord Bridge said ([1988] 1 All ER 871 at 881–882, [1988] AC 1074 at 1090) that it represented a 'robust and pragmatic approach' to the facts which had enabled the House to draw a 'legitimate inference of fact' that the 'defenders' negligence had materially contributed to the pursuer's injury'. My Lords, however robust or pragmatic the tribunal may be, it cannot draw inferences of fact in the teeth of the undisputed medical evidence. My noble and learned friend Lord Bingham has demonstrated that such an analysis of *McGhee*'s case is untenable.

[71] An alternative ground of distinction is to be found in a passage in the dissenting judgment of Browne-Wilkinson V-C in the Court of Appeal, which was approved by the House. He said that the difference was that in *McGhee*'s case the agent of injury was the same—brick dust—and the only question was whether it happened before or after it should have been washed off. In *Wilsher*'s case, the fibroplasia could have been caused by a number of different agencies.

[72] That distinction would leave the present case on the right side of the line because the agent of injury was the same—asbestos dust. But I do not think it is a principled distinction. What if Mr Matthews had been exposed to two different agents—asbestos dust and some other dust—both of which created a material risk of the same cancer and it was equally impossible to say which had caused the fatal cell mutation? I cannot see why this should make a difference.

[73] The question is how narrowly the principle developed in *McGhee*'s case and applied in this case should be confined. In my opinion, caution is advisable. *Wilsher*'s case shows the dangers of over-generalisation. In *Rutherford v Owens-Illinois Inc* (1997) 67 Cal Rptr 2d 16 the Supreme Court of California, in a valuable and lucid judgment, said that in cases of asbestos-related cancer, the causal requirements of the tort were satisfied by proving that exposure to a particular product was a substantial factor contributing to the 'plaintiff's or decedent's risk of developing cancer' (at 32). That is precisely the rule your Lordships are being invited to apply in this case. The Californian Supreme Court stated the principle specifically in relation to asbestos-related cancer cases. No doubt it could also apply in other cases which were thought to have sufficient common features, but that was left for decision on a case-by-case basis. Likewise I would suggest that the rule now laid down by the House should be limited to cases which have the five features I have described.

[74] That does not mean that the principle is not capable of development and application in new situations. As my noble and learned friend Lord Rodger of Earlsferry has demonstrated, problems of uncertainty as to which of a number of possible agents caused an injury have required special treatment of one kind or another since the time of the Romans. But the problems differ quite widely and the fair and just answer will not always be the same. For example, in the famous case of *Sindell v Abbott Laboratories* (1980) 26 Cal 3d 588 the plaintiff had suffered pre-natal injuries from exposure to a drug which had been manufactured by any one of a potentially large number of defendants. The case bears some resemblance to the present but the problem is not the same. For one thing, the existence of the additional manufacturers did not materially increase the risk of injury. The risk from consuming a drug bought in one shop is not increased by the fact that it can also be bought in another shop. So the case would not fall within the *McGhee*'s case principle. But the Supreme Court of California laid down the imaginative rule that each manufacturer should be liable in proportion to his market share. Cases like this are not before the House and should in my

a view be left for consideration when they arise. For present purposes, the *McGhee* principle is sufficient. I would therefore allow the appeals.

LORD HUTTON.

[75] My Lords, in these three cases the deceased husbands of two of the appellants, Mrs Fox and Mrs Fairchild, contracted the disease of mesothelioma
b from the conditions in which they worked and the disease caused their deaths. The third appellant, Mr Matthews, also contracted that disease from the conditions in which he worked and he is now very gravely ill.

[76] Mesothelioma is caused by the inhalation of tiny fibres of asbestos contained in asbestos dust. The nature of the disease, the way in which it
c develops and the extent of medical knowledge in relation to it, and a description of the working conditions which caused the disease in these three cases are set out in the judgment of my noble and learned friend Lord Bingham of Cornhill and I gratefully adopt that account.

[77] In order for a claimant to recover damages against his employer for injury
d or disease suffered by him he must prove a breach of duty owed to him by his employer and that the breach was a cause of the injury or disease. The defendants have not disputed that they were each in breach of the respective duties which they owed to the husbands of Mrs Fox and Mrs Fairchild and to Mr Matthews. It is the requirement of the law that a claimant must prove causation in order to recover damages which has given rise to the issue in these
e cases. If Mr Fox, Mr Fairchild and Mr Matthews had each been employed throughout their working lives by a single employer each of them (or his widow) would have been entitled to recover damages against that employer. The dispute in these cases arises because Mr Fox, Mr Fairchild and Mr Matthews were each employed by a number of different employers throughout their working lives
f and in the present state of medical knowledge and on the basis of the medical evidence given in the High Court it is possible that the disease suffered by each employee could have been caused solely by the breach of duty of one employer. Accordingly each of the defendants has argued that each claimant cannot establish that it was its breach of duty which was a cause of the disease and that it is as probable as not that the disease was caused by the breach or breaches of
g duty of one or more other employers.

[78] In considering the argument advanced on behalf of the defendants there are two parts of the medical evidence (which did not differ in any material respect between the three cases) which are of particular importance and which are summarised as follows in the agreed statement of facts in the case of Matthews:

h
'5. The risk of mesothelioma increases in proportion to the dose of asbestos received and each successive period of exposure augments the risk that mesothelioma will occur. There is no evidence of a threshold dose below which there is no risk but at low levels of exposure the risk is very small, whereas a lagger with his high level of exposure has a 10% chance of
j dying from mesothelioma. Mesothelioma usually occurs in persons who have inhaled millions of asbestos fibres in the course of their work ...

7. The mechanism by which asbestos causes mesothelioma being unknown, the transformation of a normal mesothelial to a cancerous cell could be due to the action of a single fibre, a few fibres or multiple fibres. It is believed that carcinogenesis of mesothelioma is a multi-stage process involving a sequence of 6 or 7 genetic changes which together result in a

normal mesothelial cell being transformed into a malignant mesothelioma cell. Asbestos is probably involved at one or more stages of this process.'

[79] The claimants rely on the decision of this House in *McGhee v National Coal Board* [1972] 3 All ER 1008, [1973] 1 WLR 1; rvsg 1973 SC(HL) 37 to counter the arguments of the defendants on the issue of causation and submit that they are entitled to succeed by reason of that decision. In that case a workman contracted dermatitis after working in the hot and dusty brick kilns of his employer. The dermatitis was caused by quantities of abrasive brick dust adhering to his skin softened by sweating, and exertion would cause the dust to injure the horny layer exposing the tender cells below to injury or infection from which dermatitis would develop. Washing was the only practicable way of removing the danger, and if the skin was not thoroughly washed as soon as the workman ceased work the process could continue for some considerable time. The workman, cycling home caked with sweat and dust, was liable to further injury until he could wash himself thoroughly.

[80] The Lord Ordinary found that there was no breach of duty by the employer in requiring the pursuer to work in the hot and dusty brick kilns, but that there was a breach of duty in failing to provide a shower for him to use after his work. On the issue of causation the pursuer's doctor said in evidence that he could not say that the provision of showers would probably have prevented the dermatitis. He said that showers would have reduced the risk materially but he would not go further than that. On this evidence the Lord Ordinary found that the pursuer had failed to prove that the breach of duty had caused the dermatitis and he held that he could not succeed if the only inference from the evidence was that lack of shower baths was a possibility as a cause of his having contracted the disease. His decision was upheld by the First Division, the Lord President stating that risk of dermatitis and causation of dermatitis are two quite separate matters.

[81] On appeal to this House the pursuer relied on the decision of the House in *Bonnington Castings Ltd v Wardlaw* [1956] 1 All ER 615, [1956] AC 613 where it was held that if there are two causes of the disease each materially contributing to it such as dust from two sources, and the defendant company is responsible for only one of them, it is liable notwithstanding that the dust for which it was responsible was not in itself sufficient to cause the disease. Part of the pursuer's argument is reported at 1973 SC(HL) 37 at 51:

> 'Reliance was placed on *Wardlaw v Bonnington Castings* ([1956] 1 All ER 615, [1956] AC 613) and *Nicholson v Atlas Steel Foundry and Engineering Co* ([1957] 1 All ER 776, [1957] 1 WLR 613). The dicta in these cases were followed in *Gardiner v Motherwell Machinery and Scrap Co* ([1961] 3 All ER 831, [1961] 1 WLR 1424) which applied the principles of the two earlier cases. Where there were a number of contributory factors to an injury, it was enough to bring the case within the dicta if the employers were guilty in relation to one.'

The defender sought to distinguish *Wardlaw's* case by arguing that in that case every particle of dust inhaled played its part in causing the onset of the disease whereas in the case of *McGhee's* case the disease might have been started by a single abrasion.

[82] In considering this point Lord Reid stated in his speech ([1972] 3 All ER 1008 at 1010, [1973] 1 WLR 1 at 4) that the evidence did not show how the dermatitis began. It might be a necessary precondition for the onset of the disease that there should be an accumulation of minor abrasions of the skin, or it might

a be that the disease started at one particular abrasion and then spread, so that multiplication of abrasions merely increased the number of places where the disease could start and in that way increased the risk of its occurrence. Lord Reid stated that he could not hold that it was probable that an accumulation of minor abrasions was a necessary precondition; if this had been proved the case would have been indistinguishable from *Wardlaw*'s case. He then stated:

b 'But I think that in cases like this we must take a broader view of causation. The medical evidence is to the effect that the fact that the man had to cycle home caked with grime and sweat added materially to the risk that this disease might develop. It does not and could not explain just why that is so. But experience shews that it is so. Plainly that must be because what happens while the man remains unwashed can have a causative effect, although just how the cause operates is uncertain. I cannot accept the view expressed in the Inner House that once the man left the brick kiln he left behind the causes which made him liable to develop dermatitis. That seems to me quite inconsistent with a proper interpretation of the medical evidence. Nor can I accept the distinction drawn by the Lord Ordinary between materially increasing the risk that the disease will occur and making a material contribution to its occurrence. There may be some logical ground for such a distinction where our knowledge of all the material factors is complete. But it has often been said that the legal concept of causation is not based on logic or philosophy. It is based on the practical way in which the ordinary man's mind works in the every-day affairs of life. From a broad and practical viewpoint I can see no substantial difference between saying that what the respondents did materially increased the risk of injury to the appellant and saying that what the respondents did made a material contribution to his injury.' (See [1972] 3 All ER 1008 at 1011, [1973] 1 WLR 1 at 4–5.)

f [83] Lord Wilberforce stated:

'My Lords, I agree with the judge below to the extent that merely to show that a breach of duty increases the risk of harm is not, in abstracto, enough to enable the pursuer to succeed. He might, on this basis, still be met by successful defences. Thus, it was open to the respondents, while admitting, or being unable to contest that their failure had increased the risk, to prove, if they could, as they tried to do, that the appellant's dermatitis was "non-occupational". But the question remains whether a pursuer must necessarily fail if, after he has shown a breach of duty, involving an increase of risk of disease, he cannot positively prove that this increase of risk caused or materially contributed to the disease while his employers cannot positively prove the contrary. In this intermediate case there is an appearance of logic in the view that the pursuer, on whom the onus lies, should fail—a logic which dictated the judgments below. The question is whether we should be satisfied in factual situations like the present, with this logical approach. In my opinion, there are further considerations of importance. First, it is a sound principle that where a person has, by breach of duty of care, created a risk, and injury occurs within the area of that risk, the loss should be borne by him unless he shows that it had some other cause. Secondly, from the evidential point of view, one may ask, why should a man who is able to show that his employer should have taken certain precautions, because without them there is a risk, or an added risk, of injury

or disease, and who in fact sustains exactly that injury or disease, have to
assume the burden of proving more: namely, that it was the addition to the
risk, caused by the breach of duty, which caused or materially contributed to
the injury? In many cases of which the present is typical, this is impossible to
prove, just because honest medical opinion cannot segregate the causes of an
illness between compound causes. And if one asks which of the parties, the
workman or the employers should suffer from this inherent evidential
difficulty, the answer as a matter in policy or justice should be that it is the
creator of the risk who, ex hypothesi, must be taken to have foreseen the
possibility of damage, who should bear its consequences.' (See [1972] 3 All
ER 1008 at 1012, [1973] 1 WLR 1 at 6.)

[84] Lord Simon of Glaisdale stated:

'But *Bonnington Castings Ltd v Wardlaw* and *Nicholson v Atlas Steel Foundry &*
Engineering Co Ltd ([1957] 1 All ER 776, [1957] 1 WLR 613) establish, in my
view, that where an injury is caused by two (or more) factors operating
cumulatively, one (or more) of which factors is a breach of duty and one (or
more) is not so, in such a way that it is impossible to ascertain the proportion
in which the factors were effective in producing the injury or which factor
was decisive, the law does not require a pursuer or plaintiff to prove the
impossible, but holds that he is entitled to damages for the injury if he proves
on a balance of probabilities that the breach or breaches of duty contributed
substantially to causing the injury. If such factors so operate cumulatively, it
is, in my judgment, immaterial whether they do so concurrently or
successively. The question, then, is whether on the evidence the appellant
brought himself within this rule. In my view, a failure to take steps which
would bring about a material reduction of the risk involves, in this type of
case, a substantial contribution to the injury. In this type of case a stark
distinction between breach of duty and causation is unreal. If the provision
of shower baths was (as the evidence showed) a precaution which any
reasonable employer in the respondents' position would take, it means that
such employer should have foreseen that failure to take the precaution
would, more probably than not, substantially contribute towards injury; this
is sufficient prima facie evidence.' (See [1972] 3 All ER 1008 at 1014, [1973] 1
WLR 1 at 8.)

[85] Lord Kilbrandon stated:

'In the present case, the appellant's body was vulnerable, while he was
bicycling home, to the dirt which had been deposited on it during his
working hours. It would not have been if he had had a shower. If showers
had been provided he would have used them. It is admittedly more probable
that disease will be contracted if a shower is not taken. In these
circumstances I cannot accept the argument that nevertheless it is not more
probable than not that, if the duty to provide a shower had been neglected,
he would not have contracted the disease. The appellant has, after all, only
to satisfy the court of a probability, not to demonstrate an irrefragable chain
of causation, which in a case of dermatitis, in the present state of medical
knowledge, he could probably never do.' (See [1972] 3 All ER 1008 at 1016,
[1973] 1 WLR 1 at 10.)

[86] Lord Salmon stated:

> 'In the circumstances of the present case it seems to me unrealistic and contrary to ordinary common sense to hold that the negligence which materially increased the risk of injury did not materially contribute to causing the injury.' (See [1972] 3 All ER 1008 at 1017, [1973] 1 WLR 1 at 11–12.)

And:

> 'In the circumstances of the present case, the possibility of a distinction existing between (a) having materially increased the risk of contracting the disease, and (b) having materially contributed to causing the disease may no doubt be a fruitful source of interesting academic discussions between students of philosophy. Such a distinction is, however, far too unreal to be recognised by the common law.' (See [1972] 3 All ER 1008 at 1018, [1973] 1 WLR 1 at 12–13.)

[87] In *Wilsher v Essex Area Health Authority* [1988] 1 All ER 871, [1988] AC 1074 the plaintiff was born prematurely and due to the negligence of a doctor excessive amounts of oxygen were administered to him. The plaintiff developed retrolental fibroplasia, a condition of the eyes, which resulted in blindness. The administration of the excessive amounts of oxygen was a possible cause of the retrolental fibroplasia but there were a number of other possible causes of the condition which were in no way related to the negligence of the doctor. At first instance the judge gave judgment for the plaintiff and awarded damages. The defendant appealed and the appeal was dismissed by the Court of Appeal (Mustill and Glidewell LJJ, Browne-Wilkinson V-C dissenting). Mustill LJ recognised that the case differed from *McGhee*'s case in that in the latter case there was only one risk operating, which was that the contact of brick dust with a sweaty skin would lead to dermatitis, whereas in *Wilsher*'s case there was a list of risk factors, any one of which might have caused the injury. However he came to the conclusion that the approach taken in *McGhee*'s case could be adopted in the case before him and stated:

> 'Reading all the speeches together, the principle applied by the House of Lords seems to me to amount to this. If it is an established fact that conduct of a particular kind creates a risk that injury will be caused to another or increases an existing risk that injury will ensue, and if the two parties stand in such a relationship that the one party owes a duty not to conduct himself in that way, and if one party does conduct himself in that way, and if the other party does suffer injury of the kind to which the injury related, then the first party is taken to have caused the injury by his breach of duty, even though the existence and extent of the contribution made by the breach cannot be ascertained. If this is the right analysis, it seems to me that the shape taken by the enhancement of the risk ought not to be of crucial significance. In *McGhee* the conduct of the employers made it more likely that the pursuer would contract dermatitis, and he did contract dermatitis. Here, the conduct of those for whom the defendants are liable made it more likely that Martin would contract RLF, and he did contract RLF. If considerations of justice demanded that the pursuer succeed in the one case, I can see no reason why the plaintiff should not succeed in the other.' (See [1986] 3 All ER 801 at 829, [1987] QB 730 at 771–772.)

[88] In his dissenting judgment Browne-Wilkinson V-C stated:

'The position, to my mind, is wholly different from that in *McGhee*, where there was only one candidate (brick dust) which could have caused the dermatitis, and the failure to take a precaution against brick dust causing dermatitis was followed by dermatitis caused by brick dust. In such a case, I can see the common sense, if not the logic, of holding that, in the absence of any other evidence, the failure to take the precaution caused or contributed to the dermatitis. To the extent that certain members of the House of Lords decided the question on inferences from evidence or presumptions, I do not consider that the present case falls within their reasoning. A failure to take preventive measures against one out of five possible causes is no evidence as to which of those five caused the injury.' (See [1986] 3 All ER 801 at 835, [1987] QB 730 at 779.)

[89] The defendant appealed to this House and the appeal was allowed ([1988] 1 All ER 871, [1988] AC 1074). The ground on which the appeal was allowed was the ground stated by Browne-Wilkinson V-C in his dissenting judgment, and in his speech with which the other members of the House concurred, Lord Bridge of Harwich ([1988] 1 All ER 871 at 881–882, 883, [1988] AC 1074 at 1090, 1091) set out the relevant passage in the judgment of Browne-Wilkinson V-C and stated that he was quite unable to find any fault with it.

[90] The House also considered the passages in the speech of Lord Wilberforce in *McGhee's* case [1972] 3 All ER 1008 at 1012–1013, [1973] 1 WLR 1 at 6–7 which the House considered constituted a reversal of the burden of proof. Lord Bridge stated:

'My Lords, it seems to me that both these paragraphs, particularly in the words I have emphasised, amount to saying that, in the circumstances, the burden of proof of causation is reversed and thereby to run counter to the unanimous and emphatic opinions expressed in *Bonnington Castings Ltd v Wardlaw* [1956] 1 All ER 615, [1956] AC 613 to the contrary effect. I find no support in any of the other speeches for the view that the burden of proof is reversed and, in this respect, I think Lord Wilberforce's reasoning must be regarded as expressing a minority opinion.' (See [1988] 1 All ER 871 at 879, [1988] AC 1074 at 1087.)

[91] In his speech Lord Bridge also stated that in his opinion the decision of Lord Reid, Lord Simon, Lord Kilbrandon and Lord Salmon was based on the drawing of an inference. He said:

'A distinction is, of course, apparent between the facts of *Bonnington Castings Ltd v Wardlaw* where the "innocent" and "guilty" silica dust particles which together caused the pursuer's lung disease were inhaled concurrently and the facts of *McGhee v National Coal Board* where the "innocent" and "guilty" brick dust was present on the pursuer's body for consecutive periods. In the one case the concurrent inhalation of "innocent" and "guilty" dust must both have contributed to the cause of the disease. In the other case the consecutive periods when "innocent" and "guilty" brick dust was present on the pursuer's body may both have contributed to the cause of the disease or, theoretically at least, one or other may have been the sole cause. But where the layman is told by the doctors that the longer the brick dust remains on the body, the greater the risk of dermatitis, although the doctors cannot identify the process of causation scientifically, there seems to be

a

nothing irrational in drawing the inference, as a matter of common sense, that the consecutive periods when brick dust remained on the body probably contributed cumulatively to the causation of the dermatitis. I believe that a process of inferential reasoning on these general lines underlies the decision of the majority in *McGhee*'s case.' (See [1988] 1 All ER 871 at 879–880, [1988] AC 1074 at 1087–1088.)

b

After citing passages from the four speeches he said:

'The conclusion I draw from these passages is that *McGhee v National Coal Board* laid down no new principle of law whatever. On the contrary, it affirmed the principle that the onus of proving causation lies on the pursuer or plaintiff. Adopting a robust and pragmatic approach to the undisputed
c
primary facts of the case, the majority concluded that it was a legitimate inference of fact that the defenders' negligence had materially contributed to the pursuer's injury. The decision, in my opinion, is of no greater significance than that and the attempt to extract from it some esoteric principle which in some way modifies, as a matter of law, the nature of the
d
burden of proof of causation which a plaintiff or pursuer must discharge once he has established a relevant breach of duty is a fruitless one.' (See [1988] 1 All ER 871 at 881–882, [1988] AC 1074 at 1090.)

[**92**] Mr Stewart QC, in an impressive argument on behalf of two of the defendants, advanced submissions which I summarise as follows. (1) The
e
fundamental principle of English law in relation to industrial injury cases which has been constantly followed and applied by this House is that stated by Lord Reid in *Bonnington Castings Ltd v Wardlaw* [1956] 1 All ER 615 at 618, [1956] AC 613 at 620:

'It would seem obvious in principle that a pursuer or plaintiff must prove
f
not only negligence or breach of duty but also that such fault caused, or materially contributed to, his injury, and there is ample authority for that proposition both in Scotland and in England. I can find neither reason nor authority for the rule being different where there is breach of a statutory duty. The fact that Parliament imposes a duty for the protection of employees has been held to entitle an employee to sue if he is injured as a
g
result of a breach of that duty, but it would be going a great deal further to hold that it can be inferred from the enactment of a duty that Parliament intended that any employee suffering injury can sue his employer merely because there was a breach of duty and it is shown to be possible that his injury may have been caused by it. In my judgment, the employee must, in
h
all cases, prove his case by the ordinary standard of proof in civil actions; he must make it appear at least that, on a balance of probabilities, the breach of duty caused, or materially contributed to, his injury.'

(2) *Wardlaw*'s case was a case where the inhalation of 'innocent' and 'guilty' dust contributed cumulatively over a period of time to the pursuer's lung disease, and
j
therefore the inhalation of the 'guilty' dust was properly regarded as making a material contribution to the disease. Mr Stewart submitted that *McGhee*'s case was also a case where it was established that there had been a cumulative causative process because the 'innocent' and 'guilty' brick dust had been present on the pursuer's body for consecutive periods. In support of this submission he relied on the passage in Lord Bridge's speech in *Wilsher*'s case [1988] 1 All ER 871 at 879, [1988] AC 1074 at 1087–1088, where he referred to the cumulative

contribution to the causation of the dermatitis. He further submitted that the present case was not governed by the decision in *McGhee's* case because in this case the medical evidence was that it was as probable as not that the onset of the disease was not due to a cumulative process occurring during the entire period when an employee was employed by different employers but was due to the inhalation of a single fibre or a number of fibres during the course of employment with only one employer. (3) This House held in *Wilsher's* case that the decision in *McGhee's* case had not laid down a new principle of law that proof of a material increase in risk constitutes proof of causation: rather the decision was based on the robust drawing of an inference. But in the present case it was not open to draw such an inference because the medical evidence established that it was as likely as not that the cause of the onset of the disease was the inhalation of a single fibre or a small number of fibres. (4) If this House were to hold that the decision in *McGhee's* case laid down a principle of law that proof of a material increase of risk constitutes proof of causation, such a decision would reverse the burden of proof contrary to the decision in *Wardlaw's* case where the House overruled the decision of the Court of Appeal in *Vyner v Waldenberg Bros Ltd* [1945] 2 All ER 547, [1946] KB 50 that the onus is on an employer to show that the breach of a safety regulation was not the cause of an accident. Moreover if the House were to hold that there was such a principle of law, it would not be possible to confine the principle to cases such as the present ones where there is only one possible cause, and the principle would be extended to cases of medical negligence (as was done by the Court of Appeal in *Wilsher's* case) and to other cases.

[93] I do not accept Mr Stewart's submission that *McGhee's* case was a case where there was a cumulative process analogous to that in *Wardlaw's* case, and that the present case is not governed by *McGhee's* case and is distinguishable from it because in this case it was as probable as not that the disease developed from the inhalation of one fibre or a small number of fibres. Lord Reid stated in his speech in *McGhee's* case [1972] 3 All ER 1008 at 1010, [1973] 1 WLR 1 at 4 that whilst it was possible that the pursuer's disease started with an accumulation of minor abrasions this was not proved and that it was possible that the disease started at one particular abrasion. Therefore it is clear that Lord Reid held that the defender was liable even if the onset of the disease had not been due to an accumulation of abrasions but had started at one particular abrasion.

[94] My Lords, I consider that the question whether the decision in *McGhee's* case was based on an inference raises an issue of some difficulty. There does not appear to be a clear statement in the speeches that the House was formulating a new principle of law rather than basing its decision on an inference from the evidence. The case was one in which there was no real conflict between the medical witnesses and therefore the House was in as good a position to evaluate the evidence and to come to a factual conclusion on causation as were the trial judge and the Inner House: see *Benmax v Austin Motor Co Ltd* [1955] 1 All ER 326 at 329, [1955] AC 370 at 376 per Lord Reid. Moreover the issue of causation is one to be decided ultimately by the tribunal of fact and not by the medical witnesses (see *Sentilles v Inter-Caribbean Shipping Corp* (1959) 361 US 107 cited in [100], below), although the tribunal of fact must give proper weight to their opinions.

[95] Although at the commencement of his speech Lord Reid said ([1972] 3 All ER 1008 at 1009, [1973] 1 WLR 1 at 3) that the allegation that the defender was at fault in not providing adequate washing facilities 'raises a difficult question of law', there are other passages in the speeches which I think can be read as pointing to the decision being based on the drawing of an inference.

[96] Lord Simon, referring to *Wardlaw*'s case and *Nicholson v Atlas Steel Foundry & Engineering Co Ltd* [1957] 1 All ER 776, [1957] 1 WLR 613, said:

'... the law does not require a pursuer or plaintiff to prove the impossible, but holds that he is entitled to damages for the injury *if he proves on a balance of probabilities* that the breach or breaches of duty contributed substantially to causing the injury ... The question, then, is whether *on the evidence* the appellant brought himself within this rule. In my view, a failure to take steps which would bring about a material reduction of the risk involves, in this type of case, a substantial contribution to the injury. In this type of case a stark distinction between breach of duty and causation is unreal. If the provision of shower baths was (as the evidence showed) a precaution which any reasonable employer in the respondents' position would take, it means that such employer should have foreseen that failure to take the precaution would, more probably than not, substantially contribute towards injury; *this is sufficient prima facie evidence.*' (See [1972] 3 All ER 1008 at 1014, [1973] 1 WLR 1 at 8; my emphasis.)

It is also relevant to note that at the conclusion of his speech ([1972] 3 All ER 1008 at 1014–1015, [1973] 1 WLR 1 at 9) Lord Simon cited with approval the decision in *Gardiner v Motherwell Machinery and Scrap Co Ltd* [1961] 3 All ER 831, [1961] 1 WLR 1424 where Lord Reid stated:

'In my opinion, when a man who has not previously suffered from a disease contracts that disease after being subjected to conditions likely to cause it, and when he shows that it starts in a way typical of disease caused by such conditions, he establishes a prima facie presumption that his disease was caused by those conditions. I think that the facts proved in this case do establish such a presumption. That presumption could be displaced in many ways.' (See [1961] 3 All ER 831 at 832–833, [1961] 1 WLR 1424 at 1429.)

In my opinion in the context of *Gardiner*'s case and *McGhee*'s case there is little, if any, difference between a prima facie presumption and an inference.

[97] Lord Kilbrandon said:

'The appellant has, after all, only to satisfy the court of a probability, not to demonstrate an irrefragable chain of causation, which in a case of dermatitis, in the present state of medical knowledge, he could probably never do.' (See [1972] 3 All ER 1008 at 1016, [1973] 1 WLR 1 at 10.)

And Lord Salmon said:

'In the circumstances of the present case it seems to me unrealistic and contrary to ordinary common sense to hold that the negligence which materially increased the risk of injury did not materially contribute to causing the injury.' (See [1972] 3 All ER 1008 at 1017, [1973] 1 WLR 1 at 11–12.)

I incline to the view that these statements by Lord Simon, Lord Kilbrandon and Lord Salmon point more to the drawing of an inference in a commonsense way from the evidence than to the formulation of a principle of law.

[98] In *Hotson v East Berkshire Area Health Authority* [1987] 2 All ER 909, [1987] AC 750, Lord Mackay of Clashfern (who was counsel for the defender in *McGhee*) referring to that case, said:

'... the decision of this House may be taken as holding that in the circumstances of that case it was reasonable to infer that there was a relationship between contraction of dermatitis in these conditions and the absence of washing facilities and therefore it was reasonable to hold that absence of washing facilities was likely to have made a material contribution to the causation of the dermatitis.' (See [1987] 2 All ER 909 at 916, [1987] AC 750 at 786.)

[99] It is clear that this House in *Wilsher*'s case considered that a new principle of law was not laid down in *McGhee*'s case and that the decision of the majority was based on the drawing of an inference from the evidence in a robust and commonsense way. And in the Court of Appeal ([1986] 3 All ER 801 at 835, [1987] QB 730 at 779) Browne-Wilkinson V-C said:

'To the extent that certain members of the House of Lords decided the question on inferences from evidence or presumptions, I do not consider that the present case falls within their reasoning.'

[100] In describing in *Wilsher*'s case the manner in which, in his opinion, the House drew an inference in *McGhee*'s case, Lord Bridge said:

'But where the layman is told by the doctors that the longer the brick dust remains on the body, the greater the risk of dermatitis, although the doctors cannot identify the process of causation scientifically, there seems to be nothing irrational in drawing the inference, as a matter of common sense, that the consecutive periods when brick dust remained on the body probably contributed cumulatively to the causation of the dermatitis.' (See [1988] 1 All ER 871 at 880, [1988] AC 1074 at 1088.)

I consider that this approach, whereby the layman applying broad common sense draws an inference which the doctors as scientific witnesses are not prepared to draw, is one which is permissible. In the United States Supreme Court in *Sentilles v Inter-Caribbean Shipping Corp* (1959) 361 US 107 at 109 Brennan J stated:

'The jury's power to draw the inference that the aggravation of petitioner's tubercular condition, evident so shortly after the accident, was in fact caused by that accident, was not impaired by the failure of any medical witness to testify that it was in fact the cause. Neither can it be impaired by the lack of medical unanimity as to the respective likelihood of the potential causes of the aggravation, or by the fact that other potential causes of the aggravation existed and were not conclusively negated by the proofs. The matter does not turn on the use of a particular form of words by the physicians in giving their testimony. The members of the jury, not the medical witnesses, were sworn to make a legal determination of the question of causation.'

[101] It is apparent from his judgment in the action brought by Mr Matthews in which he found that the breaches of duty by the defendants caused his mesothelioma that Mitting J based his decision on an inference from the evidence. He referred to the judgment of Lord Bridge in *Wilsher*'s case and stated:

'Adopting that robust approach, my firm conclusion in this case is that the claimant's exposure to asbestos fibres in the employment of the two defendants, did materially contribute to, and so cause his mesothelioma. I reach that conclusion by a simple, direct process of reasoning, readily understandable to a layman. The claimant was exposed by each defendant and by both defendants, to asbestos fibres, in quantities sufficient greatly to increase his risk of contracting mesothelioma, on the evidence of Dr Rudd, by up to a thousand times the general population risk. They owed him statutory and common law duties to take steps to minimise that risk. They failed to do so. He contracted the very disease against which it was their duty to take those steps. In those circumstances, like Lord Reid in *McGhee*'s case, I can see no substantial difference between saying that what the defendant did materially increased the risk of injury to the claimant and saying that what the defendants did made a material contribution to his injury. It seems to me wholly artificial to require a claimant to prove which fibre, or fibres, inhaled in whose employment in precisely what circumstances, caused or set off or contributed to the process by which one or more mesothelial cells became malignant. In principle, it is just as artificial as requiring proof in a case in which a pool of liquid, collected from separate sources, has caused injury, of precisely which molecule was the mechanical cause of injury. Even though the precise mechanism by which the claimant's mesothelioma was caused or set off cannot be established, those conclusions point, inexorably, to the finding that the defendants' breaches of duty materially contributed to his contracting the disease. In other words, the evidence which I have heard proves, on the balance of probabilities, that their breach of duty caused his injury.'

[102] The courts in Canada have taken the view that the majority decision in *McGhee*'s case was based on an inference. In *Snell v Farrell* (1990) 72 DLR (4th) 289 Sopinka J, in delivering the judgment of the Supreme Court, stated (at 296) with reference to *McGhee*'s case:

'Two theories of causation emerge from an analysis of the speeches of the Lords in this case. The first, firmly espoused by Lord Wilberforce, is that the plaintiff need only prove that the defendant created a risk of harm and that the injury occurred within the area of the risk. The second is that in these circumstances, an inference of causation was warranted in that there is no practical difference between materially contributing to the risk of harm and materially contributing to the harm itself.'

[103] The judgment of Lambert JA in the British Columbia Court of Appeal in *Haag v Marshall* (1989) 61 DLR (4th) 371 contains, in my respectful opinion, an illuminating discussion of the decision in *McGhee*'s case. He stated (at 378–379):

'*McGhee v. National Coal Board* was considered by the House of Lords in *Kay v. Ayrshire and Arran Health Board* [1987] 2 All ER 417; *Hotson v. East Berkshire Area Health Authority* ([1987] 2 All ER 909, [1987] AC 750), and *Wilsher v. Essex Area Health Authority* ([1988] 1 All ER 871, [1988] AC 1074). It is clear from those decisions that *McGhee* is not now, and never was, authority for the legally adventurous proposition that if a breach of duty is shown, and damage is proven within the area of risk that brought about the duty, and if the breach of duty materially increases the risk of damage of that type, then the onus of proof shifts from the plaintiff to the defendant to disprove the causal connection. That proposition could be derived only from the speech of Lord Wilberforce and it is now clear that it was never a binding principle emerging from the *McGhee* case. But *McGhee* remains a worthwhile study. And there is a somewhat more cautious principle underlying the decision in that case. However, it is not an "onus" principle but an "inference" principle ... The "inference" principle derived from *McGhee*, and from the three

Canadian cases to which I have referred, is this: Where a breach of duty has occurred, and damage is shown to have arisen within the area of risk which brought the duty into being, and where the breach of duty materially increased the risk that damage of that type would occur, and where it is impossible, in a practical sense, for either party to lead evidence which would establish either that the breach of duty caused the loss or that it did not, then it is permissible to infer, as a matter of legal, though not necessarily logical, inference, that the material increase in risk arising from the breach of duty constituted a material contributing cause of the loss and as such a foundation for a finding of liability ... Whether the inference of causation should in fact be made in any particular case depends on whether it is in accordance with common sense and justice in that case to say that the breach of duty which materially increased the risk ought reasonably to be considered as having materially contributed to the loss.'

[104] Courts in Australia have also taken the view that the decision in *McGhee's* case was arrived at on the basis of an inference. In the Supreme Court of South Australia in *Birkholtz v R J Gilbertson Pty Ltd* (1985) 38 SASR 121 at 130 King CJ stated:

'Has the failure to take those precautions been shown to have caused or materially contributed to the contracting of the disease by the appellant? It might be argued as a matter of strict logic, that the fact that given precautions would substantially diminish the risk, does not prove that failure to take those precautions materially contributed to the appellant's infection unless it can be established how that infection occurred. But the law's view of causation is less concerned with logical and philosophical considerations than with the need to produce a just result to the parties involved. Where a defendant is under a legal duty to take precautions to protect the plaintiff from the risk of contracting disease, and, by omitting those precautions, he substantially increases the risk of the plaintiff contracting that disease, the law treats that increase in risk as a sufficient basis, in the absence of evidence showing how the infection occurred, for an inference that the omission of the precautions materially contributed to the contracting of the disease. Justice requires such an approach to the problem of causation and it is the approach which was taken by the House of Lords in *McGhee v National Coal Board*.'

[105] Another illuminating discussion of the proper approach to the issue of causation where a claimant seeks to recover damages for an asbestos-related cancer is contained in the judgment of Baxter J in the Supreme Court of California (with which the majority of the court agreed) in *Rutherford v Owens-Illinois Inc* (1997) 67 Cal Rptr 2d 16 at 32 where he stated:

'In refining the concept of legal cause we must also ensure that the triers of fact in asbestos-related cancer cases know the precise contours of the plaintiff's burden. The generally applicable standard instructions on causation are insufficient for this purpose. Those instructions tell the jury that every "substantial factor in bringing about an injury" is a legal cause (BAJI No. 3.76), even when more than one such factor "contributes concurrently as a cause of the injury" (BAJI No. 3.77). They say nothing, however, to inform the jury that, in asbestos-related cancer cases, a particular asbestos-containing product is deemed to be a substantial factor in bringing about the injury if its contribution to the plaintiff or decedent's *risk* or *probability* of developing cancer was substantial. Without such guidance, a juror might well conclude that the plaintiff needed to prove that fibers from the defendant's product were a substantial factor *actually contributing* to the development of the plaintiff's or decedent's cancer. In many cases, such a burden will be medically impossible to sustain, even with the greatest possible effort by the plaintiff, because of irreducible uncertainty regarding the cellular formation of an asbestos-related cancer. We therefore hold that, in the trial of an asbestos-related cancer case, although no instruction "shifting the burden of proof as to causation" to defendant is warranted, the jury should be told that the plaintiff's or decedent's exposure to a particular product was a substantial factor in causing or bringing about the disease if in reasonable medical probability it was a substantial factor contributing to plaintiff's or decedent's *risk* of developing cancer.'

[106] As I have stated, I think that there is no clear statement in the speeches in *McGhee*'s case as to the underlying basis of the decision. The preponderance of subsequent judicial opinion has been that the decision was based on an inference from the facts. On the evidence before it in *McGhee*'s case I think that the House was entitled to draw an inference in the way described by Lord Bridge in *Wilsher*'s case. But some authorities suggest that in cases where the claimant can prove that a breach of duty materially increased the risk of the contraction of a particular disease and the disease occurred, the law should treat this as giving rise to the inference that the breach of duty was a cause of the disease rather than that the judge as the tribunal of fact should draw a factual inference. I think this was the view of Lambert JA in *Haag v Marshall* when he said ((1989) 61 DLR (4th) 371 at 379) 'it is permissible to infer, as a matter of legal, though not necessarily logical, inference, that the material increase in risk arising from the breach of duty constituted a material contributing cause of the loss'. I think that King CJ was expressing the same view when he said in *Birkholtz v RJ Gilbertson Pty Ltd* (1985) 38 SASR 121 at 130 that 'the law treats that increase in risk as a sufficient basis, in the absence of evidence showing how the infection occurred, for an inference that the omission of the precautions materially contributed to the contracting of the disease'.

[107] A rule that such a legal inference should or can arise is, in effect, a principle of law. I consider that such a rule is virtually indistinguishable from the approach of the Supreme Court of California in *Rutherford*'s case where Baxter J stated that a jury should be directed that—

'a particular asbestos-containing product is *deemed* to be a substantial factor in bringing about the injury if its contribution to the plaintiff or decedent's risk or probability of developing cancer was substantial ... the jury *should be told* that the plaintiff's or decedent's exposure to a particular product *was* a substantial factor in causing or bringing about the disease if in reasonable medical probability it was a substantial factor contributing to plaintiff's or decedent's risk of developing cancer.' (See (1997) 67 Cal Rptr 2d 16 at 32; my emphasis.)

[108] Therefore, whilst the decision taken by the House in *McGhee*'s case may have been based on an inference of fact, I consider that it is in the interests of justice that it should now be held as a matter of law that the approach taken by the House in *McGhee*'s case is one which should be followed by trial judges in cases such as the present ones where the claimant can prove that the employer's

breach of duty materially increased the risk of him contracting a particular disease
and the disease occurred, but where in the state of existing medical knowledge he
is unable to prove by medical evidence that the breach was a cause of the disease.

[109] Whilst there is very little practical difference between the two views I
prefer, with respect, to take the view that the *McGhee* approach is based on the
drawing of a factual or legal inference leading to the conclusion that the breach
of duty was a cause of the disease rather than that the decision in *McGhee* laid
down a new principle that, in cases where medical evidence as to the precise
nature of the causation cannot be adduced, the material increase in the risk is
taken in law to be a cause of the disease without reliance on a factual or legal
inference. As well as the passages in the speeches of Lord Simon of Glaisdale,
Lord Kilbrandon and Lord Salmon to which I have referred in [96], [97], above I
incline to the view that Lord Reid's references to the legal concept of causation
being based 'on the practical way in which the ordinary man's mind works in the
everyday affairs of life' and to a 'broad and practical viewpoint' (see [1972] 3 All
ER 1008 at 1011, [1973] 1 WLR 1 at 5) point more to the drawing of an inference
than to the laying down of a new principle of law. Moreover I think that in his
speech in *McGhee*'s case [1972] 3 All ER 1008 at 1013, [1973] 1 WLR 1 at 7 Lord
Wilberforce recognised that there were two ways in which injustice to the
pursuer could be avoided: one way was by drawing an inference (which he
rejected in that case as a fiction), and the other way was, in effect, by reversing
the burden of proof on causation. But as Lord Bridge observed in *Wilsher*'s case
[1988] 1 All ER 871 at 879, [1988] AC 1074 at 1087, there was no support for the
reversal of the burden of proof in the other speeches.

[110] In some cases in other jurisdictions (as in the hunting cases where two
hunters fire negligently at the same time and the claimant, struck by one shot,
cannot prove which shot struck him) the courts, in order to avoid injustice, have
expressly held that the burden of proof on causation should be reversed. In
Summers v Tice (1948) 199 P 2d 1 Carter J delivering the judgment of the Supreme
Court of California stated (at 4) 'a requirement that the burden of proof on that
subject be shifted to defendants becomes manifest'; see also the majority
judgment of the Supreme Court of Canada in *Cook v Lewis* [1952] 1 DLR 1 at 18.
In the hunting cases and in cases analogous to them justice may well require that
the burden of proof be reversed, but in relation to cases of industrial disease there
appears to be no support in the English authorities, other than in Lord
Wilberforce's speech in *McGhee*'s case, for the reversal of the burden of proof as
a matter of law.

[111] Where the claimant proves that the breach of duty materially increased
the risk of the onset of the disease from which he suffers, it will be open to the
defendant to adduce evidence and to argue that even though the breach of duty
materially increased the risk, nevertheless the evidence adduced on its behalf
displaces the inference of causation. Therefore I turn to consider whether the
medical evidence relied on by the defendants displaces the inference which
should otherwise be drawn that the prolonged exposure to asbestos dust which
increased the risk of contracting mesothelioma materially contributed to the
onset of the disease in the three employees. The evidence upon which the
defendants rely is that it is as probable as not that the transformation of a normal
mesothelial cell to a cancerous cell could be due to the action of a single asbestos
fibre or of a few asbestos fibres. In the light of this evidence the defendants
submit that it was as probable as not that each employee contracted the disease
during the course of his employment with only one employer who cannot be
identified. Therefore the evidence that each successive period of exposure

augments the risk that the disease will occur should not give rise to the inference that the exposure to asbestos dust created by the default of each employer was the cause of the disease.

[112] I am unable to accept that submission. The other part of the evidence as to the mechanism by which asbestos causes mesothelioma is that it is as probable as not that the onset of the disease could be due to the action of multiple fibres. When this is added to the evidence that each successive period of exposure augments the risk that the disease will occur, and that mesothelioma usually occurs in persons who have inhaled millions of asbestos fibres in the course of their work, I think that the inference of causation is not displaced by the evidence upon which the defendants rely.

[113] In the course of his evidence in the trial of the action brought by Mrs Fairchild her medical witness, Dr Rudd, referred to the common sense conclusion on the question whether Mr Fairchild's mesothelioma was caused by one fibre or by prolonged exposure to many fibres. I set out a portion of the transcript so that his observation on common sense can be seen in its context. I add that I do not think that his evidence departs from the agreed statement of facts in any of the three cases:

'Re-examined by MR HOGARTH

MR HOGARTH: (To the witness) Dr Rudd, you are (inaudible) deal with the situation (?) put to you by Mr Stewart, where he suggested that if you assume that there are two equal exposers it is impossible to say which one produced or exposed to the fatal fibre. Can you say that one or other, or both?

A. It's not possible to say it was one or another, or both. It could have been one. It could have been the other. It could have been both if there was more than one fibre involved.

Q. It has to be one, or the other, or both?

A. What is known for certain is that together they were responsible for the malignant transformation. The situation is analogous to causation of lung cancer by cigarette smoking. The cigarette smoke causes a [series] of mutations which, together, give rise to the lung cancer. One could say, theoretically, that last mutation was caused by a molecule of tar from one cigarette, but it would not be in accordance with common sense to suggest that the man who had smoked for thirty years and developed lung cancer got it as a result of smoking one cigarette rather than another. The cancer is the end result of the sum total of smoking. Mesothelioma is the end result of the sum total of asbestos exposure.

Cross-examined by MR STEWART

MR STEWART: My Lord, I am a little concerned your Lordship may possibly be misled by that last answer. I wonder if I may clarify it? (To the witness) Dr Rudd, that last statement, that it is the sum total of the exposure to asbestos, is strictly on the hypothesis that more (inaudible) which was not proven that as asbestos fibres, as opposed to one asbestos fibre, is more likely to have caused it?

A. It's a statement based upon the facts which can be known with certainty. The facts which can be known with certainty are that asbestos causes mesothelioma. The risk that mesothelioma will occur increases with the quantity of asbestos inhaled. Mr Fairchild was exposed to a quantity of asbestos from various sources. As a result, he developed mesothelioma. The rest is speculation.

Q. You are not, I assume, [resiling from] the fact that you agreed that it is possible that the risk lies with exposure simply because each fibre has a chance in initiating the fatal (?) mutation?

A. That's possible.

Q. That is equally likely, as you said before, that it is the one fibre out of all those millions that it is equally likely to be that, as more than one fibre?

A. Yes, we're moving on to mechanisms, now, as opposed to observable facts.'

I consider that the common sense view expressed by Dr Rudd is the one which a court should take and is in conformity with the opinion of Lord Reid in *McGhee's* case [1972] 3 All ER 1008 at 1011, [1973] 1 WLR 1 at 5 that the issue of causation in cases such as these should be assessed from a broad and practical viewpoint.

[114] The application of the *McGhee* principle in these cases and in similar cases, where successive employers of an employee have been in breach of duty to take steps to guard against an industrial disease which the employee contracts, may mean that an employer may be held liable when in reality, if medical science were able to be certain as to how the employee's disease started, it was not fibres inhaled during the employment with it which caused the onset of the disease. But if the *McGhee* principle is not applied the consequence will be that an employee who undoubtedly sustained the disease because one or some or all of his employers were in breach of duty to take steps to guard against the onset of the disease, will recover no damages because in the present state of medical knowledge the doctors are unable to say which breach of duty by an employer caused the disease. In these circumstances I have no doubt that justice is better served by requiring an employer, who has been in breach of duty and who has materially increased the risk of its innocent employee incurring the disease, to pay damages than by ruling that the employee who has sustained a grievous disease can recover nothing. Therefore I am in respectful agreement with the opinion of Lord Wilberforce in *McGhee's* case [1972] 3 All ER 1008 at 1012, [1973] 1 WLR 1 at 6:

'And if one asks which of the parties, the workman or the employers should suffer from this inherent evidential difficulty, the answer as a matter in policy or justice should be that it is the creator of the risk who, ex hypothesi, must be taken to have foreseen the possibility of damage, who should bear its consequences.'

This view is also well put by Lambert JA in *Haag v Marshall* (1989) 61 DLR (4th) 371 at 379:

'... as between an innocent plaintiff and a defendant who has committed a breach of duty to the plaintiff and by so doing materially increased the risk of loss to the plaintiff, in a situation where it is impossible, as a practical matter, to prove whether the breach of duty caused the loss, it is more in keeping with a common sense approach to causation as a tool of justice, to let the liability fall on the defendant.'

[115] In its judgment the Court of Appeal stated ([2001] EWCA Civ 1881 at [103], [2002] 1 WLR 1052):

'... the claimant is wholly unable to prove on the balance of probabilities that that period of employment had any causative relationship with the inception of the disease. This is far too weighty an edifice to build on the slender a foundations of *McGhee v. National Coal Board*, and Lord Bridge has told us in *Wilsher v. Essex Area Health Authority* that *McGhee* established no new principle of law at all. If we were to accede to the claimants' arguments, we would be distorting the law to accommodate the exigencies of a very hard case. We would be yielding to a contention that all those who have suffered injury after being exposed to a risk of that injury from which someone else b should have protected them should be able to recover compensation even when they are quite unable to prove who was the culprit.'

For the reasons which I have given I am unable, with respect, to agree with the opinion of the Court of Appeal that the claimants were unable to prove on the balance of probabilities that there was a causative relationship between a period c of employment during which there was exposure to asbestos dust at the onset of the disease. The Court of Appeal also stated (at [104]):

d 'In our judgment, what Lord Reid said in *McGhee* ([1972] 3 All ER 1008 at 1011, [1973] 1 WLR 1 at 4–5), in the passage of his speech which forms the basis of Mr Langstaff's argument, must be read in the context of that case. There was only one causative agent, brick dust, and only one possible tortfeasor, Mr McGhee's employer. In that situation Lord Reid was prepared to find causation established in the absence of scientific proof. Lord Bridge in *Wilsher* has made it clear that the same technique cannot be used where there is more than one causative agent. It seems to us that for the e same reasons the same technique cannot be used where there is more than one tortfeasor, unless of course the evidence establishes, on the balance of probabilities, that the disease was caused by cumulative exposure.'

I am unable to agree with this view because I consider that where there is only one causative agent (in this case asbestos dust) the *McGhee* principle can apply f notwithstanding that there are a number of tortfeasors.

[116] Therefore applying the *McGhee* principle I concluded that the breach of duty by each defendant materially increasing the risk of the onset of mesothelioma in Mr Fox, Mr Fairchild and Mr Matthews involved a substantial contribution to the disease suffered by them and it was for this reason that I g allowed the appeals.

[117] I observe that no argument was addressed to the House that in the event of the claimants succeeding there should be an apportionment of damages because the breaches of duty of a number of employers had contributed to cause the disease and therefore the damages awarded against a defendant should be a proportion of the full sum of damages which the claimant would have recovered h if he (or the claimant's husband) had been employed by only one employer for the whole of his working life. Therefore each defendant is liable in full for a claimant's damages, although a defendant can seek contribution against another employer liable for causing the disease.

j [118] In my respectful opinion in *Wilsher's* case the House was right to hold that the majority of the Court of Appeal should not have extended the *McGhee* principle to apply where there were five possible candidates which could have caused the plaintiff's blindness. I consider that, as Browne-Wilkinson V-C observed ([1986] 3 All ER 801 at 835, [1987] QB 730 at 780) the justification for holding a defendant liable is that the defendant created a risk and that the injury suffered by the plaintiff fell squarely within that risk. Subject to this observation on the decision in *Wilsher's* case, I wish to confine my opinion to the circumstances of these cases. It may be necessary in the future to consider whether the *McGhee* principle should be applied to other cases, but such decisions will have to be taken when such cases arise.

LORD RODGER OF EARLSFERRY.

[119] My Lords, these appeals concern the liability of employers for mesothelioma which employees developed as a result of being exposed to asbestos dust in the course of their employment with more than one employer. The Court of Appeal held ([2001] EWCA Civ 1881, [2002] 1 WLR 1052) that the claimants had not proved that the defendants whom they had sued had caused or materially contributed to the mesothelioma afflicting the men in respect of whom the actions had been raised. Their claims accordingly failed, as all similar claims in courts throughout the United Kingdom would have failed if the Court of Appeal's approach had prevailed. On 16 May 2002, however, your Lordships reported to the House that the appeals should be allowed. I agree with the reasons given in the speech of my noble and learned friend, Lord Bingham of Cornhill, for allowing the appeals, but I have thought it right to explain in my own words why I differed from the unanimous judgment of the Court of Appeal on this important matter.

[120] I gratefully adopt the account of the facts and issues given by Lord Bingham of Cornhill. As he has explained, the Court of Appeal reached their conclusion on the basis of the expert medical evidence, which was essentially the same in each of the cases. Mesothelioma arises when one of the mesothelial cells in the pleura is damaged and undergoes a malignant transformation. While it is certain that asbestos fibres play a role in triggering this transformation, it is not known whether the triggering mechanism involves a single asbestos fibre or multiple asbestos fibres. In the state of medical knowledge today, the one is as likely as the other. Once the malignant transformation has been triggered, the malignancy develops in a process that may involve some six or seven genetic changes. Asbestos may have a role to play at one or more of these stages, but again there is no evidence that the action of asbestos is more or less likely at one stage than at another. In summary therefore—

> 'it could not be said whether a single fibre of asbestos was more or less likely to have caused the disease, alternatively whether more than one fibre was more or less likely to have caused the disease. In the latter event, it could not be shown that it was more likely than not that those fibres came from more than one source. In other words, none of these scenarios could be proved on the balance of probabilities. Similarly, it could not be proved on the balance of probabilities that any one man's mesothelioma was caused cumulatively by exposure to asbestos dust in more than one employment.' (See [2002] 1 WLR 1052 at [26].)

[121] Since it is possible that mesothelioma is triggered by a single fibre of asbestos and since the disease, once contracted, is not made worse by the extent of any subsequent exposure to asbestos dust, the disease differs, for example, from pneumoconiosis or asbestosis where the severity of the condition will depend, to some extent at least, on the amount of dust to which the victim has been exposed. In pneumoconiosis and asbestosis, therefore, by contrast with mesothelioma, it can be said in an appropriate case that the severity of the particular victim's condition will have been caused cumulatively by exposure to dust in more than one employment.

a
[122] Equally importantly, however, 'the risk that mesothelioma will occur increases in relation to the total dose of asbestos received' ([2002] 1 WLR 1052 at [25]). Why this should be so is not known. It may be because the build-up of asbestos progressively weakens and eventually overwhelms the body's defences, with the result that a mesothelioma then develops. But this is now thought to be unlikely. The alternative explanation would seem to be that the greater the

b
number of asbestos fibres taken into the body, the greater are the chances that one of them will trigger a malignant transformation. Whatever may be the reason for the increase in risk, since all the defendants exposed the men concerned to an atmosphere containing a substantial amount of asbestos dust, they all increased the risk that the men would develop mesothelioma.

[123] All of the men were employed by more than one employer. This is, of

c
course, typical of the employment patterns of men who have been exposed to asbestos, whether in fitting out or stripping buildings and ships or in casual dock labour, handling cargoes of asbestos. Mesothelioma takes at least ten, and up to 40, years to manifest itself. When the disease does eventually show itself, therefore, the men inevitably find it difficult to identify more than a few of the

d
employers for whom they worked; after so many years employment records tend to be relatively few and far between. The claimants in these cases accordingly sued only those employers whom they could identify and who—or whose successors—were still in existence. They could do no more.

[124] Because of the current state of medical knowledge about the aetiology of mesothelioma, it was impossible for the claimants to prove on the balance of

e
probabilities that the men's illness had been triggered by a fibre or fibres inhaled while working with any particular employer and, more especially, while working with the particular defendants whom they had sued. For that reason the Court of Appeal rejected their claims. The claimants thus failed because of the particular stage which medical science has reached. Research has gone far enough for

f
scientists to be able to see, at a microscopic level, what the possible mechanisms may be, but not far enough for them to determine which is the one that actually operates. In future more may be known. As Mr Stewart rightly observed, in the course of submissions that were both helpful and sensitive, this may change the way in which the law treats such cases. But the House must deal with these appeals on the basis of the evidence as to medical knowledge today and leave the

g
problems of the future to be resolved in the future.

[125] At the hearing counsel for the appellants simply contended that the appeals should be allowed and that the respondents should be found liable in damages. The contentions for the respondents were to the opposite effect. No argument was advanced to the effect that, if they were held liable, the defendants'

h
liability should be reduced or apportioned in some way to reflect an assessment of the chances that the particular defendants, rather than other employers, were actually responsible for the exposure that led to the development of the claimants' mesothelioma. Indeed it was said that no such assessment, even on a rough basis, was possible. Counsel accepted accordingly that, if liable at all, the defendants would be jointly and severally liable for the whole of the damage done

j
to the claimants.

[126] Cases on the liability of employers to their employees who develop industrial diseases have been coming before the courts for many years. At the hearing counsel cited a number of well-known decisions of your Lordships' House in this sphere. Although the battles in those cases were hard fought, both for the employees and for the employers, for the most part the descendants of the protagonists now acknowledge in tranquillity what was won and what was lost

in the struggle: the resulting decisions have long been accepted as shaping the law
that governs these matters. *McGhee v National Coal Board* [1972] 3 All ER 1008,
[1973] 1 WLR 1; *rvsg* 1973 SC(HL) 37 is an exception. It dealt with the issue of
causation in a case where, as here, the medical experts could not fully explain
how the pursuer's condition had started. Controversy persists as to why the
pursuer, having lost his claim for damages for dermatitis in the Court of Session,
won it in this House. In *Wilsher v Essex Area Health Authority* [1988] 1 All ER 871,
[1988] AC 1074 the House sought, with only limited success, to put an end to that
controversy. Giving the unanimous views of the Appellate Committee, Lord
Bridge indicated that in *McGhee's* case the pursuer had won his case simply
because the House had been prepared to draw from the primary facts an
inference that the defenders' wrongful failure to provide showers had materially
contributed to the onset of his dermatitis. On that basis *McGhee's* case laid down
no new legal principle and was nothing more than a decision on a matter of fact,
of no relevance for the present case. On behalf of the appellants Sir Sydney
Kentridge and Mr Langstaff questioned that explanation of *McGhee's* case,
however. They submitted that the majority of their Lordships had proceeded on
the principle that, in the circumstances of that case, proof that the defenders'
wrongdoing had increased the risk of the pursuer developing dermatitis was to
be equated with proof that the defenders had materially contributed to his
dermatitis. If applied to the facts in the present cases, that principle would
determine the appeals in favour of the appellants. For their part, counsel for the
respondents frankly, and in my view correctly, acknowledged that if the House
applied that approach in these cases, then the appeals must indeed succeed.
Counsel contended, however, that the House should follow the interpretation of
McGhee's case adopted in *Wilsher's* case. On that basis the appeals must fail since,
on the evidence, the claimants had not proved that the defendants had caused or
materially contributed to their mesothelioma. The proper interpretation of
McGhee's case is therefore critical to the disposal of these appeals.

[127] To appreciate the novelty of the issue confronting the House in
McGhee's case and the possible significance of that decision for the present
proceedings, it is necessary to go back to *Bonnington Castings Ltd v Wardlaw* [1956]
1 All ER 615, [1956] AC 613, the starting-point of much of the law in this field.
The pursuer sued his employers for damages for contracting pneumoconiosis as
a result of inhaling air containing minute particles of silica. The evidence showed
that the dust in the workshop was caused by the operation of two types of
equipment, the pneumatic hammer at which the pursuer worked and certain
swing grinders. Given the technology available at the time, the defenders were
not at fault in the operation of the pneumatic hammer nor in failing to extract the
dust which it threw off. They were, however, at fault in as much as the apparatus
for intercepting the dust from the swing grinders was choked. The First Division
of the Court of Session (Lord President Clyde, Lord Carmont and Lord Russell)
held that the pursuer could succeed only if he could show that the sole source of
his disease was the dust from the swing grinders. The majority (the Lord
President dissenting) applied a reverse onus of proof and so held that the pursuer
had indeed proved this (1955 SC 320). The defenders appealed and the House
held that the majority had been wrong to apply the reverse onus of proof. Lord
Reid said:

'In my judgment, the employee must, in all cases, prove his case by the
ordinary standard of proof in civil actions; he must make it appear at least

a

that, on a balance of probabilities, the breach of duty caused, or materially contributed to, his injury.' (See [1956] 1 All ER 615 at 618, [1956] AC 613 at 620.)

He went on, however, to hold that the pursuer did not need to show that the dust from the swing grinders had been the sole source of his illness. It appeared to Lord Reid that—

b

'the source of his disease was the dust from both sources, and the real question is whether the dust from the swing grinders materially contributed to the disease. What is a material contribution must be a question of degree. A contribution which comes within the exception de minimis non curat lex is not material, but I think that any contribution which does not fall within

c

that exception must be material. I do not see how there can be something too large to come within the de minimis principle, but yet too small to be material.' (See [1956] 1 All ER 615 at 618–619, [1956] AC 613 at 621.)

Lord Keith of Avonholm observed:

d

'It was the atmosphere inhaled by the respondent that caused his illness, and it is impossible, in my opinion, to resolve the components of that atmosphere into particles caused by the fault of the appellants and particles not caused by the fault of the appellants, as if they were separate and independent factors in his illness. Prima facie the particles inhaled are acting cumulatively, and I think the natural inference is that, had it not been for the

e

cumulative effect, the respondent would not have developed pneumoconiosis when he did, and might not have developed it at all.' (See [1956] 1 All ER 615 at 622, [1956] AC 613 at 626.)

The House held that it had been established that the swing grinders had indeed contributed a quota of dust that was not negligible and that they had therefore

f

helped to produce his disease. On that footing the House dismissed the appeal.

[128] As Lord Reid noted ([1956] 1 All ER 615 at 618, [1956] AC 613 at 620), there was nothing new in the idea that the pursuer required to prove no more than that the defenders' wrongful act had materially contributed to his injury. Although he did not refer to it, there was ample authority for the proposition in both English and Scots law. For instance, in *Senior v Ward* (1859) 1 E & E 385 at

g

392, 120 ER 954 at 957 where the owner of a coal mine who superintended its operation had failed to test the cable of a cage as required by statutorily approved rules, Lord Campbell CJ, sitting in the Queen's Bench, would have held him liable, even though the banksman had also been at fault, because the mine owner's own negligence had 'materially contributed to the death of the

h

deceased'. In fact, however, the court held that the plaintiff's action failed because the deceased's own negligence had 'materially contributed to his death'. In *Wakelin v London and South Western Rly Co* (1886) 12 App Cas 41 at 47 Lord Watson stated that the liability of a defendant must rest in the first place on there being—

j

'some negligent act or omission on the part of the company or their servants which materially contributed to the injury or death complained of … Mere allegation or proof that the company were guilty of negligence is altogether irrelevant; they might be guilty of many negligent acts or omissions, which might possibly have occasioned injury to somebody, but had no connection whatever with the injury for which redress is sought, and therefore the plaintiff must allege and prove, not merely that they were negligent, but that their negligence caused or materially contributed to the injury.'

Similarly, in *Craig v Glasgow Corp* 1919 SC(HL) 1 at 6 where the pursuer sought damages for personal injuries caused by a tramcar driven by one of the defenders' employees, Lord Buckmaster said:

'It is a common and familiar principle that in an action seeking such relief it is incumbent upon the pursuer to prove both that the defenders were guilty of negligence, and that such negligence caused, or materially contributed to, the injuries received.'

[129] The idea of liability based on wrongful conduct that had materially contributed to an injury was therefore well established long before *Wardlaw's* case. But *Wardlaw's* case became a convenient point of reference, especially in cases of industrial disease. In such cases this basis of liability is of considerable importance. Since it is enough that the defendant's wrongful act materially contributed to the claimant's injury, the law is not applying the causa sine qua non or 'but for' test of causation. In *Wardlaw's* case, for instance, the pursuer did not need to prove that, but for the dust from the swing hammers, he would not have developed pneumoconiosis. All he needed to prove was that the dust from the swing hammers contributed materially to the dusty atmosphere which he breathed and which caused his illness. As will be seen below, in the Court of Session in *McGhee's* case the judges lost sight of this important point.

[130] The House quickly applied this approach in two Scottish appeals that were heard one after the other: *Quinn v Cameron & Robertson Ltd* [1957] 1 All ER 760 at 764, 771, [1958] AC 9 at 23, 34 per Viscount Simonds and Lord Morton of Henryton respectively, and *Nicholson v Atlas Steel Foundry & Engineering Co Ltd* [1957] 1 All ER 776, [1957] 1 WLR 613. The second is of particular importance for present purposes. The action was at the instance of the relatives of a workman who had died from pneumoconiosis. The man had worked in the defenders' dressing shop where there was a pneumatic hammer the operation of which, lawfully at the time, gave rise to siliceous dust in the atmosphere. There were also two swing grinders, but it was unclear on the evidence whether they had given off dust. The House therefore proceeded on the basis that all the dust in the atmosphere had been caused by the lawful operation of the pneumatic hammer. It was proved, however, that the ventilation in the dressing shop was inadequate in terms of the relevant statutory provisions. As a result the dust remained in the atmosphere for longer than would have been the case if the ventilation had met the statutory requirements. The House followed the decision in *Wardlaw's* case and held the defenders liable on the ground that the inadequate ventilation had materially contributed to the man's pneumoconiosis.

[131] Viscount Simonds, with whom Lord Oaksey and Lord Morton of Henryton concurred, set out his approach in these terms:

'My Lords, I do not think that it can be wrong to approach this question from the angle that, if the statute prescribes a proper system of ventilation by the circulation of fresh air so as to render harmless so far as practicable all fumes, dust and other impurities that may be injurious to health generated in the course of work carried on in the factory, and if it is proved that there is no system, or only an inadequate system, of ventilation, it requires little further to establish a causal link between that default and the illness due to noxious dust of a person employed in the shop. Something is required as was a held in *Wardlaw*'s case. I was a party to that decision and would not in any way resile from it. But it must not be pressed too far. In the present case there was, in my opinion, ample evidence to support the appellants' case. The appellants rightly or wrongly by their pleadings assumed the burden not only of proving that there was a causal link between default and disease but also of proving that it was practicable for the respondents to have reduced

b the risk by the provision of additional roof ventilations and openings in the walls for the admission of fresh air.' (See [1957] 1 All ER 776 at 779, [1957] 1 WLR 613 at 618.)

Viscount Simonds thus firmly adhered to the decision in *Wardlaw*'s case, that there could be no question of reversing the burden of proof which lay on a

c pursuer to establish the necessary causal link between the employer's default and his illness. Nevertheless, he considered that, where a statutory provision prescribed a system of ventilation to remove elements in the atmosphere that might be injurious to health and the employer had no ventilation or only an inadequate system, these factors were relevant in considering how much more the pursuer required to prove in order to establish the causal link between the

d employer's default and the pursuer's disease due to noxious dust. In other words, these factors were relevant to *what* or *how much* the pursuer had to prove in order to establish the causal link, rather than to the attitude that the court should take when assessing the evidence adduced for that purpose. Viscount Simonds went on to consider whether it was practicable for the defenders to have provided a

e better system of ventilation. He concluded that it was. Therefore the dust containing dangerous particles had hung about in the air in a concentrated form for longer than it would have done if there had been that better system of ventilation. He continued:

f 'It follows that, owing to the default of the respondents, the deceased was exposed to a greater degree of risk than he should have been, and, though it is impossible even approximately to quantify the particles which he must in any event have inhaled and those which he inhaled but need not have, I cannot regard the excess as something so negligible that the maxim "de minimis" is applicable. Accordingly, following the decision in *Wardlaw*'s

g case, I must hold the respondents liable.' (See [1957] 1 All ER 776 at 781, [1957] 1 WLR 613 at 620.)

[132] Similarly Lord Cohen said:

'The respondents are, admittedly, not to blame for the generation of this cloud, but any failure to provide proper ventilation must, I think, lengthen

h the period during which the cloud remains intense. It seems to me to follow that the respondents' failure to provide adequate ventilation must increase the risk to which the workmen are exposed. Reading the evidence as a whole, I think it establishes that (to use the language of Lord Reid in *Wardlaw*'s case ... "on a balance of probabilities, the breach of duty caused,

j or materially contributed to", the injury.' (See [1957] 1 All ER 776 at 782, [1957] 1 WLR 613 at 622.)

[133] Questions of the risk or increased risk of causing harm are more frequently considered in relation to issues of foreseeability and fault. But these passages are important precisely because they show that the House was proceeding on the basis that, in considering whether the pursuers in *Nicholson*'s case had proved that the defenders had materially contributed to the deceased's

condition, it was relevant to consider whether the defenders' wrongful act had *a*
exposed him to an increased risk of disease. In other words, in that case proof of
increased risk of harm to the deceased was relevant to proof of causation of that
harm.

[134] In *McGhee*'s case Lord Simon of Glaisdale suggested ([1972] 3 All ER 1008
at 1014, [1973] 1 WLR 1 at 8) that the same had been said in the opinion of the
Lord Ordinary (Kilbrandon) in another dermatitis case, *Gardiner v Motherwell* *b*
Machinery and Scrap Co Ltd 1961 SC(HL) 1 at 3. Lord Kilbrandon recorded the
argument on behalf of the pursuer in these terms:

> '... that the washing facilities which were provided were inadequate and
> primitive, and that, if they had been up to standard, the risk of dermatitis
> would have been very much reduced.'   *c*

As Lord Simon noted, Lord Kilbrandon accepted that argument. He did so
towards the end of his opinion (1961 SC(HL) 1 at 4):

> 'In my opinion, the defenders neglected to supply reasonable washing
> facilities in the circumstances, and thereby exposed the pursuer to an *d*
> enhanced risk of contracting industrial dermatitis. They are accordingly
> liable to him in damages.'

It appears, however, that, both when recording the argument and when giving
his decision on it, Lord Kilbrandon was concerned with fault rather than with
causation, since he had already held (1961 SC(HL) 1 at 3), on the basis of the *e*
dermatologists' evidence, that the pursuer had established the necessary causal
link between his work with the defenders and the onset of his dermatitis. In these
later passages Lord Kilbrandon seems to have been making the point that the
defenders' failure to provide adequate washing facilities amounted to legally
relevant fault where it was foreseeable that this would lead to an enhanced risk *f*
of dermatitis.

[135] Be that as it may, the statements in the speeches of Viscount Simonds
and Lord Cohen in *Nicholson*'s case had stood unchallenged for some 15 years
when the House came to consider *McGhee*'s case, again an appeal from the Court
of Session. The case involved a claim for dermatitis which the pursuer had
developed after working in a hot and dusty atmosphere, pulling bricks out of the *g*
defenders' kiln. At the relevant time there were no showers at the works and so,
when his working day was over, the pursuer had to cycle home without washing
the sweat, dust and grit from his body. As indeed often happens, the point upon
which the decision was ultimately to turn emerged only after the Lord Ordinary
had rejected much of the rest of the pursuer's case. The pursuer began the proof *h*
before answer with both a common law and a statutory case to the effect that the
defenders should have provided a system of ventilating the kiln. He disclaimed
the statutory case at the hearing on evidence. The Lord Ordinary (Kissen)
rejected the common law case. He also rejected the pursuer's case that the
defenders should have taken reasonable care to see that the kiln had cooled *j*
sufficiently before the pursuer and his colleagues were sent to work in it.

[136] The pursuer had a further common law case which he set out at the end
of art 3 of condescendence in these terms:

> 'It was their duty to take reasonable care to provide adequate washing
> facilities including showers, soap and towels to enable men to remove dust
> from their bodies. In each and all of said duties the defenders failed and so

a   caused said disease. Had the defenders fulfilled said duties incumbent on
them the pursuer would not have contracted said disease.'

The final averments in this passage relate, of course, to the alleged failure by the
defenders to perform all the common law duties averred by the pursuer,
including those that the Lord Ordinary had rejected. The Lord Ordinary held
that the pursuer had indeed contracted his dermatitis in the course of his work in
b   the brick kiln and as a result of his exposure to dust and ashes there (1973 SC(HL)
37 at 39). He also held that the defenders were at fault in not providing showers
but that the pursuer had failed to prove on the balance of probabilities that this
fault on the part of the defenders had caused or materially contributed to his
injury (1973 SC(HL) 37 at 42–43). Lord Kissen put the point in this way:

c
'Dr Hannay's evidence was that he could not say that the provision of
showers would probably have prevented the disease. He said that it would
have reduced the risk materially but he would not go further than that. Dr
Ferguson said that washing reduces the risk. Pursuer's counsel maintained
that a material increase in the risk of contracting a disease was the same as a
d   material contribution to contracting the disease and that Dr Hannay
established this by his evidence. I think that defenders' counsel was correct
when he said that the distinction drawn by Dr Hannay was correct and that
an increase in risk did not necessarily mean a material contribution to the
contracting of the disease. The two concepts are entirely different. A
material increase in risk may refer only to possibilities and may not make a
e   possibility into a probability. It may strengthen the possibility but that
cannot mean that in all such cases the possibility has become a probability.
What the pursuer has to show is that, *as he avers*, he would not have
contracted the disease but for the defenders' breach of duty. He has to show
that this was probable and the degrees of risk have no relevance unless they
f   make the contraction of the disease more probable than not contracting the
disease. He cannot succeed if the only inference from the evidence is that
lack of shower baths is a possibility as a cause of his having contracted the
disease and that the provision of shower baths would have increased the
possibility but not made it a probability. That is the only inference which I
can draw from Dr Hannay's evidence and that was the best evidence for the
g   pursuer. Causal connection between fault and the contraction of the disease
has not been established.' (My emphasis.)

[137] The pursuer reclaimed but the First Division (Lord President Clyde,
Lord Migdale and Lord Johnston) refused the reclaiming motion. The Division
h   proceeded on the basis that, in accordance with his averments in article 3 of
condescendence, the pursuer had to prove that the provision of showers would
have prevented his dermatitis (1973 SC(HL) 37 at 43, 46–47 per Lord President
Clyde and Lord Migdale respectively). They also took the view that the effects of
the heat and dust had come to an end when the pursuer left the kiln so that the
failure to provide washing facilities could have played no part in the development
j   of the pursuer's condition (1973 SC(HL) 37 at 44, 47 per Lord President Clyde and
Lord Migdale respectively, with whom Lord Johnston somewhat hesitantly
agreed). Since all the damage had been done in the kiln, a shower could not have
obviated or lessened that damage (1973 SC(HL) 37 at 48 per Lord Migdale). In
addition, however, in a passage (1973 SC(HL) 37 at 45) that Lord Salmon was
specifically to disapprove ([1972] 3 All ER 1008 at 1017, [1973] 1 WLR 1 at 11) the
Lord President held:

'Even if the pursuer had established (as he did not) that the absence of washing facilities increased the risk of the pursuer getting dermatitis, that would clearly not prove that the absence of these facilities caused the disease, nor indeed would it go any distance towards proving it. For risk of dermatitis and causation of dermatitis are two quite separate matters.'

[138] This House analysed both the evidence and the pursuer's case rather differently from the Court of Session. The medical witnesses were agreed that the defenders' failure to provide washing facilities increased the risk of the pursuer developing dermatitis. In this sense, and in this sense only, the abrasion to the pursuer's skin was cumulative 'the longer a subject is exposed to injury the greater the chance of his developing dermatitis' ([1972] 3 All ER 1008 at 1010, [1973] 1 WLR 1 at 3–4 per Lord Reid). The fact that the risk did increase in this way if no washing facilities were provided was important because it showed that, contrary to the view taken by the First Division, the pursuer had not left behind the causes which made him liable to develop dermatitis when he left the brick kiln ([1972] 3 All ER 1008 at 1011, [1973] 1 WLR 1 at 4–5 per Lord Reid).

[139] On the other hand, the evidence did not show just how the type of dermatitis affecting the pursuer began. Lord Reid summarised the effect of the evidence in this way:

'It suggests to me that there are two possible ways. It may be that an accumulation of minor abrasions of the horny layer of the skin is a necessary precondition for the onset of the disease. Or it may be that the disease starts at one particular abrasion and then spreads, so that multiplication of abrasions merely increases the number of places where the disease can start and in that way increases the risk of its occurrence. I am inclined to think that the evidence points to the former view. But in a field were so little appears to be known with certainty I could not say that that is proved. If it were then this case would be indistinguishable from *Wardlaw*'s case.' (See [1972] 3 All ER 1008 at 1010–1011, [1973] 1 WLR 1 at 4.)

In this passage Lord Reid goes into more of the detail of the medical evidence than either the Lord Ordinary or the First Division. From what he says here and elsewhere ([1972] 3 All ER 1008 at 1010, [1973] 1 WLR 1 at 3) it is clear, of course, that the pursuer's condition would not have developed but for his work in the kiln. It was there that he was exposed to the heat that made him sweat profusely and so softened his skin and made it easily injured. It was there also that he was exposed to the cloud of brick dust, with the result that the particles adhered to his skin. Exertion then caused the dust to injure the horny layer of his skin and so exposed the tender cells below to injury or infection. The most significant exertion would, presumably, have occurred while the pursuer was working in the kiln, pulling out the bricks. But the pursuer would also have exerted himself while cycling home and, perhaps, when he got home. So any abrasions on his softened skin could have been caused either by the exertion in the kiln or else by the exertion during his ride home or by a combination of the two. For the consequences of the exertion in the kiln alone the defenders would not have been liable since they were not at fault in that respect. For the consequences of the exertion during his cycle ride, the defenders would, on the other hand, have been liable since the pursuer would not have been open to injury due to dust on his skin at that stage if the defenders had fulfilled their duty to provide showers.

[140] On this analysis the pursuer could succeed in his claim only if he could connect his dermatitis with his ride home while unwashed, rather than simply

a
with his work in the kiln. Lord Reid pointed out, however, that the pursuer's pleadings in respect of the duty to provide showers were potentially misleading ([1972] 3 All ER 1008 at 1010, [1973] 1 WLR 1 at 4). He did not elaborate the point, but he clearly had in mind the standard-form averment at the end of art 3 of condescendence in which the pursuer offered to prove that, if the defenders had fulfilled their duty to provide showers, he would not have contracted

b
dermatitis. Even though both the Lord Ordinary and the First Division had judged his case on that basis, the pursuer's self-imposed goal was too tough. He did not need to go that far. It would be sufficient and relevant in law if the pursuer showed that the defenders' failure had materially contributed to the development of his dermatitis, whether or not the dermatitis would have developed but for that failure. So, despite the terms of the pursuer's averment,

c
Lord Reid considered his case by simply asking whether the defenders' failure to provide showers had materially contributed to the development of the pursuer's dermatitis. It was at this point that the difficulty in the case came into focus.

[141] According to the medical evidence, the pursuer's dermatitis might have occurred either as a result of an accumulation of abrasions or as a result of a single

d
abrasion. If the former were the case, then one could say that the accumulation of abrasions had resulted from the effects of the pursuer's exertions as a whole. Just as it had been right in *Wardlaw*'s case to consider the effects of the cloud of dust as a whole and not to break it down into 'innocent' and 'guilty' particles, so in *McGhee*'s case it would have been right to consider the effects of the exertion as a whole acting on the dust particles on his skin and not to break the exertion

e
down into 'innocent' exertion in the kiln and 'guilty' exertion on the way home. Provided that the exertion on the way home was material, it would be proper to hold that the effects of that exertion on the dust still on his unwashed skin materially contributed to cause the pursuer's illness. But the pursuer had only proved that the accumulation of abrasions was one possible mechanism for

f
triggering his dermatitis. The evidence showed that another possibility was that the disease had started from a single abrasion. If that were the case, liability could not be based on the cumulative effect of the pursuer's exertions in producing an accumulation of abrasions. So the analogy of *Wardlaw*'s case would not apply. But, furthermore, the pursuer could not prove that this hypothetical single abrasion had been caused by his exertion when riding home with the dust

g
adhering to his skin, rather than by his exertions in the kiln. The defenders argued that the pursuer's case must therefore fail because he had not proved, and could not prove, that the defenders' failure to provide showers had caused or materially contributed to the onset of his illness.

[142] Lord Reid dealt with that argument in this way:

h
'But I think that in cases like this we must take a broader view of causation. The medical evidence is to the effect that the fact that the man had to cycle home caked with grime and sweat added materially to the risk that this disease might develop. It does not and could not explain just why that is so. But experience shews that it is so. Plainly that must be because what

j
happens while the man remains unwashed can have a causative effect, although just how the cause operates is uncertain. I cannot accept the view expressed in the Inner House that once the man left the brick kiln he left behind the causes which made him liable to develop dermatitis. That seems to me quite inconsistent with a proper interpretation of the medical evidence. Nor can I accept the distinction drawn by the Lord Ordinary between materially increasing the risk that the disease will occur and making

a material contribution to its occurrence. There may be some logical ground
for such a distinction where our knowledge of all the material factors is
complete. But it has often been said that the legal concept of causation is not
based on logic or philosophy. It is based on the practical way in which the
ordinary man's mind works in the every-day affairs of life. From a broad and
practical viewpoint I can see no substantial difference between saying that
what the respondents did materially increased the risk of injury to the
appellant and saying that what the respondents did made a material
contribution to his injury.' (See [1972] 3 All ER 1008 at 1011, [1973] 1 WLR
1 at 4–5.)

Lord Reid holds that, even though the evidence leaves open the two possible
causes of his illness, the pursuer succeeds because the court takes a broader view
of causation. There is nothing whatever to suggest that, in reaching this
conclusion, Lord Reid was simply adopting a robust and pragmatic approach to
the primary facts and holding that it could somehow be inferred—in the face of
the expert evidence which he had just narrated and which gave rise to the very
problem that had to be resolved—that, if the pursuer's dermatitis was caused by
a single abrasion, that particular abrasion was caused by his exertion while riding
home. What Lord Reid does, rather, is to accept that the pursuer must prove that
the defender's conduct materially contributed to the onset of his illness but also,
like Viscount Simonds and Lord Cohen in *Nicholson's* case, he considers what it is
that the pursuer must prove in order to establish that material contribution.
Taking the 'broader view of causation', he holds that, in these particular
circumstances, there is no substantial difference between saying that what the
defenders did materially increased the risk of injury to the pursuer and saying that
it made a material contribution to his injury. This is his decision on the point of
law posed in the case. Proof that the defenders' failure to provide showers had
materially increased the risk that the pursuer would develop dermatitis would
therefore be, as a matter of law, sufficient to prove that the defenders had
materially contributed to the onset of his condition. And, of course, the pursuer
had actually proved that their failure had increased that risk. Lord Reid
accordingly allowed the appeal.

[143] My Lords, I have analysed the leading speech of Lord Reid at
considerable length. Happily, it is unnecessary to go into the other speeches in
the same detail, since it is in my view clear that Lord Wilberforce, Lord Simon of
Glaisdale and Lord Salmon all took essentially the same approach as Lord Reid.
They were prepared to hold, under reference to the speeches of Viscount
Simonds and Lord Cohen in *Nicholson's* case, that in the particular circumstances,
by proving that the defenders' negligent failure to provide showers had increased
the risk that he would develop dermatitis, the pursuer had proved that the
defenders' failure had materially contributed to his dermatitis. I do not take up
space by repeating the relevant passages, all of which have been set out by Lord
Bingham of Cornhill. I refer in particular to the long passage towards the end of
the speech of Lord Wilberforce ([1972] 3 All ER 1008 at 1012–1013, [1973] 1 WLR
1 at 6–7), which is by no means predicated on the reference to a possible reversal
of the onus of proof that the House detected and disapproved in *Wilsher's* case
[1988] 1 All ER 871 at 879, [1988] AC 1074 at 1087. In *McGhee's* case indeed any
reference to the possibility of proof by the defenders was necessarily obiter since,
ex hypothesi, there was no relevant medical evidence which they could have led.
Despite his reference to 'sufficient prima facie evidence', Lord Simon's approach
is similar ([1972] 3 All ER 1008 at 1014–1015, [1973] 1 WLR 1 at 8–9). The same

a goes for two passages in Lord Salmon's speech where he specifically rejects the distinction between materially increasing the risk of contracting industrial disease and materially contributing to causing it ([1972] 3 All ER 1008 at 1017, 1018, [1973] 1 WLR 1 at 11–12, 12–13). Although Lord Kilbrandon reached the same conclusion as the rest of the House, his exact approach is harder to determine. Like the judges in the Court of Session, however, he appears to have taken the

b view that the pursuer needed to prove that, but for the defenders' failure to provide showers, he would not have contracted dermatitis ([1972] 3 All ER 1008 at 1016, [1973] 1 WLR 1 at 10). For present purposes it is unnecessary to investigate his minority view in more detail.

[144] While Lord Wilberforce's observations on the burden of proof have been disapproved, the decision itself in *McGhee*'s case has not been overruled.

c Nor indeed did counsel for the respondents suggest that it should now be overruled. It may well be that in *McGhee*'s case the members of the House could have proclaimed more clearly and more openly that they were stating a new principle. If so, the possible virtues of a certain reticence in such matters were famously recognised by Lord Devlin (*The Judge* (1979) p 12). But the risk was, of

d course, that opinions couched in this way might be misconstrued. As, in my view, did indeed happen. In *Wilsher*'s case the House examined *McGhee*'s case and came to the conclusion that the decision rested not on any legal principle but on nothing more than 'a robust and pragmatic approach' to the facts of the case. In my respectful opinion, that conclusion was inconsistent with the terms of the speeches in *McGhee*'s case.

e [145] Lord Bridge, with whom the other members of the House agreed, said that in *McGhee*'s case—

> 'the consecutive periods when "innocent" and "guilty" brick dust was present on the pursuer's body may both have contributed to the cause of the
f > disease or, theoretically at least, one or other may have been the sole cause. But where the layman is told by the doctors that the longer the brick dust remains on the body, the greater the risk of dermatitis, although the doctors cannot identify the process of causation scientifically, there seems to be nothing irrational in drawing the inference, as a matter of common sense, that the consecutive periods when brick dust remained on the body probably
g > contributed cumulatively to the causation of the dermatitis. I believe that a process of inferential reasoning on these general lines underlies the decision of the majority in *McGhee*'s case.' (See [1988] 1 All ER 871 at 880, [1988] AC 1074 at 1088.)

h Lord Bridge then quoted the relevant passages from the speeches of their Lordships, apart from Lord Wilberforce, in *McGhee*'s case and went on:

> 'The conclusion I draw from these passages is that *McGhee v National Coal Board* laid down no new principle of law whatever. On the contrary, it affirmed the principle that the onus of proving causation lies on the pursuer
j > or plaintiff. Adopting a robust and pragmatic approach to the undisputed primary facts of the case, the majority concluded that it was a legitimate inference of fact that the defenders' negligence had materially contributed to the pursuer's injury. The decision, in my opinion, is of no greater significance than that and the attempt to extract from it some esoteric principle which in some way modifies, as a matter of law, the nature of the burden of proof of causation which a plaintiff or pursuer must discharge once

he has established a relevant breach of duty is a fruitless one.' (See [1988] 1
All ER 871 at 881–882, [1988] AC 1074 at 1090.) a

In the present case the Court of Appeal naturally had regard to what Lord Bridge
said in this passage ([2002] 1 WLR 1052 at [103]).

[146] Although Lord Bridge took the opportunity of the appeal in *Wilsher's*
case to comment on *McGhee's* case, the two cases were very different. In b
Wilsher's case the plaintiff had been born prematurely and placed in a special unit
in a hospital managed by the defendants. It was necessary for him to be given
extra oxygen but, unfortunately, due to mistakes on their part the staff
administered too much oxygen. The plaintiff developed retrolental fibroplasia,
which resulted in blindness. He claimed damages from the defendants on the
basis that his condition had been caused by the unduly high level of oxygen. The c
evidence in the case showed that exposure to such a high level of oxygen
increased the risk that the plaintiff would suffer retrolental fibroplasia. The
evidence also showed, however, that the condition could occur in premature
babies without any artificial administration of oxygen. More particularly, there
was evidence to indicate a correlation between the occurrence of retrolental d
fibroplasia and four other conditions from which the plaintiff, like many other
premature babies, suffered. Medical science had not, however, positively
identified any causal mechanism linking those conditions and the development of
retrolental fibroplasia.

[147] In the Court of Appeal Mustill LJ, with whom Glidewell LJ agreed,
found in favour of the plaintiff. He acknowledged that the facts of *Wilsher's* case e
differed from those of *McGhee's* case in an important respect:

> 'In *McGhee* there was only one risk operating, namely that contact of a
> sweaty skin with brick dust would lead to dermatitis. The fact that such
> contact did cause the injury was not in dispute. Just as in *Bonnington Castings* f
> *Ltd v Wardlaw* the defenders' fault lay in not in taking proper steps to reduce
> that single risk. The uncertainty was whether the fault had tipped the scale.
> In the present case there is a greater uncertainty. Instead of a single risk
> factor known to have caused the injury there is a list of factors, which cannot
> be fully enumerated in the current state of medical science, any one of which
> might have caused the injury. What the defendants did was not to enhance g
> the risk that the known factors would lead to injury, but to add to the list of
> factors which might do so. I acknowledge that this is much further from the
> facts of *Bonnington Castings Ltd v Wardlaw*, which was the springboard for
> *McGhee*, than were the facts of *McGhee* itself. The question is whether this
> makes a crucial difference. The root of the problem lies in the fact that, for h
> reasons of policy, the House of Lords mitigated the rigour of the rule that the
> plaintiff must prove that the breach caused the loss in the interests of
> achieving a result which was considered to be just. Given that this was a
> decision based on policy, rather than a chain of direct reasoning, the
> difficulty is to know whether a similar approach can properly be adopted in
> the different circumstances of the present case. After much hesitation I have j
> come to the conclusion that it can. Reading all the speeches together, the
> principle applied by the House of Lords seems to me to amount to this. If it
> is an established fact that conduct of a particular kind creates a risk that injury
> will be caused to another or increases an existing risk that injury will ensue,
> and if the two parties stand in such a relationship that the one party owes a
> duty not to conduct himself in that way, and if one party does conduct

himself in that way, and if the other party does suffer injury of the kind to which the injury related, then the first party is taken to have caused the injury by his breach of duty, even though the existence and extent of the contribution made by the breach cannot be ascertained. If this is the right analysis, it seems to me that the shape taken by the enhancement of the risk ought not to be of crucial significance. In *McGhee* the conduct of the employers made it more likely that the pursuer would contract dermatitis, and he did contract dermatitis. Here, the conduct of those for whom the defendants are liable made it more likely that Martin would contract RLF, and he did contract RLF. If considerations of justice demanded that the pursuer succeed in the one case, I can see no reason why the plaintiff should not succeed in the other.' (See [1986] 3 All ER 801 at 828–829, [1987] QB 730 at 771–772.)

[148] Browne-Wilkinson V-C dissented. In a passage with which Lord Bridge ([1988] 1 All ER 871 at 881–882, [1988] AC 1074 at 1090) was quite unable to find any fault he pointed out that to apply the 'principle' in *McGhee's* case to the facts of *Wilsher's* case would constitute an extension of that principle. He then summarised the facts of *McGhee's* case in this way:

'In *McGhee* there was no doubt that the pursuer's dermatitis was physically caused by brick dust; the only question was whether the continued presence of such brick dust on the pursuer's skin after the time when he sould have been provided with a shower caused or materially contributed to the dermatitis which he contracted. There was only one possible agent which could have caused the dermatitis, viz brick dust, and there was no doubt that the dermatitis from which he suffered was caused by that brick dust.' (See [1986] 3 All ER 801 at 834, [1987] QB 730 at 779.)

Having stated the issues in *Wilsher's* case, Browne-Wilkinson V-C continued:

'The position, to my mind, is wholly different from that in *McGhee*, where there was only one candidate (brick dust) which could have caused the dermatitis, and the failure to take a precaution against brick dust causing dermatitis was followed by dermatitis caused by brick dust. In such a case, I can see the common sense, if not the logic, of holding that, in the absence of any other evidence, the failure to take the precaution caused or contributed to the dermatitis. To the extent that certain members of the House of Lords decided the question on inferences from evidence or presumptions, I do not consider that the present case falls within their reasoning. A failure to take preventive measures against one out of five possible causes is no evidence as to which of those five caused the injury.' (See [1986] 3 All ER 801 at 835, [1987] QB 730 at 779.)

[149] Adopting the reasoning of Browne-Wilkinson V-C, the House reversed the decision of the Court of Appeal—and rightly so. Mustill LJ's extension of the approach in *McGhee's* case to a situation where there were all kinds of other possible causes of the plaintiff's condition, resulted in obvious injustice to the defendants. In particular, there was nothing to show that the risk which the defendants' staff had created—that the plaintiff would develop retrolental fibroplasia because of an unduly highly level of oxygen—had eventuated. That being so, there was no proper basis for applying the principle in *McGhee's* case. As Browne-Wilkinson decisively observed, a failure to take preventive measures against one of five possible causes was no evidence as to which of those five had

caused the injury. The reasoning of Browne-Wilkinson V-C, which the House adopted, provided a sound and satisfactory basis for distinguishing *McGhee*'s case and for allowing the appeal. The year before indeed, the House had distinguished *McGhee*'s case on the basis that a pursuer had not proved that the junior house officer's mistake had materially increased the risk of the particular kind of neurological damage suffered by his son: *Kay v Ayrshire and Arran Health Board* [1987] 2 All ER 417.

[150] Instead of distinguishing the decision in *McGhee*'s case, however, Lord Bridge chose to gloss it in a way that does not do justice to the reasoning in the speeches, with the possible exception of Lord Kilbrandon's. Contrary to Lord Bridge's view that nothing more was involved than an issue of fact, Lord Reid had expressly stated that the pursuer's case raised 'a difficult question of law' ([1972] 3 All ER 1008 at 1009, [1973] 1 WLR 1 at 3). Even with the benefit of the further analysis of my noble and learned friend, Lord Hutton, I am satisfied that it was this question of law that Lord Reid and the other judges proceeded to elucidate and to determine, having regard to the various policy issues that arose. Taking account of such matters in formulating a legal test is usual and legitimate. By contrast, using them as a basis for modifying the way in which a court assesses evidence and finds facts, as Lord Bridge appears to suggest, is at best questionable. A judge applying 'a robust and pragmatic approach to the undisputed primary facts' may all too readily stray beyond the realm of inference into the wilderness of 'mere speculation or conjecture' *Caswell v Powell Duffryn Associated Collieries Ltd* [1939] 3 All ER 722 at 734, [1940] AC 152 at 169–170 per Lord Wright. In particular, even though it is always for the judge rather than for the expert witness to determine matters of fact, the judge must do so on the basis of the evidence, including the expert evidence. The mere application of 'common sense' cannot conjure up a proper basis for inferring that an injury must have been caused in one way rather than another when the only relevant evidence is undisputed scientific evidence which says that either way is equally possible. In my respectful opinion, therefore, despite the criticism of Sopinka J in *Snell v Farrell* [1990] 2 SCR 311 at 331, Lord Wilberforce was right to say that using inference to bridge the evidential gap in *McGhee*'s case would have been something of a fiction since it was precisely that inference which the medical expert had declined to make ([1972] 3 All ER 1008 at 1013, [1973] 1 WLR 1 at 7). In any event, the gloss added by the House in *Wilsher*'s case, highly influential though it has subsequently proved to be, cannot in itself supplant the reasoning of the judges in *McGhee*'s case. In the circumstances, I too take the view that these observations in *Wilsher*'s case should no longer be regarded as authoritative.

[151] Although counsel for the respondents accepted that, if reinstated, the principle in *McGhee*'s case would govern the present appeals and would mean that the appeals would have to be allowed, it is worth noticing why that should be so.

[152] The parallels between the cases are striking. In *McGhee*'s case the defenders had negligently failed to provide showers to remove sweat and dust; in these cases the defendants had negligently failed to provide protection from asbestos dust. In *McGhee*'s case, by removing the sweat and dust, the showers would have been intended to guard the workmen against suffering skin diseases such as dermatitis; here the protection against inhaling asbestos dust would have been intended to guard the workmen against suffering asbestos-related illnesses such as mesothelioma. In *McGhee*'s case the failure to provide the showers materially increased the risk of the pursuer developing dermatitis; in these cases the failure to protect against inhaling asbestos dust materially increased the risk of the claimants developing mesothelioma. In *McGhee*'s case the pursuer

a developed dermatitis due to the presence of dust and sweat on his skin, while in these cases the claimants developed mesothelioma due to inhaling asbestos dust. In *McGhee's* case it was not possible in the state of medical knowledge for the pursuer to prove in the usual way whether the dermatitis started because of a single abrasion or because of multiple abrasions. Here in the state of medical knowledge it is not possible for the claimants to prove whether the mesothelioma

b started from the effect of a single fibre or from the effect of multiple fibres. In *McGhee's* case it was simply not possible for the pursuer to prove that his dermatitis was caused by an accumulation of abrasions; similarly, here it is simply not possible for the claimants to prove that their mesothelioma was caused by an accumulation of asbestos fibres. In *McGhee's* case it was not possible for the pursuer to prove that the hypothetical single abrasion had been caused at a time

c after he should have had a shower and was cycling home. Here it is not possible for the claimants to prove that the hypothetical single fibre had been inhaled while they were working with any particular employer and especially while they were working with any of the defendants.

[153] In one respect, of course, the cases diverge. In *McGhee's* case the only

d possible source of the dust and sweat was the National Coal Board's kiln and the only possible wrongdoers were the coal board. Here, by contrast, the defendants are simply some among a number of employers who negligently exposed the claimants to asbestos dust. The Court of Appeal ([2002] 1 WLR 1052 at [104]) attached some importance to this distinction. On closer inspection, however, the distinction does not appear to be material for present purposes. The important

e point is that in both cases the state of scientific knowledge makes it impossible for the victim to prove on the balance of probabilities that his injury was caused by the defenders' or defendants' wrongdoing rather than by events of a similar nature which would not constitute wrongdoing on their part. Therefore, if the principle applies to permit the pursuer to recover in *McGhee's* case, it should

f similarly apply to allow the claimants to recover in these cases. Indeed, on one view the principle is easier to apply in the present cases than in *McGhee's* case since it is not disputed that the men developed mesothelioma as a result of a tort by one of their employers. The claimants thus have all the necessary elements for a successful claim except, it is argued, proof of causation. In *McGhee's* case, on the other hand, it was possible that the pursuer's dermatitis had been prompted

g purely by his exposure to dust in the kiln and by his exertions there, for which the employers would not have been liable in delict. So, application of the principle was crucial to connect the pursuer's illness not just with the defenders' legal wrong but with any legal wrong at all. In that sense these cases are a fortiori *McGhee's* case.

h [154] The decision in *McGhee's* case undoubtedly involved a development of the law relating to causation. The context within which that development falls to be evaluated is described in the observations on principle in the speeches of my noble and learned friends, Lord Nicholls of Birkenhead and Lord Hoffmann, to which I respectfully refer.

[155] As counsel for the defendants submitted, the principle in *McGhee's* case

j involves an element of rough justice, since it is possible that a defendant may be found liable when, if science permitted the matter to be clarified completely, it would turn out that the defendant's wrongdoing did not in fact lead to the men's illness. That consideration weighed with the Court of Appeal ([2002] 1 WLR 1052 at [103]). It must be faced squarely. The opposing potential injustice to claimants should also be addressed squarely. If defendants are not held liable in such circumstances, then claimants have no claim, even though, similarly, if the

matter could be clarified completely, it might turn out that the defendants were
indeed the authors of the men's illness. Other considerations colour the picture.   *a*
The men did nothing wrong, whereas all the defendants wrongly exposed them
to the risk of developing a fatal cancer, a risk that has eventuated in these cases.
At best, it was only good luck if any particular defendant's negligence did not
trigger the victim's mesothelioma. The defendants, in effect, say that it is because
they are all wrongdoers that the claimants have no case. In other words: the   *b*
greater the risk that the men have run at the hands of successive negligent
employers, the smaller the claimants' chances of obtaining damages. In these
circumstances, one might think, in dubio the law should favour the claimants.
Moreover, in *McGhee's* case the House did nothing more than set the
requirement of proof at the highest that the pursuer could possibly attain—hardly
a relaxation in any real sense. He had proved all that he could and had established   *c*
that the defenders' wrongdoing had put him at risk of the very kind of injury
which befell him. To require more would have been to say that he could never
recover for his injury—unless he achieved the impossible. Finally, as was
recognised in *McGhee* ([1972] 3 All ER 1008 at 1015, 1018, [1973] 1 WLR 1 at 9, 12
per Lord Simon and Lord Salmon respectively), if the law did indeed impose a   *d*
standard of proof that no pursuer could ever satisfy, then, so far as the civil law is
concerned, employers could with impunity negligently expose their workmen to
the risk of dermatitis—or, far worse, of mesothelioma. The substantive duty of
care would be emptied of all practical content so far as victims are concerned. In
my view considerations of these kinds justified the House in developing the
approach of Viscount Simonds and Lord Cohen in *Nicholson's* case to fashion and   *e*
apply the principle in *McGhee's* case. A fortiori they justify the application of that
principle in the present case where the risk to the men was so much worse.

[156] I derive support for that conclusion from what has been done in other
legal systems. In the course of the hearing counsel for both sides referred to
authorities from a number of different jurisdictions. It would be impossible to do   *f*
justice to all of them in this opinion. Broadly speaking, they appear to me to
demonstrate two things: first, that other systems have identified the need to
adopt special rules or principles to cope with situations where the claimant
cannot establish which of a number of wrongdoers actually caused his injury;
secondly, that there are considerable divergences of view and indeed uncertainty
as to the proper area within which any such special rules or principles should   *g*
apply. I have simply selected a few among the many authorities cited by counsel.

[157] Perhaps the most telling illustration of the universality of the problem
with which the House is faced comes from two passages in the digest cited by Sir
Sydney Kentridge QC. The issues in the texts have been helpfully analysed in a
recent study by Mr Jeroen Kortmann 'Ab alio ictu(s): Misconceptions about   *h*
Julian's View of Causation' (1999) 20 Journal of Legal History 95. The texts show
that, in a certain form, problems with unidentifiable wrongdoers had begun to
exercise the minds of Roman jurists not later than the first century BC.

[158] D 9 2 51 Julian 86 digesta contains a substantial extract from one of the
most important works on Roman law, written in the second century AD, the high
classical period of Roman law. In the principium Julian is discussing ch 1 of the   *j*
Lex Aquilia, which gives the owner of a slave the right to claim damages if
someone wrongfully 'kills' the slave. Julian considers whether someone 'kills' a
slave for these purposes if he mortally wounds him and later someone else attacks
the slave who dies more quickly as a result. Julian takes the view, which was
probably not shared by all the jurists, that both persons who attacked the slave
should be liable for 'killing' him. In support of that view, he says in D 9 2 51 1 that

a it follows from the authoritative rulings of the old, Republican, jurists who held
that, where a slave was wounded by a number of people in such a way that it was
impossible to say whose blow had caused his death, then all of them were liable
under the lex Aquilia:

b '... idque est consequens auctoritati veterum qui, cum a pluribus idem
servus ita vulneratus esset ut non appareret cuius ictu perisset, omnes lege
Aquilia teneri iudicaverunt.'

The old translation in CH Monro *The Digest of Justinian* (1909) vol 2, pp 140–141
is reliable, with the addition of the words in square brackets:

c 'This is in keeping with the view handed down from the old lawyers, who,
where the same slave was wounded by several persons under such
circumstances that it did not appear by whose hand it was that he died, came
to the conclusion that they were all liable [under the lex Aquilia].'

The text does not state expressly whether the case involved a concerted attack or
simply a series of blows inflicted by different people, perhaps at different times.
d But the context of this particular passage, at least as preserved by Justinian's
compilers, would suggest that, even if the case involves a concerted attack, Julian
is thinking in terms of the liability of the participants as individuals, striking their
own separate blows. Otherwise, Julian would not quote it as support for his view
on a case which plainly involved blows delivered by different people in the course
e of quite separate attacks. In any event, the underlying doctrine must be that, in
the kind of attack in question, in principle only the actual person who kills the
slave is liable for killing. Were that not so, the old jurists would not have needed
to make this special ruling that all the participants are liable under the lex Aquilia
for killing the slave when it is unclear whose blow actually killed him. The reason
for the ruling was, obviously, to make the statutory remedy of damages under
f ch 1 available to the owner of the slave in these circumstances.

[159] This passage in Julian's digesta is referred to by the later writer Ulpian in
D 9 2 11 2 Ulpian 18 ad edictum:

g '... sed si plures servum percusserint, utrum omnes quasi occiderint
teneantur, videamus. et si quidem apparet, cuius ictu perierit, ille quasi
occiderit tenetur: quod si non apparet, omnes quasi occiderint teneri Iulianus
ait, et si cum uno agatur, ceteri non liberantur: nam ex lege Aquilia quod
alius praestitit, alium non relevat, cum sit poena.'

Again the translation by Monro *The Digest of Justinian* vol 2, pp 121–122 is
h satisfactory for present purposes, with the omission of the word in square
brackets:

'But if a number of persons struck him, it is a point to consider whether all
are not liable, as having [all] killed him. As to this, if it is known who struck
the fatal blow, that one is liable, as having killed him; but, if it is not known,
j then, according to Julianus, all are liable, as having slain, and if an action is
brought against one, this does not release the others, because, under the *lex
Aquilia*, payment by one man is no discharge to another, as it is a case of penal
damages.'

Ulpian considers whether, if several people strike a slave, all of them are liable for
killing him. He says that, if it is clear who struck the blow from which the slave
died, that person is liable for killing him. But he reports Julian's view that, if this

is not clear, then all of them are liable for killing him. Again the precise factual
situation is not spelled out, but it looks as if Ulpian is considering the case of an
attack on the slave by several people at once. Since only the actual person whose
blow killed the slave is liable if his identity is known, Ulpian must, however, be
thinking primarily in terms of the individual liability of the person who does the
killing: it is only if you cannot tell whose blow proved fatal that Julian holds that
all are liable for killing the slave. A separate rule is adopted for that situation.

[160] I would take from these passages the clear implication that classical
Roman jurists of the greatest distinction saw the need for the law to deal specially
with the situation where it was impossible to ascertain the identity of the actual
killer among a number of wrongdoers. If strict proof of causation were required,
the plaintiff would be deprived of his remedy in damages for the death of his
slave. In that situation, some jurists at least were prepared, exceptionally, to hold
all of the wrongdoers liable and so afford a remedy to the owner whose slave had
been killed. The exact scope of these decisions can, of course, no longer be
ascertained and it is likely that different jurists held differing views: the sixth
century compilers of the digest may well have altered the texts to some extent, if
only by abbreviation, cutting out the cut and thrust of debate. Nor could the
decisions, as recorded, furnish any guidance on the formulation of any equivalent
rule today. The point remains, however, that all these centuries ago
considerations of policy plainly led to a departure from what the law would
usually require by way of proof of causation.

[161] Among slightly more recent authorities the decision of the Supreme
Court of California in *Rutherford v Owens-Illinois Inc* (1997) 67 Cal Rptr 2d 16
stands out both as being directly in point and as providing powerful support for
applying the principle in *McGhee*'s case to the circumstances of the present cases.
Mr Rutherford had worked with asbestos products on board ships at Mare Island
Naval Shipyard. He developed, and died from, lung cancer caused by inhaling
asbestos fibres. Proceedings were raised against some 19 manufacturers and
distributors of asbestos products, including Owens-Illinois. Before the issues of
liability and damages fell to be determined, all of the defendants except
Owens-Illinois settled. In the trial the judge gave the jury an instruction that the
burden was on Owens-Illinois to prove that their products were not a legal cause
of the deceased's injuries. The Supreme Court held that this direction should not
have been given, but further held that the plaintiffs need do no more than prove
that exposure to the company's asbestos products was, in reasonable medical
probability, a substantial factor in causing or contributing to his risk of developing
cancer ((1997) 67 Cal Rptr 2d 16 at 19).

[162] The Supreme Court were satisfied that the plaintiffs bore the burden of
proving which exposures to asbestos were substantial factors increasing the risk
(at 32–33). For their part Owens-Illinois conceded that plaintiffs in asbestos cases
were not required to identify the manufacturer of specific fibres that caused the
cancer. Giving the judgment of the Supreme Court, Baxter J agreed (at 31–32):

'Plaintiffs cannot be expected to prove the scientifically unknown details of
carcinogenesis, or trace the unknowable path of a given asbestos fiber. But
the impossibility of such proof does not dictate use of a burden shift. Instead,
we can bridge this gap in the humanly knowable by holding that plaintiffs
may prove causation in asbestos-related cancer cases by demonstrating that
the plaintiff's exposure to defendant's asbestos-containing product in
reasonable medical probability was a substantial factor in contributing to the
aggregate *dose* of asbestos the plaintiff or decedent inhaled or ingested, and

a hence to the *risk* of developing asbestos-related cancer, without the need to demonstrate that fibers from the defendant's particular product were the ones, or among the ones, that *actually* produced the malignant growth.'

The judge considered the standard jury instructions but commented (at 32):

b 'They say nothing, however, to inform the jury that, in asbestos-related cancer cases, a particular asbestos-containing product is deemed to be a substantial factor in bringing about the injury if its contribution to the plaintiff or decedent's *risk* or *probability* of developing cancer was substantial. Without such guidance, a juror might well conclude that the plaintiff needed to prove that fibers from the defendant's product were a substantial factor *actually contributing* to the development of the plaintiff's or decedent's cancer. In many cases, such a burden will be medically impossible to sustain, even with the greatest possible effort by the plaintiff, because of irreducible uncertainty regarding the cellular formation of an asbestos-related cancer. We therefore hold that, in the trial of an asbestos-related cancer case, although no instruction "shifting the burden of proof as to causation" to defendant is warranted, the jury should be told that the plaintiff's or decedent's exposure to a particular product was a substantial factor in causing or bringing about the disease if in reasonable medical probability it was a substantial factor contributing to plaintiff's or decedent's *risk* of developing cancer.'

e [163] The court held that proof, that exposure to a defendant's product was a substantial factor contributing to the risk of developing cancer, was to be equated with proof that the exposure was a substantial factor in causing or bringing about the disease. Mr Stewart accepted that analysis of the decision. Allowing for slight differences in terminology, the doctrine espoused by the Californian court is similar to the principle to be derived from *McGhee*'s case which the appellants f contend should be applied in these cases. There is nothing in the report of the judgment to show that the Supreme Court of California were referred to *McGhee*'s case. The fact that, apparently independently, they came to an essentially similar conclusion is powerful corroboration of the approach in *McGhee*'s case and of its applicability in the present cases. Mr Stewart criticised g *Rutherford*'s case on the ground that the law should not develop principles to be applied only in the case of asbestos-related illness. While the court's opinion is indeed couched solely in relation to cases of that kind, the reasoning itself develops from the impossibility of proof inherent in those cases. There is nothing in that reasoning to suggest that the Supreme Court would refuse to apply a similar approach in other cases where similar irremediable problems of proof of h causation arose. I would therefore reject that criticism, which in any event does not strike at the application of the reasoning in *McGhee*'s case to cases of mesothelioma.

[164] Counsel referred to many cases decided by the courts of Australia and Canada and Lord Bingham of Cornhill has analysed the most important of them. j Again, they illustrate the very real problem which confronts the law in cases of this kind. The decisions vary but, overall, they tend to reflect the same rival lines of thinking as are to be found in *McGhee*'s case and *Wilsher*'s case. I merely mention some that are favourable to plaintiffs. In the classic case of *Cook v Lewis* [1951] SCR 830 the Supreme Court of Canada were faced with a situation where the jury in a civil action had been unable to determine which of two huntsmen had fired the shot which injured the plaintiff. For the majority, Cartwright J held

(at 842) that, if the shot had been fired negligently, both should have been held liable. The fact that, otherwise, the victim would have been remediless appears to have been a factor in the court's decision. In some more recent cases examples are to be found of courts and judges applying the kind of approach adopted in *McGhee's* case: *Birkholtz v RJ Gilbertson Pty Ltd* (1985) 38 SASR 121 at 130 per King CJ; *Bendix Mintex Pty Ltd v Barnes* (1997) 42 NSWLR 307 per Stein JA dissenting; *Chappel v Hart* (1998) 195 CLR 232 at 244 (para 27) per McHugh J dissenting. I draw support for my view on the applicability of the *McGhee* principle from these judgments.

[165] The Commonwealth cases were supplemented, at your Lordships' suggestion, by a certain amount of material describing the position in European legal systems. Again I do not repeat Lord Bingham's survey. The material provides a check, from outside the common law world, that the problem identified in these appeals is genuine and is one that requires to be remedied.

[166] So, for instance, the French courts have been particularly exercised by cases, similar to *Cook v Lewis*, arising out of hunting accidents where the victim is unable to pinpoint which of a group of huntsmen caused his injury. The law has permitted the victim to recover damages, partly at least by finding that the substantial cause of the victim's injury was some negligence or recklessness of the group as a whole. The decision of the Second Chamber of the Cour de Cassation in *Litzinger v Kintzler* (Cass civ 2e, 5 June 1957, D 1957 Jur 493 note Savatier) is an early example. I refer to the discussion in W van Gerven, J Lever, P Larouche *Tort Law* (2000) pp 442–444.

[167] The German position is even more instructive. Since its inception, art 830(1) second sentence of the Bürgerliches Gesetzbuch has contained a special provision which in effect provides that, where it cannot be ascertained which of a number of individual wrongdoers caused the victim's injury, each of them is to be held liable:

> 'Haben mehrere durch eine gemeinschaftlich begangene unerlaubte Handlung einen Schaden verursacht, so ist jeder für den Schaden verantwortlich. Das Gleiche gilt, wenn sich nicht ermitteln lässt, wer von mehreren Beteiligten den Schaden durch seine Handlung verursacht hat.'

The translation is:

> 'If several persons have caused damage by an unlawful act committed in common, each is responsible for the damage. The same rule applies if it cannot be discovered which of several participants has caused the damage by his act.'

The mere fact that the draftsmen of the code identified the need for a general provision of this type shows that the problem of injury caused by unidentified wrongdoers was thought to be of some significance. It is, moreover, a problem that is not necessarily to be solved simply by leaving the loss to lie on the victim. On the other hand, it is equally plain that in Germany the policy is to resolve such difficulties in favour of the claimant on a wide front and, therefore, to do so in many cases where the law in this country would simply hold that he had failed to prove his case. See, for instance, *Motive zu dem Entwurfe eines Bürgerlichen Gesetzbuches für das Deutsche Reich* (1888) vol 2, p 738. That reflects the particular policy choice of German law, which the courts articulate: BGHZ 25, 271, 274; OLG München MDR 1967, 671, 672. A good example of this more extensive approach is the case of the lady who fell on an uneven surface and could not a establish whether the precise place where she fell was on an unfinished street belonging to the local authority or on land belonging to an individual. The Bundesgerichtshof held that the provision in art 830(1) applied and allowed her to recover damages against the individual: BGHZ 25, 271; van Gerven, *Tort Law*, pp 444–445.

b [168] At the very least, the cross-check with these systems suggests that it is not necessarily the hallmark of a civilised and sophisticated legal system that it treats cases where strict proof of causation is impossible in exactly the same way as cases where such proof is possible. As I have tried to show, there are obvious policy reasons why, in certain cases at least, a different approach is preferable in English law too. The present are among such cases. Following the approach in *McGhee*'s case I accordingly hold that, by proving that the defendants individually

c materially increased the risk that the men would develop mesothelioma due to inhaling asbestos fibres, the claimants are taken in law to have proved that the defendants materially contributed to their illness.

[169] While that is sufficient for the decision of the appeals, Mr Stewart urged that, if minded to apply some version of the principle in *McGhee*'s case, the House

d should define its scope. He pointed out that the speeches in *McGhee*'s case had left doubt as to the scope of the principle that the House had been applying and the decision of the Court of Appeal in *Wilsher*'s case had shown only too clearly that it could be extended too far. It is indeed plain that, as Lord Nicholls of Birkenhead has observed, considerable restraint is called for in using the principle. Identifying, at an abstract level, the defining characteristics of the cases

e where it is, none the less, proper to apply the principle is far from easy. The common law naturally and traditionally shies away from such generalisations especially in a developing area of the law. But, having regard to the cases cited by counsel and also, in particular, to the cases and textbooks on the German law referred to in van Gerven *Tort Law*, pp 444–447 and 459–461, I would tentatively

f suggest that certain conditions are necessary, but may not always be sufficient, for applying the principle. All the criteria are satisfied in the present cases.

[170] First, the principle is designed to resolve the difficulty that arises where it is inherently impossible for the claimant to prove exactly how his injury was caused. It applies, therefore, where the claimant has proved all that he possibly can, but the causal link could only ever be established by scientific investigation

g and the current state of the relevant science leaves it uncertain exactly how the injury was caused and, so, who caused it. *McGhee*'s case and the present cases are examples. Secondly, part of the underlying rationale of the principle is that the defendant's wrongdoing has materially increased the risk that the claimant will suffer injury. It is therefore essential not just that the defendant's conduct created

h a material risk of injury to a class of persons but that it actually created a material risk of injury to the claimant himself. Thirdly, it follows that the defendant's conduct must have been capable of causing the claimant's injury. Fourthly, the claimant must prove that his injury was caused by the eventuation of the kind of risk created by the defendant's wrongdoing. In *McGhee*'s case, for instance, the risk created by the defenders' failure was that the pursuer would develop dermatitis

j due to brick dust on his skin and he proved that he had developed dermatitis due to brick dust on his skin. By contrast, the principle does not apply where the claimant has merely proved that his injury could have been caused by a number of different events, only one of which is the eventuation of the risk created by the defendant's wrongful act or omission. *Wilsher*'s case is an example. Fifthly, this will usually mean that the claimant must prove that his injury was caused, if not by exactly the same agency as was involved in the defendant's wrongdoing, at

least by an agency that operated in substantially the same way. A possible
example would be where a workman suffered injury from exposure to dusts
coming from two sources, the dusts being particles of different substances each
of which, however, could have caused his injury in the same way. Without
having heard detailed argument on the point, I incline to the view that the
principle was properly applied by the Court of Appeal in *Fitzgerald v Lane* [1987] 2
All ER 455, [1987] QB 781. Sixthly, the principle applies where the other possible
source of the claimant's injury is a similar wrongful act or omission of another
person, but it can also apply where, as in *McGhee's* case, the other possible source
of the injury is a similar, but lawful, act or omission of the same defendant. I
reserve my opinion as to whether the principle applies where the other possible
source of injury is a similar but lawful act or omission of someone else or a natural
occurrence.

[171] For these reasons I was in favour of allowing the appeals and of making
the appropriate orders in each of the cases.

Appeals allowed.

Kate O'Hanlon   Barrister.

a # English v Emery Reimbold & Strick Ltd

DJ & C Withers (Farms) Ltd v Ambic Equipment Ltd

b ## Verrechia (trading as Freightmaster Commercials) v Commissioner of Police of the Metropolis

[2002] EWCA Civ 605

c

COURT OF APPEAL, CIVIL DIVISION

LORD PHILLIPS OF WORTH MATRAVERS MR, LATHAM AND ARDEN LJJ

25, 26 MARCH, 30 APRIL 2002

d

Judge – Reasons – Failure by judge to give reasons for conclusion essential to judgment – Appeals on ground of inadequacy of reasons – Guidance.

In the first two of three appeals to the Court of Appeal, trial judges had found for the defendants in cases in which conflicting expert evidence had been of critical
e importance. In each case, the claimant contended that he had not received a fair trial, and was entitled to a retrial, because the judge had failed to explain why he had reached his decision. In the third case, the judge expressed the provisional view that there should be no order as to the costs of proceedings in which the claimant had been partially successful. The parties then made substantial written
f submissions to the judge on that issue. Subsequently, she handed down a one-paragraph judgment affirming her provisional view, but without giving any reasons for her decision. The claimant appealed, relying, inter alia, on the judge's failure to give reasons. On the appeals, the Court of Appeal provided guidance on various issues relating to appeals on the ground of failure to give adequate reasons.
g

Held – (1) When considering the extent to which reasons should be given, it was necessary to have regard to the practical requirements of the appellate system. A judge could not be said to have done his duty if it were only after permission to appeal had been given, and the appeal had run its course, that the appeal court
h was able to conclude that the reasons for the decision were sufficiently apparent to enable it to uphold the judgment. Although the judge did not need to identify and explain every factor that had weighed with him in his appraisal of the evidence, he should identify the issues the resolution of which had been vital to his conclusion, and explain the manner in which he had resolved them. If the
j critical issue were one of fact, it might be enough to say that one witness was preferred to another because the one manifestly had a clearer recollection of the facts or the other had given answers which demonstrated that his recollection could not be relied upon. In cases involving a conflict of expert evidence, a judge simply had to provide an explanation, apparent from the judgment, as to why he had accepted the evidence of one expert and rejected that of another (see [18]–[20], below).

(2) An unsuccessful party should not seek to upset a judgment on the ground
of inadequacy of reasons unless, despite the advantage of considering the
judgment with knowledge of the evidence given and submissions made at the
trial, he was unable to understand why the judge had reached an adverse
decision. If an application for permission to appeal on the ground of lack of
reasons were made to the trial judge, he should consider whether his judgment
was defective for lack of reasons, adjourning for that purpose if necessary. If he
did find such a defect, he should remedy it by the provision of additional reasons,
refusing permission to appeal on the basis that he had adopted that course. If an
application for permission to appeal on the ground of lack of reasons were made
to the appellate court, and the application appeared to be well founded, that court
should consider adjourning the application and remitting the case to the trial
judge with an invitation to provide additional reasons for his decision or, where
appropriate, his reasons for a specific finding or findings. Where the appellate
court was in doubt as to whether the reasons were adequate, it might be
appropriate to direct that the application be adjourned to an oral hearing, on
notice to the respondent (see [25], [118], below); *Flannery v Halifax Estate
Agencies Ltd* [2000] 1 All ER 373 considered.

(3) Where permission to appeal had been granted on the grounds of
inadequate reasons, the appellate court should first review the judgment, in the
context of the material evidence and submissions at the trial, in order to consider
whether the reason why the judge had reached his decision was apparent. If the
court were satisfied that the reason was apparent and constituted a valid basis for
the judgment, the appeal would be dismissed. If, however, the reason was not
apparent, the appeal court would have to decide whether to proceed to a
rehearing or to direct a new trial (see [26], below).

(4) Although a judge need not give reasons for an order for costs where those
reasons were clearly implicit from the order made, the CPR sometimes required
a more complex approach to costs, and judgments dealing with costs would more
often need to identify the provisions of the rules that had been in play and why
they had led to the order being made. Where no express explanation had been
given for a costs order, an appellate court would approach the material facts on
the assumption that the judge would have had good reason for the award made.
Where it was apparent that there was a perfectly rational explanation for the
order made, the court was likely to draw the inference that that explanation had
motivated the judge in making the order. Thus, in practice, it was only likely to
be appropriate to give permission to appeal, on the ground of lack of reasons,
against an order that related solely to costs in those cases where the order had
been made neither with reasons nor any obvious explanation (see [14], [28]–[30],
[91], below).

(5) In the instant cases, the judgments had created uncertainty as to the
reasons for the decisions. That uncertainty had been resolved, but only after
appeals involving consideration of the underlying evidence and submissions.
Nevertheless, the claimants should have appreciated why they had not been
successful. In each case, the judge's decision was justified by the reasoning
identified on the appeal. Accordingly, the appeals would be dismissed (see [53],
[56], [57], [89], [90], [110]–[112], [117], [118], below).

Per curiam. Under the CPR, the court has wide power to make orders for
costs that reflect not just the ultimate victory, but the extent to which a party has
raised issues on which he has not succeeded. However, CPR 44.3(7)[a] requires
that an order allowing or disallowing costs by reference to certain issues should

a   be made only if other forms of order cannot be made that sufficiently reflect the justice of the case. A 'percentage' order under CPR 44.3(6)(a) will often produce a fairer result than an 'issues-based' order under CPR 44.3(6)(f). Wherever practicable, therefore, judges should endeavour to form a view as to the percentage of costs to which the winning party should be entitled or alternatively whether justice would be sufficiently done by awarding costs, under CPR 44.3(6)(c), from or until a

b   particular date only (see [113], [115], [116], below).

Notes

For a judge's duty to give reasons, see 1(1) *Halsbury's Laws* (4th edn) (2001 reissue) para 112 n12.

c   **Cases referred to in judgment**

Antaios Cia Naviera SA v Salen Rederierna AB, The Antaios [1984] 3 All ER 229, [1985] AC 191, [1984] 3 WLR 592, HL.

Balani v Spain (1994) 19 EHRR 566, [1994] ECHR 18064/91, ECt HR.

Brent London BC v Aniedobe [1999] CA Transcript 2003.

d   *Eagil Trust Co Ltd v Pigott-Brown* [1985] 3 All ER 119, CA.

Eckersley v Binnie (1987) 18 ConLR 1, QBD and CA.

Flannery v Halifax Estate Agencies Ltd [2000] 1 All ER 373, [2000] 1 WLR 377, CA.

Hadjianastassiou v Greece (1992) 16 EHRR 219, [1992] ECHR 12945/87, ECt HR.

Harrison v Bloom Camillin (4 February 2000, unreported), Ch D.

e   *Helle v Finland* (1997) 26 EHRR 159, [1997] ECHR 20772/92, ECt HR.

Knight v Clifton [1971] 2 All ER 378, [1971] Ch 700, [1971] 2 WLR 564, CA.

Lewis v Wilson & Horton Ltd [2000] 3 NZLR 546, NZ CA.

Ludlow v National Power plc [2000] All ER (D) 1868, CA.

North Range Shipping Ltd v Seatrans Shipping Corp [2002] EWCA Civ 405, [2002] All ER (D) 409 (Mar).

f   *R v Crown Court at Harrow, ex p Dave* [1994] 1 All ER 315, [1994] 1 WLR 98, DC.

R v Crown Court at Knightsbridge, ex p International Sporting Club (London) Ltd [1981] 3 All ER 417, [1982] QB 304, [1981] 3 WLR 640, DC.

Roache v News Group Newspapers Ltd [1998] EMLR 161, CA.

Robins v UK (23 September 1997, unreported), [1997] ECHR 22410/93, ECt HR.

g   *Ruiz v Spain* (2001) 31 EHRR 589, [1999] ECHR 30544/96, ECt I IR.

Soulcmezis v Dudley (Holdings) Pty Ltd (1987) 10 NSWLR 247, NSW CA.

Torija v Spain (1994) 19 EHRR 553, [1994] ECHR 18390/91, ECt HR.

Van de Hurk v The Netherlands (1994) 18 EHRR 481, [1994] ECHR 16034/90, ECt HR.

Webb v UK (1997) 24 EHRR CD 73, E Com HR.

h   *X v Federal Republic of Germany* (1982) 4 EHRR 398, E Com HR.

Appeals

English v Emery Reimbold & Strick Ltd

j   The claimant, Peter Andrew English, appealed with permission of Sedley LJ from the decision of Judge Ruberry in the High Court at Stoke-on-Trent on 5 June 2001 in respect of the issue of damages in his proceedings for personal injury against the defendant employers, Emery Reimbold & Strick Ltd. The facts are set out in the judgment of the court.

---

a   Rule 44.3, so far as material, is set out at [114], below

DJ & C Withers (Farms) Ltd v Ambic Equipment Ltd

The claimant, DJ & C Withers (Farms) Ltd (Withers), appealed with permission *a* of the Court of Appeal (Sedley and Arden LJJ) from the decision of Judge MacKay, sitting in the Technology and Construction Court in Liverpool on 4 May 2001, dismissing its proceedings against the defendant, Ambic Equipment Ltd (Ambic). The facts are set out in the judgment of the court.

b

Verrechia (t/a Freightmaster Commercials) v Commr of Police of the Metropolis

The claimant, Michael John Verrechia, appealed from the decision of Steel J on 4 April 2001 making no order as to the costs of his proceedings against the defendant, the Commissioner of Police of the Metropolis. The facts are set out in the judgment of the court.

c

Edward Pepperall (instructed by *Woolliscrofts*, Stoke-on-Trent) for Mr English.
Roger Giles (instructed by *Browne Jacobson*, Birmingham) for the employers.
Edward Bartley Jones QC and David Casement (instructed by *Bowcock Cuerden*, Nantwich) for Withers.
Robert Moxon-Browne QC and John McDonald (instructed by *Sheridans*) for Ambic. *d*
Ronald Walker QC and Alexander Hill-Smith (instructed by *Gordon Dadds*) for Mr Verrechia.
James Watson QC and Jason Beer (instructed by *David McCahon*) for the commissioner.

Cur adv vult

e

30 April 2002. The following judgment of the court, to which all of its members had contributed, was delivered.

LORD PHILLIPS OF WORTH MATRAVERS MR.

INTRODUCTION *f*

[1] In *Flannery v Halifax Estate Agencies Ltd* [2000] 1 All ER 373, [2000] 1 WLR 377 this court allowed an appeal on the sole ground that the judge had failed to give adequate reasons for his decision. This was despite the fact that his judgment was 29 pages in length. The trial had involved a stark conflict of expert evidence. The judge had preferred the expert evidence of the defendants to that of the plaintiffs, without explaining why. This court ordered a retrial. *g*

[2] *Flannery's* case has inspired a large number of applications for permission to appeal on the ground of inadequate reasons. In granting permission to appeal in one of the appeals before us, Sedley LJ remarked that they were becoming a cottage industry. It is an industry which is an unwelcome feature of English justice. The rights of appeal that are afforded under statute reflect the fact that *h* no judge is infallible. It should, however, be possible to deduce from a judgment the reason for the judge's decision. Happily the rash of applications for permission to appeal based upon the decision in *Flannery's* case does not reflect a widespread inability or disinclination on the part of the judiciary to explain the basis for their decisions. Rather it reflects uncertainty on the part of litigants and judges alike as *j* the extent to which a judgment should detail the chain of reasoning which has led to the order made by the judge.

[3] This judgment addresses three appeals which were listed for hearing together. In the event, the first two, *English v Emery Reimbold & Strick Ltd* and *DJ & C Withers (Farms) Ltd v Ambic Equipment Ltd,* were heard together, while the third, *Verrechia (t/a Freightmaster Commercials) v Commissioner of Police of the Metropolis*

a followed immediately afterwards. In *English's* case the critical issue was whether a disabling dislocation of a section of the claimant's spine was attributable to an injury for which the defendants were responsible or resulted from a congenital condition. On this issue, expert evidence was of critical importance. In the *DJ & C Withers* case the central issue was also one of causation—whether a hydraulic system for milking cows supplied by the defendants had suffered from design

b defects which had been responsible for an outbreak of mastitis in the claimant's herd. Again expert evidence was of critical importance. In each case the judge found for the defendants. In each case the claimant accepted that such a finding was one that was open to the judge on the evidence. In each case the claimant contended that, because the judge had failed to explain why he had reached his decision, he had not received a fair trial and was entitled to a retrial.

c [4] The decision challenged in the *Verrechia* case was of a different nature. In that case the claimant had sued the Commissioner of Police of the Metropolis for the return of a large number of commercial vehicle parts which had been lawfully seized in connection with criminal proceedings. He succeeded in relation to about one third of these; the remainder were shown to have been stolen—without

d complicity on the part of the claimant—and to belong to third parties. The judge made no order as to the costs of the proceedings, without explanation. The claimant obtained permission to appeal against her decision in relation to costs, not merely on the ground that she had failed to give any reason for it, but on the ground that it was wrong in principle.

e [5] Before turning to the facts of the individual appeals, we propose to examine the decision in *Flannery's* case in order to see whether it is possible to dispel the uncertainty to which it appears to have given rise.

THE DECISION IN FLANNERY'S CASE

[6] In giving the judgment of the court, Henry LJ remarked ([2000] 1 All ER
f 373 at 377, [2000] 1 WLR 377 at 381) that it was clear that today's professional judge owed a general duty to give reasons for his decision, citing *R v Crown Court at Knightsbridge, ex p International Sporting Club (London) Ltd* [1981] 3 All ER 417, [1982] QB 304 and *R v Crown Court at Harrow, ex p Dave* [1994] 1 All ER 315, [1994] 1 WLR 98. He made the following comments on the general duty to give reasons:

g '(1) The duty is a function of due process, and therefore of justice. Its rationale has two principal aspects. The first is that fairness surely requires that the parties—especially the losing party—should be left in no doubt why they have won or lost. This is especially so since without reasons the losing party will not know (as was said in *Ex p Dave*) whether the court has
h misdirected itself, and thus whether he may have an available appeal on the substance of the case. The second is that a requirement to give reasons concentrates the mind; if it is fulfilled, the resulting decision is much more likely to be soundly based on the evidence than if it is not. (2) The first of these aspects implies that want of reasons may be a good self-standing
j ground of appeal. Where because no reasons are given it is impossible to tell whether the judge has gone wrong on the law or the facts, the losing party would be altogether deprived of his chance of an appeal unless the court entertains an appeal based on the lack of reasons itself. (3) The extent of the duty, or rather the reach of what is required to fulfil it, depends on the subject matter. Where there is a straightforward factual dispute whose resolution depends simply on which witness is telling the truth about events

which he claims to recall, it is likely to be enough for the judge (having, no *a* doubt, summarised the evidence) to indicate simply that he believes X rather than Y; indeed there may be nothing else to say. But where the dispute involves something in the nature of an intellectual exchange, with reasons and analysis advanced on either side, the judge must enter into the issues canvassed before him and explain why he prefers one case over the other. This is likely to apply particularly in litigation where as here there is disputed *b* expert evidence; but it is not necessarily limited to such cases. (4) This is not to suggest that there is one rule for cases concerning the witnesses' truthfulness or recall of events, and another for cases where the issue depends on reasoning or analysis (with experts or otherwise). The rule is the same: the judge must explain *why* he has reached his decision. The question is always, what is required of the judge to do so; and that will differ from case *c* to case. Transparency should be the watchword.' (See [2000] 1 All ER 373 at 377–378, [2000] 1 WLR 377 at 381–382.)

[7] At the same page of the judgment ([2000] 1 All ER 373 at 377, [2000] 1 WLR 377 at 381), Henry LJ identified a number of exceptions to the duty to give reasons, including decisions in the magistrates' court and areas where the court's *d* decision is more often that not a summary exercise of discretion, in particular orders for costs. *Flannery*'s case was decided before the Human Rights Act 1998 came into force. It is clearly established by the Strasbourg jurisprudence that the right to a fair trial guaranteed by art 6 of the European Convention for the Protection of Human Rights and Fundamental Freedoms 1950 (as set out in Sch 1 *e* to the 1998 Act), which includes the requirement that judgment shall be pronounced publicly, normally carries with it an obligation that the judgment should be a reasoned judgment. In response to this requirement, magistrates' courts now give reasons for their decisions. Shortly before the hearing of these appeals another division of this court held that, in some circumstances, art 6 requires the Commercial Court to give at least limited reasons when refusing *f* permission to appeal against an arbitration award under s 69 of the Arbitration Act 1996, a practice which the House of Lords in *Antaios Cia Naviera SA v Salen Rederierna AB, The Antaios* [1984] 3 All ER 229, [1985] AC 191 had held should not be followed (see *North Range Shipping Ltd v Seatrans Shipping Corp* [2002] EWCA Civ 405, [2002] All ER (D) 409 (Mar)). We propose at the outset to consider the *g* extent of the requirement to give reasons that has been identified by the Strasbourg court and the nature of the decisions to which that requirement applies, before turning to consider whether our domestic law extends further than this jurisprudence.

h

THE STRASBOURG JURISPRUDENCE
[8] Both the general principle and the elusive nature of the task of encapsulating it in a test that can be applied in practice are apparent from the following passage from the judgment of the court in *Torija v Spain* (1994) 19 EHRR 553 at 562 (para 29):

j

'The Court reiterates that Article 6(1) obliges the courts to give reasons for their judgments, but cannot be understood as requiring a detailed answer to every argument. The extent to which this duty to give reasons applies may vary according to the nature of the decision. It is moreover necessary to take into account, *inter alia*, the diversity of the submissions that a litigant may bring before the courts and the differences existing in the Contracting States *a*   with regard to statutory provisions, customary rules, legal opinion and the presentation and drafting of judgments. That is why the question whether a court has failed to fulfil the obligation to state reasons, deriving from Article 6 of the Convention, can only be determined in the light of the circumstances of the case.'

b   These principles were reaffirmed by the court in *Ruiz v Spain* (2001) 31 EHRR 589.

[9] In *Van de Hurk v The Netherlands* (1994) 18 EHRR 481 at 501 (para 59) the court observed that art 6(1) placed the 'tribunal' under a duty to conduct a proper examination of the submissions, arguments and evidence adduced by the parties. The Strasbourg court will hold that art 6(1) has been violated if a judgment leaves it unclear whether the court in question has addressed a contention advanced by

c   a party that is fundamental to the resolution of the litigation (see, for instance, *Torija*'s case and *Balani v Spain* (1994) 19 EHRR 566). In each case, however, the court found it necessary to consider whether the fact that the Spanish Supreme Court had made no mention of the point in question could reasonably be construed as an 'implied rejection' of it. This might suggest that the court was only concerned to ascertain whether the Supreme Court had considered and

d   rejected the point, rather than whether it had given reasons for the rejection. However, the court went on to state in each case that it was impossible to ascertain whether the Supreme Court simply neglected to deal with the submission or whether it intended to dismiss it 'and, if that were its intention, what its reasons were for so deciding'.

e   [10] In *Helle v Finland* (1997) 26 EHRR 159 at 185 (para 60) the court emphasised:

> '... the notion of a fair procedure requires that a national court which has given sparse reasons for its decisions, whether by incorporating the reasons of a lower court or otherwise, did in fact address the essential issues which were submitted to its jurisdiction and did not merely endorse without
>
> *f*   further ado the findings reached by a lower court.'

[11] However in *Ruiz*'s case the court held that an appellate judgment was adequately reasoned which simply endorsed the factual and legal reasons for the first instance decision to the extent that these were not in conflict with the appellate judgment.

g   [12] The Strasbourg court, when considering art 6, is not concerned with the merits of the decision of the domestic court that is under attack. It is concerned to see that the procedure has been fair. It requires that a judgment contains reasons that are sufficient to demonstrate that the essential issues that have been raised by the parties have been addressed by the domestic court and how those

h   issues have been resolved. It does not seem to us that the Strasbourg jurisprudence goes further and requires a judgment to explain why one contention, or piece of evidence, has been preferred to another. The common law countries have developed a tradition of delivering judgments that detail the evidence and explain the findings in much greater detail than is to be found in the judgments of most

j   civil law jurisdictions. We do not believe that the extent of the reasoning that the Strasbourg court requires goes any further than that which is required under our domestic law, which we are about to consider. It remains to consider, however, the nature of the judicial decisions for which reasons are required under the Strasbourg jurisprudence.

[13] All of the Strasbourg decisions to which we have so far referred were considering judgments which determined the substantive dispute between the

parties. The critical issue in each case was whether the form of the judgment in question was compatible with a fair trial. Where a judicial decision affects the substantive rights of the parties we consider that the Strasbourg jurisprudence requires that the decision should be reasoned. In contrast, there are some judicial decisions where fairness does not demand that the parties should be informed of the reasoning underlying them. Interlocutory decisions in the course of case management provide an obvious example. Furthermore, the Strasbourg commission has recognised that there are some circumstances in which the reason for the decision will be implicit from the decision itself. In such circumstances art 6 will not be infringed if the reason for the decision is not expressly spelled out by the judicial tribunal (see *X v Federal Republic of Germany* (1982) 4 EHRR 398; *Webb v UK* (1997) 24 EHRR CD 73).

[14] It is an unhappy fact that awards of costs often have greater financial significance for the parties than the decision on the substance of the dispute. Decisions on liability for costs are customarily given in summary form after oral argument at the conclusion of the delivery of the judgment. Often no reasons are given. Such a practice can, we believe, only comply with art 6 if the reason for the decision in respect of costs is clearly implicit from the circumstances in which the award is made. This was almost always the case before the introduction of the new CPR, where the usual order was that costs 'followed the event'. The new rules encourage costs orders that more nicely reflect the extent to which each party has acted reasonably in the conduct of the litigation. Where the reason for an order as to costs is not obvious, the judge should explain why he or she has made the order. The explanation can usually be brief. The manner in which the Strasbourg court itself deals with applications for costs provides a model of all that is normally required.

THE REQUIREMENT TO GIVE REASONS UNDER COMMON LAW

[15] There is a general recognition in the common law jurisdictions that it is desirable for judges to give reasons for their decisions, although it is not universally accepted that this is a mandatory requirement—'There is no invariable rule established by New Zealand case law that Courts must give reasons for their decisions' (see *Lewis v Wilson & Horton Ltd* [2000] 3 NZLR 546 at 565 (para 75) per Elias CJ). While a constant refrain is that reasons must be given in order to render practicable the exercise of rights of appeal, a number of other justifications have been advanced for the requirement to give reasons. These include the requirement that justice must not only be done but be seen to be done. Reasons are required if decisions are to be acceptable to the parties and to members of the public. Henry LJ in *Flannery v Halifax Estate Agencies Ltd* [2000] 1 All ER 373, [2000] 1 WLR 377 observed that the requirement to give reasons concentrates the mind of the judge and it has even been contended that the requirement to give reasons serves a vital function in constraining the judiciary's exercise of power (see Professor Shapiro's article 'In Defence of Judicial Candor' (1987) 100 Harv L Rev 731 at 737). The function that judgments play under the common law in setting precedents for the future has also been identified as one of the justifications for the requirement to give reasons, although as Mahoney JA stated in *Soulemezis v Dudley (Holdings) Pty Ltd* (1987) 10 NSWLR 247 at 273:

'The court's order is a public act. The judgment given for it is a professional document, directed to the parties and to their professional advisers. It may, *a*   in a particular instance, delineate, develop or even decorate the law but that is peripheral and not essential to its nature.'

[16] We would put the matter at its simplest by saying that justice will not be done if it is not apparent to the parties why one has won and the other has lost.

[17] As to the adequacy of reasons, as has been said many times, this depends
b   on the nature of the case (see, for example, *Flannery's* case [2000] 1 All ER 373 at 378, [2000] 1 WLR 377 at 382). In *Eagil Trust Co Ltd v Pigott-Brown* [1985] 3 All ER 119 at 122, Griffiths LJ stated that there was no duty on a judge, in giving his reasons, to deal with every argument presented by counsel in support of his case:

> *c*   'When dealing with an application in chambers to strike out for want of prosecution, a judge should give his reasons in sufficient detail to show the Court of Appeal the principles on which he has acted and the reasons that have led him to his decision. They need not be elaborate. I cannot stress too strongly that there is no duty on a judge, in giving his reasons, to deal with every argument presented by counsel in support of his case. It is sufficient if what he says shows the parties, and if need be, the Court of Appeal the basis
> *d*   on which he has acted ... (see Sachs LJ in *Knight v Clifton* [1971] 2 AER 378 at 392–393, [1971] Ch 700 at 721).'

[18] In our judgment, these observations of Griffiths LJ apply to judgments of all descriptions. But when considering the extent to which reasons should be given it is necessary to have regard to the practical requirements of our appellate
e   system. A judge cannot be said to have done his duty if it is only after permission to appeal has been given and the appeal has run its course that the court is able to conclude that the reasons for the decision are sufficiently apparent to enable the appeal court to uphold the judgment. An appeal is an expensive step in the judicial process and one that makes an exacting claim on judicial resources. For
f   these reasons permission to appeal is now a nearly universal prerequisite to bringing an appeal. Permission to appeal will not normally be given unless the applicant can make out an arguable case that the judge was wrong. If the judgment does not make it clear why the judge has reached his decision, it may well be impossible within the summary procedure of an application for permission to appeal to form any view as to whether the judge was right or
g   wrong. In that event permission to appeal may be given simply because justice requires that the decision be subjected to the full scrutiny of an appeal.

[19] It follows that, if the appellate process is to work satisfactorily, the judgment must enable the appellate court to understand why the judge reached his decision. This does not mean that every factor which weighed with the judge
h   in his appraisal of the evidence has to be identified and explained. But the issues the resolution of which were vital to the judge's conclusion should be identified and the manner in which he resolved them explained. It is not possible to provide a template for this process. It need not involve a lengthy judgment. It does require the judge to identify and record those matters which were critical to his
j   decision. If the critical issue was one of fact, in may be enough to say that one witness was preferred to another because the one manifestly had a clearer recollection of the material facts or the other gave answers which demonstrated that his recollection could not be relied upon.

[20] The first two appeals with which we are concerned involved conflicts of expert evidence. In *Flannery's* case Henry LJ quoted from the judgment of Bingham LJ in *Eckersley v Binnie* (1987) 18 ConLR 1 at 77–78 in which he said that

'a coherent reasoned opinion expressed by a suitably qualified expert should be the subject of a coherent reasoned rebuttal'. This does not mean that the judgment should contain a passage which suggests that the judge has applied the same, or even a superior, degree of expertise to that displayed by the witness. He should simply provide an explanation as to why he has accepted the evidence of one expert and rejected that of another. It may be that the evidence of one or the other accorded more satisfactorily with facts found by the judge. It may be that the explanation of one was more inherently credible than that of the other. It may simply be that one was better qualified, or manifestly more objective, than the other. Whatever the explanation may be, it should be apparent from the judgment.

[21] When giving reasons a judge will often need to refer to a piece of evidence or to a submission which he has accepted or rejected. Provided that the reference is clear, it may be unnecessary to detail, or even summarise, the evidence or submission in question. The essential requirement is that the terms of the judgment should enable the parties and any appellate tribunal readily to analyse the reasoning that was essential to the judge's decision.

AMPLIFICATION OF REASONS

[22] In *Flannery*'s case [2000] 1 All ER 373 at 379, [2000] 1 WLR 377 at 383 the court made two suggestions with a view to preventing unnecessary appeals on the ground of the absence of reasons. It suggested that one remedy open to the appeal court would be to remit the matter to the trial judge with an invitation or requirement to give reasons. In *Flannery*'s case this was not considered appropriate because more than a year had passed since the hearing. The delay between hearing and appeal will normally be too long to make a remission to the trial judge for further reasons a desirable course. The same is not true of the position shortly after judgment has been given.

[23] The other suggestion made by the court in *Flannery*'s case was that the respondent to an application for permission to appeal on the ground of lack of reasons should consider inviting the judge to give his reasons, and his explanation as to why they were not set out in the judgment, in an affidavit for use at the leave hearing and at the hearing if leave be granted.

[24] We are not greatly attracted by the suggestion that a judge who has given inadequate reasons should be invited to have a second bite at the cherry. But we are much less attracted at the prospect of expensive appellate proceedings on the ground of lack of reasons. Where the judge who has heard the evidence has based a rational decision on it, the successful party will suffer an injustice if that decision is appealed, let alone set aside, simply because the judge has not included in his judgment adequate reasons for his decision. The appellate court will not be in as good a position to substitute its decision', should it decide that this course is viable, while an appeal followed by a rehearing will involve a hideous waste of costs.

[25] Accordingly, we recommend the following course. If an application for permission to appeal on the ground of lack of reasons is made to the trial judge, the judge should consider whether his judgment is defective for lack of reasons, adjourning for that purpose should he find this necessary. If he concludes that it is, he should set out to remedy the defect by the provision of additional reasons refusing permission to appeal on the basis that he has adopted that course. If he concludes that he has given adequate reasons, he will no doubt refuse permission to appeal. If an application for permission to appeal on the ground of lack of

a   reasons is made to the appellate court and it appears to the appellate court that
the application is well founded, it should consider adjourning the application and
remitting the case to the trial judge with an invitation to provide additional
reasons for his decision or, where appropriate, his reasons for a specific finding or
findings. Where the appellate court is in doubt as to whether the reasons are
adequate, it may be appropriate to direct that the application be adjourned to an
b   oral hearing, on notice to the respondent.

THE APPROACH OF THE APPELLATE COURT

[26] Where permission is granted to appeal on the grounds that the judgment
does not contain adequate reasons, the appellate court should first review the
judgment, in the context of the material evidence and submissions at the trial, in
c   order to determine whether, when all of these are considered, it is apparent why
the judge reached the decision that he did. If satisfied that the reason is apparent
and that it is a valid basis for the judgment, the appeal will be dismissed. This was
the approach adopted by this court, in the light of *Flannery's* case, in *Ludlow v
National Power plc* [2000] All ER (D) 1868. If despite this exercise the reason for
d   the decision is not apparent, then the appeal court will have to decide whether
itself to proceed to a rehearing, or to direct a new trial.

COSTS

[27] At the end of a trial the judge will normally do no more than direct who
is to pay the costs and upon what basis. We have found that the Strasbourg
e   jurisprudence requires the reason for an award of costs to be apparent, either
from reasons or by inference from the circumstances in which costs are awarded.
Before either the 1998 Act or the new CPR came into effect, Swinton Thomas LJ,
in a judgment with which Scott V-C, who was the other member of the court,
agreed, said this in *Brent London BC v Aniedobe* [1999] CA Transcript 2003, in
f   relation to an appeal against an order for costs:

'... this court must be slow to interfere with the exercise of a judge's
discretion, when the judge has heard the evidence and this court has not. It
is also, in my view, important not to increase the burden on overworked
judges in the county court by requiring them in every case to give reasons
g   for their orders as to costs. In the great majority of cases in all probability the
costs will follow the event, and the reasons for the judge's order are plain, in
which case there is no need for a judge to give reasons for his order.
However, having said that, if a judge does depart from the ordinary order
(that is in this case the costs following the event) it is, in my judgment,
incumbent on him to give reasons, albeit short reasons, for taking that
h   unusual course.'

[28] It is, in general, in the interests of justice that a judge should be free to
dispose of applications as to costs in a speedy and uncomplicated way and even
under the CPR this will be possible in many cases.
j   [29] However, the CPR sometimes require a more complex approach to costs
and judgments dealing with costs will more often need to identify the provisions
of the rules that have been in play and why these have led to the order made. It
is regrettable that this imposes a considerable burden on judges, but we fear that
it is inescapable.
[30] Where no express explanation is given for a costs order, an appellate
court will approach the material facts on the assumption that the judge will have

had good reason for the award made. The appellate court will seldom be as well placed as the trial judge to exercise a discretion in relation to costs. Where it is apparent that there is a perfectly rational explanation for the order made, the court is likely to draw the inference that this is what motivated the judge in making the order. This has always been the practice of the court (see the comments of Sachs LJ in *Knight v Clifton* [1971] 2 All ER 378 at 393, [1971] Ch 700 at 721). Thus, in practice, it is only in those cases where an order for costs is made with neither reasons nor any obvious explanation for the order that it is likely to be appropriate to give permission to appeal on the ground of lack of reasons against an order that relates only to costs.

[31] This concludes our general observations on the issues raised by the three appeals, and we now turn to consider each in turn in accordance with the approach that we have commended above.

ENGLISH v EMERY REIMBOLD & STRICK LTD

[32] The judgment under appeal was delivered by Judge Rubery, sitting as a deputy judge of the High Court.

The critical issue

[33] Mr English, the appellant, was born in 1964. He suffered a back injury when he slipped at work on 18 October 1994. His employers, the respondents, admitted liability for his accident. Evidence on the issue of damages was heard on 8, 11, 13 September 2000 and 12 December 2000. Closing submissions were submitted in writing by 28 January 2001. Judgment was handed down over four months later on 5 June 2001. This was a lamentable document, full of errors of spelling, punctuation and syntax. In granting permission to appeal, Sedley LJ accurately described it as a rambling and in places unintelligible document. He ruled that, in the light of *Flannery v Halifax Estate Agencies Ltd* [2000] 1 All ER 373, [2000] 1 WLR 377 the appeal had a realistic prospect of success, to the extent, at least, of securing a retrial.

[34] We had the benefit of a version of the judgment which had been edited by the judge, pursuant to the direction of Sedley LJ, to the extent of correcting the errors of spelling, punctuation and syntax. The judgment is 18 pages in length. It presents the case as turning almost exclusively on a conflict between the evidence of Mr McBride, the consultant orthopaedic surgeon instructed by the claimant, and Mr Andrew, the consultant orthopaedic surgeon instructed by the defendants.

[35] It was common ground that, on 20 February 1995, an X-ray revealed that Mr English had an 8 mm spondylolisthesis, that is an 8 mm forward displacement of a part of the vertebral column by reference to the remainder of the vertebral column below. It was also common ground that, before the spondylolisthesis developed or occurred, Mr English had a congenital condition known as spondylolysis, which involves a weakening of the spine.

[36] The expert evidence, which included a joint experts' report setting out where the experts agreed and where they differed, had further areas of common ground. (i) Approximately 10% of the population suffers from spondylolysis. Of these, approximately half subsequently develop spondylolisthesis. (ii) The development of spondylolisthesis normally occurs either as the child grows into an adult, in the first 18 years of life ('congenital spondylolisthesis') or in old age ('degenerative spondylolisthesis'). (iii) Spondylolisthesis can be sustained by a person with a healthy spine as a result of a severe accident such as being run over

a by a motor car ('traumatic spondylolisthesis'). The slipping accident experienced by Mr English would not have sufficed to cause a spondylolisthesis if his spine had been sound.

[37] Before his slipping accident Mr English had suffered from intermittent back pain. This had led on 17 November 1993 to his lumbar-sacral spine being X-rayed by Dr West, a radiologist. The X-rays had not been preserved, but b Dr West's report, dated 25 November, had been. This stated 'Lumbar-sacral spine: normal examination'.

[38] Dr West was called to give evidence. He had no recollection of taking the X-rays or writing the report. He said that it was not inconceivable that he had missed Mr English's spondylolisthesis, but that it was very unlikely that he would have done so in view of the fact that the slippage in question was almost 1 cm.

c
[39] The judge correctly recorded the central issue as being whether the spondylolisthesis was developmental in origin and was therefore present before the accident, or whether it was caused by the accident.

[40] It was Mr Andrew's opinion that Mr English must have developed his spondylolisthesis in the first 18 years of his life and that his slipping accident d merely led to a degree of temporary back sprain. Mr McBride's opinion was that the slipping accident must have caused the spondylolisthesis because Mr English's existing spondylolysis had left him more susceptible to such an injury.

[41] Mr Andrew expressed himself as amazed at Mr McBride's evidence that spondylolysis had predisposed Mr English to traumatic spondylolisthesis from an e accident which could not normally have caused this. He was taken aback because Mr McBride had not mentioned this theory in his medical report or when agreeing the joint report with Mr Andrew. Mr Andrew was firmly of the view that Mr McBride's theory was untenable because there was no record in the textbooks of an adult with spondylolysis developing spondylolisthesis in such circumstances, nor was such an event known to him or his colleagues. Having f regard to the number of adults in the population with spondylolysis he considered that it was not conceivable that the suggested potential effect of a minor trauma would not have been recorded if it existed.

[42] In these circumstances the judge was faced with a choice between two unlikely scenarios. Either Mr English had had a spondylolisthesis before his g slipping accident, and Dr West had missed this on his X-ray examination, or he had sustained a traumatic spondylolisthesis in circumstances which were without recorded or known medical precedent.

[43] We could not have formulated the central issue in this way simply from reading the judgment. We have been assisted in our understanding of the nature h of the case by the submissions of counsel and references to the evidence.

The judgment

[44] The first six pages of the judgment were devoted to an introduction and a summary of the evidence given by Mr English. This might have been thought j by the judge to be of some peripheral significance, for there were grounds for concluding that Mr English had somewhat over-egged the pudding when describing his symptoms to Mr McBride and the somewhat cursory treatment that he received at the hospital after his slipping accident could not readily be reconciled with the degree of agony he claimed to have been in. However, the judge made no comment of any kind in relation to the implications of Mr English's evidence.

[45] The judge then observed that he felt it 'would be helpful' to quote in a
little detail from the experts' joint report and proceeded to do so over the next
four pages of the judgment. The extracts quoted demonstrated, for the most
part, the difference of opinion between the experts. The judge did not explain
why the extracts that he had set out were helpful.

[46] The judge then, cryptically, interposed the following paragraph:

'Learned counsel for the defendants submits that "Not only must the court
distinguish between the medical opinions of Mr McBride and Mr Andrew
but that when doing so it is of the utmost importance to understand how
audacious is the diagnostic position adopted at the trial by Mr McBride and
how logically inconsistent is his evidence in support of it."'

Mr Giles, for the employers, explained to us that the audacity referred to was that
involved in adducing a theory at the trial to which Mr McBride had made no prior
reference.

[47] The judge then remarked that it would be helpful 'in reaching the
conclusion which I have' to look at certain parts of the evidence of Mr McBride
and Mr Andrew. Referring first to the evidence of Mr McBride, he included the
following passage:

'Put to him by Mr Pepperall so on the balance of probabilities before this
man suffered his accident in October 1994 do you take the view that there
was or was not evidence of degenerative change? He answered "I do not
believe there was on the balance of probabilities ..."'

[48] The judge then commented 'and I come back to this again later'. It is not
clear to us where he did so. A little later, however, he quoted Mr McBride as
saying: 'I believe that the evidence in this case suggests that this was a traumatic
event.'

[49] Turning to the evidence of Mr Andrew, the judge quoted repeated and
emphatic dissents from Mr McBride's evidence:

'... one would have to have a catastrophic injury to cause a traumatic
spondylolisthesis ...'
'... [this type of traumatic spondylolisthesis] is unbelievable, it is just
impossible. It is totally alien to all one can anticipate ...'
'I'd be as certain as I can be that he had [spondylolisthesis] the day before
he slipped on the floor ...'
'... it is just inconceivable that some minor trauma could cause this ...'
'... there is no scientific evidence to back up Mr McBride's theory ...'

[50] The judge then summarised shortly the evidence of Dr West to which we
referred earlier, without making any comment on it. Finally he stated his
conclusions as follows:

'As I said earlier it would have made this judgment of inordinate length if I
were to simply recite all the detailed medical evidence that the court heard
during the course of the trial. At the end of the day the court must
distinguish between the medical opinions of Mr McBride and Mr Andrew
and having considered the matter at considerable length I prefer, on the
balance of probabilities, the evidence of Mr Andrew that the spondylolisthesis
was developmental in origin and was therefore present before the accident and
not caused by the accident as is the view of Mr McBride. In preferring

a   Mr Andrew's evidence it followed that on the balance of probabilities I accept Mr Andrew's evidence that Dr West missed the spondylolisthesis which Mr Andrew considers to have been present when he X-rayed the claimant on 7 November 1993.'

(The judge plainly meant 17 November 1993.)

b
Submissions

[51] Mr Pepperall, for Mr English, attacked the judgment with vigour. He submitted that its features were indistinguishable from those of the judgment in *Flannery's* case, save that in *Flannery's* case the judge had at least referred to the benefit of hearing the witnesses. The judge had set out extracts from the
c   evidence, followed by bald conclusions. The judgment gave Mr English no better understanding of the reason behind it than had his presence at the trial. The X-ray examination carried out by Dr West had been of critical importance to Mr English's case, yet the judge had failed to weigh Dr West's evidence of fact before turning to the expert evidence.

d   [52] Mr Giles submitted that the judgment should not be disturbed. The judge had correctly identified the issue, he had set out the conflicting expert opinions and he had made his choice on balance of probabilities. He had been justified in preferring the views of Mr Andrew, which were supported by the textbooks, rather than the theory of Mr McBride, which was produced new on the day of the trial.

e   [53] Our initial impressions on reading the judgment accorded with Mr Pepperall's submissions. The judgment gave little indication of the process of reasoning that led to the result. By the end of counsel's submissions we were, however, confident that we had identified this.

[54] The clue to the judge's reasoning lies in his use of the phrase 'on the
f   balance of probabilities' in the final paragraph that we have quoted from his judgment. This is a strange phrase to use to qualify the choice between conflicting expert evidence. It reflects the fact that the conflict was not strictly between conflicting expert evidence, but between conflicting opinions of the experts in relation to the central issue of whether Mr English had developed spondylolisthesis before his slipping accident or sustained it as a result of the
g   accident. The experts' opinions had regard to evidence which fell outside the area of their expertise, in particular the fact that Dr West had not identified spondylolisthesis in the X-ray examination which he carried out before Mr English's accident.

[55] Mr McBride did not base his conclusion that Mr English suffered a traumatic
h   spondylolisthesis on professional experience that spondylolysis predisposed adults to sustaining such a condition as a consequence of a minor accident of the type suffered by Mr English. He advanced, at the trial, the theory that Mr English's spondylolysis had predisposed him to traumatic spondylolisthesis as his considered explanation of all the evidence 'on balance of probabilities'. Mr Andrew's
j   professional knowledge and experience led him firmly to reject this explanation of the evidence and thus to conclude that Dr West must have missed Mr English's congenital spondylolisthesis when he carried out his X-ray examination.

[56] Each expert gave an opinion on the issue which was ultimately for the judge. Mr Pepperall accepted that Mr English's case was largely founded on Dr West's report. He could not have hoped to succeed on the expert evidence alone, which did not provide precedents for spondylolisthesis sustained in the

manner alleged on behalf of Mr English. Ultimately the judge had to decide
whether it was more probable that Dr West had overlooked Mr English's
condition or that his spondylolisthesis resulted in a manner for which there was
no known medical precedent. He decided that the former was the more probable.

[57] The judge could have explained the issue and his reasoning process in
comparatively few words. It is regrettable that he did not do so and that it has
taken the appellate process and the assistance of counsel who appeared at the trial
to enable us to follow the judge's reasoning. Having done so we conclude that
this appeal must be dismissed.

D J & C WITHERS (FARMS) LTD v AMBIC EQUIPMENT LTD

[58] The judgment under appeal was delivered by Judge MacKay, sitting in the
Technology and Construction Court in Liverpool, on 4 May 2001. He had
provided it in draft to the parties in advance. When he delivered the judgment
he was referred to the decision in *Flannery v Halifax Estate Agencies Ltd* [2000] 1 All
ER 373, [2000] 1 WLR 377 and told that the claimants (Withers) were minded to
apply for permission to appeal on the ground that his judgment did not give
adequate reasons for his preference of the defendant's (Ambic) evidence. This led
the judge to add a short addendum to his judgment, to the substance of which we
shall revert in due course.

[59] On the paper application for permission to appeal, Sedley LJ observed
that it was arguable that the judgment did not give adequate, or indeed any,
reasons for preferring Ambic's expert evidence, but refused permission to appeal
on the ground that the judge had made findings of fact which, of themselves,
would have been capable of proving fatal to the claim.

[60] The application to appeal was renewed on notice. On this occasion Sedley
LJ, sitting with Arden LJ, acceded to the application. The court held that it was
arguable that want of analytical consideration of the evidence of Withers' expert
constituted grounds for setting the judgment aside. Sedley LJ observed:

'It ought to be visible in principle from the judgment, however succinctly
it is expressed, why it is that the judge has preferred one expert's evidence
and one party's case to the others. But I do accept that the judge had before
him, and without doubt had in mind, tenable reasons for preferring the
defendant's to the claimant's expert evidence. I accept too that if one goes
to the reports and written arguments one can find the material there.'

The critical issue

[61] Withers farmed dairy cattle on several separate farms in New Zealand. In
August 1991 Withers purchased from Ambic a system of hydraulic milking which
they started to use on one of the farms in September 1991, the start of the
1991–1992 milking season. Withers originally contended that the Ambic system
suffered from design defects which almost immediately produced an increase in
the incidence of mastitis on the farm where the equipment was used, although by
the time of the trial, it was conceded that there was no significant increase in
clincial mastitis until the 1995–1996 season. The critical issue was whether the
increase in mastitis which occurred was caused mechanically, as a result of design
defects in the Ambic system, or resulted from environmental factors attributable
to, or augmented by, poor dairy farming practices on the farm in question.

[62] Pleaded particulars of defects in the Ambic system identified mechanical
idiosyncrasies of the system and the mechanisms by which these were alleged to

a increase the propensity of the teats of the cattle to suffer bacteriological infection resulting in mastitis.

[63] Evidence bearing on the critical issue was partly evidence of fact and partly expert evidence, nor was it possible to draw the line precisely between the two. This evidence included: evidence of facts from which the incidence of mastitis on the farm using the Ambic equipment, and on another farm which was
b not, could be deduced; evidence as to the standard of the dairy farming practices observed on Withers' farms; evidence indicative of the extent to which the teats of cattle were suffering damage; veterinarian evidence of somatic cell count tests and the significance of these and evidence of whether, in theory and in practice, the allegedly idiosyncratic features of the Ambic system were liable to render the teats of cattle more susceptible to bacteriological infection.
c

The judgment

[64] The judgment, prior to the addendum, extended to 27 pages. The first seven pages were introductory. They included a short narrative, a description of mastitis, a list of witnesses of fact, which erroneously included a number of
d individuals who, while they had featured in the story, had not provided any evidence, and brief particulars of the six expert witnesses who had given evidence on different aspects of the case. The most significant of these were, for Withers, Mr Bromwell, a dairy and milking technology consultant, who had spent 27 years as a member of the Ministry of Agriculture advisory service, specialising particularly in milking machines and milking technology, and for Ambic, Dr Hillerton, a
e research scientist who, since 1990, had headed the Milk and Mastitis Centre of the Institute for Animal Health. For nearly 20 years he had specialised in the udder health of the dairy cow.

[65] The judgment then observed, correctly, that the crucial issue taken by Ambic was that of causation. Ambic relied on the fact that for four years their
f equipment had been used by Withers without any increase of mastitis in the herd. Withers' case was that during this period the mastitis was latent, in sub-clinical form, kept under control by good farming practices. Ambic contended that it was significant that Withers had experienced an outbreak of mastitis on another farm which did not use the Ambic system, and had been concerned to conceal this fact. Withers contended that events on that other farm were irrelevant. Withers
g contended that the Ambic equipment was liable to cause damage to the teats of cows and that Ambic were in breach of duty in failing to inform them of the unacceptable risk that this posed.

[66] Summarising the position, the judge held that if Withers were to succeed they had to show (i) that the Ambic system had a propensity to cause mastitis and
h (ii) that it in fact did so on Withers' farm.

[67] The judge devoted two-and-a-half pages of his judgment to quoting a lengthy section of Dr Hillerton's report, which compared the Ambic hydraulic system with conventional vacuum milking systems.

[68] The next nine pages of the judgment are devoted to the issue of
j causation. We shall shortly return to consider these in some detail. The final five pages of the judgment deal with contributory negligence, limitation and quantum and are not material to this appeal. We observe, however, that the judge found that the damages that would have been recoverable had liability been established amounted to no more than about £15,000. This emphasises how unsatisfactory it is that further substantial costs should have been incurred because of doubts about the adequacy of the judge's reasoning.

Submissions

[69] For Withers, Mr Bartley Jones QC submitted that the reasons in the judgment failed to cross the threshold that a fair trial required, as identified in *Flannery*'s case. Mr Bromwell was the only expert to address the first essential issue of whether the Ambic equipment had a propensity to cause mastitis. Dr Hillerton simply failed to deal with this, confining himself to the second issue of whether in fact the Ambic equipment had been responsible for the mastitis suffered by the Withers herd. Yet the second issue could not satisfactorily be addressed until the first had been independently resolved. The judge, for his part, had also failed to address the issue of the propensity of the Ambic equipment to cause teat damage. The judge had repeatedly accepted the evidence of Dr Hillerton without analysis or explanation.

[70] For Ambic, Mr Moxon-Browne QC responded in two ways. First he submitted that the judge had made it plain that he considered that Dr Hillerton was the more authoritative of the experts. He was right to do so and this justified his preferring Ambic's case where the expert evidence was in conflict. Secondly, he set out to demonstrate by reference to the judgment that, contrary to Mr Bartley Jones' submission, the judge had dealt with the issue of whether the Ambic equipment had a propensity to cause mastitis.

Conclusions

[71] If there were any doubt as to the judge's view of the respective merits of the expert witnesses, this was laid to rest by the addendum to his judgment. He explained:

'I accepted the evidence of the defendant's expert throughout. I was particularly impressed by Dr Hillerton. The fact that he was a research scientist and not a veterinary surgeon was not, to me, a crucial factor. He had made a deep and long lasting investigation into many of the problems connected with milking cows and mechanical milking.'

[72] We consider that the judge was entitled to form this view. Dr Hillerton was very highly qualified to give expert evidence in this case. The 150-odd publications itemised in his curriculum vitae demonstrate his particular expertise in the bovine udder and the effect of mechanical milking on mastitis. Furthermore, his expert report was a model of its kind identifying in detail and with precision the data on which his conclusions were based. Mr Bromwell was also highly qualified, but his expert report was much less disciplined and detailed. It also exhibited indications of a lack of objectivity. By way of example, it is not appropriate for an expert on milking to comment on the witness statement of a sales representative: 'In common with the statement of Mr Mills this appears to me to be a catalogue of selective recollection.'

[73] It is legitimate, where there is a direct conflict of expert evidence, for the judge to prefer the evidence of one expert to the other simply on the ground that he was better qualified to give it, or was a more authoritative witness, if the judge is unable to identify any more substantial reason for choosing between them. This should not often be the case. If this is the basis for the judge's conclusion, he should make it plain. We do not read Judge MacKay's judgment, even with its addendum, as placing that much weight on Dr Hillerton's conclusions. Plainly Dr Hillerton's authority added weight to his evidence, but the judgment indicates that the judge was also impressed with the substance of what he had to say, and

a he made clear in his addendum that his findings of fact had some bearing on his assessment of the expert evidence, as, indeed, they should have done.

[74] We turn to the section of the judgment dealing with causation. We have not found this easy to analyse. We have been able to identify a number of different reasons for the judge's conclusions, but these are not set out in logical order; they are intertwined. So far as the expert evidence is concerned, the judge
b has attempted to summarise the technical issues, but on occasion fallen between two stools, so that the relevance of the facts set out in the judgment to the particular issue is incomprehensible. We shall attempt briefly to identify each reason.

[75] *Credibility.* The judge found that Mr Withers, the proprietor of the claimants, was not a reliable witness. He had failed to provide adequate records
c (p 17). He had alleged that he had made complaints about mastitis to Ambic's representative in the years prior to 1995 when this was not true (p 17, and again at pp 19, 20 and 25). He had falsely stated that he had no problems with mastitis at his other farms (p 18).

[76] *Track record of the Ambic equipment.* While some farmers experienced
d some difficulties with Ambic equipment, many farmers were entirely satisfied: 'I do not regard the criticisms which were made by some farmers as invalidating the efficiency of the equipment' (p 19), followed by reference to trials (p 21). 'I should also say that I do not regard the settlements achieved in the previous cases as relevant or conclusive in this case ...' (p 25).

[77] *Poor standards of hygiene and dairy practice at Withers' farms.* 'More likely
e that the claimants' farms are not the ideal or perfectly run farms postulated ...' 'The evidence suggests that the other farms had environmental mastitis ...' (p 17). 'The eventual outbreak of mastitis ... had much more to do with inadequacies in cleansing and other safety measures than any fault in the equipment ...' (p 21). 'It seems likely that Mr Withers did not replace the teat
f cup liners often enough ...' (p 22). 'There may well have been a failure to use adequate dry cow therapy ...' (p 22). 'It may well be that cows were over milked and insufficient staff were employed but as I have indicated above I do not accept that the farm was as hygienically clean or as well run as the claimant contends ...' (p 22). On p 23:

g   '... a picture clearly emerges of a farm using elderly equipment, with poor milking practices and infrequent placement of essential equipment which would have resulted in the same level of mastitis whether or not the Hydra flow had been used. The fact that there were even worse mastitis problems in the key years on farm no 2 bears this out.'

h [78] *Allegation that the Ambic equipment increased hyperkeratosis, which led to mastitis.* This was one of the allegations of the propensity of the Ambic equipment to cause mastitis. The judge dealt with this allegation, initially at p 14. He rejected it on the basis of Dr Hillerton's evidence which he briefly summarised. Hyperkeratosis was always a feature of machine milking. There was no relationship
j between hyperkeratosis and mastitis. The judge referred to evidence of a test which confirmed the latter point. To this the judge added that there was an almost total absence of evidence of hyperkeratosis at the relevant farm.

[79] This brief summary did not explain the nature of hyperkeratosis. For that, it is necessary to refer to the evidence. This we did, with the help of counsel. This disclosed some confusion between the experts as to the precise nature of the phenomenon. The word describes the extrusion of keratin from the teat canal as

a result of the mechanism of milking. Withers' veterinary expert appears to have
assumed that this depleted the amount of keratin that remained, which was an
unsatisfactory feature, in that keratin seals off the teat and has antibacterial
activity. Dr Hillerton, on the other hand, considered that hyperkeratosis resulted
from an increase in the production of keratin as a result of the milking action.
What is, however, particularly material is that Dr Hillerton was able to give
evidence of participating in a study, which failed to find any relationship between
the degree of hyperkeratosis in herds and the average cell count, which was taken
as a measure of infection. The judge took an active part in the discussion. It is
clear from his judgment that he was persuaded by Dr Hillerton's evidence. When
the judgment is considered together with the evidence, the reason for his doing
so becomes clear.

[80] The allegation that the Ambic equipment resulted in 'wedging', which
led to mastitis. This suggestion was not pleaded, but was introduced in oral
evidence by Withers' veterinary expert. The judge dealt with this in a short
passage of his judgment, containing references to congestion and failure of
circulation which are not readily intelligible, standing alone. What was clear was
that the judge accepted Dr Hillerton's evidence that wedging did not increase the
risk of mastitis. Once again, reference to the evidence, with the help of counsel,
enabled us to make sense of the judgment. Again the judge took a full part in the
discussion with Dr Hillerton, and plainly followed the purport of his evidence.
The phenomenon under discussion was the deformation of the teat into a wedge
shape under pressure during the milking operation. It was suggested that this
would reduce blood circulation within the teat, thereby depriving areas of
potential infection of the therapeutic access of white cells. Dr Hillerton's answer
was that the white cells in question were carried not in the blood supply, but in
the milk. It is apparent that the judge accepted this evidence as an answer to the
allegation about wedging, though he went on to add that there was very little
evidence, if any, that wedging in fact occurred on the relevant farm.

[81] *Lack of massage leading to mastitis.* It was alleged that the mechanism of the
Ambic equipment resulted in a lack of massaging of the teats, which could lead to
mastitis. The judge referred (at p 15) to this very briefly, accepting Dr Hillerton's
evidence that it was necessary to break the skin to cause infection and that there
was no evidence that any lack of massage resulted in this. He reverted to the
topic (at p 20) where he stated that Withers' allegations in relation to lack of
massage were not made out or likely. He added that Dr Hillerton had pointed
out in his report that even a linerless milking system involving no liner
movement whatsoever did not result in any teat damage being observed.
Counsel referred us to the relevant passage in Dr Hillerton's report and to the fact
that he maintained his position under cross-examination.

[82] Mr Bartley Jones criticised this finding on the part of the judge, referring
us to evidence which indicated that Dr Hillerton's view was unorthodox, and that
the orthodox view was that massaging of the teat in the course of milking was
very important if infection was to be avoided. We do not think that this criticism
is in point. The grounds of this appeal are not that the judge's reasons were
erroneous but that he failed to give adequate reasons. The judge's reason for
rejecting this aspect of Withers' case on the propensity of the Ambic equipment
to cause mastitis is apparent.

[83] *Allegation that vacuum peaks caused damage to the teats leading to mastitis.*
The judge recorded (at p 15) the suggestion that the Ambic system caused high
vacuum levels which, in some way, caused damage to the teats, based on a

a high vacuum reading alleged to have been taken on one occasion. He recorded that Dr Hillerton had no knowledge that a high vacuum compromised the teat defence mechanism and rejected the allegation, holding that on the balance of the evidence the allegations that damage was caused by the operation of the Ambic system were not made out.

[84] Once again the judge returned to the topic at pp 20–21 of his judgment.
b The references that he there makes to the evidence are too disjointed to make sense, without reference to Dr Hillerton's evidence. What is apparent from them is that the judge had considered the technical evidence and was preferring Dr Hillerton on the basis of the evidence that he had given.

[85] *Allegation that infection was increased because milk was always in contact with the teat.* When describing the Ambic system at the start of his judgment, the judge
c observed that one significant feature was that 'the liner was completely and permanently flooded with milk'. In his judgment (at p 20), he held: 'I accept the evidence of Dr Hillerton, who I regard as a compelling and very expert witness, that milk cannot be trapped throughout the milking period.' This is all that the judge had to say in answer to the allegation that the fact that milk was always in
d contact with the teat under the Ambic system provided a pathway for bacterial infection. This did not deal adequately with this aspect of Withers' case. Dr Hillerton had accepted that milk could provide a pathway for infection from one cow to another if the milking cluster was not disinfected after milking an infected cow, as good husbandry required. He also made the point that the one-way valve system of the Ambic clusters would not allow milk return so that
e infection of one-quarter could not be transmitted to the other. We have not found it possible to reconcile this evidence with the judge's reasoning.

[86] *The nature of the pathogens.* The judge held that there was little evidence of the pathogens that caused the outbreak of mastitis in 1995, but that the best evidence was in the form of a report which he identified. This was a 'Five Year
f Summary of Milk Results' provided to Withers by Agvet Services Ltd. It showed that the most frequently found pathogen was streptococcus uberis. The judge found that this pathogen was associated with wet and dirty conditions. He found that environmental pathogens could not be machine-induced. He based these conclusions on the evidence of Dr Hillerton and on a paper which supported this.

g [87] *The significance of the somatic cell count.* It was common ground that an increase in somatic cells usually signifies infection, which the white blood cells are combating. The records showed that the somatic cell count was very similar in 1991/1992, after the installation of the Ambic system, to what it had been in 1990/1991. It rose significantly in 1992/1993, but then dropped back to its lowest level for any year in 1993/1994. It rose again in the next two years and soared in
h 1997/1998. Dr Hillerton considered the data in detail and concluded that it demonstrated that, up to 1997, there was poor dry cow management around the calving period, resulting in a high level of mastitis in the cows that were calving, whereas two-year old cows which were being milked retained a very low cell count. The evidence did not suggest any influence from the Ambic clusters.

j [88] The judge held, simply (at p 17), 'I am unconvinced that the somatic cell count indicates a machine-induced situation which only exploded in 1995.' The apparent inadequacy of this passage particularly impressed the court when giving permission to appeal. Sedley LJ commented of the judge:

> '... if he was to reject the suggestion that the somatic cell count pointed to machine-induced mastitis, the claimant can, I think, say with some legitimacy

that it is entitled to know why, and to say the same about several other places
where the judge expresses himself entirely referentially ...'   *a*

Having considered the evidence in relation to the somatic cell count it seems to
us that it was ambivalent. Having regard to the judge's other findings, we think
that it was open to him to dismiss the evidence of the somatic cell counts in the
way that he did. It would, however, have been preferable if he had given a short
explanation, even if by reference to Dr Hillerton's evidence, as to why he thought   *b*
that the evidence of somatic cell counts was inconclusive.

Summary

[89] There were shortcomings in the judgment in this case. On a number of
occasions we have had to consider the underlying material to which the judge   *c*
referred in order to understand his reasoning. On one occasion, the significance
of the fact that the milking cups were perpetually full of milk, we failed to follow
his reasoning even with the benefit of the underlying material. At the end of the
exercise, however, we have been able to identify reasons for the judge's
conclusions which cogently justify his decision. While he did not express all of   *d*
these with clarity in his judgment, he made sufficient reference to the evidence
that had weighed with him to enable us, after considering that evidence, to follow
that reasoning with confidence.

[90] It follows that the appeal based on inadequacy of the reasons fails and
must be dismissed.
          e

VERRECHIA

[91] As indicated above the appellant in this appeal challenges the order of
Steel J as to the costs. The particular point of general interest in this case is that
it raises in an acute form the questions discussed in general terms above, namely
when is it necessary to give reasons for an order for costs and what should the   *f*
approach of the appellate court be if reasons have not been expressly given for the
judge's decision? We have already concluded that reasons need not be given
where they are clearly implicit from the order made. The obvious example is an
order that the costs follow the event where neither party has urged the court to
reflect any other factor. In such a case it is self-evident why the order was made:
the court thought that the usual position should apply. On the other hand, if the   *g*
reasons for the order are not obvious, the judge should provide reasons. The
present appeal tests that principle because, following a trial lasting eight days and
having received substantial written submissions on costs, the judge announced
the court's decision on costs without giving any reasons at all.

[92] The circumstances which had given rise to the litigation have been briefly   *h*
mentioned already and were unusual. Following a raid on the appellant's
business premises between 18 and 21 April 1994, the police (the party represented
by the respondent on this appeal) held a number of vehicle engines and vehicle
spare parts which they considered to be stolen property. The appellant and his
son were charged with dishonestly handling 25 of these items which they   *j*
conceded were stolen property. In November 1995 the appellant and his son
were acquitted. The police did not however then return the property seized to
the appellant. They were clearly concerned that, although the appellant and his
son were found not guilty of handling, none the less the engines and spare parts
could represent stolen property which belonged to third parties. They were able
to identify the owners of some of the items.

a [93] In November 1998 the appellant started these proceedings seeking to recover damages under the Torts (Interference with Goods) Act 1977 in respect of 65 items which the police had failed to return to him. These items did not include the items which had been the subject of the charges brought against the appellant and his son. The amount of damages claimed was £141,500 exclusive of interest. In addition there were claims for aggravated and exemplary damages.

b [94] The police were entitled to retain the goods until the conclusion of the trial on any basis. The issue was whether they were entitled to refuse to return them to the appellant thereafter. They had established that several items were stolen property and in some cases the items had been returned to their owners. In respect of the majority of the other items the means of identification had been removed and it was not possible to trace the owners. The police case was that in

c all the circumstances the court should infer that they were stolen property. By the start of the trial the appellant had reduced his claim to 58 items. This number was reduced to 45 items in the appellant's opening and to 40 items in the appellant's closing speech.

[95] Steel J found that the claim succeeded in respect of 20 items but failed in

d respect of the remaining 20 items. The judge refused to draw the inference that where the means of identification had been removed the items were stolen property. The judge observed (for reasons with which this court has not been concerned) that the history of the case and the way in which the police had carried out their duty of care with respect to the items the subject of action gave

e rise to concern. However, apart from that observation, the judge made no comment about the conduct of the parties whether before or during the trial. The judge awarded damages in the sum of £37,300, plus interest. The claims for aggravated and exemplary damages were dismissed and it is unnecessary to say more about them as neither party considered that that claim had caused any significant additional costs.

f [96] A draft of the judge's judgment was made available to the parties before it was handed down. The last paragraph simply said: '111. No order as to costs.'

[97] This was clearly only a provisional view and, when the judgment was handed down, the judge, having been informed of various CPR Pt 36 matters, made an order that the issue of costs should be dealt with by way of written

g submissions. Unknown to the judge, there had been various offers to settle the case. On 23 November 2000 the claimants had offered to settle the case for £98,600 inclusive of interest and costs and on 29 January 2001 the police had made a payment into court in respect of the whole of the appellant's claims in the sum of £5,500. Neither party succeeded to the extent of their prior offer(s).

h [98] Counsel submitted extensive written submissions on costs to the judge. The position taken by the appellant was that there should be an order for costs in his favour. The police submitted that there should be no order as to costs. On 4 April 2001, the judge handed down the following judgment in writing:

j 'I have considered the submissions and all the authorities cited. In all the circumstances of this action, I am unpersuaded that I should vary my order that each party should pay their own costs, and that there should be no order as to costs.'

[99] The judge had not, of course, made any order which could be varied so that when the judge said 'I am unpersuaded that I should vary my order', the judge meant 'I am unpersuaded that my provisional view was incorrect.'

Submissions

[100] Mr Ronald Walker QC, for the appellant, submitted that the judge should have given reasons. The issue as to incidence of costs was important, there had been a substantial trial and the judge had had written submissions. Mr Walker relied on the jurisprudence of the European Court of Human Rights under art 6. He particularly relied on *Ruiz v Spain* (2001) 31 EHRR 589, *Hadjianastassiou v Greece* (1992) 16 EHRR 219 and *Robins v UK* (23 September 1997, unreported).

[101] Mr Walker submitted that in making the order in this case the judge departed from the usual order and should have given reasons. In support of this proposition he relied on *Eagil Trust Co Ltd v Pigott-Brown* [1985] 3 All ER 119 and *Brent London BC v Aniedobe* [1999] CA Transcript 2003. Mr Walker accepted that the judge would have had reasons for the order that was made, but he submitted that this court should not assume that those reasons were sound.

[102] Mr Walker accepted that if the result which the judge reached was the right result, the appeal should fail. However, he submitted that it would not be sufficient to show that the judge might properly have reached the result. That would be to assume that the reasons which the judge had were good reasons. It was not fair to make that assumption where no reasons at all had been given.

[103] As respects the exercise of the judge's discretion, Mr Walker referred to CPR 44.3. He relied on the fact that the appellant was the successful party and that there was no criticism of the appellant's conduct. If the appellant had accepted the payment then made by the police, the appellant would have been entitled to all the costs which he had incurred up to the date of acceptance. Mr Walker submitted that the appellant made timeous concessions. The police had all the information as to ownership. At most the appellant should be deprived of some of his costs. However, Mr Walker did not place a percentage on these costs. He submitted that if the appellant were to be deprived of any costs, it should be done on an issues basis. If the result of the case was truly a draw, then the appellant should at least get 50% of its costs with no order as to the balance. However, Mr Walker warned against treating success on 20 out of 40 items as equivalent to success which should be represented by an award of 50% of the costs.

[104] Mr Walker submitted that it is artificial to treat this case as 65 separate claims. He relied on the fact that the respondent failed to take the obvious step of applying to a judge for reasons, pursuant to the practice indicated in *Flannery*'s case [2000] 1 All ER 373, [2000] 1 WLR 377.

[105] Mr James Watson QC, for the respondent, submitted that this was not a case where reasons were required. He submitted that reasons would not have been required under the Strasbourg jurisprudence. He relied on the way in which the European Court of Human Rights itself awarded costs. Its usual course was not to give reasons.

[106] Mr Watson submitted that the proper test was that reasons are only required where an unusual order is made. In this respect he relied on the *Eagil Trust* case, above, and on *R v Crown Court at Harrow, ex p Dave* [1994] 1 All ER 315, [1994] 1 WLR 98. Mr Watson submitted that the judge must have chosen to adopt the defendant's submissions.

[107] Mr Watson submitted that the evidential burden of proving that the items in issue were stolen was on the police and that it was only by going to court that the police could avoid or reduce the liability to pay the damages sought by the claimant. The police would have lost the entire case if they had not taken any active part in the trial. Therefore, they had to go to court to protect themselves

a from liability. In those circumstances, they should be treated as a successful
party. In this respect, he relied on *Roache v News Group Newspapers Ltd* [1998]
EMLR 161 where the Court of Appeal examined the question whether a party
was really the winner or not. The three members of the court (Bingham MR,
Stuart-Smith and Simon Brown LJJ) each gave separate judgments. Mr Watson
relied on passages in each of the judgments, including the test put forward by
b Simon Brown LJ (at 178) that the party seeking to recover his costs 'must show at
least that he has obtained at the hearing something of value which he would not
otherwise have expected to get'. On this basis, Mr Watson submitted that the
police were equally the winner in these proceedings.

[108] Mr Watson also made submissions based on the conduct of the appellant
prior to trial. In particular the police had served 147 hearsay statements served
c for the purpose of the criminal trial. Originally the appellant wanted all of these
witnesses to be called. He eventually decided upon nine of these witnesses and
then at trial decided none need be cross-examined. There were other matters in
the conduct prior to trial on which Mr Watson relied, but since the judge referred
to none of these in argument, it is unnecessary to refer to them further.

d
Conclusions

[109] The judge was clearly entitled to form a provisional view as to costs in
the draft judgment. It was helpful to the parties to do so.

[110] The judge formed the provisional view that there should be no order as
to costs. A fair reading of this part of the judge's judgment leads to the conclusion
e that the judge considered that that order was the right order in the light of what
the appellant had obtained under the judgment. It is not to be supposed that the
judge took into account factors not mentioned in the judgment. In other words,
the judge clearly thought that the action had resulted in a "draw". In our view, it
was open to the judge to reach this conclusion. Although when the case was
f started there were some 65 items in issue, by the time of closing speeches there
were only 40 items in issue. The appellant won in respect of half in number of
these items. There were no criticisms relevant to costs in the conduct of either
party. Nor was there any reference to the appellant's conduct in the interim
stages of the proceedings. The judge could not have considered that there was
any aspect of the parties' conduct material to the decision on costs.
g [111] The reasons deducible for the judge's provisional order as to costs must,
therefore, be that the appellant had won half of his case and lost on the rest. In
the circumstances of the case, it was open to the judge to conclude, as Mr Watson
submitted, that the police as well as the appellant had had to come to court to win
that part of the case on which they succeeded. To this extent, the judge was
h entitled to take the view that each side was to that extent the winner.
Alternatively it was open to the judge, in the light of the wide powers conferred
by the CPR, to conclude that, in any event, the appellant should only have part
of his costs, as he had been successful in part only of his case, and that the police
should have the costs of the part of the case on which they had been successful.
j On either basis the judge could properly conclude that the proportion of costs
which each party should receive was 50% and that the net result was nil when
these two percentages were set against each other.

[112] When the judge handed down the judgment on costs on 4 April 2001, in
our judgment, the judge confirmed that, notwithstanding the submissions which
the appellant had made, in the judge's view the order originally proposed was the
correct one.

[113] In our judgment, nothing turns on the question whether for the purposes of the costs this case ought to be analysed as a trial of 65 causes of action or as a trial of a single cause of action. That issue would have been important to the payment into court made by the police if that payment played any part in resolving the incidence of costs, since the payment in was made in respect of all causes of action and not just specified causes of action. In the present circumstances it would be undesirable if the approach of the court to the appropriate order of costs turned on such technical distinctions. The court now has wide power under the CPR to make orders for costs which reflect not just the ultimate victory, but the extent to which a party raised issues on which he did not succeed. Accordingly the court could in this case make the same order whether the costs are treated as relating to a single cause of action, which was partly successful, or to series of causes of action, some only of which succeeded.

[114] In this connection we add the following observations about the appropriate form of order where a party is to be awarded some only of his costs. Mr Walker submits that the appellant should obtain all its costs of the action other than those which relate to the issues on which it failed. In support of this approach, he relies on the decision of Neuberger J in *Harrison v Bloom Camillin* (4 February 2000, unreported). In that case, the judge held that he could not do justice to the parties by placing a percentage of the costs of the hearing on the issues which either party had won. He therefore made an order that the claimants in that case should have their costs save in relation to certain specified issues. He referred to CPR 44.3(6) and (7) which provide:

'(6) The orders which the court may make under this rule include an order that a party must pay—(a) a proportion of another party's costs ... (c) costs from or until a certain date only ... (f) costs relating only to a distinct part of the proceedings ...

(7) Where the court would otherwise consider making an order under paragraph (6)(f), it must instead, if practicable, make an order under paragraph (6)(a) or (c).'

[115] We are in no position to express a view as to whether we would have made the same order as Neuberger J did in the *Bloom Camillin* case. However, we would emphasise that the CPR requires that an order which allows or disallows costs by reference to certain issues should be made *only if* other forms of order cannot be made which sufficiently reflect the justice of the case (see CPR 44.3(7), above). In our view there are good reasons for this rule. An order which allows or disallows costs of certain issues creates difficulties at the stage of the assessment of costs because the costs judge will have to master the issue in detail to understand what costs were properly incurred in dealing with it and then analyse the work done by the receiving party's legal advisors to determine whether or not it was attributable to the issue the costs of which had been disallowed. All this adds to the costs of assessment and to the amount of time absorbed in dealing with costs on this basis. The costs incurred on assessment may thus be disproportionate to the benefit gained. In all the circumstances, contrary to what might be thought to be the case, a 'percentage' order (under CPR 44.3(6)(a)) made by the judge who heard the application will often produce a fairer result than an 'issues based' order under CPR 44.3(6)(f). Moreover such an order is consistent with the overriding objective of the CPR.

[116] In general the question of what costs order is appropriate is one for the discretion of the judge and an appellate court will be slow to interfere in its

a exercise. But the considerations mentioned in the preceding paragraphs are ones which a judge should bear in mind when considering what form of order ought to be in order properly to apply CPR 44.3(7). These considerations will in most cases lead to the conclusion that an 'issues based' order ought not to be made. Wherever practicable, therefore, the judge should endeavour to form a view as to the percentage of costs to which the winning party should be entitled or

b alternatively whether justice would be sufficiently done by awarding costs from or until a particular date only, as suggested by CPR 44.3(6)(c).

[117] For the reasons that we have given, this appeal will be dismissed.

POSTSCRIPT

[118] In each of these appeals, the judgment created uncertainty as to the

c reasons for the decision. In each appeal that uncertainty was resolved, but only after an appeal which involved consideration of the underlying evidence and submissions. We feel that in each case the appellants should have appreciated why it was that they had not been successful, but may have been tempted by the example of *Flannery's* case to seek to have the decision of the trial judge set aside.

d There are two lessons to be drawn from these appeals. The first is that, while it is perfectly acceptable for reasons to be set out briefly in a judgment, it is the duty of the judge to produce a judgment that gives a clear explanation for his or her order. The second is that an unsuccessful party should not seek to upset a judgment on the ground of inadequacy of reasons unless, despite the advantage of considering the judgment with knowledge of the evidence given and

e submissions made at the trial, that party is unable to understand why it is that the judge has reached an adverse decision.

Appeals dismissed. Permission to appeal refused.

Kate O'Hanlon   Barrister.

Practice Statement

COURT OF APPEAL, CRIMINAL DIVISION
LORD WOOLF CJ
31 MAY 2002

Sentence – Murder – Life imprisonment – Minimum term – Setting of minimum terms of imprisonment for adults convicted of murder – Guidance.

Sentence – Young person – Serious criminal offence – Minimum term – Setting of minimum terms for juveniles sentenced to detention during Her Majesty's pleasure – Guidance.

LORD WOOLF CJ gave the following direction at the sitting of the court.

1. *Practice Note (juveniles: murder tariff)* [2000] 4 All ER 831, [2000] 1 WLR 1655 handed down on 27 July 2000 is replaced by this Practice Statement. This Statement comes into force immediately and should be applied by judges in cases in which they sentence or make a recommendation after today. Its primary, but not sole, purpose is to give effect to the advice of the Sentencing Advisory Panel dated 15 March 2002. It does not set out rules, but guidance from which a judge can in his discretion depart, if he considers this is necessary in view of the particular circumstances of an individual case notwithstanding the desirability of achieving consistency. Reasons for any departure from the guidance should be given.

2. The previous *Practice Note* referred to a 'tariff'. This term, in accordance with the advice of the panel, will no longer be used because it has commonly been misunderstood. The present Statement refers instead to 'minimum term' to make it clearer that, even when released, the offender has not served his sentence which continues for the remainder of his life.

3. In fact, an offender is most unlikely to be released on the expiry of the minimum term and for the purpose of calculating the earliest date of normal release on licence the minimum term is approximately the equivalent of a determinate sentence of twice its length. So a minimum term of 14 years is equivalent to a determinate sentence of approximately 28 years. (See *Re Thompson (tariff recommendations)* [2001] 1 All ER 737 at 740.)

4. When a person of 21 years or over is convicted of murder the only sentence is life imprisonment. When an offender is aged 18 to 20 the equivalent sentence is custody for life and for an offender aged 17 or under at the date of the offence the sentence is detention at Her Majesty's pleasure. In the appropriate circumstances, a judge can also pass a discretionary life sentence and an automatic life sentence. Except when sentencing an offender aged 18 or over for murder, a judge is required to announce the minimum term in public. A judge sentencing a prisoner to life imprisonment for murder has the power to make a recommendation in open court as to the 'minimum period' which should elapse before the person convicted is released on licence under s 1 of the Murder (Abolition of Death Penalty) Act 1965. This statutory power is rarely exercised. Before it is exercised the judge should carefully consider whether it would not be preferable to rely on the usual practice of making a recommendation after the trial has finished which is then forwarded to the Lord Chief Justice. The Home Secretary can then be sent the recommendation of both judges.

Announcing a minimum term

a

5. When a judge gives in public his decision as to the minimum term a prisoner is required to serve, he should make clear how that term is calculated. In particular, he should normally commence by indicating what he considers would be the appropriate determinate sentence suitable for punishment and deterrence. He should then explain that it is necessary to calculate a minimum

b term so that it will be known when the prisoner's case should be referred to the Parole Board. Finally, he should explain that if a prisoner is released on licence still, for the remainder of his life, he can be recalled to prison if he does not comply with the terms of his licence.

Adult offenders convicted of murder

c

6. In relation to adults convicted of murder, after the Lord Chief Justice, in accordance with the present practice, has received the relevant information from the trial judge including the trial judge's recommendation, he will make his own recommendation. The Home Secretary will then make the final decision as to the appropriate minimum term having considered both recommendations.

d

7. Before recommending a release date, the Parole Board, in accordance with present practice, must be satisfied that the offender is no longer a risk to the public and is ready for release into society. Following release, life sentence prisoners remain subject to the life sentence and the terms of their licence for the rest of their lives. They must comply with any conditions of their licence and are

e subject to supervision by the Probation Service and they are liable to recall to custody at any time if the terms of the licence are breached.

8. The *Practice Note* dated 27 July 2000, confirmed the starting point of 14 years, which had been increased from 12 years, as the minimum term for a case with no aggravating or mitigating factors. It also listed the factors which indicate that either a higher or a lower than normal minimum term is appropriate

f in an individual case.

9. This Statement replaces the previous single normal tariff of 14 years by substituting a higher and a normal starting point of respectively 16 (comparable to 32 years) and 12 years (comparable to 24 years). These starting points have then to be increased or reduced because of aggravating or mitigating factors such

g as those referred to in paras 10–18, below. It is emphasised that they are no more than starting points.

The normal starting point of 12 years

10. Cases falling within this starting point will normally involve the killing of

h an adult victim, arising from a quarrel or loss of temper between two people known to each other. It will not have the characteristics referred to in para 12. Exceptionally, the starting point may be reduced because of the sort of circumstances described in the next paragraph.

11. The normal starting point can be reduced because the murder is one

j where the offender's culpability is significantly reduced, for example, because: (a) the case came close to the borderline between murder and manslaughter; or (b) the offender suffered from mental disorder, or from a mental disability which lowered the degree of his criminal responsibility for the killing, although not affording a defence of diminished responsibility; or (c) the offender was provoked (in a non-technical sense), such as by prolonged and eventually unsupportable stress; or (d) the case involved an overreaction in self-defence; or (e) the offence was a mercy killing. These factors could justify a reduction to eight/nine years (equivalent to 16/18 years).

The higher starting point of 15/16 years

12. The higher starting point will apply to cases where the offender's culpability was exceptionally high or the victim was in a particularly vulnerable position. Such cases will be characterised by a feature which makes the crime especially serious, such as: (a) the killing was 'professional' or a contract killing; (b) the killing was politically motivated; (c) the killing was done for gain (in the course of a burglary, robbery etc.); (d) the killing was intended to defeat the ends of justice (as in the killing of a witness or potential witness); (e) the victim was providing a public service; (f) the victim was a child or was otherwise vulnerable; (g) the killing was racially aggravated; (h) the victim was deliberately targeted because of his or her religion or sexual orientation; (i) there was evidence of sadism, gratuitous violence or sexual maltreatment, humiliation or degradation of the victim before the killing; (j) extensive and/or multiple injuries were inflicted on the victim before death; (k) the offender committed multiple murders.

Variation of the starting point

13. Whichever starting point is selected in a particular case, it may be appropriate for the trial judge to vary the starting point upwards or downwards, to take account of aggravating or mitigating factors, which relate to either the offence or the offender, in the particular case.

14. Aggravating factors relating to the offence can include: (a) the fact that the killing was planned; (b) the use of a firearm; (c) arming with a weapon in advance; (d) concealment of the body, destruction of the crime scene and/or dismemberment of the body; (e) particularly in domestic violence cases, the fact that the murder was the culmination of cruel and violent behaviour by the offender over a period of time.

15. Aggravating factors relating to the offender will include the offender's previous record and failures to respond to previous sentences, to the extent that this is relevant to culpability rather than to risk.

16. Mitigating factors relating to the offence will include: (a) an intention to cause grievous bodily harm, rather than to kill; (b) spontaneity and lack of pre-meditation.

17. Mitigating factors relating to the offender may include: (a) the offender's age; (b) clear evidence of remorse or contrition; (c) a timely plea of guilty.

Very serious cases

18. A substantial upward adjustment may be appropriate in the most serious cases, for example, those involving a substantial number of murders, or if there are several factors identified as attracting the higher starting point present. In suitable cases, the result might even be a minimum term of 30 years (equivalent to 60 years) which would offer little or no hope of the offender's eventual release. In cases of exceptional gravity, the judge, rather than setting a whole life minimum term, can state that there is no minimum period which could properly be set in that particular case.

19. Among the categories of case referred to in para 12, some offences may be especially grave. These include cases in which the victim was performing his duties as a prison officer at the time of the crime or the offence was a terrorist or

a   sexual or sadistic murder or involved a young child. In such a case, a term of 20 years and upwards could be appropriate.

Young offenders

20. Section 60 of the Criminal Justice and Court Services Act 2000 brought sentencing procedures for those sentenced to detention during Her Majesty's

b   pleasure into line with adult offenders sentenced to discretionary and automatic (but not mandatory) life sentences. When imposing the mandatory sentence of detention at Her Majesty's pleasure on an offender convicted of murder, who was aged under 18 at the time of the offence, the sentencing judge may now order that s 28(5)–(8) of the Crime (Sentences) Act 1997 shall apply to the young offender as soon as he has served that part of the sentence which is specified by

c   the sentencer. A minimum term should be specified in all but the most exceptional circumstances. If a minimum sentence is not fixed the Home Secretary will, in due course, determine the appropriate stage for the early release provisions to apply to the young offender.

21. In setting the minimum term, sentencers are required by s 82A(3) of the

d   Powers of Criminal Courts (Sentencing) Act 2000 to take account of the same three considerations that apply to discretionary or automatic life sentences imposed on an adult, namely:

(a) the seriousness of the offence, or the combination of the offence and one or more offences associated with it;

(b) the effect which s 67 of the Criminal Justice Act 1967 would have had if he

e   had been sentenced to a term of imprisonment; and

(c) the early release provisions contained in ss 33(2) and 35(1) of the Criminal Justice Act 1991.

22. Subparagraph (b) requires the sentencer to make adjustment for any period which had been spent on remand in custody, since that period is not

f   automatically deducted from the minimum period by s 67 of the 1967 Act. The period spent by the offender in local authority secure accommodation should be deducted from the minimum term (see *R v Secretary of State for the Home Dept, ex p A* [2000] 1 All ER 651, [2000] 2 AC 276).

23. As in the case of an adult, sub-para (c) requires the sentencer to fix the minimum term at one half of the normal determinate sentence which would

g   have been imposed for the offence if a life sentence had not been passed (see *R v Secretary of State for the Home Dept, ex p Furber* [1998] 1 All ER 23).

24. In the case of young offenders, the judge should always start from the normal starting point appropriate for an adult (12 years). The judge should then reduce the starting point to take into account the maturity and age of the

h   offender. Some children are more, and others less, mature for their age and the reduction that is appropriate in order to achieve the correct starting point will very much depend on the stage of the development of the individual offender. A mechanistic approach is never appropriate. The sort of reduction from the 12-year starting point which can be used as a rough check, is about one year for

j   each year that the offender's age is below 18. So, for a child of ten, the judge should be considering a starting point in the region of five years.

25. Having arrived at the starting point the judge should then take account of the aggravating and mitigating factors in the particular case, which will take the prescribed minimum term above or below the starting point. The sliding scale proposed is intended to recognise the greater degree of understanding and capacity for normal reasoning which develops in adolescents over time as well as

the fact that young offenders are likely to have the greatest capacity for change. It cannot take into account the individual offender's responsibility for, and understanding of, the crime.

26. The welfare needs of the offender have also to be taken into account (see s 44(1) of the Children and Young Persons Act 1933). Lord Browne-Wilkinson in *R v Secretary of State for the Home Dept, ex p Venables, R v Secretary of State for the Home Dept, ex p Thompson* [1997] 3 All ER 97 at 122, [1998] AC 407 at 499 emphasised that the Home Secretary 'must at all times be free to take into account as one of the relevant factors the welfare of the child and the desirability of reintegrating the child into society'. He also pointed out that the extent this was possible—

> 'must depend, in the case of a young child at least, on the way in which that child was maturing through his formative years. If the child is making exceptional progress and it is clear that his welfare would be improved by release from detention, that is one of the factors the Secretary of State must take into account and balance against the other relevant factors of retribution, deterrence and risk. The child's welfare is not paramount but it is *one* of the factors which must be taken into account.' (See [1997] 3 All ER 97 at 122, [1998] AC 407 at 499–500.)

27. The Home Secretary does not consider that this statement as to his responsibility is relevant now that the minimum term is set by the trial judge. The trial judge can only act on the information before him in taking into account the welfare of the child at the time that he announces the minimum term. It has been suggested that in these circumstances s 44(1) of the 1933 Act requires judges to fix the lowest possible minimum term so as to ensure the Parole Board will consider the case at the correct time if a child happens to make exceptional progress. It is recommended that this suggestion is not followed although it is appreciated that the Home Secretary's view means that apparently exceptional progress by a child while in detention will not influence the date his case is considered by the Parole Board.

Kate O'Hanlon   Barrister.

Callery v Gray (Nos 1 and 2)
[2002] UKHL 28

a

HOUSE OF LORDS

LORD BINGHAM OF CORNHILL, LORD NICHOLLS OF BIRKENHEAD, LORD HOFFMANN,
LORD HOPE OF CRAIGHEAD AND LORD SCOTT OF FOSCOTE

23–25 APRIL, 27 JUNE 2002

b

Solicitor – Costs – Conditional fee agreement – Success fee uplift – After-the-event (ATE) insurance premium – Personal injury claims – Modest and straightforward claims for personal injuries arising from road traffic accidents – Claimant entering into conditional fee agreement with success uplift – Claimant taking out ATE cover at outset for premium of £350 – Court of Appeal allowing success fee of 20% and recovery of ATE premium in full – Whether ATE insurance premium recoverable from defendant as reasonable disbursement if claimant paying premium at outset – Whether amount of success fee and premium reasonable.

c

d

The claimant instructed solicitors to pursue a straightforward claim for damages against the defendant in respect of minor injuries that he had suffered in a road traffic accident. At the same time, the claimant entered into a conditional fee agreement (CFA) with his solicitors, providing for a success fee of 60%. Such agreements were part of the new regime for funding litigation, and in particular personal injury litigation, introduced by the Access to Justice Act 1999. A few days after entering into the CFA, the claimant took out an after-the-event (ATE) insurance policy, at a premium of £350, to protect himself against the risk of incurring liability for the defendant's costs. On the same day, the claimant's solicitors sent a letter before action to the defendant. The policy was therefore taken out before the claimant or his advisers could have concluded that litigation to pursue the claim would be necessary or even likely. In the event, the claim was settled without the need to issue proceedings, with the defendant agreeing to pay the claimant's reasonable costs and disbursements. When the parties proved unable to agree the amount of such costs and disbursements, the claimant commenced costs-only proceedings pursuant to CPR 44.12A. In those proceedings, the district judge reduced the success fee to 40%, but allowed the premium. The defendant's appeal was dismissed by the judge. On the defendant's further appeal, the Court of Appeal reduced the success fee to 20%, but held that the ATE premium could, in principle, be recovered as part of a claimant's costs in costs-only proceedings. In a subsequent judgment, the court held that the amount of the premium was not manifestly disproportionate to the risk. The defendant appealed to the House of Lords, challenging the reasonableness both of the 20% success fee and the premium, and contending, in particular, that the ATE policy had been taken out prematurely.

e

f

g

h

Held – (Lord Scott dissenting in part) The responsibility for monitoring and controlling the developing practice in a field such as the new regime for funding litigation lay with the Court of Appeal and not with their Lordships, who should ordinarily be slow to intervene. Their Lordships could not respond to changes in practice with the speed and sensitivity of the Court of Appeal, before which a number of cases were likely to come over time. Although the instant appeal was a final and not an interlocutory appeal, there was some analogy between appeals on matters of practice and interlocutory appeals. The latter were only exceptionally

j

allowed to come before their Lordships. Even if the instant case were such an
exceptional case, their Lordships should not intervene. The Court of Appeal had   *a*
stressed that the issues in it arose at a very early stage in the practical
development of the new funding regime, when reliable factual material was
sparse, market experience was meagre and trends hard to discern. The court had
also made it plain that it was not purporting to lay down rules applicable for all
time but was giving provisional guidance to be reviewed in the light of increased   *b*
knowledge and developing experience. Accordingly, the appeal would be
dismissed (see [8]–[11], [17], [45], [55], [56], [62], [133], below).

Decisions of the Court of Appeal [2001] 3 All ER 833 and [2001] 4 All ER 1 affirmed.

Notes
For recovery of insurance premium by way of costs, see 41 *Halsbury's Laws* (4th   *c*
edn reissue) para 922.

Cases referred to in opinions
Birkett v James [1977] 2 All ER 801, [1978] AC 297, [1977] 3 WLR 38, HL.
Girvan v Inverness Farmers Dairy (No 2) 1998 SC (HL) 1.   *d*
Gomba Holdings UK Ltd v Minories Finance Ltd (No 2) [1992] 4 All ER 588, [1993] Ch
  171, [1992] 2 WLR 723, CA.
Thai Trading Co (a firm) v Taylor [1998] 3 All ER 65, [1998] QB 781, [1998] 2 WLR
  893, CA.

Appeal   *e*
The defendant, Charles Gray, appealed with permission of the Appeal Committee
of the House of Lords given on 24 January 2002 from (i) the order of the Court of
Appeal (Lord Woolf CJ, Lord Phillips of Worth Matravers MR and Brooke LJ) on
17 July 2001 ([2001] EWCA Civ 1117, [2001] 3 All ER 833, [2001] 1 WLR 2112)
allowing, to the extent only of reducing the success fee to 20%, his appeal from   *f*
that part of the decision of Judge Edwards at Chester County Court on 29 January
2001 dismissing his appeal from that part of the order of District Judge Wallace,
made in costs-only proceedings under CPR 44.12A at Macclesfield County Court
on 7 November 2000, whereby he allowed the claimant, Stephen Callery, to
recover from Mr Gray as reasonable costs a success fee uplift of 40% under a
conditional fee agreement with his solicitors in respect of a personal injury claim   *g*
against Mr Gray, and (ii) the order of the Court of Appeal (Lord Phillips of Worth
Matravers MR and Brooke LJ) on 31 July 2001 ([2001] EWCA Civ 1246, [2001]
4 All ER 1, [2001] 1 WLR 2142) dismissing Mr Gray's appeal against that part of
the decision of Judge Edwards dismissing his appeal from that part of the order of
District Judge Wallace allowing Mr Callery to recover from him as a reasonable   *h*
disbursement a premium of £350 paid by Mr Callery for after-the-event insurance
protecting him against incurring any liability for Mr Gray's costs. The Lord
Chancellor's Department was given permission to intervene in the appeal on
17 April 2002. The facts are set out in the opinions of Lord Hoffmann and Lord
Scott of Foscote.   *j*

Anthony Temple QC, Peter Birts QC and *Deborah Taylor* (instructed by *Beachcroft
  Wansbroughs*) for Mr Gray.
Geoffrey Nice QC and *Nicholas Bacon* (instructed by *Amelans*, Manchester) for
  Mr Callery.
Jonathan Crow (instructed by the *Treasury Solicitor*) for the Lord Chancellor's
  Department.

a Their Lordships took time for consideration.

27 June 2002. The following opinions were delivered.

LORD BINGHAM OF CORNHILL.

b [1] My Lords, for nearly half a century, legal aid provided out of public funds was the main source of funding for those of modest means who sought to make or (less frequently) defend claims in the civil courts and who needed professional help to do so. By this means, access to the courts was made available to many who would otherwise, for want of means, have been denied it. But as time passed the defects of the legal aid regime established under the Legal Aid and Advice Act *c* 1949 and later statutes became more and more apparent. While the scheme served the poorest well, it left many with means above a low ceiling in an unsatisfactory position, too well-off to qualify for legal aid but too badly-off to contemplate incurring the costs of contested litigation. There was no access to the courts for them. Moreover, the effective immunity against adverse costs orders enjoyed by legally-aided claimants was always recognised to place an *d* unfair burden on a privately-funded defendant resisting a legally-aided claim, since he would be liable for both sides' costs if he lost and his own even if he won. Most seriously of all, the cost to the public purse of providing civil legal aid had risen sharply, without however showing an increase in the number of cases funded or evidence that legal aid was directed to cases which most clearly *e* justified the expenditure of public money.

[2] Recognition of these defects underpinned the Access to Justice Act 1999 which, building on the Courts and Legal Services Act 1990, introduced a new regime for funding litigation, and in particular personal injury litigation with which alone this opinion is concerned. My noble and learned friend Lord Scott of Foscote makes full reference to these Acts and the relevant subordinate *f* legislation made under them in his opinion, which I have been privileged to read in draft, and I gratefully adopt his account which I need not repeat. The 1999 Act and the accompanying regulations had (so far as relevant for present purposes) three aims. One aim was to contain the rising cost of legal aid to public funds and enable existing expenditure to be refocused on causes with the greatest need to *g* be funded at public expense, whether because of their intrinsic importance or because of the difficulty of funding them otherwise than out of public funds or for both those reasons. A second aim was to improve access to the courts for members of the public with meritorious claims. It was appreciated that the risk of incurring substantial liabilities in costs is a powerful disincentive to all but the *h* very rich from becoming involved in litigation, and it was therefore hoped that the new arrangements would enable claimants to protect themselves against liability for paying costs either to those acting for them or (if they chose) to those on the other side. A third aim was to discourage weak claims and enable successful defendants to recover their costs in actions brought against them by indigent claimants. Pursuant to the first of these aims publicly-funded assistance *j* was withdrawn from run-of-the-mill personal injury claimants. The main instruments upon which it was intended that claimants should rely to achieve the second and third of the aims are described by my noble and learned friend: they are conditional fee agreements and insurance cover obtained after the event giving rise to the claim.

[3] At the time when the 1999 Act was enacted and brought into effect, new CPR were also in the course of being implemented. The objects underlying these

rules were not new, but the rules gave a sharply increased emphasis to the need for expedition in the conduct of legal proceedings, to the need for simplicity and to the need to avoid unnecessary and disproportionate costs. To achieve these ends, new and detailed procedures were devised to moderate the traditional adversarial approach to the making and defending of claims. There was inevitably a bedding-down period during which both judges and practitioners adjusted to the practical implications of the new procedural regime to which they were required to give effect.

[4] If the objects underlying the new procedural regime were not new, those underlying the new funding regime were. Arrangements which had until relatively recently been professionally improper were to become the norm. It was, however, evident that the success of the new funding regime was threatened by two contingencies which, had they occurred, could have proved fatal. One was that lawyers, in particular solicitors, would decline to act on a conditional fee basis. To counter that risk the maximum permissible uplift, on the first introduction of conditional fees in 1995, had been fixed, despite very strong opposition, at 100% and this high level of permissible uplift was retained. It was no doubt felt, rightly as events have proved, that if solicitors were permitted in some cases to earn, as the reward for success, double the fee otherwise receivable, they would be tempted into the market. The other contingency was that no accessible market would develop in after-the-event insurance. There was at the outset very little knowledge and experience of whether or how such a market would develop.

[5] Even if these contingencies did not occur, the new funding regime was obviously open to abuse in a number of ways. One possible abuse was that lawyers would be willing to act for claimants on a conditional fee basis but would charge excessive fees for their basic costs, knowing that their own client would not have to pay them and that the burden would in all probability fall on the defendant or his liability insurers. With this expectation the claimants' lawyers would have no incentive to moderate their charges. Another possible abuse was that lawyers would be willing to act for claimants on a conditional fee basis but would contract for a success uplift grossly disproportionate to any fair assessment of the risks of failure in the litigation, again knowing that the burden of paying this uplifted fee would never fall on their client but would be borne by the defendant or his insurers. A third possible abuse was that claimants, although able to obtain after-the-event insurance, would be able to do so only at an unreasonably high price, the after-the-event insurers having no incentive to moderate a premium which would be paid by the defendant or his insurers and which might be grossly disproportionate to the risk which the insurer was underwriting. Under the new regime, a claimant who makes appropriate arrangements can litigate without any risk of ever having personally to pay costs either to those acting for him or to the other side and without any risk of ever having to pay an after-the-event insurance premium whatever the outcome: the practical result is to transfer the entire cost of funding this kind of litigation to the liability insurers of unsuccessful defendants (and defendants who settle the claims made against them) and thus, indirectly, to the wider public who pay premiums to insure themselves against liability to pay compensation for causing personal injury.

[6] The front-line responsibility for making the new funding regime work fairly and effectively and in accordance with the objects both of the 1999 Act and the new CPR lay with lawyers agreeing to act under conditional fee agreements

a and insurers offering after-the-event insurance cover. The role of watchdog would be exercised, in the first instance, by district judges and costs judges, on whose judgment and insight in assessing recoverable costs much would depend. If they were too restrictive in the level of success fees or after-the-event insurance premiums which they allowed, lawyers and clients might be deterred from acting or proceeding on this basis and the objects of the new regime would be defeated.

b If they were too generous and too uncritical, excessive fees and premiums might be allowed and an unfair and disproportionate burden placed on defendants and their liability insurers, thereby undermining one of the key objects of the CPR. The difficult task entrusted to district judges and costs judges called for a clear understanding of the object of both the 1999 Act and the CPR, an understanding how the new funding regime was developing in practice and an alert willingness

c to make appropriate orders if and when signs of abuse appeared. However carefully and attentively district judges and costs judges applied themselves to their task, it was inevitable that occasions would arise when judges misdirected themselves and made erroneous orders, and given the number of orders made by different judges in different parts of the country disparities in practice would be

d likely to arise. The responsibility for curbing errors and giving guidance to district judges and costs judges on the exercise of their powers in this context, of correcting erroneous orders and of seeking to harmonise practice between various courts rests with circuit judges and then, importantly, with the Court of Appeal.

[7] There is obvious force in the appellant's contention that even a 20%

e success uplift provided a generous level of reward for Mr Callery's solicitors given the minuscule risk of failure which his claim apparently presented, that it would have been reasonable to await a reply from Mr Gray or his liability insurers before obtaining after-the-event insurance cover and that the premium charged for such cover, on the facts of the case as they then appeared, was unreasonable

f and disproportionate. There are none the less two reasons which lead me to the conclusion that the House should not intervene.

[8] The first is that the responsibility for monitoring and controlling the developing practice in a field such as this lies with the Court of Appeal and not the House, which should ordinarily be slow to intervene. The House cannot respond to changes in practice with the speed and sensitivity of the Court of

g Appeal, before which a number of cases are likely over time to come. Although this is a final and not an interlocutory appeal, there is in my view some analogy between appeals on matters of practice and interlocutory appeals, of which Lord Diplock in *Birkett v James* [1977] 2 All ER 801 at 804, [1978] AC 297 at 317 observed that only very exceptionally are appeals upon such matters allowed to come

h before the House.

[9] Even if this were one of those exceptional cases, however, I would decline to intervene because, as the Court of Appeal repeatedly stressed, the present issues arise at a very early stage in the practical development of the new funding regime, when reliable factual material is sparse, market experience is meagre and

j trends are hard to discern. I would draw attention, in the first judgment of the Court of Appeal ([2001] EWCA Civ 1117, [2001] 3 All ER 833, [2001] 1 WLR 2112), to passages at [64], [99](v), [103], [105] and [116]. In the second judgment of the Court of Appeal ([2001] EWCA Civ 1246, [2001] 4 All ER 1, [2001] 1 WLR 2142) similar points are made at [14], [15], [17] and [69]. In the report of Master O'Hare annexed to the second judgment of the Court of Appeal, relevant passages appear at [2001] 4 All ER 1 at 22, 23, [2001] 1 WLR 2142 at 2163, 2164 (paras 19, 23). The

Court of Appeal made plain that it was not purporting to lay down rules applicable for all time but was giving provisional guidance to be reviewed in the light of increased knowledge and developing experience.

[10] For these reasons (and those given by my noble and learned friends Lord Nicholls of Birkenhead and Lord Hope of Craighead) I would dismiss this appeal. In doing so I would not wish to discount either the risk of abuse or the need to check any practices which may undermine the fairness of the new funding regime. This should operate so as to promote access to justice but not so as to confer disproportionate benefits on legal practitioners or after-the-event insurers or impose unfair burdens on defendants or their insurers. I feel sure that district and costs judges, circuit judges and in the last resort the Court of Appeal can be relied on to maintain a fair and publicly beneficial balance between competing interests.

LORD NICHOLLS OF BIRKENHEAD.

[11] My Lords, I have had the advantage of reading in draft the speeches of my noble and learned friends Lord Bingham of Cornhill and Lord Hope of Craighead. For the reasons they give I too would dismiss this appeal. I wish to emphasise only one point.

[12] All legal procedures are open to abuse. A theme running through much of the appellant's case in your Lordships' House was that the new funding arrangements for personal injuries claims in road traffic cases are unduly open to abuse and are being abused. Costs are being incurred unnecessarily and at an excessive level. The underlying problem, it was said, is that claimants now operate in a costs-free and risk-free zone.

[13] In short, this result comes about as follows. By entering into a conditional fee agreement at the outset, a claimant achieves the position that his solicitors' charges will never be payable by him or at his expense. If his claim is successful the fees, including the amount of the uplift, will be payable by the defendant's liability insurers. If his claim is unsuccessful, nothing will be due from him to his solicitor under the agreement. Likewise with the premium payable for after-the-event insurance: if the claim is successful, the premium will be payable by the other side's liability insurers. If the claim is unsuccessful, nothing will be payable by the claimant when, as frequently happens, the policy provides that no premium will be payable in that event.

[14] The consequence, it was said, of these arrangements, hugely attractive to claimants, is that claimants are entering into conditional fee agreements, and after-the-event insurance, at an inappropriately early stage. They have every incentive to do so, and no financial interest in doing otherwise. Moreover, in entering into conditional fee agreements and insurance arrangements they have no financial interest in keeping down their solicitors' fees or the amount of the uplift or the amount of the policy premiums. Further, they have no financial incentive to accept reasonable offers or payments into court: come what may, their solicitors' bills will be met by others. So will the other side's legal costs.

[15] As a result, it was said, the new arrangements, as they are currently working, are unbalanced and unfairly prejudicial to liability insurers and the general body of motorists whose insurance policy premiums provide the money with which liability insurers meet these personal injuries claims and costs. The appellant urged your Lordships to promulgate guidelines to reduce the scope for abuse in this situation.

[16] My Lords, I agree that for the two reasons given by Lord Bingham your Lordships should decline this invitation. Plainly, however, the criticisms outlined above give cause for serious concern. It is imperative that these aspects of the new funding system should be watched closely as the system develops and matures.

LORD HOFFMANN.

[17] My Lords, the Court of Appeal is traditionally and rightly responsible for supervising the administration of civil procedure. This is an area in which your Lordships have in the past seldom intervened and, it must be said, the few exceptions to this policy of self-restraint have usually tended to confirm the wisdom of the general practice. In addition, the issues in this case arise out of an interaction between the new CPR and the new conditional fee system for funding personal injury litigation. Both are in a relatively early stage of development. So I would be very reluctant to differ from a Court of Appeal which included Lord Woolf CJ, the architect of the new system, Lord Phillips of Worth Matravers MR, the Head of Civil Justice and Brooke LJ, one of the foremost experts on civil procedure. I am not satisfied that their decisions were wrong and therefore would dismiss the appeals.

[18] That said, I am bound to add that I feel considerable unease about the present state of the law. In this respect I do not think that I am alone. There seems to be widespread recognition among those involved in personal injury litigation that costs, particularly in relation to small claims, are getting out of hand. They are excessive in relation to the amounts at stake (contrary to the principle of proportionality), some elements (such as after-the-event insurance premiums) lack transparency and, perhaps in consequence, too much time, money and court resources are spent in disputes over costs. The view of the Court of Appeal, at any rate as expressed in the judgments under appeal, is that things will settle down when costs judges acquire greater experience of applying the new rules to the new system of litigation funding. But I must express some doubt as to whether the questions which arise in these appeals are capable of solution by the traditional method of adjudication by costs judges, subject to guidance from the Court of Appeal. It may be that they are not justiciable and require a legislative solution.

[19] *Callery v Gray* was a typical straightforward personal injury claim. On 2 April 2000 Mr Callery was a passenger in a car driven by Mr Wilson, which was involved in a collision in Ormskirk with a car driven by Mr Gray, insured by CGU Insurance Co (CGU). He instructed Amelans, solicitors who specialise entirely in personal injury litigation and process such claims on an industrial scale. On 28 April 2000 he signed a conditional fee agreement (CFA) which provided for a success fee of 60%. On 4 May 2000 he took out an after-the-event (ATE) insurance policy with Temple Legal Protection Ltd (Temple) for a premium of £367·50 inclusive of Insurance Premium Tax. On the same day Amelans wrote a standard letter of claim to Mr Gray, which he passed on to his insurers. On 19 May 2000 CGU wrote back admitting liability. A medical report was obtained and on 12 July 2000 Amelans made a CPR Pt 36 offer to accept £3,010 and costs. On 24 July 2000 CGU made a counter-offer of £1,200. On instructions from Mr Callery, Amelans telephoned CGU and agreed to accept £1,500 and reasonable costs. This was confirmed on 7 August 2000.

[20] There followed a dispute over costs. Amelans submitted a bill for £4,709·35. In proceedings commenced by Amelans under CPR 44.12A, District Judge

Wallace summarily assessed their costs at £1,941 (including VAT) and ordered them to pay £285 as costs of the assessment. The assessment included a 40% success fee and allowed the Temple insurance premium as a disbursement. CGU obtained permission to appeal on the question of whether it was reasonable to incur the cost of ATE insurance before sending the letter before action. At the hearing before Judge Edwards QC it also argued that a 40% success fee was far too high. The judge dismissed the appeal on both points. The Court of Appeal upheld the judge on the insurance point but reduced the success fee to 20%.

[21] There are two points in relation to the success fee. The first is whether it was reasonable to fix it without waiting to find out whether the claim would be admitted. The second is whether in any event a 20% fee was too high for a claim which was as certain of success as anything in litigation can be (the Court of Appeal described as a 'very, very low risk case' (see [2001] EWCA Civ 1117 at [131], [2001] 3 All ER 833 at [131], [2001] 1 WLR 2112)).

[22] Three arguments were given for fixing the success fee at once. The first was that it was a necessary part of a CFA and that it was natural for client and solicitors to want to agree at the first opportunity upon the terms of engagement. The client wants to be sure from the beginning that whatever happened he will not have to pay any costs and the solicitor wants to be sure that any work he did will be covered by the agreement and recoverable (in the event of success) from the defendant. The Court of Appeal recorded (at [90]) the claimants' argument:

'... the claimant will be concerned [when he first instructs a solicitor] that, by giving instructions ... he is not exposing himself to liability for costs. The solicitor for his part will be anxious to offer the claimant services on terms that, whatever the outcome, he will not find himself liable for costs.'

[23] I am sure that giving such an assurance is an important selling point (it is stressed on the Amelans website) and perhaps under the present rules an immediate CFA is the only practical way of achieving it. In a large-scale study undertaken in 1998 on behalf of the Legal Aid Board Research Unit (*Personal Injury Litigation in Practice*) Mr Pascoe Pleasence noted (at p 19) that 'it was common for clients to have their initial advice in a free consultation with a solicitor. Often firms used free first consultations as a marketing tool'. It may therefore be that if a solicitor had to wait until he received an answer to his letter before action before fixing the success fee, he would be willing for marketing purposes to take the risk of not being able to recover from anyone the relatively trivial costs already incurred. On the other hand, it may need a change to the indemnity principle to provide him with the additional incentive of being able to recover those costs from the defendant if the claim succeeds. These are empirical questions on which it is difficult for judges to form a view.

[24] The second argument was that by agreeing to a success fee at the first meeting, the client, so to speak, insures himself against having to pay a higher one later if his case turns out to be more difficult than at first appeared. (This is very similar to the argument for an early ATE insurance, which I shall come to later.) At first sight, therefore, one could say that agreeing an immediate success fee is no more than economically rational behaviour on the part of any client and that the fee should therefore be recoverable as an expense reasonably incurred.

[25] The difficulty is that while, in principle, it may be rational to agree a success fee at the earliest moment, it is extremely difficult to say whether the actual 'premium' paid by the client was reasonable or not. This is because the client does not pay the 'premium', whether the success fee is agreed at an earlier or later

stage. The transaction therefore lacks the features of a normal insurance, in which the transaction takes place against the background of an insurance market in which the economically rational client or his broker will choose the cheapest insurance suited to his needs. Since the client will in no event be paying the success fee out of his pocket or his damages, he is not concerned with economic rationality. He has no interest in what the fee is. The only persons who have such an interest are the solicitor on the one hand and the liability insurer who will be called upon to pay it on the other. And their interest centres entirely upon whether the agreed success fee will or will not exceed what the costs judge is willing to allow.

[26] Amelans in fact assessed the success fee by reference to a 'matrix' under which points were allocated between 0 (no success fee) and 20 (100%). The effect of the matrix was that virtually no personal injury cases could score less than seven (35%) and Mr Callery's scored another five because there were no witnesses (two) Amelans were funding the case (two) and it was expected to take over six months to settle (one). No doubt some kind of point system like this is essential in a firm in which large numbers of claims are processed. But it can hardly be regarded as a rational calculation and I do not think that the judge took much notice. What in fact determines the success fee solicitors charge is what costs judges have been willing to allow in more or less comparable cases, the fee being set at the level regarded as optimistic but hopefully not so optimistic as to provoke the liability insurers into contesting the amount. I shall in due course come back to the question of whether this is a sensible system.

[27] The third argument is that assessing risk at the earliest stage is logical because the success fee should be related, not to the prospects of success in a particular case, on which it might be reasonable first to find out more before making the assessment, but on the prospective success rate over the whole range of cases which the solicitor undertakes. The argument for CGU on the other hand, was that the success fee should reflect the risk in the particular case. If it was thought to be 90%, the success fee should be 11%. If it was evenly balanced, it should be 100%. If the prospects were less than even, an economically rational solicitor, faced with a statutory maximum success fee of 100%, should not undertake the case at all.

[28] The respondents on the other hand said that lawyers needed to be compensated for undertaking risks at all. If they undertook two cases with even prospects of success, they might statistically be expected to win one and lose one. But there was a 25% chance they might lose both and they were entitled to compensate for this by charging a higher success fee on cases almost certain to win. If they could not do so, they would have to decline cases which appeared less than sure fire winners and this would reduce access to justice.

[29] The Court of Appeal accepted this argument, which it described as a 'global' approach to fixing success fees. It said ([2001] 3 All ER 833 at [93]):

> 'Including success fees in recoverable costs has the general effect of shifting from the legal aid fund to defendants, or their insurers, the costs incurred by litigants whose claims fail. In the first instance the claimants' solicitors shoulder the risks in relation to these costs, in exchange for uplift. But the fact that the uplift in successful cases is transferred to the unsuccessful defendants results, if one takes a global view, in the burden of unsuccessful claimants' costs being [borne] by unsuccessful defendants.'

[30] It was therefore, said the Court of Appeal ([2001] 3 All ER 833 at [95]), an 'inevitable consequence of government policy that unsuccessful defendants should be subjected to an additional costs burden'. As between the individual parties, it might appear unjust to saddle defendants with the cost of (high) success fees without giving them a fair chance to identify cases in which success is assured, but the alternative would be to impose liability for the same overall costs in the form of higher success fees payable by defendants who (perhaps reasonably) contested liability and lost. Turning to the question of what success fee could be regarded as reasonable in a simple road accident claim, the court said in its view 20% was the maximum which a costs judge should allow in a 'modest and straightforward claim' which had no special features to suggest that the claim might not be sound ([2001] 3 All ER 833 at [102]–[104]). It acknowledged that this view was based on very limited data and might have to be revised in the light of experience.

[31] My Lords, the Court of Appeal gave this question the most anxious consideration and, as I have said, it has unrivalled knowledge of the problem. But I rather doubt whether, at any rate in their judicial capacities, they had the material on which to make a decision. The liability insurers who supported these appeals accept that the policy of the Access to Justice Act 1999 was to transfer the burden of funding unsuccessful motor accident claims from public funds to the motor liability insurers and thence to the motoring public by way of increased premiums. That is a perfectly rational social and economic policy and is not contested. The real questions are, first, whether the level of success fees chargeable by lawyers gives the motoring public reasonable value for the money it has to spend on funding litigation and, secondly, whether assessment by costs judges (with guidance from the Court of Appeal) is the best way to ensure that such value for money is obtained.

[32] The reasoning of the Court of Appeal at [93] of its judgment, which I have quoted above, assumes that the present cost of motor accident litigation is a fixed sum which must be paid by liability insurers one way or the other. But that is the very question in issue. And the reason why it is disputed is that, in the circumstances in which such litigation is funded, market forces are insufficient to keep costs within reasonable limits. As I have already said, solicitors offering motor accident personal injury CFAs have no incentive to compete on the success fees they charge. So the next question is whether a decision of a costs judge, or the Court of Appeal on appeal from a costs judge, is the best way of compensating for the absence of price competition in the market. The traditional function of the costs judge, or taxing master, as he used to be called, was to decide what fees were reasonable by reference to his experience of the general level of fees being charged for comparable work. But this approach only makes sense if the general level of fees is itself directly or indirectly determined by market forces. Otherwise the exercise becomes circular and costs judges will be deciding what is reasonable according to general levels which costs judges themselves have determined. In such circumstances there is no restraint upon a ratchet effect whereby the highest success fees obtainable from a costs judge are relied upon in subsequent assessments.

[33] The matter becomes even more difficult when a solicitor 'carrying on litigation business on a large scale' is entitled, as the Court of Appeal have said ([2001] 3 All ER 833 at [83]) to fix success fees to ensure 'that the uplifts agreed result in a reasonable return overall, having regard to his experience of the work done and the likelihood of success or failure of the particular class of litigation'.

a The costs judge has simply no way of knowing whether the solicitor is carrying on business on a large enough scale to justify such an approach, still less what level of success fees would give him a 'reasonable return overall'. Such matters are traditionally outside the consideration of costs judges. As your Lordships' Appellate Committee said in *Special Report from the Appeal Committee: the Clerk of the Parliaments' Reference Regarding Criminal Legal Aid Taxation* (HL Paper 145

b (1997–98)) at para 30:

> 'As to fixing fees by reference to a reasonable annual income, quite apart from the difficulties of making the necessary adjustments, to ask what is a reasonable annual income merely forces the question one stage back: what is a reasonable income for a barrister? £20,000 per annum, £100,000 per
> *c* annum, £500,000 per annum? As to using remuneration paid out of public funds to, for example, doctors, Mr Lawrence Collins QC for The Law Society submitted that target incomes for barristers could be set in much the same way as they are for medical and dental practitioners. But in our view it is not the function of a taxing officer to fix target incomes for barristers by reference to the earnings of other professions. He is concerned to allow the
> *d* barrister a fee which is reasonable in relation to fees which are generally allowed to barristers for comparable work and the earnings of other professions are irrelevant to this calculation. They would be proper to be taken into account (although the practical difficulties of doing so are considerable) by someone charged with fixing levels of fees for the
> *e* profession as a whole, such as the Lord Chancellor when he determines levels of graduated fees. But a taxing officer, in deciding what is a reasonable fee in a particular case, must take the general levels of fees as given and use them as the basis of his taxation.'

[**34**] I rather doubt whether difficulty is likely to be removed merely by the
f passage of time. All that costs judges will learn is what other costs judges are allowing. Solicitors will charge whatever is currently allowed and exert upward pressure to be able to charge more. But that will not tell anyone whether the fees paid to the solicitors represent reasonable value for money.

[**35**] As my noble and learned friend Lord Scott of Foscote has observed, the criteria prescribed by the CPR for determining whether costs are reasonable are
g framed entirely by reference to the facts of the particular case. Once one invokes a global approach designed to produce a reasonable overall return for solicitors, one moves away from the judicial function of the costs judge and into the territory of legislative or administrative decision.

[**36**] It seems to me likely (although reliable statistical evidence is not presently
h available) that the costs which can reasonably be expended in a small personal injury claim conducted in accordance with the protocol and which settles within the protocol period are unlikely in the great majority of cases to vary much from the statistical mean. The present case—letter before action, acknowledgment of liability, medical report and a relatively brief negotiation—must be fairly typical.
j It involves standardised legal services at a fairly low level. This would suggest that these costs—both the basic costs and the success fee—should be fixed by the rules which apply in all but exceptional circumstances. I understand that such a system is under consideration by the Civil Justice Council. A legislative decision to fix costs at levels calculated to provide adequate access to justice in the most economical way seems to me a more rational approach than to leave the matter to individual costs judges. If it is considered the most appropriate way to secure

value for money when the expenditure is borne by the public as a whole (as for example, in the fixing of graduated fees for criminal legal aid) it should be no less appropriate when the expenditure is borne by a section of the public, namely the motorists. Not only would this be more likely to keep the actual costs within reasonable levels but it would also greatly reduce the cost of disputes over costs. We were told that no less than 150,000 cases awaited the outcome of your Lordships' decision in this case.

[37] In their submissions to the Court of Appeal, the liability insurers said that what they wanted most was certainty. If the consequence of your Lordships' decision was that motor insurance premiums had to be raised, so be it. But they wanted to be able to make the calculations with reasonable certainty about what the motoring public would have to pay. This would not be the case if everything turned upon a case-by-case assessment by the costs judge.

[38] My Lords, the arguments for legislative determination of allowable costs apply even more strongly to the other two questions in these appeals, namely whether it was reasonable to take out ATE insurance before it was known whether the claim would be resisted and whether £375 was a reasonable premium in the circumstances.

[39] The arguments put forward to justify taking out an ATE insurance policy before sending the letter before action are much the same as those for fixing the success fee at the same time. The client is immediately assured that in no circumstances will he be liable for the defendant's costs. He may pay a higher premium than would be individually justifiable if it was known that the claim was admitted, but he insures himself against the possibility that a later premium might be much higher or even unobtainable. And ATE insurers say that they cannot obtain a reasonable premium income unless everyone takes out insurance when they first instruct solicitors. This was the principle upon which insurers such as Temple, in this case, delegated to solicitors the authority to issue policies.

[40] Again, as it seems to me, the Court of Appeal accepted these arguments. They said ([2001] 3 All ER 833 at [67]): 'It is hardly surprising that delegated authority arrangements will only work successfully if the solicitor does not "cherry-pick" by taking out ATE insurance only in risky cases'.

[41] Perhaps that is true. I am certainly not in a position to say that it was wrong. But neither, in my respectful opinion, was the Court of Appeal. Of course it is true that, other things being equal, premiums will rise if fewer people take out ATE insurance. And it is true that when ATE insurance made its first appearance, at a time when it could not be recovered from the defendant and claimants would take out policies only if they were seriously concerned about losing the case, underwriters burnt their fingers. But premiums were then also very low compared to current rates. Now, premiums are much higher *and* ATE insurers insist upon all claimants taking out policies. Whether the latter is necessary to keep ATE insurers in business at current premium rates is an open question.

[42] Furthermore, it is a question which costs judges are quite unable to answer. When the Court of Appeal asked for the report of Master O'Hare on the question of whether the Temple premium in this case was reasonable, he said ([2001] EWCA Civ 1246, [2001] 4 All ER 1 at 23, [2001] 1 WLR 2142 at 2163 (para 20)): '... I am not convinced these market forces impinge upon the premium levied to the ultimate consumer and claimed by him from his unsuccessful opponent.'

[43] That seems to me obviously right. ATE insurers do not compete for claimants, still less do they compete on premiums charged. They compete for solicitors who will sell or recommend their product. And they compete by offering solicitors the most profitable arrangements to enable them to attract profitable work. There is only one restraining force on the premium charged and that is how much the costs judge will allow on an assessment against the liability insurer.

[44] Again, the costs judge has absolutely no criteria to enable him to decide whether any given premium is reasonable. On the contrary, the likelihood is that whatever costs judges are prepared to allow will constitute the benchmark around which ATE insurers will tacitly collude in fixing their premiums. In its submissions to Master O'Hare, Temple said that the court 'should not arrogate to itself the functions of a financial regulator of the insurance industry' (see [2001] 4 All ER 1 at 23, [2001] 1 WLR 2142 at 2164 (para 22)). I am sure that is right, because the costs judge is wholly unequipped to perform that function. But that does not mean that some form of financial regulation is not necessary. Such regulation is normally considered necessary in those parts of the economy in which market forces are insufficient to produce an efficient use of resources. And that seems to me to be the position in ATE insurance, in which the premiums are not paid either by the claimants who take out the insurance or by the solicitors who advise or require them to do so.

[45] My Lords, these are my reservations about the exercise which your Lordships are asked to undertake. But, given that your Lordships have to say whether, on the materials before you, the Court of Appeal were right or wrong, I would dismiss the appeals.

LORD HOPE OF CRAIGHEAD.

[46] My Lords, this appeal raises important questions about the operation of a new costs regime to assist members of the public who wish to claim damages for personal injury. The facts have been fully described by my noble and learned friend Lord Scott of Foscote, and I gratefully adopt his account of them.

[47] The previous scheme was based on the provision of legal aid out of public funds. But it had become clear that it was no longer possible for the government to fund legal aid in civil cases in England and Wales across the board at the required level. So the government decided to withdraw legal aid from certain categories of proceedings including actions of damages for personal injury, and to replace it with a new system based on conditional fee and litigation funding agreements. The legislation which was required to give effect to this was enacted as Pt II of the Access to Justice Act 1999. An essential part of the new arrangement was the government's decision that claimants should not be at risk of being left out of pocket by reason of the additional liabilities which they would have to incur under this scheme. These included the cost of taking out an insurance policy against the risk of incurring a liability to the other party in the proceedings for costs.

[48] The new scheme was the subject of a consultation paper entitled *Conditional Fees: Sharing the Risks of Litigation* which was issued by the Lord Chancellor's Department in September 1999. It was based upon two recent developments in the private funding of litigation. The first was the introduction of conditional fee agreements (CFAs) under s 58 of the Courts and Legal Services Act 1990. Initially there had been concerns that these agreements would be abused and that this part of the new system would be unworkable. But experience

of its operation showed that this was not so. In *Thai Trading Co (a firm) v Taylor*
[1998] 3 All ER 65 at 73, [1998] QB 781 at 790 Millett LJ said that fears that lawyers
might be tempted by such an arrangement to act improperly were exaggerated,
and that there was a countervailing public policy in making justice readily
accessible to persons of modest means. The second was the concept of
after-the-event insurance (ATE). This was a new kind of insurance policy which
had been developed by the Law Society in conjunction with insurance brokers as
a means of protecting claimants against their liability for the other side's costs.

[49] These developments had gone a long way towards removing the barrier
to justice for prospective litigants. But they still left one problem untouched. In
its response to consultation, the government said that it recognised that a major
barrier to justice had always been the risk that litigants would have to pay the
other side's costs as well as their own if they lost the case. The policy which it
decided to pursue was to ensure that the expense of shifting the claimant's
liability in costs, whether to the solicitor under a CFA or to the insurer for the
premium payable under the ATE insurance policy, was met by the losing party
where damages were claimed for personal injury. As the consultation paper
pointed out, the purpose of the legislation was to provide the framework within
which the new system was to operate. The detail was to be informed by rules of
court and by practice directions. There was to be a division of responsibility
between the courts and the legislature.

[50] Mr Gray seeks to challenge the operation of two powers which have been
given by the legislature under the new scheme to the courts. The first is the
power to include in an award of costs in favour of the claimant an order for
payment by the losing party of the amount of the success fee payable by the
claimant under a CFA entered into with his legal representative. Section 58A(7)
of the 1990 Act, inserted by s 27(1) of the 1999 Act, provides:

'Rules of court may make provision with respect to the assessment of any
costs which include fees payable under a conditional fee agreement (including
one which provides for a success fee).'

The second is the power of the court to include in a costs order the amount of the
insurance premium for a claimant's ATE insurance policy against the risk of
incurring a liability to pay the other parties' costs in the event of his having to
raise proceedings to recover damages. Section 29 of the 1999 Act provides:

'Where in any proceedings a costs order is made in favour of any party who
has taken out an insurance policy against the risk of incurring a liability in
those proceedings, the costs payable to him may, subject in the case of court
proceedings to rules of court, include costs in respect of the premium of the
policy.'

[51] Three broad questions are raised by these new powers. The first is
whether it is right in principle that a claimant's liability for his legal
representative's success fee and the cost of his insurance premium should be
recoverable from the losing party. The second is whether it should ordinarily be
considered to be reasonable for the purposes of any costs order for the claimant
to enter into the CFA, and to take out the ATE policy at the same time, on the
occasion when he first consults his legal representative. The third is whether the
cost of insuring against a cost liability that cannot be passed on to the opposing
party should be included in the recoverable amount of the insurance premium.
In addition Mr Gray has challenged the decision of the Court of Appeal not to

a interfere with the judge's conclusion that a success fee of 20% was appropriate in this case.

[52] Answers to these questions were provided by the Court of Appeal in the two judgments which are before your Lordships in this appeal. In *Callery v Gray, Russell v Pal Pak Corrugated Ltd* [2001] EWCA Civ 1117 at [100], [2001] 3 All ER 833 at [100], [2001] 1 WLR 2112 (Lord Woolf CJ, Lord Phillips of Worth Matravers MR b and Brooke LJ) the court held that, where a reasonable uplift is agreed at the outset as part of a CFA and an ATE insurance is taken out at that stage at a reasonable premium, the costs of both the uplift and the premium are recoverable from the defendant in the event that the claim succeeds or is settled on terms that the defendant pay the claimant's costs. The court said (at [99]) that it had reached this conclusion after taking account of the legislative policy and c various practical considerations which were established by the evidence. Its conclusion on the issue as to the reasonableness of the uplift by way of a success fee was that, where a CFA is agreed at the outset in straightforward cases such as this one, 20% is the maximum uplift that can reasonably be agreed.

[53] The Court of Appeal dealt in a separate judgment with the reasonableness d of the ATE insurance premium ([2001] EWCA Civ 1246, [2001] 4 All ER 1, [2001] 1 WLR 2142 (Lord Phillips of Worth Matravers MR and Brooke LJ)). It held (at [59], [60]) that the jurisdiction which has been given to the courts by s 29 of the 1999 Act to order the defendant to pay the cost of the insurance premium extends to the cost of insurance against the risk of incurring a costs liability that cannot be passed on to the opposing party. The court said that it believed that this e interpretation of s 29 gave the words the meaning that would be attributed to them by the reasonable litigant, and that it also gave them a meaning that accorded with the legislative intention and with the overall scheme for the funding of legal costs.

[54] I accept that the new regime is not beyond criticism. It is plain that it has f transferred the burden of meeting the cost of access to justice in these cases from the taxpayer through the medium of the legal aid fund. Instead a different kind of taxation is involved. The burden of meeting the cost of access to justice now falls on liability insurers. It thus falls indirectly on their policy holders, who are likely to have to face increased premiums. Furthermore, unless the new regime is controlled very carefully, its effect may be to benefit ATE insurance providers g unreasonably and to place a burden on liability insurers which is disproportionate. It may lead to a culture of incurring additional costs which lacks any incentive on claimants to keep costs down. The circumstances of the present case add force to these criticisms. It must have been obvious from the outset that this was a claim which was almost certain to succeed on liability and that there was almost h nothing to discuss on the quantum of damages. Mr Callery's exposure to risk was, at the worst, minimal. And, as my noble and learned friend Lord Scott has pointed out, the premium which Temple Legal Protection Ltd (Temple) charged for the insurance cover was not based on an individual assessment of the risk but was a uniform premium. The costs incurred in this case by way of the success fee j and the ATE premium do indeed appear at first sight to be wholly out of line with what the case required.

[55] But it would be hard to imagine judges who were better qualified to examine these issues than the Lord Chief Justice, the Master of Rolls—who has particular responsibilities in this field as the Head of Civil Justice in England and Wales—and Brooke LJ. They are in close and regular contact with all relevant aspects of civil practice. They heard representations from a number of bodies

who have a direct interest in these issues. They also had the advantage in this case
of having a report on the reasonableness of the premiums charged for ATE
insurance from Master O'Hare. He has an unrivalled expertise in the matter of
costs. The Court of Appeal could not have been better informed. I think that
their judgment is entitled to the greatest respect in a matter of this kind. I would
be very slow to differ from the conclusions which they have reached.

[56] In *Girvan v Inverness Farmers Dairy (No 2)* 1998 SC (HL) 1 at 21 I said that
the Court of Session is far better placed than this House can ever be to assess what
changes could appropriately be made in procedure and practice relating to the
conduct of civil jury trials in that court. I drew attention to the process of
consultation that is available to it through its Statutory Rules Council, to its
ability to keep its rules under regular review and to the advantages which it can
bring to bear of speed and flexibility. I suggested that the proper approach for this
House to take was to leave it to the Court of Session to decide what changes, if
any, should be made to its own rules. This case is concerned with the role of the
court in administering the new regime in a way that seeks to do justice between
the parties within the limits that have been set by the legislative policy. For
similar reasons to those which I gave in *Girvan's* case I consider that the
responsibility for dealing with these issues lies pre-eminently with the Court of
Appeal and not with this House.

[57] Two other factors seem to me to favour the decisions which the Court of
Appeal reached in this case. The first is the fact that it was common ground that
not enough is yet known about the likely effect on CFAs of different levels of
success fees (see [2001] 3 All ER 833 at [64]). Mr Gray did not suggest to your
Lordships that the position was otherwise. The second is the state of the evidence
about the effect on the market for ATE insurance if your Lordships were to
uphold Mr Gray's argument that the taking out of these policies should be
delayed until proceedings have been issued. The Court of Appeal held ([2001]
4 All ER 1 at [99](ix)) that there was overwhelming evidence from those engaged
in the provision of ATE insurance that unless the policy is taken out before it is
known whether a defendant is going to contest liability, the premium is going to
rise substantially and cover may indeed not be available at all in such
circumstances.

[58] Ample support for the finding about the effect on ATE insurance is to be
found in witness statements provided by Christopher Ward and Christopher
Wait. Mr Ward is the managing director of Abbey Legal Protection Ltd, a
specialist legal expenses underwriting agency providing both before-the-event
and after-the-event legal expenses insurance. Mr Wait is an underwriting director
of Temple, which specialises in the same field. Mr Temple QC for Mr Gray said
that these statements were self-serving and that little weight should be attached
to them. But there was no contrary evidence.

[59] I note also that in para 27 of his report to the Court of Appeal ([2001] 4 All ER
1 at 24, [2001] 1 WLR 2142 at 2165) Master O'Hare acknowledged the risks to
which ATE providers would be exposed if increasing premiums and the need to
make inquiries were to encourage more claimants to dispense with insurance
altogether. In preparing his report he considered written and oral submissions
from many parties (see [2001] 4 All ER 1 at 18, [2001] 1 WLR 2142 at 2165
(para 2)). He also drew attention to the advantages which flow from the insurers'
practice of giving delegated authority to solicitors to offer ATE cover to their
clients (see [2001] 4 All ER 1 at 21–22, [2001] 1 WLR 2142 at 2162–2163 (para 16)).
As he explained, it is characteristic of these policies that they do not differentiate

a between cases which are strong and those which are borderline. This all-in approach reduces the administrative cost of risk assessment, and there is the further point that risk assessment at the outset of proceedings may well be imprecise or unreliable. His findings support the Court of Appeal's observation in *Callery v Gray* [2001] 3 All ER 833 at [67] that it was hardly surprising that delegated authority arrangements would only work successfully if the solicitor

b did not 'cherry-pick' by taking out ATE insurance only in risky cases. It is plain that a finding that the cost of taking out ATE insurance at the outset was in principle irrecoverable from the losing party would have a profound effect on the cost and availability of this form of insurance cover.

[60] These and the other practical considerations relied on by the Court of Appeal seem to me to point clearly in favour of allowing the ATE insurance

c policy to be taken out at the outset when the claimant first consults his legal representative. The extent to which the cost of doing so will be recoverable from the losing party will require to be watched very carefully. But a sufficient safeguard lies in the fact that it will continue to be subject to the supervision of the court on the basis described in *Callery v Gray (No 2)* [2001] 4 All ER 1 at [61]:

d 'The circumstances in which and the terms on which own costs insurance will be reasonable, so that the whole premium can be recovered as costs, will have to be determined by the courts, when dealing with individual cases, assisted, if appropriate, by the Rules Committee.'

e [61] I think that it is also worth recording that Mr Gray's counsel did not challenge the conclusions of the Court of Appeal in *Callery v Gray (No 2)* [2001] 4 All ER 1 at [60] as to how s 29 of the 1999 Act ought to be interpreted. This was an issue of law which would have been open for further consideration by your Lordships if it had been suggested that the section was not capable of bearing the meaning which the Court of Appeal said could and should be given to it. But

f Mr Birts QC accepted that it had reached a sound conclusion on this point, and for my part I think that he was right to do so. The remaining issues seem to me to be essentially issues of practice. They are best dealt with by penalising unreasonable behaviour on a case-by-case basis as the circumstances require.

[62] For these reasons, and for those given by my noble and learned friend

g Lord Bingham of Cornhill whose speech I have had the advantage of reading in draft and with which I am in entire agreement, I would dismiss the appeal.

LORD SCOTT OF FOSCOTE.

INTRODUCTION

h [63] My Lords, the civil courts of this country have power to order a party to litigation to pay to the other party his (the latter's) costs of the litigation. This power presumably owes its origin to the inherent power of the court to regulate the proceedings before it, but in modern times the power has been a statutory one, embodied in rules of court made under rule-making powers conferred by

j statute. The power to make costs orders has always been, and remains, a discretionary one. But the discretion is circumscribed by guidance laid down under rules of court and by principles established by judicial precedent.

[64] At the risk of some oversimplification, the issues that may arise in relation to costs orders fall into three groups. First, there are issues as to which, if any, of the litigants should have a costs order made in his favour and against whom the order should be made. Secondly, there may be issues as to the extent of the

receiving party's costs that the paying party should be ordered to pay. And, thirdly, there may be issues of quantification. The sum that, under the order, the paying party must pay to the receiving party will have to be quantified. A process of assessment must be carried out.

[65] For example, a successful claimant in a road traffic accident case would expect to have an order for costs made in his favour against the negligent defendant. But if the engagement by the claimant of a particular expert witness appeared to have been unnecessary, the court might exclude the fee paid to the expert witness from the costs payable under the order. And if the engagement of the expert witness appeared reasonable but the fee paid to the expert appeared to be excessive, the court might reduce to a reasonable amount the sum in respect of the fee payable under the costs order. These basic principles are very well known and understood and hardly need repeating, but, in my opinion, need to be kept in mind in considering some of the issues before the House on this appeal.

[66] The appeal relates to costs issues arising out of a very simple and commonplace type of claim. The difficulties that have led to this appeal are attributable to recent changes in the costs regime, which reflect changes in the means by which the bringing of actions can be funded. In order to deal with these issues it is necessary to set out the facts which have given rise to them and the statutory provisions that bear upon them.

THE ACCIDENT

[67] On 2 April 2000 Mr Callery, respondent before your Lordships, was a passenger in a car which was struck side-on by a vehicle driven by the appellant, Mr Gray. Mr Callery sustained minor injuries. He instructed solicitors, Amelans, to pursue a claim for damages against Mr Gray. Amelans are a firm who deal with a large number of road traffic accident claims. They are specialists in this field. I have described Mr Callery's claim as commonplace. It was. There are thousands of such claims every year. They rarely reach the courts.

THE FUNDING ARRANGEMENTS

[68] Under the Access to Justice Act 1999, legal aid to support road traffic accident claims such as Mr Callery's was no longer available. Instead the use of conditional fee agreements (CFAs) was authorised. A feature of a CFA is that, if the claim fails, the lawyer, whether solicitor or barrister, who has given his services under the CFA, receives no remuneration but, if the claim succeeds, the lawyer becomes entitled not only to the normal fee for his services but also to a success fee, calculated as a percentage of the normal fee. (see the Conditional Fee Agreements Order 1998, SI 1998/1860). The percentage uplift is required by the 1998 order to be specified in the CFA and must not exceed 100% of the normal fee.

[69] The logic of the success fee is that its size will reflect the risk the lawyer is incurring in taking on the case. The more difficult the case and the less clear that the outcome will be a successful one, the higher the percentage uplift that can be justified; and, of course, vice versa. A CFA protects the claimant who enters into it from having to remunerate his lawyers if the claim fails. A typical CFA does not, however, protect the claimant from having to reimburse his lawyers for their disbursements in pursuing the claim. These disbursements might, for example, include the fees of experts whose opinion on some issue or other had been sought. If the claim succeeds the claimant will have the expectation that the

a burden of paying for his solicitor's reasonable disbursements will fall on the defendant. If the claim fails, he will have to meet the disbursements himself.

[70] Nor does a CFA protect the claimant from the risk that if litigation is commenced he may find himself ordered to pay the costs, or some part of the costs, of the defendant. But it is important to notice that this risk cannot arise unless litigation is commenced.

b [71] In order to protect himself against the risk that he may find himself liable to pay the costs, or some of the costs, of the defendant, a claimant can take out after-the-event (ATE) insurance.

[72] In the present case Mr Callery entered into a CFA with Amelans at the same time as instructing them to pursue his damages claim. The CFA was dated 28 April 2000. It said that if Mr Callery succeeded in his claim for damages he c would pay Amelans' basic charges and a success fee. It said that, win or lose, Mr Callery would have to pay their disbursements. It set the success fee at 60% of Amelans' basic charges but provided also that in the event of an assessment of costs by the court—

d   'and the court disallows any amount of the success fee percentage on the ground that it is unreasonable in view of what we [the solicitors] knew or should have known at the time, that amount ceases to be payable under this agreement unless the court is satisfied that it should continue to be payable.'

[73] The effect of a provision in these terms would be, in practice, and save in e exceptional circumstances, to relieve the claimant of his contractual liability to pay any excess of the success fee above the amount that, on the assessment of costs, the court had decided the defendant should pay.

[74] On 4 May 2000 Mr Callery took out an ATE insurance policy with Temple Legal Protection Ltd (Temple). This was the date on which Amelans' first letter to Mr Gray, informing him of the claim, was sent. The policy was f taken out before Mr Callery or his legal advisors, Amelans, could have come to the conclusion that litigation to pursue the claim would be necessary or even likely. The premium for the policy was £350 plus £17·50 tax, a total of £367·50. Under the policy Temple agreed to indemnify Mr Callery, up to a limit of £100,000, (i) for any sum in respect of Mr Gray's costs that might be ordered by g the court to be paid by Mr Callery; and (ii) for disbursements paid out by Amelans in the event that the litigation came to an end without the disbursements becoming payable by Mr Gray. In this description of the insurance cover provided under the policy I have attempted to describe the broad scope of the cover rather than set out its exact details. The exact details are not relevant to any issue before the House.

h [75] A noteworthy feature of the policy is that the premium of £350 would not become payable until the conclusion of the legal proceedings in respect of which the policy had been taken out and, if the amount of the premium were challenged by Mr Gray in any cost assessment process, the recoverable amount of the premium would be reduced to the amount payable by Mr Gray under the j assessment.

THE PROGRESS OF MR CALLERY'S CLAIM

[76] On 4 May 2000 (the day on which the ATE policy was taken out) Amelans wrote to Mr Gray giving notice of their client's damages claim and enclosing a copy of the letter for his insurers. The letter asked for an acknowledgment within 21 days from Mr Gray or his insurers.

[77] On 19 May 2000, Mr Gray's insurers, CGU Insurance Co (CGU), replied. *a* Their reply said that they were able 'to admit liability as to negligence but not to causation'. Following an exchange of offer and counter-offer, the parties reached agreement on 2 August 2000 that Mr Callery should receive damages of £1500. Amelans wrote on 7 August 2000 to CGU confirming 'acceptance of your offer in the sum of £1,500 in respect of our client's damages' and that 'acceptance of the offer is subject to payment of our client's reasonable costs and disbursements'. *b* However, the parties were unable to agree the amount of the 'reasonable costs and disbursements'. There were two main issues.

[78] First, CGU took the view that a 60% success fee for Amelans was unreasonably high. It was always certain, they thought, that Mr Callery would succeed in recovering damages. He had been a passenger in a vehicle struck side-on by Mr Gray's vehicle. He had been injured in the accident. He was *c* bound to recover something. So this was not a case in which there was any risk that Amelans, in pursuing the claim on Mr Callery's behalf, would be working for nothing. It followed that any success fee should be very low.

[79] Second, CGU contended that the £350 premium was an item of expenditure that had not been reasonably incurred. The likelihood of litigation *d* being necessary was always very remote. At the least Mr Callery should have waited until a response to Amelans' letter of 4 May 2000 had been received before taking out a policy to protect himself against the costs consequences of litigation that was unlikely ever to materialise.

[80] In these circumstances, there being agreement as to the amount of the *e* damages and agreement that Mr Callery would be paid his reasonable costs and disbursements but no agreement as to the amount of a reasonable success fee or whether the £350 premium represented a reasonable disbursement, Mr Callery commenced 'costs only' proceedings (see CPR 44.12A) in order to have the reasonable costs and disbursements to which he was entitled under the settlement agreement quantified by the court. *f*

THE RELEVANT STATUTORY PROVISIONS

[81] The statutory provisions relevant to the recovery under a costs order of a CFA success fee or of the premium payable for ATE insurance cover have been comprehensively set out in the judgment of the Court of Appeal ([2001] EWCA *g* Civ 1117 at [24]–[39], [2001] 3 All ER 833 at [24]–[39], [2001] 1 WLR 2112) handed down by Lord Woolf CJ, sitting with Lord Phillips of Worth Matravers MR and Brooke LJ, on 17 July 2001. This was the first of the two Court of Appeal judgments from which the appeal to the House is brought. It is unnecessary for me to do more than refer to the critical provisions.

[82] Section 58A(6) of the Courts and Legal Services Act 1990, as substituted *h* by s 27 of the Access to Justice Act 1999 provides that:

'A costs order made in any proceedings may, subject in the case of court proceedings to rules of court, include provision requiring the payment of any fees payable under a conditional fee agreement which provides for a success *j* fee.'

Section 29 of the 1999 Act provides:

'Where in any proceedings a costs order is made in favour of any party who has taken out an insurance policy against the risk of incurring a liability in those proceedings, the costs payable to him may, subject in the case of court *a* proceedings to rules of court, include costs in respect of the premium of the policy.'

[83] There is, therefore, no doubt but that a costs order can require the paying party to pay a sum in respect of a success fee for which the receiving party has become contractually liable and to pay a sum in respect of the premium payable for an ATE insurance policy that the receiving party has taken out.

b [84] In the CPR, r 43.2 provides that '"costs" includes … any additional liability incurred under a funding arrangement' and that 'additional liability' includes the success fee under a CFA and the premium payable for an ATE insurance policy.

[85] Rule 44.4 sets out the basis upon which costs are to be assessed:

c
> '(1) Where the court is to assess the amounts of costs (whether by summary or detailed assessment) it will assess those costs—(a) on the standard basis; or (b) on the indemnity basis, but the court will not in either case allow costs which have been unreasonably incurred or are unreasonable in amount …
>
> *d* (2) Where the amount of the costs is to be assessed on the standard basis, the court will—(a) only allow costs which are proportionate to the matters in issue; and (b) resolve any doubt which it may have as to whether costs were reasonably incurred or reasonable and proportionate in amount in favour of the paying party.'

e [86] Rule 44.5 sets out the factors the court must take into account in assessing costs:

> '(1) The court is to have regard to all the circumstances in deciding whether costs were—(a) if it is assessing costs on the standard basis *f* (i) proportionately and reasonably incurred; or (ii) were proportionate and reasonable in amount …
>
> (3) The court must also have regard to—(a) the conduct of all the parties, including in particular—(i) conduct before, as well as during, the proceedings; and (ii) the efforts made, if any, before and during the proceedings in order to try to resolve the dispute; (b) the amount or value of any money or property *g* involved; (c) the importance of the matter to all the parties; (d) the particular complexity of the matter or the difficulty or novelty of the questions raised; (e) the skill, effort, specialised knowledge and responsibility involved; (f) the time spent on the case; and (g) the place where and the circumstances in which work or any part of it was done.'

h [87] These factors, as one would expect, concentrate on the circumstances and conduct of the parties in relation to the claim in question and on the nature of the particular claim. They are case-specific factors.

[88] The Costs Practice Direction that supplements the rules relating to costs contains further guidance on the assessment, for costs purposes, of an additional *j* liability. Section 11 of the Costs Practice Direction contains the following relevant provisions:

> '11.2 In any proceedings there will be costs which will inevitably be incurred and which are necessary for the successful conduct of the case. Solicitors are not required to conduct litigation at rates which are uneconomic. Thus in a modest claim the proportion of costs is likely to be

higher than in a large claim, and may even equal or possibly exceed the amount in dispute ...

11.5 In deciding whether the costs claimed are reasonable and (on a standard basis assessment) proportionate, the court will consider the amount of any additional liability separately from the base costs.

11.6 In deciding whether the base costs are reasonable and (if relevant) proportionate the court will consider the factors set out in rule 44.5.

11.7 Subject to paragraph 17.8(2), when the court is considering the factors to be taken into account in assessing an additional liability, it will have regard to the facts and circumstances as they reasonably appeared to the solicitor or counsel when the funding arrangement was entered into and at the time of any variation of the arrangement.

11.8(1) In deciding whether a percentage increase is reasonable relevant factors to be taken into account may include: (a) the risk that the circumstances in which the costs, fees or expenses would be payable might or might not occur; (b) the legal representative's liability for any disbursements; (c) what other methods of financing the costs were available to the receiving party ...

11.9 A percentage increase will not be reduced simply on the ground that, when added to base costs which are reasonable and (where relevant) proportionate, the total appears disproportionate ...

11.10 In deciding whether the cost of insurance cover is reasonable, relevant factors to be taken into account include ... (2) the level and extent of the cover provided; (3) the availability of any pre-existing insurance cover; (4) whether any part of the premium would be rebated in the event of early settlement ...'

[89] Rule 44.12A and section 17 of the Costs Practice Direction relate to 'costs only' proceedings. 'Costs only' proceedings may be commenced where the parties, before the commencement of litigation, have agreed in writing on all issues in the case, including which party is to pay the costs, but have been unable to agree the amount of the costs (see r 44.12A). In effect, the court is allowing its costs quantification procedures to be used to support an out-of-court settlement under which one party is to pay the reasonable costs and disbursements of another party. It is implicit in such a settlement agreement (unless the contrary is expressly stated) that the costs to be paid should be quantified on the standard basis in accordance with the rules and practice directions that would have been applicable if there had been a court order for the payment of the costs.

[90] Paragraph 17.8(2) of the Costs Practice Direction makes clear that in assessing the reasonableness of an additional liability, whether a success fee or an ATE premium, the likelihood of litigation having to be commenced is an important factor. The paragraph provides that:

'In cases in which an additional liability is claimed, the costs judge or district judge should have regard to the time when and the extent to which the claim has been settled and to the fact that the claim has been settled without the need to commence proceedings.'

THE COURSE TAKEN BY THE 'COSTS ONLY' PROCEEDINGS

[91] On 12 September 2000 Mr Callery commenced proceedings under CPR Pt 8 asking the court to assess his reasonable costs of and occasioned by his damages claim against Mr Gray. The particulars of claim pleaded the agreement

a that had been reached that Mr Gray would pay £1,500 damages and Mr Callery's reasonable costs.

[92] On 14 September an ex parte order was made in the Macclesfield County Court ordering, inter alia, that Mr Callery's costs be assessed.

[93] The assessment hearing took place before District Judge Wallace on 7 November 2000. The district judge assessed Amelans' basic charges, reduced
b the success fee from 60% to 40% of the basic charges and allowed the ATE insurance premium of £350 plus tax as a disbursement. The assessment allowed a total of £1,008, plus VAT, for fees and £617·50 for disbursements.

[94] Mr Gray (prompted by CGU) appealed to the circuit judge. The appeal was heard by Judge Edwards in the Chester County Court on 29 January 2001. Two points were taken on the appeal, one relating to Amelans' success fee under
c the CFA, the other relating to the ATE insurance premium. They are the two points to which I have already referred. The appeal was dismissed on both points.

[95] CGU took the view that important points of principle were at stake, with implications for personal injury litigants and their insurers generally, and prompted Mr Gray to apply to the Court of Appeal for permission to bring a
d second appeal to that court. On 16 March 2001 Hale LJ granted permission on condition that Mr Gray, if successful, would not seek costs from Mr Callery unless his liability to pay were covered in full by the terms of the ATE policy.

[96] Further evidence was, with the permission of the Court of Appeal, introduced at the hearing of the appeal and written and oral intervention by the Law Society, the Association of British Insurers, the After Event Insurers Group
e Forum, the Association of Personal Injury Lawyers and the Forum of Insurance Lawyers was authorised. The hearing of the appeal was directed to be conjoined with the hearing of the appeal in *Russell v Pal Pak Corrugated Ltd* under which similar success fee issues arose.

[97] The Court of Appeal heard the appeal on 5, 6 and 7 June 2001. On 17 July
f 2001 the court handed down the judgment of the court on the success fee issue ([2001] 3 All ER 833, [2001] 1 WLR 2112), reducing Amelans' success fee from the 40% fixed by the district judge to 20% (and dismissing the appeal in *Russell*'s case). In addition the court ruled that an ATE insurance premium could in principle be recovered as part of a claimant's costs in 'costs only' proceedings. But the court formed the view that, on the evidence available, it was not possible to come to a
g conclusion as to the reasonableness in amount of the £350 premium. So the court postponed judgment on the issue relating to the amount of the ATE insurance premium pending an inquiry by a costs judge, Master O'Hare. A separate judgment on that issue would await Master O'Hare's report.

[98] It is important to be clear that the court's further reservation of judgment
h regarding the ATE insurance premium related only to the reasonableness of the amount of the premium. In principle the premium was held to be recoverable notwithstanding that the policy had been taken out before the commencement of litigation for the purpose of recovering damages had become necessary, or even likely. As it was put at [2001] 3 All ER 833 at [100]:

j   '... we have concluded that where, at the outset, a reasonable uplift is agreed and ATE insurance at a reasonable premium is taken out, the costs of each are recoverable from the defendant in the event that the claim succeeds, or is settled on terms that the defendant pay the claimant's costs.'

[99] I will return later to examine the reasons why, in relation to the ATE insurance premium, the court came to this conclusion.

[100] Master O'Hare's report ([2001] 4 All ER 1 at 18–40, [2001] 1 WLR 2142 at 2159–2179) was dated 23 July 2001. The purpose of his report was expressed to be 'to enable the Court of Appeal to give guidance in its judgment as to the practice to be adopted in future in taking out [ATE] insurance' (see [2001] 4 All ER 1 at 18, [2001] 1 WLR 2142 at 2163 (para 1)).

[101] Master O'Hare had received written submissions from a number of interested parties but none the less concluded ([2001] 4 All ER 1 at 22, [2001] 1 WLR 2142 at 2163 (para 19)) that 'for several reasons it is not possible to state standard or average premiums for different classes or categories of ATE insurance. The industry is still immature'. And 'now is not the time to publish guideline figures for ATE premiums ...' (see [2001] 4 All ER 1 at 23, [2001] 1 WLR 2142 at 2164 (para 23)).

[102] On 31 July 2001 Lord Phillips of Worth Matravers MR, sitting with Brooke LJ, handed down the judgment of the court dealing with the reasonableness of the amount of Mr Callery's ATE premium. The court concluded ([2001] EWCA Civ 1246 at [70], [2001] 4 All ER 1 at [70]) that 'the amount of the premium does not strike us as manifestly disproportionate to the risk'.

[103] So the appeal on the insurance premium point was dismissed. The appeal on the success fee point had been allowed by the reduction of the percentage uplift from 40% to 20%.

THE s 29 JURISDICTION ISSUE

[104] One of the contentions argued on behalf of Mr Gray, the appellant, before the Court of Appeal was that s 29 of the 1999 Act was not applicable to a case where a settlement out of court had been reached and all that was left was the quantification of the claimant's costs and disbursements to be paid by the defendant. The point was based on the language of s 29. The 'proceedings' referred to in the section were the substantive proceedings for recovery of damages. Absent the section, ATE insurance premiums would not have been recoverable under a costs order. So, in the absence of any substantive proceedings for the recovery of damages, or any order for costs made in such proceedings, the court, it was said, had no jurisdiction to include an ATE insurance premium in the recoverable costs. This argument was advanced in the Court of Appeal but was rejected. The argument has not been raised again before your Lordships and I mention it only in order to express my respectful agreement with the Court of Appeal's rejection of it. It was a term of the settlement agreement that Mr Callery would be paid his reasonable costs and expenses. It was plainly implicit that these would be standard basis costs and that the amount, unless agreed, would be assessed by a costs judge in accordance with the relevant rules and practice directions. These rules and practice directions allow for a sum in respect of an ATE premium that has been reasonably incurred to be included in the recoverable costs. So in quantifying Mr Callery's recoverable costs on that basis the district judge was acting in accordance with the agreement the parties had made. There is no jurisdictional reason why a costs judge should not assess the costs to which a party has become contractually entitled (see *Gomba Holdings UK Ltd v Minories Finance Ltd (No 2)* [1992] 4 All ER 588 at 602, [1993] Ch 171 at 188). No issue of jurisdiction, in my opinion arises.

THE ISSUES BEFORE THE HOUSE

[105] The appellant's written case identifies ten issues:

'(1) Was the insurance premium recoverable given the stage when the policy was taken out? (prematurity). (2) Was the amount of the premium *a* reasonable having regard to the characteristics of the instant case? (3) Was the amount of the premium reasonable having regard to prematurity? (4) Was the Court of Appeal wrong not to resolve doubt—if any—as to the amount of the recoverable premium in favour of the paying party? (5) Should the defendant be liable for any part of the premium which covers adverse costs orders and all aspects of own costs, however incurred? (6) The

b success fee ("uplift"): is the full uplift recoverable given the stage when the CFA was effected? (7) Was the 20% uplift a reasonable maximum for simple accident cases? (the "reasonableness issue") (8) Was the Court of Appeal's assessment of 20% uplift for the instant case wrong? (9) Should an uplift be assessed by reference to the risk in the particular case, or on a more general, and if so what, basis? (10) Should uplift levels be conditioned, and if so how,

c by public interest considerations?'

Issues (1)–(5) relate to the ATE premium; issues (6)–(10) relate to the success fee.

THE ATE PREMIUM

d *Issue (1)—the ATE policy and prematurity*

[106] The prematurity issue was dealt with in the first Court of Appeal judgment [2001] 3 All ER 833 at [80]–[100] in relation both to the time at which a claimant could reasonably enter into a CFA and to the time at which he could reasonably take out ATE insurance. The Court of Appeal's approach to the

e prematurity issue is expressed at [91]:

> '... we consider that, from the viewpoint of both the claimant and his solicitor, it will normally be reasonable for a CFA to be concluded and ATE cover taken out on the occasion that the claimant first instructs his solicitors. What we have to decide is whether, having regard to the statutory
f > provisions, (i) the cost of the success fee and (ii) the ATE premium, when incurred at that early stage, can be recovered.'

[107] I agree with the Court of Appeal's proposition that it is reasonable for a claimant to enter into a CFA with his solicitor at their first meeting and before the defendant's reaction to the claim is known. It was not contended before your

g Lordships that Mr Callery instructed Amelans prematurely. It was plainly reasonable for him to instruct solicitors to pursue his claim and for them then to notify Mr Gray of his claim. And it was reasonable for him, having instructed Amelans, immediately to enter into a CFA with regard to their fees. After all, the fees clock begins ticking as soon as a solicitor is instructed. The issues for your

h Lordships regarding the success fee relate, in my opinion, not to the time when the CFA was entered into but to the size of the success fee and the manner in which its reasonableness should be assessed.

[108] It is otherwise with an ATE policy. The main issue, indeed I think the only real issue before the House, is whether it is reasonable, in a cost assessment

j context, for a claimant to take out an ATE policy at a time when litigation is highly unlikely. The purpose of an ATE policy is to protect the claimant against adverse costs orders. But the risk of such orders cannot arise unless and until the claimant commences litigation to pursue his damages claim. The CFA is needed as soon as he instructs his solicitors. But the ATE policy is not needed unless there is going to be litigation.

[109] The circuit judge, Judge Edwards, interpreted CGU's reply of 19 May 2000 to Amelans' letter of 4 May as a denial of liability. This led him to conclude

that it had been reasonable for Mr Callery to take out ATE insurance cover at an early stage 'because a contest was looming'. The Court of Appeal, rightly in my opinion, did not accept that view of the letter of 19 May. They commented ([2001] 3 All ER 833 at [131]):

> 'In view of that letter, the claimant's solicitors would not be justified in continuing to investigate and prepare the case on liability. Their sole concern after the letter was to establish the extent of the damages. Therefore all that was required of the claimant's solicitors was that they should proceed in accordance with the protocol to obtain a medical report and investigate the question of damages. From a practical point of view, this was, as Mr Birts contends on behalf of the appellant, a very, very low risk case.'

[110] I would respectfully agree with this analysis of the letter of 19 May and how matters stood after it had been received. But the content of the letter was not the reason why the ATE policy was taken out. The policy had been taken out well before Amelans' receipt of the 19 May letter. Indeed, it was taken out before either Mr Gray or CGU could have received the letter of 4 May notifying them of the claim.

[111] It is apparent, therefore, that the Court of Appeal's conclusion that it had been reasonable for Mr Callery to take out the ATE insurance policy on 4 May immediately on instructing Amelans was not based on any perception that, on what was then known, the policy was a reasonable precaution to be put in place in order to protect Mr Callery against the possibility of an adverse costs order in litigation. No one in Amelans was contemplating that litigation might be needed in order to obtain the payment of a satisfactory sum of damages for Mr Callery; it was not completely impossible that litigation might be needed, but it was very unlikely indeed. On what then was the Court of Appeal's conclusion based? It seems to me to have been based on the evidence placed before the court about the ATE insurance market and the Court of Appeal's concern that unless premium recovery under costs orders were allowed in such commonplace, minimal risk cases as Mr Callery's, the market in ATE insurance policies might wither. The Court of Appeal was told that if claimants in road traffic accident cases postponed taking out cover until a litigation contest seemed likely, the premiums charged would rise steeply, putting at risk the ability of those who needed the cover in risky or speculative litigation to obtain it and thereby impeding their access to justice. The court referred, in particular, to evidence from Mr Ward, managing director of Abbey Legal Protection, whose firm ran the Law Society's Accident Line Protect conditional fee insurance scheme. Under this scheme, nominated solicitors were given delegated authority to offer clients ATE insurance cover once agreement on a CFA had been reached. But, in order to ensure that the principle of 'the many paying for the few' was observed, solicitors who wished to offer the Accident Line Protect cover to their clients had to do so at the time the CFA was entered into and before notifying the proposed defendant, or his insurers, of the claim (see the first Court of Appeal judgment ([2001] 3 All ER 833 at [70]) commenting on Mr Ward's evidence). As to the policy of Temple, Mr Callery's insurers, the first judgment said (at [74]):

> 'Mr Wait [underwriting director of Temple] told us that most of the ATE insurance schemes available on the market today can only provide insurance if cover is in place before the initial letter of claim is sent. Again, the practice follows the basic insurance principle that "the many pay for the few".'

a [112] It may be noticed how, in the ATE insurance context, the 'many pay for the few' insurance principle has become distorted. The principle means that the 'many', all those who take out policies and pay premiums but many of whom do not suffer an insured risk, build up a premium fund by means of which the 'few', who likewise take out policies and pay premiums but who do suffer an insured risk, can have their insured losses met. In the ATE insurance field, however, the
b 'many', ie the defendants who are to be called upon to meet the premiums that build up the premium fund from which the insured losses of the few can be met, do not take out policies at all. The premium fund is not built up for their benefit or protection. It has been suggested that defendants, as well as claimants, benefit from ATE insurance because, in the event of costs orders in favour of a defendant being made, the claimant's insurance cover will provide a means by which this
c liability can be met. In view of the number of exclusions likely to be found in a typical ATE policy, I doubt whether this will be of much practical comfort to defendants. More importantly, the policy will come into play only in the event of litigation and in a case, such as the present, where the prospect of litigation was always highly remote, the suggested benefit to the defendant seems to me
d theoretical and illusory.

[113] Your Lordships cannot know what will be the consequence for the ATE insurance market if premiums payable under ATE policies that have been taken out where there is no real risk of litigation, and therefore no real risk of the occurrence of the event insured against, are ruled to be irrecoverable from defendants. I would for my part be prepared to accept that, if recovery of
e premiums is restricted to those premiums paid in respect of policies taken out where there is at least a fair likelihood that litigation in pursuit of the damages claim will be needed, the size of premiums will rise. But I would certainly not be prepared to accept that cover will be unavailable. In any event, however, it is, in my opinion, contrary to principle for the reasonableness of the premature taking
f out of ATE insurance to be judged by reference to arguments about the impact on the ATE insurance market if recovery of premiums in commonplace cases such as Mr Callery's is not allowed.

[114] The correct approach for costs assessment purposes to the question whether an item of expenditure by the receiving party has been reasonably incurred is to look at the circumstances of the particular case. The question
g whether the paying party should be required to meet a particular item of expenditure is a case specific question. It is not a question to which the macroeconomics of the ATE insurance market has any relevance. If the expenditure was not reasonably required for the purposes of the claim, it would, in my opinion, be contrary to long-established costs recovery principles to
h require the paying party to pay it.

[115] Section 29 of the 1999 Act allows recovery of ATE insurance premiums: '… the costs payable to him *may* … include costs in respect of the premium …' (My emphasis.) The section does not mandate the inclusion of costs in respect of the premium. And whether a particular ATE insurance premium, or part of it,
j should be included in the costs ordered to be paid in a particular case should be tested and answered by reference to the same principles of reasonableness that apply under the rules and practice directions to all other items of expenditure.

[116] There is, I think, no dispute that the likelihood of litigation being necessary in order to pursue Mr Callery's damages claim was always very remote. Amelans, with their experience in the field, knew this. They offered ATE insurance to their client on 4 May, before notifying the defendant of the

claim and obtaining his reaction to it, not on the footing that their client would
be likely to need it, but because it had become their practice to do so. The offer   *a*
was no doubt made on the footing that it would not be he who would have to
pay the premium.

[117] The argument advanced by the respondent, both in the Court of Appeal
and before your Lordships, is, in effect, that defendants to claims which are bound
to succeed and where litigation to pursue the claims is highly unlikely, must bear   *b*
the cost of ATE insurance cover that is not needed in order to enable ATE
insurance cover in cases where it is needed to be offered by insurers at lower rates
than would otherwise be commercially possible. The clear principles on which
costs recovery is based, both before and after the 1999 Act, are in my opinion
hostile to this argument. In my opinion, the Court of Appeal fell into error in
accepting it and in adopting an approach to the ATE premium that was not case   *c*
specific but was based on the evidence about the ATE insurance market to which
I have referred.

[118] Submissions made to the House on behalf of the Lord Chancellor's
Department (the Department) have contended that 'access to justice would be
restricted if claimants could not insure against liability for costs from the point   *d*
they instructed a solicitor'. This, in my opinion, misses the point. There is
nothing to prevent claimants from taking out ATE policies as soon as they
instruct a solicitor. The question is whether this is a reasonable step to take
vis-à-vis the defendant who they expect to bear the burden of paying the
premium. If there is no real risk of litigation or of adverse costs orders, the
absence of an ATE policy will not discourage access to justice for the claimant in   *e*
question. If, despite the absence of any such real risk, the claimant wants to take
out the policy, he can do so but cannot then reasonably expect the defendant to
pay for it. To describe this state of affairs as restricting access to justice seems to
me unwarranted.

[119] The Lord Chancellor's case continues by referring to—   *f*

> 'the Department's policy objective ... that successful claimants would
> ordinarily be able to recover the cost of ATE premiums from unsuccessful
> defendants even though the policy was entered into before the defendant's
> response to the claim was known.'

g

[120] The paragraph does not say that it is the Department's policy objective
that claimants would ordinarily be able to recover ATE premiums even though
there was never any likelihood that litigation in which adverse costs orders might
be made would be necessary. If that is or was the Department's policy, I would
expect your Lordships to be unimpressed by it. In any event, it is Parliament's   *h*
policy underlying s 29, not the Department's policy, that the House should take
account of and, as to that, there is nothing to lead one to suppose that expenditure
on ATE premiums was, for costs purposes, to be approached differently from any
other item of potentially recoverable expenditure.

[121] Moreover, if general policy considerations are to be brought into
account, they tend strongly, in my opinion, against allowing recovery of this ATE   *j*
premium. One of the main purposes of Lord Woolf's civil justice reforms was to
reduce the cost and the complexity of pursuing legal remedies and an important
step in that direction was the introduction of pre-action protocols. These set out
steps which parties are intended to take before the commencement of litigation
so as to confine litigation, as a means of dispute resolution, to cases where the
dispute cannot be resolved without it. Under pre-action protocols the claimant

a must write a letter to the proposed defendant giving the outline of the claim and an opportunity to the defendant to respond. Various key documents, eg a medical report in accident cases, should be supplied to the defendant. This correspondence enables the parties to ascertain what, if anything, is in issue between them and whether, or on what issues, litigation will be necessary. If litigation is shown to be unnecessary, because the defendant admits the claim and

b the parties can agree terms of settlement, the expense of unnecessary litigation is, by the parties' observance of the pre-action protocol requirements, avoided. And if a claimant fails to observe the requirements of the relevant pre-action protocol and commences litigation prematurely, the court may, even if his claim succeeds, deprive him of costs or order him to pay the defendant's costs (see paras 2.2, 2.3 of the Protocol Practice Direction).

c   [122] In the present case, Amelans' letter of 4 May 2000 corresponded with the relevant pre-action protocol requirements. So did CGU's response on 19 May. So did their ensuing correspondence which led, by early August, to a settlement agreement. Litigation was not necessary to pursue Mr Callery's claim. The pre-action protocol had served its purpose. In these circumstances the proposition that the defendant

d should have to pay by way of costs for an item of Mr Callery's expenditure that related exclusively to the litigation that the parties had succeeded in avoiding seems to me inconsistent with the purpose of the pre-action protocol. If during the pre-action protocol period the claimant incurs expenditure for the purpose of litigation that, in the event, never happens, there are, in my opinion, very sound policy reasons, consistent with those that underlie the civil justice reforms, for

e leaving the claimant to bear the cost of what, in the event, is useless expenditure.

        [123] For all these reasons I would give the answer No to the question posed in issue (1) and allow the appeal to that extent.

Issues (2), (3) and (4)

f   [124] Issues (2) and (3) are fact-dependent reasonableness issues. Your Lordships should not, in my opinion, second guess the courts below on issues such as these unless their decisions are plainly unreasonable or unless some evident error has been made. In the present case, the Court of Appeal, in the second judgment ([2001] 4 All ER 1 at [70]), concluded that the amount of the premium was not manifestly disproportionate to the risk being under taken and was reasonable.

g But in reaching this conclusion the Court of Appeal was proceeding under a misapprehension as to the basis on which the premium had been calculated. The court thought that Temple had fixed the amount of the premium, £350, having regard to the facts of this particular case. Counsel are agreed that this was an error. The £350 premium was in fact a uniform premium charged by Temple for

h ATE insurance cover in respect of every claim which carried a prospect of success of better than 50% (see the second judgment ([2001] 4 All ER 1 at [22])). This was a 'block rating' case, not an individual assessment case.

        [125] The factual basis, therefore, on which the Court of Appeal concluded that the £350 premium was reasonable in amount was erroneous. The Court of Appeal did not address the question whether in a case, like the present, where the

j percentage prospect of success is at the least in the mid-1990s, it was reasonable to charge a premium calculated on a block basis for all cases with a percentage prospect of success of better than 50. Your Lordships do not know what answer the Court of Appeal would have given. It is at this point that issue (4) becomes relevant.

        [126] The injunction in CPR 44.4(2)(b) that requires the court to resolve doubts about reasonableness or proportionality in favour of the paying party does

not mean that in every case where a decision as to reasonableness or as to proportionality is a difficult one to reach, with something to be said on each side, the paying party must win. The costs judge must endeavour to reach a conclusion on the issue, taking account of all the circumstances and of the factors that the rules and practice directions require to be taken into account. If, having done so, the costs judge remains uncertain whether the item of costs under review is reasonable and proportionate, then the paying party should win.

[127] In the present case, where a block rate calculated for use in cases with a prospect of success of above 50%, has been applied to a case with a prospect of success of well over 90%, there cannot, in my opinion, be other than doubt as to the reasonableness of the charge. It might be oversimplistic to conclude that a charge reasonable for a case with a prospect of success of, say, 70%, must be too high for a case with a prospect of success of, say, 95%. But at least there must be doubt. So r 44.4 (2)(b) comes into play and requires that the doubt be resolved in favour of the paying party. The £350 premium, and the £17·50 tax, should, in my opinion, have been disallowed on this ground as well.

Issue (5)

[128] This issue relates to adverse costs orders made against a claimant where (a) the claimant has failed to beat a CPR Pt 36 offer; or (b) the claimant has lost on some discrete issue and been ordered to pay the costs of that issue; or (c) there has been some other adverse exercise of costs discretion in the defendant's favour. It is contended that recovery of the part of an ATE premium that relates to adverse costs orders of the sort described ought not to be allowed. It is put almost as a point of public policy. The burden of adverse costs orders that reflect the court's disapprobation of some aspect of the manner in which a claimant has conducted his case ought not to be shifted to the defendant.

[129] Counsel for the appellant accepts that a premium, or more likely part of a premium, paid to protect a claimant against the risk of liability under these adverse costs orders is within the scope of s 29 but submits that it cannot be reasonable to require the defendant, who has presumably been unsuccessful on the main issue in the case and who has had a normal order for costs made against him, to reimburse the claimant for that premium, or that part.

[130] If it is reasonable for a claimant to take out ATE insurance cover in order to protect himself against incurring a costs liability in litigation, whether in respect of the other side's costs or his own costs, I can, for my part see no reason why any distinction should be drawn between the types of adverse costs orders that might be made or the circumstances in which the orders might be made. If the claimant becomes entitled to costs and the expenditure has been reasonably incurred and is reasonable in amount, the expenditure, in my opinion, ought in principle to be included in the costs to be paid.

[131] In my view, for the reasons already expressed, the expenditure on the ATE premium was not reasonably incurred. If, on the other hand, it was reasonably incurred, and is reasonable in amount, I do not think there is any principle that could justify subtracting from the recoverable premium some part of it notionally attributable to the risk of the adverse costs orders described.

THE SUCCESS FEE

Issue (6)

[132] The full contractual uplift of 60% was reduced by the district judge to 40% and then further reduced by the Court of Appeal to 20%. The full uplift was

a held to be not recoverable. There has been no cross-appeal on the point and this issue does not, therefore, arise.

Issues (7) and (8)

[133] These issues are fact-dependent reasonableness issues. Your Lordships should not, in my opinion, interfere with the decision of the Court of Appeal that

b 20% represented a reasonable uplift. The appellant has submitted that the 20% was unduly high for 'a very, very low risk case'. I think this may be so, but it is not, in my opinion, sufficiently out of line to justify your Lordships in interfering. It is reasonable, for the reasons I have given, for a would-be claimant to enter into a CFA with his solicitors as soon as he instructs them. The amount of the success fee must be stated in the CFA and, therefore, fixed before it is possible for the

c solicitors to know for certain what part, if any, of their client's story the defendant will accept.

Issue (9)

[134] I am in no doubt but that a success fee should be assessed by reference

d to the risk in the particular case. As I have said already, a costs assessment process should be case specific. I agree with the appellant that the costs rules and practice directions reflect a case-specific approach. If the risk of a claim failing is minimal then, in my opinion, the success fee should be correspondingly low.

Issue (10)

e [135] This is too general a question to enable a useful answer to be given. I would simply repeat that, in my opinion, the reasonableness of a success fee is a case-specific issue.

Conclusion

f [136] I would allow the appeal to the extent of disallowing recovery by the respondent of the £350 premium and £17·50 tax.

Appeal dismissed.

Kate O'Hanlon   Barrister.

Seray-Wurie v Hackney London Borough Council

[2002] EWCA Civ 909

COURT OF APPEAL, CIVIL DIVISION
SIMON BROWN, BROOKE AND DYSON LJJ
25 JUNE 2002

High Court – Jurisdiction – Application to reopen appeal – Whether High Court having power to reopen appeal after final judgment given and drawn up.

The claimant obtained a default costs certificate against the defendant local authority, but the certificate was set aside by a deputy costs judge on the authority's application. The claimant then applied to a High Court judge for permission to appeal against the order setting aside the certificate. Following a hearing, the judge refused permission, holding that there was no possibility of any reasonable costs judge reaching a different conclusion and that accordingly there was no realistic prospect of an appeal succeeding. Subsequently, the claimant applied to another High Court judge for an order that the case be reopened for a hearing. In a reasoned order on paper, the judge refused that application, concluding that the claimant was relying on grounds that had been argued before the first judge and that in those circumstances he had not shown good grounds for reopening the decision. At a subsequent hearing, however, the judge made an order transferring the proceedings to the Court of Appeal so that it could consider whether the High Court had jurisdiction to reopen an appeal that it had already determined.

Held – The High Court had a jurisdiction to reopen an appeal that it had already determined so as to avoid real injustice in exceptional circumstances. That power should, however, only be exercised where it was clearly established that a significant injustice had probably occurred and that there was no alternative effective remedy. Applications to reopen decisions should be handled in the High Court on paper and only allowed to proceed if the court so directed after the paper application had been considered. There would be no right to an oral hearing if the application were refused on paper. The court should exercise strong control over any such application, so as to protect those who were entitled reasonably to believe that the litigation was already at an end. In the instant case, the circumstances went nowhere near satisfying the extremely tough requirement for the exercise of the jurisdiction to reopen an appeal, and the judge had been correct when he had disposed of the application on paper in the way that he had (see [16]–[18], [21], [22], below).

Taylor v Lawrence [2002] 2 All ER 353 applied.

Notes

For appeals to a judge of the High Court, see 37 *Halsbury's Laws* (4th edn reissue) para 1519.

Cases referred to in judgments

Godwin v Swindon BC [2001] EWCA Civ 1478, [2001] 4 All ER 641, [2002] 1 WLR 997.
Taylor v Lawrence [2002] EWCA Civ 90, [2002] 2 All ER 353.

Application

a

By order made on 10 April 2002, Lloyd J transferred from the High Court to the Court of Appeal an appeal by the claimant, Dr Adu Aezick Seray-Wurie, from the order of Deputy Costs Judge Jefferson on 6 December 2001 setting aside a default costs certificate obtained by the claimant against the defendant, Hackney London Borough Council. The transferred proceedings included an application by the

b claimant for the case to be reopened notwithstanding the refusal of Gibbs J on 24 January 2002 to grant the claimant permission to appeal against the decision of the deputy costs judge. The facts are set out in the judgment of Brooke LJ.

The claimant appeared in person.
The council was not represented.

c

BROOKE LJ (giving the first judgment at the invitation of Simon Brown LJ).

[1] This court has now been involved in the latest stage of a long-running dispute between Dr Adu Seray-Wurie, who is chairman of the Hackney African Organisation (the claimant), and the London Borough of Hackney (the council).

d The matter comes before the court in an unusual way. On 6 December 2001 Deputy Costs Judge Jefferson made an order whereby he set aside a default costs certificate in the sum of £280,063 which had been obtained by the claimant on 2 October 2001. The claimant sought permission to appeal against this order to a High Court judge, and at a hearing in court on 24 January 2002 Gibbs J, in a carefully reasoned judgment, refused permission to appeal. That would ordinarily

e be the end of the matter (see s 54(4) of the Access to Justice Act 1999 and CPR PD 52, para 4.8). The claimant, however, relying on the judgment of the court in *Taylor v Lawrence* [2002] EWCA Civ 90 at [54], [2002] 2 All ER 353 at [54], applied to a High Court judge for an order that the case be 'reopened for a hearing'.

f [2] On 19 March 2002 Lloyd J made a reasoned order on paper refusing this application. The claimant then sought an oral hearing of what he now described as an 'application for permission to appeal'. At a hearing in court on 10 April Lloyd J made an order in the following terms (so far as are material):

g

'... that under CPR PD 51, para 14 the appeal from the order of Deputy Costs Judge Jefferson dated 6 December 2001 (including the claimant's application ... for an order that the case be reopened notwithstanding the refusal of permission to appeal by Gibbs J on 24 January 2002) be transferred to the Court of Appeal.'

h [3] Before he made this order Lloyd J told the claimant that he thought there was an important question as to whether the High Court had jurisdiction to entertain his application, and how the High Court should deal with cases like this if it did possess jurisdiction. He had decided that the point should be considered by the Court of Appeal, because only the Court of Appeal could give authoritative guidance on the point. It was always possible that it might take the view that he

j should not have transferred the matter, in which case there would be a regrettable delay while the case was sent back. The claimant then filed a fresh appeal notice in the Court of Appeal. I will refer to the contents of this notice, and to the question whether this court has any jurisdiction to deal with the matter, after I have described the history of this matter in rather greater detail.

[4] In these proceedings the claimant has always acted in a representative capacity on behalf of himself and the other trustees of the Hackney African

Organisation. This is a registered charity whose primary objective is the relief of
poverty by promoting schemes which are of benefit to the community, *a*
particularly the needs of the African and other ethnic minorities. It occupied
premises in Hackney under a ten-year lease granted to it by the council. In
November 1992 the council issued proceedings against it whereby it forfeited the
lease and sought possession of the premises on the grounds of arrears of rent and
insurance premium contributions. The charity put most of the arrears in issue *b*
and made a counterclaim based on the contention that the council owed it money
in relation to contracts for 52 projects which more than extinguished its claim for
arrears of rent.

[5] In the event the council repossessed the premises under powers granted to
it by a compulsory purchase order, and the long-running litigation, which came
to a head at a trial conducted by Judge Thornton QC on eight days between *c*
21 February and 7 July 2000, culminated in an order made by the judge on
31 October 2000 granting the charity nearly £300,000 on its counterclaim. The
judge decided that interest and costs should be dealt with at a subsequent hearing,
which was fixed for 1 December 2000. On 23 November 2000 the claimant filed
and served a bill of costs claiming a total sum of £279,943. *d*

[6] We have not been shown the order made by Judge Thornton, but it led to
the detailed assessment proceedings before the deputy costs judge with which we
are now concerned. On 10 September 2001 the claimant filed and served his bill
of costs in those proceedings, accompanied by a notice which stated that points
in dispute must be served by 1 October 2001. On 2 October he obtained a default
costs certificate in the sum of £280,063 he now claimed. On 5 October the council *e*
applied for an order that this certificate be set aside. It maintained that the points
of dispute had been sent by Royal Mail, Special Delivery on 28 September, and
that the guaranteed delivery date was 1 October. It said that Royal Mail had
attempted to deliver the package at the claimant's address, but nobody was at the
address to acknowledge the item. The package was therefore undelivered, and *f*
the document was held at his local Royal Mail inquiry office. The council also
said that the documentation would not have passed through the letter box at that
address, even if there had been an attempt to deliver it by hand. It appears that it
came into the claimant's possession on 6 October.

[7] September 28 was a Friday, and 1 October a Monday. The claimant has
taken the point that even if the document had been served by post on 1 October, *g*
it would have been deemed to have been served on 2 October (see *Godwin v
Swindon BC* [2001] EWCA Civ 1478, [2001] 4 All ER 641, [2002] 1 WLR 997 for the
interpretation by this court of the effect of the deeming provisions of CPR 6.7(1)).

[8] The council's application was made under CPR 47.12 which provides, so
far as is material: *h*

'(1) The court must set aside a default costs certificate if the receiving
party was not entitled to it.
(2) In any other case, the court may set aside or vary a default costs
certificate if it appears to the court that there is some good reason why the *j*
detailed assessment proceedings should continue.'

Section 38 of the Practice Direction about Costs (supplementing CPR 47.12)
contains further details about the procedure for setting aside a default costs
certificate and the matters which the court must take into account.

[9] It appears that the deputy costs judge did not give a judgment in the matter
or give specific reasons for his decision, although he was aware of the rule and the

a practice direction and referred to the overriding objective in CPR 1.1. After setting aside the default costs certificate, he set out a timetable for steps to be taken in the detailed assessment and ordered each party to bear its own costs of the application to set aside.

[10] The claimant sought permission to appeal against his order, and we have a transcript of the judgment of Gibbs J on the application. He said that the point

b at issue was whether there was any realistic prospect of a successful appeal against the setting aside of the default costs certificate. He took into consideration the fact that service of the defendants' points of dispute was not effected by 1 October and that the default certificate was rightly obtained on 2 October. On the other hand he said that an attempt had been made to serve in time, that within three days an application had been lodged to set aside the default certificate, and that

c the points of dispute in fact came into the claimant's possession on 6 October. He thought it was difficult on the facts to imagine a more prompt application to set aside the certificate (for the significance of promptness in this context see CPR PD 47, section 38.2(2)).

[11] When the judge considered the effect of the overriding objective, he said

d that there was a clearly articulated dispute about the amount of costs. For the purposes of this judgment he was content to assume that the council had been late in submitting its points of objection, but it did dispute them and there was clearly a dispute to be determined. The overriding objective necessarily implied that dealing with a case justly included actually dealing with the case. If the deputy judge had made any other order, he would have shut out the council

e entirely from pursuing the disputed points in relation to costs, and both sides agreed that the amount of costs were very substantial indeed.

[12] In these circumstances, whilst assuming that the disputed facts (some of which related to the hearing before the deputy costs judge) were found in the claimant's favour, there was no possibility of any reasonable costs judge reaching

f any other conclusion. There was therefore no realistic prospect of an appeal succeeding. Permission to appeal was accordingly refused.

[13] As I have said in [1], above, that would ordinarily be the end of the matter, because the Court of Appeal has no jurisdiction to entertain an appeal from a judge in a lower appeal court who has himself refused permission to appeal. On 1 March 2002, however, the claimant applied for an order that the case be

g reopened for a hearing because—

> 'the learned judge has impliedly overruled the Court of Appeal and had failed to take certain matters into consideration and by so doing had meted out serious injustice to the claimant. The case should be reopened. See *Taylor v*
h *Lawrence* ([2002] 2 All ER 353) and claimant's skeleton argument ...'

[14] In his skeleton argument the claimant sought to argue that the judge had been wrong in saying that the council had attempted to serve the document in time (because the effect of the decision in *Godwin*'s case was that service would have been deemed to have been out of time) and that there were procedural

j deficiencies and unfairnesses about the way which Gibbs J had dealt with the matter. It appears that the claimant had originally thought that he should be seeking redress from this court (because his skeleton argument is dated 12 February and headed 'In the Court of Appeal') but was told that this court plainly had no jurisdiction.

[15] When Lloyd J originally dealt with this application on paper he made the assumption that the High Court had the same power to reopen its own decisions

as the Court of Appeal (see *Taylor v Lawrence*). But he said that the grounds on
which the claimant relied were that he disagreed with the judge's decision on
points which were argued before him (in particular the significance of *Godwin's*
case, which was cited to him). In those circumstances no good grounds had been
shown for reopening the decision.

[16] In *Taylor v Lawrence* a litigant complained that after his appeal to the
Court of Appeal had been dismissed information had come into his possession
which showed that his appeal had been dismissed in ignorance of a material fact.
A five-judge division of the Court of Appeal, of which I was a member, was
convened to consider whether the Court of Appeal had power to reopen an
appeal after it had given a final judgment, which had been drawn up. In giving
the judgment of the court Lord Woolf CJ said that the court possessed a residual
jurisdiction to reopen an appeal it had already determined in order to avoid real
injustice in exceptional circumstances. The material part of his judgment is at
[2002] 2 All ER 353 at [54]–[57] in which he said:

> '[54] … The residual jurisdiction which we are satisfied is vested in a court
> of appeal to avoid real injustice in exceptional circumstances is linked to a
> discretion which enables the court to confine the use of that jurisdiction to
> the cases in which it is appropriate for it to be exercised. There is a tension
> between a court having a residual jurisdiction of the type to which we are
> here referring and the need to have finality in litigation. The ability to
> reopen proceedings after the ordinary appeal process has been concluded can
> also create injustice. There therefore needs to be a procedure which will
> ensure that proceedings will only be reopened when there is a real
> requirement for this to happen.
>
> [55] One situation where this can occur is a situation where it is alleged,
> as here, that a decision is invalid because the court which made it was biased.
> If bias is established, there has been a breach of natural justice. The need to
> maintain confidence in the administration of justice makes it imperative that
> there should be a remedy. The need for an effective remedy in such a case
> may justify this court in taking the exceptional course of reopening
> proceedings which it has already heard and determined. What will be of the
> greatest importance is that it should be clearly established that a significant
> injustice has probably occurred and that there is no alternative effective
> remedy. The effect of reopening the appeal on others and the extent to
> which the complaining party is the author of his own misfortune will also be
> important considerations. Where the alternative remedy would be an
> appeal to the House of Lords this court will only give permission to reopen
> an appeal which it has already determined if it is satisfied that an appeal from
> this court is one for which the House of Lords would not give leave.
>
> [56] Today, except in a few special cases, there is no right of appeal
> without permission. The residual jurisdiction which we have been considering,
> is one which should only be exercised with the permission of this court.
> Accordingly a party seeking to reopen a decision of this court, whether
> refusing permission to appeal or dismissing a substantive appeal, must apply
> in writing for permission to do so. The application will then be considered
> on paper and only allowed to proceed if after the paper application is
> considered this court so directs. Unless the court so directs, there will be no
> right to an oral hearing of the application. The court should exercise strong
> control over any such application, so as to protect those who are entitled
> reasonably to believe that the litigation is already at an end.

a

[57] In due course the Civil Procedure Rules Committee may wish to consider whether rules or a practice direction setting out the procedure should be introduced.'

[17] The question which Lloyd J referred to this court for its consideration is whether the High Court, when sitting as an appeal court, possesses a similar jurisdiction to reopen its decisions in exceptional circumstances in order to avoid

b real injustice. It appears to me that the same logic which drove the Court of Appeal in *Taylor v Lawrence* [2002] 2 All ER 353 at [51]–[53] to hold that the Court of Appeal possessed such a power must also drive us to hold that the High Court, which also possesses an inherent jurisdiction to do what it needs must have power to do in order to maintain its character as a court of justice, possesses a

c similar power. The restrictions on the exercise of the power will be precisely the same. As Lord Woolf CJ said (at [55]):

> 'What will be of the greatest importance is that it should be clearly established that a significant injustice has probably occurred and that there is no alternative effective remedy.'

d The present case, as Lloyd J correctly observed, gets nowhere near satisfying this extremely tough requirement, and in my judgment Lloyd J was right when he disposed of the application on paper in the way that he did.

[18] It is not necessary for present purposes to express any view on the question whether Lloyd J possessed the power to transfer this matter to this court

e for decision, because it was clearly desirable that we should decide the point. On any future occasion, an application of this kind should be handled in the High Court on paper along the lines described by Lord Woolf CJ in *Taylor v Lawrence* (at [56]). Whether such an application should be referred to a High Court judge or a High Court master will be a matter for the Civil Procedure Rules Committee to consider. The answer may depend on the anticipated volume of attempts

f made by litigants to have adverse decisions reopened, following this judgment and the judgment in *Taylor v Lawrence*. At all events there will be no right to an oral hearing if the application is refused on paper.

[19] Nothing in this judgment should be interpreted as having any effect in relation to the reopening of decisions made by circuit judges sitting as an appeal

g court in the county court. Different considerations, and different procedural rules, apply in the county court, and we are not concerned with them on the present occasion.

[20] For the avoidance of doubt, this judgment is free from the restrictions on citation contained in para 6.1 of the recent *Practice Note* (*citation of cases: restrictions and rules*) [2001] 2 All ER 510, [2001] 1 WLR 1001.

h

DYSON LJ.

[21] I agree.

SIMON BROWN LJ.

j   [22] I also agree.

Order accordingly.

Dilys Tausz   Barrister.

Lowe v Guise

[2002] EWCA Civ 197

COURT OF APPEAL, CIVIL DIVISION

POTTER, RIX LJJ AND MORLAND J

4 DECEMBER 2001, 26 FEBRUARY 2002

Damages – Personal injury – Carer services – Gratuitous carer services provided by claimant to relative living as part of same household – Whether claimant in personal injury action able to recover damages in respect of loss of ability to continue providing gratuitous carer services to relative living in same household.

The claimant, who lived with his mother and disabled brother, was injured in an accident caused by the defendant's negligence. In subsequent proceedings, the claimant alleged that, before the accident, he had provided gratuitous carer services to his brother, estimated at some 77 hours per week, but that after the accident his injuries had limited him to providing such services for only 35 hours per week, with the difference being made up by his mother. A preliminary issue arose as to whether, on the facts pleaded by the claimant, he was entitled to recover damages for the carer services that he was no longer able to provide. The judge determined the issue against the claimant, holding that the services had been provided for the benefit of the brother alone and that accordingly the claimant could not claim the value of those services on the basis that they had been performed for the benefit of the household at large. The claimant appealed.

Held – Where the claimant in a personal injury action had, prior to his accident, provided gratuitous care to a relative, spouse or partner, living as part of the same household, that had gone beyond the ordinary interaction of members of a household, he was entitled to recover as damages the value of the care which, as a result of the defendant's negligence, he was no longer able to provide. Such a claimant suffered the loss of being able to contribute the value of his services to the needs of his family, or he transferred the loss, by reason of his injuries, to another member of the family household who was in turn obliged to contribute his service. There was no difficulty in valuing in pecuniary terms the gratuitous service provided by such a claimant. Although the carer did not expect, or at any rate was willing to forego, compensation for the service, its value could still be assessed as his loss if he were deprived by another's fault of the ability to make that contribution or financial sacrifice. It followed in the instant case that the claimant was entitled, on the basis of the pleaded facts, to claim damages in respect of the loss of his ability to look after his brother. To the extent that the claimant's mother had, by her own additional care, mitigated his loss, it might be that the claimant would hold that recovery on trust for his mother. Accordingly, the appeal would be allowed (see [28], [38], [40], [41], [48], [49], [57], below).

Daly v General Steam Navigation Co Ltd [1980] 3 All ER 696, *Hunt v Severs* [1994] 2 All ER 385 and *Swain v London Ambulance Service NHS Trust* [1999] All ER (D) 260 considered.

Notes

For damages in respect of gratuitous services, see 12(1) *Halsbury's Laws* (4th edn reissue) para 898.

Cases referred to in judgments

Best v Samuel Fox & Co Ltd [1952] 2 All ER 394, [1952] AC 716, HL.

Cunningham v Harrison [1973] 3 All ER 463, [1973] QB 942, [1973] 3 WLR 97, CA.

Daly v General Steam Navigation Co Ltd [1980] 3 All ER 696, [1981] 1 WLR 120, CA; *affg* [1979] 1 Lloyd's Rep 257.

Donnelly v Joyce [1973] 3 All ER 475, [1974] QB 454, [1973] 3 WLR 514, CA.

Edgar v Lord Advocate 1965 SC 67, Ct of Sess.

Hunt v Severs [1994] 2 All ER 385, [1994] 2 AC 350, [1994] 2 WLR 602, HL.

Pepper (Inspector of Taxes) v Hart [1993] 1 All ER 42, [1993] AC 593, [1992] 3 WLR 1032, HL.

Swain v London Ambulance Service NHS Trust [1999] All ER (D) 260, CA.

Appeal

The appellant claimant, Richard Anthony Lowe, appealed with the permission of Potter LJ granted on 23 March 2001 from the decision of Judge MacDuff QC at the Birmingham County Court on 20 December 2000 determining in favour of the respondent defendant, Doris Guise, two preliminary issues (set out at [6], [7], below) arising in the appellant's action for negligence against the respondent. The facts are set out in the judgment of Rix LJ.

Mark Anderson (instructed by *F A Greenwood & Co*, Birmingham) for the appellant.

Simon King (instructed by *Irwin Mitchell*, Birmingham) for the respondent.

Cur adv vult

26 February 2002. The following judgments were delivered.

RIX LJ (giving the first judgment at the invitation of Potter LJ).

[1] Richard Lowe, the appellant, was riding his bicycle on 2 August 1996 when he was injured in an accident involving a car driven by Doris Guise, the respondent. On 30 March 1998 he issued his claim against her. Liability in negligence is no longer in dispute. This appeal concerns two preliminary issues of law relating to quantum decided by Judge MacDuff QC. The issues had to be decided on the assumption that the matters pleaded by the appellant were true. They would be in issue at any subsequent trial.

[2] At the time of the accident the appellant was aged 31. He lived with his mother and brother, Gary. His brother is severely disabled. Prior to the accident the appellant provided gratuitous carer services for his brother, estimated at some 77 hours per week. For two months following the accident the appellant was unable to provide any care to his brother at all. Thereafter he resumed looking after his brother, but he has been limited by his injuries to providing only 35 hours per week. That is the minimum qualifying care for entitlement to invalid care allowance benefits and he maintains that minimum in order to earn his continued entitlement to invalid care allowance, which in 1996 brought him £38 per week. That allowance does not increase with the provision of further hours of care above the minimum of 35. The difference between the hours of care which the appellant used to provide to his brother before the accident and the 35 hours to which he is limited since the accident has been provided by his mother, Mrs Helen Lowe. The appellant pleads that the services which he had provided to his brother and can no longer provide—

'benefited the Lowe household as a whole. They relieved the claimant's
mother of the need to render them herself; they benefited Gary Lowe
personally; and they also discharged a moral obligation resting upon the
claimant himself. The services should accordingly be categorised as discharging
the obligations and needs of the family as a whole.'

[3] He therefore claims, in an amount presently unparticularised, the value of
42 hours per week carer services, presumably as provided by his mother, up to
14 June 2000, the date of his reamended schedule of loss.

[4] He also claims damages for loss of employment capacity, on the basis that
now that his injuries prevent him from looking after his brother for more than 35
hours a week, his only reason for abstaining from paid employment, namely the
pressing moral obligation to care for his brother, has also been removed by the
accident: with the result that his injuries are now the sole cause of his inability to
earn wages. He values his loss at the national minimum wage for 38 hours per
week, less a discount for the possibility of unemployment.

[5] Nothing further is known from the appellant's pleadings. Thus the
circumstances in which his mother has come to take over the major part of his
role as his brother's carer is unpleaded. It is not clear whether the claim for 'carer
services' is intended to extend beyond 14 June 2000.

[6] On 20 July 1999 'the issue of whether the claimant is entitled to recover
damages [from] the defendant for carer services as pleaded' was ordered to be
determined as a preliminary issue.

[7] At the hearing of that preliminary issue before the judge an order for a
second preliminary issue was made in the following terms:

'PREAMBLE
The claimant's case is that, but for the accident, he would have continued
to afford 77 hours of care each week to his brother. He would not have been
paid for that work (save for a state allowance which he continues to receive)
and would not have been available for any other form of remunerative
employment. The claimant's case is that as a result of the accident he can
now only afford some 35 hours of care per week to his brother. His case is
that he is therefore no longer fully employed in caring for his brother and
that he is disabled (alternatively disadvantaged) from obtaining remunerative
work by reason of his injuries.

ISSUE
The claimant says that, if the facts alleged in the preamble are proved, his
claim for lost earning capacity should be assessed without reference to the
fact that, but for the accident, he would have continued to care for his
brother and would therefore have been unavailable for remunerative work.
Is the claimant correct?'

[8] The judge answered both these issues in the negative, that is to say against
the appellant and in favour of the respondent.

Further matters in evidence

[9] The wording of the issues strictly makes any further information of no
consequence. However, the following may be stated as part of the background
of this appeal.

[10] The appellant's evidence (his witness statement dated 14 August 1999)
states that his brother, who was born in 1963 and is therefore some two years
older than him, suffers inter alia from Down's Syndrome, needs to be carried and

a lifted or otherwise transported by wheelchair, and is in need of constant care and attention. The appellant had been his brother's main carer for about four years before the accident, since the appellant was 27 years old.

[11] In the witness statement of the appellant's solicitor dated 14 April 1999 it is stated that any recovery under the carer services claim is to be held by the appellant on trust for his mother: clearly a reference to *Hunt v Severs* [1994] 2 All ER

b 385, [1994] 2 AC 350. That statement was repeated in the appellant's amended schedule of special damages (attached to the solicitor's witness statement). However, as of 14 June 2000 it has dropped out of his *reamended* schedule of loss (see [2], [3], above) for which the appellant obtained permission from the judge at the hearing below.

c *The first issue: carer services.*

[12] To understand this issue it is first necessary to explain the statutory and jurisprudential background to it.

[13] It has been established for some time in England that an injured claimant is entitled to claim in respect of the value of care provided gratuitously to him by

d voluntary carers. The history of the common law's development can be found set out in *McGregor on Damages* (16th edn, 1997) p 1088 (paras 1675ff) and in the speech of Lord Bridge of Harwich in *Hunt's* case. In *Cunningham v Harrison* [1973] 3 All ER 463 at 469, [1973] QB 942 at 952 Lord Denning MR had said:

e 'It seems to me that when a husband is grievously injured—and is entitled to damages—then it is only right and just that, if his wife renders services to him, instead of a nurse, he should recover compensation for the value of the services that his wife has rendered. It should not be necessary to draw up a legal agreement for them. On recovering such an amount, the husband should hold it on trust for her and pay it over to her. She cannot herself sue

f the wrongdoer ... but she has rendered services necessitated by the wrongdoing, and should be compensated for it. If she had given up paid work to look after him, he would clearly have been entitled to recover on her behalf, because the family income would have dropped by so much ...'

[14] At almost exactly the same time in another division of this court in *Donnelly v Joyce* [1973] 3 All ER 475 at 480, [1974] QB 454 at 462 Megaw LJ

g analysed the problem of voluntary care in a different way, emphasising that the loss, consisting in the need for care, was the claimant's loss. Megaw LJ continued:

'Hence it does not matter, so far as the defendant's liability to the plaintiff is concerned, whether the needs have been supplied by the plaintiff out of his own pocket or by a charitable contribution to him from some other person

h whom we shall call the "provider"; it does not matter, for that purpose, whether the plaintiff has a legal liability, absolute or conditional, to repay to the provider what he has received, because of the general law or because of some private agreement between himself and the provider; it does not matter whether he has a moral obligation, however ascertained or defined,

j so to do.'

[15] In *Hunt's* case, however, the House of Lords preferred the reasoning of Lord Denning MR. Lord Bridge said ([1994] 2 All ER 385 at 393–394, [1994] 2 AC 350 at 361–363):

'With respect, I do not find this reasoning convincing. I accept that the basis of a plaintiff's claim for damages may consist in his need for services but

I cannot accept that the question from what source that need has been met is irrelevant. If an injured plaintiff is treated in hospital as a private patient he is entitled to recover the cost of that treatment. But if he receives free treatment under the National Health Service, his need has been met without cost to him and he cannot claim the cost of the treatment from the tortfeasor. So it cannot, I think, be right to say that in all cases the plaintiff's loss is "for the purpose of damages ... the proper and reasonable cost of supplying [his] needs". In Scotland the law on this subject has developed differently. In [*Edgar v Lord Advocate* 1965 SC 67] it was held by a majority of the Inner House of the Court of Session that the injured pursuer's averment that his accident had caused his wife to give up work to look after him and thereby lose wages was irrelevant. Having pointed out that the wife, not being a party to the action, could not recover the loss, the Lord President (Lord Clyde) continued (at 71): "If, on the other hand, the averment is intended to form the basis for a claim for domestic assistance for which the pursuer would have had to pay if he had not been able to secure it gratuitously the claim is, in my opinion, an irrelevant one. It would have been another matter altogether if the pursuer had actually paid some third party, or had entered into a contract to pay some third party for this domestic assistance. It could then have formed a relevant item in his claim for damages. But if the assistance which he got was given gratuitously and there is no undertaking or understanding by him to pay for it (and that is the situation in the present case) then I am quite unable to see how he can claim to be reimbursed for a payment he has not and cannot be compelled to make. In Scotland, damages necessarily involves a loss either actual or prospective, and the plain fact of the matter is that the pursuer has sustained no such loss at all in regard to this item." The difference in this regard between Scottish and English law was examined by the Scottish Law Commission in 1978 (Scot Law Com No 51). In para 20 they adopted the view that "the value of the services of persons who have assisted the injured person should be recoverable by the latter in his action against the wrongdoer" but considered that "the principle should apply only as between members of the injured person's family group or circle". In para 22 they criticised the reasoning used in the judgment of Megaw LJ in *Donnelly v Joyce* ([1973] 3 All ER 475, [1974] QB 454) in the following terms: "In cases where services have been rendered gratuitously to an injured person, it is artificial to regard that person as having suffered a net loss in the events which happened. The loss is in fact sustained by the person rendering the services, a point vividly illustrated in cases where he has lost earnings in the course of rendering those services. We suggest, therefore, that it is wrong in principle, in cases where services have been rendered gratuitously by another to an injured person, to regard the latter as having in fact suffered a net loss." They concluded (at para 23)—"that it would be right to devise an approach which will enable the injured person to recover in his own action the value of services which have been rendered to him by relatives but which would, at the same time, enable the relative to recover, if he so wished, the value of these services from the injured person.' The Commission's recommendations in this respect were implemented by Pt II of the Administration of Justice Act 1982, which applies to damages for personal injuries in Scotland and which by s 8 provides: "(1) Where necessary services have been rendered to the injured person by a relative in consequence of the injuries in question, then, unless the relative has

a expressly agreed in the knowledge that an action for damages has been raised
   or is in contemplation that no payment should be made in respect of those
   services, the responsible person shall be liable to pay to the injured person by
   way of damages such sum as represents reasonable remuneration for those
   services and repayment for reasonable expenses incurred in connection
   therewith. (2) The relative shall have no direct right of action in delict
b against the responsible person in respect of the services or expenses referred
   to in this section, but the injured person shall be under an obligation to
   account to the relative for any damages recovered from the responsible
   person under this section." An elaborate definition of "relative" in s 13(1),
   which I need not here set out, implements the Commission's recommendation
   that this provision should apply only if the person rendering the services and
c the injured person belong to the same "family group or circle". Thus, in both
   England and Scotland the law now ensures than an injured plaintiff may
   recover the reasonable value of gratuitous services rendered to him by way
   of voluntary care by a member of his family. Differences between the
   English common law route and the Scottish statutory route to this
d conclusion are, I think, rarely likely to be of practical importance, since in
   most cases the sum recovered will simply go to swell the family income. But
   it is nevertheless important to recognise that the underlying rationale of the
   English law, as all the cases before *Donnelly v Joyce* demonstrate, is to enable
   the voluntary carer to receive proper recompense for his or her services and
   I would think it appropriate for the House to take the opportunity so far as
e possible to bring the law of the two countries into accord by adopting the
   view of Lord Denning MR in *Cunningham v Harrison* ([1973] 3 All ER 463,
   [1973] QB 942) that in England the injured plaintiff who recovers damages
   under this head should hold them on trust for the voluntary carer.'

f [16] This account of the correct analytical basis of the claimant's recovery for
   the value of her husband's gratuitous care was of critical importance in *Hunt's*
   case, for in that case the carer was the defendant himself. The House of Lords
   ruled ([1994] 2 All ER 385 at 394, [1994] 2 AC 350 at 363) that because the claimant
   would have to hand over to the defendant the recovery made on account of his
   gratuitous care, 'there can be no ground in public policy or otherwise' for
g requiring the defendant to pay such sums to the claimant. This result has been
   described as logical but unfortunate, and liable to lead to the more expensive use
   of professional carers (see *McGregor on Damages* p 1092 (para 1682)). The Law
   Commission's report on *Damages for Personal Injury: Medical, Nursing and Other
   Expenses; Collateral Benefit* (1999) (Law Com no 262) has recommended the legislative
h reversal of the actual decision in *Hunt's* case while approving of its central reasoning,
   in particular that the loss is that of the provider of the care rather than the
   claimant's.

   [17] Lord Bridge's reference to s 8 of the Administration of Justice Act 1982
   and to its background in the recommendations of the Scottish Law Commission
j is important for present purposes, because the present claim, if it arose in
   Scotland, would have come directly within the immediately following section of
   the Act, s 9. Both sections fall, with some others, within Pt II of the Act which
   applies only to Scotland. Section 8 deals with gratuitous services rendered by a
   relative to the injured person following his injury, and s 9 deals with services
   which, prior to his injury, the injured person had (or might have been expected
   to have) rendered gratuitously to a relative. Section 9 provides:

'(1) The responsible person shall be liable to pay to the injured person a reasonable sum by way of damages in respect of the inability of the injured person to render the personal services referred to in subsection (3) below.

(2) Where the injured person has died, any relative of his entitled to damages in respect of loss of support under section 1(3) of the Damages (Scotland) Act 1976 shall be entitled to include as a head of damage under that section a reasonable sum in respect of the loss to him of the personal services mentioned in subsection (3) below.

(3) The personal services referred to in subsections (1) and (2) above are personal services—(a) which were or might have been expected to have been rendered by the injured person before the occurrence of the act or omission giving rise to liability, (b) of a kind which, when rendered by a person other than a relative, would ordinarily be obtainable on payment, and (c) which the injured person but for the injuries in question might have been expected to render gratuitously to a relative.

(4) Subject to subsection (2) above, the relative shall have no direct right of action in delict against the responsible person in respect of the personal services mentioned in subsection (3) above.'

[18] The essential question in this appeal is whether the appellant's claim in respect of additional hours of care which he used to, but can no longer, give his brother, (a claim which, as is common ground, would, on the assumed facts, succeed under s 9 in Scotland) must fail in England because Parliament has not seen fit to enact a similar provision for England. The judge concluded that it must, on the basis of the decision of this court in *Swain v London Ambulance Service NHS Trust* [1999] All ER (D) 260.

[19] In *Swain's* case the claimant was injured in the course of his employment and had to retire early. The appeal was solely concerned with the extent of his damages. The principal issue concerned matters far removed from the present subject. However, Mr Swain's cross-appeal raised a point on the cost of valeting his wife's car. The judge had awarded him £140 in respect of his own car, but had given him nothing in respect of his wife's car, for which Mr Swain sought a similar figure. He said that it was his practice to clean his wife's car before the accident and that after it he had to pay someone else to do the work. His £140 appeal failed.

[20] Beldam LJ appears to have put the matter broadly on the basis that claims by the injured person based on gratuitous services rendered to a member of his family could not be recovered. He said:

'The question whether an injured plaintiff can recover compensation for loss of his capacity to render services to others and, in particular, to members of his family has been a subject of discussion in the law of damages for personal injury for many years. Historically a husband was able to claim in respect of the loss of services performed for him by his wife but no similar cause of action was afforded a wife in respect of services performed for her by her husband (see *Best v Samuel Fox & Co Ltd* [1952] 2 All ER 394, [1952] AC 716). The reason given by Lord Goddard in his opinion ([1952] 2 All ER 394 at 398, [1952] AC 716 at 730–731) was: "Negligence, if it is to give rise to legal liability, must result from a breach of duty owed to a person who thereby suffers damage. But what duty was owed here by the employers of the husband to the wife? If she has an action in this case so must the wife of any man run over in the street by a careless driver. The duty there which gives

a

rise to the husband's cause of action arises out of what may for convenience be called proximity; the driver owes a duty not to injure other persons who are using the road on which he is driving. He owes no duty to persons not present except to those whose property may be on or adjoining the road which it is his duty to avoid injuring. It may often happen that an injury to one person may affect another. A servant whose master is killed or

b

permanently injured may lose his employment, it may be of long standing, and the misfortune may come when he is of an age when it would be very difficult for him to obtain other work, but no one would suggest that he thereby acquires a right of action against the wrongdoer. Damages for personal injury can seldom be a perfect compensation, but where injury has been caused to a husband or father it has never been the case that his wife or

c

children whose style of living or education may have radically to be curtailed, have on that account a right of action other than that which, in the case of death, the Fatal Accidents Act, 1846, has given." Thus, on policy grounds, the law denied a wife whose husband was injured a cause of action where historically it allowed a claim to the husband. But can the injured

d

husband include in his claim the value of the loss of his capacity to render services to his wife and family which, but for his performing them gratuitously, he would probably have paid for out of the family budget? This question was considered by the *Royal Commission on Civil Liability and Compensation for Personal Injury* (Cmnd 7054-I (1978)) (the Pearson Commission). In its report (ch 12) the Pearson Commission considered the question of

e

services rendered by a plaintiff to others. After stating that damages for the loss of gratuitously rendered services are not usually recoverable where the victim survives, the Pearson Commission thought that it would be right to regard the loss of the capacity to render services gratuitously as primarily the plaintiff's loss, rather than the loss of those who used to benefit from the services. It therefore considered that the damages should be recoverable by

f

the plaintiff in his own right (see para 354). The Law Commission had already recommended that such a claim should be confined to services rendered by the victim to a person within the class of dependants having a remedy under the Fatal Accidents Acts. The Pearson Commission agreed with that approach and said (para 356): "The loss of the plaintiff's capacity to

g

render services to those dependant on him could bring about substantial pecuniary loss to the family in replacing them; but the loss suffered by those not dependant on the plaintiff seems to us to be altogether more remote. There are advantages in consistency with the right to recover damages for lost services in fatal cases." The Administration of Justice Act 1982 implemented

h

some of the recommendations of the Pearson Commission. Part I contained provisions relating to England and Wales, including the abolition of an action by a husband for being deprived of the services or society of his wife. However, it did not enact the recommendation that damages should be recoverable by an injured person for the loss of his capacity gratuitously to

j

render services to his relatives. By way of contrast, Parliament did give effect to the recommendations of the Scottish Law Commission and in Pt II of the Act included in s 9 a provision giving an injured party a right to claim a reasonable sum by way of damages in respect of his inability to render personal services to a relative which he might have been expected to render gratuitously. As far as I am aware, the changes to the law in Scotland have attracted no adverse comment. As the Law Commission, supported by the

Pearson Commission, had recommended that the law in England and Wales
should be similarly changed, it is perhaps surprising that the change was
confined to Scotland; the objection founded on policy that a wrongdoer's
liability should be confined within reasonable bounds is met by confining the
claim in respect of personal services to services which might reasonably be
expected to be provided by the injured party to a dependant relative.
However, Parliament having declined the opportunity to introduce such a
provision into English law, I can see no basis for doing so in the present case.'

[21] Potter LJ, however, the only other member of that court, appears to have
put the matter on a narrow basis, thus:

'I agree. I would only add a few remarks of my own in relation to the claim
by the plaintiff for recovery of the costs of valeting his wife's car. So far as
that is concerned, my decision is a reluctant one and depends upon the
particular way in which the claim appears to have been advanced and
argued, namely the loss of the husband's capacity to render services for
others. Put in that way, the claim fell foul of what was, as it seems to me, the
logically inexplicable refusal of Parliament to import into English law the
recommendations of the Pearson Commission and the English and Scottish
Law Commissions at the time it saw fit to do so in respect of Scottish law. It
appears that the husband's case was argued and decided below on the basis
that the service of car valeting was one which he performed gratuitously for
his wife, (who was herself a wage earner) in respect of "her" car, ie a vehicle
regarded as her own separate property and used exclusively for her benefit.
On that basis it was, I accept, correct to regard the service performed by the
husband as one performed for the wife alone, so that his subsequent claim
for car valeting was in essence a claim for loss of his capacity gratuitously to
render a service to a relative. My decision would be different, if, assuming
the facts warranted it, the claim had been advanced on the basis that,
whether or not the property and principal benefit of the car lay with the wife,
this was essentially a "two-car family" in which the use of both vehicles
benefited a household in which the expenses and domestic tasks were shared
and performed, whether by husband or wife, for the benefit of both. On that
basis, it seems to me that the post-accident expense incurred by the husband
at the car wash might properly have been regarded as a claim for loss caused
to him as a result of his inability to discharge his usual functions and so to
save himself expense in relation to his own usual household tasks. It does not
seem to me that the mere fact that the claim is in respect of expenditure on
something which benefited and/or belonged to the plaintiff's wife need
necessarily be determinative. If it were, it could be argued that when a
husband claims in respect of his post-accident inability to do DIY decorations
to a property owned by his wife, but the home of both, his claim should be
disallowed as being work done for the benefit of the wife. In my view, where
the post-accident expense may properly be regarded as a household or family
expense incurred by a plaintiff spouse in discharging a function which he or
she previously performed gratuitously for the benefit of the household at
large, then it is recoverable.'

[22] In the present case the judge put the claimant's argument and his own
solution as follows:

a   'Mr Anderson first of all concedes that the reality is that the claimant here was performing gratuitous services on one view exclusively for his brother, but he seeks to bring it within Potter LJ's dictum in the following way. He says that it was a moral obligation upon the family which was in fact performed by the claimant, and that now that the claimant cannot do it—and I must assume these facts to be correct for the purpose of this submission—

b   the mother does it, and therefore what the claimant was doing pre-accident was benefiting not just the brother but the whole family ... This is an ingenious argument. It could have been applied equally to the car wash for the claimant's wife in *Swain v London Ambulance Service NHS Trust* [1999] All ER (D) 260. It relieved the wife or the children in that case of the need to wash the mother's car. It was not just a matter of pleading; it was a matter

c   of looking at the realities of the circumstances, and within any family situation it would always be possible in any given family situation to say that gratuitous services provided for a third party within the family, be it wife, brother, cousin or anybody else, was for the benefit of the family as a whole because if the claimant did not do it somebody else would do it. But in my

d   judgment, sadly and with regret because I share Potter LJ's concerns as to the state of the law, the reality is that what the claimant was here doing was providing gratuitous services for the brother and the brother alone. It was the brother's benefit, and in those circumstances I fear that in my judgment the claimant cannot claim the value of those services. If it were different it would mean that by a back door that which Parliament did not amend would

e   be enacted by me. It would mean that the judgment in *Swain*'s case lost its potency in absolutely every situation within the family situation ...'

The parties' submissions on the first issue

f   [23] On behalf of the appellant Mr Mark Anderson puts his case on this issue in two ways. First, he repeats his submission that the claim falls within Potter LJ's dicta in *Swain*'s case. If the law will compensate a claimant for the cost of the work he can no longer perform in looking after his, or his family's, car or home or garden, then it must be able to compensate him for the work he can no longer do in looking after other members of his own family. The law cannot be so mistaken as to give a remedy in respect of one's garden but not one's brother.

g   This approach should be seen not so much as a back door approach to subvert the logic of Beldam LJ's judgment, but rather as an exception or refinement to it, based on a recognised need to support family life. In this way it was still open for the English common law to develop its own s 9 type remedy.

h   [24] Secondly, but possibly not so much of his own motion as in response to questions from the court, he broadened his submission to revisit the issues discussed by Beldam LJ in *Swain*'s case. If the English common law could develop for itself the remedy which had to be rescued for Scotland by s 8 (see *Hunt v Severs* [1994] 2 All ER 385, [1994] 2 AC 350), it could follow the logic of that remedy and give relief in a s 9 situation as well. Parliament, in enacting ss 8 and 9

j   was not rejecting such relief for England so much as leaving it to the common law to follow its own path. Where the basic facts had been pleaded, the appellant's claim should not fail because of any particular way in which it had been advanced: the court could categorise it as it felt was just.

      [25] On behalf of the respondent Mr Simon King submitted that although he could not say that *Swain*'s case foreclosed the argument as a matter of binding precedent, the judge's view of that case as being determinative as a matter of

reason represented good sense. The common law could not develop a remedy
which Parliament had visited but not enacted outside Scotland. The consequences
were potentially too large to be safely contemplated. In any event, whereas a s 8
type loss was foreseeable, a s 9 type loss was not: it was therefore simply too
remote. *Hunt's* case, the s 8 situation, began with an injury to and thus a loss on
the part of a claimant; but the s 9 situation started, and ended, with the brother's
loss not with the appellant's. That was a fundamental difference. In that event,
it did not help to look at the matter in terms of the value of the mother's services
or the needs of the family. And Lord Goddard's dicta from *Best v Samuel Fox
& Co Ltd* [1952] 2 All ER 394, [1952] AC 716 were a famous and salutary reminder
that whereas proximity existed and thus a duty of care was owed in the case of an
injured claimant, neither was true in the case of a claimant's brother. In such
circumstances, the gloss put by Potter LJ on the reasoning of Beldam LJ in
Swain's case could not apply in the present case. In any event, the appellant's
moral obligation was only to do what he could. In doing that, he suffered no loss,
for he continued to earn the maximum allowance for only 35 hours' care.

Discussion

[26] As a matter of principle, I would have thought that an injured claimant
who has been prevented by his injuries from working should be entitled to say
that prima facie he has suffered loss. The most obvious form of that loss is of
course loss of earnings or loss of earning capacity where the claimant has been
employed or might be expected to be employed. It was common ground that,
contrary to that prima facie situation, a claimant who chooses not to work, either
through wealth or idleness, will in this respect have no claim, subject to any
argument that he would have altered his way of life at some point in the future.
But the appellant in the present case had worked, in caring for his brother, even
though his financial compensation for doing so was limited to the invalid care
allowance. What then has he lost, if he cannot work for more than 35 hours but
still retains the whole of that allowance? Mr King says 'nothing', and submits that
non-pecuniary loss, such as the self-fulfilment of useful work or the gratification
of helping his disabled brother, has to be and is totally compensated by his award
of general damages for pain, suffering and loss of amenity.

[27] I would not dispute that last submission: but in my judgment an injured
claimant who works albeit gratuitously for his family, a fortiori or at any rate
within the nucleus of a family home, does suffer loss, the loss of being able to
contribute the value of his service to the needs of his family. Just as the wife's care
of her injured husband, or the husband's care of his injured wife, can be and is to
be valued in pecuniary terms, even though gratuitously provided, and is to be
compensated, through the injured person's claim, as the provider's loss: so it
seems to me that the injured claimant's loss of the ability to contribute his or her
service to the needs of the family is a real loss suffered by the claimant, or
transferred by the claimant by reason of his or her injuries on to another member
of the family household who is in turn obliged to contribute his or her service. If
public policy and the law's transparent recognition of the special ties of family life
can find, as it has done (see *Hunt v Severs* [1994] 2 All ER 385, [1994] 2 AC 350 and
the cases leading up to it), a mechanism which enables it to value in pecuniary
terms the gratuitous care thus provided, then there is, in my judgment, no
difficulty in valuing in pecuniary terms the gratuitous service provided by a
claimant to his or her family household. Of course the carer does not expect or
at any rate is willing to forego compensation for the service, for he contributes it

a willingly to the family: but if he is deprived by another's fault of the ability to make that contribution or that financial sacrifice, the value of that can still be assessed as his loss.

[28] In truth this situation, what may be called the s 9 situation even if it has not been strictly recognised as such, has for at least some 20 years been more or less acknowledged in a series of cases which have compensated a claimant for the

b cost of providing by other means the gratuitous services which in the absence of his injury he would have wanted to contribute to the family. Thus in *Daly v General Steam Navigation Co Ltd* [1980] 3 All ER 696, [1981] 1 WLR 120 the claimant was a housewife whose housekeeping duties following her injury were in part performed by her husband and daughter. This court rejected the argument that the employment of outside paid domestic help was a necessary

c condition for recovery for the future. Bridge LJ said:

'Once the judge had concluded that to put the plaintiff, so far as money could do so, in the position in which she would have been if she had never been injured, she was going to need, in the future, domestic assistance for eight hours a week, it seems to me that it was entirely reasonable and

d entirely in accordance with principle in assessing damages, to say that the estimated cost of employing labour for that time ... was the proper measure of her damages under this heading. It is really quite immaterial, in my judgment, whether having received those damages the plaintiff chooses to alleviate her own housekeeping burden ... by employing the labour which

e has been taken as the basis of the estimate on which damages have been awarded, or whether she chooses to continue to struggle with the housekeeping on her own and to spend the damages which have been awarded to her on other luxuries which she would otherwise be unable to afford.' (See [1980] 3 All ER 696 at 701, [1981] 1 WLR 120 at 127.)

f [29] It is to be observed that, with respect to the period between injury and trial, when no paid help had been employed, this court said that there could be no recovery on the same basis, only an increment in general damages to compensate the claimant for the extra suffering of attempting the work by herself, and, if the claim had been maintained, compensation for the husband's assistance. The distinction between the pre-trial and post-trial period has been

g criticised as being illogical (a criticism of which Bridge LJ himself seems to have been sensible, for he commented that he looked at the matter 'as one not so much of logic as of practical reality'); and the English Law Commission (*Damages for Personal Injury: Medical, Nursing and Other Expenses; Collateral Benefits* (Consultation Paper no 144 (1996) and Law Com no 262 (1999))) has proposed that both

h pre-trial and post-trial periods should be compensated in the same way. For present purposes, however, I would emphasise a different aspect of the case. In awarding Mrs Daly damages for the housekeeping duties which she could no longer perform, the court was not deterred from compensating her in the future by the thought that the work had been conferred on her family gratuitously. In

j reality, it needed to be done, not so much for her own sake, as for her family's.

[30] In *Swain v London Ambulance Service NHS Trust* [1999] All ER (D) 260 Beldam LJ referred to the Pearson Report (*Royal Commission on Civil Liability, and Compensation for Personal Injury* (Cmnd 7054-I (1978)); ch 12). The report commented on the case of gratuitous services provided by the injured claimant as follows:

'352 Another result of an injury may be that the plaintiff loses his capacity to render services to others. The most important example is the loss suffered

by an injured housewife, who is deprived of her capacity to look after her
family. Damages for the loss of gratuitously rendered services are not
usually recoverable where the victim survives.

353 It seems to us that a person who loses the capacity to render services
to others suffers a real loss. The housewife who can no longer care for her
family has not lost money, but she has lost money's worth. If her services
are replaced by hired help, the family as a whole may suffer substantial
pecuniary loss. But we do not think her claim should be determined by the
way in which her services are replaced. Even if they are partly replaced free
of charge by a friend or relative, we consider that damages should be
recoverable ...

354 Again, we think that it is right to regard the loss of the capacity to
render services gratuitously as primarily the plaintiff's loss, rather than the
loss of those who used to benefit from the services. We consider therefore
that damages should be recoverable by the plaintiff in his own right.'

[31] The significance of that 'again' at the beginning of para 354 is that at
paras 343–349 the report had preferred the reasoning of Megaw LJ in *Donnelly v
Joyce* [1973] 3 All ER 475, [1974] QB 454 to the alternative approach in *Cunningham v
Harrison* [1973] 3 All ER 463, [1973] QB 942. That was just before the Scottish Law
Commission published its 1978 report (Scot Law Com no 51) in which it criticised
the reasoning of Megaw LJ (at para 22, referred to in *Hunt v Severs* [1994] 2 All ER
385 at 393, [1994] 2 AC 350 at 362). In the event the House of Lords in *Hunt*'s case
followed the Scottish Law Commission and has preferred the analysis of Lord
Denning MR in *Cunningham*'s case to that of Megaw LJ in *Donnelly*'s case. I do
not for myself, however, think that that undermines the reasoning of the Pearson
Report at paras 352–354 in any way.

[32] That report was published in March 1978. *Daly v General Steam Navigation
Co Ltd* [1980] 3 All ER 696, [1981] 1 WLR 120 was decided in between then and
the enactment of the 1982 Act. *Daly*'s case, if not completely in line with the
reasoning of the Pearson Report, goes a long way towards embracing it.

[33] The question arises as to why Pt II of the Act applies only to Scotland.
The judge came to his conclusion 'sadly and with regret' and with concern as to
the state of the law. In *Swain v London Ambulance Service NHS Trust* [1999] All ER
(D) 260 Beldam LJ said that it was 'perhaps surprising' that the change was
confined to Scotland; Potter LJ said that the failure (his word was in fact 'refusal',
but I wonder whether he might agree that that word overstates the position) of
Parliament to import into English law the recommendations of the Pearson
Commission and of the English and Scottish Law Commissions was 'logically
inexplicable'. There was a discussion before us as to whether it might be
appropriate, pursuant to *Pepper (Inspector of Taxes) v Hart* [1993] 1 All ER 42, [1993]
AC 593, to consult Hansard: but it was hard to say that there was any ambiguity
or absurdity in construction of the Act.

[34] The question posed nevertheless needs answering. In my judgment the
answer is most unlikely to have been that Parliament intended the law in
Scotland to differ in this major respect from that of England, and the explanation
to which I am therefore driven is that Parliament believed that in England the
common law had developed or was capable of developing along the lines
recommended by the commissions. After all, by 1982 the common law in the s 8
type situation had already been well developed in England and, albeit more
recently, *Daly*'s case had largely answered the need for reform in the s 9 type
situation. In Scotland, however, as explained in *Hunt*'s case [1994] 2 All ER 385 at

a   393, [1994] 2 AC 350 at 361 per Lord Bridge, 'the law on this subject has developed differently' because the Inner House of the Court of Session had held in *Edgar v Lord Advocate* 1965 SC 67 that gratuitous services (even in the family context, there a wife who had given up work to care for her injured husband) had no value in the eye of the law. Nevertheless, following the Act, Lord Bridge was able to say that in the s 8 situation:

b

> 'Differences between the English common law route and the Scottish statutory route to this conclusion are, I think, rarely likely to be of practical importance, since in most cases the sum recovered will simply go to swell the family income.' (See [1994] 2 All ER 385 at 394, [1994] 2 AC 350 at 363.)

c   It is clear therefore that, at any rate in the s 8 situation, Parliament intended that the English common law should continue to develop *alongside* the newly enacted Scottish statutory law. It may or may not be a matter for intriguing inquiry as to why Parliament thought that the s 8 situation should be covered in these competing ways above and below the border, but it remains clear enough that
d   that was its intention. If that was so in the s 8 situation, I do not see why a similar explanation is not to be given for the s 9 situation. The two types of situation, although of course not identical, are different strands of a knotted problem generated at least in large part by the law's difficulty in giving pecuniary form to gratuitous service.

[35] It is interesting to note in this connection that in its 1999 report on
e   *Damages for Personal Injury: Medical, Nursing and Other Expenses; Collateral Benefits* (Law Com no 262) it had not occurred to the English Law Commission that the enactment of Pt II of the 1982 Act had put a halt to the development of the English common law. It reviews (p 17 (para 2.34)) the 'loss of the claimant's ability to do work in the home' in the contemporary law by reference to *Daly's*
f   case. It comes to its own recommendation on this topic at paras 3.87–3.93 (pp 56–58). Thus it reasons as follows:

> '3.88 In our Consultation Paper we criticised the decision in *Daly* for this inconsistency between past and future loss. Although the decision recognises that it was artificial to assume that past loss was always pecuniary in nature,
g   it applies that very artificiality to the assessment of future loss. We provisionally recommended that past and future loss should be treated consistently. That is, it should be compensated as a pecuniary loss to the claimant where he or she has paid or will pay for the work to be done, as a loss to the third party where that third party has carried out, and will carry out the work for free,
h   and as an element of non-pecuniary loss where the claimant has struggled on with the work regardless and will continue to do so.
>
> 3.89 Our consultees welcomed the suggestion that the law should be consistent as between past and future loss, and there was widespread agreement with the statement of the law we had proposed ...
>
j   3.90 Where the work is done by a third party, such as a friend or a member of the claimant's family, consultees were unanimous in accepting that damages should be recovered.'

While recognising that legislation would be necessary to alter the actual decision in *Hunt's* case that an injured person could not recover in respect of the *tortfeasor's* gratuitous care, and also somewhat to amend the trust concept adopted there, the Commission nevertheless said this (p 58):

'3.92 Should the recommendation in paragraph 3.91 be implemented by
legislation? It appears from the responses we have received that litigation on
these issues is rare, and that in practice the decision in *Daly* is often
distinguished so that past and future loss can be treated consistently.
Moreover, the impact of the House of Lords' approach in *Hunt v Severs* on
this area has not yet come before the courts. We therefore think it unlikely
that the courts would consider themselves bound by the approach in *Daly*.
In general, it follows that we consider that the common law can be expected
to reach the position set out in paragraph 3.91; and that legislation is, by and
large, unnecessary.'

For the reasons set out in this judgment above I had independently come to a
similar view.

[36] What then of Lord Goddard's famous dictum in *Best v Samuel Fox
& Co Ltd* [1952] 2 All ER 394, [1952] AC 716? I would not wish to suggest that it
does not have continued vibrancy today. But it has to be understood in its
context, and it is in any event clear that it has not prevented the development of
the English common law in its journey towards *Hunt's* case. The context of
course was a wife's attempt to sue in her own name in respect of her own loss
arising out of her husband's accident. That is what gave force to his statement,
in effect, that loss without legal injury, without breach of a duty of care owed to
the particular claimant, could not give rise to a liability or a separate right of
action. That is true; but it tells you little, at any rate from the hindsight of 2001,
about whether an injured person can claim as part of his loss the value of
gratuitous care given to him by his wife. Moreover, the analysis of *Hunt's* case,
that the loss is in truth that of the wife which the husband can claim in trust for
the wife, is all the more remarkable if Lord Goddard's dictum is thought of as
determinative throughout all such areas of quantum.

[37] And what of *Swain v London Ambulance Service NHS Trust* [1999] All ER (D)
260? Mr King did not submit that it was binding on this court. I think that is
correct, not so much, as he suggested, because it only concerned a claim for £140,
but because (as he also submitted) it is not possible to derive from the judgments
of that two-judge court a clear ratio. Potter LJ clearly thought that if the claim had
been pleaded differently, or perhaps I should say, if the facts had been different,
a different result would have been obtained ('My decision would be different if ...').
In such a case the absence of s 9 in England would not have prevented a result in
favour of Mr Swain. That suggests that what was critical about *Swain's* case was,
as explained by Potter LJ, that the car in question was not in any sense a family
car, but rather one that was not only owned by the wife (that was not regarded
as determinative) but used for her exclusive benefit and at her exclusive cost.

[38] The present case, however, is one where, as must at present be assumed
to be correct, the disabled brother is part of the household and one whose care
had, prior to the accident, been the appellant's prime responsibility. That care
was not a mere gratuitous favour bestowed on a third party, but was a
responsibility of his own, adopted by him and owed to his brother, but also to his
mother with whom he shared the household. When he lost the ability to care for
his brother for more than 35 hours per week, he lost something of real value to
himself (as well as to his brother) which was his contribution to his family's
welfare, and his loss imposed a corresponding obligation on his mother to make
good by her own care what he was no longer able to provide. In my judgment
the appellant is entitled to claim in respect of the loss of his ability to look after
his brother. Since he will maintain his state allowance, he has suffered no loss so

a far as that allowance is itself concerned. But he has suffered a loss nevertheless because, even though his care was provided gratuitously, it can and ought as a matter of policy to be measured in money's worth. To the extent that his mother has by her own additional care mitigated the appellant's loss, it may be that the appellant would hold that recovery in trust for his mother.

b [39] Were it otherwise, then as Mr Anderson has submitted, the loss of an injured person's ability to look after the family garden would be compensated, but the loss of his ability to look after his brother would not be (otherwise than as might be reflected in the award of general damages). That would bring no credit on the law. In my judgment the result which I favour would be within the logic and policy of the existing state of the English common law.

c [40] In these circumstances, what is to be said against such a result? That Parliament has willed it otherwise? I have suggested that that is a misreading of the situation: Parliament has left the common law in England to take its course. That the loss is unforeseeable and thus too remote, as Mr King has submitted? But a defendant must take the injured claimant as he finds him: and there is nothing unforeseeable about a claimant having family responsibilities. That the

d loss is the brother's loss and not the injured person's, as Mr King has also submitted? In my view the loss is that of the appellant, which was also the view of the Pearson Commission. That the availability of this head of damage opens the floodgates? But s 9 has operated in Scotland for nearly 20 years without, as Beldam LJ put it and as far as is known, attracting adverse comment.

e [41] Of course, the facts of the appellant's claim have yet to be investigated. I would for the present confine myself to the assumed facts of this case: where the care is to a relative (to which I would add, a spouse or partner) living as part of the same household and goes beyond the ordinary interaction of members of a household.

f [42] The solution which I have proposed in this judgment differs somewhat from the recommendation of the Law Commission in its 1999 report, where it suggests inter alia that there should be recovery (a) for past loss where the claimant has necessarily paid someone else to do the work; (b) for future loss where the claimant establishes that he will reasonably pay someone to do it; and (c) for past or future work gratuitously and reasonably rendered by a relative or friend (see pp 57–58 (para 3.91)). In the present case, where the allegation is that

g the mother has been providing the additional hours of care that Mr Lowe cannot now provide, that difference may not be significant. It may, however, be significant if the mother has ceased or will be likely to cease being able to provide that care. The question may then arise whether that care will have to be paid for; or will have to be provided in some other way, which may further mitigate the

h loss. Those questions, however, as it seems to me, are matters of the assessment of quantum which lie outside the issues before this court and have not been touched on in argument.

The second issue: loss of earnings

j [43] Mr Anderson submitted that although, if the accident had not occurred, the appellant would have continued to look after his brother and would not have earned an employed living, nevertheless, since his injuries had taken away *both* his ability to look after his brother (for more than 35 hours per week) *and* his capacity to earn a living, he should be compensated for the latter. The fact that he had chosen, for compelling moral reasons, not to exploit his earning capacity did not mean that he had not had the capacity to earn, nor that it was valueless. His injuries were now the sole cause of his unemployment. Unlike the man who

had chosen not to work because he was rich or idle and who would remain rich
or idle after his accident, the appellant had lost, and lost by reason of his accident,
the only reason which had kept him from earning.

[44] The judge said that this was an attractive argument, and that he would
have decided it in favour of the appellant 'if the facts had been that the claimant
could not at all in any circumstance now provide care for his brother'. As it was,
he was only prevented from performing the additional 42 hours of care per week,
he continued to earn the state allowance (save for the first two months following
the accident when he could do no work at all, a period for which he should be
entitled to claim special damage), and the fact that he would have continued to
devote those extra hours to his brother without further compensation if he had
not been injured could not be ignored. However, it would in due course be a
matter for the judge of the facts to determine whether the appellant might have
changed his mind at some stage of the future and 'decided to exploit his
undoubted earning capacity which he no longer has'.

[45] For my part, I would look at this issue somewhat differently. I do not
myself think that the fact that the appellant has not been totally incapacitated
from looking after his brother is critical. The issue has rather been formulated in
such a way (see [7], above) as to ask the court to sanction the conclusion that the
(stipulated) fact that, but for his injuries he would have continued to care for his
brother, is irrelevant. As Mr King submits, the trial court of fact should not be
fettered in this way, which would require an artificial approach carrying with it
the risk of over-compensation. That court should rather be entitled to consider
the issue of loss of earnings with the aid of such reference to the pre- and
post-accident realities as may be appropriate. At that trial it would be open to the
appellant to formulate his loss of earnings claim by reference to his own (and his
brother's) prospects. After all, the essential factual question is, what is necessary
to put the appellant in the same position, so far as money can do it, as he would
have been in but for the accident?

[46] In my judgment therefore the answer to the second issue is simply 'No'.
But the trial judge can take all appropriate matters into account.

[47] Having said that, I would merely comment that it seems to me that what
the judge viewed as attractive and very nearly compelling in the appellant's
argument on this second issue is in truth the underlying force of the fact that a
person in his position has suffered a real loss when he is forced by his injuries to
give up the value of work which he has previously donated to his brother's care,
work which although carrying no income because gratuitously given nevertheless
in principle has and as a matter of policy should have a real value attached to it.
The common law should not, and need not, leave the question 'am I my brother's
keeper?' with the wrong answer.

MORLAND J.

[48] I agree on both issues.

POTTER LJ.

[49] I also agree and have nothing to add in respect of the second issue. In
relation to the first issue, I am grateful to Rix LJ for his careful exposition of the
law and his illuminating approach to the question raised, with which I also agree,
subject to a reservation in respect of the claimant's pre-trial loss. I also wish to
add a few observations of my own, not least because I was a member of the court
in the case of *Swain v London Ambulance Service NHS Trust* [1999] All ER (D) 260,

a   by reason of which decision Judge MacDuff QC felt himself bound (with regret) to reach the conclusion which he did.

[50] Upon reconsideration of what I said in that case, I do not think that the judge was so bound in respect of the instant claim which, framed as it is, raises the question of the right of an injured person to recover in respect of his consequent inability to perform 'carer' services which prior to the accident were rendered by *b*   him gratuitously to a member of his family, but which he was subsequently unable to render, those services being taken over gratuitously by another member of the family. In *Swain*'s case, I put my decision upon the narrow ground that in that case the claim had been argued and decided on the basis that, in valeting his wife's car, the claimant was performing a gratuitous service for his wife in respect of her own property used exclusively for her own benefit, rather than performing *c*   a task which benefited a household in which the expenses and domestic tasks were shared out and performed for the benefit of the family as a whole. I stated in conclusion:

> 'In my view, where the post-accident expense may properly be regarded as
> *d*   a household or family expense incurred by a plaintiff spouse in discharging a
> function which he or she previously performed gratuitously for the benefit
> of the household at large, then it is recoverable.'

[51] That seems to me to be wholly in accord with the decision in *Daly v General Steam Navigation Co Ltd* [1980] 3 All ER 696, [1981] 1 WLR 120, already *e*   referred to by Rix LJ, in which the court upheld the decision of Brandon J ([1979] 1 Lloyd's Rep 257), by which he awarded to a claimant wife damages for deprivation of housekeeping capacity. In a passage (at 265), Brandon J set out the principles in a manner subsequently approved by the Court of Appeal:

> 'I have considered first whether it is right to treat the plaintiff's partial loss
> *f*   of housekeeping capacity as a separate head of damage, or whether it should
> be regarded only as one element in the loss of the amenities of life for which
> general damages have to be awarded. Having considered the matter, I have
> reached the conclusion that this disability should be treated as a separate
> head of damage. When a person in paid employment suffers a total or partial
> loss of earnings by reason of disability, such loss is invariably treated as a
> *g*   separate head of damage, with separate assessments of past and future loss.
> Where the person concerned is a housewife, who is disabled wholly or partly
> from doing housekeeping in her own home, she does not suffer an actual loss
> of earnings, and unless a substitute is employed, she may not suffer any
> pecuniary loss at all. Nevertheless, she is just as much disabled from doing
> *h*   her unpaid job as an employed person is disabled from doing his paid one,
> and I think that she is, in principle, entitled to be compensated separately for
> her loss in a similar way.'

[52] The decision in *Daly*'s case duly established that in an appropriate case loss of the claimant's ability to do unpaid work in the home for the benefit of the *j*   family is a recoverable head of damage. It seems to me that the principle recognised is applicable to cover the position not only of a spouse, but also of a member of the family, such as the claimant in this case, who acknowledges and undertakes the obligation to carry out household and other tasks for the general benefit of the family of which he or she is a member and without which, following his or her disablement, it is necessary to obtain a substitute, whether that substitute is someone who is remunerated for such services or is another

member of the family who has not previously performed the relevant tasks but
gratuitously agrees to take them on, over and above the previous arrangements
reasonably adopted by the family. If the task in question is the care of a disabled
member of the family rather than some more humdrum family activity, it is not
thereby removed from the category of recoverability on the grounds (as the
judge put it) that the gratuitous services were for the benefit of the brother alone;
nor is there any reason in logic or humanity why that should be so.

[53] Within that head of damage, where the services have been supplied
gratuitously and are thereafter performed by another, also gratuitously, a
subsidiary problem arises as to the basis upon which the loss or value of the
services is to be assessed. In particular, if the court adopts the yardstick of a
reasonable rate of remuneration for the hours worked, does such yardstick fall to
be applied both to special damage (ie pre-trial loss) and future loss? In *Daly's* case
at first instance, Brandon J adopted a consistent approach as between the two,
treating the award of special damages as a simple matter of calculation based on
the appropriate notional cost of supplying the services and, similarly in respect of
future loss, by use of an appropriate multiplier applied to a multiplicand based on
the cost of providing the housekeeping services which the claimant would in
future be unable to perform, regardless of whether an outsider would in fact have
been employed to provide those services. Brandon J's method in respect of future
costs was approved by the Court of Appeal. The court (while acknowledging the
lack of logic involved) took the view that the figure for special (ie pre-trial)
damages had to be assessed on the basis of actual rather than notional loss, being
limited to the amount actually expended on substitute services, any part-time
earnings lost by the claimant's husband in looking after her, and an augmented
sum by way of general damages for pain, suffering and loss of amenity up to trial.

[54] In its report *Damages for Personal Injury; Medical Nursing and Other Expenses;
Collateral Benefits* (1999) (Law Com no 262), already quoted by Rix LJ, the Law
Commission recommended (inter alia) (p 58 (para 3.91)) that where a claimant
has suffered loss of, or reduction in, his or her ability to do work in the home—

> '(1) this should be compensated as past pecuniary loss where the claimant
> has reasonably paid someone to do the work, and as a future pecuniary loss
> where the claimant establishes that he or she will reasonably pay somebody
> to do it.
> (2) ... the claimant should also be able to recover damages for the cost of
> the work where the work has been or will reasonably be done gratuitously
> by a relative or friend ... and should be under a personal liability to account
> for the damages awarded in respect of *past* work, to the person ... who
> performed the work; but no legal obligation should be imposed in respect of
> damages awarded for work to be done in the *future*.'

[55] The Law Commission considered that legislation would be necessary to
reverse *Hunt v Severs* [1994] 2 All ER 385, [1994] 2 AC 350 in so far as it held that
no damages can be recovered where the person who has gratuitously carried out
domestic work is the active tortfeasor; also to modify the trust concept endorsed
in *Hunt's* case. However, the Commission expressed the view that the common
law could otherwise be expected to develop so as to reach the position recommended
by the Law Commission. I agree that it should so develop and that this case
represents a welcome opportunity to push it in that direction.

[56] In *Swain v London Ambulance Service NHS Trust* [1999] All ER (D) 260,
I expressed the view that it was inexplicable that Parliament had 'refused' to

a import into English law the recommendations of the Pearson Commission (*Royal Commission on Civil Liability and Compensation for Personal Injury* (Cmnd 7054-I (1978)); ch 12). As suggested by Rix LJ, it seems to me that I put the matter too strongly and that the failure of parliament in that respect does not constitute a barrier to a decision of the court in this case by way of expansion of the decision in *Daly v General Steam Navigation Co Ltd* [1980] 3 All ER 696, [1981] 1 WLR 120.

b I agree with Rix LJ that *Daly's* case, having been decided a year before the Administration of Justice Act 1982 was passed, may well have been regarded by parliament as marking a development which rendered less pressing the need for any specific provision in English law along the lines provided by s 9 of the Act in respect of Scottish law.

[57] Thus, I would give an affirmative answer to the first of the issues before
c the judge. At the same time, because this court is bound by its previous decision in *Daly's* case, I feel unable to follow so far as I would like in the direction in which logic and my own inclination would otherwise lead. It is therefore my reluctant conclusion that the judge who eventually has the task of assessing the claimant's damage in respect of any impaired ability to perform carer services for his brother
d will be obliged to assess the special damages and the future loss on the differing bases prescribed in respect of each by the Court of Appeal in that case.

[58] I would add one final note of reservation. The issues as drafted raised questions of broad principle for the consideration of the court on a factual basis which is assumed but not admitted. The underlying facts of the case are still wholly at large and will require careful examination in the course of the
e assessment of damages in the light of the various factual challenges briefly set out in the respondent's skeleton argument but not explored before us.

Appeal allowed in part.

Kate O'Hanlon   Barrister.

Re N T Gallagher & Son Ltd (in liquidation)
Shierson and another v Tomlinson and another

[2002] EWCA Civ 404

COURT OF APPEAL, CIVIL DIVISION
PETER GIBSON, WARD AND DYSON LJJ
17 JANUARY, 26 MARCH 2002

Insolvency – Voluntary arrangement – Company – Whether liquidation terminating trusts created by voluntary arrangement – Insolvency Act 1986, Pt I.

A company brought proceedings against its principal customer for the recovery of sums allegedly due under a contract. Subsequently, the company entered into a voluntary arrangement (CVA) with its creditors under Pt I of the Insolvency Act 1986. Under the terms of the CVA, the company retained the book debts to enable it to continue to trade and to offer the best chance of recovery of the customer debt 'for the benefit' of unsecured creditors. In return, the company agreed to make certain payments to the supervisors of the CVA 'for the benefit' of creditors. There was no provision for what was to happen to any trust created by the CVA in the event of the company going into liquidation. The company eventually did go into liquidation. At the commencement of the liquidation, the supervisors retained a substantial sum from the payments made by the company under the CVA. The company's assets included the claim against the customer, which was yet to be resolved. On an application by the liquidators for directions, the judge declared that both the sum retained by the supervisors and the cause of action against the customer were held on trust for the sole benefit of the CVA creditors, and were not therefore available for distribution to the general body of creditors, including post-CVA creditors. In the final part of his order, the judge further declared that the CVA creditors were only entitled to prove in the liquidation for the unpaid balance of their claims if they agreed to abandon their rights in relation to the cause of action against the customer. The liquidators appealed, contending that the sums retained by the supervisors were held on trust to implement the terms of the CVA as a whole; that the proceeds of the cause of action against the customer could only become subject to a trust when they were received; and that any trust created by the CVA had been brought to an end by the liquidation in the absence of any term to the contrary in the CVA. Both the liquidators and the supervisors challenged the final part of the judge's order.

Held – Where a CVA provided for moneys or other assets to be paid to or transferred or held for the benefit of CVA creditors, a trust would be created of those moneys or assets for the benefit of those creditors, and that trust would not be brought to an end by the liquidation of the company unless there was a provision in the CVA to the contrary. If the CVA specified what was to happen on liquidation, effect had to be given to it. If, however, the CVA did not so provide, the trust would continue notwithstanding the liquidation, and had to take effect according to its terms. Such a default rule furthered the purpose of Pt I of the 1986 Act, namely to encourage companies and creditors to enter into CVAs in order to provide creditors with a means of recovering what they were owed without recourse to the more expensive means provided by winding up or administration, thereby giving many companies the opportunity to continue to a   trade. Moreover, CVA creditors could prove in the liquidation for so much of their debt as remained after payment of what had been or would be recovered under the trust. It followed in the instant case that the judge had been correct except in relation to the final part of his order. In substitution for that part of the order, the court would declare that the CVA creditors were entitled to prove in the liquidation for their CVA debts after giving credit for dividends received from

b   the supervisors. Save to that extent, the appeal would be dismissed (see [28], [30], [48], [50], [51], [53]–[55], below).

Notes
For company voluntary arrangements in general, see 7(3) *Halsbury's Laws* (4th edn reissue) para 2044.

c   For the Insolvency Act 1986, Pt I, see 4 *Halsbury's Statutes* (4th edn) (1998 reissue) 736.

Cases referred to in judgment
Arthur Rathbone Kitchens Ltd, Re [1997] 2 BCLC 280.

d   *Barclays Bank Ltd v Quistclose Investments Ltd* [1968] 3 All ER 651, [1970] AC 567, [1968] 3 WLR 1097, HL.
Bradley-Hole (a bankrupt), Re [1995] 4 All ER 865, [1995] 1 WLR 1097.
Davis v Martin-Sklan [1995] 2 BCLC 483.
Excalibur Airways Ltd (in liq), Re [1998] 1 BCLC 436.
Halson Packaging Ltd, Re [1997] BCC 993.

e   *Kings v Cleghorn* [1998] BPIR 463.
Kudos Glass Ltd (in liq), Re [2001] 1 BCLC 390.
Leisure Study Group Ltd, Re [1994] 2 BCLC 65.
Maple Environmental Services Ltd, Re [2000] BCC 93.
McKeen (a debtor), Re [1995] BCC 412.

f   *Welsby v Brelec Installations Ltd (in liq)* [2000] 2 BCLC 576.

Case also cited or referred to in skeleton arguments
Glegg v Bromley [1912] 3 KB 474, [1911–13] All ER Rep 1138, CA.

g   **Appeal**
The appellants, Malcolm Shierson and Michael Horrocks, the joint liquidators of N T Gallagher & Son Ltd (in liquidation), appealed with permission of Judge Howarth from his decision on 13 June 2001 ([2002] 1 BCLC 224) whereby he declared, inter alia, that sums retained by the respondents, Alan Howard Tomlinson and Michael Horrocks, in their capacity as joint supervisors of a

h   voluntary arrangement (CVA) into which the company had entered prior to its liquidation, were held on trust for the sole benefit of the CVA creditors; that the benefit of a cause of action against Mercury Communications Ltd and the benefit of any sums that might be recovered from it were similarly held on trust for the sole benefit of the CVA creditors; and that the CVA creditors were entitled to

j   prove in the liquidation in relation to the unpaid balance of their claims only if they agreed to abandon their rights in relation to the cause of action and any sums recovered pursuant to it. The facts are set out in the judgment of the court.

Antony Zacaroli (instructed by *DLA*, Manchester) for the liquidators.
Martin Pascoe (instructed by *NJ Goodman & Co*, Altrincham) for the supervisors.

Cur adv vult

26 March 2002. The following judgment of the court was delivered.

a

PETER GIBSON LJ.

[1] This appeal gives rise to the question whether trusts which are created by
a voluntary arrangement in respect of a company (CVA) are brought to an end
by the termination of the CVA through the company going into liquidation.
There have been a number of decisions of the High Court on this and the like
question in respect of an individual voluntary arrangement (IVA) brought to an
end by a bankruptcy order being made. Not all the decisions are consistent with
each other. This is the first occasion on which this question has come before this
court for determination.

b

The statutory provisions

[2] The Insolvency Act 1986 introduced new provisions designed to make it
simpler for companies and individuals in financial difficulties to enter into
arrangements with their creditors which would be binding on dissentient
creditors if a sufficient majority approved the proposed arrangement. By the
Insolvency Act 2000, amendments have been made to those provisions but they
have yet to come into force.

c

d

[3] The applicable provisions for CVAs are contained in Pt I of the 1986 Act.
By s 1, a CVA may be proposed to the company and its creditors by the directors
of the company, not being one for which an administration order is in force or
which is being wound up. The Act also contemplates that a CVA may be
proposed by the administrator of a company for which an administration order is
in force or by the liquidator of a company which is being wound up. In each case
the proposal must be one for a composition in satisfaction of the company's debts
or a scheme of arrangement of its affairs, and it must provide for some qualified
insolvency practitioner, called 'the nominee', to act in relation to the CVA, either
as trustee or for the purpose of supervising its implementation.

e

f

[4] Sections 2, 3 and 4 set out the procedures to be followed when the directors
make a proposal: the nominee submits to the court a report stating whether
meetings of the company should be summoned to consider the proposal, and,
unless the court otherwise directs, the nominee summons those meetings; the
meetings decide whether to approve the CVA with or without modifications. By
s 5(2) the approved CVA binds every person who, in accordance with the
Insolvency Rules 1986, SI 1985/1925, had notice of, and was entitled to vote at,
the meeting whether or not he was present or represented at the meeting, as if he
were a party to the CVA. Thus the CVA, if approved, operates as a form of
statutory contract to which even dissentients and non-voters receiving notice of
and entitled to vote at the meeting are treated as parties. Section 6 provides for
challenges to the CVA to be made through applications to the court. Where a
CVA has taken effect, the person who carries out the functions conferred as the
nominee is known as the supervisor (s 7(2)). Any creditor or other person
dissatisfied with any act or omission of the supervisor may apply to the court
which may give the supervisor directions (s 7(3)). The supervisor may himself
apply to the court for directions and is included among the persons who may apply
for a winding-up or administration order (s 7(4)).

g

h

j

[5] Part I of the 1986 rules applies to CVAs. By r 1.3(1) the directors are
required to include in their proposal a short explanation why in their opinion a
CVA is desirable and give reasons why the company's creditors may be expected
to concur with the CVA. Rule 1.3(2) prescribes what must be contained in the

a directors' proposal. It must include a statement of the company's assets and the extent to which particular assets are to be excluded from the CVA (para (a)), a statement of the company's liabilities and the manner in which they are to be dealt with by the CVA (para (c)), the proposed duration of the CVA (para (e)), the manner in which funds held for the purposes of the CVA are to be banked, invested or otherwise dealt with pending distribution to creditors (para (k)), and

b the manner in which funds held for the purpose of payment to creditors, and not so paid on the termination of the arrangement, are to be dealt with (para (l)). Rule 1.19(1) provides that for any resolution to pass at the creditors' meeting approving any proposal or modification there must be a majority in excess of three-quarters in value of the creditors present in person or by proxy and voting on the resolution.

c [6] By r 4.21A (introduced by way of the Insolvency (Amendment) Rules 1987, SI 1987/1919):

'Where a winding-up order is made and there is at the time of the presentation of the petition in force for the company a voluntary arrangement under Part I of the Act, any expenses properly incurred as expenses of the

d administration of the arrangement in question shall be a first charge on the company's assets.'

It is to be noted that r 4.21A only applies to compulsory liquidations. There is no corresponding provision for a voluntary liquidation.

[7] The provisions for IVAs are contained in Pt VIII of the 1986 Act. They

e differ from the provisions for CVAs in some respects, but there is much similarity, mutatis mutandis, between the IVA provisions and the CVA provisions in the respects to which we have drawn attention. By s 264(1)(c) the supervisor or any other person bound by the IVA is empowered to present a petition for bankruptcy. Section 276(2) provides:

f 'Where a bankruptcy order is made on a petition under section 264(1)(c), any expenses properly incurred as expenses of the administration of the voluntary arrangement in question shall be a first charge on the bankrupt's estate.'

g As with r 4.21A, the limits on the applicability of this provision are to be noted. It does not apply where bankruptcy is the consequence of a petition under any paragraph of s 264(1) other than (c).

[8] Part 5 of the 1986 rules applies to IVAs. Rule 5.3 provides what should be contained in the debtor's proposal for an IVA in terms similar to the provisions in r 1.3 for CVAs. Rule 5.18(1) is in terms similar to r 1.19(1).

h [9] Unless inferences drawn from r 4.21A in relation to CVAs and from s 276(2) in relation to IVAs provide the answer to the question stated in [1], above, it is not in dispute that the statutory provisions do not state the effect of a liquidation or a bankruptcy order on trusts created by a CVA or IVA respectively.

j *The facts*

[10] The appellants, Malcolm Shierson and Michael Horrocks, are the liquidators of N T Gallagher & Son Ltd (Gallagher). Gallagher was incorporated on 26 October 1990. It was engaged in civil engineering works and cabling contracts. Its principal customer was Mercury Communications Ltd (Mercury) with whom Gallagher had a cabling contract. In March 1995 Mercury alleged that Gallagher had repudiated that contract. Gallagher promptly commenced proceedings

against Mercury, claiming £2,340,000 for sums due under the contract and damages for breach of contract. Mercury ceased to make payments to Gallagher which in consequence came under increasing financial pressure. The directors of Gallagher put forward a proposal for a CVA.

[11] In the introduction to the proposal the directors said:

'We feel that a Voluntary Arrangement would be of benefit to the creditors of the Company because they would have a much better prospect of being paid their debts under a Voluntary Arrangement rather than if the Company went into Liquidation, Administration or Administrative Receivership. The reasons for this are as follows: (i) We believe the appointment of an Administrative Receiver, Liquidator or Administrator would have a detrimental effect on the collectability of the Company's book debts. (ii) A Voluntary Arrangement would permit the Company to continue to trade and prosecute its claim against [Mercury]. (iii) A Voluntary Arrangement would enable the Company to continue as a going concern and to provide suppliers with the opportunity to conduct further business with the Company in the future and to preserve the employment of some 340 people in the business.'

[12] In paras 4.11 and 12 of the proposal the directors said that the amount the creditors would receive would depend on the success of the litigation against Mercury, and the directors believed that there was a greater likelihood of success if the company continued to trade; it was therefore proposed that the company continued to trade, agreeing credit terms with suppliers where possible and continuing to pay its employees and direct labour sub-contractors in the usual way and on the due dates. In para 4.13 it was stated that the cash flow forecast indicated that the company would be able to fund its short-term trading from its own resources.

[13] The details of the proposal included the following:

'11. (a) It is proposed that all the assets of the Company are to be included in the Voluntary Arrangement, and, with the exception of stock are to be retained by the Company for the purpose of the fulfilment of the Arrangement. (b) The Company's bank overdraft is being reduced as are credit lines from suppliers. In order for the Company to be able to continue to trade and to offer the best chance of recovery of the Mercury debt for the benefit of unsecured creditors it is proposed that the Company retain the book debts to provide working capital.

12. In consideration of clause 11(b), the Company shall make payments to the Supervisor of £15,000 per month for the first year and £35,000 per month the second year, for the benefit of creditors. If the Supervisor in his absolute discretion shall be of the opinion that the Company can afford to make a greater contribution in any one month having regard to its financial position, it will pay such additional sum as may be required by the Supervisor.

13. The Company will continue to trade and that ongoing trade will be carried on by the Directors with the Company's financial performance being monitored by the Supervisor on whatever basis he considers most appropriate but to include the submission to him no less frequently than quarterly [of] management accounts and revised forecasts.

14. It is proposed that litigation will continue to be pursued, if necessary, against Mercury to obtain payment of the monies due, for the benefit of

a creditors. Monies recovered from this source will be remitted direct to the Supervisor. All funds accumulated by the Supervisor shall be applied by him in the following order of priority: a) settlement of the cost of the arrangement; b) distribution to the creditors of the arrangement in the statutory order of priority; c) payment of interest on creditors' claims at the rate of 8% per annum; d) any surplus will be returned to the Company.

b   15. The Company will continue to incur credit in the ordinary course of its trading as illustrated in the cash flow projections. However it is proposed that all credit incurred and liabilities accrued shall be paid in full out of trading receipts.'

[14] By para 19 it was proposed that the duration of the CVA be two years.
c But by modification 1, being one of 11 modifications suggested by the Customs and Excise Commissioners as creditors and approved by the creditors' meeting, the duration was altered so that, in effect, the CVA would end on the settlement of the claim against Mercury.

[15] By para 22, preferential creditors were to be paid in full as soon as the
d supervisor was in a position to pay; all the remaining unsecured liabilities were to be dealt with by dividend payments to be made at the supervisor's discretion.

[16] Paragraph 29 provided that funds held for the purpose of the CVA should be banked by the supervisor in an account of his choice and that any funds held by him 'pending distribution to creditors may be placed on deposit or invested in recognised securities for the benefit of the creditors'.

e [17] Paragraphs 30–32 dealt with the payment to the nominee and the supervisor of fees and remuneration and the discharge of disbursements. By para 34, the supervisor was to have powers similar to those of a liquidator, including the power to bring or defend any legal proceedings in Gallagher's name and on its behalf. Paragraph 35 provided for the appointment of a creditors'
f committee to assist the supervisor.

[18] Paragraph 37 required the submission of all outstanding VAT returns and the settlement of PAYE/NIC liabilities within 30 days of the approval of the CVA, and it provided that any failure thereafter to submit returns and make payments of VAT as and when due should be a breach of the CVA, and that the supervisor should, at his discretion, petition for the winding up of Gallagher. Further, by
g para 39:

'In the event that any of the terms of the Proposal are not complied with, the Supervisor shall petition for the winding up of the company unless the Committee or if none, a meeting of creditors, shall approve his alternative proposals. The Supervisor shall at all times during the Voluntary Arrangement
h maintain sufficient funds to obtain a winding up order against the company.'

However, modification 9 provided:

'The Joint Supervisors shall petition for the winding up of the company immediately it fails in any of its obligations under the arrangement, the
j Supervisors to retain sufficient funds at all times to do so.'

[19] There are three other modifications to which we should refer. Modification 5 conferred on the joint supervisors, in conjunction with the committee, the sole power to approve any settlement of the Mercury litigation. Modification 6 provided that if the contributions to be made by Gallagher to the joint supervisors fell 60 days in arrears or below the specified level, the arrangement would be

deemed to have failed. Modification 10 provided that the joint supervisors were
to be the respondents, Alan Tomlinson and Michael Horrocks. They are licensed
insolvency practitioners.

[20] The directors' proposal, as modified by the modifications, was duly
approved at the creditors' meeting on 21 April 1995. Gallagher continued to
trade, but the claim against Mercury, although referred to arbitration, remains
unresolved. Gallagher made the required contributions for a number of months,
but by March 1997 it fell into arrears by more than 60 days so that the CVA under
modification 6 was deemed to have failed. However, the supervisors, with the
consent of the creditors' committee, allowed the CVA to continue on condition
that the company complied with a revised contribution arrangement. The view
was taken that the supervisors had a discretion whether to petition for the
winding up of Gallagher despite the failure to comply with the obligation to make
the contributions specified in para 12. The dubious correctness of that view is not
an issue in these proceedings. By September 1997, Gallagher's financial position
had grown worse. In September or October 1997 increasing pressure was placed
on Gallagher by the Crown in respect of the post-CVA tax liabilities of the
company. The directors informed the supervisors that Gallagher could only meet
its ongoing commitments if they returned to Gallagher contributions already
paid to them pursuant to the CVA.

[21] The supervisors refused to return any contributions. They, with the
directors, considered that the only options available were either that the supervisors
should petition for the winding up of Gallagher or that the directors should put
Gallagher into voluntary liquidation. The directors chose the latter because this
would result in the speedier appointment of a liquidator and because it would be
less expensive.

[22] Gallagher went into creditors' voluntary liquidation on 20 November
1997. At the date of the commencement of the liquidation: (1) the sum retained
by the supervisors from contributions made by Gallagher pursuant to the CVA
was in excess of £500,000: by 20 November 2000 that sum plus interest amounted
to £571,141·87; (2) Gallagher's post-CVA liabilities were estimated at £2,525,649;
(3) Gallagher's total liabilities were estimated at £5,066,890; (4) the assets of
Gallagher (leaving out of account the funds retained by the supervisors) were
(i) the claim against Mercury, (ii) a claim against another company, Nynex,
estimated to realise approximately £350,000, and (iii) approximately £98,000 of
other realisable assets.

The proceedings

[23] The liquidators issued an originating application, to which the supervisors
were made respondents and by which the liquidators sought a direction whether
each or any of (1) the sum of £571,141·87 retained by the supervisors, (2) the
benefit of the cause of action against Mercury and of any sums recovered
pursuant thereto, and (3) the remaining assets of Gallagher is (a) held on trust for
the sole benefit of the creditors bound by the CVA, or (b) available for the
purposes of the liquidation including (in so far as there are sufficient assets)
distribution among all the creditors of Gallagher (including creditors bound by
the CVA and post-CVA creditors) in accordance with the statutory scheme
applicable to the winding up of Gallagher.

[24] The proceedings came before Judge Howarth, sitting as a judge of the High
Court, whose judgment is now reported ([2002] 1 BCLC 224). The judge
considered first what assets were held in trust for the CVA creditors under the

a CVA before the commencement of the winding up. He decided that Gallagher held the claim against Mercury as a trustee for the CVA creditors and that the supervisors held the funds which they retained in trust for the CVA creditors, but that no other assets of Gallagher were so held. He considered secondly whether the trusts had come to an end on Gallagher's liquidation. He decided that question by reference to the authorities on CVAs and IVAs and preferred what he b called the majority view that the liquidation did not bring the trusts to an end. The judge considered thirdly the position of CVA creditors proving in the winding up. He analysed the rights of such creditors as analogous to the rights of a secured creditor who is entitled to prove if he abandons his security. He held that the CVA creditors would not be entitled to prove in the winding up unless they gave up their security in respect of the cause of action against Mercury. He c therefore declared (at 247–248) that the sum held by the supervisors and the benefit of the cause of action against Mercury and the benefit of any sums which may be recovered therefrom were held on trust for the sole benefit of the CVA creditors but that the remaining assets of Gallagher were available for the purpose of the liquidation for distribution among the creditors of Gallagher, and, d in accordance with whether or not the CVA creditors chose to surrender their rights in respect of the Mercury claim, they would or would not be able to prove in the liquidation for the balance of any claim.

[25] The appeal by the liquidators to this court is brought with the leave of the judge. We have been greatly assisted by the skilful arguments of Mr Zacaroli for e the liquidators and of Mr Pascoe for the supervisors on the questions considered by the judge.

What assets were held on trust?

[26] Mr Zacaroli points out that there is nothing in the CVA which expressly f creates a trust over any assets of Gallagher, but he accepts that the funds received by the supervisors pursuant to the CVA and held by them immediately before the liquidation were held on trust. However he submits that the relevant trust was to implement the terms of the CVA. In making that submission, he draws attention to the priority given by para 14 to the settlement of the cost of the CVA and to para 15 with its proposal for the payment in full of all credit incurred by g Gallagher in the ordinary course of its continued trading and of all accrued liabilities. He argues that such payment comes within 'the cost of the arrangement' to be paid in priority out of the moneys accumulated by the supervisors. Mr Zacaroli also points to the provisions of s 7 of the 1986 Act by which the court is empowered to give directions to the supervisors and he says that it would have h been open to the court to order the supervisors to return the contributions so that Gallagher could pay in full the liabilities accruing from its continued trading. Mr Zacaroli further submits that no assets other than the funds in the supervisors' hands were held in trust at the commencement of the liquidation, the proceeds of the litigation against Mercury only becoming subject to a trust if and when j they were received.

[27] Mr Pascoe submits that the judge was right to hold that not only the moneys in the supervisors' hands but also the benefit of the cause of action against Mercury were held at the commencement of the litigation upon trust for the benefit of the CVA creditors. Mr Pascoe does not seek to contend in this court, although he had argued below, that other assets of the company were held in trust.

[28] Section 1(2) of the 1986 Act contemplates that the nominee, who on the approval of the directors' proposal becomes the supervisor, may under the proposal act as trustee. What assets of the company are to be held on trust by the supervisor or the company must depend on the terms of the CVA. Paragraph 12 requires the payment by Gallagher of monthly sums to the supervisors 'for the benefit of creditors'. Paragraph 14 requires the supervisors to apply all funds accumulated by them, after settlement of the cost of the CVA, in distributing the moneys to the CVA creditors. The phrase 'the cost of the arrangement' in para 14 naturally covers items such as the fees and remuneration payable to the nominee and the supervisors and expenditure by and on behalf of the supervisors. It is not apt to cover what was proposed in the CVA to be paid by Gallagher out of trading receipts received by Gallagher from its continued trading. Paragraph 29 also supports the proposition that what the supervisors held, whether in a bank account or invested, was held for the benefit of the CVA creditors. There is no doubt that the court, on an application to it under s 7(3) or (4) of the Act, can give the supervisors directions. But it does not follow that the court could give a direction inconsistent with the terms on which the supervisors are required by para 14 to apply moneys in their hands. The court has no power to modify the CVA. Paragraph 14 only contemplates a return to Gallagher of any surplus after payment of the cost of the CVA and after paying off the CVA creditors with interest. In our judgment, therefore, neither the terms of the CVA nor s 7(3) and (4) support the liquidators' submission that the funds in the hands of the supervisors were held for the purpose of implementing the CVA as a whole. On the contrary. The CVA operated as an accord and satisfaction between Gallagher and the CVA creditors who gave up their rights to enforce their debts against Gallagher, including their right to seek the compulsory liquidation of Gallagher so that its assets were distributed to the CVA creditors in accordance with the statutory regime for liquidations. In return Gallagher was to pay the monthly contributions to the supervisors to be applied in accordance with para 14; in addition, any moneys recovered from the litigation against Mercury were to be treated in the same way as Gallagher's contributions. Gallagher was thereby enabled to continue to trade lawfully.

[29] Although the CVA does not expressly use the language of trusts, Mr Zacaroli was, in our view, plainly right to concede that the supervisors were trustees of the assets in their hands. In *Re Leisure Study Group Ltd* [1994] 2 BCLC 65 Harman J similarly held that a supervisor receiving contributions for distribution to the creditors of the company pursuant to a CVA was a trustee of those moneys for the CVA creditors.

[30] The fact that the supervisors have as yet received no moneys from the Mercury claim does not answer the question whether the benefit of the cause of action against Mercury was held by Gallagher as trustee. In our judgment that question must be answered in the affirmative in the light of the terms of the CVA. In para 11(b) reference is made to the 'recovery of the Mercury debt for the benefit of unsecured creditors' and para 14 provides for the entire proceeds of the litigation to be applied, subject to the settlement of the cost of the CVA, in distribution to the CVA creditors to the extent of their debts. Further by para 34.4, the supervisors could bring proceedings in the name and on behalf of Gallagher, and so could take over the conduct of the Mercury litigation. By modification 5, any settlement of that litigation required the approval of the supervisors in conjunction with the creditors' committee. In our opinion the judge was right to say that it seemed clear that Gallagher held the claim against

a Mercury as trustee for the benefit of the CVA creditors (see [2002] 1 BCLC 224 at 233).

Did the trust survive the liquidation?

[31] Before we turn to the rival arguments, it is convenient to refer to the authorities which deal with this and the like question arising in respect of IVAs.

b [32] In *Re McKeen (a debtor)* [1995] BCC 412 a post-IVA creditor obtained a bankruptcy order. The debtor applied to the court for the annulment of the order under s 282(1)(b) of the 1986 Act. This allows the court to annul the order if it appears that 'the bankruptcy debts' and expenses have been paid or secured to the satisfaction of the court. It was not argued that the IVA created a trust in favour of the IVA creditors. *Re Leisure Study Group* had not yet been decided. But c Morritt J held that the IVA was not terminated by the making of the bankruptcy order and that the debts of the IVA creditors were not 'bankruptcy debts' to which the debtor was subject. Accordingly the annulment was allowed.

[33] In *Re Bradley-Hole (a bankrupt)* [1995] 4 All ER 865, [1995] 1 WLR 1097 a post-IVA creditor obtained a bankruptcy order against the debtor. The supervisor d applied to the court for directions as to whether the bankruptcy order brought the IVA to an end. Rimer J held, applying *Re Leisure Study Group*, that the IVA created a trust of the bankrupt's assets for the benefit of the IVA creditors, that the bankruptcy order did not terminate the IVA, that the bankrupt retained no interest in the assets subject to the IVA, that those assets did not vest in the trustee e and that the trust continued notwithstanding the bankruptcy. An argument based on s 276(2) of the 1986 Act that the trust ended on the making of the bankruptcy order was not accepted.

[34] In *Davis v Martin-Sklan* [1995] 2 BCLC 483 Blackburne J considered whether trusts created by an IVA terminated on the making of a bankruptcy order on a petition under s 264(1)(c) by the supervisor. He held that the supervisor was f acting on behalf of the IVA creditors and that the trusts did terminate on the bankruptcy order. He found support in s 276(2) on the basis that Parliament appears to have assumed that the assets subject to an IVA become part of the debtor's estate.

[35] In *Re Halson Packaging Ltd* [1997] BCC 993 the facts were similar to those g of the present case. A CVA was approved by creditors on terms that the company would continue to trade, making contributions to the supervisors which would be held in trust to be applied in accordance with the CVA. This provided that after the payment of costs and of preferential debts there would be a dividend for unsecured creditors. The CVA failed and the company went into a creditors' voluntary liquidation. The question was whether the funds in the supervisors' h hand should be paid to the liquidator and distributed to the creditors. Judge Maddocks, sitting as a High Court judge, held that a valid trust had been created by the CVA and that trust had not failed nor was it revoked by the terms of the CVA nor by the winding up of the company. He distinguished *Davis'* case on its facts. He rejected an argument based on r 4.21A (incorrectly referred to as j r 4.2.1(a)), saying (at 997):

'I do not find any real assistance from that rule, which was no doubt added by the amendment rules to protect a supervisor who had not been able to collect sufficient funds for his expenses, a situation which could easily occur in a compulsory winding up, but would be unlikely to arise, or certainly less likely to arise on a voluntary liquidation.'

[36] In *Re Arthur Rathbone Kitchens Ltd* [1997] 2 BCLC 280 a CVA, under which the company was to continue trading and was to pay moneys for distribution to the CVA creditors, failed and the company went into a creditors' voluntary liquidation. The supervisor petitioned for a compulsory winding-up order. Mr Roger Kaye QC, sitting as a deputy High Court judge, made the order. He held that the implication of r 4.21A was that the assets held on trust under the CVA would no longer be held under the control of the supervisor but of the liquidator and that the CVA creditors were discharged from the CVA by the making of the order and would have to prove for their debts after giving credit for sums received under the CVA. But he expressed the view that had there been no compulsory winding-up order, the trusts would have continued.

[37] In *Re Excalibur Airways Ltd (in liq)* [1998] 1 BCLC 436 a supervisor held moneys realised under the CVA on trust. A compulsory winding-up order was then made on the petition of the directors. Jonathan Parker J distinguished between a case where a supervisor on behalf of the CVA creditors obtains a winding-up order, which was a case where the CVA creditors elect to abandon the CVA, and a case where the winding-up order was obtained by directors or by a non-CVA creditor. In the latter case he held that the CVA does not come to an end whereas in the former it did, the CVA creditors having to prove in the liquidation.

[38] In *Kings v Cleghorn* [1998] BPIR 463 Judge Behrens, sitting as a High Court judge, held that an IVA terminated on the making of a bankruptcy order on the petition of a post-CVA creditor, and that moneys held by the supervisor on trust for the CVA creditors should be handed to the trustee in bankruptcy.

[39] In *Re Maple Environmental Services Ltd* [2000] BCC 93, the CVA contained an express term that moneys paid to the supervisor should, in the event of failure of the CVA, be paid to the liquidator. Judge Boggis QC, sitting as a High Court judge, held that the CVA failed, that the supervisor should have petitioned for the winding up of the company but did not do so, and that the fact that the company went into a creditors' voluntary liquidation did not affect the conclusion that the trust of the moneys paid to the supervisor ended and that the money should be paid to the liquidator.

[40] In *Welsby v Brelec Installations Ltd (in liq)* [2000] 2 BCLC 576 a CVA provided for the payment by the company of contributions to the supervisors for distribution to creditors. The company went into a creditors' voluntary liquidation. Blackburne J held that the sums held by the supervisors in trust for the CVA creditors remained subject to that trust notwithstanding the liquidation.

[41] Finally in *Re Kudos Glass Ltd (in liq)* [2001] 1 BCLC 390 there was a CVA under which moneys came to the hands of the supervisors as trustees. The CVA provided that if it should fail, the supervisors should distribute the moneys, after deduction of fees and expenses, to the CVA creditors. Mr Richard McCombe QC, sitting as a deputy High Court judge, held that the trust continued, notwithstanding the winding-up order obtained by a post-CVA creditor. But he distilled from the authorities that it is the identity of the petitioner for the compulsory winding up that is normally crucial to the question whether the trusts arising from the scheme are held to have determined. However he rejected an argument based on r 4.21A, saying (at 401):

'It seems to me in principle to be unlikely that the rule makers intended administrative provisions such as these to affect the overall workings of schemes such as the present ...'

He accepted (at 403) an argument that the rule, like s 276(2) of the 1986 Act, was to provide the supervisor with a safety net for the event that he is unable otherwise to recover his expenses. He continued:

'It is not intended to set any premise upon which to judge whether a particular IVA or CVA, and any trust constituted under it, terminates upon the making of a bankruptcy or winding-up order.'

[42] In a number of the cases unease has been expressed at the fine distinctions drawn in the authorities. Neither counsel before us sought to derive much assistance from the authorities, both counsel being agreed that the cases display a misplaced concentration on the form of liquidation (in CVA cases) and the identity of the petitioner in IVA as well as CVA cases.

[43] We agree. Those distinctions and that concentration on the form of liquidation and the identity of the petitioner are at least in part based on the terms of r 4.21A and s 276(2). Mr Zacaroli does not suggest that in themselves those provisions establish that trusts created by a CVA or IVA must come to an end on liquidation or bankruptcy. He only says that they are consistent with that result. For our part we agree with the comments of Judge Maddocks in *Re Halson Packaging Ltd* and of Mr McCombe in *Re Kudos Glass Ltd* on the effect of those provisions. It makes little sense for the form of the liquidation to affect the question of the effect of liquidation on trusts created by a CVA. A creditors' voluntary liquidation is often preferred to a compulsory winding up on practical grounds related to expense and delay, as in this case. We would question whether the mere fact that a supervisor presents a petition entails that the CVA or IVA creditors have elected to terminate the CVA or IVA trust in their favour. Even if there is evidence that all the CVA or IVA creditors supported the presentation of a petition, it does not follow that they were thereby evincing an intention that the trust should come to an end and that the trust assets should revert to the company or debtor.

[44] Mr Zacaroli submits that the CVA, including the trust created by it, failed and terminated on the liquidation of Gallagher. He accepts that the terms of the CVA may dictate what is to happen on liquidation to a trust created by the CVA, but he submits that where the parties have failed to state clearly what is to happen, the court must apply a default rule. That rule, he says, should be that where the liquidation causes the CVA itself to fail or terminate, any trust created over assets of the company for the purpose of the CVA also terminates. He, again, submits that the trust assets are held for the purpose of implementing the CVA as a whole and he says that if the CVA cannot be implemented as a whole, the trust cannot be carried into effect and, by analogy with *Barclays Bank Ltd v Quistclose Investments Ltd* [1968] 3 All ER 651, [1970] AC 567, the trust fails. Alternatively, he argues that the court should lean against construing the CVA as extending the life of the trust beyond the termination of the CVA caused by the liquidation. He points in particular to the fact that the CVA, by para 39 and modification 9, provided that the supervisors were to petition for the winding up of Gallagher on its failure to comply with its obligations. He contends that where one set of insolvency proceedings, the CVA, is succeeded pursuant to the terms of the CVA by a second set of insolvency proceedings, liquidation, the whole of the CVA, including the trusts created thereunder, should terminate, as it must follow that the CVA creditors were intended to prove in the liquidation.

[45] Mr Zacaroli also relies on certain policy considerations. He points out that to allow a trust of assets to continue after liquidation produces in relation to

post-CVA creditors a result which is the complete opposite of that which would be produced in respect of post-liquidation, post-administration or post-administrative receivership creditors. In a liquidation, liabilities incurred after liquidation would rank as expenses of the winding up. In an administration, subsequent liabilities would have the benefit of the statutory charge in s 19(5) of the 1986 Act and would rank ahead of the administrator's own remuneration. In an administrative receivership the receiver is personally liable on each contract entered into by him unless the contract contains a contrary provision, and, if it does, the other contracting party would be aware of the risk of extending credit to the company in receivership. In contrast, Mr Zacaroli says, the post-CVA creditors may well not be alerted to the existence of the CVA or to the extent to which assets of the company are held for CVA creditors and so not available to post-CVA creditors, if the judge is right. There is no provision for putting those dealing with a company on notice through registration of the CVA. Mr Zacaroli submits that the judge's conclusion is unfair to post-CVA creditors.

[46] Mr Pascoe submits that it is essential to distinguish between the contractual and proprietary elements of a CVA, and that if the company is in breach of its obligations under the statutory contract constituted by the CVA, that provides no basis for concluding that the trust of the CVA must have failed or determined, particularly when it can be carried into effect in relation to the trust assets. He argues that the *Quistclose* case provides no analogy relevant to the present case and he argues that policy considerations point to the adoption of a default rule having the converse effect to that suggested by Mr Zacaroli. He further submits that the applicable default rule should be that the CVA trust should continue following a liquidation unless the CVA creditors evince a clear intention to abandon it and that the form of liquidation and the identity of the petitioner should not be determinative of whether the trust of the CVA continues. In the present case, he submits, there has been no abandonment by the CVA creditors of the trust in their favour, and the judge's conclusion should be affirmed, albeit for different reasons.

[47] It is common ground that the starting point is the terms of the CVA itself. Its terms can, indeed should, provide for what is to happen to assets on the termination of the CVA (r 1.3(2)(l) of the 1986 rules). It is also common ground that the CVA does not expressly nor by necessary implication provide what is to happen to the trusts assets on liquidation, though Mr Zacaroli finds significance, as we have noted, in the provisions for the supervisors to put Gallagher into liquidation, even though that is not what happened in the present case. It begs the question to assert that because liquidation was contemplated by the CVA, the CVA creditors were intended to prove in the liquidation instead of taking under the trust for their benefit. Mr Zacaroli further stresses the importance of para 15 of the CVA and its proposal that all liabilities incurred by Gallagher after the approval of the CVA should be paid in full out of trading receipts, which, he said, was entirely inconsistent with an intention that the trust should continue in the event of a subsequent insolvent liquidation. But that paragraph was directed to the circumstances attending Gallagher's intended continuing trading and merely stated that Gallagher intended to pay post-CVA creditors out of its trading receipts in the ordinary course of business. It was not directed to the question of the continuation of the trusts if Gallagher went into liquidation.

[48] The real difficulty in Mr Zacaroli's way, as it seems to us, is in showing why a fully constituted trust created by a CVA should terminate on the CVA failing or terminating in the absence of any provisions requiring the trust to

terminate and specifying what is to happen to the trust assets. It is not suggested that any moneys paid to creditors pursuant to the trust can or should be recovered. The fact that Gallagher was in breach of its obligations under the statutory contract constituted by the CVA and went into liquidation, thereby rendering it impossible to fulfil any further the purpose of the CVA, does not entail the consequence that the trust also failed when plainly it can still be carried into effect. Whilst the administration of the trust may not, by reason of Gallagher's liquidation, produce the full benefit originally envisaged for the CVA creditors, that is no reason for denying those creditors such benefit as carrying the trust into effect might still provide. The *Quistclose* case has no relevance to the present circumstances even by way of analogy. In that case money was advanced by a third-party lender to enable the company to continue to pay a declared dividend. But that purpose could not be fulfilled when the company went into liquidation and so, the House of Lords held, there was a resulting trust to the lender. In the present case the supervisors can carry the CVA trust into effect. We agree with Mr Pascoe that unless there is a provision in the CVA to the contrary, the CVA trust should continue. We doubt whether Mr Pascoe's second exception (namely, where the CVA creditors display a clear intention that the trust should determine) is a real exception. Of course all beneficiaries under a trust can combine to bring a trust to an end and dispose of the trust assets and no beneficiary can be compelled to take a benefit he does not want, but in the real commercial world such a situation is hardly likely to arise.

[49] Nor are we persuaded that the policy considerations point in favour of the default rule suggested by Mr Zacaroli. The differences between the consequences of a CVA, if the judge is right, and the other forms of insolvency proceedings reflect the differing circumstances pertaining to each. The primary purpose of the CVA was to enable Gallagher to go on trading. In contrast, liquidation does not have that purpose. Administration is only intended to be temporary. By s 8(3)(a) of the 1986 Act, a purpose for which an administration order may be made is the approval of a CVA. As for administrative receivership, the practice of administrative receivers is to exclude personal liability on contracts. Whilst we acknowledge the possibility that there will be post-CVA creditors who are unaware of the CVA and its terms, in practice there is likely to be a considerable overlap between CVA creditors and post-CVA creditors. Further, save for the Crown and local authorities in respect of fiscal liabilities (and they are likely to be CVA creditors), no one is forced to become a creditor of a company without making such inquiries as are thought appropriate to ascertain the financial position of the company. We do not, therefore, accept that to treat a trust created by a CVA as continuing notwithstanding the liquidation of the company is productive of such unfairness that the court should conclude that liquidation brings the trust to an end. Such a conclusion would run counter to the general law which leaves trusts of assets not held for a company unaffected by its liquidation.

[50] Further, as a matter of policy, in the absence of any provision in the CVA as to what should happen to trust assets on liquidation of the company, the court should prefer a default rule which furthers rather than hinders what might be taken to be the statutory purpose of Pt I of the 1986 Act. Parliament plainly intended to encourage companies and creditors to enter into CVAs so as to provide creditors with a means of recovering what they are owed without recourse to the more expensive means provided by winding up or administration, thereby giving many companies the opportunity to continue to trade. If Mr Zacaroli's

default rule were to apply, so that trust assets under the CVA which happen not to have been distributed before the liquidation would become available to meet the claims of post-CVA creditors as well as CVA creditors, that would be a disincentive to creditors to agree to a CVA and to keep the CVA in operation.

[51] We therefore conclude, in acceptance of Mr Pascoe's submissions, that the trust did survive the liquidation and that the judge was right so to hold, though our reasoning differs somewhat from the judge's.

Are the CVA creditors entitled to prove in the liquidation?

[52] Although this was not a question expressly raised in the originating application, and although the judge did not hear argument from any class of creditor who might be affected by the outcome, the judge was invited to deal with the question and para 4 of the order made by him was in this form:

'The CVA creditors are not entitled to prove in the liquidation of the company, save that:
(1) in the event that any claims of CVA creditors which would have been preferential debts of the company had the company gone into liquidation on 21 April 1995 are not paid in full out of the assets held by the supervisors, those creditors are entitled to prove in the liquidation of the company for the unpaid balance of their claims; and
(2) in the event that the CVA creditors agree to abandon their rights in relation to the cause of action against Mercury and any sums recovered pursuant thereto, they are entitled to prove in the liquidation for the unpaid balance of their claims.'

[53] As we understand Mr Zacaroli's position, he does not challenge sub-para (1) of that order in the circumstance that the court dismisses the appeal on the first two questions; but both he and Mr Pascoe criticise sub-para (2) and the judge's reasoning which led him so to order. The judge analysed the CVA creditors' rights as analogous to the rights of secured creditors who are only entitled to prove if they abandon their security. But we cannot see any sustainable basis for that analysis and in any event there would be considerable practical difficulties in determining whether the CVA creditors had given up their rights in respect of the cause of action against Mercury. In the present case the liquidation of Gallagher brought the CVA, though not the trust created thereunder, to an end and made the statutory contract incapable of further performance. In the circumstances it seems to us only just that the CVA creditors should be able to prove for the balance of their CVA debts after giving credit for dividends received from the supervisors.

Conclusions

[54] It may be helpful if we were to summarise our conclusions on the points raised on this appeal. (1) Where a CVA or IVA provides for moneys or other assets to be paid to or transferred or held for the benefit of CVA or IVA creditors, this will create a trust of those moneys or assets for those creditors. (2) The effect of the liquidation of the company or the bankruptcy of the debtor on a trust created by the CVA or IVA will depend on the provisions of the CVA or IVA relating thereto. (3) If the CVA or IVA provides what is to happen on liquidation or bankruptcy (or a failure of the CVA or IVA), effect must be given thereto. (4) If the CVA or IVA does not so provide, the trust will continue notwithstanding the liquidation, bankruptcy or failure and must take effect according to its terms.

(5) The CVA or IVA creditors can prove in the liquidation or bankruptcy for so much of their debt as remains after payment of what has been or will be recovered under the trust.

[55] We would, therefore, dismiss the appeal save in relation to para 4 of the judge's order. In substitution for that paragraph it should be declared that the CVA creditors are entitled to prove in the liquidation for their CVA debts after giving credit for dividends received from the supervisors. We would hear further submissions on whether it is necessary to incorporate in the order of this court liberty to individual creditors who are not content with this court's conclusion on para 4 to argue the point afresh.

Appeal dismissed save as specified.

Kate O'Hanlon   Barrister.

Sayers v Clarke Walker (a firm)

[2002] EWCA Civ 645

COURT OF APPEAL, CIVIL DIVISION

BROOKE, KAY LJJ AND SIR CHRISTOPHER STAUGHTON

18 APRIL, 14 MAY 2002

Court of Appeal – Time for appeal – Extension of time for appeal – Discretion – Factors to be considered in complex cases – CPR 3.9, 52.4(2).

The claimant brought proceedings for professional negligence against the defendant firm of accountants. In a judgment handed down on 12 October 2001, the judge found for the claimant in respect of part of his claim and concluded that he was entitled to damages. At a further hearing on 17 October, the judge made a ruling on costs. The order, setting out the figures that the parties agreed followed from the judge's rulings, was not drawn up and sealed until 16 November. The accountants wished to appeal against both rulings. Under CPR 52.4(2)(b)[a], they were required to file their appellant's notice within 14 days after the date of 'the decision' against which they wished to appeal. That marked a change from the previous practice under which the time limit for appealing ran from the date on which the judgment or order of the court below had been sealed or otherwise perfected. The accountants' solicitors, who seemed not to have been wholly familiar with the effect of the change of practice, telephoned the Civil Appeals Office to obtain clarification of the situation. They maintained that they had been told, mistakenly, that the 14-day time limit for appealing against a decision ran from the date that the order had been sealed. Acting on that information, the solicitors did not attempt to file an appellant's notice until 26 November. After being told that the notice was out of time, the solicitors wrote to the Civil Appeals Office. In response, the deputy master correctly directed that the 14-day time limit ran from the date of the decision, and that accordingly the appellant's notice had indeed been filed out of time. On 20 December, three days after their solicitors had received that direction, the accountants applied for an extension of time in which to appeal. That application was refused by a single Lord Justice. On a renewed application to the full Court of Appeal, the latter considered the principles to be applied in such a case and, in particular, what guidance, if any, was to be gleaned from CPR 3.9[b], which provided a checklist of the matters to be taken into account on an application for relief from any sanction imposed for a failure to comply with any rule.

---

a   Rule 52.4(2), so far as material, is set out at [5], below

b   Rule 3.9, so far as material, provides: '(1) On an application for relief from any sanction imposed for a failure to comply with any rule, practice direction or court order the court will consider all the circumstances including—(a) the interests of the administration of justice; (b) whether the application for relief had been made promptly; (c) whether the failure to comply was intentional; (d) whether there is a good explanation for the failure; (e) the extent to which the party in default has complied with other rules, practice directions, court orders and any relevant pre-action protocol; (f) whether the failure to comply was caused by the party or his legal representative; (g) whether the trial date or the likely trial date can still be met if relief is granted; (h) the effect which the failure to comply had on each party; and (i) the effect which the granting of relief would have on each party ... '

Held – When a court was considering, in a case of any complexity, an application for an extension of time for appealing, it should have regard to the checklist in CPR 3.9. That was because the applicant had not complied with CPR 52.4(2), and if the court were unwilling to grant him relief from his failure to comply through the extension of time he was seeking, the consequence would be that the order of the lower court would stand and he could not appeal against it. Even though that might not be a sanction expressly 'imposed' by the rule, the consequence would be exactly the same as if it had been, and it would be far better for courts to follow the checklist in r 3.9 in such circumstances than for judges to make their own checklists for cases where sanctions were implied and not expressly imposed. In cases where the arguments for granting or refusing an extension of time were otherwise evenly balanced, the court would have to evaluate the merits of the proposed appeal in order to form a judgment on what the appellants would be losing if time were not extended. In the instant case, having regard to the matters set out in r 3.9, the court would, in the exercise of its discretion, grant the extension of time sought by the accountants (see [21], [22], [34], [36], [40], [41], below).

Notes
For relief from sanctions, see 37 *Halsbury's Laws* (4th edn reissue) para 458.

Cases referred to in judgment
Alliance and Leicester plc v Slayford [2001] 1 All ER (Comm) 1, CA.
Audergon v La Baguette Ltd [2002] EWCA Civ 10, [2002] All ER (D) 166 (Jan).
CM Van Stillevoldt BV v El Carriers Inc [1983] 1 All ER 699, [1983] 1 WLR 297, CA.
Customs and Excise Comrs v Eastwood Care Homes (Ilkeston) Ltd (18 January 2000, unreported).
Mallory v Butler [1991] 2 All ER 889n, [1991] 1 WLR 458, CA.
Norwich & Peterborough Building Society v Steed [1991] 2 All ER 880, [1991] 1 WLR 449, CA.
Palata Investments Ltd v Burt & Sinfield Ltd [1985] 2 All ER 517, [1985] 1 WLR 942, CA.

Applications for extension of time for appealing and for permission to appeal
The defendants, Clarke Walker (a firm), applied for an extension of time for appealing and for permission to appeal from (i) the decision of Buckley J on 12 October 2001 giving judgment for the claimant, Michael Patrick Sayers, in his action for professional negligence against the defendants, and (ii) the judge's decision on 17 October 2001 in respect of the costs of the proceedings. The facts are set out in the judgment of Brooke LJ.

Robert Anderson (instructed by *Hammond Suddards Edge*) for the defendants.
Giles Goodfellow (instructed by *Thomas Eggar Church Adams*) for Mr Sayers.

Cur ad vult

14 May 2002. The following judgments were delivered.

BROOKE LJ.
[1] There was before the court a renewed application by the defendants for an extension of time for appealing and for permission to appeal against two orders made by Buckley J on 12 October and 17 October 2001, the first as to liability in this action and the second as to costs. The defendants' notice of appeal, which

included an application for an extension of time pursuant to CPR 3.1(2), was not effectively lodged at this court until 20 December 2001. On 22 January 2002 Sedley LJ refused to grant an extension of time, saying that the application appeared to him to be irretrievably out of time. This three-judge division of the court was convened because the case raised a question as to the principles on which an appeal court should grant an extension of time under the CPR appeals regime on an application made after the original time for appealing has expired.

[2] This is a professional negligence action, brought by the claimant Michael Sayers against Clarke Walker, a firm of accountants, in relation to what he claimed were shortcomings in the advice they gave him in 1989 in connection with his purchase of 90% of the issued share capital of the company which employed him. At the trial the judge found that the defendant firm had been retained by both parties to the transaction for the purpose of dealing with formalities and of acting as facilitators to implement an agreement which had already been reached.

[3] He dismissed Mr Sayers' claim that the defendants had been negligent in some informal advice they had given him about the reasonableness of the price he had agreed to pay. On the other hand, he found that their retainer had been wide enough to cover advice on a tax structure for the transaction they should have advised him to use, and that their failure to give him any such advice was negligent and sounded in damages.

[4] The judge handed down his reserved judgment on 12 October, and the defendants wish to appeal against his findings on causation. There was a further hearing on 17 October when the judge made a ruling on the costs of the action, against which the defendants also wish to appeal. He also made rulings about the amount of the award which the defendants do not wish to challenge. He directed the parties to try and reach agreement on the figures which should appear in the court order in consequence of his rulings. If they could not reach agreement, they should return to court within 28 days. In the event the figures were agreed, and the order was drawn up and sealed on 16 November 2001.

[5] CPR 52.4(2) states, uncompromisingly, so far as is material:

> 'The appellant must file the appellant's notice at the appeal court within ...
> (b) ... 14 days after *the date of the decision of the lower court* that the appellant wishes to appeal.' (My emphasis.)

This marks a change of practice from RSC Ord 59, r 4(1), which provided:

> 'Except as otherwise provided by this Order, every notice of appeal must be served under rule 3(5) not later than 4 weeks after *the date on which the judgment or order of the court below was sealed or otherwise perfected.*' (My emphasis.)

[6] The defendant's solicitor, Mr Gildener, seems to have been not wholly familiar with the effect of this change of practice. He was later to complain that the CPR gave him no guidance as to how parties were to deal with a situation whereby the 'decision' of the court was established in a piecemeal fashion over the course of a number of hearing dates, where the order was not yet perfected, and where there were still issues to be concluded. He therefore spoke to counsel, and on counsel's recommendation he telephoned the Civil Appeals Office on 22 October to clarify the situation. We do not know exactly how he described the position to the member of that office's staff to whom he spoke. He has, however, produced a contemporary attendance notice recording that she 'confirmed'

a
that the 14-day time limit for appealing a decision ran from the date the order was sealed. Mr Anderson, who appears for the defendants, rightly accepted that lawyers must do their work themselves and that they should not be able to depend on advice given to them by whoever is at the end of a telephone when they ring up an appeal court office. On the other hand, he said that this was an incident which we should take into account when we decided how we should
b
exercise our discretion on the application by his clients for an extension of time.

[7] In the mistaken belief that time for appealing did not start to run until the order was drawn up and sealed on 16 November, Mr Gildener's firm did not attempt to file the appellants' notice until 26 November. This would have been well within the 14-day period permitted under the rules. On this occasion they
c
paid the appropriate fee, only to be told that their notice was out of time. A member of his firm then telephoned the Civil Appeals Office for clarification and explained the circumstances surrounding the case. She asked whether the notice was indeed out of time, given the delayed sealing of the order. Again, we do not know exactly what she said, or how it was understood. At all events she maintains that the assistant to whom she spoke, after checking with her superior, told her
d
that the notice was not out of time, and that it could be filed within 14 days of 16 November.

[8] The firm's outdoor clerk then tried to file the notice again the following day, only to be told that it was out of time and that the defendants should make an application for an extension of time (see CPR 52.6(1)). It appears that
e
Mr Gildener was away on holiday while all this was happening, but on his return on 3 December he wrote a long letter to the Civil Appeals Office setting out the history, as he saw it, and inviting them to confirm that the notice had indeed been filed in time and that it could now be issued. On 13 December he received a reply to the effect that his letter had been referred to Deputy Master Joseph, who had made a direction in these terms:
f

'There are certain inaccuracies in [the solicitors'] letter of 3rd December. Let me deal with them first.

1. The time limit for filing an appellant's notice is clearly set out in CPR 52.4(2)(a) and (b) as being 14 days after the date of the <u>decision</u> of the
g
lower court that the appellant wishes to appeal, in the absence of any other period being directed by the Court. Therefore, it is entirely right that time is calculated from the date of the decision as shown in the order, which is 17th October 2001. If the parties felt there would be difficulties in complying with the deadline for filing an Appellant's Notice the appropriate course
h
would have been to ask the Judge to extend time pursuant to CPR 52.4(2)(a).

2. The Court will often accept an Appellant's Notice when an order has not yet been drawn on the basis of an undertaking supplied by the Solicitors lodging it ...

3. I cannot speak for what may or may not have been said in conversations
j
between the solicitors and members of staff in the Registry. It is however, quite wrong for solicitors to attempt to rely on such conversations for the purpose of interpretation of legal practice which they, as lawyers, should be expected to know. They should also be expected to realise that CPR 52 made radical changes from the old RSC Order 59, one of which was that time now runs from the date of the decision <u>NOT</u> the date of the seal on the order (paragraphs 6, 7, 8, 9, 10, 11).

For the reasons I have given this appellant's notice has been filed <u>out of</u> <u>time</u>.'

[9] The defendants' solicitors received this letter on 17 December. They did not seek a review of this decision pursuant to CPR 52.16(5). They were wise not to do so, and I take this opportunity of endorsing the correctness of the deputy master's ruling and the reasons he gave for it. Instead they filed their application for an extension of time for appealing on 20 December, nearly ten weeks after Buckley J's ruling on liability, and nine weeks after his ruling on costs.

[10] Under the pre-CPR regime the practice of this court was conveniently summarised in note 59/4/17 of the 1999 edition of the *Supreme Court Practice* in these terms:

'It is entirely in the discretion of the Court to grant or refuse an extension of time. The factors which are normally taken into account in deciding whether to grant an extension of time for serving a notice of appeal are: (1) the length of the delay; (2) the reasons for the delay; (3) the chances of the appeal succeeding if time for appealing is extended; and (4) the degree of prejudice to the potential respondent if the application is granted (see *C.M. Van Stillevoldt BV v. El Carriers Inc.* [1983] 1 All E.R. 699; [1983] 1 W.L.R. 297...) ... Where the delay in serving notice of appeal is short and there is an acceptable excuse for it, an extension of time will not be refused on the basis of the merits of the intended appeal, unless the appeal is hopeless: *Palata Investments Ltd v. Burt & Sinfield Ltd* [1985] 2 All E.R. 517; [1985] 1 W.L.R. 942, CA. In *Norwich & Peterborough Building Society v. Steed* [1991] 2 All E.R. 880, [1991] 1 W.L.R. 449 and *Mallory v. Butler* [1991] 2 All E.R. 889n, [1991] 1 W.L.R. 458 the Court of Appeal held that: ... (4) The settled practice of the Court is to assess and take into account the merits of the proposed appeal in deciding whether or not to grant an extension of time for appealing (subject to the qualification in the *Palata* case (above)).'

[11] Until October 1982 there was a six-week time limit for appealing to the Court of Appeal against final orders and a two-week time limit for appeals against interlocutory orders. This led to ancillary litigation over the status of the order being appealed, and an amendment to RSC Ord 59, r 4(1) was therefore introduced providing for a standard time limit of four weeks for appealing against all orders, except as otherwise provided.

[12] The authors of the report on the *Review of the Court of Appeal (Civil Division)* (September 1997) (the Bowman report), suggested that these arrangements should be reformed in a fairly radical way. In addition to recommending a 'common starting point'(at 82 (para 6)), being the date when the order was made (see [5], above), they expressed the view (at 82 (para 7)) that the four-week period was too short for appeals against final decisions and that it should be extended to six weeks. In this context they took into account not only their recommendation that a skeleton argument should now accompany the grounds of appeal but also the consideration that the present four-week period was often not quite long enough to allow for the preparation of transcripts. On the other hand, they recommended that the time limit for seeking leave to appeal against procedural decisions should be reduced to seven days.

[13] They also recommended a new, much tougher regime in relation to the sanctions for non-compliance with time limits for appealing. They said (at 91 (para 54)):

'For the system to work effectively, it is important that all rules and procedures are complied with strictly. In some Federal Circuits in the United States very little leeway is given if parties do not comply with the rules. Once this is clear, parties seem to find it easier to meet deadliness and other requirements. It is time this approach was applied in the [Court of Appeal].'

[14] After noting with some concern that it was relatively easy to obtain an extension of time in which to apply for leave to appeal, and after quoting the *Van Stillevoldt* criteria (see [10], above), they continued (at 92):

'56. We do not believe that whether an appeal has a realistic chance of succeeding should be relevant. There should be realistic time limits. There should be a strong presumption that time limits should not be extended save in exceptional circumstances.

57. A similar view should be taken about all the rules of the [Court of Appeal]. If they are not complied with, the applicant or appellant should be at risk of having his or her case dismissed or at least being penalised in costs.'

[15] In the event, the Civil Procedure Rules Committee decided when formulating CPR 52.4(2)(b) to pay less attention to the need to provide more realistic time limits for appeals against final decisions to the Court of Appeal and more attention to the desirability of having a single set of rules for all civil appeals governed by CPR Pt 52, whether procedural or final, and whether the 'appeal court' (see CPR 52.1(3)(b)) is a circuit judge, a High Court judge or the Court of Appeal. This approach had the merit of eliminating most of the wrangling about the status of the decision appealed against which had led to the 1982 change to RSC Ord 59, r 4(1) (for which see [11], above).

[16] In order to accommodate the difficulties which a 14-day time limit might present in heavy cases, the practice direction to CPR Pt 52 (CPR PD 52) lists (at para 5.6) the documents which must be filed with the appellant's notice but provides (para 5.7) that 'where it is not possible to file all the above documents, the appellant must indicate which documents have not yet been filed and the reasons why they are not currently available'. This procedure enables the appeal court to apply pressure on an appellant to file all the necessary documentation (including any necessary transcripts) as soon as reasonably practicable.

[17] Extensions of time are now governed by CPR 52.6 which provides that:

'(1) An application to vary the time limit for filing an appeal notice must be made to the appeal court.

(2) The parties may not agree to extend any date or time limit set by—
(a) these Rules; (b) the relevant practice direction; or (c) an order of the appeal court or a lower court.

(Rule 3.1(2)(a) provides that the court may extend or shorten the time for compliance with any rule, practice direction or court order (even if an application for an extension is made after the time for compliance has expired)) ...'

CPR PD 52, para 5.2 provides:

'If an appellant requires an extension of time for filing his notice the application must be made in the appellant's notice. The notice should state the reason for the delay and the steps taken prior to the application being made.'

[18] It must not be assumed that this provision sets out all the information a court may be likely to require in every case when deciding whether it is just to extend time for appealing in the face of non-compliance with the mandatory requirements of CPR 52.4(2). The court's general power to extend the time for compliance with a rule (even if an application for extension is made after the time for compliance had expired) is contained in CPR 3.1(2)(a), and in deciding how to exercise that power the court must of course take into account the overriding objective in CPR 1.1. The question then arises whether the CPR give any further guidance to judges as to how they should exercise their discretion when making orders under CPR 3.1(2)(a), or whether, uncharacteristically, the way is left wide open for the creation of judge-made checklists of the type recently deplored by this court in the judgment of Jonathan Parker LJ (with whom Pill and Tuckey LJJ agreed) in *Audergon v La Baguette Ltd* [2002] EWCA Civ 10 at [107], [2002] All ER (D) 166 (Jan) at [107]:

> 'Inherent in such an approach, as it seems to me, is the danger that a body of satellite authority may be built up ... leading in effect to the rewriting of the relevant rule through the medium of judicial decision. This would seem to me to be just the kind of undesirable consequence which the CPR were designed to avoid.'

[19] In very many cases a judge will be able to decide whether to extend or shorten a period of time for complying with a rule, practice or direction without undue difficulty after considering the matters set out in CPR 52PD para 5.2. In more complex cases, of which this is undoubtedly one, a more sophisticated approach will be required.

[20] The philosophy underpinning CPR Pt 3 is that rules, court orders and practice directions are there to be obeyed. If a sanction is imposed in the event of non-compliance, the defaulting party has to seek relief from the sanction on an application made under CPR 3.8, and in that event the court will consider all the matters listed in CPR 3.9, so far as relevant. Similarly, if an application is made under CPR 3.6 to set aside a judgment obtained under CPR 3.5, the court will consider all the matters listed in CPR 3.9 unless it is shown that the right to enter judgment had not arisen at the time when it was entered (see CPR 3.6(3) and (4)).

[21] In my judgment, it is equally appropriate to have regard to the checklist in CPR 3.9 when a court is considering an application for an extension of time for appealing in a case of any complexity. The reason for this is that the applicant has not complied with CPR 52.4(2), and if the court is unwilling to grant him relief from his failure to comply through the extension of time he is seeking, the consequence will be that the order of the lower court will stand and he cannot appeal it. Even though this may not be a sanction expressly 'imposed' by the rule, the consequence will be exactly the same as if it had been, and it would be far better for courts to follow the checklist contained in CPR 3.9 on this occasion, too, than for judges to make their own checklists for cases where sanctions are implied and not expressly imposed.

[22] It follows that when considering whether to grant an extension of time for an appeal against a final decision in a case of any complexity, the courts should consider 'all the circumstances of the case' including (a) the interests of the administration of justice; (b) whether the application for relief has been made promptly; (c) whether the failure to comply was intentional; (d) whether there is a good explanation for the failure; (e) the extent to which the party in default has complied with other rules, practice directions and court orders; (f) whether the

a failure to comply was caused by the party or his legal representative; (h) the effect which the failure to comply had on each party; and (i) the effect which the granting of relief would have on each party. In the case of a procedural appeal the court would also have to consider item (g), 'whether the trial date or the likely trial date can still be met if relief is granted'.

b [23] In the Autumn 2001 edition of volume 1 of *Civil Procedure* (the White Book) reference is made (at 45) to the unreported judgment of Lightman J in *Customs and Excise Comrs v Eastwood Care Homes (Ilkeston) Ltd* (18 January 2000) in which he was concerned with an application for an extension of time for appealing beyond that permitted by RSC Ord 91, r 6(3). That case was decided in the period between the introduction of the main body of the CPR in April 1999 and the introduction of the new appellate regime in CPR Pt 52 in May 2000. I can c understand why Lightman J created his own checklist of matters which should be taken into account in an application of this kind, some of which, as he said in his judgment (at para 8), were specified in the rules and some of which were not. For the reasons set out in [18], above, however, judge-made checklists of this kind are to be avoided wherever possible. Lightman J was, however, correct to say (at d para 8) that each application must be viewed by reference to the criterion of justice. He was also correct to say (at para 9) that one of the important features in deciding what justice requires is to bear in mind that time limits are there to be observed, and that justice may be seriously defeated if there is any laxity in that regard.

e [24] Having identified the criteria we must apply, I now turn to the merits of this application.

[25] I do not consider that item (a), the interests of the administration of justice cast very much light either way. On the one hand there is an interest in rules being obeyed and the resources of the court not being taken up with ancillary disputes of this kind. On the other hand, the overriding objective is to f deal with cases justly, so that resource considerations should not carry very much weight if fairness demands that an extension of time should be granted. Although the new regime has removed the absolute right to appeal against a final judgment in a case like this, they have given effect to the principle that a litigant should be allowed to have such a judgment reviewed by an appeal court provided that he can show that he has a real, and not a fanciful, prospect of success.

g [26] The application for relief (item (b)) was not made promptly in the strict sense, in that the time for appealing the order made on 12 October expired on 26 October, and the application for an extension of time was not made until 20 December. However, in the peculiar circumstances of the present case it was made very soon after the defendants' solicitors received notice of the deputy h master's direction on 17 December.

[27] The failure to comply was certainly not intentional (item (c)), and there was an explanation for the failure which even if it could not be categorised as 'good' (item (d)) was certainly one which would incline a court in these fairly early days of the CPR appellate regime to be merciful, everything else being j equal. The failure to comply was caused by the defendants' legal representative (item (f)) and not by the defendants themselves.

[28] Item (e) needs more detailed consideration on the facts of this case. It entitles the appeal court to take into account the extent to which the party seeking an extension of time has failed to comply in the past with other rules, practice directions and court orders. This introduces a factor which was never considered by the Court of Appeal in pre-CPR days.

[29] We have been furnished by Mr Goodfellow with a note describing the procedural history of this action. It seems to have been started in 1994, and in September 1994 Mr Sayers' solicitors entered judgment in default of defence. The existence of this judgment appears to have come to the attention of the defendants' solicitors by the end of 1995, but they seem to have been very dilatory in producing an affidavit and draft defence in support of an application to set aside the judgment which they eventually made in July 1996, so that the judgment was not finally set aside until March 1997, with costs being ordered in favour of Mr Sayers.

[30] The later procedural history of the action appears to have been marked by delays on the part of the defendants, in non-compliance with court orders. In June 1998 they were five-and-a-half weeks late in providing discovery by list, after two previous extensions of time had been granted. Under an order made in April 1998 witness statements were to be provided by 25 June 1998, a timetable which slipped because of the delay in providing discovery. Mr Sayers, however, was ready to exchange witness statements in March 1999, but the defendants repeatedly requested extensions of time. They eventually delivered their witness statements on 1 September 2000, the day when the guillotine imposed by an 'unless' order was due to fall. The history of the relevant events is set out in items 15–30 of the 'detailed chronology of the defendants' defaults and delays' which Mr Sayers' advisors have prepared.

[31] I would not place any great weight on the subsequent delays in the preparation and exchange of experts' reports. Although Mr Sayers' advisors complained of delay on the part of the defendants, they had been more than two months late in serving their own experts' report, apparently because one of their client's former accountants was claiming a lien on the papers he held and was only willing to make them available on terms.

[32] Mr Anderson drew our attention to certain criticisms of the claimant's conduct of the action in the judgment the judge delivered on 17 October 2001, but he made no very determined attempt to challenge any of the events set out in the detailed chronology with which we have been supplied, and it certainly appears from that chronology that the defendants, for the most part in pre-CPR days, had a bad record of non-compliance with court orders.

[33] Turning to item (h), the effect of the defendants' failure to comply with the rule has been to create a number of false dawns for Mr Sayers and his wife. The defendants evinced an early intention to seek permission to appeal and then failed to file their appeal notice (and serve it on Mr Sayers' solicitors) within the permitted time, thereby raising hopes that they would not appeal after all. They compounded this failure by informing Mr Sayers' solicitors on 6 December that they had lodged the papers at the Court of Appeal at a time when they knew the court had rejected the papers. When the true position was ascertained on 10 December Mr Sayers' hopes were raised once again, only to be dashed ten days later when they received notice that the correct papers had been lodged. So far as Mr Sayers is concerned, his life was put 'on hold' for all this time. His solicitors had estimated his costs at £290,000, and he had a judgment in his favour for over £68,000 (which was duly paid) and 60% of his costs of the action. Although the defendants had not sought any form of stay they were declining to pay him any sum on account of costs. Quite apart from the worry this continuing delay would have caused him, it was exacerbated for him by the depressive illness from which his wife is now suffering. Her general practitioner believes that the

a worries of her husband's litigation was a major precipitating cause of this illness, which is unlikely to abate until the litigation process has been resolved.

[34] So far as the defendants are concerned, the effect of their failure to comply with the rule means that they cannot appeal unless they obtain the relief they are now seeking. In cases where the arguments for granting or refusing an extension of time were otherwise evenly balanced, a court will have to evaluate
b the merits of the proposed appeal in order to form a judgment on what the defendants will be losing if time is not extended. The pre-CPR rule in *Palata Investments Ltd v Burt & Sinfield Ltd* [1985] 2 All ER 517, [1985] 1 WLR 942 (see [10], above) is no longer relevant, because the court will not now entertain any appeal unless it is satisfied that there is a real prospect of success (or there is some other compelling reason for entertaining it). The consequence of the new requirement
c for permission to appeal is that if other factors militate towards the refusal of an extension of time, the likely prospects of success will have to be weighed in the balance. In other words the consequence of the appellants' failure to comply with the rule will be more serious for them if the court thinks that it is more probable than not that their appeal will succeed if it is allowed to proceed than if
d its prospects of success are smaller, even though they are just past the threshold at which it can be said that they are 'real' rather than fanciful.

[35] Finally, so far as the checklist is concerned, the effect which the granting of relief would have on the defendants is that if they go on to obtain permission to appeal they will have a chance of challenging the judgments entered against
e them. As to Mr Sayers, on the other hand, he will not only be relieved, if relief is refused, of the additional burden imposed on him by the defendants' refusal to make him a payment on account of costs. He is also now having to borrow to finance his continuing legal costs, and the interest running on the costs order will not afford full compensation for their delayed receipt. The reason for this is that the interest on his borrowing will not be tax deductible, whereas the interest on
f the costs will be fully taxable.

[36] After taking all these matters into account, I consider that this is a case in which this court ought, in the exercise of its discretion, to grant the extension of time sought by the defendants. Although I have great sympathy for Mr Sayers, and although a number of the matters I have considered point in his favour, it
g would in my judgment be a disproportionate response for the court to deny the defendants the opportunity of seeking to persuade us that they should be permitted to appeal, given the circumstances in which they came to delay filing their appellants' notice and the other peculiar features of this history.

[37] I should add, for completeness, that we were invited by Mr Anderson to
h consider the judgment of Peter Gibson LJ in *Alliance and Leicester plc v Slayford* [2001] 1 All ER (Comm) 1. The facts of that case were so very different, and the arguments addressed to us were so very different, that the citation of this authority did not really assist us.

[38] So far as the merits of the proposed appeal are concerned, Mr Goodfellow
j has delivered to us some cogent written submissions setting out reasons why we should not grant permission to appeal. The hearing on 18 April, which lasted more than an hour, was occupied entirely with oral submissions on the matters with which this judgment is concerned. I consider that fairness demands that a further 30-minute hearing should be fixed as soon as possible at which we will hear Mr Anderson's oral submissions on the merits of the proposed appeal. We do not require Mr Goodfellow to attend this hearing. If he does attend, we will

not necessarily invite him to address us, because we have a clear understanding
of the arguments with which he seeks to resist the granting of permission.

[39] For the avoidance of doubt, this is a judgment which sets out general
guidance on matters of practice, and the restrictions on citation that are
contained in para 6.1 of the *Practice Note* (*citation of cases: restrictions and rules*)
[2001] 2 All ER 510, [2001] 1 WLR 1001 do not apply to it.

KAY LJ.

[40] I agree.

SIR CHRISTOPHER STAUGHTON.

[41] I also agree.

*Application for extension of time for appealing granted. Application for permission to
appeal adjourned for further hearing.*

Kate O'Hanlon   Barrister.

a # Needler Financial Services Ltd v Taber

CHANCERY DIVISION

SIR ANDREW MORRITT V-C

b 16–18, 31 JULY 2001

Damages – Mitigation of loss – Benefit accruing to victim of breach of duty – Pensions misselling – Financial adviser wrongfully advising defendant to transfer deferred benefits under occupational pension scheme to pension plan with mutual life assurance society – Society demutualising and defendant receiving shares in transferee of society's
c *business – Whether value of shares to be taken into account in assessing compensation payable by financial adviser for breach of duty.*

In 1990, on the advice of a representative of the claimant financial services company (the company), the defendant transferred the deferred benefits to which
d he was entitled under an occupational pension scheme to a personal pension plan (PPP) with a mutual life assurance society. In 1997 the society was demutualised in order to enable it to compete successfully in the new financial services markets that had emerged in the 1990s. As part of the scheme, the defendant received, in respect of the PPP, shares in the parent company of the subsidiary to which the society's long-term business had been transferred. He sold those shares for
e approximately £7,815 net. In April 1998, when the defendant attained the age of 65, he discovered that the pension to which he was entitled under the PPP was less than the pension to which he would have been entitled under the occupational pension scheme. He therefore brought a complaint to the Ombusdman. The latter upheld the complaint, and assessed the loss sustained by the defendant in capital
f terms as £21,322. The company subsequently offered to compensate the defendant for the consequences of its advice, but insisted that he had to give credit for the value of the shares received on the society's demutualisation. That contention was disputed by the defendant. The company sought to resolve the issue, which had also arisen in thousands of other cases, by bringing a test case against the defendant.
g

Held – Where, as a result of the negligence or wrongful advice of a financial adviser, a person transferred his deferred benefits under an occupational pension scheme to a PPP with a mutual life assurance society, the value of the shares obtained by that person on the demutualisation of the society was not to be taken
h into account as a credit in assessing the compensation payable to him by the adviser. Under the normal common law principles, the relevant question was whether the negligence that had caused the loss had also caused the profit in the sense that the latter had been part of a continuous transaction of which the former had been the inception. That was primarily a question of fact. In the
j instant case, the breach of duty had given rise to the opportunity to receive the profit, but had not caused it. The benefit had derived from the demutualisation, which had not been caused by the company's negligence. Accordingly, the demutualisation benefit had not been caused by the misselling of which the defendant had complained, and the common law principles of assessment of damages did not require the value of the benefit of the demutualisation shares to be brought into account in diminution of the compensation to be awarded to the

defendant for the company's breach of duty. It followed that the issue would be determined against the company (see [24]–[26], [28], below).

Hussey v Eels [1990] 1 All ER 449, *Dominion Mosaics and Tile Co Ltd v Trafalgar Trucking Co Ltd* [1990] 2 All ER 246 and *Gardner v Marsh & Parsons (a firm)* [1997] 3 All ER 871 considered.

Notes
For benefits arising from independent or disconnected transactions, see 12(1) *Halsbury's Laws* (4th edn reissue) para 1044.

Cases referred to in judgment
AXA Equity & Law Life Assurance Society plc, Re [2001] 1 All ER (Comm) 1010.
British Westinghouse Electric and Manufacturing Co v Underground Electric Railways Co of London Ltd [1912] AC 673, [1911–13] All ER Rep 63, HL.
Dominion Mosaics and Tile Co Ltd v Trafalgar Trucking Co Ltd [1990] 2 All ER 246, CA.
Equitable Life Assurance Society v Hyman [1999] PLR 297; *rvsd* [2000] 2 All ER 331, [2000] 2 WLR 798, CA; *affd* [2000] 3 All ER 961, [2002] 1 AC 408, [2000] 3 WLR 529, HL.
Galoo Ltd (in liq) v Bright Grahame Murray (a firm) [1995] 1 All ER 16, [1994] 1 WLR 1360, CA.
Gardner v Marsh & Parsons (a firm) [1997] 3 All ER 871, [1997] 1 WLR 489, CA.
Hodgson v Trapp [1988] 3 All ER 870, [1989] 1 AC 807, [1988] 3 WLR 1281, HL.
Hussey v Eels [1990] 1 All ER 449, [1990] 2 QB 227, [1990] 2 WLR 234, CA.
Livingstone v Rawyards Coal Co (1880) 5 App Cas 25, HL.
Parry v Cleaver [1969] 1 All ER 555, [1970] AC 1, [1969] 2 WLR 821, HL.
Quinn v Burch Brothers (Builders) Ltd [1966] 2 All ER 283, [1966] 2 QB 370, [1966] 2 WLR 1017, CA.
Smith New Court Securities Ltd v Scrimgeour Vickers (Asset Management) Ltd [1996] 4 All ER 769, [1997] AC 254, [1996] 3 WLR 1051, HL.

Cases also cited or referred to in skeleton arguments
Alcona Minerals of Jamaica Inc v Broderick [2002] 1 AC 371, [2000] 3 WLR 23, PC.
Bradburn v Great Western Railway Co (1874) LR 10 Exch 1, [1874–80] All ER Rep 195, Exch D.
Cantwell v Criminal Injuries Compensation Board [2001] UKHL 36, 2001 SLT 966.
Caswell v Dairy Produce Quota Tribunal for England and Wales [1990] 2 All ER 434, [1990] 2 AC 738, HL.
Clark v University of Lincolnshire and Humberside [2000] 3 All ER 752, [2000] 1 WLR 1988, CA.
Credit Suisse v Allerdale BC [1996] 4 All ER 129, [1997] QB 306, CA.
Johnson v Agnew [1979] 1 All ER 883, [1980] AC 367, HL.
Longden v British Coal Corp [1998] 1 All ER 289, [1998] AC 653, HL.
Mercury Communications Ltd v Director General of Telecommunications [1996] 1 All ER 575, [1996] 1 WLR 48, HL.
Miliangos v George Frank (Textiles) Ltd [1975] 3 All ER 801, [1976] AC 443, HL.
National Insurance Co of New Zealand v Espagne (1960) 105 CLR 569, Qld HC.
R v Investors Compensation Scheme Ltd, ex p Bowden [1995] 3 All ER 605, [1996] AC 261, HL.
R v Securities and Investments Board, ex p Independent Financial Advisers Association [1995] 2 BCLC 76, DC.

a *R v Securities and Investments Board, ex p Sun Life Assurance Society plc* [1996] 2 BCLC
    150.
    Redpath v Belfast and County Down Railway [1947] NI 167.
    Smoker v London Fire and Civil Defence Authority, Wood v British Coal Corp [1991]
    2 All ER 449, [1991] 2 AC 502, HL.

b **Claim**

By claim form issued on 12 April 2001 in a test case brought by the claimant,
Needler Financial Services Ltd (Needler), against the defendant, Ronald Henry
Taber, Needler sought the determination of three questions of law, set out at [3],
below. The facts are set out in the judgment.

c *AG Bompas QC* and *Charles Marquand* (instructed by *Reynolds Porter Chamberlain*)
    for Needler.
Richard Gordon QC and *Sarah Asplin* (instructed by *Norton Rose*) for Mr Taber.

Cur adv vult

d
    31 July 2001. The following judgment was delivered.

SIR ANDREW MORRITT V-C.

Introduction
e
    [1] On 10 May 1990 the defendant Mr Taber, on the advice of a representative
of the claimant Needler Financial Services Ltd (Needler), transferred the deferred
benefits to which he was entitled in the Ilford Pension Scheme to a personal
pension plan (PPP) with Norwich Union Life Assurance Society (the Society). On
14 April 1998 Mr Taber attained the age of 65. He then discovered that the
f pension to which he was entitled under the PPP was less than the pension to
which he would have been entitled under the Ilford Pension Scheme. On 24 April
1998 Mr Taber complained to the PIA Ombudsman. The Ombudsman upheld
his complaint. Needler does not dispute, for the purposes of these proceedings
only, that its representative's advice was negligent and in breach of duty. On
15 November 1999 Needler offered to compensate Mr Taber for the consequences
g of its negligent advice, an offer which, but for one matter, Mr Taber would have
accepted.

    [2] The matter to which I refer is the demutualisation of the Society in June
1997 whereby its long-term business was transferred to Norwich Union Life &
Pensions Ltd (LP), a subsidiary of Norwich Union plc (NU). As part of that
h scheme fully paid shares in NU were allotted to the holders of with-profits
policies issued by the Society. On 16 June 1997 Mr Taber received 2,441 shares in
respect of the PPP. He sold them on 21 August 1997 for a net sum of £7,815·77.
In their offer to Mr Taber of 15 November 1999 Needler insisted that the shares
so allocated to Mr Taber should be taken into account in determining how much
j he should receive by way of compensation.

    [3] Needler's offer had been copied to the PIA Ombudsman. He drew to Mr
Taber's attention a Regulatory Update no 33 issued by PIA to its members in May
1997 to the effect that the financial impact of demutualisation should be ignored
in calculations of loss or redress in cases such as his. After further correspondence,
and with the consent of both the PIA Ombudsman and Mr Taber, Needler
invoked the test-case procedure for which the Ombudsman's terms of reference

provide. The claim form was issued by Needler on 12 April 2001 and seeks the *a* determination of the court of the following questions of law:

'(1) Whether the claimant may, in assessing the compensation payable by it to the defendant pursuant to the PIA pension review, for negligence and/or breach of contract and/or pursuant to s 62 of the Financial Services Act 1986 in respect of wrongful advice given to the defendant to transfer his deferred benefits under the Ilford Occupational Pension Scheme to the *b* Norwich Union Life Insurance Society (the Society) to buy a personal pension plan take into account as a credit to the defendant the value of shares in the Society received by the defendant following the demutualisation of the Society?

(2) If the answer to the first question be in the affirmative: (a) At what date *c* is the value of the shares in the Society received by the defendant to be assessed? (b) May the claimant also take into account as a credit to the defendant dividends received or receivable by the defendant in respect of his shares in the Society?'

[4] It is apparent from those questions and the written and oral arguments of *d* counsel that the relevant issues fall into three distinct categories, namely (1) the demutualisation of the Society, (2) the consequences at common law of such demutualisation on Mr Taber's claim for compensation and (3) the effect (if any) of the pensions review procedure which was activated by Mr Taber's complaint to the PIA Ombudsman. The evidence is documentary with helpful explanations provided by the witness statements of a number of individuals including Mr Taber *e* and experts' reports from two actuaries, Mr Grenville-Jones instructed by Mr Taber and Mr Wilson instructed by Needler. There was no oral evidence. In so far as there may be material differences between the experts it is agreed that I should resolve them as best I may without cross-examination.

f

Demutualisation
[5] The Society was established by a deed of settlement dated 1 July 1808. On 10 May 1893 it registered under the Companies Act 1862 as an unlimited company. It was an insurance company authorised to transact ordinary long-term insurance business under the Insurance Companies Act 1982.
[6] The articles of association of the Society provided that its members were *g* the legal holders, whether by original grant or assignment, of policies of insurance or annuity entered into by the Society as part of its ordinary long-term insurance business falling within Classes I or III of those specified in Sch 1 to the 1982 Act. The members were entitled to attend and vote at general meetings of the Society (art 1). In the case of a member whose policy entitled him to do so he *h* was eligible to share in the profits of the Society as provided for in arts 69–72 (art 17). Those articles required the directors at least once a year to determine in the light of an actuarial investigation the amount of profit available for allocation and to distribute that profit amongst with-profit policyholders in all respects as the directors thought fit. The directors were specifically authorised to allocate *j* additional bonuses and to set up special or reserve funds.
[7] Thus, in summary, when Mr Taber took out his PPP with the Society in May 1990 he not only became entitled by contract to the sums provided for in the PPP but, in accordance with the articles of association, he became a member of the Society and an object of the fiduciary powers conferred on the directors by arts 69–71.

a [8] I should, at this stage, refer to certain concepts associated with the conduct of long-term insurance business. I do so in simple, perhaps over simple, terms because no greater precision appears to be required in this case. The first is 'the asset share' of a long-term policyholder. This is calculated by reference to the value of the investments in the insurance company's long-term business fund acquired with the accumulated premiums paid by that policyholder together

b with the accumulated profits arising from those investments and an appropriate share in the net profits made in other operations financed by the long-term business fund (see *Equitable Life Assurance Society v Hyman* [1999] PLR 297 at 303 (para 41) and *Re AXA Equity & Law Life Assurance Society plc* [2001] 1 All ER (Comm) 1010 at [12]). The second is the policyholders reasonable expectation (PRE). This is dealt with in more detail in the judgments of Scott V-C in the

c *Equitable Life* case and Evans-Lombe J in *Re AXA Equity & Law Life Assurance Society plc*. For present purposes it is the collective reasonable expectation of the relevant class of policyholder derived from a number of sources including the articles of association, the past bonus policy of the company and the current practice of the insurance industry generally. The third is 'the inherited estate'.

d This may be described as that part of the long-term business fund in excess of the sum of the asset shares of the current policyholders. It is the accumulated surplus carried forward from past operations. It is a significant resource of the company. It provides for flexibility of investment, it enables bonus declarations to be averaged over good and bad years and it is available to finance new business. It provides additional security for the benefits of policyholders in case of need.

e [9] The demutualisation of the Society arose from the wish of the board to compete successfully in the new financial services market which emerged in the 1990s. It was thought by the board and others that the structure of a mutual society was inappropriate. The demutualisation of the Society was a complicated process, but it is unnecessary to go into all the complications. In essence it

f involved the following steps. (1) The long-term business of the Society was transferred to LP, a wholly-owned subsidiary of NU. Thus the liability under Mr Taber's PPP was taken over by LP in place of the Society. (2) The long-term business fund of the Society included shares in various subsidiary companies which carried on substantial general insurance business. Those shares were transferred to NU, not LP. The rest of the assets of the long-term business fund

g of the Society were transferred to LP. Within LP two funds were created, a shareholders' fund and a long-term business fund. The latter was divided into two sub-funds, a with-profits sub-fund and a non-profits sub-fund. (3) As consideration for the transfer of the shares in the subsidiaries from the Society to NU, NU paid £1·5bn to LP having raised the same by an issue of shares to the

h public. (4) As consideration for the transfer of the long-term business fund from the Society to LP, the wholly-owned subsidiary of NU, the latter issued fully paid shares to those policyholders who had been members of the Society. (5) The issue of shares by NU to the former policyholders and members of the Society was regulated by a flotation benefit deed dated 27 April 1997 made between the

j Society (1) and NU (2). The deed provided for two benefits, with a cash alternative, namely a fixed allocation and an additional variable allocation. The fixed allocation was 150 shares for each member irrespective of the number or type of policies held. The additional variable allocation was intended to be 'fair and broadly proportional to asset share' (recital H) in respect of all with-profits policies held by a member with a minimum of 300 shares. (6) The Society re-registered as a company limited by shares all of which were issued to LP.

[10] In order to obtain the approval of the court under s 49 of and Sch 2C to the 1982 Act, without which the transfer of the long-term business of the Society could not be effected, it was necessary for the scheme to be approved by both an appointed and an independent actuary. The appointed actuary recorded (para 6.2 of his report) that the principles behind the flotation benefit share scheme were the acceptability of the scheme to the membership as a whole, the reflection of the rights of members to vote at meetings and the rights of members holding with-profits policies to share in the future profits of the Society. In his opinion (para 6.11) the immediate tangible benefits of the free share scheme provided fair compensation for the membership rights in the Society. The independent actuary considered the share scheme for members in ch 9 of his report. He pointed out (para 9.3) that the value of the free shares would broadly reflect the value of the assets and entitlements transferred from policyholders to shareholders as a result of the scheme, less the capital contribution of £1·5bn into the [LP] with-profit fund. In para 9.12 he stated:

'The fixed allocation to all members may be regarded as providing compensation for the loss of voting rights. The additional variable allocation reflects the additional interest in the distribution of surplus of members holding with profit policies.'

He considered (para 9.17) that the balance of the free share allocation between members holding with-profits policies was appropriate because—

'These members have effected policies which have a low guaranteed entitlement but which participate in the fortunes of [the Society]. They would also be the main or sole beneficiaries of any distribution of free assets in circumstances such as the closure of [the Society] to new business.'

He agreed (para 9.31) with the appointed actuary that the proposed allocation of free shares fairly reflected the interests of members of the Society.

[11] In fact Mr Taber opposed the scheme, but he was in a minority. In due course he received 3,069 shares in NU. It is agreed that 150 were his fixed allocation, 478 represented his additional allocation attributable to two other with-profit policies he held and 2,441 were his additional allocation attributable to the PPP. The shares allotted to Mr Taber were first traded on 16 June 1997 at £2·90 each. By the time Mr Taber sold his holding on 21 August 1997 the share price had risen to £3·24. Net of the expenses of sale Mr Taber received £7,815·77 for the 2,441 shares attributable to the PPP. NU did not declare any dividend before 21 August 1997.

[12] The loss sustained by Mr Taber transferring his deferred benefits from Ilford Pension Scheme to the PPP was calculated by the PIA Ombudsman as at the date of Mr Taber's 65th birthday in capital terms as £21,322. If the contentions of Needler are correct then the loss so computed would be reduced by the net sum of £7,815·77 together with interest or the dividend declared between 21 August 1997 and 14 April 1998 (7·75p per share). Not only would Mr Taber's compensation be reduced by 36·6% but the principle could affect both the 43,000 outstanding claims and the 83,000 claims already dealt with in which demutualisation benefits are involved.

Common law treatment of demutualisation benefits

[13] For the purpose of dealing with this issue it is necessary to assume that, instead of complaining to the PIA Ombudsman, Mr Taber had commenced

a proceedings seeking damages for breach of statutory duty under s 62 of the Financial Services Act 1986, breach of contract and negligence. In that event would the benefit derived from the demutualisation shares have been brought into account in assessing the damages to which Mr Taber would, on the basis of the admission of liability for the purpose of these proceedings, have been entitled? It is common ground that such assessment should be made as at the date Mr Taber

b became 65, 14 April 1998, rather than the date of the breach in April/May 1990. That it is permissible to take such a date is apparent from the speech of Lord Browne-Wilkinson in *Smith New Court Securities Ltd v Scrimgeour Vickers (Asset Management) Ltd* [1996] 4 All ER 769 at 777–778, [1997] AC 254 at 265–266.

[14] It is also common ground that the basic rule is that enunciated by Lord

c Blackburn in *Livingstone v Rawyards Coal Co* (1880) 5 App Cas 25 at 39, namely:

> '...you should as nearly as possible get at that sum of money which will put the party who has been injured, or who has suffered, in the same position as he would have been in if he had not sustained the wrong for which he is now getting his compensation ...'

d One element in the calculation is emphasised in the speech of Lord Bridge of Harwich in *Hodgson v Trapp* [1988] 3 All ER 870 at 873–874, [1989] 1 AC 807 at 819 where he said:

> '... it cannot be emphasised too often when considering the assessment of
e damages for negligence that they are intended to be purely compensatory. Where the damages claimed are essentially financial in character, being the measure on the one hand of the injured plaintiff's consequential loss of earnings, profits or other gains which he would have made if not injured, or on the other hand, of consequential expenses to which he has been and will be put which, if not injured, he would not have needed to incur, the basic
f rule is that it is the net consequential loss and expense which the court must measure. If, in consequence of the injuries sustained, the plaintiff has enjoyed receipts to which he would not otherwise have been entitled, prima facie, those receipts are to be set against the aggregate of the plaintiff's losses and expenses in arriving at the measure of his damages.'

g [15] Lord Bridge went on to point out that the classic exceptions to the general rule are (1) moneys accruing to the claimant from insurance for which he has paid, and (2) moneys received due to the benevolence of third parties. The reasons for these exceptions are explained by Lord Reid in *Parry v Cleaver* [1969] 1 All ER 555 at 557, [1970] AC 1 at 13 and depend, ultimately, on considerations

h of justice, reasonableness and public policy.

[16] Counsel for Needler submitted that the operation of the general rule required that the demutualisation benefits should be brought into account and that the rationale behind the exceptions to the general rule did not apply to any such benefits. He suggested that when Mr Taber took out his PPP with the

j Society he thereby exchanged his rights in the Ilford Pension Scheme for all the rights accruing to him in consequence of the PPP scheme. The rights so accruing were not only the contractual rights under the policy but also the further rights conferred by the articles of association, namely, the right to vote at general meetings and the right to share in the distribution of surpluses. He contended that the right to share in the distribution of surpluses was translated by the demutualisation into the 2,441 shares in NU. In summary, he argued, the policy with the Ilford Pension Scheme was replaced by the PPP and the demutualisation benefits were the product of the PPP.

[17] This was disputed by counsel for Mr Taber. He argued that the demutualisation shares came to Mr Taber under an independent transaction. There were two elements to this argument. The first was that there was insufficient causal connection with the original breach of duty to bring the demutualisation shares within the general rule expressed by Lord Bridge in *Hodgson*'s case. The second was to the effect that the requirement for a benefit to be brought into account is confined to those benefits which are similar to the loss sustained. Both elements were challenged by counsel for Needler. The challenge to the first element was to the effect that the cases on which Mr Taber relied were inapplicable to cases in which the benefit accrued to the claimant before, not after, the date at which damages are to be assessed. His challenge to the second was to the effect that the judicial statements concerning the need to compare like for like are limited to cases which are said to constitute exceptions to the general rule. For reasons which will become apparent it is unnecessary to give further consideration to the second element.

[18] Counsel for Mr Taber relied on *McGregor on Damages* (16th edn, 1997) pp 219–235 (paras 336–356) under the general heading of 'No recovery for loss which the plaintiff has avoided, unless the matter is collateral'. The principal authority to which the editors refer is the well-known case of *British Westinghouse Electric and Manufacturing Co v Underground Electric Railways Co of London Ltd* [1912] AC 673, [1911–13] All ER Rep 63. In that case, which was concerned with a breach of contract only, Viscount Haldane LC emphasised that the subsequent transaction, if it was to be taken into account, must be one arising out of the consequences of the breach and in the ordinary course of business. As the editors of *McGregor* point out a wider formulation to include cases of tort is to exclude benefits arising from a matter completely collateral and merely res inter alios acta. It is true, as pointed out by counsel for Needler, that these passages are within the general topic of a claimant's duty to mitigate his loss. I do not accept his submission that they have no wider application. There can be no recovery of damages for loss avoided by matter not collateral whether by the claimant or by the course of events triggered by the breach of duty (cf *Hussey v Eels* [1990] 1 All ER 449 at 452, [1990] 2 QB 227 at 232).

[19] Counsel for Mr Taber relied on three recent decisions of the Court of Appeal. The first in chronological order is *Dominion Mosaics and Tile Co Ltd v Trafalgar Trucking Co Ltd* [1990] 2 All ER 246. In that case the plaintiffs' factory premises were severely damaged by fire in October 1983 due to the negligence of the defendants. The diminution in the value of the premises caused by the fire was about £60,000. The cost of the rebuilding (£570,000) and loss of profits in the meantime (£300,000) led the plaintiffs to buy a lease of larger premises for a total sum of £390,000. In 1987, having acquired other factory premises, the plaintiffs sold the new premises for £690,000. At the subsequent trial the judge held that the plaintiffs were entitled to recover the sum of £390,000 spent on acquiring the new premises. On appeal it was contended that the claim of the plaintiffs should be limited to the normal measure of damages, namely diminution in value. This contention failed. As Taylor LJ explained (at 252):

'... counsel for the appellants sought to bring later dealings into account. The respondents, by the comparatively modest expenditure of £60,000 in 1986, acquired the freehold of Waterend Road and were then able to sell it

a
for £690,000 in April 1987. It is argued that, since all of this happened before trial, it should all be brought into account in the appellants' favour. There should, up to the trial, be in effect a running account between the parties so that any gain to the respondents from whatever cause in regard to their property or its proceeds can be used by the appellants to diminish their liability. The judge rejected this argument on the practical ground that the

b
gains made by the respondents were attributable simply to the inflationary rise in the value of real property during the relevant period. I agree with him; but further, as a matter of principle, I do not accept that a defendant is entitled to the benefit of any successful dealings which the plaintiff may have had up to trial.'

c
[20] The second case is *Hussey v Eels* [1990] 1 All ER 449, [1990] 2 QB 227. In that case in February 1984 the plaintiffs had bought a bungalow in reliance on a misrepresentation that it had not been subject to subsidence. It had and the remedial works required would have cost £17,000. The plaintiffs could not afford them. After several unsuccessful attempts, in August 1986 the plaintiffs obtained planning permission to demolish the bungalow and to put up two other houses.

d
In October 1986 the plaintiffs sold the land with the benefit of that planning permission for £78,500 and moved elsewhere. Their claim for damages for the initial representation went through various mutations. The first formulation was the value of the land with a sound bungalow on it (£80,000) less the net receipts after reselling and moving (£76,095). By an amendment made before trial the

e
sum of £80,000 was increased to £90,000, thereby increasing the claim for damages from £3,905 to £13,905. At the trial a further amendment was made quantifying the damages as £17,000 being the difference between the price paid by them in buying the bungalow in 1984 (£53,250) and its actual value at the time (£36,250). The judge held that the misrepresentation had been made but that the claim failed because the gain on the resale exceeded the initial loss.

f
[21] On appeal the plaintiffs raised two contentions. The first was that they owed no duty to mitigate their loss by obtaining planning permission and reselling the land with the benefit of it. The second was that the profit on the resale was not to be taken into account. The Court of Appeal accepted both arguments. With regard to the second Mustill LJ, with whom Farquharson LJ

g
and Sir Michael Kerr agreed, considered all the relevant authorities and concluded:

'I have dealt with the authorities at some length, because it was said that in one direction or another they provided a direct solution to the present problem. For the reasons already stated, I do not see them in this light. Ultimately, as with so many disputes about damages, the issue is primarily

h
one of fact. Did the negligence which caused the damage also cause the profit, if profit there was? I do not think so. It is true that in one sense there was a causal link between the inducement of the purchase by misrepresentation and the sale two and a half years later, for the sale represented a choice of one of the options with which the plaintiffs had been presented by the

j
defendants' wrongful act. But only in that sense. To my mind the reality of the situation is that the plaintiffs bought the house to live in, and did live in it for a substantial period. It was only after two years that the possibility of selling the land and moving elsewhere was explored, and six months later still that this possibility came to fruition. It seems to me that when the plaintiffs unlocked the development value of their land they did so for their own benefit, and not as part of a continuous transaction of which the

purchase of land and bungalow was the inception.' (See [1990] 1 All ER 449 at 459, [1990] 2 QB 227 at 241.)

[22] The third case is *Gardner v Marsh & Parsons (a firm)* [1997] 3 All ER 871, [1997] 1 WLR 489. In that case the plaintiffs, in reliance on a survey which had been negligently carried out, bought from the landlord a leasehold property for £114,000. Three years later they discovered the defect. Two years later still the defect was remedied by the landlord pursuant to a term in the lease. The plaintiffs sought damages from the surveyors for their negligence. The judge assessed the damages as the difference between the value of the property without the defect (£114,000) and its market value with the defect at the time of the purchase (£85,000). The Court of Appeal, Peter Gibson LJ dissenting, held that the action of the landlord in repairing the defect was collateral to the negligence and therefore not to be taken into account in reduction of the defendant's liability. Hirst LJ said:

'[Counsel for the plaintiffs], founding his argument on *Hussey v Eeels* [1990] 1 All ER 449, [1990] 2 QB 227, submitted that where as a result of the defendant's negligence a plaintiff suffers loss in the form of diminution of value of the property, that loss is not avoided by the subsequent conduct of the plaintiff unless such conduct flows inexorably from the original transaction, and can properly be seen as part of a continuous course of dealing with the situation in which the plaintiff originally found himself. Here, he submitted, the action of the landlords in repairing the property was collateral, and res inter alios acta; moreover, it did not flow inexorably from the original transaction (i e [the surveyors'] negligent valuation) and was in no sense part of a continuous course of dealing, in view of the long lapse of time and of the nature and magnitude of the intervening events. In evaluating these arguments I bear very much in mind Mustill LJ's salutary warning against laying down potentially unreliable statements of principle in the field of damages, and I respectfully adopt his approach, namely that the issue is primarily one of fact, and that the relevant considerations are mutatis mutandis those cited by him in his conclusion, which seem to me in line with [*British Westinghouse Electric and Manufacturing Co v Underground Electric Railways Co of London Ltd* [1912] AC 673, [1911–13] All ER Rep 63] (see especially the second passage quoted above from Lord Haldane LC's speech ([1912] AC 673 at 691–692, [1911–13] All ER Rep 63 at 70–71)). It follows that I accept [counsel for the plaintiffs'] analysis and reject [counsel for the surveyors'] broad brush formulation, not least because of its inconsistency with the cases dealing with sale of goods or shares cited above, which cannot in my view be segregated from the main stream of authority. In my judgment, having regard to the intervening events and to the long interval of time, the repairs executed in 1990 were not part of a continuous transaction of which the purchase of the lease as a result of [the surveyors'] negligence was the inception. Furthermore, these repairs undertaken by [the landlord] at the plaintiffs' insistence were res inter alios acta and therefore collateral to [the surveyors'] negligence.' (See [1997] 3 All ER 871 at 885–886, [1997] 1 WLR 489 at 503.)

Pill LJ reached the same conclusion. He said

'In holding that the negligence which caused the damage did not also cause the profit, Mustill LJ in *Hussey v Eels* referred to the lapse of time between

a
purchase and sale and to the fact that the plaintiffs unlocked the development value of the land. That was done for their own benefit and not as part of a continuous transaction of which the purchase following misrepresentation was the inception. In distinguishing the *British Westinghouse* case, Mustill LJ said that "there was no question of [that] case being concerned with a chain of disconnected transactions" (see [1990] 1 All ER 449 at 455, [1990] 2 QB 227 at

b
236). In my judgment, the present case, on its facts, is on the *Hussey v Eels* side of the line. Hirst LJ has described the intervening events. Years after the defendants' negligence, the freeholders performed their obligation to the plaintiffs under a contract which the plaintiffs had negotiated with them. That has the effect of rectifying the damage resulting from the defendants' negligence. The benefit came by reason of the performance of a contractual

c
obligation by a third party. The plaintiffs had to undertake protracted negotiations with that third party and other third parties, the other tenants in the building. Before that obligation was performed by the freeholder, there was a considerable lapse of time in the course of which the plaintiffs, because of the structural defect, were unable to sell the property when they

d
wished to do so in 1988. In my judgment, the facts relied upon as affecting the measure of the damages are too remote to be taken into consideration and, on the facts, the judge was entitled to find for the plaintiffs as he did. On the sequence of events as it occurred, and not as it might have occurred, I do not regard the decision reached by the judge as contrary either to principle or to common sense.' (See [1997] 3 All ER 871 at 895–896, [1997] 1 WLR 489 at 514.)

e

[23] There is no hint in any of these cases or in any others of which I am aware that the general principle is inapplicable if the benefit precedes the date at which compensation is to be assessed. Obviously the benefit must accrue from acts or events occurring at the same time as or after the negligence for which

f
compensation is sought; otherwise the benefit could not have been caused by the negligence. If the benefit accrued at the same time as or after the negligence of which complaint is made I cannot see any reason why the general principle should apply only if it accrued after the date at which the compensation is to be assessed. Accordingly I reject the submission to which I referred in [17], above.

[24] In my view the authorities to which I have referred establish two relevant

g
propositions. First, the relevant question is whether the negligence which caused the loss also caused the profit in the sense that the latter was part of a continuous transaction of which the former was the inception. Second, that question is primarily one of fact.

[25] The profit in this case is the holding of demutualisation shares issued to

h
Mr Taber, but it might just as easily have taken the form of a cash payment or an additional bonus. I can see no reason for drawing any distinction based on the form in which the benefit was received. The benefit was derived from the demutualisation. The demutualisation was not caused by the negligence of Needler. It arose from the desire of the board of directors of the Society to have

j
the corporate structure best suited to competing in the new markets for financial products they perceived to have arisen in the mid-1990s. The underlying reasons are explained in detail on ch 3 of the report of the independent actuary. They have no connection with the breaches of duty of all or any of the financial advisers which led policyholders to transfer to a mutual society.

[26] It is true that but for the negligence of Needler Mr Taber would not have taken out the PPP. It is also true that but for the PPP Mr Taber would not

have received any demutualisation benefit. Even allowing for these factors the
demutualisation benefit was not caused by and did not flow, as part of a
continuous transaction, from the negligence. In causation terms the breach of
duty gave rise to the opportunity to receive the profit, but did not cause it (see
Quinn v Burch Brothers (Builders) Ltd [1966] 2 All ER 283, [1966] 2 QB 370; *Galoo
Ltd (in liq) v Bright Grahame Murray (a firm)* [1995] 1 All ER 16 at 30, [1994] 1 WLR
1360 at 1375). The link between the negligence and the benefit was broken by all
those events in the mid-1990s and later which led to the directors of the Society
formulating and the court approving under s 49 of the 1982 Act the transfer of the
long-term insurance business of the Society to LP.

[27] The matter may be tested in this way. Would Mr Taber have received
comparable benefits from his PPP if there had been no demutualisation? The
answer is plainly in the negative. Mr Taber was contractually entitled to share in
the profits of the Society by way of bonus. Such bonus was likely to provide him
with a reasonable return on his asset share in accordance with the PRE. But in
the absence of the transfer of the long-term business under the 1982 Act or the
winding up or closure of the Society to new business it was most unlikely that he
would ever share in a distribution of the inherited estate. But by virtue of the
demutualisation he did. Thus in ch 12 of his report the independent actuary
summarised his opinions as to the consequences of the demutualisation that no
group of policyholders would suffer any reduction in reasonable benefit
expectations, some with-profits policyholders might receive slightly higher
benefits, the proposed allocation of free shares fairly reflected the interests which
the members would be giving up and that the allocation of free shares meant that
qualifying members would be better off.

[28] For these reasons I conclude that the demutualisation benefit received by
Mr Taber was not caused by the misselling by Needler of which he complained.
Thus, the common law principles for the assessment of damages do not require
the value of the benefit of the demutualisation shares issued to Mr Taber to be
brought into account in diminution of the compensation to be awarded to him
for Needler's breach of duty. It follows that the questions whether if the general
rule had applied the demutualisation benefits should be excepted by analogy with
the exceptions, as explained by Lord Reid in *Parry v Cleaver* [1969] 1 All ER 555 at
557, [1970] AC 1 at 13, and whether the pension review procedure conferred on
Mr Taber an entitlement to compensation in excess of what would have been
recoverable at law do not arise. I answer question 1 in the claim form in the
negative.

Order accordingly.

Celia Fox Barrister.

a
Matthews v Ministry of Defence
[2002] EWCA Civ 773

COURT OF APPEAL, CIVIL DIVISION

b LORD PHILLIPS OF WORTH MATRAVERS MR, MUMMERY AND HALE LJJ

22, 23 APRIL, 29 MAY 2002

Crown – Proceedings against – Liability of Crown – Immunity from suit in respect of claim in tort by serviceman for personal injury sustained during service – Whether immunity incompatible with right to fair hearing in determination of 'civil rights' –
c *Crown Proceedings Act 1947, s 10 – Human Rights Act 1998, Sch 1, Pt I, art 6(1).*

The claimant had served in the Royal Navy between 1955 and 1968. He alleged that, in the course of his duties, he had been exposed to asbestos fibres and dust; that as result he had developed asbestos-related injuries; and that his
d injuries had been caused by the negligence and breach of statutory duty of the Ministry of Defence and of fellow servicemen for whose negligence and breach of duty the Ministry was vicariously liable. As a preliminary point, the ministry contended that it was immune from liability by reason of s 10[a] of the Crown Proceedings Act 1947, a provision that had been repealed in 1987, but only prospectively. Section 10 precluded a claim against the Crown in tort by a
e serviceman for personal injury if the injury had arisen in the circumstances specified in sub-ss (1)(a) or (2)(a) and the Secretary of State certified, under sub-ss (1)(b) or (2)(b), that the injury suffered had been, or would be, treated as attributable to his service for the purposes of an entitlement to a pension. The claimant contended, inter alia, that s 10 was incompatible with art 6(1)[b] of the
f European Convention for the Protection of Human Rights and Fundamental Freedoms 1950 (as set out in Sch 1 to the Human Rights Act 1998) since it prevented him from asserting a 'civil right' within the meaning of that article, namely his entitlement to compensation for the injury caused by the ministry. The judge accepted that contention, holding, inter alia, that art 6(1) was engaged
g since s 10 was a procedural rather than a substantive measure. The ministry appealed.

Held – Section 10 of the 1947 Act was not incompatible with art 6(1) of the convention. Its effect was substantive, not procedural. If the circumstances set out in s 10(1)(a) or (2)(a) applied, the serviceman had no effective cause of action
h in negligence. Any claim that he brought would, in the normal course of events, be defeated by the issue by the Secretary of State of a certificate under s 10(1)(b) or (2)(b). The issue of that certificate was a procedural step required by the Secretary of State in order to assert the defence to the claim that was always latent. That defence existed as a matter of substantive law and not procedure. In
j those circumstances, a serviceman had no 'civil right' that engaged the provisions of art 6(1) of the convention. Accordingly, the appeal would be allowed and the action dismissed (see [67]–[69], [80], below).

---

a   Section 10, so far as material, is set out at [8], below
b   Article 6, so far as material, is set out at [15], below

Per curiam. Although disputes relating to a serviceman's conditions of service are excluded from the application of art 6 of the convention, there is no such exclusion in respect of a claim in tort by a serviceman arising from events during his period of service (see [31]–[33], below); *Pellegrin v France* (2001) 31 EHRR 651 and *Fogarty v UK* (2001) 12 BHRC 132 considered.

Notes

For the right to a fair trial and for limitations on proceedings against the Crown, see 8(2) *Halsbury's Laws* (4th edn reissue) paras 134, 383.

For the Crown Proceedings Act 1947, s 10, see 13 *Halsbury's Statutes* (4th edn) (2000 reissue) 14. Section 10 has been repealed by s 1 of the Crown Proceedings (Armed Forces) Act 1987, save in relation to anything suffered by the person in consequence of an act or omission committed before 15 May 1987.

For the Human Rights Act 1998, Sch 1, Pt I, art 6, see 7 *Halsbury's Statutes* (4th edn) (1999 reissue) 523.

Cases referred to in judgment

Ashingdane v UK (1984) 6 EHRR 69, E Com HR; (1985) 7 EHRR 528, [1985] ECHR 8225/78, ECt HR.

Bell v Secretary of State for Defence [1985] 3 All ER 661, [1986] QB 322, [1986] 2 WLR 248, CA.

Church of Scientology v Sweden (1980) 21 DR 109, E Com HR.

Devlin v UK [2002] IRLR 155, ECt HR.

Dyer v UK (1985) 7 EHRR 469, E Com HR.

Fayed v UK (1994) 18 EHRR 393, ECt HR.

Fogarty v UK (2001) 12 BHRC 132, ECt HR.

Frydlender v France (2001) 31 EHRR 1152, [2000] ECHR 30979/96, ECt HR.

Golder v UK (1975) 1 EHRR 524, [1975] ECHR 4451/70, ECt HR.

James v UK (1986) 8 EHRR 123, [1986] ECHR 8793/79, ECt HR.

Kaplan v UK (1980) 4 EHRR 64, E Com HR.

Ketterick v UK (1983) 5 EHRR 465, E Com HR.

Mulcahy v Ministry of Defence [1996] 2 All ER 758, [1996] QB 732, [1996] 2 WLR 474, CA.

Osman v UK (1998) 5 BHRC 293, ECt HR.

Pellegrin v France (2001) 31 EHRR 651, [1999] ECHR 28541/95, ECt HR.

Pepper (Inspector of Taxes) v Hart [1993] 1 All ER 42, [1993] AC 593, [1992] 3 WLR 1032, HL.

Pinder v UK (1985) 7 EHRR 464, E Com HR.

Powell v UK (1990) 12 EHRR 355, [1990] ECHR 9310/81, ECt HR.

Pressos Compania Naviera SA v Belgium (1995) 21 EHRR 301, [1995] ECHR 17849/91, ECt HR.

R v A [2001] UKHL 25, [2001] 3 All ER 1, [2002] 1 AC 45, [2001] 2 WLR 1546.

R v Belgium (27 February 2001, unreported), ECt HR.

Reid v UK (26 June 2001, unreported), ECt HR.

Sporrong v Sweden (1982) 5 EHRR 35, [1982] ECHR 7151/75, ECt HR.

Stubbings v UK (1996) 1 BHRC 316, ECt HR.

Tinnelly & Sons Ltd v UK (1998) 4 BHRC 393, ECt HR.

Waite v Germany (1999) 6 BHRC 499, ECt HR and E Com HR.

Z v UK (2001) 10 BHRC 384, ECt HR.

a
Appeal
The defendant, the Ministry of Defence, appealed from the decision of Keith J on 22 January 2002 ([2002] EWHC 12 (QB), [2002] All ER (D) 137 (Jan)) whereby, on the determination of preliminary issues in proceedings brought against the ministry by the claimant, Alan Robert Matthews, he declared that s 10 of the Crown Proceedings Act 1947 was incompatible with art 6 of the European *b* Convention for the Protection of Human Rights and Fundamental Freedoms 1950 (as set out in Sch 1 to the Human Rights Act 1998). The PTSD Group Action claimants were given permission to intervene in the appeal. The facts are set out in the judgment of the court.

c
David Pannick QC, Philip Sales and *Kate Gallafent* (instructed by the *Treasury Solicitor*) for the ministry.
Richard Gordon QC and *Robert Weir* (instructed by *Bond Pearce*) for Mr Matthews.
Conor Gearty (instructed by *Linder Myers*) for the intervenors.

Cur adv vult

d
29 May 2002. The following judgment of the court was delivered.

LORD PHILLIPS OF WORTH MATRAVERS MR.

INTRODUCTION
e   **[1]** This is an appeal from the judgment of Keith J given on 22 January 2002 ([2002] EWHC 13 (QB), [2002] All ER (D) 137 (Jan)). It raises the issue of whether s 10 of the Crown Proceedings Act 1947 is compatible with the European Convention for the Protection of Human Rights and Fundamental Freedoms 1950 (as set out in Sch 1 to the Human Rights Act 1998). That is an issue of importance to any serviceman or ex-serviceman, such as Mr Matthews the claimant, who seeks to *f* claim damages against the Ministry of Defence in respect of injuries resulting from events that occurred prior to 1987.

THE CLAIM
[2] Mr Matthews served in the Royal Navy as an electrical mechanic between *g* 1955 and 1968. During this time he served in a total of seven vessels. He alleges that during maintenance at sea and periods of refit in port he had to work in boiler rooms where boilers and pipes were lagged with asbestos, from which asbestos fibres and dust dissipated into the air. He claims that, by reason of his exposure to these fibres and dust, he has developed asbestos-related injuries, namely pleural plaques and bilateral diffuse pleural fibrosis. These conditions do not *h* carry with them significant disability, but they can lead to more serious, and indeed life-threatening, illnesses.
[3] Mr Matthews alleges that his injury was caused by the negligence and breach of statutory duty of the Ministry of Defence and of fellow servicemen for whose negligence and breach of duty the ministry is vicariously liable. *j* Mr Matthews learned of the nature of his injury in September 1999 when Dr Halpin, a consultant physician, diagnosed pleural plaques.
[4] The ministry intends, if necessary, to defend Mr Matthews' claim on the merits. It has, however, taken the preliminary point that it is immune from liability by reason of the provisions of s 10 of the 1947 Act. Mr Matthews contends that it is both possible and necessary to give s 10 an interpretation which leaves

his claim unscathed.　Alternatively, if this is not possible, he contends that s 10 is incompatible with the convention.　Keith J rejected the former contention, but upheld the latter.　Before describing the issues raised in more detail, it will be helpful to refer to the statutory regime.

THE STATUTORY REGIME

[5] Until the 1947 Act the Crown was neither directly nor vicariously liable in tort.　If a servant of the Crown was held liable in negligence for an act or omission in the course of his employment, the Crown would normally indemnify that servant, but was not legally bound to do so.　This state of affairs was pithily summarised by the statement 'the King can do no wrong' (see *Mulcahy v Ministry of Defence* [1996] 2 All ER 758 at 763, [1996] QB 732 at 740).

[6] Away from the field of war there was, prior to 1947, no bar upon one serviceman suing another for negligence in respect of events occurring while on duty.　While engaged in warfare, however, no duty of care arose between servicemen (see *Mulcahy's* case).

[7] The 1947 Act brought an end to the Crown's immunity from liability in tort.　Under the general heading 'Substantive Law', s 2 provided:

> '*Liability of the Crown in tort.*—(1) Subject to the provisions of this Act, the Crown shall be subject to all those liabilities in tort to which, if it were a private person of full age and capacity, it would be subject:—(a) in respect of torts committed by its servants or agents; (b) in respect of any breach of those duties which a person owes to his servants or agents at common law by reason of being their employer; and (c) in respect of any breach of the duties attaching at common law to the ownership, occupation, possession or control of property: Provided that no proceedings shall lie against the Crown by virtue of paragraph (a) of this subsection in respect of any act or omission of a servant or agent of the Crown unless the act or omission would apart from the provisions of this Act have given rise to a cause of action in tort against that servant or agent or his estate.'

[8] Section 10 of the 1947 Act made special provision in relation to members of the armed forces:

> '(1) Nothing done or omitted to be done by a member of the armed forces of the Crown while on duty as such shall subject either him or the Crown to liability in tort for causing the death of another person, or for causing personal injury to another person, in so far as the death or personal injury is due to anything suffered by that other person while he is a member of the armed forces of the Crown if—(a) at the time when that thing is suffered by that other person, he is either on duty as a member of the armed forces of the Crown or is, though not on duty as such, on any land, premises, ship, aircraft or vehicle for the time being used for the purposes of the armed forces of the crown; and (b) the Secretary of State certifies that his suffering that thing has been or will be treated as attributable to service for the purposes of entitlement to an award under the Royal Warrant, Order in Council or Order of His Majesty relating to the disablement or death of members of the force of which he is a member: Provided that this subsection shall not exempt a member of the said forces from liability in tort in any case in which the court is satisfied that the act or omission was not connected with the execution of his duties as a member of those forces.

(2) No proceedings in tort shall lie against the Crown for death or personal injury due to anything suffered by a member of the armed forces of the Crown if—(a) that thing is suffered by him in consequence of the nature or condition of any such land, premises, ship, aircraft or vehicle as aforesaid, or in consequence of the nature or condition of any equipment or supplies used for the purposes of those forces; and (b) [the Secretary of State] certifies as mentioned in the preceding subsection; nor shall any act or omission of an officer of the Crown subject him to liability in tort for death or personal injury, in so far as the death or personal injury is due to anything suffered by a member of the armed forces of the Crown being a thing as to which the conditions aforesaid are satisfied.

(3) … a Secretary of State, if satisfied that it is the fact:—(a) that a person was or was not on any particular occasion on duty as a member of the armed forces of the Crown; or (b) that at any particular time any land, premises, ship, aircraft, vehicle, equipment or supplies was or was not, or were or were not, used for the purposes of the said forces; may issue a certificate certifying that to be the fact; and any such certificate shall, for the purposes of this section, be conclusive as to the fact which it certifies.'

[9] Section 10 of the 1947 Act was repealed by the Crown Proceedings (Armed Forces) Act 1987, but only prospectively. Thus, s 1 provided:

'Subject to section 2 below, section 10 of the Crown Proceedings Act 1947 (exclusions from liability in tort in cases involving the armed forces) shall cease to have effect except in relation to anything suffered by a person in consequence of an act or omission committed before the date on which this Act is passed.'

[10] Section 2 of the 1987 Act gave the Secretary of State power to revive the effect of s 10 of the 1947 Act, but only where necessary or expedient:

'(2) … (a) by reason of any imminent national danger or of any great emergency that has arisen; or (b) for the purposes of any warlike operations in any part of the world outside the United Kingdom or of any other operations which are or are to be carried out in connection with the warlike activity of any persons in any such part of the world.'

THE CERTIFICATE

[11] At the time of the hearing before Keith J the Secretary of State had not issued a certificate under s 10(1)(b) of the 1947 Act. On 11 March 2002 he did so, in the following terms:

'In so far as the personal injury of former Leading Ordnance Electrical Mechanic Alan Robert Matthews (service number D/M947091) is due to anything suffered by him as a result of exposure to asbestos during his service in the Royal Navy between 29 March 1955 to 15 March 1968, I hereby certify that his suffering that thing will be treated as attributable to service for the purposes of entitlement to an award under the Naval, Military and Air Forces etc (Disablement and Death) Service Pensions Order 1983 relating to the disablement or death of members of the service of which he was a member.'

[12] Mr Matthews has not yet applied for a pension under the 1983 order. We
understand that his medical condition would not be considered to constitute
sufficient 'disablement' to entitle him to a pension.

THE IMPACT OF THE CONVENTION

Article 2

[13] Before the judge, Mr Robert Weir for Mr Matthews, advanced an argument
based on art 2 of the convention. The judge recorded this argument as follows
([2002] All ER (D) 137 (Jan) at [47]):

> 'Article 2(1) of the convention provides: "Everyone's right to life shall be
> protected by law. No one shall be deprived of his life intentionally save in
> the execution of a sentence of a court following his conviction of a crime for
> which this penalty is provided by law." In brief, the argument developed on
> behalf of the claimant was as follows. Exposure to asbestos can result in the
> onset of diseases, such as mesothelioma, which can prove fatal. Article 2(1)
> imposes a positive duty on the state to take appropriate steps to safeguard
> life. As an organ of the state, the ministry was therefore obliged to take
> appropriate steps to protect the claimant from losing his life as a result of
> exposure to asbestos while he worked on naval ships in circumstances where
> the failure to take those steps amounted to negligence or breach of statutory
> duty. As a result of the operation of s 10 and the proposed issue by the
> Secretary of State of the appropriate certificate, the claimant's conventional
> remedy for this alleged infringement of his right to life under art 2(1) has
> been removed and replaced by one which (for the reasons given earlier) is
> wholly inadequate.'

[14] The judge did not find it necessary to deal with this argument.
Mr Gordon QC did not revive it before us. We are inclined to think that he was
right not to. We cannot see how s 10 of the 1947 Act could infringe Mr Matthews'
right to life under art 2. If the events of which he complains infringed art 2, then
the effect of s 10 might be to deny him an adequate remedy. In that event,
however, it seems to us that it is art 13 of the convention which would be
infringed as a result of s 10, not art 2.

Article 6

[15] Article 6(1) of the convention provides:

> 'In the determination of his civil rights and obligations ... everyone is
> entitled to a fair and public hearing within a reasonable time by an
> independent and impartial tribunal established by law.'

[16] Mr Gordon has made the following submissions in relation to art 6.
Mr Matthews asserts a civil right in the form of his entitlement to compensation
for the injury caused by the ministry. If s 10 of the 1947 Act prevents him from
putting forward his claim it thereby infringes art 6 and is incompatible with it. In
that event he is entitled to a declaration of incompatibility. His preferred
submission is, however, that, as s 3 of the 1998 Act requires, it is possible to
interpret s 10 of the 1947 Act in a manner that is compatible with the convention.
Such interpretation will enable Mr Matthews to pursue his claim.

[17] For the Secretary of State Mr Pannick QC has submitted that the judge
was right to rule that it was impossible to interpret s 10 of the 1947 Act in such a
way as to permit Mr Matthews to pursue his claim. He has further submitted that

there is no incompatibility between s 10 and art 6 for the following reasons:
(i) art 6 does not apply to claims by servicemen. This gives rise to what the judge
has described as 'the state service issue'. (ii) Mr Matthews has no 'civil right'
which entitles him to a court hearing under art 6. This gives rise to what the
judge has described as 'the procedural bar issue'. (iii) Mr Matthews is seeking to
use the 1998 Act to create a cause of action based on events that occurred before
the Act came into force. This is not legitimate. This gives rise to what the judge
has described as 'the retrospectivity issue'. (iv) If s 10 restricts rights under art 6,
it does so in a manner which serves a legitimate aim and is proportional. This
gives rise to what the judge has described as 'the proportionality issue'. We
propose to consider these issues in a different order from that adopted by the
judge.

THE STATE SERVICE ISSUE

[18] Strasbourg jurisprudence has long recognised that certain claims by
servants of the state are not properly to be considered as claims asserting 'civil
rights' and that, in consequence, art 6 does not apply to them. This jurisprudence
reflects law and procedures of member states which are not familiar to common
law jurisdictions. Certainly we have found ourselves in unfamiliar territory when
considering this issue.

[19] Mr Pannick's submissions have been founded on two decisions of the
Strasbourg court, *Pellegrin v France* (2001) 31 EHRR 651 and *R v Belgium* (27 February
2001, unreported). He submitted that these cases established that a claim against
the state for personal injuries in tort, if brought by a serving member of the armed
forces, was not a claim in respect of a civil right to which art 6 applied.

[20] In *Pellegrin's* case the applicant was a senior technical adviser employed by
the French Ministry of Co-operation and Development. His name was removed
from the list of the establishment on psychiatric grounds. He challenged this
decision in the administrative court system. This deals with disputes of public
law and is to be distinguished from the French court system which deals with
private law disputes. These proceedings were so dilatory that he complained to
the Strasbourg court that his rights under art 6 were infringed. The government
contended that art 6 did not apply because 'the dispute manifestly concerned
termination of the applicant's employment in the civil service'.

[21] The court observed (at 662 (para 59)):

> '... in the law of many Member States of the Council of Europe there is a
> basic distinction between civil servants and employees governed by private
> law. This has led the Court to hold that "disputes relating to the recruitment,
> careers and termination of service of civil servants are as a general rule
> outside the scope of Article 6(1)".'

[22] The court went on to describe a number of cases in which there had been
difficulty in deciding whether, on the facts, the application fell within the
category of cases to which art 6 did not apply. The test appears to have been
whether the decision complained of fell within the discretionary powers of the
state or was one that related to an essentially economic right that was contractual
in nature. The court commented (at 663 (para 60)) that the case law gave rise to
uncertainty:

> 'The criterion relating to the economic nature of a dispute, for its part,
> leaves scope for a degree of arbitrariness, since a decision concerning the
> "recruitment", "career" or "termination of service" of a civil servant nearly

always has pecuniary consequences. This being so, it is difficult to draw a
distinction between proceedings of "purely" or "essentially" economic
interest and other kinds of proceedings.'

[23] After observing that the basis on which civil servants provided their
services varied in different member states, the court continued:

'3. *New criterion to be applied*

64 To that end, in order to determine the applicability of Article 6(1) to
public servants, whether established or employed under contract, the Court
considers that it should adopt a functional criterion based on the nature of
the employee's duties and responsibilities. In so doing, it must adopt a
restrictive interpretation, in accordance with the object and purpose of the
Convention, of the exceptions to the safeguards afforded by Article 6(1).

65 The Court notes that in each country's public-service sector certain
posts involve responsibilities in the general interest or participation in the
exercise of powers conferred by public law. The holders of such posts thus
wield a portion of the State's sovereign power. The State therefore has a
legitimate interest in requiring of these servants a special bond of trust and
loyalty. On the other hand, in respect of other posts which do not have this
"public administration" aspect, there is no such interest.

66 The Court therefore rules that the only disputes excluded from the
scope of Article 6(1) of the Convention are those which are raised by public
servants whose duties typify the specific activities of the public service in so
far as the latter is acting as the depository of public authority responsible for
protecting the general interests of the State or other public authorities. A
manifest example of such activities is provided by the armed forces and the
police. In practice, the Court will ascertain, in each case, whether the
applicant's post entails—in the light of the nature of the duties and
responsibilities appertaining to it—direct or indirect participation in the
exercise of powers conferred by public law and duties designed to safeguard
the general interests of the State or of other public authorities. In so doing,
the Court will have regard, for guidance, to the categories of activities and
posts listed by the European Commission in its Communication of 18 March
1988 and by the Court of Justice of the European Communities.

67 Accordingly, no disputes between administrative authorities and
employees who occupy posts involving participation in the exercise of
powers conferred by public law attract the application of Article 6(1) since
the Court intends to establish a functional criterion. Disputes concerning
pensions all come within the ambit of Article 6(1) because on retirement
employees break the special bond between themselves and the authorities;
they, and *a fortiori* those entitled through them, then find themselves in a
situation exactly comparable to that of employees under private law in that
the special relationship of trust and loyalty binding them to the State has
ceased to exist and the employee can no longer wield a portion of the State's
sovereign power.'

[24] *Pellegrin's* case was a decision of the Grand Chamber, and in a concurring
opinion (para O-I2) one member of the court described it as a 'landmark
judgment'. We have, however, had some difficulty in distinguishing the precise
nature of the landmark.

a

[**25**] Keith J observed ([2002] All ER (D) 137 (Jan) at [31]):

'... before the application of the new criterion in *Pellegrin*'s case is engaged, the claim still has to be one to which the state service exclusion is capable of applying. The state service exclusion was said in *Pellegrin*'s case (para 58) to apply "to disputes raised by servants of the State over their conditions of service". Accordingly, the preliminary question which arises is whether a claim for damages for ill-health arising from harmful conditions *at work* can be classified as a claim relating to the employee's conditions *of service*.'

b

[**26**] Thus, on the judge's reading, *Pellegrin*'s case was concerned solely with the test of who constituted 'servants of the state'. The decision left untouched the requirement, if art 6 were not to apply, that the claim in question should relate to conditions of service. He went on to hold that Mr Matthews' claim did not 'relate to his conditions of service'. He observed (at [34]):

c

'To put it bluntly, the claimant's claim is a claim in tort. It does not become a claim relating to the terms on which he is employed simply because the terms on which he is employed excludes his claim in tort.'

d

[**27**] The argument advanced below on behalf of the Secretary of State appears to have accepted that the *Pellegrin* test applied only to disputes relating to the claimant's conditions of service. Before us, Mr Pannick's submissions went wider. He submitted that the exception to the application of art 6 applied to any claim against the state by a person whose functions fell within the *Pellegrin* criterion. The armed forces were expressly identified in *Pellegrin*'s case as an example of those who fell within that criterion. Thus the exclusion of art 6 applied to claims in tort.

e

[**28**] In support of this submission Mr Pannick referred us to the decision of the Strasbourg court in *R v Belgium* (27 February 2001, unreported). In that case the court reached its conclusion without the need for an oral hearing. The applicant complained of the fact that it had taken 22 years for him to establish his entitlement to a pension in respect of injuries sustained in the course of military exercises in which he was taking part as a reserve officer. He contended that his rights under art 6 had been infringed. The court held that the applicant fell within the *Pellegrin* criterion in that there was no valid distinction between a soldier serving as a regular and a soldier serving as a reservist. The court described (para 39) the claim as one 'for the payment of a pension in reparation for the lesions suffered during the accomplishment of military obligation'. There was no discussion as to whether this claim was one relating to the claimant's 'conditions of service' or as to whether this was any longer a relevant question, having regard to the decision in *Pellegrin*'s case.

f

g

h

[**29**] Before us Mr Pannick argued that Keith J's observation that Mr Matthews' underlying claim was in tort was irrelevant. Provided that Mr Matthews fell within the *Pellegrin* criterion any claim that he brought arising from his service fell outside the application of art 6.

j

[**30**] In considering this issue it is essential to bear in mind the nature of the claim that Mr Matthews contends he is entitled, pursuant to art 6, to have decided by a court. It is not a claim to a service pension. Nor is it a claim that, on true interpretation of s 10 of the 1947 Act, he is entitled to assert a claim in tort. The nature and effect of s 10 of the 1947 Act is the subject of the present proceedings, and there is no suggestion that the present proceedings infringe art 6. Mr Matthews complains

that he has a civil right to recover damages from the ministry in tort and that, to the extent that s 10 of the 1947 Act precludes him from asserting that right in legal proceedings, art 6 is infringed.

[31] The issue is whether a member state can preclude servicemen, or any other public servants, from asserting claims against the state in tort, or, if we correctly understand the effect of Mr Pannick's submissions, any other civil claims arising from events during their period of service, without infringing art 6. For reasons which will become apparent, it is not necessary for us to resolve this question. Our firm opinion is, however, that the judge was right in restricting the effect of the decision in *Pellegrin's* case (2001) 31 EHRR 651 to disputes relating to conditions of service. We observe that the court introduced its explanation of the new criterion with the statement that it was necessary to adopt a restrictive interpretation to exceptions to the safeguards afforded by art 6. In a supplement (*First Annual Updating Supplement* (2001)) to their work on *The Law of Human Rights* (2000), which covers decisions up to October 2001, Clayton and Tomlinson identify (at pp 76–77), seven decisions of the Strasbourg court in which the criterion in *Pellegrin's* case has been applied so as to exclude the application of art 6. All appear to have related to conditions of employment. The same is true of two further decisions to which we were referred—*Frydlender v France* (2001) 31 EHRR 1152 and *Devlin v UK* [2002] IRLR 155. If the test in *Pellegrin v France* (2001) 31 EHRR 651 is of general application, then it is surprising that there is no example of its application in relation to a claim in delict.

[32] We were referred to *Fogarty v UK* (2001) 12 BHRC 132 in the context of the procedural bar issue. We have noted, however, that the following observation of the court (at 140 (para 28)) bears on the present issue:

'The court recalls that in *Pellegrin v France* it adopted a functional test for the purposes of determining the applicability of art 6(1) to employment disputes involving public servants, based on the nature of the employee's duties and responsibilities. An employment dispute is excluded from the scope of art 6(1) if it concerns a public servant whose duties typify the specific activities of the public service in so far as he or she acts as the depository of public authority responsible for protecting the general interests of the state.'

[33] This suggests that the court considers that the decision in *Pellegrin's* case applies only to 'employment disputes'. We do not believe that the Strasbourg court intended the *Pellegrin* criterion to exclude claims in tort from the application of art 6.

THE PROCEDURAL BAR ISSUE

[34] This issue is the most critical of the four identified by the judge. Article 6(1) is essentially concerned with judicial process. Its effects include an entitlement to a fair, public and reasonably prompt hearing in respect of any assertion of an infringement of a civil right. A claim that a civil right has been infringed may involve a seminal question of law of whether the civil right, which the claimant asserts has been infringed, exists at all. English civil procedure is accustomed to resolving such seminal issues as preliminary points of law, before the facts that are alleged to give rise to the infringement of the right are investigated by the court. Whether a civil right exists is a matter of the substantive law of the contracting states. If a preliminary issue as to the existence of a civil right is decided against a claimant, there will be a procedural bar to his

a exploring the facts before the court. The nature of this procedure does not appear to have been fully appreciated by the Strasbourg court in *Osman v UK* (1998) 5 BHRC 293. The court has, however, since recognised that this procedure does not infringe art 6 (see *Z v UK* (2001) 10 BHRC 384; *Reid v UK* (26 June 2001, unreported)).

b [35] Some statutory rules and regulations are clearly designed to regulate court procedure. Examples are rules relating to admissibility of evidence, burden of proof and manner of proof. The provision in s 10(3) of the 1947 Act as to the conclusiveness of a certificate issued by the Secretary of State under that subsection is a further example of such a rule. Such procedural rules are subject to the requirements of art 6.

c [36] Other statutory rules, which may preclude a successful claim for infringement of a civil right, do so because they delimit the rights and liabilities that arise under civil law. They are not procedural rules, but rules of substantive law. The Strasbourg court recognises that art 6 has no impact on such rules. In *James v UK* (1986) 8 EHRR 123 the provisions of the Leasehold Reform Act 1967, which allowed tenants to buy their freeholds, were attacked before the d Strasbourg court on the ground that they infringed art 1 of the First Protocol to the convention. That challenge failed. It was also alleged that art 6 was infringed because, once the statutory criteria were satisfied, there was no court before which a landlord could challenge a tenant's right of enfranchisement on the basis of the merits of the individual case. The court observed (at 157–158 (para 81)):

e
> 'Article 6(1) extends only to "*contestations*" (disputes) over (civil) "rights and obligations" which can be said, at least on arguable grounds, to be recognised under domestic law: it does not in itself guarantee any particular content for (civil) "rights and obligations" in the substantive law of the Contracting States. Confirmation of this analysis is to be found in the fact f that Article 6(1) does not require that there be a national court with competence to invalidate or override national law.'

[37] In some circumstances it is less easy to differentiate between procedural and substantive rules. Rules providing for limitation of actions are procedural and g subject to art 6 (see *Stubbings v UK* (1996) 1 BHRC 316). Rules limiting the liability of shipowners under the Merchant Shipping Acts have always been treated as substantive. In *Fayed v UK* (1994) 18 EHRR 393, a decision to which we shall return, the court observed (at 430 (para 67)):

h
> 'It is not always an easy matter to trace the dividing line between procedural and substantive limitations of a given entitlement under domestic law. It may sometimes be no more than a question of legislative technique whether the limitation is expressed in terms of the right or its remedy.'

j [38] In the present case Mr Gordon's primary submission is that s 10 of the 1947 Act is procedural in character. Alternatively he submits that, if it is to be characterised as substantive, it is still subject to the application of art 6. This, he says, is because the Strasbourg jurisprudence shows that art 6 will be infringed if the state confers immunity from a civil liability which exists generally on a particular category of persons.

[39] Section 10 is not an easy provision to analyse. It is of an unusual, if not unique, character. Before undertaking that exercise, we propose to consider the Strasbourg jurisprudence that bears on this issue.

[40] In *Ketterick v UK* (1983) 5 EHRR 465 the applicant had been seriously injured while taking part in military training. The Secretary of State issued a certificate under s 10 of the 1947 Act. The applicant complained that this infringed his rights under art 6. The Commission held that the complaint was 'manifestly ill founded'. Its reasoning included the following passage (at 465):

'The applicant complains that as a consequence of the issue of the Certificate under Section 10 of the Crown Proceedings Act 1947, he is effectively barred from pursuing civil proceedings against the Ministry of Defence for negligence. It is clear from Section 10 of the 1947 Act that the legislature sought to confer on the Crown immunity from liability in tort in respect of members of the armed forces who suffer injuries in the course of their service. However, such immunity only arises if *inter alia* the Minister of Pensions certifies that his injuries are attributable to service for the purposes of entitlement to an award under the Royal Warrant ... The effect of this provision is that the applicant's right to sue in tort is effectively extinguished once such a certificate is issued and replaced by a pension entitlement. In the Commission's view the substitution of a pension entitlement for an action in tort does not in principle give rise to an issue under Art. 6(1) of the Convention. Such a system, for example, in the field of workman's compensation for personal injuries may be found in the legal system of many State Parties to the Convention. These rules are commonly based on the principle that compensation should be independent of the frequently difficult proof of negligence. The Commission notes that the applicant does not allege a violation of Art. 6 in so far as access to the courts in respect of his pension rights is concerned. It may therefore be left open whether these rights replacing the eventual tort claims are to be considered as "civil rights" in the sense of Art. 6(1).'

[41] It seems to us that the Commission ruled the complaint inadmissible because the effect of s 10 and the issue of the certificate was to alter the applicant's substantive legal rights, rather than to pose an impediment to his access to the courts to enforce those rights. This decision was considered by the Commission in two similar applications which were determined in identical terms—*Pinder v UK* (1985) 7 EHRR 464 and *Dyer v UK* (1985) 7 EHRR 469. It is necessary to quote at length from these decisions.

[42] At the outset the Commission posed the following question:

'It is not in dispute between the parties that, in general, the right to compensation for negligence constitutes a "civil right" and therefore the right to bring a civil action for negligence is guaranteed by Art. 6(1). The question, however, arises whether there can be said to be a "civil right" where such a right, i.e., a right to compensation for negligence, has been expressly removed by a statutory immunity such as that conferred by s. 10 of the 1947 Act.' (See (1985) 7 EHRR 464 at 465 (para 3).)

[43] After reference to the decision in *Ketterick v UK* (1983) 5 EHRR 465, the Commission continued ((1985) 7 EHRR 464 at 465–466):

a   '5. The Commission reaffirms the above view that, the substitution of a pension entitlement for a right to compensation in tort removes the "civil right" to sue for purposes of this provision. It recalls that the concept of "civil rights" is autonomous. Thus, irrespective of whether a right is in domestic law labelled "public", "private", "civil" or something else, it is ultimately for the Convention organs to decide whether it is a "civil" right

b   within the meaning of Art. 6(1). However, in the Commission's view, Art. 6(1) does not impose requirements in respect of the nature and scope of the relevant national law governing the "right" in question. Nor does the Commission consider that it is, in principle, competent to determine or review the substantive content of the civil law which ought to obtain in the State Party any more than it could in respect of substantive criminal law. As

c   it has stated in [*Sporrong v Sweden* (1982) 5 EHRR 35]: Whether a right is at all at issue in a particular case depends primarily on the legal system of the State concerned. It is true that the concept of a "right" is itself autonomous to some degree. Thus it is not decisive for the purposes of Art. 6(1) that a given privilege or interest which exists in a domestic legal system is not classified or described as a "right" by that system. However, it is clear that the

d   Convention organs could not create by way of interpretation of Art. 6(1) a substantive right which has no legal basis whatsoever in the State concerned. (Commission's Report, para. 150; see also [*Church of Scientology v Sweden* (1980) 21 DR 109; *Kaplan v UK* (1980) 4 EHRR 64 at 82 (para 134)]). It follows, therefore, that the State does not bear the burden of justifying an immunity

e   from liability which forms part of its civil law with reference to a "pressing social need" as contended by the applicant.

6. On the other hand, the Commission recognises that Art. 6(1) must be read in the light of the rule of law referred to in the preamble, of which the principle whereby a civil claim must be capable of being submitted to a

f   judge, is an integral part (see [*Golder v UK* (1975) 1 EHRR 524 at 535–536 (para 35)]). Were Art. 6(1) to be interpreted as enabling a State Party to remove the jurisdiction of the courts to determine certain classes of civil claim or to confer immunities from liability on certain groups in respect of their actions, without any possibility of control by the Convention organs, there would exist no protection against the danger of arbitrary power (see,

g   *mutatis mutandis* GOLDER judgment, para. 35).

7. In recognition of these principles the Commission has indicated that the jurisdiction of the courts cannot be removed altogether or limited beyond a certain point ([*Kaplan v UK* (1980) 4 EHRR 64 at 90 (para 162)]). Similarly, the Commission has emphasised that "a real threat to the rule of law could

h   emerge if a State were arbitrarily to remove the jurisdiction of civil courts to determine certain classes of civil action" ([*Ashingdane v UK* (1984) 6 EHRR 69 at 74 (para 92)]). These principles apply not only in respect of procedural limitations such as the removal of the jurisdiction of the court, as in the ASHINGDANE case, but also in respect of a substantive immunity from

j   liability as in the present case. The question, therefore, arises in the present context, whether s. 10 of the 1947 Act constitutes an arbitrary limitation of the applicant's substantive civil claims.'

[44] The Commission went on to hold that the substitution of a right to a pension, irrespective of fault, for a right to claim in negligence was legitimate. It then considered a related complaint that art 14, in conjunction with art 6, was

infringed because s 10 discriminated against servicemen. This complaint was also held to be manifestly ill-founded because the differentiation between servicemen and others had an objective and reasonable justification and was proportional.

[45] The observations of the Commission, if correct, indicate that s 10 of the 1947 Act is a substantive, rather than procedural, provision but that the provision would none the less have infringed art 6 if it constituted an arbitrary limitation on the applicant's civil law rights. Mr Pannick submitted that the latter proposition was wrong and that we should so find. In order to consider that submission it is necessary to consider a number of further decisions relied upon by Mr Gordon.

[46] In *Fayed v UK* (1994) 18 EHRR 393 Mr Fayed complained of the defence of qualified privilege against liability in defamation of inspectors appointed by the government to investigate the take over of Harrods. This prevented him from challenging in court the accuracy of their report. He contended that this infringed his right of access to a court under art 6 and his right to an effective remedy under art 13 for the breach of his right to respect for family life under art 8. The government contended that there was no infringement of art 6 because qualified privilege was a defence under the substantive law of defamation. The court held that it was unnecessary to resolve this question because the same issues arose in respect of the alleged breach of arts 6 and 8. It none the less repeated, with approval, the statement of the Commission in *Pinder v UK* (1985) 7 EHRR 464 and *Dyer v UK* (1985) 7 EHRR 469 that it would not be consistent with the rule of law in a democratic society or with the basic principle underlying art 6(1) if a state could 'confer immunities from civil liability on large groups or categories of persons' (see (1994) 18 EHRR 393 at 429 (para 65)).

[47] With the exception of *Osman v UK* (1998) 5 BHRC 293, as to which see our comments at [34], above, we have not been referred to any decision where the Strasbourg court has held that a rule of substantive law conferring immunity from liability on a category of persons infringes art 6(1). In so saying we distinguish between immunity from liability, which is substantive, and immunity from suit, which is procedural, although sometimes it is not easy to distinguish between the two (see, for instance, *Ashingdane v UK* (1985) 7 EHRR 528 at 545–546 (para 54)).

[48] In *Waite v Germany* (1999) 6 BHRC 499 the Commission and the court held that a complaint about the immunity of the European Space Agency from suit in the German courts engaged art 6(1). In so concluding the Commission observed (at 272 (para 55)) that the immunity asserted was procedural, not substantive:

> '... the rules on immunity from jurisdiction of, *inter alia*, international organisations prevent claims concerning substantive rights, which exist as such under German law, from being raised and enforced against the privileged persons in German court proceedings, unless they waive their immunity. In these circumstances, it is merely a procedural bar preventing the possibilities of bringing potential claims to court.'

[49] The same point was made by the court in *Fogarty v UK* (2001) 12 BHRC 132. In that case the applicant had attempted to bring proceedings against the United States government before an industrial tribunal, claiming discrimination contrary to the Sex Discrimination Act 1975. The United States government claimed state immunity under the State Immunity Act 1978 which precluded the tribunal from entertaining her claim. She complained to the Strasbourg court

a   that this infringed her rights under art 6(1). The United Kingdom government contended that art 6(1) was not engaged because the applicant had no actionable domestic claim. The court rejected this contention. It held (at 140 (para 26)):

b   '... the proceedings which the applicant intended to pursue were for damages for a cause of action well known to English law. The court does not accept the government's plea that because of the operation of state immunity she did not have a substantive right under domestic law. It notes that an action against a state is not barred in limine: if the defendant state does not choose to claim immunity, the action will proceed to a hearing and judgment, as occurred with the first discrimination action brought by the applicant ... The court is, therefore, satisfied that the grant of immunity is to

c   be seen not as qualifying a substantive right but as a procedural bar, preventing the applicant from bringing her claim before the Industrial tribunal ...'

[50] These decisions support the observations of the Commission in *Pinder v*

d   *UK* (1985) 7 EHRR 464 and *Dyer v UK* (1985) 7 EHRR 469 in so far as they extend to the conferring of *procedural* immunities from liability on certain groups. We have concluded that the Commission was wrong to suggest that art 6(1) could be engaged by a provision of the substantive law of a member state which provides that certain groups will be under no civil liability in circumstances where others

e   would be under such liability. To conclude otherwise would be to hold that the convention is capable of rendering unlawful substantive laws of a member state on the ground that they are discriminatory, notwithstanding that no fundamental right under the convention is in play. Such a radical conclusion cannot properly be founded on what were no more than observations of the Commission which

f   were not necessary for its decision. It is significant that art 14 of the convention, which prohibits discrimination, does so only to the extent that this impacts on 'the enjoyment of the rights and freedoms set forth in this convention'.

[51] We derive support for this conclusion from the decision of the Strasbourg court in *Powell v UK* (1990) 12 EHRR 355. The applicants lived in the vicinity of Heathrow and were consequently subject to aircraft noise. They could not bring

g   an action in nuisance against the operators of the aircraft by reason of immunities from liability conferred by s 76(1) of the Civil Aviation Act 1982. This section thus conferred on a particular group an immunity from the general law of nuisance. The Commission held the complaint that art 6(1) was infringed as inadmissible. The court agreed, observing (at 366 (para 36)):

h
'The applicants' grievance under Article 6(1) is in essence directed against the limitation of liability set out in section 76(1) of the Civil Aviation Act 1982. Framed in this way their grievance does not bring into play Article 6 or Article 13. As the Commission pointed out in its admissibility decisions,

j   the effect of section 76(1) is to exclude liability in nuisance with regard to the flight of aircraft in certain circumstances, with the result that the applicants cannot claim to have a substantive right under English law to obtain relief for exposure to aircraft noise in those circumstances. To this extent there is no "civil right" recognised under domestic law to attract the application of Article 6(1).'

[52] For these reasons we have concluded that the question of whether s 10 of the 1947 Act is procedural or substantive is all important when considering whether it infringes art 6(1).

IS S 10 OF THE 1947 ACT PROCEDURAL OR SUBSTANTIVE?

[53] Mr Gordon argued that s 10 was procedural. His argument turned largely on the provision of s 10(1)(b) and (2)(b). He submitted that a serviceman in the position of Mr Matthews had a vested cause of action in negligence unless and until the Secretary of State issued a certificate under these subsections. The issue of a certificate was a procedural step which precluded the claimant from pursuing the cause of action. Mr Gordon argued that the Secretary of State had an unfettered option as to whether or not to issue a certificate. His case did not, however, turn upon that point.

[54] Mr Pannick argued that the effect of s 10 was that a serviceman had no claim against the Crown for injuries sustained in service. In substitute for a claim in negligence, in which fault would have to be proved, a pension was provided without any need to prove fault. It was, and had always been, the practice to issue a certificate whenever a claim fell within the terms of s 10. The issue of the certificate was the mechanism by which the right to claim in negligence was replaced by pension rights. The scheme was not procedural, it was one whereby the substantive right of service claimants to sue in negligence for personal injuries was removed.

[55] On this issue Keith J found in favour of Mr Matthews. He considered that his case was supported by two decisions of the Strasbourg court and by an analysis of the effect of s 10, which we shall have to consider. We turn first to the two decisions.

[56] In *Tinnelly & Sons Ltd v UK* (1998) 4 BHRC 393 two contractors in Northern Ireland complained to the Fair Employment Agency that their tenders had been rejected because of what were believed to be the religious belief and political opinions of their employees, thereby infringing the Fair Employment (Northern Ireland) Act 1976. Section 42 of that Act provided, however:

'(1) This Act shall not apply to an act done for the purpose of safeguarding national security or of protecting public safety or public order.

(2) A certificate signed by or on behalf of the Secretary of State and certifying that an act specified in the certificate was done for a purpose mentioned in subsection (1) shall be conclusive evidence that it was done for that purpose.'

[57] The Secretary of State issued such a certificate. The applicants complained that the effect of this was to prevent their access to the court to determine whether their rights under the 1976 Act had been infringed. The government argued that the effect of s 42 was that they had no such rights.

[58] The court rejected this submission, holding that s 42 merely provided a defence to a claim under the 1976 Act. Furthermore, the provision that the certificate of the Secretary of State should be conclusive had the effect of preventing a judicial determination of the merits of the applicants' complaints that they were the victims of unlawful discrimination. The right guaranteed to an applicant to submit a dispute to a court or tribunal in order to have a determination of questions of both fact and law could not be displaced by the ipse dixit of the executive (see (1998) 4 BHRC at 417 (para 77)).

a   [59] We do not find that this decision has much bearing on the question of whether the effect of the provisions of s 10(1) and (2) of the 1947 Act are procedural or substantive. Nor is the certificate for which provision is made under s 10(1)(b) and (2)(b) to be equated with the certificate for which provision was made by s 42(2) of the 1976 Act. The true comparison is between the latter certificate and the certificate for which s 10(3) of the 1947 Act makes provision.

b   The *Tinnelly* case demonstrates that the provision for the s 10(3) certificate to be conclusive is potentially incompatible with art 6(1). That is not, however, in issue in the present appeal.

[60] The decision which Keith J found weighed more strongly in favour of Mr Matthews, indeed he found it indistinguishable from the present case, was *Fogarty v UK* (2001) 12 BHRC 132. The judge considered that the claim to

c   immunity in *Fogarty*'s case was identical in effect to the issue of a certificate by the Secretary of State under s 10(1)(b) and (2)(b). In either case, absent the claim or the certificate, the substantive proceedings would go ahead. The Strasbourg court had held that the claim to immunity merely imposed a procedural bar; it followed that the same was true of the issue of a certificate by the Secretary of

d   State in the present case.

[61] In our judgment the analogy drawn by the judge is a false one. The requirement in s 10 for a certificate from the Secretary of State as a precondition to defeating a claimant's cause of action is an unusual one and not easily analysed, and it cannot be treated simply as an option to impose a procedural bar on the claim.

e

[62] In this case Mr Gordon has had resort to Hansard, without objection from the Secretary of State or the judge below, in order to identify the purpose of the s 10 exception from the provisions of the 1947 Act. Having looked at Hansard for this purpose, it is not easy to ignore the reason why provision came to be made for the s 10(1) and (2) certificate—the more so because Mr Conor Gearty, whom

f   the court permitted to intervene briefly on behalf of the PTSD Group Action claimants, drew attention to this. Indeed, it seems to us that reference to Hansard for the latter purpose comes much closer to satisfying the requirements of *Pepper (Inspector of Taxes) v Hart* [1993] 1 All ER 42, [1993] AC 593, for s 10 leaves one in some doubt as to the nature and purpose of the Secretary of State's certificate.

g   [63] The Bill, which became the 1947 Act, was introduced into the House of Lords by the Lord Chancellor. The debate there shows that the Bill was always subject to the s 10 exception, which was not initially qualified by the requirement for a certificate. Provision was made for the 'conclusive' certificates under s 10(3) and there was considerable discussion about these. The requirement for the s 10(1) and (2) certificate was introduced in the committee stage by the Attorney

h   General. In moving these amendments the Lord Chancellor explained (151 HL Official Report (5th series) col 849, 31 July 1947):

> 'The substance of these Amendments is this, and I think that it is valuable. It is quite plain that a soldier does not lose his right of action against a fellow soldier through whom he has been injured, unless the Minister of Pensions
> *j*   certifies that the injury he has sustained is attributable to war service, or that he can get a pension. In other words, we must see that before we deprive a man of his right of action we give him a co-relative right, by way of pension.'

[64] It is thus apparent that it was never intended that the question of whether or not a serviceman should enjoy a right of action against a fellow serviceman or

the Crown for personal injuries sustained in service should be at the option of the *a* Secretary of State. The requirement for a certificate was introduced as a prerequisite to the loss of the cause of action in order to establish conclusively that the circumstances which had deprived the serviceman of a cause of action had entitled him, provided other relevant criteria were satisfied, to a pension. While reference to Hansard makes this quite clear, it is the conclusion to which we would have come without that assistance. The observations of Donaldson MR *b* in *Bell v Secretary of State for Defence* [1985] 3 All ER 661 at 664–665, [1986] QB 322 at 328 are to like effect.

[65] The essence of the judge's reasoning on this issue appears in the following section of his judgment ([2002] All ER (D) 137 (Jan)). Dealing with the effect of the issue of a certificate, he said:

c

'[21] ... Plainly his right to sue, i e the claimant's right to claim his preferred remedy of damages for exposure to asbestos in circumstances amounting to negligence or breach of statutory duty, has been extinguished. But does the extinguishment of that right mean that he did not thereafter have the right not to have been exposed to asbestos in circumstances amounting to *d* negligence or breach of statutory duty? If, after the passing of the 1947 Act, he had the primary right not to be exposed to asbestos in circumstances amounting to negligence or breach of statutory duty, s 10 merely extinguished his secondary right to claim damages for its breach, and that would amount merely to a procedural bar on his secondary right to claim his preferred remedy for breach of his primary right. *e*

[22] The structure of the 1947 Act shows that after its enactment the claimant did indeed have the primary right not to be treated in a way which amounted to tortious conduct. The Crown's previous immunity from liability in tort (whatever its extent may have been) was removed by s 2 of the 1947 Act. Thereafter the Crown could be liable in tort. Not merely did the Crown *f* then owe, for example, a duty of care in appropriate circumstances, but if it broke that duty it could be sued. What s 10 did was simply to prevent the Crown being sued if it broke that duty in respect of members of the armed forces. Otherwise, s 10 would simply have provided that s 2 was not to apply to claims in tort brought by members of the armed forces against the Crown or against other members of the armed forces.' *g*

[66] We have difficulty with this reasoning, which appears to be founded on the premise that the substitution of a potential entitlement to a pension for a cause of action in negligence is necessarily a matter of procedure. It seems to us that it is a matter of substantive law. A cause of action in negligence, as a matter *h* of substantive law, requires duty, breach of duty and entitlement to a remedy. That last element is essential to the cause of action. The entitlement to a pension is some consolation for the loss of the cause of action, but it cannot properly be described as a remedy for breach of duty when it is not dependent upon proof of fault.

[67] We conclude that the effect of s 10 is substantive and not procedural. The *j* reality is that, if the circumstances set out in s 10(1)(a) or (2)(a) apply, the serviceman has no effective cause of action in negligence. Any claim that he brings will, in the normal course of events, be defeated by the issue by the Secretary of State of a certificate under s 10(1)(b) or (2)(b). The issue of that certificate is a procedural step required by the Secretary of State in order to assert the defence

a to the claim which is always latent. That defence exists as a matter of substantive law and not procedure.

[68] In these circumstances, art 6 is not engaged. If there is an issue as to whether the criteria in s 10(1)(a) or (2)(a) are satisfied, that issue is justiciable in the courts. If there is no such issue, and the Secretary of State has issued the necessary certificate, the serviceman has no civil right which engages the
b provisions of art 6(1) of the convention.

[69] It follows from this conclusion that there is no incompatibility between s 10 of the 1947 Act and art 6 of the convention.

ARTICLE 1 OF THE FIRST PROTOCOL TO THE CONVENTION

c [70] We now turn to the other way in which Mr Gordon contended that s 10 was incompatible with the convention. The relevant part of art 1 of the First Protocol to the convention reads:

d 'Every natural or legal person is entitled to the peaceful enjoyment of his possessions. No one shall be deprived of his possessions except in the public interest and subject to the conditions provided for by law and by the general principles of international law.

The preceding provisions shall not, however, in any way impair the right of a State to enforce such laws as it deems necessary to control the use of property in accordance with the general interest ...'

e
[71] Mr Gordon submitted that, up to the moment that the Secretary of State issued his certificate, Mr Matthews enjoyed a vested right to bring an action in negligence against the Ministry of Defence. This right constituted a 'possession' under art 1. The issue of the certificate deprived Mr Matthews of this possession. To do so was not 'in the public interest and subject to the conditions provided for by
f law and by the general principles of international law'. It followed that s 10, which entitled the Secretary of State to adopt this course, was incompatible with the First Protocol to the convention.

[72] The submission that a vested cause of action in tort constitutes a 'possession' for the purposes of the First Protocol receives support from the
g decision of the Strasbourg court in *Pressos Compania Naviera SA v Belgium* (1995) 21 EHRR 301 at 334–335 (para 31). However, Mr Matthews' right to claim in tort under the 1947 Act was always subject to the provisions of s 10. It was defeasible and would, in the normal course of events, be defeated by the issue of a certificate by the Secretary of State should any claim be brought. Thus, we do not consider that the issue of a certificate by the Secretary of State deprived Mr Matthews of a
h possession. If Mr Matthews' claim is to be treated as a possession, the issue of the certificate was an incident of that possession which demonstrated that it was of little value. There is no incompatibility between s 10 and the First Protocol.

SECTION 3 AND A PURPOSIVE INTERPRETATION

j [73] It is convenient now to refer to the argument of construction, which Mr Gordon, with permission from this court granted on 10 April of this year, advanced as his primary case. It was not advanced before Keith J. It was founded on this explanation for s 10 of the 1947 Act given to the House of Commons by the Attorney General, Sir Hartley Shawcross (439 HC Official Report (5th series) col 1681, July 1947):

'Clause 10 is another Clause to which the attention of the House ought to be directed, because it contains a special exemption, or exclusion, in the case of claims between members of the Armed Forces in respect of personal injury which they have sustained while on duty as members of the Forces, or on Service premises. Here, again, I think Members will appreciate the special position which exists. For instance, it is necessary in the course of Service training, in order to secure the efficiency of the Forces, to exercise them in the use of live ammunition, in flying in close formation and, in the Navy, in battle conditions, with, perhaps, destroyers dashing about with lights out, and so on. These operations are highly dangerous and, if done by private citizens, would, no doubt, be extremely blameworthy, but it is impossible to apply the ordinary law of tort in regard to them, or make the Crown liable for any injury which, unhappily, results.'

[74] Mr Gordon submitted that this explanation for s 10 could not justify conferring immunity on servicemen or the Crown in respect of tortious conduct that occurred in circumstances where warlike conditions did not pertain. Section 10 should be given a purposive interpretation in order to make it accord with Parliament's intention. This should be achieved by implying the following additional sentence at the end of s 10(1)(b):'Such certificate shall not, however, be issued in any event unless the Secretary of State is satisfied that the circumstances in which the death or personal injury occurred were those of warlike conditions.'

[75] Mr Gordon submitted that his proposed interpretation would have the effect that s 10 addressed a legitimate aim in a manner which was proportionate and thus rendered the section compatible with the convention. It was legitimate, indeed mandatory, to give the section this interpretation because of the obligation imposed on the court by s 3 of the 1998 Act. The decision of the House of Lords in *R v A* [2001] UKHL 25, [2001] 3 All ER 1, [2002] 1 AC 45 showed that the technique of 'reading down' a statutory provision so as to restrict its ambit was legitimate.

[76] We can deal with these submissions quite shortly. In the first place, we have concluded that neither art 6 nor the First Protocol is engaged by the facts of this case. It follows that s 3 has no application. In the second place, we consider that to imply the additional clause suggested by Mr Gordon would be to go beyond the bounds of what s 3 of the 1998 Act permits. The fundamental alteration of the scope of s 10, which would result from the addition of the proposed clause, would amount to legislation by this court. Such a course is not permissible. Keith J came to the same conclusion.

THE RETROSPECTIVITY ISSUE

[77] Despite Mr Pannick's eloquence we had difficulty in seeing how questions of retrospectivity provided an answer to Mr Matthews' case. This was that he was prevented from access to the court by a procedural bar at the moment when the Secretary of State issued the certificate on 11 March of this year. No retrospectivity was involved in this case.

[78] Retrospectivity might have been relevant to Mr Gordon's new submission on interpretation for, had we acceded to this, it would have altered the effect of s 10 so as to confer on Mr Matthews an indefeasible cause of action which he did not enjoy before the 1998 Act, and in particular s 3 of that Act, came into force. We did not, however, understand Mr Pannick's submissions on retrospectivity to be directed to this issue, for they were advanced in the court below at a time

a where this issue did not arise. At all events, in view of our finding that the facts of this case engage neither art 6 nor the First Protocol, no question of retrospectivity arises.

THE PROPORTIONALITY ISSUE

b [79] Because we have found no interference with a convention right, no issue of proportionality arises. In these circumstances we do not propose to consider the attack made by Mr Pannick on the judge's findings that s 10 applied too widely to serve a legitimate aim in a manner that was proportional. We would simply conclude with the observation that it does appear to us to be harsh that servicemen who are now discovering that they have sustained injury as a result of tortious conduct prior to 1987 should be treated so less favourably than c servicemen who have sustained injury in similar circumstances, but as a result of more recent events.

[80] For the reasons that we have given, this appeal will be allowed with the result that the action must be dismissed.

Appeal allowed. Permission to appeal granted.

Kate O'Hanlon   Barrister.

R v Hanratty   *a*

[2002] EWCA Crim 1141

COURT OF APPEAL, CRIMINAL DIVISION
LORD WOOLF CJ, MANTELL LJ AND LEVESON J
15–17, 22–25 APRIL, 10 MAY 2002   *b*

Criminal law – Appeal – Fresh evidence – Prosecution application to admit fresh evidence – Whether Court of Appeal having power to admit fresh evidence at request of prosecution where such evidence not intended to rebut fresh evidence adduced by appellant – Criminal Appeal Act 1968, s 23.   *c*

In 1961 H was charged with the capital murder of a man in an incident in which the assailant also raped and shot the victim's female companion. He was convicted and executed the following year. In 1999 the Criminal Cases Review Commission referred the conviction to the Court of Appeal. On the order of that court, H's body was exhumed for the purposes of obtaining specimens of his   *d* DNA. When the appeal was heard, the prosecution made an application, under s 23[a] of the Criminal Appeal Act 1968, for the admission of fresh evidence, namely a DNA analysis which showed that H's DNA matched that obtained from an item of the woman's clothing and from a handkerchief that had been found with the murder weapon. Although the DNA evidence did not directly address the   *e* grounds of appeal, which relied on alleged procedural defects in the investigation and at the trial, the prosecution contended that it proved conclusively that H was the murderer. The defence challenged the admissibility of the DNA evidence, contending that the prosecution was only entitled to adduce fresh evidence under s 23 in order to rebut fresh evidence adduced by the defence on the appeal.   *f*

Held – On an appeal against conviction, the Court of Appeal was entitled, under s 23 of the 1968 Act, to receive fresh evidence at the request of the prosecution, even though that evidence was not adduced to rebut fresh evidence introduced by the appellant. The overriding consideration for the court in deciding whether fresh evidence should be admitted on the hearing of an appeal was whether the evidence would assist it to achieve justice. Justice could equally be achieved by   *g* upholding a conviction if it were safe or setting it aside if it were unsafe. Fresh evidence that was of sufficient quality and was relevant to the question of guilt would usually contribute to the question of the safety of the conviction, and so would be legally admissible if, in its discretion, the court decided to admit it. Where, however, the issue in question was not the evidence of guilt but the   *h* procedural quality of a trial, evidence relating to guilt would usually not be admissible because it would not address the defect in the trial unless it helped to place the defect in context. In the instant case, the DNA evidence was admissible under s 23 and it would be admitted in the exercise of the court's discretion. That evidence made a strong case even stronger and established beyond doubt that H   *j* had been the murderer. In any event, the other evidence in the case was sufficient in itself to provide overwhelming proof of the safety of the conviction from an evidential perspective. As regards the procedural shortcomings, they fell far short of what was required to lead to the conclusion that the trial should be regarded

---

a   Section 23 is set out at [88], below

a as flawed and the conviction unsafe on procedural grounds. Accordingly, the appeal would be dismissed (see [94]–[96], [101], [102], [105], [127], [211]–[213], below).

R v Pendleton [2002] 1 All ER 524 considered.

Notes

b For evidence on appeal, see 11(2) *Halsbury's Laws* (4th edn reissue) para 1380.
For the Criminal Appeal Act 1968, s 23, see 12 *Halsbury's Statutes* (4th edn) (1997 reissue) 393.

Cases referred to in edited version of judgment
R v Craven [2001] 2 Cr App R 181, CA.
c *R v Gilfoyle* [1996] 3 All ER 883, CA.
R v Gordon [2001] NIJB 50, NI CA.
R v Hakala [2002] EWCA Crim 730, [2002] All ER (D) 277 (Mar).
R v Hanratty [1962] Crim LR 409, CA.
R v Pendleton [2001] UKHL 66, [2002] 1 All ER 524, [2002] 1 WLR 72.
d *Randall v R* [2002] UKPC 19, [2002] TLR 179.
Stafford v DPP, Luvaglio v DPP [1973] 3 All ER 762, [1974] AC 878, [1973] 3 WLR 719, HL.

Appeal against conviction on reference by Criminal Cases Review Commission

e By reference dated 26 March 1999, the Criminal Cases Review Commission referred to the Court of Appeal the conviction of James Hanratty who had been convicted of capital murder on 17 February 1962 after a trial before Gorman J and a jury, and executed on 4 April 1962. The facts are set out in the judgment of the court.

f
Michael Mansfield QC and *Henry Blaxland QC* (instructed by *Bindman and Partners*) for Hanratty.
Nigel Sweeney QC, Mark Dennis and *David Perry* (instructed by the *Crown Prosecution Service*) for the Crown.

g   *Cur adv vult*

10 May 2002. The following judgment of the court was delivered.

LORD WOOLF CJ.

h INTRODUCTION
[1] On the evening of Tuesday 22 August 1961, Michael Gregsten and Valerie Storie were together in a grey Morris Minor car in a cornfield at Dorney Reach, Buckinghamshire. It was getting dark, when they were approached by a man who threatened them with a gun. On his instruction, the car was driven onto the
j A6. In the early hours of the following morning, at a lay-by south of Bedford, Michael Gregsten was shot twice at close range; he died almost instantly. Valerie Storie was raped and also shot: of approximately seven bullets fired, five entered her body. Miraculously, although she was left for dead, she was not killed; she did, however, suffer a catastrophic injury which resulted in paralysis to the lower part of her body. She was later able to describe the man responsible and provide considerable detail both of the events of the night and of what had been said.

[2] On 14 October 1961, following an extensive police investigation, James Hanratty was charged with capital murder. Committal proceedings took place between 22 November and 5 December 1961. He was indicted only for capital murder; there was no charge in relation to Valerie Storie in accordance with the then practice.

[3] The trial commenced before Gorman J and a jury on 22 January 1962. Eighty-three witnesses were called as part of the prosecution case, James Hanratty and 14 others were called on behalf of the defence and three were called in rebuttal (of an alibi disclosed for the first time when Mr Michael Sherrard, for the defence, opened his case). The trial having lasted what was then a record 21 days, on 17 February, James Hanratty was convicted of capital murder and sentenced to death.

[4] An appeal was mounted before the Court of Criminal Appeal; it was heard on 13 March 1962 by Lord Parker CJ, Ashworth and Fenton Atkinson JJ (*R v Hanratty* [1962] Crim LR 409). The grounds of appeal which were pursued were that the verdict of the jury was unreasonable or could not be supported by the evidence; the learned judge failed properly or fully to put the defence to the jury; and the learned judge misdirected the jury as to the evidence and/or failed adequately or properly to sum up on the issues raised upon the evidence adduced by the prosecution. There was no application to adduce further evidence.

[5] As to the first ground, giving the judgment of the court, Lord Parker CJ observed that 'there was abundant evidence which, if accepted by the jury, would support the verdict'. In relation to the other points, Lord Parker CJ went on:

'Mr Sherrard ... referred to a number of points which he says the judge failed to make and certain evidence to which he failed to refer. This was a case lasting 21 days ... and it would indeed be remarkable if every item of the evidence were referred to and in which the judge referred to every point or comment made by counsel on either side. Indeed, we would emphasise that it is no part of the judge's duty to refer to all the evidence or to mention all the points taken and comments made. His duty is to present the case on each side fairly and impartially to the jury concentrating of course on the vital issues in the case.'

In dismissing each of the grounds advanced, he went on to observe:

'... the summing up was clear, it was impartial, it was not only fair but favourable to the prisoner and contained no misdirections of law and no misdirections in fact on any of the important issues in the case. The court is of the opinion that this was a clear case.'

[6] On 4 April 1962, just over seven weeks after his conviction and seven-and-a-half months after the killing, James Hanratty was executed. It is worth observing that he was one of the last to suffer that penalty in this country. On 9 November 1965, by the Murder (Abolition of Death Penalty) Act 1965, capital punishment was abrogated, initially until 31 July 1970, but thereafter, by affirmative resolution of both Houses, permanently. It now offends art 1 of the Sixth Protocol of the European Convention for the Protection of Human Rights and Fundamental Freedoms 1950 (as set out in Sch 1 to the Human Rights Act 1998).

[7] In the years which have followed, there has been a vigorous campaign to establish that the conviction constituted a miscarriage of justice. In July 1963, Fenner Brockway submitted a dossier to the Home Office; on 2 August 1963, during an early day motion in Parliament, the Home Secretary of the day rejected

a calls for an inquiry into the conviction. In 1967, following a Panorama television programme, the then Home Secretary appointed a senior police officer to undertake an inquiry into the alibi evidence. He reported that the conviction was safe. On 1 November 1967, the Home Secretary made a Commons statement to that effect. There were further references to the case in the Houses of Parliament in 1969, 1971 (when a new inquiry was refused) and 1972.

b [8] In 1974, the then Home Secretary, the Rt Hon Roy Jenkins, appointed Lewis Hawser QC to conduct an inquiry. Bindmans (who continue to act for the Hanratty family) forwarded submissions. On 10 April 1975, Mr Hawser concluded that the case against James Hanratty was 'overwhelming'.

[9] On 13 July 1994, further submissions were made to the Criminal Cases *c* Unit of the Home Office. On 1 April 1997, responsibility for considering alleged miscarriages of justice passed to the Criminal Cases Review Commission (the Commission) who took over responsibility for investigating the allegations as to James Hanratty's conviction. Having conducted further inquiries (including obtaining DNA evidence), on 26 March 1999, the Commission referred the conviction to this court pursuant to s 13 of the Criminal Appeal Act 1995. The *d* Commission stated, in accordance with the statutory provisions, that there was a real possibility that the conviction would not be upheld.

[10] The referral has been followed by perfected grounds of appeal which rely on 17 grounds. These grounds overlap. Eleven are based on failures by the prosecution to disclose material to the defence, one concerns the conduct of the *e* identification parade at which Valerie Storie identified James Hanratty, one relates to the interviews (and is supported by electrostatic document analysis testing of interview notes) and four deal with directions given during of the course of the summing up (all but one based on stricter standards introduced since 1962).

f [11] On 17 October 2000, in the light of the DNA evidence then available, this court ordered that the body of James Hanratty be exhumed for the purposes of obtaining specimens of his DNA. Extensive further scientific evidence has since been assembled.

[12] In addition to raising factual issues the appeal has required us to consider issues of law which are of general importance as to the role of this court in *g* relation to fresh evidence relied on by the prosecution as well as the appellant. The appeal also raises the vexed question of how the changes in standards over the years affects appeals against convictions following trials which took place prior to those changes. We will deal with these issues after we have set out the facts.

h [In [13]–[77] the court reviewed the facts in greater detail, before continuing:]

[78] From the account of the facts which we have set out, coupled with the summary of the submissions of counsel at the trial, it is apparent, that the only issue with which the jury was concerned at the trial was the identity of the person who was guilty of murdering Michael Gregsten and raping Valerie Storie. By *j* finding James Hanratty guilty the jury resolved that issue. That on the evidence which they heard, the jury were entitled to come to this conclusion was made clear by the previous decision of this court and the conclusion of Mr Hawser to which we have already referred (see [4], [5], [8], above). Mr Mansfield QC does not suggest otherwise. In addition, he accepts that judged by the standards of 1962 the summing up of Gorman J, except in one respect, was extremely fair and beyond criticism.

[79] With this background the onus must be squarely on the appellant to establish that the appeal should succeed. Why then is it said that an appeal which *a* has previously failed should now after all these years succeed? The complaints which are made are based on non-disclosure for the purposes of the trial by the prosecution, fresh evidence which was not available at the trial and, with one addition, omissions from the summing up of directions which by present day standards, as opposed to those which existed in 1962, should have been included *b* in the summing up.

[80] The prosecution do not dispute there was non-disclosure as alleged and have not relied on the substantial difference between the duties of disclosure on the prosecution today as compared with 1962. Furthermore, it is not suggested that the appellant's additional evidence is not admissible.

[81] In opposing the appeal the prosecution unusually wish to rely on fresh *c* evidence, in the form of DNA findings which do not directly address the grounds of appeal but which the prosecution contend as a result of scientific developments clearly establish the guilt of James Hanratty. The appellant challenges the admissibility and relevance of the DNA evidence which was obtained from a piece of fabric from Valerie Storie's knickers and from the handkerchief which *d* was found with the murder weapon under the back seat of the bus[b]. They also seek to give an explanation for the findings consistent with James Hanratty's innocence by alleging that the exhibits on which the tests were conducted could have been contaminated due to the failure to preserve them in the way they would be today.

e

THE LAW

The role of the Court of Appeal

[82] In support of the contention that the DNA evidence is not admissible or relevant, Mr Mansfield submits that it is the jury and not the Court of Appeal *f* which, as the tribunal of fact, has the responsibility of determining the guilt or innocence of the defendant. He contends that if this court were to rely on the DNA evidence they would be usurping the role of the jury. He adds that the Court of Appeal's role is one of review and fresh evidence which does not relate to and is independent of fresh evidence relied on by the appellant cannot assist this court in the performance of its task as a court of review. *g*

[83] On behalf of the prosecution, Mr Sweeney QC argues that the DNA evidence is admissible and we should rely on it, if we are satisfied that it establishes James Hanratty's responsibility for the murder, as part of our reasoning for rejecting each of the grounds of appeal. Mr Sweeney suggests that the DNA evidence clearly establishes the correctness of the decision of the jury and proves *h* beyond doubt that there has been no miscarriage of justice.

[84] On the hearing of the appeal we allowed the evidence as to DNA to be placed before us, but indicated that we would give our decision as to whether we would admit the evidence in the course of giving this judgment.

[85] The issues on this appeal and, in particular, the dispute as to the *j* admissibility of the DNA evidence raise in acute form the question as to what is the precise role of this court when hearing an appeal and the extent of its discretion to admit fresh evidence. This question is undoubtedly one of general

---

b   Editor's note: the murder weapon together with ammunition, wrapped in a handkerchief, was found under the back seat of a bus.

a importance, but it is also one on which the authorities now provide considerable assistance, even though Mr Mansfield is right in submitting that they do not provide binding authority as to the relevance and admissibility of the DNA evidence.

The statutory provisions

b [86] The starting point for our consideration of these issues are the relevant statutory provisions. On references by the Criminal Cases Review Commission under s 9(1)(a) of the 1995 Act, the references are to be treated in accordance with s 9(2) of that Act as an appeal against conviction under s 1 of the Criminal Appeal Act 1968.

c [87] Fortunately, the role of this court on an appeal under the 1968 Act has recently been considered by the House of Lords in *R v Pendleton* [2001] UKHL 66, [2002] 1 All ER 524, [2002] 1 WLR 72. Lord Bingham of Cornhill referred to the legislative history of that section and in particular s 4(1) of the Criminal Appeal Act 1907, which is the predecessor of s 2 of the 1968 Act. He described (at [7]) that provision as being the—

d

'core provision' and added that the section 'clearly expresses Parliament's overriding intention that the interests of justice should be served [by this court] and also its expectation that the court would have to grapple with potentially difficult factual issues ...'

e Lord Bingham then went on to state (at [8]):

'Although the 1907 Act has been repeatedly amended, the scheme of the Act has not been fundamentally altered. The most notable change has been the granting by the Criminal Appeal Act 1964 and the extension by the Criminal Justice Act 1988 of a power, on the allowing of an appeal against conviction, to order a retrial. The core provision contained in s 4 of the 1907 Act is now expressed more shortly and simply in s 2 of the 1968 Act as amended: "(1) Subject to the provisions of this Act, the Court of Appeal—(a) shall allow an appeal against conviction if they think that the conviction is unsafe; and (b) shall dismiss such an appeal in any other case."'

f

g The most important lesson to be learnt from this part of Lord Bingham's speech is that Parliament's overriding intention in the 1907 Act, and now in the 1968 Act, is that it should be this court's central role to ensure that justice has been done and to rectify injustice.

h [88] The next provision to which it is necessary to refer is s 23 of the 1968 Act as amended by ss 4(1) and 29 of, and Sch 2 para 4(1)(3) and Sch 3 to, the 1995 Act. The section is in these terms:

'(1) For the purposes of an appeal under this Part of this Act the Court of Appeal may, if they think it necessary or expedient in the interests of justice—(a) order the production of any document, exhibit or other thing connected with the proceedings, the production of which appears to them necessary for the determination of the case; (b) order any witness who would have been a compellable witness in the proceedings from which the appeal lies to attend for examination and be examined before the Court, whether or not he was called in those proceedings; and (c) receive any evidence which was not adduced in the proceedings from which the appeal lies.

j

(2) The Court of Appeal shall, in considering whether to receive any
evidence, have regard in particular to—(a) whether the evidence appears to
the Court to be capable of belief; (b) whether it appears to the court that
the evidence may afford any ground for allowing the appeal; (c) whether the
evidence would have been admissible in the proceedings from which the
appeal lies on an issue which is the subject of the appeal; and (d) whether
there is a reasonable explanation for the failure to adduce the evidence in
those proceedings.

(3) Subsection (1)(c) above applies to any evidence of a witness (including
the appellant) who is competent but not compellable.

(4) For the purposes of an appeal under this Part of this Act, the Court of
Appeal may, if they think it necessary or expedient in the interests of justice,
order the examination of any witness whose attendance might be required
under subsection (1)(b) above to be conducted, in manner provided by rules
of court, before any judge or officer of the Court or other person appointed
by the Court for the purpose, and allow the admission of any depositions so
taken as evidence before the Court.'

[89] A feature of s 23 is that it makes the discretion which the section gives to
this court to receive fresh evidence, subject to an express requirement that this
court shall consider it is 'necessary or expedient in the interests of justice' to do
so. Thus, the section echoes the 'core provision' identified by Lord Bingham
which is implicitly a part of s 2 of the 1968 Act. Subsection (2) does no more than
identify the different considerations to which the court is required to have regard
when exercising that discretion.

[90] Mr Mansfield referred us to the legislative history of s 23 in its present
form. He pointed out s 23 is derived from s 9 of the 1907 Act. He argues the
amendments which were made to s 23 restrict the discretion of the court to admit
fresh evidence. We do not accept that this is the position. The changes simplified
the language of the section but did not affect the overriding purpose of the section
which was, and is, that the power to admit fresh evidence should be to assist this
court in its task of furthering the interests of justice.

[91] In performing this task the court should have in mind that, in the same
speech ([2002] 1 All ER 524 at [17]), Lord Bingham also emphasised, that while the
Court of Appeal is entrusted 'with a power of review to guard against the
possibility of injustice', it should not intrude 'into territory which properly
belongs to the jury'. He also endorsed the approach in *Stafford v DPP, Luvaglio v
DPP* [1973] 3 All ER 762, [1974] AC 878. What made a decision 'unsafe' was to be
determined by deciding what was the effect of the fresh evidence on the minds of
the court and not by asking what might be the effect that the evidence would
have on the mind of the jury. This court has, however, to bear 'very clearly in
mind that the question for its consideration is whether the conviction is safe and
not whether the accused is guilty'. The court has also to remember that it should
not become the primary decision-maker as it has not heard the evidence which
the jury heard. So it is perfectly in order for—

'the Court of Appeal, in a case of any difficulty, to test their own
provisional view by asking whether the evidence, if given at the trial, might
reasonably have affected the decision of the trial jury to convict. If it might,
the conviction must be thought to be unsafe.' (See [2002] 1 All ER 524 at
[19].)

a To cite Lord Bingham again (at [17]):

> 'Trial by jury does not mean trial by jury in the first instance and trial by judges of the Court of Appeal in the second. The Court of Appeal is entrusted with a power of review ... to be exercised with caution, mindful that the Court of Appeal is not privy to the jury's deliberations and must not
b intrude into territory which properly belongs to the jury.'

[92] On this aspect of the law, Lord Bingham's views were endorsed by all the other members of the House and they deserve our particular attention. (Lord Hobhouse of Woodborough delivered the only other separate speech and he expressly agreed (at [35]) with this aspect of the speech of Lord Bingham.)

c **[93]** The decision in *R v Pendleton* was subsequently applied by this court in *R v Hakala* [2002] EWCA Crim 730, [2002] All ER (D) 277 (Mar). In his judgment (at [11]), Judge LJ made this statement, which is particularly relevant to the issues before us:

d > 'The judgment in "fresh evidence" cases will inevitably therefore continue to focus on the facts before the trial jury, in order to ensure that the right question—the safety, or otherwise, of the conviction—is answered. It is integral to the process that if the fresh evidence is disputed, this court must decide whether and to what extent it should be accepted or rejected, and if it is to be accepted, to evaluate its importance, or otherwise, relative to the
e > remaining material which was before the trial jury: hence the jury impact test. Indeed, although the question did not arise in *R v Pendleton*, *the fresh evidence produced by the appellant, or indeed the Crown, may serve to confirm rather than undermine the safety of the conviction.* Unless this evaluation is carried out, it is difficult to see how this court can carry out its statutory responsibility in a fresh evidence case, and exercise its "powers of review to guard against the
f > possibility of injustice". However the safety of the appellant's convictions is examined, the essential question, and ultimately the only question for this court, is whether, in the light of the fresh evidence, the convictions are unsafe.' (Our emphasis.)

g *The admissibility of fresh evidence and the two different grounds for allowing an appeal*

[94] Assisted by these authorities it is clear that the overriding consideration for this court in deciding whether fresh evidence should be admitted on the hearing of an appeal is whether the evidence will assist the court to achieve
h justice. Justice can equally be achieved by upholding a conviction if it is safe or setting it aside if it is unsafe.

[95] Here it is important to have in mind that a conviction can be unsafe for two distinct reasons that may, but do not necessarily, overlap. The first reason being that there is a doubt as to the safety of the conviction and the second being
j that the trial was materially flawed. The second reason can be independent of guilt because of the fundamental constitutional requirement that even a guilty defendant is entitled, before being found guilty, to have a trial which conforms with at least the minimum standards of what is regarded in this jurisdiction as being an acceptable criminal trial. These standards include those that safeguard a defendant from serious procedural, but not technical, unfairness. A technical flaw is excluded because it is wrong to elevate the procedural rules that govern a

trial to a level where they become an obstacle as opposed to an aid to achieving justice.

[96] Fresh evidence which is of sufficient quality and is relevant to the question of guilt will usually contribute to the question of the safety of the conviction and so will be legally admissible if in its discretion the court decides to admit it. Where what is in question is not the evidence of guilt but the procedural quality of a trial, evidence relating to guilt will usually not be admissible because it will not address the defect in the trial unless it helps to place the defect in context. Evidence as to what happened at the trial may on the other hand be very important as to the extent to which the trial is flawed. It follows that relevance of the fresh evidence may not be capable of being determined until after the purpose for which it is said to be relevant has been ascertained. The approach to procedural and evidential issues will not be the same.

[97] It is also necessary to distinguish between procedural flaws which are technical and those which are not. Clear guidance as to this distinction has also been provided by Lord Bingham in the recent Privy Council decision of *Randall v R* [2002] UKPC 19 at [28], [2002] TLR 179:

'While reference has been made above to some of the rules which should be observed in a well-conducted trial to safeguard the fairness of the proceedings, it is not every departure from good practice which renders a trial unfair. Inevitably, in the course of a long trial, things are done or said which should not be done or said. Most occurrences of that kind do not undermine the integrity of the trial, particularly if they are isolated and particularly if, where appropriate, they are the subject of a clear judicial direction. It would emasculate the trial process, and undermine public confidence in the administration of criminal justice, if a standard of perfection were imposed that was incapable of attainment in practice. But the right of a criminal defendant to a fair trial is absolute. There will come a point when the departure from good practice is so gross, or so persistent, or so prejudicial, or so irremediable that an appellate court will have no choice but to condemn a trial as unfair and quash a conviction as unsafe, however strong the grounds for believing the defendant to be guilty. The right to a fair trial is one to be enjoyed by the guilty as well as the innocent, for a defendant is presumed to be innocent until proved to be otherwise in a fairly conducted trial.'

We would also refer to the way the subject was encapsulated by Carswell LCJ in *R v Gordon* [2001] NIJB 50 at 66:

'It seems to us that it is now possible to formulate two propositions in respect of irregularities at trial, which formed the subject of a good deal of argument before us: 1. If there was a material irregularity, the conviction may be set aside even if the evidence of the appellant's guilt is clear. 2. Not every irregularity will cause a conviction to be set aside. There is room for the application of a test similar in effect to that of the former proviso, viz whether the irregularity was so serious that a miscarriage of justice has actually occurred.'

The effect of the passage of time

[98] The non-technical approach is especially important in references by the Commission such as this since standards may have changed because of the

a passage of time. For understandable reasons, it is now accepted in judging the question of fairness of a trial, and fairness is what rules of procedure are designed to achieve, we apply current standards irrespective of when the trial took place. But this does not mean that because contemporary rules have not been complied with a trial which took place in the past must be judged on the false assumption it was tried yesterday. Such an approach could achieve injustice because the non-compliance with rules does not necessarily mean that a defendant has been
b treated unfairly. In order to achieve justice, non-compliance with rules which were not current at the time of the trial may need to be treated differently from rules which were in force at the time of trial. If certain of the current requirements of, for example, a summing up are not complied with at a trial which takes place today this can almost automatically result in a conviction being
c set aside but this approach should not be adopted in relation to trials which took place before the rule was established. The fact that what has happened did not comply with a rule which was in force at the time of trial makes the non-compliance more serious than it would be if there was no rule in force. Proper standards will not be maintained unless this court can be expected, when
d appropriate, to enforce the rules by taking a serious view of a breach of the rules at the time they are in force. It is not appropriate to apply this approach to a 40-year-old case.

[99] Another difference between a case such as this and a case which has only been tried recently is that this court can expect in the latter type of case to be provided with an explanation for situations which give rise to a suspicion of
e possible impropriety. There may be an explanation for what happened which shows there is no cause for suspicion, but this may be impossible to discover due to the passage of time. This has to be borne in mind, particularly where to draw an adverse inference could reflect, as in this case, on the integrity of those who are not alive. (Here this is true of Det Supt Acott and Det Sgt Oxford.[c])

f [100] The question of whether a trial is sufficiently seriously flawed, so as to make a conviction unsafe because it does not comply with what would be regarded today as the minimum standards, must be approached in the round, taking into account all the relevant circumstances, and this is what we propose to do notwithstanding the fact that Mr Sweeney did not seek to rely on the different standards which existed at the time of the trial and the standards today.

g

Admitting fresh evidence at the request of the prosecution

[101] It is now necessary to concentrate on situations in which it can be appropriate for this court to receive fresh evidence at the request of the prosecution, such as the findings of the DNA tests on which the prosecution are
h seeking to rely in this appeal. It is Mr Mansfield's contention that if this court is not to exceed its role as a court of review it can only receive fresh evidence on behalf of the prosecution if that evidence is being relied upon to rebut fresh evidence introduced on the appeal by an appellant. In support of his contention, Mr Mansfield focuses upon s 23(2) of the 1968 Act. He points out correctly that
j the subsection contains a mandatory requirement, and that the requirement as to para (b) in particular is only likely to be complied with by an appellant and not the prosecution. The prosecution are not going to submit evidence which will undermine the conviction. He therefore submits that evidence cannot be allowed to be placed before the court by the prosecution unless the evidence on which the

---

c Editor's note: they were the interviewing police officers.

prosecution relies is to be used in order to evaluate or rebut fresh evidence that the appellant has adduced.

[102] We do not accept this submission. Subsection (2) is subordinate to sub-s (1). It is sub-s (1) which confers a general discretion on the court to be exercised in the interests of justice. Subsection (2) identifies the considerations to which this court is required to have regard when exercising its discretion under sub-s (1). If this court has regard to the matters referred to in sub-s (2), the court has done its duty irrespective of how it exercises its discretion. If it is the prosecution which wishes to introduce fresh evidence which is intended to weaken the appeal, this does not mean that the evidence cannot be admitted. All that s 23(2)(b) requires is that this court, when exercising its discretion, has regard to the fact that the evidence will not 'afford any ground for allowing the appeal' but on the contrary support the conviction. To apply sub-s (2) as Mr Mansfield contends would mean that the court would be unable to admit evidence even if the admission of that evidence is very much in accord with the interests of justice and its rejection could result in injustice. In addition, it would undermine the public's confidence in the justice system.

[103] Furthermore Mr Mansfield's approach to s 23 is inconsistent with the decisions of this court in *R v Gilfoyle* [1996] 3 All ER 883 and in *R v Craven* [2001] 2 Cr App R 181. In *R v Craven* there was a failure by the prosecution to disclose certain material which could have been of relevance to the defence at the trial, and in an important passage in the judgment (at 196–197 (para 58)), Latham LJ stressed—

> 'that this Court, empowered as it is under section 23 of the Criminal Appeal Act 1968 to consider the jury's verdict in the light of fresh evidence, should do so in the light of all the fresh evidence that is available to it. We are entitled, as it seems to us, to consider whether the material which was withheld could have affected the jury's verdict in the light of all the facts now known to this Court. If it could have done, the conviction would be unsafe. If, on the other hand, the material that has been withheld has not, on a proper analysis of the facts known to this Court, undermined in any way the verdict of the jury, then the conviction will be safe. In evaluating the significance of the evidence that has been withheld in the context of all the information now available, we consider that we properly secure the rights of the defence for the purposes of Article 6 of the [European Convention for the Protection of Human Rights and Fundamental Freedoms 1950] and serve the interests of justice. We acknowledge that in carrying out this exercise we are trespassing upon what at trial would be the function of the jury. But that is the inevitable consequence in any case involving fresh evidence. It seems to us that if on a proper analysis of the information available to this Court, the only reasonable conclusion is that the conviction is safe, in that the jury's verdict in the light of all the relevant material was correct, this Court would not be carrying out its statutory obligation if it did give effect to that conclusion.'

[104] Mr Mansfield argues that the approach of Latham LJ is inconsistent with the decision of the House of Lords in *R v Pendleton* and therefore we should not follow it. We do not agree. Latham LJ did not have the advantage that we have of the decision in *R v Pendleton* but his general approach can be satisfactorily reconciled with that of Lord Bingham. It is to be recognised that the evidence was not being introduced to remedy a trial which was fatally flawed because, for

a example, the trial was an abuse of process or should have been stopped on a submission of no case to answer for lack of evidence, but so that the question of the correctness of the conviction could be considered in the round.

[105] Applying this reasoning we came to the conclusion that the DNA evidence on this appeal is evidence which we are entitled to admit under s 23. Furthermore we conclude that in our discretion we should admit the evidence b while recognising: (1) that its weight, if any, will depend on whether the appellant may be right that the explanation for the DNA findings is contamination and (2) that if the appellant is able to show that, because of lack of disclosure or the misdirections in the summing up the trial was still fatally flawed, the DNA evidence will not rescue the conviction.

c THE DNA EVIDENCE.

[106] We turn to the DNA evidence. As already noted, seminal fluid was found on Valerie Storie's knickers and one of her slips. At the time all that could be shown was that the rapist's and hence the murderer's blood group was O secretor. So was James Hanratty's and Peter Alphon's^d together with 40% of the d male population. The handkerchief found with the murder weapon bore traces of nasal mucus. Mucus was not capable of being analysed for blood type. Evidence based upon the comparison of hairs and fibres was inconclusive. Apart from some seminal staining on James Hanratty's striped trousers, said to be part of the Hepworth suit^e, that was the extent of the scientific evidence at trial.

e [107] During the 1980s and 1990s important work was carried out in the field of genetic profiling based on a complex chemical found in cells throughout the human body, the shorthand for which is DNA. As is now well known, DNA carries genetic information which determines the physical characteristics of the individual. The information comes in equal measure from each parent. It is the same in all body fluids and tissues, so, for example, DNA from a person's blood f will be the same as that found in his or her saliva and hair roots. Identical twins apart, each individual's DNA is unique. In attributing DNA to a particular individual, however, success will depend, in part at any rate, on the completeness or otherwise of the profile obtained. Techniques for recovering genetic profiles gradually improved throughout the 1990s. Those employed in 2000 were much more sensitive than were available in 1995.
g
[108] No doubt conscious of developments in this area there came a time in 1995 when the Hanratty family were anxious to apply DNA testing to such of the exhibits as had survived and which might show one way or the other whether James Hanratty had been responsible for the murder of Michael Gregsten and the rape of Valerie Storie. Attempts made in March 1995 were unsuccessful. h However, in November 1997 after much consultation further DNA analyses were commissioned, this time using highly sensitive DNA amplification techniques. The test was conducted on the small remaining piece of fabric from the knickers (part having been used in the 1995 experiment), a piece of material from one of the slips and the areas of staining from the handkerchief. This time j the experiment did produce results in that profiles were obtained both from the fabric and from the handkerchief which could be compared with samples taken from James Hanratty's brother, Michael, and his mother, Mary. These comparisons

---

d   Editor's note: Peter Alphon had been interviewed by the police during the investigation.
e   Editor's note: this was a suit, purchased from Hepworths, which Hanratty wore during the week of the murder.

confirmed that the male contribution to the profiling from the knickers almost
certainly came from either a son of Mary or a brother of Michael. It was also
shown at a much lower level of probability that it was a son of Mary and a brother
of Michael who had been responsible for depositing the mucus stains on the
handkerchief.

[109] Following the order of the court on 17 October 2000, James Hanratty's
body was exhumed and samples taken from which it has been possible for
Dr Whitaker of the Forensic Science Laboratory to state with what a non-scientist
would regard as equivalent to absolute certainty (or almost absolute certainty as
makes no difference) that the DNA profile recovered from the fragment of
knickers and the DNA profile recovered from the mucus staining on the
handkerchief have come from James Hanratty. That is not in dispute and, indeed,
it is conceded by Mr Mansfield on behalf of the appellant that, should it transpire
that all possibility of contamination can be excluded, the DNA evidence points
conclusively to James Hanratty having been both the murderer and the rapist.

Contamination

[110] As was so clearly explained by Ms Woodroffe, an independent scientific
consultant and a most impressive witness, DNA may migrate from one surface to
another by a variety of means. Primary transfer is what happens when there is
direct contact between a donor individual and a recipient individual or surface as
might occur during sexual intercourse. Secondary transfer is what happens when
the DNA is moved via an intermediary as where a contaminated and an
uncontaminated surface are brought into contact with one another. Then there
may be movement of DNA again via an intermediary where perhaps the same
hand first touches the infected surface and then another surface which had
hitherto been uncontaminated as might happen where exhibits are handled
without proper precautions in the witness box. Having said that, usually one can
expect a greater quantity of DNA to be transferred as a result of primary as
opposed to secondary contact. But it is always necessary to allow for particular
circumstances as where the DNA is dry, as in the case of hair, or wet, as in the
case of seminal fluid. Similarly, regard must be had to the duration of the contact.
Up to the happening of the crime event, accidental movement of DNA in this
way is referred to as 'transfer'; after the crime event as 'contamination'. We are
only concerned with the latter, but for ease of expression we shall use the terms
interchangeably.

[111] In this case it may be helpful first to identify the relevant exhibits or
objects and then to trace their history through to their first examination in 1995
by which time it is accepted that there was no longer any risk of contamination.

[112] Quite clearly the knickers and later the fragment cut from the crotch
area and the handkerchief are of first importance. So too, as possible contaminators,
are James Hanratty's intimate samples and items of clothing which may have
borne traces of his DNA.

[113] The knickers arrived at the Metropolitan Police Laboratory on 23 August
1961 where they were examined by Dr Nickolls, the director and his assistant,
Henry Howard. They were found to be stained with seminal fluid in the area of
the crotch and at the back for five inches upwards from the crotch. Vaginal fluid
from Valerie Storie was also present. There were smaller quantities of seminal
fluid of blood group AB assumed to have come at some earlier stage from
Michael Gregsten. Although the laboratory records are not dated, the notes are
numbered sequentially and we are confident that the knickers were examined

a almost immediately and in any event no later than 23 September 1961 when the notes show that certain samples taken from Peter Alphon were examined at the laboratory. The handkerchief came to the laboratory on 25 August, was screened for blood and semen and, none being found, seems to have been put to one side.

[114] On 7 October 1961 a suitcase containing James Hanratty's clothing was seized from the home of his girlfriend, Louise Anderson. It was received at the

b laboratory on 9 October. Amongst other items it contained a pair of dark pinstriped trousers (part of the Hepworth suit) and a green jacket and trousers. Some hairs and fibres were removed from the outside of the dark trousers as was a sample from a seminal stain on the inside of the fly. A suggestion, which has not been contradicted, is that the seminal stain may have been washed out and retained in the form of a liquid. On 13 October, the laboratory received samples

c of James Hanratty's blood and saliva. It was only at this point that the police became aware of his blood grouping. The records are incomplete but there would seem to be no reason for any of James Hanratty's items of clothing or for his intimate samples to be present in the laboratory at the same time as the knickers or the handkerchief. There is, of course, the possibility that all the

d exhibits were stored in the same place, albeit separately packaged, which, it is submitted, might have provided the opportunity for secondary contamination. Dr Nickolls is dead. Mr Howard is still alive though in poor health. His recollection is that the dangers of contamination were recognised even in 1961 and that the practice was to take elementary precautions such as making sure that clothing from victim and suspect were not examined on the same day.

e [115] All the exhibits, including those mentioned, were produced at the committal proceedings which took place between 22 November 1961 and 5 December 1961. If the usual procedures of the time were followed it would seem doubtful that any one of the exhibits, barring possibly the gun and certain of the cartridges, would ever have been removed from its packaging or container.

f Even so, as Mr Mansfield points out and the respondent concedes, the possibility that there was contact between the various exhibits cannot be excluded altogether.

[116] As a result of correspondence between James Hanratty's then solicitors and the DPP, arrangements were made for the pathologist, Dr Grant, to have access to James Hanratty's intimate samples and also to certain of the exhibits. It appears from the records that Dr Grant examined the green jacket and trousers

g on 28 December 1961 and Valerie Storie's slips and knickers the following day. It was on this latter occasion that a portion of the crotch area of the knickers was removed and thereafter, as seems clear, stored separately from the other exhibits including the knickers from which it had been excised. As also seems clear, a fragment of the excised portion was retained by the laboratory having first been

h placed in a small envelope made of cellophane and sellotape which was in turn put into a small brown envelope and the small envelope into a larger envelope before being treasury tagged to a laboratory file. It was so placed when rediscovered in 1991.

[117] At the trial which took place between 22 January 1962 and 17 February

j 1962 all the exhibits with the exception of a portion of the slip and the fragment of the knickers referred to previously were produced and in due course, taken out by the jury on retirement. Thereafter, on 9 April 1962, James Hanratty's suitcase and clothing were returned to his father and on 22 May 1962 Valerie Storie's slips, her knickers and various samples were all destroyed.

[118] The handkerchief seems to have remained with the Bedfordshire Constabulary until September or early October 1997 when it was discovered in

the course of inquiries made on behalf of the Commission. It was in the original envelope inside another envelope marked with the exhibit number '35'.

[119] The file containing the fragment from the knickers was discovered in 1991 by Jennifer Wiles. It was still packaged as described except that the cellophane package was no longer intact. Also found in the file were some broken slides and slide holders possibly having contained hairs and fibres collected at the scene of the murder. There were also two polythene bags each containing hairs thought now to have come from Alphon. There was another polythene bag containing a number of bullets and significantly, so Mr Mansfield submits, a polythene bag containing a small rubber bung and fragments of glass including a curved piece suggesting that the polythene bag had at one time contained a glass vial or tube.

[120] Mr Mansfield submits against that background that the respondent has not been able to exclude the possibility of contamination. In making that submission, he is supported by Dr Martin Evison who is a senior lecturer in Forensic Biological Anthropology in the Department of Forensic Anthropology at the Medico-Legal Centre in Sheffield and has many academic achievements and publications to his credit. He told the court that he had not been able to exclude 'the realistic possibility of contamination'. Dr Evison seems to accept that in the case of the knicker fragment the contaminant would have to be semen. That really limits the possibilities to (1) contact between the knickers and the Hepworth trousers and (2) contact between the contents of the broken vial and the fragment held on file. That would mean, so far as the first possibility is concerned, contact between the knickers and the fly area of the trousers in the laboratory, during storage or on production at committal. The mechanics are difficult to visualise and we gain the impression that it is neither Mr Mansfield's nor Dr Evison's preferred explanation. Contact could not take place any later than that because, as we know, Dr Grant cut out the fragment from the knickers before the trial took place and the fragment itself was not exhibited. The second possibility involves a hypothesis in which the broken vial contained a solution of James Hanratty's semen (extracted from the Hepworth trousers) which upon the vial being broken escaped in such a way as to invade the insecure packaging in which the fabric from the knickers was being kept. One of the respondent's witnesses, Mr Roger Mann, who has 32 years' experience as a forensic scientist, gave evidence that he has never come across a vial or tube containing liquid being retained on a file and we are bound to say that, without having any kind of scientific experience at all, it would seem a curious method of storage. Mr Greenhalgh, who saw the file and examined the fabric in 1995, told us that he considered the risk of contamination to the fabric to be very low. We quote from his evidence:

'As I examined the item, the piece of blue material from the knickers was in a sealed packet inside the two envelopes. I did not observe any damage to that packaging which I considered likely to be a risk of contamination. As far as I was concerned they were sealed, although the outer envelopes were not sealed there was no indication of any liquid damage on the brown paper envelopes, as might have been expected if a liquid sample had leaked onto them.'

[121] That said we should also record that not one of the respondent's witnesses excluded the possibility of contamination. They have expressed themselves in different ways but the general tenor of the evidence has been that

they each considered the possibility to be remote. That, of course, has to be contrasted with the opinion of Dr Evison who never moved from his original position as stated in this judgment.

[122] As far as the handkerchief is concerned, it will be remembered that when first examined it was considered to be of no scientific interest. No blood or semen was detected. When John Bark, a forensic scientist working at the Forensic Science Laboratory in Birmingham, examined the handkerchief in 1997 he found that—

'the handkerchief appears to be stained with some body fluid, cellular material which has bonded strongly to the cotton fabric over a number of years. There is no microscopic evidence that semen is present.'

That conclusion is supported by Roger Mann who subjected the handkerchief to chemical screening though he acknowledges the test carried out would not necessarily detect semen deposited by a male who did not produce spermatozoa. Realistically, however, it would seem to follow that the contaminant would have to be something other than semen and almost certainly liquid in form.

[123] The handkerchief was placed in an open buff OHMS envelope from which, no doubt, it was produced both at the committal proceedings and at trial. It was not examined by Dr Grant. In those circumstances the opportunities for contamination would seem to be extremely limited. However, in common with the approach taken in the case of the knicker fragment, the respondent's experts are prepared to accept that there has been, at least, a theoretical risk of contamination.

[124] Making it quite clear that for the time being we are simply considering the risk of contamination of a neutral surface without regard to the DNA profiles which were eventually obtained, we, too, accept that there was at least a theoretical possibility of both the knicker fragment and the handkerchief having been in contact with a surface bearing DNA contaminants from James Hanratty.

[125] But that is to ignore the results of the DNA profiling. With regard to the knicker fragment we have what Dr Whitaker would describe as a typical distribution of male and female DNA following an act of sexual intercourse leading to the obvious inference that the male contribution came from James Hanratty. For that not to be the case we would have to suppose that the DNA of the rapist, also of blood group O, had either degraded so as to become undetectable or had been masked by James Hanratty's DNA during the course of a contaminating event. Moreover, we would also have to suppose that Valerie Storie's DNA had remained in its original state, or at least detectable, and had escaped being overridden by DNA from James Hanratty. The same would have to be true of the DNA attributed to Michael Gregsten. Finally, we must visualise a pattern which is wholly consistent with sexual intercourse having taken place in which Valerie Storie and James Hanratty were the participants.

[126] Much the same reasoning would apply to the handkerchief. The only DNA extracted from the handkerchief came from James Hanratty. The only places on the handkerchief from which his DNA was extracted were the areas of mucus staining. It is to be expected that whoever was responsible for the mucus staining would have left evidence of his DNA. If the explanation for James Hanratty's DNA being found on the handkerchief is subsequent contamination it must follow that either the original DNA had degraded so as to become undetectable or James Hanratty's DNA has in some way overwhelmed the original deposit so that the original is no longer capable of being traced. More than that the transfer

must have taken place in such a way as to affect only the areas of mucus staining and not the unstained part of the handkerchief which was not found to bear DNA from James Hanratty or anyone else. In our view the notion that such a thing might have happened in either case is fanciful. The idea that it might have happened twice over is beyond belief.

[127] Accordingly, we reject the evidence of Dr Evison where it is in conflict with the additional evidence of the respondents, agreeing as we do with the submission made by Mr Sweeney that the DNA evidence standing alone is certain proof of James Hanratty's guilt.

[128] By way of postscript we should record that it has been agreed by Mr Sweeney and Mr Mansfield that on the evidence now available Peter Alphon could not have been the murderer. It is understood that this agreement arose out of the DNA evidence.

[In [129]–[210] the court set out and rejected the 17 grounds of appeal. It continued:]

CONCLUSION

[211] We have already stressed the importance of looking at a case such as this in the round. The grounds of appeal are of differing significance and although we have dealt with them individually it is also necessary to consider them collectively in asking ourselves the critical question: is the conviction of James Hanratty of murder unsafe either on procedural or evidential grounds? As to the evidential issues they all ultimately relate to the single issue which dominated the trial and this appeal, the identity of the killer. In our judgment for reasons we have explained the DNA evidence establishes beyond doubt that James Hanratty was the murderer. The DNA evidence made what was a strong case even stronger. Equally the strength of the evidence overall pointing to the guilt of the appellant supports our conclusion as to the DNA.

[212] Mr Michael Sherrard apparently opened the defence at the trial by saying appositely that this was a case 'sagging with coincidences'. Just let us consider some of the more striking coincidences in the light of the DNA evidence if James Hanratty was not guilty. He was wrongly identified by three witnesses at identification parades; first as the person at the scene of the crime and secondly (by two witnesses) driving a vehicle close to where the vehicle in which the murder was committed was found; he had the same identifying manner of speech as the killer; he stayed in a room the night before the crime from which bullets that had been fired from the murder weapon were recovered; the murder weapon was recovered from a place on a bus which he regarded as a hiding place and the bus followed a route he could well have used; his DNA was found on a piece of material from Valerie Storie's knickers where it would be expected to be if the appellant was guilty; it was also found on the handkerchief found with the gun. The number of alleged coincidences means that they are not coincidences but overwhelming proof of the safety of the conviction from an evidential perspective.

[213] As we have seen, even by contemporary standards of the time, there are criticisms of some substance which can be made as to the procedural defects, but these criticisms have to be seen in the context of the case as a whole. On the appeal we focus on what are alleged to have been defects in the trial process. This is particularly true in relation to non-disclosure. However, when we consider whether this was a flawed trial we have to consider the sum total of the defects against the backcloth of what was undoubtedly a thorough exploration of the real

a issue, namely was James Hanratty the killer and on that issue the jury came to the right answer. In making this comment we are not ignoring the two different grounds for saying a conviction is unsafe. We are recognising those two grounds but also acknowledging that the purpose of the rules is to ensure that an individual is not wrongly convicted and in the case of the procedural errors in this case this involves taking into account whether they interfered with the ability of

b James Hanratty to defend himself by raising a doubt as to his guilt. In that context we are satisfied the procedural shortcomings fell far short of what is required to lead to the conclusion that the trial should be regarded as flawed and this conviction unsafe on procedural grounds. The trial still met the basic standards of fairness required. We are satisfied that James Hanratty suffered no real prejudice.

c [214] The appeal must therefore be dismissed. However, before we end this judgment it is right we should mention the Hanratty family and their supporters. Throughout the appeal we have observed that they have attended in significant numbers and followed the proceedings behaving impeccably. Although their cause, to establish the innocence of James Hanratty has failed, we consider they

d deserve commendation for the extraordinary loyalty and commitment they have shown to what they thought was a just cause, to right an injustice. They have also been remarkably well served by the lawyers who acted on their behalf.

[215] Finally we appreciate the immense amount of diligence shown by the Commission. We do not consider it would be right to attempt to judge the Commission with the benefit of hindsight in relation to this case. We do however

e emphasise that there have to be exceptional circumstances to justify incurring the expenditure of resources on this scale, including those of this court, on a case of this age.

Appeal dismissed. Leave to appeal refused, but court certifying that a point of law of

f *general public importance was involved in its decision, namely whether, on an appeal against conviction, the Court of Appeal was entitled under s 23 of the Criminal Appeal Act 1968 (as amended) to receive fresh evidence at the request of the prosecution, other than evidence that was received to rebut fresh evidence adduced on the appeal by the appellant.*

Lynne Townley   Barrister.

1 July 2002. The Appeal Committee of the House of Lords refused leave to appeal.

Chester v Afshar

[2002] EWCA Civ 724

a

COURT OF APPEAL, CIVIL DIVISION

HALE LJ, SIR CHRISTOPHER SLADE AND SIR DENIS HENRY

4, 5 DECEMBER 2001, 27 MAY 2002

b

Medical practitioner – Negligence – Causation – Failure to warn of risks of operation – Surgeon negligently failing to advise patient of risk inherent in operation – Patient suffering injury when risk materialising during operation – Patient establishing that she would not have had operation if properly advised but unable to show that she would never have had operation in future – Whether surgeon causing damage suffered by patient.

c

The claimant patient suffered from severe back pain. She was referred to the defendant, an eminent neurosurgeon, who advised her that three intra-vertebral discs should be removed. Although the patient had been anxious to avoid *d* surgery, she agreed to the operation, and it was performed three days later. During the operation, which was properly performed, the patient suffered nerve damage resulting in paralysis. Such damage was a very small but known risk of the operation. In subsequent proceedings for negligence, the patient alleged that the surgeon had failed to advise her of that risk, and that, if he had, she would *e* have sought at least two further opinions as to whether an operation was necessary. She did not, however, allege that she would never, at any time or under any circumstances, have consented to the surgery. After accepting the patient's evidence, the judge held that the surgeon had been negligent in failing to advise her of the risk and that, if he had given proper advice, the patient would not have had the operation when she did. On the basis of those findings, the *f* judge concluded that the patient had established the necessary causal link between the negligence and the damage suffered, and that that link had not been broken by the fact that she was unable to prove that she would never have undergone the operation at some time in the future. He therefore gave judgment for the patient for damages to be assessed. The surgeon appealed, contending that the patient could only succeed if she established that she would never have *g* undergone the surgery at any time in the future.

Held – Where, as a result of a doctor's failure properly to advise a patient about the risk involved in a surgical procedure, the patient had an operation which she would not otherwise have had at that time, and the risk materialised and caused *h* her injury, the causal connection between the negligence and the damage was not broken merely because the patient had been unable to show that she would never, at any time in the future, have had an operation of that kind, carrying the same or similar risks. If it were more likely than not that the same damage would not have been suffered, the doctor would have caused the patient to sustain it by *j* causing her to have the operation that day. A conclusion to the contrary would thwart the purpose of the rule that required a doctor to give appropriate information to his patient, namely to enable the patient to decide whether or not to run the risks of having the operation at that time. It followed that causation had been established in the instant case. Although the judge had not expressly found that the patient would probably not have suffered the same injury on a *a* different occasion, such a finding was, on the evidence, strongly arguable if not inevitable when damages came to be assessed. Accordingly, the appeal would be dismissed (see [39], [41], [42], [45], [47], [48], [50], below).

Smith v Barking, Havering and Brentwood Health Authority [1994] 5 Med LR 285 and Smith v Salford Health Authority (1994) 23 BMLR 137 distinguished.

b **Notes**

For a doctor's duty to inform the patient of the risks involved in treatment and for causation generally, see respectively 30 Halsbury's Laws (4th edn reissue) para 39 and 33 Halsbury's Laws (4th edn reissue) para 603.

Cases referred to in judgment

c Allied Maples Group Ltd v Simmons & Simmons (a firm) [1995] 4 All ER 907, [1995] 1 WLR 1602, CA.

Bolam v Friern Hospital Management Committee [1957] 2 All ER 118, [1957] 1 WLR 582.

Chappel v Hart (1998) 72 ALJR 1344, [1999] Lloyd's Rep Med 223, Aust HC.

Chatterton v Gerson [1981] 1 All ER 257, [1981] QB 432, [1980] 3 WLR 1003.

d Empress Car Co (Abertillery) Ltd v National Rivers Authority [1998] 1 All ER 481, [1999] 2 AC 22, [1998] 2 WLR 350, HL.

Hotson v East Berkshire Area Health Authority [1987] 2 All ER 909, [1987] AC 750, [1987] 3 WLR 232, HL.

March v E & M H Stramare Pty Ltd (1991) 171 CLR 506, Aust HC.

McAllister v Lewisham and North Southwark Health Authority [1994] 5 Med LR 343.

e Rahman v Arearose Ltd [2001] QB 351, [2000] 3 WLR 1184, CA.

Rogers v Whitaker (1992) 175 CLR 479, Aust HC.

Sidaway v Bethlem Royal Hospital Governors [1985] 1 All ER 643, [1985] AC 871, [1985] 2 WLR 480, HL.

Smith v Barking, Havering and Brentwood Health Authority (1988) [1994] 5 Med LR 285.

f Smith v Salford Health Authority (1994) 23 BMLR 137.

Smith v Tunbridge Wells Health Authority [1994] 5 Med LR 334.

South Australia Asset Management Corp v York Montague Ltd, United Bank of Kuwait Ltd v Prudential Property Services Ltd, Nykredit Mortgage Bank plc v Edward Erdman Group Ltd [1996] 3 All ER 365, [1997] AC 191, [1996] 3 WLR 87, HL.

Wilsher v Essex Area Health Authority [1988] 1 All ER 871, [1988] AC 1074, [1988] *g* 2 WLR 557, HL.

Cases also cited or referred to in skeleton arguments

Gwembe Valley Development Co Ltd v Koshy (No 2) [2000] TLR 247.

Harrison v Bloom Camillin (a firm) (No 2) [2000] Lloyd's Rep PN 404.

h McGhee v National Coal Board [1972] 3 All ER 1008, [1973] 1 WLR 1, HL.

Appeal

The defendant, Fari Afshar, appealed with permission of Judge Robert Taylor from his decision, sitting as a judge of the High Court on 21 December 2000, giving judgment for the claimant, Carole Gay Ogilvy Chester, for damages to be *j* assessed in her claim for medical negligence against Mr Afshar. The facts are set out in the judgment of the court.

Martin Spencer (instructed by Hempsons) for Mr Afshar.

Jacqueline Perry (instructed by Eversheds, Manchester) for Miss Chester.

Cur adv vult

27 May 2002. The following judgment of the court, to which all of its members had contributed, was delivered.

SIR DENIS HENRY.

[1] The defendant appeals against the order made by Judge Robert Taylor, sitting as a judge of the High Court in the Queen's Bench Division, on 21 December 2000 in a medical negligence action. The judge found that the defendant had not been negligent in his conduct of the operation but had been negligent in failing to warn the claimant of the risk of paralysis which in fact ensued. He held the defendant liable for the injuries sustained in the operation and gave judgment for the claimant for damages to be assessed.

[2] The appeal raises the important and difficult question, not so far considered at appellate level in this country, of when a doctor should be held to have caused the injury, the risk of which he failed to give proper warning to his patient. The judge gave permission to appeal on that issue. The defendant also wishes to challenge the judge's finding of fact that a proper warning had not been given and to argue that the allegation should not have been pursued because it was not properly pleaded. The claimant wishes to challenge the judge's finding of fact that the operation had not been negligently performed, but only should she lose the appeal on the main issue. She also has permission to appeal against the costs order made by the judge, but that has not been argued pending the determination of the current appeal.

The facts

[3] The claimant in this action, Miss Chester, was a working journalist born in 1943, who had had various episodes of back pain from April 1988. For these she was conservatively treated by Dr Wright, a consultant rheumatologist. In September of 1994 she had a fifth episode of back trouble, very shortly before she was to undertake a professional engagement in France. The episode was so severe that walking was painful. She consulted Dr Wright, who gave her an epidural injection to tide her over the trip, and on her return arranged for her to have a MRI scan.

[4] On 13 October 1994, Dr Wright saw Miss Chester again, having seen the results of the scan which showed 'a very substantial centro-lateral variation at L2/3, central canal stenosis at L3 and L4/5'. He advised the claimant to consider surgery to her back. She made it clear that she wished to avoid surgery if at all possible, expressing a general aversion to it. Accordingly, he gave a sinu-vertebral block injection at L2 level and a large volume epidural injection. As this brought about no clear improvement, Dr Wright repeated his advice as to surgery, this time recommending two practitioners, one of whom was the defendant, Mr Afshar, an eminent neurosurgeon.

[5] Miss Chester was not impressed by this choice. She wanted a consultant (a word she understood as 'adviser') to advise her on alternatives to surgery, while Dr Wright was advising surgery and sending her to a surgeon. In his letter of referral to Mr Afshar, Dr Wright wrote that she was 'anxious to avoid surgery if at all possible … I feel sure she will take a long time to recover without your assistance'. As the last sentence implied, surgery then was elective rather than necessary. She did not need emergency surgery.

[6] Miss Chester had her consultation with Mr Afshar as his last appointment on 18 November 1994, a Friday. He examined her for 15 minutes and some 30 minutes was spent in discussion. It is common ground that Mr Afshar advised

Miss Chester that the three intra-vertebral discs in question should be removed. But there was a sharp conflict of evidence as to the detail of the conversation. Mr Afshar gave an account in which he dealt with the risk of cauda equina nerve root disturbance, while according to Miss Chester there was no such explanation. Miss Chester's account was summarised thus by the judge (we have corrected clerical errors in his verbatim quotations from the witness statements but adopted his summaries of the oral evidence, taken from his notes):

'According to the claimant, she was never adequately warned of the possible risks involved in such an operation. Her account of what she was told by the defendant on 18 November 1994 is set out in the following terms in para 5 of her first witness statement, which is dated 22 September 1999: "I first met the defendant, Mr Afshar, on 18 November 1994 when I attended his Harley Street surgery for examination. On that occasion, I was accompanied by my husband and, after studying the MRI scan which was taken on 6 October 1994, Mr Afshar quite matter of factly said I needed surgery to remove three discs, which were the cause of my problem. As I was very concerned about having to undergo surgery for my problem, I asked what the success rate of such an operation was, but did not receive a clear answer from Mr Afshar, although he did tell me that he performed about 300 operations such as this per year. As I was concerned, I told him of the many horror stories I had heard about back operations and he laughed, stating that he had never crippled anybody yet. Indeed, so confident was he that I distinctly remember that, almost as an aside, he stated: 'Of course, you could be my first'. Certainly it occurred to me that removal of three discs was rather a lot, and when I put this to Mr Afshar, he almost dismissively agreed. Further, when he told me the time at which he was to perform the surgery, I did suggest that it was rather late in the evening, but Mr Afshar responded that he would not be tired and was capable of working through the night when necessary. As a result of Mr Afshar's confidence in performing the surgery, and because he was recommended by Dr Wright, I agreed to undergo the operation. However, at no time was it suggested to me that there could be serious complications which could lead to any form of paralysis or leave me in a wheelchair. Indeed, if I had been aware of the major complications associated with this surgery then, due to my fear of surgery, I would have obtained at least a second, if not a third, opinion. Unfortunately, Mr Afshar never provided me with information on the seriousness of possible complications and as a result I lost the opportunity to seek an alternative opinion." In the course of her evidence, she somewhat expanded this account in response to counsel's questions. In her evidence-in-chief, the claimant said this: "After examination Mr Afshar showed me the scan. He pointed out three bulges and said they shouldn't be there and would all have to come out. When I was told this I felt terrible because he was, in effect, saying that I would have to have surgery. I didn't want to have surgery. I asked Mr Afshar if there was any other way to escape having surgery. He didn't give me any alternatives. He said I had three discs which would have to be removed—and that in a couple of months I would be back doing the work I had always done. He said I would be eight to ten days in hospital, after which I would have to rest up a bit. I said I had heard a lot of horror stories about surgery and I wanted to know about the risks. The reply I got from Mr Afshar was: 'Well, I have never crippled anybody yet'. It was a

throw-away line. He did add: 'Of course, you could be my first'. I didn't take
this seriously, in a crippling sense. I just took it that it was a very easy
operation—Zum! Zum! Zum! One of my questions to Mr Afshar in
Miss Martin's office was: 'Isn't three discs rather a lot?' the answer was
matter-of-factly: 'Yes' ... I agreed to the surgery because Mr Afshar made it
sound really simple. He did not tell me about any downside or risks
whatever. He made it sound easy. He said he did about 300 such operations
a year, so I said: 'Let's do it'. If I had been provided with an alternative that
didn't involve surgery, as I now know them to be, I would have taken it. If
I had been told of the risks of surgery, as I now know them to be, I would not
have had the operation on Monday 21 November. I would have had a very
shaky weekend and called various journalist friends as to who I should go to
see. I would also have contacted the BMA. I would have wanted to have at
least two further opinions as to whether an operation was necessary in the
first place. Nobody had said to me that this was a life-and-death matter and
'if you don't have this operation you will end up in a wheelchair'. Dr Wright
and Mr Afshar had never said this. The operation sounded so simple and
routine." When cross-examined, she replied: "I asked a lot of questions
about the operation. Before I went to see Mr Afshar I knew surgery was a
possibility. I hadn't done any research about surgery beforehand. Mr Afshar
did not discuss any risks with me whatsoever. He didn't mention haemorrhage.
I did not mention paralysis specifically, but I may have implied this when
I spoke of horror stories. If I had learnt that, as has subsequently come out,
I was a high risk patient, I would not have gone for operation on the Monday,
nor would my husband have let me. Mr Afshar never mentioned the risk of
paralysis. He never mentioned the risk of being crippled, except in a
throw-away line at which we laughed. It was not mentioned that there was
a small risk of nerve damage, infection and bleeding. I have a good memory
for the conversation on that particular occasion."'

[7] Mr Afshar's account was that he had warned Miss Chester of the risks, as
the judge recounts:

'The defendant dealt with this issue in paras 7–9 of his first witness
statement, which is dated 23 September 1999: "I recollect that the claimant
attended the appointment on 18 November 1994 with her husband and she
asked numerous questions regarding the surgery and the risks. All matters
were discussed in great detail with her. I believe that she was the last patient
of the day and that she was continuing to ask questions when we left my
consulting room and went into my secretary's room in order to book the
operation. My secretary clearly remembers the claimant asking further
questions in the secretary's office in her presence. The claimant could
therefore be in no doubt about the procedure or the risks associated with it.
I explained to her that there was a small risk of cauda equina nerve root
disturbance. I explained that this could mean sensory disturbance leading to
reduction in power in her legs and alterations to touch, temperature and
position sense. I would have explained that the risks were not great. The
advice would be based on my own experience of having performed many
hundreds of similar operations since 1975, and I had not experienced these
problems previously. I also explained that there was a small risk of
haemorrhage and infection. Following similar operations I have experienced
a case of infection in about three or four cases, but I have never had a case of

a   haemorrhage and this is very rare. We explain that all operations carry
certain risks but that the risks of this particular operation were not great in
comparison to surgical procedures that are carried out on the brain and
spinal cord. The claimant asked a number of questions in addition to what
the operation involved and what the risks were. She asked what would
happen if nothing was done, how long she would be in hospital, and when
b   she would be able to go back to work. I went into the procedure very
thoroughly and explained that if she did not have the operation performed
then she would certainly have continual problems due to the substantial
L2/L3 disc. I would not have described the operation as straightforward,
although I may well have described it as routine as I perform up to three or
four of these operations per week. I would not have expressly stated to the
c   claimant that I was entirely competent to carry out the procedure, although
I accept that this would be implicit as the claimant would not have been
referred to me if I was not competent to carry out the procedure. I would
not have expressly said to her that she could only experience improvement
in her symptoms if she had the operation performed, and that she had
nothing to lose only to gain. However I would have told her that her pain
d   would have the optimal chance of improvement as a result of the operation
and the operation would decrease the risk of the discs causing damage in the
future. I did not tell her that there should be no delay in carrying out the
procedure. The claimant asked me when she could have it done and
I explained that I would check with my secretary. The claimant was not
e   someone who needed emergency surgery. As it was routine surgery,
I explained that she would be able to have the operation performed at the
next available slot. When we went to see my secretary it was apparent that
there was space for her on the operating list on 21 November 1994 and we
booked her in for that date." In the course of his evidence he said this in
f   chief: "With all patients who undergo neurosurgery, whatever the
procedure is, it is important to tell them of the risks. This was indelibly
imprinted on me from my one-and-a-half years' residence in the United
States. I was doing the majority of the surgery there and having to get
consents. Informed consent was then as big an issue in the United States as
it has become here. It is always my practice to explain the risks to the patient.
g   She was an articulate, highly intelligent lady. She was nervous and anxious.
She asked many questions. I explained to her about nerve damage. In
particular she asked about paralysis and leg weakness. I can't remember the
exact words but she expressed herself in terms such as 'crippling'. I tried to
reassure her. I told her that I had never caused any damage to the cauda
h   equina or nerve roots in many hundreds of operations I had carried out in
20–25 years of spinal surgery. I can't remember verbatim what I told her but,
if she had asked what the risk was, I would have told her that the risk was less
than one in 100. I would have gone on to speak of my own experiences,
which is really what she was interested in, in the terms she has said in her
j   witness statement. I do not feel that I misled her about the risks. I do not
think that I would now alter what I said to her." In cross-examination, the
defendant replied: "I can't remember verbatim what I said about the risks to
Miss Chester. I said in general terms that the risks of nerve damage in
someone who was neurologically intact were not great. I didn't think that
operating as I did would cause a high risk, or indeed any significant risk, of
cauda equina syndrome. Otherwise I would have told Miss Chester of this.

Pre-operatively I had not come across a case where disc surgery had caused
cauda equina syndrome. Before the surgery I would have said that the risks
of cauda equina syndrome were small. It was a possible risk. Every operation
has possibilities. I discussed with Miss Chester the outcomes of having
surgery or not having surgery. In order to remove any disc by any route you
have to manipulate the nerve root and dural sac. There is a small risk of
nerve damage in any routine micro-discectomy. The more compression and
the greater the prolapse, the greater the risk. The higher the disc, the bigger
the risk. I showed Miss Chester where the disc was, what it was doing to the
nerve roots and why I recommended surgery. I can't remember the
percentage terms I told her for that particular disc. Cauda equina syndrome
can lead, at one end of the spectrum, to minor disturbance of nerve roots. At
the other end there is paralysis. I thought I had spent a great deal of time
spelling out the risks. Miss Chester asked me a lot of questions about nerve
damage and I told her. I told Miss Chester that she would have continuing
problems without surgery: I meant the problems she had experienced
before. I would not have agreed before the event that she was at risk of
paralysis without surgery. There was a risk of paralysis but I did not think it
sufficient to mention it to an already nervous patient. She had a potential risk
of paralysis without surgery, but if you ask me what the degree of risk was
or when it could occur, I cannot say." He also accepted that he had not made
a note about his discussion about risks with the claimant, adding: "Certainly
since the mid-nineties we have been making notes of our discussions but
I have no note of this discussion." Finally, in re-examination, he said:
"Pre-operatively this was not an exceptional case. It was a large prolapsed
disc. It was at an unusual site. Most prolapsed discs are lower down but
prolapses at this site are not uncommon."'

[8] The operation took place when scheduled on Monday 21 November 1994,
three days after the consultation. The consent form, signed without further
explanation on the afternoon of the operation, was for an L2/3, L3/4 and L4/5
micro-discectomy. It took some two hours. At first Mr Afshar thought the
operation had been successful. His operation note reflects this. His evidence
was:

'There was no complication during the operation. When I said in my note
"roots and cauda equina fully decompressed", that is what I actually could
see using the microscope. The goals of my original operation were fully
met.'

But when Miss Chester recovered consciousness, it was clear that all was not
well. There was both motor and sensory impairment. Mr Afshar mobilised a full
radiological team, and a scan showed that full decompression had not been
achieved in the first operation. So Mr Afshar conducted a second operation. The
site was re-explored immediately. But still Mr Afshar could not, during his second
operation, find any explanation for Miss Chester's condition which satisfied him.
Accordingly, a second post-operative scan was performed the following day; this
revealed only a small fragment of material which Mr Afshar did not think would
have contributed to 'the profound change which had occurred'. In his
contemporaneous note he recorded:

'My only explanation for the current situation is one of cauda equina
contusion that may have occurred on the routine medial retraction of L3

a   root and cauda equinal dura during the L2/L3 disc removal at the first procedure.'

He said in evidence: 'Because a nerve had been damaged, I assumed that I had caused the damage by manipulation. That is only an assumption. There could be other factors, such as interruption of vascular supply.'

b   [9] Post-operatively, Miss Chester made progress in certain respects. Within two or three weeks her right leg function returned virtually to normal, but on her left side progress was much slower, and at trial, six years later, she still suffered substantial disability in a number of areas. Paragraph 8 of her statement of claim reads:

c   'Following the said surgical procedures set forth in para 7 hereinbefore, the plaintiff's condition was worse than it had been pre-operatively. She has, since that date been suffering extensive neurological deficit which has resulted in gross functional deficit, continuing pain, unemployability and every aspect of her life has been diminished if not ruined.'

d   [10] Miss Chester's claim was put in two ways. First, it was said that in breach of contractual duty and negligently, Mr Afshar failed to advise, explain or otherwise counsel her as to the real risks attached to the surgical procedure, thereby depriving her of an opportunity to reflect, consider and/or seek alternative medical or other opinion as to the options which might be open to her; second, that the first surgical procedure was negligently carried out by
e   Mr Afshar, that he used the wrong technique, and that he caused bruising (and so neural damage) to the cauda equina and/or nerve roots (no criticism is now made of the second or remedial operation). It follows that if Miss Chester succeeded in proving negligence in the first operation, she would not have to prove the issue as to warning of risks inherent in that operation.

f
The judge's findings: the operation
    [11] The judge found (at para 52) that Miss Chester had—

g   'suffered a cauda equina syndrome as a result of contusion or damage to her already compressed cauda equina occurring while the defendant was retracting or at least manipulating the relevant nerve root and theca during the L2/L3 disc removal.'

That was a known risk of the surgery advised and performed by Mr Afshar, put by him at about 0.9%. Mr Firth (the claimant's expert) described the risk as 'the terror of neurosurgery'. Mr Findlay (the defendant's expert) reported that 'nerve
h   root injury or injury to the cauda equina is a recognised risk in lumbar surgery', and said (at para 54): 'Most of us would put a figure of one to two percent on the risk of nerve damage (including both single and multiple nerves) and other serious risks.'

    [12] It was common ground that the risk of cauda equina damage from
j   microdiscectomy was no less and no greater than from other forms of lumbar surgery, such as laminectomy, and that cauda equina damage can occur during lumbar surgery without any negligence on the part of the surgeon (paras 55, 56). Mr Firth spoke of the 'irreducible minimum of risk inherent in all lumbar surgery—that one can lose movement of the legs, bowels and bladder in what can be quite a "simple" operation'. Mr Findlay confirmed that damage to the cauda equina 'does not in itself indicate a sub-standard performance of the surgery'.

[13] The judge concluded that the defendant had not been negligent in the first
operation:

> '76. I am not satisfied that any of Mr Firth's criticisms of the way in which
> the defendant performed the first operation have been made out. I accept
> that Mr Firth is very eminent in the field of neurosurgery, and that his
> research interests include microsurgery. But he was in the difficult position of
> trying to criticise the conduct of a delicate operation at which he had not been
> present. The defendant, who had sole conduct of the operation throughout,
> gave a very clear account of what he had done, supported by a detailed
> contemporaneous note. I find it improbable that a man of his undoubted
> skill and experience, performing an operation he had done many times
> before, would not have removed as much bone as he needed to give himself
> the access that he required. I also find it improbable that he would have
> concluded the first operation without achieving full decompression, when
> this had been his objective. I also accept that he confirmed this when he
> carried out the second operation. I do not think that the post-operative scans
> are a reliable guide to whether or not decompression had been achieved, for
> the reasons given by Mr Findlay (which I accept).
>
> 77. As I have already said, it is common ground that, in an operation of
> this kind, nerve damage can occur without any negligence on the part of the
> operating surgeon. I think that this was the position in the present case. In
> my judgment, the claimant has failed to establish that the defendant was in
> any [way] negligent in his conduct of her surgery.'

We have not been asked to consider and rule on that conclusion in the single issue
of causation that we have to consider. Miss Perry, for the claimant, has indicated
that she wishes this issue to be kept open in the event that she fails on the
causation issue.

The judge's findings: the warning

[14] The relevant law on the duty to warn is not controversial. The judge
summarised it in this way:

> '44. ... Effectively this claim has been pursued on the basis that the
> appropriate test to apply to the defendant's conduct was the well-known test
> enunciated by McNair J in *Bolam v Friern Hospital Management Committee*
> [1957] 2 All ER 118, [1957] 1 WLR 582 and approved by the House of Lords
> in *Sidaway v Bethlem Royal Hospital Governors* [1985] 1 All ER 643, [1985] 1 AC
> 871.
>
> 45. In *Sidaway's* case Lord Bridge of Harwich said ([1985] 1 All ER 643 at
> 661, [1985] 1 AC 871 at 898) that, when questioned by a patient of apparently
> sound mind about risks involved in a particular treatment proposed, the
> doctor's duty must be to answer both as truthfully and as fully as the
> questioner requires. That case concerned a laminectomy operation, and
> Lord Templeman said ([1985] 1 All ER 643 at 664, [1985] 1 AC 871 at 902) that
> if the plaintiff concerned had asked questions about this operation "she could
> and should have been informed that there was an aggregate risk of between
> one per cent and two per cent risk of some damage either to the spinal cord
> or to a nerve root resulting in some injury which might vary from irritation
> to paralysis."'

a [15] It was common ground at the trial that the defendant in accordance with good medical practice should have warned the claimant of the risk of damage involved in the surgery and its possible consequences, such as paralysis. In the light of the questions she asked, and the observations of Lord Bridge and Lord Templeman in *Sidaway*'s case, she should have been fully told what the risk was. The only issue was whether she was told.

b [16] That brings us back to the details of the initial discussion which took place between Miss Chester and Mr Afshar on 18 November 1994 resulting in the 'routine' operation being performed on the 21 November, the Monday after that Friday. The varying accounts given by parties are set out at [6], [7], above. The judge accepted Miss Chester's account and gave his reasons for this:

c '64. Despite all these difficulties, I am satisfied that the claimant's account of the discussions is the more accurate of the two. This is because I find it the more plausible and probable, for the following reasons: (1) she is an intelligent and articulate woman, whose work is likely to have developed her abilities to absorb and retain information; (2) to her this was a unique and extremely important event, whereas for the defendant it was one of many;
d (3) her description of the defendant's response to the possibility of her being crippled seems to me to have the ring of truth and most unlikely to be the result of either invention or reconstruction; (4) at a very early stage, albeit after the outcome of the surgery was known to her, she was telling Mr Polkey that she had not been advised about the risk of being crippled;
e (5) there can be no doubt that prior to the consultation, the claimant was very averse to the idea of any surgery, and was anxious to avoid it if at all possible: this is confirmed by Dr Wright's letter of referral to the defendant; (6) it is not in dispute that neither the defendant nor the claimant regarded the operation as a matter of urgency, and that it was fixed for the following Monday as a matter of convenience; (7) in all these circumstances I find it
f extremely improbable that, if the claimant had been adequately informed that the proposed surgery carried a recognised, albeit small, risk of nerve damage possibly resulting in paralysis, she would have agreed without demur to the operation going ahead in three days' time (with a weekend intervening). It seems to me that, given her pre-existing aversion to surgery
g and her expressed concern about being crippled, the very least that she would have done would have been (as she says) to seek a second, or even third, opinion—which would inevitably have meant that the proposed operation would not have gone ahead on 21 November 1994; (8) in reaching these conclusions, I am alert to the dangers identified by Hutchison J (as he then was) in *Smith v Barking, Havering and Brentwood Health Authority* [1994]
h 5 Med LR 285 at 289, of giving weight to assertions by a plaintiff, after the adverse outcome of an operation is known, as to what she would have decided before the operation had she been given proper advice as to the risks inherent in it. However, if I apply the suggested test of what a reasonable claimant in Miss Chester's position would have done—assuming, as I think
j I should, a reasonable person with Miss Chester's documented aversion to surgery—my conclusion is still the same.'

[17] We find those reasons compelling. Points (1) and (2) show that Miss Chester was potentially a good and reliable witness. The judge was entitled to find that points (3) to (5) had the ring of truth and that her questions as to 'horror stories' were laughed off, and not confronted. Point (6) emphasises that

there was no hurry for this elective operation, and that the claimant was unlikely to agree to a timetable which for practical purposes would have excluded the opportunity to take a second or third opinion—further supporting the downplaying of the risk (see point (7)). Lastly (point (8)), whether one takes a subjective or objective view of her aversion to surgery, the judge was fully entitled to find that her account rang true, and was consistent with reconciling Miss Chester's change from aversion to acquiescence in 72 hours. He concluded:

'66. Having accepted the claimant's account of what was said at the consultation, I am satisfied that she was never given adequate or proper advice by the defendant as to the risks involved in the proposed surgery, in particular as to the risk of nerve damage possibly resulting in paralysis. Despite her requests for information about such risks, she was given to understand in effect that there were none. Accordingly I find that in this respect the defendant's failure to advise the claimant adequately was negligent under the principle in *Bolam's* case.'

[18] Mr Spencer has asked for permission to appeal against the judge's factual findings on this issue but we do not think it appropriate to give permission. The judge saw and heard the witnesses. There is no reason to think that he did not make the most of that opportunity. He gave detailed and compelling reasons for preferring the claimant's account of the conversation. There are no grounds which would justify our interfering with his findings of fact. He also gave an explanation of why the defendant did not warn. He concluded (at para 65) that Mr Afshar would—

'naturally be anxious to avoid alarming or confusing the patient unnecessarily. In the present case, as the defendant indicated during his evidence, he clearly thought that the risk of damage to the claimant was extremely small. Furthermore he knew that he personally had never caused any nerve damage in the many hundreds of operations he had carried out over 20 to 25 years. It may be that he considered the claimant over-anxious or over-preoccupied with "horror stories" and the possibility of being crippled. In these circumstances I do not find it improbable that, in an attempt to reassure, he deflected her inquiries by answering them in the light-hearted terms she has described—and which he accepts that he may have used at some stage. However understandable such a response may have been in psychological terms, it was not an adequate response in legal terms, as Lord Templeman indicated in *Sidaway's* case.'

The judge's findings: causation

[19] The next step was for the judge to consider what would have happened if Miss Chester had been adequately warned as to the risk. The judge accepted Miss Chester's evidence that if she had known the actual risks of the proposed surgery, she would not have consented to the operation taking place on 21 November, and that before deciding what to do, she would have sought a second or possibly even a third opinion. In all the circumstances, that finding brings with it the conclusion that, on the balance of probabilities, she would not have been operated on 21 November had she been properly advised of the risks of the operation. There was no urgency about the operation, and 21 November would not have allowed time to satisfy Miss Chester's reasonable requirements of taking a second and perhaps a third opinion before making up her mind. The

a judge found that a reasonable person with her aversion to surgery would have done something. He took it as an indicator of her truthfulness that she never went further to claim that she would never at any time or under any circumstances have consented to surgery.

[20] Mr Spencer for the defendant urged the judge to find that had she sought a second opinion it would probably have been from Professor Crockard, who *b* would have advised her that she was at lesser risk of paralysis with surgery than without, and that the probable outcome would have been that Miss Chester would in due course have consented to the same surgery. However, the judge declined to make these findings. While he accepted both as possibilities, he rejected them as probabilities because had Professor Crockard given such advice as a second opinion, Miss Chester, having made her own inquiries of journalist *c* colleagues, would have sought a third opinion.

[21] The judge concluded that it would be impossible to determine whom she would have seen, what she would have been advised, and how she would have acted in response to that advice. The judge had heard a considerable amount of evidence on this topic, which revealed a considerable divergence of views as to *d* whether the claimant was in November 1994 at serious risk of paralysis without surgery. He found that, if the claimant had gone to another consultant, it was more probable than not that the consultant would have tried to meet her concerns by suggesting some alternative course presenting her with a number of different options both surgical and conservative. He concluded (at para 70):

e   'Accordingly—while it is impossible to say what the probable outcome would have been if the claimant had sought a further opinion or opinions— I think it improbable that any surgery she might eventually undergo would have been *identical* in circumstances (including the nature of the surgery, procedure and surgeon) to the operation she actually underwent on 21 November 1994.'

f The judge was entitled to his view that it was impossible for him to draw an inference as to the probable outcome if Miss Chester had sought a further opinion or opinions. If, however, this court disagreed with that view, and if the material were there, this court could draw its own inference.

[22] The judge went on to conclude that this was sufficient to prove a causal *g* link between the failure to warn and the damage suffered:

     '81. ... On the findings that I have made, the risk that materialised during the operation on 21 November 1994 was the risk about which she should have been, but was not, adequately warned. Had she been adequately warned, the operation in question would not have taken place and she would *h*   not have suffered damage. In these circumstances, and without more, it seems to me that the necessary causal link is sufficiently established. I do not see how the fact that the claimant cannot prove that at no future time would she have undergone such an operation can break the causal link thus established. This is especially so when, as I have found, it is improbable that *j*   the circumstances of any future surgery would have been identical to those in which the risk, on any view a small one, actually materialised.'

What might happen in future was relevant to quantum:

     '82. ... Of course, the possibility that the claimant might in future undergo such an operation, or even another type of lumbar operation carrying a similar risk, may well be relevant. But it seems to me that such a possibility

would be relevant to the issue of damages rather than liability (as was the
view of Gaudron and Gummow JJ in *Chappel v Hart* [1998] 72 ALJR 1344) [see
at [30] et seq, below] ... Let me suppose a case similar in type to—but more
extreme than—the present one in which the court found on the facts that,
had the claimant been adequately advised, the operation in question would
have been postponed for six months, at the end of which period she would
have undergone surgery and probably suffered the same damage ... In such
a case the claimant's damages would presumably be limited to six months
pain, suffering and consequential loss, but it seems to me that there would
be a causal link between the failure to advise and such damages.'

The issue in this appeal

[23] The issue on causation is easy to state. Miss Perry for the claimant
submits that, to establish a causal link between the defendant's failure to advise
and warn the claimant of the risk and the damage (and its consequences) which
she sustained, it is sufficient for the claimant to prove that, had she been properly
advised, she would not have consented to undergo that operation on that day.
Miss Perry relies on the majority decision of the High Court of Australia, *Chappel v
Hart* (1998) 72 ALJR 1344, [1999] Lloyd's Rep Med 223.

[24] Mr Spencer, for the defendant, submits that to establish the causal link,
the claimant must go further than that. She must prove that, had she been
properly advised, she would never have undergone the surgery in question,
either on 21 November *or on any subsequent date*. Effectively she must show that,
had the operation been postponed and had she taken a second opinion, she would
then have refused to have surgery of the type proposed at any stage. Mr Spencer
submitted that the minority view in *Chappel v Hart* was to be preferred. He drew
attention to a line of first instance decisions in this country pre-dating *Chappel v
Hart*, which are consistent with the approach for which he contends.

[25] First in time was *Smith v Barking, Havering and Brentwood Health Authority*
[1994] 5 Med LR 285, a decision of Hutchison J in 1988. The claimant was not
properly warned of the risk of tetraplegia resulting from the difficult operation
recommended by her surgeon; but without it she would have become tetraplagic
within about nine months in any event. He accepted that the question of what
the claimant would have done had she been properly warned was to be
approached subjectively rather than objectively—ie what would this particular
claimant have done rather than what would a reasonable claimant have done. He
rejected a submission that the onus was on the defendant to prove that the
claimant would not have refused the operation if properly advised. In reliance on
the House of Lords' decisions in *Hotson v East Berkshire Area Health Authority*
[1987] 2 All ER 909, [1987] AC 750 and *Wilsher v Essex Area Health Authority* [1988]
1 All ER 871, [1988] AC 1074 he held that the burden of proving causation lay with
the claimant. He accepted the submission that 'the plaintiff could only succeed if
she established on the balance of probabilities that, had she received proper
warning and advice, she would have elected against the operation'. But he found
on the balance of probabilities that she would have consented to it, even if
properly advised. This case is obviously correct as to where the burden of proof
lies. It is also correct as to the legal consequence of the factual finding reached: if
a claimant would have had the operation even if properly advised, then the lack
of a warning cannot have caused the injury. The judge did not have to address
the more subtle question at issue here.

a [26] Next in time was *McAllister v Lewisham and North Southwark Health Authority* [1994] 5 Med LR 343, a decision of Rougier J in December 1993. The claimant underwent lengthy brain surgery to correct a neurological deficit in her left leg. She was warned of the risk that it would make her leg worse rather than better but not of the general risks affecting brain surgery or of the risk of hemiplegia which in fact occurred. The judge held that this was negligent. The **b** claimant herself was reluctant to say what she would have done had she been properly warned. The judge was confident that she would not have had the operation when she did and would have seized the opportunity of postponing it at least until after she was secure in her job and could take the risk of a long period of time off. He went on to conclude that on the balance of probabilities she would have continued to decline the operation. Hence she had succeeded in **c** proving the necessary causal connection. Thus Rougier J adopted the same approach as that signalled by Hutchison J in *Smith v Barking, Havering and Brentwood Health Authority* but reached the opposite conclusion on the facts. Judge Taylor commented in this case:

d 'I acknowledge that Rougier J in *McAllister's* case decided liability on the basis that it was necessary for the plaintiff to establish that she would have continued to decline the operation in question; but it does not appear that he was ever invited to adopt any different approach to the question of causation, or that the interesting point which I have to decide was ever canvassed before him. Furthermore the decision in *Chappel v Hart* [1998] 72 ALJR 1344 **e** was several years later than *McAllister's* case.'

[27] The same comment could be made of *Smith v Tunbridge Wells Health Authority* [1994] 5 Med LR 334, in which Morland J reached a similar result. He found that the claimant had not been properly warned of the risk of impotence and bladder malfunction from rectal surgery. The major part of his judgment is **f** devoted to whether a warning should have been given and if so whether it was done sufficiently clearly. He was entirely satisfied that if a proper warning had been given, the claimant would have refused the operation.

[28] Last in the line was *Smith v Salford Health Authority* (1994) 23 BMLR 137. Potter J found that the defendant was at fault in his pre-operative investigations and assessment of the situation, in failing to give proper advice, and in his conduct **g** of the operation. He found the defendant liable on the basis of the use of an inappropriate instrument. He would not have found the defendant liable on the basis of the failure to warn, because he was not satisfied that the claimant would have declined the operation if he had been properly advised.

[29] We thus have two cases finding against the claimant on the basis that he **h** or she would have had the operation in any event and two cases finding for the claimant on the basis that he or she would have refused the operation. Not surprisingly, both parties to the present case draw some support from these decisions. Mr Spencer relies upon the way in which Hutchison, Rougier and Potter JJ asked themselves the question: had the claimant satisfied them that he **j** or she would have refused the operation? Miss Perry points out that there is no case denying liability on the basis of the factual findings in this case: ie that she would have refused this particular operation but it was impossible to predict whether she would have consented to some form of surgery in the future.

[30] We come, therefore, to the majority decision of the High Court of Australia in *Chappel v Hart* (1998) 72 ALJR 1344, [1999] Lloyd's Rep Med 223 which the judge found 'extremely persuasive'. The facts were, in his careful

words, 'reasonably similar' to this case. The claimant, a school teacher, had a strong clear voice, which was important to her, both professionally and generally. She had a 'relentlessly progressive' throat condition which would require surgery at some time, sooner or later. That surgery carried with it a very slight risk of injury which would leave her with a weak voice. Whether the operation was done well or badly, it would carry with it an inherent risk of perforation of the oesophagus, which could lead to infection and damage to her voice. She brought her anxieties as to her voice to Dr Chappel's attention, but he did not warn her of the risk inherent in the operation. In the event, he operated on the claimant with due skill and care, but perforation occurred notwithstanding, infection set in, and her voice was permanently damaged. She sued Dr Chappel both in contract and in tort for his failure to warn her. The Supreme Court of New South Wales awarded her damages. The trial judge found that had Mrs Hart received an appropriate warning, she would not have had surgery when she did, but would have had it done later by 'the most experienced surgeon with a record and a reputation in the field'. The Court of Appeal of New South Wales dismissed the doctor's appeal. He then appealed to the High Court of Australia. The appellant contended that there was no causal connection between the failure to warn and her injury, because surgery was inevitable and carried the risk which eventuated, she had not lost any real or valuable chance of the risk being diminished or avoided, and the injury resulted from a random risk that she was willing to accept. Hence she was entitled to only nominal damages. The doctor's appeal was dismissed.

[31] The majority (Gaudron, Gummow and Kirby JJ) rejected the appellant's arguments and held that his negligence had caused the injury. All three of them declined to treat the case as one involving the loss of a chance. Her loss was the physical injury suffered. Gaudron J ((1998) 72 ALJR 1344 at 1347) said this (we quote from that report because the paragraphs are numbered):

'[9] Where there is a duty to inform it is, of course, necessary for a plaintiff to give evidence as to what would or would not have happened if the information in question had been provided. If that evidence is to the effect that the injured person would have acted to avoid or minimise the risk of injury, it is to apply sophistry rather than common sense to say that, although the risk of physical injury which came about called the duty of care into existence, breach of that duty did not cause or contribute to that injury, but simply resulted in the loss of an opportunity to pursue a different course of action ...'

Further:

'[12] ... The argument proceeds on the erroneous footing that the damage sustained by Mrs Hart was simply exposure to risk, not the harm which eventuated. And to say that Mrs Hart would inevitably have been exposed to risk of the harm which she suffered is not to say that she would inevitably have suffered that harm.'

As Gaudron J also pointed out (at 1348 (para 17)), the risk may have been the same, but the likelihood of that risk eventuating in future was not the same. There was evidence that the risk diminished with the skill and experience of the surgeon concerned. It was in any event extremely rare (see para 20).

[32] Gummow J (at 1356–1358) referred to previous High Court authority in *March v E & M H Stramare Pty Ltd* (1991) 171 CLR 506 at 514, per Mason CJ:

a

'[62] ... generally speaking, a sufficient causal connection is established if it appears that the plaintiff would not have sustained the injuries complained of had the defendant not been negligent. However, the "but for" test is not a comprehensive and exclusive criterion, and the results which are yielded by its application properly may be tempered by the making of value judgments and the infusion of policy considerations ...

b

[66] In the present appeal, not only was the damage which Mrs Hart suffered reasonably foreseeable, but the fact that the relevant conjunction of circumstances could occur should have been the subject of any adequate warning and the reason for giving it. It is true that in some cases of a failure to warn by a medical practitioner an application of the "but for" test without qualification could lead to absurd or unjust results. Such would have been

c

the situation if, for example, instead of suffering damage to her laryngeal nerve, Mrs Hart had been injured through misapplication of anaesthetic. Whilst it would still be open to conclude that, but for Dr Chappel's failure to warn her of the possibility of damage to her voice, she would not have opted for the operation at that time and would not have been injured by the

d

anaesthetic, the law would not conclude that the failure to warn of the risk of injury to the laryngeal nerve caused the injury resulting from the anaesthetic.

[67] The present appeal is significantly different from the situation described. In Mrs Hart's case, the very risk of which she should have been warned materialised. In his written submissions filed by leave after the

e

hearing of the appeal, Dr Chappel conceded that, if the surgery had been performed at a different time, then "[i]n all likelihood" Mrs Hart "would not have suffered the random chance of injury". In addition, the particular risk involved had been the subject of specific inquiry by Mrs Hart of the medical practitioner who was then engaged by her to perform the surgery. She was

f

a person for whom the potential consequences of damage to her voice were more significant than the "statistical" risk. Those additional factors, combined with the satisfaction of the "but for" test were sufficient to establish causation in this case.'

[33] Kirby J (at 1369–1370) described his thought process thus:

g

'[94] ... The strongest arguments for Dr Chappel, as it seems to me, are those which lay emphasis upon a logical examination of the consequences which would have flowed had he not breached his duty to warn his patient. Dissecting the facts in that way affords a powerful argument which would banish from consideration the events which in fact occurred in the operation

h

which he carried out. All that would have happened, had he given the requisite warning, would have been a change in the timing of the operation and of the identity of the surgeon. For Dr Chappel, these were irrelevant changes as the evidence showed that, whenever the operation was performed and whoever did it, the tripartite chances which had to combine

j

to produce the misfortune which Mrs Hart suffered were extremely rare. There was thus an equivalence of unlikelihood. They were risks inherent in the procedure, not wholly avoidable even by the most skilful and experienced of surgeons. In the view which Dr Chappel urged of the case, Mrs Hart was left with nothing more than the time sequence. To burden a surgeon, in whose actual performance no fault could be found, with civil liability for randomised chance events that followed the surgery would not

be reasonable. It would penalise him for chance alone. It would do nothing
to establish a superior standard in the performance of the work of surgeons *a*
generally.

[95] For a time I was attracted to Dr Chappel's arguments. Ultimately,
I have concluded against them. The "commonsense" which guides courts in
this area of discourse supports Mrs Hart's recovery. So does the setting of
standards which uphold the importance of the legal duty that was breached *b*
here. This is the duty which all health care professionals in the position of
Dr Chappel must observe: the duty of informing patients about risks,
answering their questions candidly and respecting their rights, including
(where they so choose) to postpone medical procedures and to go elsewhere
for treatment.

[96] In [*Empress Car Co (Abertillery) Ltd v National Rivers Authority* [1998] *c*
1 All ER 481 at 487–488, [1999] 2 AC 22, at 29–31], Lord Hoffmann emphasised
that commonsense answers to questions of causation will differ according to
the purpose for which the question is asked. The answer depends upon the
purpose and scope of the rule by which responsibility is being attributed. In
Rogers v Whitaker ((1992) 175 CLR 479 at 490), this Court decided that "a *d*
doctor has a duty to warn a patient of a material risk inherent in the proposed
treatment" and that: "a risk is material if, in the circumstances of the
particular case, a reasonable person in the patient's position, if warned of the
risk, would be likely to attach significance to it or if the medical practitioner
is or should be reasonably aware that the particular patient, if warned of the
risk, would be likely to attach significance to it." These standards have fairly *e*
been described as onerous. They are. But they are the law. They are
established for good reason. When not complied with (as was held to be so
in this case) it should occasion no surprise that legal consequences follow.
This was an unusual case where the patient was found to have made very
clear her concerns. The practicalities are that, had those concerns been met *f*
as the law required, the overwhelming likelihood is that the patient would
not, in fact, have been injured. So much was eventually conceded. In such
circumstances, commonsense reinforces the attribution of legal liability. It
is true to say that the inherent risks of injury from rare and random causes
arise in every surgical procedure. A patient, duly warned about such risks,
must accept them and their consequences. Mrs Hart was ready to accept any *g*
general risks of the operation of which she was warned. However, she
declined to bear the risks about which she questioned the surgeon and
received no adequate response. When those risks so quickly eventuated,
commonsense suggests that something more than a mere coincidence or
irrelevant cause has intervened. This impression is reinforced once it is *h*
accepted that Mrs Hart, if warned, would not have undergone the operation
when she did.'

[34] English law does not impose quite such a rigorous standard upon doctors
as that in *Rogers v Whitaker*, but the policy point made by Kirby J would still apply.

[35] The minority view can be taken from the judgment of McHugh J (at 1349): *j*

'[25] The rejection [in *March v E & M H Stramare Pty Ltd* (1991) 171 CLR
506] of the "but for" test as the sole determinant of causation means that the
plaintiff in this case cannot succeed merely because she would not have
suffered injury but for the defendant's failure to warn her of the risk of injury.
However, his failure to warn her of the risk was one of the events that in

a   combination with others led to the perforation of her oesophagus and damage to the right recurrent laryngeal nerve. Without that failure, the injury would not have occurred when it did and, statistically, the chance of it occurring during an operation on another occasion was very small. Moreover, that failure was the very breach of duty which the plaintiff alleges caused her injury. The defendant's failure to warn, therefore, must be
b   regarded as the cause of the plaintiff's injury unless either common sense or legal policy requires the conclusion that, for the purposes of this action, the failure is not to be regarded as a cause of the plaintiff's injury.'

However (at 1350):

c   '[27] Before the defendant will be held responsible for the plaintiff's injury, the plaintiff must prove that the defendant's conduct materially contributed to the plaintiff suffering that injury. In the absence of a statute or undertaking to the contrary, therefore, it would seem logical to hold a person causally liable for a wrongful act or omission only when it increases the risk of injury to another person. If a wrongful act or omission results in an increased risk
d   of injury to the plaintiff and that risk eventuates, the defendant's conduct has materially contributed to the injury that the plaintiff suffers whether or not other factors also contributed to that injury occurring. If, however, the defendant's conduct does not increase the risk of injury to the plaintiff, the defendant cannot be said to have materially contributed to the injury
e   suffered by the plaintiff.'

The reasoning of Haynes J was to much the same effect.

[36] The commentaries which we have read on *Chappel v Hart* are in general supportive of the result reached by the majority, albeit not necessarily for the reasons they gave (see Adrian Whitfield QC's commentary [1999] Lloyd's Rep
f   Med 223 at 253–255; Cane 'A Warning about Causation' (1999) 115 LQR 21; and Stauch 'Taking the Consequences for Failure to Warn of Medical Risks' (2000) 63 MLR 261).

Discussion

g   [37] The divergence of views expressed in *Chappel v Hart* shows that the issue is not an easy one and may be approached in a number of different ways. It is axiomatic that it is not enough to show that the acts or omissions of the defendant caused the damage. Obviously, in this case they did that. It is not only that Mr Afshar's actions at the operating table produced the physical effects sustained. His acts and omissions during the consultation on 18 November were clearly one
h   cause, along with the claimant's own decision, of the claimant having the operation on 21 November. But the claimant must prove that the defendant's breach of his duty towards her caused the damage. Miss Chester must show that Mr Afshar's failure to warn her of the risk of the damage she sustained caused her to suffer that damage.

j   [38] In accordance with logic and authority (e g *Allied Maples Group Ltd v Simmons & Simmons (a firm)* [1995] 4 All ER 907, [1995] 1 WLR 1602) the answer to that question must considerably depend upon the answer to the further question of what would have happened if she had been properly warned. There is a spectrum of possible answers to that second question. At each end of the spectrum the solution would be plain. If the claimant would have had the same operation at the same time in any event (as in the first and third *Smith* cases), then

the defendant's failure to warn her properly would have made no difference. He
would not have caused her to do anything which she would not otherwise have
done. It would be as if she had chosen to have the operation knowing the risks
she was running. On the other hand, if the claimant would never have had the
operation had she been properly warned (as in *McAllister's* case and the second
Smith case), clearly the defendant's breach of duty would have caused her to have
it and Mr Spencer accepts that it would also have caused her to sustain the
damage. The only issue would then have become one of quantum: how does
her damaged state after the operation compare with the state she would have
been in without it?

[39] The present case lies in between the two extremes. The claimant can
show that she would not have had the operation she did, or would not have had
it when she did, or would not have had it in the circumstances in which she did,
but she cannot show that she would never have had some surgical procedure of
this kind which would have carried the same or similar risks. Can it then be said
that causing her to have the operation caused her to suffer the damage?

[40] The minority view in *Chappel v Hart* was that the defendant had not
increased the risk to which the claimant was exposed. That may have been
debatable, in that there was some evidence from which it might be inferred that
the risk would have been less at the hands of a more experienced surgeon.
But the risk was in any event so small that the difference must have been minuscule.
However, if it were only appropriate to focus attention on the risks of having the
operation whenever it took place, the claimant would never succeed, even when
she could show that she would never have had the operation. The risks were
always the same and the defendant did not increase them. But Mr Spencer
accepts that *McAllister's* case was rightly decided. In our view he is correct to do
so. The defendant does change the risk in a material way: he causes the patient
to have an operation which she would not otherwise have had then and there and
possibly not at all. Logically, the correct comparison of risk is between having
that operation on that occasion and not having it.

[41] Miss Perry put it in this way to the judge in her closing speech:

'All she has to do is to satisfy my Lord that, given the appropriate advice,
she would have gone elsewhere. Unless my Lord is satisfied that, going
elsewhere, will inevitably or on the balance of probabilities have produced
exactly the same result for her ... then ... the claimant must succeed.'

If it is more likely than not that the same damage would have been sustained in
any event, then all the defendant has done is bring forward the date when she
suffers it. If it is more likely than not that the same damage would not have been
suffered, then by causing her to have the operation that day he has caused her to
sustain it. There is no problem of remoteness because the risk was clearly
foreseeable: it was the fact that it was a foreseeable risk, albeit a small one, that
gave rise to the duty to warn which was broken. Indeed, in each of these cases,
it can be said that he has caused some damage, the question of acceleration being
one of quantum rather than causation.

[42] If that is the correct approach, then causation is established in this case.
The judge made a clear finding that the claimant would not have had the
operation when she did. The defendant therefore caused her to have the
operation. The judge did not expressly find that the likelihood was that she
would not have suffered the same injury on a different occasion. But the
evidence both as to the general and the particular risks of this procedure was such

a   that such a finding was strongly arguable if not inevitable when damages come to be assessed. At the trial it was not suggested that the well-known risk of cauda equina damage resulting from the type of surgery advised and performed by the defendant was greater than 1% to 2%. Nor do we think that there was any evidence to show that the claimant's constitution made her abnormally vulnerable to this type of surgery. But this will be a matter for the court assessing damages.

b   On the assessment it will be open to the defendant to argue (and prove so far as he may be able to do so) that (i) it is more likely than not that the claimant would have undergone an operation with the same or similar risks in the future; and (ii) it is more likely than not that the same risk would have been eventuated.

[43] Several further considerations help us to conclude that the correct approach goes at least this far. We accept that the 'but for' test is necessary but
c   not always sufficient to establish causation in law. Even if the claimant would not have been on the operating table that day if the defendant had given her a proper warning, the defendant is not liable for coincidences which have nothing to do with him, such as the anaesthetic failure referred to by Gummow J or lightning striking the operating theatre. The classic example of this point was given by
d   Lord Hoffmann in *South Australia Asset Management Corp v York Montague Ltd, United Bank of Kuwait Ltd v Prudential Property Services Ltd, Nykredit Mortgage Bank plc v Edward Erdman Group Ltd* [1996] 3 All ER 365 at 371, [1997] AC 191 at 213:

> 'A mountaineer about to undertake a difficult climb is concerned about the fitness of his knee. He goes to a doctor who negligently makes a superficial
e   > examination and pronounces the knee fit. The climber goes on the expedition, which he would not have undertaken if the doctor had told him the true state of his knee. He suffers an injury which is an entirely foreseeable consequence of mountaineering, but has nothing to do with his knee.'

f   [44] In cases such as the present, however, it simply cannot be said that the injury suffered had nothing to do with the problem which had taken the claimant to the doctor. It was a consequence of that very problem and the doctor's attempt to put it right. Furthermore it was a consequence about which the claimant had expressed her concern to the doctor and been wrongly reassured. The closer analogy is with the mountaineer who consults his doctor because he
g   is afraid that his knee will give way under the strain of mountain climbing, is wrongly reassured that it will not, and who is injured because his knee does give way. The doctor was not to blame for the knee giving way, any more than the doctor (if the first operation was not negligently performed) was to blame for the cauda equina syndrome in this case, but he was to blame for the mountaineer
h   being on the mountain at all.

[45] What if the mountaineer would not have taken the risk immediately but cannot rule out the possibility that his love of mountaineering was such that he would have been prepared to run it at some later date? Logic would again suggest that this should only make a difference if it was more likely than not that he
j   would do so: the mere possibility that his feelings would eventually get the better of him does not break the chain. Furthermore, by causing him to go up the mountain when he would not have done so the doctor had caused him to suffer the injury earlier than he would otherwise have done. He has therefore lived for longer with the consequences of a broken leg (or whatever) than he would otherwise have done. The question then becomes one of quantification rather than causation, as the judge held in this case.

[46] In *Chappel v Hart* Kirby J also referred to the observations of Lord Hoffmann in *Empress Car Co (Abertillery) Ltd v National Rivers Authority* [1998] 1 All ER 481 at 487, 488, [1999] 2 AC 22 at 29, 31:

> 'The first point to emphasise is that commonsense answers to questions of causation will differ according to the purpose for which the question is asked. Questions of causation often arise for the purpose of attributing responsibility to someone, for example, so as to blame him for something which has happened ... one cannot give a common sense answer to a question of causation for the purpose of attributing responsibility under some rule without knowing the purpose and scope of the rule.'

A somewhat similar point was made by Laws LJ in *Rahman v Arearose Ltd* [2001] QB 351 at 367, [2000] 3 WLR 1184 at 1199–1200, albeit in the different context of sharing responsibility between two different tortfeasors:

> 'So in all these cases the real question is, what is the damage for which the defendant under consideration should be held *responsible*. The nature of his duty (here, the common law duty of care) is relevant; causation, certainly, will be relevant—but it will fall to be viewed, and in truth can only be understood, in the light of the answer to the question: from what kind of harm was it the defendant's duty to guard the claimant?'

In principle there seems to be little difficulty in attributing causative responsibility to a doctor who has in breach of duty failed to draw a particular risk to his patient's attention if in the event that particular risk materialises.

[47] The purpose of the rule requiring doctors to give appropriate information to their patients is to enable the patient to exercise her right to choose whether or not to have the particular operation to which she is asked to give her consent. English law has rejected the proposition that a failure to give adequate warning vitiates the patient's consent, thus turning the operation into an assault (see *Chatterton v Gerson* [1981] 1 All ER 257, [1981] QB 432). Liability lies in negligence rather than trespass. But the patient does still have the right to choose what will and will not be done with her body and the doctor must take the care expected of a reasonable doctor in the circumstances in giving her the information relevant to that choice. The law is designed to require doctors properly to inform their patients of the risks attendant on their treatment and to answer questions put to them as to that treatment and its dangers, such answers to be judged in the context of good professional practice, which has tended to a greater degree of frankness over the years, with more respect being given to patient autonomy. The object is to enable the patient to decide whether or not to run the risks of having that operation at that time. If the doctor's failure to take that care results in her consenting to an operation to which she would not otherwise have given her consent, the purpose of that rule would be thwarted if he were not to be held responsible when the very risk about which he failed to warn her materialises and causes her an injury which she would not have suffered then and there. As Adrian Whitfield QC pointed out in his commentary on *Chappel v Hart* [1999] Lloyd's Rep Med 223 at 255:

> 'The view of the minority of the High Court, that the "but for" test works injustice and that the effective cause should be taken not as the defendant's failure to warn but the random occurrence of an inherent risk, runs counter

a   to the whole basis of informed consent cases, which are designed to protect patients against negligent failure to warn of just such risks.'

It would in our judgment be unjust to hold that the effective cause of the claimant's injury was the random occurrence of the 1% to 2% risk referred to above rather than the defendant's failure to bring such risk to her attention.

b   [48] In the end, therefore, all these considerations lead us to the same conclusion: that the conclusion of the majority in *Chappel v Hart* was right and that the judge reached the right conclusion in this case. We therefore reject the grounds of appeal which argue that the judge adopted the wrong test, failed to adopt the correct test, and therefore failed to make the necessary findings of fact to support his conclusions. We have already indicated that we see no reason to

c   disturb the judge's factual findings on the issue of whether or not an adequate warning was given and would refuse permission to appeal on that ground.

[49] That leaves the first ground of appeal, for which the defendant would also require permission. This is a pleading point. From issue of the statement of claim on 9 April 1998 until trial of the action in December 2000, the claimant's pleading was in the form complained of, para 11 of which read:

d
'In breach of his said duty and/or negligently, the defendant wholly failed to advise, explain or otherwise counsel the plaintiff as to the real risks attached to the said surgical procedure thereby depriving the plaintiff of an opportunity to reflect, consider and/or seek alternative medical or other opinion in respect of options which may be open to her which, it is averred,

e   the plaintiff would have done and so sought had the defendant acted in accordance with reasonably medical practice in the course of his said consultation and thereafter at the London Bridge Hospital.'

At the beginning of the trial Mr Spencer sought to strike out the issue on the ground that it was inadequately pleaded in terms of causation. He was

f   unsuccessful. The defendant had had more than two years to obtain whatever particulars he wanted. So far as we are aware he did nothing effective to do so. The judge held that it was too late to do so on the eve of trial. We cannot say that the exercise of his discretion was plainly wrong. In any event, the pleading was adequate to allege that the claimant would not have consented to the operation

g   which was in fact performed upon her and would at the very least have postponed the decision. That, on the law as we have held it to be, was sufficient.

[50] The defendant's appeal is dismissed.

Appeal dismissed. Permission to appeal refused.

James Brooks   Barrister.

Johnson (trading as Johnson Butchers) v BJW Property Developments Ltd

EWHC 1131 (TCC)

QUEEN'S BENCH DIVISION (TECHNOLOGY AND CONSTRUCTION COURT)

JUDGE THORNTON QC

14 NOVEMBER 2001, 30 JANUARY 2002.

Fire – Accidental fire – Vicarious liability – Defendant engaging independent contractor to carry out work on fireplace – Fire in defendant's grate escaping onto claimant's adjoining premises because of contractor's negligence in performing work – Defendant relying on statutory provision precluding proceedings against any person in whose house 'any fire shall accidentally begin' – Whether provision precluding action in respect of fire starting in domestic grate – Whether owner or occupier of land vicariously liable for escape of fire caused by independent contractor's negligence – Fires Prevention (Metropolis) Act 1774, s 86.

The parties were the owners and occupiers of adjoining premises of sixteenth century origin, separated by a party wall in which a chimney was embedded. The original chimney breast had been constructed with a number of timber fillets embedded in the brickwork. The defendant engaged Y to replace the fire surround of a fireplace which opened up into the chimney. Y performed the work negligently, removing firebrick lining to two sides of the chimney and failing to replace it with adequate fire protection. As a result, he created a potential fire path, made of timber, leading from the grate of the defendant's fireplace into the claimant's premises. Some weeks later, at least two of the timber fillets started to smoulder due to exposure to heat from a fire that had been lit in the defendant's grate. That in turn eventually resulted in a conflagration in the claimant's premises. In subsequent proceedings, the claimant contended primarily that the defendant was strictly liable for fire damage resulting from the escape of fire from its premises. He relied, inter alia, on s 86[a] of the Fires Prevention (Metropolis) Act 1774 which provided that no action could be brought against any person in whose house 'any fire shall accidentally begin'. In particular, the claimant contended that s 86 provided, by necessary implication, for liability where a fire had been started deliberately. In support of that submission, he referred to the ancient common law strict liability for fires started on an occupier's land which then escaped (liability for the escape of ignis suus). The defendant also relied on s 86, contending that the word 'accidentally' covered fires started in domestic grates, and that s 86 therefore provided it with a complete defence to the proceedings. In the event of that being wrong, a further issue arose as to whether the defendant was vicariously liable, under the liability for the escape of ignis suus, for the negligence of Y, even though it was accepted that he was an independent contractor. In submitting that it was not vicariously liable, the defendant contended, inter alia, that Y's negligence was not directly linked to the start or continuation of the fire that had escaped onto the claimant's premises.

---

a   Section 86, so far as material, is set out at [21], below

a **Held** – (1) For the purposes of s 86 of the 1774 Act, the critical question was not whether the original fire had been started accidentally, but whether the escape of fire was an accident. The words 'any fire shall accidentally begin' referred to fire damage on an adjoining occupier's land that had been caused by an escape of fire from the occupier of the land from which the fire had escaped. The word 'accidentally', which meant anything that was not

b deliberate or negligent, was clearly intended to refer to a fire which had spread or escaped without any fault or other established basis for legal liability attaching to the householder for that occurrence. Thus, in context, the Act, which narrowed the liability for the escape of ignis suus, was intended to regulate the situation that arose once a fire had escaped from a domestic grate and had damaged the adjoining occupier's premises. If that

c escape were accidental, the Act provided a defence to the defendant occupier from whose domestic grate the fire had spread and escaped. If, on the other hand, the cause of the escape onto the adjoining occupier's land was the negligence of the defendant, or negligence for which he was responsible, the Act provided no defence. In the instant case, the Act was of no relevance and

d was inapplicable to the original fire that had been started deliberately in the defendant's grate since the mere ignition of that fire gave rise to no liability, whether before or after the Act. Moreover, it provided the defendant with no defence to the claim in so far as it was based on the escape of fire onto the claimant's land as a result of negligence (see [25]–[28], [32], below); *Filliter v Phippard* [1843–60] All ER Rep 879 and *Sochacki v Sas* [1947] 1 All ER 344

e considered.

(2) An owner or occupier of land was liable for the escape of fire resulting from the non-accidental acts of anyone lawfully on the land, including the negligence of an independent contractor. That liability was the last vestige of the ancient strict liability for the escape of ignis suus, and had survived both

f the 1774 Act and the contrary trends in the general development of the law of negligence against the imposition of vicarious liability for the negligence of an independent contractor. Moreover, there was no difference in principle between the negligent failure to control a fire once started so that the fire escaped onto adjoining premises and, as in the instant case, the negligent failure to provide fire prevention measures to a domestic fireplace in

g circumstances where there was a foreseeable need for such measures to prevent the escape of a controlled domestic fire onto adjoining premises. It followed that the defendant was vicariously liable for the damage caused by the escape of the fire into and onto the claimant's premises since the fire had only escaped and caused damage because of the negligent workmanship of

h the defendant's independent contractor, for whom the defendant was to be held separately liable. Accordingly, the claimant was entitled to judgment against the defendant for damages to be assessed (see [39], [43], [44], [69], below); *Balfour v Barty-King (Hyder & Sons (Builders) Ltd, Third Parties)* [1957] 1 All ER 156 and *H&N Emanuel Ltd v Greater London Council* [1971] 2 All ER

j 835 applied.

Notes

For liability of the occupier of premises for fire, see 18(2) *Halsbury's Laws* (4th edn reissue) para 5.

For the Fires Prevention (Metropolis) Act 1774, s 86, see 22 *Halsbury's Statutes* (4th edn) (2000 reissue) 11.

Cases referred to in judgment

Alcock v Wraith (1991) 59 BLR 16, CA.

Balfour v Barty-King (Hyder & Sons (Builders) Ltd, Third Parties) [1957] 1 All ER 156, [1957] 1 QB 496, [1957] 2 WLR 84, CA.

Bar Gur v Bruton [1993] CA Transcript 981.

Beaulieu v Finglam (1401) YB 2 Hen 4, fo 18, pl 6.

Black v Christchurch Finance Co Ltd [1894] AC 48, [1891–4] All ER Rep Ext 1498, PC.

Bower v Peate (1876) 1 QBD 321, [1874–80] All ER Rep 905.

Bradburn v Lindsay [1983] 2 All ER 408.

Cambridge Water Co Ltd v Eastern Counties Leather plc [1994] 1 All ER 53, [1994] 2 AC 264, [1994] 2 WLR 53, HL.

Dalton v Henry Angus & Co, The Commissioners of HM Works and Public Buildings v Henry Angus & Co (1881) 6 App Cas 740, [1881–5] All ER Rep 1, HL.

Filliter v Phippard (1847) 11 QB 347, [1843–60] All ER Rep 879, QB.

Goldman v Hargrave [1966] 2 All ER 989, [1967] 1 AC 645, [1966] 3 WLR 513, PC.

Green v Fibreglass Ltd [1958] 2 All ER 521, [1958] 2 QB 245, [1958] 3 WLR 71.

H&N Emanuel Ltd v Greater London Council [1971] 2 All ER 835, CA.

Holbeck Hall Hotel Ltd v Scarborough BC [2000] 2 All ER 705, [2000] QB 836, [2000] 2 WLR 1396, CA.

Honeywill & Stein Ltd v Larkin Bros (London's Commercial Photographers) Ltd [1934] 1 KB 191, [1933] All ER Rep 77, CA.

Hughes v Percival (1883) 8 App Cas 443, [1881–5] All ER Rep 44, HL.

J Doltis Ltd v Issac Braithwaite & Sons (Engineers) Ltd [1957] 1 Ll L Rep 522.

Job Edwards Ltd v The Company of Proprietors of the Birmingham Navigations [1924] 1 KB 341, CA.

Leakey v National Trust for Places of Historic Interest or Natural Beauty [1980] 1 All ER 17, [1980] QB 485, [1980] 2 WLR 65, CA.

Marchant v Capital & Counties Property Co Ltd [1982] 2 EGLR 152, CA.

Mason v Levy Auto Parts of England Ltd [1967] 2 All ER 62, [1967] 2 QB 530, [1967] 2 WLR 1384.

Matania v National Provincial Bank Ltd and Elevenist Syndicate Ltd [1936] 2 All ER 633, CA.

Musgrove v Pandelis [1919] 2 KB 43, [1918–19] All ER Rep 589, CA.

Perry v Kendricks Transport Ltd [1956] 1 All ER 154, [1956] 1 WLR 85, CA.

Rees v Skerrett [2001] ECWA Civ 760, [2001] 1 WLR 1541.

Richards v Easto (1846) 15 M & W 244.

Rylands v Fletcher (1868) LR 3 HL 330, [1861–73] All ER Rep 1, HL.

Sedleigh-Denfield v O'Callagan (Trustees for St Joseph's Society for Foreign Missions) [1940] 3 All ER 349, [1940] AC 880, HL.

Sochacki v Sas [1947] 1 All ER 344.

Spicer v Smee [1946] 1 All ER 489.

Wagon Mound (No 2), The, Overseas Tankship (UK) Ltd v The Miller Steamship Co Pty Ltd [1966] 2 All ER 709, [1967] 1 AC 617, [1966] 3 WLR 498, PC.

Wringe v Cohen [1939] 4 All ER 241, [1940] 1 KB 229, CA.

Cases also cited or referred to in skeleton arguments

British Celanese Ltd v A H Hunt (Capacitors) Ltd [1969] 2 All ER 1252, [1969] 1 WLR 959.

Brooke v Bool [1928] 2 KB 578, [1928] All ER Rep 155, DC.

E Hobbs (Farms) Ltd v Baxenden Chemical Co Ltd [1992] 1 Lloyd's Rep 54.

Salsbury v Woodland [1969] 3 All ER 863, [1970] 1 QB 324, CA.

Action

a
By claim form issued on 14 February 2001 the claimant, Mr A Johnson (trading as Johnson Butchers), brought proceedings for damages against the defendant, BJW Property Developments Ltd, in respect of a fire which escaped from the defendant's premises at 49 High Street, Newington, Sittingbourne, Kent, and damaged the claimant's adjoining premises at 45/47 High Street. The facts are

b
set out in the judgment.

Richard Booth (instructed by *Hill Dickinson*) for the claimant.
Paul Staddon (instructed by *Kingsley Smith & Co*, Chatham) for the defendant.

Cur adv vult

c
30 January 2002. The following judgment was delivered.

JUDGE THORNTON QC.

(1) INTRODUCTION

d
[1] This claim arises out of a disastrous fire which started on the defendant's premises and spread to the claimant's premises causing extensive damage. The two premises are adjoining and are located in a terrace of houses at High Street, Newington, Sittingbourne, Kent. The claimant's premises at 45/47 High Street consist of a butcher's shop on the ground floor of no 45 with private living accommodation both above at no 45 and in the adjoining premises no 47, the

e
living accommodation of the two premises have been combined to form one residential unit. The adjoining premises are no 49 High Street and are owned by the defendant and were, in 1997 at the time of the fire, a vacant public house that was being refurbished, having been acquired earlier in that year by the defendant.

[2] Both premises are mid-sixteenth century in origin. They were separated

f
by a party wall consisting of two timber framework skins with the frames infilled with a lath and daub construction. This party wall was crossed by both horizontal and vertical timber beams that were embedded into the wall and which supported the floor boards and the structure of both premises. The fire had been caused by a domestic fire lit in the grate of the fireplace built into the fire breast which was itself built into the party wall in the ground floor lounge of the public

g
house and which had caused adjoining timber members to smoulder. The interconnection of the timbers of both premises was such that this smouldering eventually caused timbers in the claimant's premises to cause flames to break out under or within the floorboards of a first-floor bedroom adjoining the party wall. The fire started in the early hours of 14 February 1998. No one was injured

h
but the fire spread rapidly and eventually caused extensive damage to the claimant's premises and to their contents which caused loss of about £214,000.

[3] The claim is brought against the defendant as the owner and occupier of the premises from where the fire started, spread and escaped and as the employer of an independent contractor whose work to the chimney breast and surround of

j
the fire grate removed the fire and heat protection previously provided to certain timber structural members, thereby creating the conditions under which the fire in the grate was able to cause some timber fillets to start to smoulder. It was one of these fillets which ultimately caused the fire to start in the claimant's adjoining premises.

[4] The evidence adduced at the trial consisted of witness statements from Mr Wilson, the defendant's managing director, and Mr Johnson, the owner and occupier of the damaged premises and the proprietor of the butcher's shop *a* trading there. Mr Wilson was briefly cross-examined. The principal evidence was adduced by the claimant in the form of an expert's report from a fire expert, Mr Bourdillon of Dr JH Burgoyne and Partners. The contents and opinions expressed in this report were agreed. Mr Bourdillon had inspected both fire damaged premises on 17 February 1998, only two days after the fire. The report consisted of a thorough and conclusive account of the cause of the fire and *b* I accept and adopt those conclusions in this judgment.

(2) THE CAUSE OF THE FIRE

[5] The public house has a ground floor lounge. When the claimant acquired these premises the fireplace had a Victorian surround. Mr Wilson showed Mr Young around the premises in November 1997. Mr Young is both an old *c* acquaintance of Mr Wilson's and an antiques dealer. Mr Young mentioned that he had come across a fire surround that would be an ideal replacement for this surround. Mr Wilson inspected the proposed surround, liked it and agreed to buy it from Mr Young who also mentioned that he had installed a similar fire surround in his own home. Mr Wilson also inspected this fire surround, liked *d* what he saw and decided that Mr Young was fully capable of undertaking the apparently simple building work that would be involved in the installation of the fire surround he was buying. He therefore also contracted with Mr Young to install the fire surround and arranged to pay him £400 for the surround and a further £400 to install it. Mr Young carried out the installation work soon afterwards. *e*

[6] The existing chimney breast had an opening which was about 400 mm wide. Its sides were lined with fire bricks. The fireplace it contained opened up into the chimney which was embedded into the party wall. The rear of the fireplace was protected by a fire curtain constructed of glass fibre which had been added a few years previously as an infill into the void between the double skin of *f* the timber framed partitioning forming the party wall. This fire curtain had only been added by the previous owners of the public house in order to obtain a fire certificate. The new fire surround required, for full visual effect, a much larger opening. The surround also, again for visual effect, required the chimney breast to be widened so as to appear significantly wider than it was in its constructed *g* state. Mr Young achieved this adaptation by enlarging the fire opening and by attaching a dummy extension to each side of the chimney breast. The enlargement work involved removing the fire brick lining to the two sides of the fireplace and rendering the underlying brickwork with a render face which was taken up a short distance into the chimney itself. The dummy extension was made of a timber and stud rectangular frame which was built against the two *h* sides of the chimney breast and then plastered over. This extended piece left a void within it positioned against the existing side of the chimney breast and the existing external face of the party wall against which the chimney breast abutted. The extension, therefore, sat in the rectangular corner made by the side of the breast and the party wall. The resulting visual effect was of a chimney *j* breast which was wider than before and with a wider fireplace opening.

[7] The original chimney breast had been constructed with a number of timber fillets embedded into the brickwork. These lengths of timber were located so that they ran from the internal faces of the brickwork within the fireplace to the edges of the sides of the chimney breast with the internal end of

a the fillet abutting the fire brick lining and the external end abutting the existing plaster covering of the side wall of the chimney breast. Mr Young's installation work affected these timber fillets in two material respects. Firstly, the internal end of each fillet was exposed by the removal of the fire brick lining of the fireplace. The protection provided by those bricks was replaced with a thin layer of facing plaster. Secondly, the external end of each fillet had placed next to it part

b of the timber frame of the dummy extension that was being added to each side of the chimney breast. Embedded into the party wall were a number of structural timbers.

[8] The consequence of this arrangement was that there was a potential fire path made of timber that lead directly from the grate through the side wall of the chimney breast to the timber studwork of the extension and on to timber

c structural members embedded into the party wall which in turn connected to the timber structural members of the adjoining premises including the connecting floor boards and other internal timbers. This potential fire path was not arrested by the fire curtain since the timbers within the party wall associated with the public house were not completely separated from those of the adjoining structure

d by the fibreglass curtain infill.

[9] After Mr Young had installed the fire surround, he successfully lit a fire in the grate to demonstrate to Mr Wilson that the surround, fireplace and grate were satisfactory. The internal redecoration of the lounge and other rooms then continued. Some of this work was undertaken by a Mr Andrews who, on 13 February 1998, some weeks after Mr Young had installed the new fire

e surround, lit a fire in the grate to keep him warm whilst he was working. He ceased work in the early afternoon, extinguished the fire and left the premises unoccupied. There was no unusual smell or other untoward signs. The outbreak of fire within the adjoining premises was not first noticed until about 2.00 am the following morning.

f [10] It is now accepted how the outbreak of fire occurred. At least two of the timber fillets linking the side faces of the fire place with the cavity erected by Mr Young at each side of the chimney breast were exposed to heat sufficiently to cause them to ignite and slowly to smoulder along their entire length. This smouldering eventually caused part of the timber studwork within each cavity to

g start to smoulder, a process that was encouraged and prolonged by the airless cavity in which these timbers were located. In the case of the left hand cavity, the smouldering then advanced to and into the interconnecting timber components of the building structure located within the party wall including a joist positioned behind the chimney stack. Finally, the fire underwent a transition of flame enabling it to ignite and break through the floor boards at first floor level in the

h claimant's adjoining premises.

[11] The particular fillets providing a fire path could not be precisely identified. However, two holes, one on each side of the fireplace, were discovered which led from the fireplace through the chimney breast into each side cavity. These holes had been filled by timber fillets which had obviously

j smouldered and then been completely destroyed by fire. The left hand cavity had provided the means for the fire path to continue into and through the party wall whereas the right hand cavity, although damaged internally, had not provided a further path for the fire into the party wall. There might, however, have been further fillets which had been exposed by the removal of the fire bricks which could have provided additional fire paths through the chimney breast into each

cavity. If these existed, their ends embedded in the side of the fireplace would
have been covered by the render applied by Mr Young and their remains *a*
would not have been visible during Mr Bourdillon's subsequent inspection.

[12] The reason why the timber fillets, which were part of the original
structure of the chimney breast, ignited and smouldered along their entire length
was because of the removal of the fire brick lining on the inside side faces of the
fireplace which had provided full protection to the ends of the fillets embedded *b*
in the chimney breast. Part of the exposed brickwork face was then rendered.
The two fillet holes that were discovered that had accommodated fillets
destroyed by the fire appeared to be located just above the rendering, one on each
side of the fireplace. It was not clear whether the fillet ends had been rendered
by Mr Young and the render had subsequently been displaced or whether they
had not originally been rendered at all. However, the rendering was regarded as *c*
ineffective as a fire protection by Mr Bourdillon and any render protection would
not have precluded the ignition of a timber fillet located immediately behind it.

[13] In summary, adequate fire protection was removed by Mr Young and this
was either replaced by inadequate fire protection or, in the possible case of two
of the fillets, by no fire protection at all. *d*

(3) THE NEGLIGENCE OF MR YOUNG

[14] It is accepted by the defendant that Mr Young was negligent in the
manner in which he undertook the installation of the fire surround. He clearly
took on work and owed the adjoining owner a duty of care to carry out his work
in such a manner that the physical integrity of the adjoining premises was not *e*
damaged by his work or by the consequences of his work. The particular respects
in which he was negligent were in removing obvious fire protection from the
inside face of the fireplace and in not replacing that protection with adequate fire
protection. It is true that the presence of timber fillets within the chimney breast,
the potential fire path through the chimney breast, the potential additional fire
path created by the false extension at each side of the breast and the potential for *f*
the accessible timbers in the party wall to extend that fire path into the claimant's
premises were not known to, or foreseen by, Mr Young. However, damage by
fire to the surrounding structure from controlled fires burning within the
fireplace located within the chimney breast was clearly foreseeable, particularly
since obvious fire protection of parts of the fireplace had been removed. *g*
Moreover, the fireplace and its surrounds abutted and formed part of a party wall
and both premises were very old and contained much timber work. Mr Young
clearly had a duty to ensure that any fire bricks that he removed were replaced by
equally efficacious fire protection measures. It was not necessary, for the duty of
care to be broken, for Mr Young to have foreseen the precise path or passage of *h*
any fire emanating from or caused by a domestic fire lit in the fireplace since
damage to the structure left unprotected from that domestic fire by the removal
of fire bricks was clearly foreseeable.

(4) THE CASE AGAINST THE DEFENDANT

[15] The claimant's case is simply stated. The fire damaging his premises *j*
spread from, escaped and was caused by a fire started on the defendant's
premises. That is sufficient to give rise to a liability for the consequent damage
since the owner or occupier of premises is strictly liable for fire damage resulting
from an escape of fire from those premises. However, since liability for fire
damage arising from the starting of a fire, or from its continuation or escape,

normally requires proof of a negligent act, the claimant also relies on the negligence of Mr Young since that negligence undoubtedly caused the fire to break out from the fireplace and escape into his premises.

[16] The defendant disputes liability on two grounds. Firstly, it is alleged that liability for fire damage is not strict but requires proof of negligence. Secondly, it is alleged that, whether liability be strict or dependent upon proof of negligence, the defendant cannot be liable since the relevant negligence was that of an independent contractor. In the circumstances of this case, no vicarious liability can arise as a result of the negligence of an independent contractor. To this second line of defence, the claimant responds that fire damage, particularly where it occurs following work to a party wall, provides an exception to the independent contractor defence.

[17] It follows that this case involves a consideration of the somewhat complex interrelationship of four distinct types of common law liability or causes of action, being those relating to the escape of fire, to the escape of fire resulting from a dangerous or non-natural use of land nowadays usually known as *Rylands v Fletcher* liability (see *Rylands v Fletcher* (1868) LR 3 HL 33, [1861–73] All ER Rep 1), to negligence and to nuisance. The complexity of this area of law arises because each cause of action has moved slowly towards the others yet it remains unclear what is the extent to which all four causes of action have been assimilated, particularly as regards a defence of an occupier based on the negligence of an independent contractor.

[18] The defendant's potential liability must be considered in a somewhat blinkered way, given the way the claimant's case was developed. Firstly, the claimant's case did not seek to rely on the obvious breach of the Building Regulations that had occurred as a result of structural works being undertaken on the defendant's premises which failed to provide adequate fire protection to adjoining structures. In consequence, the potential case against the defendant building owner based on any such breach of statutory duty was not pursued. Secondly, the case did not seek to rely on the possible negligence of the defendant in selecting and contracting with an independent contractor who was possibly unsuitable to undertake structural work involving fire protection measures close to a party wall separating old buildings since Mr Young, as an antiques dealer, would not have had obvious skills as a builder, even if he had previously installed fire surrounds on a do-it-yourself basis. Thirdly, it was accepted on behalf of the claimant that Mr Young was an independent contractor as that term is used in the law of tort despite his obvious lack of qualifications or expertise to act or trade as a builder or to be able to decide what structural work should be undertaken close to a fireplace, chimney breast or party wall. Fourthly, the claimant's case did not seek to rely on the recently enacted legislation, the Party Wall etc Act 1996, which re-enacted the London party wall legislation in an amended form and extended it to the whole country and which imposes duties on an owner towards his adjoining owner when undertaking structural work on an adjoining party wall. Finally, it was accepted that Mr Young was engaged by, and contracted with, the defendant and was not in contract with Mr Wilson personally. Thus, despite the contract having been apparently made by Mr Wilson personally, the defendant may rely on the assumption that the relevant work was undertaken negligently by its own independent contractor. It should be stressed that Mr Booth, counsel for the claimant, had neither pleaded or decided upon the case to be argued on

the claimant's behalf and was, therefore, at the trial, constrained by the case pleaded by others.

(5) THE FIRES PREVENTION (METROPOLIS) ACT 1774

[19] Since Anglo-Saxon times, the common law has treated fire damage caused by an escape of fire as being actionable by an adjoining owner without proof of fault. This liability was based on custom and on the special duty imposed on householders to keep their fires safe. This liability became known in the Year Book cases as a liability for the escape of ignis suus. The strictness of this liability was the result of a land-based feudal economy with closely knit domestic housing arrangements that were susceptible to catastrophic loss from fires that got out of control. The early history was well summarised by Lord Goddard CJ in *Balfour v Barty-King (Hyder & Sons (Builders) Ltd, Third Parties)* [1957] 1 All ER 156 at 158, [1957] 1 QB 496 at 502:

> 'From very early times it seems to have been recognised in our law that there is a special duty to guard against an escape of fire. It is perhaps not without interest to observe that in dealing with the meaning and derivation of "curfew", the OXFORD DICTIONARY points out that its imposition was not an act of political repression. It was a precautionary measure, so that people should not retire for the night and leave their fires burning. The ENCYCLOPAEDIA BRITANNICA says that curfew was rung at Oxford in the days of Alfred the Great. In days when houses were built mainly of timber and when thatch was the commonest roofing, a spark might, and, indeed, in a country village may still, do almost incalculable damage.'

[20] However, the losses resulting from the Great Fire of London in 1666 fuelled the growing belief that had already started to develop that it was anomalous that a man should be liable for fire damage that had not been caused by his fault. This led to statutory intervention, first in s 6 of the Act of 1707 (6 Anne c 31) and then by the section that replaced it, s 86 of the Fires Prevention (Metropolis) Act 1774 (14 Geo 3 c 78). Despite the apparently localised ambit of this latter Act, the critical section has always been interpreted as being of general application across England and Wales (see *Richards v Easto* (1846) 15 M & W 244 at 251 per Parke B).

[21] The modification of the strict liability for the escape of fire was in these terms in s 86 of the 1774 Act:

> '... no action, suit or process whatever shall be had, maintained or prosecuted against any person in whose house, chamber, stable, barn or other building, or on whose estate any fire shall ... accidentally begin, nor shall any recompence [sic] be made by such person for any damage suffered thereby, any law, usage or custom to the contrary notwithstanding ...'

[22] The word 'accidentally' was not defined in the 1707 or 1774 Acts and its full meaning has never since been authoritatively settled. However, one of the claimant's bases of claim is that the 1774 Act, in prohibiting actions for damage caused by fires started accidentally, is by necessary implication providing for liability where a fire was started deliberately. This submission is supported by reference to the long-standing common law strict liability for fires started on an occupier's land which then escape. The defendant, on the other hand, contends that the word 'accidentally' has a special meaning and includes a reference to fires

started in domestic grates. Since this fire started in the defendant's grate, the 1774
Act would, on the defendant's case, provide a complete defence to this action.

[23] Some guidance as to the meaning and effect of s 86 of the 1774 Act is
provided by the case of *Filliter v Phippard* (1847) 11 QB 347 at 357, [1843–60]
All ER Rep 879 at 881 where Lord Denman CJ stated that the word accidentally
was used in contradistinction to the word 'wilful' and meant not only
'unintentionally' but also 'without negligence'. He stated:

> '... it may ... mean a fire produced by mere chance, or incapable of being
> traced to any cause, and so would stand opposed to the negligence of either
> servants or masters.'

This dictum would suggest that a fire started either deliberately or negligently
would not be subject to the immunity conferred by the 1774 Act. On the strength
of *Filliter*'s case, therefore, the claimant's submission would appear to have some
force since the fire was started deliberately by the defendant, the 1774 Act would
provide no protection and the defendant would be liable, given the common
law's long-standing provision for strict liability for the escape of fire.

[24] There are, however, conflicting dicta on whether a fire started in a
domestic grate is accidentally started for the purposes of the 1774 Act. In *Job
Edwards Ltd v The Company of Proprietors of the Birmingham Navigations* [1924] 1 KB
341 at 361, Scrutton LJ stated that the Act provided protection to an occupier in
such circumstances since the fire would have been started accidentally whereas
in *Musgrove v Pandelis* [1919] 2 KB 43 at 51, [1918–19] All ER Rep 589 at 593,
Duke LJ stated that the Act would provide the occupier with no protection in
such circumstances. However, neither opinion was based on any supporting
reasoning and both were provided obiter. The only other modern decision that
has any bearing on this subject is that of Lord Goddard CJ, sitting in the Queen's
Bench Division, in *Sochacki v Sas* [1947] 1 All ER 344. This decision related to a
fire started when a spark or burning lump of coal fell out of a domestic fire whilst
the room in which the fire was burning was unattended and which set fire to the
floor boards. The fire then spread to an adjoining lodger's room causing much
damage. The fire was not started or continued by any act of negligence and the
defendant was held to be not liable for the damage even though, of course, the
fire in the grate had been started deliberately. This decision can only be explained
on the basis that the fire in the adjoining lodger's room had been started
accidentally and not intentionally but the 1774 Act was not referred to in the
judgment. Certainly, some of the textbook writers have suggested that the 1774
Act provides a defence to fires started in domestic grates.[b]

[25] Since the word 'accidentally' has never been authoritatively defined, it is
necessary to consider its meaning in the historic context of the 1707 and 1774
Acts[c]. In that context, the intended meaning of the word 'accidentally' can readily
be ascertained. The 1774 Act was intended to regulate the strict liability for the
escape of fire provided for by the common law and to curtail that liability to some
extent. The reference to 'any fire shall accidentally begin' is a reference to fire
damage on an adjoining occupier's land which has been caused by an escape of
fire from the occupier of the land from which the fire has escaped. Before the

---

b   Thus, *Clerk & Lindsell on Torts* (18th edn, 2000) p 1064 (para 20-52) states that the 1774 Act would be
    a defence where fire spread without negligence from a fire started deliberately in a domestic grate.
c   In what follows, I have drawn extensively on an authoritative article, AI Ogus 'Vagaries in Liability
    for the Escape of Fire' (1969) 27 CLJ 104.

1774 Act, even if such a fire had escaped accidentally onto the adjoining
occupier's land, the occupier of the land from which the fire had escaped could *a*
have been held strictly liable. Following the 1774 Act, fires that were started by
an accidental escape were within the Act and an occupier of the land from which
the fire had escaped could not be sued and held liable for the resulting damage.
The critical question was whether the escape of fire was an accident, not whether
the original fire had been started accidentally. The Act was, therefore, narrowing *b*
the liability for the escape of ignis suus.

[26] This reading of the 1774 Act is supported by the wording of its long title
which provides that the Act is for 'the more effectually preventing mischiefs by
fire'. Thus, the Act was intending to prevent mischief caused by the combustion
of physical materials. This regulation of fire damage had been undertaken against
a background that there existed before it was enacted a strict liability for fires *c*
spreading and escaping, without any fault on the part of a householder, to
adjoining land and that that rule had become one which was regarded as being
unnecessarily harsh and anomalous. Thus, 'accidentally' is clearly intended to
refer to a fire which had spread or escaped without any fault or other established
basis for legal liability attaching to the householder for that occurrence. A fire in *d*
a domestic grate is clearly a fire that was started accidentally in that sense since it
is a harmless and controlled method of providing heat, is enclosed in a domestic
grate or fireplace and has not escaped. However, the 1774 Act is not referring to
such a fire at all since it gives rise to no liability.

[27] Thus, in context, the 1774 Act is intended to regulate the situation that
arises once a fire has escaped from a domestic grate and has damaged the *e*
adjoining occupier's premises. If, as in *Sochacki*'s case, that escape was accidental,
the 1774 Act provides a defence to the defendant occupier from whose domestic
grate the fire has spread and escaped. If, on the other hand, the cause of the
escape onto the adjoining occupier's land was the negligence of the defendant or
for which he was responsible, the Act provides no defence. In this case, the 1774 *f*
Act has no relevance and is inapplicable to the original fire that was started
deliberately in the defendant's grate since the mere ignition of that fire gives rise
to no liability, whether before or after the 1774 Act. Moreover, it provides the
defendant with no defence to the claimant's claim in so far as that claim is based
on the escape of fire onto the claimant's land as a result of negligence.

[28] This interpretation of the 1774 Act is consistent with twentieth-century *g*
fire cases. The Act has been held not to protect a householder where a fire was
started accidentally but was continued and not extinguished by the negligence of
the householder (see *Musgrove v Pandelis* [1919] 2 KB 43, [1918–19] All ER Rep
589). Further, fire resulting from a non-natural user of land or from a nuisance
has been held to be outside the protection from being sued provided by the 1774 *h*
Act since the relevant fire was not regarded as having been started accidentally
(see *Musgrove*'s case, *Spicer v Smee* [1946] 1 All ER 489 at 495 and *Perry v Kendricks
Transport Ltd* [1956] 1 All ER 154, [1956] 1 WLR 85).

[29] The narrowing of the meaning of the word 'accidentally' so as to exclude
from the protection of the 1774 Act fires for which strict *Rylands v Fletcher* liability *j*
would otherwise be applicable was criticised by MacKenna J in *Mason v Levy Auto
Parts of England Ltd* [1967] 2 All ER 62 at 68–69, [1967] 2 QB 530 at 540–541.
MacKenna J's criticism was that, if such fires were excluded from the ambit of the
Act's protection, no effect would be given to the wide words of the Act which
provided that no proceedings could be brought for fires accidentally begun 'any
law, usage or custom to the contrary notwithstanding'. However, given previous

a authority, MacKenna J excluded such a fire from the protection of the Act. With respect to MacKenna J, however, the narrow meaning given to the Act which so concerned him is one that is particularly appropriate given the Act's historical origins since the fire in question had not escaped 'accidentally' since it escaped following a dangerous or non-natural use of the land. Thus, the escape was one for which custom had long since imposed strict liability on the occupier of the *b* land.

(6) RYLANDS v FLETCHER LIABILITY

[30] The common law strict liability for damage caused by an escape of fire had developed long before the recognition of the more general strict liability imposed on occupiers of land for any escape from their land onto adjoining land *c* in the course of a dangerous or non-natural user of land, the so-called rule in *Rylands v Fletcher* (1868) LR 3 HL 330, [1861–73] All ER Rep 1. Indeed, liability for damage caused by the spread of fire has traditionally been a separate form of liability outside the traditional causes of action in negligence, nuisance or under the rule in *Rylands v Fletcher*. As Lord Denning MR explained in *H&N Emanuel Ltd v* *d* *Greater London Council* [1971] 2 All ER 835 at 839:

> *e* 'There has been much discussion about the exact legal basis of liability for fire. The liability of the occupier can be said to be a strict liability in this sense that he is liable for the negligence not only of his servants but also of independent contractors and, indeed, of anyone except a "stranger". By the same token it can be said to be a "vicarious liability", because he is liable for the defaults of others as well as his own. It can also be said to be a liability under the principle of *Rylands v Fletcher*, because fire is undoubtedly a dangerous thing which is likely to do damage if it escapes. But I do not think *f* it necessary to put it into any one of these three categories. It goes back to the time when no such categories were thought of. Suffice it to say that the extent of liability is now well defined as I have stated it. The occupier is liable for the escape of fire which is due to the negligence of anyone other than a stranger.'

g [31] Fire is an obvious 'dangerous thing' so that any escape of fire gives rise to the potential of *Rylands v Fletcher* liability if the escape was caused by, or arose out of, a dangerous or non-natural user of land. However, the burning of a domestic fire in a domestic grate has long since been regarded as falling outside the scope of this rule of strict liability. As Lord Goddard CJ put it in *Sochacki v Sas* [1947] 1 All ER 344 at 344–345:

> *h* 'I do not think the doctrine in *Rylands* v. *Fletcher* applies to a case of this sort. [The defendant] was using his room in the ordinary, natural way in which the room could be used. It is not the case of a fire starting on one owner's premises and spreading to the premises of an adjoining owner … *j* here the fire was being used by a man in a fireplace in his own room. There was an ordinary, natural, proper, everyday use of a fireplace in a room. The fireplace was there to be used.'

The inapplicability of *Rylands v Fletcher* strict liability to domestic fires started within grates and fireplaces was affirmed by Streatfield J in *J Doltis Ltd v Issac Braithwaite & Sons (Engineers) Ltd* [1957] 1 Ll L Rep 522.

(7) SUMMARY—OWNER OR OCCUPIER'S LIABILITY FOR FIRE DAMAGE

[32] In summary. (1) An owner or occupier of land was from ancient times *a*
liable at common law for damage caused by any escape of fire onto adjoining
land. This was liability for the escape of ignis suus. (2) Following the 1707 and
1774 Acts, fire damage caused by an escape of fire where that escape arose from
a deliberate or negligent act still gives rise to liability but an action against an
occupier is precluded where the escape of fire from his land was accidentally *b*
caused. 'Accidentally' means anything that is not deliberate or negligent.
(3) However, damage caused by the spread of fire from a domestic fire in a grate
or fireplace cannot give rise to strict liability since such a fire is outside the ambit
of the 1774 Act altogether and burning a domestic fire in a grate is not a
non-natural user of land. The critical question is whether any escape or spread of
fire from the grate, if such occurs, was 'accidental'. (4) Fire damage caused by the *c*
escape of fire started following a non-natural user of land or as a result of a
dangerous use of land gives rise to strict liability for the owner or occupier of the
land on which the fire started. This liability is separate and distinct from the
ancient strict liability for the escape of ignis suus and is merely an aspect of the
more general common law *Rylands v Fletcher* strict liability. (5) If a fire is started *d*
accidentally on land, the liability of the owner or occupier of the land none the
less arises for damage caused by the escape of that fire where that escape is
continued or not contained by the negligence or nuisance of the owner or
occupier. (6) The potential liability of an owner or occupier for fire damage exists
for personal injury to someone on, or for damage to another's goods stored on,
the same premises as the fire that was started there. This liability must, however, *e*
be founded on negligence since the necessary foundation for ignis suus liability,
Rylands v Fletcher liability or for nuisance, namely an escape of fire or an
interference with the enjoyment of the use of land, would not be present (see the
J Doltis Ltd case).

(8) VICARIOUS LIABILITY FOR THE ESCAPE OF FIRE   *f*

8.1 The law

[33] An owner or occupier of land has always been vicariously liable for the
damage caused by an escape of fire which has been negligently started by the acts
of others lawfully in occupation of the land. The strictness of the common law *g*
ignis suus liability for an escape of fire was such that an occupier could only
escape liability where the act of a stranger caused the escape of fire from his house
or land. This was established as early as 1401 in *Beaulieu v Finglam* (1401) YB 2
Hen 4, fo 18, pl 6. The restriction of strict liability by the 1707 and 1774 Acts did
not effect this vicarious liability save that the escape had to have occurred other *h*
than accidentally. It follows that this strict or vicarious liability for the escape of
fire developed long before the tort of negligence had developed as a separate tort.

[34] The tort of negligence developed in the nineteenth century and, with it,
there also developed the corollary doctrine that a person was not to be held liable
for damage caused by the negligence of his independent contractor. The
interrelationship of this general exemption from liability for damage caused *j*
negligently by an independent contractor with the contrary ancient vicarious
liability in fire cases where the escape was caused non-accidentally by anyone
other than a stranger was not directly addressed for nearly 150 years after the
development of negligence liability in the early nineteenth century and, when it
was, the Court of Appeal held in two important decisions in 1956 and 1971 that

the ancient strict liability for the negligence of independent contractors survived in fire cases.

[35] These cases followed a case in the Privy Council in 1893 which had held a defendant liable for fire damage caused by the negligence of its independent contractor but without a full discussion of the basis of vicarious liability. The Privy Council case was *Black v Christchurch Finance Co Ltd* [1894] AC 48, [1891–4] All ER Rep Ext 1498, an appeal from the Court of Appeal in New Zealand. The defendant had engaged an independent contractor to clear scrub land by burning and felling. This contractor negligently allowed a fire lit for this purpose to escape onto the adjoining land causing much fire damage. The defendant disputed that the fire had been lit by its independent contractor but the jury found that it had been. The only other issue argued was whether the independent contractor had been in breach of contract in lighting the fire in December when the contract apparently only allowed burning in February and, if he was in breach, whether the fire was to be treated as having been lit by a stranger. The board decided that although the independent contractor was in breach of contract, that breach did not make the act of lighting the fire one that was collateral to the contract and so held the defendant liable. The principle that a defendant may be held liable for the authorised negligent acts of its independent contractor which allows a fire to start and then to escape was not disputed. However, the board did state as follows:

'The lighting of a fire on open bush land, where it may readily spread to adjoining property and cause serious damage, is an operation necessarily attended with great danger, and a proprietor who executes such an operation is bound to use all reasonable precautions to prevent the fire extending to his neighbour's property (sic utere tuo ut alienum non lædas). And if he authorizes another to act for him he is bound, not only to stipulate that such precautions shall be taken, but also to see that they are observed, otherwise he will be responsible for the consequences. See *Hughes* v. *Pericival* ((1883) 8 App Cas 443, [1881–5] All ER Rep 44) and authorities there cited ... In any view no preventive means of any kind were adopted, and there can be no doubt as to the liability of the defendants if they are responsible for [the independent contractor's] act.' (See [1894] AC 48 at 54, [1891–4] All ER Rep Ext 1498 at 1502.)

[36] Holdsworth, in his *History of English Law*, vol XI, pp 608–609, cites this case as authority for the proposition that in English law an occupier is liable for the negligent acts of an independent contractor in starting a fire that spreads to a neighbour's property[d] but there is understandable force in the view of the Court of Appeal in *Balfour v Barty-King (Hyder & Sons (Builders) Ltd, Third Parties)* [1957] 1 All ER 156 at 159, [1957] 1 QB 496 at 504 that 'we do not get much assistance' from *Black's* case since the opinion of the board in that case was mainly concerned with whether the employer was still to be held liable for the fire damage if the independent contractor had in fact caused the fire in disregard of a special term of the contract. However, the case could only have been decided in the way that it was on the basis that the landowner was vicariously liable for the acts of an

d   See *Balfour v Barty-King (Hyder & Sons (Builders) Ltd, Third Parties)* [1957] 1 QB 496 at 499 (John Thompson QC in argument) and [1957] 1 All ER 156 at 159, [1957] 1 QB 496 at 504.

independent contractor who had negligently started a fire that had spread to an adjoining occupier's land.

[37] Other than in *Black's* case, the principle of vicarious liability for the negligent acts of an independent contractor in fire cases was not properly examined until the cases of *Balfour v Barty-King* and *H&N Emanuel Ltd v Greater London Council* [1971] 2 All ER 835 were decided by the Court of Appeal. In *Balfour's* case, a householder engaged a building contractor to unfreeze pipes in her loft which had frozen up in exceptionally hard weather. The building contractor sent a young apprentice carpenter with a blowtorch who set fire to lagging whilst attempting to thaw the pipe with the naked flame of his torch. The resulting disastrous fire severely damaged an adjoining premises and led to the householder being held liable for that damage. In giving the judgment of the court, Lord Goddard CJ stated as follows:

'… a person in whose house a fire is caused by negligence is liable if it spreads to that of his neighbour, and this is true whether the negligence is his own or that of his servant or his guest, but he is not liable if the fire is caused by a stranger. Who then is a stranger? Clearly a trespasser would be in that category, but, if a man is liable for the negligent act of his guest, it is, indeed, difficult to see why he is not liable for the act of a contractor whom he has invited to his house to do work on it, and who does the work in a negligent manner.' (See [1957] 1 All ER 156 at 159, [1957] 1 QB 496 at 504.)

[38] A similar conclusion was reached by the Court of Appeal in the *H&N Emanuel* case [1971] 2 All ER 835. Lord Denning MR made it clear (at 838) that an occupier was not only liable for the negligence of an independent contractor where the negligence of that contractor started a fire which caused damage but was also liable where the fire spread by the negligence of an independent contractor. He stated:

'After considering the cases, it is my opinion that the occupier of a house or land is liable for the escape of fire which is due to the negligence not only of his servants, but also of his independent contractors and of his guests, and of anyone who is there with his leave or licence.'

[39] Thus, an owner's or occupier's ancient vicarious liability for a fire spreading and escaping onto adjoining premises due to the non-accidental acts of anyone who is not a stranger survived both the 1707 and 1774 Acts and the contrary trends in the general development of the law of negligence in the nineteenth and twentieth centuries against the imposition of vicarious liability for negligence. Indeed, the liability of an owner or occupier for the damage caused by the escape of fire resulting from an independent contractor's negligence is the last vestige of the ancient strict liability for the escape of ignis suus.

[40] Whether this aspect of strict liability for the escape of ignis suus, namely vicarious liability for fire damage where the escape was caused other than accidentally by others, should have survived from the fifteenth century into the twenty-first century is a matter of policy. The Court of Appeal, in the two decisions already cited, clearly decided that this aspect of strict liability should survive. However, it is worth noting the views of Mr Ogus set out in his article entitled 'Vagaries in Liability for the Escape of Fire' (1969) 27 CLJ 104 at 118, 120. These are to the effect that *Balfour's* case was decided on a basis midway between negligence and strict liability and the decision has led to an undesirable result in

a a modern loss-distribution based system of tort liability. Mr Ogus would prefer that vicarious liability for the negligent acts of an independent contractor in causing an escape of fire should be replaced by a regime in which the injured party, backed by fire insurance and not the employer, should bear the risk of loss from fire damage caused to a neighbour by an impecunious negligent independent contractor.

b *8.2 Defendant's vicarious liability for the escape of fire*

[41] Two grounds are put forward by the defendant in seeking to avoid the conclusion that it should be held liable on the basis of its independent contractor's negligent workmanship. Firstly, it is argued that Mr Young was not authorised c to carry out the installation work in a negligent manner since he was on a frolic of his own. However, for an owner or occupier to escape liability on that basis, the independent contractor's acts or omissions must constitute so alien an act that he should be regarded as a trespasser (as Lord Denning MR put it in the *H&N Emanuel* case [1971] 2 All ER 835 at 839) or the act must be a casual or collateral act of negligence (as Lord Goddard CJ put it in *Balfour's* case [1957] 1 All ER 156 d at 159, [1957] 1 QB 496 at 504). Although a negligent act, Mr Young's removal of the fire bricks and their replacement by a thin coat of render formed part of the work that he was engaged to perform. Thus, this work formed part, albeit a negligent part, of the work involved in installing the new larger fire surround. The work was authorised by the defendant who cannot avoid vicarious liability e on this suggested ground of immunity.

[42] Secondly, it is argued by the defendant that Mr Young's negligence was not directly linked to the starting or continuation of the fire which escaped onto and damaged the claimant's premises. Indeed, so the argument ran, the fire that was lit in the grate was lit some weeks after Mr Young had installed the fire surround. Once the fire in the grate had been started 'accidentally', no one could f reasonably have known, nor did know, that it had ignited certain timber fillets which then smouldered undetected until a conflagration broke out on the claimant's premises. On this basis, the fire was started without anyone being aware of it and no one had had a reasonable opportunity of quelling the fire once it had started and before the damage complained of had actually been done.

g [43] This argument is unsustainable. There is no difference in principle between the negligent failure to control a fire once started so that the fire escapes to an adjoining premises and, as happened in this case, the negligent failure to provide fire prevention measures to a domestic fireplace in circumstances where there was a foreseeable need for such measures to prevent the escape of a controlled domestic fire onto adjoining premises. Indeed this case is similar to *Spicer v Smee* [1946] 1 h All ER 489 where Atkinson J held the defendant liable for the negligent workmanship of her independent contractor who had left the premises in a state of disrepair. This led to the starting of a fire which subsequently escaped to damage the adjoining occupier's premises. The defendant's electrician had failed to insulate the wiring being installed so that both it and its inflammable surroundings caught j fire. Just as one function of insulation is to prevent overheating and conflagration of surrounding materials, one function of a fire brick lining a fireplace is to prevent similar physical consequences when it has a domestic fire burning in it.

[44] It follows that the defendant in this case is to be held vicariously liable for the damage caused by the escape of fire into and onto the claimant's premises since the fire only escaped and caused damage because of the negligent

workmanship of the defendant's independent contractor for whom the defendant *a* is to be held separately liable.

(9) NEGLIGENCE AND NUISANCE

9.1 The law

[45] In the light of my findings based on the escape of the fire onto the *b* claimant's premises, it is not strictly necessary to deal with the separate and potentially additional ground of liability arising out of the negligence of Mr Young and the nuisance created by his negligent work and the defendant's potential vicarious liability for that negligence and nuisance that was also relied upon by the claimant. However, this further potential ground of liability was fully argued and the argument merits a separate finding. *c*

[46] The claimant's claims based on negligence and nuisance focus not on the fire that was started in the grate but on the spread of that fire to, and the starting of a fire within, the adjoining timber fillets that then progressed via the timber frame of the chimney breast extension into the adjoining premises. The relevant negligence relied on was the failure by the defendant's independent contractor to provide adequate fire protection to the surrounding woodwork previously *d* protected by fire bricks and which was capable of being harmed by the natural and ordinary use of the fireplace when a domestic fire was burnt. The nuisance relied on was the unjustified interference in the enjoyment of the claimant's use of his land by the spread or escape of fire from the defendant's land. The relevant spread or escape of fire was the smouldering which travelled from the timber *e* members located on the defendant's premises to the timber members located on the claimant's premises. The nuisance is said to arise since that spread or escape occurred as a result of the negligent workmanship of the defendant's independent contractor in relation to an activity on or close to the party wall which was likely to cause damage to the claimant.

[47] There is, in modern times, no significant distinction between liability in *f* negligence and nuisance where the damage in question has been caused by an escape. Liability in nuisance for such an escape requires it to be established that the escape was caused by a failure by the defendant to exercise reasonable care in allowing the circumstances giving rise to an escape, or the escape itself, to start or by a failure to exercise reasonable care to control or to stop the escape once it *g* has started. This assimilation of nuisance with negligence, in relation to an escape, has occurred following the decisions in *Goldman v Hargrave* [1966] 2 All ER 989, [1967] 1 AC 645, *H&N Emanuel Ltd v Greater London Council* [1971] 2 All ER 835, *Leakey v National Trust for Places of Historic Interest or Natural Beauty* [1980] 1 All ER 17, [1980] QB 485 and *Holbeck Hall Hotel Ltd v Scarborough BC* [2000] 2 All ER *h* 705, [2000] QB 836.

[48] The assimilation of negligence and nuisance in escape cases is an aspect of the development of a general liability imposed on an owner or occupier of land that is based on a duty to take reasonable steps to prevent or remove a risk of damaging neighbouring property. This duty has been recognised and developed in a long line of recent cases starting with *Sedleigh-Denfield v O'Callagan (Trustees* *j* *for St Joseph's Society for Foreign Missions)* [1940] 3 All ER 349, [1940] AC 880 and subsequently developed in *The Wagon Mound (No 2), Overseas Tankship (UK) Ltd v Miller Steamship Co Pty Ltd* [1966] 2 All ER 709, [1967] 1 AC 617, *Goldman's* case, *Leakey's* case, *Marchant v Capital and Counties Property Co Ltd* [1982] 2 EGLR 152, *Bradburn v Lindsay* [1983] 2 All ER 408 (Judge Blackett-Ord V-C), *Alcock v Wraith*

a (1991) 59 BLR 16, *Bar Gur v Bruton* [1993] CA Transcript 981, the *Holbeck Hall Hotel* case and *Rees v Skerrett* [2001] ECWA Civ 760, [2001] 1 WLR 1541.

[49] The law relating to liability for activities on land which cause damage to adjoining land or adjoining occupiers is still developing and the authorities have yet to finally clarify the extent to which the various types of liability giving rise to this more general liability have been assimilated. However, the nature of this

b assimilation was recently clearly stated in the Court of Appeal in *Rees'* case by Lloyd J as follows ([2001] 1 WLR 1541 at [28]):

> '[*Leakey's* case] established the proposition that an occupier of land owes a general duty of care to a neighbouring occupier, in relation to a hazard occurring on his land, whether natural or man-made ... to prevent or
>
> *c* minimise the risk of any injury or damage to the neighbour or his property of which the occupier knew or ought to have known, and that what is reasonable in all the circumstances will depend, among other things, on the cost of the steps which might usefully be taken and, viewed broadly, the resources available to the occupier and the neighbour.'

d

[50] It is, therefore, possible to regard liability for damage caused by an escape of fire as having been assimilated into this more general liability save for the surviving features of liability for an escape of ignis suus. This assimilation has been of various torts including those of negligence, nuisance, trespass, withdrawal of support and the escape of fire. In addition to this fault-based

e liability, there remains a residual category of cases where liability for damage to adjacent property or to persons on the adjacent highway remains strict, albeit that the range of situations where strict liability has survived has narrowed in recent years. This survival of strict liability may be seen in the withdrawal of support cases such as the recent decision in *Rees'* case and the survival of the

f criticised decision in *Wringe v Cohen* [1939] 4 All ER 241, [1940] 1 KB 229. Furthermore, strict liability still exists independently of this general duty where an escape occurs from a non-natural use of land so as to bring the resulting damage within the scope of *Rylands v Fletcher* liability albeit that that liability is now confined to cases where harm to an adjoining property was foreseen (see *Cambridge Water Co Ltd v Eastern Counties Leather plc* [1994] 1 All ER 53,

g [1994] 2 AC 264).

[51] Since negligence and nuisance have been assimilated in recent years both generally and in relation to liability for fire damage, it is necessary nowadays to treat the fire damage decision of Atkinson J in *Spicer v Smee* [1946] 1 All ER 489 with some caution. In that case, the judge found that the defendant was liable for

h the damage resulting from the state of disrepair left by an independent contractor. The basis of his finding was that the state of disrepair of electric wiring was itself a nuisance before it led to overheating and the subsequent fire. Liability for damage caused by that nuisance was at that time assumed to be strict so that no separate question arose as to the defendant's liability for the acts of her

j independent contractor. It would no longer be possible to hold a defendant in the position of the defendant Miss Smee in that case liable merely because the state of her premises constituted a nuisance for which she was strictly liable. However, on the strength of the judge's findings of fact, *Spicer's* case would now be decided in the same way but on the basis that the relevant liability was in nuisance resulting from the negligent wiring of the defendant's independent contractor

which caused the escape of fire to the adjoining bungalow and for which she was   *a*
vicariously liable.

9.2 Defendant's vicarious liability for negligence or nuisance

[52] The claimant can succeed in its claim against the defendant based on
either negligence or nuisance if the defendant is capable of being held vicariously
liable for the damage caused by an escape resulting from the negligence or   *b*
nuisance of its independent contractor. However, the defendant submits that it
cannot be held liable in this case since the facts do not give rise to vicarious
liability for either the negligence or nuisance of its independent contractor. It is
important to stress that this submission is based on the general immunity of an
employer for negligence or nuisance committed by an independent contractor   *c*
and not on the special status of fire cases already discussed.

[53] There would seem to be force in the defendant's submission. This is
because, in relation to the claim based in negligence, a defendant is not usually
vicariously liable for the negligence of its independent contractor. Thus, it has
been held in similar cases that there was no vicarious liability for the negligence
of an independent contractor, for example where an independent contractor was   *d*
employed to undertake a commonplace act such as the rewiring of premises by
an electrical contractor (see *Green v Fibreglass Ltd* [1958] 2 All ER 521, [1958] 2 QB
245, Salmon J). The damage in that case that was caused was not fire damage. In
relation to the claim based in nuisance, a person employing an independent
contractor is not usually vicariously liable for a nuisance resulting from the work   *e*
carried out by that independent contractor which leads to an escape onto, and
damage to, adjoining land or with an interference with its use.

[54] Vicarious liability for damage arising from the negligence or nuisance of
an independent contractor can, however, arise in certain situations. The first
essential requirement for vicarious liability is that the activity of the independent
contractor must have been authorised, instructed or adopted by the employer.   *f*
This approval will usually arise from the terms of the contract under which the
independent contractor performed the relevant work since the work in question,
or the way in which the work was performed that gave rise to the relevant escape
or interference, will usually have been instructed or not prohibited by the terms
of the relevant contract. If the act was prohibited by the contract, the resulting   *g*
escape or interference may, but not necessarily must, be regarded as one for
which there is no vicarious liability. That will depend on the nature of the breach
of contract in question.

[55] If the relevant activity was authorised and the escape was foreseeable, it
must then be determined whether or not the circumstances were of a kind that
give rise to vicarious liability for an escape or interference caused by the   *h*
negligence or nuisance of an independent contractor. The relevant test has been
expressed in a variety of ways which have included the following: the activity
causing the escape was of a kind which gave rise to a special danger (see *Matania v
National Provincial Bank Ltd and Elevenist Syndicate Ltd* [1936] 2 All ER 633), was of
an extra hazardous kind (see *Honeywill & Stein Ltd v Larkin Bros (London's*   *j*
Commercial Photographers) Ltd [1934] 1 KB 191, [1933] All ER Rep 77) or was such
as to create a special risk due of damage to the difficulties inherent in carrying out
that activity (see *Alcock v Wraith* (1991) 59 BLR 16).

[56] The work need not have been on a party wall but if it was, any resulting
escape and damage is more likely to give rise to vicarious liability. The authorities

a   suggest that the work must have been extra hazardous to give rise to vicarious
liability for damage to neighbouring land caused by work away from the
boundary or party wall (see *Matania's* and *Honeywill's* cases) whereas it need only
create a special risk of damage if work causing such damage was carried out on
or adjacent to the boundary or party wall (see *Bower v Peate* (1876) 1 QBD 321,
[1874–80] All ER Rep 905 and *Alcock's* case).

b   [57] It follows that the exceptions to the general rule that an employer is not
to be held vicariously liable for fire damage caused by the negligence or nuisance
of an independent contractor have developed piecemeal over a lengthy period. It
is therefore necessary to apply these exceptions in a somewhat mechanical way.
The test is to see whether any existing exception is applicable to the fact situation
in question or whether any relevant exception can be made applicable to that fact
c   situation by a small incremental extension of its existing boundaries.

[58] This was the approach of the Court of Appeal in *Alcock v Wraith* (1991) 59
BLR 16, a case brought in both negligence and nuisance by an adjoining
householder against his neighbour in a row of terraced houses in relation to
damage caused by water ingress and damp penetration from the defendant's to
d   the plaintiff's premises. Neill LJ stated as follows (at 23):

'Counsel for [the defendant] placed reliance on the principle that where
someone employs an independent contractor to do work on his behalf he is
not in the ordinary way responsible for any tort committed by the contractor
in the course of the execution of the work. In addition he argued that the
e   facts of this case did not fall within any of the exceptions to this principle and
in particular that the work could not be regarded as hazardous work of the
kind contemplated in *Matania's* case. It is therefore necessary to consider
some of the exceptions to the general principle. The main exceptions to the
principle fall into the following categories ... (b) Cases involving the
withdrawal of support from neighbouring land. (c) Cases involving the
f   escape of fire ... (g) Cases involving extra-hazardous acts.'

9.3 Vicarious liability for party wall work and extra-hazardous activities

[59] The claimant relies on three particular circumstances that he alleges give
rise to the defendant's vicarious liability for negligence or nuisance in this case,
g   being those relating to an escape, to extra-hazardous work carried out on land
which endangered his adjacent land and to work associated with a party wall
which gave rise to a special risk of damage.

[60] The claimant suggests that the particular basis upon which the defendant
should be held vicariously liable is that the defendant's independent contractor
h   carried out work on or adjacent to a party wall negligently and, as a direct
consequence, damage was subsequently caused to the claimant's adjoining
premises. The origins of this suggested vicarious liability lie in the law of
nuisance, particularly where support or protection provided by adjoining premises
is removed. This liability has been extended by reliance on the law of negligence
to cover work on a party wall whose nature is such that it is attendant with special
j   risks which it is foreseeable might damage the adjoining property.

[61] A good recent example of vicarious liability for party wall work of a
particular risky kind is provided by *Alcock's* case. In that case, re-roofing work was
undertaken by an independent contractor. Before the work had been started, the
whole terrace had been roofed with a continuous slate roof. The defendant's
slates were replaced with concrete interlocking tiles which intruded about

200 mm beyond the boundary wall onto the plaintiff's adjoining house. The joint
between the two types of tile was constructed negligently by first filling it with
stuffed newspapers and then covering it with an inadequate cement fillet. This
joint eventually allowed water to penetrate into the plaintiff's adjoining house.

[62] The defendant was held liable for the negligent workmanship of his
independent contractor despite the rule that, ordinarily, a defendant is not liable
for such negligence. The basis of liability was stated by Neill LJ ((1991) 59 BLR 16
at 29) as follows:

'But, as it seems to me, the true basis for the exception in the party-wall
cases [to the rule that an owner is not liable for the negligent acts of his
independent contractor] is that where the law confers a right to carry out
work on a wall or other division between two properties, and that work
involves a risk of damage to the adjoining property, the law also imposes a
duty on the party carrying out the work to ensure that it is carried out
carefully ... In the present case work had to be done on the division between
the properties at roof level. [The defendant] had the right to interfere with
the joint between the two roofs and, because of its structure, to intrude
slightly on to the slate roof of [the plaintiff's] house. But if they exercised this
right they were under a duty, as I see it, to see that reasonable skill and care
were used in the operation. Moreover, this duty could not be delegated to
an independent contractor. In this context I can see no satisfactory
distinction between interfering with a party-wall or with a floor on the one
hand and interfering with the edge of a contiguous roof on the other hand.
In each case the work involves the risk of weakening or damaging the
structure of the adjoining property. Furthermore, the risk of damage to the
adjoining property is even greater where, as here, the interference involves
the removal of a small part of the neighbouring roof.'

In reaching this conclusion, Neill LJ relied on a line of cases including *Bower v
Peate* (1876) 1 QBD 321, [1874–80] All ER Rep 905, *Dalton v Henry Angus & Co, The
Commissioners of HM Works and Public Buildings v Henry Angus & Co* (1881) 6 App
Cas 740, [1881–5] All ER Rep 1, *Hughes v Percival* (1883) 8 App Cas 443, [1881–5]
All ER Rep 44 and *Matania v National Provincial Bank Ltd and Elevenist Syndicate Ltd*
[1936] 2 All ER 633. It can be seen that the vicarious liability in question is
drawn from several separate recognised heads of vicarious liability including
negligence involving extra-hazardous activities or a particular risk of damage
and nuisance involving withdrawal of support.

[63] It is also worth noticing again the recent decision of the Court of Appeal
in *Rees v Skerrett* [2001] 1 WLR 1541. The relevant demolition work involved a
property which protected an adjoining property and which was demolished
without any works being undertaken to protect that adjoining property from the
weather in flagrant disregard of the requirements of a Building Act notice that
had been served by the local authority. The Court of Appeal held the owner of
the demolished property liable for both withdrawal of support and, more
materially for this case, in negligence. The work had been undertaken by an
independent contractor but there was no suggestion, nor was it argued, that that
afforded the owner a defence to the claim. This would have been because the
relevant work related to a party wall and involved a particular risk of damage to
the adjoining property.

a [64] Thus, for this type of vicarious liability to be established in principle, the following requirements must be shown to exist. (1) The independent contractor must be primarily liable in negligence or nuisance. This involves showing that the independent contractor undertook work on land that created a danger to adjoining property and that there was a failure to exercise reasonable care in carrying out that work or in failing to eliminate the risk of danger created by that b work once that risk was, or should have been, appreciated. (2) The occupier of land employing the independent contractor will be vicariously liable for that contractor's negligence or nuisance if the work causing an escape was to the party wall or to a similar division between two properties, was authorised or approved by the occupier and involved some special risk or was from its very nature likely to cause damage if it was poorly performed.

c

9.4 Defendant's vicarious liability in negligence

[65] I therefore turn to the facts of this case. The structure being adapted was obviously one that was capable of being significantly damaged or set light to by any fire lit in the fireplace if its fire protective properties were removed or d reduced. This was because the chimney breast with its associated chimney would be used for domestic fires. The fireplace was built against and into a party wall which was located at the back of the fire place, comprised two skins of timber framing infilled with lath and daub and was obviously inflammable. The potential for the party wall to be damaged by heat and fire was shown by the fact that relatively recently the then owners, in order to obtain a fire certificate, had been e required to install a fire curtain of glass fibre within the void created by the two skins of this wall for the obvious purpose of preventing the spread of heat and fire from the fireplace into and beyond the party wall. Moreover, the sides of the fireplace were lined with fire bricks, an obvious fire-protecting medium. Finally, the work was covered by statutory provisions in the Building Regulations f concerning the need to ensure the fire protection of the structure if work was undertaken to that structure.

[66] The installation of the new fire surround obviously involved the widening of the fireplace opening and the removal of the fire brick lining of the fireplace. This would clearly involve the removal of surfaces close to the fire g which had fire-resistant properties. Moreover, a significant quantity of timber members were to be added to the outside face of the chimney breast placing them close to a possible source of heat, namely any fire lit in the adjacent fireplace.

[67] It follows that the work to be performed by Mr Young involved special risk to the party wall and to the claimant's property given its close association with and its proximity to the potentially inflammable party wall. The work was h authorised by the defendant given the rudimentary contract which merely required Mr Young to install the new fire surround. If that work was misperformed, resulting fire damage to the claimant's adjoining property would be a real possibility. Finally, Mr Young's work, although not being carried out directly on the party wall, would affect and was carried out adjacent to, and was j associated with a party wall and with a structure that was common to both properties.

[68] I conclude that all the requirements that need to be shown to give rise to an occupier's vicarious liability for the negligence of his independent contractor have been made out. The relevant work was undertaken negligently on and adjacent to a party wall. It involved a special risk to, and by its very nature

endangered, the claimant's adjoining premises. In consequence, the defendant is liable for the fire damage that occurred.

(10) CONCLUSION

[**69**] I conclude that the claimant is entitled to judgment against the defendant for liability with damages to be assessed. That liability is in both negligence and nuisance, being both a primary liability for the fire damage and also vicarious liability for the negligence of its independent contractor in causing that damage.

[**70**] I would like to express my gratitude to the clear and helpful submissions of both counsel which illuminated a difficult and developing area of the common law.

Order accordingly.

Martyn Gurr   Barrister.

Menashe Business Mercantile Ltd and another v William Hill Organisation Ltd

[2002] EWHC 397 (Pat)

CHANCERY DIVISION (PATENTS COURT)

JACOB J

8, 15 MARCH 2002

Patent – Infringement – Indirect infringement – Supplying in United Kingdom a person with any of the means relating to essential element of invention for putting invention 'into effect' in United Kingdom – Bookmakers supplying punter with computer program making punter's computer a terminal for bookmakers' gaming system – Bookmakers' host computer held abroad – Whether host computer having to be within United Kingdom to constitute supply for purpose of putting invention 'into effect' in United Kingdom – Patents Act 1977, s 60(2).

The claimant patentees were the proprietors of a European patent registered in respect of a gaming system. The claims of the patent specified a host computer, terminal computer(s), a communication means between them and a program means for operating the terminal computer. The defendant bookmakers operated a gaming system whereby punters within the United Kingdom were supplied with a program, via compact disc or the world wide web, which turned a punter's computer into a terminal computer for the bookmakers' system. The bookmakers' host computer was held abroad. The patentees brought proceedings against the bookmakers for infringement of their patent. They contended that the supply of the computer programs in the United Kingdom fell within s 60(2)[a] of the Patents Act 1977, which provided that a person infringed a patent for an invention if, inter alia, he supplied in the United Kingdom a person with any of the means, relating to an essential element of the invention, for putting the invention 'into effect' in the United Kingdom. On the determination of a point of law, the bookmakers contended that the supply of the program was not for putting the invention 'into effect' in the United Kingdom, as that would require both the host and terminal computer to be within the United Kingdom.

Held – It was no defence to a claim under s 60(2) of the 1977 Act that the host computer claimed in the patent in suit was not present in the United Kingdom, but was otherwise connected to the rest of the apparatus claimed in the patent. A conclusion to the contrary would allow a defendant to use supposed cross-border problems to avoid infringement of the system anywhere. As a matter of construction, the double reference to the United Kingdom within s 60(2) looked to the effect within the United Kingdom, not use within the United Kingdom. No businessman would think that the effect of the invention was not within the United Kingdom when the whole point of the bookmakers' system was to get United Kingdom punters to play their system. Accordingly, the relevant paragraphs of the bookmakers' pleadings would be struck out (see [4], [20], [21], [24], [25], below).

---

a   Section 60(2) is set out at [5], below

Notes

For indirect infringement, see 35 *Halsbury's Laws* (4th edn reissue) para 595.

For the Patents Act 1977, s 60, see 33 *Halsbury's Statutes* (4th edn) (2001 reissue) 209.

Preliminary issue

The court was required to determine a preliminary issue, set out at [4], below in proceedings for patent infringement brought by the claimants, Menashe Business Mercantile Ltd and Julian Menashe, against the defendants, William Hill Organisation Ltd. The facts are set out in the judgment.

Peter Prescott QC and *Lindsay Lane* (instructed by *Laytons*, Guildford) for the claimants.
Henry Carr QC and *Benet Brandreth* (instructed by *Wragge & Co*) for the defendants.

Cur adv vult

15 March 2002. The following judgment was delivered.

JACOB J.

[1] The claimants own a patent (European Patent No 0625760) for a gaming system. The claims call for a host computer, terminal computer(s), a communication means between them and a program means for operating the terminal computer. So the two computers are connected. The claims spell out more details about each computer, the communication means and the program. For present purposes the details do not matter.

[2] The defendants are bookmakers. They operate a gaming system available to punters in the United Kingdom who have a computer. The punters are supplied with a program, either by a CD or by downloading from the Internet. This turns the punter's computer into a terminal computer for the defendants' system. When it is in communication via the Internet with the defendants' host computer the claimants say the whole system falls within the patent.

[3] Whether that is so does not, at present, matter. The defendants take a short point. They say they cannot infringe. Patent law does not catch them because they have put their host computer abroad (now in Curaçao in the Netherlands Antilles, formerly in Antigua). The claimants say 'not so'. They say the supply within the United Kingdom to the punters of the computer program amounts to infringement under s 60(2) of the Patents Act 1977.

[4] So the parties ask me to determine a point of law. The agreed point is as follows:

'Is it a defence to the claim under s 60(2) of the 1977 Act, if otherwise good, that the host computer claimed in the patent in suit is not present in the United Kingdom, but is connected to the rest of the apparatus claimed in the patent.'

[5] Section 60 is entitled 'Meaning of infringement'. Subsections (1), (2) and (3) provide as follows:

'(1) Subject to the provisions of this section, a person infringes a patent for an invention if, but only if, while the patent is in force, he does any of the following things in the United Kingdom in relation to the invention without the consent of the proprietor of the patent, that is to say—(a) where the invention is a product, he makes, disposes of, offers to dispose of, uses or a   imports the product or keeps it whether for disposal or otherwise; (b) where the invention is a process, he uses the process or he offers it for use in the United Kingdom when he knows, or it is obvious to a reasonable person in the circumstances, that its use there without the consent of the proprietor would be an infringement of the patent; (c) where the invention is a process, he disposes of, offers to dispose of, uses or imports any product obtained

b   directly by means of that process or keeps any such product whether for disposal or otherwise.

(2) Subject to the following provisions of this section, a person (other than the proprietor of the patent) also infringes a patent for an invention if, while the patent is in force and without the consent of the proprietor, he supplies or offers to supply in the United Kingdom a person other than a

c   licensee or other person entitled to work the invention with any of the means, relating to an essential element of the invention, for putting the invention into effect when he knows, or it is obvious to a reasonable person in the circumstances, that those means are suitable for putting, and are intended to put, the invention into effect in the United Kingdom.

d   (3) Subsection (2) above shall not apply to the supply or offer of a staple commercial product unless the supply or the offer is made for the purpose of inducing the person supplied or, as the case may be, the person to whom the offer is made to do an act which constitutes an infringement of the patent by virtue of subsection (1) above.'

e   [6] Section 60 is one of those sections which, by s 130(7) of the 1977 Act, is declared to be:

'so framed as to have, as nearly as practicable, the same effects in the United Kingdom as the corresponding provisions of the European Patent Convention [Convention on the Grant of European Patents 1978

f   (Munich, 5 October 1973; TS 20 (1978); Cmnd 7090) (EPC)], the Community Patent Convention [Convention for the European Patent for the Common Market (Luxembourg, 15 December 1975; EC 18 (1976); Cmnd 6553) (as amended by Council Agreement (EEC) 89/695) (OJ 1989 L 401 pp 1–27) (CPC)], and the Patent Co-operation Treaty [Washington, 19 June 1970; TS 78 (1978); Cmnd 7340 (PCT)] …'

g   Practically speaking therefore one can go directly to the corresponding PCT provision and construe that. Our provision will have the same meaning. Only if it is said that the United Kingdom provision actually departs from the PCT does one have to look at the language of the 1977 Act to see if that was really meant.

h   No one has ever found a departure from the corresponding PCT provision. Neither side suggests such a departure in this case.

[7] It also follows that one does not adopt the rather strict or linguistic approach to construction which might be called for in a free-standing United Kingdom Act. Rather one uses the approach used for the construction of international treaties. It is teleological, not strictly grammatical. What matters is

j   the spirit and intendment—the purpose. And one can have regard to authentic versions of the PCT in other languages. Also to any travaux preparatoires.

[8] The corresponding provision to s 60(2) is art 26(1) of the CPC. It is entitled 'Prohibition of indirect use of the invention.' It says:

'A Community patent shall also confer on its proprietor the right to prevent all third parties not having his consent from supplying or offering to

supply within the territories of the Contracting States a person, other than a
party entitled to exploit the patented invention, with means, relating to an
essential element of that invention, for putting it into effect therein, when
the third party knows, or it is obvious in the circumstances, that these means
are suitable and intended for putting that invention into effect.'

[9] Mr Prescott QC for the claimants says the supply of the computer
programs in the United Kingdom falls within s 60(2); that it is 'supplying ... within
the United Kingdom a person ... with means relating to an essential element of
the invention, for putting it into effect in the United Kingdom'. Mr Carr QC for
the defendants accepts (for present purposes) that the supply of the program is
within the United Kingdom and that it is an essential element of the invention.
But, says he, it is not for putting the invention into effect in the United Kingdom.
For that you would need the claimed combination (host and terminal) to be in
the United Kingdom.

[10] Mr Prescott fastens on the words 'effect in the United Kingdom'. That is
not the same as saying the invention must actually be used in the United
Kingdom. It is sufficient if there is the effect of use here. As a practical business
matter the defendants are using the effect of the invention here.

[11] Further says Mr Prescott, if he were wrong there would be an enormous
hole in the internationally agreed rules for infringement. His skeleton argument
demonstrates the hole in the following way:

'Take the case of a someone who installs and sells a telecommunications
apparatus which straddles the French-German border. Suppose the patent
claim calls for integers A + B. Both are essential integers. But A is in France
and B is in Germany. If the defendants are right, no infringement. We
respectfully submit it obviously would be infringement—else it would offend
common sense. That cannot be what the framers of the CPC intended. It is
not purposive construction. We could give many other examples, and of
great commercial and industrial importance. For instance, a constellation of
satellites, not all passing over the United Kingdom at once, and a downlink
here.'

[12] Moreover, says Mr Prescott, the other language versions of the PCT are
not inconsistent with his argument. They read as follows: French: 'de *mise en
oeuvre*, sur ce territoire, de cette invention'; German: 'zur *Benutzung* der Erfindung
in diesem Gebiet'; Italian: 'per *utilizarre*, in tale territorio, l'invenzione'; Spanish:
'para *llevarla en efecto* en dicho territorio'; Portuguese: 'para *executar*, nesse
territürio, a referida invencão'. He submits that none of these phrases compels
the notion that the complete apparatus necessarily resides in any particular
country. They are at least equally consistent with the notion of getting the
invention to work so that its *effect* is enjoyed in the appropriate territory. So,
submits Mr Prescott, no version of the PCT precludes his construction.

[13] Next Mr Prescott prays in aid a second order argument—an argument
based on working back from other provisions. He says look at the exception to
art 26(1) for the supply of staple commercial products. Article 26(2) says:
'Paragraph 1 shall not apply when the means are staple commercial products,
except when the third party induces the person supplied to commit acts
prohibited by Article 25.' Article 25 sets out the rules for direct infringement,
which are territorial. You are only liable for selling a staple commercial product
if you induce a primary infringer to infringe *within* the territory. The contrast is

a between a direct reference to primary infringement (ie art 25) and a reference to *putting the invention into effect* within the territory. The latter, submits Mr Prescott, conveys a wider notion.

[14] Mr Prescott also prays in aid the philosophy of infringement to be found in art 69 of the EPC and its well-known Protocol. The EPC and CPC were drafted at the same time and they should be construed together at least so far as
b ascertaining their general purpose. The key provision of the Protocol demands 'a fair protection for the patentee'. There would be nothing fair if United Kingdom punters were using the system yet it were held the system was not being put into effect here.

[15] He closes with a flourish: 'The system is what is claimed in the patent. It actually claims "a system". Therefore it makes sense to speak of the invention
c being put into effect in this country. If not in this country, then where?'

[16] Mr Carr for the defendants ripostes by pointing to the double reference to 'United Kingdom' in s 60(2). This corresponds to the EPC's use of 'territories of the Contracting States' and 'therein'—again a double use. Moreover he points out that the second use is particularly deliberate having received specific
d consideration during the treaty negotiations. 'Therein' was specifically added to an earlier draft on the suggestion of the AIPPI [the Association Internationale pour la Protection de la Propriété Intellectuelle].

[17] Mr Carr realised the force of Mr Prescott's 'hole' point. He sought to answer it by saying that it was a hole which, if the claimants' agent had been more ingenious, could have been plugged. All the agent had to do was to insert
e separate claims to the terminal and the host computers. Mr Carr handed me claims for the terminal and host which, he said, would have done the job. They took the form: 'A terminal (host) computer for using in a gaming system [then defined], the terminal computer comprising ...' And he answered Mr Prescott's flourish by saying that in the case of the system claim the invention was not put
f into effect in any one country.

[18] Mr Carr also had a second order argument. He relied on the ships and aircraft exemption contained in s 60(5)(d)—itself derived from art 27(d) of the CPC though it is expressed in the 1977 Act in unnecessarily different language. This exempts from infringement use of an invention on board a vessel temporarily within the waters of a contracting state. Suppose, submitted Mr Carr, a man
g supplied a 'means essential' to such a ship. There would be no infringement on board—so why would the supplier be an infringer? Yet he would be if the claimants were right.

[19] Mr Carr's main point, however, was that to give *into effect in the United Kingdom* the wide meaning suggested by the claimants would be far too
h uncertain. What effect would do? Receipt of money here? You would have to look at the effect in a wide range of cases and it would be quite uncertain what sort of effect (financial, economic, direct or indirect) would count.

[20] I have no hesitation in accepting the arguments of Mr Prescott and rejecting those of Mr Carr. I do so without regret. Any other result would be
j monstrous—allowing a defendant to use supposed cross-border problems to avoid infringement of a system anywhere. My detailed reasons for rejecting Mr Carr's argument follow.

[21] First the double reference to the United Kingdom. Mr Carr overlooks the fact that the second reference (*into effect in the United Kingdom*) looks to *effect within the United Kingdom* not *use within the United Kingdom*. The fact that second reference ('therein') was added during the negotiations is understandable but

irrelevant. All that did was to identify the territory within which the effect was *a*
to be identified—to make sure that both the supply of the essential means and its
effect were within the same territory. Mr Prescott's second order point is
telling—why speak of 'putting invention into effect in the United Kingdom' if you
simply meant 'infringe the United Kingdom patent'. I can see no purposive
construction of the PCT which would make sense in this context.

[22] Next, the hole. I do not think Mr Carr's answer is either rational or *b*
correct. The claimants' invention is in substance *the combination* of elements. It
is the system. To say that a claim to the heart of the inventive concept would not
suffice to provide protection is to suggest that patentees should play games with
the patent system. Here the game is to pretend that the invention is a terminal
when programmed whereas really the invention is a system. Moreover the
argument is flawed. It is trite patent law that individual items of a combination *c*
may be old or obvious, yet the combination not.

[23] As to Mr Carr's argument about ships, I find that fanciful. I called it a
second order argument. More accurately I think it is well down the order
to second—construing a main provision by way of a very minor exception is
hardly ever productive, especially in the context of an international treaty. In this *d*
case in any event it is wrong: the point of the exemption is to exempt the use of
the invention on board, not to exempt suppliers. A ship which came to the
United Kingdom temporarily for repairs would not infringe, but someone who
supplied a device which was an essential element of an invention used on board
would infringe.

[24] Finally there is Mr Carr's 'uncertainty' argument—that if 'effect' meant *e*
any effect it was too vague. Mr Prescott shrewdly noticed a parallel with art 5(3)
of the Brussels Convention on Jurisdiction and the Enforcement of Judgments in
Civil and Commercial Matters 1968 (as set out in Sch 1 to the Civil Jurisdiction
and Judgments Act 1982). This confers tort jurisdiction on a court in a member
state where 'the harmful event occurred'. If anything that is a vaguer test than *f*
'effect' yet it has proved reasonably workable. In any event, just because there
may be borderline cases of difficulty is no reason for not holding that an obvious
case falls within the rule. No businessman would think for a moment that the
effect of the invention is not within the United Kingdom when the whole point
of the defendants' system is to get United Kingdom punters to play their system.

[25] Accordingly I reject this defence. The answer to the question is No. *g*
I order that the appropriate paragraphs of the pleading be struck out. If the
defendants have a defence it must be that they are not using a system within the
claims of the patent or that the patent is invalid. The wheeze of putting the host
computer abroad is of no help to them.

Order accordingly.

Celia Fox   Barrister.

Practice Direction

a

FAMILY DIVISION

b *Practice – Family Division – Cases proceeding in Royal Courts of Justice – Judicial continuity – Allocated judge – Case management conference – Children Act 1989, Pt IV.*

1. This direction applies only to cases proceeding in the Family Division of the High Court at the Royal Courts of Justice in London.

c 1.1. In order to achieve as much judicial continuity as possible in the hearing of cases and to avoid delay, the procedure described in this direction will apply as from 9 April 2002.

2. *Applications within Pt IV (care and supervision) of the Children Act 1989*

d 2.1. Upon transfer to the High Court (or where applicable, commencement) the case will be allocated to a High Court judge (the allocated judge) and a date fixed for a case management conference. The clerk of the rules will notify the parties of the date for the case management conference and the name of the allocated judge as soon as practicable after receipt of the court file.

2.2. Within 24 hours of transfer to the High Court (or commencement), the applicant must lodge with the clerk of the rules, a very brief (less than one page) *e* summary of the case. This should be delivered to the office of the clerk of the rules or sent by fax (020 7947 7304).

2.3. The case management conference and all further hearings (including directions hearings) will be conducted by the allocated judge, unless the case is released to another judge or when it is impracticable for the hearing to be before *f* the allocated judge.

2.4. As soon as practicable the clerk of the rules will send to the parties a copy of the standard directions (in the form attached to this direction) completed by a judge (usually the allocated judge), notifying the parties of the steps they are required to take in preparation for the case management conference.

2.5. At the case management conference which is to be attended by all parties, *g* the allocated judge will give directions, managing the case to a final hearing.

2.6. It is of the essence of this procedure that counsel retained for the final hearing should attend the case management conference and any other directions hearings, except when all the directions have been agreed in advance. Counsel should therefore use their best endeavours to ensure attendance at these *h* hearings. On occasions when one of these hearings coincides with a hearing in another case in which counsel is engaged, counsel should, whenever possible, seek release from the judge before whom they are appearing, so as to enable them to attend the directions hearing. This requirement applies equally to a solicitor who intends to appear as advocate at the final hearing.

j 2.7. When a case is transferred to the High Court and an urgent hearing is required prior to the case management conference, the clerk of the rules should be requested to provide an immediate or early hearing date, if possible before the allocated judge. This may be obtained by telephone. Accordingly, other than to appoint a children's guardian (when required), it will not usually be necessary or appropriate for the transferring court to give any directions when transferring the case to the High Court.

2.8. The final hearing will be before the allocated judge, unless it is impracticable so to arrange.

3. *Urgent Applications Court*

3.1. Cases which have been allocated to a judge will not be taken by the Urgent Applications Court except to deal with an emergency. When the allocated judge is not in London, it will nevertheless usually be possible to communicate with the judge by telephone or by fax (or e-mail) in order to obtain directions or release of the case. A video conference may sometimes be appropriate.

4. *Applications within Pt II of the 1989 Act*

4.1. These cases (ie private law children cases) when commenced in or transferred to the High Court will not formally come within this direction except that judicial continuity will be observed whenever possible. The aim will be for the same judge to deal with the directions and other interlocutory hearings as well as the final hearing.

5. *Ancillary relief applications within matrimonial causes and applications for financial provision under the 1989 Act*

5.1. These applications when transferred to (or commenced in) the High Court will not formally come within this direction except that judicial continuity will be observed whenever possible, in particular in very complex cases and in cases where there are very substantial assets.

5.2. The above is subject to the requirement in r 2.61E of the Family Proceedings Rules 1991, SI 1991/1247, in relation to the judge before whom any financial dispute resolution (FDR) hearing takes place.

5.3. In cases which are suitable for adjudication in the High Court by a High Court judge and in which it would be appropriate for the first appointment to be listed before a judge, for example because of the likelihood of substantial dispute about the extent of financial disclosure or the desirability of using the first appointment as an FDR, it may be appropriate for the application for transfer to be made at an early stage of the proceedings, before the date initially given for the first appointment.

6. The standard directions form attached to this direction may be amended from time to time as experience requires.

DAME ELIZABETH BUTLER-SLOSS
President

22 March 2002

a

IN THE HIGH COURT OF JUSTICE   FDO2C
FAMILY DIVISION
PRINCIPAL REGISTRY

b

Application of [   ]

Re [(Child(ren))   ]

c **Standard directions by High Court Judge (Care proceedings)**

Date of this order [   ]

Upon reading the papers filed by the applicant

d

IT IS ORDERED by **The Honourable** [   ]

This case is to be allocated to **The Honourable** [

e   **Clerk's Tel:** 020 7947]

The allocated judge will be responsible for the continuous case management of this case

f *All* future hearings in this case (including all directions and other interlocutory hearings, the pre-trial review and the final and any split hearing(s)) will be conducted by the allocated judge and *not* by the urgent applications judge or by any other judge unless on application to the allocated judge (if necessary in case of urgency by telephone) the allocated judge releases the case to another judge

Case Management Conference

g There will be a Case Management Conference before the allocated judge at the

Royal Courts of Justice Strand London WC2A 2LL **at** [   ]

on the [   ]

h

Purpose of the Case Management Conference

The purpose of the Case Management Conference is to

j • Identify and consider the issues in the case
   • Consider whether there are any features requiring particular urgency
   • Identify whether there is to be a contested hearing of any application for an interim care order and (if so) when such hearing should take place
   • Consider what expert assessments and reports are required, when and in what disciplines

- Consider whether twin-track planning is appropriate
- Consider whether a split hearing is necessary
- Consider the time estimate(s) for the final and any split hearing(s)
- Consider whether any directions or other interlocutory hearings
  - should be before the allocated judge
  - can be released to another judge
- Consider whether the final and any split hearing(s)
  - should be before the allocated judge
  - can be released to another High Court judge
  - can be released to a Deputy High Court judge
- Timetable the case through to final disposal (fixing the dates of all future hearings, including all directions and other interlocutory hearings, a pre-trial review and the final and any split hearing(s) and considering the appropriate venue)
- Give directions as to
  - the format of future directions and other hearings (including where appropriate the giving of directions on paper application without the attendance of the parties or by telephone conference)
  - who is to attend future directions and other hearings
- Give directions as to the format of and the arrangements to be made for up-dating the Trial Bundle
- Give directions as to expert evidence (including, where appropriate, directions for the experts to meet and for the preparation of agreed schedules of agreement and disagreement)
- Give directions as to the filing by each of the Respondents of
  - evidence and
  - a response to the Local Authority's proposed Threshold Findings
- Give such further directions as are appropriate

NOTE: THE PARTIES and their legal representatives MUST consider each of the above matters and if appropriate liaise BEFORE the day of THE CASE MANAGEMENT CONFERENCE

STANDARD DIRECTIONS
to ensure that the Case Management Conference achieves these objectives

THE LOCAL AUTHORITY MUST not later than 2 pm 5 working days before the date of the Case Management Conference file with the

a Bundle prepared in accordance with the *Practice Direction (Family Proceedings: Court Bundles)* [2000] 1 FLR 536. The Local Authority must at the same time serve on each of the Respondents an Index to the Bundle.

The Bundle to be prepared by the Local Authority must contain in addition to any other documents referred to in the *Practice Direction*

- A clear and concise summary on one page of A4 paper of
  - the issues in the case and the Local Authority's plan(s) for the child(ren) and
  - any specific issues which may require to be determined at the Case Management Conference
- A Schedule of the Threshold Findings which the court is to be invited to make
- The witness statements upon which the Local Authority intend to rely
- The (Interim) Care Plan(s)
- A Listing Information Sheet indicating
  - whether the case is complex/standard/straightforward
  - whether there are any features requiring particular urgency
  - whether twin-track planning is being considered
  - whether a split hearing is necessary
  - what assessments are contemplated, when, by whom and for what purpose
  - what expert evidence it is proposed to obtain, when, from whom and for what purpose
  - the outline timetable proposed by the Local Authority
  - any other matters which may affect the length of any interlocutory or final hearing
- A draft of the order which the Local Authority will invite the judge to make at the conclusion of the Case Management Conference

THE RESPONDENTS MUST not later than 2 pm 2 working days before the date of the Case Management Conference file with the

and serve on the Local Authority copies of

- Any response to the documents filed by the Local Authority which the judge will be invited to consider at the Case Management Conference
- A Listing Information Sheet indicating
  - whether any assessment is to be sought and (if so) when, from whom and for what purpose
  - whether any expert evidence is proposed to be obtained and (if so) when, from whom and for what purpose
  - the outline timetable proposed by the Respondent(s)
- A draft of the order which the Respondent(s) will invite the judge to make at the conclusion of the Case Management Conference

It is the DUTY OF THE PARTIES' LEGAL REPRESENTATIVES to find out so far as is possible and notify to all other parties BEFORE THE CASE

MANAGEMENT CONFERENCE the names and the availability of anybody proposed to conduct any assessment or to provide any expert evidence

THE PARTIES' LEGAL REPRESENTATIVES and all other relevant professionals who attend the Case Management Conference MUST BRING TO THE CASE MANAGEMENT CONFERENCE

- Their professional diaries for the next 15 months and
- Details (so far as known) of the names and the availability of anybody who it is proposed should conduct any assessment or provide any expert evidence

THE PARTIES together with their legal representatives MUST ARRIVE AT COURT on the day of the Case Management Conference NO LATER THAN 1 hour before the time fixed for the hearing so that they can all meet together to discuss and if possible agree

- The outline timetable to be presented to the judge holding the Case Management Conference and
- The order which the judge will be invited to make at the conclusion of the Case Management Conference

THE LOCAL AUTHORITY MUST PREPARE so that it can be handed to the judge holding the Case Management Conference at the beginning of the hearing, a schedule listing (so far as is known) the names and contact details (professional addresses and telephone / fax / DX / e-mail numbers for)

- the lead social worker
- the Guardian ad litem
- the solicitors and counsel for each party
- any experts who have been or may be instructed

ADDITIONAL DIRECTIONS (if any)

OBSERVATIONS

Signed

A Justice of the High Court

Pumperninks of Piccadilly Ltd v Land Securities plc and others

[2002] EWCA Civ 621

COURT OF APPEAL, CIVIL DIVISION

SIMON BROWN, CHADWICK LJJ AND CHARLES J

15 MARCH, 10 MAY 2002

Landlord and tenant – Opposition to grant of new tenancy of business premises – Intention of landlord to demolish or reconstruct premises comprised in holding – 'Eggshell tenancy' – Tenant having 'eggshell' tenancy excluding load-bearing parts of building – Landlord intending to demolish 'eggshell' and opposing grant of new tenancy – Whether 'eggshell tenancy' constituting 'premises' capable of being demolished – Whether court entitled to look beyond programme of intended works when considering whether landlord could reasonably carry them out without obtaining possession – Landlord and Tenant Act 1954, ss 30(1)(f), 31A(1)(a).

The appellant tenant had an 'eggshell tenancy' of a ground floor shop in a building, ie a tenancy in which the demise consisted of the internal skin of the part of the building occupied by the tenant, with all load-bearing parts of the building excluded. The tenant applied for the grant of a new tenancy under Pt II of the Landlord and Tenant Act 1954. The landlord opposed the application on the ground set out in s 30(1)(f)[a] of the 1954 Act, namely that it intended to 'demolish' the 'premises' comprised in the holding, and that it could not reasonably do so without obtaining possession. The intended works would have removed the 'eggshell', thereby transforming the tenant's shop into part of an open space. At the hearing, the tenant contended that the intended works fell outside s 30(1)(f). Alternatively, the tenant, who hoped to reinstate the premises so as to enable it to carry on its existing business, sought to rely on s 31A(1)(a)[b]. Under that provision, the court was precluded from holding that the landlord could not reasonably carry out the demolition without obtaining possession of the holding if the tenant agreed to the inclusion, in the terms of the new tenancy, of terms giving the landlord access and other facilities for carrying out the intended work, and, given such access and facilities, the landlord could reasonably carry out the work without obtaining possession of the holding (the first condition) and without interfering to a substantial extent or for a substantial time with the use of the holding for the purpose of the business carried on by the tenant (the second condition). After concluding that the intended works fell within s 30(1)(f), the judge held that the tenant was unable to satisfy the first condition in s 31A(1)(a). On appeal, the tenant contended that the word 'premises' in s 30(1)(f) applied only to parts of a built structure that performed some structural function, and that accordingly, in the case of an 'eggshell tenancy', there were no 'premises' capable of being demolished. It further contended that, in considering whether s 31A(1)(a) applied, the court could look only at the effect on the tenant's use of the holding while the works were carried out, and that accordingly it was not entitled to look beyond the works programme.

---

a   Section 30, so far as material, is set out at [20], below
b   Section 31A, so far as material, is set out at [20], below

Held – (1) On the true construction of s 30(1)(f) of the 1954 Act, the word 'premises' was not confined to parts of a built structure that performed some structural function, and could include an 'eggshell' within a building. An 'eggshell' was capable of being demolished on the ordinary meaning of the word 'demolish'. In the instant case, the intended works did involve the demolition of premises comprising the holding or a substantial part of those premises (see [65], [69], [86], [87], [90], [97], below); *City Offices (Regent Street) Ltd v Europa Acceptance Group plc* [1990] 1 EGLR 63 applied.

(2) When considering whether s 31A(1)(a) of the 1954 Act applied, the court was entitled to look beyond the programme of the intended works. Thus if, after the intended works had been carried out, the premises would not exist precisely as they had before, that would be a relevant factor in considering whether they could be carried out without obtaining possession. Moreover, where the tenant agreed to the inclusion in the terms of the new tenancy of terms giving access and other facilities for carrying out the intended work and that work would result in the holding no longer existing, they could not be terms that enabled the landlord to carry out the works without obtaining possession of the holding. However, a tenant should be able to take advantage of s 31A in some circumstances when a landlord intended to do work that the tenant wanted to undo, and/or when the tenant would need to work after the landlord had finished his work to enable him to use the holding. In those circumstances, issues of fact and degree were likely to arise. In the instant case, however, the tenant was ultimately seeking reinstatement of something that the intended works would have destroyed and that was not reasonably compatible with the purpose and effect of those works. Accordingly, the landlord could not reasonably carry out the intended works without obtaining possession. In any event, s 31A(1)(a) could be of no assistance to the tenant since it would be a necessary consequence of carrying out the work that the holding would become unusable, indefinitely, for the purpose of the tenant's business. It followed that the appeal would be dismissed (see [39], [42], [43], [47], [48], [55], [60], [94]–[97], below); *Redfern v Reeves* [1978] 2 EGLR 52, *Price v Esso Petroleum Co Ltd* [1980] 2 EGLR 58 and *Cerex Jewels Ltd v Peachey Property Corp plc* [1986] 2 EGLR 65 distinguished; *Heath v Drown* [1972] 2 All ER 561 and *Decca Navigator Co Ltd v Greater London Council* [1974] 1 All ER 1178 considered.

Notes

For intended demolition and the need for possession, see 27(1) *Halsbury's Laws* (4th edn reissue) paras 590–593.

For the Landlord and Tenant Act 1954, ss 30, 31A, see 23 *Halsbury's Statutes* (4th edn) (1999 reissue) 152, 157.

Cases referred to in judgments

Barth v Pritchard [1990] 1 EGLR 109, CA.

Bewlay (Tobacconists) Ltd v British Bata Shoe Co Ltd [1958] 3 All ER 652, [1959] 1 WLR 45, CA.

Blackburn v Hussain [1988] 1 EGLR 77, CA.

Bracey v Read [1962] 3 All ER 472, [1963] Ch 88, [1962] 3 WLR 1194.

Cerex Jewels Ltd v Peachey Property Corp plc [1986] 2 EGLR 65, CA.

City Offices (Regent Street) Ltd v Europa Acceptance Group plc [1990] 1 EGLR 63, CA.

Cook v Mott [1961] EGD 294, CA.

Coppen v Bruce-Smith (1999) 77 P & CR 239, CA.

Decca Navigator Co Ltd v Greater London Council [1974] 1 All ER 1178, [1974] 1 WLR 748, CA.

a   *Fernandez v Walding* [1968] 1 All ER 994, [1968] 2 QB 606, [1968] 2 WLR 583, CA.
Graysim Holdings Ltd v P & O Property Holdings Ltd [1993] 1 EGLR 96; rvsd [1994]
    3 All ER 897, [1994] 1 WLR 992, CA; rvsd [1995] 4 All ER 831, [1996] AC 329,
    [1995] 3 WLR 854, HL.
Heath v Drown [1972] 2 All ER 561, [1973] AC 498, [1972] 2 WLR 1306, HL;
    rvsg [1971] 1 All ER 1011, [1971] 2 QB 1, [1971] 2 WLR 147, CA.
b   *Housleys Ltd v Bloomer-Holt Ltd* [1966] 2 All ER 966, [1966] 1 WLR 1244, CA.
Joel v Swaddle [1957] 3 All ER 325, [1957] 1 WLR 1094, CA.
Little Park Service Station Ltd v Regent Oil Co Ltd [1967] 2 All ER 257, [1967] 2 QB
    655, [1967] 2 WLR 1036, CA.
Percy E Cadle & Co Ltd v Jacmarch Properties Ltd [1957] 1 All ER 148, [1957] 1 QB
    323, [1957] 2 WLR 80, CA.
c   *Price v Esso Petroleum Co Ltd* [1980] 2 EGLR 58, CA.
Redfern v Reeves [1978] 2 EGLR 52, CA.
Romulus Trading Co Ltd v Henry Smith's Charity Trustees [1990] 2 EGLR 75, CA.

Case also cited or referred to in skeleton arguments
d   *Leathwoods Ltd v Total Oil (Great Britain) Ltd* [1985] 2 EGLR 237.

Appeal
The appellant, Pumperninks of Piccadilly Ltd (the tenant), appealed with
permission of Judge Rich QC from his decision on 18 June 2001 in Central London
County Court refusing, on the determination of a preliminary issue, its request for
e   the grant of a new tenancy under Pt II of the Landlord and Tenant Act 1954 in
proceedings brought by it against the respondents, Land Securities plc, Shaftesbury
(Piccadilly) (No 1) Ltd and Shaftesbury (Piccadilly) (No 2) Ltd (collectively the
landlord). The facts are set out in the judgment of Charles J.

f   *Kim Lewison QC* (instructed by *Samuel Phillips & Co*, Newcastle) for the tenant.
Michael Driscoll QC (instructed by *Nabarro Nathanson*) for the landlord.

Cur adv vult

10 May 2002. The following judgments were delivered.

g   **CHARLES J** (giving the first judgment at the invitation of Simon Brown LJ).

Introduction
    [1] This is an appeal with the permission of the judge from a decision of Judge
Rich QC made on the application of the appellant (the applicant in the county
h   court) for the grant of a new tenancy under Pt II of the Landlord and Tenant Act
1954. I shall refer to the appellant, Pumperninks of Piccadilly Ltd, as the tenant.
There are three respondents to the appeal. This is because during the course of
the proceedings the landlord changed. The original respondent, Land Securities plc,
was the landlord who served the s 25 notice and the additional respondents are in
j   the same group of companies. Nothing turns on the identity of the landlord and
I shall refer to the respondents as the landlord.
    [2] The issue before the judge was whether the landlord had proved its ground
of opposition to the grant of a new tenancy. The ground relied on was that set
out in s 30(1)(f) of the 1954 Act and the issues before the judge were therefore
whether that ground was satisfied having regard to the terms of that subsection
and the terms of s 31A of the 1954 Act.

Overview

[3] This case concerns what is commonly referred to as an 'eggshell tenancy' because the demise is of the internal skin of the part of the building occupied by the tenant. No load-bearing parts of the building are included in the demise. Counsel confirmed that this was not an uncommon type of business lease. However they did not refer us to any reported case under the 1954 Act relating to such a lease. The only case dealing with an eggshell tenancy to which we were referred was *City Offices (Regent Street) Ltd v Europa Acceptance Group plc* [1990] 1 EGLR 63.

[4] There is therefore no authority directly in point and this case raises points as to the application of the 1954 Act to tenancies of this type.

[5] The 1954 Act gives security to business tenants in respect of the parts of the property let to them that they occupy. This is clear from the terms of the Act itself. Further, the cases we were referred to on s 31A show that it was introduced into the 1954 Act to provide additional protection to tenants. However, as was confirmed by leading counsel for the tenant (who has considerable expertise in the field) it has often been said that the 1954 Act is not intended to stand in the way of redevelopment. As Lord Reid said in *Heath v Drown* [1972] 2 All ER 561 at 564, [1973] AC 498 at 506, when construing the Act—

> 'One must first look at the apparent policy of the Act. I think that this was to give security of tenure to business tenants so far as that was thought to be reasonably practicable. Security of tenure was no new idea. [He then refers to other examples when security of tenure has been given] In every case one has to examine the relevant Act to find the limits of that security.'

[6] This case gives rise to problems in connection with the point that work which involves the removal of the skin of a building or a part thereof (and thus the eggshell) and its later replacement could be categorised as glorified works of redecoration. The tenant says that having regard to the purposes of the 1954 Act it would be surprising if a landlord could obtain possession on the ground specified in s 30(1)(f) of that Act on the basis that such works, or works that could fairly be so described, were to be carried out. This point has considerable force. But so does the point made by the landlord that it would be surprising if a landlord intended to demolish an entire building let on an eggshell lease (or a number of eggshell leases) this work did not satisfy the ground in s 30(1)(f) in respect of each of the eggshell tenancies. In argument, the example of a third floor eggshell tenancy in a building that was to be demolished was taken. By reference to that example there are plainly a multitude of examples ranging from the position as in the example when the whole building is to be demolished, through demolition of parts of the building that support all or parts of the relevant eggshell, to removal of only the eggshell leaving all the parts of the building that support it (which could be a mixture of load-bearing and non-load-bearing walls and joists). Further the application of the 1954 Act in such situations can be complicated by reason of the terms of the relevant leases and the rights they give to a landlord to enter to carry out certain works to the building (e g to floor joists).

[7] The width of potential examples highlights the point made in many of the cases that in applying the relevant provisions of the 1954 Act the court is dealing with issues of fact and degree. This applies in the case of an eggshell tenancy just as it does in other situations.

[8] Finally by way of overview and before turning to the detail of this case I add that an eggshell tenancy such as this is a letting of an enclosed space which

the tenant will use and occupy as such. To enable such use and occupation to take place the eggshell must be supported. It follows that in using and occupying the eggshell the tenant is taking advantage of, and making use of, that support.

The lease

[9] This is an underlease dated 25 June 1976 for a term of 25 years. It therefore created a legal estate in land. Clause 1 provided (so far as relevant) as follows:

'In consideration of the respective rents and covenants by and on the part of the Lessee hereinafter reserved and contained the Lessors HEREBY DEMISE unto the Lessee ALL THAT shop and premises situate on the ground floor of the Building ... including the shopfront and fascia thereof and pavement lights (if any) or such interest as the Lessors may have therein TOGETHER with the Lessors fixtures or fittings therein or thereon and the appurtenances thereunto appertaining ... but there shall be excluded from the demise hereby made the excluded parts of the said premises (hereinafter called "the excluded parts") defined in the First Schedule hereto AND which said premises (less the excluded parts) are hereinafter referred to as the "demised premises".'

The first schedule provided that—

'"the excluded parts" shall mean the main structure of the Building of which the demised premises form part (but not the internal or external surfaces claddings finishes thereto or thereon within or contiguous to the demised premises) which main structure comprises without prejudice to the generality of the foregoing ...'

And it then particularised that general description. I use the term 'demised premises' in this judgment to refer to the demised premises as defined in the lease.

[10] The second schedule set out exceptions and reservations in favour of the lessors and included rights to enter onto the demised premises to build on or into any boundary or party wall and to repair and maintain all other parts of the remainder of the building making good any damage thereby caused.

[11] The lease includes a covenant for quiet enjoyment and a covenant by the lessors to repair the excluded parts and the remainder of the building. Additionally the lease provided by cl 5 thereof that (i) the lessors could without derogating from grant carry out works to the remainder of the building, but this was subject to the obligation that the lessors had to make good to the reasonable satisfaction of the lessee 'any physical damage occasioned to the demised premises', and (ii) if possession of the demised premises should 'be required for or in connection with any scheme or works of demolition reconstruction construction modernisation or improvement' the lessors may in the penultimate year of the term determine the underlease by notice to expire at any time during the last year.

[12] Additionally the lease contained a covenant by the lessee in cl 2(14) thereof to permit workmen employed by the lessors to enter the demised premises to carry out works to the building making good any damage done to the demised premises by such entry (this covenant essentially mirrors the reservations and obligations of the lessors). Further by cl 2(19) the lessee covenanted as follows:

'(i)(a) Not without the consent in writing of the Lessors and Superior
Lessors (such consent in the case of the Lessors not to be unreasonably
withheld) at any time during the said term to make or suffer to be made any
external projection from the demised premises or make or change the
existing design or appearance of the external decorative scheme of the
demised premises

(b) Not to cut maim injure or alter any of the excluded parts

(ii) Not at any time during the said term to make any alterations or
addition whatsoever either externally internally or otherwise in or to the
demised premises or any part thereof without first submitting to the Lessors
and (where necessary) the Superior Lessors and receiving their consent in
writing to the plans erections drawings elevations and specifications of the
proposed alteration or addition such consent in the case of the Lessors not to
be unreasonably withheld

(iii) If the Lessee shall carry out any works which are prohibited by
sub-clause (i) hereof or without such consent as is required under the
provisions of sub-clause (ii) hereof or build erect construct or place or permit
or suffer to be built erected constructed or placed any new or additional
buildings or erections or works on the demised premises the exterior of the
demised premises and/or the Building or any part or parts thereof then the
Lessee shall immediately upon notice in writing from the Lessor and/or the
Superior Lessors requiring them so to do remove all such new or additional
buildings erections works alterations or additions and make good and restore
the demised premises and/or the Building to the state and condition thereof
existing before the breach by the Lessee of subclauses (i) and/or (ii) of this
Clause and if the Lessee shall neglect to commence so to do for the space of
Seven days after such notice them it shall be lawful for the Lessors and their
servants contractors agents and workmen to enter upon the demised premises
and to remove such new or additional buildings erections works alterations
or additions and to make good and restore the same to the state and
condition existing before the breach by the Lessee of the provisions of
subclauses (i) and/or (ii) hereof ...'

[13] Standing back from the detail of the terms of the lease it provides the
tenant with a right to use and occupy a ground floor shop. To enable the tenant
to do this it is making use of the rights of support to the 'demised premises' (ie the
floor, the ceiling, and the remainder of the eggshell) provided by the covenant for
quiet enjoyment and the obligation not to derogate from grant.

The works the landlord intends to carry out

[14] There was no effective dispute as to what these were. The judge said this
about them:

'I turn first to the question of whether the intended work satisfies s 30(1)(f).
It is essential in order to determine whether the nature of the works
proposed involve the demolition of the premises comprised in the holding
for the purpose of that paragraph to identify carefully the scope of the
proposed works and the extent of the premises so comprised. I should say at
the outset that save in respect of one piece of work, to which I shall return,
the landlords rely on an intention to demolish—and only an intention to
demolish. There is no difficulty about the works which they identify
through the evidence of Mr Mortimore, their architect. They involve the

complete stripping out of all the ducts and services within the shop; the cutting back of the surfaces of the walls which contain the shop to the underlying brickwork and, in the case of the wall between nos 9 and 11 (the adjoining shop) the removal of 60–70% of the wall; replacing the support that wall gives to the upper floors by a steel column to be positioned outside the area of the demise; the removal of the roller shutter which forms the shop's frontage and its replacement by a show window extending in front of all four shops with the entrance into no 13; the removal of the existing floor and ceiling and the replacement of the load-bearing floor supporting the shop floor at a level ten inches below the existing floor; the structural floor of the mezzanine will be replaced at a different level. As Mr Driscoll QC for the landlords puts it, every physical built thing in the demise will be removed. The issue is however joined as to whether these built things are part of the premises comprised in the holding.'

The work to which the judge said he would return concerned the removal of a roller shutter and the runners to either side of it at the front of the shop. The judge returned to this when setting out his overall conclusion on whether the intended works satisfied the first part of s 30(1)(f), he said:

'The case with which I am concerned, of course, is a case in which there is no load-bearing element and it is a matter for consideration under the 1954 Act. I do not think that in the case of an eggshell demise, which includes no load-bearing element, there are for that reason no premises capable of demolition. The structure is the fabric which encloses the demise in so far as it is itself demised, in my judgment the physical boundaries of the demise, be they constituted by walls, ceiling or floor, or only their surfaces, are premises within the meaning of the paragraph at least if they are of such physical quality as to be sensibly capable in ordinary language of being constructed or part of the construction, or of being demolished. I think in the present case that the tile work which lines the wall, the wooden floorboards covered by a metallic surface which constitute the demised floor and the roller shutter which provides the enclosure of the fourth side of the shop are all capable of being described as having been constructed or at least meaningfully of being demolished, and they constitute the premises which I hold that the landlord has proved he is intending to demolish; and, in the case of the roller shutter, to reconstruct by inserting a new shop front. I take this view of the roller shutter notwithstanding that it appears to be removable from within the runners on each side, which are no doubt affixed to the building at least in part because it is a replacement of the shop front which itself constituted the envelope of the demise. It is in that sense, therefore, part of the fabric or structure of the demise. On the other hand I would not regard its replacement, as proposed, by a shop front consisting of glass within an aluminium frame which would be a day's work costing some £4,200, as "substantial work of construction" within the second limb of s 30(1)(f). The work of demolition and reconstruction, however, is to the whole of what constitutes the premises so that for the reasons set out in *Housleys Ltd v Bloomer-Holt Ltd* [1966] 2 All ER 966, [1966] 1 WLR 1244 the works intended are within the first limb of the paragraph.'

[15] Later when considering s 31A and the argument whether the landlord could reasonably carry out the intended works without obtaining possession of the holding the judge said this about the works:

'The works which the landlord intends include the substitution for the roller shutter of a new shop front, continuous across the whole frontage. If that were carried out the tenant would immediately alter the work done by substituting a new front with an access and would be entitled to expect consent so to do. The work to the floor would involve the laying of a floor of continuous level through the four shops. If the landlord carried out that work, the tenant would rely upon it although below the tenant's own demise to provide support for a new floor at the level of the existing floor. The work includes opening up the wall between nos 9 and 11. If the landlord carried out that work the tenant would construct a new wall within its own demise to obstruct the opening and be entitled to expect consent to do so.'

It is to be noted that the findings that the tenant could expect consent to carry out works do not extend to the reinstatement of a floor at the existing level.

[16] Those findings show that the effect of the intended works is: (i) the removal of the existing floor (there was evidence but no finding that the joists underneath the floor did not form part of the main structure and were thus excluded from the 'demised premises') with the result that after the works have been done to provide a floor to stand on at the present level it would have to be provided with support from outside the area contained in the demised premises, and this is so whether that support is from the new floor or from joists, (ii) the removal of about 60% of the dividing wall with the result that to provide a partition the tenant would have to build a partition wall within the area of the existing demise or a wall in the same place as the one to be removed would have to be constructed, (iii) the removal of the roller-blind at the front of the shop and its replacement with a plate glass window part of which would have to be removed if the tenant is to be able to gain access from the street, which is the only access at present, (iv) the removal of the existing ceiling, with the result that a new ceiling would have to be put in which would have to be suspended or supported from outside the present demise, and (v) all the existing wiring and all the existing plaster and tiling on the other two walls will have been removed.

[17] The work that the landlord intends to carry out is part of a substantial programme of works. As to the time that it would take to carry out the intended works the judge recorded and found that—

'They agreed that if the works were carried out as proposed in the s 31A terms "in one continuous operation" they would take between 17 and 23 working days during which the tenant would have to vacate the holding and could not use it for the purposes of its business. On the other hand, if the landlord's works were carried out in the order which their architect, Mr Mortimore, would propose such that all necessary demolition began at the beginning of the landlord's contract and no access to the building was permitted until after all the works at the building had been completed, the tenant would have to vacate for over 40 weeks. Even total vacation, which is of course the maximum possible interference with the tenant's use of the holding, if limited to 17 to 23 working days (say up to four weeks) does not appear to me to be interference for such a substantial time as to prevent the tenant relying upon s 31A if it is willing to grant the landlord appropriate rights.'

[18] The overall effect of the intended works is therefore that effectively the eggshell and thus the material enclosing the 'demised premises' will be removed

and what was the tenant's shop will become part of an open space including other parts of the ground floor. That open space will have to be fitted out by, or on behalf of, the new occupier or occupiers to provide a floor, a ceiling, plastering or other wall covering and such internal partitions as may be appropriate. The new ceiling may or may not be at the existing height. The manner in which the whole space is divided up will depend on whether it is let as a whole or in parts. The landlord's intention is that the new floor will be lower than the existing floor to avoid the small 'step up' from street level that now exists.

[19] To enable a new lease of the 'demised premises' to be granted it would be necessary for it to be provided with support from other parts of the building. Any new lease of an eggshell within the ground floor area would have such support through the operation of the covenant for quiet enjoyment and the principle that the lessor cannot derogate from his grant. This would be so whether the lessor or the lessee carried out the work to provide such support.

The most relevant provisions of the 1954 Act

[20] As the judge recognised the most important sections are ss 30(1)(f) and 31A. They are in the following terms (so far as is relevant):

> '**30.** *Opposition by landlord to application for new tenancy.*—(1) The grounds on which a landlord may oppose an application under subsection (1) of section twenty-four of this Act are such of the following grounds as may be stated in the landlord's notice under section twenty-five of this Act or, as the case may be, under subsection (6) of section twenty-six thereof, that is to say ... (f) that on the termination of the current tenancy the landlord intends to demolish or reconstruct the premises comprised in the holding or a substantial part of those premises or to carry out substantial work of construction on the holding or part thereof and that he could not reasonably do so without obtaining possession of the holding ...
>
> **31A.** *Grant of new tenancy in some cases where section 30(1)(f) applies.*—(1) Where the landlord opposes an application under section 24(1) of this Act on the ground specified in paragraph (f) of section 30(1) of this Act the court shall not hold that the landlord could not reasonably carry out the demolition, reconstruction or work of construction intended without obtaining possession of the holding if—(a) the tenant agrees to the inclusion in the terms of the new tenancy of terms giving the landlord access and other facilities for carrying out the work intended and, given that access and those facilities, the landlord could reasonably carry out the work without obtaining possession of the holding and without interfering to a substantial extent or for a substantial time with the use of the holding for the purposes of the business carried on by the tenant; or ...'

[21] In my judgment those sections should not be construed and applied in isolation and ss 23(1), (3), 32 and 35 are also of particular relevance. They are in the following terms (so far as is relevant):

> '**23.** *Tenancies to which Part II applies.*—(1) Subject to the provisions of this Act, this Part of this Act applies to any tenancy where the property comprised in the tenancy is or includes premises which are occupied by the tenant and are so occupied for the purposes of a business carried on by him or for those and other purposes ...

(3) In the following provisions of this Part of this Act the expression "the holding", in relation to a tenancy to which this Part of this Act applies, means the property comprised in the tenancy, there being excluded any part thereof which is occupied neither by the tenant nor by a person employed by the tenant and so employed for the purposes of a business by reason of which the tenancy is one to which this Part of this Act applies ...

32. Property to be comprised in new tenancy.—(1) Subject to the following provisions of this section, an order under section twenty-nine of this Act for the grant of a new tenancy shall be an order for the grant of a new tenancy of the holding; and in the absence of agreement between the landlord and the tenant as to the property which constitutes the holding the court shall in the order designate that property by reference to the circumstances existing at the date of the order ...

(3) Where the current tenancy includes rights enjoyed by the tenant in connection with the holding, those rights shall be included in a tenancy ordered to be granted under section twenty-nine of this Act except as otherwise agreed between the landlord and the tenant or, in default of such agreement, determined by the court ...

35. Other terms of new tenancy.—(1) The terms of a tenancy granted by order of the court under this Part of this Act (other than terms as to the duration thereof and as to the rent payable thereunder) shall be such as may be agreed between the landlord and the tenant or as, in default of such agreement, may be determined by the court; and in determining those terms the court shall have regard to the terms of the current tenancy and to all relevant circumstances.'

[22] The 'holding' is defined. The definition is linked to s 23(1) and the term the holding is expressly referred to in ss 30(1)(f) and 32 but words within that definition, and s 23(1), namely 'property' and 'occupied' are not defined.

[23] 'Premises' is a word used in both ss 23(1) and 30(1)(f). If the definition of 'holding' is written into s 30(1)(f) the relevant part thereof would read:

'... intends to demolish or reconstruct the premises comprised in the property comprised in the tenancy there being excluded any part thereof which is neither occupied by the tenant ...'

[24] It follows that in this case the landlord has to show that he intends to demolish or reconstruct the premises comprised in the property comprised in the tenancy that is occupied by the tenant. This is not necessarily the same as the 'demised premises' because: (i) 'property' is a word which, as its definition in s 205 of the Law of Property Act 1925 shows, is capable of a wider meaning than the extent of the 'demised premises' and thus the eggshell, and (ii) 'occupied' is also a word with a breadth of meaning. The definition of 'property' in s 205 of the 1925 Act is that it 'includes any thing in action, and any interest in real or personal property'. Naturally that definition does not apply but in my judgment it reflects the natural breadth of meaning of the word and provides a pointer to the extent of its meaning when used to describe the subject matter of a tenancy. Leading counsel for the tenant pointed out that normally a person does not 'occupy' a right or an easement; I agree. Further it seems to me that this is reflected and catered for by s 32(3) which recognises the possibility of there being 'rights enjoyed ... with the holding' and that they need to be included in the new tenancy which s 32(1) requires to be a new tenancy of the holding.

[25] I return to the possible meaning of the phrase 'the premises comprised in the holding' (as defined—and thus the property comprised in the tenancy occupied by the tenant) at the end of this judgment when considering what constitutes work of demolition or reconstruction when no structural parts of a building are included in the demise but what is demised enjoys rights of support from the building without which it cannot be used or occupied.

[26] The word 'possession' is used in ss 30(1)(f) and 31A. It has been held by the House of Lords in *Heath v Drown* [1972] 2 All ER 561, [1973] AC 498 that for the purposes of s 30(1)(f) the phrase 'obtaining possession of the holding' means obtaining legal possession which would yield physical possession rather than simply physical possession of the holding. Lord Kilbrandon gave the speech of the majority and the most relevant passages of his speech are [1972] 2 All ER 561 at 572–573, [1973] AC 498 at 515–516, 517, where he says:

'Looking at the terms of s 30(1)(f) it seems clear that what the respondent *proposes to do is not demolition, which would have caused the holding to cease to exist physically, nor is it properly described as reconstruction of the premises, since at the end of the operation the premises will exist exactly as they existed before, with the holdings now occupied by the tenant continuing to be capable of being leased out of the premises.* Conceding that the work is a "substantial work of construction" that is not inconsistent with it being, what it has always been accepted as being, a necessary repair for the carrying out of which the landlord was entitled to access in terms of the leases. If the respondent is correct in his submission that the work proposed falls under s 30(1)(f) an inexplicable situation has arisen, namely, that although the appellant could have been obliged to tolerate a substantial amount of construction, irreconcilable with her occupation of the premises for the purposes of her business, being carried out over a substantial period during the currency of the present leases, she is nevertheless disentitled from the statutory security of renewed leases, containing similar derogatory terms, on the ground that the respondent would not be able to do under the new leases what he concedes he could have done under the old. *I do not think that s 31A enters into this question. It was suggested in the Court of Appeal ([1971] 1 All ER 1011, [1971] 2 QB 1) that, if the appellant's construction of s 30(1)(f) is correct, she is in a better position under the earlier statute than under the later, which was no doubt passed for the additional security of tenants. In my view, however, it is the reservation of the landlord's right of entry in the old leases which is recognised by s 35 as being capable of importation into the new leases, that makes it unnecessary for the appellant to rely on the new s 31A. The history of the later Act seems to show that it was passed for the protection of tenants whose original leases had contained no such term, and in order to authorise the court to incorporate a term of this kind in the new lease, which would otherwise have been doubtfully competent under s 35 in default of agreement by the landlord.* It seems likely that this doubt arose from the contrasting decisions of the Court of Appeal in *Little Park Service Station Ltd v Regent Oil Co Ltd* ([1967] 2 All ER 257, [1967] 2 QB 655) and in *Fernandez v Walding* ([1968] 1 All ER 994, [1968] 2 QB 606). In the former case the tenant succeeded in his contention that the case did not fall within s 30(1)(f). It is clear from the judgments in that case that the current lease contained a clause under which the landlord could have carried out the intended work of reconstruction; and it is implicit in the reasoning of Russell LJ ([1967] 2 All ER 257 at 265, [1967] 2 QB 655 at 673) *when he paraphrased the final words of the paragraph "without obtaining possession of the holding" as meaning "if a new tenancy is granted" that he was contemplating a new tenancy incorporating similar terms as respects the landlord's right of entry for the purposes of reconstructing the premises as were contained in the current lease.* In the latter case, *Fernandez v Walding,* the current tenancy was oral. It reserved no right of entry to the landlord, and the tenant failed. *It appears to have been tacitly assumed that in these circumstances there was no power under s 35 to incorporate in the new lease a right of entry adequate for the landlord's purposes. One can see that, in such circumstances, a term which substantially and for a substantial time interfered with the use of the holding by the tenant would be inappropriate, since that interference would have been inconsistent with the very security of tenure which it is the policy of the statutory code to promote. But it is not possible to say that such a term would be thus inconsistent, or that it would be so anomalous as to be outside a reasonable relationship of landlord and tenant, when it is merely a repetition of a term, and having the same practical incidents as that term, which had been freely negotiated between the parties when the relationship was originally entered into* ... Where I differ from the Court of Appeal is on the crucial question of construction of the words "without obtaining possession of the holding". I have already indicated the *inherent improbability, on a purposive construction of the Act as a whole, that Parliament should have intended to deny security of tenure to a tenant because the landlord intended to carry out work on the premises which he was entitled to do under the terms of the existing tenancy.* That such was not the intention of Parliament appears to me to be plain from an analysis of the actual words of s 30(1)(f) themselves. The "holding" referred to in s 30(1)(f) is ex hypothesi one in respect of which there is a subsisting tenancy, since s 24(1) extends the current tenancy until the tenant's application for a new lease has been finally disposed of. *"Obtaining possession of the holding" (sc by the landlord) must, in my view, mean putting an end to such rights of possession of the holding as are vested in the tenant under the terms of his current tenancy.* This is the ordinary meaning of "obtaining possession" in the context of the relationship of landlord and tenant. Moreover, an examination of the Act shows that when the word "possession" is used it means the legal right to possession of land.' (My emphasis.)

[27] As Lord Morris of Borth-y-Gest points out in *Heath v Drown* [1972] 2 All ER 561 at 569, [1973] AC 498 at 511 to obtain possession the landlord has to terminate the current tenancy without it being followed by a new tenancy. Section 30(1)(f) is a ground of opposition to a new tenancy. The terms of the new tenancy sought by the tenant can be introduced pursuant to ss 35 or 31A and as Lord Kilbrandon points out in *Heath v Drown* [1972] 2 All ER 561 at 572, [1973] AC 498 at 516 a purpose of s 31A was to enable the court to introduce a term into the new lease equivalent to a term of the lease in question in that case (and which exists in this case) to enable the landlord to enter to do repairs. Lord Kilbrandon's approach (and thus the approach of the majority of the House of Lords) was based on the effect of a term of the existing tenancy which would be incorporated into the new tenancy by s 35 rather than s 31A, and thus the meaning of the statutory phrase 'obtaining possession of the holding' in s 30(1)(f). Additionally, and perhaps in contrast to what goes before, the last passage I have emphasised in the citation in [26], above focuses on the current tenancy rather than the new one with the relevant term included in it pursuant to s 35. However in my judgment *Heath v Drown* applies to: (i) a consideration of the effect of the relevant terms of (a) the new lease, whether they are introduced therein pursuant to s 31A or s 35, and

(b) the existing tenancy (as continued by s 24 of the 1954 Act), and (ii) the statutory phrase 'obtaining possession of the holding' in both ss 30(1)(f) and 31A. Indeed the contrary was not argued.

[28] *Heath v Drown* therefore provides that 'obtaining possession of the holding' in s 31A(1)(a) means putting an end to the tenant's legal right to possession and thus that the question to be asked under that subsection is whether given the access and other facilities provided to the landlord under the terms that the tenant agrees can be included in the new tenancy the landlord can reasonably carry out the intended works without putting an end to the tenant's legal right to possession under that new tenancy.

My approach on this appeal

[29] The judge found that the ground of opposition to the grant of a new tenancy in s 30(1)(f) was satisfied and the tenant appeals that conclusion on two bases, namely that the judge was wrong in law to conclude that: (i) the works on which the landlord relied were works of demolition or reconstruction of the premises comprised within the holding; and further or alternatively (ii) the tenant was not entitled to rely on s 31A.

[30] The landlord argues that the judge was right for the reasons he gave and that his conclusions can be supported by further and alternative reasons.

[31] Clearly a logical approach to the application of ss 30(1)(f) and 31A is firstly to consider the first part of s 30(1)(f), namely whether the landlord has an intention to demolish etc, and then to consider the second part of s 30(1)(f) and thus s 31A. This is what the judge did and was the order in which the issues were argued before us and the judge. However for the purposes of analysis I shall take the arguments under the second part of s 30(1)(f) and thus s 31A first. One of my reasons for doing so is that in argument it was asserted that s 31A provides protection to a tenant if the intended works are properly classified as 'glorified works of decoration'.

Obtaining possession of the holding

[32] It follows from the decision in *Heath v Drown* and is confirmed for example in *Cerex Jewels Ltd v Peachey Property Corp plc* [1986] 2 EGLR 65 at 68 that a first stage in the consideration of whether the landlord can reasonably carry out the work intended without obtaining possession is to consider what parts of the work the landlord can carry out pursuant to the terms of the existing lease and a new lease containing those terms and the terms of access and other facilities the tenant agrees should be included therein for carrying out the work intended. *Heath v Drown* established that if the landlord can carry out the intended work under an existing term of the tenancy he cannot satisfy the second part of s 30(1)(f). To my mind this in part prompted the remark of Templeman LJ in *Price v Esso Petroleum Co Ltd* [1980] 2 EGLR 58 at 62 that—

> 'It is also true that, if section 31A of the Landlord and Tenant Act 1954 is construed in the manner indicated in *Redfern v Reeves* ([1978] 2 EGLR 52), the legislature may, in large part, have given away, in the last portion of paragraph (a), that which they have conferred on tenants by the first part.'

In my view this remark was also prompted by the point that s 31A was introduced to give further protection to tenants (see *Redfern v Reeves* [1978] 2 EGLR 52 at 53) by, for example, adding a term to the lease such as that which existed in *Heath v Drown*, and *Price's* case to enable the landlord to enter to carry out the intended

work but then cutting down the protection it gives by the second part of
s 31A(1)(a). It follows that a landlord is, or is arguably, in a better position if the
term to enter and carry out improvements or repairs is introduced into the new
lease through s 31A than he is if it is contained in his existing lease. Indeed this is
shown by the decision in *Price's* case because in that case the effect of the decision
of the Court of Appeal was that the tenant lost on the application of s 31A in
accordance with the approach in *Redfern v Reeves* which had not been referred to
the judge (see [1980] 2 EGLR 58 at 60) but won because the landlord could carry
out the intended work under a term of the existing lease (see [1980] 2 EGLR 58 at
60, 62).

[33] It is clear that as is pointed out in the *Cerex* case [1986] 2 EGLR 65 at 72
the Court of Appeal in *Price's* case felt some difficulty with the decision in *Redfern v
Reeves* (see *Price's* case [1980] 2 EGLR 58 at 62). However the fact that it is binding
was recognised in both *Price's* case and the *Cerex* case. I too recognise that these
decisions are binding but in my judgment the difficulties in the interpretation and
application of s 31A recognised in them have the result that their extent should
be examined with care when they are being considered in a different factual
matrix.

[34] Further I comment that the point made by Templeman LJ in *Price's* case
should be read with passages from the speech of Lord Kilbrandon in *Heath v
Drown* quoted in [26], above. As to those passages I comment: (i) Lord Kilbrandon
makes it clear that he is considering premises that after the works were
completed would exist precisely as they did before, (ii) Lord Kilbrandon was of
the view that s 31A did not enter into the question and recognised the existence
of the problem identified later by Templeman LJ in *Price's* case and in a slightly
different form by the Court of Appeal in *Heath v Drown* [1971] 1 All ER 1011,
[1971] 2 QB 1 and answered it on a purposive approach by reference to the
difference between a mere repetition of a term and the introduction of a new
term in the new tenancy, and (iii) argument as to whether Lord Kilbrandon's
purposive approach (and thus the approach of the majority of the House of
Lords) fits with the decision in *Redfern v Reeves* was not advanced before us and
does not arise on this appeal.

[35] In the county court the tenant argued that the landlord could do the
intended works under the terms of the lease. The judge rejected those arguments
and there is no appeal against that conclusion. The position before us is therefore
that it is accepted that the intended works cannot be carried out in reliance on the
terms of the lease. It follows that if, as the judge found, the intended works are
within the first part of s 30(1)(f) to succeed the tenant has to rely on s 31A.

[36] The judge said that s 31A contained two conditions, and described them
as follows:

'The first is that given that access and facilities, the landlord could
reasonably carry out the work without obtaining possession; the second is
that it could carry out the work "without interfering to a substantial extent
or for a substantial time with the use of the holding for the purposes of the
business carried on by the tenant".'

He found that the second condition was satisfied on the basis of a finding that the
works could be done as a continuous operation in 17 to 23 working days (see [17],
above). However he found that the first condition was not satisfied. As to this he
said:

a   'I return, however, to the question whether the landlord could reasonably carry out the works given access and facilities without obtaining possession. Mr Lewison QC [counsel for the tenant] says I must do no more than consider the intended works and ask myself only whether the landlord could do those works without undue disruption. That is the question which I have just answered in the tenant's favour. The decision in *Decca Navigator Co Ltd v*
b   *Greater London Council* [1974] 1 All ER 1178, [1974] 1 WLR 748, says Mr Lewison, turning that authority to the tenant's advantage, is that it is no part of the inquiry of the court whether that which the landlord proposes is or is not reasonable.'

The judge then sets out the headnote in the *Decca Navigator* case and continues:

c   'It seems to me to be a far cry from questioning whether the landlord could reasonably carry out those works which he intended if the absence of possession meant that their being carried out would be rendered useless.'

He then describes the works in the terms quoted in [15], above and continues:

d   'I do not say that because some part of the work which the landlord intends to carry out would be undone by the tenant after it is done, it necessarily becomes unreasonable for the landlord to carry out the work which he intends without the legal possession which would enable him to preserve it. Indeed, I am inclined to think that work such as installation of the shop front
e   might be carried out and then replaced without its being unreasonable to carry out the work in the first place. I would, in this case, have wanted some evidence perhaps as to the aesthetic considerations before founding myself on this part of the work alone. Again, I accept that sometimes the doing of structural work to the building as a whole may reasonably be carried out even if the individual tenants do work to adapt the results to their particular
f   needs. That could be the case with the floor or even the wall between nos 9 and 11. Considered individually therefore it may be that the landlord not only could physically carry out each item of that work which he intends, but also he could reasonably carry out that intention without having possession. There must, however, in my judgment, come a point where the necessity of permitting the tenant to undo what the landlord intends would leave so little
g   purpose in the landlord's doing what he intends that he could not reasonably do that which he otherwise intends without possession. As a matter of fact and degree I think that that point is reached in this case and the tenant is not entitled to rely on s 31A as precluding a finding that the landlord could not reasonably carry out the works which I have held are within s 30(1)(f)
h   without obtaining possession.'

In taking this approach the judge had earlier stated and concluded that—

'The terms which the tenant proposes should be included in the new tenancy ("the s 31A" terms) are as follows. "The right on reasonable notice
j   to enter the demised with workmen and others to carry out the scheme of works described in the reports of Mr Graham Mortimore dated 15 December 2000 and 9 May 2001 and 31 May 2001 ('the intended works') in so far as the intended works cannot be carried out without such entry provided that (a) this right shall only be exercisable if the intended works in so far as they affect the demised premises are carried out in one operation ... (c) the exercise of this right shall not prejudice the exercise of the lessee of any easement including,

for the avoidance of doubt, the easement of support enjoyed by the floor of
the demised premises." The tenant also offers in the form of what had been
para (B) of the original draft of such terms an undertaking as follows: "The
lessee shall indemnify the lessor against the reasonable additional costs
incurred by the lessor in carrying out the intended works in so far as they
affect the demised premises in one continuous operation." Mr Lewison for
the tenant provided the court with five other proposed modifications to the
terms of the current tenancy, not being terms giving the landlord access or
other facilities for carrying out the work—that is to say not being s 31A
terms. These are modifications which the tenant would seek if this
preliminary issue were determined in the tenant's favour. I think on any of
the bases advanced by Mr Lewison for the tenant to succeed on the
preliminary issue they would be intended to secure that if the works were
carried out under the terms of any new tenancy, the tenant could reinstate
the premises in such a manner as would enable it to carry out its existing
business. They are not, however, a matter for consideration on this
preliminary issue and if I do order, on determination of the preliminary issue,
that the tenant is entitled to a new tenancy (whether upon the inclusion of
the s 31A terms or otherwise) the other terms of the tenancy would be for
later determination. If the court then refused the modification of which
Mr Lewison has given notice, the tenant may apply for revocation of the
order under s 36(2) of the Act.'

[37] I agree that s 31A contains the two conditions the judge identified and
that these are separate conditions. This flows from the language of the section
which, with my alterations and additions, reads as follows:

'... the tenant agrees to the inclusion in the terms of the new tenancy of
terms giving the landlord access and other facilities for carrying out the work
intended and given that access and those facilities, the landlord could
reasonably carry out the work: (1) without obtaining possession of the
holding (the first condition), and (2) without interfering to a substantial
extent or for a substantial time with the use of the holding for the purpose of
the business carried on by the tenant (the second condition).'

Additionally this conclusion has strong support from the statement of Templeman LJ
in *Price*'s case set out in [32], above.

[38] I agree with the conclusion of the judge that the first condition is not
satisfied. My reasoning in support of this conclusion is not on all fours with that
of the judge. But it has a substantial overlap with it and this has the consequence
that in my judgment there is no need for any further facts to be found.

[39] In reliance on (1) *Redfern v Reeves* (and its application in the *Cerex* case and
Price's case) and (2) the *Decca Navigator* case, it was argued on behalf of the tenant
that: (i) the judge erred by asking himself the question whether it was reasonable
for the landlord to carry out the intended work at all, (ii) the correct question is
that given that the landlord intends to carry out the work, can he do so in a
reasonable way which does not interfere to a substantial extent or for a substantial
time with the use of the holding by the tenant, and (iii) the judge was wrong to
look beyond the programme of works and the correct approach was to look only
at the effect on the tenant's use of the holding whilst the works intended by the
landlord were carried out. I do not accept any of these points.

[40] As to point (i), in my judgment when considering both the first and the
second condition in s 31A(1)(a) the judge did not ask himself this question.

a Rather he asked himself the correct statutory question and thus in respect of the first condition he considered whether the landlord could reasonably carry out the work it intended without obtaining possession. His references to reasonableness that are used by the tenant to found this ground of attack are addressed to the landlord's need to obtain possession and not to the issue whether it was reasonable for it to carry out the intended works. I accept, and in my judgment
b so did the judge, that as Stephenson LJ says in the *Decca Navigator* case [1974] 1 All ER 1178 at 1182, [1974] 1 WLR 748 at 753:

> 'The question for the court is not, were the landlords reasonable in intending to do the particular work defined in the drawing? but, were they, having genuinely formed that intention, reasonable in dispossessing the
c tenants completely in order to carry it out? Could they in common sense and in reason have carried out that substantial work of construction—not some different work answering to that general description—without obtaining possession of the whole of the holding, or could they have carried it out while leaving the tenant in possession of the 15 foot wide strip?'

d In this case it is accepted that the landlord has a genuine intention to carry out the works and there was no issue that it had been tailored to enable the landlord to obtain possession. In those circumstances the above passage from the judgment of Stephenson LJ (and the other judgments in the *Decca Navigator* case) show that for the purposes of s 31A the court is to look at the work the landlord intends to
e do and not some other work which might be said to achieve the same object, or additional work that the landlord might have carried out to make the ground floor ready for re-letting.

[41] As to points (ii) and (iii), in my judgment they fail to have regard to the first condition in s 31A(1)(a) and the point that none of the cases relied on were directed to that condition.

f [42] More generally, and in my judgment importantly, the arguments advanced on behalf of the tenant fail to have proper regard to the fact that in this case when the works that the landlord intends to carry out are completed: (i) the premises demised by the lease (ie the eggshell) and rights enjoyed with it and thus the holding will no longer physically exist and be capable of occupation, and
g (ii) before the tenant can occupy the holding under the new tenancy it seeks (a) some of the works carried out by the landlord will have to be undone, and (b) additional work will have to be carried out. This was not the position in any of the cases to which we were referred. Further, as I have pointed out in *Heath v Drown* [1972] 2 All ER 561, [1973] AC 498 Lord Kilbrandon mentioned that after the works had been completed the premises would exist precisely as they had
h before. To my mind this provides support for the view that if after the intended works are carried out the premises would not exist precisely as they had before this would be a relevant factor in deciding whether those works could be carried out without obtaining possession.

[43] As a matter of language the first condition in s 31A(1)(a) is separate and
j distinct from the second condition and thus in my judgment as none of *Redfern v Reeves* [1978] 2 EGLR 52, *Price v Esso Petroleum Co Ltd* [1980] 2 EGLR 58 and *Cerex Jewels Ltd v Peachey Property Corp plc* [1986] 2 EGLR 65 are concerned with the first condition they do not support an argument that when the court is considering whether a landlord can reasonably carry out the intended works without obtaining possession it should not look beyond the programme (and period) of the works the landlord intends to carry out.

[44] The terms of the new tenancy referred to in s 31A(1)(a) are for the limited purpose of giving the landlord access and other facilities to carry out the work it intends to do, and the *Decca Navigator* case makes clear that what the court has to consider is those works. Therefore the terms referred to in s 31A(1)(a) do not extend to terms that enable the landlord (or the tenant) to carry out works the landlord does not intend to do and thus, for example, replacement of support or an interior.

[45] If (as was argued on behalf of the tenant before us and the judge found) it is correct that in considering the application of s 31A the court should ignore the terms of the new lease that would make provision for: (i) some of the works carried out by the landlord being undone, and (ii) additional work being carried out so that the tenant can occupy and trade from the holding, in my judgment it is clear that the landlord cannot reasonably carry out the intended works without obtaining possession in the sense of putting an end to the tenant's legal right to possession under the new tenancy. This is because whether through the covenant for quiet enjoyment, or the principle that a landlord cannot derogate from his grant, an aspect of the tenant's legal right to possession includes the ability to occupy the holding and thus to enjoy as part of it, or ancillary to it, rights of support and access that enable the tenant to enter upon, use and occupy the holding.

[46] The point can be tested by more obvious examples, namely (i) the demolition of a building let as a whole and the construction in its place of a different building, or (ii) the demolition of a building the third floor of which is let on an 'eggshell basis' (or on the basis that some parts of the structure are included in the demise) and the construction in its place of a two-storey building. The latter was the example considered in argument. To my mind in both examples it is quite unreal to say that a landlord can reasonably carry out the intended works without obtaining possession because after those works have been done the holding simply will not exist (see for a similar view *Blackburn v Hussain* [1988] 1 EGLR 77 at 78). Further to my mind the holding cannot sensibly and reasonably be recreated on the basis of terms that could be included in a new tenancy of the holding or arrangements that were ancillary to such a tenancy.

[47] In more general terms, in my judgment when a tenant agrees to the inclusion in the terms of the new tenancy (which in broad terms has to be of the holding—see s 32 of the 1954 Act) of terms giving access and other facilities for carrying out the work intended and that work will have the result that the holding will no longer exist they cannot be terms that enable the landlord to carry out the works without obtaining possession of the holding. This is supported by dicta in the judgment of Parker LJ in *Blackburn v Hussain* [1988] 1 EGLR 77 at 78 where he said:

'That is sufficient to dispose of the issue arising on this appeal, but it was also submitted on behalf of the appellant that section 31A did not really arise at all, because it cannot have contemplated an agreement which involved the destruction of the subject-matter of the original holding. Were it otherwise it would involve a tenant's being able to say: "I agree to the destruction of my holding, but I demand that, it having been destroyed, I am granted a tenancy, not of my holding, but of some entirely different entity." Without finally deciding the matter, I should say that I accept that there is great force in that contention and that for my part I do not, as presently advised, accept that it is possible for a tenant by any such agreement to avoid the plain meaning of section 30(1)(f).'

[48] However I am of the view having regard to the terms and purpose of the 1954 Act that in some circumstances when a landlord intends to do work that the tenant wants to undo, and further or alternatively when the tenant will need to do work after the landlord has finished his work to enable him to use the holding, the tenant should be able to take advantage of s 31A and that in those circumstances issues of fact and degree are likely to arise. An example could be one in which a landlord intends to produce a shell for letting and fitting out by a tenant. This has similarities to the present case and to the situation in *Blackburn v Hussain*. In particular in my judgment (i) the point that the overall test in ss 30(1)(f) and 31A is whether the landlord could or could not reasonably do the work he intends (and not other work—see the *Decca Navigator* case) without obtaining possession, and (ii) the purposes underlying the 1954 Act have the result that in such cases, when deciding whether s 31A applies: (a) the court is not limited to considering only whether the intention of the landlord is genuine (although this would be a relevant consideration—see the judgment of Stephenson LJ in the *Decca Navigator* case), and (b) when, as here, the landlord has a genuine intention the court should consider the terms giving the landlord access and facilities to carry out the intended works together with the other relevant terms of the new lease.

[49] It follows that in my judgment the judge was wrong to conclude that the terms of the new lease suggested by the tenant providing for effective reinstatement to enable it to carry on business should not be considered at this stage, and thus that those terms should only be considered later on the basis that if the tenant did not like the terms ordered by the court it could exercise its right under s 36(2) of the 1954 Act not to take up the new tenancy. However in my judgment this error does not mean that this court should remit the case for further consideration because: (i) the findings made by the judge as to (a) the works intended by the landlord, and (b) the effect of those works and thus the work that would have to be done to recreate the holding and to enable the tenant to use and trade therefrom, (ii) the finding of the judge when he concluded that the landlord could not carry out the intended works under cl 2(14) of the lease when he said:

> 'In my judgment, the circularity of the position which would arise from the exercise of the rights under cl 2(14) means that the landlord could not reasonably carry out any work permitted thereby without having legal possession if the absence of such possession required him to reinstate as soon as he had done the work.'

And (iii) the overall finding by the judge that in this case as a matter of fact and degree the point had been reached that the tenant is not entitled to rely on s 31A have the result that it is clear that having regard to ss 32 and 35 of the 1954 Act the tenant would not be able to persuade the court to include further terms in the new lease which would enable it to argue successfully that having regard to those terms (and other offers made by the tenant) it could rely on s 31A.

[50] I am of this view notwithstanding: (i) the point that s 32(3) provides for rights enjoyed by the tenant in connection with the holding to be included in the new tenancy and thus that if terms which enabled the tenant to reinstate the floor (and the remainder of a new eggshell) could be included they would 'carry with them' rights of support, and (ii) the views of the judge, quoted in [15], above as to the tenant getting consent to do some of the works it would wish to carry out, which as I pointed out did not include the reinstatement of a floor at the existing level. I add that I have some doubt whether the views expressed by the judge concerning the giving of consent for the replacement of part of the plate glass

window and the erection of a partition within the area of the existing demise are
correct if they are considered in the context of s 35, and the intention of the
landlord to create a letting space which incorporates other units on the ground
floor. However for present purposes I shall assume that these views are correct
and could lead to terms being introduced into the new tenancy that allow such
works to be done, or a finding that consent should be given for them under
cl 2(19) of the existing lease.

[51] On that assumption, in my judgment the insuperable difficulty for the
tenant relates to reinstatement of the floor. This is recognised and confirmed by
(i) the fact that the terms offered to enable the landlord to carry out its intended
works were offered on the basis that they would not prejudice the easement of
support enjoyed by the floor, and (ii) the point made by the judge that to reinstate
the existing floor the tenant would have to use a replacement floor as support for
it. It was common ground before us that the intention was that the landlord
would leave a shell and that a new floor (with support and no doubt with
appropriate underfloor services) would be installed throughout the ground floor
and that it would be at a different level to the old floor. The difference in level is
a matter of inches but is not de minimis because the existing floor is slightly above
street level and its reintroduction would recreate the existing small 'step up'
whereas the intended new floor will be at street level.

[52] It follows that to reinstate the existing floor the tenant would have to
carry out works outside the area of the existing demise and thus work that: (i) is
not within the ambit of the work for which it can seek consent (not to be
unreasonably withheld) under cl 2(19) of the existing lease (see [12], above), and
(ii) is likely to involve work that is prohibited by cl 2(19)(i)(b). Further I do not
see why (i) reinstatement of a floor at the existing level would be regarded as an
improvement, or (ii) a court would agree to a term being included in the new
lease that enabled the tenant, or compelled the landlord, to install a floor at the
existing level because what the tenant is seeking is reinstatement of a substantial
part of the holding (together with support for it if such support is not included
within the holding as defined) in a manner which 'undoes' a substantial part of
the work carried out by the landlord and undermines its purpose.

[53] It may be that equivalent, albeit perhaps less compelling, points could be
made in respect of the ceiling but as there was no finding, and so far as I am aware
no evidence, that the ceiling would be reinstated at a different height I have not
taken such points into account.

[54] I accept that points of fact and degree arise in the above approach which
were not addressed in this context by the judge but in my judgment the findings
made by the judge, and the common ground, relating to the floor mean that it is
not necessary to remit for further consideration of the works the tenant would
have to carry out to enable it to use and occupy the holding under a new tenancy.

[55] More generally, I add that in my judgment when a court is considering
whether a landlord could reasonably carry out the work it intends and wishes to
carry out without obtaining possession and thus the terms of the new lease
(i) that would allow access and facilities to carry out those works, and (ii) that
would allow the tenant to undo some of those works and to reinstate to enable
him to use and occupy the holding, each aspect of the tenant's works should be
considered against the background that s 31A is directed to the works that the
landlord intends to do. Although this is not an essential part of my reasoning, in
this case this would mean that the court should have regard to the evidence of the
landlord that if it could not obtain possession of the holding (unit 9 of the ground

a floor) it would abandon its scheme in respect of that unit and carry it out on only units 11 and 13. In my judgment this evidence supports the view that what the tenant is ultimately seeking is reinstatement of something which the works intended by the landlord will have destroyed and which is not reasonably compatible with the purpose and effect of those works and therefore the conclusion that the landlord could not reasonably carry out the intended works

b without obtaining possession.

Further arguments on obtaining possession of the holding

[56] In reaching the above conclusion I have found that the authorities relied on by the tenant to support the assertion that when considering s 31A the court should only have regard to the period of the programme and period of works of

c demolition etc intended by the landlord do not apply to the first condition in s 31A and therefore do not have that result in respect of that condition. Additionally it was submitted on behalf of the landlord that those authorities do not have that result in respect of either the first or the second condition in a case such as this one where the works that the landlord intends to carry out do not

d result in (i) replacement of the premises as they were, or (ii) an improvement (and alteration) carried out pursuant to a term of the existing lease. Although a finding on this point is not necessary to support my conclusion set out above I record that I agree with this submission.

[57] As I have already said (see [33], above) in my judgment *Redfern v Reeves* [1978] 2 EGLR 52, *Price v Esso Petroleum Co Ltd* [1980] 2 EGLR 58 and *Cerex Jewels Ltd v*

e *Peachey Property Corp plc* [1986] 2 EGLR 65 should be examined with care when they are being considered in a different factual matrix. In *Price's* case ([1980] 2 EGLR 58 (at 60)) the intended works are described and it is made clear (e g at 60, 61, 62) that the case was decided on the basis that the works intended were works of improvement within an existing term of the lease. In reaching their

f conclusion that if that had not been the case and thus the tenant would have had to have relied on s 31A *Redfern v Reeves* meant that the tenant would fail (see [1980] 2 EGLR 58 at 60, 62) the Court of Appeal (i) were considering a case where the intended works resulted in an improved filling station that could be occupied without further work being done, and (ii) were focusing on the judge's approach that took into account interference with the business (or the goodwill of the

g business), as opposed to the point whether the physical effect of the works when completed by the landlord could or could not be taken into account. In *Redfern v Reeves* it seems that after the completion of the works intended by the landlord (some of which were covered by a term of the existing lease and some of which were not) the tenant could go back into occupation. The argument for the tenant

h was that the tenant's business could be safeguarded whilst the works were carried out by her moving her business on a temporary basis to other premises. This was rejected and the submission that was accepted was (at 53):

'... the court must look to the *physical effects of the work,* and not *to the consequences of the work from a business point of view.* [Counsel for the appellant]

j submitted that this must be so from the use of the words "with the use of the holding."' (My emphasis.)

This focuses on the issue in that case and does not address the question whether the physical effects of the work when completed can be taken into account. Indeed to my mind both the language of this submission and the phrase 'the use of the holding' in the section favour the conclusion that the physical effects of the

a

landlord's intended works after they have been completed, and thus whether at that stage and without doing more works the tenant could occupy the holding, can be taken into account.

b

[58] In the *Cerex* case [1986] 2 EGLR 65 the Court of Appeal was concerned with intended works which when they were completed resulted in the reinstatement (or effective reinstatement without a new shop front) of the holding (see 69). The works were works of demolition and reconstruction. Thus the court was not concerned with a case such as this when following completion of the works by the landlord further works have to be carried out to enable the tenant to occupy and use the holding. In my judgment the conclusions of Slade LJ (at 68, 72) have to be read with that in mind and in the context of my comments set out above on *Redfern v Reeves* and *Price's* case and the point that Slade LJ is setting out what those cases decide. I add that it is also clear that Slade LJ (at 68) was considering only the second condition in s 31A.

c

[59] On that approach to the *Cerex* case in my judgment it does not deal with and therefore is not binding authority on cases such as this one when the physical effect of the landlord's works when completed is that further work has to be done to enable the tenant to occupy and use the holding. As I have explained the citations from *Redfern v Reeves* and *Price's* case focus on the distinction between the physical effects of works which will result in premises that can be occupied and used and the overall effect of the works on the goodwill of the business and its continuation.

d

[60] In my judgment the language of s 31A supports the conclusion that when considering interference with 'the use of the holding' the physical effects of the result of the works intended by the landlord should be taken into account. The problems that then arise concerning the further works that are necessary to enable the tenant to occupy and use the holding merge with those discussed above in respect of the first condition (ie obtaining possession). In my judgment in the context of the second condition the extent and time of the interference should include consideration of the nature, extent and period of the works that would have to be done pursuant to terms of the new lease to enable the tenant to occupy and use the holding. These factual issues were not considered by the judge.

e

f

[61] Finally as to s 31A I mention that it was argued on behalf of the landlord that the judge was wrong not to apply a dictum in *Graysim Holdings Ltd v P & O Property Holdings Ltd* [1993] 1 EGLR 96 at 101 and to conclude as a matter of law that in considering how long the works it intended to carry out would take he could take into account an indemnity offered by the tenant to cover additional costs incurred by an alteration of the timetable to reduce the period to one of between 17 to 23 working days (see [17], above). The judge reached his conclusion that as a matter of law he could take such an indemnity into account (and thereby avoid it being a term of the new tenancy which has to be taken into account in determining the rent) because (and I quote) s 31A—

g

h

'requires the court to consider whether the landlord could reasonably carry out those intended works given the facilities which the tenant offers. That so clearly indicates that the landlord may have to adjust his method or sequence of work in order to carry out his intended works, as compared with that which he would adopt if he had possession instead of merely access and facilities, that I feel bound to say that this dictum is clearly wrong and I should not follow it.'

j

a As appears in [49], above I agree that as a matter of law the overall test of reasonableness gives the court this flexibility. As the judge recognises this conclusion gives rise to issues of fact and degree which have to be considered in the light of the decision in *Decca Navigator Co Ltd v Greater London Council* [1974] 1 All ER 1178, [1974] 1 WLR 748 that the works to be considered are those that the landlord intends and not some other works (see the citation in [40], above *b* from the judgment of Stephenson LJ in the *Decca Navigator* case).

[62] In my judgment the conclusion in [61], above means that in considering other aspects of the application of the two conditions within s 31A the court is not precluded from considering offers made by the tenant outside the terms of the new tenancy, for example, as to carrying out refitting works.

c
Section 30(1)(f)—the works

[63] The tenant argues that the judge was wrong to hold that works intended by the landlord were within s 30(1)(f) because in the context of works of demolition (and reconstruction) the word 'premises' in s 30(1)(f) applies only to parts of a *d* built structure which perform some structural function.

[64] In support of this argument the tenant accepts that it means giving 'premises' a narrower meaning than it has in s 23 where the tenant accepts it includes open land (see *Coppen v Bruce-Smith* (1999) 77 P & CR 239 at 245). It follows that the tenant accepts that the possible breadth of meaning of the word 'premises' in s 30(1)(f) is wide enough to include open land but points out that *e* (i) it is difficult to see how open land could be demolished or reconstructed, and (ii) the second part of s 30(1)(f) (which refers to substantial work of construction on the holding) could apply to open land and from those points argues that there is nothing odd in a result that both parts of s 30(1)(f) should not apply to the subject matter of all tenancies covered by the 1954 Act and thus that the first part *f* should apply to some tenancies and not to others. On the assumption, but without deciding, that open land cannot be demolished I agree. But this does not mean that the dividing line between what is included and excluded from the first part of s 30(1)(f) should be drawn where the tenant asserts, when as the tenant correctly accepts the word 'premises' can include open land and thus to my mind can also include an eggshell within a building.

g [65] Further in my judgment the ordinary meaning of the words demolish and reconstruct is wide enough to apply to an eggshell. In other words, in my judgment in this case the eggshell (and thus in this case the outside skin of the enclosed shop that is occupied by the tenant and includes the floor, the ceiling, the plaster and tiling and the shop front) is capable of being demolished and *h* reconstructed. In my judgment strong support for this view is found in *City Offices (Regent Street) Ltd v Europa Acceptance Group plc* [1990] 1 EGLR 63 (in particular at 65). I accept that that case was concerned with the construction of the lease in question so that the court was giving meaning to the phrase 'redevelopment or reconstruction of the demised premises' as used in the lease itself and thus in *j* circumstances in which the parties to the lease plainly intended it to apply to the eggshell demised. The *City Offices* case would therefore be a closer analogy with cl 5 of the lease in this case (see [11], above) albeit that that clause does not refer to works on, or to, the demised premises. None the less in my judgment the *City Offices* case provides clear support for the view that as a matter of language an eggshell with no structural element can, as found in that case, be reconstructed and thus, in my view, demolished.

[66] To support the argument that in the context of s 30(1)(f) of the 1954 Act 'premises' applies only to parts of a built structure which perform some structural function leading counsel for the tenant referred us to a number of authorities, these included the two cases referred to in the *City Offices* case, namely *Percy E Cadle & Co Ltd v Jacmarch Properties Ltd* [1957] 1 All ER 148, [1957] 1 QB 323 and *Joel v Swaddle* [1957] 3 All ER 325, [1957] 1 WLR 1094. They also included *Housleys Ltd v Bloomer-Holt Ltd* [1966] 2 All ER 966, [1966] 1 WLR 1244 (in particular at 1250, 1252, 1253), *Barth v Pritchard* [1990] 1 EGLR 109 (in particular at 110, 111) and *Romulus Trading Co Ltd v Henry Smith's Charity Trustees* [1990] 2 EGLR 75 (in particular at 76, 77). As he indicates the judge was referred to these, and further, cases of which he mentions *Bewlay (Tobacconists) Ltd v British Bata Shoe Co Ltd* [1958] 3 All ER 652, [1959] 1 WLR 45 and *Cook v Mott* [1961] EGD 294.

[67] As I have already mentioned, none of these cases deal with an eggshell tenancy and thus one where a part of a building is demised but the demise excludes the load-bearing structure of the building and includes nothing which performs a structural function in relation to the building. When that is taken into account, in my judgment none of the passages in those cases are authority for the proposition advanced on behalf of the tenant that in s 30(1)(f) 'premises' refers only to parts of a built structure which perform some structural function.

[68] As Nicholls LJ points out in the *City Offices* case [1990] 1 EGLR 63 at 65 the cases referred to therein (and in my judgment the other cases relied on by the tenant) may be authority for the proposition that where the demised property includes structural parts of the building there can never be reconstruction (or demolition) unless there is some demolition or alteration to a load-bearing part of the structure (or I would add, in agreement with the judge, enclosing walls, floor and ceiling even if not load-bearing or structural) included in the demised property. I respectfully agree, and in my judgment they go no further.

[69] Here any load-bearing parts of the building and its enclosing walls are excluded from the demised premises but they include the floor, ceiling and roller-blind. In my judgment having regard to the language of s 30(1)(f) and the purpose of the 1954 Act the works intended by the landlord (leaving aside the work relating to the roller-blind which involves demolition or reconstruction— see the *Bewlay* case) are works which involve demolition of the premises comprising the holding, or a substantial part of those premises, because, either: (i) as found by the judge they involve the demolition of the eggshell that was demised, or (ii) they involve the demolition of that eggshell together with the rights of support which render the eggshell demised capable of occupation and use by a tenant. For the purposes of deciding this appeal it does not matter which.

[70] Reason (ii) was raised by me during the course of the hearing but it was not adopted by leading counsel for the landlord and was not fully argued. Accordingly in my judgment I should leave the point open. I raised it in the context of the purposive arguments raised on behalf of the parties and referred to in [6], above and in particular in respect of the points made by the tenant that a tenant who had an eggshell tenancy would have less security than a tenant whose demise contained the walls enclosing his shop etc or some of those walls and all or part of the structure of the floor and the ceilings. This would be because in the latter case by reference to the authorities referred to in [66], above there is force in the points that the removal of all the plastering and wall coverings, false ceiling and floorboards leaving a shell for refitting would be properly classified as glorified works of redecoration which did not satisfy s 30(1)(f).

[71] An answer to that purposive point could be that the tenant of an eggshell would be able to rely on s 31A to give him equivalent protection when the result of the intended works was to remove the eggshell leaving a shell for refitting by or on behalf of a new tenant. However having regard to (a) the complications and difficulties relating to the application of s 31A referred to above in respect of the creation of the new eggshell, (b) the purposes of the 1954 Act and the competing interests of landlord and tenant (see [5], above) and (c) the desirability to my mind of s 30(1)(f) applying in the same way to tenancies of an enclosed shop or offices, or other business premises whether they include none of the structural parts of the building and no dividing walls or some of those parts of a building, my preliminary view remains that reason (ii) has much to recommend it.

[72] The reasoning behind it is based on the points set out in [23]–[25], above from which it would be argued that looked at pragmatically what is occupied is the shop and that as the rights to structural support that are necessary to enable the tenant to use the shop etc are based on the covenant for quiet enjoyment or non-derogation from grant and not on an express grant, in the context of the 1954 Act the premises comprised in the holding (as defined—and thus the property comprised in the tenancy occupied by the tenant) includes those rights of support. A counter-argument would be that rights of support are within, and are catered for by, s 32(3) and that 'premises comprising the holding' does not cover rights enjoyed in connection with the holding.

Overall conclusion

[73] For the reasons set out above I would dismiss this appeal.

CHADWICK LJ.

[74] Pt II of the Landlord and Tenant Act 1954 contains provisions which give some degree of security to occupying tenants of business premises. A tenancy to which Pt II applies does not come to an end unless terminated in accordance with those provisions. If the landlord gives notice under s 25 of the 1954 Act to terminate such a tenancy, the tenant may apply to the court for a new tenancy (see s 24(1) of that Act). The grounds upon which a landlord may oppose an application for a new tenancy are set out in s 30(1) of the 1954 Act. They include:

'(f) that on the termination of the current tenancy the landlord intends to demolish or reconstruct the premises comprised in the holding or a substantial part of those premises or to carry out substantial work of construction on the holding or part thereof and that he could not reasonably do so without obtaining possession of the holding ...'

[75] In that context 'the current tenancy' means the tenancy under which the tenant holds for the time being—see s 26(1) of the 1954 Act; and 'the holding' means so much of the property comprised in that tenancy as is occupied by the tenant (or by a person employed by the tenant for the purposes of the business carried on there)—see s 23(3) of that Act.

[76] It is clear that in order to rely on ground (f) of s 30(1) of the 1954 Act a landlord must establish two distinct elements: (A) that he intends either (i) to demolish or reconstruct the premises comprised in the holding or a substantial part of those premises or (ii) to carry out substantial work of construction on the holding or part thereof; and (B) in either case, that he could not reasonably do so without obtaining possession of the holding. The landlord succeeded before the judge in establishing elements (A)(i) and (B). It did not succeed in establishing

element (A)(ii)—in so far as it attempted to do so—and there is no challenge to the judge's decision on that point.

[77] The first issue on this appeal is whether, in the circumstances that the property comprised in the current tenancy was demised in terms which exclude any structural element, there are any 'premises comprised in the holding' which are capable of being demolished. The appellant submits that there are not; as it is put in the skeleton argument prepared for its appeal, in the context of s 30(1)(f) of the 1954 Act 'the word ["premises"] applies only to parts of a built structure which perform some structural function'.

[78] In order to succeed (as it did) in establishing the second of those elements—element (B)—the landlord had not only to satisfy the judge that, having regard to the terms of the current tenancy, it could not reasonably carry out the demolition intended without obtaining possession of the holding, but also to surmount the hurdle posed by para (a) in s 31A(1) of the 1954 Act. The section is in these terms (so far as material):

'(1) Where the landlord opposes an application under section 24(1) of this Act on the ground specified in paragraph (f) of section 30(1) of this Act the court shall not hold that the landlord could not reasonably carry out the demolition, reconstruction or work of construction intended without obtaining possession of the holding if—(a) the tenant agrees to the inclusion in the terms of the new tenancy of terms giving the landlord access and other facilities for carrying out the work intended and, given that access and those facilities, the landlord could reasonably carry out the work without obtaining possession of the holding and without interfering to a substantial extent or for a substantial time with the use of the holding for the purposes of the business carried on by the tenant ...'

[79] Section 31A(1) became material only if the landlord had first satisfied the judge that, under the terms of the current tenancy, it could not reasonably carry out the demolition intended without obtaining possession of the holding. The judge expressed himself satisfied of that; and there is no challenge to his conclusion on that point. It was then necessary for him to address para (a) of s 31A(1). That paragraph, also, contains two elements. The condition is that, given access and other facilities for carrying out the work intended (under the terms of the new tenancy for which the tenant has applied under Pt II of the 1954 Act) the landlord could reasonably carry out the work (A) without obtaining possession of the holding and (B) without interfering (i) to a substantial extent or (ii) for a substantial time with the use of the holding for the purposes of the business carried on by the tenant. If both elements of that condition are satisfied, then the landlord cannot succeed in establishing ground (f) of s 30(1) of the 1954 Act.

[80] The judge held that element (B) of the condition in para (a) of s 31A(1) was satisfied; but, nevertheless, held that element (A) was not satisfied. He reached the conclusion which he did on element (A) because he was satisfied that the tenant would immediately seek to undo the effect of the work which the landlord intended to carry out in relation to the building of which the holding formed a part. As he put it in his judgment:

'... there must come a point where the necessity of permitting the tenant to undo what the landlord intends would leave so little purpose in the landlord's doing what he intends that he could not reasonably do that which a he otherwise intends without possession. As a matter of fact and degree I think that that point is reached in this case ...'

[81] The appellant challenges that conclusion. It is said that the judge asked himself the wrong question. The point is put at para 6.7 of the appellant's skeleton argument:

b   'The question is not: is it reasonable for the landlord to carry out the work which he says he intends to carry out? Rather, the question is: given that the landlord intends to carry out the work, can he carry them [sic] in a reasonable way which does not interfere to a substantial extent or for a substantial time with the use of the holding by the tenant?'

c The respondent seeks to support the judge's conclusion in relation to element (A) of the condition in para (a) of s 31A(1) on other grounds (in addition to those which the judge gave). It also seeks to challenge the judge's conclusion in relation to element (B) of that condition. The scope and effect of s 31A(1) of the 1954 Act in the circumstances of the present case is the second issue raised on this appeal.

d *The first issue: are there any premises capable of being demolished?*

[82] The expression 'the premises' is not defined for the purposes of Pt II of the 1954 Act. But there are a number of indications as to its meaning. It is used, first, in s 23(1) in the context of identifying the tenancies to which Pt II of the Act e applies:

        '... this Part of this Act applies to any tenancy where the property comprised in the tenancy *is or includes premises* which are occupied by the tenant and are so occupied for the purposes of a business carried on by him ...' (My emphasis.)

f In *Bracey v Read* [1962] 3 All ER 472, [1963] Ch 88, Cross J held that, in that context, 'premises' was synonymous with 'property comprised in the tenancy'— although 'premises ... occupied by the tenant ... for the purposes of a business' would not, of course, necessarily include all the property comprised in the tenancy. He rejected ([1962] 3 All ER 472 at 475, [1963] Ch 88 at 92) the argument g that Parliament must have intended, by the use of the words 'property' and 'premises' in juxtaposition, to confine premises to what he described as its popular sense or meaning—that is to say 'buildings or buildings with land immediately adjoining them'. But he seems to have accepted ([1962] 3 All ER 472 at 476, [1963] Ch 88 at 93) that 'premises' might have the more restricted or h popular meaning in the context of s 30(1)(f) of the 1954 Act.

[83] That 'premises' does have a more restricted meaning in the context of s 30(1)(f) is confirmed by the decision of this court in *Housleys Ltd v Bloomer-Holt Ltd* [1966] 2 All ER 966, [1966] 1 WLR 1244—as Robert Walker LJ has pointed out in *Coppen v Bruce-Smith* (1999) 77 P & CR 239 at 245. In the *Housleys* case Diplock LJ j observed that:

        'It is plain, on the true construction of para. (f), that "the premises" there referred to must be limited to that part of the holding which is capable of being demolished and capable of being reconstructed.' (See [1966] 2 All ER 966 at 970, [1966] 1 WLR 1244 at 1252.)

Russell LJ agreed. He said:

'It seems clear to me that what is proposed is the demolition of the whole
premises comprised in the holding. The county court judge said that there   *a*
was to be "no demolition of a substantial part of the premises". This seems
to me to confuse the premises comprised in the holding with the holding ...
I would allow the appeal on this one ground. It has escaped the notice of the
county court judge that the proposal involves demolition not of a part, let
alone an insubstantial part, of the premises but of the whole of the premises.'   *b*
(See [1966] 2 All ER 966 at 971, [1966] 1 WLR 1244 at 1253.)

[84] As I have said 'the holding' means so much of the property comprised in
the current tenancy as is occupied by the tenant or an employee (see s 23(3) of the
1954 Act). It is, I think, reasonably clear, in the light of *Bracey v Read*, that 'the
holding' means much the same as 'premises which are occupied by the tenant ...   *c*
for the purposes of a business carried on by him' in s 23(1). Be that as it may, in
the light of the *Housleys* case, 'premises comprised in the holding' in the context
of s 30(1)(f) must be taken in this court to mean only so much of the holding as is
capable of being demolished and reconstructed.

[85] The short question, therefore, is whether the property comprised in the   *d*
current tenancy and occupied by the appellant as tenant for the purposes of its
business (the holding) comprises something capable of being demolished and
reconstructed. The judge answered that question in the affirmative; and, in my
view, he was right to do so. He said:

'The structure is the fabric which encloses the demise in so far as it is itself   *e*
demolished. In my judgment the physical boundaries of the demise, be they
constituted by walls, ceiling or floor, or only their surfaces, are premises
within the meaning of the paragraph at least if they are of such physical
quality as to be sensibly capable in ordinary language of being constructed or
part of the construction, or of being demolished. I think in the present case
that the tile work which lines the wall, the wooden floorboards covered by a   *f*
metallic surface which constitute the demised floor and the roller shutter
which provides the enclosure of the fourth side of the shop are all capable of
being described as constructed or at least meaningfully of being demolished,
and they constitute the premises which I hold the landlord has proved he is
intending to demolish; and, in the case of the roller shutter, to reconstruct by   *g*
inserting a new shop front.'

I agree.

[86] I agree, also, with the view expressed by Charles J (whose judgment I
have had the advantage of reading in draft) that there is nothing in the passages
upon which the appellant relies (*Percy E Cadle & Co Ltd v Jacmarch Properties Ltd*   *h*
[1957] 1 All ER 148 at 148–150, [1957] 1 QB 323 at 328–329, *Joel v Swaddle* [1957]
3 All ER 325 at 328–330, [1957] 1 WLR 1094 at 1099–1101, *Barth v Pritchard* [1990]
1 EGLR 109 at 111, and *Romulus Trading Co Ltd v Henry Smith's Charity Trustees*
[1990] 2 EGLR 75 at 76–77) which compels, or even supports, the conclusion for
which they were cited: that 'premises' in s 30(1)(f) of the 1954 Act is confined to   *j*
parts of a built structure which perform some structural function. What is plain,
from those passages, is that cases on the meaning of 'demolish' or 'reconstruct'
for the purposes of s 30(1)(f) turn on their particular facts. In each case the
relevant questions are: (i) what are the physical features of the property
comprised in the tenancy; (ii) what, amongst those features, is capable of being
demolished and reconstructed; (iii) is what is being done to those features which

a are capable of being demolished and reconstructed, taken as a whole, properly to be described as demolition or reconstruction of those features or a substantial part of them? It is, I think, wrong to start from the premise that physical features which are not load-bearing are incapable of being demolished and reconstructed; although it may well be that, in the particular case where there are load-bearing features, work which does not involve the demolition or reconstruction of any of those load-bearing features will not meet the test under (iii). But there is no reason why, in a case where there are physical features which are capable of being demolished and reconstructed, but none which are load-bearing, the test under (iii) should not apply, or should not be met in appropriate circumstances.

[87] In relation to the question whether the physical features of property comprised in an 'eggshell' lease—such as that in the present case—are capable of being demolished and reconstructed, I agree with Charles J that assistance can be found in the decision of this court in *City Offices (Regent Street) Ltd v Europa Acceptance Group plc* [1990] 1 EGLR 63. The issue in that case was whether notice given under a break clause in such a lease—which permitted the landlord to determine the term by notice of its desire to do so 'for the purpose of the redevelopment or reconstruction of the demised premises'—was effective. Nicholls LJ (with whose judgment Balcombe LJ agreed) described the property comprised in the lease in these terms (at 64):

'It is apparent from the plan and the terms of the definition clause that the leased property excludes the load-bearing structure of the building, in particular the steel framework structure in the walls and the floor and ceiling slabs. Essentially the demise is of an airspace with a thin enclosing skin.'

The works which the landlord proposed to carry out to the building of which the property comprised in the lease formed part did not differ in any material respect from those which are proposed in the present case (see [1990] 1 EGLR 63 at 64).

f The arguments advanced on behalf of the tenant by Mr Michael Rich QC (as he then was) were substantially the arguments advanced in this case. Two of the authorities cited to this court—the *Percy Cadle* case and *Joel v Swaddle*—were cited in that case; the others not having been decided at that date.

[88] After setting out an analysis of the effect of the works proposed, which he summarised in the sentence:

'In short, as the works proceed, the demolition work will involve the physical demolition of most of the eggshell as well as part of the larger scheme and the rebuilding of something significantly different.'

h Nicholls LJ went on to say (at 65):

'In my view, the judge was correct in deciding that works having this far-reaching physical effect on the state of the leased property satisfied the requirement of "reconstruction of the demised premises" in clause 8 [of the lease]. I do not think that this conclusion is inconsistent with either of the two authorities I have mentioned. It is a sufficient ground of distinction to note that in both those cases the demised property seems to have included structural parts of the building in question. Whether, in the case of such leases, there can never be reconstruction unless there is some alteration to a load-bearing part of the structure included in the demised property is not a point which calls for decision in the present case. I make no comment either way on that point. Even assuming (but without deciding) in the defendant's

favour that in such cases an alteration to a load-bearing part of the structure
is required before the work can constitute reconstruction, that is not this
case. Here, as I have already indicated, the demise is in terms which make
plain that the load-bearing structure is not included. Clause 8 envisaged that,
despite this, the resultant unit could be the subject of reconstruction. In that
context, in agreement with the judge, I am in no doubt that works as
extensive as those I have described qualify as "reconstruction of the demised
premises". Indeed, those works will change the identity of the leased
property and they will make the leased property wholly unusable while
being carried out. But the works involve much more than that, as I have
sought to indicate.'

[89] It is said that the *City Offices* case turned on the fact that the parties to the
lease must be taken to have intended that some effect should be given to the
expression 'reconstruction of the demised premise' in cl 8 of the lease, in
circumstances in which the demise excluded any load-bearing structure. But I am
not persuaded that the decision can be distinguished on that basis. The observations
of Nicholls LJ seem to me to be of more general application. I think that they
support the three-stage approach which I have set out above.

[90] It follows that I would reject the submission that there are no 'premises'
for the purposes of ground (f) of s 30(1) of the 1954 Act in the present case.

The second issue: the scope and effect of s 31A(1) of the 1954 Act

[91] The hypothesis which underlies the question posed by the first element
of the condition in para (a) of s 31A(1) is that the tenant agrees to the inclusion *in
the new tenancy* of terms giving the landlord access and other facilities for carrying
out the work intended. The new tenancy, in that context, is a tenancy granted
pursuant to an order made under s 29(1) of the 1954 Act on the application which
has been made by the tenant under s 24(1) of that Act. It is to be assumed that the
application has been successful and the order made in circumstances in which the
landlord has failed to establish, in the context of ground (f) in s 30(1) read with
s 31A(1)(a) of the 1954 Act, that, given the access and other facilities for carrying
out the work that he will enjoy under the terms of the new tenancy, he could not
reasonably carry out the work without obtaining possession of the holding.

[92] The property to be comprised in the new tenancy is the holding (see
s 32(1) of the 1954 Act). It is impossible for the tenant to occupy and enjoy the
holding without rights of support to a floor, to some surface covering on the walls
and to a suspended ceiling. It is pertinent, therefore, to consider the rights of
support that would be comprised in a new tenancy granted in the circumstances
which para (a) of s 31A(1) of the 1954 Act requires to be assumed. Section 32(3)
of that Act provides that:

'Where the current tenancy includes rights enjoyed by the tenant in
connection with the holding, those rights shall be included in a tenancy
ordered to be granted under section twenty-nine of this Act except as
otherwise agreed between the landlord and the tenant or, in default of such
agreement, determined by the court.'

That section has to be applied in the assumed circumstances that the tenant has
agreed to the inclusion of terms in the new tenancy which give the landlord
access and facilities for removing the floor, the existing surface covering on the
walls and the suspended ceiling; and which impose no obligation on the landlord

a   to reinstate. In those circumstances it is difficult to see any basis for the inclusion of rights of support in the new tenancy. Its terms are inconsistent with the need for such rights. Put shortly, once the landlord has carried out the permitted works and in the absence of reinstatement, there will be nothing to support.

[93] That raises the question whether the tenant would be entitled to reinstate. Section 35(1) of the 1954 Act requires that the terms of a tenancy

b   granted by order of the court (other than terms as to duration and rent) shall be such as may be agreed between the landlord and the tenant or, in default of agreement, as 'may be determined by the court; and in determining those terms the court shall have regard to the terms of the current tenancy *and to all relevant circumstances*' (my emphasis). The terms of the current tenancy are those contained in the lease under which the appellant holds the property. Clause 2(19)(i)

c   contains, at sub-para (a), a covenant by the tenant not without the consent in writing of the landlord to make any external projection from the demised premises; and, at sub-para (b), a covenant not to cut, maim, injure or alter any of the excluded parts. In that context 'the excluded parts' means the main structure of the building of which the demised premises form part and the main walls,

d   beams, floors and ceilings which run under or over the demised premises (see the first schedule to the lease). Clause 2(19)(ii) of the lease contains a covenant by the tenant not to make any alterations or additions to the demised premises without the consent of the landlord.

[94] It follows, as it seems to me, that if the proposed works were carried out with access and facilities given pursuant to the terms of a new tenancy, the

e   property comprised in that new tenancy would thereafter be unusable by the tenant for the purposes of its business. It is not, I think, in dispute that the property comprised in the new tenancy would be incapable of use without reinstatement of (at the least) a floor, and (very probably) surface covering to the walls and a suspended ceiling. The tenant could not do that work, consistently

f   with the terms of the current tenancy, without the consent of the landlord. It is, I think, inconceivable that the court would impose terms in the new tenancy (under s 35(1) of the 1954 Act) which permitted reinstatement without the consent of the landlord. The court would be required to have regard to all relevant circumstances; and those circumstances would include the tenant's agreement, to be assumed in the context of s 31A(1)(a) of the 1954 Act, to the

g   landlord having access and facilities to remove the floor, the existing surface covering to the walls and the suspended ceiling. To permit the tenant to reinstate—so as to undo the works which the landlord has been permitted to carry out—would be inconsistent with that agreement. And, in the circumstances that the tenant has agreed to the landlord carrying out works which remove the

h   need for rights of support, it seems to me impossible to say that the rights of support previously enjoyed would be continued under s 32(3) of the 1954 Act.

[95] The judge thought that there came a point where the necessity of permitting the tenant to undo what the landlord intends to do would leave so little purpose in the landlord doing what he intends to do that the correct conclusion was that he could not reasonably do what he intends to do without

j   possession of the holding. That view finds support, as it seems to me, in the observations of Parker LJ in *Blackburn v Hussain* [1988] 1 EGLR 77 at 78, to which Charles J has already referred:

'... it was also submitted ... that section 31A did not really arise at all, because it cannot have contemplated an agreement which involved the destruction of the subject-matter of the original holding. Were it otherwise it would involve a tenant's being able to say: "I agree to the destruction of my holding, but I demand that, it having been destroyed, I am granted a tenancy, not of my holding, but of some entirely different entity." Without finally deciding the matter, I should say that I accept that there is great force in that contention and that for my part I do not, as presently advised, accept that it is possible for a tenant by any such agreement to avoid the plain meaning of section 30(1)(f).'

I accept that it is possible to decide this appeal on the basis that (if s 31A(a) had any application) the landlord could not reasonably carry out the proposed works without obtaining possession of the holding—and I do not hold that the judge was wrong to take the view that he did on that point—but for my part I prefer to base my conclusion that s 31A(1)(a) of the 1954 Act can be of no assistance to the tenant on the ground that, whether or not it would be possible for the landlord to carry out the work without obtaining legal possession of the holding, it would be a necessary consequence of carrying out the work that the holding would become unusable, indefinitely, for the purpose of the tenant's business. In my view s 31A(1)(a) cannot have been intended to have any application in such a case.

Conclusion

[96] For those reasons I, too, would dismiss this appeal.

SIMON BROWN LJ.

[97] For the reasons set out by Chadwick LJ and Charles J, I, too, would dismiss this appeal.

Appeal dismissed.

Dilys Tausz   Barrister.

Hamilton v Al Fayed (No 2)

[2002] EWCA Civ 665

COURT OF APPEAL, CIVIL DIVISION

SIMON BROWN, CHADWICK AND HALE LJJ

25–27 MARCH, 17 MAY 2002

Costs – Order for costs – Payment of costs by non-party – Whether 'pure' funders generally exempt from liability for costs of successful unfunded party – Supreme Court Act 1981, s 51(3).

The claimant, an impecunious former MP, brought an action for libel against the defendant, an extremely wealthy man, arising out of the 'cash for questions' scandal. A sizeable part of the claimant's costs was contributed by a fighting fund to which several hundred donors, including the nine respondents, had made contributions. The contributors, who wished to ensure, out of sympathy for his cause, that the claimant was able to bring and fight the action, had no control over how their donations were spent and played no part in the management of the litigation. Their only expectation, in the event of the claim succeeding, was a return of their contributions. At trial, the jury found against the claimant, and he was ordered to pay the defendant's costs. Subsequently, the defendant sought to recover his unpaid costs from the respondents under s 51[a] of the Supreme Court Act 1981 which, in sub-s (3), gave the court full power to determine by whom and to what extent the costs were to be paid. On the application, the judge contrasted the position of 'pure' funders, such as the respondents, with professional funders who funded litigation under a contractual obligation, and normally exercised considerable control and supervision of the litigation. After concluding that it would be exceptional not to make a s 51 order against professional funders, the judge held that the reverse was true in the case of pure funders, and that no such order should be made against the respondents. The defendant appealed, contending that justice required that funders of litigation should normally pay the unfunded party's costs if the litigation failed.

Held – Pure funders were generally exempt from liability under s 51(3) of the 1981 Act for the costs of the successful unfunded party. Such a conclusion was consistent with the policy of the law, illustrated most conspicuously by the court's approach to conditional fee agreements and security for costs, that an unfunded party's ability to recover costs had to yield to the funded party's right of access to the courts to litigate the dispute in the first place. If solicitors acting under a conditional fee agreement were not liable for the other side's costs in the event of their client's claim failing, there was no reason why the pure funder should be so liable. Such agreements served the public interest by facilitating access to justice where publicly-funded legal assistance was not available. Similarly, the pure funding of litigation, whether claims or defences, ought generally to be regarded as being in the public interest, providing only and always that its essential motivation was to enable the funded party to litigate what the funders perceived to be a genuine case. That approach ought not to be confined

---

a   Section 51, so far as material, is set out at [4], below

merely to relatives moved by natural affection, but rather should extend to anyone, not least those responding to a fund-raising campaign, whose contribution, whether described as charitable, philanthropic, altruistic or merely sympathetic, was animated by a wish to ensure that a genuine dispute was not lost by default or inadequately contested. If pure funders were regularly exposed to liability under s 51, such funds would dry up and access to justice would thereby on occasions be lost. They should not, however, ordinarily be held liable. So long as the law continued to allow impoverished parties to litigate without having to provide security for their opponents' costs, those sympathetic to their plight should not be discouraged from assisting them to secure representation. It followed in the instant case that the judge's approach had been correct. Nor was there anything in the facts to take the case out of the general principle. Accordingly, the appeal would be dismissed (see [45], [47]–[51], [57], [58], [63], [64], [66], [67], [70]–[73], [83], [86], [87], below).

Notes

For the award of costs against non-parties, see 10 *Halsbury's Laws* (4th edn reissue) para 202.

For the Supreme Court Act 1981, s 51, see 11 *Halsbury's Statutes* (4th edn) (2000 reissue) 1094.

Cases referred to in judgments

Abraham v Thompson [1997] 4 All ER 362, CA.
Aiden Shipping Co Ltd v Interbulk Ltd, The Vimeira [1986] 2 All ER 409, [1986] AC 965, [1986] 2 WLR 1051, HL.
Broxton v McClelland (6 November 1992, unreported), QBD.
Chapman, (T G A) Ltd v Christopher [1998] 2 All ER 873, [1998] 1 WLR 12, CA.
Condliffe v Hislop [1996] 1 All ER 431, [1996] 1 WLR 753, CA.
Cooper v Maxwell [1992] CA Transcript 273.
Cormack v Washbourne [2000] Lloyd's Rep PN 459, CA.
Faryab v Smyth (Izzo, third party) [2000] CA Transcript 2090.
Globe Equities Ltd v Globe Legal Services Ltd [1999] BLR 232, CA.
Gloucestershire Health Authority v M A Torpy and Partners Ltd (t/a Torpy and Partners) [1999] Lloyd's Rep IR 203.
Hill v Archbold [1967] 3 All ER 110, [1968] 1 QB 686, [1967] 3 WLR 1218, CA.
Hodgson v Imperial Tobacco Ltd [1998] 2 All ER 673, [1998] 1 WLR 1056, CA.
McFarlane v E E Caledonia Ltd (No 2) [1995] 1 WLR 366.
Metalloy Supplies Ltd (in liq) v M A (UK) Ltd [1997] 1 All ER 418, [1997] 1 WLR 1613, CA.
Murphy v Young & Co's Brewery plc [1997] 1 All ER 518, [1997] 1 WLR 1591, CA.
Orchard v South Eastern Electricity Board [1987] 1 All ER 95, [1987] QB 565, [1987] 2 WLR 102, CA.
R v Lord Chancellor, ex p Witham [1997] 2 All ER 779, [1998] QB 575, [1998] 2 WLR 849, DC.
Roache v News Group Newspapers Ltd (1992) [1998] EMLR 161, CA.
Singh v Observer Ltd [1989] 2 All ER 751; *rvsd* [1989] 3 All ER 777n, CA.
Symphony Group plc v Hodgson [1993] 4 All ER 143, [1994] QB 179, [1993] 3 WLR 830, CA.
Tharros Shipping Co Ltd v Bias Shipping Ltd (No 3) [1995] 1 Lloyd's Rep 541.
Thistleton v Hendricks (1992) 32 Con LR 123.
Tolstoy-Miloslavsky (Count) v Lord Aldington [1996] 2 All ER 556, [1996] 1 WLR 736, CA.

Cases also cited or referred to in skeleton arguments

a

Awwad v Geraghty & Co (a firm) [2000] 1 All ER 608, [2001] QB 570, CA.

Bellenden (formerly Satterthwaite) v Satterthwaite [1948] 1 All ER 343, CA.

Bradlaugh v Newdegate (1883) 11 QBD 1.

Bristol and West plc v Bhadresa, Bristol and West plc v Mascarenhas [1999] 1 Lloyd's Rep IR 138.

b

G v G [1985] 2 All ER 225, [1985] 1 WLR 647, HL.

Giles v Thompson [1993] 3 All ER 321, [1994] 1 AC 142, HL.

Hamilton v Al Fayed [1999] 3 All ER 317, [1999] 1 WLR 1569, CA; affd [2000] 2 All ER 224, [2001] 1 AC 395, HL.

Harris v Brisco (1886) 17 QBD 504, [1886–90] All ER Rep 564, CA.

Land and Property Trust Co plc, Re [1991] 3 All ER 409, [1991] 1 WLR 601, CA.

c

Locabail (UK) Ltd v Bayfield Properties Ltd, Emmanuel v Locabail (UK) Ltd [2000] 2 Costs LR 169.

Magic Menu Systems Ltd v A F A Facilitation Pty Ltd (1996) 137 ALR 260, Aust Fed Ct.

Martell v Consett Iron Co Ltd [1955] 1 All ER 481, [1955] Ch 363, CA.

Stephenson (S B J) Ltd v Mandy [2000] IRLR 233.

d

Tanfern Ltd v Cameron-MacDonald [2000] 2 All ER 801, [2000] 1 WLR 1311, CA.

Taylor v Pace Developments Ltd [1991] BCC 406, CA.

Thai Trading Co (a firm) v Taylor [1998] 3 All ER 65, [1998] QB 781, CA.

Appeal

e

The appellant defendant, Mohamed Al Fayed, appealed with permission of the Court of Appeal from the decision Morland J on 13 July 2001 ([2001] All ER (D) 181 (Jul)) dismissing his application for orders under s 51 of the Supreme Court Act 1981 requiring the respondents, (1) Sir Robert McAlpine Ltd, (2) Lord Hanson, (3) Richard Clay, (4) the Duke of Devonshire, (5) Christopher Sharples, (6) David Wills, (7) Taki Theodoracopulos, (8) the Earl of Portsmouth and

f

(9) Henry James (Bud) Smith, to pay the unpaid costs of unsuccessful proceedings for libel brought against him by the claimant, Mostyn Neil Hamilton. The facts are set out in the judgment of Simon Brown LJ.

Elizabeth Gloster QC, James Price QC (instructed by *D J Freeman*) and *Laurence Harris* of *D J Freeman* for Mr Al Fayed.

g

Sir Sydney Kentridge QC and *Simon Salzedo* (instructed by *Mishcon de Reya*) for the first and second respondents and (instructed by *Russell Jones & Walker*) for the third to the sixth respondents.

Philip Heslop QC and *Orlando Fraser* (instructed by *Peters & Peters*) for the seventh respondent.

h

John Wardell (instructed by *Forsters*) for the eighth respondent.

The ninth respondent did not appear and was not represented.

Cur adv vult

j

17 May 2002. The following judgments were delivered.

SIMON BROWN LJ.

[1] On 21 December 1999, following a five-week trial before Morland J and a jury, Mr Neil Hamilton famously lost his libel action against Mr Al Fayed arising out of the 'cash for questions' scandal. To the question, 'are you satisfied on the balance of probabilities that Mr Al Fayed has established on highly convincing

evidence that Mr Hamilton was corrupt in his capacity as a Member of Parliament?', the jury returned the answer Yes. Mr Hamilton was ordered to pay Mr Al Fayed's costs.

[2] On 15 January 2001, following Mr Hamilton's failed application to the Court of Appeal (Lord Phillips of Worth Matravers MR, Sedley and Hale LJJ) ([2001] EMLR 15) for permission to appeal against the jury's verdict in the light of Mr Al Fayed's subsequently revealed purchase of documents stolen during the trial from Mr Hamilton's counsel's dustbin, those costs were assessed in default in the sum of £1,467,576. Some £1·19m of that sum remains unpaid, Mr Hamilton personally having paid nothing towards it and having now been bankrupted.

[3] The present proceedings relate to Mr Al Fayed's efforts to recover his unpaid costs from a number of individuals who backed Mr Hamilton's unsuccessful action. Stripped of inconsequential detail, the position is this. A sizeable part of Mr Hamilton's costs had been contributed by a fighting fund conceived and raised by Lord Harris of High Cross to enable the action to be brought. The money was raised on the understanding that if the action were successful, the money would be returned, otherwise not. The fund totalled £466,320 and consisted of 484 anonymous contributions of which 308 were for £100 or less, 153 of between £100 and £5,000, and 18 of £5,000 or more. Those 18 largest contributors paid a total of £323,500 (including £100,000 paid direct to Mr Hamilton's solicitors by the Earl of Portsmouth, the one contributor who declared himself), and against these contributors (whose names the judge required to be revealed) Mr Al Fayed sought orders for costs under s 51 of the Supreme Court Act 1981. Several of the contributors settled with Mr Al Fayed, paying him in total some £193,000. Nine, however, the respondents to this appeal, contested their liability. On 20 June 2001, for reasons given in a lengthy judgment handed down on 13 July 2001, Morland J ([2001] All ER (D) 181 (Jul)) rejected the s 51 applications. Now before us is Mr Al Fayed's appeal, brought with permission which we ourselves gave during the course of the three-day hearing last month.

[4] Section 51 (as amended by s 4 of the Courts and Legal Services Act 1990) provides:

'(1) ... the costs of and incidental to all proceedings in ... (b) the High Court ... shall be in the discretion of the court ...

(3) The court shall have full power to determine by whom and to what extent the costs are to be paid.'

[5] Pursuant to CPR 48.2(1)(a) the respondents were added as parties to Mr Hamilton's action for the purposes of costs only. That brought into play CPR 44.3 which sets out the court's discretion as to costs and the circumstances to be taken into account in its exercise:

'(1) The court has discretion as to—(a) whether costs are payable by one party to another; (b) the amount of those costs ...

(2) If the court decides to make an order about costs—(a) the general rule is that the unsuccessful party will be ordered to pay the costs of the successful party; but (b) the court may make a different order ...

(4) In deciding what order (if any) to make about costs, the court must have regard to all the circumstances, including—(a) the conduct of all the parties ...

a   (5) The conduct of the parties includes—(a) conduct before, as well as
during, the proceedings ...'

[6] At the heart of the judgment below, in a section headed 'Funding',
Morland J said:

b   '[69] The respondents to Mr Al Fayed's application are pure funders.
Their donations towards Mr Hamilton's costs were not made as the result of
any obligation owed to him but as an act of charity through sympathy with
his predicament and in some instances affinity to the Conservative Party.
They have no control over how their donation is spent. They have no part
in the management of the litigation up to and including the trial ... Their
c   only hope was that Mr Hamilton would achieve sufficient success in trial to
enable their donations to be repaid to them. Why would a pure donor be in
any more vulnerable position than a solicitor or counsel acting on a
contingency fee? (See the observations of Rose LJ in *Count Tolstoy-Miloslavsky v
Lord Aldington* [1996] 2 All ER 556 at 565–566, [1996] 1 WLR 736 at 746.)
d   [70] The position of the professional funder is very different. Almost
always the funding arises out of a contractual obligation, for example where
the funder is a trade union, an insurer or a professional or trade association.
Normally such a funder exercises considerable control, management and
supervision of the litigation ...
e   [71] ... It would be very exceptional that a situation would arise where it
would not be just and reasonable to make a s 51 order against a professional
funder.
[72] The reverse is the position in the case of a pure funder. It will be rare
or very rare that it will be just and reasonable to make an order against him.'

f   [7] Later in the judgment, in a long section entitled 'Guidance from the Court
of Appeal', in which the judge reviewed (as I shall have to review) a number of
this court's decisions, he referred to the 'exceptionality principle', a principle he
regarded not as a fetter on the exercise of his discretion but none the less as 'a very
important guideline'.

[8] It is towards those paragraphs that the main thrust of the appeal is directed.
g   Miss Gloster QC for Mr Al Fayed challenges the view that it will only rarely or
very rarely be just and reasonable to make an order against a pure funder and that
some exceptional further feature is required to warrant a s 51 order. As finally
formulated her argument is:

h   '... the correct approach ... is that, where a rich man (or company) chooses
for his own reasons (political, "philanthropic" or other) to fund a claimant of
limited means to pursue a libel action, which would not otherwise be
brought, on terms that he, the funder, will be reimbursed by the defendant
if the action succeeds, fairness and justice in general require that the funder
shall bear some responsibility for the costs to which the defendant has
j   thereby been put, if the action fails. Otherwise the funder is not made
responsible for the severe financial consequences of what he has enabled ...
the judge approached the matter from the incorrect starting point ... He was
... looking for some exceptional feature to take the case out of the ordinary
run of pure funding cases, instead of recognising that a case which is funded
as this one was is already exceptional ...'

[9] That is the central ground of appeal. The other grounds arise out of the final paragraph of the judgment under the heading 'Conclusion' which I now set out in full (not least because it contains in summary form most of the relevant factual background to this appeal):

'[115] In reaching my conclusion to dismiss Mr Al Fayed's application in addition to the facts applicable to individual respondents I considered all the circumstances of the case including in particular the following factors which are generally applicable:

(a) Mr Al Fayed had made the allegation that Mr Hamilton had received cash for questions, a matter of important and legitimate public interest and concern.

(b) By its verdict the jury had found that Mr Al Fayed had justifiably accused Mr Hamilton of being corrupt as a member of Parliament albeit that Mr Al Fayed was himself criminally corrupt.

(c) It was Mr Hamilton's choice to sue Mr Al Fayed who if he was to justify his accusation was bound to incur a very large outlay in costs which he was unlikely to recover from Mr Hamilton as the contributors to Mr Hamilton's costs should have realised if they had thought about it.

(d) There is no indication that the respondents who are rich or very rich would suffer any hardship by contributing towards Mr Al Fayed's costs.

(e) It is unfair that a successful defendant who is unable to recover his outlay of costs from the claimant should not recover his outlay from the rich backers of the claimant who is impecunious.

(f) Mr Al Fayed's solicitors took the proper step of warning Mr Hamilton's backers who were unknown to them that they were liable potentially to an application under s 51. It was no fault of Mr Al Fayed that backers were not alerted to this risk.

(g) Until the last minute emergence of the Mobil allegation Mr Hamilton had some realistic prospect of success viewed objectively.

(h) There were grounds of public interest for deciding that in any event the dispute between Mr Hamilton and Mr Al Fayed should be conclusively decided by a jury.

(i) It is in the public interest and the interest of justice that a litigant of limited means asserting a right against a very rich opponent should be afforded effective access to the courts in appropriate cases.

(j) Rich philanthropists who wish out of charity to achieve (i) above and a measure of equality of arms should not be discouraged.

(k) The respondents were entitled to have regard to (h), (i), (j) above and the honest belief of Lord Harris, the fund raiser, and Mr Hamilton's solicitors that success for Mr Hamilton was to be expected.

(l) The respondents were entitled to have regard to Mr Hamilton's persistent and consistent denial of cash for questions when having in mind Mr Al Fayed's questionable reputation for probity.

(m) Legitimate criticism was voiced as to the fairness to Mr Hamilton of the Downey Inquiry and proceedings before the select committee of the House of Commons.

(n) Mr Al Fayed's misuse of the witness box to make speeches and utterly scandalous accusations irrelevant to the dispute with Mr Hamilton.

(o) Mr Al Fayed's "discreditable" conduct after the trial in acquiring the confidential papers of Mr Hamilton's counsel.

(p) Most of the money received by Mr Hamilton's solicitors from the respondents was donated after the solicitors had taken the decision that the case would go ahead to trial irrespective of whether or not sufficient donations were received. That decision was unknown to the respondents who were led to believe that further donations were required to bring the case to trial.

(q) In contrast to (p) above the case of Mr Hamilton would not have proceeded to 10 October 1999 when the stage was reached that counsels' briefs were about to be delivered except for the existence of the fund.

(r) If Mr Hamilton were successful the respondent's only expectation was a return of their contributions.

(s) None of the respondents took any active part in the litigation or had any detailed knowledge of the merits of Mr Hamilton's claim.

(t) Mr Al Fayed's state of mind indicating resentment as expressed to the Independent journalist on 10 January 2000: "I am going for the bastards who think they are members of the Establishment who pay his fees and want to bring me down. I am going for people who encourage him, like the Lord Harris and that ... Earl of Shit".

(u) At the conclusion of the trial Mr Hamilton's counsel did not submit that costs should not follow the event or ask for a reduced costs order. I cannot with hindsight say what my reaction would have been if Mr Hamilton's counsel had made any such submissions. In any event it is irrelevant because the respondents were not then parties to the proceedings.'

[10] Miss Gloster advances three main criticisms of para 115 of the judgment. She contends, first, that it is impossible to see what weight was attached to which factors: no reasoned analysis is provided of how the judge came to his conclusion. Secondly, she submits that certain of the factors ought not to have been taken into account at all, notably the second limb of factor (b) and factors (n), (o) and (t). Thirdly, she complains that the judge left out of account what she calls 'the inequitable basis on which the funds were provided', namely, the contributors' understanding that if Mr Hamilton's claim succeeded, their contributions would be refunded, whereas if it failed they would make no contribution to Mr Al Fayed's costs.

[11] It is convenient at this stage to deal with that third criticism which Mr Al Fayed's skeleton argument puts in these terms:

'This factor is of great significance, given that the funders' primary stated motivation was to create a level playing field. What these funders have done is, on the contrary, to create an uneven playing field. Their stance is: you (the defendant) have no choice about whether to play this game; we are going to provide the means to start and continue it; if our side wins, you pay us; but if you win we will not pay you. In fact, it appears that the judge ... treated this, the basis on which the fund was raised, as a factor in the funders' favour (see factor (r)).'

[12] The reference to the funders' own motivation being 'to create a level playing field' is a reference to Lord Portsmouth's statement:

'What concerned me was that either Mr Hamilton's solicitors would be unable to conduct the case properly through a lack of funds or he would have to fight the case himself. My sole concern was to see that justice was done and, to this end, to ensure that the case was contested on a level playing field.'

[13] Other funders spoke of wanting to give Mr Hamilton the chance to clear his name. The Duke of Devonshire, who had met neither party, states that he made his contribution 'to enable a case of genuine public interest and some constitutional importance to be brought before the court'.

[14] I have no doubt that the judge did indeed regard factor (r) as being in the respondents' favour: whatever the result of the action they stood to make no profit from their contribution; at best they would get it back. Theoretically, no doubt, they could have given the money to Mr Hamilton's solicitors on terms which would have precluded Mr Hamilton, had he won, from recovering that part of his costs. That, however, is an unlikely scenario and, so far as I am aware, has not been a feature of any funding case. Arguably, moreover, such an arrangement would in fact tilt the balance in favour of the unfunded party, just as if one side's counsel were acting pro bono.

[15] Whether the funding in this case was to be regarded as 'inequitable'— whether, to use the sporting metaphor, it created an uneven as opposed to a level 'playing field'—depends no doubt upon one's point of view. The funders wanted to ensure that Mr Hamilton was able to bring and fight his claim on equal terms with Mr Al Fayed; Mr Al Fayed, given that he would have been liable for Mr Hamilton's costs (including the funders' contributions) had he lost, now wants to recover his own costs, having won.

[16] In my judgment, therefore, this point on analysis is subsumed within the central ground of appeal to which I earlier referred. Competing public interests are in play and the critical question is which of them ultimately must prevail?

[17] First, however, it is necessary to examine the existing case law to see whether, as the respondents contend, the judge below was right to conclude in effect that 'pure' funders are generally exempt from s 51(3) liability for the successful unfunded party's costs. A large number of authorities were placed before us. I propose to concentrate on those which point most helpfully to the general principles in play.

[18] My starting point must be with the single House of Lords authority on s 51, *Aiden Shipping Co Ltd v Interbulk Ltd, The Vimeira* [1986] 2 All ER 409, [1986] AC 965 in which Lord Goff of Chieveley, giving the only reasoned speech, found no justification for implying into the provision a limitation that costs were only to be paid by parties to the proceedings, but none the less recognised that 'in the vast majority of cases, it would no doubt be unjust to make an award of costs against a [non-party]', and that he could not imagine such an award being made 'against some person who has no connection with the proceedings in question'.

[19] I pass to *Symphony Group plc v Hodgson* [1993] 4 All ER 143 at 152, [1994] QB 179 at 193 in which Balcombe LJ, summarising various categories of case in which, following the *Aiden Shipping* case, costs order had been made against non-parties, included:

'(2) Where a person has maintained or financed the action. This was undoubtedly considered to be a proper case for the exercise of the discretion by Macpherson J in *Singh v Observer Ltd* [1989] 2 All ER 751, where it was alleged that a non-party was maintaining the plaintiff's libel action. However, on appeal the evidence showed that the non-party had not been maintaining the action and the appeal was allowed without going into the legal issues raised by the judge's decision: see *Singh v Observer Ltd* ([1989] 3 All ER 777n).'

[20] In deference to Miss Gloster's argument, I should, I think, cite just one paragraph from Macpherson J's judgment in *Singh's* case [1989] 2 All ER 751 at 757:

'During argument reference was made to common circumstances in which others pay for the litigation of a party, for example, legally aided cases, insurance cases and union-assisted cases which make up much of today's non-jury list. But legal aid is statutory and so are the restrictions on recovery of costs from the fund. The legal aid authorities can control the hardship which may be caused to successful litigants, who may not recover their costs, by requiring counsel to give fearless opinions as to the merits of the case as a condition of continuing legal aid. Insurance companies are subrogated to their insured's rights, and both they and unions invariably pay the costs of unsuccessful litigation. Otherwise, injustice would certainly result and I do not believe that if, for example, unions decided simply to refuse to pay costs in these cases, the court would not step in.'

[21] Balcombe LJ identified in the *Symphony Group* case a number of material considerations to have in mind in the exercise of the section 51(3) power. For present purposes only the first need be noted:

'An order for the payment of costs by a non-party will always be exceptional: see the *Aiden Shipping* case ... per Lord Goff. The judge should treat any application for such an order with considerable caution.' (See [1993] 4 All ER 143 at 152–153, [1994] QB 179 at 192–193.)

[22] As to what is meant in this context by 'exceptional' (a word used in most of the cases which followed the *Symphony Group* case) let me turn next, out of chronological sequence, to Morritt LJ's judgment in *Globe Equities Ltd v Globe Legal Services Ltd* [1999] BLR 232 at 239–240, the final, and as I think compelling, authority on the point:

'21. The principal argument was directed to the question whether the circumstances in these applications could properly be regarded as "exceptional". Counsel for Miller Gardner [a firm of solicitors] submitted that they could not. In addition to the judgment of Balcombe LJ in *Symphony Group plc v Hodgson* ([1993] 4 All ER 143, [1994] QB 179) he referred to similar statements in [a series of further cases]. But these statements left open the question by what standard the circumstances are to be judged in ascertaining whether they are exceptional. That question was answered by Phillips LJ in [*T G A Chapman Ltd v Christopher* [1998] 2 All ER 873 at 881, [1998] 1 WLR 12 at 20] where he said: "The test is whether they [sc the features relied on] are extraordinary in the context of the entire range of litigation that comes to the courts." I would also comment that there appears to me to be a danger of treating the requirement that the circumstances are "exceptional" as being part of the statute to be applied. It is not. The epithet originates in the first proposition enunciated by Balcombe LJ in *Symphony Group plc v Hodgson* but it is based on what Lord Goff said in [*Aiden Shipping Co Ltd v Interbulk Ltd, The Vimeira* [1986] 2 All ER 409 at 416, [1986] AC 965 at 980]. In none of the cases to which I have referred have "exceptional circumstances" been elevated into a pre-condition to the exercise of the power; nor should they be.

Ultimately the test is whether in all the circumstances it is just to exercise the power conferred by subsections (1) and (3) of section 51 Supreme Court Act 1981 to make a non-party pay the costs of the proceedings. Plainly in the ordinary run of cases where the party is pursuing or defending the claim for his own benefit through solicitors acting as such there is not usually any justification for making someone else pay the costs. But there will be cases where either or both these two features are absent. In such cases it will be a matter for judgment and the exercise by the judge of his discretion to decide whether the circumstances relied on are such as to make it just to order some non-party to pay the costs. Thus, as it seems to me, the exceptional case is one to be recognised by comparison with the ordinary run of cases not defined in advance by reference to any further characteristic.'

[23] A s 51 order was duly made in that case. Put simply, the firm of solicitors against whom it was made had created a limited liability company through whom to lease their office premises. The company litigated with the freeholder and lost. The case did not accordingly fall 'in the ordinary run of cases where the party is pursuing the claim for his own benefit through solicitors acting as such'. No more, submits Miss Gloster, does a funding case like the present. Given that 'the test is whether [funding as here] [is] extraordinary in the context of the entire range of litigation that comes to the courts' (see the *Chapman* case [1998] 2 All ER 873 at 881, [1998] 1 WLR 12 at 20) and that 'the exceptional case is one to be recognised by comparison with the ordinary run of cases' (see the *Globe Equities* case [1999] BLR 232 at 240), a funded case, by the very fact of it being such, is, Mr Al Fayed submits, exceptional. The present appeal, therefore, cannot be decided by reference to 'the exceptionality principle'; rather, as Morritt LJ put it in the passage already cited, 'the test is whether in all the circumstances it is just to exercise the power'.

[24] I turn, therefore, to the funding cases themselves, the first of which to come before the Court of Appeal was *Cooper v Maxwell* [1992] CA Transcript 273. In that case provisional liquidators, having successfully resisted Mr Kevin Maxwell's application to be excused from answering their questions on the ground of privilege against self-incrimination, sought a s 51 order against Mr Maxwell's mother who had funded his costs both at first instance and on appeal. Rejecting their application, Dillon LJ in the leading judgment said this:

'The development of the authorities has not been that there will automatically be an order for costs against a person who is not a party to the proceedings if that person has funded the litigation. More is required. It is not suggested that a bank which funded litigation by providing an overdraft for a party's litigation on commercial terms would automatically be ordered to pay the other side's costs if the litigation was unsuccessful. The position could be different with a trade union which has an interest in funding the litigation of a member in the industrial field and habitually does pay the costs if the litigation fails. I do not see that there is anything in the circumstances of Mrs Maxwell in the present case which makes it right that the court should make an order against her to pay the costs of Mr Kevin Maxwell's unsuccessful appeal.'

[25] I come next to *Murphy v Young & Co's Brewery plc* [1997] 1 All ER 518, [1997] 1 WLR 1591 in which the court had to address—

a
'The critical question ... whether the mere fact that Sun Alliance have funded the Murphys' legal expenses under a policy of insurance, up to the limit of the cover under that policy, makes it reasonable and just that Sun Alliance should be ordered to pay Youngs' costs.' (See [1997] 1 All ER 518 at 529, [1997] 1 WLR 1591 at 1603.)

b In giving the leading judgment in this court, Phillips LJ dealt first with *Thistleton v Hendricks* (1992) 32 Con LR 123, a first instance decision much relied upon by the successful defendant there (as, indeed, it has been by Miss Gloster before us):

c

d

'That case involved a claim by a builder against a house-owner and a counterclaim by the house-owner. The latter was successful and recovered damages of some £19,000 on the counterclaim. The builder's costs had been funded by his mother under loans motivated by maternal affection and made in the belief that her son's claim was bona fide. Judge Hicks QC, sitting as an Official Referee, ordered the mother to contribute £7,000 towards the house-owner's costs. In so doing he had particular regard to the following facts: (i) the mother knew that her son would be unlikely to be able to pay any costs ordered in favour of the house-owner; (ii) the builder was the plaintiff in the litigation; and (iii) the house-owner was a private individual. Judge Hicks considered that these circumstances justified his reaching a different conclusion from that of the Court of Appeal in *Cooper v Maxwell* ...' (See [1997] 1 All ER 518 at 529–530, [1997] 1 WLR 1591 at 1603.)

e

[26] Phillips LJ then outlined the circumstances of *Cooper v Maxwell*, cited (as I have already done) from Dillon LJ's judgment in that case, and continued:

f

g

h

j

'This decision demonstrates a proposition that [counsel] has not sought to challenge. Funding alone will not justify an order against the funder under s 51. I do not consider that an order under s 51 will normally be appropriate where a disinterested relative has, out of natural affection, funded costs of a claim or a defence that is reasonably advanced. [Counsel] has urged that the special feature that makes it reasonable and just to make an order under s 51 in the present case is that Sun Alliance has funded the Murphys' costs under a commercial agreement. This, it seems to me, reduces the central issue in this case to the following: Should a legal expense insurer be permitted to cap its liability, or should the provision of such cover render the insurer liable to pay the costs of the successful adverse party, regardless of any contractual limit of liability? ... I accept the submission that legal expenses insurance is in the public interest, particularly if it is on the terms of the cover in the present case [terms which required the assured to satisfy the insurers that they had reasonable grounds for pursuing or defending the proceedings]. Such insurance not only provides desirable protection to the assured, it is of benefit to the adverse party in that (i) it is likely to ensure that careful consideration is given to the merits of the litigation at an early stage, and (ii) it provides a potential source of funding of the adverse party's costs, should the assured be unsuccessful. The latter has proved illusory in the present case because of the limit of cover, but evidence before the court suggests that it is unusual for the limit of cover to be exceeded. That very evidence leaves me uncertain what the effect on the availability of such cover would be if legal expense insurers were exposed to costs orders under s 51, but I do not believe that that question is critical to the answer in this case.' (See [1997] 1 All ER 518 at 530, 531, [1997] 1 WLR 1591 at 1603–1604.)

[27] Sir John Balcombe added:

'... the legal expenses insurance with which we are here concerned did not relate to a specific piece of litigation, and this distinguishes this case from one where a third party funds a particular claim and has a direct commercial interest in the outcome of that claim.' (See [1997] 1 All ER 518 at 531, [1997] 1 WLR 1591 at 1604.)

[28] It is convenient at this stage to mention two further insurance cases, *T G A Chapman Ltd v Christopher* [1998] 2 All ER 873, [1998] 1 WLR 12 (the case mentioned by Morritt LJ in the context of exceptionality) and *Cormack v Washbourne* [2000] Lloyd's Rep PN 459. The insurers in both those cases, unlike the Sun Alliance in *Murphy's* case, gave cover against specific liability and therefore had a direct commercial interest in the outcome of the litigation. In each case the insured defendant failed to defeat the claim and in each his liability to the plaintiff exceeded the limit of the indemnity provided. In the *Chapman* case the insurers were held liable under s 51 for the successful plaintiff's costs; in *Cormack's* case they were not. In the *Chapman* case Phillips LJ, again giving the leading judgment, described the underwriters as 'the defendants in all but name', having earlier observed that 'it must be rare for litigation to be funded, controlled and directed by a third party motivated entirely by its own interests'. In those circumstances he regarded it as 'a paradigm case' for a s 51 order.

[29] In *Cormack's* case [2000] Lloyd's Rep PN 459, for reasons which are not presently material, a different view was taken of the insurers' role and consequent liability. There is, however, one passage in Auld LJ's leading judgment (at 464) which is relied on by both sides in the present appeal, and which I must, therefore, cite:

'[Counsel for the successful uninsured plaintiffs] submitted [that] where a non-party funds an unsuccessful action, particularly one who has an interest in its outcome, there is a strong public policy reason for making a section 51 order the norm. He referred to Phillips LJ's citation in [*T G A Chapman Ltd v Christopher* [1998] 2 All ER 873 at 883, [1998] 1 WLR 12 at 22] of Sir Thomas Bingham MR's words in [*Roache v News Group Newspapers Ltd* (1992) [1998] EMLR 161 at 166], that the principle that costs normally follow the event is "of fundamental importance in deterring plaintiffs from bringing and defendants from defending actions which they are likely to lose". [He] referred also to what he propounded as a general principle, that a maintainer of unsuccessful litigation, particularly one who has an interest in its outcome, should normally pay the costs of the adverse successful party.

However, the authorities and passages from the judgments on which [counsel] relied for those propositions indicate only that they may, depending on the circumstances, be relevant and justify such an outcome, not that they necessarily do ... Moreover, as His Honour Judge Bowsher QC, observed in [*Gloucestershire Health Authority v M A Torpy and Partners Ltd (t/a Torpy and Partners)* [1999] Lloyd's Rep IR 203 at 205], such a public policy consideration may not be so strong in the case of insured defendants as it is for insured plaintiffs. A plaintiff can choose whether to sue, the cause of a   action, the amount to claim and when to sue. A defendant has no choice in those matters.'

The respondents rely on the first of those paragraphs in which, they say, the court can be seen to have rejected Miss Gloster's central argument. She, however, relies on the second paragraph which, she submits, goes some way towards b   reinstating the relevance of the successful party being, as here, the defendant and unable therefore to escape the costs of the litigation.

[30] I now leave the insurance cases and turn to two cases touching upon the exercise of the s 51 discretion in the context of applications for the stay of funded proceedings. The first of these is *Condliffe v Hislop* [1996] 1 All ER 431, [1996] 1 WLR 753, where the court refused to stay a libel action being brought against c   Private Eye by a bankrupt plaintiff with the financial support of his mother. The following passages in Kennedy LJ's leading judgment are helpful:

'... we have looked at a number of cases decided since 1986, but none of them has led me to conclude that the court has any right to fetter the plaintiff because of the assistance which his mother has given him and the stance d   which she has taken in relation to this case. A number of the cases have been concerned with orders for costs at the conclusion of litigation, an issue with which we are not concerned ... it has become the practice in defamation actions for the defendants, if they discover that the plaintiff has financial support, to seek an undertaking that the supporter will pay the defendant's e   costs if his claim fails. That of course leads on to the question of how defendants are to discover if a plaintiff has financial support, a point considered in 1991 in a *Report On Practice and Procedure in Defamation* prepared by a committee chaired by Sir Brian Neill. There is also the further question of how a court should react if an acceptable undertaking is not forthcoming. In *Broxton v McClelland* (6 November 1992, unreported) an undertaking was f   offered on behalf of the plaintiff which the defendant considered to be unsuitable. In that case the plaintiff in a libel action was being maintained by a French company which offered a limited undertaking as to costs, and Drake J, being satisfied that an order for costs against the company would be difficult to enforce, upheld an order made by a deputy master that the action g   be stayed until a fuller undertaking was given. That decision, as I shall endeavour to explain in due course, may well have been correct on its facts, but in my view it is of no assistance to the defendant in the present case. In *McFarlane v E E Caledonia Ltd (No 2)* [1995] 1 WLR 366 Longmore J, at the request of the successful defendants, ordered that costs be paid by a h   commercial organisation which had funded the plaintiff under the terms of a contract which would have given the organisation 12·5% of the plaintiff's damages. Having referred to *Hill v Archbold* ([1967] 3 All ER 110, [1968] 1 QB 686) he said (at 373): "It may well be that it is not necessary to every case of lawful maintenance that the maintainer should accept a liability for a successful adverse party's costs; for example, a member of a family or a j   religious fraternity may well have a sufficient interest in maintaining an action to save such maintenance from contractual illegality, even without any acceptance of liability for such costs. But in what one may call a business context (e.g. insurance, trade union activity, or commercial litigation support for remuneration) the acceptance of such liability will always, in my view, be a highly relevant consideration." That seems to me to be the

correct approach. The existence of a business relationship will not always
lead the court to expect acceptance for liability for costs (eg if the financial
backer is a bank lending money to a plaintiff, or in some cases an insurer (see
Tharros Shipping Co Ltd v Bias Shipping Ltd (No 3) [1995] 1 Lloyd's Rep 541) but
it will be a highly relevant consideration.' (See [1996] 1 All ER 431 at 439–440,
[1996] 1 WLR 753 at 761–762.)

[31] Having then observed that there is at present no power to require a party
who is maintained but who does not satisfy the requirements of RSC Ord 23 to
give security for costs, Kennedy LJ continued ([1996] 1 All ER 431 at 440, [1996]
1 WLR 753 at 762):

'Nevertheless, the court is entitled to protect its own procedures, and as
Sir Thomas Bingham MR said in [*Roache v News Group Newspapers Ltd* (1992)
[1998] EMLR 161 at 166] the principle that in the ordinary way costs follow
the event "is of fundamental importance in deterring plaintiffs from bringing
and defendants from defending actions they are likely to lose". If that
principle is threatened, as for example if an insurer or a trade union were
known to be giving financial support to a party without accepting liability for
the costs of the other side if the supported party were to lose, then, as it
seems to me, the court might, at least in some cases, be prepared to order
that the action be stayed … Normally the better course will be to let the
action proceed to trial and then, if need be, consider the powers of the court
under s 51 of the Supreme Court Act 1981 (as in *McFarlane*'s case) but if the
circumstances suggest that the litigating party or the maintainer may not be
bona fide, or that if that party were to lose, an order for costs would be
difficult to enforce against the maintainer then, as it seems to me, a stay
could be imposed.'

[32] He concluded, however, that, even were there a discretion to stay the
case, he would not exercise it:

'No one has suggested that the plaintiff's claim is not bona fide. His
mother is not a lady of great wealth, and there is no reason to suspect that
when giving financial support to her son she has any ulterior motive to
serve.' (See [1996] 1 All ER 431 at 440, [1996] 1 WLR 753 at 762.)

That conclusion notwithstanding, Miss Gloster seeks to rely on the judgment as
a whole. Underlying it, she submits, is the assumption that ordinarily speaking
the funder of proceedings is on risk as to costs.

[33] Before turning to the second of the 'stay' cases, I should mention *Metalloy
Supplies Ltd (in liq) v M A (UK) Ltd* [1997] 1 All ER 418, [1997] 1 WLR 1613 in which
this court allowed a liquidator's appeal against a s 51(3) order, Millett LJ observing:

'It is not an abuse of the process of the court or in any way improper or
unreasonable for an impecunious plaintiff to bring proceedings which are
otherwise proper and bona fide while lacking the means to pay the
defendant's costs if they should fail. Litigants do it every day, with or
without legal aid. If the plaintiff is an individual, the defendant's only
recourse is to threaten the plaintiff with bankruptcy. If the plaintiff is a
limited company, the defendant may apply for security for costs and have the
proceedings dismissed if the plaintiff fails to provide whatever security is
ordered. The court has a discretion to make a costs order against a non-party.

Such an order is, however, exceptional, since it is rarely appropriate. It may be made in a wide variety of circumstances where the third party is considered to be the real party interested in the outcome of the suit. It may also be made where the third party has been responsible for bringing the proceedings and they have been brought in bad faith or for an ulterior purpose or there is some other conduct on his part which makes it just and reasonable to make the order against him. It is not, however, sufficient to render a director liable for costs that he was a director of the company and caused it to bring or defend proceedings which he funded and which ultimately failed. Where such proceedings are brought bona fide and for the benefit of the company, the company is the real plaintiff. If in such a case an order for costs could be made against a director in the absence of some impropriety or bad faith on his part, the doctrine of the separate liability of the company would be eroded and the principle that such orders should be exceptional would be nullified. The position of a liquidator is a fortiori.' (See [1997] 1 All ER 418 at 424–425, [1997] 1 WLR 1613 at 1619–1620.)

That passage is, of course, strongly relied on by the respondents.

[34] Millett LJ next had to consider s 51 in *Abraham v Thompson* [1997] 4 All ER 362, the other case, like *Condliffe v Hislop* [1996] 1 All ER 431, [1996] 1 WLR 753, in which the defendant was attempting to stay a funded action—in *Abraham's* case until the plaintiff agreed to disclose the identity of the third party funders. The first paragraph of Millett LJ's supporting judgment ([1997] 4 All ER 362 at 377), in part echoing what he had said in the *Metalloy* case, is again relied on by the respondents:

'It is not an abuse of the process of the court for an impecunious plaintiff to bring proceedings for a proper purpose and in good faith while being unable to pay the defendant's costs if the proceedings fail. If the plaintiff is an individual the court has no jurisdiction to order him to provide security for the defendant's costs and to stay the proceedings if he does not do so. It may be unjust to a successful defendant to be left with unrecovered costs, but the plaintiff's freedom of access to the courts has priority. The risk of an adverse order for costs and consequent bankruptcy has always been regarded as a sufficient deterrent to the bringing of proceedings which are likely to fail. Where there is no risk of personal bankruptcy, as in the case of a plaintiff which is a limited company, the court has a statutory jurisdiction to award security for costs; but even in this case it will frequently not do so if this will have the effect of stifling bona fide proceedings. It is preferable that a successful defendant should suffer the injustice of irrecoverable costs than that a plaintiff with a genuine claim should be prevented from pursuing it.'

[35] There is, however, a later passage in Millett LJ's judgment (at 378, 379) upon which Mr Al Fayed seeks to rely:

'In a number of cases starting with *Hill v Archbold* [1967] 3 All ER 110, [1968] 1 QB 686 Lord Denning MR suggested that a stranger who funded litigation should be required to undertake to pay the costs of the other side, and that the proceedings could be struck out if such an undertaking was not forthcoming. Lord Denning did not, however, suggest that the court should require the undertaking to be fortified or order the third party to provide security for costs. Thus the mischief which he identified was not the risk that the successful party might be left with unrecovered costs, but that proceedings might be financed by a party who was immune from personal liability for an adverse order for costs. This mischief has now been remedied by s 51 of the Supreme Court Act 1981. The jurisdiction conferred by s 51, however, is normally exercised after trial, and then with caution and only after proper consideration of all the circumstances. It is inappropriate to pre-empt the decision by exacting an undertaking from a third party at an interlocutory hearing before the outcome of the proceedings is known ... In making the order for disclosure in the present case the judge was adopting the approach foreshadowed by Kennedy LJ in *Condliffe v Hislop* [1996] 1 All ER 431 at 439, [1996] 1 WLR 753 at 761. In my judgment such an approach would not be justified unless there was clear evidence of an abuse of the process of the court and, for the reasons I have given, the presence of unlawful maintenance is not by itself such an abuse.'

[36] The next pair of authorities to which I must refer are *Count Tolstoy-Miloslavsky v Lord Aldington* [1996] 2 All ER 556, [1996] 1 WLR 73 (the case referred to in para 69 of Morland J's judgment below) and *Hodgson v Imperial Tobacco Ltd* [1998] 2 All ER 673, [1998] 1 WLR 1056. Both were concerned with the liability to s 51 orders of solicitors acting as such, in *Count Tolstoy-Miloslavsy's* case on a pro bono basis and in *Hodgson's* case under a conditional fee agreement (CFA).

[37] In *Count Tolstoy-Miloslavsy's* case the Court of Appeal held that the judge below had been wrong to make a costs order against the solicitors under s 51(3) but upheld the order on the very different ground that their conduct had been so unreasonable as to found a wasted costs order under s 51(6) of the 1981 Act. The relevant passage in Rose LJ's leading judgment is for present purposes this ([1996] 2 All ER 556 at 565–566, [1996] 1 WLR 736 at 745–746):

'In my judgment [counsel for the solicitors] is correct in his submission that there are only three categories of conduct which can give rise to an order for costs against a solicitor: (i) if it is within the wasted costs jurisdiction of s 51(6) and (7); (ii) if it is otherwise a breach of duty to the court ... ; (iii) if he acts outside the role of solicitor (eg in a private capacity or as a true third party funder for someone else). There is in my judgment no jurisdiction to make an order for costs against a solicitor solely on the ground that he acted without fee. It is in the public interest and it has always been recognised that it is proper for counsel and solicitors to act without fee. The access to justice which this can provide, for example in cases outside the scope of legal aid, confers a benefit on the public. Section 58 of the [Courts and Legal Services Act 1990], which legitimises conditional fees, inferentially demonstrates Parliament's recognition of this principle. For it would be very curious if a legal representative on a contingent fee and, therefore, with a financial interest in the outcome of litigation, could resist an order for costs against himself but one acting for no fee could not. Whether a solicitor is acting for remuneration or not does not alter the existence or nature of his duty to his client and the court, or affect the absence of any duty to protect the opposing party in the litigation from exposure to the expense of a hopeless claim. In neither case does he have to "impose a pre-trial screen through which a litigant must pass": see *Orchard v South Eastern Electricity Board* [1987] 1 All ER 95 at 100–101, [1987] QB 565 at 572–574 per Donaldson MR.'

a
[**38**] The Court of Appeal in *Hodgson's* case, albeit dismissing the solicitors' appeal against the refusal to make a pre-emptive order in their favour relating to costs, nevertheless made plain that no adverse order could be made by reference to their having entered into a lawful CFA:

b
'There is no reason why the circumstances in which a lawyer, acting under a CFA, can be made personally liable for the costs of a party other than his client should differ from those in which a lawyer who is not acting under a CFA would be so liable. Any suggestion by the defendants' lawyers, and any concern of the plaintiff's lawyers, that the position of the plaintiff's lawyers is different from that of any other legal adviser is misconceived. The existence of a CFA should make a legal advisers' position as a matter of law

c
no worse, so far as being ordered to pay costs is concerned, than it would be if there was no CFA. This is unless, of course, the CFA is outside the statutory protection ... Just as in *Count Tolstoy-Miloslavsky's* case it was made clear that it is in the public interest and perfectly proper for counsel and solicitors to act without fee, so it must now be taken to be in the public interest, and should be recognised as such, for counsel and solicitors to act

d
under a CFA. There are no grounds for treating the party who is or has been represented under a CFA differently [from] any other party. The same is true of their lawyers.' (See [1998] 2 All ER 673 at 681, 683, [1998] 1 WLR at 1065, 1067.)

[**39**] The final Court of Appeal decision in point is *Faryab v Smyth (Izzo, third*

e
party) [2000] CA Transcript 2090 in which the successful respondent in this court applied for a s 51 order against four individuals who in varying amounts had put up the £40,000 which the appellant, Mr Faryab, had been required to pay into court as security for costs in the appeal. Although the moneys had been loaned to Mr Faryab on terms that they would be repayable together with a substantial premium (in practice, although not in law, dependent upon the outcome of the

f
appeal), the court found that 'in fact the lenders were helping Mr Faryab for motives other than the hope of gain'. In giving the leading judgment, Robert Walker LJ noted that the most important statements of principle are those in *Symphony Group plc v Hodgson* [1993] 4 All ER 143, [1994] QB 179 and, in relation to insurers, *Murphy v Young & Co's Brewery plc* [1997] 1 All ER 518, [1997] 1 WLR 1591 and *T G A Chapman Ltd v Christopher* [1998] 2 All ER 873, [1998] 1 WLR 12; he stated

g
that 'a costs order of this sort will always be exceptional and must always be based on a substantial connection between the litigation and the person against whom the costs order is sought' and concluded:

'... I do not consider that it would be fair, just or reasonable to make any

h
costs order against [the named lenders]. To do so would have the practical effect of giving Ms Smyth a larger layer of security than that which this court thought fit to order for her.'

[**40**] Within that substantial body of Court of Appeal authority, submit the respondents, the immunity of 'pure' funders from s 51 liability is clearly to be

j
seen established—pure funders being those with no personal interest in the litigation, who do not stand to benefit from it, are not funding it as a matter of business, and in no way seek to control its course. *Cooper v Maxwell* [1992] CA Transcript 273 is directly in point, there being no logical distinction between a disinterested relative and other funders. That case clearly prevails over Judge Hicks' decision in *Thistleton v Hendricks* (1992) 32 Con LR 123, a decision about

which Phillips LJ in *Murphy's* case clearly had reservations if, indeed, he did not
implicitly overrule it—see in particular his reference to a disinterested relative
funding 'costs of *a claim or* a defence that is reasonably advanced' (my emphasis).
The facts of *Murphy's* case itself support the view that mere funders (as opposed
to those with a direct commercial interest in the litigation) ought not to be liable
for costs. Auld LJ in *Cormack v Washbourne* [2000] Lloyd's Rep PN 459 rejected the
contended-for principle that the funder of unsuccessful litigation, even one who
had an interest in its outcome, should normally pay the other side's costs (see [29],
above). Millett LJ in *Metalloy Supplies Ltd (in liq) v M A (UK) Ltd* [1997] 1 All ER 418,
[1997] 1 WLR 1613 held that neither a director nor a liquidator is liable for costs
merely for causing a company 'to bring or defend proceedings which he fund[s]'
(see [33], above). The governing principle is as stated by Millett LJ (see [34],
above) in *Abraham v Thompson* [1997] 4 All ER 362 at 377:

> 'It may be unjust to a successful defendant to be left with unrecovered
> costs, but the plaintiff's freedom of access to the courts has priority ... It is
> preferable that a successful defendant should suffer the injustice of irrecoverable
> costs than that a plaintiff with a genuine claim should be prevented from
> pursuing it.'

[41] That principle should encompass funded claims no less than claims
advanced without providing security for the defendant's costs. 'Genuine' for this
purpose must mean in good faith as perceived by the funders. Furthermore,
argue the respondents, if lawyers acting under CFAs are not amenable to s 51(3)
orders, no more should pure funders be liable. Finally, they contend, the present
case is a fortiori to *Faryab v Smyth*: there, after all, the funders stood to make a
substantial profit (see [39], above).

[42] Miss Gloster for Mr Al Fayed contends the contrary. She submits that the
most that the Court of Appeal authorities establish is, as was held in *Cooper v
Maxwell* and stated by Phillips LJ in *Murphy's* case [1997] 1 All ER 518 at 530,
[1997] 1 WLR 1591 at 1603–1604:

> 'Funding alone will not justify an order against the funder under s 51. I do
> not consider that an order under s 51 will normally be appropriate where a
> disinterested relative has, out of natural affection, funded costs of a claim or
> a defence that is reasonably advanced.'

[43] To exempt ('normally') from liability a 'disinterested relative' moved by
'natural affection' (like Mrs Maxwell) is one thing; to exempt backers like the
present respondents whose motives are likely to be less pure is another. *Faryab v
Smyth* was a very different case, the critical feature there being that the funders'
contributions had gone to meet a specific order for security for costs. Dicta in
certain of the cases strongly support the view that the funder of a losing party
ought in principle to carry liability for the other side's costs. That appears to have
been the underlying assumption in *Condliffe v Hislop* [1996] 1 All ER 431, [1996]
1 WLR 753 (consider not least Kennedy LJ's reference to the practice in defamation
cases of seeking the funder's undertaking to pay the defendant's costs if the claim
fails). Some suggestion of that approach is also to be found in Millett LJ's
judgment in *Abraham v Thompson* (cited at [35], above). Certainly Lord Denning MR
in *Hill v Archbold* [1967] 3 All ER 110, [1968] 1 QB 686 (the authority to which
Millett LJ there referred) only regarded the maintenance of claims and defences
respectively by unions and insurers as justified 'provided always that the one who

a supports the litigation, if it fails, pays the costs of the other side'. The ruling principle, she submits, is that articulated by Bingham MR in *Roache v News Group Newspapers Ltd* (1992) [1998] EMLR 161 at 166 'that in the ordinary way costs follow the event ... [a] principle ... of fundamental importance in deterring plaintiffs from bringing and defendants from defending actions they are likely to lose'. Justice requires that funders who enable litigation to be fought, and who in

b a real sense, therefore, may be regarded as responsible for it, should pay the unfunded party's costs if it fails.

[44] It is time to state my conclusions on the appeal. As I observed earlier (see [16], above) conflicting principles are here in play and only one can prevail. Should the law accord priority to the funded party gaining access to justice or to the unfunded party recovering his costs if he wins?

c

[45] Although none of the authorities to my mind precisely dictates the result of this appeal, I conclude that on balance they clearly favour the respondents' argument and that the unfunded party's ability to recover his costs must yield to the funded party's right of access to the courts to litigate the dispute in the first place. That seems to me to be the essential policy underlying the cases. Perhaps

d most conspicuously this is so in two of the categories of case discussed above: the CFA cases and those concerning security for costs. The respondents' argument arising out of the CFA ruling is really a very powerful one: if in these cases solicitors (or, indeed, barristers) are not to be liable for the other side's costs if their client's claim fails, why should the pure funder be? True, the client may

e obtain insurance and secure the other side's costs in that way, but this will not always be so and is certainly not a condition of acting under a CFA. True too, the lawyers will generally not be prepared to act under a CFA unless the claim has reasonable prospects of success thus arguably securing in a different way the public interest referred to by Bingham MR in *Roache*'s case (of deterring actions likely to be lost), deterrence perhaps less likely to be achieved in funding cases

f where the backers will probably not be exercising the same careful judgment as the CFA lawyers. As against that, however, it must be remembered that in CFA cases the lawyers are entitled to a substantial uplift in costs if the claim succeeds, and for this the defendant will be liable. The defendant's potential liability for costs in a CFA case is therefore greater than in an ordinary case and, of course, greater still than if the claimant is either unrepresented or represented pro bono.

g It could, indeed, be argued that unless both sides' costs are (a) the same and (b) actually able to be recovered in the event of success, the playing field of justice is uneven. That, however, is very plainly not the approach taken by the law. Rather, the law's policy with regard to CFAs is plainly to favour access to justice.

h [46] The court's approach to security for costs is similar (see in particular Millett LJ's judgment in *Abraham v Thompson* cited at [34], above). The law allows a claimant to litigate, at any rate at first instance, however clear it is that the defendant's costs could not be met—even, indeed, if the claimant can be shown to be expending all his assets in meeting his own costs. This same policy, moreover, underlies the legal aid scheme as it applies at first instance: the only

j circumstances in which the successful unfunded party can recover his costs from the fund are (a) if he is the defendant and (b) if he would otherwise suffer hardship. True it is that in a legal aid case—as Macpherson J pointed out in *Singh v Observer Ltd* [1989] 2 All ER 751 at 757 (see [20], above)—counsel are required 'to give fearless opinions as to the merits of the case as a condition of continuing legal aid'. Against that, however, it should be borne in mind that in legal aid cases the sanction of bankrupting the unsuccessful funded party—which Millett LJ in *Abraham v Thompson* [1997] 4 All ER 362 at 377 said 'has always been regarded as a sufficient deterrent to the bringing of proceedings which are likely to fail'—is unavailable.

[47] By the same token that Phillips LJ in *Murphy's* case found legal expenses insurance to be in the public interest (see [26], above) so too in my judgment the pure funding of litigation (whether of claims or defences) ought generally to be regarded as being in the public interest providing only and always that its essential motivation is to enable the party funded to litigate what the funders perceive to be a genuine case. This approach ought not to be confined merely to relatives moved by natural affection but rather should extend to anyone—not least those responding to a fund-raising campaign—whose contribution (whether described as charitable, philanthropic, altruistic or merely sympathetic) is animated by a wish to ensure that a genuine dispute is not lost by default (or, as concerned Lord Portsmouth here, inadequately contested). I recognise, of course, the very real differences between *Murphy's* case and the present, not least in that the two specific benefits identified by Phillips LJ as likely to accrue to the other party from legal expenses insurance—the early consideration of the claim's merits and the provision of funds which may cover an adverse costs order—are substantially less likely to accrue in the case of pure funding (although it is by no means impossible that the funds provided may enable the funded party to meet at least part of his costs liability if he loses). Whereas in *Murphy's* case, however, the court expressed itself unconcerned as to whether or not the making of s 51 orders against insurers would reduce the availability of such cover, here it seems to me plain beyond question that if pure funders are regularly exposed to liability under s 51, such funds will dry up and access to justice will thereby on occasions be lost.

[48] In expressing my conclusions thus far I have intentionally spoken in very general terms and sought to deal with pure funding cases as a broad category. It seems to me that nothing could be more inconvenient and productive of satellite litigation than to hold that some pure funding cases are likely to attract s 51 orders, others not, depending merely on the sort of considerations which moved Judge Hicks to decide against the funder in *Thistleton v Hendricks* (1992) 32 Con LR 123. For my part, therefore, whilst I am disposed to accept Miss Gloster's argument that hitherto the courts have not clearly laid down a rule that pure funders are generally to be regarded as exempt from s 51 orders, I am against her submission that they should ordinarily be held liable. So long as the law continues to allow impoverished parties to litigate without their having to provide security for their opponent's costs, those sympathetic to their plight should not be discouraged from assisting them to secure representation. Thus is access to justice promoted and, another benefit too—fewer litigants in person.

[49] It follows that I would support the approach taken by the judge below as expressed in paras 69–72 of his judgment (see [6], above) and would accordingly reject the central ground of this appeal (see [8], above).

[50] As to Miss Gloster's three criticisms of para 115 of the judgment below, I have already dealt with the third (see [11]–[16], above) and can take the other two really very shortly. The first criticism—that in para 115 the judge merely catalogued the factors (some in favour of Mr Al Fayed, some against him) to which he had regard, without explaining how he reached his conclusion—seems to me misplaced. Essentially the judge decided that there was nothing so

a exceptional in the circumstances of this case to justify making s 51 orders against the respondent funders. Paragraph 115 was designed merely to demonstrate that in so deciding he had overlooked nothing which could be thought to compel a different conclusion. What, however, this criticism does highlight is, I would suggest, the enormity of the exercise that would need to be undertaken in every case of pure funding were the court not to lay down a clear and strong

b presumption either for or (as I think) against s 51 liability generally in these cases.

[51] The second criticism—that the judge took into account against Mr Al Fayed certain matters which should not strictly have counted against him (at any rate as to liability for costs as opposed to quantum)—I find altogether more persuasive. Take, for example, sub-para (t): it seems to me quite wrong that Mr Al Fayed should be penalised for expressing, however abusively, his no doubt heartfelt

c views about this funding campaign. It is not, I think, necessary for present purposes to discuss the other sub-paragraphs individually. Overall, indeed, I have some considerable sympathy for Mr Al Fayed however obviously open to criticism some aspects of his conduct may have been. He was, after all, resoundingly vindicated by the jury in his contest with Mr Hamilton—and that

d despite the strong prejudice which a jury might initially have been expected to feel against him—and yet at the end of the day he has been left hugely out of pocket. Even though, as I have sought to explain, the policy of the law in these cases favours access to justice over the recoverability of costs, I think it right to recognise that it is Mr Al Fayed and others in his position who are required to pay the price of that policy. The court should rather sympathise with their predicament

e than rub salt into their wounds. But even acceding to this particular criticism of the judgment and exercising our discretion afresh, we must, I believe, inevitably reach the same ultimate conclusion as the judge below. This was a case of pure funding by contributors whose essential motive was to allow Mr Hamilton to litigate his claim. They acted rather through sympathy with his cause than out of

f malice towards Mr Al Fayed. (The contrary case advanced against Mr Taki Theodoracopulos who had battled with Mr Al Fayed down the years was rejected by the judge who was satisfied that 'Mr Theodoracopulos' main motive for contributing was charity', a finding not challenged on this appeal.) Although, moreover, Miss Gloster, in a supplementary skeleton argument, sought to contend that the contributors were 'at best reckless' in supporting a claim so

g conspicuously lacking in merit, in the course of the appeal hearing she expressly withdrew that allegation of recklessness together with any suggestion that the contributors should have read any of the documentation underlying the litigation (most particularly Sir Gordon Downey's July 1997 report on the cash for questions inquiry). There is in short nothing in the facts of this case to take it out

h of the general principle which for my part I would lay down: that pure funders generally are exempt from s 51 liability.

[52] This conclusion makes it strictly unnecessary to deal with the arguments, advanced by way of the respondents' notice, that the judge ought in any event to have dismissed these applications on grounds of causation. I propose nevertheless

j to deal with it briefly since it illustrates the sort of difficulty likely to arise in these cases if funders are ordinarily to be held liable under s 51.

[53] The argument was advanced most strongly on behalf of Lord Portsmouth whose £100,000 contribution was made on 26 October 1999, after Mr Hamilton's solicitors had taken the decision to proceed with the case irrespective of whether any further donations were made—after, as the judge put it, 'the Rubicon was

crossed' with the delivery of counsel's briefs on 10 October 1999 (see sub-paras (p) *a* and (q) of para 115).

[54] Given that proof of causation is a necessary pre-condition of the making of a s 51 order against a non-party—as to which there is ample authority and, as I understand it, no dispute—Mr Wardell submits that the bare facts just recited demonstrate of themselves that in Lord Portsmouth's case such proof was wanting—that, indeed, Lord Portsmouth's contribution plainly did not cause *b* Mr Al Fayed to incur any costs which he would not otherwise have incurred.

[55] The judge dealt with this argument in his judgment as follows:

'[110] Argument about causation has featured extensively in this case. In my judgment but for the existence of the fund Mr Hamilton's case would not have proceeded so that by 10 October 1999 the case was almost ready for trial *c* the following month. The subsequent large donations were made in the belief that without further substantial funding the trial might not take place. Unknown to the donors the decision to cross the Rubicon had been taken whether or not further funding was forthcoming by Mr Hamilton's solicitors.

[111] If it had been just and reasonable to make a s 51 order against those *d* funders who contributed before 10 October 1999, in my judgment it would have been unjust and unreasonable not to have made an order against those who contributed after 10 October 1999. The distinction is artificial. The fund-raising by Lord Harris was ongoing and repeated. Mr Hamilton's claim to clear his name could not be prosecuted and brought to a conclusion at trial without continual funding.' *e*

[56] That reasoning, submits Mr Wardell, is unsustainable. In particular the last sentence of para 111 is belied by the judge's earlier finding in para 33 of his judgment that 'the probabilities are that the case would have proceeded to trial and concluded as it did irrespective of whether or not there had been further funding after 10 October 1999'. The mere fact that the later contributors knew *f* nothing of the Rubicon having been crossed cannot logically avail Mr Al Fayed. Nor can the fact that the solicitors no doubt hoped for and perhaps even expected further contributions to be made.

[57] The argument, I have to say, appears to me not merely irresistible but also to demonstrate that there would need to be further factual exploration along *g* these lines in all pure funding cases were they not to be subject to a general presumption against s 51 liability in any event. As already indicated, it is upon such a presumption—not displaced on the facts of this case—that I would dispose of the present appeal. It is accordingly unnecessary to follow up the conclusion I have reached on the separate issue of causation by relating it to the various contributions made here by the individual respondents. *h*

[58] I would dismiss this appeal.

CHADWICK LJ.

[59] The power of the High Court to determine by whom the costs of proceedings in that court are to be paid is conferred by s 51(3) of the Supreme *j* Court Act 1981. Whether or not that power should be exercised (and, if so, in what manner) is, subject to the provisions of the 1981 Act or any other enactment and to rules of court, in the discretion of the court—see s 51(1) of that Act. An appellate court should not interfere with an order of the trial judge in respect of costs unless satisfied that he has erred in the exercise of that discretionary power.

a   [60] In the present case, following the trial of defamation proceedings brought by Mr Hamilton, an impecunious claimant, the judge dismissed an application by the defendant, Mr Al Fayed, as the successful party in those proceedings, for orders that the respondents to that application (who were amongst those who had provided funding towards Mr Hamilton's costs) should contribute towards his costs. Mr Al Fayed appeals to this court. It is submitted on his behalf that the

b   judge erred in the three respects to which Simon Brown LJ has referred: that is to say, (i) that, in exercising his discretion, he took into account factors which ought not to have been taken into account, (ii) that he failed to take into account what is described as 'the inequitable basis on which the fund was raised and the money contributed'; and (iii) that, in relation to the factors which he was entitled to and did take into account, he failed to give any sufficient indication as to the weight

c   which he attributed to each—or, indeed, whether some were weighed in favour of, or against, the orders sought.

[61] I agree with Simon Brown LJ that there is force in the criticism that the judge took into account factors which should have had no place in the exercise of discretion in which he was engaged. The judge should not have allowed the

d   factors which he listed under sub-paras (o) (Mr Al Fayed's 'discreditable' conduct after the trial) and (t) (Mr Al Fayed's state of mind indicating resentment as expressed to a journalist from The Independent after the trial) in para 115 of his judgment to affect his decision. If he intended to list those factors only to discount them, he should have said so. Nor could factor (n) (Mr Al Fayed's misuse of the witness box to make speeches and 'utterly scandalous allegations') have any

e   relevance to the question whether an order for costs should be made against those who had funded Mr Hamilton; although, as Simon Brown LJ has pointed out, that factor—if it had led to the waste of court time at the trial—might have been relevant to the amount of any such order.

[62] In those circumstances, whether or not there is also force in the other

f   criticisms made of the judgment below, it is necessary for this court to consider, for itself, whether this was a case in which an order for the payment of the successful defendant's costs should have been made against those who had funded the claimant. In order to answer that question it is necessary to address the issue which lies at the heart of Mr Al Fayed's submissions: whether fairness and justice will, in general, require that where C, for reasons of his own, funds the

g   litigation costs of A, an impecunious claimant, in defamation proceedings brought by A against B in which B is successful, C should contribute to the costs which B will (by reason of A's impecuniosity) be unable to recover under an order for costs against A alone?

[63] The starting point, as it seems to me, is to recognise that, where there is

h   tension between the principle that a party who is successful in defending a claim made against him ought not to be required to bear the costs of his defence and the principle that a claimant should not be denied access to the courts on the grounds of impecuniosity, that tension has to be resolved in favour of the second of those principles (see the observations of Millett LJ in Metalloy Supplies Ltd

j   (in liq) v M A (UK) Ltd [1997] 1 All ER 418 at 424, [1997] 1 WLR 1613 at 1619, and Abraham v Thompson [1997] 4 All ER 362 at 377). As it was put in the second of those cases:

'It may be unjust to a successful defendant to be left with unrecovered costs, but the plaintiff's freedom of access to the courts has priority ... It is preferable that a successful defendant should suffer the injustice of irrecoverable costs than that a plaintiff with a genuine claim should be prevented from pursuing it.'

It is true that the rule that the costs of litigation generally follow the event— which gives effect to the first of those principles—was described by Bingham MR in *Roache v News Group Newspapers Ltd* (1992) [1998] EMLR 161 at 166 as 'of fundamental importance in deterring plaintiffs from bringing and defendants from defending actions they are likely to lose'. But 'the risk of an adverse order for costs and consequent bankruptcy has always been regarded as a sufficient deterrent to the bringing of proceedings which are likely to fail' (see *Abraham v Thompson* [1997] 4 All ER 362 at 377). An impecunious claimant who is not deterred by the risk of bankruptcy is not to be prevented from pursuing a genuine claim.

[64] It may be said that a defendant does not choose to be sued. It may be said that, if he is obliged to incur costs in the successful defence of a claim brought against him, it is unjust that he should suffer financially because he is unable to recover those costs from an impecunious claimant. It may be said that it is unjust that a defendant should have to face a claim brought by a claimant who, if unsuccessful, will not be in a position to meet an order for costs made against him. But the courts have had to balance the risk of injustice to the defendant in those circumstances against the risk of injustice to a claimant who is denied access to the courts to pursue a genuine claim; and the scales have come down in favour of the latter.

[65] Access to the courts is one thing; effective access with the benefit of legal representation is another. That is not to suggest that those who choose to represent themselves—or who are forced by circumstances to do so—do not receive a full and fair hearing. The need to ensure, so far as possible, that whatever points can properly be made in support of the case advanced by an unrepresented claimant are identified and considered is well recognised; and judges should be, and almost universally are, scrupulous in seeking to meet that need. But it would be idle to pretend that an unrepresented claimant in complex proceedings will not be at some disadvantage against a skilled and experienced advocate. In some cases the perception of disadvantage may be so overwhelming that the unrepresented claimant will be deterred from bringing his claim at all. Defamation proceedings before a jury may be regarded as a paradigm example of such a case. It is of little consolation to an impecunious claimant to learn that he has access to the courts to pursue his claim—notwithstanding his inability to meet an order for payment of the defendant's costs if that claim is unsuccessful—if he perceives, rightly or wrongly, that the claim has no reasonable prospect of success in the absence of an 'equality of arms'. The need to promote 'equality of arms' in civil litigation, where practical, may be seen as a necessary adjunct to the need to afford access to the courts in pursuit of genuine claims. The point is recognised by the principle, set out in CPR 1.1(2)(a), that dealing with a case justly includes, so far as practical, ensuring that the parties are on an equal footing.

[66] It is important, therefore, that a court which is invited to make an order for costs against persons who have, in one way or another, assisted a claimant to obtain the legal representation which will put him on an equal footing with the defendant should recognise that, if such orders become commonplace, the form of assistance which has led to the making of the order is unlikely to be forthcoming in future cases. It is one thing to make a finite monetary contribution to the claimant's fighting fund or to contribute time and skill pro bono or under a

a no-win/no-fee arrangement; it is quite another thing to accept an unlimited liability to contribute to the defendant's costs if the claim fails.

[67] The courts have recognised the need to protect legal advisers who have acted for a claimant on a pro bono basis from exposure to orders, made under s 51(3) of the 1981 Act, for payment of the successful defendant's costs (see *Count Tolstoy-Miloslavsky v Lord Aldington* [1996] 2 All ER 556, [1996] 1 WLR 736). It is,
b I think, instructive to note the basis upon which Rose LJ rejected the application in that case:

> 'It is in the public interest ... for counsel and solicitors to act without fee. The access to justice which this can provide, for example in cases outside the scope of legal aid, confers a benefit on the public.' (See [1996] 2 All ER 556
c at 565, [1996] 1 WLR 736 at 746.)

That protection has been extended to those who act under a conditional fee arrangement which satisfies the conditions applicable to such an agreement by virtue of s 58 of the Courts and Legal Services Act 1990 (see *Hodgson v Imperial Tobacco Ltd* [1998] 2 All ER 673, [1998] 1 WLR 1056). In giving the judgment of
d the court, Lord Woolf MR said this:

> 'Just as in *Count Tolstoy-Miloslavsky*'s case it was made clear that it is in the public interest ... for counsel and solicitors to act without fee, so it must now be taken to be in the public interest ... for counsel and solicitors to act under a CFA.' (See [1998] 2 All ER 673 at 683, [1998] 1 WLR 1056 at 1067.)

e Parliament having enacted that conditional fee agreements which satisfy the applicable conditions are not to be unenforceable, notwithstanding that those providing legal representation under such agreements have a direct interest in the outcome of litigation to which they are not party, the courts must accept that it is in the public interest that legal representation should be available on no-win/
f no-fee terms. The public interest is served by facilitating access to justice by such arrangements in cases where publicly funded legal assistance is not available.

[68] It may be said that the potential injustice to the successful defendant in a case where the claimant has been represented under a conditional fee agreement is avoided—or, at the least, mitigated—by the feature that such claimants are almost invariably advised to purchase 'after the event' insurance cover against
g their own liability for the successful defendant's costs. After the event insurance cover is a sensible protection for the claimant against the risk of personal bankruptcy; and, when in place, it provides a source from which the successful defendant's costs can be met. But insurance cover is not a requirement under the 1990 Act, nor—so far as appears from the material which has been shown to
h us—is the existence of such cover a pre-condition imposed by the General Council of the Bar or the Law Society before barristers or solicitors may accept instructions under conditional fee agreements. There is no reason to think that a barrister or solicitor who accepted such instructions in circumstances in which the claimant was unable to obtain—or refused to obtain—after the event
j insurance cover would, on that ground alone, be exposed to liability for the costs of a successful defendant.

[69] Mr Al Fayed relies heavily on what is said to be the unfairness inherent in a funding arrangement which has the consequence that, if the claim succeeds, the funders will be reimbursed out of costs which the claimant will recover from him but that, if the claim fails, he will not recover his costs from the funders. But that is a feature inherent also in a conditional fee agreement. And it is accepted that

it is in the public interest to facilitate access to justice by an agreement which has that effect. Indeed, it is accepted that it remains in the public interest to fund litigation by that means notwithstanding that the other party to the proceedings—usually a defendant—is exposed to the risk of liability for the uplifted fees payable under the conditional fee agreement if the claim succeeds.

[70] For my part I can see no difference in principle, in the context of facilitating access to justice, between the lawyer who provides his services pro bono or under a conditional fee arrangement, the expert (say an accountant, a valuer or a medical practitioner) who provides his services on a no-win/no-fee basis, and the supporter who—having no skill which he can offer in kind—provides support in the form of funding to meet the fees of those who have. In each case the provision of support—whether in kind or in cash—facilitates access to justice by enabling the impecunious claimant to meet the defendant on an equal footing.

[71] It follows that I would hold that—in the interests of justice generally—fairness to the successful defendant does not, as a general rule, require that where a pure funder provides financial support towards the litigation costs of an impecunious claimant, he should contribute to the costs which that defendant will (by reason of the claimant's impecuniosity) be unable to recover under an order for costs against the claimant alone. In that context I use the expression 'pure funder' to denote a person who provides funds to meet the litigation costs of a claimant in circumstances in which he, himself, has no collateral interest in the outcome of the claim—other than as a source of reimbursement of the funds which he has provided.

[72] It follows, also, that I would dismiss this appeal. As Simon Brown LJ has pointed out, on the evidence before the judge the respondents were 'pure funders' in the sense which I have described.

HALE LJ.

[73] I am reluctantly persuaded to agree. This is a situation in which the greater good of the community must prevail over considerations of justice to the individuals concerned. If we were simply concerned with the individuals in this case, I would have concluded that the injustice to Mr Al Fayed in not making the orders he seeks was much greater than the injustice to the respondents in making them.

[74] It is unjust to Mr Al Fayed because the normal principle is that the successful party to litigation is entitled to his costs. There are at least two reasons for this. The principled reason is that a person should not have to bear the cost of vindicating his rights. In practice, he will often be considerably out of pocket in doing so, because a standard costs order will not allow him to recover all that he has had to pay his own lawyers. But the courts do not take the view taken in other countries, and in some tribunals in this country, that litigants should bear their own costs. The pragmatic reason for this is that the risk of an adverse costs order is seen as a deterrent to bringing bad claims or defending good ones (see *Roache v News Group Newspapers Ltd* (1992) [1998] EMLR 161 at 166 per Bingham MR, *T G A Chapman Ltd v Christopher* [1998] 2 All ER 873 at 883, [1998] 1 WLR 12 per Phillips LJ).

[75] The courts do accept that an impecunious individual cannot be prevented from litigating just because he may not be able to pay the other side's costs if he loses (see *Metalloy Supplies Ltd (in liq) v M A (UK) Ltd* [1997] 1 All ER 418 at 424,

a [1997] 1 WLR 1613 at 1619–1620 per Millett LJ, *Abraham v Thompson* [1997] 4 All ER 362 at 377 per Millett LJ). But it does not follow that those who assist such a person to bring a claim which he would not otherwise have been able to bring should not generally be placed in the same position in which he would have been had the resources been his. As I understand it, costs orders are not normally made against trade unions who fund their members' claims against employers,

b but it is taken for granted that they will in fact meet the costs ordered against their members. The same is true of liability insurers, because the costs are included in the cover. In both cases, the court would otherwise probably make a costs order against them unless there was a good reason not to do so (see *Singh v Observer Ltd* [1989] 2 All ER 751 at 757 per Macpherson J; exceeding the limits of cover may sometimes be a good reason, cf the *Chapman* case and *Cormack v Washbourne*

c [2000] Lloyd's Rep PN 459). This is so, even though the trade union is simply providing a service for its members and does not stand to gain anything directly from the litigation, whereas the liability insurer is protecting his own interests at least as much as those of his insured.

[76] It is quite difficult to understand why there should be any difference

d between 'pure' funders such as those in this case and trade union funders. It is true that trade unions will not fund cases which they consider unmeritorious and exercise a degree of control over the litigation they do fund. But it could well be said that 'pure' funders ought to be more discriminating in deciding what to fund. They should not be able to put their heads in the sand and support unmeritorious

e litigation at no risk of further cost to themselves just because they happen to sympathise with the unsuccessful litigant. Sympathy for a person or his cause may be understood: but we would not in other contexts regard it as any substitute for a hard-headed assessment of the legal and factual merits of his case.

[77] There is no reason in principle why those who fund other people's

f litigation should not be expected to put sums aside to cover against the risk of failure or take the risk of an adverse costs order. One can only speculate as to why those funders who have already settled with Mr Al Fayed were persuaded to do so, but it is at least possible that they recognised the justice of his claim. The only possible injustice to the funders in this case was that they were not warned of the risk. That, as the judge accepted, was not the fault of Mr Al Fayed or his advisers.

g They did everything they could to warn of their intention to make these applications. Those warnings were not passed on. Given the present uncertainty in this area of the law, they should have been.

[78] Simon Brown LJ has set out the authorities. To make a costs order against a person who is neither a party to the proceedings nor directly interested

h in the outcome is of course exceptional (see *Aiden Shipping Co Ltd v Interbulk Ltd, The Vimeira* [1986] 2 All ER 409, [1986] AC 965, *Symphony Group plc v Hodgson* [1993] 4 All ER 143, [1994] QB 179). But outside funding other than from liability insurers, trade unions or statutory sources is exceptional, in the sense that it is outside the general run of cases coming before the courts (see *T G A Chapman Ltd v*

j *Christopher* [1998] 2 All ER 873 at 881, [1998] 1 WLR 12 at 20 per Phillips LJ, *Globe Equities Ltd v Globe Legal Services Ltd* [1999] BLR 232 at 239–240 (para 21) per Morritt LJ). Only two authorities have been cited to us which clearly deal with private funders, mothers in each case, one going one way (*Cooper v Maxwell* (20 March 1992, unreported)) and one going the other (*Thistleton v Hendricks* (1992) 32 Con LR 123). There is no case dealing with a public campaign such as this.

[79] I do not find the comparison with legal aid particularly helpful. This was *a* a statutory scheme involving public funds in which Parliament had to make some difficult policy choices. It was decided that the fund should be able to recover the costs of successful litigation but should not have to pay the costs of unsuccessful litigation save in cases of hardship or on appeal. The fact that Parliament made those choices does not necessarily indicate where justice lies in cases where public funds are not involved or how the courts should exercise the open discretion *b* given them by s 51 of the Supreme Court Act 1981.

[80] Nor do I find the comparison with lawyers who offer their services free or under conditional fee agreements (CFAs) particularly helpful (see *Count Tolstoy-Miloslavsky v Lord Aldington* [1996] 2 All ER 556, [1996] 1 WLR 736, *Hodgson v Imperial Tobacco Ltd* [1998] 2 All ER 673, [1998] 1 WLR 1056). There is a distinction *c* between those who provide legal services for the litigant and those who provide the money to pay for those legal services. In the case of pro bono lawyers, this is pure altruism. They do not expect to get their costs from the other side even if they win. In the case of CFAs, there is no altruism, rather a cold calculation of the risks, but there is a risk. Parliament decided that their clients should then be able to recover not only the standard costs but also the uplift from *d* the other side. That again is a controversial policy choice. As part of the CFA package, the client normally takes out after the event insurance to cover against the risk of having to the pay the other side's costs, and that premium is also recoverable from the other side. This too is a policy choice made by Parliament.

[81] The relevance of those developments, it seems to me, is not so much in *e* their detail as in the clear evidence they give of a trend in public policy towards funding access to the courts (I would not be so presumptuous as to assume that access to the courts and access to justice were synonymous, although of course it is always the courts' aim to achieve both procedural and substantive justice). Access to the courts is a fundamental aspect of the rule of law in a democratic society, guaranteed to everyone by art 6(1) of the European Convention on *f* Human Rights and Fundamental Freedoms 1950 (as set out in Sch 1 to the Human Rights Act 1998). It should not be denied to those who cannot afford to pay the court's fees (see *R v Lord Chancellor, ex p Witham* [1997] 2 All ER 779, [1998] QB 57).

[82] But our system of adversarial justice depends heavily upon the use of lawyers to conduct litigation. We do have tribunals which are, or were originally *g* intended to be, more specialist in their knowledge of the law, more inquisitorial in their approach to the facts and thus less heavily dependent upon lawyers to assist them, where costs orders are accordingly rare or entirely unknown. But these are outside the ordinary court system. However hard the courts try to accommodate litigants in person it is unrealistic to suggest that such litigants are not often at a considerable disadvantage. It is also a disadvantage for the court. *h*

[83] It used to be thought that the answer to this problem lay in public funding for those who had a reasonable case to bring or defend but were unable to afford lawyers to help them do so. Parliament no longer takes that view. The eligibility criteria for public funding have been much restricted, as has its scope. The gap has been filled by permitting methods of funding which were previously not *j* allowed, principally conditional fee arrangements, and by encouraging greater use of other methods, such as legal expenses insurance (as in *Murphy v Young & Co's Brewery plc* [1997] 1 All ER 518, [1997] 1 WLR 1591), which were previously uncommon. Private or voluntary funding from people with no direct interest in the outcome of the case must now be seen as part of this picture. If the policy of

a the law is now to encourage such alternative methods of securing access to the courts, then the funders should not be discouraged by the fear of having to pay more. I am prepared to assume that the risk of adverse costs orders would make the task of raising such funds a great deal more difficult.

[84] If the general policy is accepted, the court cannot start drawing distinctions according to whether or not it approves of the litigation in question. It could not, *b* for example, say that it was right to fund Private Eye in defending a libel action but wrong to fund Mr Hamilton in bringing this one, or right to fund an environmental challenge to a major development but wrong to fund patients pressing for an inquiry into medical incompetence. Still less would it be proper to distinguish on the basis of whether the court approved or disapproved of the individual parties to the litigation. Justice should be blind to such things. It is *c* regrettable indeed if Mr Al Fayed has gained the impression that the outcome of his application was in any way influenced by the court's views about him personally.

[85] It might be more practicable to distinguish on the basis of whether the party funded had a reasonable prospect of success in the litigation. But experience *d* with legal aid has shown that this is difficult to predict in advance, particularly where the outcome depends upon credibility or the impression made in the witness box. Lawyers give advice on the basis that what their client tells them is honest and accurate (although they should draw attention to the difficulties which a court may have in accepting the evidence). It is unreasonable to expect funders to be any more sceptical. In practice, there has to be a general approach, *e* whether for or against making such orders, even if there may sometimes be exceptions.

[86] On balance, the arguments in favour of a general approach that 'pure' funders should not be expected also to fund the opposing party's costs outweigh the arguments in favour of a general approach that they should. There must, *f* however, be exceptional cases where it would be quite unjust not to make an order: principally where the litigation was oppressive or malicious or pursued for some other ulterior motive. The fact that it was quite unmeritorious would be powerful evidence of ulterior motive but neither a necessary nor a sufficient criterion in itself.

[87] In the end, I am driven to the view that the law must protect the people who club together to support someone who would not otherwise be able to fund his case, so that such a person is not denied access to the courts, even though the result will be unfair to the other side if he loses. The costs sanction will still be a deterrent to the actual party funded, who will stand to lose a great deal more than his case, as indeed has Mr Hamilton here.

Appeal dismissed. Permission to appeal refused.

Dilys Tausz   Barrister.

Woodland-Ferrari v UCL Group Retirement Benefits Scheme

[2002] EWHC 1354 (Ch)

CHANCERY DIVISION

FERRIS J

18 JUNE, 5 JULY 2002

Insolvency – Bankruptcy – Discharge – Release of bankruptcy debts by discharge – Fraudulent breach of trust – Whether dishonesty essential ingredient of 'fraudulent breach of trust' for purposes of exception to release of bankruptcy debts by discharge – Insolvency Act 1986, s 281(3).

By a deed made in 1990, the applicant was appointed one of the two trustees of the respondent pension scheme. The terms of the scheme contained a provision exonerating a trustee from liability in respect of any loss arising upon any investments, save where there had been 'wilful default' on the trustee's part. In 1992 both trustees were replaced by order of the court. The applicant was made bankrupt in 1993, but was discharged from bankruptcy in 1996. In 2001, following a complaint by two members of the scheme, the Pensions Ombudsman delivered a determination in which he found that the two former trustees had made certain investments in breach of trust; that there had been wilful default; that accordingly the trustees were not entitled to rely on the exoneration provision; and that, as a result of the investments made in breach of trust, the scheme had suffered a shortfall of approximately £874,000. He directed that the former trustees should pay that sum to the current trustee for the benefit of the scheme. Subsequently, a statutory demand was served on the applicant for the sum due. On his application to have the demand set aside, the applicant contended that his liability to make good his breaches of trust, all of which had been committed before his bankruptcy, were bankruptcy debts for the purposes of s 281(1)[a] of the Insolvency Act 1986, and that he was discharged from those debts by virtue of that provision. The respondent relied on s 281(3) which provided that discharge did not release the bankrupt from any bankruptcy debt which he had incurred in respect, inter alia, of any 'fraudulent breach of trust' to which he had been a party. When found in earlier provisions dealing with discharge, including ss 26 and 28 of the Bankruptcy Act 1914, the phrase 'fraudulent breach of trust' had been construed as requiring deliberate conduct involving an element of dishonesty. The respondent nevertheless contended that conduct that was unconscionable, though not dishonest, was sufficient to constitute fraudulent breach of trust for the purposes of s 281(3) of the 1986 Act. Alternatively, the respondent contended that the Ombudsman's determination established dishonesty on the part of the applicant and therefore gave rise to an issue estoppel sufficient to substantiate the statutory demand.

Held – For the purposes of s 281(3) of the 1986 Act, dishonesty was an essential ingredient of fraudulent breach of trust. There was nothing in the policy of the 1986 Act which suggested that Parliament was intending to give the words 'fraudulent breach of trust' in s 281(3) a different meaning from that which they had borne for the purposes of ss 26 and 28 of the 1914 Act and their predecessor

---

a Section 281, so far as material, is set out at [7], below

a sections. If dishonesty were not required, there would be a considerable narrowing of release from debts by comparison with the old law. That would be contrary to the legislative and social changes which underlay the 1986 Act, namely the abandonment of a retributive approach and the giving of a new emphasis to rehabilitation. Furthermore, the narrowing would be of uncertain, although probably very substantial, extent since it was arguable that virtually all breaches

b of trust involved an element of unconscionable conduct. In the instant case, the Ombudsman's decision had not given rise to an issue estoppel which established that the applicant was guilty of fraudulent breaches of trust. 'Wilful default' was not precisely the same as 'fraudulent breach of trust' so that a finding of the first necessarily involved a finding of the second as well, and the Ombudsman's decision had not unequivocally established conduct of the requisite character.

c Accordingly, the application would be granted and the statutory demand set aside (see [42], [43], [48]–[50], [68]–[70], below).

Re Freeman, ex p Freeman (1890) 7 Morr 38 and Re Waldron (a bankrupt), ex p the bankrupt v Official Receiver (1985) 129 SJ 171 applied.

d **Notes**
For debts and liabilities for which discharge is no release, see 3(2) *Halsbury's Laws* (4th edn) (2002 reissue) para 643.

For the Insolvency Act 1986, s 281, see 4 *Halsbury's Statutes* (4th edn) (1998 reissue) 947.

e **Cases referred to in judgment**
Armitage v Nurse [1997] 2 All ER 705, [1998] Ch 241, [1997] 3 WLR 1046, CA.
Castle Mail Packets Co, ex p, Re Payne (1886) 18 QBD 154, CA.
Davy Bros Ltd v Garrett (1878) 7 Ch D 473, CA.
Debtor (No 1 of 1987, Lancaster), Re a, ex p the debtor v Royal Bank of Scotland [1989] 2 All ER 46, [1989] 1 WLR 271, CA.

f *Debtor (No 784 of 1991), Re a, ex p the debtor v IRC* [1992] 3 All ER 376, [1992] Ch 554, [1992] 3 WLR 119.
Derry v Peek (1889) 14 App Cas 337, [1886–90] All ER Rep 1, HL.
Edgcome, Re, ex p Edgcome [1902] 2 KB 403, [1900–3] All ER Rep 862, CA.
Freeman, Re, ex p Freeman (1890) 7 Morr 38, DC.

g *Kitchen v Royal Air Forces Association* [1958] 2 All ER 241, [1958] 1 WLR 563, CA.
Perrins v Bellamy [1899] 1 Ch 797, CA.
Royal Brunei Airlines Sdn Bhd v Tan [1995] 3 All ER 97, [1995] 2 AC 378, [1995] 3 WLR 64, PC.
Smith v Braintree DC [1989] 3 All ER 897, [1990] 2 AC 215, [1989] 3 WLR 1317, HL; rvsg

h sub nom *Smith (a bankrupt), Re, ex p Braintree DC v The Bankrupt* [1988] 3 All ER 203, [1988] Ch 457, [1988] 2 WLR 327.
Twinsectra Ltd v Yardley [2002] UKHL 12, [2002] 2 All ER 377, [2002] 2 WLR 802.
Vickery, Re, Vickery v Stephens [1931] 1 Ch 572, [1931] All ER Rep 562.
Waldron (a bankrupt), Re, ex p the bankrupt v Official Receiver [1985] CA Transcript 28,

j (1985) 129 SJ 171.
Walker v Stones [2000] 4 All ER 412, [2001] QB 902, [2001] 2 WLR 623, CA.

Cases also cited or referred to in skeleton arguments
Mander v Evans [2001] 3 All ER 811, [2001] 1 WLR 2378.
Masters v Leaver [2000] BPIR 284, CA.
Seifert v Pensions Ombudsman, Lynch v Pensions Ombudsman [1997] 1 All ER 214; rvsd [1997] 4 All ER 947, CA.

Application

The applicant, Robert Woodland-Ferrari (Mr Woodland), applied to set aside a
statutory demand in the sum of £877,887.03 served on him by the respondent,
UCL Group Retirement Benefits Scheme. The facts are set out in the judgment.

Andreas Gledhill (instructed by *Lawrence Graham*) for Mr Woodland.
Mark Arnold (instructed by *Taylor Joynson Garrett*) for the respondent.

Cur adv vult

5 July 2002. The following judgment was delivered.

FERRIS J.

[1] This application to set aside a statutory demand has been transferred to me
from Guildford County Court under r 7.11(2) of the Insolvency Rules 1986,
SI 1986/1925 by a consent order dated 23 April 2002. Accordingly it comes before
me for hearing at first instance instead of coming to a High Court judge only
upon appeal, as is more usual. The reason for dealing with the matter in this way
was the perceived importance and difficulty of the point in issue.

[2] The statutory demand in question is for the sum of £877,887·03, being the
amount, including interest, said to be due from the applicant, Mr Robert
Woodland-Ferrari (Mr Woodland) by reason of a determination of the Pensions
Ombudsman dated 29 August 2001.

[3] The essential facts can be stated quite shortly. Mr Woodland and a Mr Lewis
were appointed trustees of a pension scheme known as the UCL Group Retirement
Plan (the scheme) by a deed dated 20 February 1990. They ceased to be trustees
when they were replaced by GMBC Pension Ltd (now Abbey National Pension
Trustees Ltd, which I shall refer to as ANPTL) by an order of the High Court
made on 9 December 1992. In the intervening period Mr Woodland and Mr Lewis
were the only trustees of the scheme.

[4] After Mr Woodland and Mr Lewis had been removed as trustees two
members of the scheme, Mr Robson and Mr Boswell, made a complaint to the
Pensions Ombudsman about the loss or diminution in the value of the assets of
the scheme during the period that Mr Woodland and Mr Lewis were trustees.
Mr Robson also made complaints against a company named Acorn Pensions and
Financial Services (Acorn) which acted as adviser to and administrator of the
scheme. The Pensions Ombudsman delivered his determination on 29 August
2001. He found that Acorn had been guilty of maladministration in certain
respects but that this maladministration had not caused Mr Robson injustice. He
found also that certain investments had been made by Mr Woodland and
Mr Lewis in breach of trust and that neither of them was entitled to rely upon an
exoneration clause contained in the scheme to excuse personal liability.

[5] As to quantum, the Pensions Ombudsman found that the shortfall suffered
by the scheme as a result of the making of investments in breach of trust,
including interest down to the date of the determination, was £874,482·33. He
directed that Mr Woodland and Mr Lewis should between them pay this sum to
ANPTL for the benefit of the scheme within 28 days of the date of the
determination. Neither of them has paid this sum or any part of it. Interest for
the period between 29 August 2001 and 28 September 2001 (the date of the
statutory demand) brings the amount due to the £877,887·03 referred to in
the statutory demand.

[6] If this were all Mr Woodland would have no defence to the claim made in the statutory demand (see s 151 of the Pension Schemes Act 1993, particularly sub-s (5)). What is said to make the difference is that Mr Woodland was made bankrupt on 7 June 1993. He was discharged from bankruptcy on 19 September 1996. The breaches of trust giving rise to the liability found by the Pensions Ombudsman were all committed before the date of the bankruptcy order. Accordingly he claims that he was discharged from all the bankruptcy debts, which included his liability to make good his breaches of trust, by virtue of s 281(1) of the Insolvency Act 1986.

[7] In these proceedings it has not been disputed that Mr Woodland's liability for breach of trust was part of his bankruptcy debts for the purposes of s 281(1). But it is argued that Mr Woodland is not discharged from this particular liability by reason of s 281(3), which so far as material provides: 'Discharge does not release the bankrupt from any bankruptcy debt which he incurred in respect of … any fraud or fraudulent breach of trust to which he was a party.'

[8] The only material which is relied upon in these proceedings in support of the contention that Mr Woodland's liability in respect of the debt referred to in the statutory demand was incurred in respect of 'fraud or fraudulent breach of trust' is the determination of the Pensions Ombudsman.

[9] On these facts two main questions arise, namely: (a) What are the ingredients of 'fraudulent breach of trust' for the purpose of s 281(3)? In particular does dishonesty have to be shown? (b) Are these ingredients proved to exist by the Pensions Ombudsman's determination? In addition there is a question on the form of the statutory demand which may need to be determined. I will come to this at the end of this judgment.

What are the ingredients of 'fraudulent breach of trust'?

[10] It is not submitted that the Pensions Ombudsman's determination establishes actual fraud on the part of Mr Woodland in the *Derry v Peek* sense (see *Derry v Peek* (1889) 14 App Cas 337, [1886–90] All ER Rep 1). It is for this reason that I am concerned only with the limb of s 281(3) which refers to 'fraudulent breach of trust'.

[11] In order to elucidate the meaning of this expression I was referred to the old law from 1869 onwards. One of the matters which I shall have to consider is whether this, and the decisions under it, constitute a guide to the meaning of a provision in the 1986 Act. But first I must explain what emerges from the old law.

[12] The first piece of legislation to which I was referred was the Bankruptcy Act 1869. Section 48 of this Act gave the court a discretion, on the application of the bankrupt, to discharge the bankrupt from bankruptcy provided certain conditions were fulfilled. Section 49 provided, so far as material:

> 'An order of discharge shall not release the bankrupt from any debt or liability incurred by means of any fraud or breach of trust … but it shall release the bankrupt from all other debts provable under the bankruptcy with the exception of [certain specified debts].'

[13] On the face of it the s 49 release did not extend to any debt incurred by reason of any breach of trust, whether or not it was occasioned by fraud. However there does not appear to be any decision in which this point was put to the test.

[14] The Bankruptcy Act 1883 adopted a somewhat more elaborate scheme in respect of discharge from bankruptcy. By s 28 provision was made, as before, for

a bankrupt to apply to the court for discharge. It was, however, specifically provided that on the hearing of the application the court was to take into account a report of the Official Receiver in respect of the bankrupt's affairs. Section 28(3) contained a list of eight facts which were to be taken into account. These included, in para (h): 'That the bankrupt has been guilty of any fraud or fraudulent breach of trust.' On proof of any of the enumerated facts the court was obliged either to refuse the application, or to suspend its operation for a specified time or to attach conditions to it.

[15] Release from bankruptcy debts was dealt with by s 30 of the 1883 Act. This begins with a provision specifying certain debts which were not released by an order of discharge. In particular the latter part of s 30(1) provides:

'An order of discharge shall not release the bankrupt from any debt or liability incurred by means of any fraud or fraudulent breach of trust to which he was a party, nor from any debt or liability whereof he has obtained forbearance by any fraud to which he was a party.'

Subsection (2) then provides that an order of discharge 'shall release the bankrupt from all other debts provable in bankruptcy'.

[16] I was referred to two decisions under these provisions of the 1883 Act. The first was *Ex p Castle Mail Packets Co, Re Payne* (1886) 18 QBD 154. This was an appeal by a creditor against an order granting two bankrupts a suspended order of discharge. The creditor contended that no order of discharge should have been granted because, amongst other things, the bankrupts had committed, in the slightly tentative words of counsel for the creditor, 'a fraudulent breach of trust, or, at any rate, a fraud'.

[17] Lord Esher MR graphically described (at 157–158) the conduct complained of as follows:

'When this application for a discharge was made the first thing shewn by the opposing creditors was that the bankrupts had continued to trade after knowing themselves to be insolvent. That is no light offence. The opposing creditors also shewed that the bankrupts, acting as brokers, had received money from time to time for freights largely in excess of any deduction which they were entitled to make; that they did not merely neglect to send in accounts to their principals, but that they sent in misleading accounts, and that before doing so they had misappropriated to their own private use money for which they ought to have accounted; and that, therefore, the inevitable inference was that they had knowingly misused these moneys for which they ought to have accounted; that they knew they had done wrong, and that they sent in these misleading accounts in order to conceal what they had thus done. And, still worse, when they did send in a final account, in order to get rid of that which they knew to be a valid claim against them, they knowingly, falsely, and wickedly asserted that they had a counter-claim, which they knew to be wholly unfounded. What offences, then, have they been guilty of? Besides trading after they knew they were insolvent, they have for their own purposes, and in order to conceal a fraud, made an improper and fraudulent entry in their books. I will not say that they have been in the strict sense of the words guilty of a fraudulent breach of trust, but any more fraudulent conduct in business as between principal and agent I cannot conceive. I come, therefore, to the clear conclusion that these bankrupts have been guilty of three offences against the Bankruptcy Act: by *a* trading after they knew that they were insolvent; by sending in misleading accounts and making misleading entries in their books; and by committing a wicked fraud upon their employers. Under these circumstances the bankrupt Payne applied for his discharge, and in my opinion the only proper course is to refuse the application altogether.'

b [18] The other two members of the Court of Appeal, Lindley and Lopes LJJ, agreed with Lord Esher MR. Lindley LJ said (at 159):

c 'I am compelled to say that he has been guilty of a gross fraud. Whether technically there has been a "fraudulent breach of trust" may be open to question. I am inclined to think that a man who, knowing that he has a balance to pay over to his employers, embezzles it, may fairly be said to be guilty of fraudulent conduct as a trustee. But, at any rate, it is clear that he comes within sub-s. 3(h) of s. 28 as having been guilty of fraud. In my opinion, therefore, the order of discharge ought to be refused.'

d [19] The second case under the 1883 Act to which I was referred was *Re Freeman, ex p Freeman* (1890) 7 Morr 38, decided by a Divisional Court consisting of Cave and AL Smith JJ. There a county court judge had refused an order of discharge on the ground that the bankrupt was guilty of a fraudulent preference, was guilty of a fraudulent breach of trust and had sold his business before the date of the receiving order without the consent of his creditors. As to the breach of trust, it *e* appears that the bankrupt had used a sum of £130, which was held by him as a trustee, for the purposes of his own business. As to this Cave J said (at 44–45):

f 'The main ground for alleging that he has been guilty of a breach of trust at all was the statement which he himself made in his previous affidavit, that he had been advised by his solicitor that he had been guilty of a breach of trust; that the consequences might be distressing to him, and that he therefore desired to repay the money which he had so diverted from its original purpose. Now all that is perfectly consistent with the breach of trust not having been in any sense a fraudulent breach of trust. The difference between the two things, of course, is very considerable. A man is guilty of a *g* breach of trust whenever he applies trust money to any purpose which is not warranted by the deed which creates the trust, and breaches of trust of that kind undoubtedly do exist to a considerable extent, leading to civil remedies against the trustees but not necessarily involving any dishonour in them or any conduct which in a moral point of view can be said to be blameable. A trustee is very frequently induced at the solicitation of the *cestui que trust* to *h* consent to invest the trust funds, for the purpose of getting a higher rate of interest, in a class of security which is not warranted by the deed of trust, for which trustees not unfrequently are made to pay out of their own pocket. But no one goes the length of saying that if a thing of that kind is proved to have existed in the case of a man who afterwards became bankrupt, that *j* ought to be taken into account in considering whether he ought or ought not to have his discharge.'

He then referred to the evidence of a Mrs Harvey, a beneficiary of the trust, which had not been before the county court, to the effect that the breach of trust had been committed with her knowledge and acquiesced in by her. He went on (at 45–46):

'I think, therefore, the learned County Court Judge, while warranted in coming to the conclusion that there was a breach of trust, was not warranted in coming to the conclusion that the breach of trust had been fraudulent. That no doubt is the point which weighs most heavily against the debtor in this case. A breach of trust is always a serious matter in a civil point of view, but when in addition it becomes a fraudulent breach of trust it assumes a criminal aspect, and is undoubtedly a matter of serious consequence which ought properly to be taken into consideration by the judge when he is considering an application for discharge.'

[20] The 1883 Act was replaced by the Bankruptcy Act 1914, the material parts of which were amended by the Bankruptcy (Amendment) Act 1926. Discharge was dealt with by s 26 of the 1914 Act, the general scheme of which was similar to s 28 of the 1883 Act. The list of facts proof of which limits the discretion of the court to grant the order has been somewhat expanded, from 8 items to 12, the last of them being '(l) That the bankrupt has been guilty of any fraud or fraudulent breach of trust'. This reproduces without change the wording of the equivalent provision in the 1883 Act.

[21] Release from bankruptcy debts was governed by s 28 of the 1914 Act, as amended, which was, for all practical purposes, in the same terms as s 30 of the 1883 Act.

[22] A further change in the law was made by the Insolvency Act 1976, which greatly enlarged the scope for discharging bankrupts, in particular by providing for automatic or semi-automatic discharge in a wide range of cases. Discharge under the provisions for automatic discharge after a period of time was to have the same effect as if the court had made an absolute order of discharge on the relevant date under s 26 of the 1914 Act (see s 7(2) of the 1976 Act).

[23] I was referred to one decision under s 26 of the 1914 Act, namely that of the Court of Appeal consisting of Oliver and Neill LJJ and Sir David Cairns in the case of *Re Waldron (a bankrupt), ex p the bankrupt v Official Receiver* [1985] CA Transcript 28 given on 30 January 1985. The decision is unreported, except very briefly at (1985) 129 SJ 171, but I was provided with a full transcript of the judgments. The appeal was from a decision of Mr Registrar Dewhurst who had refused a bankrupt an order of discharge on a number of grounds, including a finding that he had been guilty of fraudulent breach of trust. The bankrupt did not seek to reverse the registrar's refusal to make an order of discharge, but he sought an order setting aside the finding of guilt of fraudulent breach of trust.

[24] Early on in his judgment Oliver LJ explained the importance of the finding of fraudulent breach of trust, saying:

'The significance of that is emphasised by the provisions of s 28 of the Bankruptcy Act 1914 which deals with the effects of discharge. The effect of the discharge, as appears from sub-ss (1), (2) of that section, is that the bankrupt is released from all indebtedness provable in the bankruptcy except for a number of specified exceptions, and (b) is as follows: "from any debt or liability incurred by means of any fraud or fraudulent breach of trust to which he was a party ..." So one can see that the finding against the bankrupt which is contained in the order I have recited is a very important one from the bankrupt's point of view.'

[25] The facts relied upon in support of the finding of fraudulent breach of trust in *Re Waldron* were that the bankrupt, who had carried on the business of

insurance broker in partnership with another, had (i) failed to pay over a sum of £32,000 which had been paid to him for the purpose of being invested in a policy of some sort with an insurance company; and (ii) had failed to pay over to insurers some £17,000 received by him in respect of the premiums due under motor insurance policies issued by the insurers.

[26] In his decision Mr Registrar Dewhurst had cited what was said by Cave J in *Re Freeman* (1890) 7 Morr 38 from which he held that it followed—

'that in order to prove fraudulent breach of trust the conduct of the bankrupt must have been (i) blameable in a moral sense, (ii) against the wishes and without the knowledge of the persons to whom the money was due, and (iii) with a criminal aspect.'

As to the case before him he concluded:

'I accept [counsel's] submission that the bankrupt's conduct was not deliberate and that he was not guilty of dishonesty, but it seems to me plain from the evidence that it meets the test which I conceive to be the right one.'

On the appeal the contention was that, on the test propounded by Cave J, it was impossible for the bankrupt to have been guilty of fraudulent breach of trust if, as the registrar had held, his conduct was not deliberate and he was not guilty of dishonesty.

[27] In seeking to uphold the registrar's decision, counsel for the Official Receiver submitted that, although the word 'fraud' in s 26 of the 1914 Act did not mean anything other than common law fraud, the words 'fraudulent breach of trust' must mean something different because they appear in the section as an alternative to 'fraud' simpliciter. He relied upon cases under s 26 of the Limitation Act 1939 in which the expression 'fraudulent breach of trust' had been given a meaning which extended to equitable fraud and covers conduct which 'having regard to some special relationship between the two parties concerned, is an unconscionable thing for the one to do towards the other' (see *Kitchen v Royal Air Forces Association* [1958] 2 All ER 241 at 249, [1958] 1 WLR 563 at 572–573 per Lord Evershed MR).

[28] As to this attempted reliance upon the Limitation Act authorities Oliver LJ said:

'It does not seem to me that one can really treat the two sections as being pari materia, and as it seems to me the true construction of the section with which we are concerned here, namely s 26 of the 1914 Act, is that which is contained in the judgment of Cave J in [*Re Freeman*].'

[29] Oliver LJ expressed his conclusion in *Re Waldron* as follows:

'What [counsel] has submitted is that when the learned judge, Cave J ((1890) 7 Morr 38 at 46), used the expression "but when in addition it becomes a fraudulent breach of trust it assumes a criminal aspect", he was not there meaning that the fraud involved dishonesty or was equivalent to a crime but merely that it was something more serious than a mere civil wrong, and that what he was indicating was what indeed the learned registrar understood by the phrase, namely that criminal aspect meant something that was not in fact criminal but which might be considered otherwise blameworthy in some respect, or unconscionable. For my part I find myself quite unable to accept that submission as being a correct analysis of what Cave J was saying in the judgment under consideration. In my judgment, where one is looking at a case of this sort, but particularly having regard to the very serious consequences which are involved in the finding of fraud or fraudulent breach of trust in the 1914 Act, one has to interpret the phrase strictly and in its ordinary sense, and in my judgment the finding of the learned registrar that the bankrupt was not acting deliberately and that he was not guilty of dishonesty is in itself quite contrary to the concept of his being guilty of a fraudulent breach of trust, though undoubtedly he was guilty of a breach of trust. In those circumstances it seems to me inevitable that the appeal must be allowed and that the order asked for in the notice of appeal should be made, namely the same order as the learned registrar made but with the omission of the critical finding (1).'

[30] Neill LJ agreed with Oliver LJ. Sir David Cairns also agreed but expressed his own reasons as follows:

'I have no doubt that in s 26(3)(1) of the Bankruptcy Act 1914 the expression "fraudulent breach of trust" means breach of trust which, among other things, is dishonest. In common parlance and in common law the words "fraudulent" and "fraud" certainly connote dishonesty. There are other contexts in which conduct which has not been held to be dishonest has nevertheless been held to be fraudulent. That is true of the Limitation Act 1939 in connection with concealment by fraud—s 26 of that Act. And indeed it is true of the 1914 Act itself in relation to the expression "fraudulent preference". But in my judgment there is no reason for giving an exceptional and extended meaning to the words "fraud" and "fraudulent", or either of them, in s 26 of the 1914 Act. My reasons may be summarised as follows: (1) No positive ground is advanced for giving any extended meaning to the words. (2) The consequence of a finding of fraudulent breach of trust are very serious to a bankrupt, because under s 28(1)(b) of the Act any debt or liability incurred by such a breach is excepted from the release effected in general by an order of discharge. (3) In s 26(3) there are set out 12 types of fact on the ground of which the court may refuse or suspend an order for discharge. Many of the facts so listed are of such a character as would usually amount to unconscionable conduct, but it is only in connection with fact (1), fraud or fraudulent breach of trust, that debts incurred in connection therewith are picked out as being an absolute bar to discharge. (4) The judgment of Cave J in [*Re Freeman*] supports the natural and ordinary interpretation of the word in this section.'

[31] I was at one stage a little puzzled by Sir David Cairns' third reason. Section 26 does not, so far as I can see, make a finding of fraudulent breach of trust an absolute bar to discharge. But I think he must have been considering the joint effect of ss 26 and 28, which is that any discharge from bankruptcy is of no substantive effect in relation to debts attributable to fraudulent breach of trust. Moreover, although ' fraudulent breach of trust' does not mean the same thing in s 26 of the 1914 Act as it meant in s 26 of the 1939 Act, conduct which is found to amount to 'fraudulent breach of trust' for the purposes of s 26 of the 1914 Act must be within the scope of 'fraudulent breach of trust' for the purposes of s 26 of the 1939 Act. Accordingly a finding of fraudulent breach of trust for the purposes of the 1914 Act means that the bankrupt is indefinitely liable for the consequential debt, regardless of any lapse of time.

[32] In the light of these authorities there can be no doubt that for conduct to amount to fraudulent breach of trust within the meaning of s 26 of the 1914 Act and its predecessor there must have been deliberate conduct involving an element of dishonesty.

[33] In relation to the present case, however, the relevant legislation is not the 1914 Act as amended but the 1986 Act. This Act, as is well known, made a number of fundamental changes in the law relating to bankruptcy. In particular, in relation to matters relevant to the present case, the old machinery for discharge was swept away. In most cases (the exception being cases of a second or subsequent bankruptcy within a 15-year period which fall within s 279(1)(a)) no court order for discharge is now required. Discharge is automatic at the expiration of the specified relevant period unless the Official Receiver applies successfully under s 279(3). The commission of a fraudulent breach of trust is therefore now irrelevant to discharge from bankruptcy.

[34] Under the regime established by the 1986 Act it is, however, still necessary for the legislation to prescribe the effect of discharge. This is done by s 281. While this is very different in form from s 28 of the 1914 Act it retains many of the old concepts. Thus the section prescribes (in sub-ss (2)–(6)) a number of debts from which the bankrupt is not released by discharge. The list is more extensive than the corresponding list in s 28 of the 1914 Act, but sub-s (3) deals with debts incurred in respect of fraud or fraudulent breach of trust in language which is substantially indistinguishable from the equivalent part of s 28 of the 1914 Act. Subject to these exceptions discharge has the effect of releasing the bankrupt from all 'bankruptcy debts' (see s 281(1)). This is a more extensive release than that which was provided for by s 28 of the 1914 Act, since 'bankruptcy debts' are defined in s 382 more widely than 'debts provable in bankruptcy' which were the only debts from which the bankrupt was released by s 28(2). This difference is not material in the present case, but it probably explains why the exceptions to the release provided for by s 281(1) are more extensive than the exceptions to the release provided for by the old s 28.

[35] On this application the first question which I have to consider is whether 'fraudulent breach of trust' in s 281(3) of the 1986 Act has the same meaning as the same expression in s 26 of the 1914 Act. It was contended on behalf of Mr Woodland that it does and that dishonesty must therefore be established. In support of the statutory demand, however, it was argued that it has a more extended meaning, similar to that unsuccessfully contended for in *Re Waldron (a bankrupt), ex p the bankrupt v Official Receiver* [1985] CA Transcript 28, (1985) 129 SJ 171 so that conduct which is unconscionable, though not dishonest, is enough.

[36] In support of this latter argument Mr Mark Arnold, seeking to uphold the statutory demand, relied upon two main contentions. First he said that all the old authorities concerned the meaning of 'fraudulent breach of trust' only in relation to the power of the court to make an order for discharge, not in relation to the effect of the statutory release. In terms of the 1914 Act they are authorities on s 26, not on s 28. It is s 28, not s 26, which was the predecessor of s 281(3). Secondly he said that the 1986 Act represents a new code and the cases decided on the previous legislation provide no guidance as to its true construction.

[37] As to the first contention, it is true that the applications leading to the authorities I have mentioned were applications for discharge, not attempts to enforce a bankruptcy debt against a discharged bankrupt. But where one has the same expression used in a single statute in sections which not only closely follow each other as a matter of arrangement but deal with the same general subject

matter, the strong likelihood is that parliament intended that expression to have the same meaning in each case.

[38] Moreover the Court of Appeal in *Re Waldron* plainly assumed that the registrar's finding of fraudulent breach of trust in the application for discharge under s 26 would prevent the bankrupt being released from the relevant debts under s 28. If this had not been so there would have been little purpose in the appeal in *Re Waldron*. The registrar had, in that case, refused an order for discharge on a number of grounds besides fraudulent breach of trust and there was no challenge to his decision on these other grounds. Oliver LJ, with whose reasons the other two members of the court agreed, expressly referred to s 28 early on in his judgment and Sir David Cairns specifically based the second of his own reasons on s 28(3).

[39] I therefore reject the argument that the pre-1986 authorities provide no guidance as to the meaning of 'fraudulent breach of trust' in the context of a provision denying a discharged bankrupt a release from certain debts.

[40] As to the second contention, it is true that the 1986 Act is an entirely new code in relation to the 1914 Act. In *Smith v Braintree DC* [1989] 3 All ER 241, [1990] 2 AC 215 a question was raised as to the power of the court to restrain proceedings against a bankrupt under s 285(1) of the 1986 Act. The decision of the Court of Appeal in *Re Edgcome, ex p Edgcome* [1902] 2 KB 403, [1900–3] All ER Rep 862 was that the equivalent legislation at that time precluded the debtor's application and this was applied by the High Court in *Smith's* case (see *Smith (a bankrupt), Re, ex p Braintree DC v The Bankrupt* [1988] 3 All ER 203, [1988] Ch 457). On appeal to the House of Lords it was held that *Re Edgcome* and a case which preceded it were wrongly decided. But Lord Jauncey of Tullichettle, with whom the rest of their Lordships agreed, gave a second reason for allowing the appeal. He said ([1989] 3 All ER 897 at 907, [1990] 2 AC 215 at 237–238):

'... the 1986 Act, although re-enacting many provisions from earlier statutes, contains a good deal of fresh material derived from the Insolvency Act 1985. In particular, the legislation now emphasises the importance of the rehabilitation of the individual insolvent, it provides for automatic discharge from bankruptcy in many cases and it abolishes mandatory public examinations as well as enabling a bankrupt to be discharged without public examination. Thus, not only has the legislative approach to individual bankruptcy altered since the mid-nineteenth century, but social views as to what conduct involves delinquency, as to punishment and as to the desirability of imprisonment have drastically changed. It is, for example, most unlikely that anyone today analysing the six exceptions in s 4 of the 1869 Act would conclude, as did Lord Hatherley LC in 1871, that they all involved an element of delinquency. In these circumstances, I feel justified in construing s 285 of the 1986 Act as a piece of new legislation without regard to nineteenth century authorities or similar provisions of repealed Bankruptcy Acts, an approach which was, in my view, correctly adopted by the Court of Appeal in *Re a debtor (No 1 of 1987, Lancaster)* [1989] 2 All ER 46, [1989] 1 WLR 271. So construed, I have no doubt that, for reasons which I have already given, the words "or other legal process" in s 285(1) covered the proceedings in the magistrates' court for the issue of a warrant of committal, and that accordingly the registrar had jurisdiction to stay those proceedings.'

[41] What was said in *Smith's* case does not, however, lead to the result that pre-1986 authority must always be disregarded in construing the 1986 Act.

Hoffmann J dealt with the matter in what has become a well-known passage in his judgment in *Re a debtor (No 784 of 1991), ex p the debtor v IRC* [1992] 3 All ER 376 at 378, [1992] Ch 554 at 558–559. Having referred to *Smith's* case and other authorities he said:

'Those authorities show that, in approaching the language of the 1986 Act, one must pay particular attention to the purposes and policies of its own provisions and be wary of simply carrying over uncritically meanings which had been given to similar words in the earlier Act. It does not, however, mean that the language of the new Act comes to one entirely free of any of the intellectual freight which was carried by words and phrases in earlier bankruptcy or other legislation. Decisions of the court on the meanings of phrases used in Acts of Parliament may come in the course of time to give them the quality of terms of art which Parliament may well be assumed to have intended them to bring with them when used in subsequent legislation. In s 265, for example, terms such as "domiciled", "personally present", "ordinarily resident", have had attributed to them, both in the context of bankruptcy and in that of civil procedure generally, a wealth of refined construction which it is difficult to suppose Parliament did not intend equally to apply when those words were used in the 1986 Act. Is there any reason why that should not apply equally to the words "has carried on business"? There does not seem to me to be anything in the policy of the new Act which suggests that in this provision Parliament was intending to give those words a different meaning from those which they had been held to bear under the 1914 Act.'

[42] Applying the test which is implicit in the last two sentences of the passage quoted from Hoffmann J's judgment, I ask myself whether there is anything in the policy of the 1986 Act which suggests that in s 281(3) of the Act Parliament was intending to give the words 'fraudulent breach of trust' a different meaning from that which they had for the purposes of ss 26 and 28 of the 1914 Act and their predecessor sections. In my judgment this question must be answered in the negative.

[43] The main changes in legislative approach and social views as to the relevant conduct in respect of the law of bankruptcy which occurred between 1914 and 1986 were the abandonment of a retributive approach and the giving of a new emphasis to rehabilitation. This explains why there is no direct equivalent of s 26 of the 1914 Act in the 1986 Act. Discharge from bankruptcy as the result of the exercise of discretion by the court has now in most cases been replaced by automatic discharge after the lapse of the prescribed time. However s 281 still provides, as had s 28 of the 1914 Act, exceptions to the scope of the release from debts consequential upon discharge. One would expect, however, that the effect of the new climate would be to limit the scope of the exceptions rather than to enlarge them.

[44] This expectation is, I think, supported by the fact that s 281 begins by providing the release from debts, subject to exceptions, while s 28 had begun by listing the cases in which discharge did not release the bankrupt and only later provided for a release in respect of all other debts. I do not consider that the fact that s 281(2)–(7) contain a rather longer list of exceptional cases than s 28 had contained is of significance. The additional cases referred to in sub-ss (4) and (5) (fines, personal injury damages and debts arising from orders made in family proceedings) are, I think, included because of the widening in the extent of the

general release by the reference to 'bankruptcy debts' instead of to 'debts provable in the bankruptcy'.

[45] Mr Arnold argued that 'fraudulent breach of trust' must mean something different from 'fraud' because it appears in s 281(3) as an alternative to fraud. However the same juxtaposition appeared in ss 26 and 28 of the 1914 Act and this same argument was raised by counsel in *Re Waldron (a bankrupt), ex p the bankrupt v Official Receiver* [1985] CA Transcript 28, (1985) 129 SJ 171 and rejected by the Court of Appeal. In my view there is no substance in it.

[46] The reason why s 281(3) refers to both fraud and fraudulent breach of trust appears, I think, from the judgment of Millett LJ in *Armitage v Nurse* [1997] 2 All ER 705 at 710–711, [1998] Ch 241 at 250–251 where he said:

> 'The common law knows no generalised tort of fraud. *Derry v Peek* ((1889) 14 App Cas 337, [1886–90] All ER Rep 1) was an action for damages for deceit, that is to say, for fraudulent misrepresentation. In such a case fraud must be proved by showing that the false representation was made knowingly, that is to say, without an honest belief in its truth; or recklessly, that is to say, not caring whether it was true or false. Care needs to be taken when these concepts are applied not to a representation but to a breach of trust. Breaches of trust are of many different kinds. A breach of trust may be deliberate or inadvertent; it may consist of an actual misappropriation or misapplication of the trust property or merely of an investment or other dealing which is outside the trustees' powers; it may consist of a failure to carry out a positive obligation of the trustees or merely of a want of skill and care on their part in the management of the trust property; it may be injurious to the interests of the beneficiaries or be actually to their benefit. By consciously acting beyond their powers (as, for example, by making an investment which they know to be unauthorised) the trustees may deliberately commit a breach of trust; but if they do so in good faith and in the honest belief that they are acting in the interest of the beneficiaries their conduct is not fraudulent. So a deliberate breach of trust is not necessarily fraudulent. Hence the remark famously attributed to Selwyn LJ by Lindley MR in the course of argument in *Perrins v Bellamy* [1899] 1 Ch 797 at 798: "My old master, the late Lord Justice Selwyn, used to say, 'The main duty of a trustee is to commit *judicious* breaches of trust' ..."'

[47] It appears to me that the use of the concept of 'fraudulent breach of trust' in addition to that of fraud shows an appreciation by the draftsman of the need for care later articulated by Millett LJ.

[48] The interpretation of 'fraudulent breach of trust' which was urged upon me in this case would, if accepted, result in a considerable narrowing of the release from debts by comparison with the old law. This seems to me to be contrary to the legislative and social changes which underlie the 1986 Act.

[49] Further the narrowing which was contended for would, in my view, be of uncertain, although probably very substantial, extent. If the requirement of an element of dishonesty, or 'criminal aspect', is no longer an essential ingredient of fraudulent breach of trust, where, if anywhere, is a dividing line to be drawn between these breaches of trust which are fraudulent and those which are not? Mr Arnold suggested that the test should be one of unconscionability. But it seems to me to be arguable that all, or virtually all, breaches of trust involve an element of unconscionable conduct. A trustee acts in breach of trust when he deals with trust property in a manner inconsistent with the terms of the trust,

even though he would be fully entitled to deal with the property in that way if the trust property were his own, as indeed it is in the eyes of the common law. In such a case equity intervenes because it regards the trustee as behaving unconscionably when he deals with the trust property as if it were his own.

[50] I see no reason for regarding 'fraudulent breach of trust' in s 281(3) of the 1986 Act as meaning anything different from what the same expression meant in s 28 of the 1914 Act. Dishonesty therefore remains an essential ingredient.

Is dishonesty proved by the Pensions Ombudsman's determination?

[51] As I have already observed, the only material relied upon as establishing fraudulent breach of trust in the present case is the findings of the Pensions Ombudsman in his determination. It was accepted that an issue estoppel would be capable of arising from those findings, so that if the Ombudsman has found a fraudulent breach of trust that would be sufficient to substantiate the statutory demand. The question is whether the Ombudsman made such a finding.

[52] The starting point must, I think, be to consider what functions the Pensions Ombudsman was discharging when making his determination. The functions of the Ombudsman are set out in s 146 of the Pension Schemes Act 1993. Section 146(1), which is the only material part of the section for present purposes, gives the Ombudsman jurisdiction to investigate and determine certain specified matters. The only matters which are potentially relevant to the present case are those set out in paras (a) and (c). Paragraph (a) relates to complaints by a beneficiary of a pension scheme resulting from injustice in consequence of maladministration of the scheme. Paragraph (c) includes—

'any dispute of fact or law ... in relation to an occupational or personal pension scheme between—(i) a person responsible for the management of the scheme, and (ii) an actual or potential beneficiary ...'

[53] There is no dispute that Mr Woodland and Mr Lewis were persons responsible for the management of the scheme and that the complainants, Mr Robson and Mr Boswell, were beneficiaries under it. No complaint of maladministration as such was made against the trustees. The complaint against them was that they had—

'removed assets from the scheme and reinvested them in companies in which they had personal interests and, in doing so, they had failed to act prudently, did not take advice and were influenced by their personal interests.'

[54] What the Ombudsman considered in relation to the conduct of the trustees was first whether this amounted to a breach of trust and secondly, if it was a breach of trust, whether the trustees, or either of them, were exonerated from liability by means of a clause which provided:

'No trustee shall be responsible chargeable or liable in any manner whatsoever for or in respect of any loss of or any depreciation in or default upon any of the investments ... in which the moneys and assets of the fund or any part thereof may at any time be invested ... or by reason of any other matter or thing except wilful default on the part of the trustee who is sought to be made liable.'

[55] In paras 12–24 of the determination the Ombudsman set out his findings in respect of 'the investments', namely the investments which were the subject

of the complaint, and in paras 25–31 he dealt with certain matters concerning the
conduct of the trustees. Paragraphs 32–46 relate to a complaint of maladministration
against Acorn.   In para 47 the Ombudsman returned to the conduct of the
trustees. His first conclusion on this is stated in para 59, where he says:

'For the reasons set out in paras 47–58 above, I find that the investments
were made by the trustees in breach of trust. They are, subject to my
comments below on the exoneration clause, jointly and severally liable to
the scheme for all losses caused by those breaches.'

[56] To some extent the Ombudsman's reasons are clear. Of the paragraphs
of the determination which are said to set out his reasons, paras 48–52 are
preliminary. Paragraph 53 contains a clear finding that it was a breach of trust for
the trustees to move the majority of the assets of the scheme from the low risk
investments in which they were held when the trustees took office into high
risk investments, without taking any investment advice and contrary to the
previous advice of Acorn. Paragraph 54 finds that the trustees did not seek legal
or investment advice in respect of the new investments, save in one limited case.
Paragraph 55 finds that the trustees were in breach of their duties to diversify
investments. Paragraph 58 states, quite correctly, that it was of no relevance that
the trustees may not have relished their duties.

[57] Paragraphs 56 and 57 are less straightforward. The two paragraphs must,
I think, be read together. Although all the steps in the Ombudsman's reasoning
are set out, I think it may be more helpful to take them in a slightly different order
from that in which they are stated. The Ombudsman found that the trustees had
placed themselves in a position where their duties to members of the scheme
conflicted with their own personal interests in the companies in which they
invested. He found also that a clause to the effect that no decision of the trustees
should be invalidated on the ground that the trustees had a personal interest in the
result of such decision did not relieve the trustees from their obligations to
consider the matters which trustees ought to consider when making or varying
investments. He accepted that the fact that the trustees had a personal interest in
the new investments which they made did not automatically make those
investments improper. But he considered that the existence of the trustees'
personal interest cast upon them the burden of showing that the transactions
which they had entered into were reasonable and proper, and he found that the
trustees had not done this.

[58] Neither in paras 56 and 57, which I have sought to explain in some detail,
nor in paras 48–55, which I have dealt with in less detail, does the Ombudsman's
determination as to breach of trust (as distinct from exoneration) appear to me to
demonstrate anything capable of being regarded as dishonest or having a criminal
aspect.

[59] The Ombudsman next turned to the question whether the trustees could
claim to be exonerated from personal liability in respect of the breaches of trust
which he found they had committed. The question which he asked himself was
whether the trustees could satisfy him that they were not in wilful default.

[60] The meaning of 'wilful default' was considered by the Court of Appeal in
Armitage v Nurse [1997] 2 All ER 705, [1998] Ch 241. Millett LJ, with whom the
other members of the court agreed, pointed out ([1997] 2 All ER 705 at 711, [1998]
Ch 241 at 252) that the expression is used in two senses. The first is when a trustee
is said to be accountable on the footing of wilful default, meaning that he is
accountable not only for money which he has in fact received but also for money

which he could with reasonable diligence have received. In such a case it is sufficient that the trustee has been guilty of a want of ordinary prudence. Millett LJ went on to deal with the second sense of the expression as follows:

'In the context of a trustee exclusion clause, however, such as s 30 of the Trustee Act 1925, it means a deliberate breach of trust (*Re Vickery, Vickery v Stephens* [1931] 1 Ch 572, [1931] All ER Rep 562) ... Nothing less than conscious and wilful misconduct is sufficient. The trustee must be— "conscious that, in doing the act which is complained of or in omitting to do the act which it is said he ought to have done, he is committing a breach of his duty, or is recklessly careless whether it is a breach of his duty or not." (See *Re Vickery* [1931] 1 Ch 572 at 583, [1931] All ER Rep 562 at 567 per Maugham J.) A trustee who is guilty of such conduct either consciously takes a risk that loss will result, or is recklessly indifferent whether it will or not. If the risk eventuates he is personally liable. But if he consciously takes the risk in good faith and with the best intentions, honestly believing that the risk is one which ought to be taken in the interests of the beneficiaries, there is no reason why he should not be protected by an exemption clause which excludes liability for wilful default.' (See [1997] 2 All ER 705 at 711, 712, [1998] Ch 241 at 252.)

[61] In his determination the Ombudsman based himself on what was said in *Re Vickery*, as quoted in the passage set out above, and on the paragraph from the judgment of Millett LJ which follows that quotation. He addressed a submission of the trustees, who were not legally represented before him, to the effect that they honestly believed that the Investments were in the best interests of the beneficiaries. In the case of Mr Woodland he did so after Mr Woodland had attended an oral hearing. (Mr Lewis declined to attend such a hearing.)

[62] The Ombudsman's conclusion in respect of Mr Woodland is stated in para 73 of the determination, which reads as follows:

'I find from the documentary evidence and from oral evidence given by Mr Woodland, that he acted with a dual motivation. One, instinctive, motivation was to gain a good investment return. Having heard Mr Woodland give evidence, I find that this motivation came from his own commercial instincts and ambitions rather than any duty he felt to members of the scheme. I find that his other, conscious, motivation was the personal advantages he and his family would gain as a result of his involvement in the investment companies as directors and shareholders. Whilst I do not find that he was actually aware that he was committing a breach of trust I do find that he was recklessly indifferent in blindly following suggestions made by Mr Lewis in not taking legal advice and in not taking advice on the suitability of the investments as assets of a pension scheme. I do not find that Mr Woodland gave any significant thought to his duties as a trustee or to the interests of the members. Whilst I do not find that he deliberately set out to defraud members he was reckless in failing to take advice and recklessly indifferent in relying on Mr Lewis. There is no firm evidence that Mr Woodland genuinely took into account members' interests. Had he done so I do not accept that, in a scheme in winding up, Mr Woodland could have come to the conclusion that the investments were appropriate for the scheme and that he would have decided to invest a large proportion of scheme assets in them. I therefore do not accept his evidence that he considered the interests of the scheme members when making the investments. I find that he deliberately acted as he would have done had the scheme money been his own. I therefore find that the investments made in breach of trust resulted in losses caused by wilful default on the part of Mr Woodland. Accordingly he may not rely on the exoneration clause to excuse his personal liability to the scheme.'

[63] Mr Arnold argued that this conclusion was sufficient not only to prevent Mr Woodland relying on the exoneration clause but also to establish that Mr Woodland was guilty of a fraudulent breach of trust. In advancing this argument he relied upon a number of matters.

[64] First he pointed out that in *Armitage v Nurse* [1997] 2 All ER 705 at 711, [1998] Ch 241 at 251 Millett LJ accepted a formulation advanced by counsel that 'actual fraud' (the expression at the heart of the dispute in *Armitage*'s case)—

'connotes at the minimum an intention on the part of the trustee to pursue a particular course of action, either knowing that it is contrary to the interests of the beneficiaries or being recklessly indifferent whether it is contrary to their interests or not.'

To this Millett LJ added:

'It is the duty of a trustee to manage the trust property and deal with it in the interests of the beneficiaries. If he acts in a way which he does not honestly believe is in their interests then he is acting dishonestly. It does not matter whether he stands or thinks he stands to gain personally from his actions.'

[65] Secondly, in *Walker v Stones* [2000] 4 All ER 412, [2001] QB 902 the Court of Appeal held that the test of dishonesty in relation to reliance upon a trustee exoneration claim should be the same as the test applicable in the case of accessory liability in accordance with *Royal Brunei Airlines Sdn Bhd v Tan* [1995] 3 All ER 97, [1995] 2 AC 378. In particular the subjective state of mind of the trustee cannot be determinative where his conduct is dishonest according to objective standards. On this Mr Arnold referred also to *Twinsectra Ltd v Yardley* [2002] UKHL 12 at [36], [2002] 2 All ER 377 at [36], [2002] 2 WLR 802 per Lord Hutton.

[66] Thirdly he maintained that the facts found by the Ombudsman showed that Mr Woodland acted dishonestly in that (a) he intentionally pursued the course of causing funds belonging to the scheme to be applied in making the investments; (b) the Ombudsman rejected the trustees' claim that they had honestly believed that the investments were in the best interests of the beneficiaries; (c) he also rejected the trustees' claim that they took legal and investment advice; (d) he found that Mr Woodland treated the funds with which he dealt as if they were his own property without considering the interests of the beneficiaries and was thus recklessly indifferent whether his action was contrary to their interests, with the result that he cannot honestly have believed that his actions were in their interests; and (e) he acted not with any intention of benefiting the beneficiaries but so as to benefit himself and his family.

[67] I do not think that the last of these factors emerges with clarity from the Ombudsman's decision, although it is clear that Mr Woodland and his family were interested in the making of the investments. The other factors are, I think, fairly established by the Ombudsman's decision.

a
[68] Nevertheless I am not persuaded that the Ombudsman's decision gives rise to an issue estoppel which establishes that Mr Woodland was not only guilty of breaches of trust but that these breaches were fraudulent. I do not think that the issue which the Ombudsman had to consider was the same as that which has to be considered in relation to s 281(3). It does not appear to me that 'wilful default' is precisely the same as 'fraudulent breach of trust' so that a finding of the

b
first necessarily involves a finding of the second as well.

[69] Fraudulent breach of trust, like any other fraudulent conduct, must be distinctly alleged and as distinctly proved (see *Davy Bros Ltd v Garrett* (1878) 7 Ch D 473 at 489 and *Armitage v Nurse* [1997] 2 All ER 705 at 715, [1998] Ch 241 at 256). There are no formal pleadings in the present case and the only claim which can be taken to be impliedly pleaded is that the Ombudsman's decision establishes

c
fraudulent breach of trust. Unless this decision can be said to establish conduct which can only be characterised as fraudulent conduct it is not enough to support the plea, because if the facts pleaded are consistent with innocence it is not open to the court to find fraud (see *Armitage's* case [1997] 2 All ER 705 at 715, [1998] Ch 241 at 256). I do not consider that the decision establishes unequivocally conduct

d
of the requisite character.

[70] In my view therefore the statutory demand ought to be set aside on the ground that the debt is disputed on grounds which appear to be substantial. This decision will not, of course, prevent ANPTL, as the present trustee of the scheme, commencing a new action in which the claim of fraudulent breach of trust is duly pleaded with the necessary particularity and, if it is possible to do so, proved with

e
the necessary degree of certainty.

[71] I mentioned earlier that I would return, at the end of my judgment, to a point on the form of the statutory demand. In the demand the creditor is described as 'UCL Group Retirement Benefits Scheme'. It asserts that the Pensions Ombudsman determined that Mr Woodland must pay the sum in issue

f
to 'the creditor'. The scheme as such has, however, no separate legal personality enabling it to sue or be sued. The Ombudsman's direction was for the payment of the specified sum not to the scheme as such but to ANPTL for the benefit of the scheme. It appears to me, therefore, that any statutory demand ought to have been served by ANPTL and that ANPTL would be the correct petitioner if a bankruptcy petition were to ensue. As the statutory demand must, in my

g
judgment, be set aside the point is one of no practical importance. But if I had taken a different view on the substantive issues it might nevertheless have been necessary to set aside the statutory demand even though there would be no answer to a new statutory demand served by ANPTL. In that event, of course, the outcome in respect of costs would be likely to be very different.

h
Order accordingly.

Celia Fox   Barrister.

Peet v Mid-Kent Healthcare NHS Trust

[2001] EWCA Civ 1703

COURT OF APPEAL, CIVIL DIVISION

LORD WOOLF CJ, SIMON BROWN AND BUXTON LJJ

5 NOVEMBER 2001

Practice – Evidence – Expert evidence – Jointly-instructed sole expert – Whether permissible for party to have conference with jointly-instructed expert in other party's absence – CPR 35.7.

In proceedings for medical negligence brought on behalf of the claimant, a child born with cerebral palsy, the court approved a settlement whereby the defendant NHS trust agreed to pay 95% of the damages which were to be assessed. With the consent of the parties, the court subsequently made an order for the joint instruction of seven non-medical experts to deal with different issues in relation to quantum. CPR 35.7[a] gave the court power to direct that evidence in relation to a particular issue be given by one expert only, while other provisions of Pt 35 dealt, inter alia, with the mutual disclosure of instructions given by the instructing parties to a single joint expert and the putting of written questions to such an expert by a party. The claimant's parents and their lawyers wished to have a conference with the joint experts, in the absence of the trust's representatives, so that they could discuss the experts' evidence and test its strength. After the trust objected, the master ordered that no such conference should take place without the trust's written consent. The claimant appealed.

Held – Where the parties had instructed a single joint expert, it was not permissible for one party to have a conference with the expert in the absence of the other party without the latter's prior written consent. A conclusion to the contrary would be inconsistent with the whole concept of the single expert. The framework found in CPR Pt 35 was designed to ensure an open process so that both parties knew what information had been placed before the single expert. It would be wholly inconsistent with that structure to allow one party to conduct a conference where the evidence of the experts was in effect tested in the course of discussions with them. There could be no point in a unilateral meeting or conference unless what transpired between the party enjoying sole access and the expert was, at least in part, intended to be hidden from the expert's other client. That was necessarily inconsistent with the very concept of a jointly-instructed expert, owing an equal duty of openness and confidence to both parties. Accordingly, the appeal would be dismissed (see [21], [24], [25], [32], [34]–[36], [39], below).

Per curiam. (1) Where non-medical expert evidence is required in a medical negligence case, the court should, in the absence of special circumstances, direct that the evidence be given by a single expert rather than an expert from each party. Only by doing so can the court exercise control over the costs involved (see [5], [7], [36], below).

(2) There will normally be no need for the report of a single joint expert to be amplified or tested by cross-examination. Although the court has a discretion to

a Rule 35.7 is set out at [13], below

a permit such amplification or cross-examination, either before or during the hearing, the assumption should be that the single joint expert's report is the evidence (see [28], [36], below).

Notes

b For the court's power to direct that evidence be given to a single joint expert and for instructions to such an expert, see 37 *Halsbury's Laws* (4th edn reissue) paras 998–999.

Cases cited or referred to in skeleton arguments

Daniels v Walker [2000] 1 WLR 1382n, CA.

Smith v Stephens (26 January 2001, unreported).

c *Swallow v Jackson* (26 April 2001, unreported).

Appeal

The claimant, Matthew Peet, suing through his father and litigation friend, Robert James Peet, appealed with permission of Master Ungley from his order on *d* 28 September 2001 that the claimant should conduct no conference in the presence of experts jointly instructed by the claimant and the defendant, Mid-Kent Healthcare NHS Trust, without the defendant's written consent. The facts are set out in the judgment of Lord Woolf CJ.

Simon Taylor (instructed by *Alexander Harris*) for the claimant.

e *Jane Mishcon* (instructed by *Bevan Ashford*) for the defendant.

LORD WOOLF CJ.

[1] This appeal comes before this court with the permission of Master Ungley from whose order dated 28 September 2001 it arises. It was correctly considered *f* by him that the issue is one which requires the attention of this court.

[2] The appeal raises a point of general significance in relation to expert evidence. It arises in the context of a claim for medical negligence following the birth of one of two twins to Major and Mrs Peet on 3 October 1996. Tragically that twin was born suffering from four limb cerebral palsy of a mixed type with hypertonia and writhing movements which meant that the child had limited mobility.

g [3] The history of the proceedings can be summarised shortly as follows. The letter before action was sent in October 1997. Proceedings were issued in March 1998. The trial of liability was fixed to start on 10 May 1999. Following the exchange of experts' reports, the claimant made an application for summary judgment. It was originally returnable on 5 March 1999, but on 25 March, after *h* the matter had been adjourned, the defendant offered to pay 95% of the full liability quantum of damages which were to be assessed. That offer was accepted and the proposed settlement was approved by Turner J on 23 April 1999.

[4] In due course, on 17 February 2000, an order was made by the senior master, Master Turner. He gave directions designed to ensure the proportionate *j* disposal of the proceedings. He ordered simultaneous mutual exchange of medical expert evidence. He subsequently required the parties to serve a schedule of loss with supporting documentation, the first schedule to be served by the claimant by 30 November 2001, and that to be followed by a counter-schedule not later than 28 February 2002. The object of the exercise was that a trial should take place in approximately March 2002. In addition, the master ordered that there should be jointly instructed non-medical expert evidence dealing with quantum

limited to seven such witnesses who were identified as follows: an educational
psychologist, an employment consultant, a nursing specialist, an occupational
therapist, a physiotherapist, an architect and a speech therapist. In addition, a
video of the claimant was to be seen by the trial judge.

[5] The parties were in agreement that there should be non-medical evidence
from experts in their respective fields. That part of the order was therefore made
by consent. I will return to that aspect of the order later in this judgment. In the
absence of special circumstances, evidence by a single expert witness is the
appropriate course to be adopted when giving directions in a case of this nature
as to non-medical experts.

[6] The scale of litigation over medical mishaps of the sort that occurred to the
claimant in this case is a matter of considerable concern. In addition, this area of
litigation tends to be peculiarly adversarial: both sides, unless they are careful, can
allow the litigation to become disproportionate. The issues may be made more
difficult to resolve. The costs of litigation may be extremely high. Claims can be
very large indeed. The amount of costs incurred, when the size of the claim is
considered, may be a relatively small percentage of the amount in issue.
However, it has to be realised by those who are involved in litigation in this area
that almost invariably the costs fall upon those who are responsible for providing
for the health of the nation through the National Health Service. In these
circumstances it is the duty of the lawyers on both sides to use their best
endeavour to keep those costs under control. It is not only the lawyers who are
under a duty, the courts too are under a duty to restrain those costs. A way of
doing so is by ensuring that the medical and non-medical expert evidence is
restricted so far as possible. In some cases it is difficult to restrict the medical
evidence because there can be difficult issues as to the appropriate form of
treatment in the particular case and also problems as to the standard of treatment
which is required.

[7] However, this appeal arises in relation to the non-medical evidence.
Although the amount of the claim can be significantly influenced by non-medical
evidence, in my view, in the great majority of cases where there is the need for
such non-medical evidence, that evidence should be given by a single expert
rather than by experts called on behalf of the respective parties. As we will see
when we come to the framework which is provided by the CPR, the CPR permit
the court to require the parties to use a single expert. This is not a matter of
choice for the parties. In the absence of special circumstances I consider that the
appropriate way that the power should be exercised is to require a single expert
rather than an expert from each party. It is only by so doing that control can be
exercised over the costs involved. I have already referred to the number of
non-medical experts that were required in this particular case. To have contested
issues over the evidence given by those non-medical experts would make the
litigation disproportionate.

[8] It does not help the parties to a dispute to have contests over such an issue.
Quite apart from the additional costs which are incurred, the stress and anxiety
which is caused to the claimant or the claimant's parents has to be borne in mind.
Also to be borne in mind is the delay which arises. Finally, it has to be recognised
that litigation of this sort has an adverse effect upon the resources of the health
service, not only in costs but also in the manpower which has to be deployed in
providing the information to those who are responsible for conducting this class
of litigation on behalf of hospitals and other parts of the health service. It is
therefore to be hoped that parties will exercise the degree of responsibility

a required to control those costs, and it is also to be hoped that the courts will use their powers as far as they can to restrict those costs.

[9] The framework provided by the CPR with regard to expert evidence and the practice direction in support of the CPR is designed to provide a flexible framework. There will always be cases which require special treatment because of particular issues which arise thereunder. But in general the CPR should cater
b satisfactorily for the great majority of situations where expert evidence, particularly in a medical context, is required. CPR 35.3 makes clear that experts in general owe an overriding duty to the courts. It provides:

> '(1) It is the duty of an expert to help the court on the matters within his expertise.
c
> (2) This duty overrides any obligation to the person from whom he has received instructions or by whom he is paid.'

[10] The power of the court to restrict expert evidence is contained in r 35.4 which provides: '(1) No party may call an expert or put in evidence an expert's report without the court's permission …'.

d [11] The court therefore is in a position to control the way that expert evidence is provided. Rule 35.5 contains general requirements: '(1) Expert evidence is to be given in a written report unless the court directs otherwise …'. Rule 35.6 enables written questions to be addressed to experts. It provides:

> '(1) A party may put to—(a) an expert instructed by another party; or (b) a
e single joint expert appointed under rule 35.7, written questions about his report.
> (2) Written questions under paragraph (1)—(a) may be put once only; (b) must be put within 28 days of service of the expert's report; and (c) must be for the purpose only of clarification of the report, unless in any case—(i) the court gives permission; or (ii) the other party agrees …'
f

[12] The requirement that questions may only be put once is a general requirement. If the circumstances require the questions to be put more than once, then the court may permit that to happen. If the parties accept that questions should be put on an additional occasion, normally the court will be content to allow them to do so. There is no need for applications to be made to
g the court in the absence of disagreement.

[13] It is apparent from rr 35.5 and 35.6 that the process with regard to the obtaining of expert evidence depends upon the use of written instructions, followed by a written report. Rule 35.7 is particularly relevant to the issue which is before the court on this appeal. It provides:

h
> '(1) Where two or more parties wish to submit expert evidence on a particular issue, the court may direct that the evidence on that issue is to be given by one expert only.
> (2) The parties wishing to submit the expert evidence are called "the instructing parties".
j
> (3) Where the instructing parties cannot agree who should be the expert, the court may—(a) select the expert from a list prepared or identified by the instructing parties; or (b) direct that the expert be selected in such other manner as the court may direct.'

[14] In relation to r 35.7 I would emphasise that the power of the court to direct that the evidence be given by a single joint expert is unrestricted. The court

has a wide discretion and that discretion has to be used in order to further the overriding principles set out in CPR Pt 1.

[15] When it comes to instructions to a single joint expert, r 35.8 provides:

'(1) Where the court gives a direction under rule 35.7 for a single joint expert to be used, each instructing party may give instructions to the expert.

(2) When an instructing party gives instructions to the expert he must, at the same time, send a copy of the instructions to the other instructing parties.

(3) The court may give directions about—(a) the payment of the expert's fees ...'

Rule 35.9 anticipates that written instructions will be given to the single expert, although that is not said explicitly in terms. Rule 35.10 provides in sub-para (4):

'The instructions referred to in paragraph (3) shall not be privileged against disclosure but the court will not, in relation to those instructions—(a) order disclosure of any specific document; or (b) permit any questioning in court, other than by the party who instructed the expert, unless it is satisfied that there are reasonable grounds to consider the statement of instructions given under paragraph (3) to be inaccurate or incomplete.'

Rule 35.11 provides: 'Where a party has disclosed an expert's report, any party may use that expert's report as evidence at the trial.' Rule 35.12 gives the court power at any stage to direct discussions between experts.

[16] The provisions of Pt 35 are supported by a practice direction (CPR PD 35) which deals with the form and content of the expert's report. One of the matters required to be referred to in an expert's report to which the practice direction applies is a summary of the range of opinions of matters dealt with in the report. Paragraph 3[b] of the practice direction deals with the question of privilege. Paragraph 4 amplifies the contents of r 35.6 as to questions, and states specifically: 'Questions asked for the purpose of clarifying the expert's report ... should be put, in writing, to the expert not later than 28 days after receipt of the expert's report ...'

[17] Paragraph 5 provides:

'Where the court has directed that the evidence on a particular issue is to be given by one expert only ... but there are a number of disciplines relevant to that issue, a leading expert in the dominant discipline should be identified as the single expert. He should prepare the general part of the report and be responsible for annexing or incorporating the contents of any reports from experts in other disciplines.'

[18] The problem that arose in the present case is that, although the master had ordered single experts to prepare reports, there came a stage where the claimant's parents wished to have a conference with the experts. They wanted that conference to take place without there being any representative of the defendant present because they wished the experts' evidence to be discussed. The proposal was not one which was acceptable to the defendant. Accordingly, the master was asked to give a ruling upon this. The master took the view that it would not be appropriate for a conference of that nature to take place. He ordered, inter alia, that: (1) the application for the defendant's solicitor to be

---

b   Editor's note: on 25 March 2002 the paragraph numbering of CPR PD 35 was renumbered. Paragraphs 3, 4 and 5 are now paras 4, 5.1 and 6 respectively.

a present at the claimant's conference be refused; (2) no conference be conducted by the claimant with the presence of joint experts and those separately instructed by the claimant or save with written consent by any party with any joint single expert.

[19] The father of the claimant, who is the litigant's friend, was unhappy about that order. Thus we have this appeal.

b [20] On 20 July 2001 he wrote a letter to his solicitors in which he said:

> 'I am writing to express my deep dismay at this prospect. For both [my wife] and myself, a crucial part of such conferences is our ability to express ourselves freely, without fear that any of our comments might be used or c taken up by "the other side", in what is still an adversarial process of deciding the final quantum. The presence of [the defendant's solicitors'] representative would severely inhibit this. Indeed we would find such a presence intimidating and distressing and are vehemently opposed to it. When we originally agreed to having joint experts, there was no suggestion that it would be necessary to have a conference with [the defendant's solicitors] present. We would not d have agreed to such arrangements and would not have agreed to joint experts if [the defendant's solicitors] had stipulated that we would be obliged to have them present at such a conference. In a similar vein we are keen that the experts are allowed to discuss their opinions and reports with us separately from the Health Authority's solicitors. We do understand they e may be required to do this again separately with [the defendant's solicitors], but feel it is vital that they are allowed to give advice to us and our representatives without the presence of the defendant's legal representatives.'

[21] Unfortunately, because of the initial delays which occurred in the defendant admitting liability, the claimant's parents feel traumatised by their f experience. There is no doubt that they were already highly distressed at the fact that the claimant was extremely disabled as a result of what occurred during his birth. In those circumstances litigation which is prolonged adds to that distress. This court fully understands and sympathises with their position. However, litigation of this sort cannot be conducted in a particular way because of distress of this nature. One of the experts whose expertise is nursing has interviewed the g parents of the claimant for the purposes of the preparation of her report. There can be no objection to that. A single expert is perfectly entitled to interview the parents for the purposes of preparing a satisfactory report. There was no suggestion, as I understand it, for the defendant to be represented when instructions of that sort were being taken by the expert, and I would not expect h the defendant to raise any objection to what happened in this case. That is one thing; but the idea of having an experts' conference including lawyers without there being a representative of the defendant present, as was suggested by the claimant's solicitors, in my judgment is inconsistent with the whole concept of the single expert. The framework to which I have made reference is designed to j ensure an open process so that both sides know exactly what information is placed before the single expert. It would be totally inconsistent with the whole of that structure to allow one party to conduct a conference where the evidence of the experts is in effect tested in the course of discussions which take place with that expert. I emphasise that what I have just said does not prevent one expert from communicating with another expert in order to obtain any information which that expert requires to include in his or her report.

[22] In support of this appeal, Mr Taylor sets out the reasons why he considers that the proposed consultation should take place. He says that in many cases of maximum or near-maximum severity a conference or consultation with experts on quantum issues is important. If that be so, speaking for myself, I would see no objection to consultation, as long as it takes place where both sides are aware of what happens within that consultation. Mr Taylor goes on to submit that the discussion is necessary for the lawyers to understand and to test fully the views of each individual expert so as to discover the strengths and weaknesses of their views and to understand the reasonable range of opinion on any important issues. There is nothing objectionable, subject to both sides being present, in such a discussion taking place. But the idea that one side should be able to test the views of an expert in the absence of the other party is clearly impermissible. It is said that it is necessary for the experts to understand each other fully and to raise any concerns that they may have about the impact of the proposals. For the reasons I have indicated, as long as the matter takes place in a way where one party is not in any way disadvantaged, again there is no difficulty.

[23] The other reasons put forward by Mr Taylor are variations to those with which I have already dealt, and I do not need to deal with them separately.

[24] There is a helpful protocol which has been prepared by the Academy of Experts as a guide for those who are instructing experts (*Code of Guidance for Experts and Those Instructing Them* (1 June 2001 revision)). In relation to the conduct of the single joint expert, it specifically states in para 19.9: 'A single joint expert should not attend any meeting or conference that is not a joint one, unless all the parties have first agreed in writing.'

[25] It seems to me that that admirably summarises the position whether it is the claimants or the defendants who wish to have a conference of that nature. I therefore consider that the master came to the right conclusion in his decision.

[26] We have been referred to two cases, one of which was decided by a deputy High Court judge, and the other by a county court judge, which are to the same effect. No authority has been placed before us which suggests that the position might be otherwise. In my judgment it would be surprising indeed if there was any such authority.

[27] Certain subsidiary matters arose in the course of argument in this appeal to which the court should briefly refer to avoid uncertainty in the future. We were referred to a passage in the White Book (*Civil Procedure* (Autumn 2001) vol 1), para 35.7.1 which is in these terms:

'If a single joint expert is called to give oral evidence at trial, it is submitted, although the rule and the practice direction do not make this clear, that both parties will have the opportunity to cross-examine him/her, but with a degree of restraint, given that the expert has been instructed by the parties.'

[28] That paragraph may be applicable in some cases, but it certainly should not be regarded as being of general application. I summarise my reasons for so saying. The starting point is: unless there is reason for not having a single expert, there should be only a single expert. If there is no reason which justifies more evidence than that from a single expert on any particular topic, then again in the normal way the report prepared by the single expert should be the evidence in the case on the issues covered by that expert's report. In the normal way, therefore, there should be no need for that report to be amplified or tested by cross-examination. If it needs amplification, or if it should be subject to cross-examination, the court has a discretion to allow that to happen. The court may permit that to

a happen either prior to the hearing or at the hearing. But the assumption should be that the single joint expert's report is the evidence. Any amplification or any cross-examination should be restricted as far as possible. Equally, where parties agree that there should be a single joint expert, and a single joint expert produces a report, it is possible for the court still to permit a party to instruct his or her own expert and for that expert to be called at the hearing. However, there must be

b good reason for that course to be adopted. Normally, where the issue is of the sort that is covered by non-medical evidence, as in this case, the court should be slow to allow a second expert to be instructed.

[29] It was understandably said by Mr Taylor that the sums at stake in this case as a result of the non-expert evidence may be substantial. However, the fact that the sums at stake may be substantial does not justify the departure from the

c general approach in relation to single experts which I have just sought to indicate. If there is an issue which requires cross-examination, or requires additional evidence, that is one thing. But the court should seek to avoid that situation arising, otherwise the objectives of having a single expert will in many situations be defeated.

d [30] In litigation of this nature the need for co-operation and openness on both sides is critical. Co-operation and openness will go a long way to meet the concerns of a person in the position of the claimant's father in this case. An unnecessarily adversarial approach will cause the sort of concerns that this father apparently has to fester and grow in intensity. It is very important that that is avoided.

e [31] It is fortunate that this case came before this court, as the master desired. In the future there will be a clearer understanding as to the correct approach in a case of this nature in relation to expert evidence.

SIMON BROWN LJ.

f [32] When, if at all, should one party, without the consent of the other party, be permitted to have sole access to a single joint expert, ie an expert instructed and retained by both parties? In common with Lord Woolf CJ, I believe that the answer to this question must be an unequivocal Never. Not merely is there nothing in CPR Pt 35, the practice direction supplementing Pt 35, and the relevant Queen's Bench guide suggesting that such access should be permitted, but

g the implications of the CPR are all the other way: see particularly CPR 35.6 and 35.8.

[33] As Lord Woolf CJ has pointed out, the one document drawn to our attention which specifically addresses the point is the *Code of Guidance for Experts and Those Instructing Them* (1 June 2001 revision) published by the Academy of

h Experts which in part states:

> '19.8 Any meeting or conference attended by a single joint expert must be proportionate to the case. Any such meeting will normally be a joint one with all his instructing parties and/or their advisers.
>
> 19.9 A single joint expert should not attend any meeting or conference

j that is not a joint one, unless all the parties have first agreed in writing: (1) that such a meeting may be held; and (2) who will pay the expert's fees for the meeting.'

[34] The good sense of this is surely plain. There can be no point in a unilateral meeting or conference unless what transpires between the party enjoying sole access and the expert is, at least in part, intended to be hidden from the expert's

other client. What is to be hidden will necessarily be either the information which the party enjoying access is giving the expert, ie part of the expert's instructions, or the expert's view expressed in the light of that information, or more likely both.

[35] The hiding of such material seems to me necessarily inconsistent with the very concept of a jointly-instructed expert, owing, as such an expert does, an equal duty of openness and confidence to both parties, besides his overriding duty to the court. That, in short, is the fundamental objection in principle to what the claimant seeks to achieve by this appeal. I too would dismiss it.

BUXTON LJ.

[36] I agree with both judgments. I add simply one point of my own. Counsel for the claimant said that one reason why a conference such as he sought was desirable, indeed in his view required, was not in order to persuade the expert to improve his or her report in favour of the claimant, but to enable the claimant's lawyers the better to assess the strength and range of the expert's report: with a view to their being able better to advise their client and to fulfil their duty to report to the court about the reasonableness of any proposed settlement, it being borne in mind that this was an infant's case.

[37] That, as it seemed to me, was the only even arguable practicable reason why such a conference should take place. But the argument is, in my view, clearly unsound. The machinery of the CPR enables clarification of the report to be sought by way of questions under CPR 35.6. That process, together with informed reading of the report, should be amply sufficient to enable advisers with any experience of this area of litigation to judge the likely outcome of the case in the context of the expert's report. In my view, that process of reflection upon written material is likely to be much more reliable than probing viva voce at a conference. The desire for the latter process to be introduced into this part of the procedure reveals a scepticism about the efficacy of written procedure and clarification of issues on paper, which represents what perhaps was an earlier position of English law that the CPR have gone a long way towards displacing.

[38] However, even if there were force in this particular requirement on the part of the claimant, I would not in any event agree to its being indulged. It will be noted that these arguments would apply equally in any case where a child was involved. Further, the whole idea of separate and private approaches (and I emphasise private) to a joint expert is wholly inconsistent with the reasons for the introduction of a regime of joint expert evidence. It is unfair to the expert himself, who cannot properly judge how he should deal with the matters in the consultation. And if it is known to have been engaged in, it is likely to undermine the reliability which the court itself can place upon the evidence which the expert eventually gives.

[39] In my judgment, those are powerful and conclusive reasons, even taking into account the practical reasons asserted by the claimant in this case, why such separate meetings should never take place. I also would dismiss this appeal.

Appeal dismissed.

Melanie Martyn   Barrister.

a
Montrod Ltd v Grundkötter Fleischvertriebs GmbH and another

COURT OF APPEAL, CIVIL DIVISION

b THORPE, POTTER LJJ AND SIR MARTIN NOURSE

16, 17 OCTOBER, 20 DECEMBER 2001

Bank – Documentary credit – Irrevocable credit – Duty of bank – Documents presented complying on their face but including certificates signed without authority – Bank
c *arguing documents a 'nullity' – Whether 'nullity' exception existing in addition to 'fraud' exception to obligation of bank to pay on presentation of apparently complying documents – Whether beneficiary to letter of credit owing duty of care to applicant merely by reason of having agreed to terms of credit.*

d The seller entered into a contract of sale with the purchaser for the sale of a consignment of frozen pork. Payment was to be made by documentary credit, expressed to be subject to UCP 500, issued by SCB, a London bank, in favour of the seller at the request of another bank, F, acting on the instructions of the claimant, a finance company engaged by the buyer for the purposes of the transaction. One of the documents to be presented under the credit was an
e inspection certificate to be signed by the claimant. In the course of communications with the buyer, the seller was led to understand that one of its employees should sign the inspection certificate on the claimant's behalf and that that would be authorised by the claimant. The seller acted accordingly although, unknown to it, the buyer was not entitled to speak for the claimant as to the conduct of the
f credit. The documents under the credit were subsequently presented to and accepted by the banks. The documents were then presented to the claimant, which told the seller and SCB that it had not issued or authorised the inspection certificate and so ought not be required to pay. On advice, SCB paid the total of the invoices and sought reimbursement from F, while F sought summary judgment against the claimant if it were to be found liable to SCB. The judge
g found that the inspection certificate had been signed without the claimant's authority but that the seller had not been fraudulent and was accordingly entitled to payment by SCB, which was in turn entitled to payment by F, which was in turn entitled to reimbursement from the claimant. In reaching that conclusion, the judge rejected a contention by the claimant that SCB was entitled to refuse
h payment to the seller on the grounds that, even if the seller was not fraudulent, SCB and the seller had been made aware prior to payment that the inspection certificate had not been signed or authorised by the claimant and as such was either a 'nullity' or a non-conforming document or both. The claimant and F appealed. The claimant also applied for permission to appeal from the judge's refusal to allow it to plead Pt 20 claims against the seller (i) for negligence on the
j basis that, by agreeing to the terms of the letter of credit, the seller had assumed a duty to the claimant to exercise reasonable care and skill in the presentation of the documents to SCB (the primary negligence claim), and (ii) for breach of fiduciary duty. The seller applied for permission to appeal from the judge's decision allowing the claimant to plead a claim in negligence based on the assumption by the seller of the right and responsibility to issue and sign certificates of inspection (the narrower negligence claim).

Held – (1) There was no general nullity exception based upon the concept of a document being fraudulent in itself or devoid of commercial value. The fraud exception to the autonomy principle recognised in English law should remain based upon the fraud or knowledge of fraud on the part of the beneficiary or other party seeking payment under and in accordance with the terms of the letter of credit. That exception should not be avoided or extended by the argument that a document presented which conformed on its face with the terms of the letter of credit was none the less of a character which disentitled the person making the demand to payment because it was fraudulent in itself independently of the knowledge and bona fides of the demanding party. A conclusion to the contrary would make undesirable inroads into the principles of autonomy and negotiability universally recognised in relation to letter of credit transactions. In the instant case, the judge had been correct to find that the seller was entitled to payment. Accordingly, the appeals on the nullity issue would be dismissed (see [56]–[61], [81], [82], below); *GKN Contractors Ltd v Lloyds Bank plc* (1985) 30 Build LR 48 and *Consolidated Oil Ltd v American Express Bank Ltd* [2000] CA Transcript 85 distinguished; *Gian Singh & Co Ltd v Banque de l'Indochine* [1974] 2 All ER 754 and *United City Merchants (Investments) Ltd v Royal Bank of Canada* [1982] 2 All ER 720 considered.

(2) A beneficiary to a credit did not owe a duty of care to the applicant with regard to the documents which it presented merely by reason of having agreed to the terms of the letter of credit. In seeking to ensure that documents presented to the issuing bank complied with the terms of the letter of credit, a beneficiary was pursuing its own commercial interests. It sought to present compliant documents in order to be paid in the context of a transaction in which the commercial interests of the issuing bank and other parties involved were dealt with in the manner provided for by UCP 500, subject to the provisions of which they were aware that the transactions would be conducted and the commercial risk distributed. It followed in the instant case that the judge had been right to refuse the claimant permission to plead the primary negligence claim, and accordingly the claimant's application for permission to appeal on that issue would be dismissed. He had also been right to allow the claimant permission to plead the narrower negligence claim, and accordingly the seller's application for permission to appeal would also be dismissed. However, he had erred in refusing to allow the claimant to plead a claim for breach of fiduciary duty, and accordingly the application for permission to appeal on that matter would be granted and the appeal allowed (see [66]–[68], [75], [80]–[82], below).

Decision of Judge Raymond Jack QC [2001] 1 All ER (Comm) 368 reversed in part.

Notes

For liability for forged documents and for the scope of the fraud exception, see 3(1) *Halsbury's Laws* (4th edn reissue) paras 286, 289.

Cases referred to in judgments

Bristol and West Building Society v Mothew (t/a Stapley & Co) [1996] 4 All ER 698, [1998] Ch 1, [1997] 2 WLR 436, CA.

Caparo Industries plc v Dickman [1990] 1 All ER 568, [1990] 2 AC 605, [1990] 2 WLR 358, HL.

Consolidated Oil Ltd v American Express Bank Ltd [2000] CA Transcript 85.

Czarnikow-Rionda Sugar Trading Inc v Standard Chartered Bank London Ltd [1999] 1 All ER (Comm) 890.

a *Deutsche Ruckversicherung AG v Walbrook Insurance Co Ltd, Group Josi Re (formerly known as Group Josi Reassurance SA) v Walbrook Insurance Co Ltd* [1996] 1 All ER 791, [1996] 1 WLR 1152, CA.

English v Dedham Vale Properties Ltd [1978] 1 All ER 382, [1978] 1 WLR 93.

Gian Singh & Co Ltd v Banque de l'Indochine [1974] 2 All ER 754, [1974] 1 WLR 1234, PC.

GKN Contractors Ltd v Lloyds Bank plc (1985) 30 Build LR 48, CA.

b *Hamble Fisheries Ltd v L Gardner & Sons Ltd, The Rebecca Flame* [1999] 2 Lloyd's Rep 1, CA.

Hedley Byrne & Co Ltd v Heller & Partners Ltd [1963] 2 All ER 575, [1964] AC 465, [1963] 3 WLR 101, HL.

Henderson v Merrett Syndicates Ltd, Hallam-Eames v Merrett Syndicates Ltd, Hughes v Merrett Syndicates Ltd, Arbuthnott v Feltrim Underwriting Agencies Ltd, Deeny v Gooda Walker Ltd (in liq) [1994] 3 All ER 506, [1995] 2 AC 145, [1994] 3 WLR 761, HL.

c

Lambias (Importers and Exporters) Co PTE Ltd v Hong Kong & Shanghai Banking Corp [1993] 2 SLR 751, Sing HC.

Owen (Edward) Engineering Ltd v Barclays Bank International Ltd [1978] 1 All ER 976, [1978] QB 159, [1977] 3 WLR 764, CA.

d

Phipps v Boardman [1965] 1 All ER 849, [1965] Ch 992, [1965] 2 WLR 839, CA; *affd* [1966] 3 All ER 721, [1967] 2 AC 46, [1966] 3 WLR 1009, HL.

Sztejn v J Henry Schroder Banking Corp (1941) 31 NYS 2d 631, NY SC.

Turkiye Is Bankasi AS v Bank of China [1996] 2 Lloyd's Rep 611; *affd* [1998] 1 Lloyd's Rep 250, CA.

e

United City Merchants (Investments) Ltd v Royal Bank of Canada [1982] 2 All ER 720, [1983] 1 AC 168, [1982] 2 WLR 1039, HL; *rvsg* [1981] 3 All ER 142, [1982] QB 208, [1981] 3 WLR 242, CA; *affg* [1979] 1 Lloyd's Rep 267.

Cases also cited or referred to in skeleton arguments

f *Anns v Merton London Borough* [1977] 2 All ER 492, [1978] AC 728, HL.

Chaudhry v Prabhakar [1988] 3 All ER 718, [1989] 1 WLR 29, CA.

Euro-Diam Ltd v Bathurst [1988] 2 All ER 23, [1990] 1 QB 1, CA.

Galoo Ltd (in liq) v Bright Grahame Murray (a firm) [1995] 1 All ER 16, [1994] 1 WLR 1360, CA.

g *Group Josi Re (formerly known as Group Josi Reassurance SA) v Walbrook Insurance Co Ltd* [1996] 1 All ER 791, [1996] 1 WLR 1152, CA.

IE Contractors Ltd v Lloyds Bank plc [1990] 2 Lloyd's Rep 496, CA.

Kwei Tek Chao (t/a Zung Fu Co) v British Traders and Shippers Ltd [1954] 1 All ER 779, [1954] 2 QB 459.

h *Lombard Finance Ltd v Brookplain Trading Ltd* [1991] 2 All ER 762, [1991] 1 WLR 271, CA.

Malas (t/a Hamzeh Malas & Sons) v British Imex Industries Ltd [1958] 1 All ER 262, [1958] 2 QB 127, CA.

Saunders v Edwards [1987] 2 All ER 651, [1987] 1 WLR 1116, CA.

Scott v Brown Doering McNab & Co [1892] 2 QB 724, [1891–4] All ER Rep 654, CA.

j *South Pacific Manufacturing Co Ltd v New Zealand Security Consultants & Investigations Ltd* [1992] 2 NZLR 282, NZ CA.

Target Holdings Ltd v Redferns (a firm) [1995] 3 All ER 785, [1996] AC 421, HL.

Thackwell v Barclays Bank plc [1986] 1 All ER 676.

Tinsley v Milligan [1993] 3 All ER 65, [1994] 1 AC 340, HL; *affg* [1992] 2 All ER 391, [1992] Ch 310, CA.

United Trading Corp SA v Allied Arab Bank Ltd [1985] 2 Lloyd's Rep 554, CA.

White v Jones [1995] 1 All ER 691, [1995] 2 AC 207, HL.
Yorkshire Water Services Ltd v Sun Alliance & London Insurance Ltd [1997] 2 Lloyd's   *a*
     Rep 21, CA.

Appeals and applications for permission to appeal

The claimant, Montrod Ltd, and the second defendant, Fibi Bank (UK) plc,
appealed with permission of Judge Raymond Jack QC from his decision on 28   *b*
November 2001 ([2001] 1 All ER (Comm) 368) giving judgment for the third
defendant, Standard Chartered Bank (SCB), against Fibi Bank in the sum of
$US 498,311.51, and for Fibi Bank against Montrod for the same sum. Montrod
also applied for permission to appeal from the judge's refusal to allow it to plead
new claims under CPR Pt 20 for negligence and breach of fiduciary duty on the
part of the first defendant, Grundkötter Fleischvertriebs GmbH, in the event that   *c*
Montrod was found liable to Fibi Bank. Grundkötter applied for permission to
appeal from the judge's decision to allow Montrod to add a new claim for
negligence on a narrower ground. Fibi Bank, with the agreement of the other
parties, was not represented, having agreed to be bound by the decision of the
court. The facts are set out in the judgment of Potter LJ.   *d*

Nigel Jones QC and *Sara Benbow* (instructed by *Simmons Stein & Co*) for Montrod.
Alain Choo Choy (instructed by *Sherrards*, St Albans) for Grundkötter.
Ali Malek QC and *Michael Kay* (instructed by *Lawrence Jones*) for SCB.

Cur adv vult   *e*

20 December 2001. The following judgments were delivered.

POTTER LJ.

   f

INTRODUCTION

[1] The various appeals and applications for permission to appeal before us
arise from orders made by Judge Raymond Jack QC (sitting as a judge of the
Commercial Court) on 28 November 2000 ([2001] 1 All ER (Comm) 368) following
his judgment in relation to the liability of the various parties arising from
payment made by Standard Chartered Bank (SCB) in London pursuant to a   *g*
documentary credit issued by SCB in favour of Grundkötter Fleischvertriebs
GmbH (GK), a German company named as beneficiary, through the advice of its
German bank, Commerzbank. That credit had been issued at the request of Fibi
Bank (UK) plc (Fibi) acting on the instructions of Montrod Ltd (Montrod), the
claimants in the action, who were named as applicants in the credit. The   *h*
underlying contract was a contract of sale made between GK as sellers and
Ballaris, a Russian entity of uncertain status, as buyers of a consignment of 400 mt
of frozen pork sides sold cif Moscow. The credit called inter alia for the
presentation of certificates of inspection signed by Montrod.

[2] There were before the court applications whereby: (a) GK sought summary   *j*
judgment under CPR Pt 24 against Montrod on Montrod's claim against GK for
a declaration that no valid certificates of inspection had been issued by Montrod
capable of satisfying the requirements of the letter of credit; (b) SCB sought
summary judgment under CPR Pt 24 against Fibi in respect of its claim for
reimbursement of moneys paid to GK pursuant to the letter of credit; (c) Fibi
similarly applied for summary judgment against Montrod in the event of it being
found liable to SCB; and (d) Montrod sought reconstitution of the action with

a SCB claiming against Fibi, Fibi claiming under CPR Pt 20 against Montrod, and Montrod claiming against GK in the form of a new Pt 20 claim against GK for reimbursement in the event of being found liable to Fibi. So far as the issues between SCB, Fibi and Montrod were concerned, it was agreed between the parties that the judge should not decide simply whether or not the defences put forward by Fibi and Montrod had any real prospect of success, but should give

b final judgment on the basis of the statements and documentary evidence before the court. So far as Montrod's application to add a CPR Pt 20 claim against GK was concerned, it was resisted by GK on the basis that Montrod's claim as formulated in a draft statement of case before the court had no realistic prospect of success. However, there was no agreement limiting the court in relation to its consideration of that issue to the evidence then available to the court.

c   [3] Montrod, a company carrying on a finance and investment business in England, was engaged through an intermediary to provide the necessary documentary credit which GK required if the matter was to proceed. The credit was payable by SCB '45 days sight' on presentation by GK of various specified documents which included: 'Certificate of Inspection issued and signed by the

d credit applicant at his discretion on the goods quality and quantity in good order before shipment.'

   [4] The credit was expressed to be subject to the Uniform Customs and Practice for Documentary Credits 500 (UCP 500). In circumstances to which I will turn in more detail below, GK presented to SCB documents, including an inspection certificate apparently signed by Montrod, which on their face complied with the

e terms of the credit. SCB paid the credit in the face of an assertion by Montrod that the inspection certificate which GK presented had not been signed or authorised by Montrod and that the document was fraudulently created. The judge found that the inspection certificate had indeed been signed without the authority of Montrod but that GK was not fraudulent and was entitled to payment by SCB

f which was entitled to payment from Fibi, which was in turn entitled to reimbursement by Montrod. In the course of his judgment the judge rejected Montrod's alternative argument that SCB was entitled to refuse payment on the grounds that, even if GK was not fraudulent, SCB and GK had prior to payment been made aware that the inspection certificate had not been signed or authorised by Montrod and as such was a 'nullity' and/or a non-conforming document.

g   [5] Montrod and Fibi appeal with the permission of the judge. Their appeals raise identical issues and Fibi has not appeared to present any separate argument. The finding of the judge that GK was innocent of any fraud has not been challenged and the success of the appeal depends upon the correctness of the 'nullity' argument, as to which there is no clear previous authority.

h   [6] In relation to Montrod's application for permission to add a CPR Pt 20 claim against GK, Montrod's draft case raised various causes of action which were the subject of applications by GK for summary relief and/or to strike out. The judge's decision on those matters, in respect of which he refused leave to appeal, has given rise to applications to this court for leave to appeal, to which I shall turn

j in due course.

THE BACKGROUND FACTS

   [7] GK had prior experience of export business but this was its first letter of credit transaction. It opened a new account with Commerzbank which it used as its adviser in connection with the credit. In the course of its communications with Ballaris when negotiating the contract of sale and the putting in place of the letter of credit, GK (who never had direct contact with Montrod) dealt with

Ballaris in good faith on the basis that Ballaris could speak as to Montrod's intentions so far as signature of the inspection certificate was concerned. GK were led to understand that Mr Wieler, an employee of GK, should sign the inspection certificates on behalf of Montrod and GK agreed that he would do so, receiving through the post a Montrod company stamp as proof of Montrod's authorisation of GK. GK acted accordingly. The full circumstances in which that unusual situation came about, and the judge's reasons for accepting that GK, who at all times acted on the advice of Commerzbank, were entirely innocent of fraud, appear in the report of the judge's decision ([2001] 1 All ER (Comm) 368 at 377–378 and 379). As already indicated there is no appeal against those findings.

[8] Unknown to GK, Ballaris were not entitled to speak for Montrod as to the contents of the credit. The negotiations between Montrod and Ballaris were conducted entirely between Mr Hoory on behalf of Montrod and a Mr Bernard Choo of Frankfort Trade Credit Agencies of Singapore who (as apparent agent/intermediary for Ballaris) had approached Mr Hoory to provide the credit. Mr Hoory had no direct contact with either Ballaris or GK. The precise relationship and the content of any communications between Mr Choo and Ballaris or GK remain to be determined. However, it was in fact the case (and it is not in dispute) that Montrod did not wish or intend to inspect the goods. So far as Mr Hoory was concerned, the requirement for presentation of a signed certificate was no more than a device, or 'locking' clause, intended to ensure that, by withholding its signature, Montrod could ensure that the credit would not be operable until it had been put in funds by Ballaris. That purpose was never disclosed to GK who were unaware of it and would never have agreed to the inclusion of such a term had it been so aware. GK duly despatched the goods by means of 20 lorry shipments to Moscow where they were delivered to Ballaris without any subsequent complaint. GK did so on the understanding that it was entitled to sign the inspection certificates for each truckload on behalf of Montrod and believing that, in any event, the goods were also to be inspected by an agency on arrival in Moscow. Having signed the certificates in those circumstances, GK duly presented 20 sets of documents under the credit to SCB in London, which accepted them as conforming with the credit.

THE RELEVANT CHRONOLOGY

[9] In February 2000, Montrod requested Fibi to obtain a letter of credit to be issued by the London branch of SCB in respect of the price of the goods agreed to be sold by GK which was to be named as the beneficiary. On 17 February 2000 Fibi wrote to SCB forwarding Montrod's request and stating:

'[Fibi] shall reimburse you two working days after receipt of your tested Telex/Swift claim confirming that documents have been presented to yourselves strictly in accordance with the LC terms and are being forwarded to us ...'

[10] In fact, since the letter of credit was '45 days sight', the notice period for reimbursement was considerably longer. However, nothing turns upon that.

[11] On 21 February 2000 SCB issued the letter of credit in accordance with Fibi's instructions, stating that Montrod was the applicant. SCB then requested Commerzbank to advise the letter of credit to GK, Commerzbank acknowledging receipt by SWIFT message on 24 February 2000.

[12] On 20 March 2000 two sets of documents were presented to SCB by Commerzbank and were followed by a further four sets on 22 March 2000. Between 23 and 27 March, SCB sent notification to Fibi that six sets of

a conforming documents had been received, together with the documents themselves. On 27 March 2000, Montrod informed Fibi that the certificates of inspection 'are not issued by the applicant Montrod Ltd [and] no payment is to be executed'. Fibi in turn passed a SWIFT message to SCB, adding later that day that 'Montrod Ltd has informed us that they have not issued any certificates of inspection and that the certificates of inspection presented are apparently
b forgeries'.

[13] On 28 March 2000, SCB contacted Fibi and confirmed that the documents complied on their face with the terms of the letter of credit. On the same day Fibi confirmed that SCB was obliged to pay against the documents at their maturity date. Thereafter, 14 further sets of documents were presented to SCB by Commerzbank on 31 March 2000 (four sets) and 6 April 2000 (ten sets). They
c were accepted by SCB as conforming on their face to the terms of the letter of credit and were duly forwarded to Fibi who were informed that the documents had been checked and found in order, SCB requesting reimbursement on an appropriate date.

[14] By a SWIFT message of 29 March 2000 Fibi, in acknowledging the
d documents received to date, confirmed that the documents appeared on their face to be in strict conformity with the terms of the letter of credit and confirmed that they would remit to SCB the relevant amounts on the value dates shown. Fibi added:

> *e* 'However, as the applicants claim that certificates of origin presented were not issued by themselves, we have informed them that we shall require either instructions from the beneficiary's bank, or a court order if payment is not to be effected. In the absence of either of these, we shall effect payments of all 6 drawings as stated above.'

[15] On 7 April 2000 Fibi acknowledged four sets of documents recently
f received and confirmed that payment would be made in due course without qualification.

[16] On 10 April 2000, SCB presented a further ten sets of documents to Fibi, but Fibi was not prepared to confirm that payment would be made in due course.

[17] On 11 April 2000, solicitors for Montrod sent a fax letter to GK asserting
g that the signature attached to the certificate of inspection delivered to SCB was a forgery. They requested confirmation that GK would not seek payment failing which they would apply to the High Court for an injunction and, on the same date, commenced proceedings against GK, Fibi and SCB for an injunction until trial or further order to prevent them from paying according to the terms of the
h letter of credit, supported by an affidavit from Mr Hoory.

[18] On 13 April 2000, Fibi accepted the ten sets of documents recently presented.

[19] Montrod's application was heard inter partes before David Steel J, who dismissed it for reasons set out in his judgment dated 19 April 2000. He found that, upon the evidence then before him, Montrod fell 'miserably short' of
j establishing a case of fraud on the part of GK as seller/beneficiary, or of notice of such fraud on the part of SCB, while acknowledging the right of Montrod to renew the application before a commercial judge if and when further evidence became available.

[20] By the end of May a further witness statement by Mr Hoory had expanded on his allegations. On various dates between 4 May and 22 May 2000 inclusive, the maturity dates for payment in respect of the various sets of

documents matured. At the end of May, witness statements for GK were served
to the effect that GK had at all relevant times dealt with persons whom they   *a*
believed to be acting on behalf of Ballaris as buyers, that they believed Montrod
had been involved in the transaction by Ballaris in relation to the opening of the
credit, and that Montrod had appropriate funds or security from Ballaris. They
had been unaware that the requirement for a certificate inspection was intended
to act as a 'locking clause' which was not an arrangement they would have   *b*
accepted had they known of it. They believed that, as a result of communications
between Ballaris and GK, one of GK's employees could properly sign the
inspection certificates. The consignments of pork had been despatched and
delivered to the Russian buyers between 7 and 24 March 2000 and no complaints
had been raised by the buyer. In respect of half the deliveries, GK had sold its
right to payment under the credit to Commerzbank in accordance with the   *c*
discount arrangement.

[21] On 7 June SCB made payment to Commerzbank of $US 498,311·51 in the
light of the failure of Montrod's application before David Steel J and the absence
of any renewed application upon the basis of such further evidence which had
become available. In relation to that evidence, it was the evidence of Mr Thompson,   *d*
SCB's operations manager, that he considered on any view it could not be said
that it was clear and established fraud, having concluded that there was no
evidence of any dishonesty on the part of GK and Commerzbank.

THE NULLITY ISSUE

[22] Following his judgment, the judge made an order by which he (i) struck   *e*
out Montrod's particulars of claim in which Montrod sought a declaration against
SCB and Fibi that no certificates of inspection had been issued and signed which
were capable of satisfying the relevant condition in the letter of credit; (ii) gave
judgment for SCB against Fibi for $US 498,311·51 plus interest (to date of
judgment) of $US 18,196·92; (iii) gave judgment for Fibi against Montrod in the   *f*
like sums. That result inevitably followed from his finding that there was no
proof of fraud on the part of GK and that the so-called 'nullity exception' argued
for by Montrod was not an exception recognised by English law as entitling a
bank to refuse payment under a letter of credit in the face of documents
conforming 'on their face' with those stipulated for under the terms of the credit.
As already indicated, the judge's finding of 'no fraud' on the part of GK is not   *g*
challenged on this appeal; the sole issue before us in respect of paras 1–3 of the
judge's order is whether or not he was correct in his understanding and
application of the law so far as the nullity exception is concerned.

[23] The formulation of the so-called 'nullity exception' as advanced before
the judge was as follows: *h*

'If, by the time of full payment (or the time when a bank irrevocably
commits itself to a third party who has taken in good faith, if earlier), the only
reasonable inference is that one (or more) of the documents [...] presented
under the credit is not what it appears on its face to be, but is a nullity, then
the bank is not obliged to make payment under the credit.'   *j*

[24] Mr Jones QC, on behalf of Montrod, has acknowledged that, if the court
regards that formulation as unnecessarily wide to do justice in the instant case,
his purpose would be equally well served if there were inserted within the square
brackets indicated in the quotation above the additional words 'created by the
beneficiary and'. Mr Jones submits that the broad issue of importance is whether
a beneficiary should be entitled to insist upon payment under a letter of credit in

a circumstances where he has presented a document which, prior to payment, he knows is not a genuine document issued under the authority of the person purporting to make it. On the alternative formulation, the issue narrows to the question whether a beneficiary who is himself responsible for the (albeit bona fide) presentation of a false document should nevertheless be able to insist on payment once he is aware of its falsity and/or unauthorised nature.

b

THE DECISION BELOW

[25] The judge rejected Montrod's arguments. He held that there was no authority which supported the existence of such a nullity exception, apart from certain dicta of Lord Diplock in *United City Merchants (Investments) Ltd v Royal Bank of Canada* [1982] 2 All ER 720, [1983] 1 AC 168 which he described as 'very *c* slender support' for the proposition advanced. He also made clear that the 'nullity exception' was not supported by UCP 500, the terms of which were imported into the letter of credit. Finally he stated that it did not form part of English law, observing that—

d
> 'It is unsupported by authority. It provides a further complication where simplicity and clarity are needed. There are problems in defining when a document is a nullity. The exception could have unfortunate consequences in relation to the rights of third parties.' (See [2001] 1 All ER (Comm) 368 at 381.)

e UCP 500

[26] Before turning to the submissions of the parties, it is convenient to set out the relevant provisions of UCP 500 which, by their incorporation into the credit, became binding upon all the parties.

[27] Article 3 (Credits v Contracts) spells out the principle of autonomy whereby a documentary credit operates independently of the underlying transaction. It *f* provides:

> 'a. Credits, by their nature, are separate transactions from the sales or other contract(s) on which they may be based and banks are in no way concerned with or bound by such contract(s), even if any reference whatsoever to such contract(s) is included in the Credit. Consequently, the *g* undertaking of a bank to pay, accept and pay Draft(s), or negotiate and/or to fulfil any other obligation under the Credit, is not subject to claims or defences by the Applicant resulting from his relationships with the Issuing Bank or the Beneficiary.
>
> b. A beneficiary can in no case avail himself of the contractual *h* relationships existing between the banks or between the Applicant and the Issuing Bank.'

[28] Article 4 (Documents v Goods/Services/Performances) provides that the parties concerned deal with documents and not with goods, services or other *j* performances to which the documents may relate.

[29] Article 9 (Liability of Issuing and Confirming Banks) provides:

> 'a. An irrevocable Credit constitutes a definite undertaking of the Issuing Bank, provided that the stipulated documents are presented to the Nominated Bank or to the Issuing Bank and that the terms and conditions of the Credit are complied with:
>
> (i) if the Credit provides for sight payment to pay at sight:

(ii) if the Credit provides for deferred payment—to pay on the maturity
date(s) determinable in accordance with the stipulations of the Credit ...

b. A confirmation of an irrevocable Credit by another bank (the
"Confirming Bank") upon the authorisation or request of the Issuing Bank,
constitutes a definite undertaking of the Confirming Bank, in addition to that
of the Issuing Bank, provided that the stipulated documents are presented to
the Confirming Bank or to any other Nominated Bank and that the terms
and conditions of the Credit are complied with:

(i) if the Credit provides for sight payment—to pay at sight;

(ii) if the Credit provides for deferred payment—to pay on the maturity
date(s) determinable in accordance with the stipulations of the Credit ...'

[30] Article 13 (Standard for Examination of Documents) provides:

'a. Banks must examine all documents stipulated in the Credit with
reasonable care, to ascertain whether or not they appear, on their face, to be
in compliance with the terms and conditions of the Credit ...

b. The Issuing Bank, the Confirming Bank, if any, or a Nominated Bank
acting on their behalf, shall each have a reasonable time, not to exceed seven
banking days following the day of receipt of the documents, to examine the
documents and determine whether to take up or refuse the documents and
to inform the party from which it received the documents accordingly ...

c. If a Credit contains conditions without stating the document(s) to be
presented in compliance therewith, banks will deem such conditions as not
stated and will disregard them.'

[31] Article 14 (Discrepant Documents and Notice) provides by paragraph (a)
that an issuing bank must reimburse any other bank which it has authorised to
pay 'against documents which appear on their face to be in compliance with the
terms and conditions of the Credit'.

[32] Article 14b provides:

'Upon receipt of the documents the Issuing Bank and/or Confirming Bank,
if any, or a Nominated Bank acting on their behalf, must determine on the
basis of the documents alone whether or not they appear on their face to be
in compliance with the terms and conditions of the Credit. If the documents
appear on their face not to be in compliance with the terms and conditions
of the Credit, such banks may refuse to take up the documents.'

[33] Article 14c provides:

'If the Issuing Bank determines that the documents appear on their face not
to be in compliance with the terms and conditions of the Credit, it may in its
sole judgment approach the Applicant for a waiver of the discrepancy (ies).
This does not, however, extend the period mentioned in sub-Article 13b.'

[34] Article 14d provides:

'(i) If the Issuing Bank and/or Confirming Bank, if any, or a Nominated
Bank acting on their behalf, decides to refuse the documents, it must give
notice to that effect by telecommunication or, if that is not possible, by other
expeditious means, without delay but no later than the close of the seventh
banking day following the day of receipt of the documents. Such notice shall
be given to the bank from which it received the documents, or to the
Beneficiary, if it received the documents directly from him.

(ii) Such notice must state all discrepancies in respect of which the bank refuses the documents ...'

[35] Article 14e provides:

'If the Issuing Bank and/or Confirming Bank, if any, fails to act in accordance with the provisions of this article [it] shall be precluded from claiming that the documents are not in compliance with the terms and conditions of the Credit.'

[36] Article 15 (Disclaimer on Effectiveness of Documents) provides that banks assume 'no liability or responsibility for the form, sufficiency, accuracy, genuineness, falsification or legal effect of any document ... or for the good faith or acts or omissions, solvency, performance or standing of ... any other person whomsoever'.

[37] The combination of the autonomy principle and the rule that the banks concerned deal in documents and not in goods (arts 3 and 4), together with the issuing bank's undertaking of payment if the stipulated documents presented conform with the terms of the credit (see art 9) plainly entitled GK as beneficiary to obtain, and obliged SCB as issuing bank to make, payment against the documents presented, provided that they complied 'on their face' with the requirements of the credit (see arts 13a, 14a, 14b and 14c). It has not been, and plainly could not be, argued on this appeal that the documents presented and, in particular, the inspection certificates were other than compliant *on their face* with the requirements of the credit. Leaving aside for a moment the exception of fraud on the part of the beneficiary (which the judge held not to exist) the liability of SCB to make payment under the UCP 500 terms is clear.

[38] Neither as a matter of general principle, nor under UCP 500, is an issuing bank obliged to question or investigate the genuineness of documents which appear on their face to be documents the nature and content of which comply with the requirements of the credit. So far as the common law is concerned, the position has been clearly stated in the House of Lords in *Gian Singh & Co Ltd v Banque de l'Indochine* [1974] 2 All ER 754 at 757–758, [1974] 1 WLR 1234 at 1238 per Lord Diplock:

'The fact that a document presented by the beneficiary under a documentary credit, which otherwise conforms to the requirements of the credit, is in fact a forgery does not, of itself, prevent the issuing bank from recovering from its customer moneys paid under the credit. The duty of the issuing bank, which it may perform either by itself, or by its agent, the notifying bank, is to examine documents with reasonable care to ascertain that they appear on their face to be in accordance with the terms and conditions of the credit. The express provision to this effect in art 7 of the Uniform Customs and Practice for Documentary Credits does no more than restate the duty of the bank at common law.'

[39] Article 7 referred to by Lord Diplock is now art 13 of UCP 500. Not only is the necessity to examine the documents presented by the beneficiary limited to an examination of the documents alone (art 14b) but, under art 15, the bank assumes no liability or responsibility for the genuineness or legal effect of any such document. Finally, it is clear that there is a timetable laid down (a reasonable time not to exceed seven banking days following receipt of documents: see art 13b and 14d) in which the issuing bank must examine the

documents and indicate to the party submitting them whether it accepts or refuses them: see art 14d(ii). If it does not refuse the documents within the seven days specified, then it is precluded from claiming that the documents are not in compliance with the terms and conditions of the credit (art 14e). Thus, in this case, once the documents had been presented and accepted, or at any rate no intimation of rejection for discrepancy had been given within seven days of receipt, SCB were prima facie liable to pay under the credit on its maturity date. Accordingly, upon a straightforward application of the provisions of UCP 500, the liability of SCB as issuing bank to pay on maturity accrued seven days after presentation of the various sets of documents, well before the end of April 2000, such payments falling due on various dates in May 2000 (see para [20], above).

[40] As already made clear, Montrod's original allegation of fraud on the part of GK as beneficiary has not been pursued before us. There is no issue between the parties that, so far as the state of the authorities is concerned, no English court has yet held an issuing bank entitled to withhold payment under a letter of credit, against documents which on their face conform with the requirements of the credit, save on the ground of fraud of the beneficiary himself, or the person seeking payment. Nor is it in dispute that in England the fraud exception is part of the common law and that it is apt to apply despite the fact that UCP 500 makes no reference to, nor makes allowance for, such an exception. As was made clear by Lord Diplock in *United City Merchants (Investments) Ltd v Royal Bank of Canada* [1982] 2 All ER 720 at 725, [1983] 1 AC 168 at 184:

> 'The exception for fraud on the part of the beneficiary seeking to avail himself of the credit is a clear application of the maxim ex turpi causa non oritur actio or, if plain English is to be preferred, "fraud unravels all". The courts will not allow their process to be used by a dishonest person to carry out a fraud.'

[41] The rationale of the fraud exception was more recently considered by Rix J in *Czarnikow-Rionda Sugar Trading Inc v Standard Chartered Bank London Ltd* [1999] 1 All ER (Comm) 890 at 914. In that case, in the course of his consideration of the claim for the grant of an injunction against an issuing bank and the prima facie need to find a substantive cause of action against the party enjoined, he put the basis of the fraud exception, at least as between the issuing bank and its customer, on the basis of an implied contractual term. He stated:

> 'The fact that the rationale of the fraud exception is the law's prohibition on the use of its process to carry out fraud (per Lord Diplock in the *UCM* case) may appropriately be viewed as an authoritative expression of the source in law of the implied limitation on a bank's mandate ... If the source of the power to injunct were purely the law's interest in preventing the beneficiary from benefiting from his own fraud, I do not see why there should be the added requirement that the fraud be patent to the bank.'

[42] Finally, it is not in dispute in respect of the fraud exception that—

> 'it is nothing to the point that at the time of trial the beneficiary knows, and the bank knows, that the documents presented under the letter of credit were not truthful in a material respect. *It is the time of presentation that is critical.*' (See *Deutsche Ruckversicherung AG v Walbrook Insurance Co Ltd, Group Josi Re (formerly known as Group Josi Reassurance SA) v Walbrook Insurance Co*

a   *Ltd* [1996] 1 All ER 791 at 800, [1996] 1 WLR 1152 at 1161 per Staughton LJ; my emphasis.)

[43] The argument for Montrod that, where fraud on the part of the beneficiary cannot be established, there should none the less be room for a nullity exception in the case of a document which is worthless in the sense that it is not genuine and has no commercial value, whether as a security for the goods or
b   otherwise, involves an undoubted extension of the fraud exception as hitherto propounded in the English authorities. If the basis of a fraud exception is that the court will only intervene in breach of the autonomy principle for the purpose of preventing or discouraging the perpetration of fraud on the part of the beneficiary or other presenting party, it is a clear extension to hold that
c   presentation of a document which is itself a nullity for reasons which are *not* known to the beneficiary or issuing bank at the time of presentation, are none the less to be similarly treated.

[44] The leading authority on the question is the *United City Merchants* case [1979] 1 Lloyd's Rep 267 in which the court was concerned with a bill of lading
d   which showed that shipment of the goods had been made on 15 December 1976, when it had in fact been made on 16 December, the last date for shipment provided by the credit being 15 December. That date had been inserted by an employee of the loading brokers to the carriers who acted fraudulently, knowing that the date inserted was false. Neither the sellers, nor their bankers (to whom they had assigned their interest under the credit), were aware of the fraud.
e   Mocatta J found in favour of the seller's assignees at first instance, having found no fraud on the part of the plaintiffs in the documents. Having considered, inter alia, the decision in *Sztejn v J Henry Schroder Banking Corp* (1941) 31 NYS 2d 631, which authority is historically the foundation stone of English law in this regard (see *Edward Owen Engineering Ltd v Barclays Bank International Ltd* [1978] 1 All ER 976 at
f   981, [1978] QB 159 at 169), he observed:

> 'The case is, therefore vitally different from the *Sztejn v. Schroder* case approved by the Court of Appeal in the recent *Edward Owen v. Barclays Bank* case. Where there has been personal fraud or unscrupulous conduct by the seller presenting the documents under the letter of credit, it is right that a
g   > bank should be entitled to refuse payment against apparently conforming documents on the principle ex turpi causa non oritur actio. But here I have held that there was no fraud on the part of the plaintiffs, nor can I, as a matter of fact, find that they knew the date on the bills of lading to be false when they presented the documents.' (See [1979] 1 Lloyd's Rep 267 at 278.)

h   [45] In the House of Lords, the argument against the sellers was—

> 'that a confirming bank is not under any obligation, legally enforceable against it by the seller/beneficiary of a documentary credit, to pay to him the sum stipulated in the credit against presentation of documents, if the documents presented, although conforming on their face with the terms of
j   > the credit, nevertheless contain some statement of material fact that is not accurate.' (See [1982] 2 All ER 720 at 726, [1983] 1 AC 168 at 184.)

This argument was rejected by Lord Diplock. He resoundingly affirmed the autonomous nature of the contracts arising in connection with the letter of credit and their independence of any dispute in relation to the underlying contract as affecting the right of a seller/beneficiary to payment under the letter of credit on presentation of conforming documents and stated ([1982] 2 All ER 720 at 725, [1983] 1 AC 168 at 183):

> 'To this general statement of principle as to the contractual obligations of the confirming bank to the seller, there is one established exception: that is, where the seller, for the purpose of drawing on the credit, fraudulently presents to the confirming bank documents that contain, expressly or by implication, material representations of fact that to his knowledge are untrue.'

[46] He went on to state the 'ex turpi causa' basis of the exception, as already quoted at para [40], above and stated that acceptance of a proposition 'which does not call for knowledge on the part of the seller/beneficiary of the existence of any inaccuracy would embrace the fraud exception and render it superfluous' ([1982] 2 All ER 720 at 726, [1983] 1 AC 168 at 184).

[47] For reasons which he subsequently elaborated, Lord Diplock stated 'to assent to it would, in my view, undermine the whole system of financing international trade by means of documentary credits'.

[48] Having referred to art 9 of the Uniform Customs (now to be found in art 15 of UCP 500) he observed:

> 'It would be strange from the commercial point of view, although not theoretically impossible in law, if the contractual duty owed by confirming and issuing banks to the buyer to honour the credit on presentation of apparently conforming documents despite the fact that they contain inaccuracies or even are forged were not matched by a corresponding contractual liability of the confirming bank to the seller/beneficiary (in the absence, of course, of any fraud on his part) to pay the sum stipulated in the credit on presentation of apparently conforming documents.' (See [1982] 2 All ER 720 at 726, [1983] 1 AC 168 at 184.)

[49] Lord Diplock went on to deal with what he characterised as the 'halfway house' involved in the proposition accepted by the Court of Appeal which he said lay—

> '... not only halfway between the unqualified liability of the confirming bank to honour a documentary credit on presentation of documents which on reasonably careful examination appear to conform to the terms and conditions of the credit and what I have referred to as the fraud exception to this unqualified liability which is available to the confirming bank where the seller/beneficiary presents to the confirming bank documents that contain, expressly or by implication, material representations of fact that to his own knowledge are untrue; but it also lies halfway between the fraud exception and the broad proposition favoured by the confirming bank with which I have hitherto been dealing. The halfway house is erected on the narrower proposition that, if any of the documents presented under the credit by the seller/beneficiary contain a material misrepresentation of fact that was *false to the knowledge of the person who issued the document* and intended by him to deceive persons into whose hands the document might come, the confirming bank is under no liability to honour the credit, even though, as in the instant case, the persons whom the issuer of the document intended to, and did, deceive included the seller/beneficiary himself ... what rational ground can there be for drawing any distinction between apparently conforming documents that, unknown to the seller, in fact contain a statement of fact

a
that is inaccurate where the inaccuracy was due to inadvertence by the maker of the document, and the like documents where the same inaccuracy had been inserted by the maker of the document with intent to deceive, among others, the seller/beneficiary himself?' (See [1982] 2 All ER 720 at 728, [1983] 1 AC 168 at 186–187.)

b
[50] Lord Diplock observed that the Court of Appeal had reached its halfway house by starting from the premise that a confirming bank could refuse to pay against a document that it knew to be forged even though the seller/beneficiary had no knowledge of that fact, and by reasoning from that premise that, if forgery by a third party relieved the confirming bank of liability to pay the seller/beneficiary, then fraud by a third party ought to have the same consequence. He went on to
c state:

> 'I would not wish to be taken as accepting that the premise as to forged documents is correct, even where the fact that the document is forged deprives it of all legal effect and makes it a nullity, and so worthless to the confirming bank as security for its advances to the buyer. This is certainly
> d not so under the Uniform Commercial Code as against a person who has taken a draft drawn under the credit in circumstances that would make him a holder in due course, and I see no reason why, and there is nothing in the Uniform Commercial Code to suggest that, a seller/beneficiary who is ignorant of the forgery should be in any worse position because he has not negotiated the draft before presentation. *I would prefer to leave open the*
> e *question of the rights of an innocent seller/beneficiary against the confirming bank when a document presented by him is a nullity because unknown to him it was forged by some third party, for that question does not arise in the instant case.* The bill of lading with the wrong date of loading placed on it by the carrier's agents was far from being a nullity. It was a valid transferable receipt for the goods
> f giving the holder a right to claim them at their destination, Callao, and was evidence of the terms of the contract under which they were being carried.' (See [1982] 2 All ER 720 at 728, [1983] 1 AC 168 at 187–188; my emphasis.)

[51] In addition to the passage emphasised in italics above, which Mr Jones relies on in support of Montrod's argument, he cites also various dicta culled from
g the authorities. In particular he relies upon the observation of Ackner LJ in the *United City Merchants* case [1981] 3 All ER 142 at 170, [1982] QB 208 at 246:

> 'A banker cannot be compelled to honour a credit unless all the conditions precedent have been performed, and he ought not to be under an obligation to accept or pay against documents which he knows to be waste paper. To
> h hold otherwise would be to deprive the banker of that security for his advances, which is a cardinal feature of the process of financing carried out by means of the credit: see *Gutteridge and Megrah on the Law of Bankers' Commercial Credits* (6th Edn, 1979, p 142).'

j [52] Mr Jones has also referred us to the observation of Parker LJ in *GKN Contractors Ltd v Lloyds Bank plc* (1985) 30 Build LR 48 at 63:

> 'There can, however, clearly be cases where, albeit the ultimate beneficiary was not fraudulent, the bank itself may have been fraudulent. The claim presented by the ultimate beneficiary may have been presented in good faith and honesty albeit owing to some mistake [it] was an invalid claim. In such a case, if the invalidity of the claim was known to the bank

which received it, it appears to me that, if that bank were to pass on the claim
as a valid claim and demand payment, it would be guilty of fraud which
would justify non-payment of the demand, notwithstanding that the
demand on its face appeared to be valid.'

[53] Finally, in the recent unreported case of *Consolidated Oil Ltd v American
Express Bank Ltd* [2000] CA Transcript 85, a case in which the validity of a demand
made under a performance guarantee was in issue on the basis that the
committee in whose name the demand was made was no longer in existence,
Clarke LJ observed:

'In addition, it (the bank) could not properly pay if the only realistic
inference on the material available was that M Brou could not honestly have
believed in the validity of the demand or that the committee no longer
existed, or that M Brou no longer had the authority of the committee even if
it did exist.'

[54] It is also to be noted that, immediately following the passage quoted,
Clarke LJ added:

'However, as I have already indicated, the claimant cannot show that that
is the only realistic inference. It is well settled in cases of this kind that a bank
is under no duty to investigate whether there is fraud. To impose such a duty
upon a bank in the position of the bank here would, as I see it, deal a serious
blow to the ordinary processes of international banking and international
commerce. In all the circumstances, I have reached the conclusion that the
claimant has not established a sufficiently arguable case that the bank would
be in breach of any duty owed to it if it were to pay.'

[55] In the context in which they were uttered, it does not seem to me that the
dicta relied on in those cases, other than the *United City Merchants* case, provide
any assistance in relation to the argument placed before us. All arise in cases
where the argument raised and considered related to the fraud exception; no
nullity exception, as such, was under discussion. In the *GKN* case, Parker LJ was
considering fraud by a bank rather than by a beneficiary and was envisaging the
case of a demand made under a performance guarantee by a party whom the
bank knew not to be the party named as the beneficiary entitled to make the
demand. He was thus not considering the case of a document which, at the time
it was tendered and accepted was, *unknown* to the bank, false or made without
authority, but a case involving fraudulent conduct by the bank itself in accepting
a claim known to be made by a person not entitled to make it and passing it on as
a valid claim without disclosing the position to the bank's principal. In the
Consolidated Oil case, Clarke LJ was, in the passage relied on, dealing with a not
dissimilar point going to the existence and entitlement of the named beneficiary
at the time of making his demand and was in any event propounding an exception
where the only realistic inference was one of fraud on the part of the beneficiary.

[56] I consider that the judge was correct in the decision to which he came.
The fraud exception to the autonomy principle recognised in English law has
hitherto been restricted to, and it is in my view desirable that it should remain
based upon, the fraud or knowledge of fraud on the part of the beneficiary or
other party seeking payment under and in accordance with the terms of the letter
of credit. It should not be avoided or extended by the argument that a document
presented, which conforms on its face with the terms of the letter of the credit, is
none the less of a character which disentitles the person making the demand to

a payment because it is fraudulent *in itself*, independently of the knowledge and bona fides of the demanding party. In my view, that is the clear import of Lord Diplock's observations in *Gian Singh* and in the *United City Merchants* case, in which all their Lordships concurred. As I understand it, Lord Diplock was of the view that a seller/beneficiary who was ignorant of forgery by a third party of one of the documents presented, or of the fact that the document contained a

b representation false to the knowledge of the person who created it, should not be in a worse position than someone who has taken a draft drawn under a letter of credit in circumstances which rendered him a holder in due course. While he left open the position in relation to a forged document where the effect of the forgery was to render the document a 'nullity', there is nothing to suggest that he would have recognised any nullity exception as extending to a document which was not

c forged (ie fraudulently produced) but was signed by the creator in honest error as to his authority; nor do I consider that such an exception should be recognised.

[57] That being so, I do not consider that the fact that in this case it was the seller/beneficiary himself who created the document said to be a nullity should *of itself* disentitle him to payment, assuming (as the judge found) that such

d creation was devoid of any fraudulent intent and was effected in the belief that GK enjoyed the authority of Montrod, as applicant for the credit, to sign and issue the certificate. Although the circumstances were highly unusual, they may none the less be regarded as no more than an illustration of the wide variety of circumstances in which documents come into existence in a commercial context which do not necessarily reflect the factual situation but which parties may none

e the less employ as a convenient means of progressing a particular transaction. If, in the circumstances of a multipartite transaction, a seller/beneficiary is indeed led to believe that he has authority to create and present a certificate of inspection for the purpose of triggering payment by letter of credit, I do not see why he should be regarded as any less entitled to payment in accordance with UCP 500

f than in a case where he receives from a third party a document regular on its face which has, unknown to him, been created without authority.

[58] In my view there are sound policy reasons for not extending the law by creation of a general nullity exception. Most documentary credits issued in the United Kingdom incorporate the UCP by reference. Various revisions of the UCP have been widely adopted in the United States and by United Kingdom and

g Commonwealth banks. They are intended to embody international banking practice and to create certainty in an area of law where the need for precision and certainty are paramount. The creation of a general nullity exception, the formulation of which does not seem to me susceptible of precision, involves making undesirable inroads into the principles of autonomy and negotiability universally recognised in relation to letter of credit transactions. In the context

h of the fraud exception, the courts have made clear how difficult it is to invoke the exception and have been at pains to point out that banks deal in documents and questions of apparent conformity. In that context they have made clear that it is not for a bank to make its own inquiries about allegations of fraud brought to its notice; if a party wishes to establish that a demand is fraudulent it must place

j before the bank evidence of clear and obvious fraud (see the *Edward Owen Engineering Ltd* case [1978] 1 All ER 976 cf *Turkiye Is Bankasi AS v Bank of China* [1996] 2 Lloyd's Rep 611 at 617 per Waller J). If a general nullity exception were to be introduced as part of English law it would place banks in a further dilemma as to the necessity to investigate facts, which they are not competent to do and from which UCP 500 is plainly concerned to exempt them. Further, such an exception would be likely to act unfairly upon beneficiaries participating in a chain of contracts in cases where their good faith is not in question. Such a development would thus undermine the system of financing international trade by means of documentary credits.

[59] I have concluded that there is and should be no general nullity exception based upon the concept of a document being fraudulent *in itself* or devoid of commercial value. I would only add, with reference to Lord Diplock's reservation, that I would not seek to exclude the possibility that, in an individual case, the conduct of a beneficiary in connection with the creation and/or presentation of a document forged by a third party might, though itself not amounting to fraud, be of such character as not to deserve the protection available to a holder in due course. In this connection, I note the reference by Mocatta J in the *United City Merchants* case [1979] 1 Lloyd's Rep 267 to 'personal fraud' or 'unscrupulous conduct' on the part of the seller presenting documents for payment, a remark upon which Lord Diplock made no adverse comment when approving the original judgment on the documentary credit point. In this connection, we have had brought to our attention the decision of the High Court of Singapore in *Lambias (Importers and Exporters) Co PTE Ltd v Hong Kong & Shanghai Banking Corp* [1993] 2 SLR 751, in which the defendant bank rejected documents tendered under a letter of credit which included a quality and weight inspection certificate required to be countersigned by a named individual. The court held that the certificate contained discrepancies which entitled the bank to refuse the documents tendered and went on to find that the inspection certificate was in any event a nullity in that, not only did it fail to state the particulars of the goods and their quality and weight, but that, having been issued by the beneficiary instead of the applicant, it had been countersigned by an impostor. Having considered the observations, and in particular the reservation, of Lord Diplock in the *United City Merchants* case and the particular facts before the court in relation to the plaintiffs, who had themselves introduced the countersignatory to the bank as the person named, the court observed:

'The law cannot condone actions which, although not amounting to fraud per se, are of such recklessness and haste that the documents produced as a result are clearly not in conformity with the requirements of the credit. The plaintiffs in the present case are not guilty of fraud, but they were unknowingly responsible for having aided in the perpetration of the fraud. In such a case, where the fraud was discovered even before all other documents were tendered, I think it is right and proper that the plaintiffs should not be permitted to claim under the letter of credit.' (see [1993] 2 SLR 751 at 765–766.)

[60] While such a finding was not necessary to the outcome of the case, it fell within the reservation of Lord Diplock in the *United City Merchants* case and has certain attractions. However, it is not necessary for us to decide in this case whether it is correct. This is a case where the judge found neither recklessness, haste, nor blame in the conduct of GK. Furthermore, in the *Lambias* case the bank rejected the documents as non-compliant, whereas in this case SCB accepted the documents as compliant, having raised Montrod's observations and reservations with Fibi before it did so. Fibi in turn accepted the documents when sent to them, making clear to Montrod that payment would be made unless a court order to prevent it were obtained.

[61] In those circumstances, I consider that GK were entitled to payment and I would affirm the decision of the judge. Consequently, I would dismiss the

a appeal of Fibi in respect of the claim of SCB for reimbursement of the sum of $US 498,311·51 paid to Commerzbank and the appeal of Montrod against the judgment obtained by Fibi for indemnity against the claim of SCB.

MONTROD'S NEW CLAIMS AGAINST GK

[62] By the judge's decision that Fibi was obliged to reimburse SCB and that
b Montrod must pay Fibi, the proposed reconstitution of the action with SCB as claimant against Fibi, Fibi claiming in turn against Montrod, was rendered unnecessary. However, that left outstanding Montrod's application to make new claims against GK to recover what it had paid to Fibi. The judge therefore treated Montrod's application to file a claim against GK under CPR Pt 20 as an application for permission to amend its existing claim for a declaration against GK to include
c new claims as set out in a draft amended statement of case. Permission was opposed by GK on the grounds that the proposed claims had no real prospect of success.

[63] The claims sought to be made in the draft case were various and some fell by the wayside as a result of the judge's decision in relation to the nullity
d exception. However, the pleas relevant to this appeal were the following.

(1) A claim in negligence to the effect that—

'By its agreement to the terms of the letter of credit Grundkotter assumed a duty to Montrod to exercise reasonable skill and care in the presentation to SCB of documents intended to induce a payment thereunder.'

e
This claim has been referred to as the primary claim in negligence.

(2) A further claim in negligence that:

'16 ... Alternatively, by its assumption of the right and responsibility to
f issue and sign the certificates of inspection purportedly on behalf of Montrod and thereafter to present the same to SCB without qualification, Grundkotter assumed a duty to take reasonable care to ensure that it had Montrod's instructions so to do and that the documents so issued, signed and presented were valid.

17. Grundkotter failed to take reasonable or any care to ensure that it had
g such instructions prior to the issue, signature and presentation of each certificate of inspection to SCB. In the premiss it was in breach of the said duty of care on each such occasion.'

This has been referred to as the narrower negligence claim.
h (3) A claim for breach of fiduciary duty pleaded as follows:

'18. Further or in the alternative, by holding itself out to third parties, in particular SCB, as Montrod's agent for the purposes of issuing and signing the certificates of inspection, Grundkotter assumed a fiduciary duty to Montrod to act only in accordance with Montrod's instructions to do so,
j alternatively to take reasonable care to ensure that it was acting only in accordance with such instructions. No such instructions were given by Montrod or by an authorised agent of Montrod. Grundkotter failed to take reasonable care to ensure that relevant instructions had been given to it by Montrod. In the premises, Grundkotter's issue, signature and presentation to SCB of each certificate of inspection was a breach of the said fiduciary duty.'

The primary claim in negligence

[64] The judge rejected the alleged duty of care in the following terms ([2001] 1 All ER (Comm) 368 at 383):

'It cannot be argued that the beneficiary to a credit owes a duty to the applicant with regard to the documents which he presents. If the documents accord with the credit, the beneficiary is entitled to be paid. If they do not, they will be rejected unless the applicant agrees to waive the discrepancy. If the documents accord with the credit but there is none the less a breach of the underlying contract, which breach arises in connection with the documents, the buyer has a right of action against the seller/beneficiary arising from their contract. If the buyer is not the applicant, when the documents came through he will have had to reimburse the applicant just as he would have had to reimburse the issuing bank if he had been the applicant. The beneficiary does not owe a duty of care to the issuing bank. In the present case Montrod simply stands in the chain as a finance house. Its position is the same as that of Fibi Bank save that Fibi Bank is one further up the chain. Grundkotter owed no duty of care to Standard Chartered in the presentation of documents. Nor did it owe such a duty to Fibi Bank or to Montrod.'

[65] Montrod seek permission to appeal against that decision.

[66] In my view the judge was right to refuse Montrod permission to advance the primary claim in negligence. The only fact pleaded in support of the duty of care was GK's 'agreement to the terms of a letter of credit', the duty of care being expressed as a duty relating to all of the documents required to be produced by GK to SCB in order to obtain payment under the letter of credit. Montrod did not plead any *express* assumption of responsibility or duty; its case was simply based on an implied assumption of responsibility, arising by reason of GK's agreement to the terms of the credit. So far as GK was concerned, the letter of credit (albeit issued on Montrod's application) was procured by Ballaris pursuant to its obligation to pay GK under the supply contract by this form of payment. GK agreed to its terms as part of Ballaris' performance of its payment obligation. GK's acceptance of that performance did not imply or give rise to any assumption of responsibility by GK vis-à-vis Montrod. In seeking to ensure that documents presented to the issuing bank comply with the terms of the letter of credit, a beneficiary is pursuing his own commercial interests. He seeks to present compliant documents in order himself to be paid in the context of a transaction in which the commercial interests of the issuing bank and other parties involved in connection with the letter of credit are dealt with in the manner provided for under UCP 500, subject to the provisions of which they are aware that the transactions will be conducted and the commercial risk distributed.

[67] Montrod's arguments before us have not been based upon a *Hedley Byrne*-type assumption of duty or responsibility as pleaded (*Hedley Byrne & Co Ltd v Heller & Partners Ltd* [1963] 2 All ER 575, [1964] AC 465; see *Henderson v Merrett Syndicates Ltd* [1994] 3 All ER 506 at 518–521, [1995] 2 AC 145 at 178–181 per Lord Goff) but upon foresight, proximity and the 'fair, just and reasonable' test in *Caparo Industries plc v Dickman* [1990] 1 All ER 568, [1990] 2 AC 605. In relation to that test, it has been submitted that it is both proper and appropriate to impose a duty of care on a beneficiary in respect of the presentation of documents intended to induce payment under a letter of credit in circumstances where the credit applicant (not being the buyer) has no alternative contractual relationship with

the beneficiary through which any injustice can be addressed. However, that ignores the fact that the applicant for a credit who is not the buyer may normally be expected to have secured his position, and to be reliant upon a remedy against his buyer in respect of any of his liabilities arising from the letter of credit transaction. Further, on the assumption that Montrod did not confer, or authorise those who purported to confer, authority upon GK to sign the inspection certificates, it follows that those individuals were engaged in a conspiracy to defraud in respect of which Montrod could, if it saw fit, pursue legal remedies. The fact that it may not be practicable or financially expedient to pursue those remedies does not point to a lacuna in the law to be filled by implying a duty of care in a situation in which no responsibility was assumed by GK.

[68] The real issue is which of two innocent parties should bear the risk of the fraud of a third party in a case of this kind. It is not the function of the law of negligence to provide a general remedy for the recovery of purely economic losses resulting from such a fraud. In any given situation, the remedy will only exist if the ingredients of a voluntary assumption of responsibility of the relevant type can be established: see *Hamble Fisheries Ltd v L Gardner & Sons Ltd, The Rebecca Flame* [1999] 2 Lloyd's Rep 1 at 8 (paras 3 and 4 of the judgment of Mummery LJ). In my view the mere fact that GK agreed to the terms of the letter of credit is insufficient material from which to imply any such assumption of responsibility. I would therefore affirm the judge's decision in that respect.

The narrower negligence claim

[69] In relation to the narrower negligence claim based on GK's 'assumption of the right and responsibility to issue and sign the certificates of inspection', the judge granted Montrod permission to amend its claim in order to advance that case at trial. He stated his reasons as follows ([2001] 1 All ER (Comm) 368 at 383):

'I approach the novel and unusual situation in the present case by considering first the position of a party who is the agent of another in the sense that he regularly receives instructions from him and acts for him. It is not difficult to foresee circumstances in which such an agent should as part of the performance of his duty to his principal check or clarify his instructions. The checking of instructions where the circumstances call for it is one of the ordinary incidents of an agency situation. If the agent fails to do so, then he may be liable in damages if as a result his principal suffers damage. If the party is not an agent in the sense I have mentioned, but believes that he has authority to act for a principal which he does not in fact have, it seems to me arguable with a real chance of success that he would come under a similar duty. So, on this application, so far as the existence of a duty in this form is concerned, I am in Montrod's favour.'

[70] GK asserts the judge's conclusion was wrong for the following reasons. (1) He was wrong to start with, or treat as analogous, the position of an agent who regularly acts for a particular principal. The duty of such agent to check his instructions arises from a real and pre-existing agency, and then only if the instructions are ambiguous. In the case of clear 'ad hoc' and first-time instructions as in this case, there was no duty or occasion to check further. From GK's point of view the instructions were not ambiguous. On GK's state of knowledge the signature on the certificate was simply a written confirmation and assurance of the quality of the goods, GK having no knowledge of the 'blocking' purpose underlying Montrod's stipulation in respect of such certificates. (2) Montrod's claim for negligence must be categorised either as performance of a negligent

service by GK or the making of a negligent statement. It is not put on the latter basis and, as to the former, GK were not negligent in that they properly fulfilled the only task of which they were aware, ie to certify the quality of the goods, being ignorant of any need to check whether Montrod had been placed in funds.(3) Causation cannot be established. SCB did not pay because GK had failed to check whether it had Montrod's authority. The real cause of the loss was that Montrod had failed to obtain cash cover from Ballaris, which contingency was not foreseeable by GK. Thus GK's failure to check merely provided the occasion for Montrod's loss but did not cause it. (4) For the same reasons that it would not be fair, just or reasonable to impose the wider duty of care, it would be wrong to impose the narrower duty, given that GK acted honestly at all times in agreeing to sign for Montrod and in presenting the documents under the letter of credit. It was not party to any information which might lead it to suspect the underlying purpose of Montrod, either from the buyers or on the face of the documents. Thus, however it is put, the negligence claim has no prospect of success.

[71] The above submissions have considerable force and may well lead to success at trial. However, they ignore the fact that the only material so far before the court consists of the untested statements of the various witnesses, in particular those for GK, who will plainly be the subject of probing examination as to their experience, competence and state of knowledge as to letter of credit transactions, and what precisely they were told by the buyers or their representatives.

[72] As to GK's first submission, it is no part of GK's case that Ballaris had any apparent authority to act or speak for Montrod, let alone to give instructions that GK should check the goods and exercise Montrod's stated discretion to issue and sign the certificates in respect of which GK assumed authority. Thus, vis-à-vis Montrod, GK acted in the role of self-appointed agents. That being so it is well arguable that, in carrying out the role and exercising the authority they had assumed, they owed Montrod duties analogous to those of an agent. Whether or not it was helpful for the judge to consider the position where there was a pre-existing agency, it does not seem to me possible to say that, in the circumstances of the case as they may emerge at trial, Montrod has no prospect of successfully establishing that, before shipping and/or exercising the role of agent in relation to the certificates of quality, GK should have checked the fact that, and the circumstances in which, they should exercise such authority, in the light of the (somewhat ambiguous) provision that Montrod had a discretion in respect of the issue and signature of the certificates.

[73] As to GK's second submission, the negligence complained of is GK's breach of the duty as purported agent to check and clarify its authority and/or the extent of its instructions in the circumstances of doubt and ambiguity which, on Montrod's case, existed (in respect of which it is noteworthy that GK in part sought advice from Commerzbank); Montrod does not allege negligence in the course of rendering a specific service. Honesty is not relevant to the question of negligence in that respect.

[74] As to GK's third submission, it seems to me at least arguable that it was foreseeable that Montrod would not exercise its discretion to sign and issue a certificate unless it was in funds, or at least adequately secured, vis-à-vis Ballaris and that the damage was therefore not too remote.

[75] As to GK's fourth submission, depending upon the position as it emerges at trial, I do not consider that it can at this stage be decided that it would not be fair, just and reasonable to impose liability on GK for breach of duty in a situation in which (ex hypothesi) by its own incompetence it created a document without

a authority and thereby procured a payment to which it was entitled at the expense of the person in whose name the document was executed. The question in respect of the narrower duty is not whether, simply by agreeing to the letter of credit transaction, GK assumed a duty, but whether, by agreeing to an unusual procedure in respect of certification at the request of the buyer without enquiry as to whether the procedure requested engaged the authority and consent of the

b applicant for credit, GK both assumed and failed to discharge its responsibility vis-à-vis the applicant. Short of agreement between the parties, it does not seem to me that that issue can or should be disposed of without a trial. I therefore would refuse GK's application for leave to appeal in this respect.

FIDUCIARY DUTY

c [76] The judge rejected Montrod's pleaded claim for breach of fiduciary duty in the following terms ([2001] 1 All ER (Comm) 368 at 384):

'If this claim is intended to give the same remedy as the claim in negligence, then it adds nothing. In *Bristol and West Building Society v Mothew (t/a Stapley & Co)* [1996] 4 All ER 698 at 710, [1998] Ch 1 at 16 Millett LJ

d stated: "The expression 'fiduciary duty' is properly confined to those duties which are peculiar to fiduciaries and the breach of which attracts legal consequences differing from those consequent upon the breach of other duties." In *Henderson v Merrett Syndicates Ltd, Hallam-Eames v Merrett Syndicates Ltd, Hughes v Merrett Syndicates Ltd, Arbuthnott v Feltrim Underwriting Agencies Ltd, Deeny v Goods Walker Ltd (in liq)* [1994] 3 All ER 506 at 543, [1995]

e 2 AC 145 at 205 Lord Browne-Wilkinson stated: "The liability of a fiduciary for the negligent transaction of his duties is not a separate head of liability but the paradigm of the general duty to act with care imposed by law on those who take it upon themselves to act for or advise others." Mr Jones referred to *Phipps v Boardman* [1965] 1 All ER 849, [1965] Ch 992, Court of Appeal, and

f [1966] 3 All ER 721, [1967] 2 AC 46, House of Lords. But I do not think that the principles considered there have any application to the present circumstances.'

[77] Thus it is apparent that the judge dismissed the claim for breach of fiduciary duty on the basis that it added nothing to the claim in negligence.

g [78] Before turning to the question of whether that was an appropriate course, it seems to me clear that, where someone puts himself in the position of a self-appointed agent in relation to the affairs and interests of another, he is liable to be regarded as a fiduciary in respect of the exercise of his powers in the name of that other. That seems to me inherent in the judgments of the Court of Appeal

h in *Phipps v Boardman* [1965] 1 All ER 849 at 855, 864, [1965] Ch 992 at 1017–1018, 1030 per Lord Denning MR and Pearson LJ respectively; see also *English v Dedham Vale Properties Ltd* [1978] 1 All ER 382, [1978] 1 WLR 93. Montrod argues that this is such a case. Reliance is placed on GK's purported exercise of Montrod's discretion, its representation to SCB that its signature was that of Montrod in order to demand money from a bank which ultimately Montrod was liable to reimburse,

j and its continued demand for payment even when it knew and accepted that it had submitted false certificates; all are said to be breaches of duty of a fiduciary nature. While the judge held that GK were not guilty of fraud, it seems to me that those are arguments which are in principle open to Montrod in the circumstances of this case and, since the application was made at an early stage in the proceedings and did not raise matters which would not require to be investigated in any event in relation to the narrower claim in negligence, it is difficult to see why amendment was not permitted. In the event the judge rejected the plea on the basis that it would add *e* nothing to the remedy sought in negligence.

[79] We have received lengthy submissions from Mr Choo-Choy for GK as to why the judge was correct to take that view. He has argued that, since there is no claim for a secret profit (the matter of principle concerned in *Phipps*'s case and *English*'s case) nothing useful can be added to the case via the fiduciary duty route. None the less, Montrod seeks to claim not only damages for common law *b* negligence in the amount of the sum which it is liable to pay Fibi, but also lays claim to the sum paid by, or at the direction of, SCB to GK as a sum held in trust for Montrod for which GK is liable to account. It is at least arguable that recovery on the basis of breach of fiduciary duty will lead to a more beneficial interest rate. In my view, the only vice of this amendment is that if, in truth, it adds nothing to the plea in negligence, argument upon the point of principle will lead to a *c* relatively short increase in court time and (it may be) an increase in costs. I do not think that the former consideration is sufficient to outweigh the opportunity for Montrod to air its case fully and the latter may be compensated for within the order for costs made at trial, should the court think it appropriate to do so.

[80] I would therefore grant Montrod's application for permission to appeal, *d* allow the appeal and permit the amendment sought to be made together with any appropriate adjustment to the claim for relief.

SIR MARTIN NOURSE.
[81] I agree with the judgment of Potter LJ and with the orders proposed by him. *e*

THORPE LJ.
[82] I agree.

Montrod's and Fibi's appeal on the nullity issue dismissed. Montrod's application for permission to appeal on the primary negligence issue dismissed, but its application for f permission to appeal granted, and appeal allowed, on the breach of fiduciary duty issue. Grundkötter's application for permission to appeal dismissed.

James Brooks   Barrister.

30 May 2002. The Appeal Committee of the House of Lords dismissed a petition by Montrod for permission to appeal.

a
Medcalf v Mardell and others
[2002] UKHL 27

HOUSE OF LORDS

LORD BINGHAM OF CORNHILL, LORD STEYN, LORD HOFFMANN, LORD HOBHOUSE OF
b WOODBOROUGH AND LORD RODGER OF EARLSFERRY

16–18 APRIL, 27 JUNE 2002

*Counsel – Payment of costs by counsel personally – Costs incurred improperly,
unreasonably or negligently – Whether court having power to make wasted costs orders
c only against lawyers of party applying for such an order – Whether liability of
barristers for wasted costs limited to conduct of case in court – Whether rule of
professional conduct precluding counsel from pleading allegation of fraud in absence of
admissible evidence – Circumstances in which court may make wasted costs orders
where barristers precluded by legal professional privilege from answering complaints
made against them – Supreme Court Act 1981, s 51 – Code of Conduct of the Bar of
d England and Wales, para 606(c).*

The appellant barristers acted as advocates for two defendants in an appeal to the
Court of Appeal against a judgment in the claimant's favour. The first day-and-a-half
of the four-day hearing was taken up by an application by the defendants to
amend their notice of appeal in order to make serious allegations of fraud and
e other impropriety against the claimant. Those allegations had been set out in a
draft amended notice of appeal, bearing the names of both barristers, and a
skeleton argument in support of the application to amend, signed by both
barristers. The court rejected the application to amend in respect of the allegations
of fraud and impropriety, and also dismissed the appeal. The claimant then
f sought wasted costs orders against the barristers under s 51(6)[a] of the Supreme
Court Act 1981, seeking to recover the costs said to have been incurred in
investigating and rebutting the allegations of fraud and impropriety. Section 51(7)
of the 1981 Act defined 'wasted costs' as, inter alia, any costs incurred by a party
as a result of any improper, unreasonable or negligent act or omission on the part
of any legal representative, while s 51(13) provided that 'legal representative', in
g relation to a party to the proceedings, meant any person exercising a right of
audience or 'right to conduct litigation on his behalf'. The claimant contended
that the barristers had acted improperly by breaching para 606(c)[b] of the Code of
Conduct of the Bar of England and Wales (the Code), which precluded a barrister
from drafting any notice of appeal containing any allegation of fraud unless, inter
h alia, he 'has before him reasonably credible material which as it stands establishes
a prima facie case of fraud'. The barristers denied that allegation, but claimed that
legal professional privilege precluded them from putting before the court full
details of the material that had been available to them, and that accordingly it
would be unfair of the court to draw inferences as to the available material or to
j exercise its discretion to make an order. That contention was rejected by the
majority of the Court of Appeal which held that para 606(c) of the Code
precluded a barrister from putting his signature to an allegation of fraud unless he
had before him evidence in a form to be put before the court to make good the

---

a   Section 51, so far as material, is set out at [12], below
b   Paragraph 606, so far as material, is set out at [11], below

allegation; that there was no reasonably credible admissible evidence before the
court to substantiate most of the allegations of fraud; that the barristers could have
had no such admissible evidence before them when signing the draft amended
notice of appeal and the skeleton argument; and that in those circumstances a
wasted costs order should be made against them. The barristers appealed,
challenging those conclusions. They also relied on the words 'right to conduct
litigation on his behalf' in s 51(13) to contend that the court had no power to make
a wasted costs order against the legal representative of any opposing party, and that
such an order could only be made against barristers in relation to their conduct
when exercising a right of audience in court.

Held – (1) On the true construction of s 51 of the 1981 Act, the court did have power
to make a wasted costs order in favour of one party to proceedings against the legal
representative of any other party to the same proceedings, and the liability of a
barrister for such an order was not limited to his conduct when exercising a right
of audience in court. Subsection (13) was intended simply to make plain that no
liability could attach to any practitioner not involved in the litigation giving rise to the
claim. It would stultify the section if a barrister were not potentially liable for
conduct immediately relevant to the exercise of a right of audience but not
involving advocacy in open court. It followed in the instant case that the Court of
Appeal had had jurisdiction to make the wasted costs order against the barristers (see
[19], [20], [45], [46], [74], [75], below); *Brown v Bennett* [2002] 2 All ER 273 approved.

(2) On the true construction of para 606(c) of the Code, counsel was not
required, when putting his signature to an allegation of fraud, to have before him
evidence in a form to put before the court to make good the allegation.
Although, at the hearing stage, counsel could not properly make or persist in an
allegation that was unsupported by admissible evidence, it was sufficient at the
preparatory stage that he had material of such a character as to lead responsible
counsel to conclude that serious allegations could properly be based upon it. It
followed in the instant case that the majority of the Court of Appeal had applied
too stringent a test (see [22], [26], [45], [46], [75], [79], below).

(3) Where a wasted costs order was sought against a practitioner precluded by
legal professional privilege from giving his full answer to the application, the
court should not make an order unless, proceeding with extreme care, it was
(a) satisfied that there was nothing the practitioner could say, if unconstrained, to
resist the order and (b) that it was in all the circumstances fair to make the order.
Only rarely would the court be able to make full allowance for the inability of the
practitioner to tell the whole story or to conclude that that there was no room for
doubt in a situation in which, of necessity, the court was deprived of access to the
full facts on which, in the ordinary way, any sound judicial decision had to be
based. Even if the court were able properly to be sure that the practitioner could
have no answer to the substantive complaint, it could not fairly make an order
unless satisfied that nothing could be said to influence the exercise of its
discretion. In the instant case, the court did not know, and could not be told,
whether the barristers, when signing the draft amended notice of appeal and the
skeleton argument, had had before them material of any kind which justified the
making of the allegations. Hunch and suspicion were not enough, and the
barristers had to be given the benefit of the doubt. In a case of such complexity,
it would be unfair and contrary to the appearance of justice to condemn them
unheard. Accordingly, the appeal would be allowed (see [23], [25]–[27], [41]–[46],
[74]–[76], below); *Ridehalgh v Horsefield* [1994] 3 All ER 848 approved.

Notes

a For personal liability of legal representatives for costs in civil proceedings, see 44(1) *Halsbury's Laws* (4th edn reissue) para 171.

For the Supreme Court Act 1981, s 51, see 11 *Halsbury's Statutes* (4th edn) (2000 reissue) 1094.

b Cases referred to in opinions

Associated Leisure Ltd v Associated Newspapers Ltd [1970] 2 All ER 754, [1970] 2 QB 450, [1970] 3 WLR 101, CA.

Brown v Bennett [2002] 2 All ER 273, [2002] 1 WLR 713.

Byrne v South Sefton (Merseyside) Health Authority [2001] EWCA Civ 1904, [2002] 1 WLR 775.

c *Campbell v UK* (1992) 15 EHRR 137, [1992] ECHR 13590/88, ECt HR.

De Haes v Belgium (1997) 25 EHRR 1, [1997] ECHR 19983/99, ECt HR.

Drums and Packaging Ltd v Freeman [1999] All ER (D) 964.

Foxley v UK (2000) 8 BHRC 571, ECt HR.

General Mediterranean Holdings SA v Patel [1999] 3 All ER 673, [2000] 1 WLR 272.

d *Hall (Arthur J S) & Co (a firm) v Simons, Barratt v Ansell (t/a Woolf Seddon (a firm)), Harris v Scholfield Roberts & Hill (a firm)* [2000] 3 All ER 673, [2002] 1 AC 615, [2000] 3 WLR 543, HL.

Harley v McDonald, Glasgow Harley (a firm) v McDonald [2001] UKPC 18, [2001] 2 AC 678, [2001] 2 WLR 1749.

Kelly v London Transport Executive [1982] 2 All ER 842, [1982] 1 WLR 1055, CA.

e *Ladd v Marshall* [1954] 3 All ER 745, [1954] 1 WLR 1489, CA.

Lillicrap v Nalder & Son (a firm) [1993] 1 All ER 724, [1993] 1 WLR 94, CA.

Myers v Elman [1939] 4 All ER 484, [1940] AC 282, HL.

Oldfield v Keogh (1941) 41 SR (NSW) 206, NSW SC.

Orchard v South Eastern Electricity Board [1987] 1 All ER 95, [1987] QB 565, [1987] 2 WLR 102, CA.

f *Parry-Jones v Law Society* [1968] 1 All ER 177, [1969] 1 Ch 1, [1968] 2 WLR 397, CA.

R v Derby Magistrates' Court, ex p B [1995] 4 All ER 526, [1996] AC 487, [1995] 3 WLR 681, HL.

R v IRC, ex p Taylor (No 2) [1989] 3 All ER 353, DC; *affd* [1990] 2 All ER 409, CA.

g *Ridehalgh v Horsefield* [1994] 3 All ER 848, [1994] Ch 205, [1994] 3 WLR 462, CA.

Symphony Group plc v Hodgson [1993] 4 All ER 143, [1994] QB 179, [1993] 3 WLR 830, CA.

Worsley v Tambrands Ltd (8 November 2000, unreported), QBD.

Appeal

h The appellant barristers, Bernard Richard Weatherill QC and Josephine Mary Hayes, appealed with permission of the Appeal Committee of the House of Lords given on 15 May 2001 from the order of the Court of Appeal (Peter Gibson and Schiemann LJJ, Wilson J dissenting) on 24 November 2000 ([2001] Lloyd's Rep PN 146) requiring them to pay the wasted costs incurred by the claimant, Roger Keith

j Medcalf, flowing from the pleading and pursuit of allegations set out in certain paragraphs of a draft amended notice of appeal, signed by the barristers as counsel for the first and fourth defendants, Terence Mardell and the Terry Mardell Organisation Ltd (TMO), from the order of Lloyd J on 29 June 1998 giving judgment for Mr Medcalf in his proceedings against Mr Mardell, TMO and the second defendant, Michael Kemp. That appeal, in which Mr Kemp played no part, had been dismissed by the Court of Appeal on 2 March 2000. Proceedings

against the third defendant, the British Broadcasting Corp, had been settled
before the trial of the action. The facts are set out in the opinion of Lord Bingham
of Cornhill.

Nicholas Davidson QC and *Leigh Ann Mulcahy* (instructed by *Clyde & Co*) for the
barristers.
Romie Tager QC and *Edward Rowntree* (instructed by *Gordon Dadds*) for Mr Medcalf.

Their Lordships took time for consideration.

27 June 2002. The following opinions were delivered.

LORD BINGHAM OF CORNHILL.
[1] My Lords, in this appeal two barristers (Mr Bernard Weatherill QC and
Ms Josephine Hayes) challenge a wasted costs order made against them by the
Court of Appeal. They do so on two grounds: first, that the court had no
jurisdiction to make the order; and second, that such an order should not have
been made when they were precluded by legal professional privilege from
answering the complaints made against them. The appeal requires the House,
for the first time, to consider the wasted costs order regime introduced by s 4 of
the Courts and Legal Services Act 1990 and expressed in s 51(6), (7) and (13) of the
Supreme Court Act 1981.

The proceedings
[2] The proceedings in which the wasted costs order was made against the
barristers concerned a snooker-based television quiz game, originally conceived
by Mr Michael Kemp in about 1984 and developed in its early stages in 1987, first by
Mr Kemp and Mr Roger Medcalf and then by these two with the addition of
Mr Mardell, who had professional experience of developing and exploiting television
game shows and was involved both personally and through his company,
originally named Createl Ltd and then the Terry Mardell Organisation Ltd (the
TMO). The plans for this new game show went through various different
versions and were the subject of much discussion and refinement. Presentations
were made on several occasions to the BBC, which was slow to respond. In the end,
however, the BBC did respond. It bought the new game show and programmes
were transmitted. They have proved to be a continuing success. But from about
the end of 1987 Mr Medcalf was excluded from any part in the development and
exploitation of the project, which were handled by Mr Mardell and his company
and Mr Kemp.
[3] In July 1993 Mr Medcalf issued proceedings against Mr Mardell, Mr Kemp,
the BBC (which settled before the action came to trial and played no further part)
and the TMO. Mr Medcalf's claim at that stage was based on alleged infringement
of copyright and breach of confidence. The action came on for trial before
Lightman J in January 1997 but was aborted on the third day of trial to enable
Mr Medcalf's advisers to re-plead his case so as to include an additional claim in
partnership. A stringent order in costs was made against Mr Medcalf as a condition
of the postponement. Mr Medcalf's case was then re-pleaded and a second trial
took place before Lloyd J in May 1998. At this trial the judge preferred the
evidence of Mr Medcalf to that of Mr Mardell and Mr Kemp. He found that there
had been a partnership between the three men to be inferred from their conduct
and that there had also been a breach of confidence. The defendants were ordered

a to provide an account of the profits of the partnership and to make an interim
payment of £100,000 into court.

[4] Mr Mardell and the TMO (but not Mr Kemp) at once appealed against the
judge's decision and there was a second appeal against certain orders made by the
judge in a later decision on the taking of the partnership accounts. No satisfactory
account was provided in compliance with the judge's order and in July 1999
b Mr Medcalf applied to strike out the defendants' third attempt to provide the
account ordered. In response the defendants served witness statements making,
for the first time, serious allegations of fraud against Mr Medcalf and his solicitors
in connection with the conduct of the action before Lloyd J. It was alleged that
Mr Medcalf or his solicitors had tampered with the transcripts of evidence given
at the trial, that Mr Medcalf's solicitors had attempted to pervert the course of
c justice during without prejudice discussions with Mr Kemp and that Mr Medcalf's
signature on his witness statement had been forged. No transcripts of evidence
had been available to the judge when he had given judgment and Mr Medcalf in
evidence had vouched the proof of his witness statement, but these points were
relied on as impugning the credibility of Mr Medcalf, and the reliability of his
d evidence had been an important issue at the trial. The master referred the striking
out application to Lloyd J, who was to have heard it on 26 November 1999 but
who was in the event unable to hear it until 2 December 1999.

[5] Neither of the appellant barristers had up to then represented Mr Mardell or
the TMO. Ms Hayes was instructed shortly before 24 November. On 25 November
she informed leading counsel for Mr Medcalf (Mr Romie Tager QC) of an application
e she intended to make (and shortly thereafter did make) to the judge, that he should
direct the police to investigate the allegations made concerning the transcripts and the
perversion of the course of justice and that Mr Medcalf's application to strike out the
account should meanwhile be stayed. Mr Medcalf's solicitors intimated an intention
to apply for a wasted costs order against the defendants' solicitors, although this
f was not pursued. In her skeleton argument for the hearing before Lloyd J on
2 December Ms Hayes included the allegations of misconduct already mentioned
but with the addition of certain serious allegations of a similar character. An
amended notice of appeal was drafted, although not formally served, including
these and additional allegations of impropriety.

[6] On 6 December 1999 Lloyd J rejected the defendants' application and
g refused permission to appeal. He went on to hear Mr Medcalf's application to
strike out the defendants' third partnership account. Mr Weatherill, appeared
before the judge with Ms Hayes on 8 December 1999 (having been instructed on
that date or shortly before) when application was made that the judge should
defer giving judgment on the striking out application pending receipt of evidence
h from the United States Department of Justice which might substantiate one of the
allegations of fraud made against Mr Medcalf. This application was refused. On
Mr Medcalf's application to strike out, the judge refused to make the order
sought, but held that the third account which the defendants had given did not
comply with his order and that they should have a last opportunity to comply.

j [7] There was intense interlocutory activity on the part of Mr Medcalf and the
defendants over the next two months. Relevantly for present purposes, the
defendants' appeal against the judge's substantive decision in favour of Mr Medcalf,
coupled with an application by the defendants to amend their notice of appeal so
as to include the allegations of impropriety against Mr Medcalf already referred
to, were due to be heard by the Court of Appeal on 14 February 2000. At a
hearing on 28 January 2000 Clarke LJ gave directions to ensure that that date

would be effective: among other things he ordered that evidence in the defendants' possession relevant to matters raised in the draft amended notice of appeal be served that day, with an indication in writing of any further evidence the defendants might wish to put before the court, and that the defendants should by 4 February 2000 issue and serve an application to amend their notice of appeal and to introduce fresh evidence, serve and file a bundle comprising all witness statements and evidence intended to be relied on, and serve and file a draft amended notice of appeal and supporting skeleton arguments covering those of the existing grounds of appeal still advanced and identifying any which were abandoned.

[8] In response to that order of Clarke LJ, the defendants served certain reports and listed evidence which was not in their possession but which they hoped would follow. A draft amended notice of appeal dated 3 February 2000, bearing the names of both barristers, was served on the following day. Skeleton arguments dated 4 February 2000, including a supplementary skeleton argument in support of the application to amend the notice of appeal signed by both the barristers, were also served on 4 February. The supplementary skeleton argument advanced submissions in support of each of the new allegations of fraud, forgery and other impropriety. Two additional bundles of evidence were served on Mr Medcalf. In the course of Friday 4 February 2000, for reasons which have not been disclosed, instructions were withdrawn from the defendants' solicitors. The barristers ceased to be instructed and the solicitors came off the record on Monday 7 February. During the following week Mr Medcalf's advisers prepared and filed evidence to rebut the allegations of fraud and impropriety raised in the draft amended notice of appeal. This evidence was not served on the barristers, who were no longer acting, but they were again instructed at about midday on Friday 11 February and the evidence was then made available to them.

[9] At the hearing before the Court of Appeal (Peter Gibson and Schiemann LJJ and Wilson J) on Monday, 14 February, Mr Weatherill and Ms Hayes, acting (as it is accepted that they did throughout) on instructions, opened the defendants' application to amend the notice of appeal and to adduce new evidence. The application to amend failed in respect of the allegations of impropriety. In the course of argument Mr Weatherill abandoned some of the allegations in the face of judicial hostility. In relation to the remaining allegations, the Court of Appeal rejected the application to amend (although other parts of the application to amend were conceded or were successful). This application occupied about one-and-a-half days of court time, although no oral answer on behalf of Mr Medcalf was called for. A further two-and-a-half days were devoted to argument on the substantive appeal. On 2 March 2000 the Court of Appeal handed down a unanimous reserved judgment, giving its reasons for rejecting the application to amend in respect of the defendants' allegations of fraud and impropriety and dismissing the substantive appeal. Counsel for Mr Medcalf indicated that he would be seeking a wasted costs order against the barristers. This matter was adjourned to enable Mr Medcalf to state his case and to enable the barristers to respond. At a hearing on 2 July 2000 the Court of Appeal ordered that this application proceed to a second stage.

[10] Before that application was resolved, Mr Medcalf compromised his action against Mr Mardell, Mr Kemp and the TMO. The terms of the compromise are not material, save to note that it expressly preserved and excluded Mr Medcalf's claim for wasted costs against the barristers. The principal basis upon which counsel for Mr Medcalf advanced the application for wasted costs against the

a   barristers was that it had been improper of them as counsel for the defendants to have advanced allegations of fraud and other improprieties in the draft amended notice of appeal, in the supplementary skeleton argument and at the hearing of the appeal when, in contravention of para 606 of the Code of Conduct of the Bar of England and Wales, they could not have had before them reasonably credible material establishing a prima facie case of fraud. Mr Medcalf sought to recover as

b   wasted costs the costs said to have been incurred in investigating and rebutting the allegations made, both by way of written evidence and oral argument at the hearing.

Paragraph 606 of the Code of Conduct

c   [**11**] Paragraph 606 of the Code of Conduct, headed 'Drafting pleadings and other documents', at the relevant time provided:

> 'A practising barrister must not devise facts which will assist in advancing his lay client's case and must not draft any originating process pleading affidavit witness statement or notice of appeal containing ... (c) any
d   allegation of fraud unless he has clear instructions to make such allegation and has before him reasonably credible material which as it stands establishes a prima facie case of fraud ... provided that nothing in this paragraph shall prevent a barrister drafting a pleading affidavit or witness statement containing specific facts matters or contentions included by the barrister
e   subject to the lay client's confirmation as to their accuracy.'

Section 51 of the Supreme Court Act 1981

[**12**] So far as relevant to this appeal, s 51 of the Supreme Court Act 1981, as substituted by s 4 of the Courts and Legal Services Act 1990, provides:

f
> '(1) Subject to the provisions of this or any other enactment and to rules of court, the costs of and incidental to all proceedings in—(a) the civil division of the Court of Appeal; (b) the High Court; and (c) any county court, shall be in the discretion of the court ...
>
> (3) The court shall have full power to determine by whom and to what
g   extent the costs are to be paid ...
>
> (6) In any proceedings mentioned in subsection (1), the court may disallow, or (as the case may be) order the legal or other representative concerned to meet, the whole of any wasted costs or such part of them as may be determined in accordance with rules of court.
>
h   (7) In subsection (6), "wasted costs" means any costs incurred by a party—(a) as a result of any improper, unreasonable or negligent act or omission on the part of any legal or other representative or any employee of such a representative; or (b) which, in the light of any such act or omission occurring after they were incurred, the court considers it is unreasonable to
j   expect that party to pay ...
>
> (13) In this section "legal or any other representative", in relation to a party to proceedings, means any person exercising a right of audience or right to conduct litigation on his behalf.'

Sections 111 and 112 of the 1990 Act make provision for wasted costs to be awarded in criminal proceedings and civil proceedings in the magistrates' court.

The wasted costs jurisdiction

a

[13] In *Ridehalgh v Horsefield* [1994] 3 All ER 848, [1994] Ch 205 the Court of
Appeal heard a composite group of six test appeals. Both the Bar and the Law
Society were represented by leading counsel. At the invitation of the court, the
Attorney General nominated two counsel to represent the general public
interest. In a reserved judgment of the court, the Court of Appeal (Bingham MR,
Rose and Waite LJJ) reviewed at some length the history of the court's b
jurisdiction to order payment of costs by legal practitioners whose conduct had
led to the incurring of unnecessary costs, made detailed reference to the rules and
legislation governing the exercise of this jurisdiction, drew attention to certain
obvious dangers to which the jurisdiction was subject and gave guidance on the
future handling of such applications. Save that this judgment must now be read
subject to the decision of the House in *Arthur J S Hall & Co (a firm) v Simons, Barratt v* c
Ansell (t/a Woolf Seddon (a firm)), Harris v Scholfield Roberts & Hill (a firm) [2000]
3 All ER 673, [2002] 1 AC 615, and subject to what is said in para [23], below,
I would endorse and need not repeat what the Court of Appeal said in *Ridehalgh's*
case. It does however appear, from material laid before the House, that the clear
warnings given in that case have not proved sufficient to deter parties from d
incurring large and disproportionate sums of costs in pursuing protracted claims
for wasted costs, many of which have proved unsuccessful. The House is grateful
for the perceptive commentary on the weaknesses of this jurisdiction made by
Hugh Evans 'The Wasted Costs Jurisdiction' (2001) 64 MLR 51.

e

The decision under appeal

[14] The decision of the Court of Appeal now under appeal is reported at
[2001] Lloyd's Rep PN 146. Opinion was divided. Peter Gibson and Schiemann LJJ
(for reasons given by Peter Gibson LJ on behalf of both) held that a wasted costs
order should be made against the barristers. Wilson J dissented.

[15] In the majority judgment (at 152 (para 25)), Peter Gibson LJ recorded that f
there was no dispute as to the jurisdiction to make a wasted costs order nor as to
the principles to be applied. Full reference was made to *Ridehalgh's* case. The
crux of Mr Tager's case (for Mr Medcalf) was that the barristers had acted
improperly, in breach of para 606 of the Code of Conduct, in making allegations
of fraud unsupported by any reasonably credible material establishing a prima g
facie case (see 153–154 (para 35)). The defence advanced by Mr Davidson QC on
behalf of the barristers was summarised (at 154 (para 39)):

'He says that the fundamental point was that this was a case in which it
appeared that the court had been deceived at the trial and that it was right
and in the public interest for advocates to bring that point forward for h
adjudication. His main line of defence, however, was based on the fact that,
despite the best efforts of the solicitors acting for the barristers, the defendants
have not responded to requests that they waive privilege so as to enable the
barristers to refer to privileged material in defending the wasted costs claim.
The barristers have put in evidence that they were fully aware of their duties j
under the Code of Conduct and believed that they complied with those
duties. They say that they would like to put before the court full details of
what material was available, their own consideration of it and their
reasoning but are prevented by the law of privilege and confidentiality from
doing so. They believe that if they could do so, no wasted costs order would
be made. Mr Davidson submits that it is impossible for this court to know

a on what material the barristers acted, that it is unfair to the barristers, who are unable to give evidence on privileged and confidential matters, for us to draw inferences as to the available material or to exercise our discretion as to whether an order should be made. He and his junior, Miss Mulcahy, have drawn our attention to Article 6 of the European Convention on Human Rights and to the cases decided thereunder. They submit that it would be a

b contravention of that Article to decide this case in circumstances where the barristers cannot give evidence on material matters whereas Mr Medcalf is able to bring forward all the evidence in his possession on what they call "the key issue of fact".'

c [16] The majority began by considering the allegations of fraud in the draft amended notice of appeal in order to assess whether there was a possibility that the barristers had had other material. This review was prefaced by certain preliminary observations. First, the majority emphasised the importance of para 606, which gave litigating parties a measure of redress against potentially very damaging allegations for which (because of the law of absolute privilege) they could obtain no redress. Thus a barrister must be instructed to make the

d allegation in question, and should have reasonably credible material establishing a prima facie case before drafting such an allegation. The judgment continued (at 154 (para 40)):

e 'The material must be evidence which can be put before the court to make good the allegation. If there is material before counsel which cannot be used in court, the existence of that material cannot justify the actions of counsel in putting their names to the allegation.'

Secondly, it was said that para 606 applied not only to allegations of fraud but also to other allegations of dishonest or dishonourable conduct. Thirdly, the majority

f made plain that counsel must maintain his independence and not compromise his professional standards in order to please the client. In its review of ten allegations made by the defendants, the majority held that no reasonably credible material had been produced to the court to justify seven, while concluding that there was some evidence to support the remaining three. In considering whether, on the material put before the court, the conduct of the barristers had been shown to be

g improper, unreasonable or negligent, the majority commented on the peripheral character of these allegations in relation to the main issues in the action (157 (para 54)) and based its finding against the barristers primarily on the failure to produce evidence to the court to support the allegations made. The majority said (at 158 (para 58)):

h 'Second, the barristers could not have allowed the draft amended notice of appeal to go out under their names to Mr Medcalf containing allegations of impropriety reliant on the expected contents of the witness statements without the barristers satisfying themselves of the existence of that evidence in a form to be put before the court. We emphasise that the duty under

j paragraph 606 is one personal to counsel and cannot be delegated to his solicitors. He has to satisfy himself that he has reasonable credible material *before him* which *as it stands* establishes a prima facie case of fraud when he drafts the notice of appeal.'

The majority held (at 158 (para 59)) that the propriety of the pleading had to be assessed in the light of the material put before the court. It was not persuaded

(158 (para 60)) that the inability of the barristers to reveal privileged or confidential material made the hearing of the application unfair or contrary to art 6 of the European Convention on Human Rights and Fundamental Freedoms 1950 (as set out in Sch 1 to the Human Rights Act 1998). While acknowledging the high professional standing of the barristers, the majority found no reasons why, in the exercise of the court's discretion, it should deny Mr Medcalf the order he sought (see 159 (para 64)).

[17] In his dissenting judgment Wilson J compressed into six the seven allegations on which the majority had found against the barristers. He agreed that, at the hearing, no reasonably credible evidence had been placed before the court which prima facie established the validity of those six allegations made against Mr Medcalf (see 160 (para 72)). But in his opinion that was not the point. The point was whether the barristers had had such material before them. Wilson J first considered the barristers' position on 3–4 February when the draft amended notice of appeal had been finalised and the skeleton arguments delivered. He said (at 161):

'78. I harbour doubts whether on 3 and 4 February the barristers had before them the material which justified their making the six allegations. All six of them had figured in drafts of Ms Hayes dating back to early December 1999 so there had already been two months in which to collect the evidence to justify them. In the drafting of the jointly signed notice dated 3 February it is hard to discern selection, as opposed to blanket repetition, of (to use Mr Weatherill's own description at the hearing) the gallimaufry of allegations which on instructions had been assembled in the drafts of Ms Hayes.

79. But, in the complete absence of evidence as to what the barristers actually had before them on 3 and 4 February, I have insufficient confidence in the fertility of my imagination to come to a positive conclusion that they could not have had before them whatever paragraph 606 required.

80. There is an initial question as to what paragraph 606 did require to be before them. The words refer to "reasonably credible material which as it stands establishes a prima facie case of fraud". In paragraph 58 above my Lords so construe those words as to require the barristers to have before them reasonably credible evidence, in a form to be put before the court, which establishes the prima facie case. My view is that the word "material" goes wider than evidence in proper form; that the phrase "as it stands" just means "at face value"; and that to construe the word "establishes" as something which can be achieved only by evidence admissible in court is, in this context, arguably to read too much into it. My own preference would be not to adopt any such paraphrase.'

Wilson J raised a series of questions relating to the material which might have been before the barristers on 3–4 February and concluded (at 162):

'84. Answers to such questions might well have enabled me to concur in the conclusion of my Lords. Or they might have had the reverse effect. Lacking the answers, I remain in doubt as to whether on 3 and 4 February the barristers were guilty of professional impropriety. It is doubt of which, pursuant to the same passage in *Ridehalgh v Horsefield*, they must have the benefit. It is better that in certain circumstances the wasted costs jurisdiction should be emasculated by the principle of legal professional privilege than vice versa.'

a Of the hearing on 14–15 February he said (at 163 (para 85)) that 'There was therefore an element of professional impropriety in articulation of these serious allegations at the hearing' in the absence of evidence to support them. In the exercise of his discretion, however, Wilson J would have declined to make an order against the barristers on this limited ground. In reaching this conclusion he was impressed by the extremely difficult circumstances in which both barristers,
b but particularly Mr Weatherill, had been called upon to act in this complex and highly contentious matter.

Jurisdiction

[18] The barristers' argument on jurisdiction was first raised in the House. It was said, first, that s 51 conferred no right on a party to seek a wasted costs order against any legal representative other than his own. Thus the court had no power
c to make an order against the legal representative of any opposing party. This submission was based on the wording of s 51(13) quoted above, and in particular the words 'on his behalf': it was argued that a party could only seek a wasted costs order against a person exercising a right of audience or a right to conduct
d litigation on his behalf or any employee of such a person.

[19] There are in my opinion very compelling reasons why this construction cannot reflect the intention of Parliament. It is clear that in the exercise of its inherent jurisdiction the court could order a solicitor to compensate a party who was not the client of that solicitor, as it did in *Myers v Elman* [1939] 4 All ER 484,
e [1940] AC 282. In *Orchard v South Eastern Electricity Board* [1987] 1 All ER 95 at 99, 106, [1987] QB 565 at 571, 581, the Court of Appeal expressly dissented from the view, advanced obiter by Lord Denning MR in *Kelly v London Transport Executive* [1982] 2 All ER 842 at 851, [1982] 1 WLR 1055 at 1065, that this jurisdiction could be exercised against counsel also. In the context of the 1990 Act, which among other things provided for a substantial extension of solicitors' rights of audience
f in the higher courts, this inequality of treatment as between advocates performing the same professional function was plainly indefensible, and the object of s 51(6) and (7) was to put barristers and solicitors, for this purpose, effectively in the same position. Section 51 only applies in civil proceedings, but (as was accepted on behalf of the barristers) it is quite clear from s 111 of the 1990 Act (amending the Prosecution of Offences Act 1985) and s 112 of the 1990 Act
g (amending the Magistrates' Courts Act 1980) that in criminal proceedings in the Court of Appeal, the Crown Court or a magistrates' court and civil proceedings in a magistrates' court a wasted costs order may be made in favour of a party to the proceedings against the legal representative of any other party. No reason has been advanced why Parliament should have wished to lay down a different rule
h governing barristers in civil proceedings in the High Court, and it is to my mind inconceivable in the context of the 1990 Act that Parliament should have wished to afford to barristers in civil proceedings (otherwise than in a magistrates' court) a ground of exemption not enjoyed by solicitors. Against arguments of this weight, any submission based on the wording of sub-s (13) would have to be
j irresistible. The barristers' argument is not. The subsection is intended to make plain that no liability can attach to any practitioner not involved in the litigation giving rise to the claim. I note without surprise that a similar conclusion was reached by Neuberger J in *Brown v Bennett* [2002] 2 All ER 273, [2002] 1 WLR 713.

[20] The barristers' second argument on jurisdiction was also based on the language of sub-s (13). It was to the effect that any order made against them could only relate to their conduct when exercising a right of audience in court.

This was because they had no right to conduct litigation, as defined in ss 28 and 119(1) of the 1990 Act. Thus (it was said) they could not be liable in wasted costs for anything done when settling the draft amended notice of appeal or the skeleton arguments, the activities which had in fact given rise to most of the wasted costs claimed against them. A similar argument was advanced to, and rejected by, Leveson J in *Worsley v Tambrands Ltd* (8 November 2000, unreported) and also by Neuberger J in *Brown v Bennett*. Both judges were right to reject it. Section 4 of the 1990 Act substituted a new s 51 in the 1981 Act. Once inserted that section was to be read as part of the 1981 Act. Its interpretation was to be governed by its own terms and any other terms of the 1981 Act. I would question whether it would be permissible in principle to construe sub-s (13) in the light of definitions imported into the 1990 Act for quite different purposes: see Bennion *Statutory Interpretation* (3rd edn, 1997) p 213. The section was intended, as already stated, simply to make plain that no liability could attach to any practitioner not involved in the litigation giving rise to the claim. For the reasons convincingly given by Leveson J it would stultify the section if a barrister were not potentially liable for conduct immediately relevant to the exercise of a right of audience but not involving advocacy in open court. If one might have thought sub-s (13) to be unnecessary, the facts of *Byrne v South Sefton (Merseyside) Health Authority* [2001] EWCA Civ 1904, [2002] 1 WLR 775 show that it was not.

The construction of para 606 of the Code of Conduct

[21] As is evident from the quotations from the judgments of the majority and the minority in the Court of Appeal set out in [16], [17], above, there was a difference of opinion on the interpretation of para 606. The majority held that, when putting his signature to an allegation of fraud or dishonesty, counsel must have before him evidence in a form to be put before the court to make good the allegation. Wilson J held that counsel must have 'material' but that it need not be evidence in admissible form.

[22] Paragraph 606(c) lays down an important and salutary principle. The parties to contested actions are often at daggers drawn, and the litigious process serves to exacerbate the hostility between them. Such clients are only too ready to make allegations of the most damaging kind against each other. While counsel should never lend his name to such allegations unless instructed to do so, the receipt of instructions is not of itself enough. Counsel is bound to exercise an objective professional judgment whether it is in all the circumstances proper to lend his name to the allegation. As the rule recognises, counsel could not properly judge it proper to make such an allegation unless he had material before him which he judged to be reasonably credible and which appeared to justify the allegation. At the hearing stage, counsel cannot properly make or persist in an allegation which is unsupported by admissible evidence, since if there is not admissible evidence to support the allegation the court cannot be invited to find that it has been proved, and if the court cannot be invited to find that the allegation has been proved the allegation should not be made or should be withdrawn. I would however agree with Wilson J that at the preparatory stage the requirement is not that counsel should necessarily have before him evidence in admissible form but that he should have material of such a character as to lead responsible counsel to conclude that serious allegations could properly be based upon it. I could not think, for example, that it would be professionally improper for counsel to plead allegations, however serious, based on the documented conclusions of a DTI inspector or a public inquiry, even though counsel had no access to the

a   documents referred to and the findings in question were inadmissible hearsay. On this point I would accept the judgment of Wilson J.

Legal professional privilege

[23] In *Ridehalgh v Horsefield* [1994] 3 All ER 848, [1994] Ch 205 the Court of Appeal addressed the issue of legal professional privilege which may arise where an *b* applicant seeks a wasted costs order against lawyers acting for an opposing party and it said:

> 'The respondent lawyers are in a different position. The privilege is not theirs to waive. In the usual case where a waiver would not benefit their client they will be slow to advise the client to waive his privilege, and they *c* may well feel bound to advise that the client should take independent advice before doing so. The client may be unwilling to do that, and may be unwilling to waive if he does. So the respondent lawyers may find themselves at a grave disadvantage in defending their conduct of proceedings, unable to reveal what advice and warnings they gave, what instructions they received. In some cases this potential source of injustice may be mitigated by reference *d* to the taxing master, where different rules apply, but only in a small minority of cases can this procedure be appropriate. Judges who are invited to make or contemplate making a wasted costs order must make full allowance for the inability of respondent lawyers to tell the whole story. Where there is room for doubt, the respondent lawyers are entitled to the benefit of it. It is *e* again only when, with all allowances made, a lawyer's conduct of proceedings is quite plainly unjustifiable that it can be appropriate to make a wasted costs order.' (See [1994] 3 All ER 848 at 866, [1994] Ch 205 at 237.)

I do not for my part consider this passage to be inaccurate or misleading, and counsel did not criticise it. Read literally and applied with extreme care, it ought *f* to offer appropriate protection to a practitioner against whom a wasted costs order is sought in these circumstances. But with the benefit of experience over the intervening years it seems clear that the passage should be strengthened by emphasising two matters in particular. First, in a situation in which the practitioner is of necessity precluded (in the absence of a waiver by the client) from giving his account of the instructions he received and the material before him at the time of *g* settling the impugned document, the court must be very slow to conclude that a practitioner could have had no sufficient material. Speculation is one thing, the drawing of inferences sufficiently strong to support orders potentially very damaging to the practitioner concerned is another. The point was well put by Mr George Laurence QC sitting as a deputy High Court judge in *Drums and* *h* *Packaging Ltd v Freeman* [1999] All ER (D) 964 when he said (at para 43):

> 'As it happens, privilege having been waived, the whole story has been told. I cannot help wondering whether I would have arrived at the same conclusion had privilege not been waived. It would not have been particularly easy, in that event, to make the necessary full allowance for the firm's *j* inability to tell the whole story. On the facts known to D3 at the time it launched this application, D3 might very well have concluded that the firm would not be able to avoid a wasted costs order, even on the "every allowance" basis recommended by [Bingham MR].'

Only rarely will the court be able to make 'full allowance' for the inability of the practitioner to tell the whole story or to conclude that there is no room for doubt in a situation in which, of necessity, the court is deprived of access to the full facts on which, in the ordinary way, any sound judicial decision must be based. The second qualification is no less important. The court should not make an order against a practitioner precluded by legal professional privilege from advancing his full answer to the complaint made against him without satisfying itself that it is in all the circumstances fair to do so. This reflects the old rule, applicable in civil and criminal proceedings alike, that a party should not be condemned without an adequate opportunity to be heard. Even if the court were able properly to be sure that the practitioner could have no answer to the substantive complaint, it could not fairly make an order unless satisfied that nothing could be said to influence the exercise of its discretion. Only exceptionally could these exacting conditions be satisfied. Where a wasted costs order is sought against a practitioner precluded by legal professional privilege from giving his full answer to the application, the court should not make an order unless, proceeding with extreme care, it is (a) satisfied that there is nothing the practitioner could say, if unconstrained, to resist the order and (b) that it is in all the circumstances fair to make the order.

[24] It was not submitted to the House that a relaxation of the existing rules on legal professional privilege could or should be permitted in a case such as the present: the decision of the House in *R v Derby Magistrates' Court, ex p B* [1995] 4 All ER 526, [1996] AC 487 gave no encouragement to such a submission, and subordinate legislation introduced to modify that decision for purposes of the wasted costs jurisdiction was held to be ultra vires in *General Mediterranean Holdings SA v Patel* [1999] 3 All ER 673, [2000] 1 WLR 272 and was revoked. No attempt has been made to modify the rule by primary legislation. The result no doubt is that in a context such as the present the scope for making wasted costs orders is very limited. This is not necessarily to be regretted. In *Ridehalgh*'s case [1994] 3 All ER 848 at 867–868, [1994] Ch 205 at 238–239 the Court of Appeal considered that wasted costs hearings should be measured in hours and urged the courts to be astute to control what threatened to become a new and costly form of satellite litigation. In *Harley v McDonald, Glasgow Harley (a firm) v McDonald* [2001] UKPC 18, [2001] 2 AC 678, [2001] 2 WLR 1749, reviewing the exercise by the New Zealand courts of the inherent jurisdiction to order barristers and solicitors to pay costs unnecessarily incurred, the Judicial Committee of the Privy Council observed ([2001] 2 AC 678 at [50], [2001] 2 WLR 1749):

'As a general rule allegations of breach of duty relating to the conduct of the case by a barrister or solicitor with a view to the making of a costs order should be confined strictly to questions which are apt for summary disposal by the court. Failures to appear, conduct which leads to an otherwise avoidable step in the proceedings or the prolongation of a hearing by gross repetition or extreme slowness in the presentation of evidence or argument are typical examples. The factual basis for the exercise of the jurisdiction in such circumstances is likely to be found in facts which are within judicial knowledge because the relevant events took place in court or are facts that can easily be verified. Wasting the time of the court or an abuse of its processes which results in excessive or unnecessary cost to litigants can thus be dealt with summarily on agreed facts or after a brief inquiry if the facts are not all agreed.'

Save in the clearest case, applications against the lawyers acting for an opposing party are unlikely to be apt for summary determination, since any hearing to investigate the conduct of a complex action is itself likely to be expensive and a time-consuming. The desirability of compensating litigating parties who have been put to unnecessary expense by the unjustified conduct of their opponents' lawyers is, without doubt, an important public interest, but it is, as the Court of Appeal pointed out in *Ridehalgh*'s case [1994] 3 All ER 848 at 856, [1994] Ch 205 at 226, only one of the public interests which have to be considered.

b *The present appeal*

[25] Proceeding from the undoubted fact (with which Wilson J agreed) that at the hearing on 14–15 February there was no reasonably credible admissible evidence before the court to substantiate the seven allegations held to be improperly made, the majority of the Court of Appeal concluded that the barristers could

c have had no such admissible evidence before them when signing the draft amended notice of appeal and the skeleton arguments. It would seem likely that they did not. But this was to apply too stringent a test. The question is whether, at that stage, the barristers had material of any kind before them which justified the making of the allegations. This is something which the court does not know and cannot be told. Hunch and suspicion are not enough. Like Wilson J, and for

d the reasons given in his persuasive judgment, I remain in doubt, and the barristers must have the benefit of that doubt. In a case of this complexity, I would moreover think it unfair and contrary to the appearance of justice to condemn them unheard. While the Strasbourg jurisprudence to which the House was referred fortifies that conclusion (see, for example, *De Haes v Belgium* (1997) 25 EHRR

e 1 at 48 (paras 80–81)) I do not think it relies on any principle not recognised by the common law. Again like Wilson J, I would not think it right to base even a partial order on the barristers' failure to abandon the objectionable allegations at the outset of the proceedings on 14 February. They do not appear to have clung to these allegations with undue tenacity, and the matters relied on by Wilson J as influencing the exercise of discretion cannot be lightly discounted.

f [26] I am in full agreement with the reasons given by my noble and learned friends Lord Steyn and Lord Rodger of Earlsferry. Save in relation to the transcript allegation, I am also in full agreement with the opinion of my noble and learned friend Lord Hobhouse of Woodborough: on that matter I differ from him because the transcript allegation, although weaker on its face than the other

g allegations, was not different in kind; and also because I share the view expressed by Lord Rodger in [76], below.

[27] Despite the highly regrettable outcome for Mr Medcalf, whose successful proceedings have had severe financial consequences for him, I would allow the barristers' appeal, quash the wasted costs order made by the Court of Appeal and

h award the barristers the costs of and occasioned by the wasted costs application both in the Court of Appeal and before the House (such order not to be enforced without leave of the Court of Appeal in relation to any period when Mr Medcalf was legally-aided).

[28] Well after the conclusion of argument, at a stage when the opinions of the

j committee were in final draft, material was received from the barristers suggesting that Mr Mardell and the TMO were or might be willing after all to waive their entitlement to legal professional privilege. The committee met informally (without reviewing this material in detail) to consider whether it should explore this material further or remit the matter to the Court of Appeal. It was unanimously resolved that the appeal should be decided on the basis upon which it had been argued both in the Court of Appeal and before the House. It would be inconsistent with the clear objectives of the wasted costs regime to permit this issue to be the subject of yet further litigation.

LORD STEYN.

[29] My Lords, I limit my remarks to the question whether the two barristers against whom wasted costs orders were made by a majority in the Court of Appeal [2001] Lloyd's Rep PN 146 had a fair opportunity to deploy their side of the case.

[30] The legislation empowering the making of wasted costs orders did not expressly address the problem which arises where a barrister is prevented by legal professional privilege from explaining what instructions and material he received from his client: s 51 of the Supreme Court Act 1981. Subsequently, the decision of the House of Lords in *R v Derby Magistrates' Court, ex p B* [1995] 4 All ER 526 at 540–541, [1996] AC 487 at 507, ascribed to legal professional privilege an absolute character. It appears to pre-empt the creation of exceptions in the interests of justice. Doubts have been expressed about a perceived rigidity of the law: AAS Zuckerman 'Legal Professional Privilege—the Cost of Absolutism' (1996) 112 LQR 535; Colin Tapper 'Prosecution and Privilege' (1997) 1 E & P 5; Colin Passmore 'The Legal Professional Privilege' (1999) 3 E & P 71.

[31] It was common ground before the House that in the wasted costs jurisdiction under s 51, the court had no power to relax the privilege so as to enable a barrister to defend himself against allegations of improper conduct. Where a client seeks a wasted costs order against his barrister, a waiver of privilege in relation to all relevant matters will be implied by law: *Lillicrap v Nalder & Son (a firm)* [1993] 1 All ER 724, [1993] 1 WLR 94; Matthews and Malek *Disclosure* (2nd edn, 2000) p 297. Sometimes the jurisdiction will be invoked against a barrister by the opposite party in the proceedings. In that situation the barrister's client will usually have no incentive to waive privilege and will refuse to do so. Here lies the root of a systemic problem.

[32] The jurisdiction provides compensation for an aggrieved litigant. It has, however, a penal effect on the practitioner against whom it is exercised: see *Myers v Elman* [1939] 4 All ER 484 at 508–509, [1940] AC 282 at 319; *Harley v McDonald, Glasgow Harley (a firm) v McDonald* [2001] UKPC 18 at [49], [2001] 2 AC 678 at [49], [2001] 2 WLR 1749. In wasted costs proceedings a barrister is therefore entitled to defend himself by placing before the court, without restriction, all logically relevant material about his side of the story.

[33] The wasted costs jurisdiction is available in respect of costs incurred by a party 'as a result of any improper, unreasonable or negligent act or omission': s 51(7). An allegation of 'improper' conduct is the most serious charge. The case against the barristers was throughout advanced and considered by the Court of Appeal on the basis that they had committed improper conduct.

[34] The substance of the case against the barristers was that, contrary to para 606 of the Code of Conduct, they made allegations of dishonesty against a litigant without having before them 'reasonably credible material which as it stands establishes a prima facie case of [dishonesty]'.

[35] This particular professional duty sometimes poses difficult problems for practitioners. Making allegations of dishonesty without adequate grounds for doing so may be improper conduct. Not making allegation of dishonesty where it is proper to make such allegations may amount to dereliction of duty. The barrister must promote and protect fearlessly and by all proper and lawful means his lay clients interests: para 203 of the Code of Conduct. Often the decision will

a depend on circumstantial evidence. It may sometimes be finely balanced. What the decision should be may be a difficult matter of judgment on which reasonable minds may differ.

[36] In the case before the House evidence is that the barristers were aware of the need for caution.

[37] By their signatures to documents submitted to the court they vouched for *b* the fact that they had before them material justifying the making of allegations of dishonesty.

[38] Improper conduct under s 51(7) does not require proof of bad faith. Nevertheless, it is a highly material circumstance that the Court of Appeal accepted that the barristers believed in good faith that they had material which *c* justified the making of the allegations: [2001] Lloyd's Rep PN 146 at 158 (para 60).

[39] Furthermore, it is relevant that both barristers were acknowledged to be competent and experienced practitioners. Their bona fide views that there were materials before them justifying the allegations they made are therefore entitled to some weight. But, despite their best endeavours they failed to obtain a waiver of privilege from their client, and they were therefore unable to explain the *d* grounds for their beliefs.

[40] In these circumstances the question is whether the barristers' beliefs that they had material which objectively justified the allegations unquestionably fell outside the range of views which could reasonably be entertained. The burden of proof is on the party applying for the wasted costs order. In *Ridehalgh v* *e* *Horsefield* [1994] 3 All ER 848 at 867, [1994] Ch 205 at 239, Bingham MR observed that the wasted cost jurisdiction 'recognises a shift in the evidential burden'. This observation was plainly not intended to have any application where barristers are prevented by professional privilege from telling their side of the story.

[41] The point narrows down to the question whether it has been proved that *f* the materials on which the barristers in fact relied did not objectively justify their decision. The majority in the Court of Appeal (Peter Gibson and Schiemann LLJ), disagreeing with a strong dissenting judgment of Wilson J, answered this question in the affirmative. In doing so the Court of Appeal made a judgment, based on inference, as to the nature and contents of the materials *before the barristers*. What exactly those materials included was and is unknown. Nevertheless, *g* the majority in the Court of Appeal decided that even if the barristers had been permitted to tell their side of the story about the materials, which were before them, it would not have availed them in any way.

[42] I cannot accept the view of the majority. The law reports are replete with cases which were thought to be hopeless before investigation but were decided *h* the other way after the court allowed the matter to be tried. Without knowing the barristers' side of the story, I am unwilling to speculate about the nature of the documents before them. In these circumstances it is unnecessary to examine the particulars of the allegations against the barristers which they had no opportunity to answer. Lawyers are also entitled to procedural justice. Due *j* process enhances the possibility of arriving at a just decision. Where due process cannot be observed it places in jeopardy the substantive justice of the outcome. In my view the analysis of Wilson J was realistic and correct.

[43] It was impossible to determine the issue fairly. It follows that the wasted costs orders must be quashed.

[44] This conclusion has relevance for other cases involving the wasted costs procedure where the privilege prevents barristers from explaining their conduct.

I am in full agreement with the guidance given by my noble and learned friend, *a*
Lord Bingham of Cornhill of his reasons (at [23], above).

[45] For the reasons given by Lord Bingham and Lord Rodger of Earlsferry, as
well as the reasons contained in this opinion, I would allow the appeals.

LORD HOFFMANN.

[46] My Lords, I have had the advantage of reading in draft the speeches of my *b*
noble and learned friends Lord Bingham of Cornhill and Lord Steyn. For the
reasons they have given I too would also allow the appeals.

LORD HOBHOUSE OF WOODBOROUGH.

[47] My Lords, this appeal has raised for consideration the wasted costs
jurisdiction of civil courts under s 51 of the Supreme Court Act 1981 as amended *c*
by the Courts and Legal Services Act 1990. The 1990 Act restructured the legal
professions and the interrelation between the roles of solicitors and barristers. It
recognised that advocacy functions could be carried out by both branches and
extended the power to make orders for costs not only against solicitors exercising
the right to conduct litigation on behalf of a party but also against any advocate *d*
exercising a right of audience: s 51(13). Section 51 is a provision dealing generally
with the jurisdiction to make orders as to costs including a general power to
determine by whom and to what extent costs of the proceedings are to be paid:
s 51(3). The 'wasted costs' jurisdiction is supplementary and sub-s (6) empowers the
court both to disallow costs which have been wasted by a legal representative as
between the lawyer and his own client and to order that the legal representative meet *e*
the whole or part of any wasted costs.

[48] The present appeal is concerned only with the problems arising from the
second limb of this power. The order in the present case was an order made on
the application of the claimant in the action, Mr Medcalf, against the two
barristers who had acted as the advocates for the defendant, Mr Mardell, and his *f*
company on their unsuccessful appeal to the Court of Appeal from a judgment
given by Lloyd J in favour of Mr Medcalf. The complaint against the barristers
made by Mr Medcalf and substantially upheld by the majority of the Court of
Appeal (Peter Gibson and Schiemann LJJ, Wilson J dissenting) was that the
barristers had caused him, Mr Medcalf, to incur wasted costs which the barristers
ought to be ordered to meet. *g*

[49] 'Wasted costs' is a defined expression. Subsection (7) provides that it
means—

> 'any costs incurred by a party—(a) as a result of any improper,
> unreasonable or negligent act or omission on the part of any legal or other *h*
> representative or any employee of such a representative; or (b) which, in the
> light of any such act or omission occurring after they were incurred, the
> court considers it is unreasonable to expect that party to pay.'

The phrase 'legal or other representative' is that to which I have already referred;
it is defined as covering those who, in respect to a party, are exercising either a *j*
right of audience or a right to conduct litigation on the party's behalf. The aspect
of these provisions with which this appeal is concerned is therefore alleged
improper, unreasonable or negligent conduct by someone exercising rights of
audience (ie acting as an advocate) on behalf of one party which the opposing
party says should lead the court to make an order that the advocate should bear
part of the costs incurred by that opposing party.

[50] At first sight, this power to make costs orders against such advocates seems sensible and straightforward. However this simplicity is deceptive as the subsequent history of the exercise of this jurisdiction has shown. These complications and pitfalls were discussed in the judgment of the Court of Appeal in the group of cases reported as *Ridehalgh v Horsefield* [1994] 3 All ER 848, [1994] Ch 205 (a judgment to which my noble and learned friend Lord Bingham of Cornhill was, as the then Master of the Rolls, a party) and principled and authoritative solutions provided. It is apparent from what your Lordships have been told from the bar that, notwithstanding that judgment, many of the adverse consequences have persisted. The same message is given in the valuable article 'The Wasted Costs Jurisdiction' by Mr Hugh Evans published at (2001) 64 MLR 51. In the present case the Court of Appeal, both the majority and the minority, were following the *Ridehalgh* judgment although this led them to different conclusions. For myself, I would wish to take this opportunity to endorse and reaffirm what was said in that judgment. But it is clearly necessary to emphasise again some of its features.

The constitutional aspect

[51] The starting point must be a recognition of the role of the advocate in our system of justice. It is fundamental to a just and fair judicial system that there be available to a litigant (criminal or civil), in substantial cases, competent and independent legal representation. The duty of the advocate is with proper competence to represent his lay client and promote and protect fearlessly and by all proper and lawful means his lay client's best interests. This is a duty which the advocate owes to his client but it is also in the public interest that the duty should be performed. The judicial system exists to administer justice and it is integral to such a system that it provide within a society a means by which rights, obligations and liabilities can be recognised and given effect to in accordance with the law and disputes be justly (and efficiently) resolved. The role of the independent professional advocate is central to achieving this outcome, particularly where the judicial system uses adversarial procedures.

[52] It follows that the willingness of professional advocates to represent litigants should not be undermined either by creating conflicts of interest or by exposing the advocates to pressures which will tend to deter them from representing certain clients or from doing so effectively. In England the professional rule that a barrister must be prepared to represent any client within his field of practice and competence and the principles of professional independence underwrite in a manner too often taken for granted this constitutional safeguard. Unpopular and seemingly unmeritorious litigants must be capable of being represented without the advocate being penalised or harassed whether by the executive, the judiciary or by anyone else. Similarly, situations must be avoided where the advocate's conduct of a case is influenced not by his duty to his client but by concerns about his own self-interest.

[53] Thus the advocate owes no duty to his client's opponent; inevitably, the proper discharge by the advocate of his duty to his own client will more often than not be disadvantageous to the interests of his client's opponent (*Orchard v South Eastern Electricity Board* [1987] 1 All ER 95 at 99, [1987] QB 565 at 571). At times, the proper discharge by the advocate of his duties to his client will be liable to bring him into conflict with the court. This does not alter the duty of the advocate. It may require more courage to represent a client in the face of a hostile court but the advocate must still be prepared to act fearlessly. It is part of the duty

of an advocate, where necessary, appropriately to protect his client from the
court as well as from the opposing party. Similarly, the advocate acting in good
faith is entitled to protection from outside pressures for what he does as an
advocate. Thus, what the advocate says in the course of the legal proceedings is
privileged and he cannot be sued for defamation. For similar reasons the others
involved in the proceedings (e g the judge, the witness) have a similar immunity.

[54] The professional advocate is in a privileged position. He is granted rights
of audience. He enjoys certain immunities. In return he owes certain duties to
the court and is bound by certain standards of professional conduct in accordance
with the code of conduct of his profession. This again reflects the public interest
in the proper administration of justice; the public interest, covering the litigants
themselves as well, is now also expressed in CPR Pt I (see also CPR PD 16(9)).
The advocate must respect and uphold the authority of the court. He must not
be a knowing party to an abuse of process or a deceit of the court. He must
conduct himself with reasonable competence. He must take reasonable and
practicable steps to avoid unnecessary expense or waste of the court's time. The
codes of conduct of the advocate's profession spell out the detailed provisions to
be derived from the general principles. These include the provisions relevant to
barristers which preclude them from making allegations, whether orally or in
writing, of fraud or criminal guilt unless he has a proper basis for so doing.
Paragraph 606(c) of the Code of Conduct of the Bar of England and Wales, which
has already been quoted by my noble and learned friend, requires express
instructions and reasonably credible material which as it stands establishes a
prima facie case of fraud. All this fits in well with an appropriate constitutional
structure for a judicial system for the administration of justice.

[55] The introduction of a wasted costs jurisdiction makes an inroad into this
structure. It creates a risk of a conflict of interest for the advocate. It is intended
and designed to affect the conduct of the advocate and to do so by penalising him
economically. Ideally a conflict should not arise. The advocate's duty to his own
client is subject to his duty to the court: the advocate's proper discharge of his
duty to his client should not cause him to be accused of being in breach of his duty
to the court (*Arthur J S Hall & Co (a firm) v Simons, Barratt v Ansell (t/a Woolf Seddon
(a firm)), Harris v Scholfield Roberts & Hill (a firm)* [2000] 3 All ER 673, [2002] 1 AC
615). But the situation in which the advocate finds himself may not be so clear
cut. Difficult tactical decisions may have to be made, maybe in difficult
circumstances. Opinions can differ, particularly in the heated and stressed arena
of litigation. Once an opposing party is entitled to apply for an order against the
other party's legal representatives, the situation becomes much more unpredictable
and hazardous for the advocate. Adversarial perceptions are introduced. This is
a feature of what happened in the present case. The factors which may motivate
a hostile application by an opponent are liable to be very different from those
which would properly motivate a court.

[56] In my judgment, the jurisdiction must be approached with considerable
caution and the relevant provisions of s 51 construed and applied so as not to
impinge upon the constitutional position of the advocate and the contribution he
is required to make on behalf of his client in the administration of civil justice.
The judgment in *Ridehalgh*'s case referred to most of the relevant points. First,
from the point of view of the advocate the jurisdiction is penal. It involves
making a finding of fault against the advocate and visiting upon him a financial
sanction. Unlike the position between the advocate and his own client where the
potential for liability will encourage the performance of the advocate's duty to his

a client (see *Arthur J S Hall & Co (a firm) v Simons*) and the order would be truly compensatory, the jurisdiction to make orders at the instance of and in favour of the opposing party gives rise to wholly different considerations for the advocate. The risk of such an application can, at best, only provide a distraction in the proper representation of his own client and, at worst, may cause him to put his own interests above those of his client. The construction of the section and the

b application of the jurisdiction should accordingly be no wider than is clearly required by the statute. Secondly, the fault must, in the present context, relate clearly to a fault in relation to the advocate's duty to the court not in relation to the opposing party, to whom he owes no duty. Thirdly, the terms used in sub-s (7) should receive an appropriately restrictive interpretation in relation to advocates. The judgment in *Ridehalgh's* case ([1994] 3 All ER 848 at 862, [1994]

c Ch 205 at 232) spelled this out. The use of the first two terms, *improper* and *unreasonable*, call for no further explanation. The word *negligent* raises additional problems of interpretation which are not material to the present appeal since the respondents' allegation against the appellants is impropriety not negligence. But it would appear that the inclusion of the word *negligent* in substitution for

d 'reasonable competence', is directed primarily to the jurisdiction as between a legal representative and his own client. It is possible to visualise situations where the negligence of an advocate might justify the making of a wasted costs order which included both parties, such as where an advocate fails to turn up on an adjourned hearing so that a hearing date is lost. The breach of the advocate's duty to the court will be clear and if the breach was not deliberate, the term *negligent*

e would best describe it. For a person exercising a right to conduct litigation (ie a litigation agent) it is less difficult to think of apt examples affecting the other side as was the situation in *Myers v Elman* [1939] 4 All ER 484, [1940] AC 282. The use of the same language in sub-s (7) in relation to both categories of legal representative does not mean that it will have the same breadth of application for

f both categories. Fourthly, it is the duty of the advocate to present his client's case even though he may think that it is hopeless and even though he may have advised his client that it is (*Ridehalgh's* case [1994] 3 All ER 848 at 863–864, [1994] Ch 205 at 233–234). So it is not enough that the court considers that the advocate has been arguing a hopeless case. The litigant is entitled to be heard; to penalise the advocate for presenting his client's case to the court would be contrary to the

g constitutional principles to which I have referred. The position is different if the court concludes that there has been improper time-wasting by the advocate or the advocate has knowingly lent himself to an abuse of process. However it is relevant to bear in mind that, if a party is raising issues or is taking steps which have no reasonable prospect of success or are scandalous or an abuse of process,

h both the aggrieved party and the court have powers to remedy the situation by invoking summary remedies—striking out—summary judgment— peremptory orders etc. The making of a wasted costs order should not be the primary remedy; by definition it only arises once the damage has been done. It is a last resort.

j *Practical consequences*

[**57**] The practical consequences of the wider use of the jurisdiction, particularly where the client's opponent is the applicant, were also commented upon in *Ridehalgh's* case. The first and most striking is that it creates satellite litigation which too easily gets out of proportion to the litigation which has spawned it. The present case provides an educational but far from extreme

illustration. The principal trial was not wholly straightforward, involving successive
amendments of the pleadings, questions of legal analysis and bitterly
contradictory oral evidence but the trial judge was able to deliver his judgment at
the end of the trial without having to reserve it. He held in favour of the existence
of a partnership and ordered an account of profits. After various contested
interlocutory applications both to the judge and to the Court of Appeal, the Court
of Appeal, in March 2000, unanimously dismissed Mr Mardell's appeal, dismissing
also his application to amend the notice of appeal and adduce fresh evidence. A
month later the main action was settled. The wasted costs application has
occupied the following two years with a further full hearing in the Court of
Appeal and an appeal to your Lordships' House. If the policy of the wasted costs
jurisdiction is to reduce the costs of litigation and to save court time, it too often
fails to achieve this objective (as is confirmed by the Modern Law Review article
already referred to). The jurisdiction is discretionary and should be reserved for
those cases where the unjustifiable conduct can be demonstrated without
recourse to disproportionate procedures. (See also *Harley v McDonald, Glasgow
Harley (a firm) v McDonald* [2001] UKPC 18, [2001] 2 AC 678, [2001] 2 WLR 1749.)
The jurisdiction does not exist as an end in itself; it is distinct from the professional
disciplinary structures. The procedures appropriate for wasted costs applications
were discussed in *Ridehalgh*'s case [1994] 3 All ER 848 at 867–868, [1994] Ch 205
at 238–239.

[58] Once the power to initiate wasted costs procedures is extended to the
opposite party in the litigation, that party is provided with a weapon which it is
too much to expect he will not on occasions attempt to use to his own advantage
in unacceptable ways. It must not be used as a threat to intimidate the lawyers
on the other side (*Ridehalgh*'s case [1994] 3 All ER 848 at 866, [1994] Ch 205 at 237,
citing *Orchard*'s case). It should not be motivated simply by resentment at an
inability to obtain an effective order for costs against an assisted or impecunious
litigant (*Ridehalgh*'s case [1994] 3 All ER 848 at 864, [1994] Ch 205 at 231, citing
Symphony Group plc v Hodgson [1993] 4 All ER 143, [1994] QB 179). Nor should it
be used as a means of continuing contentious litigation by other means or to
obtain from a party's lawyers what cannot be obtained from the party himself.
The legitimate interest of an applicant for a wasted costs order is financial, a
reduction in the costs he has to bear, but the application must be merits based and
clearly made out; it must not raise a suspicion of being itself abusive.

[59] A further consequence of exercising the jurisdiction on the application of
an opposite party is that it raises questions of the legal professional privilege
of the lawyer's client. The client very probably will have no interest in waiving
the privilege. Indeed the client may stand to gain if his opponent can look to the
client's lawyer for an indemnity rather than to the client himself. This situation
creates a serious problem which may lead to the emasculation of the wasted costs
jurisdiction as between the opposing party and the advocate. The appellants
argue that in cases such as the present it should do so: fairness requires that the
privileged material should be before the court; if it cannot be, the application for
wasted costs should fail. They submit that this argument must be conclusive.

Legal professional privilege

[60] As already observed by my noble and learned friend Lord Steyn, the
nature and extent of legal professional privilege has not been in question on this
appeal nor has it been the subject of any argument. Its absolute and paramount
character has been accepted by the respondents, citing *R v Derby Magistrates' Court,*

a *ex p B* [1995] 4 All ER 526, [1996] AC 487 and *General Mediterranean Holdings SA v Patel* [1999] 3 All ER 673, [2000] 1 WLR 272. However, the need of a lawyer to be able to ask a court to look at privileged material when a lawyer's conduct is in question may not be so intractable. The material in question may be confidential rather than absolutely privileged (*Parry-Jones v Law Society* [1968] 1 All ER 177, [1969] 1 Ch 1). It may be possible to restrict the use which can be made of the disclosed material so as to reduce or remove the infringement of the client's privilege (see *R v IRC, ex p Taylor (No 2)* [1989] 3 All ER 353 at 361 per Glidewell LJ). It may be that partially inquisitorial procedures can be adopted, as in the inter partes taxation of costs. It should be remembered that the subject matter of the wasted costs application is an alleged breach of the lawyer's duty *to the court* and it is not unique that a lawyer may have to refer to privileged material in the context of explaining himself to the court and defining his relationship to the court as, for example, when a litigation agent is applying to come off the record or a barrister is ceasing to represent an assisted defendant during the course of a criminal trial. It may be that, as in the context of arts 6 and 8 of the European Convention on Human Rights and Fundamental Freedoms 1950 (as set out in Sch 1 to the Human Rights Act 1998), the privilege may not always be absolute and a balancing exercise may sometimes be necessary (*Campbell v UK* (1992) 15 EHRR 137 and *Foxley v UK* (2000) 8 BHRC 571). But on the present appeal it must be taken that the material which the appellants say is relevant may not directly or indirectly be made available to the court with the result that it is open to the appellants to argue that the Court of Appeal must have acted unfairly in making a wasted costs order against them..

[61] The point was specifically considered in *Ridehalgh*'s case ([1994] 3 All ER 848 at 866, [1994] Ch 205 at 236–237):

> 'The privilege is not theirs to waive ... So the respondent lawyers may find themselves at a grave disadvantage in defending their conduct of proceedings, unable to reveal what advice and warnings they gave, what instructions they received. In some cases this potential source of injustice may be mitigated by reference to the taxing master, where different rules apply, but only in a small minority of cases can this procedure be appropriate. Judges who are invited to make or contemplate making a wasted costs order must make full allowance for the inability of respondent lawyers to tell the whole story. *Where there is room for doubt, the respondent lawyers are entitled to the benefit of it.* It is again only when, with all allowances made, a lawyer's conduct of proceedings is quite plainly unjustifiable that it can be appropriate to make a wasted costs order.' (My emphasis.)

The answer given therefore was not to treat the existence of privileged material as an absolute bar to any claim by an opposite party for a wasted costs order but to require the court to take into account the possibility of the existence of such material and to give the lawyers the benefit of every reasonably conceivable doubt that it might raise. So, all that the lawyer has to do is to raise a doubt in the mind of the court whether there might not be privileged material which could affect its decision whether or not to make a wasted costs order and, if so, in what terms and the court must give the lawyer the benefit of that doubt in reaching its decision, including the exercise of its statutory discretion. I see nothing unfair about this approach. Further, if the use of the jurisdiction on the application of an opposite party is kept within the proper bounds, the frequency with which the problem arises of taking into account the existence of possibly relevant but unseen privileged material should be much reduced.

[62] The contrary submission of the appellants on this appeal treats the existence of privileged material as a kind of trump card which will always preclude the making of a wasted costs order on the application of an opposite party. They ask how can a court evaluate whether privileged material which, ex hypothesi, it has not seen would affect its decision without first seeing that material. But this argument does not reflect what was said in *Ridehalgh's* case. Once the lawyer is given the benefit of any doubt, any element of unfairness is removed. It must depend upon the circumstances of each particular case. For example, a lawyer who has to ask for an extension of time or an adjournment because, say, he has forgotten about a time-limit or has accidentally left his papers at home, would not be able to say that any privileged material could possibly excuse his incompetent mistake. To make a wasted costs order against him would not (absent some additional factor) be inappropriate or unfair. In other situations privileged material may have a possible relevance and therefore require assumptions favourable to the lawyer to be made. Thus, in the present case it is assumed that in all respects the appellant barristers were acting on the express instructions of their lay clients although a finding of fact to that effect could only be made after the consideration of privileged material. The assumption removes the unfairness which might otherwise, in this respect, exist.

[63] Therefore, for myself, I would not qualify what was said in *Ridehalgh's* case. But I agree that it may be salutary to remind parties that each case must depend upon its own facts and that the power to make an order is discretionary and material which could affect the exercise of that discretion is also relevant. I agree with my noble and learned friend Lord Bingham of Cornhill that the court must be satisfied before it makes the wasted costs order that there is nothing that the lawyer could say, if unconstrained, to resist the order and that it is in all the circumstances fair to make the order.

The present case

[64] The facts leading up to the making by the Court of Appeal of the wasted costs order against the barristers are fully set out in the Court of Appeal judgments and have been summarised in the opinion of my noble and learned friend. The difference between the majority and the minority in the Court of Appeal was not in the test to be applied. All agreed that the barristers should be given the benefit of any doubt: see [2001] Lloyd's Rep PN 146 at 153 (para 30) and 157 (para 52) per Peter Gibson LJ. The difference lay in the outcome of applying the test. Thus Peter Gibson LJ said (at 158 (para 58)) on behalf of himself and Schiemann LJ:

'Try though we might, we have not found it possible to conceive of any circumstances in which the barristers in putting their names to the particular allegations of impropriety in the draft amended notice of appeal and supporting them in their skeleton and at the hearing had relevant privileged or confidential material which justified their conduct as compliant with [paragraph] 606 but had been withheld from the court.'

On the other hand, Wilson J said (at 162 (para 84)):

'I remain in doubt whether on 3 and 4 February the barristers were guilty of professional impropriety. It is doubt of which, pursuant to the same passage in *Ridehalgh v Horsefield*, they must have the benefit. It is better that

in certain circumstances the wasted costs jurisdiction should be emasculated
by the principle of legal professional privilege than vice versa.'

[65] With the one exception of the transcripts allegation, I agree that the
preferable view is that the wasted costs order should not have been made. The
complaint made on behalf of Mr Medcalf was that an application had been made
to the Court of Appeal to allow the amendment of the notice of appeal and for
the admission of fresh evidence which included allegations which could not
properly be made. The application for a wasted costs order was based upon the
draft amended notice and the accompanying skeleton argument. These documents
were effectively simultaneous although dated one day apart (3 and 4 February 2000)
and they were signed by the barristers. It was a consequence of these documents
that additional time was taken up on the first two days (14 and 15 February) at the
hearing of the appeal but there was not any additional waste of time caused by
counsel taking excessive time to argue Mr Mardell's case. All the relevant points
upon which the applications to amend and admit fresh evidence were based were
hopeless and were roundly rejected by the Court of Appeal both at the time and
in their unanimous written judgment dismissing the appeal. With the one
exception already mentioned, I would put these points into the category of
arguing a hopeless case. How they would ever persuade the Court of Appeal to
allow the appeal and reverse the judge's judgment escapes me. They related to
peripheral matters and, although the credibility of Mr Medcalf was central to the
judge's decision and the attempt to upset it on appeal, they could not be thought
sufficient, nor were they all novel. Speaking for myself, I would put these points
into the category, not of impropriety, but of counsel discharging their duty to
present even a hopeless case if instructed to do so, in which case no question of
making a wasted costs order against them should have arisen. It must be
remembered that the good faith of the barristers and their consciousness of the
rules of their profession are not challenged nor is their statement that they acted
upon their clients' express instructions. If it is considered that the barristers'
inclusion of these points was improper, I would not arrive at that conclusion
without feeling doubts which I would not wish to resolve without knowledge of
the surrounding circumstances and the privileged material covering the relationship
between the advocates and their client. I do not believe that in these circumstances
it would be fair to exercise the discretion against the appellants.

The transcripts allegation

[66] This allegation was included in ground 45 of the proposed amendments
to the notice of appeal. It was in the following terms:

'The First and Fourth Defendants have fresh evidence that since the trial
there has been interference with the official transcript of the trial. The First
and Fourth Defendants have caused a second set of transcripts to be prepared
by different transcribers. The first set of transcripts contain alterations,
deletions, interpolations, and false certifications tending to the detriment of
the First and Fourth Defendants' already disclosed grounds of appeal and
attempting to buttress the learned Judge's Judgment, obscure perjured
testimony and prevent the discovery of additional substantive grounds of
appeal. The said interference casts such fundamental doubt upon the
integrity of the plaintiff and the process of the court in this case that a new
trial should be ordered ex debito justitiae.'

This is an allegation of serious fraud and conspiracy involving not only Mr Medcalf but also the official court transcribers and, presumably, the plaintiffs' solicitors. The accompanying skeleton argument in 12 paragraphs identified the evidential material relied on, going back to the previous summer.

[67] There are three important features which are essential to the proper evaluation of the allegation made in the proposed ground 45. The appellants' argument failed to have any regard to them and the same could fairly be said of the dissenting judgment of Wilson J.

[68] The first and most important is that the allegation was made as part of and was dependant upon a *Ladd v Marshall* application to admit fresh evidence in the Court of Appeal on appeal from a final judgment (see *Ladd v Marshall* [1954] 3 All ER 745, [1954] 1 WLR 1489). The applicant has to identify and place before the Court of Appeal in documentary form the fresh evidence the subject of the application. The fresh evidence to support the relevant ground of appeal has thus to be fully disclosed. There is no room for the applicant to say that if you grant my application to adduce the fresh evidence then there is other evidence not adduced at the trial and not included in my application upon which I will also want to rely. The application is exhaustive of the opportunity to adduce fresh evidence in the Court of Appeal. In any event, the position was put beyond argument by an order of Clarke LJ on 28 January directing that any evidence to be relied on should be served by 4 February. The evidence placed before the Court of Appeal on behalf of Mr Mardell was the only evidence upon which Mr Mardell could rely in support of ground 45 and upon which the advocates could rely as justifying the allegation in ground 45 in compliance with para 606 of the Code of Conduct.

[69] There has been a discussion whether para 606 is satisfied by an expectation of obtaining admissible evidence which has not yet been obtained. I do not wish to enter upon this discussion save to say that it is misconceived: the emphasis should be upon whether the existing material discloses a prima facie case, which is a concept well understood in many areas of procedural law, not least in the criminal law. The question which the advocate must ask is: is there a prima facie case of the fraud which I am going to allege? It is important not in any way to devalue the important principle encapsulated in para 606. But, in any event the 'expectation' excuse cannot, and could not on any hypothesis, assist the appellants here. At the early stages of litigation, before the close of pleadings, some of the relevant evidence supporting an allegation may not yet have been put into a form which can actually be used at the trial; discovery may yet have to take place but a party may know what documents will have to be produced on discovery. At the stage of trial, evidence which has not been given and the advocate cannot adduce cannot be relied upon to justify an allegation. After trial and judgment, the situation is even more clear cut. Only evidence already adduced in the action or for which leave to adduce is given by the Court of Appeal under *Ladd v Marshall* can be relied upon as justification. This was the position here in relation to ground 45. Ground 45 and the accompanying skeleton argument made allegations which came within the scope of para 606 and clearly should have been (and the barristers say it was) seen as engaging the professional responsibility of an advocate to the court. Since the allegations related to matters occurring after trial and judgment, the principle in *Ladd v Marshall* was inevitably critical to the ability to sustain the allegation. A specific application to admit fresh evidence had to be made. The allegation had to be made on the evidence which Mr Mardell as the appellant was asking the Court of Appeal to admit. If that

a evidence did not disclose even a prima facie case against Mr Medcalf, it follows that a breach of para 606 and the advocates' duty to the court occurred.

[70] The second feature is partly a consequence of the first. It is not possible to make a *Ladd v Marshall* application without waiving any privilege in the material which is the subject of the application. Ground 45 starts with the words 'the ... Defendants have fresh evidence that since the trial there has been
b interference with the official transcripts of the trial'. They cannot at the same time claim any privilege against disclosing what that evidence is. The suggestion that there was material capable of justifying the allegation which Mr Mardell could rely on without waiving any privilege and disclosing the material to the opposite side and the court is patently unsustainable.

c [71] The third feature is peculiar to the present case. The allegation of fraudulent interference with the transcript had been unsuccessfully relied upon by junior counsel for Mr Mardell on previous occasions using the same material. In particular, on 2 December, she applied to Lloyd J for an order that proceedings on the account should be stayed and the police should be directed to investigate the transcript question as an attempt to pervert the course of justice. The judge
d dismissed the applications and refused leave to appeal. The reaction of the Court of Appeal on the hearing of the substantive appeal should have come as no surprise to the barristers. It was entirely in line with what had been said by the judge earlier. There was no evidence whatever that Mr Medcalf or anyone acting for him had anything to do with the defective transcripts. The evidence disclosed
e regrettably familiar deficiencies in the system whereby mechanical recordings and transcripts are made in the Royal Courts of Justice in London. The primary tape is in the courtroom where the trial is taking place and depends upon a court official each day keeping a log of the proceedings and switching the tape on and off at the right times. The tape recording should be of a reasonably good quality
f but the transcriber, who has no independent knowledge of the proceedings, is entirely dependant upon what the court officials have done. (The court officials may indeed have had to look after several courts at the same time.) What happened in the present case was that the court officials did not keep a complete log and did not always switch on or off the tape recorder at the times they should. Also, at times the voice on the tape was not clear. All this was confirmed by the
g investigations carried out and the statements and affidavits lodged. In the Royal Courts of Justice there is also a back-up multi-track tape which runs throughout the working day covering all courts. Inevitably its quality is not as good as the primary tape. A transcript is not made unless asked for. The transcript will normally be made by one of the Lord Chancellor's Department contractors from
h the daily court-room tapes if available. This was what was done initially in the present case. When the defects in the first transcript and, hence, in the tapes from the court room were discovered and the solicitors complained, the senior contractors were called in and a further complete transcript was made using both types of tape. This is the second transcript to which ground 45 refers and which
j those representing Mr Mardell consider to be satisfactory.

[72] It was an unhappy incident but it was fully explored and explained in the evidence which was put before the Court of Appeal. In my judgment no competent and reasonably experienced advocate or litigator should have seen anything remotely sinister about it let alone treat it as evidence of a conspiracy to pervert the course of justice. As previously stated, there was nothing to implicate Mr Medcalf or any one acting for him in any wrong doing in this connection whatever. It

disclosed no prima facie case against him. Yet the advocates put their signature to ground 45 and to the supporting skeleton argument.

[73] In my judgment this was just the type of situation para 606 was designed to prevent. Unjustifiable allegations of fraud have been made. Like Peter Gibson LJ and Schiemann LJ, I cannot conceive of any privileged material which could possibly make any difference to the culpability of making this irresponsible allegation or justify it. The allegation is on its face implausible and suggests an abandonment of the objectivity and sense of proportion which a court is entitled to require of an advocate. Further it was the duty of the advocate to put before the court on the *Ladd v Marshall* application the material which was said to justify the allegation. If the material was not reasonably capable of justifying it, even on a prima facie basis, the allegation should not have been made.

[74] Therefore I would for myself only allow the appeal in part. But your Lordships consider otherwise and would allow the appeal wholly. Since matters of discretion are involved and since I do not feel confident that, if the transcript allegation had stood alone, the Court of Appeal would still have thought that a wasted costs order was appropriate, or at least felt no doubt about it, I will with reluctance concur in the order proposed. Subject to what I have said in this opinion, I agree with what has been said by my noble and learned friends Lord Bingham of Cornhill and Lord Steyn; I also agree with what the former has said in his opinion (at [28], above).

LORD RODGER OF EARLSFERRY.

[75] My Lords, I have had the advantage of considering the speeches of my noble and learned friends, Lord Bingham of Cornhill and Lord Steyn, in draft. I agree with them and, for the reasons they give, I too would allow the appeal.

[76] Like my noble and learned friend, Lord Hobhouse of Woodborough, I was much troubled by the allegation, in ground 45 of the proposed amendments to the notice of appeal, of fraudulent interference with the transcript. None the less, the appellants have not been able to tell their side of the story. A court making a wasted costs order under s 51 of the Supreme Court Act 1981 exercises a discretion. All kinds of mitigatory circumstances may be relevant to the exercise of that discretion. In my view, therefore, it was wrong for the Court of Appeal to make an order against the appellants in a situation where the full facts about the circumstances in which the appellants had been instructed and had prepared the relevant documents were not known and where the appellants were prevented from putting them before the court.

[77] The majority of the Court of Appeal held that the appellants' conduct, in drafting the amended notice of appeal on 3 February 2000 and in preparing the skeleton arguments the following day, had been 'improper' in terms of s 51(7)(a). That decision was based on the view that their conduct on those dates was governed by para 606 of the Code of Conduct of the Bar of England and Wales (6th edn, 1998). Paragraph 606 provides that, before making any allegation of fraud, counsel should have before him 'reasonably credible material which as it stands establishes a prima facie case of fraud'. The majority held that, in terms of the rule, the 'material' had to be 'evidence which can be put before the court to make good the allegation' ([2001] Lloyd's Rep PN 146 at 154 (para 40) per Peter Gibson LJ). Since it was clear from what happened subsequently that no such evidence had been available to counsel on 3 and 4 February, the majority held that counsel had breached the rule in para 606.

[78] The interpretation of the para 606 that the majority adopted is, perhaps, not surprising since the rule of professional conduct was formerly understood to be to that effect. For instance, in *Associated Leisure Ltd v Associated Newspapers Ltd* [1970] 2 All ER 754 at 757–758, [1970] 2 QB 450 at 456 Lord Denning MR indicated his understanding that the duty of counsel was not to put a charge of fraud on the record 'unless he has clear and sufficient evidence to support it'. The passage is cited in Bullen, Leake and Jacob *Precedents of Pleadings* (13th edn, 1990) p 428. The same approach is to be found in the extrajudicial remark of Lord Macmillan that, where a person's reputation is at stake, the pleader should not 'trespass … a hair's breadth beyond what the facts as laid before him and duly vouched and tested, will justify': 'The Ethics of Advocacy' in *Law and Other Things* (1937) p 192, approved in *Oldfield v Keogh* (1941) 41 SR (NSW) 206 at 211 per Jordan CJ.

[79] But the current rule is that stated in para 606. Wilson J held ([2001] Lloyd's Rep PN 146 at 161 (para 80)) that the term 'material' in para 606 went wider than evidence in proper form. The paragraph states a rule of professional conduct rather than a rule of law, but I agree with his interpretation of it. The current rule of conduct is slightly less strict than the rule as at one time understood. While, usually, the material before counsel will comprise evidence in an admissible form, something less can satisfy the requirements of the current rule, provided that it establishes a prima facie case of fraud. A report of an official inquiry, or accurate reports of evidence given in a civil or criminal trial, are examples that come to mind. A professional rule that permits counsel to draft pleadings on such a basis, before the actual evidence is to hand, achieves a sensible balance: it gives due protection to defendants, while not putting unnecessary obstacles in the way of claimants and their counsel raising proceedings promptly. So interpreting the rule, I am unable to infer from the circumstances that the appellants were necessarily in breach of it on 3 or 4 February 2000.

Appeal allowed.

Celia Fox   Barrister.

Bank of Credit and Commerce International SA (in liquidation) v Ali and others (No 2)

[2002] EWCA Civ 82

COURT OF APPEAL, CIVIL DIVISION

PILL, ROBERT WALKER AND JONATHAN PARKER LJJ

20–23 NOVEMBER 2001, 31 JANUARY 2002

Employment – Contract of service – Implied term of trust and confidence – Bank breaching implied term of trust and confidence in employees' contracts of employment by operating corrupt business – Former employees claiming damages for stigma suffered in search for future employment – Whether breach of implied term of trust and confidence causing employees financial loss.

When the respondent bank collapsed in 1991, it was discovered that it had been conducting a dishonest and corrupt business for many years. That discovery was widely publicised. Subsequently, several hundred former employees of the bank, who had lost their jobs as a result of its collapse and had failed to find further employment, brought claims for damages against it. They contended that the dishonest conduct of the bank's business had constituted a breach of the implied term of trust and confidence in their employment contracts, and that, by placing a stigma on them, the breach had been the cause of their failure to find further employment. Five of the claims, including those of the two appellants, were tried as test cases. After considering expert and statistical evidence, the judge concluded that there was no general prejudice against former employees of the bank; rejected the contention that loss or damage should necessarily be assumed or inferred; and held that the attitude of a prospective employer had to be proved in every particular case. In the appellants' cases, he found that there were compelling reasons why they had remained unemployed, and that stigma was not one of them. He therefore dismissed their claims. On their appeals, the appellants contended that the judge should not have conducted a 'job-specific exercise', and that loss should necessarily have been inferred from the evidence of corruption and the widespread publicity given to it or, failing that, from the evidence of the appellants' failed job applications.

Held – In a claim for stigma damages, the onus was on the claimant to prove, on a balance of probabilities, that the breach of the trust and confidence term had caused the failure to obtain employment. In many cases a loss of business resulting from a breach of contract would be readily assumed or inferred, and it was not necessary, as a matter of law, for claimants to obtain evidence from prospective employers as to the effect of the stigma on particular job applications. Nevertheless, causation had to be proved, and in a stigma case the defendant was entitled to subject the claims to a job-specific exercise. The judge was entitled to draw conclusions from that exercise, but in considering evidence specific to particular jobs, he was not to lose sight of the overall picture, and had to reach a conclusion about loss based on the evidence as a whole. In the instant case, the judge had been entitled to make the findings that he had. Accordingly, the appeals *a* would be dismissed (see [14], [16], [17], [42], [43], [57], [58], [60], [93], [94], [98], [99], below).

    Spring v Guardian Assurance plc [1994] 3 All ER 129 and *Allied Maples Group Ltd v Simmons & Simmons (a firm)* [1995] 4 All ER 907 considered.

    Decision of Lightman J [1999] 4 All ER 83 affirmed.

b **Notes**

For the implied term of trust and confidence and for stigma damages, see 16 *Halsbury's Laws* (4th edn) (2000 reissue) paras 47, 455 n5.

Cases referred to in judgments

c *Aerial Advertising Co v Batchelors Peas Ltd (Manchester)* [1938] 2 All ER 788.

Allied Maples Group Ltd v Simmons & Simmons (a firm) [1995] 4 All ER 907, [1995] 1 WLR 1602, CA.

Balfour v A-G [1991] 1 NZLR 519, NZ CA.

Bolitho (administratrix of the estate of Bolitho (decd)) v City and Hackney Health Authority [1997] 4 All ER 771, [1998] AC 232, [1997] 3 WLR 1151, HL.

d *Chaplin v Hicks* [1911] 2 KB 786, [1911–13] All ER Rep 224, CA.

Cummings (or McWilliams) v Sir William Arrol & Co Ltd [1962] 1 All ER 623, [1962] 1 WLR 295, HL.

Davies v Taylor [1972] 3 All ER 836, [1974] AC 207, [1972] 3 WLR 801, HL.

Gerber Garment Technology Inc v Lectra Systems Ltd [1997] RPC 443, CA.

e *Hedley Byrne & Co Ltd v Heller & Partners Ltd* [1963] 2 All ER 575, [1964] AC 465, [1963] 3 WLR 101, HL.

Hotson v East Berkshire Area Health Authority [1987] 2 All ER 909, [1987] AC 750, [1987] 3 WLR 232, HL.

Joyce v Merton Sutton and Wandsworth Health Authority (1995) 27 BMLR 124, CA.

f *Kitchen v Royal Air Forces Association* [1958] 2 All ER 241, [1958] 1 WLR 563, CA.

Malik v Bank of Credit and Commerce International SA (in liq), Mahmud v Bank of Credit and Commerce International SA (in liq) [1997] 3 All ER 1, [1998] AC 20, [1997] 3 WLR 95, HL.

McGhee v National Coal Board [1972] 3 All ER 1008, [1973] 1 WLR 1, HL.

Nestle v National Westminster Bank plc [1994] 1 All ER 118, [1993] 1 WLR 1260, CA.

g *Pickford v Imperial Chemical Industries plc* [1998] 3 All ER 462, [1998] 1 WLR 1189, HL.

Ratcliffe v Evans [1892] 2 QB 524, [1891–4] All ER Rep 699, CA.

Robinson v Harman (1848) 1 Exch 850, [1843–60] All ER Rep 383, 154 ER 363, Exch.

South Australia Asset Management Corp v York Montague Ltd, United Bank of Kuwait plc v Prudential Property Services Ltd, Nykredit Mortgage Bank plc v Edward Erdman

h   *Group Ltd* [1996] 3 All ER 365, [1997] AC 191, [1996] 3 WLR 87, HL.

Spring v Guardian Assurance plc [1994] 3 All ER 129, [1995] 2 AC 296, [1994] 3 WLR 354, HL.

Stovold v Barlows (a firm) [1996] 1 PNLR 91, CA.

Sykes v Midland Bank Executor and Trustee Co Ltd [1970] 2 All ER 471, [1971] 1 QB 113, [1970] 3 WLR 273, CA.

j *Wilsher v Essex Area Health Authority* [1988] 1 All ER 871, [1988] AC 1074, [1988] 2 WLR 557, HL.

Cases also cited or referred to in skeleton arguments

100 Old Broad Street Ltd v Sidley [1999] CA Transcript 717.

Addis v Gramophone Co Ltd [1909] AC 488, [1908–10] All ER Rep 1, HL.

Anglo-Continental Holidays Ltd v Typaldos Lines (London) Ltd [1967] 2 Lloyd's
　　Rep 61, CA.
Ashmore v Corp of Lloyd's [1992] 2 All ER 486, [1992] 1 WLR 446, HL.
Benmax v Austin Motor Co Ltd [1955] 1 All ER 326, [1955] AC 370, HL.
Biogen Inc v Medeva plc (1996) 38 BMLR 149, HL.
Cartonneries de Thulin SA v CTP White Knight Ltd [2000] CA Transcript 938.
Cook v Consolidated Fisheries Ltd [1977] ICR 635, CA.
Davis v Galmoye (1888) 39 ChD 322, CA.
Doyle v Wallace [1998] PIQR Q146, CA.
English Exporters (London) Ltd v Eldonwall Ltd [1973] 1 All ER 726, [1973] Ch 415.
G v G [1985] 2 All ER 225, [1985] 1 WLR 647, HL.
Hall v Woolston Hall Leisure Ltd [2000] 4 All ER 787, [2001] 1 WLR 225, CA.
Hickman v Kent or Romney Marsh Sheepbreeders' Association (1920) 37 TLR 163, CA.
Hunter v Chief Constable of West Midlands Police [1981] 3 All ER 727, [1982] AC 529, HL.
Johnson v Unisys Ltd [2001] UKHL 13, [2001] 2 All ER 801, [2001] 2 WLR 1076.
Ley v Hamilton (1935) 153 LT 384, HL.
Mallett v McMonagle [1969] 2 All ER 178, [1970] AC 166, HL.
Marbe v George Edwardes (Daly's Theatre) Ltd [1928] 1 KB 269, [1927] All ER Rep
　　253, CA.
Maw v Jones (1890) 25 QBD 107, DC.
Ministry of Defence v Cannock [1995] 2 All ER 449, EAT.
Moeliker v A Reyrolle & Co Ltd [1977] 1 All ER 9, [1977] 1 WLR 132, CA.
Mood Music Publishing Co Ltd v De Wolfe Ltd [1976] 1 All ER 763, [1976] Ch 119, CA.
Norton Tool Co Ltd v Tewson [1973] 1 All ER 183, [1973] 1 WLR 45, NIRC.
Piglowska v Piglowski [1999] 3 All ER 632, [1999] 1 WLR 1360, HL.
Rashid v Ayub [2000] CA Transcript 1891.
Smith v Manchester Corp (1974) 17 KIR 1, CA.
Solo Industries UK Ltd v Canara Bank [2001] EWCA Civ 1041, [2001] 2 All ER (Comm)
　　217, [2001] 1 WLR 1800.
Standard Chartered Bank v Pakistan National Shipping Corp (No 2) [2000] 1 All ER
　　(Comm) 1, CA.
Tanfern Ltd v Cameron-Macdonald [2000] 2 All ER 801, [2000] 1 WLR 1311, CA.
Vernon v Bosley [1994] PIQR P337, CA.
Watt (or Thomas) v Thomas [1947] 1 All ER 582, [1947] AC 484, HL.
Withers v General Theatre Corp Ltd [1933] 2 KB 536, [1933] All ER Rep 385, CA.

Appeals

The appellants, Syed Badshah Nawab Husain and Iqbal Zafar, former employees
of the respondent, the Bank of Credit and Commerce International SA (in liquidation)
(BCCI), appealed with permission of the Court of Appeal (Chadwick and Arden LJJ)
granted on 4 May 2001 from the decision of Lightman J on 25 June 1999 ([1999]
4 All ER 83, [1999] IRLR 508) dismissing their claims for damages for stigma in
the labour market arising from the breach by BCCI of the implied term of trust
and confidence in their contracts of employment. Their claims were tried as two
of five test cases for similar claims brought against BCCI by a further 364 former
employees, including the named defendant, Munawar Ali, who had either
brought proceedings against BCCI, had brought counterclaims in proceedings
brought against them by BCCI, or had attempted to prove in the liquidation. The
facts are set out in the judgment of Pill LJ.

a *Michael Kent QC* and *Isaac Jacob* (instructed by *Finers Stephens Innocent*) for the appellants.

Christopher Jeans QC and *Annie Hockaday* (instructed by *Lovells*) for BCCI.

Robin Allen QC (instructed by *Beale & Co*) for former employees not involved in the test cases.

b   *Cur adv vult*

31 January 2002. The following judgments were delivered.

PILL LJ.

c *The appeals*

[1] This is an appeal against the judgment of Lightman J given on 25 June 1999 ([1999] 4 All ER 83, [1999] IRLR 508) whereby he dismissed claims for damages, known as the stigma claims, against Bank of Credit and Commerce International SA (BCCI) by former employees. There are over 300 stigma claims. The litigation is managed by Lightman J and on 29 July 1998 he made an order for the trial of

d five test cases, including those of Mr Syed Badshah Nawab Husain and Mr Iqbal Zafar (the appellants). His order provided that any determination or finding as to the law or the facts common to cases not before the court as test cases should be binding on the other employees who were listed in a schedule to the order.

[2] The claims of Mr Husain and Mr Zafar and three others were considered

e by the judge at a hearing which lasted nine weeks with hearings on 36 days. The judge rejected their claims. On 4 May 2001, Chadwick and Arden LJJ granted a limited permission to appeal to the appellants.

Malik v Bank of Credit and Commerce International SA (in liq), Mahmud v Bank of Credit and Commerce International SA (in liq)

f [3] The claims arise out of the conclusion of the House of Lords in *Malik v Bank of Credit and Commerce International SA (in liq), Mahmud v Bank of Credit and Commerce International SA (in liq)* [1997] 3 All ER 1, [1998] AC 20 that, in a contract of employment, there is an implied obligation on an employer not to carry on a dishonest or corrupt business. If there is a breach of that obligation as a result of

g which an employee's future employment prospects are handicapped, damages may be recoverable for financial losses sustained. Further, it makes no difference if the employee only heard of the employer's conduct after leaving the employment. Dealing with an entitlement to damages for financial loss, Lord Steyn, with whom Lord Goff of Chieveley, Lord Mackay of Clashfern and Lord Mustill agreed, stated:

h

'The principled position is as follows. Provided that a relevant breach of contract can be established, and the requirements of causation, remoteness and mitigation can be satisfied, there is no good reason why in the field of employment law recovery of financial loss in respect of damage to

j reputation caused by breach of contract is necessarily excluded.' (See [1997] 3 All ER 1 at 21, [1998] AC 20 at 52.)

[4] Lord Steyn referred to difficulties of proof and continued:

'It is, therefore, improbable that many employees would be able to prove "stigma compensation". The limiting principles of causation, remoteness and mitigation present formidable practical obstacles to such claims succeeding.

But difficulties of proof cannot alter the legal principles which permit, in appropriate cases, such claims for financial loss caused by breach of contract being put forward for consideration.' (See [1997] 3 All ER 1 at 22, [1998] AC 20 at 53.)

[5] Lord Nicholls of Birkenhead, with whom Lord Goff and Lord Mackay agreed, also referred to the difficulties involved. Among them was:

'Finally, although the implied term that the business will not be conducted dishonestly is a term which avails all employees, proof of consequential handicap in the labour market may well be much more difficult for some classes of employees than others. An employer seeking to employ a messenger, for instance, might be wholly unconcerned by an applicant's former employment in a dishonest business, whereas he might take a different view if he were seeking a senior executive.' (See [1997] 3 All ER 1 at 12, [1998] AC 20 at 42.)

The business of BCCI

[6] The present claims are to be approached on the basis that, in the words of Lord Nicholls, the employer 'was conducting a dishonest and corrupt business'. There was before the judge a statement of 'agreed misconduct'. In his summary of that misconduct, the judge stated ([1999] 4 All ER 83 at 98, 99, [1999] IRLR 508 at 515, 516):

'44. It is agreed that the bank was hopelessly insolvent from at least 1986, and the proper inference must be that it was insolvent (or at least of doubtful solvency) from the mid-1970s, for it is agreed that the wrongdoing during the period from the mid-1970s on was designed to conceal the true financial position of the group and its insolvency or doubtful solvency.

45. The fraudulent activities were not isolated, but systematic over a very long period of years. They took on a life of their own. They formed, or related to, part of the bank's banking activities. The wrongdoing included payments of bribes and kickbacks (to employees of the bank, officers of other banks and public officials), the preparation of false records (including the recording of sham and fictitious transactions) and the creation of fictitious (ie forged) documentation; the unlawful purchase of its own shares; money laundering (including the laundering of drug money); defalcations; and the preparation and filing of false annual accounts vastly overstating assets and understating liabilities. Even today the liquidators cannot say what is the full extent of the frauds. The sums involved in the frauds were massive running into billions of dollars. Such was the bank's wrongdoing that, when the house of cards collapsed, the insolvency of the bank ran into billions of pounds causing huge losses to customers. The fraudulent activities were recorded principally in the Cayman Islands and in other off-shore locations, but were orchestrated, and sometimes conducted, from London ...

48. The wrongdoing and consequent collapse were likely to be (as they were) the greatest banking scandal ever and to cast a cloud (in the eyes of the public) on those of the employees of the bank who were perceived to be involved in or party to the wrongdoing ...'

[7] It was in July 1991 that the scandal broke and BCCI entered into provisional liquidation. In January 1992 the company was ordered to be wound up compulsorily. Mr Husain was a payroll officer in the personnel department

a and was dismissed on the liquidation of BCCI. Mr Zafar had a more senior and expert position. He was regional manager for southern Africa and a relatively senior officer. He had been dismissed by BCCI in 1990. He obtained a job in June 1991 with Albaraka International Bank Ltd (AIBL) but was dismissed from it in August 1991. Both men were in their 40s. Neither of them has since been employed. They seek damages on the basis that it has been the breach by BCCI

b of the trust and confidence clause which has caused their failure to obtain employment.

The issues

[8] In making their submissions, the parties agree that in deciding the test to be applied, nothing turns on whether the claim is in contract or in tort. The

c underlying rule of the common law is that 'where a party sustains a loss by reason of a breach of contract, he is, so far as money can do it, to be placed in the same situation, with respect to damages, as if the contract had been performed' (*Robinson v Harman* (1848) 1 Exch 850 at 855, [1843–60] All ER Rep 383 at 385 per Parke B), a statement since frequently cited with approval. The judge considered

d in great detail the events between the appellants' dismissal and the trial. He concluded that their failure to find work was not caused by BCCI's breach of the trust and confidence term.

[9] It will be necessary to consider the evidence in more detail but the appellants' basic complaint about the judge's approach can be put simply. The appellants challenge the judge's treatment of the evidence and his failure to draw

e inferences. They also submit that the judge was wrong to conduct a 'job-specific exercise'. He should have adopted a 'broad brush' approach by which he evaluated the diminished chance of work and put a value on it. Loss should necessarily have been inferred from the evidence of corruption and the widespread publicity given to it. Failing that, loss should in the circumstances have been

f inferred from the evidence of the appellants' failed job applications. It was not a necessary requirement (and was unrealistic) to have to call prospective employers to give evidence as to why they did not offer employment to the appellants.

[10] An issue arises as to whether the judge wrongly excluded evidence known

g as the 'anecdotal' evidence. Subject to that, two issues on which permission to appeal has been granted arise. The first is whether the judge selected the correct legal test to be satisfied by the appellants in order to establish financial loss consequent on breach of the trust and confidence term. The second is whether, whichever legal test is applied, the judge was wrong in failing to draw inferences of financial loss in the case of each appellant from the evidence as a whole. It

h included evidence of the publicity given to wrongdoing at BCCI, evidence of the appellants' previous employment histories and their efforts to obtain employment since the relevant dismissals, statistical evidence and the evidence of experts and witnesses from Coutts' Career Consultants Ltd (Coutts). Mr Zafar also challenges the judge's finding of primary fact that his dismissal from AIBL was not, wholly

j or even in part, caused by the breach by BCCI of the trust and confidence term.

[11] In his approach to the issues in the case, the judge did not minimise the scandalous way in which BCCI had been operated. He set out the statement of agreed misconduct. The judge referred in some detail to the publicity given to the misconduct. Mr Kent QC, for the appellants, relies on that sustained bad publicity in support of the submission that the appellants were at a serious disadvantage in their job applications. The publicity suggested endemic

corruption on a vast scale and for a long time. Articles in national newspapers referred to fraud being manifest in BCCI 'from top to bottom'. The bad publicity was sustained; as late as April 1993 an article in a national newspaper included the allegation that 'there was corruption at every level of their [BCCI] operation'. It is submitted that the bad publicity is an important component in the case. The appellants were inevitably prejudiced by that publicity and their standing on the labour market was reduced. The effect of the stigma was compounded by the appellants' lengthening period of unemployment and by their increasing age. The judge failed to take into account long-term and cumulative effects of the existence of the stigma. The possible becomes probable if repeated often enough, it is submitted. The disadvantages resulting from the breach of the trust and confidence term were such that, at lowest, a lost chance of employment entitling the appellants to damages had on balance of probabilities been established. The judge adopted too high a threshold, it is submitted, in converting that disadvantage into an actionable loss.

The legal test

[12] In his judgment, which I have had the opportunity to read in draft, Robert Walker LJ has considered the judge's approach to the consequences of a breach of contract in circumstances such as the present. I agree with him that the judge has adopted an over-elaborate approach to the legal issue. I agree with the approach set out by Robert Walker LJ at [88], below. I do not consider that cases such as *Aerial Advertising Co v Batchelors Peas Ltd (Manchester)* [1938] 2 All ER 788 and *Ratcliffe v Evans* [1892] 2 QB 524, [1891–4] All ER Rep 699 assist the appellants. In those cases, loss of business by reason of the wrong was proved, and the issue was as to quantification.

[13] Neither do I consider that the decision of the House of Lords in *McGhee v National Coal Board* [1972] 3 All ER 1008, [1973] 1 WLR 1 assists them. Complex factual issues may arise when deciding whether a particular loss has been caused by a breach of contract or breach of duty in tort. Having referred to the speeches in *McGhee*'s case, Lord Bridge of Harwich, in *Wilsher v Essex Area Health Authority* [1988] 1 All ER 871 at 881–882, [1988] AC 1074 at 1090, stated:

'The conclusion I draw from these passages is that *McGhee v National Coal Board* laid down no new principle of law whatever. On the contrary, it affirmed the principle that the onus of proving causation lies on the pursuer or plaintiff. Adopting a robust and pragmatic approach to the undisputed primary facts of the case, the majority concluded that it was a legitimate inference of fact that the defenders' negligence had materially contributed to the pursuer's injury. The decision, in my opinion, is of no greater significance than that and the attempt to extract from it some esoteric principle which in some way modifies, as a matter of law, the nature of the burden of proof of causation which a plaintiff or pursuer must discharge once he has established a relevant breach of duty is a fruitless one.'

[14] To obtain substantial damages the claimant must prove, on a balance of probabilities, loss resulting from the breach of contract. The loss alleged in the present cases results from the failure to obtain employment. It is for the appellants to establish that the breach of the trust and confidence term is a cause of that failure. The parties called a very substantial amount of evidence about causation, the respondents attempting to defeat the appellants' case that there was a causal link and also the appellants' submission that an inference should be

a drawn that a loss had occurred. The respondents were entitled to do that and to subject to close scrutiny the appellants' case that it is stigma resulting from their employment with BCCI which has caused their failure to obtain work. They were entitled to subject the claims to what has been called a job-specific exercise. It is for the judge to decide whether, on the evidence, loss results from the breach (or in a negligence action from the breach of duty (see *Wilsher's* case)).

b [15] In deciding that issue, the trial judge may draw inferences in a commonsense way. The fact that the loss cannot be quantified precisely need not be a barrier either to a finding that it was caused by the breach or to an assessment of the loss in a commonsense way (see *Ratcliffe v Evans* and the *Aerial Advertising* case).

[16] In many cases a loss of business resulting from a breach of contract will c readily be assumed, inferred or proved. It will not always be necessary to call a prospective customer to say that, but for the breach by the defendant, he would have done business with the claimant. In personal injury cases, a court may be very ready to infer that a manual worker who has lost, for example, a limb is likely to suffer loss of earnings as a result. Causation must, however, be proved and it is open to a defendant to put the claimant to proof and to call evidence with d a view to disputing the alleged causal link between breach and loss, the loss in the present cases being the absence of paid employment.

[17] The judge is entitled to draw conclusions from the results of that exercise though, in considering evidence specific to particular jobs, he must not lose sight of the overall picture and must reach a conclusion about loss on the basis of the e evidence as a whole. The evidence of the parties has been carefully scrutinised in the course of a long trial. In his judgment, the judge has summarised the evidence, commented upon it and made clear and detailed findings of fact.

[18] One way the appellants put their case is on the basis of the loss of a chance of employment. They rely on the decision of this court in *Allied Maples Group Ltd v* f *Simmons & Simmons (a firm)* [1995] 4 All ER 907, [1995] 1 WLR 1602. Solicitors failed to advise the plaintiffs sufficiently in a property transaction. A warranty against liability for a former tenant's obligations under leases was not obtained. The trial judge held that, on a balance of probabilities, there was a real and not a mere speculative chance that the plaintiffs, had they been properly advised, would have successfully renegotiated with the vendor to obtain proper protection. g The decision was upheld in this court. It was held that where the defendant's negligence consisted of an omission, causation depended upon the answer to the hypothetical question as to what the plaintiff would have done if the defendant had not been guilty of the omission, which was a matter of inference to be determined from all the circumstances. Where the plaintiff's loss depended on h the hypothetical action of a third party, he was entitled to succeed if he could show that there was a real or substantial, rather than a speculative, chance that the third party would have acted so as to confer the benefit or avoid the risk to the plaintiff ([1995] 4 All ER 907 at 915–916, [1995] 1 WLR 1602 at 1611 per Stuart-Smith LJ, expressed as his category (3)). Stuart-Smith LJ stated:

j 'In many cases the plaintiff's loss depends on the hypothetical action of a third party, either in addition to action by the plaintiff, as in this case, or independently of it. In such a case does the plaintiff have to prove on balance of probability ... that the third party would have acted so as to confer the benefit or avoid the risk to the plaintiff, or can the plaintiff succeed provided he shows that he had a substantial chance rather than a speculative one, the

evaluation of the substantial chance being a question of quantification of
damages ... I have no doubt that ... the second alternative is correct.'

[19] Reliance is also placed on a statement of Lord Lowry in *Spring v Guardian
Assurance plc* [1994] 3 All ER 129 at 154, [1995] 2 AC 296 at 327, a case in which a
reference given by an employer about a former employee constituted a negligent
misstatement. Lord Lowry stated:

'Once the duty of care is held to exist and the defendants' negligence is proved,
the plaintiff only has to show that by reason of that negligence he has lost a
reasonable chance of employment (which would have to be evaluated) and has
thereby sustained loss: *McGregor on Damages* (14th edn, 1980) paras 276–278,
pp 198–202 and *Chaplin v Hicks* [1911] 2 KB 786, [1911–13] All ER Rep 224.'

Stuart-Smith LJ in the *Allied Maples* case expressed agreement with that statement.

[20] In *Chaplin v Hicks*, the plaintiff was one of 50 finalists in a competition for
12 prizes and was held entitled to damages for wrongfully being deprived of the
opportunity to take part in the final. On the evidence, it was impossible to decide
whether she would have won a prize; she was entitled to damages for loss of the
chance. In *Kitchen v Royal Air Forces Association* [1958] 2 All ER 241, [1958] 1 WLR
563, the plaintiff lost the opportunity to bring an action against the original
wrongdoer. He was entitled to damages on the basis of the court's assessment of
the prospect of success he would have had against that wrongdoer (see [1958]
2 All ER 241 at 252, [1958] 1 WLR 563 at 576 per Parker LJ). In the *Allied Maples*
case the majority held that it was possible to make 'an informed judgment of
what the chances were of achieving certain results' (see [1995] 4 All ER 907 at 925,
[1995] 1 WLR 1602 at 1620 per Hobhouse LJ). Millett LJ, dissenting, would not
have allowed damages because 'the outcome of such negotiations is a matter of
pure speculation' ([1995] 4 All ER 907 at 929–930, [1995] 1 WLR 1602 at 1625).

[21] I do not consider that Lord Lowry in *Spring*'s case was proposing to
deprive judges of the opportunity to make findings of fact on causation on the
basis of evidence before them. Lord Lowry made the statement in the context of
a finding of fact by the trial judge that one of a number of named companies
would probably have employed the plaintiff. Moreover, in the absence of a
favourable reference, the job application could not, under the rules of the
regulatory body LAUTRO (the Life Assurance and Unit Trust Regulatory
Organisation), be considered on the merits so that consideration on the merits
was a hypothetical event.

[22] In *Gerber Garment Technology Inc v Lectra Systems Ltd* [1997] RPC 443, a
business was held entitled to damages for infringement of a patent. The judge
awarded damages on the basis that the patentees would have achieved 15 sales if
the infringers had not made their 25 wrongful sales. A loss was claimed on 25 sales
and the judge did not identify the 15 which would in fact have been achieved by
the patentees. In upholding the finding of the judge, Staughton LJ relied on the
Allied Maples case. He stated (at 460):

'In my judgment the issue as to the amount of the patentees' loss in the
present case was a question in the second class; it depended on the
hypothetical actions of third parties, that is to say the buyers of the infringing
machines (or spare parts, servicing and CAD systems). The judge was
entitled to conclude that the patentees had lost a chance of making sales to
those buyers—no doubt a chance of differing probability in each case. He

a was entitled to evaluate the chances as a whole, rather than separately, if he chose to do so. The contrary view, that if the judge found 25 chances of a sale, each of 49 per cent probability, he should award nothing is absurd.'

Staughton LJ must in my view have been referring to the third of Stuart-Smith LJ's classes in the *Allied Maples* case, that dealing with the hypothetical action of a
b third party.

[23] With respect, the *Gerber* case was not a loss of a chance case in quite the sense the expression was used in class 3 in the *Allied Maples* case. The loss, if any, suffered by the parties by reason of the infringement was capable of analysis in the light of actual events. The decision is, however, entirely explicable on the conventional basis already considered. It was open to the judge to infer, on an
c evaluation of the evidence, that 15 sales were lost. The absurdity contemplated by Staughton LJ would have been an absurdity on an analysis of the evidence using common sense. Hutchison LJ stated (at 487) that there was in his view 'evidence sufficient to enable [the judge] to reach an assessment of lost profits'. The judge in the *Gerber* case was entitled to infer that 15 sales were probably lost
d without identifying 15 specific transactions. On different evidence he would have been entitled to reach a different conclusion.

[24] I do not consider that the judge was obliged to apply the loss of a chance principle in the present case. It is a useful tool for applying the general principle, that it is for the claimant to prove causation, in circumstances in which the consequences of the breach cannot easily be determined because it is impossible
e or extremely difficult to reconstruct events on the basis that there had been no breach.

[25] In the present cases it may be said that it cannot be known with certainty what would have happened if the appellants had applied for jobs without having the alleged stigma of previous employment by BCCI. The relevance of that alleged
f stigma to the events in question was, however, analysed in the most detailed and comprehensive way at the trial. The effect, if any, upon their employment prospects of the appellants having previously been employed by a corrupt employer was capable of analysis and was thoroughly analysed. Upon the judge's findings, to which it will be necessary to refer in some detail, he was not obliged to assess the
g loss of a chance; he found on the evidence that stigma played no part in the failure to obtain employment. Had there been evidence in *Kitchen's* case that the claim against the original wrongdoer had no chance of success or in the *Allied Maples* case that the vendor would in no circumstances have renegotiated, the judges in those cases need not have applied the loss of a chance principle as they did.

h *The facts and findings*

[26] Having set out the legal principles on which he proposed to rely, the judge first set out the factual background to the dispute. He then summarised and commented upon what he described as the expert evidence. That included three experts on the labour market, Mr Langman for the appellants and Professor
j Rajan and Mr Davies for the respondents. It included the evidence of Coutts, a specialist consultancy engaged by BCCI to assist employees and former employees to find other employment. Evidence was given by Mrs Docker, Ms Tsoflias, Mr Parker and Mr Charlesworth. Evidence was also given by witnesses from prospective employers and recruitment agencies. Many former BCCI employees did obtain other work. There was evidence that, of those registered with Coutts,

almost half had found employment by spring 1992, well over half if the
self-employed and those in education and training were included.

[27] In the next section of his judgment, the judge set out the different ways in
which the appellants' case was put and commented upon them. He then
considered the individual cases of the five employees chosen as test cases. They
included the present appellants. Finally the judge expressed his general conclusions.
At each stage the evidence was considered in considerable detail. The sections of
the judgment dealing with the facts cover over 170 paragraphs and, on a rough
calculation, about 40,000 words.

[28] Having considered the expert and statistical evidence, the judge rejected
the notion that loss and damage should necessarily be assumed or inferred in
stigma cases. He stated that it was the 'direct evidence of loss suffered by each of
the employees due to stigma' which was the 'real case which calls for detailed
consideration'.

[29] The judge stated that he felt able to 'place only limited reliance on the
evidence of Mr Langman and where it is in conflict with that of Professor Rajan
and Mr Davies, I incline to prefer the evidence of the latter'. The judge stated that
he found Professor Rajan 'a most impressive witness' and that the views of
Mr Davies merited 'great weight'. The judge's criticisms of Mr Langman's evidence
and the approach he had adopted to employees and to statistical material are
clearly set out. We have been referred to a good deal of the statistical material
and to the transcript of evidence and the criticisms were in my view criticisms the
judge was entitled to make. The judge's summary was ([1999] IRLR 508 at 533):

'146. I would summarise the evidence of the three experts as to the effect
that in the difficult labour market to which the employees were exposed,
there were a multitude of factors affecting their prospects. Stigma was a
potential handicap if they chanced to apply for a job to a prospective employer
who took the view that their previous employment by the bank placed a
cloud over the former employees of the bank which could not be dispelled
by the liquidators' references, but such an attitude on the part of prospective
employers is not to be assumed.'

[30] The judge found the evidence of the Coutts witnesses helpful. He stated
([1999] IRLR 508 at 534 (para 159)) that 'Ms Tsoflias was the witness whose evidence
I found to be of the greatest value, weight and assistance'. As summarised by the
judge, Ms Tsoflias stated, amongst other things (at 535):

'Coutts sent mailshots to some 1,300 prospective employers about job
vacancies specifically for former employees of the bank. One of her jobs was
to contact employers to whom mailshots were sent to follow up the mailshots.
She never received any indication whatsoever from these employers that they
regarded former employees of the bank in a less favourable light than any
other potential employees as a result of the circumstances surrounding the
bank's collapse, and in her frequent discussions with her colleagues they
never mentioned any such indication. If there had been any such indication,
there would have been a huge problem apparent to everyone ...'

Mr Charlesworth did accept that BCCI employees were marginally disadvantaged.

[31] The judge concluded ([1999] IRLR 508 at 536):

'162. I can summarise the Coutts evidence by saying that the prospects of
obtaining fresh employment very much depended on the attitude of the

a   individual client; past employment by the bank though a cause of anxiety on
     the part of clients and a possible ground for a prospective employer
     preferring another candidate with equal skills, did not deter prospective
     employers approaching Coutts to fill their vacancies and was not seen or
     experienced by Coutts to be a problem or at any rate a substantial problem.
     A prejudice against former employees on the ground of stigma was very
b   much the exception to the general rule. There were other more pressing
     problems for the clients, eg problems with English, age, market conditions
     and unrealistic expectations and demands.'

     [32] The judge summarised the evidence of employers and recruitment
     agencies:

c
     '164. In short, whilst stigma is capable of attaching to a former employee
     of the bank in the eyes of particular prospective employers and (to a greater
     or less extent) handicapping that former employee vis-à-vis that prospective
     employer, that can only be tested on a case by case examination of each
d   prospective employer. Stigma (like a multitude of other factors) may come
     into play to the prejudice of a particular job applicant depending on the
     identity of the prospective employer: there can be no presumption that it has
     come into play or will come into play on any particular application.'

     [33] Under the heading 'Status of stigma as a consideration' ([1999] IRLR 508
e   at 537) the judge stated:

     '168. The prospective employers may be assumed to have known that the
     candidate was previously employed by the bank and have had some
     recollection of the collapse of the bank and that there had been fraud at the
     bank. But beyond this it is not possible to make any assumption as to the
f   extent of the impact of the media publicity on them or whether this led to
     their having any preconception as to the integrity of employees of the bank
     generally. It would not be fair for a prospective employer to adopt the
     attitude that previous employment by the bank placed a candidate under a
     cloud; something more must be necessary to implicate the candidate. It is
g   not possible to assume that any particular prospective employer took the
     (unfair) view that all former employees of the bank were "under a cloud".
     Some prospective employers may have held this view and for them that
     stigma may have been a consideration in their thinking when the employees'
     job applications were before them, but this would have been exceptional. In
     every particular case that attitude of the particular employer has to be
h   proved: it cannot be presumed. It is merely one of the possible reasons for
     an adverse decision. The onus is upon the employees to prove that it was in
     fact a reason for an adverse decision in his case. It is important to bear in
     mind that there are not (as repeatedly maintained on behalf of the employees)
     only two alternative explanations for the employees' unemployment, namely
j   their unemployability and stigma. I have already indicated some of the
     multitude of other alternative explanations.'

     [34] On behalf of Mr Husain, reliance is placed on the fact that between July 1991
     and August 1998 he made 471 job applications. In 1990, he was 53 years old. He
     was called for interview only eight times and received no offers of work. He had,
     prior to 1991, been in regular employment with BCCI. For 11 years he was in the

personnel department and ran the salary section. Stress is placed on the very small number of occasions on which Mr Husain was called for interview.

[35] Mr Zafar had been employed by BCCI for 16 years in a senior position including regional manager for the southern Africa region. In 1990 he was 45 years old. He made 860 job applications between October 1991 and August 1998 and was called for interview on only 17 occasions. Stress is again placed on the number of times the appellant was not called for interview.

[36] Of Mr Husain, the judge stated ([1999] IRLR 508 at 545):

> '206. I should first say a few words on my impression of the witness ... But though he frequently reminded me of his duty as a Muslim to speak the truth, I regret to say that his evidence revealed him to be thoroughly dishonest, untruthful and unreliable. In his evidence (as in his applications for employment), he said whatever he thought best served his purpose. He lied (for example) about his work experience, his position at the bank, his performance and disciplinary record, his involvement in his charity, the time devoted to his book, his job search and his written applications to [Post Office Counters Ltd] ... By reason of the frequency of contradictory statements by him on so many topics, it is often difficult to decide which is true and which is false. His spoken English was not fluent. His difficulties with the English language are apparent on his application forms.'

[37] The judge commented that Mr Husain was not willing to engage in temporary or part-time work though this can often lead to permanent employment. While he made 43 applications in January 1992, in the four-and-a-half years between April 1992 and September 1996 he made only 49 applications. Many applications were made after that date but the judge concluded ([1999] IRLR 508 at 546):

> '212. ... This burst of activity is plainly attributable to his desire to show willingness to take a job in his anticipated claim for stigma damages against the bank, though I do not think that he seriously intended to take up any of them.'

The judge considered some of the job applications to be 'hopeless'. Applications were supported by 'deliberately false statements as to his means and stated or implied (again quite falsely) that he had banking facilities'. In some applications, Mr Husain 'set out deliberately to exaggerate (and thereby falsify) his experience and qualifications'. The judge (at 545) noted:

> '210. ... In a number of applications for jobs in 1997 and 1998 he explained the gap in his employment between leaving the bank and the dates of the job applications as a period expended in writing the book and in his activities for the charity. I believe that this is essentially true and that this was the priority in his life throughout this period, though Mr Husain tried to explain these statements in his job applications as falsehoods justified by his need to obtain the jobs in question.'

The judge stated (at 546 (para 215)) that he was 'not surprised that Mr Husain has remained unemployed: there were ample compelling reasons of which stigma is not one'.

[38] The judge's conclusion ([1999] IRLR 508 at 546–547) in relation to Mr Husain was:

'216. Mr Husain has not discharged the burden of proof that stigma was a cause of the failure of any job application or the loss of a chance on such an application, or that there is any real possibility that it will be such a cause in the future. I am not satisfied that stigma played any part in Mr Husain's failure to obtain employment. This was at least part attributable to his limited efforts to find a job (on several occasions interrupted by lengthy trips abroad, trips to which no reference was made in his witness statement); in the case of the applications which he did make, he had the handicaps of poor English, the poor quality of his completed application forms, the contraction in the payroll industry and the fact that he had a limited amount to offer prospective employers. Mr Langman himself commented on his weak qualifications and the problem he had with his written English. Age must have increasingly become a handicap. The falsehoods in his applications might well have been exposed at interviews with draconian consequences. By October 1996 he was almost 50 years' old and already long-term unemployed, and accordingly any prospect of employment thereafter was extremely limited. Any of these, as well as questions of personality, ethnicity and the quality of the competition may have decided the outcome of his applications. Questions of mitigation accordingly do not arise, but if they did I would have had difficulty holding that he made reasonable effort to mitigate.'

[39] The judge stated his impression of Mr Zafar. It included these comments ([1999] IRLR 508 at 549):

'226. ... Neither his spoken nor written English is fluent ... He has a very inflated opinion of himself and his abilities and is apt to adopt a very critical indeed jaundiced, view of fellow employees, and he cannot and will not keep such views to himself. He is arrogant and quite unable in a dispute to see or understand the other party's point of view ... He is a totally unreliable witness, unwilling or unable to distinguish falsehood from the truth and who lies whenever it suits his purpose.'

The judge referred to an occasion when the appellant 'quite deliberately set out to mislead the court'.

[40] The judge described Mr Zafar's applications for employment and his dismissal by AIBL, which I will consider separately. The judge set out his conclusions in relation to Mr Zafar in a sub-paragraph entitled 'Reasons for unemployment' ([1999] IRLR 508 at 557–558):

'267. I have given the most anxious consideration to the questions whether Mr Zafar has satisfied me on the balance of probabilities that stigma was an effective cause (whether sole or contributing) of (a) any of the rejections I have considered or (b) the loss of a chance of getting such jobs. I have concluded that the answer is firmly in the negative. His case has been handicapped by the fact that he has called none of those who interviewed and rejected him, compounded by the facts where such witnesses have been called by the bank they have refuted his evidence and that his own account of interviews lack evidential weight because he is not a credible witness. There were a multitude of potential candidates as causes: though stigma could have played a part, the evidence does not satisfy me that stigma did play a part or was a cause. Factors to which the various employers (or their agents) in rejecting Mr Zafar may have given varying weight include:

(1) Mr Zafar had an exaggerated view of the "catch" that he was to any prospective employer; (2) his banking skills and experience were generalist and his knowledge and experience in Islamic banking was limited; (3) the recession and the diminution in the banking market in the early 1990s (with the shrinking opportunities for generalists) made his job search more onerous, a fact reflected in his inability to find a job before he joined AIBL; (4) his written English was poor (reflected in his poorly presented applications) and his spoken English was far from fluent, a potential handicap in the senior positions to which he aspired; (5) his personality was not impressive or immediately attractive and (under pressure) becomes highly unattractive. He is prone to lecture and bully. He is not a person who would create a favourable impression at an interview: he is neither impressive nor straightforward. The character revealed in the course of his cross-examination was of a man who cannot and will not give a direct (let alone truthful) answer to questions and that may be expected to come over to an experienced interviewer; (6) he was not a good "team member". This would have come across (as Mr Davies said in evidence) surprisingly quickly at an interview; (7) he does not come over as straightforward. His unwillingness and inability to distinguish truth from falsehood were at risk of revealing itself (e g as to his "clients", his CV, his knowledge of Islamic banking). Prevarication is second nature to him; (8) his age (45 in October 1990) increasingly made him too senior for posts which were a match for his talents. Age was a serious factor from 1995; (9) his ethnic group; (10) the absence of readily available references; and (11) added to the above with the passage of time after September 1991 was the length of his unemployment and his dependence on benefits.'

[41] The judge expressed his general conclusions ([1999] 4 All ER 83 at 123–124, [1999] IRLR 508 at 558) in relation to the five claims before him, only two of which for present purposes it has been appropriate to consider in detail:

'269. The Employees have established that the bank was in breach of the [trust and confidence term] of their contracts of employment, but they have not established that this breach caused financial loss to any of them. In (*Malik v Bank of Credit and Commerce International SA (in liq)*, *Mahmud v Bank of Credit and Commerce International SA (in liq)*) [1997] 3 All ER 1, [1998] AC 20 Lord Steyn gave the clearest warning that because of difficulties of proof it was improbable that many employees would be able to prove their entitlement to stigma compensation. This trial underlines that warning and the critical importance in cases such as this of credible evidence by the prospective employer or his agent of the impact of stigma on his decision to reject the job application in question.

270. The Employees' cases consisted of three elements: (a) they relied on their long-term failure to obtain employment and they invited the court to infer that stigma was the likely cause. But stigma was not a likely cause and there were alternative more impelling causes. There is no room for any presumption that stigma played a part in the adverse decisions made on their job applications. (Subject to one proviso) only a small minority of prospective employers are likely to have adopted the view that any stigma attached to job applicants who were former employees of the bank and that this placed them under a cloud. The proviso is that there was not present any substantial reason to believe that the individual job applicant was personally implicated

a in the wrongdoing. No such reason could have existed in respect of the general body of former employees of the bank. Accordingly there can be no presumption that any particular prospective employer who was approached viewed former employees of the bank as under a cloud, and the onus was on the Employees to establish that the prospective employers to whom they made job applications held this view and rejected their applications on this

b ground (whether on this ground alone or on this and other grounds). The Employees were unable to discharge this onus. (b) The Employees gave evidence that on occasion the prospective employers expressly or impliedly stated that they were rejecting their job applications on grounds of stigma. But if the court is to accept such evidence the witness must be credible and the evidence must be clearly and reliably recollected; and even if the

c evidence is accepted, it is not necessarily enough to entitle the Employees to succeed, for the reasons given to an applicant by a prospective employer may be of limited guidance as to his true reasons. The evidence adduced by the Employees generally was not credible and did not establish that stigma had the effect claimed. (c) The Employees have also adduced evidence from some three prospective employers that stigma prompted their decisions to

d refuse the Employees' job applications, but their evidence was plainly concocted.

271. The evidential hurdles in the way of success in claims for stigma damages are substantial and any litigation is likely to prove protracted and expensive. Accordingly the greatest caution is called for before any such

e proceedings are instituted and the continuing viability of such proceedings must be the subject of continuing review. The prospects may be expected rarely to attain the required level to justify proceedings in the absence of reliable and tested evidence of the prospective employer or his agent. In any exceptional case when consideration is given to bringing proceedings

f without calling the prospective employer or his agent, at the very least the prospective employer and his agent should be approached before any proceedings are commenced to discover their account of events and see what evidence they can and will give; and the prospects of success must be assessed in the light of the response or absence of response by them. This precaution does not appear to have been taken in this case.'

g

Conclusions on general issue

[42] The conclusions with respect to Mr Husain and Mr Zafar are fatal to their claims. The judge was entitled to make the findings he did. We have been referred to many parts of the transcript of evidence and doubt has not in my view

h been cast upon the validity of the findings. The judge did not deal specifically with the point that both men were called for interview on very few occasions. It is, however, clear from his comments and reasoning that he had reached the conclusion that stigma was not the cause of their failure to obtain employment, which was the relevant conclusion. The fact that some only of the factors he

j relied on would have been relevant at the stage of deciding whether to call for interview does not defeat that conclusion. Even assuming (without accepting) that the BCCI link may have reduced the number of interviews, the judge was clearly of the view that the eventual outcome of the applications was unaffected by stigma.

[43] The judge was entitled not to assume or to infer, in either case, that loss resulted from BCCI's breach of the trust and confidence term in the contracts of

employment and to conclude in terms that it did not. I bear in mind the
submission that some of the factors mentioned by the judge, such as increasing
age and the increasing length of unemployment, are capable of operating
cumulatively with a stigma to cause a loss or increase a proved loss. The inclusion
of these factors as reasons for unemployment does not, however, affect the
validity of the judge's conclusion that stigma did not 'play a part or was a cause'
of the unemployment or the validity of the reasoning which led to it.

[44] In his general conclusion, the judge gave guidance as to what a successful
claim is likely to involve. Having regard to the length of the hearing before him
and the evidence and submissions he had heard, he was entitled to give that
guidance and was well placed to do so. The guidance requires most careful
consideration by claimants. I only add that it cannot be said as a matter of law,
and the judge was not putting it as such, that it is necessary to call, or approach,
the prospective employer or employers. On the judge's findings of fact, which
I find no reason to disturb, there can, as Mr Jeans QC for BCCI put it, be no
general inference of loss in these cases from the fact of unemployment. The onus
is on a claimant to establish a loss of employment by reason of stigma in his
particular case.

Mr Zafar's dismissal by AIBL

[45] Mr Kent rightly puts the subject of Mr Zafar's loss of employment with
AIBL as requiring separate consideration. Mr Zafar was appointed assistant
managing director of that company as from 1 June 1991. It was agreed that he
should receive a mandate specifying his duties. The judge has set out in
considerable detail in his judgment the short but eventful history of Mr Zafar's
employment. It was terminated with immediate effect on 16 August 1991 shortly
after the BCCI scandal broke. He was paid the equivalent of three months' pay
in respect of the termination. On 4 November 1991 he issued a writ against AIBL
claiming damages for breach of contract. On 28 November 1997, it was ordered
by consent that £26,000 in court be paid to Mr Zafar together with a contribution
of £10,000 towards his costs in full and final settlement of his claims.

[46] The judge's conclusion about the termination was:

'245. Generally, I am satisfied that Mr Zafar's employment by AIBL was
always under threat because of the opposition of the resident directors to his
appointment and was doomed by reason of his personal incompatibility with
them and finally brought to an end by reason of his refusal to sign a contract
to accept the position of assistant general manager. His previous employment
by the bank was a matter ventilated about the time of his dismissal, but this
was not a ground for his dismissal. It was referred to by [a non-executive
member of AIBL] and by [the vice-chairman of AIBL] as a matter which
might be taken into account, but I do not think that it was or in any way
affected the outcome. The resident directors and shareholders could reach
no agreement with Mr Zafar as to the post Mr Zafar should occupy. Despite
his protestations to [the vice-chairman] to the contrary, Mr Zafar insisted on
the elevated status of assistant managing director: and that was not
acceptable to the resident directors or the shareholders. The resident directors
had had enough of him for the other reasons I have mentioned, and the
shareholders (as they decided to go along with the resident directors on
19 June 1991 on the question of Mr Zafar's job title) decided to go along with
those directors on his dismissal. When it came to the crunch, those directors
had the shareholders' trust more than Mr Zafar did, and the shareholders did

not want a war with the resident directors over Mr Zafar. Some insight into the shareholders' attitude to his former employment by the bank may be found in Mr Zafar's evidence to the effect that (1) though the lights were flashing regarding the bank before his appointment, they were no barrier to his original appointment; and (2) after the collapse of the bank the shareholders told him they still wanted to appoint him managing director. The resident directors had long intended to rid AIBL of him for other reasons. I do not think that stigma played any part in his dismissal or was an effective or contributing cause of it or of the loss of a chance of his remaining with AIBL. I should add that, even if I had held that stigma was a cause, I would have held that it was only a minor contributory cause, that it did not affect the outcome and that if it did have any impact that impact was limited to marginally accelerating the inevitable; and that, since in any event Mr Zafar's employment would have been terminated for the other reasons I have given in a matter of weeks, if not days, and he received substantial compensation for this termination from AIBL no substantial award of damages was appropriate.' (See [1999] IRLR 508 at 553–554.)

[47] Mr Kent submits that the finding that stigma was not an effective or contributory cause of the dismissal was, on the evidence, perverse. The documentary evidence referred to by the judge pointed to stigma being the cause of dismissal and there was no oral evidence from those involved in the relevant events to defeat that conclusion. The credibility or lack of credibility of Mr Zafar could have no bearing upon the conclusion on this issue, it is submitted.

[48] Mr Jeans submits that the opinion the judge formed of Mr Zafar is relevant to this issue. It enabled the judge to form a view as to the relationship and dealings between Mr Zafar and other officers and employees of AIBL. The contemporaneous documents reveal considerable differences between Mr Zafar and the others. In evidence Mr Zafar denied such problems until his first written statement and the contents of a telephone conversation recorded on 20 July 1991 were put to him. Mr Jeans submits that the BCCI connection was only a peg on which to hang a decision taken on other grounds. The documents reveal a dispute as to whether Mr Zafar should be assistant managing director or assistant general manager. The minutes of the board meeting of 14 August 1991, to which the judge referred, referred to Mr Zafar's not accepting the offer of employment with the changed designation. It was resolved that 'Mr Zafar, having refused to accept the offer of employment as conveyed to him in writing by the Managing Director, as per instructions of the Vice-Chairman, be dismissed with immediate effect'. There is no reference in that minute to BCCI being a factor and there is no reference to it in Mr Zafar's forceful response to the dismissal in his letter of 18 August.

[49] There is force in the submission that the contradiction between the resolution adopted at the board meeting and other documents containing a reference to the BCCI factor is unresolved. However, on the evidence as a whole, the judge was in my view entitled to come to the conclusion he did on this issue. An AIBL internal minute dated 9 July 1991, in which the position of Mr Zafar was reviewed, included the statement: 'We had hoped to resolve this tiresome matter quietly but believe the BCCI events have overtaken this strategy.' That, however, is not necessarily inconsistent with the respondents' 'peg-hanging' submission. There is no justification for reversing the judge's finding of fact. Mr Zafar's oral

evidence, and the view taken of it by the judge, is a relevant factor in interpreting
and assessing the significance of the events in the summer of 1991.

Exclusion of anecdotal evidence

[50] The judge refused an application to admit at the trial evidence of 15 witnesses
directed to the experiences of other former employees of BCCI seeking work
following closure. The application had a curious history. It was first made before
the trial on 20 November 1998. The judge declined to admit the evidence but
ordered that Mr Langman, the claimants' expert witness, be at liberty to annex
the witness statements to his report. Miss Booth QC had stated, in the course of
argument before the judge, that the claimants were perfectly happy for the
statements to go in and for the judge to attach to them what weight he wanted
to attach.

[51] On 11 December 1998 Miss Booth sought permission to call Mr Vaz MP
'to give factual evidence about the market place'. A question arose as to whether
Mr Vaz was prepared to name people referred to in his statement. Miss Booth
stated that he would be spoken to and 'if he is prepared to give names we will
renew our application at that point'. That application was not renewed.

[52] On 25 February 1999, eight days into the trial, the claimants renewed
their application to call witnesses and also, and for the first time, submitted that
the Coutts witnesses should be excluded. There had been no change in circumstance
between the renewed application and the earlier one. The judge refused the
application to exclude the Coutts witness. The judge referred to the lateness of
the application and to the fact that the Coutts evidence related to their own
experience when acting as consultants for BCCI in this very matter.

[53] No objection is now taken to that decision but it is submitted that the
'anecdotal' evidence should also have been admitted. The judge declined to
review his decision, giving reasons. The admissibility of the material was the
subject of a further submission later in the trial. In his judgment, the judge gave
his reasons for excluding the evidence and did so in terms substantially the same
as those given on 25 February:

'I refused the applications for two reasons. The first was because such
evidence does not satisfy the test of admissible similar fact evidence: it was
not logically probative of the employees' case: the fact (if established) that
another person was refused work by one prospective employer because of
stigma was no evidence that the employees were likewise refused work on
this ground by prospective employers whom they approached. The second
was that, even if such evidence could have some probative value, in my
discretion it would be unjust to allow such evidence, for it would be the
occasion for a disproportionate increase in the length of trial and costs. The
evidence of witnesses alleging that they have been refused employment on
grounds of stigma (like the evidence of the employees in this case) requires
the most careful examination, and can only properly be evaluated in the light
of discovery and investigation of the incidents in question (and this includes
contact with, and often evidence by, the prospective employer in question).
To undertake this exercise in respect of each anecdotal incident would heap
trial upon trial and would involve a disproportionate expenditure of time and
cost for (at best) a marginal return.'

The judge also expressed his conclusion that, though Mr Langman had
permission to consider the 15 witness statements, Mr Langman had not in the
event based his opinions in evidence upon the contents of those statements.

[54] The judge's decision was in my view entirely justified on the second ground given, if not the first. I do not accept his conclusion that the proposed evidence could not logically be probative of the claimants' case as presented. It was capable of assisting the judge in deciding whether to draw an inference favourable to the claimants. However, the decision was justified as a decision, in the interests of justice, to limit the scope of the trial. A limited number of test cases had been chosen for investigation with a view to a manageable trial. The contents of the statements of other claimants, and the letters they say they had received, opened very broad areas for inquiry, if the evidence was to be assessed fairly. Putting in statements without cross-examination and further inquiries would have been of very limited value. Inquiries as to the credibility of the proposed witnesses and of material they claimed to have received from prospective employees would have been necessary, especially in the context of a case in which the judge found that other such material had been concocted. Quite apart from the possibility of dishonesty, extensive inquiries would have been necessary into the activities of persons who had not been selected for test purposes. Indeed, one of the statements was from a woman who had declined to be a test case because she did not want the strain of that responsibility. In the context of a case in which a broad range of evidence was before him, the judge was also entitled to conclude that the bearing of the experience of other employees upon the test cases to be considered in great detail was 'marginal'.

Mr Allen QC for other claimants

[55] Mr Allen QC was present at the hearing of the appeal on behalf of claimants not involved in the test cases. Given constraints of time, the court was not prepared to hear Mr Allen cover the ground which had been covered by Mr Kent nor, in the event, did he seek to do so. Mr Allen was invited to identify any point which the court ought to have in mind which it would not have in mind in relation to the appeals but which was distinctive to his clients. He did not do so. Mr Allen was offered the opportunity to put in a written submission when he had heard the submissions of the parties to the appeal but did not take that opportunity. Mr Allen did propose that the court should hand down a provisional judgment on which he should have the opportunity to make submissions on behalf of other parties before a final judgment was delivered. We refused that application.

[56] This account is not given by way of adverse comment upon Mr Allen's presence at the hearing of the appeal. It may well prove to have been of assistance to his clients. The court's duty is, however, to consider the two appeals before it and not cases not before it.

Result

[57] I would dismiss these appeals.

ROBERT WALKER LJ.

[58] I agree that these appeals should be dismissed for the reasons set out in the judgment of Pill LJ, which I have had the advantage of reading.

[59] If these two appeals stood alone, I would not wish to add anything. But as the judge's conclusions on issues of law and fact are to be binding in relation to other claims within this managed litigation, I wish to add a short comment on one evidential point, and some rather more extensive comments on the topic of loss of a chance.

[60] The evidential point is whether it was necessary, as a matter of law, for the claimants to call evidence from prospective employers as to the effect of BCCI stigma on particular job applications made to them. Credible evidence of that sort from an independent source would no doubt give powerful support to a claim. But I respectfully agree with Pill LJ that it was not necessary as a matter of law. To impose that requirement would put a large (and in many cases insuperable) obstacle in the way of stigma claims.

[61] In paras 64ff of his judgment ([1999] 4 All ER 83 at 108ff, [1999] IRLR 508 at 520ff) the judge considered (under the heading 'Loss of job or loss of chance of job') what the stigmatised employees had to prove in order to establish loss. The judge rightly noted that the relevant principles are discussed at length in the decision of this court in *Allied Maples Group Ltd v Simmons & Simmons (a firm)* [1995] 4 All ER 907, [1995] 1 WLR 1602 (Stuart-Smith and Hobhouse LJJ, with Millett LJ agreeing on the law but dissenting on the facts). I am far from confident of adding to the clarity of the exposition in the *Allied Maples* case but I venture to make some observations of my own.

[62] Two points should be noted at the outset. The expression 'loss of a chance' (which may have been first used in *Chaplin v Hicks* [1911] 2 KB 786 at 791, [1911–13] All ER Rep 224 at 227) has over the years been used to cover a variety of situations, some of which may be thought to stretch and distort its original meaning. It is most apt to cover the loss of a single identifiable opportunity which, although difficult to evaluate, was 'something which had a monetary value' (the words used by Vaughan Williams LJ in *Chaplin v Hicks* [1911] 2 KB 786 at 793, [1911–13] All ER Rep 224 at 228). The clearest example is when the claimant's right of action for damages against a third party is lost through the negligence of a solicitor who fails to commence proceedings in time. *Kitchen v Royal Air Forces Association* [1958] 2 All ER 241, [1958] 1 WLR 563 was such a case. In it Lord Evershed MR said:

'In my judgment, assuming that the plaintiff has established negligence, what the court has to do in such a case as the present is to determine what the plaintiff has lost by that negligence. The question is: Has the plaintiff lost some right of value, some chose in action of reality and substance? In such a case it may be that its value is not easy to determine, but it is the duty of the court to determine that value as best it can.' (See [1958] 2 All ER 241 at 251, [1958] 1 WLR 563 at 575.)

[63] *Chaplin v Hicks* itself is often referred to as another example of the loss of a chance, but it is hardly a good example of a third party decision which must be 'justifiable by objective criteria' (Millett LJ's description in the *Allied Maples* case [1995] 4 All ER 907 at 928, [1995] 1 WLR 1602 at 1623). Study of the facts shows that Mr Hicks, the actor-manager who organised the talent competition, changed the rules so that the final selection of 12 winners was to be made, not by the votes of newspaper readers, but by Mr Hicks himself, at interviews at the Aldwych Theatre in London. So it was not ultimately a case of third party volition at all, but it seems to have been treated as if it was.

[64] In other cases the label 'loss of a chance' has been used much more loosely. As is said in *McGregor on Damages* (16th edn, 1997) p 246, para 375, at the beginning of the section dealing with loss of a chance—

'All cases dealing with loss of business and professional profits depend upon the chance and contingency that other parties will act so as to bring *a*   profits in to the plaintiff; customers must come to the shop, audiences to the theatre, fish to the hook.'

The author then proceeds to consider the case where there is 'one particular chance that the plaintiff loses, one particular contingency upon which a gain to him has depended'.

b   [65] The other preliminary point to be made is that both in the true 'loss of a chance' case (exemplified by a solicitor's negligence in allowing a claim to become statute-barred) and in other more debatable 'loss of chance' cases the question arises both on the issue of causation and (if the claimant gets that far) on the issue of quantum. That point is very clearly made in the judgment of Millett LJ in the *Allied Maples* case [1995] 4 All ER 907 at 926–927, [1995] 1 WLR
c   1602 at 1622, 1623. Similarly Stuart-Smith LJ said:

'... the plaintiff must prove as a matter of causation that he has a real or substantial chance as opposed to a speculative one. If he succeeds in doing so, the evaluation of the chance is part of the assessment of the quantum of damage, the range lying somewhere between something that just qualifies as
d   real or substantial on the one hand and near certainty on the other.' (See [1995] 4 All ER 907 at 919, [1995] 1 WLR 1602 at 1614.)

The order for a split trial of the issues of liability and quantum led to some confusion in the *Allied Maples* case (see [1995] 4 All ER 907 at 926, [1995] 1 WLR 1602 at 1621 per Hobhouse LJ).
e   [66] In para 66 of his judgment ([1999] 4 All ER 83 at 109–110, [1999] IRLR 508 at 520) the judge set out most of the important statement of principle in the judgment of Stuart-Smith LJ at [1995] 4 All ER 907 at 914–919, [1995] 1 WLR 1602 at 1614 at 1609–1611. Stuart-Smith LJ's threefold classification can be briefly summarised as follows. (1) In the typical case of personal injury through a
f   positive act of negligence, causation must be decided on the balance of probability. But so far as quantum depends on what will actually happen in the future (such as whether the claimant will develop arthritis as a result of his injury) the court makes an assessment, often in percentage terms. (2) Where the defendant's breach of duty is an omission (such as a failure to give correct legal advice, or to provide proper safety equipment) the court has to decide what the
g   claimant would have done had the duty been performed. Would the claimant have followed correct advice, or used the proper equipment? These are hypothetical questions, but they are decided on the balance of probability as to what the claimant himself would have done. (3) Where proof of loss depends on the hypothetical action of a third party, the claimant can succeed if he shows that
h   there was a real or substantial chance of that third party action taking place, the evaluation of the chance being a question of quantification of damage.

[67] The process of assessment of the risk of complications mentioned in Stuart-Smith LJ's first category (see [66](1), above) can perhaps be explained by recognising that the court is not really concerned with predicting the future. It is
j   concerned with answering a present question: what is the prognosis for this claimant?

[68] Examples of the type of case in the second category (see [66](2), above) are the well-known cases of *Sykes v Midland Bank Executor and Trustee Co Ltd* [1970] 2 All ER 471, [1971] 1 QB 113 and *Cummings (or McWilliams) v Sir William Arrol & Co Ltd* [1962] 1 All ER 623, [1962] 1 WLR 295. In *Sykes'* case the claimant (a professional man whose firm had been given inadequate advice as to the terms

of a lease) failed, despite being pressed by the judge, to give any positive evidence about what his firm would have done had they been given adequate advice. In *Cummings'* case the judge found that a steel erector who had fallen to his death would not have used a safety belt (which the employer, in breach of statutory duty, failed to provide). Both claims failed because causation had not been established on the balance of probability.

[69] The type of case in the third category (see [66](3), above) is similar to the second category in that it raises a hypothetical question: what would have happened in the past, or would be likely to happen in the future, if some event (that is, the defendant's breach of duty) had not occurred? The question is hypothetical because the actual course of events took a different turning. As Lord Browne-Wilkinson put it in *Bolitho (administratrix of the estate of Bolitho (decd)) v City and Hackney Health Authority* [1997] 4 All ER 771 at 776, [1998] AC 232 at 239: 'The question is what would have happened if an event which by definition did not occur had occurred.'

[70] *Bolitho's* case was a medical negligence case. Cases of that type often raise particularly difficult questions of causation, and this court was referred to several decisions of the House of Lords on complex questions as to the causation of physical injuries, some in the context of medical negligence: see *McGhee v National Coal Board* [1972] 3 All ER 1008, [1973] 1 WLR 1, *Hotson v East Berkshire Area Health Authority* [1987] 2 All ER 909, [1987] AC 750, *Wilsher v Essex Area Health Authority* [1988] 1 All ER 871, [1988] AC 1074 and *Pickford v Imperial Chemical Industries plc* [1998] 3 All ER 462, [1998] 1 WLR 1189. These cases do not, I think, give much direct assistance on the issues which have to be decided on this appeal.

[71] It is, however, worth noting that in *Hotson's* case, although Lord Bridge of Harwich saw formidable difficulties in the concept of 'the lost chance of a better medical result which might have been achieved by prompt diagnosis and correct treatment' ([1987] 2 All ER 909 at 914, [1987] AC 750 at 782), Lord Mackay of Clashfern considered ([1987] 2 All ER 909 at 916, [1987] AC 750 at 786) that it would be unwise to lay down a rule that a claimant could never succeed by proving loss of a chance in a medical negligence case.

[72] It is also worth noting, before leaving the medical causation cases on one side, that in the typical case where treatment is given under the National Health Service a single defendant is generally responsible for a number of different healthcare professionals whose acts or omissions (in a medical emergency which may last for hours or days) are alleged to have brought about a bad outcome. If all these healthcare professionals are employed by the defendant, any question as to what one of them (for instance, a registrar or consultant who should have been called sooner) would have done but for an antecedent breach of duty by someone less highly qualified, must, it seems, be decided on the balance of probability, since in the eyes of the law no third party is involved. That seems to be the approach of Hobhouse LJ in *Joyce v Merton Sutton and Wandsworth Health Authority* (1995) 27 BMLR 124 at 156 in a passage expressly approved by the House of Lords in *Bolitho's* case:

'Thus, a plaintiff can discharge the burden of proof on causation by satisfying the court *either* that the relevant person would in fact have taken the requisite action (although she would not have been at fault if she had not) *or* that the proper discharge of the relevant person's duty towards the plaintiff required that she take that action. The former alternative calls for no explanation since it is simply the factual proof of the causative effect of the original fault. The latter is slightly more sophisticated: it involves the factual situation that the original fault did not itself cause the injury but that this was because there would have been some further fault on the part of the defendants; the plaintiff proves his case by proving that his injuries would have been avoided if proper care had continued to be taken.' (See [1997] 4 All ER 771 at 777, [1998] AC 232 at 240.)

[73] The distinguishing feature of Stuart-Smith LJ's third category is that the uncertainty in the last element of causation is as to what would have been decided or done by a third party whose decision or conduct is to some degree capable of assessment on rational grounds. In the paradigm case of the claim which legal advisors have allowed to become statute-barred (*Kitchen v Royal Air Forces Association* [1958] 2 All ER 241, [1958] 1 WLR 563) the question was whether Mrs Kitchen would have succeeded in her claim after her husband had been killed by a defective electric cooker. The third party in cases of that sort is the court, an impersonal abstraction which would (but for the failure to commence proceedings) have determined the claim in an objective and impartial manner. In other cases the third party may be expected to act in his own best interests and his conduct may in that way be predictable (see Millett LJ in the *Allied Maples* case [1995] 4 All ER 907 at 928, [1995] 1 WLR 1602 at 1623–1624).

[74] After his citation of the *Allied Maples* case the judge referred to the very well-known observations of Lord Reid in *Davies v Taylor* [1972] 3 All ER 836, [1974] AC 207 (on which Stuart-Smith LJ relied in the *Allied Maples* case) and to the decision of this court in *Nestle v National Westminster Bank plc* [1994] 1 All ER 118, [1993] 1 WLR 1260. The *Nestle* case was a claim for equitable compensation for breach of trust in the investment of trust funds, and I do not think it is of much help here.

[75] Then the judge stated ([1999] 4 All ER 83 at 111, [1999] IRLR 508 at 521 (para 70)) that the test must be whether the court can decide 'as a matter of historical fact' whether the claimant would, in the absence of the defendant's breach of duty, have obtained an advantage or avoided a detriment (in other words, whether the chance would have turned out in his favour).

[76] The judge distinguished two situations: where the defendant's wrongdoing has made it impossible to carry out that exercise of ascertaining historical fact, and where the exercise has remained possible and has in fact been carried out, but in a way which is, from the claimant's point of view, flawed. The second half of my last sentence is a paraphrase of para 70(2) of the judgment, and for the sake of accuracy I will set it out in the judge's own words:

'The wrongdoing may be such that, whilst the relevant decision-making process was completed and a decision made on the merits, by reason of the wrongdoing the decision-maker may have taken into account matters which (but for the wrongdoing) he would not have done. In that case it is possible (albeit it may be difficult) to investigate as a matter of historical fact what, if any, part the matters in question played in the decision-making. Where this is the situation the claimant must prove that the matters in question were a cause of the absence of a decision in his favour.'

[77] I have no difficulty with the first of the two situations envisaged by the judge. As Mrs Kitchen's claim never got to court, it is plainly impossible to ascertain, as a question of historical fact, what the outcome would have been.

But what if the negligence of the legal advisers (assumed not to be protected by advocate's immunity) had consisted of an obviously culpable failure to engage and call an expert witness? Then the trial judge who heard (and dismissed) the claim might make clear in his judgment that he regarded the failure as fatal to the success of the claim; but he would be unlikely to state unequivocally that the claim would otherwise have succeeded. Even if he were to go that far, I am not sure how far his statement would establish anything as a matter of historical fact, unless that means no more than a strong probability.

[78] In considering whether his view accorded with the authorities the judge then referred to the decision of this court in *Stovold v Barlows (a firm)* [1996] 1 PNLR 91, to the decision of the Court of Appeal of New Zealand in *Balfour v A-G* [1991] 1 NZLR 519, and to the decision of the House of Lords in *Spring v Guardian Assurance plc* [1994] 3 All ER 129, [1995] 2 AC 296.

[79] *Stovold v Barlows* is a case of some interest. It was heard at first instance before the *Allied Maples* case but reached this court after that case. It was a claim for solicitor's negligence arising out of the failure of a solicitor, Mr Campbell of Barlows, in despatching documents which were urgently needed in order to achieve the sale of a house belonging to his client, Mr Stovold. On Thursday 14 September 1989 Mr Dunn, the solicitor acting for the prospective purchaser, asked for the documents (the Land Registry entry and a draft contract) to be sent to him as a matter of urgency. Both solicitors had offices in Surrey. Mr Campbell said that he would post them that evening. In fact (without Mr Dunn having been asked whether he was in the DX system) Mr Campbell's secretary lodged them in the DX for the attention of Dunn & Co, a firm of tailors and outfitters.

[80] Had the documents been sent by first class post they would probably, but not certainly, have arrived on the Friday. When they had not arrived on that day Mr Susans looked at another house and made an offer for it. When the documents had not arrived by the Monday Mr Susans told Mr Dunn to proceed with the purchase of the new house, but not to tell Mr Campbell until he was ready to exchange contracts on the new house.

[81] At first instance Jowitt J held that Mr Campbell was in breach of duty and (on the balance of probability) that but for the breach Mr Susans would have proceeded with the original purchase. The case is of particular interest because Mr Susans gave evidence and there was an issue as to the credibility of his evidence. The trial judge accepted him as a witness of truth and relied on his evidence (in re-examination) that even if the documents had arrived on the Tuesday, he and his wife would probably have carried on with the original purchase.

[82] In this court that conclusion was challenged. Mr Susans' evidence was closely analysed and shown to contain inconsistencies. This court (Stuart-Smith, Pill and Otton LJJ) differed from the trial judge and concluded (in Pill LJ's words at [1996] 1 PNLR 91 at 105) that Mr Stovold's chance disappeared on the Friday. That focused attention on another imponderable, that is whether (if posted by first class post on the Thursday evening) the documents would have arrived on Friday morning. This court concluded that there was a reasonable chance that they would have done and that there was no reason to interfere with the judge's finding that in that event Mr Susans would not have gone to see the new house on Friday afternoon. So the claim succeeded but the award was reduced by half.

[83] In my view *Stovold v Barlows* illustrates (especially with the doubts about the reliability both of the first class post and of the third party's evidence) that these questions of causation and quantum cannot be reduced to a single comprehensive test, however convenient that would be. There are too many variables in play.

[84] The decision of the Court of Appeal of New Zealand in *Balfour's* case does not offer much assistance on the issue of causation. The facts were complicated and obscure, covering a period of over ten years during which Mr Balfour's attempts to make a career in working with disadvantaged children were dogged by widespread rumours about his sexual orientation. The evidence as a whole suggested that the particular file note (on his personal file at the Department of Education) on which Mr Balfour based his claim was a reflection (rather than a significant source) of the rumours (which no one sought to justify at trial). There is in the judgment of the court no discussion of principles of causation.

[85] *Spring's* case is an important case on the application of the *Hedley Byrne* principle to references given by employers in respect of former employees or representatives (see *Hedley Byrne & Co Ltd v Heller & Partners Ltd* [1963] 2 All ER 575, [1964] AC 465). Mr Spring had been an estate agent and also an appointed representative (within s 44 of the Financial Services Act 1986) for Guardian. Guardian bought the estate agency (Corinium) and Mr Spring was dismissed by Corinium's newly appointed chief executive. He wished to become an appointed representative with Scottish Amicable and two other life offices. Guardian negligently provided Scottish Amicable with a reference which could hardly have been less encouraging. It said among other things 'his former superior has further stated that he is a man of little or no integrity and could not be regarded as honest'. The 'former superior' was the newly appointed chief executive who had sacked him. The reference was written by an assistant chief compliance officer who was not actuated by malice. Scottish Amicable refused Mr Spring's application and so did the other two companies, which had received similar references.

[86] For present purposes the main importance of the case lies in a passage towards the end of Lord Lowry's speech ([1994] 3 All ER 129 at 154, [1995] 2 AC 296 at 327):

> 'Once the duty of care is held to exist and the defendants' negligence is proved, the plaintiff only has to show that by reason of that negligence he has lost a reasonable chance of employment (which would have to be evaluated) and has thereby sustained loss: *McGregor on Damages* (14th edn, 1980) paras 276–278, pp 198–202 and *Chaplin v Hicks* [1911] 2 KB 786, [1911–13] All ER Rep 224. He does not have to prove that, but for the negligent reference, Scottish Amicable *would* have employed him.'

Lord Lowry then set out quite a long passage from the judgment of the trial judge discussing submissions that Mr Spring would not have been appointed even if he had received a careful and accurate reference. This passage ended:

> 'As I observed in argument, the only person capable of giving an authoritative answer to the hypothetical question posed would have been somebody in [the Scottish Amicable compliance officer's] position who had sat in this courtroom throughout the many days of evidence and heard all the facts about the plaintiff and his career at Corinium. As it is, having done so myself, I can only say that, in my judgment, on balance, had the plaintiff received the careful and accurate reference he was entitled to, he would probably have obtained employment with one of these companies.' (See [1994] 3 All ER 129 at 154–155, [1995] 2 AC 296 at 328.)

Lord Lowry indicated that the trial judge's finding of fact might be irreversible, but that the House of Lords had not heard argument on the point. He did not comment on the trial judge's apparent reliance on a balance of probability test. The *Allied Maples* case had not then reached this court.

[87] The facts of *Spring*'s case were fairly extreme and the trial judge accepted the description (by Mr Spring's counsel) of the reference having been the 'kiss of death' to his career in insurance. There was, however, room for debate as to whether he would have been appointed on the basis of a true reference (there was evidence of some inexperience and some misselling, not involving dishonesty, on Mr Spring's part). The 'kiss of death' point (that is, the decisive negative effect of the untrue reference) led Lightman J to conclude that *Spring*'s case fell within his first category, where the ascertainment of historical fact is impossible. I infer that if Mr Spring's reference had been only mildly discouraging (but still negligent) the judge would have allocated it to his second category (in which it is in principle possible, although it may be difficult, to decide an issue of causation as a matter of historical fact).

[88] In my respectful view the judge was wrong in discerning any real difference in principle between his two categories. I consider that in all these cases there is a single question: but for the defendant's breach of duty, what would the third party have done (and what would have been the outcome for the claimant)? This question is necessarily hypothetical because the breach of duty has sent the actual course of events down a different turning. The court may sometimes be able to answer the hypothetical question with a high degree of confidence and some precision. In other cases it may have to take a broad view on a number of imponderables. But the sharp distinction between 'no decision' and a (flawed) 'decision made on the merits' cannot in my view be supported either on principle or on authority. It is, I think, akin to the distinction between 'no transaction' and 'successful transaction' cases which was rejected by the House of Lords in *South Australia Asset Management Corp v York Montague Ltd, United Bank of Kuwait plc v Prudential Property Services Ltd, Nykredit Mortgage Bank plc v Edward Erdman Group Ltd* [1996] 3 All ER 365, [1997] AC 191 (see the speech of Lord Hoffmann [1996] 3 All ER 365 at 376, [1997] AC 191 at 218).

[89] Whether that is right or not, the judge did in my respectful view err in the way in which he approached the facts of the cases before him. The way in which he had instructed himself on the law led him to distinguish between cases in which past applications to prospective employers had, or had not, been considered on their merits ([1999] 4 All ER 83 at 113–114, [1999] IRLR 508 at 522 (para 76)). He then considered future applications and (in case he were wrong on the law) past applications on a 'loss of a chance' basis ([1999] 4 All ER 83 at 114ff, [1999] IRLR 508 at 522ff (paras 77ff)). His conclusion in this part of his judgment ([1999] 4 All ER 83 at 116, [1999] IRLR 508 at 523 (para 81)) was that no applicant for a job can be said to have, in respect of any application, a real or measurable chance of obtaining it. He regarded that as conclusive against the claimants' claims (although he still went on to consider other points).

[90] I think the judge's approach was over-elaborate and that he overlooked some mundane facts. Apart perhaps from those near the very top of the employment ladder (who may aspire only to be chairman, or director-general, or permanent secretary) jobseekers do not usually set their hearts on a single job vacancy. They expect (especially in an overcrowded industry suffering serious recession) to have to make many job applications. They hope to be shortlisted for interview for some vacancies and eventually to be successful in obtaining the offer of a job on satisfactory terms.

[91] That was the position of most of those made redundant by BCCI's liquidators. It is clear from the evidence that they reacted in different ways to their predicament. Some were resentful and negative about seeking new employment. Some were overambitious (or simply unrealistic) in applying for posts for which they were insufficiently qualified. A large number of them did avail themselves of the services of Coutts' Career Consultants Ltd (Coutts) and many of them were successful in obtaining a job within a reasonably short time. But in every case the question to be answered was whether stigma from a jobseeker's previous employment with BCCI had (i) a real (or substantial) effect and (ii) if so, how great an effect on his obtaining employment. This is not an easy question to answer, and the whole history of an individual's search for employment is relevant to answering it: how many jobs he applied for, whether the applications were sensibly targeted and well presented, how many interviews he obtained, how each interview went, and any stated reasons (which would not necessarily be the only reasons or even the true reasons) for rejection. Each application is therefore relevant, but the question must be answered on the job search as a whole.

[92] That view is supported by the judgment of Staughton LJ (with which Hobhouse and Hutchison LJJ agreed on this point) in *Gerber Garment Technology Inc v Lectra Systems Ltd* [1997] RPC 443. The issue was as to the proof and computation of loss of profits caused by a patent infringement. After citing the *Allied Maples* case [1995] 4 All ER 907, [1995] 1 WLR 1602, Staughton LJ said (at 460):

'In my judgment the issue as to the amount of the patentees' loss in the present case was a question in the second class [Stuart-Smith LJ's third category]; it depended on the hypothetical actions of third parties, that is to say the buyers of the infringing machines (or spare parts, servicing and CAD systems). The judge was entitled to conclude that the patentees had lost a chance of making sales to those buyers—no doubt a chance of differing probability in each case. He was entitled to evaluate the chances as a whole, rather than separately, if he chose to do so. The contrary view, that if the judge found 25 chances of a sale, each of 49 per cent probability, he should award nothing is absurd.'

[93] In my view the same approach would be appropriate in this case. If in relation to any particular claim the trial judge was satisfied that a job search which was successful after (say) 12 months would (but for the jobseeker's stigma) have been successful after six months then damages would in my view be recoverable for that six months' loss of employment, even if it was impossible to identify which particular job application would, but for stigma, have been successful. But the judge's finding that there was no general prejudice (a finding which he was entitled to make, especially on the evidence of Ms Tsoflias and the other Coutts' witnesses) must make it much more difficult for any claimant to prove that stigma was the cause of any significant postponement of re-employment.

JONATHAN PARKER LJ.

[94] I also agree that this appeal should be dismissed, for the reasons which Pill LJ has given.

[95] I add a few observations of my own in relation to the arguments addressed to us on the question of loss of a chance, as it arises in the instant case.

[96] A former employee who claims damages against his former employer for breach of what the judge described as the trust and confidence term must prove

not merely that by reason of that breach his prospects of future employment were diminished ('stigma'), but also that the stigma caused him to suffer financial loss (see *Malik v Bank of Credit and Commerce International SA (in liq)*, *Mahmud v Bank of Credit and Commerce International SA (in liq)* [1997] 3 All ER 1, [1998] AC 20, in particular [1997] 3 All ER 1 at 10, [1998] AC 20 at 40 per Lord Nicholls of Birkenhead, where he equates such loss with special damage in a defamation action).

[97] Where the financial loss alleged takes the form of, or includes, loss of a chance, causation of damage is not to be confused with assessment of damage. On ordinary principles, causation must be proved on the balance of probabilities. In the instant case, either the stigma was an effective cause of the alleged loss or it was not (see *Nestle v National Westminster Bank plc* [1994] 1 All ER 118 at 141, [1993] 1 WLR 1260 at 1283–1284 per Leggatt LJ, a passage quoted by the judge [1999] 4 All ER 83 at 111, [1999] IRLR 508 at 521 (para 69)). There is no room for any half-way house in relation to causation: no room, that is to say, for any percentage calculation to reflect the chance (possibility) that the stigma may have been an effective cause of the alleged loss.

[98] Where causation is proved, the court may, if and to the extent that it is appropriate to do so on the facts of the particular case, assess the resulting loss by adopting a percentage figure to reflect loss of a chance. Such an approach to the assessment of damage is likely to be appropriate in relation to future events, and it may, depending on the facts of the particular case, be appropriate in relation to past events (see Stuart-Smith LJ's exposition in *Allied Maples Group Ltd v Simmons & Simmons (a firm)* [1995] 4 All ER 907 at 914–916, [1995] 1 WLR 1602 at 1609–1611). Examples of cases in which this approach has been adopted in relation to past events are the well-known cases of *Chaplin v Hicks* [1911] 2 KB 786, [1911–13] All ER Rep 224 and *Kitchen v Royal Air Forces Association* [1958] 2 All ER 241, [1958] 1 WLR 563.

[99] In the instant case, I accept the submissions of Mr Jeans QC (for the Bank of Credit and Commerce International SA (BCCI)) that had the appellants succeeded in establishing a general prejudice in the employment market against former employees of BCCI as a result of stigma, it would have been open to them to invite the court to infer that but for that general prejudice a claimant would have succeeded in obtaining—albeit not a particular job—a job of a particular type or at a particular level of salary. In the event, however, the judge found as a fact (as in my judgment he was entitled to do) that no such general prejudice existed. Absent general prejudice, it was necessary for the appellants to prove that stigma was an effective cause of the failure of their job applications on what the judge described as a 'job-specific' basis. In other words, it was necessary for them to show that stigma was an effective cause of the failure of a particular job application. That too they failed to do on the findings of the judge (findings which, once again, he was in my judgment entitled to make).

Appeals dismissed.

Dilys Tausz   Barrister.

a
South Coast Shipping Co Ltd v Havant Borough Council

CHANCERY DIVISION

PUMFREY J SITTING WITH MASTER O'HARE AND MICHAEL SEYMOUR AS ASSESSORS

b   25 OCTOBER, 21 DECEMBER 2001

Costs – Assessment – Detailed assessment – Privileged documents – Whether procedure relating to use of privileged documents in detailed assessments of costs compatible with human rights – Human Rights Act 1998, Sch 1, Pt I, arts 6, 8 – CPR Practice Direction
c   *about Costs, para 40.14.*

On the determination of a preliminary issue in a detailed assessment of costs, the paying party alleged that there had been no retainer between the receiving party and the solicitors whose costs were being claimed, and that accordingly those costs were being claimed in breach of the indemnity principle. The bills of costs
d   to be assessed were signed and certified by a partner in the firm of solicitors, and further evidence of the retainer was given in witness statements by the solicitors. The costs judge was also shown material that was said to be subject to legal professional privilege, namely interim bills submitted by the solicitors, copies of cheques paying them and letters from the correspondence file. Under para 40.14[a] of the CPR Practice Direction about Costs, the court could ask a receiving party
e   to elect whether to disclose a particular document to the paying party in order to rely on its contents, or whether to decline disclosure and instead rely on other evidence. Although the receiving party declined to waive its privilege in the documents, the costs judge declined to put that party to its election. Instead, relying, inter alia, on the interim bills and solicitors' files, he held that there were
f   no matters meriting further investigation and that there had been no breach of the indemnity principle. The paying party appealed, contending, inter alia, that it had been deprived of a fair hearing because it had not been provided with the material necessary to enable it to make submissions on the original documents as to the existence of the retainer. On the appeal, the court considered (i) the compatibility of the para 40.14 procedure with the right to a fair hearing and the
g   right to respect for private life and correspondence under, respectively, arts 6[b] and 8[c] of the European Convention for the Protection of Human Rights and Fundamental Freedoms 1950 (as set out in Sch 1 to the Human Rights Act 1998); and (ii) whether the costs judge had properly applied para 40.14.

h   **Held** – Paragraph 40.14 of the CPR Practice Direction about Costs was consistent with the requirements of the convention. The privilege would not be overridden by the court, and had to be waived by the party entitled to assert it. Once, however, the document was of sufficient importance to be taken into account in arriving at a conclusion as to recoverability, then, unless otherwise agreed, it had
j   to be shown to the paying party, or the receiving party would have to content itself with other evidence. That did not mean that the costs judge could potentially put the receiving party to its election in respect of every document relied on, regardless of its degree of relevance. Only where it was necessary and

---

a   Paragraph 40.14 is set out at [11], below
b   Article 6, so far as material, is set out at [19], below
c   Article 8 is set out at [19], below

proportionate should the receiving party be put to his election. Nor was there any requirement that privileged material available to the receiving party be disclosed for the purpose of testing the evidence given. The need for equality of arms might place on the party unwilling to waive the privilege the burden of adducing evidence without using the privileged material, but did not confer on the other party a right to see the material anyway. Given the existence of the privilege, the fairest result was that either both or neither could deploy the privileged material. In the instant case, the costs judge should have put the receiving party to its election, but he had been right to conclude on the strength of the interim bills, the cheques and the correspondence that there was nothing deserving of further investigation. Accordingly, the appeal would be dismissed (see [29]–[32], [60], below).

Pamplin v Express Newspapers Ltd [1985] 2 All ER 185 and *Bailey v IBC Vehicles Ltd* [1998] 3 All ER 570 considered.

Notes

For putting a party to his election in respect of documents produced to the court on a detailed assessment of costs, see 10 *Halsbury's Laws* (4th edn reissue) para 165.

Cases referred to in judgment

AM & S Europe Ltd v Commission of the European Communities Case 155/79 [1983] 1 All ER 705, [1983] QB 878, [1983] 3 WLR 17, [1982] ECR 1575, ECJ.
Bailey v IBC Vehicles Ltd [1998] 3 All ER 570, CA.
Bourns Inc v Raychem Corp [1999] 3 All ER 154, CA.
Campbell v UK (1992) 15 EHRR 137, ECt HR.
Carter v The Managing Partner, Northmore Hale Davy & Leake (1995) 183 CLR 121, Aus HC.
Dombo Beheer BV v Netherlands (1993) 18 EHRR 213, ECt HR.
Feldbrugge v Netherlands (1986) 8 EHRR 425, ECHR 8562/79, ECt HR.
General Mediterranean Holdings SA v Patel [1999] 3 All ER 673, [2000] 1 WLR 272.
Goldman v Hesper [1988] 3 All ER 97, [1988] 1 WLR 1238, CA.
Hobbs v Hobbs [1959] 3 All ER 827, [1960] P 112, [1959] 3 WLR 942.
Krcmár v Czech Republic (2000) 31 EHRR 953, ECHR 35376/97, ECt HR.
Niemietz v Germany (1992) 16 EHRR 97, ECHR 13710/88, ECt HR.
Pamplin v Express Newspapers Ltd [1985] 2 All ER 185, [1985] 1 WLR 689.
R v Derby Magistrates' Court, ex p B [1995] 4 All ER 526, [1996] AC 487, [1995] 3 WLR 681, HL.
R v Miller (Raymond) [1983] 3 All ER 186, [1983] 1 WLR 1056, DC.
Science Research Council v Nassé, BL Cars Ltd (formerly Leyland Cars) v Vyas [1979] 3 All ER 673, [1980] AC 1028, [1979] 3 WLR 762, HL.
Silver v UK (1983) 5 EHRR 347, ECHR 5947/72, ECt HR.
WEA Records Ltd v Visions Channel 4 Ltd [1983] 2 All ER 589, [1983] 1 WLR 721, CA.

Appeal

The appellant, Havant Borough Council (Havant), appealed with permission of Rimer J granted on 2 April 2001 from the decision of Master Campbell on 21 January 2001 whereby, on the determination of a preliminary issue in a detailed assessment of costs, he held that there had been a retainer between the respondent, South Coast Shipping Co Ltd (South Coast), and the firm of solicitors whose costs South Coast was claiming. The hearing and judgment were heard and delivered in private and the judgment is reported with the permission of Pumfrey J. The facts are set out in the judgment.

a   *Simon Jonathan Brown* (instructed by *Lewis Silkin*) for Havant.
Alexander Hutton (instructed by *Goldberg Linde*) for South Coast.

Cur adv vult

21 December 2001. The following judgment was delivered.

b   **PUMFREY J.**

Introduction

[1] This is an appeal from Master Campbell, who has held on a preliminary issue in relation to the detailed assessment of costs pursuant to three orders in
c   favour of the respondents, South Coast Shipping Company (South Coast), that there has been no breach of the indemnity principle and that they are entitled to claim the costs from the appellants, Havant Borough Council (Havant). The costs judge gave judgment disposing of the preliminary issue on 21 January 2001 with costs in favour of South Coast. Leave to appeal was refused by the costs
d   judge but was granted by Rimer J on 2 April 2001.

[2] The orders for costs arise in the context of an arbitration concerning coastal works carried out at Hayling Island. The costs claimed in respect of the three orders is £219,356·04 before interest. Notice to arbitrate was given by South Coast in July 1986. The arbitrator was not appointed until October 1992, and his final award was published on 24 November 1994: an appeal to the official referee
e   was heard in 1995 and 1996, and resulted in the remission of part of the claim to the arbitrator, who affirmed his award on 28 August 1996. Further applications to the court were made resulting in a further order of the official referee and of the Court of Appeal. Havant were in substance unsuccessful and the assessment of the costs in relation to the various appeals to the official referee and to the
f   Court of Appeal was started on 21 June 2000. The costs have still not been assessed. This detailed assessment has thus been on foot for nearly 18 months, and follows proceedings concerning liability which have lasted nearly 10 years.

[3] The allegation made by Havant before the costs judge, and repeated before me, was that there was no retainer between Howard Kennedy, the solicitors whose costs were being claimed, and South Coast. Master Campbell held that
g   there was a rebuttable presumption, raised by (1) the solicitor's signature to the bills and (2) the fact that the solicitors agreed to act for the respondent in the appeals from the arbitrators' decision that there was an agreement between South Coast and Howard Kennedy to pay Howard Kennedy the costs, and thus no breach of the indemnity principle. He held, therefore, that the onus lay upon
h   Havant, the paying party, to demonstrate that there had been such a breach, and that it had failed to discharge that onus. In the course of the investigation of the relationship between South Coast and Howard Kennedy, the costs judge was shown certain documents for which privilege was claimed. Havant were not shown these documents, but were shown certain witness statements only.

j   [4] Havant complain that the costs judge should not have concluded the case upon the footing of a presumption. They further contend that the procedure followed by the costs judge was unfair because they were never provided with the material necessary to enable them to make submissions on the original documents as to the existence or otherwise of a retainer of Howard Kennedy by South Coast. Thus, they say, they were deprived of a fair hearing before the costs judge, albeit that he was following a practice which is well established in detailed assessments.

The nature of this appeal

[5] This appeal is a review rather than a rehearing. Where, as here, the legal
basis of the costs judge's decision is under scrutiny, this has little relevance.
However, in matters of procedure, I will give proper weight to the experience of
the costs judge in considering the correctness of the course which he adopted.

The indemnity principle

[6] The indemnity principle is, for the time being, at the centre of the law
relating to the recoverability of costs. It states that the liability of the paying party
is limited to the amount that the receiving party is obliged to pay to the latter's
solicitors. Any sum claimed which the receiving party is not obliged to pay to
his solicitor is not recoverable.

[7] The existence and scope of the receiving party's contractual obligation to
pay his solicitors is thus central to his ability to recover costs. The paying party is
obviously concerned to limit his obligation to pay, and to this end will investigate
the scope of the retainer. His ability to do so will in many cases be frustrated by
the fact that documents which evidence the retainer, or from which the inference
of a retainer and its scope may be drawn, are the subject of legal professional
privilege. The question is whether, and to what extent, the obvious conflict
between the privilege and the need for fairness towards the paying party require
the relaxation of the privilege, and how. The practice is stated as follows in the
White Book (*Civil Procedure* (Autumn 2001) vol 1, p 581 (para 31.3.27)):

'There is a statutory requirement for a claimant for costs to disclose
privileged documents to the Court on taxation, and, when this is done, part
of the privilege attaching to such documents is temporarily relaxed. The
taxing officer, however, has a duty to be fair to both parties and to ensure
that privilege is maintained as far as possible without preventing the other
party from having an opportunity to challenge the taxation. In rare
circumstances the taxing officer may have to disclose privileged documents
in order to strike an appropriate balance, but any disclosure will only be for
the purposes of the taxation; the privilege can subsequently be reasserted
(*Goldman v Hesper* [1988] 3 All ER 97, [1988] 1 WLR 1238, CA; see also *Hobbs v
Hobbs* [1959] 3 All ER 827, [1960] P 112, and *Pamplin v Express Newspapers Ltd*
[1985] 2 All ER 185, [1985] 1 WLR 689).'

The need for procedural fairness in assessment proceedings is fully recognised in
Goldman's case, the effect of which is accurately summarised in this passage.
Pamplin's case was a case in which Hobhouse J had held that the interest of
fairness was capable of prevailing over the privilege, to the extent that it was
possible to put the receiving party to its election. In *Goldman's* case [1988] 3 All ER
97 at 101–102, [1998] 1 WLR 1238 at 1243–1244, Taylor LJ said:

'The starting point in considering how far privilege extends in this context
is in my judgment to look at the procedure for lodging documents on
taxation. This is now laid down in RSC Ord 62, which dates from April 1986
and is therefore later in time than the cases cited. Previously procedure was
governed by a practice direction only (see *Practice Direction* [1979] 1 All ER
958). Order 62, r 29(7), so far as is relevant, reads as follows: "A party who
begins proceedings for taxation must, at the same time, lodge in the
appropriate office ... (c) unless the taxing officer otherwise orders, a bill of
costs ... and (d) unless the taxing officer otherwise orders, the papers and
vouchers specified below in the order mentioned ... (iii) a bundle comprising

a fee notes of counsel and accounts for other disbursements ... (v) cases to counsel to advise with his advice and opinions, and instructions to counsel to settle documents and briefs to counsel with enclosures, arranged in chronological order ... (vii) the solicitor's correspondence and attendance notes ..." It is therefore clear that there is now a statutory requirement on a claimant for costs to disclose privileged documents to the court. Normally,

b where [privilege] exists it applies to protect disclosure not only to the opposing party, but also to the court. So the rule clearly makes inroads into that general protection. It follows that once a party puts forward privileged documents as part of his case for costs some measure of their privilege is temporarily and pro hac vice relaxed. In most cases, as Hobhouse J observed, no problem would arise on taxation about privilege. However, when the

c problem does arise the taxing officer has the duty of being fair to both parties: on the one hand, to maintain privilege so far as possible and not disclose the contents of a privileged document to the paying party unnecessarily; on the other hand, he has to see that that party is treated fairly and given a proper opportunity to raise a bona fide challenge. The contents of documents will

d almost always be irrelevant to considerations of taxation, which are more concerned with time taken, the length of documents, the frequency of correspondence and other aspects reflecting on costs. In my judgment, the approach adopted by Stevenson J in *Hobbs v Hobbs and Cousens* [1959] 3 All ER 827, [1960] P 112 was too rigid and uncompromising. There may be instances

e in which taxing officers may need to disclose part, if not all, of the contents of a privileged document in striking the appropriate balance. He will no doubt use all his expertise and tact in seeking to avoid that situation wherever he can. I do not envisage it occurring, except very rarely. Of course it is always open to the claimant not to rely on privileged documents which he regards as peculiarly sensitive. It would not be practicable or helpful

f for this court to seek to lay down any firm criteria as to the circumstances in which such an extreme course may be necessary. All will depend on the facts of the individual case. One factor which may affect the course taken by the taxing officer may be whether the party is represented by a lawyer or costs clerk, or whether he appears in person. Clearly, in the former case there would be more opportunity for flexibility in the approach adopted by the

g taxing officer. He might, for example, think it appropriate to allow disclosure of privileged documents to the paying party's lawyer, but not to be divulged to his client. Although the approach suggested by Hobhouse J may only rarely be practicable, it too may in a proper case be a useful resort.'

h [8] The relevant provisions are now to be found in CPR Pt 47 and in the Practice Direction about Costs (CPD). This practice direction is concerned with CPR Pts 43–48, and the relevant sections are printed in the White Book immediately following the relevant CPR. The sections of this practice direction concerned with detailed assessment are found in CPD sections 28–49, and, so far

j as they relate to the filing of documents for a detailed assessment hearing derive their force from CPR 47.14.

[9] A request for a detailed assessment hearing, which is made on a prescribed form (N258), is required by para 40.2 of CPD to be accompanied by certain prescribed documents, including a copy of the notice of commencement of detailed assessment proceedings, a copy of the bill of costs, the document giving the right to detailed assessment (normally an order), a copy of the points of

dispute appropriately annotated and so forth. By CPD para 40.2(i), the request must be accompanied—

'where there is a dispute as to the receiving party's liability to pay costs to the solicitors who acted for the receiving party, [by] any agreement, letter or other written information provided by the solicitor to his client explaining how the solicitor's charges are to be calculated ...'

In the modern context, this will normally be a copy of the 'client care letter'. This must be the latest available copy of the letter (see para 40.3(1)). The present case is of such antiquity that there was no general requirement for such letters to be sent, and, in fact, there was no such letter.

[10] CPD para 40.11 contains detailed requirements for the documents to be filed in support of a bill. They include (where the claim is for base costs): (i) instructions and briefs to counsel arranged in chronological order together with all advices, opinions and drafts received and responses to such instructions; (ii) reports and opinions of medical and other experts; (iii) any other relevant papers; (iv) a full set of any relevant pleadings to the extent that they have not already been filed in court; (v) correspondence, files and attendance notes.

[11] The decision of the Court of Appeal in *Goldman*'s case [1988] 3 All ER 97, [1988] 1 WLR 1238 is now to be found reflected in para 40.14 of CPD:

'The court may direct the receiving party to produce any document which in the opinion of the court is necessary to enable it to reach its decision. These documents will in the first instance be produced to the court, but the court may ask the receiving party to elect whether to disclose the particular document to the paying party in order to rely on the contents of the document, or whether to decline disclosure and instead rely on other evidence.'

The way in which 'other evidence' might be given is described by Hobhouse J in *Pamplin v Express Newspapers Ltd* [1985] 2 All ER 185 at 190–191, [1985] 1 WLR 689 at 696–697 in a passage implicitly approved by the Court of Appeal in the passage I have quoted from the judgment of Taylor LJ in *Goldman*'s case:

'At the taxation a problem may arise. An issue of fact may emerge which necessitates the master making formally or informally a finding of fact. In such a situation, the master may have to ask the claimant what evidence he wishes to rely on in support of the contested allegation of fact. The respondent may then take the stand that, if the claimant wishes to adduce evidence, he (the respondent) wishes to see it and comment on or contradict it. This will mean that the claimant will then have to elect whether he wants to use the evidence and waive his privilege or seek to prove what he needs in some other way. The type of situation which this visualises is where, in the ordinary course, the claimant would seek to prove his allegation by simply producing a document. If, however, the respondent objects to the claimant using the document without his seeing it as well, the claimant may prove the allegation in another way; for example, if it is the solicitor who conducted the litigation who is attending the taxation, by that solicitor formally or informally giving oral evidence. The respondent could then formally or informally cross-examine the solicitor. The master would then decide, having taken into account any counter-evidence relied on by the respondent, whether he accepted the claimant's allegation. I do not visualise that this would happen, at least not often, but it does serve to illustrate the essentials of the situation. The master does not have any power to order discovery to be given; he does not have any power to override a right of privilege. But it is the duty of the master, if the respondent raises a factual issue, which is real and relevant and not a sham or fanciful dispute, to require the claimant to prove the facts on which he relies. The claimant then has to choose what evidence he will adduce and to what extent he will waive his privilege. That is a choice for the claimant alone. The master then has to decide the issue of fact on the evidence. In considering whether he is satisfied by the evidence, the master will no doubt take into account that the claimant may have a legitimate interest in not adducing the most obvious or complete evidence, and may prefer to rely on oral evidence rather than producing privileged legal documents. What I have said about the essentials of the situation mirrors what was said by Sir John Donaldson MR in *WEA Records Ltd v Visions Channel 4 Ltd* [1983] 2 All ER 589 at 591, [1983] 1 WLR 721 at 724 … I expect that it will remain, as heretofore, very rare for the full formality of these steps to be gone through. Most respondents appreciate that once they have drawn to the master's attention the possibility that an item of charge may be unnecessary or may be being over-valued, their interests are best served by allowing the master to look at the relevant documents and form his own judgment. The respondent will normally achieve little or nothing by asking to see the documents as well. The master is well aware of the criteria he has to apply and is highly experienced in the exercise of assessment he has to undertake. The insistence by a respondent on a more formal approach could well lead to a less favourable outcome for him.'

[12] What Hobhouse J said is as true now as it was under the previous regime for the assessment of costs. I draw the following from these cases: (1) while in many respects the assessment of costs resembles ordinary litigation, it differs in important respects, among which are the lack of any provision for disclosure of documents to the opposing party. The ordinary rules of natural justice none the less apply. (2) The question is, what evidence may be adduced by the receiving party to establish a disputed fact. (3) Where there is a disputed issue of fact to be decided, the receiving party may seek to rely upon a document otherwise privileged that has been filed in support of the bill. (4) Furthermore, the costs judge may require the receiving party to produce to the costs judge any document which the costs judge may specify which he considers is necessary for him to reach a decision. (5) In either case, the costs judge has no power to order disclosure of a privileged document to the paying party, but he may put the receiving party to his election between (a) not relying upon the document and offering to prove the fact of which the document is evidence by some other means, and (b) showing it to the paying party. (6) The costs judge will exercise his discretion to put the receiving party to his election having regard to what the requirements of fairness and justice require. He may in particular consider whether the disclosure could be made to the party's legal representatives only; whether irrelevant privileged matter can be excised; and the importance of the document in establishing the disputed fact. (7) Disclosure in the context of assessment proceedings of a document otherwise privileged will not be viewed as a waiver of the privilege. Voluntary waiver or disclosure by a taxing officer on a taxation would not prevent the owner of the document from reasserting his privilege in any subsequent context. This fact is relevant to the exercise of a discretion to put the receiving party to his election, but it must be remembered that a *voluntary* disclosure made relying upon this principle is capable of giving

rise to serious difficulties (see, for example, *Bourns Inc v Raychem Corp* [1999] 3 All ER 154).

[13] The last case to which I should refer is *Bailey v IBC Vehicles Ltd* [1998] 3 All ER 570. This was a case in which a breach of the indemnity principle was alleged. The Court of Appeal approved (at 573–574) Lloyd J's statement of the burden of proof and procedure in *R v Miller (Raymond)* [1983] 3 All ER 186 at 190–191, [1983] 1 WLR 1056 at 1061–1062:

> 'Once it was shown, as is now conceded, that [the appellant] was indeed the client, then a presumption arose that he was to be personally liable for the costs. That presumption could, however, be rebutted if it were established that there was an express or implied agreement, binding on the solicitors, that [the appellant] would not have to pay those costs in any circumstances. In practice, of course, the taxing officer will have before him on the taxation the whole of the solicitor's file. If it appears to the taxing officer that there is doubt whether there was an express or implied agreement, binding on the solicitors, not to seek to recover the costs from the client, the taxing officer should ask for further evidence. It must then be for the taxing officer to come to a conclusion on the whole of the facts presented to him. Unless those facts establish a firm agreement, express or implied, that in no circumstances will the solicitors seek to obtain payment from their client, then the basic presumption stands …'

Judge LJ continued ([1998] 3 All ER 570 at 574–575):

> 'In my judgment the information available to us indicates that the union and Rowley Ashworth [the union solicitors] were agreed that the union should be charged a "full solicitor/client charge". In other words no special reduction or discount applied. The only relevant limitation, plainly implied, was that these charges should themselves be reasonable. I can see no basis for doubting the accuracy of this information. In fact, while maintaining her client's entitlement as a matter of principle to refuse to give any information additional to that set out in the letter, [counsel for the plaintiff] informed us on direct instructions that there was no "cap" in this case. That confirmed my reading of the letter dated 19 September 1997. As officers of the court, solicitors are trusted not to mislead or to allow the court to be misled. This elementary principle applies to the submission of a bill of costs. If a cap or similar arrangement had applied in this case, I should have expected Rowley Ashworth to have disclosed that fact and to have ensured that the union letter either represented a comprehensive rather than a partial explanation of the facts, or to supplement it with information of their own. They would not have produced and signed a bill of costs which included a claim for "reasonable costs" which would have fallen foul of the indemnity principle. The defendants' request that the plaintiff be required to provide information proving that the indemnity principle had been observed represents pointless satellite litigation. As there is nothing to suggest that the relationship between the union and the solicitors would have resulted in some form of capping of the fees which the solicitors would have submitted to the union if the claim had failed, the information is sufficient to enable the taxation to proceed on the basis that the figures claimed in the bill of costs do not represent an unacceptable breach of the indemnity principle.'

a This may be seen as a robust application of the principles set out by Hobhouse J. It is notable for the court's willingness to proceed upon partial material, and for the importance which is attached to the solicitor's certificate that there has been no breach of the indemnity principle. Henry LJ ([1998] 3 All ER 570 at 576) added that in this area, 'an ounce of openness is cheaper than any argument', an observation which the present case goes some distance to support.

b

The impact of the European Convention on Human Rights

[14] Thus far, I have discussed the question in the context of domestic law as it was before the incorporation of the European Convention for the Protection of Human Rights and Fundamental Freedoms 1950 (as set out in Sch 1 to the Human c Rights Act 1998). The essential question is what are the convention rights of the paying and receiving parties in the present case, how they are to be reconciled, and whether that reconciliation requires me to depart from the statement of the applicable principles which I have set out above.

[15] I can start with legal professional privilege. The confidentiality of communications with lawyers is regarded as an absolute privilege in English law d which the court has no power to override, except in the case of fraud. So far as European law is concerned, in *AM & S Europe Ltd v Commission of the European Communities* Case 155/79 [1983] 1 All ER 705, [1982] ECR 1575, Advocate-General Sir JP Warner considered that the right to confidential communication between lawyer and client is not a fundamental human right; it is a right that the laws of e civilised countries generally recognise, a right not lightly to be denied, but not one so entrenched that, in the Community, the Council could never legislate to override or modify it. It is none the less a jealously-guarded privilege and one to which only well-defined exceptions are recognised in English law. It is recognised by the Court of Justice of the European Communities as appearing in all the states of the Union, being more or less associated with the principle of fair treatment of f litigants, or *'les droits de la défense'*. As the CCBE (Consultative Committee of the Bars and Law Societies of the European Community) remarked in that case, in a phrase later repeated, it is 'a practical guarantee of fundamental, constitutional or human rights'.

[16] In the *AM & S Europe* case ([1983] 1 All ER 705 at 732–733, [1982] ECR 1575 g at 1654), Advocate-General Sir Gordon Slynn considered that the right should be recognised as a right of community law:

'... the public interest and the proper administration of justice demand as a general rule that a client should be able to speak freely, frankly and fully to his lawyer ... Whether it is described as the right of the client or the duty of h the lawyer, this principle has nothing to do with the protection or privilege of the lawyer. It springs essentially from the basic need of a man in a civilised society to be able to turn to his lawyer for advice and help, and, if proceedings begin, for representation; it springs no less from the advantages to a society which involves complex law reaching into all the business affairs of persons, j real and legal, that they should be able to know what they can do under the law, what is forbidden, where they must tread circumspectly, where they run risks. The fact that this principle of confidentiality between lawyer and client may be given effect to in different ways, and that it is not coextensive in its application at any point in time, in all the member states, does not mean that the principle does not exist. In my opinion it should be declared to be a rule of Community law.'

[17] In its judgment, the European Court of Justice said ([1983] 1 All ER 705 at 742, [1982] ECR 1575 at 1610):

'18. However, the above rules [in EEC Council Regulation 17 of 6 February 1962] do not exclude the possibility of recognising, subject to certain conditions, that certain business records are of a confidential nature. Community law, which derives from not only the economic but also the legal interpenetration of the member states, must take into account the principles and concepts common to the laws of those states concerning the observance of confidentiality, in particular, as regards certain communications between lawyer and client. That confidentiality serves the requirement, the importance of which is recognised in all of the member states, that any person must be able, without constraint, to consult a lawyer whose profession entails the giving of independent legal advice to all those in need of it.

19. As far as the protection of written communications between lawyer and client is concerned, it is apparent from the legal systems of the member states that, although the principle of such protection is generally recognised, its scope and the criteria for applying it vary, as has, indeed, been conceded both by the applicant and by the parties who have intervened in support of its conclusions ...

21. Apart from these differences, however, there are to be found in the national laws of the member states common criteria inasmuch as those laws protect, in similar circumstances, the confidentiality of written communications between lawyer and client provided that, on the one hand, such communications are made for the purposes and in the interests of the client's rights of defence and, on the other hand, they emanate from independent lawyers, that is to say lawyers who are not bound to the client by a relationship of employment ...

24. As regards the second condition, it should be stated that the requirement as to the position and status as an independent lawyer, which must be fulfilled by the legal advisor from whom the written communications which may be protected emanate, is based on a conception of the lawyer's role as collaborating in the administration of justice by the courts and as being required to provide, in full independence, and in the overriding interests of that cause, such legal assistance as the client needs. The counterpart of that protection lies in the rules of professional ethics and discipline which are laid down and enforced in the general interest by institutions endowed with the requisite powers for that purpose. Such a conception reflects the legal traditions common to the member states and is also to be found in legal order of the Community ...'

[18] The nature of the privilege in the context of the convention is, if I may respectfully say so, convincingly analysed by Toulson J in *General Mediterranean Holdings SA v Patel* [1999] 3 All ER 673, [2000] 1 WLR 272. In that case, the defendants were accused of fraudulent misrepresentation made in the course of a sale of a business to the claimant concerning the nature of the business. The defendants denied fraud. Shortly before the trial, it became clear that the defendants' case was that the claimant was fully aware of the nature of the business, and that if a representation had been made it was not effective. A wasted costs application was made against the defendants' solicitors on the footing that they had knowingly conducted the defence upon the false basis that the representation had not been made. The solicitors sought to disclose their instructions from their

a client, relying on CPR 48.7(3) (now revoked). This rule provided that for the purposes of an application made in respect of wasted costs, the court 'may direct that privileged documents are to be disclosed to the court, and, if the court so directs, to the other party to the application for an order'. Toulson J held that the privilege owed its existence to a substantive rule of law, not to a rule of evidence or procedure, that the relevant rule-making power did not extend to the modification

b of substantive rules of law and that accordingly the court could not override the assertion of privilege by the defendants in their communications with their solicitors except in the one circumstance (furtherance of fraud) which is an acknowledged exception. It followed that the provision of the CPR which gave the court power to override the privilege was ultra vires and void.

[19] Toulson J reached his conclusion on consideration purely of English

c domestic law. But he also considers the factors which would be relevant to the exercise of a discretion to override the privilege had such a discretion existed. For this purpose, he identified the two relevant convention rights as those arising under art 6(1):

d 'In the determination of his civil rights and obligations or of any criminal charge against him, everyone is entitled to a fair and public hearing within a reasonable time by an independent and impartial tribunal established by law.'

And art 8:

e '1. Everyone has the right to respect for his private and family life, his home and his correspondence.

2. There should be no interference by a public authority with the exercise of this right except such as is in accordance with the law and is necessary in a democratic society in the interests of national security, public safety or the economic well-being of the country, for the prevention of disorder or crime,

f for the protection of health or morals, or for the protection of the rights and freedoms of others.'

The decisions of the European Court of Human Rights in *Silver v UK* (1983) 5 EHRR 347, *Campbell v UK* (1992) 15 EHRR 137 and *Niemietz v Germany* (1992) 16 EHRR 97 are of some relevance. *Silver's* and *Campbell's* cases are cases concerned with

g prisoners' correspondence. In *Campbell's* case (1992) 15 EHRR 137 at 160, 161, the European Court of Human Rights said:

'46. It is clearly in the general interest that any person who wishes to consult a lawyer should be free to do so under conditions which favour full and uninhibited discussion. It is for this reason that the lawyer–client

h relationship is, in principle, privileged ...

48. ... the Court sees no reason to distinguish between the different categories of correspondence with lawyers which, whatever their purpose, concern matters of a private and confidential character. In principle, such letters are privileged under Article 8. This means that the prison authorities

j may open a letter from a lawyer to a prisoner when they have reasonable cause to believe that it contains an illicit enclosure which the normal means of detection have failed to disclose. The letter should, however, only be opened and should not be read. Suitable guarantees preventing the reading of the letter should be provided, e.g. opening the letter in the presence of the prisoner. The reading of a prisoner's mail to and from a lawyer, on the other hand, should only be permitted in exceptional circumstances when the authorities have reasonable cause to believe that the privilege is being *a* abused in that the contents of the letter endanger prison security or the safety of others or are otherwise of a criminal nature.'

[20] *Niemitz's* case (1992) 16 EHRR 97 concerned a search of a lawyer's offices by police looking for information to reveal the identity and possible whereabouts of a person who was the subject of a criminal investigation. In holding that the *b* search violated art 8, the court recognised that activities of a professional character could fall within the notions of private life and correspondence. It also recognised (at 113–114) that, where a lawyer was involved, an encroachment on professional secrecy might have repercussions on the proper administration of justice and hence on the rights guaranteed by art 6:

c

'37. ... It is true that the offence in connection with which the search was effected ... cannot be classified as no more than minor. On the other hand, the warrant was drawn in broad terms, in that it ordered a search for and seizure of "documents," without any limitation, revealing the identity of the author of the offensive letter; this point is of special significance where, as in Germany, the search of a lawyer's office is not accompanied by any special *d* procedural safeguards, such as the presence of an independent observer. More importantly, having regard to the materials that were in fact inspected, the search impinged on professional secrecy to an extent that appears disproportionate in the circumstances; it has, in this connection, to be recalled that, where a lawyer is involved, an encroachment on professional *e* secrecy may have repercussions on the proper administration of justice and hence on the rights guaranteed by Article 6 of the Convention.'

[21] The decision of the European Court of Human Rights in *Silver's* case is to much the same effect as the decision in *Campbell's* case.

[22] In *General Mediterranean Holdings SA v Patel* [1999] 3 All ER 673 at 695, *f* [2000] 1 WLR 272 at 295–296, Toulson J's conclusion was:

'Article 6 gives every person a right to a fair trial, but I do not accept that it follows as a general proposition that this gives a right to interfere with another person's right to legal confidentiality. If that were generally so, the right to legal confidentiality recognised by the court would be useless, since *g* its very purpose is to enable a person to communicate with his lawyer secure in the knowledge that such communications cannot be used without his consent to further another person's cause. In the absence of a general right under art 6 to make use of another person's confidential communications with his lawyer, I do not see how solicitors have a particular right to do so *h* under that article for the purpose of defending a wasted costs application. It may be argued that this is to adopt too inflexible an approach, and that in principle the proper solution in such cases would be to treat a person's right under art 8 to confidentiality in respect of communications with his lawyer as subject to a qualification of the kind proposed by Toohey J in *Carter's* case.' *j*

(This is a reference to *Carter v The Managing Partner, Northmore Hale Davy & Leake* (1995) 183 CLR 121 at 156 where Toohey J proposed a qualification to the principle in the following terms: 'Where an accused facing trial satisfies the court that the production of documents subpoenaed by the accused is necessary for the proper conduct of his or her defence, then, subject to any proper objection that may be taken, other than on the ground of legal professional privilege, the court

a may order the production of those documents.') Toulson J continues ([1999]
3 All ER 673 at 696, [2000] 1 WLR 272 at 296):

> 'Toohey J himself recognised that his proposal presented problems, even
> looking at the matter only in the context of a criminal trial. I have already
> cited the passage in [*R v Derby Magistrates' Court, ex p B* [1995] 4 All ER 526,
> *b* [1996] AC 487] in which Lord Nicholls considered the matter also in the
> context of other types of claim and concluded that there was no principled
> way by which judges could "ascribe an appropriate weight, on each side of
> the scale, to the diverse multitude of various claims, civil and criminal, and
> other interests of the client on the one hand and the person seeking
> disclosure on the other hand" (see [1995] 4 All ER 526 at 545, [1996] AC 487
> *c* at 512). I do not accept the submission that the approach of the House of
> Lords in that case was in violation of art 6, or that the convention requires a
> balancing exercise in individual cases of the kind which the House of Lords
> considered and rejected as a matter of English law. However if I am wrong,
> I have considerable doubt whether a general discretion to order the
> *d* disclosure of privileged material on an application for a wasted costs order is
> necessary and proportionate for the purpose of doing justice to the legal
> profession, particularly bearing in mind the point that the courts have been
> used on hearing wasted costs applications to making allowance for the
> lawyer's inability to disclose privileged information without the client's
> consent. I repeat the comment that if such a discretion were perceived by
> *e* legal practitioners as necessary for their protection, one might have expected
> the Law Society to be making opposite submissions to those which it has
> advanced on this application. On the material and arguments which I have
> heard, I would have felt driven to the view that an insufficient case had been
> made under art 8(2) to justify the interference with the right to legal
> confidentiality which r 48.7(3) involves, and that for that reason the
> *f* application should be refused.'

[23] Toulson J takes the view that the problems identified in *Ex p B* prevent
any balancing operation of the kind which is suggested to be possible in this case.
It seems to me that there is no halfway house. Either the requirements of a fair
g trial override the privilege or they do not. He refers elsewhere in the judgment
to the remarks of Lord Wilberforce in *Science Research Council v Nassé, BL Cars Ltd
(formerly Leyland Cars) v Vyas* [1979] 3 All ER 673, [1980] AC 1028. There is no
power in the court to override the privilege in a document, but there is no reason
why other means of proof, particularly oral evidence from the solicitor, may not
be relied on to prove a particular fact in respect of the retainer. The opposing
h party may not obtain disclosure of privileged material in order to challenge the
recollection of the witness.

[24] I conclude that the European Court of Human Rights considers that legal
professional privilege is a 'strong' privilege which will not be overridden in a case
in which the lawyer holds documents suggesting that his client is guilty of a
j crime. In my judgment, there is no power to override the privilege. Accordingly
the question becomes one of what the requirements of fairness require, given
that the privilege will not be overridden.

[25] The decisions in *Goldman v Hesper* [1988] 3 All ER 97, [1988] 1 WLR 1238
and in *Pamplin v Express Newspapers Ltd* [1985] 2 All ER 185, [1985] 1 WLR 689 also
respect the privilege. There comes a point at which the receiving party must be
put to its election. If the privilege is waived, the waiver will be for the purposes

of the proceedings before the costs judge only. It is not every document where
this will arise: many documents on the file will be examined by the costs judge
alone and such will be his experience that his examination will suffice for the
paying party. But where that is not possible, then secondary evidence will be
given. That evidence will not be capable of being tested without the documents,
at least in the sense that an English lawyer would give to the word 'tested'. What
then is the position?

[26] In *Dombo Beheer v Netherlands* (1993) 18 EHRR 213, the European Court of
Human Rights had to consider an exclusionary rule in the then law of evidence
in the Netherlands which prevented an interested party from giving evidence in
his own cause. The applicant (Dombo) had a dispute with its bankers concerning
the overdraft limit on an account. Dombo said that the manager of its Nijmegen
branch had agreed to increase its overdraft limit from NLG 500,000 to
NLG 2,100,000. After various transactions, the bank decided that it no longer had
confidence in Dombo, and froze its accounts without warning, although the debit
balance of NLG 783,436 was well within the overdraft limit that Dombo said had
been agreed. The bank denied the alleged agreement, which had never been
reduced into writing. It also denied that the account had been frozen. It is not
necessary to discuss in detail the procedure which was followed. Dombo eventually
proffered Mr van Reijendam, who had been its managing director at the material
times and had negotiated with the bank, as a witness. It was said that he was now
unemployed, having been dismissed. The judge refused to take his evidence,
finding that his dismissal had been a sham entered into with a view to enabling
him to give evidence. The bank proffered the manager of the Nijmegen branch
who had negotiated with Mr van Reijendam. Dombo objected on the basis that
it was unfair to hear the manager but not Mr van Reijendam. The judge rejected
this objection. Dombo sought review of the decision against it, basing itself in
part on the rejection of Mr van Reijendam as a witness. Although its Advocate-
General considered that the appeal should be allowed, the Hoge Raad rejected it.

[27] Having observed that the requirements inherent in the concept of 'fair
hearing' are not necessarily the same in criminal cases as they are in cases
concerning the determination of civil rights and obligations, the European Court
of Human Rights continued (at 229–230):

'33. Nevertheless, certain principles concerning the notion of a "fair hearing"
in cases concerning civil rights and obligations emerge from the Court's case
law. Most significantly for the present case, it is clear that the requirement
of "equality of arms," in the sense of a "fair balance" between the parties,
applies in principle to such cases as well as to criminal cases [citing *Feldbrugge
v Netherlands* (1986) 8 EHRR 425]. The Court agrees with the Commission
that as regards litigation involving opposing private interests, "equality of
arms" implies that each party must be afforded a reasonable opportunity to
present his case—including his evidence—under conditions that do not place
him at a substantial disadvantage *vis-à-vis* his opponent. It is left to the
national authorities to ensure in each individual case that the requirements
of a "fair hearing" are met.

34. In the instant case, it was incumbent upon the applicant company to
prove that there was an oral agreement between it and the Bank to extend
certain credit facilities. Only two persons had been present [at] the meeting at
which this agreement had allegedly been reached, namely Mr van Reijendam
representing the company and [the manager] representing the Bank. Yet
only one of these two key persons was permitted to be heard, namely the

a person who had represented the Bank. The applicant company was denied the possibility of calling the person who had represented it, because the Court of Appeal identified him with the applicant company itself.

35. During the relevant negotiations, Mr van Reijendam and [the manager] acted on an equal footing, both being empowered to negotiate on behalf of their respective parties. It is therefore difficult to see why they should not

b both have been allowed to give evidence. The applicant company was thus placed at a substantial disadvantage *vis-à-vis* the Bank and there has accordingly been a violation of Article 6(1).'

To a common lawyer's eyes the disparity between the parties in this case looks rather substantial, but exclusionary rules of this kind may operate in an

c environment where there is no cross-examination, and they were (and are) not unique to the Netherlands. But the principle is clearly stated. 'Equality of arms' implies an equality in access to evidence.

[28] The point is emphasised in *Krcmár v Czech Republic* (2000) 31 EHRR 953, where the Czech Constitutional Court delivered a decision based in part on documents which were not considered at the hearing and not shown to or

d discussed by the parties. There was no breach of the principal of equality of arms, but the European Court of Human Rights held (at 963) that there was a breach of the principle of fairness:

'40 However, the concept of a fair hearing also implies the right to adversarial proceedings, according to which the parties must have the opportunity not only

e to make known any evidence needed for their claims to succeed, but also to have knowledge of, and comment on, all evidence adduced or observations filed, with a view to influencing the court's decision ...

42 From the record of the oral hearing before the Constitutional Court, it does not appear that the documentary evidence in issue was read out. The

f Court considers, however, that even if such evidence was submitted and read during the oral hearing, this would not have satisfied the right of the applicants to adversarial proceedings, given the character and importance of this evidence. A party to the proceedings must have the possibility to familiarise itself with the evidence before the court, as well as the possibility

g to comment on its existence, contents and authenticity in an appropriate form and within an appropriate time, if need be, in a written form and in advance.'

This statement of principle does not seem to me to be in any way exceptionable or surprising. A party must know what forces are marshalled against it.

h [29] What, then, if the costs judge follows the guidance in *Pamplin's* case and that of *Bailey v IBC Vehicles Ltd* [1998] 3 All ER 570, as now expressed in CPD para 40.14, and having seen the documents in question, requires the receiving party to elect between giving secondary evidence of the retainer and waiving the privilege? It seems to me that there is no incompatibility with the principles articulated by the European Court of Human Rights in such circumstances. Once the document is

j of sufficient importance to be taken into account in arriving at a conclusion as to recoverability, then, unless otherwise agreed, it must be shown to the paying party or the receiving party must content itself with other evidence.

[30] This is not intended to suggest that the costs judge may potentially put the receiving party to its election in respect of every document relied on, regardless of its degree of relevance. I would expect that in the great majority of cases the paying party would be content to agree that the costs judge alone should see privileged

documents. Only where it is necessary and proportionate should the receiving
party be put to his election. The redaction and production of privileged
documents, or the adducing of further evidence, will lead to additional delay and
increase costs.

[31] The final difficulty lies in the use of other evidence in the manner
contemplated by CPD para 40.14. It does not seem to me that the principles set
out above require privileged material available to the receiving party to be
disclosed for the purpose of testing the evidence given. This is litigation without
discovery or disclosure, familiar to all from legal backgrounds which do not lie in
the common law. I do not consider that the need for equality of arms requires an
invasion of a privilege: it may place on the party unwilling to waive the privilege
the burden of adducing evidence without using the privileged material, but does
not confer on the other party a right to see the material anyway. The solution is
imperfect, but is dictated by the existence of the privilege: the fairest result given
the existence of the privilege is that either both or neither can deploy the
privileged material. The familiar rule that the other party is entitled to see the
disclosable material even if the party which possesses it does not deploy it can
have no application when the material is privileged.

[32] I do not consider that there is any balancing act to be carried out here.
The applicable principle is an absolute one. The privilege will not be overridden
by the court, and must be waived by the party entitled to assert it. It follows that
the terms of para 40.14 of CPD are consistent with the requirements of the
convention. At the same time, I think that the protection which is afforded to the
receiving party by the rule that the waiver is for the purpose of the assessment
only and that the document remains otherwise privileged should play a much
more significant role than it appears to in the decision whether or not to waive
privilege in a proper case.

The facts of the present case

[33] I take the following statement of facts broadly from the judgment of the
costs judge.

[34] South Coast has three costs orders in its favour. Their origins lie in arbitration
awards made by Mr IW Menzies on 24 November 1994 and on 28 November 1996
which were appealed to Judge Fox-Andrews QC sitting on Official Referees'
business on 20 June 1996 and 16 September 1997 and thereafter to the Court of
Appeal on 14 July 1998.

[35] The facts giving rise to the arbitration were these. On 29 January 1985
South Coast was awarded a contract by Havant to replenish the beach at Hayling
Island with shingle and armour. Part of the work was subcontracted by South
Coast to John Howard & Co. On 5 September 1984 they had formed a joint
venture whereby (by cl 6.1) South Coast was to be responsible for dredging of
marine aggregates and John Howard for all other activities. Clause 5.5 provided
that each would—

'indemnify the other against all actions claims demands liabilities expenses
and costs arising in any way whatsoever in respect of those items or those
sections of the Works or any part or parts thereof comprised in any Works
Contract and agreed to be so executed completed and maintained by it
pursuant to Clause 1.1 and all variations thereto.'

[36] The work generated considerable noise to the discomfort of local
residents. On 26 September 1985, a resident obtained an interim junction restraining
Howard from working during particular hours or within a certain area. On

a 31 October 1985, those injunction proceedings were compromised by a consent order in terms which were similar to, but not identical to those of the earlier injunction.

[37] Practical completion of the contract was certified on 22 November 1985, but the parties remained in dispute on a number of issues arising from the injunction proceedings. At an extraordinary general meeting on 16 December

b 1985 South Coast assigned its business as a going concern to a sister wholly-owned subsidiary of RMC Group plc called Rombus Materials Ltd (Rombus) with effect from 1 January 1986. It continued to trade as agent for Rombus, who indemnified it against all liabilities it incurred in pursuing its activities as an agent. It appears that South Coast continues to trade as an agent. The 1999 return (the latest in the bundles) states that the company's principal activity—

c

'is the dredging and selling of marine dredged aggregates as agent for and on behalf of RMC (UK) Ltd (formerly RMS Rombus Materials Ltd) which indemnifies the company against all losses and liabilities it may incur in pursuing that activity as agent.'

d The balance sheet reveals a loan to the parent undertaking equal to the issued and called-up share capital, there being no other assets, liabilities or reserves. The report suggests that the company holds land, but as trustee for its parent undertaking.

[38] On 29 July 1986, South Coast served notice of arbitration on Havant

e together with a request to concur in the appointment of an arbitrator. South Coast also instructed Berkeley Surveying Management Service (Berkeley) to act for it in the arbitration.

[39] On 13 May 1987, there was a meeting between South Coast and John Howard in respect of the dispute with Havant. At that meeting it was agreed that the external costs and all income relating to the arbitration claims would be split

f 40% to South Coast and 60% to John Howard. John Howard was ultimately taken over by AMEC.

[40] It was not until 15 October 1992 that Mr IW Menzies was appointed as arbitrator. Initially AMEC was a party to the arbitration until the arbitrator determined that it was not a party to the agreement with Havant. The arbitrator

g allowed eight claims to be pursued before him: (a) littoral drift, (b) injunction and instructions, (c) varied profiles, (b) trimming, batters, (e) under-measurement, (f) groyne repairs, (g) extension of time, (h) interest.

[41] In his first interim award, the arbitrator resolved various preliminary issues in favour of Havant from which there was no appeal. On 2 August 1994,

h he published his second interim award, finding in favour of South Coast in respect of claims (b), (d) and (e). He awarded respectively £251,544·15, £45,837·60 and £3,863·34 together with statutory interest under s 19A of the Arbitration Act 1950. This award was amended by his third interim award published on 19 August 1994, which reduced claim (b) to £248,514·15 under the slip rule. They are collectively known as 'the original award'. On 24 November 1994, the arbitrator published

j his final award which dealt solely with the costs of the main arbitration hearing. On 22 August 1994, Anthony Feldman & Co were instructed to act for South Coast in relation to the proceedings which arose from the awards. On 1 September 1994, Anthony Feldman & Co merged with Howard Kennedy, Mr Feldman remaining the partner with conduct of the case. There was no letter setting out the terms of the retainer, either when Anthony Feldman & Co were instructed nor when they merged with Howard Kennedy.

[42] On 10 March 1995, Judge Anthony Thornton QC granted Havant leave to appeal against the arbitrator's award in respect of claims (b) and (d). Those appeals were heard by Judge Fox-Andrews QC on various dates between 6 November 1995 and 1 April 1996 with judgment being handed down on 20 June 1996. By orders of that date, the judge allowed Havant's appeal under claim (d) and ordered repayment of the sum of £45,837·60 (plus interest thereon of £8,820·46) together with interest on those amounts and costs. The orders further provided that claim (b) be remitted to the arbitrator for reconsideration and that—

> 'If the arbitrator makes a more favourable award on the costs in any respect to the applicant than his final award then the applicant shall have the costs of the application for leave to appeal and the appeal. If the final award remains the same then the respondent shall have costs.'

[43] The order made other costs orders adverse to South Coast but they are not material to the issue before the costs judge. Permission to appeal was refused. The arbitrator published his further award (the further award) on 28 August 1996 which upheld the original award. He expressed his conclusions in these terms:

> '11.13. I therefore conclude that after the court order of 31 October 1985, it was not possible to complete the works in accordance with the contract and the claimant, was, therefore, entitled to a variation order under cl 51, as necessary for the completion of the works, to be valued in accordance with cl 53. Bearing in mind the judge's decision on the first question of law dealt with in the judgment of 13 May 1996, my second interim award of 2 August as amended by my third interim award of 19 August 1994 correctly states my determination on claim (b) and is hereby affirmed.'

[44] The effect of this award was to confirm the award in respect of claim (b) in the sum of £248,544·15. Under the order of 20 June 1996, Havant also became liable for the costs of the application for leave to appeal and the appeal to Judge Fox-Andrews QC in respect of this item.

[45] Havant was dissatisfied with the arbitrator's reconsideration. It contended that the sum awarded ought to have been calculated not from the date of the injunction (26 September 1985) but from the date of the consent order (31 October 1985). Had the assessment been made from the later date, South Coast's loss under claim (b) would have been limited to £78,763·53. Following the further award, Havant issued two further motions under s 27 of the Arbitration Act 1950 on 18 September 1986 respectively, numbered 1996 folio 1839 and 140. Havant also applied to the arbitrator on 27 September 1996 for a correction under s 17 of the Arbitration Act (the slip rule). This application was met by another by South Coast inviting the arbitrator to make clear in a further award that the material date was September 1985. In December 1996, the arbitrator declined to make either of the amendments sought.

[46] Havant's motions were heard by Judge Fox-Andrews QC ((1998) 14 Const LJ 430) on 11 April 1997 (adjourned from 21 February 1997). They sought orders that the award be set aside, alternatively declared a nullity, alternatively be remitted for reconsideration. The ground relied upon was that Mr Menzies had misconducted himself. Judgment was given on 11 June 1997 and the order dated 16 September 1997. This dismissed Havant's application and made the following orders for costs:

'(1) The applicant do pay the respondent's costs of the application to be taxed if not agreed as to 75% on the standard basis and as to 25% on the indemnity basis; (2) the applicant is refused leave to appeal this order for costs; (3) the applicant do pay the respondent's costs of today.'

In respect of the second motion:

'(1) The application be dismissed and the applicant do pay the respondent's costs to be taxed if not agreed on a standard basis; (2) the applicant is refused leave to appeal this order; (3) the applicant do pay the respondent's costs of today.'

[47] Havant appealed to the Court of Appeal with leave of Hobhouse and Chadwick LJJ dated 17 February 1998. On 14 July 1998 the Court of Appeal dismissed the appeal, affirmed the order of Judge Fox-Andrews QC and made the following costs order:

'(2) ... the respondent's costs of this appeal save the costs of the transcripts in respect of the proceedings on 11 April and 16 September 1997 be paid by the applicant [Havant] such costs to be taxed if not agreed.'

[48] South Coast commenced proceedings for detailed assessment of the three awards in its favour. These amount (before interest) to £76,793·64 (order of 20 June 1996), £88,211·51 (order of 16 September 1997) and £54,350·89 (order of 14 July 1998), making £219,356·04 in total. The three bills of costs are signed by Mr Emden, a partner in Howard Kennedy, and carry four certificates. The last certificate is in the usual form:

'I certify that his Bill is both accurate and complete and that in relation to the [terms] it covers the costs claimed herein do not [exceed] the costs which the receiving party/parties is/are required to pay me/my firm.'

The hearing before the costs judge

[49] The costs judge gave directions on 13 September 2000 which included a direction for evidence from a partner of Howard Kennedy setting out the terms of the retainer. The points of dispute raised the question of the indemnity principle, and this was taken as a preliminary issue. There was extensive evidence before the costs judge in the form of four witness statements from Mr Emden, from Mr Foster, a partner in Havant's solicitors Lewis Silkin, and in reply from Ms Bakshi a non-practising barrister and head of the construction department at Howard Kennedy and Mr Stokes, the commercial manager of South Coast. Ms Bakshi had been concerned in the matter from the beginning, having been employed by Berkeley before Anthony Feldman & Co were instructed. She was the one witness who had been involved in the proceedings throughout. Her evidence refers to invoices rendered to South Coast by Howard Kennedy throughout the proceedings, which she declines to show to Havant but offers to show to the costs judge.

[50] At the hearing before the costs judge, Havant contended that South Coast were obliged to pay only 40% of the costs of the proceedings to Howard Kennedy, the remainder being AMEC's responsibility. The costs judge carefully sets out the submissions of Havant on this question, including their submissions upon the contents of the 'supplemental bundle' which was made available at the hearing.

[51] There is no doubt that the evidence of Mr Emden and Ms Bakshi, together with Mr Emden's certificate on the bills, was evidence that there was no breach of the indemnity principle. The position on other material documents was described by the costs judge:

'8.2.2 The material over which South Coast declined to waive privilege were interim bills submitted by Howard Kennedy, copies of cheques paying them and various management accounts. Having examined the bills and cheques I could not discern anything sensitive or private about them. On the contrary, their disclosure might have satisfied Havant and thereby avoided two expensive days of argument. The same result might have been achieved if South Coast had made available their correspondence file to Havant for the period when Mr Feldman and then Howard Kennedy were first instructed. Unfortunately, as remains their right, South Coast declined to waive privilege.'

[52] Having summarised the arguments of counsel, the costs judge did not put South Coast to their election:

'8.2.6 My view is that there is a tension between art 5 and art 8 [of the convention]. So far as this decision is concerned, I consider the safeguards laid down in [Bailey v IBC Vehicles Ltd [1998] 3 All ER 570] and CPD [para 40.14] have been sufficient to enable me to decide the preliminary with no loss of fairness. Had I been alerted to any matters which merited investigation, further evidence or disclosure could have been called for. However, I cannot say with certainty that this would necessarily be the position in other cases and it is open to question whether it can be just following the introduction of the Human Rights Act 1998 for a party paying costs to have no entitlement whatsoever to see any papers belonging to the party receiving costs, especially when the sums involved, as here, may be large.'

[53] The costs judge then considers the law, and concludes that the signature, the fact of the retainer and the absence of any grounds of suspicion that the whole truth may not have been told, raise a presumption that there was an enforceable agreement between South Coast and Howard Kennedy to pay costs. Given the submissions made for Havant by Mr Simon Jonathan Brown, who also appeared before me, he proceeded to read Howard Kennedy's files and concluded that the retainer did not find its origin in Ms Bakshi's relationship with AMEC, as was Mr Brown's first contention. The costs judge finds that the relationship of solicitor and client began with the instructions to Mr Feldman. He refers to the interim bills, concludes that there is no reason why they should not have been shown to Havant, observes that they were addressed to South Coast and concludes that South Coast contracted with Howard Kennedy.

[54] Mr Brown's second contention was that South Coast contracted as agent for Havant, and was not liable to Howard Kennedy as principal, although it would no doubt have been liable for Havant's costs as a party to the action. The costs judge rejects this contention on the footing that the original retainer had been by South Coast on its own behalf, and nothing had changed. Thus, although South Coast was now merely an agent for RMC, it had contracted as principal and not as agent and was accordingly liable to pay the bills.

[55] Next, Mr Brown relied upon the insolvency of South Coast. The costs judge rejected this contention on the basis, as he put it, that the fact that the client has no money to discharge the solicitor's bill is irrelevant. Having rejected certain

a points based on the apparent lack of a final bill and the fact that there had been an apparent uplift applied to the interim bills, the costs judge dealt with the final point, which was based on the 40/60 split between South Coast and AMEC. On this point, he found that it derived from the agreement between South Coast and AMEC of 13 May 1987, and did not relate to any arrangement affecting liability to pay Howard Kennedy. So all the evidence pointed to compliance with the

b indemnity principle, and the costs judge decided the point in favour of South Coast.

The course of the appeal

[56] The position on the appeal was complicated by the statement in open court by Mr Hutton for South Coast that it was being indemnified in relation to
c costs, and by the disclosure of additional documents both before and at the hearing. Before turning to the effect of these documents, I should deal with the position as it was before the costs judge.

[57] It seems plain that the costs judge put pressure on Mr Hutton to waive privilege on the bills and cheques, but Mr Hutton declined. Since it is assumed
d by the parties that the bills and cheques were privileged, I will make the same assumption, although it is arguably incorrect at least in so far as the cheques are concerned. It seems to me that once the costs judge decided to rely upon the interim bills and upon the solicitors' files, he should have asked Havant if they had any objection. If an objection was stated, he should have asked South Coast whether they were willing to waive the privilege in the bills, the cheques and the
e relevant documents in the files. If they were not willing to do so, he should have followed para 40.14 of CPD , declined to accept the material for which privilege was claimed in evidence and invited South Coast to indicate whether they wished to adduce further evidence in respect of the manner in which interim bills had been rendered and paid. If South Coast sought to adduce further evidence, he should have considered it and decided whether to admit it. The same goes for
f any item of correspondence which he considered potentially relevant. Had disclosure been requested but resisted, he would have to put the document out of his head, but that is not a difficult task.

The waiver of privilege

g [58] Shortly before the hearing of the appeal, South Coast made available the bills from Howard Kennedy. All are addressed to South Coast. One is marked with '40%', and one bears the comment 'Recharge 60% to AMEC'. Some of these bills are stamped paid, others not. There are also four copy cheques totalling some £144,565·94 paid by South Coast to Howard Kennedy at various dates in the
h year 2000. The profit costs actually billed down to 30 June 2000 appear to be of the order of £170,000, excluding VAT and disbursements. There are 22 interim bills and a number of disbursement-only bills. At the hearing of the appeal, Howard Kennedy produced part of their correspondence file, waiving the privilege. Since it was produced so late, I gave Mr Brown an opportunity to address me on it in writing. The file includes documents from Mr Feldman's
j early file. It seems clear that that Mr Feldman relies heavily on instructions from Berkeley and South Coast, but reports to AMEC quarterly as to progress. He copies his correspondence with Mr Stokes of South Coast to Mr Harding of AMEC. South Coast receives copies of the legal documents such as the notice of appeal and the application for leave to appeal, not AMEC. It seems clear that this correspondence file is not complete. Of particular relevance is a letter from Mr Feldman of 5 September 1994 to Mr Harding asking who is to be giving

instructions in the matter. The reply to this letter is not included, but all attendance notes are headed 'South Coast Shipping'. There are letters of advice from Berkeley to South Coast. The letters written to counsel clearly indicate that South Coast is the client.

[59] The sums recovered in the arbitration were all paid to South Coast. Since they do not appear in the accounts at the year end, they were obviously paid over to RMC and AMEC, no doubt in a ratio 40/60. No doubt both these parties funded the claim. This does not mean or suggest that South Coast was not liable for the costs, which is the only issue. It seems to me quite probable that South Coast were, as Mr Brown submits, a vessel for the action. This does not matter. Mr Brown contends that it is clear that South Coast were acting as a commercial agent for AMEC (and RMC). This is not an acceptable analysis. It gave the retainer to the solicitor, in its own name. Thus it was the client. It seems to me clear that regardless of the arrangements between the companies, so far as the solicitors were concerned South Coast was the client, and it was to South Coast that the solicitors looked for their fees. What cannot be found is any hint of an agreement that South Coast were not to be so liable.

Conclusion

[60] While I accept the appellant's contention that in principle the costs judge should have put South Coast to the election for which para 40.14 of CPD provides, I consider that the material before the cost judge as a whole (including the certificates on the bills to be assessed and the witness statements, but not the privileged material) did not raise sufficient doubt to make it necessary to go further into the matter. There never was any real material to suggest that South Coast was not liable for the solicitors' costs, albeit that it was reliant upon RMC and AMEC for its funding. But it is not possible to draw the inference that it was not itself liable for the costs from that fact. Mr Brown submits that there should be further disclosure, or that it is appropriate to call for further documents. I disagree. There is nothing in all this. I consider that this is a piece of satellite litigation which has swallowed up enough costs, and that the time has now come to bring it to an end. In my judgment, the costs judge was right when he concluded on the strength of the interim bills, the cheques and the correspondence that there was nothing deserving of investigation. Albeit that I consider that he did not apply para 40.14 of CPD quite correctly, I consider that the appeal must be dismissed. I will hear counsel on the form of order.

Appeal dismissed.

Victoria Parkin   Barrister.

Sealy v Consignia plc

[2002] EWCA Civ 878

COURT OF APPEAL, CIVIL DIVISION

BROOKE, LATHAM LJJ AND HART J

22 MAY, 19 JUNE 2002

Employment tribunal – Procedure – Complaint of unfair dismissal – Presentation of complaint to tribunal – Presentation of complaint by first class post – Guidance for purposes of application of time limit provisions – Employment Rights Act 1996, s 111(2).

Following a disciplinary hearing on 9 July 2000, the respondent employee was summarily dismissed from his employment as a postman. He wished to bring a complaint of unfair dismissal against the appellant employer. Under s 111(2)[a] of the Employment Rights Act 1996, such a complaint had to be 'presented' to the employment tribunal (a) before the end of the period of three months beginning with the effective date of termination of employment, or (b) within such further period as the tribunal considered reasonable in a case where it was satisfied that it was not reasonably practicable for the complaint to be presented before the end of that period. The employee sent his complaint form to the tribunal by first class post on Friday, 6 October 2000, but it was not received until Tuesday, 10 October. In their summary reasons, the tribunal found that the last day of the three-month period was Sunday, 8 October; that if the post had run its normal course it would have arrived, if not within the time period, then immediately after its end, ie on the Monday morning; that its arrival on Tuesday was beyond the employee's control and outside his reasonable expectation; and that in those circumstances his case fell within s 111(2)(b) of the 1996 Act. In reaching that conclusion, the tribunal held, erroneously, that delivery first thing on Monday could properly have been treated as in time because there was no post on a Sunday. Subsequently, the tribunal gave extended reasons in which it expressly found that, when posting the form, the employee had had a reasonable expectation that it would be delivered the next day in the course of post, ie on the Saturday. The employer appealed, but the Employment Appeal Tribunal refused to direct that the appeal should proceed to a full hearing. The employer appealed to the Court of Appeal, contending, inter alia, that the tribunal had erred in promulgating extended reasons that were in conflict with its summary reasons. It further relied on the tribunal's failure to make any finding as to why the employee had delayed making his application until the very end of the three-month period.

Held – For the purposes of s 111(2)(b) of the 1996 Act, a complainant was entitled to rely on the ordinary course of the post, and accordingly there was no reason to penalise a complainant who had so relied for not having tried to present his complaint at some earlier point in the three-month period. Giving the applicant the benefit of the ordinary course of post provided a workable (if generous) test of what was reasonably practicable. It followed in the instant case that the question was whether there had been evidence before the tribunal on which it could conclude that the employee had posted a letter which, in the ordinary

---

a   Section 111, so far as material, is set out at [2], below

course of the post, could reasonably have been expected to arrive on the Saturday
(as opposed to the Saturday or the Monday). In its summary reasons, however,
there seemed to be an unambiguous finding that, in the ordinary course of post,
the complaint would have arrived either on the Saturday or the Monday. In
seeking to correct the error of law displayed by its summary reasons in respect of
the timeousness of a Monday delivery, the tribunal had simply substituted a
finding of fact which was both inconsistent with that made in the summary
reasons and not supported by adequate evidence. Accordingly, the appeal would
be allowed, the decision set aside and the matter remitted to a differently-constituted
tribunal for re-determination (see [20]–[22], [24], [27], [28], [34], below); *Burton v
Field Sons & Co Ltd* [1977] ICR 106 applied.

Per curiam. A complaint is 'presented' within the terms of s 111(2) of the 1996
Act when it arrives at the Central Office of Employment Tribunals or an Office
of the Tribunals. If a complainant proves that it was impossible to present a
complaint in that way before the end of the time prescribed by s 111(2)(a), it will
be possible to argue that it was not reasonably practicable for the complaint to be
presented within the prescribed period. If a complainant sends a complaint by
post, presentation will be assumed to have been effected, unless the contrary is
proved, at the time when the letter would have been delivered in the ordinary
course of post. If the letter is sent by first class post, it is legitimate to adapt the
approach contained in CPR 6.7 and conclude that, in the ordinary course of post,
it will be delivered on the second day after it was posted (excluding Sundays, Bank
Holidays, Christmas Day and Good Friday). If a letter does not arrive at the time
when it would be expected to in the ordinary course of post, a tribunal may
conclude that it is not reasonably practicable for the complaint to be presented
within the prescribed period. If a form is date-stamped on a Monday by a tribunal
office so as to be outside a three-month period which ends on the Saturday or
Sunday, a tribunal may find as a fact that it was posted by first class post not later
than the Thursday and arrived on the Saturday, or alternatively to extend time as
a matter of discretion if satisfied that the letter was posted by first class post not
later than the Thursday. The normal and expected result of posting a letter must
be objectively, not subjectively, assessed, and it is that the letter will arrive at its
destination in the ordinary course of post. For the avoidance of doubt, the strict
litigation rule on the irrebuttability of the deemed day of service does not apply
in employment tribunal cases (see [26], [27], [31], [32], below).

Notes

For the time limit for bringing a complaint to the employment tribunal, see
16 *Halsbury's Laws* (4th edn) (2000 reissue) para 513.

For the Employment Rights Act 1996, s 111, see 16 *Halsbury's Statutes* (4th edn)
(2000 reissue) 714.

Cases referred to in judgments

Anglo Continental School of English (Bournemouth) Ltd v Gardiner [1973] ICR 261, NIRC.
Beanstalk Shelving Ltd v Horn [1980] ICR 273, EAT.
Birmingham Midshires Building Society v Horton [1991] ICR 648, EAT.
Burton v Field Sons & Co Ltd [1977] ICR 106, EAT.
Dedman v British Building and Engineering Appliances Ltd [1974] 1 All ER 520, [1974]
   1 WLR 171, CA.
Godwin v Swindon BC [2001] EWCA Civ 1478, [2001] 4 All ER 641, [2002] 1 WLR 997.
Pritam Kaur (administratrix of Bikar Singh (decd)) v S Russell & Sons Ltd [1973] 1 All ER
   617, [1973] QB 336, [1973] 2 WLR 147, CA.

a   St Basil's Centre v McCrossan [1992] ICR 140, EAT.
Swainston v Hetton Victory Club Ltd [1983] 1 All ER 1170, EAT and CA.
Wall's Meat Co Ltd v Khan [1979] ICR 52, CA.

Cases also cited or referred to in skeleton arguments
Dobie v Burns International Security Services (UK) Ltd [1984] 3 All ER 333, [1985] 1 WLR
b   43, CA.
Meek v City of Birmingham DC [1987] IRLR 250, CA.
Palmer v Southend-on-Sea BC [1984] 1 All ER 945, [1984] 1 WLR 1129, CA.
Piggott Bros & Co Ltd v Jackson [1992] ICR 85, CA.
Porter v Bandridge Ltd [1978] 1 WLR 1145, CA.
c   Retarded Children's Aid Society Ltd v Day [1978] 1 WLR 763, CA.
Riley v Tesco Stores Ltd [1980] ICR 323, CA.
Sturges v A E Farr Ltd [1975] ICR 356.
Taylorplan Services Ltd v Jackson [1996] IRLR 184, EAT.

d   **Appeal**
The appellant, Consignia plc, appealed with permission of the Employment Appeal
Tribunal (Mr Commissioner Howell QC, Mr BR Gibbs and Mrs JM Matthias)
from its decision on 11 June 2001 refusing to direct a full hearing of Consignia's
proposed appeal from the decision of an employment tribunal for the London
North-West region, promulgated on 2 February 2001, that a claim for unfair
e   dismissal brought by the respondent, Russell Sealy, should be listed for a
substantive hearing. The facts are set out in the judgment of Hart J.

Lydia Seymour (instructed by *Catherine Churchyard*) for Consignia.
Marc Jones of *Underwoods*, Hemel Hempstead, acting pro bono for Mr Sealy.
f
Cur adv vult

19 June 2002. The following judgments were delivered.

g   **HART J** (giving the first judgment at the invitation of Brooke LJ).
[1] This is an appeal by Consignia plc (formerly the Post Office) from a
decision of the Employment Appeal Tribunal (EAT) on 11 June 2001 whereby it
refused to direct that Consignia's proposed appeal from a decision of an employment
tribunal (ET) promulgated on 2 February 2001 should proceed to a full hearing.
The EAT was not satisfied that the proposed appeal raised sufficiently arguable
h   points of law.
[2] Mr Sealy was employed as a postman for nearly four years. He was
summarily dismissed from his employment on the basis of gross misconduct,
following a disciplinary hearing, on 9 July 2000. An internal appeal was due to be
heard on 16 November 2000. The earlier date, however, was the effective date
j   of termination for the purposes of employment legislation, if he wished to make
a complaint that he had been unfairly dismissed. Section 111(2) of the Employment
Rights Act 1996 provides in this context that—

'an employment tribunal shall not consider a complaint under this section
unless it is presented to the tribunal—(a) before the end of the period of three
months beginning with the effective date of termination, or (b) within such
further period as the tribunal considers reasonable in a case where it is

satisfied that it was not reasonably practicable for the complaint to be presented before the end of three months.'

[3] In their summary reasons (given pursuant to para 10(3) of Sch 1 to the Employment Tribunals (Constitution and Rules of Procedure) Regulations 1993, SI 1993/2687), dated 2 February 2001, the ET found that the complaint on form IT1 ought to have been presented on Sunday, 8 October in order to be presented within the requisite three-month period, but that it was not in fact received by the tribunal office until Tuesday, 10 October 2000. They concluded therefore that 'the claim is nearly two days out of time'. The summary reasons then proceed as follows:

'5. The next issue (applying s 111) was whether it was reasonably practicable for the applicant to have presented this within time. We find that it was not reasonably practicable for him to have presented it within time because although he posted it with [sic] time on Friday, 6 October 2000 (which we find as a fact), once he posted it, it was beyond his control when it was delivered. In the event it was not delivered in course of first class mail and did not arrive until Tuesday, 10 October. The fact that it did not arrive within time therefore was something which the applicant could not control. The delay in its arrival was caused by delay in the post. He was not unreasonable in relying on the post.

6. There is no requirement on a party to present a claim earlier in the three month period rather than later, ie he is simply given a three month period in which to present the claim.

7. In this case, because of the way the dates fall, the last day in the three month period was a Sunday. The IT1 could not of course have been presented on the Sunday because there were no deliveries on a Sunday. Nevertheless if it had at least been delivered first thing on the Monday morning in view of the absence of deliveries on a Sunday it would then have been proper to treat it as in time. Otherwise applicant is effectively denied the full three month's time period and given instead three months less one day in any case where the final day of the period falls on a Sunday. In circumstances where it makes no substantive difference (as here because nothing would have happened to it on a Sunday) this would amount to denying access to the hearing of a substantive right for purely procedural reasons.

8. In this case therefore, we accept that the IT1 was posted within time and that if the post had run its normal course it would have arrived if not within the time period, immediately after the end of the time period, and that end being a Sunday would have been reasonable and proper to process it first thing Monday morning.

9. The fact that it did not arrive until the Tuesday was quite beyond the applicant's control and not within his reasonable expectation.

10. For that reason the claim should be considered and the matter should be listed for a substantive hearing.'

[4] In extended reasons, dated 21 March 2001, which were not very much longer than their summary reasons, the tribunal made an express finding that when Mr Sealy posted the IT1, properly addressed and pre-paid by first class post, on Friday, 6 October, he had a reasonable expectation that it would be delivered next day in the course of post. The ET justified this finding in the following terms:

'6. We accept on the facts of this case that he had expected it to be delivered the next day, 7 October. The applicant worked himself in the post office and knew the procedures. The respondents did not give evidence in this case of the performance of the postal delivery service in the area at the time, nor of any factor or circumstance that should have alerted the applicant to any different view. This expectation was therefore reasonable. It was suggested to him in cross-examination that he should not have left his application so late, but again his evidence as to his expectation was calm and clear, and we accepted that evidence.'

[5] The tribunal continued:

'7. The reason why the application was not received within the time limits was the postal delay. This of course was something beyond the applicant's control. Once he had posted the item he could do no more than rely on the postal service to perform in accordance with his reasonable expectation.

8. There is no requirement on an applicant to present his claim any earlier than by the end of the statutory limit. To leave it towards the end may be "an extremely dangerous practice" (*Beanstalk Shelving Ltd v Horn* [1980] ICR 273 at 277), but whether that means that it was not reasonably practicable to present in time must depend upon the facts of the case (*Birmingham Midshires Building Society v Horton* [1991] ICR 648). On the above facts found in this case it was not reasonably practical for the applicant to have presented his claim in time.

9. In this case, even if we had accepted that the applicant could not reasonably have relied upon next day delivery of the application (in spite of evidence before us), there would still have been the possibility of Monday delivery. Though that would strictly have been out of time by one day, the practical reality would have been that nothing would have been lost by that and no party disadvantaged. Not to accept the claim might then be considered to prevent him from having access to the hearing of his claim as to his substantive rights for a purely procedural reason. In the event, in this case the delivery was beyond that and was late, in terms of the applicant's expectations, by two days.'

[6] The grounds of appeal advanced before us were (i) that the tribunal had erred in finding that the applicant had a reasonable expectation of his letter posted on the Friday arriving on the Saturday, (ii) that it erred in making that finding without any finding as to the time or place at which the application was posted, (iii) that it erred in promulgating extended reasons which were in conflict with its summary reasons, (iv) that it had applied the wrong test in para 9 of its extended reasons in considering the issue of prejudice to the respondent, and (v) that it erred in considering the date of postage and expected date of receipt in isolation when they ought to have considered these matters as only part of the wider test of reasonable practicability.

[7] In support of the third of those grounds it was submitted by Miss Seymour on behalf of Consignia that the extended reasons wholly changed the basis of the tribunal's decision by adding a finding that Mr Sealy reasonably expected the application to arrive on the following day. While Consignia accepted that a tribunal is entitled to review its own decision where it realises that an error has been made, it was submitted that it can only do so effectively by making it clear that this is what has been done. In the absence of evidence that the tribunal ever met again to reconsider its decision it was (submitted Consignia) impossible to

say which set of reasons governed the tribunal's, and the decision should therefore be set aside.

[8] It was further submitted on behalf of Consignia that the EAT was wrong in this case to hold that it should have regard only to the extended reasons for the purposes of the appeal.

[9] These submissions proceed on the basis that the extended reasons did represent a significantly different process of reasoning from the summary reasons. I was in the end persuaded by Miss Seymour on behalf of Consignia that this was the case. The summary reasons state, as a finding, that if the post had run its normal course, the IT1 would have arrived 'if not within the time period, immediately after the end of the time period' (see para 8). The tribunal was also then clearly proceeding on the erroneous assumption that delivery first thing on the Monday could properly have been treated as within time (see para 7). That assumption was plainly wrong having regard to the decision of this court in *Swainston v Hetton Victory Club Ltd* [1983] 1 All ER 1170 that the principle in *Pritam Kaur (administratrix of Bikar Singh (decd)) v S Russell & Sons Ltd* [1973] 1 All ER 617, [1973] QB 336 had no application to s 67(2) of the Employment Protection (Consolidation) Act 1978 (the statutory predecessor of s 111). In holding in para 5 of the summary reasons that Mr Sealy was 'not unreasonable in relying on the post' the tribunal cannot be read as having decided that he was reasonably relying on the post to achieve delivery on the Saturday.

[10] In the final analysis the question before this court appears to me to be whether the tribunal had evidence before it which justified the further finding made in the extended reasons as to what Mr Sealy's reasonable expectations had been. Before examining that issue, it is necessary to address the question why those expectations are relevant in the first place when applying s 111 of the 1996 Act. The answer lies in the construction which has been placed by a consistent stream of authority on s 111 and its statutory predecessors (see s 67(2) of 1978 Act, para 21(4) of Sch 1 to the Trade Union and Labour Relations Act 1974, and r 2(1) of the Schedule to the Industrial Tribunals (Industrial Relations etc) Regulations 1972, SI 1972/38, made under Sch 6 to the Industrial Relations Act 1971).

[11] The relevant authorities can be summarised by referring to the reviews contained in the judgments of the EAT in *Burton v Field Sons & Co Ltd* [1977] ICR 106, in *Birmingham Midshires Building Society v Horton* [1991] ICR 648, and in *St Basil's Centre v McCrossan* [1992] ICR 140.

[12] In *Burton's* case the applicant had posted his application by first class recorded post the very day before the period expired and it arrived late. The tribunal held that since the applicant had deliberately delayed posting his complaint it had been 'reasonably practicable' for him to have presented the application in time and they therefore held that they had no jurisdiction. The EAT allowed an appeal and remitted the case for rehearing. It held that, provided that the applicant had posted the application within the period so that in the normal course of post and except for unforeseen circumstances it would have been received in time, a tribunal ought to find that it was 'not reasonably practicable' for the complaint to have been presented within the three-month period. Giving judgment, Phillips J said (at 108–109):

'The words "reasonably practicable" have received a wide interpretation in the decision of the Court of Appeal in *Dedman* v. *British Building & Engineering Appliances Ltd* ([1974] 1 All ER 520, [1974] 1 WLR 171). The Court of Appeal by a majority, Stamp L.J. dissenting, gave to those words a meaning which they would not ordinarily hold; and, as Lord Denning M.R. pointed out, it is difficult to give a dictionary definition to the meaning which the Court of Appeal has ascribed to the words and it is easier to go by way of example. Amongst the examples which he gives is this ([1974] 1 All ER 520 at 525, [1974] 1 WLR 171 at 176): "Strictly speaking it is nearly always 'practicable' for a man to present his claim within four weeks"—the time then in force—"unless he is so ill as not to be able to write and has no one to do it for him. Take a case when he posts his complaint two days before the four weeks are up, and it is delayed in the post, so that it arrives one day too late. Strictly speaking it was 'practicable' for him to have presented it in time, because he could have posted it one day earlier. But the English court would hold him saved by the escape clause on the ground that it was 'not practicable': see *Anglo Continental School of English (Bournemouth) Ltd* v. *Gardiner* [1973] I.C.R 261." He approves the view expressed as an obiter dictum by Sir Hugh Griffiths in that case who said (at 267): "If an applicant shows that he posted his application in time to arrive in the ordinary course of post within the four week period but for some reason unknown to him it is not delivered to the offices of the tribunal until after the expiry of the four week period, we should expect the tribunal to be satisfied that it was not practicable to present the complaint within this four week period and to extend the time." So, Lord Denning M.R. said, and Scarman L.J. agreed, that if you have a case where a claimant does an act within the period prescribed, which in the ordinary event would result in the complaint being made within the specified period, and that is prevented from having its normal and expected result by some unforeseen circumstance, it can be said that the case is one, and indeed it ought to be said that the case is one, where it was not "reasonably practicable" for the complaint to be presented within the period of three months.'

[13] After noting that the tribunal had proceeded on the basis that the applicant had deliberately, for his own purposes, delayed making the application, Phillips J said that this was the wrong approach, and continued (at 110):

'The important question then surely is this: whether he or his solicitors (which for present purposes means him) could reasonably have expected, on Thursday, January 22, that a letter which was posted that day would have been received in the central office of the industrial tribunals in London on Friday, January 23 ... [I]f that expectation of the employee and of his solicitors was a reasonable one, then it follows necessarily, from what we have said earlier, based on the judgment of the Court of Appeal in *Dedman's* case ... that the case would have been one where it was not reasonably practicable to present it within the period of three months, because it would have been a case where the solicitors had done what was necessary to ensure that the notice was received in time, and it was by reason of unexpected events outside their control that that did not come about. And, for the reasons already given, it is in our judgment irrelevant that, for reasons which seemed good to the employee, although he could have acted very much earlier, he had decided to postpone acting until towards the end of the period.'

[14] Phillips J went on to hold that the question was not a matter for judicial notice but a question to be determined as a matter of fact by evidence. He referred to the *Practice Direction (post: first and second class mail)* [1968] 3 All ER 319, [1968] 1 WLR 1489—which provided for a rebuttable presumption that court

documents would be deemed to have been delivered in accordance with what the
Post Office had announced would be the usual delivery times for first and second
class mail from 16 September 1968—but pointed out that that view of the Post
Office might no longer be the case. The case was therefore remitted to the
tribunal. Phillips J concluded (at 111):

> 'It seems to us ... that the tribunal require to hear evidence from the
> solicitors about their normal practice and expectation in these matters and,
> in particular, evidence from the Post Office. It is not a question of what can
> be guaranteed of the postal services; it is a question of what a reasonable
> solicitor would have expected, or might reasonably have expected, at the
> time, date and place in question.'

[15] *Birmingham Midshires Building Society v Horton* [1991] ICR 648 was another
case of posting by first class post on the penultimate day. There the EAT (Wood J
presiding) dismissed an appeal from the tribunal's finding that it had not been
reasonably practicable for the application to have been presented in time. The
applicant's solicitor had given evidence that he believed that 99% of first class post
arrived the day after it was posted, and the tribunal had believed him. The EAT,
while repeating warnings that it had previously given as to the dangers of late
posting (in particular in *Beanstalk Shelving Ltd v Horn* [1980] ICR 273) refused to
accept that the decision was perverse. The EAT indicated that they would
probably have reached a different decision, but reminded themselves of what had
been said by Shaw LJ in *Wall's Meat Co Ltd v Khan* [1979] ICR 52 at 57:

> 'The test is empirical and involves no legal concept. Practical common
> sense is the keynote and legalistic footnotes may have no better result than
> to introduce a lawyer's complications into what should be a layman's
> pristine province. These considerations prompt me to express the emphatic
> view that the proper forum to decide such questions is the industrial tribunal,
> and that their decision should prevail unless it is plainly perverse or
> oppressive.'

[16] However, the EAT went on to add ([1991] ICR 648 at 652):

> '... it is open to an industrial tribunal to examine the procedures within a
> solicitor's office to see whether the tribunal feel that they are reasonable in
> the circumstances. In the present case, the originating application which is,
> in its substantial part, extremely short, was dictated on Friday, 9 March but
> it was not typed out until Tuesday, 13 and then it was signed and included in
> that day's post. There was a gap between the dictation and the typing and
> posting, and it might have been that that was open to criticism. However, in
> the future these matters will, no doubt, be carefully considered by industrial
> tribunals and we would venture to think that the mere evidence of
> expectation of delivery of a first-class post may not, in the future, provide an
> adequate explanation.'

[17] Miss Seymour submitted that in this passage the EAT was expressing a
significantly different view from that expressed by Phillips J in *Burton*'s case. That
is a matter to which I return.

[18] In *St Basil's Centre v McCrossan* [1992] ICR 140 the critical date had been a
Monday and the application posted to London from Birmingham by first class
mail the previous Friday. It had arrived late, on the Tuesday. The applicant relied
before the tribunal on his personal experience of receiving first class letters from

a his mother in Northern Ireland the day after posting, and the tribunal had believed him. They also formed the view (contrary to the applicant's own evidence) that he had deliberately delayed making his application until the last possible moment with the intention of causing maximum uncertainty and inconvenience to the respondents. The EAT declined to interfere with the decision, finding that there had been some evidence before the tribunal on which
b it could have concluded that the applicant had a reasonable expectation of delivery on the Monday. However the EAT indicated that in considering the question of reasonable expectation in future cases it would be reasonable for tribunals to look to the guidance given by the Queen's Bench *Practice Direction (post: first and second class)* [1985] 1 All ER 889, [1985] 1 WLR 489 made on 8 March 1985. That provided for a rebuttable presumption in the case of first class mail of
c delivery on the second working day after posting. The explanatory note to that practice direction had noted:

d 'It is no longer safe to assume that letters posted by first class mail will always be delivered on the following day. To reduce the number of applications by companies to set aside default judgments on the grounds of late service, more realistic assumptions are now prescribed.'

[19] This line of authority stands for three propositions: first, that 'where a claimant does an act within the period prescribed, which in the ordinary event would result in the complaint being made within the specified period, and that is
e prevented from having its normal and expected result by some unforeseen circumstance' the escape clause is available: see *Burton v Field Sons & Co Ltd* [1977] ICR 106 at 109; secondly that, if that condition is satisfied, it does not matter why the applicant has waited until the last moment; and, thirdly, that the question whether the condition has been satisfied is a question of fact, to be determined by the tribunal on the evidence before it.

f [20] Miss Seymour on behalf of Consignia invited us to review these authorities and submitted in particular that the second of the above propositions was wrong. In the present case she pointed out that the tribunal had made no finding as to why Mr Sealy had delayed making his application until the very end of the three-month period, and that in evidence before the tribunal he had not
g sought to proffer any explanation. In my judgment, however, the second proposition follows from the first: the effect of the first proposition is that a complainant is entitled to rely on the ordinary course of post. If that is correct there is no reason to penalise a complainant who has so relied for not having tried to present his complaint at some earlier point in the three-month period. I do not
h think that Wood J's remarks in the *Birmingham Midshires* case as to the possible need to examine the progress of the application in the solicitor's office were intended to do more than encourage tribunals to be sceptical as to evidence before them of particular expectations as to the ordinary course of post.

[21] There seems to me no reason to disturb the long-standing line of authority in support of the first proposition (no controversy exists as to the third).
j It is true that Lord Denning MR's observations in *Dedman v British Building and Engineering Appliances Ltd* [1974] 1 All ER 520, [1974] 1 WLR 171 were obiter, and their effect, as Phillips J noted in *Burton's* case, is to give the words 'not reasonably practicable' a meaning which they would not ordinarily hold. Parliament has, however, re-enacted the relevant provisions on more than one occasion in the intervening period. Giving the applicant the benefit of the ordinary course of post provides a workable (if generous) test of what is reasonably practicable, and

one which is familiar in analogous contexts (cf s 7 of the Interpretation Act 1978). At the same time, however, the interpretation thus placed on the statutory words should not itself be glossed in such a way as to allow all sight to be lost of the ordinary meaning of those words.

[22] The question therefore resolves into this: did the tribunal have evidence before it on which it could conclude that Mr Sealy had posted a letter which in the ordinary course of post could reasonably have been expected to arrive on the Saturday? Once the necessary findings have been made as to when the application was posted (a matter also under challenge in this case) the starting point for the inquiry must be what was the ordinary course of post. Miss Seymour submitted, on the basis of the 1985 Queen's Bench practice direction referred to by Wood J in the *St Basil's* case, that there was a rebuttable presumption that first class mail is delivered on the second working day after posting. I have difficulty in seeing the relevance of that practice direction (which is in any event no longer operative) to the question which the tribunal had before it. At best it provides evidence as to the experience of the Queen's Bench Division of the ordinary course of post in 1985. She was, however, on stronger ground in being able to point to an actual finding of fact by the tribunal as to what would have happened in the ordinary course of post. That is to be found in para 8 of the summary reasons where the tribunal had said 'if the post had run its normal course it would have arrived if not within the time period, immediately after the end of the time period'. That certainly seems to be an unambiguous finding that in the ordinary course of post the complaint would have arrived either on the Saturday or on the Monday. There undoubtedly was evidence before the tribunal on which it could reach that conclusion. Mr Sealy's own evidence (as recorded in the chairman's notes of evidence) had been that 'a first class letter should be delivered on 7 if posted 6' and, later, that 'If 6 October had been Monday—I would have posted that day and it would have got there Tuesday or Wednesday'.

[23] Given that finding, it appears to me that the tribunal could only find a reasonable expectation of delivery on the Saturday (as opposed to the Saturday or the Monday) on the basis of evidence of an expectation that something other than the normal course of post would apply in this case. In giving their extended reasons they appeared to be conscious of this difficulty, since they invoked the fact that the respondent had 'worked himself in the post office and knew the procedures'. The suggestion appears to be that Mr Sealy had some special knowledge which entitled him to assume that the risks inherent in the ordinary course of post would not obtain in his case. There was however no evidence before the tribunal supporting that suggestion and, in those circumstances, the tribunal was not entitled to draw any inference from the absence of evidence to the contrary from Consignia. The burden of establishing the facts necessary to give the tribunal jurisdiction notwithstanding the late presentation lay on Mr Sealy.

[24] In giving its extended reasons the tribunal would in my judgment have been entitled, had the evidence justified such a course, to re-visit the finding made in the summary reasons as to the normal course of post. They did not do so, no doubt for the very good reason that the evidence they had heard supported that finding. It is impossible to resist the conclusion that the tribunal, in seeking to correct the error of law displayed by the summary reasons, simply substituted a finding of fact, which was both inconsistent with that made in the summary reasons and supported by no evidence other than the bare statements recorded in the chairman's notes and quoted above. The first of those statements could possibly have supported a finding as to Mr Sealy's actual expectation, but not, without more, a finding that the expectation was a reasonable one. The second

of those statements, and the tribunal's own finding as to the normal course of post, was inconsistent with a finding that the expectation was a reasonable one. Accordingly I consider that the decision should be set aside and the matter remitted to a differently constituted tribunal for re-determination.

[25] Having come to that conclusion, it is unnecessary to consider the other grounds of appeal relied upon.

[26] I add that I agree with the guidance given by Brooke LJ in his judgment, which I have seen in draft.

LATHAM LJ.

[27] I agree. I have also read in draft the judgment of Brooke LJ with which I also agree.

BROOKE LJ.

[28] I also agree.

[29] CPR Pt 6 has introduced into the conduct of civil litigation in this country a clear set of principles governing the service of documents by post. Documents may be served by first class post (CPR 6.2(1)(b)). If a document is served by post, it is deemed to be served on the second day after it was posted (r 6.7(1)). Saturdays, Sundays, Bank Holidays, Christmas Day and Good Friday are excluded from this computation (CPR 2.8). In *Godwin v Swindon BC* [2001] EWCA Civ 1478, [2001] 4 All ER 641, [2002] 1 WLR 997 this court interpreted these provisions as meaning that even if it could be proved that the document had arrived by post on a day earlier than the deemed date of service, it must nevertheless be deemed to have been served on the deemed date of service. May LJ, with whom Pill LJ agreed, said ([2001] 4 All ER 641 at [46]) that uncertainties in the postal system made it sensible that there should be a date of service which was certain and not subject to challenge on grounds of uncertain and potentially contentious fact, particularly where claimants are wanting to serve a claim form at the very end of the period available to do so.

[30] So far as tribunals are concerned, if we are moving towards a regime in which there is a unified tribunal service along the lines recommended by Sir Andrew Leggatt in his recent report, it would appear desirable that there should be a unified regime for the service of documents of the same simplicity as that which is now available to the courts. It appears to me to be quite wrong that tribunals should be troubled with the volume of case law with which we have had to contend in this case, and I am not surprised that the employment tribunal got the law wrong when it first issued its summary reasons: I agree with what Hart J says about this aspect of the matter in his judgment (at [9], above) which I have read in draft.

[31] Until a simpler regime is introduced, the following guidance may be helpful. (1) Section 111(2) of the Employment Rights Act 1996 speaks of 'presenting' a complaint to a tribunal. It is now well established that a complaint is 'presented' when it arrives at the Central Office of Employment Tribunals or an Office of the Tribunals (the Office). (2) If a complainant or his/her agent proves that it was impossible to present a complaint in this way before the end of the time prescribed by s 111(2)(a)—for example because the Office was found to be locked at a weekend and it did not have a letter box—then it will be possible to argue that it was not reasonably practicable for the complaint to be presented within the prescribed period. (3) If a complainant chooses to present a complaint by sending it by post, presentation will be assumed to have been effected, unless the contrary is proved, at the time when the letter would be delivered in the ordinary course of post (see, by analogy, s 7 of the Interpretation Act 1978). (4) If the letter

is sent by first class post, it is now legitimate to adapt the approach contained in
CPR 6.7 and conclude that in the ordinary course of post it will be delivered on
the second day after it was posted (excluding Sundays, Bank Holidays, Christmas
Day and Good Friday, being days when post is not normally delivered). (5) If the
letter does not arrive at the time when it would be expected to arrive in the
ordinary course of post, but is unexpectedly delayed, a tribunal may conclude
that it was not reasonably practicable for the complaint to be presented within
the prescribed period. (6) If a form is date-stamped on a Monday by a tribunal
office so as to be outside a three-month period which ends on the Saturday or
Sunday, it will be open to a tribunal to find as a fact that it was posted by first class
post not later than the Thursday and arrived on the Saturday, alternatively to
extend time as a matter of discretion if satisfied that the letter was posted by first
class post not later than the Thursday. (7) This regime does not allow for any
unusual subjective expectation, whether based on inside knowledge of the postal
system or on lay experience of what happens in practice, to the effect that a letter
posted by first class post may arrive earlier than the second day (excluding
Sundays etc: see (4), above) after it is posted. The 'normal and expected' result of
posting a letter must be objectively, not subjectively, assessed and it is that the
letter will arrive at its destination in the *ordinary* course of post. As the present
case shows, a complainant knows that he/she is taking a risk if the complaint is
posted by first class post on the day before the guillotine falls, and it would be
absurd to hold that it was not reasonably practicable for it to be presented in time
if it arrives in the ordinary course of post on the second day after it was posted.
Nothing unexpected will have occurred. The post will have taken its usual
course.

[32] For the avoidance of doubt, the strict litigation rule in *Godwin's* case does
not apply in employment tribunal cases. If in such a case a complainant takes a
chance and the letter containing the complaint happens to arrive at the Office on
the day after it was posted and therefore within the permitted three-month
period, it will have been presented in time.

[33] It would be helpful if the effect of this guidance could be incorporated in
the booklet published by the Employment Tribunal Service to prospective
applicants.

[34] Applying the principles set out in this judgment to the facts of the present
case, I agree that the appeal must be allowed, and the matter remitted to a
differently-constituted employment tribunal for rehearing. It will be a matter for
that tribunal to decide whether in all the circumstances of this particular case it
would be just to extend time pursuant to its powers under s 111(2)(b) of the 1996
Act.

Appeal allowed.

Kate O'Hanlon   Barrister.

Anderton v Clwyd County Council
and other appeals
[2002] EWCA Civ 933

COURT OF APPEAL, CIVIL DIVISION
LORD PHILLIPS OF WORTH MATRAVERS MR, MUMMERY AND HALE LJJ
29, 30 APRIL, 1 MAY, 3 JULY 2002

Claim form – Service – Deemed day of service – Rule of procedure establishing deemed day of service of documents – Whether irrebuttability of deemed day of service incompatible with right of access to court – Whether Saturday and Sunday excluded from calculation of deemed day of service by first class post – Human Rights Act 1998, Sch 1, Pt I, art 6 – CPR 2.8, 6.7(1).

Claim form – Service – Dispensing with service – Whether court having power to dispense with service of claim form in circumstances where retrospective extension of time prohibited – CPR 6.9, 7.6(3).

Claim form – Service – Service out of the jurisdiction – Claimant issuing claim form marked 'Not to be served out of the jurisdiction' – Claimant applying for permission to serve out of jurisdiction before expiry of six-month period for such service but after expiry of four-month period for service of claim form within jurisdiction – Whether application governed by general provisions of CPR or by special provisions relating to service out of jurisdiction – CPR Pt 6, section III, 7.6(3).

Five appeals to the Court of Appeal all concerned the construction and application of provisions in CPR Pts 6 and 7 relating to the service of a claim form. In the first four appeals (the deemed service appeals), the claimants contended that CPR 6.7(1)[a], which established the deemed day of service for documents served, inter alia, by first class post and fax, was incompatible with the right of access to the court under art 6[b] of the European Convention for the Protection of Human Rights and Fundamental Freedoms 1950 (as set out in Sch 1 to the Human Rights Act 1998) in so far as it prevented a claimant from proving that the defendant had actually received the claim form before the deemed day of service. As well as challenging that contention, the defendants contended that Saturdays and Sundays were excluded from the calculation of the deemed day of service by first class post (the second day after posting) since, in two of the appeals, deemed service would have taken place before the expiry of the four-month period for serving the claim form if those days were included. The defendants relied on r 2.8[c], which was referred to in r 6.7 and provided that a Saturday or Sunday did not count in the calculation of any period of time for doing any act specified by the CPR where the specified period was five days or less. A further issue arose as

---

a   Rule 6.7, so far as material, is set out at [15], below
b   Article 6, so far as material, provides: '1.   In the determination of his civil rights and obligations ... everyone is entitled to a fair ... hearing ... '
c   Rule 2.8, so far as material, provides: '(1)   This rule shows how to calculate any period of time for doing any act which is specified—(a) by these Rules ...
   (4)   Where the specified period—(a) is 5 days or less; and (b) includes—(i) a Saturday or Sunday ... that day does not count ... '

to whether the court had power to dispense with service of a claim form under CPR 6.9[d] in cases where such a dispensation would constitute a retrospective extension of time for service specifically forbidden by CPR 7.6(3)[e]. In one of the appeals, the defendant appealed against an order granting such a dispensation. In the other appeals, the claimants appealed against orders striking out their claims on the ground that deemed service had taken place after the expiry of the claim form.

In the fifth appeal, the claimant issued a claim form stamped 'Not for service out of the jurisdiction'. He subsequently applied for permission to serve the claim form out of the jurisdiction. That application was made after the expiry of the four-month period for the service of the claim form within the jurisdiction, but within the six-month period permitted for service out of the jurisdiction. The master granted the application, but the defendant's appeal was allowed by the judge who applied by analogy the strict criteria governing extensions of time under CPR 7.6(3). On the claimant's appeal, the issue was whether the exercise of the court's discretion in such a case was governed by the criteria contained in r 7.6(3) or by the special provisions about service out of the jurisdiction in section III of CPR Pt 6.

Held – (1) The deemed day of service of a claim form under CPR 6.7 was not rebuttable by evidence of actual receipt of the claim form by the defendant, and that position was not incompatible with art 6 of the convention. The aim of r 6.7 was to achieve procedural certainty in the interests of both the claimant and the defendant. Certainty in the time of service of a claim form was an important requirement for the efficient performance of the case management functions of the court. It was legitimate to promote that aim by setting a deadline of four months from issue for service of the claim form by one of the permitted methods and by using the legal technique of deemed service to bolster the certainty. The requirement for service of the claim form within four months of issue, the range of permissible methods of service available and the days of permissible service or deemed service did not impair the very essence of a claimant's right of access to the court to enforce his civil rights. Moreover, justice and proportionality required that there were firm procedural rules which should be observed, not that general rules should be construed to create exceptions and excuses whenever those who could easily have complied with the rules had slipped up and mistakenly failed to do so (see [3], [36], below); *Godwin v Swindon BC* [2001] 4 All ER 641 applied in part.

(2) On the natural and ordinary meaning of CPR 6.7, Saturday and Sunday were not excluded from the calculation of the deemed day of service by first class post. Rule 2.8 did not in terms apply whenever there was a reference in the CPR to the calculation of a period of time of five days or less. It only applied to the calculation of any period 'for doing any act' that was specified by the CPR. Rule 6.7 did not specify a period of time for doing any act under the CPR. It set out the methods of calculating the days on which the event of service was deemed to happen as a result of doing acts under other rules involving the use of the various available methods for service of a claim form. It followed that two of the deemed service appeals would be allowed on the ground that deemed service had occurred before the expiry of the claim form (see [43], [63], [76], below);

---

d   Rule 6.9, so far as material, provides: '(1) The court may dispense with service of a document ... '
e   Rule 7.6, so far as material, is set out at [7], below

a   dicta of May LJ, Rimer J and Pill LJ in *Godwin v Swindon BC* [2001] 4 All ER 641 at [47], [59], [73], and of Brooke LJ in *Sealy v Consignia plc* [2002] 3 All ER 801 at [29] disapproved.

(3) The court had power under CPR 6.9 to dispense with service of the claim form, retrospectively as well as prospectively, but that power was exercisable retrospectively only in exceptional circumstances. There was a sensible and

b   relevant distinction between two kinds of case, namely (i) an application by a claimant, who had not even attempted to serve a claim form by one of the permitted methods, for an order retrospectively dispensing with service under r 6.9, and (ii) an application by a claimant, who had already made an ineffective attempt to serve a claim form by one of the permitted methods, for an order dispensing with service of the claim form. The first case would constitute an

c   impermissible attempt to circumvent the limitations in r 7.6(3) on the grant of extensions of time for service of the claim form. In the second case, the claimant did not need to serve the claim form on the defendant in order to bring it to his attention, but had failed to comply with the rules for service and was seeking to be excused from the need to prove service in accordance with those rules. In

d   exercising the dispensing discretion, it might also be legitimate to take into account other relevant circumstances, such as the explanation for late service, whether any criticism could be made of the claimant or his advisers in their conduct of the proceedings and any possible prejudice to the defendant on dispensing with service of the claim form. In the remaining deemed service appeals, the circumstances were appropriate for the making of orders dispensing

e   with service under r 6.9. Accordingly, the claimant's appeal would be allowed in one case, while the defendant's appeal would be dismissed in the other (see [3], [50], [55]–[59], [67], [84], below); *Godwin v Swindon BC* [2001] 4 All ER 641 distinguished in part.

(4) On an application for permission to serve a claim form out of the

f   jurisdiction after the expiry of four months from the issue of a claim form marked 'not to be served out of the jurisdiction', but before the end of the six-month period allowed for service out of the jurisdiction, the discretion of the court was governed by the special provisions about service out of the jurisdiction in section III of CPR Pt 6. The discretion was not governed directly or indirectly by CPR 7.6(3), nor by the criteria set out in that rule. On that basis, the fifth appeal

g   would be allowed (see [85], [97]–[99], below); *National Bank of Greece SA v RM Outhwaite 317 Syndicate at Lloyds* [2001] Lloyd's Rep IR 652 distinguished.

Notes

For calculation of time, extensions of time for service of the claim form, deemed

h   service and applications for permission to serve the claim form out of the jurisdiction, see 37 *Halsbury's Laws* (4th edn reissue) paras 143, 306, 323, 347.

For the convention right of access to a court, see 8(2) *Halsbury's Laws* (4th edn reissue) para 141.

For the Human Rights Act 1998, Sch 1, Pt I, art 6, see 7 *Halsbury's Statutes* (4th edn) (1999 reissue) 523.

j

Cases referred to in judgment

Ashingdane v UK (1985) 7 EHRR 528, [1985] ECHR 8225/78, ECt HR.
Dong Wha Enterprise Co Ltd v Crownson Shipping Ltd [1995] 1 Lloyd's Rep 113.
East End Dwellings Co Ltd v Finsbury BC [1951] 2 All ER 587, [1952] AC 109, HL.
Elmes v Hygrade Food Products plc [2001] EWCA Civ 121, [2001] All ER (D) 158 (Jan).

Fremont Insurance Co Ltd v Fremont Indemnity Co [1997] CLC 1428.

Godwin v Swindon BC [2001] EWCA Civ 1478, [2001] 4 All ER 641, [2002] 1 WLR 997.

Golder v UK (1975) 1 EHRR 524, [1975] ECHR 4451/70, ECt HR.

Infantino v MacLean [2001] 3 All ER 802.

International Bottling Co Ltd v Collector of Customs [1995] 2 NZLR 579, NZ HC.

IRC v Metrolands (Property Finance) Ltd [1981] 2 All ER 166, [1981] 1 WLR 637; *rvsd*
    [1982] 2 All ER 557, [1982] 1 WLR 341, HL.

Miragall Escalano v Spain App no 38366/97 (25 January 2000, unreported), ECt HR.

National Bank of Greece SA v RM Outhwaite 317 Syndicate at Lloyds [2001] Lloyd's
    Rep IR 652.

Phelps v Hillingdon LBC, Anderton v Clwyd CC, Jarvis v Hampshire CC, Re G (a minor)
    [2000] 4 All ER 504, [2001] 2 AC 619, [2000] 3 WLR 776, HL.

Sealy v Consignia plc [2002] EWCA Civ 878, [2002] 3 All ER 801.

Stubbings v UK (1996) 23 EHRR 213, ECt HR.

Totty v Snowden, Hewitt v Wirral and West Cheshire Community NHS Trust [2001]
    EWCA Civ 1415, [2001] 4 All ER 577, [2002] 1 WLR 1384.

Vinos v Marks & Spencer plc [2001] 3 All ER 784, CA.

Vitol Energy (Bermuda) Ltd v Pisco Shipping Co Ltd [1998] 1 Lloyd's Rep 509, CA.

Appeals

Anderton v Clwyd CC

The claimant, Rhiannon Anderton, appealed with permission of the Court of
Appeal from the decision of McCombe J on 25 July 2001 ([2001] CP Rep 110)
dismissing her appeal from the order of Master Ungley on 12 April 2001 striking
out her claim for negligence against the defendant, Clwyd County Council, on
the ground that it had not been served in time. The facts are set out in the
judgment of the court.

Bryant v Mike Beer Transport Ltd

The claimant, Andrew Bryant, appealed with permission of Judge Holman from
his order in Manchester County Court on 10 January 2002 striking out his claim
for personal injuries against the defendant, Mike Beer Transport Ltd, on the
ground that it had been served out of time. The facts are set out in the judgment
of the court.

Dorgan v Home Office

The defendant, the Home Office, appealed with permission of Judge Marcus
Edwards QC from his order made under CPR 6.9 in Brentford County Court on
11 October 2001 dispensing with service of the claim form in proceedings
brought against it by the claimant, John Dorgan. The facts are set out in the
judgment of the court.

Chambers v Southern Domestic Electrical Services Ltd

The claimant, Tina Wendy Chambers, suing as widow and administratrix of the
estate of her late husband Stephen John Chambers, appealed with permission of
Judge Graham Jones granted on 7 March 2002 from the order of District Judge
Wyn Rees in Cardiff County Court on 30 January 2002 striking out her claim
against the defendant, Southern Domestic Electrical Services Ltd, on the ground

a that it had been served out of time. The facts are set out in the judgment of the court.

Cummins v Shell International Manning Services Ltd

The claimant, Gregory Cummins, appealed with permission of Gray J from his decision on 5 September 2001 allowing an appeal by the defendant, Shell International

b Manning Services Ltd (Shell International Manning), from the order of Master Murray on 8 June 2001 granting Mr Cummins permission to serve the claim form on Shell International Manning out of the jurisdiction. The facts are set out in the judgment of the court.

c Nicholas Bowen (instructed by Teacher Stern Selby) for Ms Anderton.
Edward Bishop (instructed by Berrymans Lace Mawer, Manchester) for the council.
Simon Monty (instructed by Lyons Wilson, Manchester) for Mr Bryant.
Adrian Palmer QC (instructed by Hugh James Ford Simey, Bristol) for Mike Beer Transport.

d Christina Michalos (instructed by the Treasury Solicitor) for the Home Office.
Barry Coulter (instructed by JR Jones) for Mr Dorgan.
Nicholas Vineall (instructed by Robertsons, Cardiff) for Mrs Chambers.
Adrian Palmer QC (instructed by Hugh James Ford Simey, Cardiff) for Southern Domestic Electrical Services.

John Ross QC and Julian Waters (instructed by Dawson & Co) for Mr Cummins.
e Timothy Young QC and Edwin Buckett (instructed by Hill Taylor Dickinson) for Shell International Manning.

Cur adv vult

f 3 July 2002. The following judgment of the court was delivered.

MUMMERY LJ.

(A) INTRODUCTION

g *The five appeals*
    [1] The five appeals all concern the construction and application of provisions in CPR Pt 6 (Service of Documents) and Pt 7 (How to Start Proceedings—The Claim Form) relating to the service of a claim form. Four of the appeals (*Anderton v Clwyd CC, Bryant v Mike Beer Transport Ltd, Chambers v Southern Domestic Electrical*

h *Services Ltd* and *Home Office v Dorgan*) were heard together. They are about the effect of the provisions in r 6.7 for the calculation of the 'deemed day of service' of a claim form sent by first class post or by fax and the scope of the discretion under r 6.9 to dispense with service of the claim form in the light of (a) the recent decision of this court in *Godwin v Swindon BC* [2001] EWCA Civ 1478, [2001] 4 All ER 641, [2002] 1 WLR 997 (Pill and May LJJ and Rimer J); and (b) s 3 of the Human

j Rights Act 1998 and art 6 of the European Convention for the Protection of Human Rights and Fundamental Freedoms 1950 (as set out in Sch 1 to the 1998 Act). The fifth appeal (*Cummins v Shell International Manning Services*) was heard separately, following immediately the first four appeals. It is about the discretion to grant permission to serve a claim form out of the jurisdiction within the period of six months allowed for service by r 7.5(3).

Non-compliance with rules for service: warnings

[2] The consequences of failure to comply with the rules governing service of
a claim form are extremely serious for a claimant and for his legal advisers. The
situation becomes fraught with procedural perils when a claimant or his solicitor
leaves the service of a claim form, which has been issued just before the end of
the relevant statutory limitation period, until the last day or two of the period
of four months allowed for service by r 7.5(2) or, even worse, almost to the end
of an extension of time granted by the court. If the claim form is then served by
first class post, by fax or in another manner permitted by the CPR there is high
risk, demonstrated by *Godwin's* case and by the cases under appeal, of a successful
application by the defendant to strike out the claim on the ground of non-
compliance with the rules and of the cause of action then being statute-barred. The
risks never need to be run: they can easily be avoided by progressing the
proceedings in accordance with the spirit and letter of the CPR. Now that the
disputed interpretations of the CPR have been resolved by *Godwin's* case and by
this judgment, there will be very few (if any) acceptable excuses for future failures
to observe the rules for service of a claim form. The courts will be entitled to
adopt a strict approach, even though the consequences may sometimes appear to
be harsh in individual cases.

[3] Later in this judgment we explain our conclusions on the contested points
of interpretation, and we state the facts and outcomes of the individual cases
under appeal. In summary the legal position is that: (a) service of a claim form,
which has been sent by first class post or fax before the end of the period for
service, may, as a result of 'deemed service' under r 6.7, occur after the end of that
period; (b) the fact that the claim form has actually been received by, and come
to the attention of, the defendant or his solicitor through the post, by fax or by
means other than personal service within the period of four months allowed by
r 7.5(2) is legally irrelevant to ascertaining the day of service, as deemed by r 6.7;
(c) if an application for an extension of time is issued by the claimant after the end
of the period of service, the court will rarely have power under r 7.6(3) to grant
an extension of time and only in the most exceptional circumstances will it be
proper to exercise its discretion under r 6.9 to dispense with service; (d) the
limitation period applicable to the cause of action may by then have run out, so
that the claimant cannot issue and serve fresh proceedings against the defendant;
and (e) the claimant may have suffered substantial economic loss in consequence
of the claim becoming statute-barred, for which the only possible remedy left,
years after the original cause of action arose, is proceedings for professional
negligence against his legal adviser. That claim may be contested. Even more
substantial costs are bound to be incurred on both sides. If fought, the case will
inevitably take even longer to come to trial.

(B) THE RELEVANT PROVISIONS OF THE CPR

Time for service of a claim form

[4] Under r 7.5(1) and (2) the general rule is that, after a claim form has been
issued, it must be served on the defendant within four months after the date of
issue.

[5] Where the claim form is to be served out of the jurisdiction the period for
service is six months (see r 7.5(3)). Special provisions about service of the claim
form out of the jurisdiction and the circumstances in which the permission of the
court is or is not required are set out in section III of Pt 6 (rr 6.17–6.31).

Extension of time for serving a claim form

a

[**6**] Under r 7.6 the claimant may apply for an order extending the period within which the claim form may be served. The general rule is that an application to extend the time for service must be made within the period for serving the claim form specified by r 7.5 or, where an order has been made under r 7.6, within the extended period for service specified by that order.

b   [**7**] Only in restricted circumstances can the court grant an extension of time for service on an application made after the end of the specified period (see r 7.6(3)). On such an application, which must be supported by evidence, the court may make—

c

'such an order only if—(a) the court has been unable to serve the claim form; or (b) the claimant has taken all reasonable steps to serve the claim form but has been unable to do so; and, (c) in either case, the claimant has acted promptly in making the application.'

Methods of service

d

[**8**] Under r 6.2 a document may be served by any of the specified methods including, as well as personal service in accordance with r 6.4, first class post and fax. Under r 6.8 the court may make an order permitting service by an alternative method where it appears to the court that there is a good reason to authorise service by a method not permitted by the rules (such an order may be made prospectively, but not retrospectively: see *Elmes v Hygrade Food Products plc* [2001]

e   EWCA Civ 121, [2001] All ER (D) 158 (Jan)).

Deemed service

[**9**] Rule 6.7(1) tabulates in two columns the method of calculating the day of service. In the right-hand column there is the 'Deemed day of service', which is attached to the corresponding 'Method of service' in the left-hand column. Five

f   methods of service are covered. The provisions apply to a document served in accordance with the rules or any relevant practice direction. The two methods of service relevant to the appeals are first class post and fax.

[**10**] In the case of first class post the deemed day of service of a document is the second day after it was posted.

g   [**11**] In the case of fax the deemed day of service differs according to whether it is transmitted on a 'business day before 4 p.m.', in which case the deemed day of service is on that day, and in any other case, in which case the deemed day of service is on 'the business day' after the day on which it is transmitted.

[**12**] Rule 6.7(2) provides:

h

'If a document is served personally—(a) After 5 p.m., on a business day; or (b) At any time on a Saturday, Sunday or a Bank Holiday, It will be treated as being served on the next business day.'

[**13**] (In r 6.7(3) 'business day' in this rule is defined as meaning any day except Saturday, Sunday or a bank holiday; and 'bank holiday' includes Christmas Day

j   and Good Friday.)

Calculation of period of time

[**14**] Rule 2.8 in Pt 2 (Application and Interpretation of the Rules) is about the calculation of any period of time for doing any act which is specified by the rules or by a practice direction or by a judgment or order of the court. Under r 2.8(4)

where the specified period is five days or less and includes a Saturday or Sunday or a Bank Holiday, Christmas Day or Good Friday, that day does not count.

[15] In the rules, as originally drafted, r 2.8 was not mentioned at all in r 6.7. As a result of amendments (made by r 4(4) of the Civil Procedure Amendment Rules 2000, SI 2000/221), it is now expressly mentioned in r 6.7 in the following manner, immediately preceding the table:

'(1) A document which is served in accordance with these rules or any relevant practice direction shall be deemed to be served on the day shown in the following table ...

(Rule 2.8 excludes a Saturday, Sunday, a Bank Holiday, Christmas Day or Good Friday from calculations of periods of 5 days or less) ...'

Service of documents generally

[16] It is provided by r 6.1 that the rules in Pt 6 apply to the service of documents, except where '(a) any other enactment, a rule in another Part, or a practice direction makes a different provision; or (b) the court orders otherwise'.

Power of court to dispense with service

[17] The court may, on an application without notice, make an order dispensing with service of a document (see r 6.9). No criteria are specified in the rule for the exercise of discretion.

(C) GODWIN

[18] *Godwin v Swindon BC* [2001] 4 All ER 641, in which three judgments were handed down on 10 October 2001, is an important decision on the resolution of the 'deemed service' appeals. Its facts neatly disclose the disputed interpretations of the CPR and demonstrate the dire practical consequences for unfortunate litigants. Subject to the provisions of the 1998 Act, which were not mentioned in any of the judgments, the ratio of *Godwin*'s case is binding on this court.

[19] The claimant in *Godwin*'s case suffered a back injury on 26 February 1997. His claim form was issued on 17 February 2000, shortly before the end of the statutory three-year limitation period. Under r 7.5(2) the claim form was required to be served within four months. The court extended the time for service of the claim form until 8 September 2000. On Thursday 7 September 2000 the claimant sent the claim form and the particulars of claim to the defendant, who was his employer, by first class post. The documents were in fact received in the post by, and came to the attention of, the defendant on the next day, Friday 8 September 2000. That was the last day for service. The claimant contended that he had served the claim form in time. The defendant successfully persuaded the Court of Appeal that there was no valid service, as the effect of r 6.7(1) was that there was 'deemed service' of the claim form on Monday 11 September. That was three days after the last day for service. The court held that no extension of time for service of the claim form could be granted under r 7.6(3) and no order dispensing with service could be made under r 6.9. The result was that Mr Godwin's claim was struck out. No fresh claim form could be validly issued by him against his employer, as the cause of action was by then statute-barred.

[20] The court, in allowing an appeal by the defendant, concluded that—(a) the deemed day of service of a document derived from the table in r 6.7(1) was not rebuttable by evidence proving that the claim form had actually been received by the defendant on a different day; and (b) the court could not dispense with service

a   under r 6.1(b) or r 6.9, where such a dispensation would constitute a retrospective extension of time for service specifically forbidden by r 7.6(3).

Deeming point under r 6.7

[21] In order to grapple with the many points debated at the hearing of these appeals it is necessary to examine the judgments in *Godwin's* case more closely.
b   May LJ gave the leading judgment. Pill LJ concurred, though with some misgivings about the adoption of the legal fiction in r 6.7. Rimer J reached the same conclusion by a rather different route. May LJ said (at [46]) that r 6.7(1) clearly meant that—

> 'for each of the five methods of service, the day to be derived from the second column is to be treated as the day on which the document is served.
c   It is a fiction in the sense that you do not look to the day on which the document actually arrived, be it earlier or later than the date to be derived from the table. Thus in the present case, the claim form and other documents were posted a day late and the fact that they arrived earlier than the deemed day of service is no more help to the claimant than it would be
d   help to the defendant if they had arrived later.'

[22] In rejecting the submission that the deemed day of service was rebuttable by evidence of earlier actual receipt of the claim form, May LJ explained (at [46]) that his construction did not offend the overriding objective of the CPR:

> *e*   'Granted that the purpose of service is to bring the document to the attention of the person to be served, these are all methods of service other than personal service which are not bound to put the document literally into the hands of the person to be served on any particular day. All these methods of service will not achieve this unless the person to be served is there to receive the document or takes steps to do so by, for example, going to the
f   document exchange or checking the e-mail ... Uncertainties in the postal system and considerations of this kind make it sensible that there should be a date of service which is certain and not subject to challenge on grounds of uncertain and potentially contentious fact. It seems to me that parties serving documents by these means are in a better position if the deemed date for service is certain than if it is open to challenge on factual grounds. This
g   particularly applies to claimants wanting to serve a claim form at the very end of the period available to do so. The deemed day of service is finite and they will not be caught by a limitation defence where the last day for service is a Friday, if they post the claim form by first class post on the preceding Wednesday whenever it in fact arrives.'

h

[23] May LJ added (at [48]) that this interpretation of r 6.7(1) accorded with the general structure of the relevant rules. He observed that many of the documents to which the rule applies will be served by the court; that the practical working of the timetables by the court depends on secure dates, which are not liable to be challenged by evidence of when documents actually arrive; that potentially
j   variable dates for service of documents are likely to give rise to disputes assuming greater apparent importance than they deserve; that for the large majority of stipulated time periods the court has power, except where the rules otherwise provide, to grant discretionary extensions of time under r 3.1(2); and that a claimant serving a claim form is not disadvantaged by a deemed day of service which is irrebuttable by evidence.

Dispensing with service point: rr 7.6(3) and 6.9

[24] May LJ concluded that Mr Godwin could not be extricated from the consequences of late service of his claim form, where limitation was critical, by the use of the rule governing extensions of time for service of a claim form or by the rule governing dispensing with service. He explained (at [50]) that a person who has mistakenly failed to serve the claim form within the period permitted by r 7.5(2) in substance needs an extension of time to serve it. Rule 7.6(3) expressly restricts the power of the court to grant an extension. On the facts of *Godwin's* case an extension of time was not available to the claimant. The power to dispense with service of a document under rr 6.1(b) and 6.9 did not enable the court to order what was in substance an extension of time for service of a claim form, which was forbidden by r 7.6(3). Pill LJ agreed with May LJ.

(D) THE ISSUES

Deemed service

[25] Is the deemed day of service of the claim form under r 6.7 rebuttable by evidence of actual receipt of the claim form by the defendant? In our judgment, it is not. The reasoning in *Godwin's* case applies. The position is unaffected by the 1998 Act and art 6 of the convention.

[26] The ratio of *Godwin's* case was that the deemed day of service was irrebuttable by evidence. There was, however, no consideration of the impact of s 3 of the 1998 Act and art 6 of the convention on the construction of r 6.7. This is no doubt explicable by the fact that the proceedings in *Godwin's* case were commenced before the 1998 Act came into force on 2 October 2000. All the relevant events concerning the posting, receipt and deemed day of service of the claim form happened in September 2000.

[27] In the case of a deeming provision it is important to identify and take account of its purpose. In *IRC v Metrolands (Property Finance) Ltd* [1981] 2 All ER 166 at 180–182, [1981] 1 WLR 637 at 646, Nourse J reviewed the leading authorities, including *East End Dwellings Co Ltd v Finsbury BC* [1951] 2 All ER 587 at 598–599, [1952] AC 109 at 132–133, and summarised their effect:

'When considering the extent to which a deeming provision should be applied, the court is entitled and bound to ascertain for what purposes and between what persons the fiction is to be resorted to. It will not always be clear what those purposes are. If the application of the provision would lead to an unjust, anomalous or absurd result, then, unless its application would clearly be within the purposes of the fiction, it should not be applied. If, on the other hand, its application would not lead to any such result then, unless that would clearly be outside the purposes of the fiction, it should be applied.'

[28] On the deeming point Mr Vineall, appearing for the claimant in *Chambers'* case, made such clear and concise submissions that they were sensibly adopted without repetition or elaboration by counsel arguing against deemed service in the other three appeals. Mr Vineall accepted that, in the context of Pt 6, certainty as to the date of service of a claim form is important, as marking both the end of a period of time and the beginning of a forward timetable. He submitted that the purpose of the deemed day of service under r 6.7 is to protect the claimant from 'attention uncertainty' by preventing the defendant from seeking to prove that the claim form has not come to his attention within the time for service, either

a because he has not received the claim form at all or because he has received it late. It is, however, no part of that protective purpose to prevent the claimant from contradicting the fiction of deemed service by giving evidence to prove the fact that the claim form was actually received by, and came to the attention of, the defendant prior to the deemed day of service. The effect of the construction of r 6.7 in *Godwin's* case [2001] 4 All ER 641 produces, he argued, an absurd and
b potentially unjust situation, in which a defendant has not been validly served until a day or more after the day on which he admits to having received and seen the claim form. This result cannot have been intended by the draftsmen of the CPR, which refer to a glossary of expressions used in the rules (see *Civil Procedure* (Spring 2002) vol 1, p 1905 (G1.1): see also r 2.2(1)) including a description of 'Service' as 'Steps required by rules of court to bring documents used in court
c proceedings to a person's attention'.

[29] Mr Vineall submitted that the admission of uncontradicted evidence of receipt of a document to rebut the 'deemed day' of service would not detract from the legitimate aim of promoting procedural certainty. He cited s 7 of the Interpretation Act 1978 as an example of the deeming technique, which is used to
d achieve certainty in the service of documents, but at the same time allows the deemed service of a document to be rebutted by proof to the contrary. It provides:

'Where an Act authorises or requires any document to be served by post (whether the expression "serve" or the expression "give" or "send" or any
e other expression is used) then, unless the contrary intention appears, the service is deemed to be effected by properly addressing, pre-paying and posting a letter containing the document and, unless the contrary is proved, to have been effected at the time at which the letter would be delivered in the ordinary course of post.'

f [30] As Mr Vineall pointed out, Pill LJ observed in *Godwin's* case (at [72]) that the word 'deemed', as a matter of construction, is capable of meaning 'presumed until the contrary is proved' (see *International Bottling Co Ltd v Collector of Customs* [1995] 2 NZLR 579 at 584). It is submitted that it is possible to construe r 6.7, so as to allow the admission of uncontroversial evidence of actual receipt of the
g claim form by the defendant before the 'deemed day' of service, consistently with the evident protective purpose of the provision. If, as was recognised in *Godwin's* case, it is possible to read and give effect to r 6.7 in two different ways on the question of the rebuttability of the deemed day of service, this court is bound by s 3 of the 1998 Act to adopt the interpretation which is compatible with art 6 of
h the convention. The court is also bound by s 6 of the Act not to act in a way that is incompatible with the convention right.

[31] Mr Vineall contended that the construction adopted in *Godwin's* case is incompatible with art 6 of the convention, that it was reached per incuriam and that it should not be followed by this court. By preventing proof of the fact that the defendant received the claim form before the end of the period for service and
j before a 'deemed day' of service, which occurred after the end of the period, the claimant asserting a civil right is precluded from access to the court and the very essence of his right is impaired. It is accepted that the right of access to the courts is not absolute and that it may be subject to implied limitations (see *Golder v UK* (1975) 1 EHRR 524 at 537 (para 38)). Thus, procedural rules setting time limits that cannot be waived or extended and laying down timetables for the conduct of

litigation can, and often will, be lawful limitations on the art 6 right imposed in pursuit of the legitimate aim of the good administration of justice. The limitations are allowed by the margin of appreciation afforded to states in regulating the right of access to a court, provided, however, that the limitations (a) do not restrict or reduce the access in such a way or to such an extent that the very essence of the right is impaired; (b) pursue a legitimate aim; and (c) represent a reasonable relationship of proportionality between the means employed and the aim sought to be achieved (see *Stubbings v UK* (1996) 23 EHRR 213 at 233 (paras 48 and 52); *Ashingdane v UK* (1985) 7 EHRR 528 at 546 (para 57)). Subject, however, to those safeguards of the art 6 right, it is no part of the function of the Strasbourg court to substitute for the assessment of national authorities any other assessment of what might be the best policy in this field.

[32] Particular reliance was placed by Mr Vineall on the recent decision of the Strasbourg court in the case of *Miragall Escalano v Spain* App no 38366/97 (25 January 2000, unreported) (paras 37 and 38), in which the court concluded (at 38) that the domestic court's—

'particularly strict interpretation of a procedural rule deprived the applicants of the right of access to a court to have their claims for compensation examined ...'

[33] The case concerned the unreasonable construction of the domestic law procedural provisions as to the date from which time ran for the purpose of bringing an application for judicial review and so as to prevent a claim against the administrative authorities for compensation from being examined on its merits. The applicants lodged their claim against the administrative authorities one year and two days after delivery of judgment by the Supreme Court in proceedings to which they were not parties. The Supreme Court, which examined the applicants' claims as a court of first and last instance, held that the limitation period of one year ran not, as the applicants contended, from the date of the publication of the court's judgment in the *Official Gazette*, but from a date four months earlier when the judgment was delivered. The Strasbourg court held that the applicants could not be said to have acted negligently or to have erred in lodging their administrative law claims within one year and two days of the date of delivery of the judgment of the Supreme Court.

[34] It was argued before us that, although the provisions as to the 'deemed day' of service have the legitimate aim of achieving procedural certainty, the *Godwin* interpretation is unreasonably strict: it is disproportionate; it causes fiction to reign over fact; and it deprives the claimant of his art 6 right to have his claim determined by the court on its merits. A procedural rule designed to protect claimants by bringing certainty to postal and other permissible methods of non-personal service available to them, has been erected into an insurmountable barrier for the claimant: service on a day, which is out of time, is inflexibly and fictitiously imposed on claimants when the undisputed fact is that the claim form was received by the defendant in time.

[35] So, it is said, the decision in *Godwin's* case operates against the claimants and for the benefit of the defendants: it prevents a claimant, if he wishes to do so, from waiving his right to rely on the 'deemed day' of service and from relying on the day of actual service. That is not a legitimate aim. Its consequences for the claimant are unjust and disproportionate. Allowing the deemed day of service to be rebutted would not prejudice the defendant, who has in fact received the claim

a form before the end of the period: he is in the same position whether the claim form was posted by first class post on the day before or two days before.

[36] Despite the eloquence of the arguments we are not persuaded that the decision of this court in *Godwin*'s case is incompatible with art 6. We are therefore bound to follow it. The aim of r 6.7 is to achieve procedural certainty in the interests of both the claimant and of the defendant. Certainty in the time of

b service of a claim form is an important requirement for the efficient performance of the case management functions of the court. It is legitimate to promote that aim by setting a deadline of four months from issue for the service of the claim form by one of the permitted methods and by using the legal technique of deemed service to bolster the certainty. The rules employ a carefully and clearly defined

c concept of the 'service' of a document, which focuses on the stated consequences of the sending of the document by the claimant, rather than on evidence of the time of its actual receipt by the defendant. The objective is to minimise the unnecessary uncertainties, expense and delays in satellite litigation involving factual disputes and statutory discretions on purely procedural points. The requirement for service of the claim form within four months of issue, the range of permissible

d methods of service available at the option of the claimant and the days of service or deemed service specified for the different methods of service do not impair the very essence of the claimant's right of access to the court to enforce his civil rights. Under the Limitation Act 1980 and the CPR the claimant has full access to the court for the enforcement of his civil rights for a period, in the case

e of personal injury claims, of three years and four months (plus any further extension granted by the court). If the claimants in these cases are debarred from access to the court, it is not in consequence of a system of disproportionately strict procedural rules, which violate the fundamental right of access to the courts: it is as a result of the claimant, or of the claimant's legal adviser, waiting until almost the end of the generous period allowed for issuing and for serving

f the claim form, and then choosing at that last moment to use a method of service, such as postal service, without regard to the provision of the rules as to when service will be deemed to be effected if this method is used. The arguments appealing to proportionality, to justice and to the CPR's overriding objective of enabling the court to deal with cases justly lend no support to the case against an irrebuttable deemed day of service. Procedural rules are necessary to achieve

g justice. Justice and proportionality require that there are firm procedural rules which should be observed, not that general rules should be construed to create exceptions and excuses whenever those, who could easily have complied with the rules, have slipped up and mistakenly failed to do so.

h *Calculation of deemed service*

[37] Are Saturday and Sunday excluded from the calculation of the day of deemed service? In our judgment, they are not excluded. Neither r 2.8 nor the bracketed summary of its effect inserted in r 6.7 produces that result.

j [38] It is submitted on behalf of the defendants that the later amendment of the rules by the insertion in r 6.7 of the reference to r 2.8 must have been intended either to clarify and highlight the existing effect of r 2.8 or to achieve a new effect on the calculation of the day of deemed service. The intention must have been that Saturdays and Sundays should be excluded from the calculation of the day of deemed service, thereby reinforcing the objectives of certainty and consistency. It is sensible that service by first class post should only be deemed to occur on a day on which there is in fact postal delivery (ie a 'business day'), thereby facilitating immediate legal assistance for the defendant.

[39] The claimants' response is that the insertion of an incomplete summary of the text of r 2.8 is only informal and parenthetical: it is intended to be by way of a helpful cross-reference, reminding the reader of the existence and effect of the rule. This technique is used in other parts of the CPR in circumstances falling short of express incorporation and substantive effect. So, r 6.7 is not thereby expressly subjected to r 2.8 when, as a matter of the construction of the rules as a whole, it does not otherwise apply. The language of r 2.8 is quite simply not apt to cover or control r 6.7. Rule 2.8 relates to the time for the doing of an act. Rule 6.7 does not relate to the doing of an act at all: it is a deeming provision identifying the days, on which events are deemed to happen as the result of the doing of the act of service of the claim form under other rules eg under rr 6.2 and 7.5. So, Saturdays and Sundays and Bank Holidays are not excluded from the calculation of the day of deemed service by first class post under r 6.7.

[40] It was pointed out that, if the draftsman of the rules and of the amendments to them had intended to exclude Saturday and Sunday from the calculation of the day of deemed service by first class post, an obvious and more apposite way of achieving the exclusion was not to invoke r 2.8 nor to insert a parenthetical summary of it into r 6.7, but to make deft use of the available expression 'business day', as defined and used within the same rule; for example, in relation to the deemed day of service of the claim form by fax.

[41] On this point we conclude that Saturday and Sunday are not excluded from the calculation of the deemed day of service. There are obiter passages to the contrary effect in the judgments in *Godwin's* case (see May LJ (at [47]), Pill LJ (at [73]) and Rimer J (at [59])). May LJ said that McCombe J in *Anderton's* case (one of the other cases under appeal) was 'obviously correct to hold that r.2.8 applies to the periods in r.6.7 for the reasons he gave'. While commenting that 'the drafting is somewhat difficult to unravel', McCombe J concluded that the question was not resolved by the use of the defined expression 'business day' in r 6.7 and that (at [29])—

'the clear intention behind the reference to r 2.8 in r 6.7(1) is to indicate that Saturdays and Sundays etc should be similarly excluded from calculations of all kinds of deemed service, save those where express provision is otherwise made.'

[42] The point did not, however, need to be decided in *Godwin's* case, because deemed service on the Saturday in that case would in any event have been outside the period for service of the claim form. We disagree with the obiter statements on this point in *Godwin's* case and, more recently, in *Sealy v Consignia plc* [2002] EWCA Civ 878 at [29], [2002] 3 All ER 801 at [29].

[43] The court has had the benefit of fuller argument on the point than in *Godwin's* case and we conclude that, on the natural and ordinary meaning of the language of r 6.7, Saturday and Sunday are not excluded from the calculation of the day of deemed service by first class post. Rule 2.8 does not in terms apply whenever there is a reference in the CPR to the calculation of a period of time of five days or less. It is in restricted terms. It only applies to the calculation of any period of time 'for doing any act' which is specified by the CPR, by a practice direction or by a court order. Rule 6.7 does not specify a period of time for doing any act under the CPR. It sets out the methods of calculating the days on which

a the event of service is deemed to happen as a result of doing acts under other rules involving the use of the various available methods for service of a claim form. Service of a claim form is an act done under rules other than r 6.7.

[44] The fact that the express mention of r 2.8 is by way of a seemingly informal cross-reference in brackets is beside the point. What matters is the language of r 2.8, whether in or out of brackets, and whether it is apt to apply to r 6.7. In our

b judgment, the language of r 2.8 is not applicable to r 6.7, even if it had been the wish of the draftsman that it should apply. If it had been intended to exclude Saturdays and Sundays from the calculation of the deemed day of service by first class post, the draftsman would probably have used and, if he wanted to make the position clear, he ought to have used, the specially defined expression 'business day' to be found in and used in other parts of r 6.7. As it is, the word 'day', not

c the defined expression 'business day', is used in the part of the table in r 6.7 dealing with service by first class post. Saturday is a 'day' and so is Sunday. The fact that there is, or may be, no postal delivery to the defendant or to his legal adviser on either of those days or that there may be no one at the premises of the defendant or of his legal adviser to deal with documents that are delivered on

d those days is legally irrelevant to the operation of the fiction of deemed service. The deemed consequences inexorably follow from the method of service of the claim form selected by the claimant: they are not dependent on the particular circumstances of the defendant to whom the claim form has been posted.

[45] We are aware that this construction of r 6.7 appears to produce a surprising mismatch of the different times of deemed service of a claim form: if a

e claim form is sent by first class post at 5.15 pm on Friday, it is deemed to be served on Sunday; but, if it is faxed at 5.15 pm on Friday, it is deemed to be served on Monday; and if it is served personally at 5.15 pm on Friday, it is treated as being served on Monday. It is a matter for consideration whether r 6.7 should be amended. Surprising results are not uncommon, however, when a court obediently

f observes a legislative direction to leave behind the facts of the real world and to move into a fictional legal world, as deemed to exist by enactment. It is not argued that ss 3 and 6 of the 1998 Act require or entitle the court to reach a different construction.

Power to extend time for service

g [46] It is not contended that the court has power in any of the cases under appeal to extend the time for service of the claim form, but the reasons for this situation need to be stated as an introduction to the important arguments on the ambit of the power to dispense with service under r 6.9, which is invoked.

[47] In *Vinos v Marks & Spencer plc* [2001] 3 All ER 784, which was decided

h before the 1998 Act came into force, the Court of Appeal decided that the general power of the court in r 3.1 to extend the time for compliance with any rule 'Except where these Rules provide otherwise' does not extend to enable the court to do what is expressly forbidden by r 7.6(3). May LJ, with whom Peter Gibson LJ agreed, foreshadowed what he later said in *Godwin's* case when he concluded

j (at 789–790):

> 'The meaning of r 7.6(3) is plain. The court has power to extend the time for serving the claim form after the period for its service has run out "only if" the stipulated conditions are fulfilled. That means that the court does not have power to do so otherwise ... Interpretation to achieve the overriding objective does not enable the court to say that provisions which are quite

plain mean what they do not mean, nor that the plain meaning should be ignored ... There is nothing unjust in a system which says that, if you leave issuing proceedings to the last moment and then do not comply with this particular time requirement and do not satisfy the conditions in r 7.6(3), your claim is lost and a new claim will be statute-barred.'

[48] After the end of hearing oral argument our attention was drawn to the judgments in the very recently reported case of *Totty v Snowden, Hewitt v Wirral and West Cheshire Community NHS Trust* [2001] EWCA Civ 1415, [2001] 4 All ER 577, [2002] 1 WLR 1384, which was decided after the conclusion of argument in *Godwin's* case [2001] 4 All ER 641, [2002] 1 WLR 997, but before the judgments in *Godwin's* case were handed down. Kay LJ said (at [31]): '... those responsible for drafting the rules were singling out the claim form for exceptional treatment.'

[49] The Court of Appeal held that the 'exceptionally strict provision' in r 7.6(3) applicable to service of the claim form did not extend to service of the particulars of claim, which are not an integral part of the claim form and are subject to a discretionary power in Pt 3 to extend the time for service. The rationale for the distinction in the treatment of the claim form and the particulars of claim was explained by Kay LJ (at [37]) and concurred in by Chadwick LJ (at [46]) and by Peter Gibson LJ (at [48]):

'Until the claim form is served, the defendant may be wholly unaware of the proceedings. He may, therefore, because of his ignorance, be deprived of the opportunity to take any steps to advance the case. The same would not be true if the claim form had been served but the particulars of claim were outstanding. In such circumstances, it would be open to a defendant either to seek an order for immediate delivery of the particulars of claim, or, if it was justified, to seek to strike out the claim. Thus a very strict regime in relation to the claim form and a discretionary regime subject to the overriding objective is a perfectly sensible approach to the differing problems raised by the two types of failure to comply with the rules as to service.'

Dispensing with service

[50] Is there power under r 6.9 to dispense with service of the claim form? In our judgment, there is a power to do so retrospectively as well as prospectively, but it is only exercisable retrospectively in exceptional circumstances.

[51] It is submitted on behalf of the claimants that under r 6.9 the court has a broad discretion to dispense with service which can and should be exercised where the claim form has in fact been received by, and come to the attention of, the defendant or his legal advisers within the four-month period, even though service of the claim form is deemed by r 6.7 to have occurred on a day after that period has expired. They argue that there could be no better ground for dispensing with service of the claim form than that it has become unnecessary to serve it in order to bring it to the attention of the defendant.

[52] The decision of Douglas Brown J in *Infantino v MacLean* [2001] 3 All ER 802 was cited by the claimants for the proposition that r 6.9 gave the court power to dispense with service of a claim form, if that were necessary to give effect to the overriding objective of the CPR to deal justly with a case and to enable the court to achieve a just result. It was held (at [56]) that to strike out the claim in that case would be 'an affront to justice': the solicitors for the claimant had behaved impeccably; it was doubtful whether any claim for professional

a negligence would succeed against them, even though they had left service until
the last day; and the claim form was received only one day late as a result of
inserting the wrong DX number due to a computer error.

[53] The decision in *Infantino*'s case was, however, disapproved in *Godwin*'s
case (see [2001] 4 All ER 641 at [50] per May LJ). *Godwin*'s case is relied on for the
contrary argument that the claimants, who have failed to serve the claim form in
b time, are in need of, and are in reality seeking, an extension of time for service to
extricate themselves from the consequences of late service. Such applications are
governed by r 7.6(3). As already explained, in the circumstances of these cases no
extension of time could be granted. It was argued that an order dispensing with
service should not be granted, if it is in fact for the purpose of treating late
c ineffective service of the claim form as effective service. Rule 7.6(3) is a complete
procedural code for an extension of time for service of the claim form after the
end of the four-month period. The discretionary power to dispense with service
under r 6.9 should not be used as a means of circumventing and rendering
nugatory the statutory limitation provisions and to do what is forbidden by the
clear provisions of r 7.6(3). The court should only dispense with service where
d there is a possibility of effective service, which is capable of being dispensed with.
There is no possibility of effective service where, as is the case in some of the
appeals, the time for service of the claim form has already expired.

[54] It was also pointed out that the rules in Pt 6 apply to the service of
documents, except where a rule in another Part of the CPR makes 'different
e provision'. Rule 7.6 makes different provision. The power to dispense with service
cannot properly be used to validate late service of a claim form where no
extension of time is available under r 7.6(3). It is also submitted that r 7.5(2)
makes 'different provision' in that it is mandatory. It requires that a claim form,
which has been issued, 'must' be served on the defendant. So it must prevail in
f all cases and there is no power to dispense with service of the claim form.

[55] On this point we conclude that the r 6.9 is sufficiently widely worded to
entitle the court to dispense retrospectively with service of the claim form in an
appropriate case (cf the obiter view of Simon Brown LJ in *Elmes v Hygrade Food
Products plc* [2001] All ER (D) 158 (Jan)). The vast majority of applications, in
which it will be appropriate to make an order to dispense with service, will be for
g prospective orders sought and granted before the end of the period for service.
As a general rule applications made for retrospective orders to dispense with
service will be caught by the reasoning in *Godwin*'s case. There may, however,
be exceptional cases in which it is appropriate to dispense with service without
undermining the principle in *Godwin*'s case that r 6.9 should not be used to
h circumvent the restrictions on granting extensions of time for service as laid
down in r 7.6(3) and thereby validate late service of the claim form.

[56] In our judgment there is a sensible and relevant distinction, which was
not analysed or recognised in *Godwin*'s case, between two different kinds of case.

[57] First, an application by a claimant, who has not even attempted to serve
j a claim form in time by one of the methods permitted by r 6.2, for an order
retrospectively dispensing with service under r 6.9. The claimant still needs to
serve the claim form in order to comply with the rules and to bring it to the
attention of the defendant. That case is clearly caught by *Godwin*'s case as an
attempt to circumvent the limitations in r 7.6(3) on the grant of extensions of time
for service of the claim form.

[58] Second, an application by a claimant, who has in fact already made an ineffective attempt in time to serve a claim form by one of the methods allowed by r 6.2, for an order dispensing with service of the claim form. The ground of the application is that the defendant does not dispute that he or his legal adviser has in fact received, and had his attention drawn to, the claim form by a permitted method of service within the period of four months, or an extension thereof. In the circumstances of the second case the claimant does not need to serve the claim form on the defendant in order to bring it to his attention, but he has failed to comply with the rules for service of the claim form. His case is not that he needs to obtain permission to serve the defendant out of time in accordance with the rules, but rather that he should be excused altogether from the need to prove service of the claim form in accordance with the rules. The basis of his application to dispense with service is that there is no point in requiring him go through the motions of a second attempt to complete in law what he has already achieved in fact. The defendant accepts that he has received the claim form before the end of the period for service of the claim form. Apart from losing the opportunity to take advantage of the point that service was not in time in accordance with the rules, the defendant will not usually suffer prejudice as a result of the court dispensing with the formality of service of a document, which has already come into his hands before the end of the period for service. The claimant, on the other hand, will be prejudiced by the refusal of an order dispensing with service as, if he is still required to serve the claim form, he will be unable to do so because he cannot obtain an extension of time for service under r 7.6(3).

[59] In the exercise of the dispensing discretion it may also be legitimate to take into account other relevant circumstances, such as the explanation for late service, whether any criticism could be made of the claimant or his advisers in their conduct of the proceedings and any possible prejudice to the defendant on dispensing with service of the claim form.

(E) THE INDIVIDUAL APPEALS IN THE DEEMED SERVICE CASES

(I) *Bryant*

[60] On 27 July 1998 Mr Andrew Bryant was injured in a road traffic accident while driving his car near Otford in Kent. On 9 August 2000 liability was agreed 65%/35% in favour of Mr Bryant. On 18 July 2001 a claim form was issued in the Manchester County Court just before the expiration of the limitation period. The defendants were Mr Stephen Pech, the driver of a heavy goods vehicle involved in the accident, and his employers, Mike Beer Transport Ltd. There were four months in which to effect service of the claim form on them. The period would expire on Sunday 18 November 2001. On Thursday 15 November 2001 the claim form was sent by Mr Bryant's solicitors by first class post and recorded delivery. It was actually received by the defendants' solicitors at 11 am on Friday 16 November 2001. They contended that service was deemed to have been effected out of time and applied to strike out the claim.

[61] On 10 January 2002 Judge Holman in the Manchester County Court struck out the claim on the basis that it had not been served in time: the day of service deemed by the CPR was Monday 19 November 2001. He held that Saturday and Sunday were excluded from the calculation of the deemed day of service by first class post under r 6.7, read in conjunction with parenthetical reference to r 2.8. He applied the ruling in *Godwin's* case, by which he was bound, that the deemed day for service is not rebuttable by evidence of prior actual

a   receipt of the claim form. He declined to dispense with service under r 6.9. He granted permission to appeal.

[62] Permission was granted to amend the grounds of appeal to include additional arguments advanced in the cases of *Anderton* and *Chambers* on the rebuttability of deemed service in the light of the 1998 Act and art 6 of the Human Rights Convention and the power to dispense with service of the claim form.

b   [63] Applying the rulings above on the construction of r 6.7 to these facts we reject the arguments on the rebuttability point, but allow the appeal on the ground that the deemed day of service of the claim form was Saturday 17 November 2001 and that that was valid service within the period of four months allowed by r 7.5(2). In those circumstances it is unnecessary to consider whether this is a case in which it would be appropriate to exercise the discretion to dispense with
c   service under r 6.9.

(II) *Chambers*

[64] On 25 February 1998 Mr Chambers was fatally injured in a road traffic accident. Mr Chambers, who was riding a motorcycle, was involved in a collision
d   with a van driven by Mr Austin Emery, an employee of the defendant, Southern Domestic Electrical Services Ltd. He left a widow, Mrs Tina Chambers, and three children. Following the conviction of the defendant's employee in the magistrates' court, liability for negligence was admitted. Experts' reports on the quantum of damages were exchanged. A claim form was issued under the Fatal
e   Accidents Act 1976 and the Law Reform (Miscellaneous Provisions) Act 1934 on 15 February 2001, shortly before the limitation period was due to expire. There was a meeting between the experts. A joint statement was prepared. On the claimant's estimate the claim is worth £477,963.

[65] On 14 June 2001 District Judge Wyn Rees extended the time for service of the claim form to 13 July 2001. On Thursday 12 July 2001 the claim form was
f   sent by first class post to the defendant's solicitors. It actually arrived on the following day, Friday 13 July 2001, being the last day for service.

[66] By his order dated 30 January 2002 District Judge Wyn Rees struck out the claim, as the form had not been validly served within the prescribed period and the court had no jurisdiction to entertain the claim. The hearing had taken place
g   on 11 October 2001. Almost immediately after the hearing the district judge became aware of the decision in *Godwin's* case. He invited further submissions, which were made in writing. In a careful reserved judgment dated 21 January 2002 he held that under r 6.7 the claim form was deemed to be served on Monday 16 July, the second day after posting, as the intervening Saturday and Sunday were excluded by r 2.8. He applied the ruling in *Godwin's* case that the date of
h   deemed service is not rebuttable by evidence of actual service at an earlier date. He refused to make an order under r 6.9 to dispense with service, observing that the decision in *Infantino v MacLean* [2001] 3 All ER 802 relied on by the claimant was not followed in *Godwin's* case. Permission to appeal was granted by Judge Graham Jones on 7 March 2002.
j   [67] In the light of the above rulings on construction we conclude that, although the appeal fails on the rebuttability of deemed service point and is not saved by including Saturday 14 July 2001 as a deemed day of service, the appeal succeeds on the r 6.9 point. We consider that this is an appropriate case for an order dispensing with service of the claim form, as it can fairly be regarded as an exceptional case. The facts speak for themselves. It is agreed that the claim form

was in fact received by, and had come to the attention of, the defendant's
solicitors before the end of the four-month period for service. There has never   *a*
been any dispute on that point. By that time the defendant had admitted liability
(it was admitted as early as January 2000); negotiations on quantum had started;
the defendant was aware of the issues on quantum; attempts had been made to
settle the claim; and the defendant had made an offer to settle the claim for
£400,000. If the discretion is not exercised the prejudice to the claimant would be   *b*
very serious. If the discretion is exercised, the only prejudice to the defendant is
one contemplated by the power to dispense with service ie depriving it of the
potential point that service of a claim form, which it has already received in time,
in respect of a cause of action, on which it has already admitted liability, was
deemed to occur one day late on Saturday 14 July 2001.

c

(III) *Anderton*

[68] This case already has a long litigation history. On 5 July 2000, just before
the expiration of the limitation period on 6 July 2000, a claim form was issued by
Ms Rhiannon Anderton (who was born on 7 July 1979) seeking damages against
Clwyd County Council (the council). The claim is for the alleged negligence of   *d*
teachers employed by the council at primary schools attended by her between
1983 and 1990 in failing to identify her learning difficulties. On 27 July 2000 the
House of Lords gave judgment relating to pre-action disclosure in respect of
Ms Anderton's proceedings (see *Phelps v Hillingdon LBC, Anderton v Clwyd CC,
Jarvis v Hampshire CC, Re G (a minor)* [2000] 4 All ER 504, [2001] 2 AC 619). An order   *e*
for disclosure was made. Extensions of time were agreed for service of the
documents and for the service of the particulars of claim, but not for the service
of the claim form. The period of four months for service of the claim form expired
on Sunday 5 November 2000.

[69] It is first necessary to deal with two short factual points on the service of
the claim form arising from the judgment of McCombe J handed down on 25 July   *f*
2001 ([2001] CP Rep 110), against which permission to appeal is sought by
Ms Anderton on the r 6.7 point and the r 6.9 point and permission to cross-appeal
is sought by the council. McCombe J inferred that the claim form was posted on
Friday 3 November 2000, but it was only received by the council's solicitors on
Tuesday 7 November. The defendant council seeks permission to cross-appeal   *g*
on the date of posting, contending that the claim form actually received on the
Tuesday was not posted until Monday 6 November, after the expiry of the period
for service.

[70] The other factual dispute is whether the claim form was sent by first class
post. There was no evidence before the judge whether the claim form was sent   *h*
by first or second class post. He said that he could not infer that the claim form
was sent by first class post. On that view r 6.7 did not apply at all, the claim form
was not served in accordance with the rules and the appeal to him from the master
would fail on that ground alone.

[71] There is, however, an application dated 9 April 2002 seeking permission   .
to rely on fresh evidence in a witness statement of Ms Laura Berman that all   *j*
letters sent by the solicitors for the claimant are automatically sent as a matter of
routine procedure by franked first class post. The application, which was opposed
by the defendant council on the ground that the evidence could have been
obtained with reasonable diligence for use at the hearing below, was granted. It
appears that the council had not even taken the first class post point in argument

a at the hearing. If it had, the claimant would then have had an opportunity to make representations on it and to seek to serve further evidence, if required. In the light of the further evidence this court has no difficulty in finding that (a) the judge was entitled to find that the claim form was posted on Friday 3 November (permission to cross-appeal on that point is accordingly refused); and (b) the proper inference in all the circumstances is that it was sent by first class post (Ms Anderton's appeal on that point is accordingly allowed).

b [72] There remain the points of interpretation of rr 6.7 and 6.9 arising on the application for permission to appeal against the decision of the judge, dismissing an appeal from an order of Master Ungley dated 12 April 2001 and holding that, on the application of rr 2.8 and 6.7, that the claim form was deemed to have been served on Tuesday 7 November 2000 and that that was out of time. Permission c to appeal to a second tier was granted in view of the important points of principle and practice raised in this and the related appeals. Permission was also given to amend the notice of appeal to include grounds based on ss 3 and 6 of the 1998 Act and art 6 of the convention.

d [73] On the deemed service point the judge held that (a) the deemed day of service was rebuttable by evidence (in this case to show that the claim form was not received until Tuesday 7 November, after the expiration of the period of four months on Sunday 5 November); and that (b) deemed service could not occur on Sunday 5 November, which would have been just in time under the rules, because the clear intention behind the reference to r 2.8 in r 6.7(1) was to indicate e that Saturday and Sunday should be excluded from calculations of all kinds of deemed service, save where express provision was otherwise made. The result was that the deemed day of service and the day of receipt of the claim form were both Tuesday 7 November, which was out of time. As already indicated, the judge's view on (a) was not approved by the Court of Appeal in *Godwin*'s case f [2001] 4 All ER 641, but his view on (b) was approved in *Godwin*'s case.

[74] The judge also held, having referred to *Infantino v MacLean* [2001] 3 All ER 802, that the court had a general power to dispense with service under r 6.9 (a ruling which is challenged in the council's respondent's notice in the light of *Godwin*'s case), but went on to decide that it was not fair, just or reasonable on the facts of the case to dispense with service. He said that the claim was very old g indeed; that the claim form had been issued on the very edge of the limitation period; that the solicitors were well aware of both the time limit for service and that no extension had been agreed; that there was no evidence that the council was acquainted with the details of the claim to be made; and that the claimant had not adduced evidence that the defendants had suffered no prejudice.

h [75] It was submitted on behalf of the claimant that the facts were very similar to those in *Infantino*'s case and that his refusal to dispense with service was based on a failure to appreciate the reasons for the passage of time in proceeding with a claim of that kind. The council submitted that, if, which it disputed, the judge had a power to dispense with service of the claim form, this court should not j interfere with the judge's exercise of his discretion, as it could not be said that it was plainly wrong.

[76] In view of the earlier rulings on construction we allow this appeal on the short ground that, as the claim form was sent by first class post on Friday 3 November, the deemed day of service is Sunday 5 November. That was in time, being on the last day for service. We also allow the appeal to the extent that

the judge was wrong in holding that the claim form was not sent by first class post on Friday 3 November 2000.

(IV) *Dorgan*

[77] Mr Dorgan alleges that, while he was an inmate in Wormwood Scrubs Prison, he was assaulted by prison officers on 14 April 1995. The claim was investigated by the Home Office in May 1995, shortly after it was brought to its notice. He issued proceedings against the Home Office on 11 April 2000, just before the expiration of the limitation period. The claim form was not served. The period of four months for the service of the claim form expired on 11 August 2001 (a Saturday).

[78] At 4.02 pm on Friday 10 August 2001 the claim form and the particulars of claim were sent by fax by the claimant's solicitor. The receipt of the fax by the defendant's solicitor was recorded as commencing at 4.03 pm. The defendant's solicitors read it and made a telephone call about it to the claimant's solicitors soon after. They contended that the fax was not deemed to be served until the next business day, Monday 13 August 2001, after the expiration of the four-month period for service.

[79] On 11 October 2001 Judge Marcus Edwards QC sitting in the Brentford County Court held that he had no power to make an order for an extension of time under r 7.6(3), but, following the decision of Douglas Brown J in *Infantino*'s case, he granted an application under r 6.9 dispensing with service of the claim form. The judgments in *Godwin*'s case were handed down after the oral argument before the judge had concluded, so that he did not have the benefit of them. He granted the defendant permission to appeal. This court granted permission to amend the respondent's notice to rely on the 1998 Act and the convention.

[80] We reject the submission of Mr Coulter, who appeared for Mr Dorgan, that the methods of service contained in r 6.2 or as permitted by the court under r 6.8 are not exhaustive and that service of the claim form by one of the specified methods of service in Pt 6 does not have to be proved by the claimant in a case where, as here, there is no dispute that the claim form has been received by, and come to the attention of, the defendant's solicitor. He submitted that fiction should not be allowed to prevail over fact, leading to an injustice under rules, which had as their overriding objective that of 'enabling the court to deal with cases justly'.

[81] He emphasised that under r 6.2 a document 'may' be served by any of the specified methods and that the rule did not provide that a document 'shall' be served by one of those methods. They are not the only methods of serving documents. What mattered was that the recipient of the document was put in the position of ascertaining the contents of the document or that it was reasonably likely that he would be enabled to do so within a relevant time period.

[82] It is clear to us that r 6.2 does provide an exhaustive list of the methods of service unless the court permits an alternative under r 6.8. The word 'may' is used only to indicate that the person serving the document may choose between them. Mr Coulter's submissions confuse the legal concept of the 'service' of documents, as defined by the CPR, with the fact of receipt and the purpose of requiring documents to be served. It is true that the claim form was brought to the attention of the defendant's solicitors within the period of four months, as the fax was received on the Friday and its receipt was admitted, but the rules clearly provide that a fax sent after 4 pm is not deemed to have been 'served' until the

a   next 'business day', in this case the following Monday, which is after the expiry of
      the four-month period. For the reasons given earlier, it is not open to Mr Dorgan
      to adduce evidence of actual receipt in order to contradict the deemed day of
      service under r 6.7.

      [83] We have, however, concluded that the appeal should be dismissed on the
      ground that the judge was entitled in the exceptional circumstances of this case
b   to make an order dispensing with service of the claim form. It was submitted on
      behalf of the defendant Home Office that there was no material on which the
      judge could properly have exercised his discretion in favour of Mr Dorgan and
      that his order should be set aside: in particular, there was no explanation for late
      service of the claim form; the claim is stale, the alleged events having occurred in
      1995; and the effect of the order would be to deprive the defendant of the benefit
c   of an accrued limitation defence.

      [84] In our judgment, the judge was entitled to exercise his discretion under
      r 6.9 to dispense with service of the claim form. The judge inferred that the
      reason for the delay in the service of the claim form was that the claimant's
      solicitors erroneously believed that they had to serve the particulars of claim and
d   the medical report, as well as the claim form, within the period of four months.
      It is agreed that the claim form was received by fax on Friday 10 August only
      3 minutes after the 4 pm deadline for service by fax on that day and it came to the
      attention of the defendant's solicitor shortly thereafter. The period for service of
      the claim form did not expire until the following day, Saturday 11 August.
      Within minutes the defendant's solicitor faxed back to the claimant's solicitor
e   requesting that five more pages of the medical report, which had not come
      through, be faxed. That was then done. The application to dispense with service
      was made promptly after the claimant's solicitors were notified that it was not
      accepted that there had been effective service of the claim form. An order
      dispensing with service will not prejudice the defendant, other than depriving it
f   of a time point on the rules which may be removed by the exercise of the
      discretion under r 6.9. The defendant had already been notified of the claim and
      had been supplied with details of it in correspondence. On the other hand, the
      claimant will be prejudiced by a refusal to dispense with service, in that his claim
      will be statute-barred and he will be deprived of a trial on the merits of a claim.

g   (F) CUMMINS

      [85] The question on this appeal is whether, on an application for permission
      to serve a claim form out of the jurisdiction after the expiration of four months
      from the issue of a claim form marked 'not to be served out of the jurisdiction',
      the discretion of the court is governed by the criteria contained in r 7.6(3) relating
h   to the extension of time for serving a claim form? In our judgment, the discretion
      exercisable on an application made before the end of the six months period
      allowed for service of the claim form out of the jurisdiction is governed by the
      'Special Provisions about Service out of the Jurisdiction' in section III of Pt 6
      (rr 6.17 to 6.31). The discretion is not governed directly or indirectly by r 7.6(3),
      which does not form part of the 'Special Provisions', or by the criteria set out in
j   that rule. We allow the appeal from the order made by Gray J on 5 September
      2001 setting aside an earlier order of Master Murray, who gave permission to
      serve the claim form out of the jurisdiction, and striking out the claim against the
      second defendants.

      [86] On 10 February 1998 Mr Gregory Cummins, a seagoing marine engineer,
      was injured in an accident at work on a vessel, MS Halia, on which he was

employed as a third engineer. The claim is said to be substantial. On 2 February
2001, a week before the expiration of the limitation period, he issued a claim form
pleading negligence and breach of statutory duty and claiming damages for his
injuries and for loss of earnings. The claim form was stamped: 'Not for service
out of the jurisdiction.'

[87] The defendants were named as (1) Shell International Trading & Shipping
Co Ltd, an English registered company which owned and operated the vessel on
which the accident occurred, and (2) Shell International Manning Services Ltd, a
Singaporean company, which employed Mr Cummins and was stated to have an
address in the Isle of Man, which is outside the jurisdiction of the court as defined
in the CPR (see r 2.3(1)). A memorandum of agreement with Shell International
Manning expressly provided that the conditions of employment of British
Officers 'shall be governed by and construed in accordance with English law and
the parties submit to the jurisdiction of the English courts'.

[88] No attempt was made to serve the claim form on either defendant within
the period of four months mentioned in r 7.5(2). The time for service of the claim
form in the jurisdiction expired on 1 June 2001. Under r 7.5(3) there was six
months in which to serve the claim form out of the jurisdiction, but permission
to do so was required under r 6.20. Neither r 7.5(3) nor the 'Special Provisions'
in section III of Pt 6 about service out of the jurisdiction, as set out in rr 6.17–6.31,
expressly state the time within which an application for permission to serve out
of the jurisdiction must be made nor do they identify particular criteria applicable
to an application for permission to serve out of the jurisdiction made after the end
of the period of four months from the issue of the claim form.

[89] On 8 June 2001 Master Murray granted permission to serve on Shell
International Manning in the Isle of Man as a 'necessary or proper party to that
claim' under r 6.20(3)(b) on an application issued on the same day. He also gave
permission to renew the claim form, extended for 21 days the time for serving the
claim form on both defendants and provided for service to be effected on them at
the registered office of the first defendants (by way of substituted service on the
second defendants) by 6 pm on Sunday 10 June 2001. Service of the claim form
on the first defendants was the premiss in the rule under which the application for
permission was made and granted. An extension of time was accordingly
required under r 7.6(3) for service of the claim form on the first defendants in the
jurisdiction.

[90] On 20 June 2001 the claim form was served on the first defendants. The
claim against them is no longer pursued and has been struck out by consent. Shell
International Manning was unwilling to accept service within the jurisdiction.
On 25 June 2001 the claim form was served on Shell International Manning in the
Isle of Man. It was deemed to have been served on 26 June 2001.

[91] Thus the claim form was served out of the jurisdiction within the period
of six months from its issue, but pursuant to permission granted on an application
made after the expiration of the period of four months from issue of the claim
form.

[92] On 29 June 2001 an application notice was issued by the defendants to set
aside the orders. The application was ordered to be referred to the judge. On
5 September 2001 Gray J set aside the orders of Master Murray granting permission
to serve the claim form out of the jurisdiction on the first defendants as 'a necessary
or proper party' and the extension of time for service on both defendants. He struck
out the claim against Shell International Manning on the basis that the CPR

a required the application for permission to serve out of the jurisdiction to be made within four months of the date of the issue of a claim form marked 'Not for service out of the jurisdiction', even though the second defendants' address on the claim form is outside the jurisdiction, and that the court's discretion to extend the time for service should not be exercised. The claim form was not served on the first defendants within the four-month period prescribed by r 7.5(2). The application to
b extend the time for service was not made until after the expiration of the four-month period. There is a discretion to extend the time for service of the claim form, but it is a limited discretion. There was no explanation for the non-service of the claim form on either of the defendants within the period of four months. The judge applied by analogy the strict criteria governing extensions of time under r 7.6(3) to an application for permission to serve out a claim form out of the
c jurisdiction after the end of the period of four months. He noted the strict approach taken by the courts in cases such as *Vinos v Marks & Spencer plc* [2001] 3 All ER 784 to extensions of time for the service of claim forms. He gave permission to appeal.

d [93] Mr Young QC made it clear that Shell International Manning, for whom he appeared, accept that there was a submission to the jurisdiction in the memorandum of agreement and that he was not relying on any argument that the master's order granting permission to serve out of the jurisdiction was made on the wrong basis in the absence of service of the claim form on the first defendants in the jurisdiction within the period of four months from its issue.

e [94] He also explained that it was not now contended, as it had been before Gray J, that the application for permission to serve the claim form out of the jurisdiction must be issued before the end of the period of four months from the issue of the claim form. His submissions on the appeal focused on the criteria to be applied to the exercise of the discretion to grant permission to serve a claim form out of the jurisdiction after the expiration of the four months from the issue.
f He submitted that the criteria to be applied are by analogy those contained in r 7.6(3). Gray J had adopted that approach in his refusal to exercise his discretion to grant permission, in the absence of any satisfactory explanation for the delay in service. On well-settled principles, this court should decline to interfere with that decision.

g [95] Mr Young developed his submissions on the effect of the CPR by reference to the position under the RSC, as amended with effect from 16 December 1996 by art 4 of the Rules of the Supreme Court (Amendment) 1996, SI 1996/2892 relating to the duration and renewal of writs and concurrent writs in RSC Ord 6, rr 8(1) and (1A). The position following the amendments was
h that, for the purposes of service, a writ (other than an Admiralty writ in rem, which was valid in the first instance for 12 months) was valid in the first instance for four months, unless issued with leave to issue and serve out of the jurisdiction or for service out of the jurisdiction and duly indorsed, in which cases the writ was valid for six months. If an original writ had not been issued for service out of
j the jurisdiction, then, provided a concurrent writ for service out of the jurisdiction had been issued within four months from the date of issue of the original writ, such concurrent writ should in the first instance be valid for service out of the jurisdiction for a period of six months beginning with the date of issue of the original writ. The background to the changes was explained by reference to what Mr Young described as 'the old, old law' discussed in the judgment of Mance J in *Dong Wha Enterprise Co Ltd v Crownson Shipping Ltd* [1995] 1 Lloyd's Rep 113; to

the 'old law' discussed in his judgment in *Fremont Insurance Co Ltd v Fremont Indemnity Co* [1997] CLC 1,428; and to the decision of the Court of Appeal in *Vitol Energy (Bermuda) Ltd v Pisco Shipping Co Ltd* [1998] 1 Lloyd's Rep 509.

[96] The position under the CPR, it was submitted, was that a claim form was required by r 7.5(2) to be served within four months of issue, unless and until the claimant had established the right to serve it out of the jurisdiction in accordance with the provisions of rr 6.19 or 6.20. If permission to serve the claim form out of the jurisdiction was not obtained within four months of its issue, the criteria guiding the exercise of the court's discretion, when an application was made for permission to serve it out of the jurisdiction, would generally include those set out in r 7.6(3), especially when a limitation defence might otherwise be material. In support of this approach the recent decision of Andrew Smith J in *National Bank of Greece SA v RM Outhwaite 317 Syndicate at Lloyds* [2001] Lloyd's Rep IR 652 (a case of proceedings against a representative defendant, representing persons within the jurisdiction) was cited. He held (at 663 (para 46)):

'... if the effect of permission for service out of the jurisdiction is to breathe new life into a Claim Form after the four-month period, this will always be an important consideration in deciding whether or not permission to serve out of the jurisdiction should be given. CPR 7.6(3) restricts the circumstances in which a court may make an order allowing service of a Claim Form which has expired. Although CPR 7.6(3) does not, I think, directly apply to an application for permission to serve out of the jurisdiction in these circumstances, in deciding whether or not such permission should be given in a case such as this, the court should not ignore the strict approach stipulated in CPR 7.6(3) to extending service periods which have expired. If the effect of the order is to set aside the general rule of a four–month period and to extend it to six months and an application is made after the end of the four-month period, it would only be in rare cases that the court would permit service out of the jurisdiction unless the conditions stipulated in CPR 7.6(3) are satisfied. If, because the proceedings are representative proceedings, the effect of the order is to set aside the general rule and expose to a claim persons within the jurisdiction who are represented by the nominated defendant, the reasons for requiring the conditions of 7.6(3) to be satisfied upon the application for permission to serve out are all the more powerful.'

(The judge went on to hold that the conditions of r 7.6(3) were not satisfied in that case and that the discretion to permit service out of the jurisdiction should not be exercised to save the claimants from the consequences of not issuing and serving the proceedings more promptly.)

[97] Our conclusion on the construction of the relevant provisions of the CPR is that, on their natural and ordinary meaning, the discretion to grant permission to serve a claim form out of the jurisdiction is not subject to any express or implied requirement or condition (1) that the application must be made before the end of the period of four months from the issue of a claim form marked 'not for service out of the jurisdiction'; or that (2) different discretionary criteria apply to an application for such permission made after the end of the period of four months from the issue of the claim form than apply to an application made within that period; or that (3) the criteria set out in r 7.6(3) apply directly or indirectly to the exercise of the discretion, whether the application is made before or after the end of the period of four months from the issue of such a claim form.

[98] The relevant provisions governing permission to serve a claim form out of the jurisdiction are in the 'Special Provisions' in section III of Pt 6 (see also r 6.5(1)), not in the general provisions in Pt 7, save for the time for service of the claim form out of the jurisdiction in 7.5(3), as to which no extension of time was required, as the six-month period for such service had not expired. In those circumstances it would require clear words to restrict, in the manner contended for by Mr Young, the exercise of the discretion to grant permission to serve the claim form out of the jurisdiction. There are no such restrictive words in Pts 6 or 7 nor are there any strong contextual indicators that the discretion was intended to be so circumscribed. The historical context relied on in the references to the RSC concerning the duration and validity of writs and concurrent writs and the authorities on them throws little light on the construction of the language of the relevant CPR. The CPR on this point are modelled upon the previous County Court Rules rather than the RSC. In our view the decision in the *National Bank of Greece* case is plainly explicable by the special feature of the representative character of the proceedings. In the circumstances Master Murray was entitled to exercise his discretion to grant permission to serve the claim form on Shell International Manning out of the jurisdiction.

[99] For the above reasons we allow this appeal.

The Home Office's appeal dismissed. Other appeals allowed. Permission to appeal refused.

Kate O'Hanlon   Barrister.

Attorney General's Reference (No 1 of 2001)

[2002] EWCA Crim 1768

COURT OF APPEAL, CRIMINAL DIVISION

KENNEDY LJ, CURTIS AND PITCHFORD JJ

1, 11 JULY 2002

Criminal law – False accounting – Using false instrument – Whether prosecution having to prove that accused had no legal entitlement to money where he had used false instrument or furnished false information with a view to obtaining such money – Theft Act 1968, s 17(1)(b) – Forgery and Counterfeiting Act 1981, s 3.

The defendants were a married couple whose daughter had been arrested abroad and charged with a criminal offence. Their friends and neighbours launched an appeal, principally to meet the travelling and other expenses which it was foreseen the defendants would incur. The money raised was held in a bank account in the appeal's name. Without the defendants' consent, mail that was addressed to them was delivered to the fund organisers and opened by volunteers. The latter placed all moneys received into the account, without any consideration of the expressed intention of the donors. Some months later, a trust deed was executed, naming the defendants as beneficiaries and defining the trust fund as, inter alia, all money that had already been given in response to the appeal. In fact, a great deal of the money in the fund might well have consisted of money that had been donated to the defendants without qualification as to how it was to be used. Subsequently, the wife presented the trustees with an invoice apparently relating to accommodation expenses incurred by her and her husband. The trustees passed the invoice for payment and a cheque was duly made payable to the wife for the sum claimed. It was subsequently alleged that the invoice was false. The defendants were charged with an offence contrary to s 3[a] of the Forgery and Counterfeiting Act 1981, which made it an offence to use an instrument known or believed to be false with the intention of inducing somebody to accept it as genuine 'and by reason of accepting it to do ... some act to his own or any other person's prejudice'. They were also charged with dishonestly furnishing false information with a view 'to gain' for themselves contrary to s 17(1)(b)[b] of the Theft Act 1968. At trial, the judge accepted the defence submission that the jury could not convict on either count unless they were sure that no money had found its way into the trust fund when it ought to have gone to the defendants. He therefore directed the defendants' acquittal. In response to that ruling, the Attorney General referred a point of law to the Court of Appeal, seeking its opinion as to whether it had been necessary for the prosecution to prove that the defendants had had no legal entitlement to the money.

---

a   Section 3 is set out at [16], below

b   Section 17, so far as material, provides: '(1) Where a person dishonestly, with a view to gain for himself or another ... (b) in furnishing information for any purpose produces or makes use of any account, or any such record or document as aforesaid, which to his knowledge is or may be misleading, false or deceptive in a material particular; he shall, on conviction on indictment, be liable to imprisonment for a term not exceeding seven years.'

Held – Where an accused had used a false instrument or furnished false information with a view to obtaining money or other property, the prosecution did not have to prove, on charges under s 3 of the 1981 Act and s 17(1)(b) of the 1968 Act, that the accused had had no legal entitlement to the money or other property in question. In relation to an offence contrary to s 3 of the 1981 Act, the prosecution had to show that when the false document was used the defendant had been aware of the alleged prejudice and had intended it. In some cases the demonstrated existence of a claim of right at the time when the false document was used might negative an intent to cause another to act to his prejudice, but where, as in the instant case, the prosecution evidence had shown both an intention to induce the trustees to accept the false invoice as genuine, and the intention to cause them by reason of so accepting it to authorise and execute a cheque in the sum alleged, which in the circumstances it was their duty not to do, both elements of the mens rea were present. There was also clear evidence that the defendants had been acting with a view to gain for themselves within the meaning of s 17(1)(b) of the 1968 Act. Even if they had had a valid claim to some of the money in the trust fund on the basis that it should never have gone into the fund, and even recognising that they were beneficiaries under the trust, that made no difference because it did not relate to what they were doing at the relevant time. They were seeking to obtain hard cash as opposed to a mere right to claim. It followed that the defence submission should not have been allowed (see [1], [16], [26], [28], [29], below).

R v Garcia (1987) 87 Cr App R 175 applied.

R v Parkes [1973] Crim LR 358 approved.

Notes

For false accounting and using a false instrument, see 11(1) *Halsbury's Laws* (4th edn reissue) paras 572, 608.

For the Theft Act 1968, s 17, see 12 *Halsbury's Statutes* (4th edn) (1997 reissue) 507.

For the Forgery and Counterfeiting Act 1981, s 3, see 12 *Halsbury's Statutes* (4th edn) (1997 reissue) 719.

Cases referred to in judgment

R v Campbell (1984) 80 Cr App R 47, CA.

R v Garcia (1987) 87 Cr App R 175, CA.

R v Lawrence, R v Pomroy (1971) 57 Cr App R 64, CA.

R v Ondhia [1998] 2 Cr App R 150, CA.

R v Parker [1910] 74 JP 208.

R v Parkes [1973] Crim LR 358.

R v Tobierre [1986] 1 All ER 346, [1986] 1 WLR 125, CA.

R v Winston (1998) 1 Cr App R 337, CA.

Reference

Pursuant to s 36 of the Criminal Justice Act 1972, the Attorney General referred to the Court of Appeal for its opinion a point of law, set out at [1], below, arising on the acquittal of the defendants, on the judge's direction in the Crown Court at Chester in July 2000, on an indictment containing counts of using a false instrument contrary to s 3 of the Forgery and Counterfeiting Act 1981 and furnishing false information contrary s 17(1)(b) of the Theft Act 1968. The facts are set out in the opinion of the court.

David Perry (instructed by the *Crown Prosecution Service*) for the Attorney General.
The defendants did not appear and were not represented.

At the conclusion of argument, the court announced that the point of law would
be answered in the negative for reasons to be given later.

11 July 2002. The following opinion of the court was delivered.

KENNEDY LJ.

The reference

[1] When persons tried on indictment have been acquitted (in the present case
on the direction of the trial judge) the Attorney General may, if he desires the
opinion of the Court of Appeal on a point of law which has arisen in the case, refer
the point to this court, pursuant to s 36 of the Criminal Justice Act 1972, and this
court is then required to consider the point, and to give its opinion upon it. The
point of law which the Attorney General has referred to the court in this case is—

'Whether on (a) a charge under section 3 of the Forgery and Counterfeiting
Act 1981 and (b) a charge under section 17(1)(b) of the Theft Act 1968, where
the accused has used a false instrument or furnished false information with a
view to obtaining money or other property it is necessary for the prosecution
to prove that the accused had no legal entitlement to the money or other
property in question.'

Facts

[2] Before turning to the law it is necessary to summarise the relevant facts as
they emerged during the prosecution case at trial.

[3] G and S are husband and wife. In February 1997 their daughter X was
arrested abroad and was charged with a criminal offence. An appeal was launched
by their friends and neighbours, principally to meet the travelling and other
expenses which it was foreseen that the parents of X would incur. Initially an
appeal committee was formed and most of the money came from fund-raising
activities in the locality. At first the money was held in an account at the Post
Office. It was then transferred to 'the X Appeal' account at the Co-operative
Bank plc, and two members of the appeal committee were signatories to that
account. From February 1997 onwards G and S spent much of their time abroad.
They paid expenses by credit card, and were reimbursed from the bank account
on production of their credit card documentation.

[4] In late October 1997 X was convicted by the verdict of a jury, but in early
November the decision of the jury was set aside by the trial judge, who
substituted a conviction for a lesser offence, and X was released. There remained
an appeal against conviction, which was not determined until mid-1998. After
October 1997 approximately £250,000 was sent by members of the public to
either the organisers of the fund, G, S, X or Y (the youngest child of G and S).
Unbeknown to both G and S, and without their consent, mail addressed to them,
or either of them, was delivered by the Post Office to the organisers of the fund
and opened by volunteers, who placed all moneys received, without any
consideration to the expressed intention of the donors, into the fund's bank
account. S then approached an accountant, Michael Jackson, who suggested the
formation of a trust, and put her in contact with a solicitor, Paul Barrow. S met

a the solicitor on 18 November 1997. He then prepared a draft trust deed which she approved when she met him again on 2 December 1997. On 7 December 1997 the trust deed was executed by the five original trustees (the accountant and four others, who did not include either G or S). The declaration of trust begins with a reference to the arrest and trial, and the launch of the appeal, and it continues:

b   '4. The terms of the appeal as publicised in the news media and the appeal literature made it clear that the money raised by the appeal was to be used for the personal support of X and her family and (among other things) to meet travelling and other expenses, living expenses both abroad and in England, the cost of providing security against intrusion into their personal

c   lives, and generally to give practical help to a hard-working family devastated by the misfortune which had happened to them.

         5. Large sums of money have already been given in response to the appeal and it is expected that further sums will be given in the future.

         6. The Original Trustees have agreed to act as trustees of the funds collected by the appeal, and they wish to set out in this Deed the trusts on

d   which those funds are to be held.'

The trust was named 'the X and Family Trust' and 'the Trust Fund' was defined by cl 2.1.4 as—

         'All money which has already been given in response to the appeal; any

e   additional monies or investments or other assets which may hereafter be paid or transferred to the Trustees to be held upon the trust and with and subject to the powers and provisions of this Deed; all accumulations of income and other capital accretions; and the money investments and assets from time to time representing the same respectively ...'

f The beneficiaries were named as X, G and S and 'such other relatives or dependants of X or her mother or father as the Trustees from time to time determine'.

   [5] By cl 4.1 the trustees were authorised to hold the trust fund and income from it upon trust to pay or apply the same—

g   'to or for the benefit of all or any of the beneficiaries in such shares and in such manner as the Trustees in their absolute discretion shall from time to time decide and think fit.'

The trustees were given the additional power in cl 5 to hold the trust fund or any part of it—

h   'to or for the benefit of such organisations, institutions or purposes, whether or not charitable, as the Trustees in their discretion may select and think appropriate as serving such needs and purposes in the spirit in which the Trust Fund was raised by the Appeal.'

j [6] Clause 7 entitled 'Ultimate trusts for charity' provided that if the trustees determined that no further provision needed to be made for the beneficiaries out of the trust fund they—

       'shall thereafter hold the Trust Fund (or such part of it) upon trust for such charitable purposes as the Trustees shall determine (and in the selection of such charitable purposes it is desirable that the Trustees, without being

under any legal obligation in this respect, should select charitable purposes
in ways consistent with and commemorative of the generosity of those who
responded to the Appeal or otherwise contributed to the Trust Fund).'

When cross-examined Mr Barrow said that when the trust was set up there was
no way of discriminating between personal donations made to X or to her parents
and payments made to the appeal fund. The trial judge also found that at that
stage no one warned G and S that they were entitled to some of the money which
was transferred because it had 'come directly to them'. Mr Perry, who has
appeared before us for the Attorney General, accepted that the evidence was
silent as to whether S and G specifically consented to the transfer of all that had
been collected into the trust fund, but, as he pointed out, S purported to act for
herself and her husband, and she was kept fully informed. In discussion with
Mr Barrow she expressed some concern that money sent for personal use was
being mixed with appeal funds, but there was no evidence that she did more than
express concern, and where S and G were able to produce documents to show
that particular donations were for their unfettered use the trustees released that
money from the trust fund. The total thus released was only about £200, but it
was and is accepted by the Crown that a great deal of the money in the trust fund
may well have been donated to G and S without any qualification as to how the
money was to be used.

[7] On 21 January 1998 S provided the accountant Michael Jackson, in his
capacity as one of the trustees, with documents to support a claim for expenses
incurred in 1997. The documents included an invoice apparently relating to
accommodation expenses incurred by G and S between February and November
1997. At the trial the prosecution led evidence to show that the invoice was
misleading, false or deceptive in that—

'(1) It stated that accommodation had been charged for at the rate of $2200
per calendar month. (2) It stated that accommodation had been provided
from 1st April 1997 to 15th November 1997. (3) It (together with the entry
on the envelope accompanying it) implied by the stamp dated 27th
November 1997 that the sum of $15,400 had been paid to Elaine Whitfield
Sharp in settlement of the said invoice.'

On 29 January 1998, at a meeting of the trustees, the invoice was passed for
payment without comment, and a cheque was then made payable to G in the
sum claimed, £9,113·50.

Interview and arrest

[8] Seventeen months later, in May 1999, as a result of a complaint made by
persons abroad who claimed to have provided accommodation without charge,
G and S were interviewed under caution, in the presence of their solicitor, and
denied that the invoice was a forgery. As Mr Perry pointed out, they did not say
that they were entitled to the money because it was really theirs to use as they
chose. Criminal proceedings were then commenced, and in July 2000, in the
Crown Court at Chester, they stood trial on an indictment which contained two
counts.

[9] In count 1 the offence was using a false instrument contrary to s 3 of the
Forgery and Counterfeiting Act 1981 and the particulars alleged that they—

'On or about the 21st day of January 1998 used an instrument, namely a
document purporting to be an invoice, which was and which they knew to

be false, with the intention of inducing Michael Jackson and other trustees of the X and Family Trust to accept it as genuine and by reason of so accepting to authorise and execute a cheque in the sum of £9,113.50.'

Count 2 alleged furnishing false information contrary to s 17(1)(b) of the Theft Act 1968, and the particulars stated that on that day they—

'Dishonestly and with a view to gain for themselves, furnished information in a document produced to Michael Jackson, which to their knowledge was misleading, false or deceptive in material particulars namely ...'

The three particulars set out are those reproduced in [7], above.

Submissions

[10] At the conclusion of the prosecution case, counsel for G accepted for the purposes of his submission that there was evidence that the invoice was false in the respects alleged in count 2, but he invited the court to concentrate on the allegation that the defendants acted 'with a view to gain for themselves'. He contended that because some money transferred to the trust was money originally donated to G and S to use as they chose, the prosecution could not prove that the amount of money that was obtained on the invoice was not the money of G and S. Attention was invited to the definition of 'gain' to be found in s 34(2)(a) of the 1968 Act. Counsel submitted that—

'Even if the invoice is fraudulent they have not gained anything by the fraudulent invoice because all that has happened is that the trustees have passed over money which in fact is theirs.'

[11] As to count 1 counsel relied upon the wording of s 3 of the 1981 Act which makes it an offence to use an instrument known or believed to be false with the intention of inducing somebody to accept it as genuine 'and by reason of so accepting it to do ... some act to his own or any other person's prejudice'. The act specified in the indictment was the authorising and executing of the cheque for £9,113·50. Prejudice is defined by s 10(1) of the 1981 Act, and counsel referred to that subsection before submitting that if the money—

'is theirs to start with in law and becomes theirs as a result of any act done by the trustees then they have not gained because it was always theirs and there was no advantage.'

Ruling

[12] The judge was persuaded that the jury could not convict of either count unless they were sure that 'no money had found its way into the trust fund when in fact it ought to have gone to G and S'. Having briefly reviewed the evidence he concluded that some of the money in the trust fund 'must have belonged' to G and S. He continued:

'It follows in my judgment that the invoice could not be said to have induced the trustees to act to the prejudice of the trust fund. They, on the evidence, were returning money which G and S were entitled to in any event. Nor could it be said that what G and S did was with a view to gain for themselves, on the evidence. It may well be that they were entitled to the sum in the indictment or even a greater sum, one does not know, but in the

end my conclusion is that there is no evidence upon which the jury could *a*
properly convict upon either of these two counts.'

General comment

[13] Both the submissions made to the trial judge and the ruling seem to us to
betray some lack of appreciation of the legal effect of the creation of the trust and
the payment into the trust fund of money some of which, perhaps even most of *b*
which, we accept, could have been withheld on the basis that it was donated to
G or S or X to use as they chose. Once the money went into the trust fund it could
not realistically be described as money which was owned by any member of the
family. It was trust money, which, subject to the supervision of the court, was
under the exclusive control of the trustees. That remained the position even
though it would have been open to G and S to either (a) seek to persuade the *c*
trustees, or the court, to release part of the fund on the basis that it should never
have formed part of the fund or (b) seek from the trustees an advance of trust
funds in their capacity of beneficiaries.

[14] On the facts this is not a case in which the trustees were administering a
mixed fund, only part of which consisted of money subject to the trust. *d*

Law

[15] Having clarified the status of the fund from which G and S were seeking
to extract payment we turn now to the law, and look first at count 1.

[16] Section 3 of the 1981 Act provides: *e*

'It is an offence for a person to use an instrument which is, and which he
knows or believes to be, false, with the intention of inducing somebody to
accept it as genuine, and by reason of so accepting it to do or not to do some
act to his own or any other person's prejudice.'

In this case no issue was raised as to the meaning of the section. It was accepted, *f*
at least for the purposes of the relevant submission, that G and S did use an
instrument, namely an invoice, which they knew to be false, with the intention
of inducing the trustees to accept it as genuine, and by reason of accepting it to
do an act, namely authorising and executing a cheque in the sum of £9,113·50.
The only issue raised was whether there was evidence to show that it was an act *g*
to their own or any other person's prejudice, but as Mr Perry points out, there has
been some dispute as to the intention that has to be shown. Is it sufficient for the
prosecution to show that the defendant intended to induce somebody to accept
the false document as genuine, or must the prosecution also show that the
defendant intended his victim, by reason of accepting the document, to do or not *h*
to do some act to his own or any other person's prejudice? The authorities, as we
shall see, show that the double intention must be demonstrated.

[17] Section 10(1) of the 1981 Act, so far as is material, provides that an act
intended to be induced is to a person's prejudice if and only if it is one which
if it occurs— *j*

'(a) will result—(i) in his temporary or permanent loss of property; or
... (b) will result in somebody being given an opportunity—(i) to earn
remuneration or greater remuneration from him; or (ii) to gain a financial
advantage from him otherwise than by way of remuneration; or (c) will be
the result of his having accepted a false instrument as genuine, or a copy of a

a
false instrument as a copy of a genuine one, in connection with his performance of any duty.'

In the circumstances of this case it is sufficient to focus on s 10(1)(c) because when the cheque was authorised and executed that was the result of the trustees having accepted a false invoice as genuine in connection with their performance of their duty as trustees (cf R v Campbell (1984) 80 Cr App R 47).

b
[18] Two other subsections of s 10 need to be considered, namely:

'(2) An act which a person has an enforceable duty to do and an omission to do an act which a person is not entitled to do shall be disregarded for the purposes of this Part of this Act ...
(5) In this section "loss" includes not getting what one might get as well as parting with what one has.'

c

The relevance of s 10(2) is not immediately apparent, but it seems that it was probably inserted to meet the point made at p 17, para 34 of the Law Commission's *Report on Forgery and Counterfeit Currency* (Law Com no 55) (1973) which referred to R v Parker [1910] 74 JP 208—a case in which a naval rating was convicted of having forged a letter from the Admiralty urging a fellow rating who owed him money to pay the debt. Paragraph 34 continued:

d

'... in our view it should not be forgery to make a false instrument to induce another to do what he is obliged to do or refrain from doing what he is not entitled to do. Cases where the forged instrument contained menaces would be caught in appropriate cases by section 21 of the Theft Act 1968 as blackmail if the instrument were used. That we think is the stage at which such an offence should be prosecuted, the determining factor being whether the person believed that the use of the menaces was a proper means of reinforcing the demand.'

e

f
[19] Having regard to the way in which the trust fund came into existence, and to the terms of the declaration of trust, we find it difficult to see how, at the close of the prosecution case, it could be said that the authorisation and execution of the cheque should be disregarded because it was an act which the trustees had an enforceable duty to do.

g
Authorities
[20] Returning to the question of double intention, which the prosecution must show to have existed for the purposes of s 3, the first authority which we need to consider is R v Tobierre [1986] 1 All ER 346, [1986] 1 WLR 125. There the defendant had a wife and children living in St Lucia. He claimed child allowance, signed the child allowance vouchers in his wife's name and received payments. He was charged with the offence set out in s 3. His defence was that he believed that he was entitled to the money, and on appeal he contended that the trial judge should have directed the jury that the Crown had to prove that he intended the Secretary of State to act to his prejudice. Tudor Evans J, giving the judgment of the court, said ([1986] 1 All ER 346 at 349, [1986] 1 WLR 125 at 129) that when ss 3 and 10 are read together it is clear that proof of a double intention is necessary.

h

j
[21] In R v Campbell (see [17], above) the appellant was given a cheque by a friend, the cheque having been made out to a third party. She endorsed the cheque to herself and paid it into her account. When it was cleared she paid the proceeds in cash to her friend, who she believed to be entitled to the money. She

was charged with forgery contrary to s 1 of the 1981 Act in that she forged the
cheque with the intention that it should be accepted by the bank and with the
intention that another person should thereby be prejudiced. Ackner LJ, giving the
judgment of the court, reiterated the need for the double intention. In relation
to s 10(2) he said ((1984) 80 Cr App R 47 at 49):

> 'In our judgment, that subsection provides no assistance to the appellant
> for this simple reason, that it was the bank's duty to pay out only on a valid
> instrument and it is common ground in this case that that which was
> presented to the bank, and which was accepted by the bank, was a false
> instrument which it was not part of the bank's duty to honour. On the
> contrary, had the bank known of the true status of that document, they
> would have wholly rejected it.'

The same could be said of the trustees had they been under an enforceable duty
to meet a valid claim for expenses, but in fact no such duty was imposed upon
them.

[22] In *R v Garcia* (1987) 87 Cr App R 175 the need for the double intention was
underlined. First there must be an intention to induce the victim to accept the
false document as genuine, then, as Russell LJ put it (at 179) the question for the
jury should have been whether the appellant was aware of the prejudice alleged,
and whether he intended it.

[23] The appellant in *R v Ondhia* [1998] 2 Cr App R 150 used false documents
to obtain the release of goods from a pharmaceutical manufacturer. One issue
raised on appeal was whether it had to be proved that the intended act resulted
in actual prejudice to the manufacturer. That was rejected by this court, Judge LJ
saying (at 158) that the language of s 10 addresses 'the intended impact on the
recipient of the document, and the intended result defined in section 10 rather
than the achievement of that result'.

[24] In the present case it could be argued that in order to prove the second
intention (ie the intention to cause prejudice) the Crown had to displace the
defence raised at trial (but not at interview) that G and S only intended to obtain
the release of funds which were lawfully theirs, but the weakness of that
argument, as it seems to us, is that it fails to have sufficient regard to the prejudice
alleged, namely inducing by means of the false document the authorisation and
execution of the cheque for £9,113·50. The fact that had there been a properly
substantiated claim of right to a share in the trust fund, the trustees might have
authorised and executed a cheque in that or some other sum cannot mean that
they were not prejudiced by being induced to authorise and execute this
particular cheque in reliance on a false document, and that, as it seems to us, must
have been the prejudice which G and S intended.

[25] In *R v Winston* (1998) 1 Cr App R 337 the defendant when claiming
housing benefit used forged documents to show the rent he was paying. At trial
he contended that although the documents did not emanate from his landlord the
information in the documents was correct, and the local authority was therefore
under an obligation to pay him the housing benefit claimed, so there was no
prejudice. That was rejected both at trial and on appeal. Hobhouse LJ said (at 343):

> 'It is necessary in every case of an offence charged under section 1 to follow
> through the steps required by that section—(1) did the defendant make a
> false instrument, (2) with the intention that it be used to induce another to
> accept it as genuine, (3) and by reason of so accepting it to do or not to do

a some act, (4) to that person or some other person's prejudice? At step (3) it must be asked whether the act is an act which must be disregarded under section 10(2). If it is, then no offence has been committed under section 1. At step (4) it must be asked whether the prejudice comes within the definition in section 10(1). If section 10(1)(c) is relied upon, it is the act and duty of the person whom the defendant intended to induce to accept the

b document as genuine and act upon such acceptance which must be looked at.'

[26] As in the present case the offence alleged was contrary to s 3 of the 1981 Act and steps (1) and (2) can be reformulated as: '(1) did the defendant use an instrument which he knew or believed to be false, (2) with the intention of inducing another to accept it as genuine.' As to steps (3) and (4), in the light of

c the earlier authorities, which do not appear to have been cited in *R v Winston*, it needs to be emphasised that the Crown must prove the double intention. As Russell LJ put it in *R v Garcia*, the Crown must show that when the false document was used the defendant was aware of the prejudice alleged and intended it. In some cases the demonstrated existence of a claim of right at the time when the false document was used may negative an intent to cause another

d to act to his prejudice, but where, as here, the prosecution evidence showed both an intention to induce the trustees to accept the false invoice as genuine, and an intention to cause them by reason of so accepting it to authorise and execute a cheque in the sum of £9,113·50, which in the circumstances it was their duty not to do, then, as it seems to us, both elements of the mens rea were present, and

e the defence submission should have not been allowed to succeed. It was irrelevant that G and S may have intended to deprive the trust fund of no more than they would have obtained if they had pursued their claim in another way.

Count 2

f [27] The offence contrary to s 17(1) of the 1968 Act is committed where persons dishonestly, with the view to gain for themselves, in furnishing information for any purpose, make use of a document which they know to be misleading, false or deceptive in material particulars. The successful submission focused on the words 'with a view to gain for themselves'. Gain is defined in s 34(2)(a) as including 'a gain by keeping what one has, as well as a gain by getting

g what one has not'. In relation to blackmail, which is also governed by s 34, the question has arisen whether a person demanding money undoubtedly owed to him did have a view to gain. In *R v Parkes* [1973] Crim LR 358 that question was answered by Judge Dean QC in the affirmative. As he put it, by intending to obtain hard cash as opposed to a mere right of action in respect of the debt the

h defendant was getting more than he already had, and in his commentary on that case Professor Smith submitted that gain means acquisition, whether at a profit or not. That was the intention of the Criminal Law Revision Committee which at p 59, para 121 of its report *Theft and Related Offences* (Cmnd 2977 (1966)) stated: '... the person with a genuine claim will be guilty unless he believes that it is proper to use the menaces to enforce his claim.' In *R v Lawrence, R v Pomroy* (1971)

j 57 Cr App R 64 the point does not seem to have been argued, but convictions were upheld where threats were made to recover a debt.

[28] In our judgment *R v Parkes* was rightly decided, and it follows that on the facts of the present case, contrary to what was decided by the trial judge, there was clear evidence that G and S were acting with a gain for themselves. Even if they had a valid claim to some of the money in the trust fund on the basis that the

money should never have gone into the fund, and even recognising that they
were beneficiaries under the trust, makes no difference, because none of that
relates to what they were doing at the material time. They were dishonestly
making use of a false invoice to substantiate a claim for expenses, and thus to
extract from the trustees a cheque for £9,113·50. As Judge Dean put it in *R v
Parkes*, they were seeking to obtain hard cash as opposed to a mere right to claim.

Conclusion

[29] Accordingly, as we indicated after hearing the submissions which were
made to us, we answer in the negative the point of law which we have been asked
to consider and we do so for the reasons set out in this judgment.

Opinion accordingly.

                                        Lynne Townley   Barrister.

a
R (on the application of Theophilus) v Lewisham London Borough Council
[2002] EWHC 1371 (Admin)

b QUEEN'S BENCH DIVISION (ADMINISTRATIVE COURT)

SILBER J

24 JUNE, 8 JULY 2002

c *Local authority – Powers – Power of local authority to do anything it considers likely to achieve promotion or improvement of economic and social well-being of its area – Whether power including provision of student assistance – Local Government Act 2000, s 2.*

The claimant, who resided in the area of the defendant local authority, applied to the authority for student support to study at a college in Dublin. In April 2001 the
d authority told her that it would require further information before determining whether it would be possible for the authority to offer her financial assistance. A month later the authority informed the claimant that she was eligible to be considered for student support, and gave her a formal offer letter to that effect. She subsequently received confirmation of the level of fees that would be paid to
e the college on her behalf and of the amount of student support that she would receive. The claimant commenced her studies at the college in September 2001, and in October she received the first of the three instalments for her student loan. She later received a notice, again confirming that college fees and student loans would be paid to her, but also showing that she would receive a dependant's allowance in respect of her daughter. However, in December 2001 the authority
f informed the claimant that it had made an error and that she was not entitled to student support at all, whether in the form of fees or loans. She applied for judicial review, contending that the authority's statements had given rise to a legitimate expectation that she would receive financial assistance from the authority. That claim could succeed only if the authority had power to provide
g the claimant with student support under s 2(1)[a] of the Local Government Act 2000, a provision that empowered a local authority to do anything which it considered likely to achieve the promotion or improvement of, inter alia, the economic and social well-being of its area. By virtue of sub-s (2)(b), that power could be exercised in relation to, or for the benefit of, any person resident in its area. Subsection (4)(b) provided that the power under sub-s (1) included power
h for a local authority to give financial assistance to any person, while sub-s (5) provided that the sub-s (1) power included power to do anything in relation to, or for the benefit of, any person situated outside its area if an authority considered that it was likely to achieve any one or more of the objects of that subsection.

j **Held** – A local authority was entitled under s 2(1) of the 2000 Act to give financial assistance to any person resident in its area if it considered that it was likely to achieve the object of promoting or improving the economic or social well-being of any of its residents, and that would include giving student assistance.

a   Section 2, so far as material, is set out at [17], below

Subsections (4) and (5) gave sub-s (1) a much wider ambit than would appear
from reading that subsection alone. Furthermore, the extended meaning given
to s 2(1)(a) was such that it would cover a loan for student fees and student
support as well. It followed in the instant case that the authority did have power
to give student support to the claimant under s 2(1), but had not invoked or
considered that power. It had made clear and unambiguous statements to the
effect that it would be paying financial assistance to the claimant. In light of that
conclusion, the authority had acted unlawfully, especially since the claimant had
relied on the authority's representations. Accordingly, a declaration would be
granted that the authority was obliged to consider the claimant's claim in the
light of its representations to her (see [15], [16], [18], [21], [22], [25], [26], below).

Notes

For promotion of economic and social well-being, see 29(1) *Halsbury's Laws*
(4th edn reissue) para 412.

For the Local Government Act 2000, s 2, see 25 *Halsbury's Statutes* (4th edn)
(2001 reissue) 1475.

Cases referred to in judgment

Brown v Secretary of State for Scotland Case 197/86 [1988] ECR 3205.
Kohll v Union des Caisses de Maladie Case C-158/96 [1998] All ER (EC) 673, [1998]
    ECR I-1931, ECJ.
Factortame Ltd v Secretary of State for Transport (No 2) Case C-213/89 [1991] 1 All ER
    70, [1991] 1 AC 603, [1990] 3 WLR 818, [1990] ECR I-2433, ECJ.
*R (on the application of Bibi) v Newham London BC, R (on the application of Al-Nashed)
    v Newham London BC* [2001] EWCA Civ 607, [2002] 1 WLR 237.
R (on the application of J) v Enfield London BC, Secretary of State for Health intervening
    [2002] EWHC 432 (Admin), [2002] 2 FLR 1.
R v A [2001] UKHL 25, [2001] 3 All ER 1, [2002] 1 AC 45, [2001] 2 WLR 1546.
R v Board of the Inland Revenue, ex p MFK Underwriting Agencies Ltd [1990] 1 All ER
    91, [1990] 1 WLR 1545, DC.
Säger v Dennemeyer & Co Ltd Case C-76/90 [1991] ECR I-4221.
Van Binsbergen v Bestuur van de Bedrijfsvereniging voor de Metaalnijverheid Case 33/74
    [1974] ECR 1299.
Watson Case 118/75 [1976] ECR 1185.

Application for judicial review

The claimant, Abimbola Elizabeth Theophilus, applied for judicial review of the
decision of the defendant, Lewisham London Borough Council, on 10 December
2001 that she was not entitled to student support. She also applied for permission
to apply for judicial review of reg 5(4) of the Education (Student Support) Regulations
2001 on the grounds that it contravened art 49 of the EC Treaty and should be
disapplied. The Secretary of State for Education and Skills was joined to the
proceedings as an interested party. The facts are set out in the judgment.

John Walsh (instructed by *Straker Holford*) for the claimant.
Harini Iyengar (instructed by *Kath Nicholson*) for Lewisham.
Martin Chamberlain (instructed by the *Treasury Solicitor*) for the Secretary of State.

Cur adv vult

SILBER J.

a

INTRODUCTION

[1] Ms Abimbola Elizabeth Theophilus (the claimant) seeks to judicially review a decision of the London Borough of Lewisham (Lewisham) communicated to the claimant on 10 December 2001 that 'central government funding through the Education (Student Support) Regulations 2001 is not available' for her LLB

b course at Griffith College in Dublin. Sir Oliver Popplewell sitting as a deputy High Court judge gave the claimant permission to make this application, which then included a claim to enforce an alleged legitimate expectation that she would receive funding as a result of a representation made to her by Lewisham. The claimant now also seeks to claim that r 5(4) of the Education (Student Support)

c Regulations 2001, SI 2001/951 contravenes art 49 of the EC Treaty but she needs permission both to amend her claim form and to pursue that claim.

[2] The claimant is a citizen of the United Kingdom, who resides within the local authority area of Lewisham. In early 2001, the claimant first approached the Student Pupil Support Department of Lewisham to enquire whether she would

d receive student support if she studied law abroad. The claimant wished to study law abroad rather than in England because she had recently been through a stressful and traumatic episode in her personal life and she wished to make a fresh start. Her intention was to obtain a Bachelor of Laws degree and then to practise as a barrister in England.

e [3] The claimant was initially told by Lewisham that she would receive student support provided she studied anywhere in the European Union, but she chose to study at Griffith College in Dublin because its courses are accepted for qualification purposes by the Bar Council of England and Wales. In about April 2001, she made a formal application for student support to study law at Griffith College. By a letter dated 10 May 2001, Lewisham informed the claimant that she

f would be entitled to student support. Initially the claimant planned to study business and law, but she later decided to study law as a single subject instead. Lewisham was aware of the change in her course and it agreed that she would be eligible for student support for this law course.

[4] Having been told that she would receive student support, the claimant

g duly accepted a place on the course at Griffith College and she commenced her studies there on 24 September 2001. Before the claimant started the course, a financial assessment of higher education student support was sent to the claimant confirming the level of fees that would be paid on her behalf to Griffith College and the amount of student support that she herself could be paid. The claimant duly received, in October 2001, the first of the three instalments for her student

h loan for the academic year, which commenced on 24 September 2001. The claimant later received a further financial assessment for assistance form, again confirming that college fees and student loans would be paid to the claimant, but it also included additionally a grant for her young dependent daughter.

[5] In late October and early November 2001, the claimant became increasingly

j concerned that her college fees had not been paid and she telephoned Lewisham's Student Pupil Support Office on several occasions to enquire on the progress of the payment for those fees. The claimant was told that there were various technical problems in processing information, but that there was nothing for her to worry about. After previously warning the claimant on the telephone, on 10 December 2001, Lewisham wrote to the claimant informing her that it had

made an error and that she was not entitled to student support at all, whether in   *a*
the form of fees or loans. It is that decision that the claimant is seeking to
judicially review in these proceedings. The claimant has not received any student
support but to her credit, she has struggled by using her credit cards to complete
the first year of her course at Griffith College. She hopes by succeeding on this
application to be able to complete her course, which she started in the genuinely-
held expectation that she would be funded for it.   *b*

THE ISSUES

[6] In support of the claim to quash Lewisham's decision not to pay her student
support, Mr Walsh on the claimant's behalf, makes two submissions, which are,
in his words, that:

> *c*
> '(i) Lewisham acted unlawfully in (a) not abiding by legitimate expectation
> she had to be paid an amount of money equivalent to what she would be
> entitled to under the 2001 regulations in the form of support towards
> payment of her tuition fees, dependant's allowance and student loan and
> (b) not providing the claimant with this sum in the exercise of their discretionary
> powers under s 2 of the Local Government Act 2000 and s 137 of the Local   *d*
> Government Act 1972 to make such a payment in view of the manifest
> unfairness to the claimant because of the prior incorrect advice given by
> Lewisham that the claimant was entitled to support under the 2001
> Regulations (claim 1—legitimate expectation); and (ii) the 2001 Regulations
> in so far as they deny the claimant support that the claimant would be   *e*
> entitled to, were she to pursue her course of studies within the United
> Kingdom should be disapplied as they restrict the claimant's right to enjoy
> the freedom to receive cross-frontier services pursuant to art 49 of the EC
> Treaty (claim 2—art 49).'

[7] The second claim was introduced into the proceedings by the claimant as   *f*
a proposed amendment on 20 June 2002, just before the present hearing started.
No objection has been made to the amendment by Lewisham or by the Secretary
of State for Education and Skills, who has been joined as an interested party; so
I grant permission to make the amendment. Both Lewisham and the Secretary
of State contend, however, that permission should not be granted to pursue the
second claim and I will consider that issue when I analyse the second claim.   *g*

CLAIM 1—LEGITIMATE EXPECTATION

[8] The claimant contends that by reason of the statements made in
documents sent to her by Lewisham, she had a legitimate expectation that she
would receive financial assistance from Lewisham. This claim is disputed by   *h*
Lewisham, which contends that it did not make a statement or representation to
the claimant that it would provide her with student support and that in any event,
there has been no abuse of power by it for which judicial review would be the
appropriate remedy. It is also submitted by Lewisham that there could be no
claim for legitimate expectation of student support as it did not have the power
to provide the claimant with student support, but Mr Walsh contends that   *j*
Lewisham did have that power under s 2(1) of the Local Government Act 2000;
that submission is disputed by Lewisham. The Secretary of State was not directly
interested in or affected by claim 1 but Mr Chamberlain, her counsel, has made a
number of submissions almost as an amicus curiae on this issue, which were
supportive of the claimant's case.

a **[9]** Therefore there are four sub-issues to be considered, namely first whether Lewisham made a statement that was sufficiently clear that it would pay her student support, second, whether Lewisham had the power to provide the claimant with student support, third, whether Lewisham acted unlawfully in relation to that commitment in the letter of 10 December 2001, and finally, if she is successful on the previously mentioned issues, what remedy should be granted b to the claimant.

(i) Was a sufficiently clear statement or representation made to the claimant relating to the provision of student support for her?

[10] The claimant contends first that a representation was made that student support would be provided and that Lewisham would arrange it and second that c this representation is to be found in the correspondence to which I now turn. On 11 April 2001, Lewisham referred to the claimant's application for student support when its student support officer wrote to the claimant stating, with my italicised emphasis added, that 'before I may determine whether it will be *possible for* [*Lewisham*] *to offer you financial assistance,* you will need to submit the following d information and/or documentation'.

[11] On 10 May 2001, Lewisham wrote to the claimant and told her again with my italicised emphasis added that 'Lewisham Education is satisfied that that you are *eligible to be considered* for student support for ... studies at Griffith College. I enclose a formal offer letter to that effect.'

e **[12]** On 13 September 2001, Lewisham wrote again to the claimant enclosing a 'manual financial notification setting out the non means tested elements of student support'. It stated that the fees would be paid on her behalf of £1,075 and that a loan would be made available to her of £4,755. The claimant was also told in an accompanying letter to specify the amount of the loan required and to send that information to the student loans company as soon as possible. The claimant f then moved to Ireland and duly started her course later in September 2001.

[13] On 19 October 2001, Lewisham explained in a letter to the claimant that it had now 'reassessed your student support entitlement to include a dependant's allowance in respect of your daughter'. A new support notice was sent under cover of that letter showing that the claimant would receive not merely these g sums referred to in the previous notice, but also a dependent grant in respect of the daughter of £2,925; the claimant was told to write on the reverse of the notice the amount of the loan that she wished to take up. She had previously been asked on 19 September 2001 for information relating to her daughter who would be with her. While the claimant was studying on her course at Griffith College, she received oral notification followed by the letter of 10 December 2001, which, as h I have explained, terminated her student support, even though she was in the middle of the first year of her course.

[14] Lewisham contend that for there to be a legitimate expectation 'it is necessary that the ruling or statement relied on should be clear, unambiguous and devoid of relevant qualification' (per Bingham LJ in *R v Board of the Inland* j *Revenue, ex p MFK Underwriting Agencies Ltd* [1990] 1 All ER 91 at 110, [1990] 1 WLR 1545 at 1569). Mr Walsh does not dispute this contention or Lewisham's further contention that, as in the same judgment Bingham LJ also explained, 'in assessing the meaning, weight and effect reasonably to be given to statements of the [representor] the factual context, including the position of the [representor] itself, is all important'.

[15] Lewisham contend that they did not make any such statements to the effect that it would be paying financial assistance to the claimant. I am unable to accept that submission because the first relevant letter from Lewisham of 11 April 2001 stated that they 'may determine whether it will be possible for London Borough of Lewisham to offer you financial assistance'. That letter indicates clearly that Lewisham was to be the sole potential offering and paying party. The next letter of 10 May 2001 states that the only reason why a full offer was not then made was because the term dates for that course had not been provided by Griffith College. There is nothing in that letter or in the subsequent letter of 13 September 2001 to indicate that Lewisham would not be the paying party as had been envisaged in the letter of 11 April 2001. Indeed, as I have explained, the letter of 13 September 2001 actually gives details of financial support for the claimant.

[16] The clear implication from those letters of 11 April and 10 May 2001 was that once the dates were supplied, a formal offer of financial support would be made to the claimant and in the light of the letter of 11 April 2000, the clear and unambiguous implication would be that this offer of financial support would be from Lewisham. The later letter says that financial assistance would be forthcoming so that the position was that Lewisham represented that it would give financial assistance to the claimant. The subsequent letter of 13 September 2001 sets out details of payment and it fortifies my view that it had been represented that financial assistance would be available from Lewisham. The mere fact that there is subsequent reference to Student Support Regulations in correspondence does not negative that point, as there is no cogent evidence that it would have affected the offer or, if it did, that the claimant knew or ought to have known of this fact. By the same token, the letter of 19 October 2001 does not indicate that Lewisham would not be the paying party but in any event, by that time, the claimant had moved to Ireland and had already started her course. I have no doubt that she took those steps in reliance on the statements by Lewisham providing student support. It is clear from the forms that the claimant had completed in order to obtain assistance that she had no other assets.

(ii) *Did Lewisham have the power to make payment?*

[17] It is common ground that first the claim based on legitimate expectation must fail if Lewisham did not have the power to provide the claimant with student support and second that Lewisham is not empowered to pay student support under the 2001 regulations. The claimant, however, contends that Lewisham did have power to provide her with student support pursuant to the provisions of s (2)(1)(a) of the 2000 Act. The relevant provisions of s 2 state that:

'(1) Every local authority are to have power to do anything which they consider is likely to achieve any one or more of the following objects —(a) the promotion or improvement of the economic well-being of their area, (b) the promotion or improvement of the social well-being of their area, and (c) the promotion or improvement of the environmental well-being of their area.

(2) The power under subsection (1) may be exercised in relation to or for the benefit of—(a) the whole or any part of a local authority's area, or (b) all or any persons resident or present in a local authority's area ...

(4) The power under subsection (1) includes power for a local authority to—(a) incur expenditure, (b) give financial assistance to any person, (c) enter

a   into arrangements or agreements with any person, (d) co-operate with, or facilitate or co-ordinate the activities of, any person, (e) exercise on behalf of any person any functions of that person ...

(5) The power under subsection (1) includes power for a local authority to do anything in relation to, or for the benefit of, any person or area situated outside their area if they consider that it is likely to achieve any one or more b   of the objects in that subsection.

(6) Nothing in subsection (4) or (5) affects the generality of the power under subsection (1).'

[18] In support of his contention that Lewisham had power to provide student support under s 2(1) of the 2000 Act, Mr Walsh for the claimant places emphasis c   on sub-s (2), as the claimant was resident in Lewisham to show that the power in that section can be used for her benefit. He also points to s 2(5) which enables Lewisham to give benefit for the claimant outside the area 'if they consider that it is likely to achieve any one or more of the objects' in sub-s (1) and so he contends that Lewisham was empowered under s 2 to provide student support to d   the claimant. Subsection (4) also enables Lewisham to give financial assistance to an individual. Thus, I agree with Mr Walsh that sub-ss (4) and (5) give s 2(1) of the 2000 Act a much wider ambit than would appear from only reading s 2(1) of the 2000 Act.

[19] I was concerned as to whether s 2 gave the council a free-standing power to pay student support, which was independent of and not complementary to e   other legislation or other powers, and I asked counsel to see if they could derive any assistance from anything said in Parliamentary debates about the purpose and effect of s 2(1) but they were unable to find anything of assistance. The explanatory notes to the 2000 Act provide some useful material and as Lord Hope of Craighead stated in *R v A* [2001] UKHL 25 at [82], [2001] 3 All ER 1 at [82], f   [2002] 1 AC 45, 'it is legitimate to refer for the purposes of clarification' to these notes when construing legislation. Paragraph 15 of the explanatory notes states, with my italicised emphasis added, that—

'Together, these sections allow local authorities to undertake a wide range of activities for the benefit of their local area and to improve the quality of g   life of local residents, businesses and those who commute to or visit the area. This is intended to clear up much of the uncertainty which currently exists about what authorities can do. Sections 2 and 3 allow authorities to take any action, unless it is subject to statutory prohibitions, restrictions or limitations *specifically* set out in legislation. The intention is to *broaden the scope for local* h   *authority action* while reducing the scope for challenge on the grounds that local authorities lack specific powers.'

[20] Thus, it is said by Mr Walsh and Mr Chamberlain that this passage confirms that the power of this legislation is to confer very broad and general powers upon local authorities to be able to respond to the needs of local residents j   and businesses as also is shown in certain paragraphs in the guidance issued by the Secretary of State for the Environment, Transport and the Regions, which is entitled *Power to Improve or Promote Economic, Social, or Environmental Well-Being.* Paragraph 7 of this states that 'the new power is wide-ranging and enables local authorities to improve the quality of life, opportunity and health of their local communities', while in para 10, it is stated that—

'The breadth of the power is such that councils can regard it as a "power of first resort". Rather than searching for a specific power elsewhere in statute in order to take a particular action, councils can instead look to the well-being power in the first instance ...'

[21] In R (on the application of J) v Enfield London BC, Secretary of State for Health intervening [2002] EWHC 432 (Admin) at [53], [2002] 2 FLR 1 at [53], Elias J used these guidance notes and the statement of Lord Hope to reach a conclusion that the power conferred by s 2 was 'capable of extending to the grant of financial assistance for acquiring accommodation'. I respectfully agree with Elias J. No cogent reason was put forward by Ms Iyengar on behalf of Lewisham to show why a different decision from that arrived at in the Enfield case should be reached in the present case in respect of financial assistance for the claimant and her daughter while she was studying at Griffith College. Furthermore, in any event, the extended meaning given to s 2(1)(a) by other parts of s 2 of the 2000 Act is such that I consider that it would cover a loan for student fees and student support as well.

[22] In other words, Lewisham is entitled under s 2(1) of the 2000 Act, subject to the s 3 point raised at [23], below, to give financial assistance to any person resident in Lewisham (s 2(2)(b) and 2(4)(b) of the 2000 Act) if they consider that it is likely to achieve the object of promoting or improving the economic or social well-being of any resident of Lewisham (s 2(5), 2(1)(a) and (b) and 2(2)(b) of the 2000 Act). This would include giving student assistance to the claimant.

[23] Ms Iyengar submitted that Lewisham's powers under s 2(1) were limited by s 3(1) of the 2000 Act which states that s 2(1) powers do 'not enable a local authority to do anything which they are unable to do by virtue of any prohibition, restriction or limitation on their powers which is contained in any enactment (whenever passed or made)'. Elias J also had to consider this provision in the Enfield London BC case and he explained (at [57]) in relation to s 3:

'It is drafted in very broad terms which provide a source of power enabling authorities to do many things which they could not hitherto have done. In my view, a "prohibition, restriction or limitation" is one which will almost always be found in an express legislature provision. I do not discount the possibility that such might arise by necessary implication, but I would have thought that would be very rare.'

[24] I respectfully agree and it will be recalled that as I explained at [19], above, para 15 of the explanatory notes refers with my italicised emphasis added in relation to s 3 refers to 'statutory prohibitions, restrictions or limitations specifically set out in legislation'. Lewisham contends that there is a 'restriction or limitation' in this case as the Teaching and Higher Education Act 1998 contains provisions enabling the Secretary of State to transfer or delegate functions relating to student support to a Local Education Authority, who would then have to comply with any directions given by the Secretary of State in exercise of their functions (ss 22 and 23). No such power has been delegated to Lewisham but it is said that these provisions in the 1998 Act amount to a 'prohibition, restriction or limitation' of the kind envisaged by s 3 of the 2000 Act on the powers of Lewisham to invoke s 2(1) for providing student support to the claimant.

[25] I am unable to agree as the powers under the 1998 Act come from a different financing regime for which the Secretary of State, and not Lewisham, is responsible. I cannot discover any express or implied statement in the 1998 Act

a that it is an exclusive and comprehensive form of funding for students so as to limit or restrict the funding powers of Lewisham. In any event, I would have difficulty in finding that the 1998 Act contained a 'prohibition, restriction or limitation' affecting the subsequent 2000 Act especially as there is no reference in the 1998 Act, whether by later amendment or otherwise, to the 2000 Act or it being the only way in which funding could be made available to students. In

b addition, as I have already explained, s 2 of the 2000 Act is a free-standing and separate source of power given to local authorities such as Lewisham. Thus, I conclude that Lewisham did have power to give student support to the claimant pursuant to s 2(1) of the 2000 Act.

c *(iii) Did Lewisham act unlawfully in relation to its commitment?*

[26] It is clear that Lewisham did not invoke its powers under s 2(1) of the 2000 Act for providing funding for the claimant. As Schiemann LJ explained in giving the judgment of the Court of Appeal in *R (on the application of Bibi) v Newham London BC, R (on the application of Al-Nashed) v Newham London BC* [2001] EWCA Civ 607 at [39], [2002] 1 WLR 237 at [39]:

d

> '... on any view, if an authority without even considering the fact that it is in breach of a promise which has given rise to a legitimate expectation that it will be honoured, makes a decision to adopt a course of action at variance with the promise then the authority is abusing its powers.'

e The evidence adduced by Lewisham indicates that this is the position in this case, as there is nothing to indicate that it considered the promise. Lewisham clearly did not even appreciate what powers it had under those provisions and so it did not consider them. In the light of my conclusions about the representations made, it follows that Lewisham acted unlawfully, especially as the claimant relied

f on Lewisham's representations.

(iv) What remedy should be given to the claimant?

[27] In *Bibi's* case, Schiemann LJ specified (at [19]) the conditions that have to be satisfied, namely that the court should intervene:

g

> 'In all legitimate expectation cases, whether substantive or procedural, three practical questions arise. The first question is to what has the public authority, whether by practice or by promise, committed itself; the second is whether the authority has acted or proposes to act unlawfully in relation to that commitment; the third is what the court should do.'

h

[28] At the hearing, I deferred hearing submissions on the relief that should be given to the claimant until, as has turned out to be the case, she was successful on the first claim. So I await those submissions after handing down judgment if convenient from counsel for the parties interested in that claim, namely the claimant and for Lewisham, on, in particular, whether I should follow the guidance of

j the Court of Appeal in *Bibi's* case in which Schiemann LJ said (at [41]):

> 'The court, even where it finds that the applicant has a legitimate expectation of some benefit, will not order the authority to honour its promise where to do so would be to assume the powers of the executive. Once the court has established such an abuse it may ask the decision taker to

take the legitimate expectation properly into account in the decision making process.'

[29] In *Bibi*'s case, remission to the decision-maker was the course adopted by the Court of Appeal (at [69]). This might be the appropriate course for the claimant in this case but I await submissions. If the matter is remitted to Lewisham, it would be expected to reach a speedy decision as the claimant's second year course starts soon and it might appear appropriate in those circumstances for me to give the claimant liberty to apply. Nevertheless, Lewisham might consider that the proper course for them to adopt on receiving this judgment is to agree to pay for the claimant's future student support, especially as she has now completed one year of her degree course.

CLAIM 2—ART 49

The claimant's submissions

[30] The claimant contends that the court should disapply the 2001 regulations in so far as they deny the claimant support that the claimant would have been entitled to, were she to pursue her course of studies within the United Kingdom. The reason is that the regulations restrict the claimant's right to enjoy the freedom to receive cross-frontier services in the form of student support in breach of art 49 of the EC Treaty. Mr Walsh develops this point by saying that the claimant is a citizen of the European Economic Area, who is in receipt of services in another member state and that the restrictions on both the provision and the receipt of services across frontiers are prohibited by art 49 (ex art 59) of the EC Treaty, which provides that:

'Within the framework of the provisions set out below, restrictions on freedom to provide services within the Community shall be prohibited in respect of nationals of Member States who are established in a State of the Community other than that of the person for whom the services are intended.'

[31] The Secretary of State disputes this second claim and Mr Chamberlain on her behalf contends that permission to pursue this claim is required but that it should not be given. Lewisham support the Secretary of State, although it made no separate submissions probably because this dispute did not affect it relating as it does to the regulations for which the Secretary of State alone is responsible financially.

[32] There are a number of background matters that are agreed by the parties and which I must now record. It is common ground between them first, that art 49 has direct effect (see *Van Binsbergen v Bestuur van de Bedrijfsvereniging voor de Metaalnijverheid* Case 33/74 [1974] ECR 1299), second, that art 49 embraces the freedom to receive services (see *Watson* Case 118/75 [1976] ECR 1185) and third that the provision of student support (at least so far as tuition fees are concerned) comes within the material scope of art 49 (see *Brown v Secretary of State for Scotland* Case 197/86 [1988] ECR 3205). The House of Lords has explained that it is the duty of the United Kingdom courts 'to override any rule of national law found to be in conflict with any directly enforceable rule of community law' (per Lord Bridge of Harwich in *Factortame Ltd v Secretary of State for Transport (No 2)* Case C-213/89 [1991] 1 All ER 70 at 108, [1991] 1 AC 603 at 659). My task is to see if, as the claimant contends, art 49 overrides the relevant provisions in the

a regulations, to which I now turn, in order to show how they prevent the claimant from obtaining assistance for her course at Griffith College.

[33] The Secretary of State contends that the 2001 regulations provide the conditions that have to be satisfied in relation to a course before a student can obtain support while attending such a course. Griffith College is a private institution and so a student attending its course can only obtain assistance if the

b teaching and supervision which comprise the course was provided by a United Kingdom institution. No support is however payable to the claimant under the regulations because of reg 5(4) as her course at that college is not provided by an educational institution in the United Kingdom. It is of crucial importance that although Nottingham Trent University validates the relevant law course in Griffith College, it does not provide in the words of reg 5(4) the 'teaching and

c supervision which comprise the course'. Thus the Secretary of State cannot provide student support to the claimant for her course at Griffith College under the 2001 regulations.

[34] It is reg 5(4) which the claimant contends should be disapplied in order to obtain compliance with art 49 and to ensure that the claimant receives student

d support. To show the impact and significance of reg 5(4), it is now necessary to set out its terms and those of some of the other relevant regulations, which provide that:

'**Eligible students.**

e **4.** (1) Subject to and in accordance with these Regulations a person shall be eligible for support in connection with his attendance at a designated course if he is a person mentioned in Schedule 1…

Designated courses.

5. (1) A course shall be designated for the purposes of section 22(1) of the Act and regulation if it is—(a) mentioned in Schedule 2; (b) a full-time course

f … (c) of at least one academic year's duration; and (d) wholly provided by an educational institution or institutions in the United Kingdom which are maintained or assisted by recurrent grants out of public funds or is provided by such an institution or institutions in conjunction with an institution or institutions outside the United Kingdom…

g (4) For the purposes of these Regulations a course is provided by an institution if it provides the teaching and supervision which comprise the course, whether it has entered an agreement with the student to provide the course.'

[35] Mr Walsh contends that the interpretation of reg 5(1) which is advanced

h by the Secretary of State, relying on the definition in reg 5(4), restricts the freedom of the claimant to receive services in another member state. He submits that this restriction would not apply were she to pursue her course of studies in the United Kingdom.

[36] He points out that the effect of art 49 is far-reaching and that it affects rules which make the provision of services more difficult. Thus, in *Kohll v Union*

j *des Caisses de Maladie* Case C-158/96 [1998] All ER (EC) 673 at 719, [1998] ECR I-1931 at 1947 (para 33), the European Court of Justice stated that art 49—

'precludes the application of any national rules which have the effect of making the provision of services purely between member states more difficult than the provision of services purely within one member state …'

Mr Walsh explains that it is also established law that—

> 'article 59 [now 49] of the Treaty requires not only the elimination of all
> discrimination against a person providing services on the ground of his
> nationality but also the abolition of any restriction, even if it applies without
> distinction to national providers of services and to those of other Member
> States, when it is liable to prohibit or otherwise impede the activities of a
> provider of services established in another Member State where he lawfully
> provides similar services.' (See *Säger v Dennemeyer & Co Ltd* Case C-76/90
> [1991] ECR I-4221 at 4243 (para 12).)

[37] Mr Walsh submits that the failure to provide the claimant with student
support for her course at Griffith College constitutes an unlawful restriction on
her freedom to receive services, given that such support would be provided to her
if she studied within the United Kingdom. So he says that reg 5(1) should be
construed so as to ensure compliance with art 49.

The Secretary of State's submissions

[38] Mr Chamberlain for the Secretary of State accepts that as a consequence
of the authorities to which I have referred, member states are prohibited from
discriminating between their own nationals and those of other EU member states
in respect of funding for tuition fees.

[39] The principle prohibiting discrimination in respect of student funding on
grounds of nationality has two important consequences. First, a national of any
EU member state, who gains a place at a university in the United Kingdom must
be offered funding for tuition fees by the United Kingdom government on the
same basis as funding is made available to United Kingdom nationals. Second, a
United Kingdom national who gains a place at a university in another member
state of the EU must be offered funding for tuition fees by the government of that
state on the same basis as funding is made available at that university to nationals
of that state.

[40] The result is that courses undertaken by EU nationals at universities in
the United Kingdom are subject to United Kingdom funding rules, regardless of
the nationality of the student. With certain exceptions relating principally to the
European University Institute, the effect of reg 5(1) is that the United Kingdom
government does not fund courses at universities outside the United Kingdom,
unless the course is being provided in conjunction with a publicly-funded
educational institution in the United Kingdom, which significantly must provide
the 'teaching and supervision which comprise the course' (reg 5(1)(d) and 5(4)).

[41] The thrust of the claimant's case is that art 49 precludes the application by
a member state of any rule, which makes it more difficult for nationals of that
state to receive services abroad than at home. Mr Chamberlain disputes the
claimant's contention that reg 5(1) read with reg 5(4) is such a rule because it
deprives her of funding for her course in Ireland when 'it would have been
provided to her if she studied within the United Kingdom'.

Conclusions on claim 2

[42] I cannot accept that argument of the claimant for at least three reasons.
First, even if Griffith College was in England, the claimant would not have been
entitled to funding under the regulations as reg 5(1)(d) precludes funding for
courses at private institutions, which are not provided by the United Kingdom

institution which provides 'the teaching and supervision which comprise the course'. This means that the claimant is not entitled to assistance at Griffith College wherever it was situated, as I have explained at [33], above. In essence, Griffith College does not provide a designated course and so its precise location is irrelevant. That answers the complaint of the claimant to which I have just referred. It also means that permission must be refused.

[43] Second, there is no evidence of any discrimination or impediment imposed by the Secretary of State of the kind envisaged by art 49 on the provision of student support to the claimant. It must not be forgotten that, as the European Court of Justice has stated, the effect of art 49 is to 'abolish all discrimination against the person providing the service by reason of his nationality or the fact he is established in a Member State other than that in which the service is to be provided' (see *Van Binsbergen v Bestuur van de Bedrijfsvereniging voor de Metaalnijverheid* Case 33/74 [1974] ECR 1299 at 1311 (para 25)).

[44] As I have already explained, the provision of student support, at least in the form of fees, falls within that provision with the result that the claim must fail as there is no discrimination against the claimant on any provision of the regulations by reason of her nationality or the place where she is to receive the services. In essence the regulations do not permit or cause such discrimination. Thus there is no arguable case for a breach of art 49 and so permission must be refused. Third, the claimant's complaint on closer analysis is about the very principle of limited funding to courses provided at least in part, by United Kingdom institutions rather than about the interpretation of the word 'provided'. The claimant's complaint is about the policy behind reg 5 but that policy is not based on any form of discrimination.

[45] The unavailability of funding *from the United Kingdom government* for a course in Ireland does not, of itself, make it more difficult for a United Kingdom national to receive educational services in Ireland than in the United Kingdom as that funding might be available from the Irish authorities. The existence of any difficulty for the claimant would also depend on the relevant Irish rules for receiving funding in respect of courses at Irish institutions. The Irish authorities are subject to art 49 and so are no more permitted than is the United Kingdom government to deny funding to any student doing a course in Ireland on the ground of his or her nationality. In the present case, there is no evidence that the claimant has investigated whether funding is available to her from the Irish authorities. In any event, if a comparison of the relevant United Kingdom rules with those applicable in Ireland meant that the claimant would receive student support here, but not in Ireland—about which there is no evidence whatsoever— that would be because of the differences in funding arrangements as between different member states in an area which, as I understand it, has yet to undergo Community harmonisation. Significantly for this claim and fatally for the claimant, the lack of student support for the claimant is not because of any rule of national law which infringes art 49.

[46] During his submissions, Mr Walsh said that the claimant is suffering hardship and that indicates that the Secretary of State's policy is restrictive. I cannot accept that point, although I totally sympathise with the claimant in her predicament as she was misled by Lewisham into thinking that she would receive student assistance. Lewisham's conduct merits serious criticism but even an arguable breach of art 49 has not been established.

CONCLUSION

[47] The second claim under art 49 requires permission from the court, but the arguments in support of this claim fail to reach the prescribed threshold and so permission to proceed on it must be refused. I await submissions from counsel for the claimant and Lewisham on the order that I should make on the legitimate expectation claim in the light of my suggestion at [29], above.[b]

Order accordingly.

Dilys Tausz   Barrister.

---

b   Judge's note inserted when the judgment was handed down: The parties agreed to a declaration that Lewisham is obliged to consider the claimant's claim to assistance in the light of its representation to the claimant and upon the undertaking of Lewisham to consider this claim of the claimant by 12 noon on Friday 12 July 2002; liberty to apply has been given.

JA Pye (Oxford) Ltd and another v Graham and another

[2002] UKHL 30

HOUSE OF LORDS

LORD BINGHAM OF CORNHILL, LORD MACKAY OF CLASHFERN, LORD BROWNE-WILKINSON, LORD HOPE OF CRAIGHEAD AND LORD HUTTON

20, 21 MARCH, 4 JULY 2002

Limitation of action – Land – Acquisition of title by squatter – Dispossession of true owner – Requirements of 'dispossession' and 'possession' – Limitation Act 1980, s 15, Sch 1, para 1.

The claimant was the owner of the paper title to certain agricultural land. The land was fully enclosed, and vehicular access was controlled by a neighbouring farmer. Until 31 August 1984, the farmer had used the land, with the owner's permission, for grazing and grass-cutting. Thereafter, he had been willing to pay for grazing rights if requested to do so. In the absence of any such request, however, he farmed the land all year round for the next 14 years without the owner's permission, using it in any way he thought best and treating it as part of his farm. During that whole period, the owner did nothing on the land, and it did not bring proceedings in connection with the land until 30 April 1998. The issue therefore arose whether the owner's action was barred by s 15[a] of the Limitation Act 1980 which provided that no action to recover land could be brought after the expiration of 12 years from the date on which the right of action accrued. By virtue of para 1[b] of Sch 1 to the 1980 Act, the right of action was treated as having accrued on the date of the 'dispossession' of the person who, having been in possession of the land, had been 'dispossessed' while entitled to it. The case therefore turned upon whether, at any time between 31 August 1984 and 30 April 1986, the owner had been dispossessed of the land. The judge concluded that the farmer had obtained title under the 1980 Act, but his decision was reversed by the Court of Appeal which held that the farmer had lacked the intention of possessing the land to the exclusion of the owner. On an appeal to the House of Lords by the administrators of the farmer's estate, their Lordships considered what constituted 'dispossession'.

Held – (1) For the purposes of para 1 of Sch 1 to the 1980 Act, there would be 'dispossession' of the paper owner in any case where (there having been no discontinuance of possession by the paper owner) a squatter assumed possession in the ordinary sense of the word. Except in the case of joint possessors, possession was single and exclusive. The paper owner could not therefore be in possession if the squatter was in possession. If the paper owner had at one stage been in possession of the land, but the squatter's occupation of it constituted possession in law, the squatter had to have 'dispossessed' the true owner for the purposes of para 1. It followed in the instant case that the relevant question was whether the farmer had been in possession of the land without the owner's consent before

---

a Section 15, so far as material, is set out at [25], below
b Paragraph 1 is set out at [25], below

30 April 1986, and accordingly it was necessary to consider what constituted 'possession' in the ordinary sense of the word (see [1], [3], [38], [39], [67], [74], below); dictum of Slade J in *Powell v McFarlane* (1977) 38 P&CR 452 at 469 approved.

(2) Legal possession required (i) a sufficient degree of physical custody and control (factual possession), and (ii) an intention to exercise such custody and control on one's own behalf and for one's own benefit (intention to possess). As regards factual possession, everything depended on the circumstances, but, broadly, such possession was constituted where the alleged possessor had been dealing with the land as an occupying owner might have been expected to deal with it, and nobody else had done so. The necessary intent was one to possess, not to own, and an intention to exclude the paper owner only so far as was reasonably possible. There was therefore no inconsistency between a squatter being willing to pay the paper owner if asked and his being in possession in the meantime. In the instant case, the farmer had plainly been in factual possession before 30 April 1986, and he had manifestly intended to assert his possession against the owner when he had remained in factual possession of the fully enclosed land after the expiry of the permission. Accordingly, the appeal would be allowed (see [1], [3], [40]–[43], [46], [64], [67], [72], [78], [80], below); *Buckinghamshire CC v Moran* [1989] 2 All ER 225 and dicta of Slade J in *Powell v McFarlane* (1977) 38 P&CR 452 at 470–472 approved; *Ocean Estates Ltd v Pinder* [1969] 2 AC 19 adopted; *R v Secretary of State for the Environment, ex p Davies* (1990) 61 P&CR 487 overruled.

Notes

For dispossession and intention to possess, see 28 *Halsbury's Laws* (4th edn reissue) paras 978–979.

For the Limitation Act 1980, s 15, Sch 1, para 1, see 24 *Halsbury's Statutes* (4th edn) (1998 reissue) 716, 745.

Cases referred to in opinions

Buckinghamshire CC v Moran [1989] 2 All ER 225, [1990] Ch 623, [1989] 3 WLR 152, CA; *affg* (1988) 56 P&CR 372.

Culley v Doe d Taylerson (1840) 11 Ad & El 1008.

George Wimpey & Co Ltd v Sohn [1966] 1 All ER 232, [1967] Ch 487, [1966] 2 WLR 414, CA.

Lambeth London BC v Blackburn [2001] EWCA Civ 912, (2001) 82 P&CR 494.

Leigh v Jack (1879) 5 Ex D 264, CA.

Littledale v Liverpool College [1900] 1 Ch 19, CA.

Nepean v Doe d Knight (1837) 2 M&W 894.

Ocean Estates Ltd v Pinder [1969] 2 AC 19, [1969] 2 WLR 1359, PC.

Paradise Beach and Transportation Co Ltd v Price-Robinson [1968] 1 All ER 530, [1968] AC 1072, [1968] 2 WLR 873, PC.

Powell v McFarlane (1977) 38 P&CR 452.

R v Kansal (No 2) [2001] UKHL 62, [2002] 1 All ER 257, [2002] 2 AC 69, [2001] 3 WLR 1562.

R v Secretary of State for the Environment, ex p Davies (1990) 61 P&CR 487, CA.

Rains v Buxton (1880) 14 Ch D 537.

Treloar v Nute [1977] 1 All ER 230, [1976] 1 WLR 1295, CA.

Wallis's Cayton Bay Holiday Camp Ltd v Shell-Mex and BP Ltd [1974] 3 All ER 575, [1975] QB 94, [1974] 3 WLR 387, CA.

Appeal

a

The defendants, Caroline Mary Graham and Charles Graeme Denton, the personal representatives of the estate of Michael John Graham (deceased), appealed with permission of the Appeal Committee of the House of Lords given on 24 July 2001 from the order of the Court of Appeal (Mummery, Keene LJJ and Sir Martin Nourse) on 6 February 2001 ([2001] EWCA Civ 117, [2001] Ch 804,

b [2001] 2 WLR 1293) allowing an appeal from the order of Neuberger J on 4 February 2000 ([2000] Ch 676, [2000] 3 WLR 242) dismissing proceedings brought by the claimants, JA Pye (Oxford) Ltd and JA Pye (Oxford) Land Ltd (Pye), for the recovery of agricultural land at Henwick, Thatcham, Berkshire. The facts are set out in the opinion of Lord Browne-Wilkinson.

c

> *Kim Lewison QC, Martin Dray* and *Jane Mulcahy* (instructed by *Burges Salmon,* Bristol) for the defendants.
> *Jonathan Gaunt QC, David Pannick QC* and *Jonathan Small* (instructed by *Darby's,* Oxford) for Pye.

d

Their Lordships took time for consideration.

4 July 2002. The following opinions were delivered.

e **LORD BINGHAM OF CORNHILL.**

[1] My Lords, for the reasons given by my noble and learned friend Lord Browne-Wilkinson, which I have had the privilege of reading in draft, I would allow this appeal and restore the order of the judge. In doing so, I would echo the misgivings expressed by the judge in the closing paragraph of his judgment

f ([2000] Ch 676 at 709–710, [2000] 3 WLR 242 at 271–272).

[2] The Grahams have acted honourably throughout. They sought rights to graze or cut grass on the land after the summer of 1984, and were quite prepared to pay. When Pye failed to respond they did what any other farmer in their position would have done: they continued to farm the land. They were not at

g fault. But the result of Pye's inaction was that they enjoyed the full use of the land without payment for 12 years. As if that were not gain enough, they are then rewarded by obtaining title to this considerable area of valuable land without any obligation to compensate the former owner in any way at all. In the case of unregistered land, and in the days before registration became the norm, such a

h result could no doubt be justified as avoiding protracted uncertainty where the title to land lay. But where land is registered it is difficult to see any justification for a legal rule which compels such an apparently unjust result, and even harder to see why the party gaining title should not be required to pay some compensation at least to the party losing it. It is reassuring to learn that the Land

j Registration Act 2002 has addressed the risk that a registered owner may lose his title through inadvertence. But the main provisions of that Act have not yet been brought into effect, and even if they had it would not assist Pye, whose title had been lost before the passing of the Act. While I am satisfied that the appeal must be allowed for the reasons given by my noble and learned friend, this is a conclusion which I (like the judge ([2000] Ch 676 at 709, [2000] 3 WLR 242 at 271)) 'arrive at with no enthusiasm'.

LORD MACKAY OF CLASHFERN.

[3] My Lords, I have had the advantage of reading in draft the speech prepared by my noble and learned friend Lord Browne-Wilkinson. I agree that this appeal should be allowed for the reasons which he gives.

LORD BROWNE-WILKINSON.

[4] My Lords, in this case the defendants, as personal representatives of the late Michael John Graham, seek to establish a possessory title to 25 hectares of agricultural land at Henwick, Thatcham, Berkshire (the disputed land). At all material times the paper title to that land has undoubtedly been vested in the second claimant JA Pye (Oxford) Land Ltd and its predecessor in title in the same group JA Pye (Oxford) Ltd (Pye) as registered proprietors of the disputed land at Her Majesty's Land Registry. At the trial Neuberger J ([2000] Ch 676, [2000] 3 WLR 242) held that the defendants had established title by possession but his decision was reversed by the Court of Appeal ([2001] EWCA Civ 117, [2001] Ch 804, [2001] 2 WLR 1293) (Mummery, Keene LJJ and Sir Martin Nourse). The defendants appealed to your Lordships' House.

[5] I will later have to deal with the law at some length but at this stage it is sufficient to highlight the essential issue. The Grahams, in order to succeed, will have to show that they 'dispossessed' Pye more than 12 years before Pye started proceedings on 30 April 1998. As will appear, this requires the Grahams to prove that Pye were dispossessed between 31 August 1984 (when the Grahams' occupation ceased to be with the permission of Pye) and 30 April 1986. It is the actions and intentions of the parties during this period that will determine the proper outcome of the case.

FACTS

[6] Until 1977 Pye was the owner of Henwick Manor together with a substantial amount of surrounding land. In 1977 Pye sold the farmhouse and approximately 67 hectares of the land (Manor Farm) but retained the disputed land which was considered to have development potential. It was, and remains, Pye's intention to retain the disputed land until planning permission can be obtained for development.

[7] The disputed land consists of four fields, the Drive Field, Hill Field, Paddocks and Wallis Field. The farmhouse at Manor Farm is approached by a private drive owned with Manor Farm which runs from a public highway to the farmhouse. Abutting the southern side of the drive is the northern boundary of the disputed land. There is a further part of the disputed land to the west of the driveway and immediately south of the farmhouse and farm buildings. The eastern boundary of the disputed land abuts the public highway. Apart from the gates I shall mention, all the boundaries of the disputed land are separated from the adjoining land by hedges.

[8] On the eastern boundary, there is a gate from the public highway into Drive Field. That gate has been padlocked at all material times, the key to that padlock being held by Mrs Michael Graham. The hedge between the driveway and Drive Field and the Paddocks has three gates. Pye has no rights of access over the driveway. There is a fourth gate on to the disputed land on its northern boundary from the farmhouse into Hill Field. There is a public footpath going through Manor Farm and then, over a stile, through Hill Field.

ACQUISITION OF MANOR FARM

[9] In 1982 Mr John Graham and his wife purchased Manor Farm. From then on, until his unhappy death in 1998, the farming activities at Manor Farm were the day-to-day responsibility of their son Michael Graham. Initially he was farming the land for the benefit of a family partnership but later on behalf of himself and his wife Caroline Graham.

[10] At the time the Grahams acquired Manor Farm, they were aware that the disputed land had been used as grazing land under agreements between the owners of Manor Farm and Pye. The Grahams were aware that this disputed land was owned by Pye and had been acquired by Pye in the hope of being able to develop it in the future. As I have said, the disputed land was fully enclosed so as to exclude the whole world except for access with the use of the key held by the Grahams from the public highway and by foot over the footway that I have mentioned.

GRAZING AGREEMENT

[11] On 1 February 1983 Pye entered into a written agreement with John Graham who is described as 'the grazier'. That agreement permitted use of the disputed land until 31 December 1983 in return for a payment of £2,000. It limited the use of the disputed land to grazing or mowing for one cut of grass and the grazier was obliged to restrict the use of the disputed land to the grazing of sheep, cattle and horses. He was also obliged to keep the disputed land free of weeds, the gates, fences and ditches in good order, and to use the land in a good and husband-like manner. It further provided that Mr Graham would not permit any trespass upon the land and further that he would not part with 'possession' of the disputed land. It further reserved to Pye the right to terminate the agreement and gain 'possession' on the service of six months' notice. It also expressly provided that any grazing after its expiry would have to be by a new and distinct contract.

[12] The Grahams had previously enjoyed an informal licence to graze the disputed land from September 1982 until 1 February 1983. It is not clear whether the Grahams vacated the land prior to the commencement of the 1983 agreement on 1 February 1983. The Grahams occupied the land under the grazing agreement until 31 December 1983. On 30 December 1983 Mr Evans, a chartered surveyor acting for Pye, wrote to Pye suggesting that Mr John Graham be granted a fresh grazing agreement for 1984. On the same day he wrote to Mr John Graham noting that the grazing agreement was on the verge of expiration and requiring the Grahams to vacate the land. In January 1984 Pye refused the request for a grazing agreement for 1984 because they anticipated seeking planning permission for the development of all or part of the disputed land and were firmly advised that it would be sensible for them to have the disputed land in hand at the time of the proposed planning application and the planning appeal which would almost certainly ensue. The Grahams were also led to believe that Pye would soon be making an application for planning permission and did not want the disputed land to be grazed because such grazing, in Pye's view, might damage the prospects of obtaining permission. No change of attitude on the part of Pye was ever communicated to the Grahams.

[13] Notwithstanding the requirement to vacate the land at the expiry of the 1983 agreement on 31 December 1983, the Grahams remained in occupation on 1 January 1984 and have remained in occupation at all times since that date. Even though there was no grazing agreement in place in 1984, Michael Graham spread dung and loose housing straw on the disputed land during the winter of

1983–1984. He was aware at the time he was spreading the dung that he was doing so at his own risk as a grazing agreement for 1984 might not be forthcoming.

[14] In approximately March 1984 the Grahams turned cattle out on to the disputed land and left them to graze until about November 1984. He harrowed, rolled and fertilised the land and spread dung and straw in February and March 1984. He did this on the basis that it was his intention to carry on using the land for grazing until requested not to do so. No request to vacate or to pay for the grazing which was taking place was made. If it had been made, Michael Graham would happily have paid. He took advantage of the ability to use the disputed land as no one challenged him and he was keen not to waste the effort that he had put into preparing the grazing during 1983 and over the winter of 1983–1984.

[15] In June 1984 an agreement was reached whereby Pye agreed to sell to John Graham the standing crop of grass on the disputed land for £1,100. That grass was cut by the Grahams and the judge made a finding that the cut was completed by 31 August 1984. The charge of £1,100 was paid in November 1984. In the circumstances, all use of the disputed land by the Grahams from 1 September 1984 onwards was made without the permission of Pye.

[16] In December 1984, pursuant to a request from the Grahams an inquiry was made of Pye whether the Grahams could take another cut of hay or preferably have a grazing agreement in 1985. There was no answer to this letter from Pye or to subsequent letters sent to Pye in May 1985. Thereafter, the Grahams did not attempt to make contact with Pye.

[17] From September 1984 onwards until 1999 the Grahams used the whole of the disputed land for farming. The Grahams never vacated the disputed land: they kept farming all the year round. Dry cattle and yearlings were kept in a shed on part of the disputed land throughout the year. Dung was spread two or three times during 1984/1985 and the disputed land was harrowed and rolled in February/March 1985, fertilised at Easter 1985 and limed in early 1985. In doing this Michael Graham was aware that there was a risk that he would not obtain the benefit of the work as there was no grazing agreement or agreement to take a cut of hay. He would have been prepared to pay Pye for a grazing licence or the hay but in the absence of any agreement he was willing to take a chance that an agreement would be forthcoming later.

[18] The same use and management of the whole of the disputed land for grazing was maintained until 1994 when the use of the Drive Field changed to arable. Save during the mid-winter months there would be between 80 and 140 cattle grazing on the disputed land. In addition part of the disputed land was limed in 1985 and re-seeded in 1988. The boundary hedges were trimmed every year from 1983 onwards by someone employed by the Grahams, and from 1984 onwards the boundary fencing was maintained by the Grahams as were the ditches on the disputed land.

[19] Various witnesses confirmed that the disputed land appeared to them to be part of Manor Farm and some gave evidence that they believed that Michael Graham owned it. When asked in cross-examination what an occupying owner of the disputed land might have done, over and above what had been done by the Grahams between 1984 and 1997, Mr Evans, an experienced chartered surveyor, was unable to think of anything.

[20] In his draft witness statement Michael Graham said that in the light of the lack of interest shown by Pye in the land he continued to use the land for what he considered to be its best use. He hoped a further agreement would be forthcoming in 1984. After he received no replies to his inquiries in 1985 he 'gave

a up trying' and waited to see if Pye contacted him. He anticipated that Pye would contact him at some point and was happy to leave matters until they did. From May 1985 at the latest, his attitude was simply that he would have preferred to have obtained a formal agreement and, if Pye had asked him to pay for his occupation, he would have done so. In his draft witness statement he says that at the time he believed that it was possible to obtain ownership of land after it had

b been occupied for a sufficient number of years, which he mistakenly thought to be seven years.

[21] As to the activities of Pye on the disputed land between 1984 and 1999, there were none. In 1993 a representative of Pye visited the disputed land to inspect it but even then he only viewed it from the road and from the drive; he did not actually go on to the land. Pye showed no interest in the agricultural

c management of the land. Pye carried out certain paper transactions during this period relating to the disputed land. But it is not suggested that they were sufficient to constitute possession. Indeed nothing was done by or on behalf of Pye to the land itself from 1 January 1984 onwards.

[22] In 1997 Michael Graham registered cautions at the Land Registry against

d Pye's title on the grounds that he had obtained 'squatter's title' by adverse possession. Pye's solicitors sought to warn off those cautions. In early February 1998 Michael Graham agreed to release the cautions in relation to certain land needed for a relief road. Shortly thereafter his draft statement was prepared. On 19 February 1998 Michael Graham was most unhappily killed in a shooting accident.

e [23] On 30 April 1998 Pye issued the originating summons seeking cancellation of the caution. A week or so later, further cautions were registered on behalf of Caroline Graham, Michael's widow, and in September 1998 letters of administration to Michael's estate were granted to Caroline Graham and her father. On 20 January 1999 Pye issued further proceedings seeking possession of the

f disputed land.

[24] At first instance there was an issue whether time should be reckoned back from the date of the issue of the originating summons or from the date of the writ action commenced on 20 January. Before the Court of Appeal it was agreed that nothing turned on the point since there was no material change in the parties' actions or states of mind between 30 April 1986 and 20 January 1987 (12 years

g before the commencement of the two actions respectively).

THE LIMITATION ACT 1980

[25] Section 15 of the 1980 Act provides:

h '(1) No action shall be brought by any person to recover any land after the expiration of twelve years from the date on which the right of action accrued to him or, if it first accrued to some person through whom he claims, to that person ...

(6) Part I of Schedule 1 to this Act contains provisions for determining the date of accrual of rights of action to recover land in the cases there mentioned.'

j Paragraph 1 of Sch 1 provides:

'Where the person bringing an action to recover land, or some person through whom he claims, has been in possession of the land, and has while entitled to the land been dispossessed or discontinued his possession, the right of action shall be treated as having accrued on the date of the dispossession or discontinuance.'

Paragraph 8 of Sch 1 provides:

> '(1) No right of action to recover land shall be treated as accruing unless the land is in the possession of some person in whose favour the period of limitation can run (referred to below in this paragraph as "adverse possession"); and where under the preceding provisions of this Schedule any such right of action is treated as accruing on a certain date and no person is in adverse possession on that date, the right of action shall not be treated as accruing unless and until adverse possession is taken of the land ...
>
> (4) For the purpose of determining whether a person occupying any land is in adverse possession of the land it shall not be assumed by implication of law that his occupation is by permission of the person entitled to the land merely by virtue of the fact that his occupation is not inconsistent with the latter's present or future enjoyment of the land. This provision shall not be taken as prejudicing a finding to the effect that a person's occupation of any land is by implied permission of the person entitled to the land in any case where such a finding is justified on the actual facts of the case.'

[26] It is to be noted that the right of action to recover the land is barred whenever 12 years have elapsed from the time when any right of action accrued: it does not have to be a period immediately before action brought. In the case of unregistered land, on the expiration of the limitation period regulating the recovery of the land, the title of the paper owner is extinguished (see s 17 of the 1980 Act). In the case of registered land, under s 75(1) of the Land Registration Act 1925 on the expiry of the limitation period the title is not extinguished but the registered proprietor is deemed to hold the land thereafter in trust for the squatter. The provisions as to registered land have been fundamentally altered by the Land Registration Act 2002 but that Act does not apply to the present case.

THE ISSUES

[27] The action was brought by Pye at the earliest on 30 April 1998. The question therefore is whether, prior to that date, there was a period of 12 years during which the Grahams were in possession of the disputed land to the exclusion of Pye. More accurately, there are two questions: (1) did Pye discontinue possession or was it 'dispossessed' of the disputed land (within the meaning of para 1 of Sch 1 to the 1980 Act) before 30 April 1986; and if so (2) did the Grahams thereafter remain in possession of the land for a period of 12 years?

[28] It is common ground that Pye did not 'discontinue' possession within the meaning of the Act. Further I did not understand there to be any claim by Pye that, if the Grahams had at any time prior to 30 April 1986 dispossessed Pye, the Grahams thereafter ceased to be in possession for the purposes of the Act.

[29] It was further common ground that so long as the Grahams were occupying the disputed land with Pye's consent, they could not be treated as having dispossessed Pye. Accordingly no relevant right of action can have accrued to Pye under para 1 of Sch 1 until after the expiry on or about 31 August 1984 of the grass-cutting permission.

[30] The relevant question therefore is whether at some time between 1 September 1984 and 30 April 1986 Pye were 'dispossessed' of the disputed land so that, at that date, Pye's right of action accrued for the purposes of para 1 of Sch 1 to the 1980 Act.

THE LAW

a [31] The apparently straightforward statutory provisions have given rise to considerable difficulties, most of which flow from the remarks of the Court of Appeal in *Leigh v Jack* (1879) 5 Ex D 264 and *Littledale v Liverpool College* [1900] 1 Ch 19. In a remarkable judgment at first instance, *Powell v McFarlane* (1977) 38 P&CR 452, Slade J traced his way successfully through a number of Court of Appeal judgments which were binding on him so as to restore a degree of order
b to the subject and to state clearly the relevant principles. Although there are one or two minor points on which (unlike Slade J) your Lordships are not bound by authority and can therefore make necessary adjustments, for the most part the principles set out by Slade J, as subsequently approved by the Court of Appeal in *Buckinghamshire CC v Moran* [1989] 2 All ER 225, [1990] Ch 623, cannot be
c improved upon. Hereafter I adopt them without specific recognition beyond marking with inverted commas those passages which I have quoted verbatim.

POSSESSION, DISPOSSESSION, OUSTER AND ADVERSE POSSESSION

[32] In *Powell's* case (1977) 38 P&CR 452 Slade J was considering the
d Limitation Act 1939. However, apart from para 8(4) of Sch 1 to the 1980 Act the statutory provisions applicable in the present case are identical in the 1939 Act and the 1980 Act. Slade J first addressed himself to the question what was the meaning of possession and dispossession in the statutory provisions. After noticing that possession and dispossession were not defined in the 1939 Act, he continued (at 469):

e

> 'Possession of land, however, is a concept which has long been familiar and of importance to English lawyers, because (*inter alia*) it entitles the person in possession, whether rightfully or wrongfully, to maintain an action of trespass against any other person who enters the land without his consent, unless such other person has himself a better right to possession. In the
f > absence of authority, therefore, I would for my own part have regarded the word "possession" in the 1939 Act as bearing the traditional sense of that degree of occupation or physical control, coupled with the requisite intention commonly referred to as *animus possidendi*, that would entitle a person to maintain an action of trespass in relation to the relevant land;
g > likewise I would have regarded the word "dispossession" in the Act as denoting simply the taking of possession in such sense from another without the other's licence or consent; likewise I would have regarded a person who has "dispossessed" another in the sense just stated as being in "adverse possession" for the purposes of the Act.'

h Save as to the last sentence I have quoted (as to which I will make certain further comments below), I entirely agree with that statement of the law. Slade J felt doubts whether, in the light of certain Court of Appeal judgments then binding on him, he could properly adhere to the view that he expressed. Decisions (for example *Wallis's Cayton Bay Holiday Camp Ltd v Shell-Mex and BP Ltd* [1974] 3 All ER
j 575, [1975] QB 94) appeared to hold that use of the land by a squatter which would have been sufficient to constitute possession in the ordinary sense of the word was not enough: it was said that such use by the squatter did not constitute 'adverse possession' which was required for the purposes of limitation unless the squatter's use conflicted with the intentions of the paper title owner as to his present or future use of the disputed land. In those cases it was held that the use by the squatter was, as a matter of law, to be treated as enjoyed with the implied

consent of the paper owner. Not surprisingly, Slade J found this line of reasoning difficult to follow. It is hard to see how the intentions of the paper title owner (unless known to the squatter) can affect the intention of the squatter to possess the land. In my judgment, Slade J was right and the decision of the Court of Appeal in those cases wrong. In any event Parliament (on the advice of the Law Reform Committee) has intervened to reverse the principle of implied licence (see para 8(4) of Sch 1 to the 1980 Act). However there remains a long-standing confusion as to what constitutes 'dispossession' and the place, if any, of 'adverse possession' in the modern law.

[33] The root of the problem is caused by the concept of 'non-adverse possession'. This was a concept engrafted by the common law and equity onto the limitation statute of James I (21 Jac 1, Ch 16). Before the passing of the Real Property Limitation Acts 1833 and 1874, the rights of the paper owner were not taken away save by a 'disseisin' or an ouster and use of the land by the squatter of a kind which was clearly inconsistent with the paper title. Such inconsistent use was called adverse possession (see Professor Dockray 'Adverse Possession and Intention' [1982] Conv 256 at 260). Under the 1833 Act (ss 2 and 3 of which were substantially to the same effect as s 15(1) of, and para 1 of Sch 1 to, the 1980 Act) the right of action was barred 20 years after 'the Right ... to bring such Action shall have first accrued' and 'such Right shall be deemed to have first accrued at the Time of such Dispossession or Discontinuance of Possession'. Soon after the passing of the 1833 Act it was held that 'the second and third sections of that act ... have done away with the doctrine of non-adverse possession, and ... the question is whether twenty years have elapsed *since the right accrued*, whatever the nature of the possession' (*Nepean v Doe d Knight* (1837) 2 M&W 894 at 911 per Denman CJ). The same statement of the new law was made in *Culley v Doe d Taylerson* (1840) 11 Ad & El 1008 at 1015 where Denman CJ said:

'The effect of [s 2] is to put an end to all questions and discussions, whether the possession of lands, &c., be adverse or not; and, if one party has been in the actual possession for twenty years, whether adversely or not, the claimant, whose original right of entry accrued above twenty years before bringing the ejectment, is barred by this section.'

[34] The same was held to be the law by the Privy Council in a carefully reasoned advice delivered by Lord Upjohn in *Paradise Beach and Transportation Co Ltd v Price-Robinson* [1968] 1 All ER 530, [1968] AC 1072 (see also Professor Dockray (supra)).

[35] From 1833 onwards, therefore, old notions of adverse possession, disseisin or ouster from possession should not have formed part of judicial decisions. From 1833 onwards the only question was whether the squatter had been in possession in the ordinary sense of the word. That is still the law, as Slade J rightly said. After 1833 the phrase 'adverse possession' did not appear in the statutes until, to my mind unfortunately, it was reintroduced by the 1939 Act, s 10 of which is in virtually the same words as para 8(1) of Sch 1 to the 1980 Act. In my judgment the references to 'adverse possession' in the 1939 and 1980 Acts did not reintroduce by a side wind after over 100 years the old notions of adverse possession in force before 1833. Paragraph 8(1) of Sch 1 to the 1980 Act defines what is meant by adverse possession in that paragraph as being the case where land is in the possession of a person in whose favour time 'can run'. It is directed not to the nature of the possession but to the capacity of the squatter. Thus a trustee who is unable to acquire a title by lapse of time against the trust estate (see

s 21) is not in adverse possession for the purposes of para 8. Although it is
convenient to refer to possession by a squatter without the consent of the true
owner as being 'adverse possession' the convenience of this must not be allowed
to reintroduce by the back door that which for so long has not formed part of the
law.

[36] Many of the difficulties with these sections which I will have to consider
are due to a conscious or subconscious feeling that in order for a squatter to gain
title by lapse of time he has to act adversely to the paper title owner. It is said that
he has to 'oust' the true owner in order to dispossess him; that he has to intend
to exclude the whole world including the true owner; that the squatter's use of
the land has to be inconsistent with any present or future use by the true owner.
In my judgment much confusion and complication would be avoided if reference
to adverse possession were to be avoided so far as possible and effect given to the
clear words of the Acts. The question is simply whether the defendant squatter
has dispossessed the paper owner by going into ordinary possession of the land
for the requisite period without the consent of the owner.

[37] It is clearly established that the taking or continuation of possession by a
squatter with the actual consent of the paper title owner does not constitute
dispossession or possession by the squatter for the purposes of the Act. Beyond
that, as Slade J said, the words possess and dispossess are to be given their
ordinary meaning.

[38] It is sometimes said that ouster by the squatter is necessary to constitute
dispossession (see for example *Rains v Buxton* (1880) 14 Ch D 537 at 539 per Fry J).
The word 'ouster' is derived from the old law of adverse possession and has
overtones of confrontational, knowing removal of the true owner from possession.
Such an approach is quite incorrect. There will be a 'dispossession' of the paper
owner in any case where (there being no discontinuance of possession by the
paper owner) a squatter assumes possession in the ordinary sense of the word.
Except in the case of joint possessors, possession is single and exclusive.
Therefore if the squatter is in possession, the paper owner cannot be. If the paper
owner was at one stage in possession of the land but the squatter's subsequent
occupation of it in law constitutes possession, the squatter must have
'dispossessed' the true owner for the purposes of para 1 of Sch 1 (see *Treloar v Nute*
[1977] 1 All ER 230 at 234, [1976] 1 WLR 1295 at 1300; and Professor Dockray
'Adverse Possession and Intention' [1982] Conv 256). Therefore in the present
case the relevant question can be narrowed down to asking whether the Grahams
were in possession of the disputed land, without the consent of Pye, before
30 April 1986. If they were, they will have 'dispossessed' Pye within the meaning
of para 1 of Sch 1 to the 1980 Act.

[39] What then constitutes 'possession' in the ordinary sense of the word?

POSSESSION
[40] In *Powell v McFarlane* (1977) 38 P&CR 452 at 470 Slade J said:

'(1) In the absence of evidence to the contrary, the owner of land with the
paper title is deemed to be in possession of the land, as being the person with
the prime facie right to possession. The law will thus, without reluctance,
ascribe possession either to the paper owner or to persons who can establish
a title as claiming through the paper owner. (2) If the law is to attribute
possession of land to a person who can establish no paper title to possession,
he must be shown to have both factual possession and the requisite intention
to possess (*"animus possidendi"*).'

Counsel for both parties criticised this definition as being unhelpful since it used the word being defined—possession—in the definition itself. This is true: but Slade J was only adopting a definition used by Roman law and by all judges and writers in the past. To be pedantic, the problem could be avoided by saying there are two elements necessary for legal possession: (1) a sufficient degree of physical custody and control ('factual possession'); (2) an intention to exercise such custody and control on one's own behalf and for one's own benefit ('intention to possess'). What is crucial is to understand that, without the requisite intention, in law there can be no possession. Remarks made by Clarke LJ in *Lambeth London BC v Blackburn* [2001] EWCA Civ 912 at [18], (2001) 82 P&CR 494 ('it is not perhaps immediately obvious why the authorities have required a trespasser to establish an intention to possess as well as actual possession in order to prove the relevant adverse possession') provided the starting point for a submission by Mr Lewison QC for the Grahams that there was no need, in order to show possession in law, to show separately an intention to possess. I do not think that Clarke LJ was under any misapprehension. But in any event there has always, both in Roman law and in common law, been a requirement to show an intention to possess in addition to objective acts of physical possession. Such intention may be, and frequently is, deduced from the physical acts themselves. But there is no doubt in my judgment that there are two separate elements in legal possession. So far as English law is concerned, intention as a separate element is obviously necessary. Suppose a case where A is found to be in occupation of a locked house. He may be there as a squatter, as an overnight trespasser, or as a friend looking after the house of the paper owner during his absence on holiday. The acts done by A in any given period do not tell you whether there is legal possession. If A is there as a squatter he intends to stay as long as he can for his own benefit: his intention is an intention to possess. But if he only intends to trespass for the night or has expressly agreed to look after the house for his friend he does not have possession. It is not the nature of the acts which A does, but the intention with which he does them which determines whether or not he is in possession.

FACTUAL POSSESSION

[41] In *Powell's* case (1977) 38 P&CR 452 at 470–471 Slade J said:

'(3) Factual possession signifies an appropriate degree of physical control. It must be a single and [exclusive] possession, though there can be a single possession exercised by or on behalf of several persons jointly. Thus an owner of land and a person intruding on that land without his consent cannot both be in possession of the land at the same time. The question what acts constitute a sufficient degree of exclusive physical control must depend on the circumstances, in particular the nature of the land and the manner in which land of that nature is commonly used or enjoyed ... Everything must depend on the particular circumstances, but broadly, I think what must be shown as constituting factual possession is that the alleged possessor has been dealing with the land in question as an occupying owner might have been expected to deal with it and that no-one else has done so.'

I agree with this statement of the law which is all that is necessary in the present case. The Grahams were in occupation of the land which was within their exclusive physical control. The paper owner, Pye, was physically excluded from the land by the hedges and the lack of any key to the road gate. The Grahams farmed it in conjunction with Manor Farm and in exactly the same way. They were plainly in factual possession before 30 April 1986.

INTENTION TO POSSESS

(a) *To own or to possess?*

[42] There are cases in which judges have apparently treated it as being necessary that the squatter should have an intention to own the land in order to be in possession. In *Littledale v Liverpool College* [1900] 1 Ch 19 at 24 Lindley MR referred to the plaintiff relying on 'acts of ownership' (see also *George Wimpey & Co Ltd v Sohn* [1966] 1 All ER 232 at 240, [1967] Ch 487 at 510). Even Slade J in *Powell v McFarlane* (1977) 38 P&CR 452 at 476, 478, referred to the necessary intention as being an intention to 'own'. In *Buckinghamshire CC v Moran* (1988) 56 P&CR 372 at 378–379 the trial judge (Hoffmann J) had pointed out that what is required is 'not an intention to own or even an intention to acquire ownership but an intention to possess'. The Court of Appeal in that case ([1989] 2 All ER 225 at 238, [1990] Ch 623 at 643) adopted this proposition which in my judgment is manifestly correct. Once it is accepted that in the Limitation Acts, the word 'possession' has its ordinary meaning (being the same as in the law of trespass or conversion) it is clear that, at any given moment, the only relevant question is whether the person in factual possession also has an intention to possess: if a stranger enters onto land occupied by a squatter, the entry is a trespass against the possession of the squatter whether or not the squatter has any long-term intention to acquire a title.

[43] A similar manifestation of the same heresy is the statement by Lindley MR in *Littledale v Liverpool College* [1900] 1 Ch 19 at 23 that the paper owners—

> 'could not be dispossessed unless the plaintiffs obtained possession themselves; and possession by the plaintiffs involves an animus possidendi—i.e., occupation with the intention of excluding the owner as well as other people.'

This requirement of an intention to exclude the owner as well as everybody else has been repeated in subsequent cases. In *Powell v McFarlane* (1977) 38 P&CR 452 at 471–472 Slade J found difficulty in understanding what was meant by this dictum since a squatter will normally know that until the full time has run, the paper owner can recover the land from him. Slade J reformulated the requirement (to my mind correctly) as requiring an—

> 'intention, in one's own name and on one's own behalf, to exclude the world at large, including the owner with the paper title if he be not himself the possessor, so far as is reasonably practicable and so far as the processes of the law will allow.'

(b) *Must the acts of the squatter be inconsistent with the intentions of the paper owner?*

[44] The decision of the Court of Appeal in *Leigh v Jack* (1879) 5 Ex D 264 has given rise to repeated trouble in later cases. In that case the plaintiff's predecessor in title (Mr Leigh) had laid out part of his estate as proposed streets to be known as Grundy Street and Napier Place. He conveyed to the defendant certain land described as being 'bounded by' Grundy Street and Napier Place: therefore the intention to use the adjoining land for streets was known to all parties. Within the 20-year limitation period, both Mr Leigh and the defendant had carried out

work on a fence separating Grundy Street from other land of Mr Leigh, Regent Road. From 1854 onwards the defendant had placed on Grundy Street and Napier Place old graving dock materials, screw propellers, boilers and refuse from his foundry. In 1872 (four years before action brought) the defendant completely enclosed Grundy Street and Napier Place. The Court of Appeal held that the defendant had not acquired title to the enclosed land under the 1833 Act.

[45] The decision on the facts is not a surprising one. Quite apart from anything else, during the 20-year limitation period relied on, the paper owner (Mr Leigh) carried out works on the fence separating Grundy Street from Regent Road. This was inconsistent with a claim that he had either discontinued possession or been dispossessed. Unfortunately, other reasons were given. Cockburn CJ said that the defendant's storage of goods on the disputed land was not 'done with the view of defeating the purpose of the parties to the conveyances'. It will be noted that the defendant was well aware of Mr Leigh's intention to use the land as a public road since he was party to the conveyance so stating. Cotton LJ relied solely on the repair of the fence by Mr Leigh which I have mentioned as showing that there had been possession by him during the limitation period. The real difficulty has arisen from the judgment of Bramwell LJ. He said (at 273):

'I do not think that there was any dispossession of the plaintiff by the acts of the defendant: acts of user are not enough to take the soil out of the plaintiff and her predecessors in title and to vest it in the defendant; in order to defeat a title by dispossessing the former owner, acts must be done which are inconsistent with his enjoyment of the soil for the purposes for which he intended to use it ...'

The suggestion that the sufficiency of the possession can depend on the intention not of the squatter but of the true owner is heretical and wrong. It reflects an attempt to revive the pre-1833 concept of adverse possession requiring inconsistent user. Bramwell LJ's heresy led directly to the heresy in the *Wallis's Cayton Bay* line of cases to which I have referred, which heresy was abolished by statute. It has been suggested that the heresy of Bramwell LJ survived this statutory reversal but in *Buckinghamshire CC v Moran* [1989] 2 All ER 225, [1990] Ch 623 the Court of Appeal rightly held that however one formulated the proposition of Bramwell LJ as a proposition of law it was wrong. The highest it can be put is that, if the squatter is aware of a special purpose for which the paper owner uses or intends to use the land and the use made by the squatter does not conflict with that use, that may provide some support for a finding as a question of fact that the squatter had no intention to possess the land in the ordinary sense but only an intention to occupy it until needed by the paper owner. For myself I think there will be few occasions in which such inference could properly be drawn in cases where the true owner has been physically excluded from the land. But it remains a possible, if improbable, inference in some cases.

(c) *Squatters' willingness to pay if asked*

[46] In a number of cases (such as the present case) squatters have given evidence that if they had been asked by the paper owner to pay for their occupation of the disputed land or to take a lease they would have been prepared to do so. In *Ocean Estates Ltd v Pinder* [1969] 2 AC 19 at 24, [1969] 2 WLR 1359 at 1363 Lord Diplock, giving the advice of the Privy Council, said that an admission by the squatter to that effect 'which any candid squatter hoping in due course to

a acquire a possessory title would be almost bound to make' did not indicate an absence of an intention to possess. In my judgment in the present case the Court of Appeal did not give full weight to that decision. In my judgment the decision of the Court of Appeal in *R v Secretary of State for the Environment, ex p Davies* (1990) 61 P&CR 487 (the decision in *Pinder's* case not having been cited) was wrong. The decision in *Pinder's* case is to be preferred because it is consistent with

b principle. Once it is accepted that the necessary intent is an intent to possess not to own, and an intention to exclude the paper owner only so far as is reasonably possible, there is no inconsistency between a squatter being willing to pay the paper owner if asked and his being in the meantime in possession. An admission of title by the squatter is not inconsistent with the squatter being in possession in the meantime.

c

THE DECISION OF NEUBERGER J

[47] The learned judge in a very full and careful judgment set out all the facts I have stated above. There are two points which I need to stress. First, although the judge referred to the grazing agreement of 1 February 1983, he did not set it

d out or indeed appear to treat it as being of major importance beyond showing that, during its continuance, the Grahams were in possession with permission of the paper owner. As will be seen, the Court of Appeal took quite a different view of the importance of that agreement. Second, the judge found that the Grahams 'never vacated the disputed land' but 'just kept farming all the year round'. In addition to grazing the 80 to 140 head of cattle from February to November in

e every year, as I have said, the Grahams overwintered dry cattle and yearlings on the disputed land. In addition, in the years 1984/1985 they dunged the land and in 1985 harrowed, rolled and fertilised the disputed land.

[48] After considering the law and, broadly, directing himself in accordance with the decisions in *Powell v McFarlane* (1977) 38 P&CR 452 and *Buckinghamshire CC v*

f *Moran* [1989] 2 All ER 225, [1990] Ch 623 the judge first held that, because of the hay-cutting agreement, the Grahams had been on the disputed land with permission of Pye until 31 August 1984: time therefore could not start to run until after that date. He then dealt with the question (which is no longer in issue) as to when time ceased to run. Thirdly, he considered whether the Grahams had been in possession ie factual possession with an intention to possess. He held that the

g acts done by the Grahams on the land from 31 August 1984 onwards, and in particular the exclusion of the whole world from any access to the disputed land save on foot, constituted factual possession. As to the intention to possess, the judge reviewed the evidence and in particular took into account six factors. First, what the Grahams had done on the land. Second, for many years before 1984 the

h disputed land had been used for grazing purposes ie grazing was a normal farming use of that land. Third, that although the Grahams had not themselves enclosed the disputed land in fact the whole world (including Pye) was excluded from it save on foot: the Grahams controlled all vehicular access to it. Fourth, the Grahams tended the land in the same way as the rest of their farm by rolling,

j harrowing, fertilising and maintaining the hedges and ditches. Fifth, the emphatic refusal by Pye to grant a further grazing licence prevented Pye from alleging that anything done on the land thereafter by Graham had been done with the intention of obtaining a further grazing licence. Sixth, the judge dealt with the argument that since the Grahams knew of Pye's intention to obtain planning permission, the Grahams should be taken as not intending to be in possession. The judge pointed out that the Grahams had been refused a further grazing licence expressly on the grounds that Pye did not want anyone using the land at that time when planning permission was to be applied for and that accordingly any agricultural use of the land by the Grahams thereafter was inconsistent with such intended future use by Pye.

[49] Considering all these factors together, the judge with considerable reluctance held that the Grahams had the necessary intention to possess and had accordingly obtained title under the 1980 Act.

THE DECISION OF THE COURT OF APPEAL

[50] The Court of Appeal attached great importance to the grazing agreement of 1 February 1983 which Mummery LJ (giving the lead judgment) described as a contemporaneous and irrefutable record of the common intention of Pye and the Grahams regarding possession of the disputed land. Given that importance, I must follow the example of the Court of Appeal and set out the agreement virtually in full.

[51] By the agreement Pye agreed to grant to John Graham (the grazier) and he agreed to take a 'right to graze' the disputed land on the following terms:

'1. THE GRAZIER shall have the right to occupy and graze or mow the said land from the first day of February 1983 until the thirty-first day of December 1983 and shall have the use of the said land only for grazing or one cut of grass.

2. THE GRAZIER shall pay to the Owner the sum of £2000 ... in respect of the period of occupation mentioned in Clause 1 above ...

3. THE GRAZIER shall use the said land for the purpose only of grazing or mowing the same.

4. THE GRAZIER shall use only sheep/cattle/horses and–or ponies for the purpose of grazing the said land and shall not allow the said land to be entered upon or in any way used by goats, pigs, poultry or any diseased animals.

5. THE GRAZIER agrees to the following conditions (a) That he will not permit any trespass upon the said land (b) That he will keep the said land clean and free from [weeds] (c) That he will keep the gates, fences and ditches in good order (d) That he will not pasture on the said land any but his own animals (e) That he will graze and use the said land in a good and husbandlike manner (f) That he will not assign the benefit of this agreement or part with possession of the land ...

8. THIS AGREEMENT is not a contract of tenancy for the purposes of the Agricultural Holdings Act 1948.

9. IT IS EXPRESSLY agreed and understood that the Owner does not undertake to repeat this grazing licence for another period but if he agrees to do so a fresh agreement will have to be entered into by the Grazier to operate from a date subsequent to the agreed period such fresh agreement to operate as a new and distinct contract.

10. THE OWNER RESERVES the right to terminate this agreement and gain possession of the land on service of six months notice at any time during the period of the agreement with a proportional refund of the licence fee to the tenant but without any other form of compensation.'

[52] The Court of Appeal considered that this agreement constituted a licence, not a tenancy, and that it did not give possession of the land to the Grahams. In reciting the facts, they stated that there was little change in the use of the land

from the date of the expiry of that licence and the expiry of the cutting agreement right down to 1999: the Grahams continued to graze between 80 and 140 cattle on the land for nine or ten months. They then set out the 'seven' factors which the judge relied upon in finding that the Grahams had an intention to possess. It is not clear to me where the Court of Appeal discerned the seventh factor beyond the six enumerated by the judge. They held that the judge significantly underestimated certain uncontradicted oral evidence as to the Grahams' intentions which consequently led him to a conclusion justified neither by the facts nor by a proper application of the 1980 Act.

[53] In outline their process of reasoning was as follows. The parties to the grazing agreement 'plainly did not intend that the Grahams should have exclusive possession of the disputed land'. When that agreement came to an end on 31 December 1983 and the right to cut the grass had been exhausted by August 1984 the Grahams' intention in relation to the land did not change: their intention remained to continue to graze, fertilise and maintain the land in just the same way as under the licence, ie not as possessors of the land of which Pye remained in possession. Although their occupation was no longer permissive, it still lacked the intention to possess. In finding that this was the intention of the Grahams, the Court of Appeal relied on evidence given in the witness statement of Mr Michael Graham. He said of the year 1984:

'My intention was to carry on using the land for grazing until I was requested not to. However, no request was ever made to me or my father to vacate the land or to pay for the grazing which was taking place. Had Pye requested payment I would have happily paid them. In short I took advantage of the ability to use the land as no one challenged me ... I farmed the land during the autumn of 1984 through to the spring of 1985 in the same way as I had in the previous year ... I was aware that there was a risk that I would not obtain the benefit of that work as again in 1984 like 1983 there was no formal grazing licence or an agreement to take a cut of hay. I would have paid Pye for a grazing licence or a cut of hay but in the absence of any formal agreement I was willing to take a chance that an agreement would be forthcoming later. In light of the lack of interest shown by Pye during the 1984 grazing season I continued to use the land [for] what I considered to be its best use ... During the spring of 1985 I believe I made one or two telephone calls to Tim Evans to ask for a grazing licence for the 1985 season. I would have preferred to have obtained a formal agreement, but in the absence of one I continued to farm the land in the same fashion as I had in the 1984 and 1983 seasons. I did not receive a response from Tim Evans to my request and after a couple of attempts I gave up trying and decided to leave matters until I heard from him or from Pye directly. I believed at that time that it was possible to obtain ownership of land after it had been occupied for a sufficient number of years which I mistakenly thought was a period of seven years.'

[54] The Court of Appeal expressed their conclusions:

'34 ... (8) In my judgment, Mr Michael Graham's account of his state of mind, when considered in the context of the circumstances of an initial permissive use under licence and the continuation of the same use after the expiration of the licence, is not that of a person who is using the land with the intention of possessing it to the exclusion of Pye. It is that of a person who, having obtained the agreement of Pye to the limited use of the land in the past, continues to use it for the time being in exactly the same fashion in the hope that in the future Pye will again be willing to accede to his requests to enter an agreement authorising him to use it. (9) In brief, there was no direct evidence that the Grahams ever changed their intentions regarding the use of the land after the end of August 1984 from what it had been when they first started to use it under licence in September 1982. That initial use was on the basis of a common intention that Pye should retain possession of it (ie as part of a land bank for future development, if planning permission were granted) and that the Grahams should use it only for the limited purpose of grazing it and without any intention to possess it to the exclusion of Pye. After 31 August 1984 they did not do anything on the disputed land which they could not have done, and had not in fact done, under the grazing agreement. Their attitude to the land remained the same. Such direct evidence as there was on the intention issue positively indicated that there was probably no change in the intentions of the Grahams or of Pye.'

CONCLUSION

[55] It will be seen that the chain of reasoning of the Court of Appeal is as follows: first, the grazing agreement of 1 February 1983 'plainly' did not give possession to the Grahams; second, after the expiry of the grazing agreement the Grahams continued to use the land for grazing in the same way. They said that 'both the nature and extent of the Grahams' use of the disputed land, which did not amount to factual possession of it during the period of the licence, remained the same'; third, that Mr Michael Graham made admissions against interest that he continued to farm the disputed land in just the same way as in 1983.

[56] In my judgment each of the steps in that reasoning is suspect. First, did the Grahams obtain possession under the grazing agreement? It is important to construe that agreement against its background. In allowing the Grahams to use the land it was essential to Pye that the Grahams did not obtain security of tenure under the Agricultural Holdings Act 1948. Such security would have been obtained in any case where the rights granted over the land (whether by way of tenancy or licence is irrelevant) endured for a full year. Accordingly, in the present case it was of minor importance to the parties whether the Grahams were given possession of the land: what was important was that they did not enjoy whatever rights they had for a full year. Hence the grant of the grazing right for 11 months only and the express provision in cl 9 that a further term would only be granted by a new and distinct contract starting after the termination of the 1 February 1983 agreement. It is against this background that the question whether the Grahams obtained possession or not has to be determined. The fact that cl 5 contains a covenant by the Grahams 'not to part with possession' and cl 10 expressly makes Pye's right to regain 'possession' during the term dependent on serving a notice does not provide a promising basis for the holding of the Court of Appeal that the 'parties plainly did not intend that the Grahams should have exclusive possession'. However, I accept that there are substantial arguments that the document did create only a licence. Under the agreement the right granted is only a 'right to graze'; the land could only be used for grazing or mowing; the right is described as a 'grazing licence' in cl 9 and the payment for the grazing is described in cl 10 as a 'licence fee'.

[57] I do not find it necessary to decide whether the Grahams obtained exclusive possession under the agreement of 1 February 1983: I will assume that

a the Court of Appeal was right in holding that they did not. But even on that assumption it must be borne in mind that, ignorant of the legal niceties, the parties as lay people plainly thought that the Grahams were obtaining 'possession' for 11 months and in order to regain 'possession' during the currency of the agreement Pye would have had to serve notice. In my judgment the form of the agreement is inconsistent with any clear distinction being drawn by the

b parties between possession on the one hand and occupation without possession on the other.

[58] The second stage of the Court of Appeal reasoning was that, after the termination of the licence on 31 December 1983, and of the mowing agreement in August 1984, the Grahams continued to use the land in just the same way as they had during the currency of the grazing agreement: all that changed was that

c use was no longer permissive. In my view the facts as found by the judge or agreed do not support this view. The grazing agreement expired on 31 December 1983. In a letter from Pye's agents dated 30 December 1983 the Grahams were expressly required to vacate the disputed land. But the Grahams did not vacate the disputed land either then or at any later date. They spread dung on the land,

d harrowed it and rolled it. They overwintered dry cattle and yearlings in a shed on the land. From 1 January 1984 onwards the Grahams repeatedly did things on the disputed land which they would have had no right to do under the old grazing agreement even if it had still been in force. The objective facts demonstrate that the Grahams made such use of the disputed land as they wished irrespective of whether it fell within the terms of any hypothetical grazing agreement.

e [59] To this must be added another factor of some importance. When in January 1984 Pye refused to grant a further grazing licence they did so expressly on the grounds of the advice which they had received that, for planning purposes, they should have all the land in hand. Therefore, as the judge pointed out, the Grahams by grazing the land during 1984 and thereafter were not only acting

f without permission of the paper owner: they were acting in a way which, to their knowledge, was directly contrary to the wishes of the proprietors.

[60] The third limb of the Court of Appeal reasoning is that Michael Graham's evidence, contrary to his interest, was consistent with the Grahams' intention being not to possess the land on their own behalf but only to graze it as though there continued to be a grazing licence. In expressing this view the Court of

g Appeal was selective in its choice of the evidence in Michael Graham's witness statement, relying only on such evidence as was contrary to his interest. It is true that from the decision in *Powell's* case onwards judges have stressed the commonsense caution to be shown towards self-serving evidence such as that which can be given by a squatter as to his own intention at a past time. But this

h case is different: the Court of Appeal is relying on part of Mr Michael Graham's evidence as to his attitude whilst ignoring other parts of the evidence. In my judgment a proper view can only be formed by looking at the whole of his evidence on the subject. The judge specifically accepted his evidence that the disputed land was farmed together with Manor Farm effectively as a single unit.

j As the judge pointed out, there was independent evidence that Michael Graham 'treated the [disputed] land' as his own. When all the evidence is looked at in my judgment it is wholly consistent with the judge's view that, although the Grahams would have been willing to pay for the use of the disputed land if asked, such willingness is not inconsistent with them intending to possess the land in the meantime as demonstrated by them treating the land as part of Manor Farm and maintaining it on the same basis as the rest of the farm.

[61] If the view of the Court of Appeal were to be correct, the result would be anomalous. Although from 1984 to 1997 the Grahams were the only people who did anything on the disputed land and Pye had throughout that period been physically excluded from the land, nevertheless Pye was throughout to be treated as in possession. In my judgment, however favourably one approaches the claim of a paper owner to possession, such a conclusion would be so unrealistic as to be an impossible one. For all practical purposes the Grahams used the land as their own and in a way normal for an owner to use it throughout the period from August 1984 onwards. During that whole period Pye did nothing on the disputed land from which they were wholly excluded, save on foot.

[62] Therefore I cannot accept the reasoning on which the Court of Appeal and Pye in their submissions before your Lordships sought to demonstrate that the Grahams did not intend to possess the land.

[63] In his persuasive submissions for Pye Mr Gaunt QC, whilst adopting the general tenor of the Court of Appeal reasoning, sought to concentrate attention on the first two-and-a-half years, ie from 31 December 1983 to 30 April 1986. He was inclined to concede that at a later stage the Grahams might have been in possession. But, he submitted correctly, the Grahams had to demonstrate that they had dispossessed Pye before 30 April 1986. He submitted that this had not been done: from the date of the end of the grazing agreement the Grahams were seeking to obtain further grazing licences from Pye. Although this was initially refused they were granted the right to cut hay in 1984. Then in 1984 they again sought to obtain grazing licences but there was no response from Pye. Therefore, he submitted, whatever may have been the position in the later stages, the Grahams had not demonstrated an intention to possess the disputed land on their own behalf before 30 April 1986 and accordingly had not demonstrated that Pye had been dispossessed before that date.

[64] This is the most persuasive way of formulating Pye's case but I do not accept it. Despite Pye's notification to quit the land in December 1983, its peremptory refusal of a further grazing licence in 1984 and the totally ignored later requests for a grazing licence, after 31 December 1983 the Grahams stayed in occupation of the disputed land using it for what purposes they thought fit. Some of those purposes (ie the grazing) would have fallen within a hypothetical grazing agreement. But the rest are only consistent with an intention, verified by Mr Michael Graham, to use the land as they thought best. That approach was adopted from the outset. In my judgment, when the Grahams remained in factual possession of the fully enclosed land after the expiry of the mowing licence they manifestly intended to assert their possession against Pye.

[65] Finally I should mention one further point. In the Court of Appeal Pye unsuccessfully contended that the Human Rights Act 1998 affected the appeal which came on for hearing on 4 December 2000, ie after the Act had come into effect on 2 October 2000. Before your Lordships' House, it was conceded that the 1998 Act did not have a retrospective effect. But Pye submitted that, even under the common law principles of construction applicable before the 1998 Act came into effect, the court should seek to apply the law so as to make it consistent with the European Convention for the Protection of Human Rights and Fundamental Freedoms 1950 (as set out in Sch 1 to the 1998 Act). Any such old principle of construction only applied where there was an ambiguity in the language of a statute. No such ambiguity in the 1980 Act was demonstrated to your Lordships.

[66] For these reasons I would allow the appeal and restore the judgment of Neuberger J.

LORD HOPE OF CRAIGHEAD.

a   **[67]** My Lords, I have had the advantage of reading in draft the speech of my noble and learned friend Lord Browne-Wilkinson. I agree with it, and for the reasons which he has given I, too, would allow the appeal. I should like however to add a few brief observations on the concept of 'adverse possession' and on the apparent injustice of the result.

b   **[68]** Where a person in whose favour the period of limitation can run under s 15 of the Limitation Act 1980 is in the possession of land, he is described in para 8(1) of Sch 1 to that Act as being in 'adverse possession'. This use of the expression 'adverse possession' has been followed in the Land Registration Act 2002, which has introduced a new regime for the registration of an adverse possessor of an estate in land or rent charge (see s 97). The details are set out in *c*   Sch 6 to that Act. Paragraph 1(1) of the Schedule provides that a person may apply to the registrar to be registered as the proprietor of a registered estate in land if he has been in adverse possession of the estate for a period of ten years ending on the date of the application. The phrase 'adverse possession' is defined in para 11 of the Schedule. In brief, a person is in adverse possession for the *d*   purposes of the 2002 Act if, but for the disapplication by s 96 of that Act of periods of limitation against a registered proprietor, a period of limitation would run in his favour in relation to the estate under s 15 of the 1980 Act.

   [69] It is plainly of some importance, both now and for the future, to understand what the use of the word 'adverse' in the context of s 15 of the 1980 Act was intended to convey. At first sight, it might be thought that the word *e*   'adverse' describes the nature of the possession that the squatter needs to demonstrate. It suggests that an element of aggression, hostility or subterfuge is required. But an examination of the context makes it clear that this is not so. It is used as a convenient label only, in recognition simply of the fact that the possession is adverse to the interests of the paper owner or, in the case of *f*   registered land, of the registered proprietor. The context is that of a person bringing an action to recover land who has been in possession of land but has been dispossessed or has discontinued his possession (see para 8 of Sch 1 to the 1980 Act). His right of action is treated as accruing as soon as the land is in the possession of some other person in whose favour the limitation period can run. In that sense, and for that purpose, the other person's possession is adverse to his. *g*   But the question whether that other person is in fact in possession of the land is a separate question on which the word 'adverse' casts no light.

   [70] The general rule, which English law has derived from the Roman law, is that only one person can be in possession at any one time. Exclusivity is of the essence of possession. The same rule applies in cases where two or more persons *h*   are entitled to the enjoyment of property simultaneously. As between themselves they have separate rights, but as against everyone else they are in the position of a single owner. Once possession has begun, as in the case of the owner of land with a paper title who has entered into occupation of it, his possession is presumed to continue. But it can be transferred from one person to *j*   another, and it can also be lost when it is given up or discontinued. When that happens, possession can be acquired by someone else. The acquisition of possession requires both an intention to take or occupy the land ('animus') and some act of the body ('corpus') which gives effect to that intention. Occupation of the land alone is not enough, nor is an intention to occupy which is not put into effect by action. Both aspects must be examined, and each is bound up with the other. But acts of the mind can be, and sometimes can only be, demonstrated by acts of the body. In practice, the best evidence of intention is frequently found in the acts which have taken place.

[71] The question as to the nature of the intention that has to be demonstrated to establish possession was controversial, particularly among jurists in Germany (see, for example, Henry Bond 'Possession in the Roman Law' (1890) 6 LQR 259). But it is reasonably clear that the animus which is required is the intent to exercise exclusive control over the thing for oneself (see Bond (1890) 6 LQR 259 at 270). The important point for present purposes is that it is not necessary to show that there was a deliberate intention to exclude the paper owner or the registered proprietor. The word 'adverse' in the context of s 15(1) of the 1980 Act does not carry this implication. The only intention which has to be demonstrated is an intention to occupy and use the land as one's own. This is a concept which Rankine *The Law of Land-Ownership in Scotland* (4th edn, 1909) p 4, captured in his use of the Latin phrase 'cum animo rem sibi habendi' (see his reference in footnote 1 to Savigny *Das Recht des Besitzes*, translated by Perry (1848) (paras 1–11)). It is similar to that which was introduced into the law of Scotland by the Prescription Act 1617, Ch 12 relating to the acquisition of an interest in land by positive prescription. The possession that is required for that purpose is possession 'openly, peaceably and without any judicial interruption' on a competing title for the requisite period (see s 1(1)(a) of the Prescription and Limitation (Scotland) Act 1973). So I would hold that, if the evidence shows that the person was using the land in the way one would expect him to use it if he were the true owner, that is enough.

[72] I agree that the only conclusion that can reasonably be drawn from the evidence is that the Grahams occupied and used the disputed land as their own for 12 years before these actions were brought. The limitation provision in s 15 of the 1980 Act applies. The case has to be treated as one where the registered owner, having been dispossessed, has lost the right to recover the land.

[73] The question whether this result is incompatible with the Pye's rights under art 1 of the First Protocol to the European Convention for the Protection of Human Rights and Fundamental Freedoms 1950 (as set out in Sch 1 to the Human Rights Act 1998) was answered by the Court of Appeal ([2001] Ch 804, [2001] 2 WLR 1293) in the negative. It was not pursued before your Lordships. This is a civil and not a criminal case (see my observations in *R v Kansal (No 2)* [2001] UKHL 62 at [76], [2002] 1 All ER 257 at [76], [2002] 2 AC 69). Nevertheless it was conceded that s 22(4) of the 1998 Act did not apply as this was an appeal against a decision of a court or tribunal which was made before 2 October 2000. The question itself however is not an easy one, as one might have expected the law—in the context of a statutory regime where compensation is not available—to lean in favour of the protection of a registered proprietor against the actions of persons who cannot show a competing title on the register. Fortunately, as my noble and learned friend Lord Bingham of Cornhill has pointed out, a much more rigorous regime has now been enacted in Sch 6 to the 2002 Act. Its effect will be to make it much harder for a squatter who is in possession of registered land to obtain a title to it against the wishes of the proprietor. The unfairness in the old regime which this case has demonstrated lies not in the absence of compensation, although that is an important factor, but in the lack of safeguards against oversight or inadvertence on the part of the registered proprietor.

LORD HUTTON.

[74] My Lords, I have had the advantage of reading in draft the speech of my noble and learned friend Lord Browne-Wilkinson. I would allow this appeal for

a the reasons which he gives and with which I am in full agreement. I wish only to make some brief observations in relation to the proof of intention to possess which is referred to by Slade J in his classic judgment in *Powell v MacFarlane* (1977) 38 P&CR 452 at 470:

b
> 'If the law is to attribute possession of land to a person who can establish no paper title to possession, he must be shown to have both factual possession and the requisite intention to possess (*"animus possidendi"*).'

[75] In the present case from August 1984 onwards the Grahams made full use of the disputed land as if they were the owners—they did everything which an owner of the land would have done and when an experienced chartered surveyor, called on behalf of the claimants, was asked in cross-examination what

c an occupying owner of the disputed land might have done over and above what was done by the Grahams between 1984 and 1997, he was unable to think of anything.

[76] I consider that such use of land by a person who is occupying it will normally make it clear that he has the requisite intention to possess and that such

d conduct should be viewed by a court as establishing that intention, unless the claimant with the paper title can adduce other evidence which points to a contrary conclusion. Where the evidence establishes that the person claiming title under the Limitation Act 1980 has occupied the land and made full use of it in the way in which an owner would, I consider that in the normal case he will not have to adduce additional evidence to establish that he had the intention to

e possess. It is in cases where the acts in relation to the land of a person claiming title by adverse possession are equivocal and are open to more than one interpretation, that those acts will be insufficient to establish the intention to possess. But it is different if the actions of the occupier make it clear that he is using the land in the way in which a full owner would and in such a way that the

f owner is excluded.

[77] The conclusion to be drawn from such acts by an occupier is recognised by Slade J in *Powell's* case (1977) 38 P&CR 452 at 472:

g
> 'If his acts are open to more than one interpretation and he has not made it perfectly plain to the world at large by his actions or words that he has intended to exclude the owner as best he can, the courts will treat him as not having had the requisite *animus possidendi* and consequently as not having dispossessed the owner.'

And (at 476):

h
> 'In my judgment it is consistent with principle as well as authority that a person who originally entered another's land as a trespasser, but later seeks to show that he has dispossessed the owner, should be required to adduce compelling evidence that he had the requisite *animus possidendi* in any case where his use of the land was equivocal, in the sense that it did not

j necessarily, by itself, betoken an intention on his part to claim the land as his own and exclude the true owner.'

In another passage of his judgment (at 471–472) Slade J explains what is meant by 'an intention on his part to ... exclude the true owner':

> 'What is really meant, in my judgment, is that the *animus possidendi* involves the intention, in one's own name and on one's own behalf, to

exclude the world at large, including the owner with the paper title if he be not himself the possessor, so far as is reasonably practicable and so far as the processes of the law will allow.'

[78] It is clear that the fact that the Grahams would have given up occupation to the claimants or would have made payment for their occupation to the claimants, if requested to do so, does not prevent the existence of the intention to possess (see the judgment of the Privy Council delivered by Lord Diplock in *Ocean Estates Ltd v Pinder* [1969] 2 AC 19 at 24, [1969] 2 WLR 1359 at 1363).

[79] Therefore I consider that Clarke LJ was right to state in *Lambeth London BC v Blackburn* [2001] EWCA Civ 912 at [36], (2001) 82 P&CR 494:

'... I would not for my part think it appropriate to strain to hold that a trespasser who had established factual possession of the property for the necessary 12 years did not have the *animus possidendi* identified in the cases. I express that view for two reasons. The first is that the requirement that there be a sufficient manifestation of the intention provides protection for landowners and the second is that once it is held that the trespasser has factual possession it will very often be the case that he can establish the manifested intention. Indeed it is difficult to find a case in which there has been a clear finding of factual possession in which the claim to adverse possession has failed for lack of intention.'

[80] In the present case I am of the opinion that the manner in which the Grahams occupied and used the land points unequivocally to the intention to possess and I further consider, for the reasons given by Lord Browne-Wilkinson, that the witness statement of the late Mr Michael Graham, when it is considered as a whole and together with the other evidence, does not lead to a different conclusion.

Appeal allowed.

Kate O'Hanlon   Barrister.

a

R v Pope
[2002] UKHL 26

HOUSE OF LORDS
LORD NICHOLLS OF BIRKENHEAD, LORD BROWNE-WILKINSON, LORD HOBHOUSE OF
b WOODBOROUGH, LORD MILLETT AND LORD SCOTT OF FOSCOTE
20 FEBRUARY, 20 JUNE 2002

Sentence – Confiscation order – Crown Court – Jurisdiction – Whether Crown Court having jurisdiction to make confiscation order on committal for sentence from a magistrates' court in respect of offences committed before 30 September 1998 – Powers
c of Criminal Courts Act 1973, s 42(1) – Magistrates' Courts Act 1980, s 38 – Criminal Justice Act 1988, s 71.

The defendant was charged with several offences of procuring the execution of a valuable security by deception. The offences charged, which had been committed
d between March 1993 and September 1997, were triable 'either way', ie summarily in the magistrates' court or on indictment in the Crown Court. The defendant pleaded guilty to all the charges in the magistrates' court, and convictions were duly entered against him. The magistrates committed the defendant to the Crown Court for sentencing pursuant to s 38 of the Magistrates' Courts Act 1980.
e On such a committal, the Crown Court had the power, under s 42(1) of the Powers of Criminal Courts Act 1973, 'to deal with the offender in any manner in which it could deal with him if he had just been convicted of the offence on indictment before the court'. In addition to imposing a custodial sentence, the Crown Court made a confiscation order against the defendant pursuant to s 71 of the Criminal Justice Act 1988, as amended in 1995. Section 71(1E), which had been
f inserted in 1995, distinguished between 'an offence of which a person is convicted in any proceedings before the Crown Court' (sub-s (1E)(a)) and 'an offence of which a person is convicted in any proceedings in a magistrates' court' (sub-s (1E)(b)). The defendant appealed against the confiscation order, contending that the Crown Court had exceeded its powers in making it since the power in s 71(1E) only arose in the court where a defendant had been convicted, ie in the magistrates' court in
g his case. In so contending, the defendant submitted that the introduction of sub-s (1E) had created an unintentional lacuna which had not been remedied until the introduction of s 71(9A) on 30 September 1998, a provision that did not apply to offences committed before it came into force. Although the Court of Appeal disagreed with that argument, it allowed the appeal on the basis that it
h was bound to do so by one of its previous decisions. The Crown appealed.

Held – On committal for sentence from a magistrates' court in respect of offences committed before 30 September 1998, the Crown Court had the power to make a confiscation order under s 71 of the 1988 Act. The supposed lacuna in the powers of the Crown Court to make confiscation orders did not exist, even for
j the short period between 1995 and 30 September 1998. Section 42 of the 1973 Act was clear and so was the function of the scheme under s 38 of the 1980 Act of which it formed part. The purpose was to enable the question of guilt in 'either way' cases to be settled in the magistrates' court where the defendant did not opt for trial on indictment, and for the Crown Court to deal with sentence where it was necessary by ensuring that the sentencing court had the appropriate

sentencing powers to reflect the gravity of the case. Section 42 of the 1973 Act used
wholly appropriate words to achieve that result. Section 71 of the 1988 Act,
as originally enacted, had no words which could even raise an argument that s 42
was to be qualified, and it was scarcely arguable that the amendments made to
s 71 in 1995 and the inclusion of sub-s (1E) were intended to qualify s 42 and
undermine s 38. Accordingly, the appeal would be allowed (see [1], [2], [16], [18],
[20], [21], below).

R v Whellem [2000] 1 Cr App R (S) 200 overruled.

Notes

For confiscation orders made by the Crown Court and for sentencing powers on
committal for sentence, see 11(2) *Halsbury's Laws* (4th edn reissue) paras 1289,
1350.

    For the Powers of Criminal Courts Act 1973, s 42, see 12 *Halsbury's Statutes* (4th
edn) (1997 reissue) 594. Section 42 of the 1973 Act was repealed by the Powers of
Criminal Courts (Sentencing) Act 2000, s 165(4), Sch 12, Pt I, with effect from
25 August 2000.

    For the Magistrates' Courts Act 1980, s 38, see 27 *Halsbury's Statutes* (4th edn)
(2000 reissue) 116.

    For the Criminal Justice Act 1988, s 71, see 12 *Halsbury's Statutes* (4th edn) (1997
reissue) 1025.

Cases referred to in opinions

F, Re (22 June 1998, unreported).
R v Stephenson [1999] 1 Cr App R (S) 177, CA.
R v Whellem [2000] 1 Cr App R (S) 200, CA.

Appeal

The Crown appealed with leave of the Appeal Committee of the House of Lords
given on 17 July 2001 from the decision of the Court of Appeal (Buxton LJ, Scott
Baker and Holman JJ) on 5 April 2001 allowing an appeal by the defendant, Alan
Pope, from a confiscation order made against him on 26 May 2000 by Judge
Morell (sitting with two justices) in the Crown Court at Peterborough following
his conviction at Huntingdon Magistrates' Court on 20 January 2000 for offences
under s 20(2) of the Theft Act 1968. The Court of Appeal certified that a question
of law of general public importance, set out at [5], below, was involved in its
decision. The facts are set out in the opinion of Lord Hobhouse of Woodborough.

Victor Temple QC and *Kennedy Talbot* (instructed by the *Crown Prosecution Service*)
    for the Crown.
Jeffrey Pegden QC and *Geoffrey Birch* (instructed by *Brignalls Balderston Warren*,
    Stevenage) for the defendant.

Their Lordships took time for consideration.

20 June 2002. The following opinions were delivered.

LORD NICHOLLS OF BIRKENHEAD.

    [1] My Lords, I have had the advantage of reading a draft of the speech of my
noble and learned friend Lord Hobhouse of Woodborough. For the reasons he
gives, with which I agree, I would allow this appeal.

LORD BROWNE-WILKINSON.

a

[2] My Lords, I have had the advantage of reading in draft the speech of my noble and learned friend, Lord Hobhouse of Woodborough. I agree with it, and for the reasons he gives I too would allow the appeal and make the order which he proposes.

b **LORD HOBHOUSE OF WOODBOROUGH.**

[3] My Lords, this appeal has been necessary to resolve a difference of opinion concerning the sentencing powers of the Crown Court under s 71 of the Criminal Justice Act 1988. The sentencing power in question is the power of the Crown Court to make a confiscation order in respect of a defendant who has been convicted in the magistrates' court and committed to the Crown Court for

c sentence under s 38 of the Magistrates' Court Act 1980.

[4] The relevant facts are that the defendant, Alan Pope, was charged with 17 offences of procuring the execution of a valuable security by deception contrary to s 20(2) of the Theft Act 1968. The offences charged spanned the period between March 1993 and September 1997 and involved in all the diversion

d of some £220,000 of his employers' money into his own bank account. The offences were indictable offences triable 'either way', ie either summarily in the magistrates' court or on indictment in the Crown Court. On 20 January 2000, in the Huntingdon Magistrates' Court, the defendant elected to plead guilty to all the charges and, in view of these pleas, convictions were duly entered against

e him. In exercise of their powers under s 38 of the Magistrates' Court Act 1980, the magistrates committed him to the Crown Court for sentence. On 26 May 2000, the Crown Court sitting at Peterborough (Judge Morrell sitting with two justices) sentenced him to two years' imprisonment concurrent on all counts and, after making the relevant assessments, made a confiscation order against him in the sum of £127,000 (with a further period of two years' imprisonment in default

f of payment within six months).

[5] The defendant appealed to the Court of Appeal on the ground that the Crown Court had exceeded its powers in making the confiscation order and the further grounds that the Crown Court had not assessed his realisable assets and exercised its discretion on the right basis and in a fair manner. The Court of

g Appeal, Buxton LJ, Scott Baker and Holman JJ, allowed the appeal and quashed the confiscation order. They held that they were bound by the previous decision of the court in *R v Whellem* [2000] 1 Cr App R (S) 200 to hold that the Crown Court had not had the jurisdiction to make the confiscation order. The Court of Appeal certified a question of law of general public importance:

h   'Whether the Crown Court on committal for sentence from a magistrates' court in respect of offences committed before 30 September 1998 has the power to make an order for confiscation pursuant to s 71 of the 1988 Act?'

The Crown has appealed to your Lordships' House with your Lordships' leave.

j It was agreed by counsel for both parties that, if the certified question is answered favourably to the Crown, the appeal should be allowed and the case remitted to the Court of Appeal.

The statutory material

[6] The question of statutory construction arises from the manner in which the 1988 Act and the other relevant Acts have been amended from time to time.

The 1988 Act as originally enacted provided in Pt VI under the heading 'Confiscation of the Proceeds of an Offence':

> '**71.**—(1) The Crown Court and a magistrates' court shall each have power, in addition to dealing with an offender in any other way, to make an order under this section requiring him to pay such sum as the court thinks fit.
>
> (2) The Crown Court may make such an order against an offender where—(a) he is found guilty of an offence to which this Part of this Act applies; and ...
>
> (3) A magistrates' court may make such an order against an offender where—(a) he is convicted of an offence listed in Schedule 4 to this Act; and ...
>
> (9) In this Part of this Act ... (c) references to an offence to which this Part of this Act applies are references to any offence which—(i) is listed in Schedule 4 to this Act; or (ii) if not so listed, is an indictable offence, other than a drug trafficking offence ...'

Schedule 4 to the 1988 Act contains a limited list of offences connected with places of entertainment and cognate activities and breach of copyright etc. The offences with which the defendant was charged and for which he was convicted were indictable offences not involving drug trafficking.

[7] The 1988 Act was amended by the Proceeds of Crime Act 1995. This provided, so far as material, that there should be substituted for the original s 71(1)–(3) new sub-ss (1)–(1E).

> '(1) Where an offender is convicted, in any proceedings before the Crown Court or a magistrates' court, of an offence of a relevant description, it shall be the duty of the court ... to [follow the prescribed procedure for possibly making a confiscation order] ...
>
> (1E) For the purposes of this Part of this Act an offence is an offence of a relevant description—(a) in the case of an offence of which a person is convicted in any proceedings before the Crown Court or which is or will be taken into consideration by the Crown Court in determining any sentence, if it is an offence to which this Part of this Act applies; and (b) in the case of an offence of which a person is convicted in any proceedings in a magistrates' court or which is or will be taken into consideration by a magistrates' court in determining any sentence, if it is an offence listed in Schedule 4 to this Act.'

Major changes were made in the 1995 Act to the confiscation order regime but they are not presently relevant. One such change had already been made by s 28 of the Criminal Justice Act 1993 which amended the 1988 Act so that the confiscation order and the other sentences, eg imprisonment or fine, no longer all had to be imposed at the same time on the same occasion but the decision upon the confiscation order and its imposition could be postponed without holding up the other parts of the sentencing process (see s 72A). In 1998, by s 83 of the Crime and Disorder Act 1998, a further subsection was added to s 71 of the 1988 Act:

> '(9A) Where an offender is committed by a magistrates' court for sentence under section 38 or 38A of the Magistrates' Court Act 1980 or section 56 of the Criminal Justice Act 1967, this section and sections 72 to 74C below shall have effect as if the offender had been convicted of the offence in the proceedings before the Crown Court and not the proceedings before the magistrates' court.'

a This provision did not apply to offences committed before it came into force, ie before 30 September 1998 (see para 8 of Sch 9). This is why that date is referred to in the certified question.

[8] This amendment refers to the 1980 Act. Section 38 was part of that Act as originally drafted. It provided:

b 'Where on the summary trial of an offence triable either way ... if ... the court is of opinion that [the defendant's character and antecedents] are such that greater punishment should be inflicted for the offence than the court has power to inflict, the court may ... commit him in custody or on bail to the Crown Court for sentence in accordance with the provisions of section 42 of the Powers of Criminal Courts Act 1973.'

c In 1991 this section was amplified in a section which was substituted by s 25 of the Criminal Justice Act 1991. The powers to commit for sentence were expanded. The cross-reference to s 42 of the Powers of Criminal Courts Act 1973 was preserved.

[9] Section 42 of the 1973 Act, as amended by the 1980 Act provided:

d 'Where an offender is committed by a magistrates' court for sentence under section 38 of the Magistrates' Court Act 1980 or section 62 of the Criminal Justice Act 1967, the Crown Court shall enquire into the circumstances of the case and shall have power to deal with the offender in any manner in which it could deal with him if he had just been convicted of

e the offence on indictment before the court.'

Later amendments have been made to s 42 but are not material to this appeal.

[10] It will be appreciated that these provisions do distinguish between the jurisdiction of the magistrates' court on the one hand and that of the Crown Court on the other to make confiscation orders. But it will likewise be

f appreciated that s 42 of the 1973 Act makes special provision for the sentencing of offenders who have been committed to the Crown Court for sentence under s 38 of the 1980 Act. The magistrates' court would not have had the power to make the confiscation order against the defendant (the offences were not offences falling within Sch 4) any more than it could have sentenced him to two years' imprisonment. But if he had just been convicted of the offences on indictment

g before the Crown Court, the Crown Court would undoubtedly have had jurisdiction to make a confiscation order against him.

R v Whellem

[11] *R v Whellem* [2000] 1 Cr App R (S) 200 was decided on 11 June 1999 by a

h Court of Appeal consisting of Tuckey LJ, Gage J and Judge Rivlin QC. The judgment of the court was delivered by Gage J. Mr Whellem had pleaded guilty in the magistrates' court to three counts of having been knowingly concerned in dealing with wine, cigarettes and tobacco with intent to defraud the Crown of the duty payable. He was committed for sentence to the Crown Court under s 38 of

j the 1980 Act. In the Crown Court he was sentenced to 12 months' imprisonment and a confiscation order was made against him in the sum of £35,243·08. The relevant evasion of duty had taken place over the period June 1996 to May 1998. Mr Whellem appealed to the Court of Appeal on the ground that, since he had pleaded guilty in the magistrates' court and had been convicted there, he was not a person who had been convicted in any proceedings before the Crown Court (s 71(1E)) the confiscation order had been made without jurisdiction. This argument was accepted and the confiscation order was quashed; but the Court of Appeal substituted a compensation order in the like amount.

[12] The argument of Mr Whellem was based upon the wording of s 71(1E) read with s 71(9A) introduced by the 1998 Act. It was submitted that the introduction of the new sub-s (1E) in 1995 had created an unintentional lacuna which had not been remedied until the introduction of sub-s (9A) in 1998 which did not have retrospective effect. Subsection (9A) had only been necessary because of the discovery of the lacuna. It was this lacuna which invalidated the order made against Mr Whellem. The argument of the Crown was that s 42 of the 1973 Act had throughout given the Crown Court the requisite power on a committal for sentence. The argument of the Crown was supported by *Re F* (22 June 1998, unreported (Jowitt J)) that the requisite power was given by s 42 read with s 71. The Court of Appeal rejected the argument of the Crown. They gave a construction to sub-s (1E) which overrode s 42 and required an actual conviction in the Crown Court. They were not impressed by the decision of Jowitt J since his attention had not been drawn to the new sub-s (9A).

[13] The decision in *R v Whellem* has been criticised in a case note in the Criminal Law Review ([1999] Crim LR 1000 at 1001). Understandably describing the relevant legislation as a 'tangled mess', the writer, Dr Thomas, points out the relevance of the confiscation legislation being drafted by reference to indictable offences which include offences triable either way and the absurdity then of failing to give effect to the clear provisions of s 42. Dr Thomas also draws attention to the case of *R v Stephenson* [1999] 1 Cr App R (S) 177 at 179, and to the view that the need for sub-s (9A) was not to fill a non-existent lacuna in the powers of the Crown Court but to enable the prosecutor, by serving a notice under the amended s 71(1), to place the Crown Court under a *duty* to follow the confiscation procedures on a s 38 (or s 38A) committal.

[14] The defendant submits nevertheless that *R v Whellem* [2000] 1 Cr App R (S) 200 was rightly decided for the reasons given in the judgment delivered by Gage J (at 204–205):

'In our judgment where a defendant pleads guilty in a magistrates' court it cannot be said that he has been convicted before the Crown Court. Section 42(1)(a) of the Powers of [Criminal] Court[s] Act 1973 gives the court power to deal with such a defendant in any manner as if he had been convicted on indictment, but the power in section 71(1E) does not arise save in the court where he was convicted; in this case that is the magistrates' court.'

The Court of Appeal

[15] In the present case Buxton LJ reviewed the law and the criticisms made of *R v Whellem* by Dr Thomas. He disagreed with the decision in *R v Whellem* but held that it was not decided per incuriam and that the court was bound to follow it. Buxton LJ pointed out that s 71(1E) was a definition section and that the relevant power was to be derived from s 71(1), that s 42 was clear and seemingly conclusive and supported by *R v Stephenson*, and that the argument of redundancy from s 71(9A) was unimpressive; he broadly agreed with the criticisms of *R v Whellem* made by Dr Thomas.

Discussion

[16] The arguments in your Lordships' House were those which had been considered by the Court of Appeal in *R v Whellem* and the present case. For the

a reasons given by Buxton LJ I prefer the argument of the Crown. Section 42 of the 1973 Act is clear and so is the function of the s 38 scheme of which it forms part. The purpose is to enable the question of guilt in an either way case to be settled in the magistrates' court where the defendant does not opt for a trial on indictment and for the Crown Court to deal with sentence where it is necessary to ensure that the sentencing court has the appropriate sentencing powers to *b* reflect the gravity of the case. Section 42 uses wholly-appropriate words to achieve this result:

> '... the Crown Court ... shall have power to deal with the offender in any manner in which it could deal with him if he had just been convicted of the offence on indictment before the court.'

c Section 71 of the 1988 Act as originally enacted had no words which could even raise an argument that s 42 of the 1973 Act was to be qualified. It is scarcely arguable that the amendments made to s 71 in 1995 and the inclusion of sub-s (1E) was intended to qualify s 42 and undermine s 38. Apparently, the factor which is thought to make it arguable and persuasive is the 1998 amendment and the *d* inclusion of sub-s (9A). But this is an unimpressive argument: it seeks to construe and determine the import of a statutory provision by reference to something which occurred three years after it was enacted and became law; it is founded on one of the weakest of arguments, the argument of redundancy; it is in any event questionable whether the premise from which the redundancy argument proceeded was made out as is demonstrated by the comments of Dr Thomas *e* already referred to.

[17] The only additional argument advanced in support of the defendant's case on this appeal was an attempt to rely upon Parliamentary material. I do not consider that this attempt was proper. Section 42 of the 1973 Act is clear and the arguments considered by Buxton LJ and the Court of Appeal do not raise any *f* ambiguity. The material sought to be relied on was the report of what was said by Lord Williams of Mostyn when inviting the House of Lords to agree to the Commons amendment which was to become s 83 of the Crime and Disorder Act 1998. He said that the amendment and that to Sch 9—

> '... are technical amendments which are designed to deal with an unintended
> *g* effect of s 49 of the Criminal Procedure and Investigations Act 1996 on the courts' powers to confiscate the proceeds of crime. Under the 1988 Act, the magistrates' court, except for a very limited range of offences, has no power to make confiscation orders. The Crown Court has extensive powers to order confiscation when it convicts a defendant, but its powers of
> *h* confiscation are not presently available where an offender is committed for sentence, which happens quite often. Amendment No. 61, with its brother, is designed to deal with that anomaly.' (See 592 HL Official Report (5th series) col 1002.)

At the best from the point of view of the defendant, this quotation does no more *j* than raise a question whether what Dr Thomas said about the motivation for the 1998 amendment was correct. The critical point is whether Lord Williams was right in the belief that there was a lacuna. For the reasons which I have already given, and those given by Buxton LJ, I do not agree that he was right. What he says is further open to question in that he believes that the problem arises from s 49 of the Criminal Procedure and Investigations Act 1996. That was the section which introduced the scheme of an initial procedure for offences triable either

way and an indication of intention as to plea. This might have raised problems
for the operation of s 38 but it did not because it was anticipated by the draftsman
who expressly provided in the new s 17A(6) that, if the accused indicates that he
would plead guilty, 'the court shall proceed as if—(a) the proceedings constituted
from the beginning the summary trial of the information; and (b) ... he pleaded
guilty'. The s 38 procedure is therefore, available as was accepted in both *R v
Whellem* and the present case, and s 42 continued to apply.

Conclusion

[18] It follows that in my opinion the supposed lacuna in the powers of the
Crown Court to make confiscation orders did not exist even for the short period
between 1995 and 30 September 1998 and that the certified question should be
answered in the affirmative. *R v Whellem* should be overruled. The appeal should
be allowed accordingly and the case remitted to the Court of Appeal.

[19] In the Court of Appeal, the defendant criticised the amount of the
confiscation order made in the Crown Court and submitted as a further ground
of appeal that it had been arrived at on the wrong basis and the proper procedures
had not been followed. The Court of Appeal indicated that, if they had not
quashed the confiscation order on the jurisdiction point, they would have
remitted the order to the Crown Court (sic). The parties' printed cases addressed
these matters but your Lordships have not heard argument upon them because,
as previously stated, counsel for both parties agreed that in the event of the appeal
on the certified question being allowed, the case should be remitted to the Court
of Appeal, the Crown having now conceded that it could not rely upon the
£585,000 figure said to be available to the defendant outside the jurisdiction (see
para 49 of the Crown's printed case).

LORD MILLETT

[20] My Lords, I have had the advantage of reading in draft the speech of my
noble and learned friend, Lord Hobhouse of Woodborough. I agree with it, and
for the reasons he gives I too would allow the appeal and make the order which
he proposes.

LORD SCOTT OF FOSCOTE

[21] My Lords, I have had the advantage of reading in draft the opinion of my
noble and learned friend, Lord Hobhouse of Woodborough. I agree with it, and
for the reasons he gives I too would allow the appeal and make the order which
he proposes.

Appeal allowed.

Kate O'Hanlon   Barrister.

a

Athletic Union of Constantinople v National Basketball Association and others (No 2)
[2002] EWCA Civ 830

b

COURT OF APPEAL, CIVIL DIVISION
LORD PHILLIPS OF WORTH MATRAVERS MR, ROBERT WALKER AND CLARKE LJJ
28 MAY 2002

c *Arbitration – Award – Challenge to award on grounds of lack of jurisdiction – Whether Court of Appeal having jurisdiction to grant permission to appeal from decision of High Court on such a challenge – Arbitration Act 1996, s 67(4).*

d A party to arbitration proceedings made an unsuccessful application to the Commercial Court for an order under s 67[a] of the Arbitration Act 1996 setting aside an arbitral award on the ground that the arbitrator had had no jurisdiction. Section 67(4) of the 1996 Act provided that the leave of 'the court' was required for any appeal from a decision of 'the court' under s 67. Similar provisions were contained in ss 68[b] and 69[c] in respect of appeals from decisions by 'the court' under those sections, while s 105(1)[d] provided that 'the court' meant the High *e* Court or the county court. The Commercial Court judge refused permission to appeal to the Court of Appeal from his decision on the s 67 application, but such permission was granted on paper by a single Lord Justice. In a subsequent application to set aside that permission, the Court of Appeal was required to determine whether it had jurisdiction to grant permission to appeal from a *f* decision of the Commercial Court under s 67.

Held – The Court of Appeal had no jurisdiction to grant permission to appeal from a decision of the Commercial Court under s 67 of the 1996 Act. The 'court' referred to twice in s 67(4) was, in each instance, the Commercial Court which had made the decision against which an appeal was sought. The natural *g* construction of s 67(4) accorded to the word 'court' the same meaning on each occasion that it was used. On the second occasion that it was used, it manifestly, indeed expressly, meant the court which had made the decision under s 67. Moreover, it was natural, and in accordance with the established approach to statutory construction, to give the words 'the court' the same meaning wherever *h* they appeared in ss 67, 68 and 69 of the Act unless the context otherwise required. The context did not so require. Section 105(1) required that 'the court' meant the Commercial Court in the present context. Furthermore, ss 67, 68 and 69 demonstrated a consistent legislative policy that no appeal should be made against the decision of a court without the permission of that court. It followed *j* in the instant case that the single Lord Justice had had no jurisdiction to grant

---

a   Section 67 is set out at [10], below
b   Sections 68 is set out at [10], below
c   Section 69 are set out at [10], below
d   Section 105(1) is set out at [11], below

permission to appeal. Accordingly, the application would be granted (see [12], *a*
[13], [17]–[19], below).

Henry Boot Construction (UK) Ltd v Malmaison Hotel (Manchester) Ltd [2001] 1 All
ER 257 applied.

Notes

For the requirement of permission to appeal from a decision of the court on a *b*
challenge to an award on the grounds of lack of jurisdiction, see Supp to
2 *Halsbury's Laws* (4th edn reissue) para 690–713.2 n3.

For the Arbitration Act 1996, ss 67, 68, 69, 105, see 2 *Halsbury's Statutes* (4th
edn) (1999 reissue) 607, 608, 609, 629.

c

Case referred to in judgments

Henry Boot Construction (UK) Ltd v Malmaison Hotel (Manchester) Ltd [2001] 1 All ER
    257, [2001] QB 388, [2000] 3 WLR 1824, CA.

Application

The National Basketball Association (NBA), the Phoenix Suns (Phoenix) and the *d*
Federation Internationale de Basketball eV (FIBA) applied pursuant to CPR 52.9
for an order setting aside the order of Rix LJ on 22 November 2001 granting the
Athletic Union of Constantinople (AEK) permission to appeal from the decision
of Richard Field QC, sitting as a deputy judge of the Queen's Bench Division in
the Commercial Court on 7 August 2001 ([2002] 1 All ER (Comm) 70), whereby *e*
he dismissed AEK's application for an order under s 67 of the Arbitration Act 1996
setting aside an arbitral award made by Ian Patrick Travers on 2 October 2000 on
the ground that he had had no substantive jurisdiction. The facts are set out in
the judgment of Lord Phillips of Worth Matravers MR.

Richard Spearman QC (instructed by *Theodore Goddard*) for NBA and Phoenix. *f*
Murray Shanks (instructed by *Farrer & Co*) for FIBA.
AEK was not represented.

LORD PHILLIPS OF WORTH MATRAVERS MR.

g

Introduction

[1] The three applicants, the National Basketball Association (NBA), Phoenix
Suns (Phoenix) and Federation International de Basketball eV (FIBA), are
respondents to an appeal, which the Athletic Union of Constantinople (AEK) has
obtained permission to bring against a judgment of Mr Richard Field QC, sitting *h*
in the Commercial Court as a deputy judge of the Queen's Bench Division
delivered on 7 August 2001 ([2002] 1 All ER (Comm) 70). Permission to appeal
was granted by Rix LJ on 22 November 2001 in response to a paper application.

[2] The applicants apply to strike out AEK's appellant's notice and to set aside
the grant of permission to appeal. They do so pursuant to CPR 52.9, which gives
the court powers to take such action where permission to appeal has been given *j*
in the absence of the respondents, but provides that the court will only exercise
those powers in exceptional circumstances.

[3] The first ground advanced by the applicants undoubtedly constitutes
exceptional circumstances. It is that this court has no jurisdiction to hear the

a appeal that Rix LJ has given permission to bring. I propose to consider that ground first. AEK are not represented at this hearing. On 22 May 2002 Master Venne ordered that Messrs Thomas Eggar Church Adams be removed from the record as acting on their behalf.

Background

b [4] On 2 October 2000 Mr Ian Patrick Travers handed down what purported to be an arbitral award in relation to an arbitration between NBA and Phoenix on the one hand and AEK on the other. The arbitration was initiated under an agreement in writing dated 14 March 1997 between NBA and FIBA. NBA is the American Association of Professional Basketball Players and FIBA is the international association. The agreement provided an umbrella under which *c* clubs' members of either association could take part in arbitrations to resolve disputes as to the employment of professional basketball players and, no doubt, other matters.

[5] The agreement made provision that FIBA and NBA could take part in the arbitrations and would be bound by the consequences, but on this occasion FIBA *d* did not choose to take part in the arbitration. When the matter came before the Commercial Court, in the circumstances which I shall describe, they intervened, as being interested in upholding the award made by Mr Travers. They have appeared before us on the same basis.

[6] The subject matter of the arbitration related to the services of a professional basketball player called Mr Tsakelidis. Phoenix wished to engage *e* him to play for them, but AEK contended that he was already contracted to them. As I understand it, the issue was whether this contention was well founded.

[7] The details of the dispute are not material. I should record, however, that, while AEK took part in the arbitration proceedings, they challenged the jurisdiction of Mr Travers. Mr Travers ruled that he had substantive jurisdiction *f* over AEK and he proceeded to make an award in favour of Phoenix and NBA. AEK then applied to the Commercial Court seeking the following relief: (1) an order pursuant to s 67 of the Arbitration Act 1996 setting aside the award, or declaring it of no effect, on the ground that the arbitrator had no jurisdiction; and in the event of the first application not succeeding, (2) permission to appeal against the award on a point of law pursuant to s 69 of the Act.

g [8] The deputy judge dismissed the first application and refused permission to appeal to the Court of Appeal against his decision. He also refused permission to appeal to the Commercial Court on a point of law under s 69.

The issue

h [9] AEK have not sought to challenge the refusal of leave under s 69. Their application for permission to appeal is only in relation to the deputy judge's decision under s 67. The applicants contend that no appeal lay either against the s 67 decision or against the s 69 decision. They submit that the provision of each section required permission to be given by the deputy judge as a precondition to *j* any right to appeal to the Court of Appeal.

The statutory provisions

[10] Sections 67, 68 and 69 of the Act make provision for different circumstances in which an award can be challenged before the court. The relevant provisions of each section are as follows:

'**67. *Challenging the award: substantive jurisdiction.*—**(1) A party to arbitral
proceedings may (upon notice to the other parties and to the tribunal) apply
to *the court*—(a) challenging any award of the arbitral tribunal as to its
substantive jurisdiction; or (b) for an order declaring an award made by the
tribunal on the merits to be of no effect, in whole or in part, because the
tribunal did not have substantive jurisdiction. A party may lose the right to
object (see section 73) and the right to apply is subject to the restrictions in
section 70(2) and (3).

(2) The arbitral tribunal may continue the arbitral proceedings and make
a further award while an application to *the court* under this section is pending
in relation to an award as to jurisdiction.

(3) On an application under this section challenging an award of the
arbitral tribunal as to its substantive jurisdiction, *the court* may by order—
(a) confirm the award, (b) vary the award, or (c) set aside the award in whole
or in part.

(4) *The leave of the court is required for any appeal from a decision of the court
under this section.*

68. *Challenging the award: serious irregularity.*—(1) A party to arbitral
proceedings may (upon notice to the other parties and to the tribunal) apply
to *the court* challenging an award in the proceedings on the ground of serious
irregularity affecting the tribunal, the proceedings or the award ...

(3) If there is shown to be serious irregularity affecting the tribunal, the
proceedings or the award, *the court* may—(a) remit the award to the tribunal,
in whole or in part, for reconsideration, (b) set the award aside in whole or
in part, or (c) declare the award to be of no effect, in whole or in part. *The
court* shall not exercise its power to set aside or to declare an award to be of
no effect, in whole or in part, unless it is satisfied that it would be inappropriate
to remit the matters in question to the tribunal for reconsideration.

(4) *The leave of the court is required for any appeal from a decision of the court
under this section.*

69. *Appeal on point of law.*—(1) Unless otherwise agreed by the parties, a
party to arbitral proceedings may (upon notice to the other parties and to the
tribunal) appeal to *the court* on a question of law arising out of an award made
in the proceedings. An agreement to dispense with reasons for the tribunal's
award shall be considered an agreement to exclude *the court's* jurisdiction
under this section.

(2) An appeal shall not be brought under this section except—(a) with the
agreement of all the other parties to the proceedings, or (b) with the leave of
the court. The right to appeal is also subject to the restrictions in section 70(2)
and (3).

(3) Leave to appeal shall be given only if *the court* is satisfied—(a) that the
determination of the question will substantially affect the rights of one or
more of the parties, (b) that the question is one which the tribunal was asked
to determine, (c) that, on the basis of the findings of fact in the award—(i) the
decision of the tribunal on the question is obviously wrong, or (ii) the question
is one of general public importance and the decision of the tribunal is at least
open to serious doubt, and (d) that, despite the agreement of the parties to
resolve the matter by arbitration, it is just and proper in all the circumstances
for *the court* to determine the question.

(4) An application for leave to appeal under this section shall identify the question of law to be determined and state the grounds on which it is alleged that leave to appeal should be granted.

(5) *The court* shall determine an application for leave to appeal under this section without a hearing unless it appears to the court that a hearing is required.

(6) *The leave of the court is required for any appeal from a decision of the court under this section to grant or refuse leave to appeal.*

(7) On an appeal under this section *the court* may by order—(a) confirm the award, (b) vary the award, (c) remit the award to the tribunal, in whole or in part, for reconsideration in the light of *the court's* determination, or (d) set aside the award in whole or in part. *The court* shall not exercise its power to set aside an award, in whole or in part, unless it is satisfied that it would be inappropriate to remit the matters in question to the tribunal for reconsideration.

(8) The decision of the court on an appeal under this section shall be treated as a judgment of the court for the purposes of a further appeal. *But no such appeal lies without the leave of the court which shall not be given unless the court considers that the question is one of general importance or is one which for some other special reason should be considered by the Court of Appeal.'* (My emphasis.)

[11] Section 105 of the Act provides, in so far as material:

'*Meaning of "the court": jurisdiction of High Court and county court.*—(1) In this Act "the court" means the High Court or a county court, subject to the following provisions.

(2) The Lord Chancellor may by order make provision—(a) allocating proceedings under this Act to the High Court or to county courts; or (b) specifying proceedings under this Act which may be commenced or taken only in the High Court or in a county court.'

Conclusion

[12] The applicants rely on the provision of s 67(4). They submit that in the present context 'the court' that is referred to twice in that subsection is, in each instance, the Commercial Court which has made the decision against which it sought to appeal. I am in no doubt that this submission is correct for the following reasons. (1) The natural construction of the subsection accords to the word 'court' the same meaning on each occasion that it is used. On the second occasion that it is used, it manifestly, indeed expressly, means the court which has given the decision under s 67. (2) It is natural, and in accordance with the established approach to statutory construction, to give the words 'the court' the same meaning wherever they appear in ss 67, 68 and 69 unless the context otherwise requires. The context does not otherwise require; on the contrary, it usually requires that 'the court' mean the Commercial Court in the present context and universally strongly suggests that 'the court' carry that meaning. (3) Section 105(1) requires that 'the court' mean the Commercial Court in the present context. (4) Sections 67, 68 and 69 demonstrate a consistent legislative policy that no appeal shall be made against the decision of a court without the permission of that court. In this respect, there is no logical reason for

distinguishing between the effects of ss 67(4) and 68(4) on the one hand, and the effect of s 69(8) on the other hand. (5) In reserved judgments, this court has recently unanimously held that, on the true construction of s 69(8), a party who wishes to appeal from the decision of the High Court or the county court on appeal from an arbitration award requires the permission of the High Court or the county court, as the case may be, and that the Court of Appeal has no jurisdiction either to grant permission itself or to review a refusal of the High Court or county court to grant permission (see *Henry Boot Construction (UK) Ltd v Malmaison Hotel (Manchester) Ltd* [2001] 1 All ER 257, [2001] QB 388). Much of the reasoning of Waller LJ, who gave the leading judgment in that case, can be applied to s 67(4).

[13] It follows that Rix LJ had no jurisdiction to grant permission to AEK to appeal against the deputy judge's decision under s 67, and the applicants are entitled to the relief they seek. In those circumstances, I do not propose to explore their alternative grounds for the application.

Postscript

[14] It is right that I should put on record some of the circumstances in which Rix LJ came to grant permission to appeal.

[15] On 27 September 2001, after AEK's application had been received in the Civil Appeals Office Registry, the deputy manager of the registry wrote to AEK's solicitors in the following terms, so far as material:

> 'Your application has been referred to the Deputy Master of Civil Appeals who has asked that I convey his direction to you in this letter. Please advise this Court whether the effect of the decision in *Henry Boot Construction (UK) Ltd v Malmaison Hotel Ltd* (which was decided in May 2000) does not preclude you from seeking permission to appeal (?) from the Court of Appeal. Additionally, please separately address the issue of what jurisdiction this Court has to grant permission.'

To this letter Thomas Eggar replied on 9 October 2001, in so far as material:

> 'In response to the queries raised by the Deputy Master of Civil Appeals we have discussed this matter with our counsel. Looking at the report of *Henry Boot Construction v Malmaison Hotel* ... it seems that the case revolved around a s 69 application that had been made, and from which decision an appeal was attempted. In this case AEK did make both a s 69 and a s 67 application to the High Court, but only sought from the judge leave to appeal on the s 67 point, and only makes application to the Court of Appeal for leave to appeal on the s 67 point. The wording of s 69 and s 67 is different, for understandable reasons. Section 69 goes to the "merits" decision of the arbitrator or arbitral tribunal, whereas s 67 in essence goes to the issue as to whether there was a valid arbitration. There is no equivalent of s 69(8) in s 67. Thus, there is no similar bar as existed in the *Henry Boot* case.'

[16] I make no comment on this passage save to state that I find the assertion in the last two sentences surprising. It appears to us that when the papers thereafter were placed before Rix LJ, the issue as to the jurisdiction of this court cannot have come to his attention.

[17] For the reasons that I have given I would grant this application.

ROBERT WALKER LJ.

[18] I agree.

CLARKE LJ.

[19] I also agree.

Application granted.

Kate O'Hanlon   Barrister.

Practice Direction

COURT OF APPEAL, CRIMINAL DIVISION
LORD WOOLF CJ
8 JULY 2002

Practice – Criminal proceedings – Consolidation of existing practice directions, practice statements and practice notes.

LORD WOOLF CJ gave the following direction at the sitting of the court.

This is a consolidation, with some amendments, of existing practice directions, practice statements and practice notes as they affect proceedings in the Court of Appeal, Criminal Division, the Crown Court and the magistrates' courts, with the exception of the practice directions which relate to costs. These are likely to be revised in the near future.

The following practice directions are included by way of cross-reference only:

(a) *Practice Direction (ECJ references: procedure)* [1999] 1 WLR 260, [1999] 1 Cr App R 452 relating to references to the European Court of Justice by the Court of Appeal and the High Court under art 177 of the European Communities Treaty.

(b) *Practice Note (devolution issues: Wales)* [1999] 3 All ER 466, [1999] 1 WLR 1592, [1999] 2 Cr App R 486 relating to devolution issues.

(c) *Practice Direction (Court of Appeal: procedure)* [1999] 2 All ER 490 at 517, [1999] 1 WLR 1027 at 1055 (para 9) (relating to the availability of judgments given in the Court of Appeal and the High Court) and para 10.1 (relating to the citation of judgments in court).

Guidelines issued by the Attorney General are not included.

Also excluded is the guidance given by the Court of Appeal, Civil Division in *C v S* [1999] 2 All ER 343, [1999] 1 WLR 1551, which deals with the conflict which can arise between the interests of the state in combating crime on the one hand and, on the other hand, the entitlement of private bodies to obtain redress from the courts and the principles that justice should be administered in public and that a party should know the case advanced against him, should have the opportunity to reply to it and should know the reasons for the decision of the court. Though arising from crime, this was civil litigation.

Reference should also be made to the following Civil Procedure Practice Directions:

(a) Such parts of Practice Direction 19—Addition and Substitution of Parties, supplementary to CPR Pt 19, as may apply where a defendant makes a claim for a declaration of incompatibility in accordance with s 4 of the Human Rights Act 1998.

(b) Practice Direction 39B—Court Sittings, supplementary to CPR Pt 39.

This consolidation is not a comprehensive statement of the practice and procedure of the criminal courts. For this reference must be made to the relevant Acts and rules to which this direction is supplementary and to the Attorney General's guidelines.

A list of the practice directions which are consolidated *for the purpose of criminal proceedings* is at Annex A. Where appropriate, these practice directions have been brought up to date. Any changes were of a relatively minor nature.

The consolidation does not affect proceedings in the Court of Appeal, Civil Division or in any division of the High Court. So, for example, in the Family a Division, reference should still be made to such directions, etc as affect proceedings there. Some criminal cases come before the Administrative Court. These form a small part of the work of that court and are not affected by this consolidation. The Administrative Court Office has a list of the relatively few practice directions which apply there.

This practice direction is divided into the following parts:

b

Part I	Directions of general application
Part II	Further directions applying in the Court of Appeal, Criminal Division
Part III	Further directions applying in the Crown Court and in magistrates' courts
Part IV	Further directions applying in the Crown Court
Part V	Further directions applying in magistrates' courts
Annex A	List of practice directions, practice notes and practice statements included in this consolidation
Annex B	List of practice directions, practice notes and practice statements not included in this consolidation, but no longer applicable in criminal proceedings
Annex C	Form of words recommended for use in explanations for the imposition of custodial sentences
Annex D	Recommended questionnaire for judicial use in conducting plea and directions hearings

c

d

e Note: throughout this document words connoting the masculine include the feminine.

CONTENTS

PART I: DIRECTIONS OF GENERAL APPLICATION

a

1. *Court dress*

1.1. In magistrates' courts, advocates appear without robes or wigs. In all other courts, Queen's Counsel wear a short wig and a silk (or stuff) gown over a court coat with bands, junior counsel wear a short wig and stuff gown with *b* bands, and solicitors and other advocates authorised under the Courts and Legal Services Act 1990 wear a black stuff gown with bands.

2. *Unofficial tape recording of proceedings*

2.1. Section 9 of the Contempt of Court Act 1981 contains provisions governing the unofficial use of tape recorders in court. Section 9(1) provides that it is a *c* contempt of court:

(a) to use in court, or bring into court for use, any tape recorder or other instrument for recording sound, except with the leave of the court;

(b) to publish a recording of legal proceedings made by means of any such instrument, or any recording derived directly or indirectly from it, by playing it *d* in the hearing of the public or any section of the public, or to dispose of it or any recording so derived, with a view to such publication;

(c) to use any such recording in contravention of any conditions of leave granted under para (a). These provisions do not apply to the making or use of sound recordings for purposes of official transcripts of the proceedings, upon *e* which the Act imposes no restriction whatever.

2.2. The discretion given to the court to grant, withhold or withdraw leave to use tape recorders or to impose conditions as to the use of the recording is unlimited, but the following factors may be relevant to its exercise: (a) the existence of any reasonable need on the part of the applicant for leave, whether a litigant or a person connected with the press or broadcasting, for the recording to *f* be made; (b) the risk that the recording could be used for the purpose of briefing witnesses out of court; (c) any possibility that the use of the recorder would disturb the proceedings or distract or worry any witnesses or other participants.

2.3. Consideration should always be given whether conditions as to the use of a recording made pursuant to leave should be imposed. The identity and role of *g* the applicant for leave and the nature of the subject matter of the proceedings may be relevant to this.

2.4. The particular restriction imposed by s 9(1)(b) applies in every case, but may not be present to the mind of every applicant to whom leave is given. It may therefore be desirable on occasion for this provision to be drawn to the attention *h* of those to whom leave is given.

2.5. The transcript of a permitted recording is intended for the use of the person given leave to make it and is not intended to be used as, or to compete with, the official transcript mentioned in s 9(4).

j 3. *Restrictions on reporting proceedings*

3.1. Under s 4(2) of the Contempt of Court Act 1981 a court may, where it appears necessary for avoiding a substantial risk of prejudice to the administration of justice in the proceedings before it or in any others pending or imminent, order that publication of any report of the proceedings or part thereof be postponed for such time as the court thinks necessary for that purpose. Section 11 of the 1981 Act provides that a court may prohibit the publication of

any name or other matter in connection with the proceedings before it which it
has allowed to be withheld from the public.

3.2. When considering whether to make such an order there is nothing which
precludes the court from hearing a representative of the press. Indeed it is likely
that the court will wish to do so.

3.3. It is necessary to keep a permanent record of such orders for later
reference. For this purpose all orders made under s 4(2) must be formulated in
precise terms having regard to the decision in *R v Horsham JJ, ex p Farquharson*
[1982] 2 All ER 269, [1982] QB 762, (1982) 76 Cr App R 87, and orders under both
sections must be committed to writing either by the judge personally or by the
clerk of the court under the judge's directions. An order must state (a) its precise
scope, (b) the time at which it shall cease to have effect, if appropriate, and (c) the
specific purpose of making the order. Courts will normally give notice to the
press in some form that an order has been made under either section of the 1981
Act and the court staff should be prepared to answer any inquiry about a specific
case, but it is, and will remain, the responsibility of those reporting cases, and
their editors, to ensure that no breach of any orders occurs and the onus rests on
them to make inquiry in any case of doubt.

4. Availability of judgments given in the Court of Appeal and the High Court

4.1. Reference should be made to para 9 of *Practice Direction (Court of Appeal:
procedure)* [1999] 2 All ER 490 at 517, [1999] 1 WLR 1027 at 1055.

5. Wards of court

5.1. Where a child has been interviewed by the police in connection with
contemplated criminal proceedings and the child subsequently becomes a ward
of court, no leave of the wardship court is required for the child to be called as a
witness in those proceedings. Where, however, the police desire to interview a
child who is already a ward of court, application must, other than in the
exceptional cases referred to in para 5.3, be made to the wardship court, on
summons and on notice to all parties, for leave for the police to do so. Where,
however, a party may become the subject of a criminal investigation and it is
considered necessary for the ward to be interviewed without that party knowing
that the police are making inquiries, the application for leave may be made ex
parte to a judge without notice to that party. Notice, should, where practicable,
be given to the reporting officer.

5.2. Where leave is given the order should, unless some special reason
requires the contrary, give leave for any number of interviews which may be
required by the prosecution or the police. If it is desired to conduct any interview
beyond what has been permitted by the order, a further application should be
made.

5.3. The exceptional cases are those where the police need to deal with
complaints or alleged offences concerning wards and it is appropriate, if not
essential, for action to be taken straight away without the prior leave of the
wardship court. Typical examples may be: (a) serious offences against the ward,
such as rape, where medical examination and the collection of scientific evidence
ought to be carried out promptly; (b) where the ward is suspected by the police
of having committed a criminal act and the police wish to interview him about it;
(c) where the police wish to interview the ward as a potential witness. The list is
not exhaustive; there will inevitably be other instances where immediate action
is appropriate. In such cases the police should notify the parent or foster parent

a with whom the ward is living or other 'appropriate adult' within the *Code of Practice for the Detention, Treatment and Questioning of Persons by Police Officers,* so that that adult has the opportunity of being present when the police interview the child. Additionally, if practicable, the reporting officer (if one has been appointed) should be notified and invited to attend the police interview or to nominate a third party to attend on his behalf. A record of the interview or a copy of any

b statement made by the ward should be supplied to the reporting officer. Where the ward has been interviewed without the reporting officer's knowledge, he should be informed at the earliest opportunity. So too, if it be the case that the police wish to conduct further interviews. The wardship court should be appraised of the situation at the earliest possible opportunity thereafter by the reporting officer, the parent, foster parent (through the local authority) or other

c responsible adult.

5.4. No evidence or documents in the wardship proceedings or information about the proceedings should be disclosed in the criminal proceedings without leave of the wardship court.

d ### 6. Spent convictions

6.1. The effect of s 4(1) of the Rehabilitation of Offenders Act 1974 is that a person who has become a rehabilitated person for the purpose of the Act in respect of a conviction (known as a 'spent' conviction) shall be treated for all purposes in law as a person who has not committed or been charged with or prosecuted for or convicted of or sentenced for the offence or offences which were the subject of

e that conviction.

6.2. Section 4(1) of the 1974 Act does not apply, however, to evidence given in criminal proceedings (see s 7(2)(a)). Convictions are often disclosed in such criminal proceedings. When the Bill was before the House of Commons on 28 June 1974 the hope was expressed that the Lord Chief Justice would issue a practice

f direction for the guidance of the Crown Court with a view to reducing disclosure of spent convictions to a minimum and securing uniformity of approach. The direction is set out in the following paragraphs. The same approach should be adopted in all courts of criminal jurisdiction.

6.3. During the trial of a criminal charge, reference to previous convictions (and therefore to spent convictions) can arise in a number of ways. The most

g common is when the character of the accused or a witness is sought to be attacked by reference to his criminal record, but there are, of course, cases where previous convictions are relevant and admissible as, for instance, to prove system.

6.4. It is not possible to give general directions which will govern all these different situations, but it is recommended that both court and advocates should

h give effect to the general intention of Parliament by never referring to a spent conviction when such reference can reasonably be avoided.

6.5. After a verdict of guilty the court must be provided with a statement of the defendant's record for the purposes of sentence. The record supplied should contain all previous convictions, but those which are spent should, so far as

j practicable, be marked as such.

6.6. No one should refer in open court to a spent conviction without the authority of the judge, which authority should not be given unless the interests of justice so require.

6.7. When passing sentence the judge should make no reference to a spent conviction unless it is necessary to do so for the purpose of explaining the sentence to be passed.

7. Explanations for the imposition of custodial sentences

7.1. The practical effect of custodial sentences imposed by the courts is almost entirely governed by statutory provisions. Those statutory provisions, changed by Parliament from time to time, are not widely understood by the general public. It is desirable that when sentence is passed the practical effect of the sentence should be understood by the defendant, any victim and any member of the public who is present in court or reads a full report of the proceedings.

7.2. Whenever a custodial sentence is imposed on an offender the court should explain the practical effect of the sentence in addition to complying with existing statutory requirements. This will be no more than an explanation; the sentence will be that pronounced by the court.

7.3. Sentencers should give the explanation in terms of their own choosing, taking care to ensure that the explanation is clear and accurate. No form of words is prescribed. Annexed to this Practice Direction are short statements which may, adapted as necessary, be of value as models (see Annex C). These statements are based on the statutory provisions in force on 1 January 1998 and will, of course, require modification if those provisions are materially amended.

7.4. Sentencers will continue to give such explanation as they judge necessary of ancillary orders relating to matters such as disqualification, compensation, confiscation, costs and so on.

8. Words to be used when passing sentence

8.1. Where a court passes on a defendant more than one term of imprisonment the court should state in the presence of the defendant whether the terms are to be concurrent or consecutive. Should this not be done the court clerk should ask the court, before the defendant leaves court, to do so.

8.2. If a prisoner is, at the time of sentence, already serving two or more consecutive terms of imprisonment and the court intends to increase the total period of imprisonment, it should use the expression 'consecutive to the total period of imprisonment to which you are already subject' rather than 'at the expiration of the term of imprisonment you are now serving', lest the prisoner be not then serving the last of the terms to which he is already subject.

9. Substitution of suspended sentences for immediate custodial sentences

9.1. Where an appellate court substitutes a suspended sentence of imprisonment for one having immediate effect, the court should have in mind any period the appellant has spent in custody. If the court is of the opinion that it would be fair to do so, an approximate adjustment to the term of the suspended sentence should be made. Whether or not the court makes such adjustment, it should state that it had that period in mind. The court should further indicate that the operational period of suspension runs from the date the court passes the suspended sentence.

10. References to the Court of Justice of the European Communities

10.1. These are the subject of *Practice Direction (ECJ references: procedure)* [1999] 1 WLR 260, [1999] 1 Cr App R 452, to which reference should be made.

11. Devolution issues

11.1. These are the subject of *Practice Note (devolution issues: Wales)* [1999] 3 All ER 466, [1999] 1 WLR 1592, [1999] 2 Cr App R 486, to which reference should be made.

12. *Preparation of judgments: neutral citation*

a

12.1. Since 11 January 2001 every judgment of the Court of Appeal, and of the Administrative Court, and since 14 January 2002 every judgment of the High Court, has been prepared and issued as approved with single spacing, paragraph numbering (in the margins) and no page numbers. In courts with more than one judge the paragraph numbering continues sequentially through each judgment

b and does not start again at the beginning of each judgment. Indented paragraphs are not numbered. A unique reference number is given to each judgment. For judgments of the Court of Appeal this number is given by the official shorthand writers. For judgments of the High Court it is provided by the Mechanical Recording Department at the Royal Courts of Justice. Such a number will also be furnished, on request to the Mechanical Recording Department, Royal Courts

c of Justice, Strand, London WC2A 2LL (Tel: 020 7947 7771), to High Court judgments delivered outside London.

12.2. Each Court of Appeal judgment starts with the year, followed by EW (for England and Wales), then CA (for Court of Appeal), followed by Civ or Crim and finally the sequential number. For example *Smith v Jones* [2001] EWCA Civ 10.

d 12.3. In the High Court, represented by HC, the number comes before the divisional abbreviation and, unlike Court of Appeal judgments, the latter is bracketed: (Ch), (Pat), (QB), (Admin), (Comm), (Admlty), (TCC) or (Fam) as appropriate. For example, [2002] EWHC 123 (Fam) or [2002] EWHC 124 (QB) or [2002] EWHC 125 (Ch).

e 12.4. This 'neutral citation', as it is called, is the official number attributed to the judgment and must always be used at least once when the judgment is cited in a later judgment. Once the judgment is reported this neutral citation appears in front of the familiar citation from the law reports series. Thus: *Smith v Jones* [2001] EWCA Civ 10, [2001] QB 124, [2001] 2 All ER 364, etc.

12.5. Paragraph numbers are referred to in square brackets. When citing a

f paragraph from a High Court judgment it is unnecessary to include the descriptive word in brackets: (Admin), (QB) or whatever. When citing a paragraph from a Court of Appeal judgment, however, Civ or Crim is included. If it is desired to cite more than one paragraph of a judgment each numbered paragraph should be enclosed with a square bracket. Thus para 59 in *Green v*

g *White* [2002] EWHC 124 (QB) would be cited: *Green v White* [2002] EWHC 124 at [59], paras 30–35 in *Smith v Jones* would be *Smith v Jones* [2001] EWCA Civ 10 at [30]–[35]; similarly, where a number of paragraphs are cited: *Smith v Jones* [2001] EWCA Civ 10 at [30], [35] and [40]–[43].

12.6. If a judgment is cited more than once in a later judgment it is helpful if only one abbreviation is used, e g *Smith v Jones* or *Smith's* case, but preferably not

h both (in the same judgment).

PART II: FURTHER DIRECTIONS APPLYING IN THE COURT OF APPEAL, CRIMINAL DIVISION

13. *Mode of addressing the court*

j 13.1. Judges of the Court of Appeal and of the High Court are addressed as 'My Lord' or 'My Lady'; so are circuit judges sitting as judges of the High Court under s 9 of the Supreme Court Act 1981.

14. *Notices of appeal and of applications for leave to appeal*

14.1. These are to be served on the Crown Court at the centre where the proceedings took place. The Crown Court will forward them to the Criminal

Appeal Office together with the trial documents and any others which may be required.

15. *Grounds of appeal*

15.1. Advocates should not settle grounds or support them with written advice unless they consider that they are properly arguable. Grounds should be carefully drafted and properly particularised. Advocates should not assume that the court will entertain any ground of appeal not set out and properly particularised. Should leave to amend the grounds be granted it is most unlikely that further grounds will be entertained.

15.2. A copy of the advocate's positive advice about the merits should be attached as part of the grounds.

16. *Loss of time*

16.1. Both the court and the single judge have power in their discretion to direct that part of the time during which an applicant is in custody after putting in his notice of application for leave to appeal should not count towards sentence. Those who contemplate putting in such a notice and their legal advisers should bear this in mind. It is important that those contemplating an appeal should seek advice and should remember that it is useless to appeal without grounds and that grounds should be substantial and particularised and not a mere formula. Where an application devoid of merit has been refused by the single judge and a direction for loss of time has been made, the full court, on renewal of the application, may direct that additional time shall be lost if it, once again, thinks it right so to exercise its discretion in all the circumstances of the case.

17. *Skeleton arguments*

17.1. In all appeals against conviction a skeleton argument from the advocate for the appellant is to be lodged with the Registrar of Criminal Appeals and served on the prosecuting authority within 14 days of receipt by the advocate of the notification of the grant of leave to appeal against conviction or such longer period as the registrar or the court may direct. The skeleton may refer to an advice, which should be annexed with an indication of which parts of it are relied upon, and should include any additional arguments to be advanced.

17.2. The advocate for the prosecuting authority should lodge with the registrar and the advocate for the appellant his skeleton argument within 14 days of the receipt of the skeleton argument for the appellant or such longer (or, in exceptional cases, shorter) period as the registrar or the court may direct.

17.3. Practitioners should ensure that, where reliance is placed upon unreported cases in skeleton arguments, short headnotes are included.

17.4. Advocates should ensure that the correct Criminal Appeal Office number appears at the beginning of their skeleton arguments and that their names are at the end.

17.5. A skeleton argument should contain a numbered list of the points the advocate intends to argue, grouped under each ground of appeal, and stated in no more than one or two sentences. It should be as succinct as possible, the object being to identify each point, not to argue it or elaborate on it. Each listed point should be followed by full references to the material to which the advocate will refer in support of it, ie the relevant passages in the transcripts, authorities, etc. It should also contain anything the advocate would expect to be taken down by the court during the hearing, such as propositions of law, chronologies, etc. If a   more convenient, these can be annexed to the skeletons rather than included in it. For points of law, the skeleton should state the point and cite the principal authority or authorities in support with reference to the passages where the principle is enunciated. Chronologies should, if possible, be agreed with the opposing advocate before the hearing. Respondents' skeletons should follow the same principles.

b   **18. *Criminal Appeal Office summaries***

18.1. To assist the court the Criminal Appeal Office prepares summaries of the cases coming before it. These are entirely objective and do not contain any advice about how the court should deal with the case or any view about its merits. They consist of two parts.

c   18.2. Part I, which is provided to all of the advocates in the case, generally contains (a) particulars of the proceedings in the Crown Court, including representation and details of any co-accused, (b) particulars of the proceedings in the Court of Appeal, Criminal Division, (c) the facts of the case, as drawn from the transcripts, advice of the advocates, witness statements and/or the exhibits, d   (d) the submissions and rulings, summing up and sentencing remarks. Should an advocate not want any factual material in his advice taken into account this should be stated in the advice.

18.3. The contents of the summary are a matter for the professional judgment of the writer, but an advocate wishing to suggest any significant alteration to part I should write to the Registrar of Criminal Appeals. If the registrar does not e   agree, the summary and the letter will be put to the court for decision. The court will not generally be willing to hear oral argument about the content of the summary.

18.4. Advocates may show part I of the summary to their professional or lay clients (but to no one else) if they believe it would help to check facts or formulate f   arguments, but summaries are not to be copied or reproduced without the permission of the Criminal Appeal Office; permission for this will not normally be given in cases involving children or sexual offences or where the Crown Court has made an order restricting reporting.

18.5. Unless a judge of the High Court or the Registrar of Criminal Appeals gives a direction to the contrary in any particular case involving material of an g   explicitly salacious or sadistic nature, part I will also be supplied to appellants who seek to represent themselves before the full court or who renew to the full court their applications for leave to appeal against conviction or sentence.

18.6. Part II, which is supplied to the court alone, contains (a) a summary of the grounds of appeal and (b) in appeals against sentence (and applications for h   such leave), summaries of the antecedent histories of the parties and of any relevant pre-sentence, medical or other reports.

18.7. All of the source material is provided to the court and advocates are able to draw attention to anything in it which may be of particular relevance.

j   **19. *Citation of judgments in court***

19.1. Reference should be made to para 10.1 of *Practice Direction (Court of Appeal: procedure)* [1999] 2 All ER 490, [1999] 1 WLR 1027.

20. *Citation of Hansard*

20.1. Where any party intends to refer to the reports of Parliamentary proceedings as reported in the official reports of either House of Parliament

(Hansard) in support of any such argument as is permitted by the decisions in *a* *Pepper (Inspector of Taxes) v Hart* [1993] 1 All ER 42, [1993] AC 593 and *Pickstone v Freemans plc* [1988] 2 All ER 803, [1989] AC 66 or otherwise he must, unless the court otherwise directs, serve upon all other parties and the court copies of any such extract together with a brief summary of the argument intended to be based upon such extract. No other report of Parliamentary proceedings may be cited.

20.2. Unless the court otherwise directs, service of the extract and summary of *b* the argument shall be effected not less than five clear working days before the first day of the hearing, whether or not it has a fixed date. Advocates must keep themselves informed as to the state of the lists where no fixed date has been given. Service on the court shall be effected by sending three copies to the Registrar of Criminal Appeals, Room C212, Royal Courts of Justice, Strand, London WC2A 2LL. If any party fails to do so the court may make such order *c* (relating to costs or otherwise) as is in all the circumstances appropriate.

PART III: FURTHER DIRECTIONS APPLYING IN THE CROWN COURT AND MAGISTRATES' COURTS

21. *Classification of Crown Court business and allocation to Crown Court centres*   *d*

Classification

21.1. For the purposes of trial in the Crown Court offences are classified as follows:

Class 1: (a) misprision of treason and treason felony; (b) murder; (c) genocide; *e* (d) torture, hostage-taking and offences under the War Crimes Act 1991; (e) an offence under the Official Secrets Acts; (f) soliciting, incitement, attempt or conspiracy to commit any of the above offences.

Class 2: (a) manslaughter; (b) infanticide; (c) child destruction; (d) abortion (s 58 of the Offences against the Person Act 1861); (e) rape; (f) sexual intercourse with a girl under 13; (g) incest with girl under 13; (h) sedition; (i) an offence under *f* s 1 of the Geneva Conventions Act 1957; (j) mutiny; (k) piracy; (l) soliciting, incitement, attempt or conspiracy to commit any of the above offences.

Class 3: (a) all offences triable only on indictment other than those in classes 1, 2 and 4; (b) soliciting, incitement, attempt or conspiracy to commit any of the above offences.   *g*

Class 4: (a) wounding or causing grievous bodily harm with intent (s 18 of the Offences against the Person Act 1861); (b) robbery or assault with intent to rob (s 8 of the Theft Act 1968); (c) soliciting, incitement or attempt to commit any of the above offences; (d) conspiracy at common law, or conspiracy to commit any offence other than those included in classes 1, 2 and 3; (e) all offences which are *h* triable either way.

Cases committed, transferred or sent for trial

21.2. Save as provided in para 21.3, for certain offences in class 2 and offences in class 3(a), the magistrates' court, upon either committing a person for trial under s 6 of the Magistrates' Courts Act 1980, transferring a person under either *j* s 4 of the Criminal Justice Act 1987 or s 53 of the Criminal Justice Act 1991 or sending a person under s 51 of the Crime and Disorder Act 1998, shall, if the offence or any of the offences is included in classes 1 or 2, specify the most convenient location of the Crown Court where a High Court judge, or, where the case is included in class 1, where a circuit judge duly approved for that purpose by the Lord Chief Justice regularly sits. These courts will be identified *a* by the presiding judges on each circuit. Where an offence is in class 4 the magistrates' court shall specify the most convenient location of the Crown Court.

21.3. Where a presiding judge has directed that cases of rape, sexual intercourse with a girl under 13, incest with a girl under 13 or soliciting, incitement, attempt or conspiracy to commit any of these offences (all of which are within class 2) or class 3 offences, may be committed, transferred or sent from

b a specified magistrates' court or courts to a specified location of the Crown Court at which a High Court judge does not regularly sit, the magistrates' court shall specify that location.

21.4. In selecting the most convenient location of the Crown Court the justices shall have regard to the considerations referred to in s 7 of the

c Magistrates' Courts Act 1980 and s 51(10) of the Crime and Disorder Act 1998 and the location or locations of the Crown Court designated by a presiding judge as the location to which cases should normally be committed from their petty sessions area.

21.5. Where on one occasion a person is committed in respect of a number of offences all the committals shall be to the same location of the Crown Court and

d that location shall be the one where a High Court judge regularly sits if such a location is appropriate for any of the offences.

Committals for sentence or to be dealt with

21.6. Where a community rehabilitation order, an order for conditional

e discharge or a community punishment order has been made, or suspended sentence has been passed, and the offender is committed to be dealt with for the original offence or in respect of the suspended sentence, he shall be committed in accordance with paras 21.7–21.10.

21.7. If the order was made or the sentence was passed by the Crown Court he shall be committed to the location of the Crown Court where the order was

f made or suspended sentence was passed unless it is inconvenient or impracticable to do so.

21.8. If he is not so committed and the order was made by a High Court judge he shall be committed to the most convenient location of the Crown Court where a High Court judge regularly sits.

g 21.9. In all other cases where a person is committed for sentence or to be dealt with he shall be committed to the most convenient location of the Crown Court.

21.10. In selecting the most convenient location of the Crown Court the justices shall have regard to the locations of the Crown Court designated by a presiding judge as the locations to which cases should normally be committed

h from their petty sessions area.

Notice of transfer in cases of serious or complex fraud

21.11. Where a notice of transfer is served under s 4 of the Criminal Justice Act 1987 (cases of serious or complex fraud) the proposed place of trial to be specified

j in the notice shall be one of the following Crown Court centres: (a) Midland Circuit: Birmingham (also sitting at West Midlands trial centre), Leicester, Northampton, Nottingham, Wolverhampton (also sitting at West Midlands trial centre); (b) North Eastern: Bradford, Leeds, Newcastle, Sheffield, Teesside; (c) Northern: Liverpool, Manchester; (d) South Eastern: Central Criminal Court, Chelmsford, Harrow, Kingston, Knightsbridge, Luton, Maidstone, Middlesex Guildhall, Norwich, Oxford, Reading, Snaresbrook, Southwark, Wood Green;

(e) Wales and Chester: Cardiff, Chester, Mold, Swansea, Warrington; (f) Western: Bristol, Plymouth, Portsmouth, Truro, Winchester.

Notice of transfer in child witness cases

21.12. Where a notice of transfer is served under s 53 of the Criminal Justice Act 1991 (child witness cases) the proposed place of trial to be specified in accordance with para 1(1) of Sch 6 to the 1991 Act shall be a Crown Court centre which is equipped with live television link facilities. The following Crown Court centres are so equipped: Birmingham, Bradford, Bristol, Caernarfon, Cardiff, Carlisle, Central Criminal Court, Chelmsford, Croydon, Exeter, Gloucester, Grimsby, Guildford, Harrow, Hull, Leeds, Leicester, Lewes, Lincoln, Liverpool, Maidstone, Manchester, Mold, Newcastle, Northampton, Norwich, Nottingham, Plymouth, Portsmouth, Preston, Reading, Sheffield, Southwark, St Albans, Stafford, Swansea, Teesside, Truro, Winchester, Wolverhampton.

22. *Applications for evidence to be given in Welsh*

22.1. If a defendant in a court in England asks to give or call evidence in the Welsh language the case should not be transferred to Wales. In ordinary circumstances interpreters can be provided on request.

23. *Use of the Welsh language in courts in Wales*

23.1. The purpose of this direction is to reflect the principle of the Welsh Language Act 1993 that in the administration of justice in Wales, the English and Welsh languages should be treated on a basis of equality.

General

23.2. It is the responsibility of the legal representatives in every case in which the Welsh language may be used by any witness or party or in any document which may be placed before the court to inform the court of that fact so that appropriate arrangements can be made for the listing of the case.

23.3. If the possible use of the Welsh language is known at the time of committal, transfer or appeal to the Crown Court, the court should be informed immediately after committal or transfer or when the notice of appeal is lodged. Otherwise the court should be informed as soon as possible use of the Welsh language becomes known.

23.4. If costs are incurred as a result of failure to comply with these directions, a wasted costs order may be made against the defaulting party and/or his legal representatives.

23.5. The law does not permit the selection of jurors in a manner which enables the court to discover whether a juror does or does not speak Welsh or to secure a jury whose members are bilingual to try a case in which the Welsh language may be used.

Plea and directions hearings

23.6. An advocate in a case in which the Welsh language may be used must raise that matter at the plea and directions hearing and endorse details of it on the judge's questionnaire so that appropriate directions may be given for the progress of the case.

Listing

23.7. The listing officer, in consultation with the resident judge, should ensure that a case in which the Welsh language may be used is listed (a) wherever a practicable before a Welsh speaking judge, and (b) in a court in Wales with simultaneous translation facilities.

Interpreters

23.8. Whenever an interpreter is needed to translate evidence from English into Welsh or from Welsh into English, the court manager in whose court the b case is to be heard shall ensure that the attendance is secured of an interpreter whose name is included in the list of approved court interpreters.

Jurors

23.9. The jury bailiff when addressing the jurors at the start of their period of c jury service shall inform them that each juror may take an oath or affirm in Welsh or English as he wishes.

23.10. After the jury has been selected to try a case, and before it is sworn, the court officer swearing in the jury shall inform the jurors in open court that each juror may take an oath or affirm in Welsh or English as he wishes.

d
Witnesses

23.11. When each witness is called the court officer administering the oath or affirmation shall inform the witness that he may be sworn or affirm Welsh or English as he wishes.

e
Opening/closing of courts

23.12. Unless it is not reasonably practicable to do so, the opening and closing of the court should be performed in Welsh and English.

Role of liaison judge
f
23.13. If any question or problem arises concerning the implementation of paras 23.1–23.12, contact should in the first place be made with the liaison judge for Welsh language matters on circuit.

24. Evidence by written statement
g
24.1. Where the prosecution proposes to tender written statements in evidence either under ss 5A and 5B of the Magistrates' Courts Act 1980 or s 9 of the Criminal Justice Act 1967 it will frequently be not only proper, but also necessary for the orderly presentation of the evidence, for certain statements to be edited. This will occur either because a witness has made more than one h statement whose contents should conveniently be reduced into a single, comprehensive statement or where a statement contains inadmissible, prejudicial or irrelevant material. Editing of statements should in all circumstances be done by a Crown Prosecutor (or by a legal representative, if any, of the prosecutor if the case is not being conducted by the Crown Prosecution Service) and not by a j police officer.

Composite statements

24.2. A composite statement giving the combined effect of two or more earlier statements or settled by a person referred to in para 24.1 must be prepared in compliance with the requirements of ss 5A and 5B of the 1980 Act or s 9 of the 1967 Act as appropriate and must then be signed by the witness.

Editing single statements

24.3. There are two acceptable methods of editing single statements. (a) By marking *copies* of the statement in a way which indicates the passages on which the prosecution will not rely. This merely indicates that the prosecution will not seek to adduce the evidence so marked. The *original signed statement* to be tendered to the court is not marked in any way. The marking on the copy statement is done by lightly striking out the passages to be edited so that what appears beneath can still be read, or by bracketing, or by a combination of both. It is not permissible to produce a photocopy with the deleted material obliterated, since this would be contrary to the requirement that the defence and the court should be served with copies of the signed original statement. Whenever the striking out/bracketing method is used, it will assist if the following words appear at the foot of the frontispiece or index to any bundle of copy statements to be tendered:

> 'The prosecution does not propose to adduce evidence of those passages of the attached copy statements which have been struck out and/or bracketed (nor will it seek to do so at the trial unless a notice of further evidence is served).'

(b) By obtaining a fresh statement, signed by the witness, which omits the offending material, applying the procedure in para 24.2.

24.4. In most cases where a single statement is to be edited, the striking out/bracketing method will be the more appropriate, but the taking of a fresh statement is preferable in the following circumstances. (a) When a police (or other investigating) officer's statement contains details of interviews with more suspects than are eventually charged, a fresh statement should be prepared and signed omitting all details of interview with those not charged except, in so far as it is relevant, for the bald fact that a certain named person was interviewed at a particular time, date and place. (b) When a suspect is interviewed about more offences than are eventually made the subject of committal charges, a fresh statement should be prepared and signed omitting all questions and answers about the uncharged offences unless either they might appropriately be taken into consideration or evidence about those offences is admissible on the charges preferred, such as evidence of system. It may, however, be desirable to replace the omitted questions and answers with a phrase such as: 'After referring to some other matters, I then said ...', so as to make it clear that part of the interview has been omitted. (c) A fresh statement should normally be prepared and signed if the only part of the original on which the prosecution is relying is only a small proportion of the whole, although it remains desirable to use the alternative method if there is reason to believe that the defence might itself wish to rely, in mitigation or for any other purpose, on at least some of those parts which the prosecution does not propose to adduce. (d) When the passages contain material which the prosecution is entitled to withhold from disclosure to the defence.

24.5. Prosecutors should also be aware that, where statements are to be tendered under s 9 of the 1967 Act in the course of *summary* proceedings, there will be a need to prepare fresh statements excluding inadmissible or prejudicial material rather than using the striking out or bracketing method.

24.6. None of the above principles applies, in respect of committal proceedings, to documents which are exhibited (including statements under caution and signed contemporaneous notes). Nor do they apply to oral statements of a defendant which are recorded in the witness statements of interviewing police *a*   officers, except in the circumstances referred to in para 24.4(b). All this material should remain in its original state in the committal bundles, any editing being left to prosecuting counsel at the Crown Court (after discussion with defence counsel and, if appropriate, the trial judge).

24.7. Whenever a fresh statement is taken from a witness, a copy of the earlier, unedited statement(s) of that witness will be given to the defence in accordance
b   with the Attorney General's guidelines on the disclosure of unused material (*Practice Note (criminal evidence: unused material)* [1982] 1 All ER 734, (1982) 74 Cr App R 302) unless there are grounds under para 6 of the guidelines for withholding such disclosure.

25. Bail during trial

c   25.1. Paragraphs 25.2–25.5. are to be read subject to the Bail Act 1976, especially s 4.

25.2. Once a trial has begun the further grant of bail, whether during the short adjournment or overnight, is in the discretion of the trial judge. It may be a proper exercise of this discretion to refuse bail during the short adjournment if
d   the accused cannot otherwise be segregated from witnesses and jurors.

25.3. An accused who was on bail while on remand should not be refused overnight bail during the trial unless in the opinion of the judge there are positive reasons to justify this refusal. Such reasons are likely to be: (a) that a point has been reached where there is a real danger that the accused will abscond, either because the case is going badly for him, or for any other reason; (b) that there is
e   a real danger that he may interfere with witnesses or jurors.

25.4. There is no universal rule of practice that bail shall not be renewed when the summing-up has begun. Each case must be decided in the light of its own circumstances and having regard to the judge's assessment from time to time of the risks involved.

f   25.5. Once the jury has returned a verdict a further renewal of bail should be decided in the light of the gravity of the offence and the likely sentence to be passed in all the circumstances of the case.

26. Facts to be stated on pleas of guilty

g   26.1. To enable the press and the public to know the circumstances of an offence of which an accused has been convicted and for which he is to be sentenced, in relation to each offence to which an accused has pleaded guilty the prosecution shall state those facts in open court before sentence is imposed.

27. Antecedents

h

Standard for the provision of information of antecedents in the Crown Court and magistrates' courts

27.1. In the Crown Court the police will provide brief details of the circumstances of the last three similar convictions and/or of convictions likely to be of interest
j   to the court, the latter being judged on a case-by-case basis. This information should be provided separately and attached to the antecedents as set out below.

27.2. Where the current alleged offence could constitute a breach of an existing community order, e g community rehabilitation order, and it is known that that order is still in force then, to enable the court to consider the possibility of revoking that order, details of the circumstances of the offence leading to the community order should be included in the antecedents as set out below.

Preparation of antecedents and standard formats to be used

27.3. In magistrates' courts and the Crown Court: personal details and summary of convictions and cautions—Police National Computer [PNC] court/defence/probation summary sheet; previous convictions—PNC court/defence/probation printout, supplemented by Form MG 16 if the police force holds convictions not shown on PNC; recorded cautions—PNC court/defence/probation printout, supplemented by Form MG 17 if the police force holds cautions not shown on PNC; and, in addition, in the Crown Court: circumstances of the last three similar convictions; circumstances of offence leading to a community order still in force; Form MG(c). The detail should be brief and include the date of the offence.

Provision of antecedents to the court and parties

Crown Court

27.4. The Crown Court antecedents will be prepared by the police immediately following committal proceedings, including committals for sentence, transfers under s 4 of the Criminal Justice Act 1987 or s 53 of the Criminal Justice Act 1991 or upon receipt of a notice of appeal, excluding non-imprisonable motoring offences.

27.5. Seven copies of the antecedents will be prepared in respect of each defendant. Two copies are to be provided to the Crown Prosecution Service (CPS) direct, the remaining five to be sent to the Crown Court. The court will send one copy to the defence and one to the Probation Service. The remaining copies are for the court's use. Where following conviction a custodial order is made one copy is to be attached to the order sent to the prison.

27.6. The antecedents must be provided, as above, within 21 days of committal or transfer in each case. Any points arising from them are to be raised with the police by the defence solicitor as soon as possible and, where there is time, at least seven days before the hearing date so that the matter can be resolved prior to that hearing.

27.7. Seven days before the hearing date the police will check the record of convictions. Details of any additional convictions will be provided using the standard format above. These will be provided as above and attached to the documents already supplied. Details of any additional outstanding cases will also be provided at this stage.

Magistrates' courts

27.8. The magistrates' court antecedents will be prepared by the police and submitted to the CPS with the case file.

27.9. Five copies of the antecedents will be prepared in respect of each defendant and provided to the CPS who will be responsible for distributing them to others at the sentencing hearing. Normally two copies will be provided to the court, one to the defence and one to the Probation Service when appropriate. Where following conviction a custodial order is made, one of the court's copies is to be attached to the order sent to the prison.

27.10. In instances where antecedents have been provided to the court some time before the hearing the police will, if requested to do so by the CPS, check the record of convictions. Details of any additional convictions will be provided using the standard format above. These will be provided as above and attached

a
to the documents already supplied. Details of any additional outstanding cases will also be provided at this stage.

27.11. The above arrangements whereby the police provide the antecedents to the CPS for passing on to others will apply unless there is a local agreement between the CPS and the court that alters that arrangement.

b
28. Personal statements of victims

28.1. This section draws attention to a scheme, which started on 1 October 2001, to give victims a more formal opportunity to say how a crime has affected them. It may help to identify whether they have a particular need for information, support and protection. It will also enable the court to take the statement into account when determining sentence.

c
28.2. When a police officer takes a statement from a victim the victim will be told about the scheme and given the chance to make a victim personal statement. A victim personal statement may be made or updated at any time prior to the disposal of the case. The decision about whether or not to make a victim personal statement is entirely for the victim. If the court is presented with a victim personal

d
statement the following approach should be adopted. (a) The victim personal statement and any evidence in support should be considered and taken into account by the court prior to passing sentence. (b) Evidence of the effects of an offence on the victim contained in the victim personal statement or other statement, must be in proper form, that is a witness statement made under s 9 of the Criminal Justice Act 1967 or an expert's report, and served upon the

e
defendant's solicitor or the defendant, if he is not represented, prior to sentence. Except where inferences can properly be drawn from the nature of or circumstances surrounding the offence, a sentencer must not make assumptions unsupported by evidence about the effects of an offence on the victim. (c) The court must pass what it judges to be the appropriate sentence having regard to

f
the circumstances of the offence and of the offender, taking into account, so far as the court considers it appropriate, the consequences to the victim. The opinions of the victim or the victim's close relatives as to what the sentence should be are therefore not relevant, unlike the consequence of the offence on them. Victims should be advised of this. If, despite the advice, opinions as to sentence are included in the statement, the court should pay no attention to

g
them. (d) The court should consider whether it is desirable in its sentencing remarks to refer to the evidence provided on behalf of the victim.

29. Support for witnesses giving evidence by live television link

29.1. This section of the Practice Direction is made pursuant to r 7 of the Crown

h
Court (Special Measures Directions and Directions Prohibiting Cross-examination) Rules 2002, SI 2002/1688, and r 7 of the Magistrates' Courts (Special Measures Directions) Rules 2002, SI 2002/1687, and supersedes previous guidance given by the senior presiding judges, Watkins LJ in 1991 and Auld LJ in 1998.

29.2. An increased degree of flexibility is now appropriate as to who can act as

j
supporter of a witness giving evidence by live television link. Where a special measures direction is made enabling a vulnerable, intimidated or child witness to give evidence by means of a live television link, the trial judge will make a direction as to the identity of the witness supporter. Where practical, the direction will be made before the trial commences. In giving the direction, the trial judge will balance all relevant interests—see para 1.11 of the guidance *Achieving Best Evidence in Criminal Proceedings: Guidance for Vulnerable or Intimated Witnesses,*

including Children. The witness supporter should be completely independent of
the witness and his or her family and have no previous knowledge of or personal   *a*
involvement in the case. The supporter should also be suitably trained so as to
understand the obligations of, and comply with, the national standards relating
to witness supporters. Providing these criteria are met, the witness supporter need
not be an usher or court official. Thus, for example, the functions of the witness
supporter may be performed by a representative of the Witness Service.   *b*

29.3. Where the witness supporter is someone other than the court usher, the
usher should continue to be available both to assist the witness and the witness
supporter, and to ensure that the judge's requirements are properly complied
with in the CCTV room.

PART IV: FURTHER DIRECTIONS APPLYING IN THE CROWN COURT   *c*

30. *Modes of address and titles of judges*

Mode of address

30.1. The following judges, when sitting in court, should be addressed as 'My   *d*
Lord' or 'My Lady', as the case may be, whatever their personal status: (a) any
circuit judge sitting as a judge of the High Court under s 9(1) of the Supreme
Court Act 1981; (b) any judge sitting at the Central Criminal Court; (c) any senior
circuit judge who is the honorary recorder of the city in which he sits.

30.2. Subject to para 30.1, circuit judges, recorders and deputy circuit judges
should be addressed as 'Your Honour' when sitting in court.   *e*

Description

30.3. In cause lists, forms and orders members of the judiciary should be
described as follows: (a) circuit judges, as 'His [or Her] Honour Judge A' (when
the judge is sitting as a judge of the High Court under s 9(1) of the Supreme Court   *f*
Act 1981 the words 'sitting as a judge of the High Court' should be added);
(b) recorders, as 'Mr [or Mrs] Recorder B'. This style is appropriate irrespective
of any honour or title which the recorder might possess, but if in any case it is
desired to include an honour or title the alternative description 'Sir CD, Recorder'
or 'The Lord D, Recorder' may be used; (c) deputy circuit judges, as 'His [or Her]
Honour EF, sitting as a Deputy Circuit Judge'.   *g*

31. *Transfer of cases from one circuit to another*

31.1. An application that a case be transferred from one circuit to another
should not be granted unless the judge is satisfied that: (a) the approval of the
presiding judges and circuit administrator for each circuit has been obtained, or   *h*
(b) the case may be transferred under general arrangements approved by the
presiding judges and circuit administrators.

32. *Transfer of proceedings between locations of the Crown Court*

32.1. Without prejudice to the provisions of s 76 of the Supreme Court Act   *j*
1981 (committal for trial: alteration of place of trial) directions may be given for
the transfer from one location of the Crown Court to another of: (a) appeals;
(b) proceedings on committal for sentence or to be dealt with.

32.2. Such directions may be given in a particular case by an officer of the
Crown Court, or generally, in relation to a class or classes of case, by the presiding
judge or a judge acting on his behalf.

a   32.3. If dissatisfied with such directions given by an officer of the Crown Court, any party to the proceedings may apply to a judge of the Crown Court who may hear the application in chambers.

33. *Allocation of business within the Crown Court*

b   General

33.1. Cases in class 1 are to be tried by a High Court judge. A case of murder or soliciting, incitement, attempt or conspiracy to commit murder, may be released, by or on the authority of a presiding judge, for trial by a deputy High Court judge, a circuit judge or a deputy circuit judge approved for the purpose by *c*   the Lord Chief Justice.

33.2. Cases in class 2 are to be tried by a High Court judge unless a particular case is released by or on the authority of a presiding judge for trial by a deputy High Court judge, circuit judge or a deputy circuit judge. A case of rape, or of a serious sexual offence of any class, may be released by a presiding judge for trial *d*   only by a circuit judge, deputy circuit judge or recorder approved for the purpose by the senior presiding judge with the concurrence of the Lord Chief Justice.

33.3. Cases in class 3 may be tried by a High Court judge or, in accordance with general or particular directions given by a presiding judge, by a circuit judge, a deputy circuit judge or a recorder who has attended a Judicial Studies Board Continuation Seminar and has been duly authorised by a presiding judge.
e

33.4. Cases in class 4 may be tried by a High Court judge, a deputy High Court judge, a circuit judge, a deputy circuit judge or a recorder. A case in class 4 shall not be listed for trial by a High Court judge except with the consent of that judge or of a presiding judge.

f   33.5. Appeals from decisions of magistrates shall be heard by: (a) a resident judge, or (b) a circuit judge, nominated by the resident judge, who regularly sits at the Crown Court centre, or (c) an experienced recorder specifically approved by the presiding judges for the purpose, or (d) where no circuit judge or recorder satisfying the requirements above is available and it is not practicable to obtain the approval of the presiding judges, by a circuit judge or recorder selected by the *g*   resident judge to hear a specific case or cases.

33.6. With the exception of courts operating the plea and directions scheme referred to in paras 41.1ff, the following arrangements for pre-trial proceedings shall apply. (a) Applications or matters arising before trial (including those relating to bail) should be listed where possible before the judge by whom the *h*   case is expected to be tried. Where a case is to be tried by a High Court judge who is not available the application or matter should be listed before any other High Court judge then sitting at the Crown Court centre at which the matter has arisen, before a presiding judge, before the resident judge for the centre, or, with the consent of the presiding judge, before a circuit judge nominated for the *j*   purpose. (b) In other cases, if the circuit judge or recorder who is expected to try the case is not available, the matter shall be referred to the resident judge or, if he is not available, to any judge or recorder then sitting at the centre.

33.7. Matters to be dealt with (eg in which a community rehabilitation order has been made or a suspended sentence passed) should, where possible, be listed before the judge who originally dealt with the matter, or, if not, before a judge of the same or higher status.

Allocation of proceedings to a court comprising lay justices

33.8. In addition to the classes of case specified in s 74 of the Supreme Court Act 1981 (appeals), any other proceedings, apart from cases listed for pleas of not guilty which, in accordance with these directions are listed for hearing by a circuit judge or recorder, are suitable for allocation to a court comprising Justices of the Peace.

Absence of resident judge

33.9. When a resident judge is absent from his centre, the presiding judges may authorise another judge who sits regularly at the same centre to exercise his responsibility.

Applications for removal of a driving disqualification

33.10. Application should be made to the location of the Crown Court where the order of disqualification was made.

Presiding judges' directions

33.11. For the just, speedy and economical disposal of the business of a circuit, presiding judges shall, with the approval of the senior presiding judge, issue directions as to the need, where appropriate, to reserve a case for trial by a High Court judge (or Deputy High Court judge) and as to the allocation of work between circuit judges, (deputy circuit judges) and recorders and where necessary the devolved responsibility of resident judges for such allocation. In such directions specific provision should be made for cases in the following categories. (a) Cases where death or serious risk to life, or the infliction of grave injury is involved, including motoring cases of this category arising from dangerous driving and/or excess alcohol. (b) Cases where loaded firearms are alleged to have been used. (c) Cases of arson or criminal damage with intent to endanger life. (d) Cases of defrauding government departments or local authorities or other public bodies of amounts in excess of £25,000. (e) Offences under the Forgery and Counterfeiting Act 1981 where the amount of money or the value of goods exceeds £10,000. (f) Offences involving violence to a police officer which result in the officer being unfit for duty for more than 28 days. (g) Any offence involving loss to any person or body of a sum in excess of £100,000. (h) Cases where there is a risk of substantial political or racial feeling being excited by the offence or the trial. (i) Cases which have given rise to widespread public concern. (j) Cases of robbery or assault with intent to rob where gross violence was used, or serious injury was caused, or where the accused was armed with a dangerous weapon for the purpose of the robbery, or where the theft was intended to be from a bank, a building society or a post office. (k) Cases involving the manufacture or distribution of substantial quantities of drugs. (l) Cases the trial of which is likely to last more than ten days. (m) Cases involving the trial of more than five defendants. (n) Cases in which the accused holds a senior public office, or is a member of a profession or other person carrying a special duty or responsibility to the public, including a police officer when acting as such. (o) Cases where a difficult issue of law is likely to be involved or a prosecution for the offence is rare or novel.

33.12. With the approval of the senior presiding judge, general directions may be given by the presiding judges of the South Eastern Circuit concerning the distribution and allocation of business of all classes at the Central Criminal Court.

34. *Settling the indictment*

34.1. Where an indictment contains counts which differ materially from, or are additional to, the charges on which an accused was committed for trial, the CPS shall notify the accused of the fact and shall, in any event, send a copy of the indictment to the accused.

34.2. There is no rule of law or practice which prohibits two indictments being in existence at the same time for the same offence against the same person on the same facts. But the court will not allow the prosecution to proceed on both such indictments. They cannot in law be tried together and the court will insist that the prosecution elect the one on which the trial shall proceed. Where different persons have been separately committed for trial for offences which can lawfully be charged in the same indictment it is permissible to join in one indictment the counts founded on the separate committals despite the fact that an indictment in respect of one of those committals has already been signed.

34.3. It is undesirable that a large number of counts should be contained in one indictment. Where defendants on trial have a variety of offences alleged against them the prosecution should be put to their election and compelled to proceed on a certain number only, leaving a decision to be taken later whether to try any of the remainder. Where an indictment contains substantive counts and one or more related conspiracy counts the judge should require the prosecution to justify the joinder. Failing justification the Crown should be required to elect whether to proceed on the substantive counts or the conspiracy counts. A joinder is justified for this purpose if the judge considers that the interests of justice demand it. In either event, if there is a conviction, the other count(s) can remain on the file marked 'Not to be proceeded with without leave of the court'. Should such conviction(s) be quashed, the others can be tried. It is possible to split an indictment and put some counts into another indictment.

35. *Voluntary bills of indictment*

35.1. Section 2(2)(b) of the Administration of Justice (Miscellaneous Provisions) Act 1933 allows the preferment of a bill of indictment by the direction or with the consent of a judge of the High Court. Bills so preferred are known as voluntary bills.

35.2. Applications for such consent must not only comply with each paragraph of the Indictments (Procedure) Rules 1971, SI 1971/2084, but must also be accompanied by: (a) a copy of any charges on which the defendant has been committed for trial; (b) a copy of any charges on which his committal for trial was refused by the magistrates' court; (c) a copy of any existing indictment which has been preferred in consequence of his committal; (d) a summary of the evidence or other document which (i) identifies the counts in the proposed indictment on which he has been committed for trial (or which are substantially the same as charges on which he has been so committed), and (ii) in relation to each other count in the proposed indictment, identifies the pages in the accompanying statements and exhibits where the essential evidence said to support that count is to be found; (e) marginal markings of the relevant passages on the pages of the statements and exhibits identified under (d)(ii). These requirements should be complied with in relation to each defendant named in the indictment for which consent is sought, whether or not it is proposed to prefer any new count against him.

35.3. The preferment of a voluntary bill is an exceptional procedure. Consent should only be granted where good reason to depart from the normal procedure is clearly shown and only where the interests of justice, rather than considerations of administrative convenience, require it.

35.4. Neither the 1933 Act nor the 1971 rules expressly require a prosecuting authority applying for consent to the preferment of a voluntary bill to give notice of the application to the prospective defendant or to serve on him a copy of documents delivered to the judge; nor is it expressly required that the prospective defendant have any opportunity to make any submissions to the judge, whether in writing or orally.

35.5. The prosecuting authorities for England and Wales have issued revised guidance to prosecutors on the procedures to be adopted in seeking judicial consent to the preferment of voluntary bills. These procedures direct prosecutors: (a) on the making of application for consent to preferment of a voluntary bill, forthwith to give notice to the prospective defendant that such application has been made; (b) at about the same time, to serve on the prospective defendant a copy of all the documents delivered to the judge (save to the extent that these have already been served on him); (c) to inform the prospective defendant that he may make submissions in writing to the judge, provided that he does so within nine working days of the giving of notice under (a) above. Prosecutors will be directed that these procedures should be followed unless there are good grounds for not doing so, in which case prosecutors will inform the judge that the procedures have not been followed and seek his leave to dispense with all or any of them. Judges should not give leave to dispense unless good grounds are shown.

35.6. A judge to whom application for consent to the preferment of a voluntary bill is made will, of course, wish to consider carefully the documents submitted by the prosecutor and any written submissions timeously made by the prospective defendant, and may properly seek any necessary amplification. The judge may invite oral submissions from either party, or accede to a request for an opportunity to make such oral submissions, if the judge considers it necessary or desirable to receive such oral submissions in order to make a sound and fair decision on the application. Any such oral submissions should be made on notice to the other party, who should be allowed to attend.

36. *Abuse of process stay applications*

36.1. In all cases where a defendant in the Crown Court proposes to make an application to stay an indictment on the grounds of abuse of process, written notice of such application must be given to the prosecuting authority and to any co-defendant not later than 14 days before the date fixed or warned for trial (the relevant date). Such notice must: (a) give the name of the case and the indictment number; (b) state the fixed date or the warned date as appropriate; (c) specify the nature of the application; (d) set out in numbered subparagraphs the grounds upon which the application is to be made; (e) be copied to the chief listing officer at the court centre where the case is due to be heard.

36.2. Any co-defendant who wishes to make a like application must give a like notice not later than seven days before the relevant date, setting out any additional grounds relied upon.

36.3. In relation to such applications, the following automatic directions shall apply. (a) the advocate for the applicant(s) must lodge with the court and serve on all other parties a skeleton argument in support of the application at least five clear working days before the relevant date. If reference is to be made to any document not in the existing trial documents, a paginated and indexed bundle of *a* such documents is to be provided with the skeleton argument. (b) The advocate for the prosecution must lodge with the court and serve on all other parties a responsive skeleton argument at least two clear working days before the relevant date, together with a supplementary bundle if appropriate.

36.4. All skeleton arguments must specify any propositions of law to be advanced (together with the authorities relied upon in support, with page

b references to passages relied upon) and, where appropriate, include a chronology of events and a list of dramatis personae. In all instances where reference is made to a document, the reference in the trial documents or supplementary bundle is to be given.

36.5. The above time limits are minimum time limits. In appropriate cases the court will order longer lead times. To this end in all cases where defence

c advocates are, at the time of the plea and directions hearing, considering the possibility of an abuse of process application, this must be raised with the judge dealing with the matter, who will order a different timetable if appropriate, and may wish, in any event, to give additional directions about the conduct of the application.

d

37. Citation of Hansard

37.1. Where any party intends to refer to the reports of Parliamentary proceedings as reported in the Official Reports of either House of Parliament (Hansard) in support of any such argument as is permitted by the decisions in *Pepper (Inspector of Taxes) v Hart* [1993] 1 All ER 42, [1993] AC 593 and *Pickstone v*

e *Freemans plc* [1988] 2 All ER 803, [1989] AC 66 or otherwise must, unless the court otherwise directs, serve upon all other parties and the court copies of any such extract together with a brief summary of the argument intended to be based upon such extract. No other report of Parliamentary proceedings may be cited.

37.2. Unless the court otherwise directs, service of the extract and summary of

f the argument shall be effected not less than five clear working days before the first day of the hearing, whether or not it has a fixed date. Advocates must keep themselves informed as to the state of the lists where no fixed date has been given. Service on the court shall be effected by sending three copies to the chief clerk of the relevant Crown Court centre. If any party fails to do so the court may make such order (relating to costs or otherwise) as is in all the circumstances

g appropriate.

38. Applications for representation orders

38.1. Applications for representation by a Queen's Counsel alone or by more than one advocate under Pt IV of the Criminal Defence Service (General) (No 2)

h Regulations 2001, SI 2001/1437, made to the Crown Court shall be placed before the resident judge of that Crown Court (or, in his absence, a judge nominated for that purpose by a presiding judge of the circuit) who shall determine the application, save that, where the application relates to a case which is to be heard before a named High Court judge or a named circuit judge, he should refer the

j application to the named judge for determination.

38.2. This does not apply where an application is made in the course of a trial or of a preliminary hearing, pre-trial review, or plea and directions hearing by the judge presiding at that trial or hearing.

38.3. In the event of any doubt as to the proper application of this direction, reference shall be made by the judge concerned to a presiding judge of the circuit, who shall give such directions as he thinks fit.

39. *Trial of children and young persons*

39.1. This direction applies to trials of children and young persons in the Crown Court. In it children and young persons are together called 'young defendants'.

39.2. The steps which should be taken to comply with paras 39.3–39.17 should be judged, in any given case, taking account of the age, maturity and development (intellectual and emotional) of the young defendant on trial and all other circumstances of the case.

The overriding principle

39.3. Some young defendants accused of committing serious crimes may be very young and very immature when standing trial in the Crown Court. The purpose of such trial is to determine guilt (if that is in issue) and decide the appropriate sentence if the young defendant pleads guilty or is convicted. The trial process should not itself expose the young defendant to avoidable intimidation, humiliation or distress. All possible steps should be taken to assist the young defendant to understand and participate in the proceedings. The ordinary trial process should, so far as necessary, be adapted to meet those ends. Regard should be had to the welfare of the young defendant as required by s 44 of the Children and Young Persons Act 1933.

Before trial

39.4. If a young defendant is indicted jointly with an adult defendant, the court should consider at the plea and directions hearing whether the young defendant should be tried on his own and should ordinarily so order unless of opinion that a joint trial would be in the interests of justice and would not be unduly prejudicial to the welfare of the young defendant. If a young defendant is tried jointly with an adult the ordinary procedures will apply subject to such modifications (if any) as the court may see fit to order.

39.5. At the plea and directions hearing before trial of a young defendant, the court should consider and so far as practicable give directions on the matters covered in paras 39.9–39.15.

39.6. It may be appropriate to arrange that a young defendant should visit, out of court hours and before the trial, the courtroom in which the trial is to be held so that he can familiarise himself with it.

39.7. If any case against a young defendant has attracted or may attract widespread public or media interest, the assistance of the police should be enlisted to try and ensure that a young defendant is not, when attending for the trial, exposed to intimidation, vilification or abuse.

39.8. The court should be ready at this stage (if it has not already done so) to give a direction under s 39 of the 1933 Act or, as the case may be, s 45 of the Youth Justice and Criminal Evidence Act 1999. Any such order, once made, should be reduced to writing and copies should on request be made available to anyone affected or potentially affected by it.

The trial

39.9. The trial should, if practicable, be held in a courtroom in which all the participants are on the same or almost the same level.

39.10. A young defendant should normally, if he wishes, be free to sit with members of his family or others in a like relationship and in a place which permits easy, informal communication with his legal representatives and others with whom he wants or needs to communicate.

39.11. The court should explain the course of proceedings to a young defendant in terms he can understand, should remind those representing a young defendant of their continuing duty to explain each step of the trial to him and should ensure, so far as practicable, that the trial is conducted in language which the young defendant can understand.

39.12. The trial should be conducted according to a timetable which takes full account of a young defendant's inability to concentrate for long periods. Frequent and regular breaks will often be appropriate.

39.13. Robes and wigs should not be worn unless the young defendant asks that they should or the court for good reason orders that they should. Any person responsible for the security of a young defendant who is in custody should not be in uniform. There should be no recognisable police presence in the courtroom save for good reason.

39.14. The court should be prepared to restrict attendance at the trial to a small number, perhaps limited to some of those with an immediate and direct interest in the outcome of the trial. The court should rule on any challenged claim to attend.

39.15. Facilities for reporting the trial (subject to any direction given under s 39 of the 1933 Act or s 45 of the 1999 Act) must be provided. But the court may restrict the number of those attending in the courtroom to report the trial to such number as is judged practicable and desirable. In ruling on any challenged claim to attend the courtroom for the purpose of reporting the trial the court should be mindful of the public's general right to be informed about the administration of justice in the Crown Court. Where access to the courtroom by reporters is restricted, arrangements should be made for the proceedings to be relayed, audibly and if possible visually, to another room in the same court complex to which the media have free access if it appears that there will be a need for such additional facilities.

39.16. Where the court is called upon to exercise its discretion in relation to any procedural matter failing within the scope of this practice direction but not the subject of specific reference, such discretion should be exercised having regard to the principles in para 39.3.

Appeal and committals for sentence

39.17. This practice direction does not in terms apply to appeals and committals for sentence, but regard should be paid to the effect of it if the arrangements for hearing any appeal or committal might otherwise be prejudicial to the welfare of a young defendant.

40. Video recorded evidence-in-chief

40.1. The procedure for making application for leave to adduce a video recording of testimony from a witness under s 27 of the Youth Justice and Criminal Evidence Act 1999 is laid down in r 8 of the Crown Court (Special Measures Directions and Directions Prohibiting Cross-Examination) Rules 2002, SI 2002/1688.

40.2. Where a court, on application by a party to the proceedings or of its own motion, grants leave to admit a video recording in evidence under s 27(1) of the 1999 Act it may direct that any part of the recording be excluded (s 27(2) and (3)). When such direction is given, the party who made application to admit the video recording must edit the recording in accordance with the judge's directions and send a copy of the edited recording to the appropriate officer of the Crown Court and to every other party to the proceedings.

40.3. Where a video recording is to be adduced during proceedings before the Crown Court, it should be produced and proved by the interviewer, or any other person who was present at the interview with the witness at which the recording was made. The applicant should ensure that such a person will be available for this purpose, unless the parties have agreed to accept a written statement in lieu of attendance by that person.

40.4. Once a trial has begun if, by reason of faulty or inadequate preparation or for some other cause, the procedures set out above have not been properly complied with and an application is made to edit the video recording, thereby making necessary an adjournment for the work to be carried out, the court may make at its discretion an appropriate award of costs.

41. *Plea and directions hearings*

41.1. These rules apply to all cases (other than serious fraud) in Crown Court centres which have notified the magistrates' courts that plea and directions hearings (PDHs) have been introduced.

41.2. At the PDH pleas will be taken and, in contested cases, prosecution and defence will be expected to assist the judge in identifying the key issues and to provide any additional information required for the proper listing of the case.

41.3. The detailed operation of the rules will be a matter for the judiciary at each Crown Court centre, taking the views of other agencies and the legal profession into account.

41.4. In every case, other than serious fraud cases in relation to which a notice of transfer to the Crown Court is given under s 4 of the Criminal Justice Act 1987 and child abuse cases transferred under s 53 of the Criminal Justice Act 1991 the magistrates' court should commit the defendant to appear in the Crown Court on a specific date fixed in liaison with the Crown Court listing officer for an initial PDH. The PDH provisions will apply equally to child abuse cases, for which special arrangements will need to be made for the Crown Court to fix a PDH date on receipt of the case papers.

41.5. The purpose of the PDH will be to ensure that all necessary steps have been taken in preparation for trial and to provide sufficient information for a trial date to be arranged. It is expected that the advocate briefed in the case will appear in the PDH wherever practicable.

41.6. At least 14 days' notice of the PDH shall be given unless the parties agree to shorter notice. The PDH should be within six weeks of committal in cases where the defendant is on bail and four weeks where the defendant is in custody.

Preparation for the PDH

41.7. Where the defendant intends to plead guilty to all or part of the indictment the defence must notify the Probation Service, the prosecution and the court as soon as this is known.

41.8. The defence must supply the court and the prosecution with a full list of the prosecution witnesses they require to attend at the trial. This must be provided at least 14 days prior to the PDH or within three working days of the notice of the hearing where the PDH is fixed less than 17 days ahead.

41.9. For all class 1 offences and for lengthy and complex cases a case summary should be prepared by the prosecution for use by the judge at the PDH. All class 2 cases should be scrutinised by the prosecution to determine whether *a*   the provision of a summary is appropriate in any particular case. The summary will assist the judge by indicating the nature of the case and focusing on the issues of fact and/or law likely to be involved. The summary should also assist the judge in estimating the trial length.

Form of hearing

b   41.10. The PDH should normally be held, and orders made, in open court and all defendants should be present (except with the leave of the court). It shall be conducted: (a) in all cases other than those in class 1 or class 2 and serious sexual offences of any class against a child, by the trial judge or such judge as the presiding judge or resident judge shall appoint; (b) in cases in class 1 or class 2 and serious sexual offences of any class against a child, by a High Court judge or by a
c   circuit judge or recorder to whom the case has been specifically released in accordance with the directions for the allocation of business within the Crown Court (see paras 33.1–33.12), or by a directions judge authorised by the presiding judges to conduct such hearings, but: (i) pleas of guilty when entered before a directions judge in such cases will be adjourned for sentencing by a High Court
d   judge, circuit judge or recorder to whom the case has been specifically released; and (ii) a directions judge will deal only with those matters necessary to see that such cases are prepared conveniently for trial, including identifying any issues suitable for a preliminary hearing before the trial judge, and making such necessary directions as may facilitate the conduct of such a preliminary hearing.

e   Conduct of the hearing

    41.11. At the PDH arraignment will normally take place.

    41.12. If the defendant pleads guilty, the judge should proceed to sentencing whenever possible.

    41.13. Following a not guilty plea, and where part or alternative pleas have not
f   been accepted, the prosecution and defence will be expected to inform the court of: (a) the issues in the case (identifying any human rights issue); (b) issues, if any, as to the mental or medical condition of any defendant or witness; (c) the number of witnesses whose evidence will be placed before the court either orally or in writing; (d) the defence witnesses in (c) above whose statements have been
g   served and whose evidence the prosecution will agree and accept in writing; (e) any additional witnesses who may be called by the prosecution and the evidence that they are expected to give; (f) facts which are to be admitted and which can be reduced into writing in accordance with s 10(2)(b) of the Criminal Justice Act 1967, within such time as may be directed at the hearing, and of the witnesses whose attendance will not be required at trial; (g) exhibits and
h   schedules which are to be admitted; (h) the order and pagination of the papers to be used by the prosecution at the trial; (i) any alibi which should already have been disclosed; (j) any point of law which it is anticipated will arise at trial, any questions as to the admissibility of evidence which appear on the face of the papers, and of any authority on which the party intends to rely; (k) any
j   applications to be made for evidence to be given through live television links by child witnesses; (l) any applications to submit pre-recorded interviews with a child witness as evidence-in-chief; (m) any applications for screens, for use by witnesses seeking a visual break between themselves and any relevant parties: whether any video, tape recorder or other technical equipment will be required during a trial; where tape recorded interviews have taken place, of any dispute or agreement as to the accuracy of any transcript or summary; (n) any other

significant matter which might affect the proper and convenient trial of the case, and whether any additional work needs to be done by the parties; (o) the estimated length of the trial, to be agreed more precisely taking account of any views expressed by the judge and the other parties; (p) witness availability and the approximate length of witness evidence so that attendance can be staggered during lengthy trials, agreeing likely dates and times of attendance, taking into consideration real hardship and inconvenience to a witness where applicable; (q) availability of advocates; (r) whether there is a need for any further directions.

41.14. Subject to the provisions of ss 9 and 10 of the Criminal Justice Act 1967, admissions under para 41.13(f) may be used at the trial.

41.15. The judge may make such order or orders as lie within his powers as appear to be necessary to secure the proper and efficient trial of the case. Each party shall, at least 14 days before the date of trial, confirm to the court in writing that all such orders have been fully complied with.

41.16. The questionnaire in Annex D, below provides a recommended structure for use by the judiciary in conducting a PDH. A single copy of the questionnaire, completed as far as possible with the agreement of both advocates, is to be handed in to the court prior to the commencement of the PDH.

41.17. The defence shall apply to the court for the case to be listed for mention if they are unable to obtain instructions from the defendant. If the defendant fails to attend court the judge will wish to consider whether a warrant of arrest should be issued.

42. *Juries*

Excusal from jury service

42.1. Jury service is an important public duty which individual members of the public are chosen at random to undertake. The normal presumption is that, unless a person is excusable as of right from jury service under Pt III of Sch 1 to the Juries Act 1974, he or she will be required to serve when summoned to do so. There will, however, be circumstances where a juror should be excused, for instance where he is personally concerned in the facts of the particular case or is closely connected with a party or prospective witness.

42.2. He may also be excused on grounds of personal hardship or conscientious objection to jury service. Each such application should be dealt with sensitively and sympathetically.

42.3. Any person who appeals to the court against a refusal by the appropriate officer to excuse him from jury service must be given an opportunity to make representations in support of his appeal.

Jury oath

42.4. The wording of the oath to be taken by jurors is: 'I swear by Almighty God that I will faithfully try the defendant and give a true verdict according to the evidence.' Any person who objects to being sworn shall be permitted to make his solemn affirmation instead. The wording of the affirmation is: 'I do solemnly, sincerely and truly declare and affirm that I will faithfully try the defendant and give a true verdict according to the evidence.'

43. *Evidence of tape recorded interviews*

43.1. Where a suspect is to be interviewed by the police, the *Code of Practice on Tape Recording of Interviews with Suspects* effective from 10 April 1995 and issued under s 60 of the Police and Criminal Evidence Act 1984 applies. Where a record of the interview is to be prepared this should be in accordance with the national guidelines approved by the Secretary of State, as envisaged by note E:5A of the Code.

43.2. Where the prosecution intends to adduce evidence of the interview-in-evidence, and agreement between the parties has not been reached about the record, sufficient notice must be given to allow consideration of any amendment to the record or the preparation of any transcript of the interview or any editing of a tape for the purpose of playing it back in court. To that end, the following practice should be followed. (a) Where the defence is unable to agree a record of interview or transcript (where one is already available) the prosecution should be notified no more than 21 days from the date of committal or date of transfer, or at the PDH if earlier, with a view to securing agreement to amend. The notice should specify the part to which objection is taken or the part omitted which the defence consider should be included. A copy of the notice should be supplied to the court within the period specified above. (b) If agreement is not reached and it is proposed that the tape or part of it be played in court, notice should be given to the prosecution by the defence no more than 14 days after the expiry of the period in (a), or as ordered at the PDH, in order that counsel for the parties may agree those parts of the tape that should not be adduced and that arrangements may be made, by editing or in some other way, to exclude that material. A copy of the notice should be supplied to the court within the period specified above. (c) Notice of any agreement reached under (a) or (b) should be supplied to the court by the prosecution as soon as is practicable. (d) Alternatively, if, in any event, prosecuting counsel proposes to play the tape or part of it, the prosecution should, within 28 days of the date of committal or date of transfer or, if earlier, at the PDH, notify the defence and the court. The defence should notify the prosecution and the court within 14 days of receiving the notice if they object to the production of the tape on the basis that a part of it should be excluded. If the objections raised by the defence are accepted, the prosecution should prepare an edited tape or make other arrangements to exclude the material part and should notify the court of the arrangements made. (e) Whenever editing or amendment of a record of interview or of a tape or of a transcript takes place, the following general principles should be followed: (i) where a defendant has made a statement which includes an admission of one or more other offences, the portion relating to other offences should be omitted unless it is or becomes admissible in evidence; (ii) where the statement of one defendant contains a portion which is partly in his favour and partly implicatory of a co-defendant in the trial, the defendant making the statement has the right to insist that everything relevant which is in his favour goes before the jury. In such a case the judge must be consulted about how best to protect the position of the co-defendant.

43.3. If there is a failure to agree between counsel under para 43.2(a)–(e), or there is a challenge to the integrity of the master tape, notice and particulars should be given to the court and to the prosecution by the defence as soon as is practicable. The court may then, at its discretion, order a pre-trial review or give such other directions as may be appropriate.

43.4. If a tape is to be adduced during proceedings before the Crown Court it should be produced and proved by the interviewing officer or any other officer who was present at the interview at which the recording was made. The prosecution should ensure that such an officer will be available for this purpose.

43.5. Where such an officer is unable to act as the tape machine operator it is for the prosecution to make some other arrangement.

43.6. In order to avoid the necessity for the court to listen to lengthy or irrelevant material before the relevant part of a tape recording is reached, counsel shall indicate to the tape machine operator those parts of a recording which it may be necessary to play. Such an indication should, so far as possible, be expressed in terms of the time track or other identifying process used by the interviewing police force and should be given in time for the operator to have located those parts by the appropriate point in the trial.

43.7. Once a trial has begun, if, by reason of faulty preparation or for some other cause, the procedures above have not been properly complied with, and an application is made to amend the record of interview or transcript or to edit the tape, as the case may be, thereby making necessary an adjournment for the work to be carried out, the court may make at its discretion an appropriate award of costs.

43.8. Where a case is listed for hearing on a date which falls within the time limits set out above, it is the responsibility of the parties to ensure that all the necessary steps are taken to comply with this practice direction within such shorter period as is available.

43.9. In para 43.2(a) and (d), 'date of transfer' is the date on which notice of transfer is given in accordance with the provisions of s 4(1)(c) of the Criminal Justice Act 1987.

43.10. This direction should be read in conjunction with the *Code of Practice on Tape Recording* referred to in para 43.1 and with Home Office circular 26/1995.

44. *Defendant's right to give or not to give evidence*

44.1. At the conclusion of the evidence for the prosecution, s 35(2) of the Criminal Justice and Public Order Act 1994 requires the court to satisfy itself that the accused is aware that the stage has been reached at which evidence can be given for the defence and that he can, if he wishes, give evidence and that, if he chooses not to give evidence, or having been sworn, without good cause refuses to answer any question, it will be permissible for the jury to draw such inferences as appear proper from his failure to give evidence or his refusal, without good cause, to answer any question.

If the accused is legally represented

44.2. Section 35(1) provides that s 35(2) does not apply if at the conclusion of the evidence for the prosecution the accused's legal representative informs the court that the accused will give evidence. This should be done in the presence of the jury. If the representative indicates that the accused will give evidence the case should proceed in the usual way.

44.3. If the court is not so informed, or if the court is informed that the accused does not intend to give evidence, the judge should in the presence of the jury inquire of the representative in these terms:

'Have you advised your client that the stage has now been reached at which he may give evidence and, if he chooses not to do so or, having been sworn, without good cause refuses to answer any question, the jury may draw such inferences as appear proper from his failure to do so?'

44.4. If the representative replies to the judge that the accused has been so advised, then the case shall proceed. If counsel replies that the accused has not been so advised, then the judge shall direct the representative to advise his client of the consequences set out in para 44.3 and should adjourn briefly for this purpose before proceeding further.

If the accused is not legally represented

44.5. If the accused is not represented, the judge shall at the conclusion of the evidence for the prosecution and in the presence of the jury say to the accused:

> 'You have heard the evidence against you. Now is the time for you to make your defence. You may give evidence on oath, and be cross-examined like any other witness. If you do not give evidence or, having been sworn, without good cause refuse to answer any question the jury may draw such inferences as appear proper. That means they may hold it against you. You may also call any witness or witnesses whom you have arranged to attend court. Afterwards you may also, if you wish, address the jury by arguing your case from the dock. But you cannot at that stage give evidence. Do you now intend to give evidence?'

45. *Discussions about sentence*

45.1. An advocate must be free to do what is his duty, namely to give the accused the best advice he can and, if need be, in strong terms. It will often include advice that a guilty plea, showing an element of remorse, is a mitigating factor which may well enable the court to give a lesser sentence than would otherwise be the case. The advocate will, of course, emphasise that the accused must not plead guilty unless he has committed the acts constituting the offence(s) charged.

45.2. The accused, having considered the advocate's advice, must have complete freedom of choice whether to plead guilty or not guilty.

45.3. There must be freedom of access between advocate and judge. Any discussion must, however, be between the judge and the advocates on both sides. If counsel is instructed by a solicitor who is in court, he too should be allowed to attend the discussion. This freedom of access is important because there may be matters calling for communication or discussion of such a nature that the advocate cannot, in his client's interest, mention them in open court, eg the advocate, by way of mitigation, may wish to tell the judge that the accused has not long to live because he is suffering maybe from cancer of which he is and should remain ignorant. Again, the advocates on both sides may wish to discuss with the judge whether it would be proper, in a particular case, for the prosecution to accept a plea to a lesser offence. It is imperative that, so far as possible, justice must be administered in open court. Advocates should, therefore, only ask to see the judge when it is felt to be really necessary. The judge must be careful only to treat such communications as private where, in fairness to the accused, this is necessary.

45.4. The judge should, subject to one exception, never indicate the sentence he is minded to impose. The exception is that it should be permissible for a judge to say, if it be the case that, whatever happens, whether the accused pleads guilty or not guilty, the sentence will or will not take a particular form. Where any such discussion on sentence has taken place, the advocate for the defence should disclose it to the accused and, subject to the exception of those matters of which he should remain ignorant, such as cancer, of which he is unaware, inform him of what took place.

45.5. Where any such discussion takes place it should be recorded either by a tape recorder or a shorthand writer.

46. *Majority verdicts*

46.1. It is important that all those trying indictable offences should so far as possible adopt a uniform practice when complying with s 17 of the Juries Act 1974, both in directing the jury in summing-up and also in receiving the verdict or giving further directions after retirement. So far as the summing-up is concerned, it is inadvisable for the judge, and indeed for advocates, to attempt an explanation of the section for fear that the jury will be confused. Before the jury retire, however, the judge should direct the jury in some such words as the following:

> 'As you may know, the law permits me, in certain circumstances, to accept a verdict which is not the verdict of you all. Those circumstances have not as yet arisen, so that when you retire I must ask you to reach a verdict upon which each one of you is agreed. Should, however, the time come when it is possible for me to accept a majority verdict, I will give you a further direction.'

46.2. Thereafter the practice should be as follows: should the jury return *before* two hours and ten minutes since the last member of the jury left the jury box to go to the jury room (or such longer time as the judge thinks reasonable) has elapsed (see s 17(4)), they should be asked: (a) 'Have you reached a verdict upon which you are all agreed? Please answer Yes or No'; (b)(i) if unanimous, 'What is your verdict?'; (ii) if not unanimous, the jury should be sent out again for further deliberation with a further direction to arrive if possible at an unanimous verdict.

46.3. Should the jury return (whether for the first time or subsequently) or be sent for *after* the two hours and ten minutes (or the longer period) has elapsed; questions (a) and (b)(i) in para 46.2 should be put to them and, if it appears that they are not unanimous, they should be asked to retire once more and told that they should continue to endeavour to reach an unanimous verdict but that, if they cannot, the judge will accept a majority verdict as in s 17(1).

46.4. When the jury finally return they should be asked: (a) 'Have at least ten (or nine as the case may be) of you agreed on your verdict?'; (b) if 'Yes', 'What is your verdict? Please only answer Guilty or Not Guilty'; (c)(i) if 'Not Guilty', accept the verdict without more ado; (ii) if 'Guilty', is that the verdict of you all or by a majority?'; (d) if 'Guilty' by a majority, 'How many of you agreed to the verdict and how many dissented?'

46.5. At whatever stage the jury return, before question (a) is asked, the senior officer of the court present shall state in open court, for each period when the jury was out of court for the purpose of considering their verdict(s), the time at which the last member of the jury left the jury box to go to the jury room and the time of their return to the jury box and will additionally state in open court the total of such periods.

46.6. The reason why s 17(3) is confined to a majority verdict of guilty and for the somewhat complicated procedure set out in para 46.3 and para 46.4 is to prevent it being known that a verdict of 'Not Guilty' is a majority verdict. If the final direction in para 46.3 continues to require the jury to arrive, if possible, at an unanimous verdict and the verdict is received as in para 46.4, it will not be known for certain that the acquittal is not unanimous.

46.7. Where there are several counts (or alternative verdicts) left to the jury the above practice will, of course, need to be adapted to the circumstances. The procedure will have to be repeated in respect of each count (or alternative verdict), the verdict being accepted in those cases where the jury are unanimous and the further direction in para 46.3 being given in cases in which they are not unanimous. Should the jury in the end be unable to agree on a verdict by the required majority (ie if the answer to the question in para 46.4(a) be in the negative) the judge in his discretion will either ask them to deliberate further or discharge them.

46.8. Section 17 will, of course, apply also to verdicts other than 'Guilty' or 'Not Guilty', e g to special verdicts under the Criminal Procedure (Insanity) Act 1964, verdicts under that Act as to fitness to be tried, and special verdicts on findings of fact. Accordingly in such cases the questions to jurors will have to be suitably adjusted.

47. *Imposition of discretionary life sentences*

47.1. Section 82A of the Powers of Criminal Courts (Sentencing) Act 2000 empowers a judge when passing a sentence of life imprisonment, where such a sentence is not fixed by law, to specify by order such part of the sentence (the relevant part) as shall be served before the prisoner may require the Secretary of State to refer his case to the Parole Board.

47.2. Thus the discretionary life sentence falls into two parts: (a) the relevant part, which consists of the period of detention imposed for punishment and deterrence, taking into account the seriousness of the offence; and (b) the remaining part of the sentence, during which the prisoner's detention will be governed by considerations of risk to the public.

47.3. The judge is not obliged by statute to make use of the provisions of s 82A when passing a discretionary life sentence. However, the judge should do so, save in the very exceptional case where the judge considers that the offence is so serious that detention for life is justified by the seriousness of the offence alone, irrespective of the risk to the public. In such a case, the judge should state this in open court when passing sentence.

47.4. In cases where the judge is to specify the relevant part of the sentence under s 82A, the judge should permit the advocate for the defendant to address the court as to the appropriate length of the relevant part. Where no relevant part is to be specified, the advocate for the defendant should be permitted to address the court as to the appropriateness of this course of action.

47.5. In specifying the relevant part of the sentence, the judge should have regard to the specific terms of s 82A and should indicate the reasons for reaching his decision as to the length of the relevant part.

47.6. Whether or not the court orders that s 82A should apply, the judge shall not, following the imposition of a discretionary life sentence, make a written report to the Secretary of State through the Lord Chief Justice as was the practice until 8 February 1993.

Note: reference should also be made to the section on life sentences below.

48. *Life sentences for juveniles convicted of murder*

48.1. When a person is convicted of a murder committed when under the age of 18 the determination of the minimum term (previously tariff) applicable to his sentence has since 30 November 2000 been set by the trial judge, as it was and is for adults subject to discretionary life sentences: see s 82A of the Powers of Criminal Courts (Sentencing) Act 2000.

49. *Life sentences*

49.1. Practice Note (juveniles: murder tariff) [2000] 4 All ER 831, [2000] 1 WLR 1655 handed down on 27 July 2000 was replaced by *Practice Statement (crime: life sentences)* [2002] 3 All ER 412, [2002] 1 WLR 1789 handed down on 31 May 2002 and reproduced in paras 49.2–49.28 below. That Statement came into force immediately and is to be applied by judges in cases in which they sentence or make a recommendation after 31 May 2002. Its primary, but not sole, purpose is to give effect to the advice of the Sentencing Advisory Panel dated 15 March 2002. It does not set out rules, but guidance from which a judge can in his discretion depart, if he considers this is necessary in view of the particular circumstances of an individual case notwithstanding the desirability of achieving consistency. Reasons for any departure from the guidance should be given.

49.2. The previous *Practice Note* referred to a 'tariff'. This term, in accordance with the advice of the panel, will no longer be used because it has commonly been misunderstood. The present Statement refers instead to 'minimum term' to make it clearer that, even when released, the offender has not served his sentence which continues for the remainder of his life.

49.3. In fact, an offender is most unlikely to be released on the expiry of the minimum term and for the purpose of calculating the earliest date of normal release on licence the minimum term is approximately the equivalent of a determinate sentence of twice its length. So a minimum term of 14 years is equivalent to a determinate sentence of approximately 28 years. (See *Re Thompson (tariff recommendations)* [2001] All ER 737 at 740, [2001] 1 Cr App R 401 at 404.)

49.4. When a person of 21 years or over is convicted of murder the only sentence is life imprisonment. When an offender is aged 18 to 20 the equivalent sentence is custody for life and for an offender aged 17 or under at the date of the offence the sentence is detention at Her Majesty's pleasure. In the appropriate circumstances, a judge can also pass a discretionary life sentence and an automatic life sentence. Except when sentencing an offender aged 18 or over for murder, a judge is required to announce the minimum term in public. A judge sentencing a prisoner to life imprisonment for murder has the power to make a recommendation in open court as to the 'minimum period' which should elapse before the person convicted is released on licence under s 1 of Murder (Abolition of Death Penalty) Act 1965. This statutory power is rarely exercised. Before it is exercised the judge should carefully consider whether it would not be preferable to rely on the usual practice of making a recommendation after the trial has finished which is then forwarded to the Lord Chief Justice. The Home Secretary can then be sent the recommendation of both judges.

Announcing a minimum term

49.5. When a judge gives in public his decision as to the minimum term a prisoner is required to serve, he should make clear how that term is calculated. In particular, he should normally commence by indicating what he considers would be the appropriate determinate sentence suitable for punishment and deterrence. He should then explain that it is necessary to calculate a minimum term so that it will be known when the prisoner's case should be referred to the Parole Board. Finally, he should explain that if a prisoner is released on licence still, for the remainder of his life, he can be recalled to prison if he does not comply with the terms of his licence.

Adult offenders convicted of murder

49.6. In relation to adults convicted of murder, after the Lord Chief Justice, in accordance with the present practice, has received the relevant information from the trial judge including the trial judge's recommendation, he will make his own recommendation. The Home Secretary will then make the final decision as to the appropriate minimum term having considered both recommendations.

49.7. Before recommending a release date, the Parole Board, in accordance with present practice, must be satisfied that the offender is no longer a risk to the public and is ready for release into society. Following release, life sentence prisoners remain subject to the life sentence and the terms of their licence for the rest of their lives. They must comply with any conditions of their licence and are subject to supervision by the Probation Service and they are liable to recall to custody at any time if the terms of the licence are breached.

49.8. The *Practice Note* dated 27 July 2000, confirmed the starting point of 14 years, which had been increased from 12 years, as the minimum term for a case with no aggravating or mitigating factors. It also listed the factors which indicate that either a higher or a lower than normal minimum term is appropriate in an individual case.

49.9. This statement replaces the previous single normal tariff of 14 years by substituting; a higher and a normal starting point of respectively 16 (comparable to 32 years) and 12 years (comparable to 24 years). These starting points have then to be increased or reduced because of aggravating or mitigating factors such as those referred to in paras 49.10–49.18, below. It is emphasised that they are no more than starting points.

The normal starting point of 12 years

49.10. Cases falling within this starting point will normally involve the killing of an adult victim, arising from a quarrel or loss of temper between two people known to each other. It will not have the characteristics referred to in para 49.13. Exceptionally, the starting point may be reduced because of the sort of circumstances described in the next paragraph.

49.11. The normal starting point can be reduced because the murder is one where the offender's culpability is significantly reduced, for example, because: (a) the case came close to the borderline between murder and manslaughter; or (b) the offender suffered from mental disorder, or from a mental disability which lowered the degree of his criminal responsibility for the killing, although not affording a defence of diminished responsibility; or (c) the offender was provoked (in a non-technical sense), such as by prolonged and eventually unsupportable stress; or (d) the case involved an over reaction in self-defence; or (e) the offence was a mercy killing.

49.12. These factors could justify a reduction to eight/nine years (equivalent to 16/18 years).

The higher starting point of 15/16 years

49.13. The higher starting point will apply to cases where the offender's culpability was exceptionally high or the victim was in a particularly vulnerable position. Such cases will be characterised by a feature which makes the crime especially serious, such as: (a) the killing was 'professional' or a contract killing;

(b) the killing was politically motivated; (c) the killing was done for gain (in the course of a burglary, robbery etc); (d) the killing was intended to defeat the ends of justice (as in the killing of a witness or potential witness); (e) the victim was providing a public service; (f) the victim was a child or was otherwise vulnerable; (g) the killing was racially aggravated; (h) the victim was deliberately targeted because of his or her religion or sexual orientation; (i) there was evidence of sadism, gratuitous violence or sexual maltreatment, humiliation or degradation of the victim before the killing; (j) extensive and/or multiple injuries were inflicted on the victim before death; (k) the offender committed multiple murders.

Variation of the starting point

49.14. Whichever starting point is selected in a particular case, it may be appropriate for the trial judge to vary the starting point upwards or downwards, to take account of aggravating or mitigating factors, which relate to either the offence or the offender, in the particular case.

49.15. Aggravating factors relating to the offence can include: (a) the fact that the killing was planned; (b) the use of a firearm; (c) arming with a weapon in advance; (d) concealment of the body, destruction of the crime scene and/or dismemberment of the body; (e) particularly in domestic violence cases, the fact that the murder was the culmination of cruel and violent behaviour by the offender over a period of time.

49.16. Aggravating factors relating to the offender will include the offender's previous record and failures to respond to previous sentences, to the extent that this is relevant to culpability rather than to risk.

49.17. Mitigating factors relating to the offence will include: (a) an intention to cause grievous bodily harm, rather than to kill; (b) spontaneity and lack of pre-meditation.

49.18. Mitigating factors relating to the offender may include: (a) the offender's age; (b) clear evidence of remorse or contrition; (c) a timely plea of guilty.

Very serious cases

49.19. A substantial upward adjustment may be appropriate in the most serious cases, for example, those involving a substantial number of murders, or if there are several factors identified as attracting the higher starting point present. In suitable cases, the result might even be a minimum term of 30 years (equivalent to 60 years) which would offer little or no hope of the offender's eventual release. In cases of exceptional gravity, the judge, rather than setting a whole life minimum term, can state that there is no minimum period which could properly be set in that particular case.

49.20. Among the categories of case referred to in para 49.13, some offences may be especially grave. These include cases in which the victim was performing his duties as a prison officer at the time of the crime or the offence was a terrorist or sexual or sadistic murder or involved a young child. In such a case, a term of 20 years and upwards could be appropriate.

Young offenders

49.21. Section 60 of the Criminal Justice and Court Services Act 2000 brought sentencing procedures for those sentenced to detention during Her Majesty's pleasure into line with adult offenders sentenced to discretionary and automatic (but not mandatory) life sentences. When imposing the mandatory sentence of detention at Her Majesty's pleasure on an offender convicted of murder, who was aged under 18 at the time of the offence, the sentencing judge may now order that ss 28(5)–(8) of the Crime (Sentences) Act 1997 shall apply to the young offender as soon as he has served that part of the sentence which is specified by the sentencer. A minimum term should be specified in all but the most exceptional circumstances. If a minimum sentence is not fixed the Home Secretary will, in due course, determine the appropriate stage for the early release provisions to apply to the young offender.

49.22. In setting the minimum term, sentencers are required by s 82A(3) of the Powers of Criminal Courts (Sentencing) Act 2000 to take account of the same three considerations that apply to discretionary or automatic life sentences imposed on an adult, namely:

(a) the seriousness of the offence, or the combination of the offence and one or more offences associated with it;

(b) the effect which s 67 of the Criminal Justice Act 1967 would have had if he had been sentenced to a term of imprisonment; and

(c) the early release provisions contained in ss 33(2) and 35(1) of the Criminal Justice Act 1991.

49.23. Subparagraph (b) requires the sentencer to make adjustment for any period which had been spent on remand in custody, since that period is not automatically deducted from the minimum period by s 67 of the 1967 Act. The period spent by the offender in local authority secure accommodation should be deducted from the minimum term (see *R v Secretary of State for the Home Dept, ex p A* [2000] 1 All ER 651, [2000] 2 AC 276).

49.24. As in the case of an adult, sub-para (c) requires the sentencer to fix the minimum term at one half of the normal determinate sentence which would have been imposed for the offence if a life sentence had not been passed (see *R v Secretary of State for the Home Dept, ex p Furber* [1998] 1 All ER 23, [1998] 1 Cr App R (S) 208).

49.25. In the case of young offenders, the judge should always start from the normal starting point appropriate for an adult (12 years). The judge should then reduce the starting point to take into account the maturity and age of the offender. Some children are more, and others less, mature for their age and the reduction that is appropriate in order to achieve the correct starting point will very much depend on the stage of the development of the individual offender. A mechanistic approach is never appropriate. The sort of reduction from the 12-year starting point which can be used as a rough check, is about one year for each year that the offender's age is below 18. So, for a child of ten, the judge should be considering a starting point in the region of five years.

49.26. Having arrived at the starting point the judge should then take account of the aggravating and mitigating factors in the particular case, which will take the prescribed minimum term above or below the starting point. The sliding scale proposed is intended to recognise the greater degree of understanding and capacity for normal reasoning which develops in adolescents over time as well as the fact that young offenders are likely to have the greatest capacity for change. It cannot take account of the individual offender's responsibility for, and understanding of the crime.

49.27. The welfare needs of the offender have also to be taken into account (see s 44(1) of the Children and Young Persons Act 1933). Lord Browne-Wilkinson in *R v Secretary of State for the Home Dept, ex p Venables, R v Secretary of State for the Home Dept, ex p Thompson* [1997] 3 All ER 97 at 122, [1998] AC 407 at

499 emphasised that the Home Secretary 'must at all times be free to take into account as one of the relevant factors the welfare of the child and the desirability of reintegrating the child into society'. He also pointed out that the extent this was possible—

> 'must depend, in the case of a young child at least, on the way in which that child was maturing through his formative year. If the child is making exceptional progress and it is clear that his welfare would be improved by release from detention, that is one of the factors the Secretary of State must take into account and balance against the other relevant factors of retribution, deterrence and risk. The child's welfare is not paramount but is *one* of the factors which must be taken into account.' (See [1997] 3 All ER 97 at 122, [1998] AC 407 at 499–500.)

49.28. The Home Secretary does not consider that this statement as to his responsibility is relevant now that the minimum term is set by the trial judge. The trial judge can only act on the information before him in taking into account the welfare of the child at the time that he announces the minimum term. It has been suggested that in these circumstances s 44(1) of the 1933 Act requires judges to fix the lowest possible minimum term so as to ensure the Parole Board will consider the case at the correct time if a child happens to make exceptional progress. It is recommended that this suggestion is not followed although it is appreciated that the Home Secretary's view means that apparently exceptional progress by a child while in detention will not influence the date his case is considered by the Parole Board.

50. *Bail pending appeal*

50.1. The procedure for granting bail by a judge of the Crown Court pending an appeal to the Court of Appeal, Criminal Division (see ss 1(2) and 11(1A) of the Criminal Appeal Act 1968, and s 81(1B) of the Supreme Court Act 1981) is described in the *Guide to Proceedings in the Court of Appeal, Criminal Division*. This is available at Crown Courts and is to be found at (1983) 77 Cr App R 138 and [1983] Crim LR 145.

50.2. The procedure is also set out in outline on Criminal Appeal Office Form C (Crown Court judge's certificate of fitness for appeal) and Form BC (Crown Court judge's order granting bail), copies of which are held by the Crown Court. The court clerk will ensure that these forms are always available when a judge hears an application under these provisions.

50.3. The judge may well think it right: (a) to hear the application for a certificate in chambers with a shorthand writer present; (b) to invite the defendant's advocate to submit before the hearing of the application a draft of the grounds of appeal which he will ask the judge to certify on Form C. The advocate for the Crown will be better able to assist the judge at the hearing if the draft ground is sent beforehand to him also.

50.4. The first question for the judge is then whether there exists a particular and cogent ground of appeal. If there is no such ground there can be no certificate, and if there is no certificate there can be no bail. A judge should not grant a certificate with regard to sentence merely in the light of mitigation to which he has, in his opinion, given due weight, nor in regard to conviction on a ground where he considers the chance of a successful appeal is not substantial. The judge should bear in mind that, where a certificate is refused, application may be made to the Court of Appeal for leave to appeal and for bail.

50.5. The length of the period which might elapse before the hearing of any appeal is not relevant to the grant of a certificate, but, if the judge does decide to grant a certificate, it may be one factor in the decision whether or not to grant bail. A judge who is minded to take this factor into account may find it advisable to have the court clerk contact the Criminal Appeal Office Listing Co-ordinator in order that he may have an accurate and up-to-date assessment of the likely waiting time. This can be very short. The co-ordinator will require a general account of the weight and urgency of the case.

50.6. Where the defendant's representative considers that bail should be applied for as a matter of urgency, the application should normally be made, in the first instance, to the trial judge, and the Court of Appeal may decline to treat such an application as urgent if there is no good reason why it has not been made to the trial judge.

PART V: FURTHER DIRECTIONS APPLYING IN THE MAGISTRATES' COURTS

51. Mode of trial

51.1. The purpose of these guidelines is to help magistrates decide whether or not to commit defendants charged with 'either way' offences for trial in the Crown Court. Their object is to provide guidance not direction. They are not intended to impinge on a magistrate's duty to consider each case individually and on its own particular facts. These guidelines apply to all defendants aged 18 and above.

General mode of trial considerations

51.2. Section 19 of the Magistrates' Courts Act 1980 requires magistrates to have regard to the following matters in deciding whether an offence is more suitable for summary trial or trial on indictment: (a) the nature of the case; (b) whether the circumstances make the offence one of a serious character; (c) whether the punishment which a magistrates' court would have power to inflict for it would be adequate; (d) any other circumstances which appear to the court to make it more suitable for the offence to be tried in one way rather than the other; (e) any representations made by the prosecution or the defence.

51.3. Certain general observations can be made: (a) the court should never make its decision on the grounds of convenience or expedition; (b) the court should assume for the purpose of deciding mode of trial that the prosecution version of the facts is correct; (c) the fact that the offences are alleged to be specimens is a relevant consideration (although, it has to be borne in mind that difficulties can arise in sentencing in relation to specimen counts, see *R v Clark* [1996] 2 Cr App R (S) 351 and *R v Kidd, R v Canavan, R v Shaw* [1998] 1 All ER 42, [1998] 1 Cr App R (S) 243); the fact that the defendant will be asking for other offences to be taken into consideration, if convicted, is not; (d) where cases involve complex questions of fact or difficult questions of law, including difficult issues of disclosure of sensitive material, the court should consider committal for trial; (e) where two or more defendants are jointly charged with an offence each has an individual right to elect his mode of trial; (f) in general, except where otherwise stated, either way offences should be tried summarily unless the court considers that the particular case has one or more of the features set out in paras 51.4–51.18 and that its sentencing powers are insufficient; (g) the court should also consider its power to commit an offender for sentence under ss 3 and 4 of the Powers of Criminal Courts (Sentencing) Act 2000, if information emerges during the course of the hearing which leads it to conclude that the offence is so serious, or the offender such a risk to the public, that its powers to sentence him are inadequate. This means that committal for sentence is no longer determined by reference to the character and antecedents of the offender.

Features relevant to individual offences

51.4. Where reference is made in these guidelines to property or damage of 'high value' it means a figure equal to at least twice the amount of the limit (currently £5,000) imposed by statute on a magistrates' court when making a compensation order.

Burglary: dwelling house

51.5. Cases should be tried summarily unless the court considers that one or more of the following features is present in the case *and* that its sentencing powers are insufficient. Magistrates should take account of their powers under ss 3 and 4 of the Powers of Criminal Courts (Sentencing) Act 2000 to commit for sentence, see para 51.3(g): (a) entry in the daytime when the occupier (or another) is present; (b) entry at night of a house which is normally occupied, whether or not the occupier (or another) is present; (c) the offence is alleged to be one of a series of similar offences; (d) when soiling, ransacking, damage or vandalism occurs; (e) the offence has professional hallmarks; (f) the unrecovered property is of high value: see para 51.4 for definition of high value; (g) the offence is racially motivated.

Note: attention is drawn to para 28(c) of Sch 1 to the Magistrates' Courts Act 1980 by which offences of burglary in a dwelling cannot be tried summarily if any person in the dwelling was subjected to violence or the threat of violence.

Burglary: non-dwelling

51.6. Cases should be tried summarily unless the court considers that one or more of the following features is present in the case *and* that its sentencing powers are insufficient. Magistrates should take account of their powers under ss 3 and 4 of the 2000 Act to commit for sentence, see para 51.3(g): (a) entry of a pharmacy or doctor's surgery; (b) fear is caused or violence is done to anyone lawfully on the premises (e g night-watchman, security guard); (c) the offence has professional hallmarks; (d) vandalism on a substantial scale; (e) the unrecovered property is of high value: see para 51.4 for definition of high value; (f) the offence is racially motivated.

Theft and fraud

51.7. Cases should be tried summarily unless the court considers that one or more of the following features is present in the case *and* that its sentencing powers are insufficient. Magistrates should take account of their powers under ss 3 and 4 of the 2000 Act to commit for sentence, see para 51.3(g): (a) breach of trust by a person in a position of substantial authority, or in whom a high degree of trust is placed; (b) theft or fraud which has been committed or disguised in a sophisticated manner; (c) theft or fraud committed by an organised gang; (d) the victim is particularly vulnerable to theft or fraud, e g the elderly or infirm; (e) the unrecovered property is of high value: see para 51.4 for definition of high value.

Handling

51.8. Cases should be tried summarily unless the court considers that one or more of the following features is present in the case *and* that its sentencing *a* powers are insufficient. Magistrates should take account of their powers under ss 3 and 4 of the 2000 Act to commit for sentence, see para 51.3(g): (a) dishonest handling of stolen property by a receiver who has commissioned the theft; (b) the offence has professional hallmarks; (c) the property is of high value: see para 51.4 for definition of high value.

b Social security frauds

51.9. Cases should be tried summarily unless the court considers that one or more of the following features is present in the case *and* that its sentencing powers are insufficient. Magistrates should take account of their powers under ss 3 and 4 of the 2000 Act to commit for sentence, see para 51.3(g): (a) organised fraud on a large scale; (b) the frauds are substantial and carried out over a long *c* period of time.

Violence (ss 20 and 47 of the Offences against the Person Act 1861)

51.10. Cases should be tried summarily unless the court considers that one or more of the following features is present in the case *and* that its sentencing *d* powers are insufficient. Magistrates should take account of their powers under ss 3 and 4 of the 2000 Act to commit for sentence, see para 51.3(g): (a) the use of a weapon of a kind likely to cause serious injury; (b) a weapon is used and serious injury is caused; (c) more than minor injury is caused by kicking or head-butting; (d) serious violence is caused to those whose work has to be done in contact with the public or are likely to face violence in the course of their work; (e) violence to *e* vulnerable people, e g the elderly and infirm; (f) the offence has clear racial motivation.

Note: the same considerations apply to cases of domestic violence.

Public Order Act offences

f 51.11. Cases should be tried summarily unless the court considers that one or more of the following features is present in the case *and* that its sentencing powers are insufficient. Magistrates should take account of their powers under ss 3 and 4 of the 2000 Act to commit for sentence, see para 51.3(g): (a) cases of *violent disorder* should generally be committed for trial; (b) *affray*; (i) organised violence or use of weapons; (ii) significant injury or substantial damage; (iii) the *g* offence has clear racial motivation; (iv) an attack on police officers, ambulance staff, fire-fighters and the like.

Violence to and neglect of children

51.12. Cases should be tried summarily unless the court considers that one or more of the following features is present in the case *and* that its sentencing *h* powers are insufficient. Magistrates should take account of their powers under ss 3 and 4 of the 2000 Act to commit for sentence, see para 51.3(g): (a) substantial injury; (b) repeated violence or serious neglect, even if the physical harm is slight; (c) sadistic violence, e g deliberate burning or scalding.

j Indecent assault

51.13. Cases should be tried summarily unless the court considers that one or more of the following features is present in the case *and* that its sentencing powers are insufficient. Magistrates should take account of their powers under ss 3 and 4 of the 2000 Act to commit for sentence, see para 51.3(g): (a) substantial disparity in age between victim and defendant, and a more serious assault; (b) violence or threats of violence; (c) relationship of trust or responsibility between defendant and victim; (d) several more serious similar offences; (e) the victim is particularly vulnerable; (f) serious nature of the assault.

Unlawful sexual intercourse

51.14. Cases should be tried summarily unless the court considers that one or more of the following features is present in the case *and* that its sentencing powers are insufficient. Magistrates should take account of their powers under ss 3 and 4 of the 2000 Act to commit for sentence, see para 51.3(g): (a) wide disparity of age; (b) breach of position of trust; (c) the victim is particularly vulnerable.

Note: unlawful sexual intercourse with a girl *under* 13 is triable only on indictment.

Drugs

51.15. Class A: (a) supply; possession with intent to supply: these cases should be committed for trial; (b) possession: should be committed for trial unless the amount is consistent only with personal use.

51.16. Class B: (a) supply; possession with intent to supply: should be committed for trial unless there is only small scale supply for no payment: (b) possession: should be committed for trial when the quantity is substantial and not consistent only with personal use.

Dangerous driving and aggravated vehicle taking

51.17. Cases should be tried summarily unless the court considers that one or more of the following features is present in the case *and* that its sentencing powers are insufficient. Magistrates should take account of their powers under ss 3 and 4 of the 2000 Act to commit for sentence, see para 51.3(g): (a) alcohol or drugs contributing to the dangerous driving; (b) grossly excessive speed; (c) racing; (d) prolonged course of dangerous driving; (e) other related offences; (f) significant injury or damage sustained.

Criminal damage

51.18. Cases should be tried summarily unless the court considers that one or more of the following features is present in the case *and* that its sentencing powers are insufficient. Magistrates should take account of their powers under ss 3 and 4 of the 2000 Act to commit for sentence, see para 51.3(g): (a) deliberate fire-raising; (b) committed by a group; (c) damage of a high value; (d) the offence has clear racial motivation.

Note: offences set out in Sch 2 to the Magistrates' Courts Act 1980 (which includes offences of criminal damage which do not amount to arson) *must* be tried summarily if the value of the property damaged or destroyed is £5,000 or less.

52. *Committal for sentence and appeals to Crown Court*

52.1. Any case notes should be sent to the Crown Court when there is an appeal, thereby making them available to the judge if the judge requires them in order to decide before the hearing questions of listing or representation or the like. They will also be available to the court during the hearing if it becomes necessary or desirable for the court to see what happened in the lower court. On a committal for sentence or an appeal, any reasons given by the magistrates for their decision should be included with the notes.

53. Bail before committal for trial

53.1. Rules 19 and 20 of the Crown Court Rules 1982, SI 1982/1109, apply to these applications.

53.2. Before the Crown Court can deal with an application it must be satisfied that the magistrates' court has issued a certificate under s 5(6A) of the Bail Act 1976 that it heard full argument on the application for bail before it refused the application. A copy of the certificate will be issued to the applicant and not sent directly to the Crown Court. It will therefore be necessary for the applicant's solicitors to attach a copy of the certificate to the bail application form. If the certificate is not enclosed with the application form it will be difficult to avoid some delay in listing.

Venue

53.3. Applications should be made to the court to which the defendant will be or would have been committed for trial. In the event of an application in a purely summary case, it should be made to the Crown Court centre which normally receives class 4 work. The hearing will be listed as a chambers matter unless a judge has directed otherwise.

54. Contempt in the face of the magistrates' court

General

54.1. Section 12 of the Contempt of Court Act 1981 gives magistrates' courts the power to detain until the court rises, someone, whether a defendant or another person present in court, who wilfully insults anyone specified in s 12 or who interrupts proceedings. In any such case, the court may order any officer of the court, or any constable, to take the offender into custody and detain him until the rising of the court; and the court may, if it thinks fit, commit the offender to custody for a specified period not exceeding one month or impose a fine not exceeding level 4 on the standard scale or both. This power can be used to stop disruption of their proceedings. Detention is until the person can be conveniently dealt with without disruption of the proceedings. Prior to the court using the power the offender should be warned to desist or face the prospect of being detained.

54.2. Magistrates' courts also have the power to commit to custody any person attending or brought before a magistrates' court who refuses without just cause to be sworn or to give evidence under s 97(4) of the Magistrates' Courts Act 1980, until the expiration of such period not exceeding one month as may be specified in the warrant or until he sooner gives evidence or produces the document or thing, or impose on him a fine not exceeding £2,500, or both.

54.3. In the exercise of any of these powers, as soon as is practical, and in any event prior to an offender being proceeded against, an offender should be told of the conduct which it is alleged to constitute his offending in clear terms. When making an order under s 12 the justices should state their findings of fact as to the contempt.

54.4. Exceptional situations require exceptional treatment. While this direction deals with the generality of situations, there will be a minority of situations where the application of the direction will not be consistent with achieving justice in the special circumstances of the particular case. Where this is the situation, the compliance with the direction should be modified so far as is necessary so as to accord with the interests of justice.

54.5. The power to bind persons over to be of good behaviour in respect of *a*
their conduct in court should cease to be exercised.

Contempt consisting of wilfully insulting anyone specified in s 12 or interrupting proceedings

54.6. In the case of someone who wilfully insults anyone specified in s 12 of
the 1981 Act or interrupts proceedings, if an offender expresses a willingness to *b*
apologise for his misconduct, he should be brought back before the court at the
earliest convenient moment in order to make the apology and to give
undertakings to the court to refrain from further misbehaviour.

54.7. In the majority of cases, an apology and a promise as to future conduct
should be sufficient for justices to order an offender's release. However, there are *c*
likely to be certain cases where the nature and seriousness of the misconduct
requires the justices to consider using their powers under s 12(2) of the 1981 Act
either to fine or to order the offender's committal to custody.

Where an offender is detained for contempt of court   *d*

54.8. Anyone detained under either of these provisions in paras 54.1 or 54.2
should be seen by the duty solicitor or another legal representative and be
represented in proceedings if they so wish. Public funding should generally be
granted to cover representation. The offender must be afforded adequate time
and facilities in order to prepare his case. The matter should be resolved the same *e*
day if at all possible.

54.9. The offender should be brought back before the court before the justices
conclude their daily business. The justices should ensure that he understands the
nature of the proceedings, including his opportunity to apologise or give
evidence and the alternative of them exercising their powers.   *f*

54.10. Having heard from the offender's solicitor, the justices should decide
whether to take further action.

Sentencing of an offender who admits being in contempt

54.11. If an offence of contempt is admitted the justices should consider *g*
whether they are able to proceed on the day or whether to adjourn to allow
further reflection. The matter should be dealt with on the same day if at all
possible. If the justices are of the view to adjourn they should generally grant the
offender bail unless one or more of the exceptions to the right to bail in the Bail
Act 1976 are made out.   *h*

54.12. When they come to sentence the offender where the offence has been
admitted, the justices should first ask the offender if he has any objection to them
dealing with the matter. If there is any objection to the justices dealing with the
matter a differently-constituted panel should hear the proceedings. If the
offender's conduct was directed to the justices, it will not be appropriate for the *j*
same bench to deal with the matter.

54.13. The justices should consider whether an order for the offender's
discharge is appropriate, taking into account any time spent on remand, whether
the offence was admitted and the seriousness of the contempt. Any period of
committal should be for the shortest time commensurate with the interests of
preserving good order in the administration of justice.

a Trial of the issue where the contempt is not admitted

54.14. Where the contempt is not admitted the justices' powers are limited to making arrangements for a trial to take place. They should not at this stage make findings against the offender.

54.15. In the case of a contested contempt the trial should take place at the earliest opportunity and should be before a bench of justices other than those *b* before whom the alleged contempt took place. If a trial of the issue can take place on the day such arrangements should be made taking into account the offender's rights under art 6 of the European Convention for the Protection of Human Rights and Fundamental Freedoms 1950 (as set out in Sch 1 to the Human Rights Act 1998). If the trial cannot take place that day the justices should again bail the *c* offender unless there are grounds under the 1976 Act to remand him in custody.

54.16. The offender is entitled to call and examine witnesses where evidence is relevant. If the offender is found by the court to have committed contempt the court should again consider first whether an order for his discharge from custody is sufficient to bring proceedings to an end. The justices should also allow the *d* offender a further opportunity to apologise for his contempt or to make representations. If the justices are of the view that they must exercise their powers to commit to custody under s 12(2) of the 1981 Act, they must take into account any time spent on remand and the nature and seriousness of the contempt. Any period of committal should be for the shortest period of time commensurate with the interests of preserving good order in the administration *e* of justice.

55. Clerk retiring with justices

55.1. A justices' clerk is responsible for: (a) the legal advice tendered to the justices within the area; (b) the performance of any of the functions set out below *f* by any member of his staff acting as legal adviser; (c) ensuring that competent advice is available to justices when the justices' clerk is not personally present in court; and (d) the effective delivery of case management and the reduction of unnecessary delay.

55.2. Where a person other than the justices' clerk (a legal adviser), who is authorised to do so, performs any of the functions referred to in this direction he *g* will have the same responsibilities as the justices' clerk. The legal adviser may consult the justices' clerk or other person authorised by the justices' clerk for that purpose before tendering advice to the bench. If the justices' clerk or that person gives any advice directly to the bench, he should give the parties or their advocates an opportunity of repeating any relevant submissions prior to the *h* advice being given.

55.3. It shall be the responsibility of the legal adviser to provide the justices with any advice they require properly to perform their functions, whether or not the justices have requested that advice, on: (a) questions of law (including European Court of Human Rights jurisprudence and those matters set out in *j* s 2(1) of the Human Rights Act 1998); (b) questions of mixed law and fact; (c) matters of practice and procedure; (d) the range of penalties available; (e) any relevant decisions of the superior courts or other guidelines; (f) other issues relevant to the matter before the court; and (g) the appropriate decision-making structure to be applied in any given case. In addition to advising the justices it shall be the legal adviser's responsibility to assist the court, where appropriate, as to the formulation of reasons and the recording of those reasons.

55.4. A justices' clerk or legal adviser must not play any part in making findings of fact, but may assist the bench by reminding them of the evidence, using any notes of the proceedings for this purpose.

55.5. A justices' clerk or legal adviser may ask questions of witnesses and the parties in order to clarify the evidence and any issues in the case. A legal adviser has a duty to ensure that every case is conducted fairly.

55.6. When advising the justices, the justices' clerk or legal adviser, whether or not previously in court, should: (a) ensure that he is aware of the relevant facts; and (b) provide the parties with the information necessary to enable the parties to make any representations they wish as to the advice before it is given.

55.7. At any time justices are entitled to receive advice to assist them in discharging their responsibilities. If they are in any doubt as to the evidence which has been given, they should seek the aid of their legal adviser, referring to his notes as appropriate. This should ordinarily be done in open court. Where the justices request their adviser to join them in the retiring room, this request should be made in the presence of the parties in court. Any legal advice given to the justices other than in open court should be clearly stated to be provisional and the adviser should subsequently repeat the substance of the advice in open court and give the parties an opportunity to make any representations they wish on that provisional advice. The legal adviser should then state in open court whether the provisional advice is confirmed or if it is varied the nature of the variation.

55.8. The performance of a legal adviser may be appraised by a person authorised by the magistrates' courts committee to do so. For that purpose the appraiser may be present in the justices' retiring room. The content of the appraisal is confidential, but the fact that an appraisal has taken place, and the presence of the appraiser in the retiring room, should be briefly explained in open court.

55.9. The legal adviser is under a duty to assist unrepresented parties to present their case, but must do so without appearing to become an advocate for the party concerned.

55.10. The role of legal advisers in fine default proceedings or any other proceedings for the enforcement of financial orders, obligations or penalties is to assist the court. They must not act in an adversarial or partisan manner. With the agreement of the justices a legal adviser may ask questions of the defaulter to elicit information which the justices will require to make an adjudication, for example to facilitate his explanation for the default. A legal adviser may also advise the justices in the normal way as to the options open to them in dealing with the case. It would be inappropriate for the legal adviser to set out to establish wilful refusal or neglect or any other type of culpable behaviour, to offer an opinion on the facts, or to urge a particular course of action upon the justices. The duty of impartiality is the paramount consideration for the legal adviser at all times, and this takes precedence over any role he may have as a collecting officer. The appointment of other staff to 'prosecute' the case for the collecting officer is not essential to ensure compliance with the law, including the Human Rights Act 1998. Whether to make such appointments is a matter for the justices' chief executive.

56. Failure to surrender

Bail granted by a magistrates' court

56.1. Where a person has been granted bail by a court and subsequently fails to surrender to custody as contemplated by s 6(1) or (2) of the Bail Act 1976, on *a*   arrest that person should be brought before the court at which the proceedings in respect of which bail was granted are to be heard. It is neither necessary nor desirable to lay an information in order to commence proceedings for the failure to surrender. Having regard to the nature of the offence, which is tantamount to the defiance of a court order, it is more appropriate that the court itself should initiate the proceedings by its own motion, following an express invitation by the

b   prosecutor. The court will only be invited so to move if, having considered all the circumstances, the prosecutor considers proceedings are appropriate. Where a court complies with such an invitation, the prosecutor will naturally conduct the proceedings and, where the matter is contested, call the evidence. Any trial should normally take place immediately following the disposal of the proceedings in respect of which bail was granted.

c

Bail granted by a police officer

56.2. Where a person has been bailed from a police station subject to a duty to appear before a magistrates' court or to attend a police station on an appointed date and/or time, a failure so to appear or attend cannot be said to be tantamount

d   to the defiance of a court order. There does not exist the same compelling justification for the court to act by its own motion. Where bail has been granted by a police officer, any proceedings for a failure to surrender to custody, whether at a court or a police station, should accordingly be initiated by charging the accused or by the laying of an information.

e

Kate O'Hanlon   Barrister.

ANNEX A

Practice Note (criminal law: time to elapse before majority verdict of jury accepted)
[1970] 2 All ER 215, [1970] 1 WLR 916, (1970) 54 Cr App R 373, CA; 11/5/70.

R v Upton, R v Hendry [1973] 3 All ER 318n, (1973) 57 Cr App R 838; 28/6/73.

Practice Direction (deferred sentences) (1974) 59 Cr App R 130, CA; 22/3/74.

Practice Note (criminal law: bail) [1974] 2 All ER 794, [1974] 1 WLR 770, (1974) 59 Cr App R 159, CA; 4/6/74.

Practice Note (criminal law: rehabilitation of offenders) [1975] 2 All ER 1072, [1975] 1 WLR 1065, (1975) 61 Cr App R 260, DC; 30/6/75.

Practice Note (indictment: joinder of accused) [1976] 2 All ER 326, [1976] 1 WLR 409, (1976) 62 Cr App R 251, CA; 9/3/76.

Practice Direction (crime: inconsistent decisions) [1976] 1 WLR 799, [1976] Crim LR 561, CA; 26/7/76.

Practice Note (indictment: joinder of charges) [1977] 2 All ER 540, [1977] 1 WLR 537, (1977) 64 Cr App R 258; 9/5/77.

Practice Note (criminal law: unmeritorious appeals) [1980] 1 All ER 555, [1980] 1 WLR 270, CA; 14/2/80.

Practice Direction (tape recorder) [1981] 3 All ER 848, [1981] 1 WLR 1526, (1982) 74 Cr App R 73, CA; 19/11/81.

Practice Note (criminal evidence: unused material) [1982] 1 All ER 734, (1982) 74 Cr App R 302; 12/81.

Practice Direction (judge: modes of address) [1982] 1 All ER 320, [1982] 1 WLR 101, (1982) 74 Cr App R 193, CA; 12/1/82.

Practice Note (contempt of court: reports of proceedings) [1983] 1 All ER 64, [1982] 1 WLR 1475, (1983) 76 Cr App R 78, DC; 6/12/82.

Practice Direction (Crown Court: bail) [1983] 2 All ER 261, (1983) 77 Cr App R 69, 26/4/83.

Practice Note (Crown Court: bail pending appeal) [1983] 3 All ER 608, [1983] 1 WLR 1292, (1983) 78 Cr App R 40, CA; 10/11/83.

Practice Note (crime: jury oath) [1984] 3 All ER 528, [1984] 1 WLR 1217, (1984) 80 Cr App R 13, CA; 12/10/84.

Practice Note (criminal law: written statements) [1986] 2 All ER 511, [1986] 1 WLR 805, (1986) 83 Cr App R 212, DC; 3/6/86.

Practice Note (bail: failure to surrender) [1987] 1 All ER 128, [1987] 1 WLR 79, (1987) 84 Cr App R 137, DC; 19/12/86.

Practice Direction (ward of court: witness in criminal proceedings) [1988] 1 All ER 223, [1987] 1 WLR 1739; 11/11/87.

Practice Note (criminal law: appeal) [1988] 1 All ER 244, [1988] 1 WLR 34, (1987) 86 Cr App R 195, CA; 18/12/87.

Practice Direction (ward of court: witness in criminal proceedings) [1988] 2 All ER 1015, [1988] 1 WLR 989; 18/7/88.

Practice Note (jury: excuse) [1988] 3 All ER 177, [1988] 1 WLR 1162, (1988) 87 Cr App R 294, DC; 19/9/88.

Practice Note (criminal law: tape recording of police interview) [1989] 2 All ER 415, [1989] 1 WLR 631, (1989) 89 Cr App R 132; 26/5/89.

Practice Note (offences triable either way: mode of trial) [1990] 3 All ER 979, [1990] 1 WLR 1439, (1990) 92 Cr App R 142, DC; 26/10/90.

Practice Note (Crown Courts: television link) [1992] 3 All ER 922, [1992] 1 WLR 838, (1992) 95 Cr App R 354, CA; 31/7/92.

Practice Note (criminal evidence: video recording of child's testimony) [1992] 3 All ER 909, [1992] 1 WLR 839, (1992) 95 Cr App R 354, CA; 31/7/92.

a   *Practice Note (Criminal Appeal Office summaries)* [1992] 4 All ER 408, [1992] 1 WLR 938, (1992) 95 Cr App R 455, CA; 1/10/92.

Practice Note (sentence: early release of prisoners) [1992] 4 All ER 307, [1992] 1 WLR 948, (1992) 95 Cr App R 456, CA; 1/10/92.

Practice Note (discretionary life sentences) [1993] 1 All ER 747, [1993] 1 WLR 223, (1993) 96 Cr App R 397, CA; 8/2/93.

b   *Practice Direction (court dress)* [1994] 1 WLR 1056, [1995] 1 Cr App R 13; 19/7/94.

Practice Note (procedure: reference to Hansard) [1995] 1 All ER 234, [1995] 1 WLR 192; 20/12/94.

Practice Note (legal aid: representation by counsel) [1995] 1 All ER 307, [1995] 1 WLR 261, [1995] 1 Cr App R 576; 12/1/95.

c   *Practice Note (Crown Court: defendants' evidence)* [1995] 2 All ER 499, [1995] 1 WLR 657, [1995] 2 Cr App R 192, CA; 10/4/95.

Practice Direction (court dress) (No 2) [1995] 1 WLR 648, [1995] 2 Cr App R 191; 11/4/95.

Practice Direction (Crown Court: plea and directions hearings) [1995] 4 All ER 379, [1995] 1 WLR 1318, [1995] 2 Cr App R 600; 25/7/95.

d   *Practice Note (crime: antecedents)* [1997] 4 All ER 350, [1997] 1 WLR 1482, [1998] 1 Cr App R 213, CA; 9/10/97.

Practice Note (custodial sentences: explanation) [1998] 1 All ER 733, [1998] 1 WLR 278, [1998] 1 Cr App R 397, CA; 22/1/98.

e   *Practice Statement (Royal Courts of Justice: judgments)* [1998] 2 All ER 667, [1998] 1 WLR 825, [1998] 2 Cr App R 144; 22/4/98.

Practice Direction (Crown Court: Welsh language) [1999] 1 All ER 575, [1998] 1 WLR 1677, [1999] 2 Cr App R 32; 16/10/98.

Practice Note (Crown Court: serious and complex fraud cases) [1998] 4 All ER 1023, [1998] 1 WLR 1692, [1999] 1 Cr App R 142, CA; 28/10/98.

f   *Practice Direction (court dress) (No 3)* [1998] 1 WLR 1764, [1999] 1 Cr App R 336; 25/11/98.

Practice Note (Royal Courts of Justice: judgments) [1999] 1 All ER 125, [1999] 1 WLR 1, [1999] 1 Cr App R 333; 25/11/98.

Practice Note (Court of Appeal, Criminal Division: skeleton arguments) [1999] 1 All ER 669, [1999] 1 WLR 146, CA; 15/12/98.

g   *Practice Direction (ECJ references: procedure)* [1999] 1 WLR 260, [1999] 1 Cr App R 452; 14/1/99.

Practice Direction (recorder of Cardiff: mode of address) [1999] 2 All ER 352, [1999] 1 WLR 597, [1999] 2 Cr App R 187; 18/2/99.

h   *Practice Direction (Court of Appeal: procedure)* [1999] 2 All ER 490, [1999] 1 WLR 1027, CA; paras 9, 10.1, 10.2; 19/4/99.

Practice Note (devolution issues: Wales) [1999] 3 All ER 466, [1999] 1 WLR 1592, [1999] 2 Cr App R 486; 30/6/99.

Practice Direction (crime: voluntary bills) [1999] 4 All ER 62, [1999] 1 WLR 1613, [1999] 2 Cr App R 442; 29/7/99.

j   *Practice Note (trial of children and young persons: procedure)* [2000] 2 All ER 285, [2000] 1 WLR 659, [2000] 1 Cr App R 483, DC; 16/2/00.

Practice Direction (criminal appeals: summaries) (No 2) [2000] 1 WLR 1177, [2000] Cr App R 178, CA; 15/05/00.

Practice Note (Crown Court: abuse of process) [2000] 3 All ER 384, [2000] 1 WLR 1322, [2000] 2 Cr App R 179, CA; 23/5/00.

Practice Note (juveniles: murder tariff) [2000] 4 All ER 831, [2000] 1 WLR 1655, *a*
[2000] 2 Cr App R 457, CA; 27/7/00.

Practice Note (magistrates: clerk and authorised legal advisor) [2000] 4 All ER 895,
[2000] 1 WLR 1886; 2/10/00.

Practice Note (judgments: neutral citation) [2001] 1 All ER 193, [2001] 1 WLR 194,
[2001] 1 Cr App R 426; 11 /01 /01.

Practice Note (magistrates' court: contempt in face of court) [2001] 3 All ER 94, [2001] *b*
1 WLR 1254, [2001] 2 Cr App R 272; 23/5/01.

Practice Note (Crown Court: allocation of court business) [2001] 4 All ER 635, [2001]
1 WLR 1996, CA; 16/10/01.

Practice Direction (criminal proceedings: victim personal statements) [2001] 4 All ER
640, [2001] 1 WLR 2038, CA; 16/10/01.   *c*

Practice Direction (High Court judgments: neutral citation) [2002] 1 All ER 351,
[2002] 1 WLR 346; 14/01/02.

Practice Statement (crime: life sentences) [2002] 3 All ER 412, [2002] 1 WLR 1789;
31/05/02.

ANNEX B   *d*

L*IST OF* P*RACTICE* D*IRECTIONS,* P*RACTICE* N*OTES AND* P*RACTICE* S*TATEMENTS NOT*
I*NCLUDED IN THIS CONSOLIDATION, BUT NO LONGER APPLICABLE IN CRIMINAL*
P*ROCEEDINGS (IN CHRONOLOGICAL ORDER)*

Practice Note (onus of proof charge of receiving stolen goods) [1946] WN 101; 1/6/46. *e*

Practice Statement (probation orders) (1952) 35 Cr App R 207; 25/2/52.

Practice Note (applications for leave to appeal) (1952) 36 Cr App R 145; 6/10/52.

Practice Note (non-capital murder: no appeal against sentence) [1957] 2 All ER 378,
CA; 13/5/57.

Practice Note (criminal law: conditional binding over: entry on depositions) [1961] *f*
1 All ER 875, [1961] 1 WLR 502, CA; 6/3/61.

Practice Note (appeal: form of order) [1961] 3 All ER 522, [1961] 1 WLR 1321, CA;
5/10/61.

Practice Note (justices: submission of no case to answer) [1962] 1 All ER 448, [1962]
1 WLR 227, DC; 9/2/62.   *g*

Practice Note (criminal law: sentence) [1962] 1 All ER 671, [1962] 1 WLR 402, CA;
26/2/62.

Practice Direction (criminal law: indictment: joinder of counts) [1964] 3 All ER 509,
[1964] 1 WLR 1244, CA; 12/10/64.

Practice Note (criminal law: sentence: corrective training) [1966] 2 All ER 905, [1966] *h*
1 WLR 1218, CA; 21/6/66.

Practice Note (criminal law: practice: trial on indictment) [1969] 1 All ER 1042,
[1969] 1 WLR 603, CA; 20/3/69.

Practice Direction (Crown Court: solicitor: right of audience) [1972] 1 All ER 608,
[1972] 1 WLR 307; 9/2/72.   *j*

Practice Note (prison: release on licence) [1976] 1 All ER 271, [1976] 1 WLR 122,
(1975) 62 Cr App R 130, CA; 19/12/75.

Practice Direction (solicitor: right of audience) [1986] 2 All ER 226, [1986] 1 WLR
545, (1986) 83 Cr App R 6; 9/5/86.

Practice Direction (Crown Court: solicitor: right of audience) [1988] 3 All ER 717,
[1988] 1 WLR 1427, (1988) 88 Cr App R 179; 26/8/88.

a   *Practice Direction (western circuit: allocation of business to Crown Court centres)*; 1/00.
Practice Direction (Wales and Chester Circuit: appeals from the magistrates' courts against conviction); 5/01.

ANNEX C

b   EXPLANATIONS FOR THE IMPOSITION OF CUSTODIAL SENTENCES: FORMS OF WORDS

The following forms may need to be adapted in the light of such provisions or practices as are in force affecting possible earlier release.

Forms of words are provided for use where the offender (a) will be a short-term prisoner not subject to licence; (b) will be a short-term prisoner subject to licence; (c) will be a long-term prisoner; (d) will be subject to a discretionary sentence of life imprisonment.

Sentencers will bear in mind that where an offender is sentenced to terms which are consecutive, or wholly or partly concurrent, they are to be treated as a single term: s 51(2) of the Criminal Justice Act 1991.

d   (a) Total term less than 12 months:

'The sentence is (...) months.'

'You will serve half that sentence in prison/a young offender institution. After that time you will be released.'

e   'Your release will not bring this sentence to an end. If after your release and before the end of the period covered by the sentence you commit any further offence, you may be ordered to return to custody to serve the balance of the original sentence outstanding at the date of the further offence, as well as being punished for that new offence.'

f   'Any time you have spent on remand in custody in connection with the offence(s) for which you are now being sentenced will count as part of the sentence to be served, unless it has already been counted.'

(b) Total term of 12 months and less than four years:

'The sentence is (...) (months/years).'

g   'You will serve half that sentence in a prison/a young offender institution. After that time you will be released.'

'Your release will not bring this sentence to an end. If after your release and before the end of the period covered by the sentence you commit any

h   further offence you may be ordered to return to custody to serve the balance of the original sentence outstanding at the date of the further offence, as well as being punished for that new offence.'

'Any time you have spent on remand in custody in connection with the offence(s) for which you are now being sentenced will count as part of the

j   sentence to be served, unless it has already been counted.'

'After your release you will also be subject to supervision on licence until the end of three-quarters of the total sentence. (If an order has been made under s 85 of the Powers of Criminal Courts (Sentencing) Act 2000: After your release you will also be subject to supervision on licence for the remainder of the licence period.) If you fail to comply with any of the requirements of your licence then again you may be brought before a court which will have power to suspend your licence and order your return to custody.'

(c) Total term of four years or more:

'The sentence is (…) (years/months).'

'Your case will not be considered by the Parole Board until you have served at least half that period in custody. Unless the Parole Board recommends earlier release, you will not be released until you have served two-thirds of that sentence.'

'Your release will not bring the sentence to an end. If after your release and before the end of the period covered by the sentence you commit any further offence you may be ordered to return to custody to serve the balance of the original sentence outstanding at the date of the new offence, as well as being punished for that new offence.'

'Any time you have spent in custody on remand in connection with the offence(s) for which you are now being sentenced will count as part of the sentence to be served, unless it has already been counted.'

'After your release you will also be subject to supervision on licence until the end of three-quarters of the total sentence. (If an order has been made under s 85 of the Powers of Criminal Courts (Sentencing) Act 2000: After your release you will also be subject to supervision on licence for the remainder of the licence period.) You will be liable to be recalled to prison if your licence is revoked, either on the recommendation of the Parole Board, or, if it is thought expedient in the public interest, by the Secretary of State.'

(d) Discretionary life sentence:

'The sentence of the court is life imprisonment/custody for life/detention for life under s 91 of the Powers of Criminal Courts (Sentencing) Act 2000. For the purposes of s 82A of that Act the court specifies a period of (x) years. That means that your case will not be considered by the Parole Board until you have served at least (x) years in custody. After that time the Parole Board will be entitled to consider your release. When it is satisfied that you need no longer be confined in custody for the protection of the public it will be able to direct your release. Until it is so satisfied you will remain in custody.'

'If you are released, it will be on terms that you are subject to a licence for the rest of your life and liable to be recalled to prison at any time if your licence is revoked, either on the recommendation of the Parole Board, or, if it is thought expedient in the public interest, by the Secretary of State.'

ANNEX D

a

Plea and Directions Hearing

The Crown Court at

Judge's Questionnaire

In accordance with the practice rules issued

b *by the Lord Chief Justice.*

A copy of this questionnaire, completed as far as possible with the agreement of both advocates, is to be handed in to the court prior to the commencement of the Plea and Directions Hearing.

c

The Crown Court at	
Case No. **T**	
PTI URN	
R v	
Date of PDH	
Name of Prosecution Advocate at PDH	
Name of Defence Advocate at PDH	

---

1 a Are the actual/proposed not guilty pleas definitely to be maintained through to a jury trial?   Yes ☐   No ☐

d

b Has the defence advocate advised his client of section 152 Powers of Criminal Courts (Sentencing) Act 2000? (*Reductions in sentence for guilty pleas*)   Yes ☐   No ☐

e

c Will the prosecution accept part guilty or alternative pleas?   Yes ☐   No ☐

2 How long is the trial likely to take?

f

3 a Are there Human Rights issues to be relied upon?   Yes ☐   No ☐

If **Yes**, what are the Human Rights

g issues?

b What are the other issues in the case?

h

4 Issues as to the mental or medical condition of any defendant or witness.

j 5 Prosecution witnesses whose evidence will be given.   To be read (number) ☐

To be called (number) ☐

Can any statement be read instead of calling the witnesses?   Names:

6 a Number of Defence witnesses whose evidence will be placed before the Court.	Defendant + [ ] *a*
b Any whose statements have been served which can be agreed and accepted in writing.	
7 Is the prosecution intending to serve any further evidence?	Yes ☐ No ☐ *b*
If **Yes**, what area(s) will it cover?	
What are the witnesses' names?	*c*
8 Facts which are admitted and can be reduced into writing. (*s10(2)(b) CJA 1967*)	*d*
9 Exhibits and schedules which are to be admitted.	*e*
10 Is the order and pagination of the prosecution papers agreed?	*f*
11 Any alibi which should have been disclosed in accordance with CJA 1967?	Yes ☐ No ☐
12 a Any points of law likely to arise at trial?	*g*
b Any questions of admissibility of evidence together with any authorities it is intended to rely upon.	
13 a Has the defence notified the prosecution of any issue arising out of the record of interview? (*Practice Direction Crime: Tape Recording of police interview 26 May 1989*)	Yes ☐ No ☐ *h*
b What efforts have been made to agree verbatim records or summaries and have they been successful?	*j*

a

14 Any applications granted/pending for:

    (i) evidence to be given through live television links?   Yes ☐ No ☐

    (ii) evidence to be given by pre-recorded video interviews with children?   Yes ☐ No ☐

b

    (iii) screens?   Yes ☐ No ☐

    (iv) the use of video equipment during the trial?   Yes ☐ No ☐

    (v) use of tape playback equipment?   Yes ☐ No ☐

c

15 Any other significant matter which might affect the proper and convenient trial of the case?
(*e.g. expert witnesses or other cases outstanding against the defendant*)

d

16 Any other work which needs to be done.   Prosecution

    Orders of the Court with time limits should be noted on page 4.

    Defence

e

17 a Witness avaiability and approximate length of witness evidence.   Prosecution

f

    Defence

    b Can any witness attendance be staggered?   Yes ☐ No ☐

g

    If **Yes**, have any arrangements been agreed?   Yes ☐ No ☐

h

18 Advocates' availability?   Prosecution

j

    Defence

Case listing arrangements

Name of Trial Judge:

Custody Cases *Fix or warned list within 16 weeks of committal*

Fixed for trial on _____

Place in warned list for trial   for week beginning _____

Further directions fixed for   _____

Not fixed or put in warned list within
16 weeks because: _____

Date of expiry of custody time limit   _____

Application to extend custody time limit?   Yes ☐   Extended to

No ☐

Bail Cases

Further directions fixed for   _____

Fixed for trial on   _____

Fixed as a floater / backer on   _____

Place in a reserve / warned list for trial   for week beginning _____

List officer to allocate   ☐ within ⬚ days / weeks
☐ before

Sentence

Adjourned for sentence on   _____

(to follow trial of R v

Other directions, orders, comments

Signed: *Judge*   Date:

Re Toshoku Finance UK plc (in liquidation)
Kahn and another v Inland Revenue Commissioners
[2002] UKHL 6

HOUSE OF LORDS

LORD HOFFMANN, LORD WOOLF CJ, LORD HUTTON, LORD HOBHOUSE OF WOODBOROUGH
AND LORD RODGER OF EARLSFERRY

10, 11 DECEMBER 2001, 20 FEBRUARY 2002

Company – Winding up – Expenses of liquidation – Statutory provision establishing priority of payment of 'expenses' of liquidation – Whether liability falling within provision payable as expense of liquidation only if satisfying test of fairness – Insolvency Rules 1986, r 4.218(1).

The appellants were the liquidators of a company whose only substantial asset was a debt owed to it by another company in the same group. After going into liquidation, the company agreed to accept a payment in full and final settlement of its claim. Although nothing was paid in respect of interest that had accrued after the liquidation date, the company was liable to pay corporation tax as if it had received such interest. The liquidators applied to the court for directions as to whether such a liability constituted an expense properly incurred in the winding up and which they were therefore required to pay out of the company's assets in priority to other claims. Under r 4.218(1)[a] of the Insolvency Rules 1986, the 'expenses' of the liquidation were payable out of the assets in the order of priority specified in that rule. The Revenue contended that the company's corporation tax liability fell within r 4.218(1)(m), namely any necessary disbursements by the liquidator in the course of his administration. The judge rejected that contention, but his decision was reversed by the Court of Appeal. On their appeal to the House of Lords, the liquidators contended that the terms of r 4.218(1) did not in themselves determine whether a liability counted as an expense of the liquidation; that a liability falling within that rule was payable as an expense only if it satisfied a test of fairness; and that it was not fair that creditors should have to bear the burden of corporation tax on fictitious credits.

Held – Rule 4.218(1) of the 1986 rules was intended to be a definitive statement of liquidation expenses (subject only to the qualification contained in the rules themselves). The heads of expense listed in r 4.218(1) were not subject to any implied qualification. Nor was it a matter for the discretion of the court whether debts should count as expenses of the liquidation. That depended upon whether a debt came within one of the paragraphs of r 4.218(1). In the instant case, it was expressly enacted that a company was chargeable to corporation tax on profits or gains arising in the winding up. It followed that the tax was a post-liquidation liability which the liquidators were bound to discharge and was therefore a 'necessary disbursement' within the meaning of r 4.218(1)(m) of the 1986 rules.

---

a   Rule 4.218, so far as material, is set out at [6], below

Accordingly, the appeal would be dismissed (see [13], [15], [17], [38], [41], [42], [47]–[51], below).

Re Mesco Properties Ltd [1980] 1 All ER 117 approved.

Re Kentish Homes Ltd [1993] BCLC 1375 overruled.

Decision of the Court of Appeal [2000] 3 All ER 938 affirmed.

Notes

For expenses of the liquidation, see 7(3) *Halsbury's Laws* (4th edn reissue) para 2569.

For the Insolvency Rules 1986, r 4.218, see 3 *Halsbury's Statutory Instruments* (2001 issue) 516.

Cases referred to in opinions

ABC Coupler and Engineering Co Ltd (No 3), Re [1970] 1 All ER 650, [1970] 1 WLR 702.

Atlantic Computer Systems plc, Re [1992] 1 All ER 476, [1992] Ch 505, [1992] 2 WLR 367, CA.

Bacon (MC) Ltd, Re [1991] Ch 127, [1990] 3 WLR 646.

Blazer Fire Lighter Ltd, Re [1895] 1 Ch 402, [1891–4] All ER Rep 1174.

Downer Enterprises Ltd, Re [1974] 2 All ER 1074, [1974] 1 WLR 1460.

Exhall Coal Mining Co Ltd, Re (1864) 4 De GJ & Sm 377, 46 ER 964.

Floor Fourteen Ltd, Re, Lewis v IRC [2001] 3 All ER 499, CA.

Hardy v Fothergill (1888) 13 App Cas 351, [1886–90] All ER Rep 597, HL.

Kentish Homes Ltd, Re [1993] BCLC 1375.

London Metallurgical Co, Re [1895] 1 Ch 758.

Lundy Granite Co, Re, ex p Heavan (1871) 6 Ch App 462.

Mesco Properties Ltd, Re [1979] 1 All ER 302, [1979] 1 WLR 558; *affd* [1980] 1 All ER 117, [1980] 1 WLR 96, CA.

Mineral Resources Ltd, Re, Environment Agency v Stout [1999] 1 All ER 746.

National Arms and Ammunition Co, Re (1885) 28 Ch D 474, CA.

Oak Pitts Colliery Co, Re (1882) 21 Ch D 322, [1881–5] All ER Rep 1157, CA.

Progress Assurance Co, Re, ex p Liverpool Exchange Co (1870) LR 9 Eq 370.

Realisations (HH) Ltd, Re (1975) 31 P&CR 249.

Watson, Kipling & Co, Re (1883) 23 Ch D 500.

Appeal

Neville Barry Kahn and Nigel John Vooght, the liquidators of Toshoku Finance UK plc, appealed with permission of the Appeal Committee of the House of Lords given on 6 December 2000 from the decision of the Court of Appeal (Scott V-C, Chadwick and Buxton LJJ) on 23 March 2000 ([2000] 3 All ER 938, [2000] 1 WLR 2478) allowing an appeal by the respondents, the Commissioners of Inland Revenue, from the decision of Evans-Lombe J on 30 July 1999 ([1999] STC 922) whereby he held that the liquidators were not required to discharge out of the company's assets, as an expense of the liquidation, any liability for corporation tax on the company's post-liquidation income. The facts are set out in the opinion of Lord Hoffmann.

Mark Phillips QC and *Felicity Toube* (instructed by *Linklaters*) for the liquidators.

Michael Briggs QC and *Philip Jones* (instructed by the *Solicitor of Inland Revenue*) for the Crown.

a Their Lordships took time for consideration.

20 February 2002. The following opinions were delivered.

LORD HOFFMANN.

b [1] My Lords, Toshoku Finance UK plc (the company) is in creditors' voluntary liquidation. It was a subsidiary of a Japanese corporation called Toshoku Ltd, which went into liquidation in December 1997. The resolution to wind up the company was passed on 26 January 1998 (the liquidation date). Two partners in PwC (the liquidators) were appointed joint liquidators. The only substantial asset was a debt owing by another Toshoku subsidiary called Toshoku Europa Establishment (TEE)
c under a loan facility agreement. TEE's indebtedness to the company on the liquidation date (including arrears of interest at the contractual rate) was $US156·3m. But TEE was itself heavily insolvent. It had realisable assets of only about $US43m and total liabilities (mainly to other group companies) of $US381·75m. Negotiations took place for the distribution of TEE's assets among its creditors.
d On 25 November 1998 the company agreed to accept about $US21·5m in full and final settlement of its claim. Nothing was paid in respect of interest which had accrued after the liquidation date.

[2] Despite the fact that the company received no interest from TEE after the liquidation date, it is in principle liable to pay corporation tax as if it had. Section 8(2) of the Income and Corporation Taxes Act 1988 provides that a company is
e 'chargeable to corporation tax on profits arising in the winding up of the company'. It may be assessed in respect of an accounting period deemed to commence on the liquidation date (s 12(7)) and the liquidator is the proper officer liable to pay the tax (see s 108(2) of the Taxes Management Act 1970). Chapter II of the Finance Act 1996 provides that, in the case of companies between which there is a
f 'connection' as defined in s 87(3), profits from a 'loan relationship' must be computed on an accruals basis (see s 87(2)). In addition, the computation must be made on the assumption that 'every amount payable under the relationship will be paid in full as it becomes due' (see s 85(3)(c), read with s 85(5)(a) and paras 5 and 6 of Sch 9). No allowance may be made for bad debts.

g [3] There was at the relevant time a connection between the company and TEE because they had both been under the control of the Japanese holding company. In principle, therefore, the company was liable in respect of the accounting period after the liquidation date for corporation tax on profits computed on the assumption that it received all interest contractually payable by
h TEE. The liquidators do not admit liability to tax because they may wish to dispute whether TEE's obligation to pay interest continued after the liquidation date. But they applied to court for directions as to whether, assuming that there was such a liability, it was an 'expense properly incurred in the winding up' which they were required by s 115 of the Insolvency Act 1986 to pay out of the company's assets in priority to other claims. The Inland Revenue was joined as a defendant
j to the application. Evans-Lombe J ([1999] STC 922) held that the liability would not be an expense incurred in the winding up, but the Court of Appeal ([2000] 3 All ER 938, [2000] 1 WLR 2478) reversed his decision. The liquidators appeal to your Lordships' House.

[4] The case for the Crown is extremely simple. Section 115 provides that in a voluntary winding up such as this:

'All expenses properly incurred in the winding up, including the
remuneration of the liquidator, are payable out of the company's assets in
priority to all other claims.'

[5] Mr Briggs QC, who appeared for the Crown, submits that r 4.218 of the
Insolvency Rules 1986, SI 1986/1925 determines both what counts as an expense
in the winding up and the priorities of such expenses between themselves. The
rule was made under both the general power in s 411 of the 1986 Act (to make
rules 'for the purpose of giving effect to' the winding up provisions of the Act) and
a specific power in para 17 of Sch 8 to make 'Provision as to the fees, costs,
charges and other expenses that may be treated as the expenses of a winding up'.

[6] Rule 4.218(1), with the omission of irrelevant items of expense, provides:

'The expenses of the liquidation are payable out of the assets in the
following order of priority—(a) expenses properly chargeable or incurred by
the official receiver or the liquidator in preserving, realising or getting in any
of the assets of the company ... (m) any necessary disbursements by the
liquidator in the course of his administration (... but not including any
payment of corporation tax in circumstances referred to in sub-paragraph (p)
below) ... (o) the remuneration of the liquidator, up to any amount not
exceeding that which is payable to the official receiver under general
regulations; (p) the amount of any corporation tax on chargeable gains
accruing on the realisation of any asset of the company (without regard to
whether the realisation is effected by the liquidator, a secured creditor, or a
receiver or manager appointed to deal with a security); (q) the balance, after
payment of any sums due under sub-paragraph (o) above, of any
remuneration due to the liquidator.'

[7] Mr Briggs says that the only question is whether the liability to corporation
tax falls within one, and if so which, of these paragraphs. He submits that it
plainly falls within (m). It is a sum which by statute is payable by a company in
respect of profits or gains arising during a winding up. The liquidator is obliged
to pay it. It is therefore a 'necessary disbursement' which the liquidator has to
make in the course of his administration. That is an end of the matter.

[8] This approach is supported by high authority. In *Re Mesco Properties Ltd*
[1979] 1 All ER 302, [1979] 1 WLR 558 the question was also whether corporation
tax had to be paid as an expense of the liquidation in priority to other claims. In
that case it had arisen not on profits but on chargeable gains, on sales of the
company's properties after the commencement of the winding up. Some of the
properties had been sold by an administrative receiver appointed by a mortgagee,
one by the mortgagee itself and the others by the liquidator. Under s 22(7) of the
Finance Act 1965 a sale by a mortgagee or receiver was treated as if it had been a
sale by a nominee for the mortgagor. The company was therefore assessed to
corporation tax on chargeable gains realised on all the dispositions.

[9] At that time the relevant rule was r 195(1) of the Companies (Winding-up)
Rules 1949, SI 1949/330. It provided that the assets of a company in a winding up
which remained after 'payment of the fees and expenses properly incurred in
preserving, realising or getting in the assets' should 'be liable to the following
payments' and there followed an earlier version of the list of items which are now
in r 4.218. At that time, however, the rules did not specifically refer to corporation
tax. The fifth paragraph, corresponding to para (m) of the current rule, simply

said: 'The necessary disbursements of any Liquidator appointed in the
winding-up by the Court ...' Brightman J said:

> '... s 243(2) of the Income and Corporation Taxes Act 1970 [now s 8(2) of
> the 1988 Act] expressly enacts that a company is chargeable to corporation
> tax on a capital gain arising in the winding-up. It follows that the tax is a
> charge which the liquidator is bound to discharge by payment, to the extent
> that assets are available. It is, therefore, to my mind, beyond argument that
> the payment of the tax is a "necessary disbursement" of the liquidator and
> must come within the fifth paragraph of r 195(1) ...' (See [1979] 1 All ER 302
> at 304–305, [1979] 1 WLR 558 at 561.)

[10] This is a clear and uncompromising statement. When the case went to
the Court of Appeal, Buckley LJ ([1980] 1 All ER 117 at 120, [1980] 1 WLR 96 at
100), quoted it and said that he agreed. Bridge LJ ([1980] 1 All ER 117 at 121,
[1980] 1 WLR 96 at 101) said expressly that he agreed with the judgment of
Brightman J and Templeman LJ also agreed. Mr Briggs says that it formed the
basis upon which paras (m) and (p) were drafted. Paragraph (m), in excepting
corporation tax on chargeable gains, assumes that it would otherwise have fallen
within the general description of a 'necessary disbursement'. It follows that
corporation tax on profits remains within (m). Chadwick LJ suggested in the
Court of Appeal ([2000] 3 All ER 938 at 951, [2000] 1 WLR 2478 at 2496) that the
reason for giving tax on chargeable gains a lower priority (below the first tranche
of the liquidator's remuneration) was because it was thought unfair to give the
higher priority to tax on gains which did not necessarily accrue during the
liquidation period but may have been latent in the company's assets at the liquidation
date. This seems a plausible explanation. The consequence is that, as a matter of
construction, the corporation tax chargeable in this case falls within (m).

[11] Both Evans-Lombe J and the Court of Appeal accepted the Crown's
submission that whether the liability counted as an expense turned upon the
construction of r 4.218. But the judge thought that corporation tax did not come
within (m). It was mentioned in (p) and so in his view could not come within
another paragraph as well. The Court of Appeal disagreed and Mr Phillips QC,
who appeared for the liquidators, did not support the construction adopted by
the judge.

[12] Instead, Mr Phillips put forward a more radical argument. He said that
the terms of r 4.218(1) did not in themselves determine whether a liability counted
as an expense of the liquidation. The rule was made, as I have said, under a power
to make provision as to the expenses which 'may be treated as the expenses of a
winding up'. Mr Phillips laid stress upon the word 'may'. He said that the rule
created only an outer envelope within which expenses were contained. If they
could not be brought within one of the paragraphs of the rule, they could not
count as expenses. But the reverse was not necessarily true. In order to be
treated as liquidation expenses, they also had to pass a judge-made test which
Nicholls LJ in *Re Atlantic Computer Systems plc* [1992] 1 All ER 476 at 482, [1992] Ch
505 at 520 called the 'liquidation expenses' principle. That principle was one of
fairness. If a liability was incurred as a result of a step taken for the benefit of the
insolvent estate, it was fair that the burden should be borne by the persons for
whose benefit the estate was being administered. So Mr Phillips said that a
liability falling within r 4.218(1) was payable as an expense only if it arose as a
result of a step taken with a view to, or for the purposes of, obtaining a benefit for

the estate. If the corporation tax had been chargeable on profits arising from carrying on the business of the company in liquidation, it would have satisfied the liquidation expenses principle. In the present case, however, the liquidator had neither received interest nor taken any steps to recover it. It was therefore not fair that the creditors should have to bear the burden of corporation tax on fictitious credits.

[13] My Lords, I do not think that, as a matter of statutory construction, r 4.218(1) is capable of being given the gloss for which Mr Phillips contends. It was in my opinion intended to be (subject to certain express qualifications and a well-established rule of construction to which I shall later return) a definitive statement of what counted as an expense of the liquidation. Until 1890, this question was answered by reference to the practice of the Companies Court. But the practice was codified by the Companies (Winding-up) Rules 1890. Rule 31 was the lineal ancestor of r 4.218(1). It provided:

'The assets of a company which is being wound up, remaining after payment of the fees, and actual expenses incurred in realising or getting in the assets, shall, subject to any order of the court ... be liable to the following payments, which shall be made in the following order of priority ...'

[14] There followed a list of items. My Lords, the language of the rule is mandatory. The assets 'shall' be liable to the payments listed. There may have been room for an argument (which I shall touch upon later) over whether the list was exhaustive. But the language is inconsistent with there being any ground upon which an item expressly mentioned in the rule can be denied the status of an expense. Similar language was used in the successive rules which were in force until 1986. Rule 4.218(1) uses slightly different language. It says 'The expenses of the liquidation are payable out of the assets in the following order of priority' and then sets out the list. But I do not think that any change of meaning was intended.

[15] The courts have treated the rule as a complete statement of liquidation expenses, subject only to the qualifications contained in the rules themselves. In *Re MC Bacon Ltd* [1991] Ch 127 at 136, [1990] 3 WLR 646 at 650 Millett J said: 'The expenses of the winding up and the order in which they are payable out of the assets are listed in rule 4.218 ...' Giving the judgment of the Court of Appeal in *Re Floor Fourteen Ltd, Lewis v IRC* [2001] 3 All ER 499 at 510 (para 32) Peter Gibson LJ said: 'Rule 4.218 tells one both what are the expenses to be treated as the expenses of a winding up and what priority they have inter se.' In *Re London Metallurgical Co* [1895] 1 Ch 758, decided soon after the first rules had been made, it was noted that the list said nothing about the costs of litigation incurred by the liquidator or awarded against him. Under the pre-1890 practice, costs awarded to a successful litigant had been recoverable in priority to the general costs of the liquidation. Vaughan Williams J said that r 31 of the 1890 rules did not change this practice. But he did not say that this was because the rule was not intended to be a complete statement of the law. He said that the practice on costs was preserved by the words 'subject to any order of the court'. When the 1890 rules were replaced by the Companies (Winding-up) Rules 1903, SR & O 1903/1103, it was specifically provided in r 170(3):

'Nothing contained in this rule shall apply to or affect costs which, in the course of legal proceedings by or against a company which is being wound up by the court, are ordered by the court in which such proceedings are a pending or a judge thereof to be paid by the company or the liquidator, or the rights of the person to whom such costs are payable.'

[16] This provision is now r 4.220(2) of the 1986 rules. No head of liquidation expense not mentioned in the rules has been discovered since the *London Metallurgical Co* case. And the general provision that the rules are 'subject to any order of the court' has gone. The only power reserved to the court is that conferred b by s 156 of the 1986 Act, which gives it a discretion to rearrange the priorities of the listed expenses inter se. This power is expressly reserved by r 4.220(1).

[17] In my opinion, therefore, both as a matter of construction and on authority, the heads of expense listed in r 4.218(1) are not subject to any implied qualification. And I do not think that the use of the word 'may' in the power in c para 17 of Sch 8 to make provision for expenses which 'may be treated as the expenses of a winding up', will bear the weight which Mr Phillips wants to put upon it. I think that the word 'may' does no more than indicate that the liquidator has a right to reimburse himself out of the assets in respect of his liabilities which fall within the rule. Whether they fall within the rule is a question of construction and no more.

d [18] Mr Phillips accepts that, with the exception of the case of *Re Kentish Homes Ltd* [1993] BCLC 1375, there is no case which supports a qualification of the statutory language. But that case has the authority of being a decision of Nicholls V-C and is based upon his own dicta when sitting as Nicholls LJ in *Re Atlantic Computer Systems plc* [1992] 1 All ER 476, [1992] Ch 505. For that reason, and in deference e to the able argument of Mr Phillips, I must examine the true scope of what Nicholls LJ called the 'liquidation expenses' principle.

[19] The rule has somewhat obscure origins in *Re Exhall Coal Mining Co Ltd* (1864) 4 De GJ & Sm 377, 46 ER 964, a briefly reported case in the Chancery Court of Appeal. Section 163 of the Companies Act 1862 provided 'any ... distress or execution put in force against the estate or effects of the company after the f commencement of the winding up shall be void to all intents'. After the presentation of a petition (which is deemed to be the commencement of a compulsory winding up) but before the winding-up order, the lessor of land of which the company was the beneficial tenant levied a distress upon the company's goods for arrears of rent. The liquidator claimed that the distress was void under the g statute. The court nevertheless said that it had a discretionary power to validate the distress. It derived this power from s 87, which provided that after a winding-up order, no 'suit, action, or other proceeding' should be proceeded with or commenced against the company without the leave of the court. The judgment of Turner LJ ((1864) 4 De GJ & Sm 377 at 379, 46 ER 964 at 965) has h usually been cited in later cases. It reads (in its entirety) as follows:

'I also concur in the decision of the Master of the Rolls. I think the 163rd section of the Act must be construed as only avoiding attachments, sequestrations, distresses or executions when leave to put them in force has not been given under the 87th section.'

j [20] Thus was created a discretion to allow a creditor to use a process of execution to recover in full a debt for which he would otherwise have had to prove in the liquidation. In subsequent years a body of precedent on the exercise of the discretion developed. In *Re Progress Assurance Co, ex p Liverpool Exchange Co* (1870) LR 9 Eq 370 the lessors of a company in liquidation levied a distress for unpaid rent upon its office furniture three months after the winding-up order.

Lord Romilly MR said (at 372–373) that a distress after the winding-up order would be allowed to proceed only where the company 'has retained, not merely formal, but actual possession of the property for the purpose of carrying on the business of the liquidation'.

[21] This principle was restated in the influential case of *Re Lundy Granite Co, ex p Heavan* (1871) 6 Ch App 462. The landlord of Lundy Island, which was let to a third party, distrained upon goods of the company which had been left upon the tenant's property. The distraint was for rent which had fallen due more than a year after the winding-up order. The tenant had agreed to assign the lease to the company but had not actually done so. He had however allowed the company into possession and the company had brought its goods upon the land. After the winding-up order the liquidator retained possession with a view to a sale of the company's assets on the land.

[22] The Lords Justices gave two reasons for allowing the distress to proceed. The first was that the distress was not in respect of a claim for rent against the company, for which the landlord could have proved in the liquidation. The company was not his tenant. The landlord was exercising his ancient right to distrain upon any goods on the land, whether they belonged to his tenant or not. It should not make a difference that the third party to whom the goods belonged happened to be a company in liquidation.

[23] The second and, for present purposes, more important reason, was that even if the rent had been owing by the company, the liquidator had retained possession of the land for the purposes of the liquidation. Following the *Progress Assurance Co* case, James LJ said ((1871) 6 Ch App 462 at 466):

'… if the company for its own purposes, and with a view to the realization of the property to better advantage, remains in possession of the estate, which the lessor is therefore not able to obtain possession of, common sense and ordinary justice require the Court to see that the landlord receives the full value of the property.'

[24] Although these principles were evolved in relation to a statutory discretion to allow a process of execution to proceed, it was obvious to everyone that there could be no practical difference between allowing a landlord to levy a distress for rent falling due after the winding up and directing the liquidator that he should be paid in full. It is important to bear in mind that the rent was a future debt for which the landlord could have proved in the liquidation (see *Hardy v Fothergill* (1888) 13 App Cas 351, [1886–90] All ER Rep 597). Under r 12.3(1) of the 1986 rules, all claims by creditors are provable as debts against the company 'whether they are present or future, certain or contingent, ascertained or sounding only in damages'. But a 'debt' is defined by r 13.12(1) as—

'(a) any debt or liability to which the company is subject at the date on which it goes into liquidation; [and] (b) any debt or liability to which the company may become subject after that date by reason of any obligation incurred before that date …'

[25] Thus debts arising out of pre-liquidation contracts such as leases, whether they accrue before or after the liquidation, can and prima facie should be proved in the liquidation. In this respect they are crucially different from normal liquidation expenses, which are incurred after the liquidation date and cannot be proved for. In the *Lundy Granite Co* case the court was therefore exercising the discretion

a conferred by s 87 of the 1862 Act to decide that, contrary to the normal pari passu rule, a creditor who had a debt which was capable of proof at the date of liquidation should be paid in priority to other creditors. What was the justification for the exercise of such a discretion?

[26] A reason, or at any rate a rationalisation, was put forward by Lindley LJ, giving the judgment of the Court of Appeal in *Re Oak Pitts Colliery Co* (1882) 21 Ch D

b 322 at 330–331, [1881–5] All ER Rep 1157 at 1162. He said:

'When the liquidator retains the property for the purpose of advantageously disposing of it, or when he continues to use it, the rent of it ought to be regarded as a debt contracted for the purpose of winding up the company, and ought to be paid in full like any other debt or expense properly incurred

c by the liquidator for the same purpose ...'

[27] My Lords, it is important to notice Lindley LJ was not saying that the liability to pay rent had been incurred as an expense of the winding up. It plainly had not. The liability had been incurred by the company before the winding up

d for the whole term of the lease. Lindley LJ was saying that it would be just and equitable, in the circumstances to which he refers, to treat the rent liability as if it were an expense of the winding up and to accord it the same priority. The conditions under which a pre-liquidation creditor would be allowed to be paid in full were cautiously stated. Lindley LJ said ((1882) 21 Ch D 322 at 329, [1881–5] All ER Rep 1157 at 1161) that the landlord 'must shew why he should have such

e an advantage over the other creditors'. It was not sufficient that the liquidator retained possession for the benefit of the estate if it was also for the benefit of the landlord. Not offering to surrender or simply doing nothing was not regarded as retaining possession for the benefit of the estate.

[28] I give two modern examples which illustrate this restrictive application of

f the principle. In *Re ABC Coupler and Engineering Co Ltd (No 3)* [1970] 1 All ER 650, [1970] 1 WLR 702, the liquidator on appointment closed down the business which had been conducted on the premises, had the company's plant and machinery valued and thought about what he should do. It was only from the time he decided to put the lease on the market that Plowman J held that he was retaining the premises for the benefit of the winding up and was liable to pay the

g rent in full. In *Re HH Realisations Ltd* (1975) 31 P&CR 249 Templeman J held that a company ceased to be liable to pay the rent in full from the time it gave notice to the landlord that it was seeking authority to disclaim the lease, even though it remained in occupation for nearly two months longer (see also *Re Downer Enterprises Ltd* [1974] 2 All ER 1074, [1974] 1 WLR 1460).

h [29] The principle evolved from *Re Exhall Coal Mining Co Ltd* (1864) 4 De GJ & Sm 377, 46 ER 964, and the *Lundy Granite Co* case (1871) 6 Ch App 462 is thus one which permits, on equitable grounds, the concept of a liability incurred as an expense of the liquidation to be expanded to include liabilities incurred before the liquidation in respect of property afterwards retained by the liquidator for the benefit of the insolvent estate. Although it was originally based upon a statutory

j discretion to allow a distress or execution against the company's assets, the courts quickly recognised that its effect could be to promote a creditor from merely having a claim in the liquidation to having a prior right to payment in full. As in the case of other equitable doctrines, the discretion hardened into principle. By the end of the nineteenth century, the scope of the *Lundy Granite Co* principle was well settled.

[30] It was not, however, a general test for deciding what counted as an expense of the liquidation. Expenses incurred after the liquidation date need no further equitable reason why they should be paid. Of course it will generally be true that such expenses will have been incurred by the liquidator for the purposes of the liquidation. It is not the business of the liquidator to incur expenses for any other purpose. But this is not at all the same thing as saying that the expenses will necessarily be for the benefit of estate. They may simply be liabilities which, as liquidator, he has to pay. For example, there will be the fees payable to fund the Insolvency Service, ranking as para (c) in r 4.218(1), where the benefit to the estate may seem somewhat remote. There would be little point in a statute which specifically imposed liabilities upon a company in liquidation if they were payable only in the rare case in which it emerged with all other creditors having been paid.

[31] The difference between the treatment of pre-liquidation debts under the *Lundy Granite Co* principle and the treatment of post-liquidation liabilities emerges clearly from the nineteenth-century cases on rates. In *Re Watson, Kipling & Co* (1883) 23 Ch D 500, which concerned an assessment for rates made after the liquidation upon property occupied by the company, Kay J rejected (at 506) the submission of counsel for the rating authority that—

'where a liability is incurred during the winding-up, that liability ought to be paid in full, and therefore these rates ought to be paid in full because they were made during the winding-up ...'

[32] He applied instead the *Lundy Granite Co* principle and said that it was not enough that the company was in rateable occupation. It must have retained occupation for the benefit of the estate. But in *Re National Arms and Ammunition Co* (1885) 28 Ch D 474 Bowen and Fry LJJ said that this was wrong. Bowen LJ said (at 480, 482):

'If the company retains the possession of property which would be rateable in the hands of anyone else, it is only reasonable that it should be rateable in the hands of the company ... [T]he true test is whether there has been a beneficial occupation within the ordinary meaning of those words in cases as to rating ...'

[33] This test was applied by Vaughan Williams J in *Re Blazer Fire Lighter Ltd* [1895] 1 Ch 402, [1891–4] All ER Rep 1174. The liquidator had closed the business and done nothing on the premises except to install a caretaker to protect them from vandalism. That was sufficient to continue the company in rateable occupation. So the rates were an expense of the liquidation.

[34] It therefore did not follow that because a liquidator might in certain circumstances retain possession of leased property without having to pay the rent as an expense of the liquidation, he did not in the same circumstances have to pay the rates. In the *ABC Coupler* case [1970] 1 All ER 650, [1970] 1 WLR 702, for example, the rent did not become a liquidation expense until some time after the winding-up order, notwithstanding that the company remained in occupation. And in the *HH Realisations* case (1975) 31 P&CR 249 the company remained in occupation for some time after the rent had ceased to be a liquidation expense. But in both cases the company would in my opinion have been liable to pay rates on the simple ground that it was in rateable occupation. The rates would have

a been an obligation incurred after the liquidation which (unlike the rent) was not provable and was therefore payable in full.

[35] My Lords, I have spent some time examining the origins and scope of the 'liquidation expenses' principle because it formed the basis of the two recent authorities upon which Mr Phillips particularly relied. *Re Atlantic Computer Systems plc* [1992] 1 All ER 476, [1992] Ch 505 was about whether rental due under hire-

b purchaser agreements should be treated as an expense of administration. But the judgment of Nicholls LJ contains a discussion of the principles upon which obligations based upon pre-liquidation agreements should be treated as expenses in a liquidation. He said ([1992] 1 All ER 476 at 484, [1992] Ch 505 at 522) that a creditor could ordinarily be given leave to execute against the company's assets for a 'new debt incurred by the liquidator for the purposes of the liquidation': 'it

c is just and equitable that the burden of the debt should be borne by those for whose benefit the insolvent estate is being administered.' It was, he said, a corollary of this principle that a debt was incurred for the purposes of the liquidation ought to be paid in full as an expense of the liquidation.

[36] Nicholls LJ then went on to say:

d
'The latter principle is not confined to new debts incurred by the liquidator. It applies also to continuing obligations under existing contracts such as leases which the liquidator chooses to continue for the benefit of the winding up.'

e In this connection he discussed the *Lundy Granite Co* case (1871) 6 Ch App 462, the *Oak Pits Colliery* case (1882) 21 Ch D 322, [1881–5] All ER Rep 1157 and others in the same line of authority. He then said:

'It is important to keep in mind that this principle, relating to outgoings on property retained by a liquidator for the purposes of the winding up, is no

f more than a principle applied by the court when exercising its discretion in a winding up. The principle, which it will be convenient to call the "liquidation expenses" principle, is a statement of how, in general, the court will exercise its discretion in a common-form set of circumstances. The liquidator himself has power, in a suitable case, to pay the relevant outgoings. But the court retains an overriding discretion to give leave under s 130(2) [of the 1986 Act]

g or to give directions to a liquidator that the relevant outgoings shall be paid by him as an expense of the liquidation.' (See [1992] 1 All ER 476 at 485, [1992] Ch 505 at 523.)

[37] Two points arise out of these passages. First, Mr Phillips is entitled to say

h that Nicholls LJ assimilates the grounds upon which post-liquidation debts count as expenses with the grounds upon which a continuing obligation which has arisen under a pre-liquidation contract may be treated as a liquidation expense. This certainly provides support for his submission that post-liquidation expenses must satisfy the 'liquidation expenses' principle. But in my respectful opinion the two categories of expenses cannot be assimilated in this way. The considerations

j which determine whether they should count as expenses are different. Assimilation is inconsistent with the authorities to which I have referred and with the statutory regime which has existed since 1890.

[38] The second point is the proposition that whether debts should count as expenses of the liquidation is a matter for the discretion of the court. In my opinion there is no such discretion. Rule 4.218 determines what counts as

expenses, subject only to the limited discretion under s 156 of the 1986 Act to
re-arrange the priorities of expenses inter se. The court will of course interpret
r 4.218 to include debts which, under the *Lundy Granite Co* principle, are deemed
to be expenses of the liquidation. Ordinarily this means that debts such as rents
under a lease will be treated as coming within para (a), but the principle may
possibly enlarge the scope of other paragraphs as well. But the application of that
principle does not involve an exercise of discretion any more than the application
of any other legal principle to the particular facts of the case. I should say that
Mr Phillips made it clear that he also did not suggest that the court was able to
exercise what would ordinarily be called a discretion.

[39] There is of course no question that s 130(2) of the 1986 Act (the lineal
descendant of s 87 of the 1862 Act upon which the *Lundy Granite Co* principle was
originally constructed) confers a statutory discretion. But the discretion is as to
the remedy which the creditor should be allowed to exercise; whether he should
be able to bring proceedings, levy distress or execution or should have to wait for
the distribution of the assets in due course of liquidation. The fact that a debt
counts as an expense of the liquidation does not necessarily mean that the
creditor should be allowed immediately to bring proceedings or levy execution.
The order of priorities under r 4.218(1) may mean that if he is paid at once, the
assets to satisfy prior expense claims may be insufficient. So the question of
remedy is entirely a matter of discretion. But the discretion does not determine
whether a claim is a liquidation expense or not. It is rather the other way
round; the claim must be a liquidation expense before the court can have any
discretion to grant a remedy which will enable the creditor to obtain payment in
priority to other claims.

[40] Nicholls V-C applied the two propositions in the *Atlantic Computer Systems*
case [1992] 1 All ER 476, [1992] Ch 505 to arrive at his decision in *Re Kentish Homes Ltd*
[1993] BCLC 1375. The question there was whether a post-liquidation liability to
community charge on empty flats was an expense of the liquidation. He recorded
(at 1380) that it was common ground that 'the company is the chargeable person
in respect of the flats for the relevant periods'. But he said that the liability was
nevertheless not a liquidation expense. In his opinion, it would rank as such only
if the court, as a matter of discretion, directed the liquidators to discharge the
obligation out of the assets in their hands. And in his view there was no ground
upon which the court should do so. The case did not fall within the *Lundy Granite Co*
principle because the liquidators had not retained possession of the flats for the
purpose of the winding up. An administrative receiver had taken possession. Nor
was there any other equitable ground upon which the liquidators should pay.

[41] The Court of Appeal said that they were driven to the conclusion that this
case was wrongly decided. I respectfully agree. In the first place, the question of
whether the community charge should count as an expense of the liquidation was
not a matter for the judge's discretion. It depended upon whether it came within
one of the paragraphs of r 4.218. In my opinion if, as was common ground, the
company was the chargeable person, it was a necessary expense which came
within (m). If, therefore, the liquidator had sufficient assets after satisfying the
liabilities coming within paras (a) to (l), he was obliged to pay it. Secondly, the
Lundy Granite Co principle had no relevance. The liability did not arise out of a
pre-liquidation obligation. If it came within the language of para (m), it was a
liquidation expense.

[42] I therefore respectfully adopt the simple approach of Brightman J in
Re Mesco Properties Ltd [1979] 1 All ER 302 at 304–305, [1979] 1 WLR 558 at 561. The

a statute expressly enacts that a company is chargeable to corporation tax on profits or gains arising in the winding up. It follows that the tax is a post-liquidation liability which the liquidator is bound to discharge and it is therefore a 'necessary disbursement' within the meaning of the 1986 rules.

[43] My Lords, I accept that it may be possible to characterise the liquidator's 'retention' of the debt from TEE as an act for the benefit of the estate which could b be brought within an attenuated version of Mr Phillips' liquidation expenses principle. But I think that such an exercise, suggesting a gloss on the language of r 4.218 in respect of post-liquidation liabilities, could only cast doubt upon law which has been perfectly clear since the *Mesco Properties* case. It should in my opinion be left that way.

[44] Everyone agrees that this is a hard case for the company's creditors. The c provisions of the 1996 Act which exclude bad debt relief in loan relationships between connected companies are to prevent groups of companies from manipulating their tax liabilities. But it does not seem fair to visit the consequences upon creditors in a winding up. The present case was specifically considered in *Corporate Debt, Financial Instruments and Foreign Exchange Gains and Losses*, a consultative document issued by d the Inland Revenue on 26 July 2001. The government said that it proposed to introduce legislation to make an exception to the bad debt rule where a creditor goes into liquidation.

[45] Mr Phillips said that the problem was not specific to this particular form of tax liability but existed in every case in which a liability might be imposed upon a company in liquidation. The answer, he said, was the adoption of a general e liquidation expenses rule. I do not agree. The injustice, if any, does not arise because liabilities imposed upon a company in liquidation have priority as expenses of the liquidation, but because it may be unjust to impose certain liabilities upon companies in liquidation. Mr Phillips mentioned liabilities under environmental legislation which might also take precedence over other claims if f there were no liquidation expenses principle. But in *Re Mineral Resources Ltd, Environment Agency v Stout* [1999] 1 All ER 746 Neuberger J carefully considered the consequences for creditors of his decision that a company in liquidation could not disclaim a waste management licence. He recognised that this might result in post-liquidation liabilities which would rank ahead of other creditors. But he decided that the legislation, on grounds of public interest, required that the claims g of the environment should be preferred.

[46] In my opinion, the question of whether such liabilities should be imposed upon companies in liquidation is a legislative decision which will depend upon the particular liability in question. It should not be ruled out by an illegitimate extension of the liquidation expenses principle, which was devised more than a h century ago for an altogether different purpose.

[47] I would therefore dismiss the appeal.

LORD WOOLF CJ.

[48] My Lords, I have had the advantage of reading in draft the speech j prepared by my noble and learned friend Lord Hoffmann. I agree with him and for the reasons, which he has given, I too, would dismiss this appeal.

LORD HUTTON.

[49] My Lords, I have had the advantage of reading in draft the speech of my noble and learned friend, Lord Hoffmann. I agree with it, and for the reasons which he gives I too would dismiss the appeal.

LORD HOBHOUSE OF WOODBOROUGH.

[50] My Lords, with some reluctance, both for reasons given by my noble and *a*
learned friend Lord Hoffmann towards the end of his opinion and because
I found the arguments of Mr Phillips QC and judgments of Nicholls LJ (*Re Atlantic
Computer Systems plc* [1992] 1 All ER 476, [1992] Ch 505) and Nicholls V-C (*Re Kentish
Homes Ltd* [1993] BCLC 1375) more persuasive than have your Lordships and
would not have accepted that the authorities are incapable of reconciliation, but, in *b*
deference to the unanimity of your Lordships' opinions, I concur in the order
proposed.

LORD RODGER OF EARLSFERRY.

[51] My Lords, I have had the privilege of studying the speech of my noble and
learned friend, Lord Hoffmann, in draft. I agree with it and, for the reasons which *c*
he gives, I too would dismiss the appeal.

Appeal dismissed.

Celia Fox   Barrister.

a
Bell v Tuohy and another
[2002] EWCA Civ 423

COURT OF APPEAL, CIVIL DIVISION

b
KENNEDY, MANTELL LJJ AND NEUBERGER J

7 MARCH, 27 MARCH 2002

Contempt of court – Committal – Jurisdiction – Execution of warrant for possession –
Whether warrant for possession a nullity if issued before date on which possession to be
given up – Whether penal notice having to be attached to possession order as matter of
c *course – Whether defects in committal application precluding committal – CPR Sch 2,*
CCR Ord 26, r 17(2), Ord 29, r 1(3), PD 29, para 2.6(5).

On 11 July 2001 the respondent trustee in bankruptcy obtained a possession
order, requiring the appellant bankrupt to deliver up possession of his premises
d to the trustee on or before 11 October. That order did not contain a notice
specifically warning the bankrupt that he would be at risk of being sent to prison
for contempt if he failed to comply with it. Such a notice was required in an
order, enforceable by committal, if the order were 'in the nature of an injunction'
(CCR Ord 29, r 1(3)[a] (as set out in CPR Sch 2)). Anticipating that the bankrupt
would not vacate, the trustee applied to the county court on 14 August for a
e warrant for possession in the prescribed form, N325. That application was
premature since CCR Ord 26, r 17(2)[b] required the person seeking a warrant for
possession to certify that the land 'has not been vacated in accordance' with the
order for recovery of the land, while form N325 itself required the claimant to
sign a statement on its face certifying that the defendant 'has not vacated the land
f as ordered'. Nevertheless, an officially sealed warrant for possession was issued
the following day. The operative part of such a warrant contained instructions to
the bailiffs, stating that the defendant 'has failed' to obey the order and that the
bailiffs were 'now' required to give possession of the land to the claimant. On
15 October, the bailiffs attended the premises to execute the warrant, but the
bankrupt refused to let them in, despite being told that failure to give up
g possession would result in an application for his committal. The trustee duly
made an application for the bankrupt's committal for contempt of court in
refusing to comply with the possession order and the warrant for possession.
That application contained various defects, including a failure to comply with the
requirement, in para 2.6(5)[c] of CCR PD 29, that such an application contain a
h prominent notice stating the possible consequences of the court making a
committal order. The judge adjourned the application, but not before warning
the bankrupt that a failure to comply with the possession order could result in
committal. At the adjourned hearing, the bankrupt said that he would not
comply with the order, and that he would not leave unless he was thrown out or
j sent to prison. The judge decided to commit the bankrupt to prison for contempt
for seven days to provide an opportunity for possession to be obtained peacefully,
relying, inter alia, on the bankrupt's failure to comply with the possession order
and to co-operate with the bailiffs. In the course of reaching that conclusion, the

---

a   Rule 1, so far as material, is set out at [32], [36], below
b   Rule 17, so far as material, is set out at [17], below
c   Paragraph 2.6, so far as material, is set out at [45], below

judge held that the court could have set aside the warrant for possession if an application had been made to that effect, but that the warrant was valid until such an application succeeded. The bankrupt challenged that ruling on his appeal against the committal order. He further relied on the lack of a penal notice in the possession order and on the defects in the contempt application.

Held – (1) (Mantell LJ dissenting) A warrant for possession was a nullity if it had been issued before the date on which possession was to be given up pursuant to the court order. CCR Ord 26, r 17(2) was expressed in a way that indicated that there was simply no right in a claimant to seek a warrant until the date for possession had passed and possession had not been delivered up. Moreover, the prescribed forms could not have made clearer the importance of the date for possession having passed before a warrant could be issued. It was impossible to marry up the mandatory direction to the bailiffs in the operative part of the warrant with the notion that the warrant would be valid if it had been issued before it was lawful for the bailiff to deliver possession to the claimant. It followed in the instant case that the warrant was invalid and that the bankrupt could not have been in contempt of court for having obstructed its execution (see [21], [25], [26], [28], [30], [59], [67], [72], below).

(2) An order for possession was not an order 'in the nature of an injunction' within the meaning of CCR Ord 29, r 1(3), and there was no requirement for every possession order to have a penal notice attached as a matter of course. Indeed, it was generally undesirable that a penal notice should be attached to such an order, unless there were good and exceptional grounds. The normal way to enforce a possession order was by requesting and obtaining the issue of a warrant for possession. If the last resort of a contempt application appeared necessary, then it would normally be more appropriate for the contempt application to be based primarily on the defendant's obstruction of the bailiff when executing the warrant for possession. In such a case, it would then be sensible to serve a copy of the order for possession with a penal notice, albeit only once the warrant had not been successfully executed due to the defendant's obstruction. In the instant case, it would not have been open to the judge to commit the bankrupt to prison for breach of the possession order unless it would have been proper for him to have exercised his power, under Ord 29, r 1(7), to dispense with the requirement that the possession order should have been served with a penal notice before the bankrupt could have been committed for breach of it (see [37], [44], [59], [71], [72], below).

(3) Although care should be taken to ensure that any committal proceedings complied with the rules and CCR PD 29, a person who was in contempt of court, and should otherwise be committed to prison, could not expect to avoid being committed simply because of some defect in the procedure that had not prejudiced him. Even where there were many defects, the proper approach was to consider each of the defects relied on, and to decide whether they had caused any prejudice or unfairness to the defendant, taken separately or together. In the instant case, there was no such prejudice or unfairness. The bankrupt had been well aware of the existence of the possession order, and had been clearly warned of the risk of committal if he did not comply with it. In the light of his obdurate and expressed determination not to give up possession, the court had been left with little alternative but to commit him to prison simply for the purpose of enabling its order to be executed effectively and peacefully. Accordingly, the appeal would be dismissed (see [46], [49]–[51], [53]–[59], [67], [68], [71], [72], below); *Nicholls v Nicholls* [1997] 2 All ER 97 applied.

a   Per curiam. It is impossible to state as a general proposition whether or not a statement by a defendant in open court that he will not comply with a court order amounts to 'wilfully insult[ing]' the judge for the purposes of s 118^d of the County Courts Act 1984. At one extreme is a statement by a person against whom a judge has just made an order for possession of his home, saying that he will not go voluntarily and will have to be evicted. Such a statement, particularly made in

b the heat of the moment, will fall outside the scope of s 118 since it cannot of itself seriously be said to risk bringing the court into disrepute, or to amount to a serious challenge to its authority, or to constitute an interruption to its orderly conduct. At the other end of the scale is a case where the possession order has expired, the execution of a valid warrant has been unlawfully impeded and the defendant, having been properly warned of the consequences, rudely and

c unambiguously maintains in court his intention to thwart any attempts to execute the possession order. Such behaviour will fall within the ambit of s 118 (see [63], [64], [71], [72], below).

Notes

d For penal notices, disobedience of a possession order and applications to commit for civil contempt, see 9(1) *Halsbury's Laws* (4th edn reissue) paras 468, 473, 498.

    For the County Courts Act 1984, s 118, see 11 *Halsbury's Statutes* (4th edn) (2000 reissue) 775.

Cases referred to in judgments

e *Alliance Building Society v Austen* [1951] 2 All ER 1068.
Danchevsky v Danchevsky [1974] 3 All ER 934, [1975] Fam 17, [1974] 3 WLR 709, CA.
Isaacs v Robertson [1984] 3 All ER 140, [1985] AC 97, [1984] 3 WLR 705, PC.
Jolly v Hull, Jolly v Jolly [2000] 2 FLR 69, CA.
Lacon v De Groat (1893) 10 TLR 24.
f *Nicholls v Nicholls* [1997] 2 All ER 97, [1997] 1 WLR 314, CA.
P (Minors) (Custody Order: Penal Notice), Re [1990] 1 WLR 613, CA.
Secretary of State for Trade and Industry v Langridge [1991] 3 All ER 591, [1991] Ch 402, [1991] 2 WLR 1343, CA.
Sofroniou v Szgetti [1991] FCR 332, CA.
Szczepanski v Szczepanski [1985] FLR 468, CA.
g

Appeal

Robert Arnold Tuohy, a bankrupt, appealed from the order of Judge Marshall Evans QC, made at Liverpool County Court on 5 November 2001, committing him to prison for seven days for contempt of court for, inter alia, failing to comply

h with an order requiring him to give possession of property known as 25C St Andrew's Gardens, Liverpool, to the respondent trustee in bankruptcy, Gary Bell, and for impeding the bailiffs in executing a warrant for possession of the property. Committal proceedings had also been brought against Mr Tuohy's wife, Margaret Mary Tuohy, but no committal order had been made against her. The facts are

j set out in the judgment of Neuberger J.

Graeme Wood (instructed by *Cobleys*, Liverpool) for Mr Tuohy.
Graham Sellers (instructed by *Brabners*, Liverpool) for the trustee.

Cur adv vult

---

d   Section 118, so far as material, is set out at [62], below

27 March 2002. The following judgments were delivered.

a

NEUBERGER J (giving the first judgment at the invitation of Kennedy LJ).

[1] This is an appeal by Mr Robert Tuohy, against an order made by Judge Marshall Evans QC in the Liverpool County Court on 5 November 2001, committing Mr Tuohy to prison for contempt of court for a period of seven days.

b

The facts

[2] Mr and Mrs Tuohy started living at 25C St Andrew's Gardens, Liverpool (the premises) in about 1976. They were both declared bankrupt in 2000. As a consequence, their interest in the premises vested in their trustee in bankruptcy, Mr Gary Bell, pursuant to s 306 of the Insolvency Act 1986. The trustee asked Mr and Mrs Tuohy to give him possession of the premises, so that he could sell the premises with a view to the proceeds of sale being distributed to their creditors. However, they refused to vacate, and the trustee applied to the Liverpool County Court for an order for sale and an order for possession.

c

[3] On 11 July 2001, District Judge Sykes made an order for the sale of the premises with vacant possession, and she also ordered that Mr and Mrs Tuohy 'deliver up possession of the [premises] to the trustee on or before 11 October 2001'. Because the trustee anticipated that Mr and Mrs Tuohy would not in fact vacate, his solicitor applied to the Liverpool County Court for a warrant for possession on 14 August 2001, in the appropriate form, N325, Request for Warrant for Possession of Land, apparently after discussing the matter with Miss Cooper, a member of the court staff.

d

e

[4] An officially sealed warrant for possession in the appropriate form, form N49, Warrant for Possession of Land, was issued, apparently the following day, 15 August 2001. On 3 October 2001, Mr and Mrs Tuohy made an application to suspend the warrant. That application was dismissed on 10 October by District Judge Smedley. (An appeal was launched, but it was dismissed on 20 November, and no stay was applied for or granted in the meantime.)

f

[5] On 15 October 2001, three county court bailiffs, two police officers, a locksmith and an observer attended at the premises to execute the warrant. Although Mr and Mrs Tuohy were at home, they refused to let the bailiffs into the premises. Mr Tuohy was told by one of the bailiffs that his failure to give up possession would result in an application for his committal to prison because of his failure to comply with the order for possession and because he was impeding the bailiffs. Although possession was not obtained on 15 October, because of Mr and Mrs Tuohy's refusal to leave the premises or to afford the bailiffs entry, Mrs Tuohy moved out shortly thereafter.

g

h

[6] On the same day as the failed attempt to execute the warrant, 15 October, the trustee applied in the county court for the committal of Mr and Mrs Tuohy—

'for contempt of court because they have refused to comply with the court's order of 11 July 2001 and have refused to comply with the warrant for possession when bailiffs attempted to execute the warrant on 15 October 2001.'

j

The application came before Judge Marshall Evans QC on 22 October, and he decided to adjourn the application to 5 November. This was partly because the application was supported by witness statements, rather than by affidavits, as required by para 3.1 of the Practice Direction—Committal Applications (CCR PD 29) (as set out in Sch 2 to the CPR).

a   [7] However, the judge's decision to adjourn the application was also influenced by the fact that, although they were present in court, Mr and Mrs Tuohy were not legally represented. The judge took the opportunity to tell Mr Tuohy that the order for possession was an order of the court which was to be obeyed. The judge also explained to Mr Tuohy in clear terms that failure to comply with the order could result in penalties, including committal to prison.

b   [8] At the adjourned hearing of the contempt application on 5 November 2001, Mr and Mrs Tuohy were represented by counsel. The judge read the affidavits, heard some evidence from Mr Tuohy, and entertained argument from counsel for the trustee and for Mr and Mrs Tuohy. He accepted that there were various defects in the application, but he was of the view that he could and should waive them. He decided not to make any order against Mrs Tuohy on the basis she had
c   moved out of the premises and 'her present position is co-operative'. He therefore adjourned the application against her.

     [9] However, the judge decided to commit Mr Tuohy to prison for seven days on the basis of Mr Tuohy's contempt. He concluded that he was entitled to commit Mr Tuohy to prison for contempt for three reasons. The first reason
d   was Mr Tuohy's failure to comply with the order of 11 July; the second was Mr Tuohy's failure to co-operate with the bailiffs on 15 October; the third reason was Mr Tuohy's patent refusal in open court on 5 November to comply with the order of 11 July. In connection with this last reason, Mr Tuohy said at that hearing: 'I am not willing to comply with the order of the court. I won't leave unless I am thrown out ... or sent to prison ... that is my carefully considered and
e   final decision.'

     [10] Having satisfied himself that he had jurisdiction to commit Mr Tuohy to prison, the judge decided that it was appropriate to do so, albeit only for seven days. He described this as 'a short period which will give an opportunity for possession to be taken peacefully' and 'the best solution to the problem'. He
f   emphasised that there was no question of 'vengeance' and that the purpose of the committal was 'merely to see that the order is obeyed'. In the event, Mr Tuohy served one-and-a-half days in prison, during which time the order for possession was executed.

     [11] Mr Tuohy now appeals against the decision to commit him to prison, contending that each of the three grounds relied on by the judge were flawed, and
g   did not justify his imprisonment. I propose to consider first the impeding of the execution of the warrant.

Contempt and the warrant for possession
     [12] Impeding a bailiff of the county court in executing a warrant can lead to
h   prosecution by virtue of the provisions of s 10 of the Criminal Law Act 1977. That does not of itself mean that it constitutes civil contempt, nor, indeed, does it mean that it could not constitute civil contempt—see *Szczepanski v Szczepanski* [1985] FLR 468. Indeed, that case shows that a civil court can deal with a contempt where it is appropriate to do so (as the judge thought here) even if there
j   is a risk of criminal proceedings.

     [13] A warrant for possession is not addressed to a defendant or any other person in occupation of premises: it is issued out of the county court office 'to the district judge and the bailiffs of the court'. Accordingly, as pointed out by Mantell LJ, it cannot be said that by failing to comply with a warrant for possession of certain property, a person in occupation of the property is refusing to comply with a court order directed to him or served on him. However, at least in the absence

of authority, it would seem to me pretty clear that impeding an officer of the
court who is in the course of lawfully executing an order of the court, which is *a*
what a bailiff is doing when executing a lawful warrant for possession, would
constitute contempt of court, at least where the person concerned knows or
clearly ought to know that what he is impeding is the proper execution of an
order of the court.

[14] There is relatively limited authority on the topic. In two cases, it has been *b*
held that, where an order for possession has been made in the High Court and has
been executed through the medium of a writ of possession, a defendant who
subsequently breaks back into the premises is in contempt of court. In *Lacon v
De Groat* (1893) 10 TLR 24 at 25, Pollock B said:

> 'Whenever, the writ being put in force, the defendant ... does not fully and *c*
> honestly give up possession, but only colourably does so, the Judge applied
> to may and ought to find that the process of the Court had not been obeyed,
> and that there had been a contempt of Court.'

This observation was quoted and applied by Roxburgh J in *Alliance Building
Society v Austen* [1951] 2 All ER 1068. *d*

[15] While each of those two cases was concerned with a writ of possession in
the High Court, which was, as it were, subsequently thwarted, it seems to me
that they support the proposition that obstruction of a bailiff seeking to execute
an order for possession, pursuant to a lawful warrant for possession, would
constitute a contempt. None the less, as was emphasised in the *Alliance* case *e*
(at 1069), the contempt procedure should be invoked very rarely in such a
context, a view supported by subsequent observations of the Court of Appeal in
Danchevsky v Danchevsky [1974] 3 All ER 934, [1975] Fam 17.

[16] The point relied on by Mr Tuohy in support of his contention that he was
not in contempt by impeding the execution, is that the warrant was invalid. This *f*
is on the basis that it is only possible for a claimant, with the benefit of an order
for possession in the county court, to apply for a warrant for possession after the
order for possession has taken effect (ie in this case, after 11 October 2001), and
that it is correspondingly only open to the court to grant a warrant for possession
after that date. Consequently, because the warrant in the present case was
applied for and granted well before the date on which possession was ordered to *g*
be given up, it is said that the warrant was a nullity.

[17] There is no doubt that the warrant was applied for and issued
prematurely. CCR Order 26, r 17(2) provides:

> '... the person desiring a warrant of possession to be issued shall file a *h*
> request in that behalf certifying that the land has not been vacated in
> accordance with the judgment or order for the recovery of the said land.'

[18] The closing words of that rule make it clear, to my mind, that a warrant
for possession can only be applied for after the date fixed for possession in the
order. That is reflected in form N325 which requires the claimant or his solicitor *j*
to sign a statement on the face of the form certifying 'that the defendant has not
vacated the land *as ordered*' (my emphasis). It is also clear from the form of
warrant itself, N49, on which, among other things, requires the insertion of the
date on which possession has been ordered to be given. Towards the end of the
form of warrant there is the operative part in capital letters, being the instruction
to the bailiffs:

a 'THE DEFENDANT *HAS FAILED* TO OBEY THE ORDER AND AT THE PLAINTIFF'S REQUEST THIS WARRANT HAS BEEN ISSUED. YOU ARE *NOW* REQUIRED TO GIVE POSSESSION OF THE LAND TO THE PLAINTIFF.' (My emphasis.)

[19] The past tense in the first sentence and the present tense in the last sentence make it as clear as one could wish that such a warrant can only be issued b after the date ordered for possession has passed. The importance of timing in relation to a warrant of possession is also emphasised by the fact that at the very end of the warrant there is this provision to be filled in: 'Application was made to this court for this warrant at ... minutes past the hour of ... o'clock on ...' It is, I believe very unusual for any legal document, whether emanating from the court or otherwise, to contain a precise time, as opposed to a day, on which c something was done.

[20] The judge thought that the fact that the warrant was applied for and issued before the date on which possession had been ordered to be given, 11 October 2001, did not render the warrant invalid. He took the view that the court would have had power to set aside the warrant if an application had been made to that d effect, but that, unless and until such an application succeeded, the warrant was valid. He also pointed out that no complaint could be made about the execution in any event, because the bailiff did not attend at the premises until after 11 October, the date on which he should have given up possession pursuant to the terms of the order.

[21] Although there is much to be said for that view, I have come to the e conclusion that it is wrong, and that a warrant for possession issued before the date on which possession is to be given up pursuant to the court order is a nullity.

[22] An order made by a judge of unlimited jurisdiction, for instance in the High Court, must be obeyed, and failure to observe it can amount to contempt of court, however irregular it might be, unless and until it is reversed or set aside f (see *Isaacs v Robertson* [1984] 3 All ER 140 at 142–143, [1985] AC 97 at 101–103). However, a warrant for possession is, in my judgment, of a very different nature from an order made by a High Court judge. First, the county court is not a court of unlimited jurisdiction. Secondly, a warrant for possession is not issued pursuant to a judicial act; its issue is an administrative act. It appears clear that, if a claimant applies for a warrant for possession after the date for possession has expired, and g fills in form N325, the county court office will then issue a warrant for possession. There is no question of any hearing, of any party being entitled to make any representation, or of any judicial discretion, or even any judicial involvement.

[23] However, the fact that the issue of a warrant for possession is an administrative act by the staff of the county court is not of itself conclusive as to h the issue of whether a warrant issued before the date ordered for possession is a nullity (as is contended on behalf of Mr Tuohy) or irregular (as the judge thought, and as is submitted on behalf of the trustee). The question of whether the issue of a document in a manner or at a time which fails to comply with the requirement of a statute, a statutory instrument, or rules of court, renders the document void j (in which case it is wholly ineffective) or irregular (in which case it can, but not necessarily will, none the less be valid) inevitably depends upon the language used and the purpose of the document and the requirement, and the provisions of which the relevant provisions form part.

[24] Some guidance to the correct approach can be gathered from the decision of this court in *Secretary of State for Trade and Industry v Langridge* [1991] 3 All ER 591, [1991] Ch 402. In that case, Balcombe LJ suggested that a useful approach in

the context of a statutory requirement was to consider the following four
questions:

> '(1) What is the scope and purpose of the ... Act? (2) What is the importance
> of the [the requirement as I have called it]? (3) What is the relation of that
> requirement to the general object intended to be secured by the ... Act?
> (4) What are the relevant circumstances of the present case?' (See [1991]
> 3 All ER 591 at 596, [1991] Ch 402 at 411–412.)

The fourth question must, I think, only relate to the issue of how the court should
exercise its discretion if the document is irregular, rather than to the question of
whether it is irregular or a nullity.

[25] In the present case, it appears to me that the language of the relevant rule
and of the prescribed forms, the purpose of the time limit, and policy
considerations all point in favour of a warrant which has been issued prematurely
being a nullity rather than irregular. The way in which CCR Ord 26, r 17(2) is
worded makes it clear that there is no question of a claimant having a contingent
right to a warrant as soon as the possession order is made, with a fetter on that
right, namely having to wait until the date for possession comes up. It is expressed
in a way that indicates that there is simply no right in a claimant to seek a warrant
until the date for possession has passed and possession has not been delivered up.
To my mind, that is a different position from that in *Langridge's* case, where a
ten-day notice had to be served before proceedings could be issued. The effect of
the statutory language, as construed by the majority of the Court of Appeal, was
that, at the date of issue, the right to issue proceedings had indeed arisen, but that
a prior procedural step should have been taken. However, that step, the service
of the ten-day notice, was not mandatory. In this case on the other hand, it is, as
it were, of the essence of a warrant for possession that it only can be brought into
existence after the date ordered for possession has passed.

[26] So far as the prescribed forms are concerned, the importance of the date
for possession having passed before a warrant can be issued could not be clearer.
On the face of the application for the warrant, form N325, the claimant must
formally and unambiguously certify that possession has not been given up in
accordance with the order. Even more crucially, in the most important part of
the warrant itself, form N49, the bailiff is ordered to deliver possession to the
claimant 'now'. In other words, the warrant for possession, which is essentially
an internal document passing within the court office, from a member of the court
issuing staff to the bailiffs' department, requires possession to be delivered by the
bailiff effectively at once. In my view, it is not possible to marry up that
mandatory direction in the operative part of the warrant with the notion that the
warrant would be valid if it was issued before it was lawful for the bailiff to deliver
possession to the claimant.

[27] Further, it appears to me that it would be inconvenient and unsatisfactory
if a claimant could apply for a warrant before the date for possession had arrived.
It would mean that the bailiffs' diary at every county court would be taken up
with appointments which would turn out to be unnecessary because the
defendant subsequently vacates on the date fixed for possession. That would
have the undesirable effects of decreasing the efficiency of the county court
bailiffs, and of penalising claimants who observe the CCR and wait until the
possession date had passed before applying for a warrant. Furthermore, as
Kennedy LJ pointed out during argument, if a warrant for possession can be
issued before the defendant has failed to comply with the possession order, it

a could work unfairly on a defendant, because the issue of the warrant might be picked up by a credit agency. That point is reinforced when one considers that, if a warrant for possession can be issued before the defendant is in breach of the order for possession, then it would seem to follow that a warrant for failure to deliver up goods, or a warrant of execution in the case of a debt could be issued prematurely. In this context, CCR Ord 26, r 16, and forms N323 and N46, for

b delivery up of goods, and CCR Ord 26, r 1 and forms N323 and N42, for execution on a debt appear to raise the same points as those I have raised in relation to CCR Ord 26, r 17 and forms N325 and N49. The consequences in terms of credit rating are, I would have thought, even more apparent in those other types of cases.

c [28] In light of these considerations, I do not accept that a warrant, which was plainly invalid and also unenforceable in accordance with its terms when issued, can or should subsequently achieve validity. It also seems to me unfair to impose on the defendant an obligation to apply to set aside an invalid warrant, failing which it would be enforceable against him, but that is what the judge's conclusion on this point would involve. After all, the majority of orders for possession made

d in the county court are in respect of homes belonging to relatively poor and unsophisticated individuals, in favour of landlords who are frequently substantial reasonably sophisticated organisations, and who will almost always have access to legal advice.

[29] It is true that it would appear to flow from the conclusion, that a prematurely issued warrant is invalid, that a bailiff purporting to execute such a

e warrant may be liable for wrongful execution. In the first place, it is not easy to see what damages could normally be claimed, if the premature warrant was executed after the date possession had been ordered. The defendant would have had no right to remain in the premises, and while the warrant would be, in my view, void, he would be very unlikely, as I see it, to suffer any damage by the

f mere fact of having been evicted pursuant to an invalid warrant. Secondly, if no claim could be made against a bailiff because the warrant was invalid, it might lead to the conclusion that a defendant would have no claim if the warrant was not merely issued prematurely, but was also executed prematurely (which is perfectly possible given that the warrant directs the bailiff to execute possession straight away). That would be a surprising and unfair outcome. Thirdly, if, as

g I think, no county court should ever issue a warrant for possession until the date for possession has passed, it appears to me that, while the bailiffs are entitled to all the protection the courts can properly give them, their complaint if they are sued as a result of executing an invalid warrant is not against the state of the law, but against the county court for wrongly issuing such a warrant. Fourthly, as the

h warrant must record the day, indeed the time, on which the warrant was applied for, the bailiff can see from the face of the warrant whether it was applied for prematurely.

[30] For these reasons, I am of the view that the warrant in the present case was invalid, and that it must follow that Mr Tuohy could not have been in

j contempt of court for having obstructed its execution. It should be added that if I had thought that the warrant was merely irregular, then the judge would have been right in concluding that Mr Tuohy's behaviour, namely keeping the door to the premises locked, refusing to let the bailiffs into the premises, and refusing to vacate the premises, constituted contempt of court, particularly as the evidence establishes that he was plainly warned at the time that the bailiffs were executing a court order.

Contempt and the order for possession

[31] I turn to consider whether the judge was entitled to commit Mr Tuohy on the grounds of his failure to comply with the order for possession. In this connection, it appears to me that, at least where an order for possession requires a defendant to deliver up possession of a particular property on or before a particular date, a defendant who fails to comply with such an order may be guilty of contempt of court. That is the effect of the CCR. CCR Order 26, r 18 states that the provisions of rr 16 and 17 (which provide for orders for delivery of goods and orders for possession of land to be enforceable by warrants) 'shall [not] prejudice any power to enforce a judgment or order for the delivery of goods or the recovery of land by an order of committal.'

[32] Further, CCR Ord 29, r 1(1) provides:

> 'Where a person required by a judgment or order to do an act refuses or neglects to do it within the time fixed by the judgment or order ... then, subject ... to the provisions of these rules, the judgment or order may be enforced, by order of the judge, by a committal order against that person ...'

Particularly in light of the way in which the possession order was phrased in the present case, I think that it is plain from the language of the rule that CCR Ord 29, r 1(1) applies to that order.

[33] Quite apart from this, the fact that a defendant's failure to comply with an order which requires him to give possession by a certain date can amount to contempt is supported by a number of matrimonial cases, where one of the spouses or former spouses has obtained an order for sale with vacant possession of the former matrimonial home. A comparatively recent example is the decision of this court in *Jolly v Hull, Jolly v Jolly* [2000] 2 FLR 69. An earlier case, to which I have already referred, is *Danchevsky v Danchevsky* [1974] 3 All ER 934, [1975] Fam 17, where, although the Court of Appeal reversed the judge's order committing the husband to prison, it is clear that all three members of the Court of Appeal considered that he was in contempt of court. The only issue was the appropriate way of dealing with the problem. The case is also important in the present context because it emphasises that committing a defendant for failing to deliver up possession in accordance with a court order is very much of a last resort, and is only appropriate in exceptional cases. Lord Denning MR said ([1974] 3 All ER 934 at 937, [1975] Fam 17 at 22): 'Whenever there is a reasonable alternative available instead of committal to prison, that alternative must be taken.'

[34] The principal grounds for attacking the judge's decision to commit Mr Tuohy to prison on the basis of his failure to deliver up possession in accordance with the order of 11 July may be characterised as technical or procedural. I do not intend that description to be pejorative: particularly in the context of an application for a committal order, the respondent, whose liberty is under threat, is entitled to expect the requirements laid down in the rules of court and practice directions to be complied with.

[35] The first point taken on behalf of Mr Tuohy in this connection is that there was no penal notice attached to the possession order, ie no notice specifically warning him that, in the event of his failing to comply with the order, he would be at risk of being fined or sent to prison for contempt of court. In this connection, it is necessary to consider the provisions of CCR Ord 29 in a little detail.

[36] I have already referred to r 1(1). Order 29, r 1 continues:

a '(2) Subject to paragraphs (6) and (7), a judgment or order shall not be enforced under paragraph (1) unless—(a) a copy of the judgment or order has been served personally on the person required to do or abstain from doing the act in question ...

(3) Where a judgment or order enforceable by a committal order under paragraph (1) has been given or made, the court officer shall, if the judgment
b or order is in the nature of an injunction, at the time when the judgment or order is drawn up, and in any other case on the request of the judgment creditor, issue a copy of the judgment or order, indorsed with or incorporating a notice as to the consequences of disobedience, for service in accordance with paragraph (2).

c (4) If the person served with the judgment or order fails to obey it, the judgment creditor may issue ... an application notice seeking the committal for contempt of court of that person and subject to paragraph (7), the claim form or application notice shall be served on him personally ...

(6) A judgment or order requiring a person to abstain from doing an act may be enforced under paragraph (1) notwithstanding that service of a copy
d of the judgment or order has not been effected in accordance with paragraph (2) if the judge is satisfied that, pending such service, the person against whom it is sought to enforce the judgment or order has had notice thereof either—(a) by being present when the judgment or order was given or made; or (b) by being notified of the terms of the judgment or order whether by
e telephone, telegram or otherwise.

(7) ... the court may dispense with service of a copy of a judgment or order under paragraph (2) or a claim form or application notice under paragraph (4) if the court thinks it just to do so.'

[37] These provisions appear to me to raise a number of relevant questions.
f First, it is somewhat difficult to identify what is meant by a 'judgment or order ... in the nature of an injunction' in para (3): it appears to extend more widely than injunctions, but it is a little difficult to discern how much further it goes. It was suggested in argument that it would cover all orders which required a defendant to do or not to do something, but that cannot be right. It is inconsistent with the opening words of CCR Ord 29, r 1(1). Further, with the exception of a declaration,
g any order of the court against a defendant requires him to do something or to abstain from doing something. In any event such a wide meaning would leave no room for 'any other case'. In my view, at least in the context of para (3), the words 'in the nature of an injunction' should be interpreted relatively narrowly, and they do not include an order for possession. The notion that the expression
h is to be construed narrowly is supported by the decision of this court in Re P (Minors) (Custody Order: Penal Notice) [1990] 1 WLR 613. In that case, the county court had made a consent order giving joint custody of two children to the parents, with care and control to the mother. The order directed that the children should not be removed from England and Wales, and, on the basis of that provision, the
j county court judge ordered the inclusion of a penal notice pursuant to CCR Ord 29, r 1(3). The Court of Appeal (at 615 per Lloyd LJ) held that, although the provision was part of a court order, and it clearly prohibited the parties to the proceedings from doing something, it was 'neither an injunction nor in the nature of an injunction'.

[38] More specifically in relation to the present case, if an order for possession is an order 'in the nature of an injunction', then it would seem to follow from the

plain words of para (3) that every order for possession should, as a matter of course, have a penal notice attached. Such a suggestion would, I believe, cause surprise, even consternation, in every county court in England and Wales. It would mean that, for over 15 years, virtually every possession order that has been issued out of a county court has failed to comply with the CCR. Quite apart from this, I cannot believe that it could have been the intention of those who drafted the CCR that every possession order made by the county court should routinely contain a penal notice. The majority, indeed I suspect the great majority, of possession orders made in the county court are in respect of the defendant's home. It is upsetting enough for a person to receive a court order requiring him to leave his home; it would add to the pressure if he was warned that, if he did not leave on the date specified in the order, he would be liable to be put in prison. Many people against whom possession orders are made hope, expect, or are entitled, to be re-housed by the council, and I believe that it often happens that their re-housing cannot be arranged until after the date on which the possession order is to take effect. The worry of a person who has been served with an order with a penal notice in that situation is self-evident. Further, the notion that a penal notice should routinely be attached to a possession order also appears to me to be inconsistent with the view expressed by Lord Denning MR in *Danchevsky v Danchevsky* [1974] 3 All ER 934 at 937, [1975] Fam 17 at 22.

[39] The second difficulty with CCR Ord 29 is that it is unclear from para (3) whether a judgment creditor can require a judgment or order to be reissued with a penal notice, if it was originally issued without a penal notice. I would have thought that the answer is in the affirmative, although there is an argument for saying that, once a judgment has been issued, it cannot be issued again.

[40] A third problem is that the consequence of there being no penal notice, appears to be rather left in the air. There is obviously a strong argument for saying that the intention of CCR Ord 29, r 1, read as a whole, is that if a claimant wishes to apply to commit a defendant for contempt under CCR Ord 29, r 1, then, subject to the dispensing provisions in that rule, the order must have a penal notice attached, and the purpose of para (3) is to ensure that a penal notice is attached on every order 'in the nature of an injunction' and to leave it to the claimant to apply for the attachment of a penal notice in any other case. While I consider that view is correct, and seems to have been assumed to be correct in previous cases (eg *Jolly v Hull, Jolly v Jolly* [2000] 2 FLR 69), it involves implying words into CCR Ord 29 which are not, strictly speaking, there.

[41] A fourth unsatisfactory feature of CCR Ord 29 is the strange relationship between paras (6) and (7). The former paragraph appears to give the court the power to dispense with service of a copy of the judgment, but only in a case where the order is prohibitory and only where the defendant has been appropriately notified of the order. It is not entirely easy to see the point of that limited exception given that there is a general power to dispense with service of a judgment, as appears to be the effect of para (7). To my mind, the way to reconcile the provisions, is that the terms of para (6) emphasise that the more general power in para (7) is to be exercised relatively sparingly, but it is fair to say that para (7) is expressed in terms of a wide and unfettered discretion.

[42] In *Sofroniou v Szgetti* [1991] FCR 332 at 334, McCowan LJ suggested that 'the dispensing power provided by para (7) is intended to be exercised prospectively'. However, that obiter observation cannot stand in light of the decision of this court in *Jolly's* case [2000] 2 FLR 69 at 75, where it was stated (per Judge LJ) that the paragraph entitled the court 'to proceed to consider a proper notice of

a application to commit notwithstanding the absence of a penal notice on the judgment itself'.

[43] A fifth point which can be made about CCR Ord 29 is that it seems curious that service of the copy judgment under para (2) and service of the application under para (4) can be dispensed with, but there is nothing which specifically provides that service of the penal notice under para (3) can be dispensed *b* with. Given the way in which para (3) is worded, it appears to me that the answer is that, given that the order is to be 'endorsed with or incorporating' the penal notice, dispensation with the service of the order carries with it dispensation of service of the penal notice. That still leaves one with the conundrum that, if the order is served without a penal notice, then it could be said that there can be no need to dispense under para (7) with service of the order, and therefore there is *c* no power to dispense with service of the penal notice, because there is no express reference to para (3) in para (7). While, as a matter of pure language, that point has force, I do not consider that it is right, and, even if I thought it was right, it seems to me that we would be bound to reject it on the basis that the point was considered and rejected by this court in *Jolly's* case [2000] 2 FLR 69 at 77 per Peter *d* Gibson LJ.

[44] In these circumstances, I consider that it would not have been open to the judge to commit Mr Tuohy to prison for breach of the order for possession, unless it was proper for him to have exercised his power, under CCR Ord 29, r 1(7), to dispense with the requirement that the possession order should have been served with a penal notice before Mr Tuohy could have been committed for *e* breaching it.

[45] I now turn to the defects relied on by Mr Tuohy in connection with the contempt application. They are as follows: (1) The wrong form was used for the contempt application: because these were insolvency proceedings, a form of application prescribed by the Insolvency Rules 1986, SI 1985/1925, and not by the *f* CCR, should have been used. (2) The contempt application did not state that the application was made in the proceedings in question and contain the same 'title and reference number' as that on the order for possession, contrary to para 2.2(3) of CCR PD 29. (3) The application failed to 'set out in full the grounds on which the committal application is made', and it failed to 'identify, separately ... each alleged act of contempt' as required by r 2.6(2) of PD 29: thus, it failed specifically *g* to identify the refusal to unlock the door, the keeping out of the bailiffs, and the refusal to vacate the premises. (4) Also in breach of para 2.6(2) of PD 29, the trustee failed to 'identify ... numerically, each alleged act of contempt'. (5) The application did not comply with para 2.6(5) of PD 29, which requires such an application to 'contain a prominent notice stating the possible consequences of the *h* court making a committal order and of the respondent not attending the hearing'.

[46] Where an application is made to commit a defendant for contempt of court, it is obviously important that great care is taken by the applicant and his advisers to ensure that all the procedural requirements are met. As the respondent's liberty is at risk, there will always be a substantial risk that the court will not be *j* prepared to commit him to prison, however much he may be in contempt of court, on the basis of an application which is procedurally defective. On the other hand, a person who is in contempt of court and who should otherwise be committed to prison, cannot expect to avoid being committed simply because of some defect in the procedure which in no way has prejudiced him.

[47] In this connection, the modern approach of the court to the exercise of its discretion to waive technical and procedural defects in contempt applications has

been authoritatively described by Lord Woolf MR in *Nicholls v Nicholls* [1997] 2 All ER 97 at 108, [1997] 1 WLR 314 at 326, in the following terms:

> 'Like any other discretion, the discretion provided by the statutory provisions must be exercised in a way which in all the circumstances best reflects the requirements of justice. In determining this the court must not only take into account the interests of the contemnor but also the interests of the other parties and the interests of upholding the reputation of civil justice in general. Today it is no longer appropriate to regard an order for committal as being no more than a form of execution available to another party against an alleged contemnor. The court itself has a very substantial interest in seeing that its orders are upheld. If committal orders are to be set aside on purely technical grounds which have nothing to do with the justice of the case, then this has the effect of undermining the system of justice and the credibility of the court orders. While the procedural requirements in relation to applications to commit and committal orders are there to be obeyed and to protect the contemnor, if there is non-compliance with the requirements which does not prejudice the contemnor, to set aside the order purely on the grounds of technicality is contrary to the interests of justice. As long as the order made by the judge was a valid order, the approach of this court will be to uphold the order in the absence of any prejudice or injustice to the contemnor as a consequence of doing so.'

[48] Consistently with this approach, there is the general dispensing power given to the court under CCR Ord 29, r 1(7) so far as compliance with paras (2), (3) and (4) of Ord 29, r 1 are concerned. As to compliance with the provisions of CCR PD 29, para 10 is in these terms:

> 'The court may waive any procedural defect in the commencement or conduct of a committal application if satisfied that no injustice has been caused to the respondent by the defect.'

[49] It is always a cause for concern if there are any technical or procedural defects in a contempt application. In the present case, it is of particular concern that counsel on behalf of Mr Tuohy has been able to identify so many different defects, and it is not surprising that he advances the argument that the combination of defects in the present case are such that the judge should not have committed Mr Tuohy. However, at least for my part, I think it is wrong simply to conclude that, because there are so many defects in the application, it must have been unsafe to commit Mr Tuohy to prison. The proper approach is to consider each of the defects relied on by Mr Tuohy, and to describe whether they caused any prejudice or unfairness to him, taken separately or together.

[50] The failure to use the right form can have caused no conceivable prejudice to Mr Tuohy: the information on the two forms is the same. The difference in the action number does not seem to me to be a good point. Both the order for possession and the committal application were headed with the reference numbers of the bankruptcy proceedings of Mr Tuohy and Mrs Tuohy (albeit in a different order). The fact that the application has an additional reference does not appear to me to represent a breach of para 2.2(3) of CCR PD 29. If that is wrong, it cannot be, and has not been, suggested that any conceivable prejudice was thereby caused to Mr Tuohy.

[51] As to the failure to identify in the application the precise nature of the breaches of the order relied on, and the failure to number those breaches, I believe

a that is also a complaint with no real merit. The words in the application identify what is relied on, namely that Mr Tuohy failed to comply with the order of 11 July, and the reference to his failure to comply with the warrant for possession made it clear what was being complained of, namely his failure to deliver up possession. As it is conceded, quite rightly in my view, that the failure to deliver up possession was a continuing breach of the court order with effect from

b 11 October, it appears to me that the reference in the contempt application to failing to deliver up possession on 15 October was perfectly apt. In any event, on the facts of this case, there is not the slightest possibility of Mr Tuohy having been in any doubt at all as to what was being complained of when he was served with the contempt application.

c [52] The strongest points available to Mr Tuohy are based on CCR Ord 29, r 1(3) and para 2.6(5) of CCR PD 29. Mr Tuohy was not given notice when first served with the possession order or thereafter (if the order should have been reissued with a penal notice, after it was first served on him) or in the committal application itself, that non-compliance with the possession order could lead to his being committed to prison for contempt of court. Those are serious defects, the

d combination of which would often be easily enough on their own to persuade the court that it would be quite wrong to commit a respondent. However, on the unusual facts of this case, I am satisfied that there is nothing in those failures which prejudiced Mr Tuohy in any way.

[53] The purpose of giving notice in writing to a defendant to the effect that

e his failure to comply with a court order could lead to his being sent to prison, is to bring home to him the terms of the court order and the seriousness of his failing to comply with that order, and to give him a proper opportunity to consider his position, to take advice, and to make appropriate arrangements. In the present case, I think that, by the time the judge decided to commit Mr Tuohy, he had had every possible opportunity to appreciate and consider his position,

f and it is quite unrealistic to think that he would have been any better off on 5 November, if he had been served with a penal notice on the possession order or on the application, or, indeed, if any of the other defects had not occurred.

[54] First, Mr Tuohy was very well aware of the existence of the order for possession, the fact that it required him to give up possession of the premises on

g 11 October, and his duty to comply with it. He was in court when the order for possession was made by the district judge on 11 July. He was, I think, served with the order for possession. He knew of the warrant and its effect, because he made an application to set aside the warrant for possession on 3 October. He was specifically told that he should give up possession by the bailiff on 15 October. It

h was clear from terms of the contempt application that this was his obligation. The judge made it very clear to him on 22 October that he was obliged to vacate the premises, and, indeed, repeated the point to him in very clear terms at the hearing of 5 November.

[55] Secondly, Mr Tuohy was very well aware, and had been very clearly

j warned, of the risk of his being committed to prison if he did not comply with the court order, and in particular if he did not vacate the premises. That was spelt out to him in terms by the bailiff on 15 October. It would also have been clear to him from the contempt application which specifically asked for him to be committed to prison for contempt because he had failed to comply with the order. Further, it was spelt out to him unambiguously by the judge at the hearing of 22 October, and, more than once on 5 November.

[56] Thirdly, as is stated in the judgment, Mr Tuohy himself had told the judge on 5 November that he had well understood the position, and, indeed, had had every opportunity to consider it. Not only had his obligations and the risks he was running been pointed out on a number of occasions, most obviously by the judge himself on 22 October, but Mr Tuohy had the benefit of counsel's advice. In the passage I have already quoted from the judgment, the judge recorded that Mr Tuohy said on 5 November that he would not leave the premises without being thrown out or being sent to prison, and that this was not merely his 'final decision' but that it had been 'carefully considered'.

[57] In my opinion the judge was right not to seek to deal with the contempt application on 22 October. Not only was it sensible to adjourn the application to enable Mr Tuohy to obtain legal representation and advice; it was also correct to give Mr Tuohy a clear and unambiguous warning that he should comply with the order for possession and that, if he did not do so, he would risk being sent to prison when the application was renewed, namely on 5 November. In light of the procedural defects, and in particular the absence of penal notices on the possession order and the application, it may well have been wrong for the judge to have committed Mr Tuohy on 22 October. However, by 5 November, any conceivable prejudice to Mr Tuohy arising out of the absence of written notice of the risks he was running had been wholly dissipated.

[58] In these circumstances, I consider that it would have been inconsistent with the approach laid down by the Court of Appeal in *Nicholls v Nicholls* [1997] 2 All ER 97, [1997] 1 WLR 314, if on 5 November the judge had decided that he did not have jurisdiction to commit Mr Tuohy for not having complied with the order for possession, if only for a short period for the purpose of enabling possession to be obtained. Indeed, in light of Mr Tuohy's obdurate and expressed determination not to give up possession, it seems to me that the judge was reasonable in his conclusion that he should send Mr Tuohy to prison for a short time to enable possession to be obtained without the risk of violence.

[59] Thus, it appears to me that this was one of those exceptional cases where the court was left with little alternative but to commit a defendant to prison simply for the purpose of enabling the court's order to be executed effectively and peacefully. In this connection, we were told that many county courts do not now encourage or even permit their bailiffs to resort to physical coercion against the people in possession of premises when executing a warrant for possession. If that is right, then it may mean that applications to commit defendants against whom possession orders have been made, and who thwart execution of such orders, will, or already have, become more common. I think it is sensible to take this opportunity to emphasise that, at any rate in my view, the appropriate points to bear in mind in such cases are as follows. First, committal for contempt of court in any such case is a last resort. Secondly, it is generally undesirable that a penal notice should be attached to a possession order, unless there are good and exceptional grounds. Thirdly, the normal way to enforce a possession order is by requesting and obtaining the issue of a warrant for possession. Fourthly, as this case shows, a warrant should be applied for only after the date for possession has gone without the defendant vacating. Fifthly, if the last resort of a contempt application appears necessary, then it is normally more appropriate for the contempt application to be based primarily on the defendant's obstruction of the bailiff when executing the warrant for possession, albeit that in some cases it may be right to rely on the possession order itself. In such a case, it would then be sensible to serve a copy of the order for possession with a penal notice, albeit only

once the warrant has not been successfully executed due to the defendant's obstruction. Sixthly, to avoid the risk of wasting costs or of unfairness on a defendant, care should be taken to ensure that any committal proceedings comply with the requirements of the rules and PD 29.

Contempt and the refusal to vacate on 5 November

[60] The fact that Mr Tuohy said in court in the clearest possible terms on 5 November that he would not vacate the premises was a factor which the judge was entitled, indeed obliged, to take into account when considering whether committal was an appropriate way of dealing with Mr Tuohy's contempt in failing to give up possession in accordance with the order of 11 July 2001. In effect, the judge was entitled to treat his behaviour as an aggravating factor, in the same way as he was entitled to treat Mrs Tuohy's change of heart as a mitigating factor.

[61] However, the narrower point which has to be considered is whether, taken on its own as it were, Mr Tuohy's statement in court on 5 November, to the effect that he would continue not to comply with the court order requiring him to give up possession of the premises, itself constituted a contempt of court for which he should have been committed.

[62] On behalf of the trustee, it is contended that the judge had power to commit Mr Tuohy for his statement on 5 November in court that he would not comply with the order for possession, by virtue of s 118(1) of the County Courts Act 1984. This provides:

> 'If any person—(a) wilfully insults the judge of a county court ... during his sitting or attendance in court ... or (b) wilfully interrupts the proceedings of a county court or otherwise misbehaves in court; any officer of the court, with or without the assistance of any other person, may, by order of the judge, take the offender into custody and detain him until the rising of the court, and the judge may, if he thinks fit ... (i) ... [commit] the offender for a specified period not exceeding one month ... or (ii) impose upon the offender ... a fine ... or may both make such an order and impose such a fine.'

[63] In my judgment, it is impossible to state as a general proposition whether or not a statement by a defendant in open court that he will not comply with a court order amounts to 'wilfully insult[ing]' the judge. At one extreme, one could conceive of a defendant, against whom the judge has just made an order for possession of his home in 28 days, saying that he will not go voluntarily, and will have to be evicted. To my mind, it would be wrong to regard such a statement, particularly made in the heat of the moment, as amounting to more than a statement of a present intention to do what could amount to a contempt. Of itself, it could not seriously be said to risk bringing the court into disrepute, or even to amount to a serious challenge to the authority of the court, let alone to constitute an interruption to the orderly conduct of the court, which are the sort of considerations which lie behind s 118. As I see it, such an outburst should, at the most, be met by a warning from the judge that failing to comply with a court order, and in particular obstructing the bailiff executing a valid warrant, could amount to a contempt of court and could lead to the defendant's committal.

[64] At the other end of the scale, one can envisage a case where the order for possession has expired, the execution of a valid warrant has been unlawfully impeded, and the defendant having been properly warned of the consequences, rudely and unambiguously maintains in open court his intention to thwart any

attempts to execute the order for possession. In my judgment, such behaviour would fall within the ambit of s 118 because the circumstances and manner of the refusal to comply with the court order would be such that the defendant would be insulting the court; the defendant would be openly and wilfully challenging and denying the authority of the judge in open court.

[65] I think that the right conclusion in the circumstances of this particular case, is that Mr Tuohy's behaviour in court on 5 November fell on what, from his point of view, was the wrong side of the line. It is true that, although the circumstances were such that Mr Tuohy had apparently impeded the execution of a warrant for possession, the warrant was in fact invalid, and that Mr Tuohy was not noisy or disruptive in court. However, it had been made clear to him on a number of previous occasions that his failure to deliver up possession after 11 October not only involved him being in persistent breach of the order for possession, but also put him in contempt of court, and liable to be imprisoned. Having considered the matter carefully, he maintained his defiance of the court, not merely in refusing to deliver up possession, but in telling the judge that he would continue to do so and risk going to prison, even though the judge gave him a number of opportunities at the hearing of 5 November to reconsider his position. In my view, that behaviour brought Mr Tuohy within the ambit of s 118 of the 1984 Act.

[66] Having said that, if this had been the only ground for committing Mr Tuohy to prison, either on the assumption that there had been no application to commit for breach of the order for possession or because the judge had concluded that the defects in the committal application had prejudiced Mr Tuohy, I rather doubt that it would have been appropriate to commit Mr Tuohy to prison there and then for what, on this hypothesis, would have been his only contempt, namely his open and defiant refusal to comply with the court order. On this hypothesis, I think it would have been appropriate for the judge to have adjourned the matter for a further period with a view to a proper application to commit being prepared and served on Mr Tuohy.

Conclusion

[67] In these circumstances, I do not consider that the judge was entitled to commit Mr Tuohy to prison for impeding the execution of the warrant, and I rather doubt that it would have been appropriate to commit Mr Tuohy solely for his defiance of the court on 5 November. However, on the very unusual facts of this case, I am of the view that the judge was entitled, indeed right, to commit Mr Tuohy to prison for a very short period for his contempt in refusing to comply with the order for possession, notwithstanding the trustee's failure to comply in a number of respects with the provisions of the CCR and PD 29.

[68] In these circumstances, I would dismiss this appeal

MANTELL LJ.

[69] As was shown by *Nicholls v Nicholls* [1997] 2 All ER 97 at 103, [1997] 1 WLR 314 at 321 per Lord Woolf MR (as he then was):

'While these requirements on Ord 29, r 1 are there to be observed, in the absence of authority to the contrary, even though the liberty of the subject is involved, we would not expect the requirements to be mandatory, in the sense that any non-compliance with the rule means that a committal for contempt is irremediably invalid.'

[70] And since I would regard the procedure required under CCR Ord 29, r 1 (as set out in CPR Sch 2) as being at least as fundamental as any contained in CCR Ord 26, I would not consider the warrant for possession to be a nullity, irregular though it certainly was. The warrant was never set aside and no application to have it set aside was ever made. As its execution after due date occasioned no prejudice to Mr and Mrs Tuohy I would uphold the judge's ruling that to resist the bailiff as was done in this case amounted to a contempt of court. To that extent I would respectfully differ from Neuberger J.

[71] Otherwise I am in total agreement with his conclusions and the reasons for them. Accordingly, I too, would dismiss this appeal.

KENNEDY LJ.

[72] I agree with the judgment of Neuberger J, and I too would dismiss this appeal.

Appeal dismissed.

Dilys Tausz　Barrister.

R (on the application of Carson) v Secretary of State for Work and Pensions

[2002] EWHC 978 (Admin)

ADMINISTRATIVE COURT

STANLEY BURNTON J

15, 16 APRIL, 8, 22 MAY 2002

Social security – Retirement pension – Inflation uprating – Claimant not entitled to inflation uprating of state pension because of residence in South Africa – Whether freeze on claimant's pension infringing her human rights – Human Rights Act 1998, Sch 1, Pt I, art 14, Pt II, art 1.

The claimant, who was resident in South Africa, had spent most of her working life in England and was in receipt of a United Kingdom state retirement pension. Like other United Kingdom pensioners resident in the countries of the so-called Old Commonwealth, the claimant was disqualified by the relevant domestic legislation from receiving the annual inflation uprating of her pension to which she would have been entitled if she had still been living in the United Kingdom. Such increases were payable, however, to United Kingdom pensioners living in certain other countries under the provisions of reciprocal agreements between those countries and the United Kingdom. The claimant brought proceedings for judicial review against the Secretary of State, contending that her state pension, or its uprating, were pecuniary rights; that they therefore constituted 'possessions' within the meaning of art 1[a] of the First Protocol to the European Convention for the Protection of Human Rights and Fundamental Freedoms 1950 (as set out in Sch 1 to the Human Rights Act 1998); and that the failure to pay the uprating breached that provision by wrongfully depriving her of her 'possessions'. She further contended that the freezing of her pension infringed art 14[b] of the convention, which prohibited discrimination in the enjoyment of convention rights on grounds 'such as sex, race ... or other status'. In particular, she contended that she been the subject of discrimination, on the ground of her residence in South Africa, as compared with pensioners resident in the United Kingdom and in other countries in which the uprating was paid.

Held – The failure to pay the claimant the inflation uprating of her United Kingdom state pension did not contravene the convention. A pecuniary right that might qualify as a possession for the purposes of art 1 of the First Protocol was defined by domestic law, and in the instant case United Kingdom legislation had never conferred a right on the claimant to the uprating of her pension while she lived in South Africa. There could therefore be no question of her having been deprived of any such right, and accordingly there had been no infringement of art 1. As for art 14, that provision would be infringed by a domestic law which disqualified an individual from enjoyment of a pecuniary right of a kind protected by art 1 on grounds prohibited by art 14 without objective and reasonable

---

a   Article 1 is set out at [8], below
b   Article 14 is set out at [11], below

a justification, and in the instant case there was clearly a difference in treatment based on residence, which was a ground within the scope of art 14. However, taking into account their social and economic circumstances and needs, the chosen comparators were not in an analogous situation to the claimant. Accordingly, the application would be dismissed (see [45], [48], [49], [54], [57], [59], [65]–[67], [77], below); *Gaygusuz v Austria* (1996) 23 EHRR 365 considered.

b   Per curiam. A government may lawfully decide to restrict the payment of benefits of any kind to those living within it territorial jurisdiction. Such a restriction may be based wholly or partly on considerations of cost, but it is not unreasonable or lacking in objective justification having regard to the wide margin of discretion that must be accorded to the government. Similarly, the government is entitled to consider the payment of uprated pensions to those living abroad on a country-
c by-country basis, taking into account the interests of the United Kingdom in each case (see [73], [74], below).

Notes

For the convention prohibition of discrimination and the right to property, see
d 8(2) *Halsbury's Laws* (4th edn reissue) paras 164, 165.

For the Human Rights Act 1998, Sch 1, Pt I, art 14, Pt II, art 1, see 7 *Halsbury's Statutes* (4th edn) (1999 reissue) 525.

Cases referred to in judgment

Air Canada v UK (1995) 20 EHRR 150, [1995] ECHR 18465/91, ECt HR.
e *Bankovic v Belgium* (2001) 11 BHRC 435, ECt HR.
Bell v Todd [2002] Lloyd's Rep Med 12.
Bellet v France App no 23805/94 (4 December 1995, unreported), ECt HR.
Blackburn v A-G [1971] 2 All ER 1380, [1971] 1 WLR 1037, CA.
Brunswick (Duke of) v King of Hanover (1844) 6 Beav 1.
f *Coke v UK* App no 38696/97 (9 September 1998, unreported), E Com HR.
Corner v UK App no 11271/84 (17 May 1985, unreported), E Com HR.
Darby v Sweden (1990) 13 EHRR 774, [1990] ECHR 11581/85, ECt HR.
Drozd v France (1992) 14 EHRR 745, ECt HR.
Gaygusuz v Austria (1996) 23 EHRR 365, ECt HR.
g *Havard v UK* App no 38882/97 (22 October 1998, unreported), E Com HR.
Inze v Austria (1987) 10 EHRR 394, [1987] ECHR 8695/79, ECt HR.
Jankovic v Croatia App no 43440/98 (12 October 2000, unreported), ECt HR.
JW v UK (1983) 34 DR 153, E Com HR.
Maclaine Watson & Co Ltd v Dept of Trade and Industry, Maclaine Watson & Co Ltd v
       International Tin Council [1989] 3 All ER 523, sub nom *JH Rayner (Mincing*
h   *Lane) Ltd v Dept of Trade and Industry, Maclaine Watson & Co Ltd v Dept of Trade*
       and Industry, Maclaine Watson & Co Ltd v International Tin Council [1990] 2 AC
       418, [1989] 3 WLR 969, HL.
Matthews v UK App no 40302/98 (15 July 2002, unreported), ECt HR.
Mellacher v Austria (1989) 12 EHRR 391, ECt HR.
j *Müller v Austria* (1975) 3 DR 25, E Com HR.
Murray v UK (1996) 22 EHRR 29, E Com HR.
N v UK App no 11077/84 (13 October 1986, unreported), E Com HR.
P v UK App no 14751/89 (12 December 1990, unreported), E Com HR.
R (on the application of Alconbury Ltd) v Secretary of State for the Environment, Transport
       and the Regions [2001] UKHL 23, [2001] 2 All ER 929, [2001] 2 WLR 1389.

R (on the application of Hooper) v Secretary of State for Work and Pensions [2002]
EWHC 191 (Admin), [2002] All ER (D) 193 (Feb).
R (on the application of Reynolds) v Secretary of State for Work and Pensions [2002]
EWHC 426 (Admin), [2002] All ER (D) 64 (Mar).
R (on the application of Waite) v Hammersmith and Fulham London BC [2002] EWCA
Civ 482.
R v DPP, ex p Kebeline, R v DPP, ex p Rechachi [1999] 4 All ER 801, [2000] 2 AC 326,
[1999] 3 WLR 486, HL.
Ryan v Liverpool Health Authority [2002] Lloyd's Rep Med 23.
Shackell v UK App no 45851/99 (27 April 2000, unreported), ECt HR.
Skorkiewicz v Poland App no 39860/98 (1 June 1999, unreported), ECt HR.
Steele Ford & Newton (a firm) v CPS [1993] 2 All ER 769, [1994] 1 AC 22, [1993]
2 WLR 934, HL.
T v Sweden (1986) 8 EHRR 269, E Com HR.
Walden v Liechtenstein App no 33916/96 (16 March 2000, unreported), ECt HR.
Wandsworth London BC v Michalak [2002] EWCA Civ 271, [2002] All ER (D) 56 (Mar).
X v Federal Republic of Germany (1981) 4 EHRR 398, E Com HR.
X v Italy (1977) 11 DR 114, E Com HR.

Application for judicial review

The claimant, Annette Carson, applied for judicial review against the defendant,
the Secretary of State for Works and Pensions, in respect of the failure to pay her,
on the grounds of her residence in South Africa, the annual inflation uprating to
her United Kingdom state pension. The government of the Commonwealth of
Australia intervened in the proceedings. The facts are set out in the judgment.

Richard Drabble QC, Helen Mountfield and Murray Hunt (instructed by Thomas Eggar
Church Adams) for the claimant.
James Eadie and Khawar Qureshi (instructed by the Solicitor to the Department of Health)
for the Secretary of State.
Thomas de la Mare (instructed by Lovells) for the Australian government.

Cur adv vult

22 May 2002. The following judgment was delivered.

STANLEY BURNTON J.

INTRODUCTION

[1] These proceedings raise the important question whether the failure of the
government of the United Kingdom to pay to pensioners resident in certain
countries abroad, in the case of the claimant South Africa, the inflation uprating
of their United Kingdom state pensions contravenes the European Convention
for the Protection of Human Rights and Fundamental Freedoms 1950 (as set out
in Sch 1 to the Human Rights Act 1998).
[2] The claimant is resident in South Africa. She spent most of her working
life in England, and while she was employed she and her employer, and while she
was self-employed she alone, paid full National Insurance contributions. She has
been resident in South Africa since 1990. When she was working in South Africa

she paid voluntary contributions to protect her right to a United Kingdom state
pension. She began to draw her pension in September 2000. She receives a British
retirement pension of £103·62 per week, comprising a basic pension of £67·50, an
additional pension (under the State Earnings Related Pension Scheme, or SERPS)
of £32·17 and graduated pension of £3·95. She has not received the increase in the
basic retirement pension of £5 (from £67·50 to £72·50) that has been paid since
9 April 2001 to those entitled to it; nor has she received the percentage increase
in the additional pension and graduated pension that has been paid since that
date. It is accepted on her behalf that she is not qualified for these increases by
reason of the relevant provisions of United Kingdom legislation and delegated
legislation, apart from the 1998 Act. While the claimant remains in South Africa,
her total British pension will remain frozen at £103·62 irrespective of inflation-
based uprating of pensions for those who live in Great Britain and certain other
countries referred to below.

[3] The position of the claimant, as a recipient of a 'frozen' pension, is
representative of United Kingdom pensioners not only in South Africa, but in all
the countries of the so-called Old Commonwealth, including Australia, Canada
and New Zealand.

[4] Pensioners living in other countries, such as the United States of America,
European Union countries, the states of the former Yugoslavia, Japan, Mauritius,
Turkey, Bermuda, Jamaica and Israel, receive the same pension from the United
Kingdom government as they would receive if they lived here: ie, their basic
retirement pensions are uprated. Of some 760,000 pensioners and widow
beneficiaries who live abroad, some 330,000 receive the annual uprating. The
remainder do not. The great majority of the remainder live in the Old
Commonwealth countries mentioned above.

[5] In some respects, the position of the claimant is not representative. A
pensioner who lives abroad receives initially the full pension that he would have
received if he had remained in this country. He is denied the uprating for inflation
from the date of his emigration or if earlier the date of his qualifying for his
pension: in effect, his pension is frozen at the amount payable when he reached
65 if he had already emigrated or when he emigrated if he did so subsequently.
(If he returns to Great Britain, his uprated pension is paid while he is here, but if
he leaves his pension reverts to its previous amount.) The effect on the claimant
has so far been relatively minor: she has not received the small percentage
uprating applied in 2001. The effect on those who retired long ago is more
substantial and may be dramatic. Mr William Hayes, who lives in Australia,
reached 65 in 1972. He receives a pension of the inconsiderable sum of £6·75 a
week, less than one-tenth of the sum of £72·50 that would be paid to a pensioner
with a complete contribution record who retired last year. Someone who retired
as recently as 1990 receives only £46·90 a week.

[6] Very many of the expatriate United Kingdom pensioners who do not
receive uprated pensions have a strong and understandable sense of grievance.
They paid their contributions calculated in the same way as pensioners now
living here and in, say, the United States, yet they do not receive the same
pension. They feel that they have been deprived of an increasingly substantial
part of the fruit of their contributions. The real value, at least in the United
Kingdom, of their pensions is declining from year to year. As a result, they have
formed associations to press their cause for equal treatment. As will be seen,
before the coming into force of the 1998 Act a number of them made applications

to the European Commission of Human Rights, complaining that their rights
under art 1 of the First Protocol and under art 14 had been infringed. Their
applications were unsuccessful. However, they contend that recent developments
in the jurisprudence of the European Court of Human Rights establish that the
United Kingdom government has indeed infringed their rights under those
articles.

[7] In her second witness statement, the claimant suggested that she had not
been informed that her pension would be frozen when she decided to pay her
voluntary contributions from South Africa. That allegation has not been pursued
on her behalf. Indeed, it is clear that the literature distributed by the Department
of Social Security (and sent to her) was explicit and clear as to the position of
United Kingdom pensioners who live in South Africa. The issues pursued on
behalf of the claimant are not dependent on her individual facts, and turn on the
provisions of the applicable United Kingdom legislation and of art 1 of the First
Protocol and art 14 of the convention.

THE ISSUES

[8] Article 1 of the First Protocol is as follows:

'*Protection of Property*

Every natural or legal person is entitled to the peaceful enjoyment of his
possessions. No one shall be deprived of his possessions except in the public
interest and subject to the conditions provided for by law and by the general
principles of international law.

The preceding provisions shall not, however, in any way impair the right
of a State to enforce such laws as it deems necessary to control the use of
property in accordance with the general interest or to secure the payment of
taxes or other contributions or penalties.'

[9] In summary, the claimant's contentions under art 1 are as follows. (a) Her
state pension, or alternatively its uprating, are pecuniary rights, and therefore
'possessions' within the meaning of art 1 of the First Protocol. (b) The failure of
the United Kingdom government to pay her the amount of the annual uprating
wrongfully deprives her partly or wholly of one or other of those possessions, ie,
part of her pension and the entirety of the uprating.

[10] Mr Eadie, on behalf of the Secretary of State, accepted that the right to a
contributory pension is protected by art 1 of the First Protocol. However, he
submitted as follows. (a) Article 1 does not confer a right to a pension in any
particular amount, and is therefore not infringed by the failure to pay uprating to
the claimant. (b) The right protected by art 1 of the First Protocol is defined by
domestic law. Since United Kingdom law does not confer (and has never
conferred) a right to an uprated pension on pensioners living in South Africa, the
claimant has not been deprived of any right, and therefore of any possession,
within the meaning of art 1. (c) The decision of the government not to pay uprating
to the claimant and to those in her position is objectively and reasonably justified
and is therefore a permissible deprivation of such possession as she may have.

[11] Article 14 is as follows:

'*Prohibition of discrimination*

The enjoyment of the rights and freedoms set forth in this Convention
shall be secured without discrimination on any ground such as sex, race,

colour, language, religion, political or other opinion, national or social origin, association with a national minority, property, birth or other status.'

[12] It is common ground that there may be a breach of art 14 without there having been a breach of any other article of the convention. Clearly, art 14 adds to the protection conferred by the other provisions of the convention. It is not however every act of discrimination that is within the scope of art 14: it protects only 'the enjoyment of the rights and freedoms set forth in this Convention ...' In *Gaygusuz v Austria* (1996) 23 EHRR 365 at 380 (para 36), the court put the matter in terms that constitute a virtual formula applied in other cases:

'According to the Court's established case law, Article 14 of the Convention complements the other substantive provisions of the Convention and the Protocols. It has no independent existence since it has effect solely in relation to "the enjoyment of the rights and freedoms" safeguarded by those provisions. Although the application of Article 14 does not presuppose a breach of those provisions—and to this extent it is autonomous—there can be no room for its application unless the facts at issue fall within the ambit of one or more of them.'

[13] Mr Drabble submitted that the complaint in the present case is 'within the ambit' of art 1 of the First Protocol, not least because the right to a state pension is a right protected by art 1. He submitted that the claimant has been the subject of discrimination, on the ground of her residence in South Africa, as compared with United Kingdom pensioners living in this country and in those other countries in which uprating is paid.

[14] Mr Eadie submitted: (a) if the claimant has no possession within the meaning of art 1 of the First Protocol (as he submitted), she has no claim within the ambit of art 14 read with art 1 of the First Protocol; (b) the basis of the differential treatment of the claimant and others to whom comparison was made was not 'any ground such as sex, race ... or other status' to which art 14 applies; (c) in any event, the decision of the government not to pay uprating to the claimant and to those in her position is objectively and reasonably justified.

[15] The above submissions of the parties raise the following issues. (a) Is the state pension or the uprating a possession of the claimant within the meaning of art 1 of the First Protocol? (b) If so, is the failure or refusal of the government to pay an uprated pension to the claimant a deprivation of that possession for the purposes of art 1 of the First Protocol? (c) If so, is that deprivation justified? (d) If uprating is not a possession for the purposes of art 1 of the First Protocol, is the payment of uprating to some, but not all, pensioners none the less within the scope of art 14? ie, does the claimant's complaint relate to 'the enjoyment of the rights and freedoms set forth in [the] Convention'? (e) If so, what is the criterion applied to determine the differential treatment of pensioners? (f) Is that criterion a ground 'such as sex, race ... or other status' that is, unless objectively justified, prohibited by art 14? (g) If so, is the differential treatment of the claimant as compared with: (i) pensioners living in this country, or (ii) pensioners living in states such as the USA, whose residents are paid uprated pensions, wrongful discrimination in breach of art 14?

[16] In addition, in the course of my consideration of my judgment in this case, I concluded that an additional, and more fundamental, issue must be considered, namely whether the provisions of the convention apply to persons,

such as the claimant, who are outside the jurisdiction. That question arises by reason of the terms of art 1 of the convention, which is as follows:

'The High Contracting Parties shall secure to everyone within their jurisdiction the rights and freedoms defined in Section 1 of this Convention.'

The claimant and those like her are of course not within the territorial jurisdiction of the United Kingdom.

[17] The express jurisdictional qualification in art 1 of the convention is not expressly reflected in the provisions of the 1998 Act. If the Act is to be construed as subject to the same qualification, and art 1 refers to presence within the territorial jurisdiction of the state, the claimant is not entitled to any of the rights conferred by the convention, and she has no rights under either art 1 of the First Protocol or art 14.

[18] In these circumstances a further hearing took place on 8 May 2002 to enable the parties to make submissions on the jurisdictional issue raised by art 1. In view of its importance I consider it first.

THE JURISDICTIONAL ISSUE

[19] The natural reading of art 1 of the convention limits convention rights to persons within the territorial jurisdiction of the High Contracting Parties. Prima facie, the jurisdiction of states in international law is territorial. This presumption is part of English law: Parliament is presumed to intend an Act to extend to each territory of the United Kingdom, but not to any territory outside the United Kingdom (see Bennion *Statutory Interpretation* (3rd edn, 1997) p 252, Section 106). The comity of nations is doubtless one basis for this presumption: one state should not be taken to interfere with the sovereignty of another state by enacting legislation extending to its territory. Another is practicality: most legislation cannot practically be applied to those present in another state.

[20] However, jurisdiction need not refer simply to personal presence within the territory of a state. Rights and property may be within the jurisdiction of a state, though the owner of the right or of the property may be outside the state. The French version of art 1 of the convention differs from the English: 'Les Hautes Parties contractantes reconnaissent à toute personne *relevant de leur juridiction* les droits et libertés définis au titre I de la présente Convention' (my emphasis). The French text suggests that the High Contracting Parties undertook to accord convention rights to all persons relevant to their jurisdiction. On this basis, a person whose rights or property are within the jurisdiction of a state is entitled to such of the convention rights as apply to those rights or property. On this basis, art 1 refers not to the presence of persons within the territorial jurisdiction, but to jurisdiction in a legal sense.

[21] That this is the correct meaning to be given to art 1 is confirmed by the jurisprudence of the court as well as state practice. In none of the cases in which expatriate state pensioners have made applications to the Commission has the territorial limitation of the convention been explicitly referred to. In *Air Canada v UK* (1995) 20 EHRR 150, the European Court of Human Rights held that the seizure of an aircraft belonging to the Canadian applicant had not infringed art 1 of the First Protocol. It was not suggested that the fact that the applicant was resident in Canada affected its rights under that provision. (However, it may well be that Air Canada carried on business in the United Kingdom, and was present within

the jurisdiction in any event.) In *Drozd v France* (1992) 14 EHRR 745 at 788 (para 91),
the court said in its judgment:

> 'The term "jurisdiction" is not limited to the national territory of the High
> Contracting Parties; their responsibility can be involved because of acts of
> their authorities producing effects outside their own territory.'

In *Bankovic v Belgium* (2001) 11 BHRC 435, the court rejected as inadmissible the
complaint of the applicants that the NATO bombing in Belgrade was in breach
of, principally, art 2 of the convention. The state respondents relied on art 1 of
the convention. They submitted that jurisdiction in that provision referred to
'the assertion or exercise of legal authority, actual or purported, over persons'
(see (2001) 11 BHRC 435 at 444 (para 36) of the judgment). The court accepted
this interpretation: it referred in para 80 (at 453) of the judgment, to the convention
operating in the legal space (espace juridique) of the contracting states.

[22] In the present case, the object of the application of the convention is
legislation that confers benefits on individuals. It clearly operates in (and only in)
the 'legal space' of the United Kingdom, and is therefore within the scope of the
convention. There is no question of any possible infringement of the sovereignty
of another state or the exercise of sovereignty over those present in another state.
Mr Eadie, on behalf of the Secretary of State, did not submit that the claimant's
case fell to be rejected on the basis of jurisdiction, and it was therefore common
ground between the parties that it falls to be considered on the merits.

[23] Article 1 of the convention is not part of English law: it was not included
in Sch 1 to the 1998 Act. In the circumstances, it is unnecessary to consider the
question whether the ambit of the rights and freedoms legislated by the Act differ
from those of the convention. I am bound to say that I should be surprised if
there were any such difference.

THE UNITED KINGDOM STATUTORY PROVISIONS ON PENSIONS

[24] Of all legislation, that relating to social security should be clear and accessible.
Regrettably, the relevant provisions are typically and unnecessarily complex,
involving the application and disapplication of other provisions: compare the
comments of Munby J in *Ryan v Liverpool Health Authority* [2002] Lloyd's Rep Med 23,
and of myself in *Bell v Todd* [2002] Lloyd's Rep Med 12. The relevant provisions
are summarised and so far as necessary set out in Annex 1 to this judgment. For
present purposes, the effect of the statutory provisions may be summarised as
follows. (a) Contrary to popular perception, a person's contributions do not in
whole or in part constitute a fund from which her pension is later paid: there is
nothing in the legislation to warrant such a conclusion. (b) The basic state pension
is contributory only in the sense that the payment of sufficient contributions is a
condition of entitlement. In addition, if more than a quarter but less than the full
number of qualifying years has been achieved, a reduced rate pension is payable.
(c) Provided Parliament approves the statutory instrument that the Secretary of
State is required to put before it by virtue of s 150(9) of the Social Security and
Administration Act 1992, the basic state pension is uprated annually in line with
United Kingdom inflation. (d) However, a person who is both absent from, and
ordinarily resident outside, Great Britain is disqualified from receiving any additional
benefit payable as a result of uprating after the date she reaches retirement age or
her emigration, whichever is later. (e) It follows from (d) that a person who is
ordinarily resident abroad who returns to this country temporarily receives her

uprated pension while here; when she returns to her country of residence
however her pension reverts to its previous sum. (f) However, uprated pensions
are paid to those living in the countries referred to in [4], above, with whom the
United Kingdom has entered into reciprocal agreements and in respect of whom
appropriate Orders in Council have been made. Where it is paid, no regard is had
to inflation in the country of residence.

FINANCE AND HISTORY
   [25] The National Insurance scheme, including the payment of state pensions,
is financed on a 'pay as you go' basis, that is, current National Insurance contributions
to the National Insurance Fund (NIF), mainly from employers, employees and
the self-employed, fund current benefits. Thus a person's contributions fund not
her own benefits, but those of others. As the Social Security Committee of the
House of Commons stated in its Third Report of January 1997 (*Uprating of State
Retirement Pensions Payable to People Resident Abroad*; HC Paper 143 (the Social
Security Committee Report)) (p ix):

> '13. The reality is that National Insurance operates as a form of taxation,
> with the benefits being paid out on a pay as you go basis from a notional fund
> topped up as required by grants from the Exchequer. The record of contributions
> still serves as a control for determining the amount of pension payable, but
> even this principle has been blurred by the introduction of home responsibilities
> protection and credits, while the availability of means tested Income Support
> and Housing Benefit has to some extent replaced the old age pension itself as
> the principal defence against poverty in old age.'

   [26] The rates and levels of contributions are set each year to ensure so far as
practicable that the overall income to the NIF is sufficient to pay for the various
benefits. When necessary, the income from contributions is supplemented by a
Treasury grant, ie from general taxation. The current contribution rates naturally
do not include an allowance for uprating all retirement pensions paid to those
who have chosen to reside abroad. Given the amount required to fund payment
of pension uprating to those living in South Africa, New Zealand, Australia and
Canada, it follows that, if uprating were applicable to their pensions, either
contributions would have to be increased or the additional cost financed out of
other taxation. (I ignore, for present purposes, the possibility of borrowing to
fund the cost.)
   [27] Provision could be made by United Kingdom legislation for the payment
of uprated pensions to pensioners living abroad without the necessity of any
reciprocal agreement with their country of residence. In practice, however, uprated
pensions are paid only to those living in countries with which the United
Kingdom government has entered into a reciprocal agreement requiring their
payment.
   [28] According to the DSS Memorandum on the uprating of state retirement
pensions payable to people resident abroad submitted to the Social Security
Committee of the House of Commons (p 41):

> '17. The main purpose of reciprocal agreements so far has been to provide
> a measure of social protection for workers, and the immediate members of their
> families, when moving from one to country to the other during their
> working lives. In effect, they generally prevent such workers from having to
> contribute to both countries' Social Security schemes at the same time while
> ensuring that they retain benefit cover from either one country or the other.

On reaching pensionable age, such workers who have been insured in two or more countries' schemes can receive a pension from each which reflects the amount of their insurance in each.

18. Whether a reciprocal Social Security agreement with another country is entered into depends on various factors, among them the numbers of people moving from one country to the other, the benefits available under the other country's scheme, how far reciprocity is possible and the extent to which the advantages to be gained by an agreement outweigh the additional expenditure likely to be incurred by the UK in negotiating and implementing it. Where an agreement is in place, the flow of funds may differ depending on the level of each country's benefits and the number of people going in each direction.

19. Since June 1996, the Government's policy has been that future reciprocal agreements should normally be limited to resolving questions of liability for social security contributions.'

[29] Between 1948 and 1992 the United Kingdom entered into reciprocal social security agreements with a number of foreign states. With one minor exception, the agreements entered into after 1979 fulfilled earlier commitments made by the United Kingdom government. Agreements with Australia, New Zealand and Canada came into force in 1953, 1956 and 1959 respectively, but these did not require payment of uprated pensions. The agreement with Australia was terminated by it with effect from 1 March 2001, because of the refusal of the United Kingdom government to pay uprated pensions to its pensioners living in Australia.

[30] Uprating has never been applied to those living in South Africa, or indeed to the residents of any of Australia, Canada and New Zealand. They have never had a statutory entitlement to uprating of their pensions. According to the Social Security Committee Report (p xviii (para 38)): 'It is impossible to discern any pattern behind the selection of countries with whom bilateral agreements have been made providing for uprating.'

[31] The EC Regulations on social security for migrant workers require uprating of benefits throughout the European Union. In practice, the entry of the United Kingdom into the EC had little effect on the provision for uprating pensions in the member states, because there were pre-existing reciprocal agreements with all of them except Denmark providing for their payment.

[32] A responsible United Kingdom minister has admitted that there is no consistent or coherent pattern for these differences other than the intention to save cost. The then Minister of State, Mr Jeff Rooker, stated in the House of Commons on 13 November 2000 (356 HC Official Report (6th Series) col 628):

'I have already said that I am not prepared to defend the logic of the present situation. It is illogical. There is no consistent pattern. It does not matter whether a country is in the Commonwealth or outside it. We have arrangements with some Commonwealth countries and not with others. Indeed, there are differences among Caribbean countries. This is an historical issue and the situation has existed for years. It would cost some £300 million to change the policy for all concerned.'

[33] The cost of comprehensive uprating would presumably now exceed that figure of £300m. The 1996 DSS Memorandum stated (p 40):

'11. Agreeing to additional expenditure on pensions paid overseas would be incompatible with the government's policy of containing the long term costs of the social security system to ensure that it remains affordable.

12. In June and July 1995, during the passage of the Pensions Bill, amendments were tabled in both Houses calling for upratings to be paid. All were defeated by large majorities.'

[34] According to the evidence filed on behalf of the Secretary of State:

'Successive Governments have taken the view that the level of increases in retirement pensions relates to conditions in the UK and that it would not be right to impose an additional burden on contributors and taxpayers in the UK in order to pay pension increases to people who have chosen to become resident elsewhere in the world.'

STATE PRACTICE

[35] There is relatively little material before me to show the practice of other states in relation to payment of pensions to expatriates. Information contained in the appendix to the DSS Memorandum (Annex G, p 4) was drawn from a 1993 research report, and is set out as Annex 2 to my judgment (supplemented, in the case of Australia, by the information in para 27 (p 42) of the Memorandum). It will be seen that there was no consistent practice among the seven states referred to.

[36] The United Kingdom is the only Organisation for Economic Co-operation and Development country that discriminates between pensioners in different overseas countries.

CONVENTION RIGHTS

[37] The parties' submissions referred to above reflect the jurisprudence of the European Court of Human Rights and the decisions and opinions of the Commission, to which I refer below. The European jurisprudence was reviewed by Moses J in *R (on the application of Hooper) v Secretary of State for Work and Pensions* [2002] EWHC 191 (Admin), [2002] All ER (D) 193 (Feb) and Wilson J in *R (on the application of Reynolds) v Secretary of State for Work and Pensions* [2002] EWHC 426 (Admin), [2002] All ER (D) 64 (Mar), and I do not propose to consider all of the material that has been put before me.

[38] In *R (on the application of Alconbury Ltd) v Secretary of State for the Environment, Transport and the Regions* [2001] UKHL 23 at [26], [2001] 2 All ER 929 at [26], [2001] 2 WLR 1389, Lord Slynn of Hadley said:

'Although the 1998 Act does not provide that a national court is bound by these decisions it is obliged to take account of them so far as they are relevant. In the absence of some special circumstances it seems to me that the court should follow any clear and constant jurisprudence of the European Court of Human Rights. If it does not do so there is at least a possibility that the case will go to that court which is likely in the ordinary case to follow its own constant jurisprudence.'

Decisions of the Commission are not of the same level as those of the court. Where, however, there is a clear and constant line of decisions of the Commission that are not inconsistent with those of the court, good reason is required if this court is to decline to follow them.

a **[39]** The starting point is the opinion of the Commission in *Müller v Austria* (1975) 3 DR 25. The position was subsequently helpfully summarised by the Commission in *T v Sweden* (1986) 8 EHRR 269:

b

c

> 'The Commission recalls its consistent case law, according to which the right to a pension is not as such guaranteed by the Convention. At the same time the Commission has frequently held that the payment of contributions to a pension fund may in certain circumstances create a property right in a portion of such a fund and a modification of the pension rights under such a system could therefore in principle raise an issue under Prot. No. 1 Art. 1. The Commission has added, however, that "even if it is assumed that Prot. No. 1 Art. 1 guarantees persons who have paid contributions to a special insurance system the right to derive benefit from the system, it cannot be interpreted as entitling that person to a pension of a particular amount" (see *Müller v Austria* ((1975) 3 DR 25)).'

d **[40]** In *X v Italy* (1977) 11 DR 114, the Commission rejected as manifestly ill-founded a claim of infringement of art 1 of the First Protocol on the basis that the applicant had not satisfied the requirements under his domestic law for the payment of a pension.

e **[41]** *JW v UK* (1983) 34 DR 153 was the first of the cases in which the Commission considered a complaint that the United Kingdom government's failure to pay an uprated pension infringed the pensioner's convention rights. The applicants were emigrating to Australia. The Commission rejected the complaint as inadmissible. In view of the relevance of their decision I shall set out the reported extract in full (at 154–155):

f

g

h

j

> '3. The Commission has considered the applicants' complaint under Article 1 of the Protocol. It first recalls that it has previously held that although this provision does not as such guarantee a right to a pension, the right to benefit from a social security system to which a person has contributed may in some circumstances be a property right protected by it. However the Commission also held that Article 1 does not guarantee a right to a pension of any particular amount, but that the right safeguarded by Article 1 consists, at most, "in being entitled as a beneficiary of the social insurance scheme to any payments made by the fund" ([*Müller v Austria* (1975) 3 DR 25 at 31]). It has further held that before the right to benefit protected by Article 1 can be established, it is necessary that the interested party should have satisfied domestic legal requirements governing the right ([*X v Italy* (1977) 11 DR 114]). In the present case when the applicants emigrate to Australia their entitlement to benefit from the United Kingdom pension scheme will come to be regulated by different rules of domestic law, under which they will cease to qualify for payment of future pension increases contemplated by the relevant legislation. To that extent they will not satisfy domestic legal requirements to benefit from the United Kingdom pension scheme. Even if the right to benefit from a scheme will normally also apply to the regular increases this is not necessarily the case where a person leaves the country where the specific scheme operates. The Commission notes that in many countries specific restrictions as to the payment of social security benefits to foreign countries exist or have existed ([cf *X v Federal Republic of Germany* (1981) 4 EHRR 398]). In the Commission's view such operation of domestic

law does not amount to a deprivation of possessions infringing Article 1 of the Protocol and there is thus no appearance of any breach of this provision.

4. The Commission has nevertheless further considered the applicants' complaints in the light of Article 14 of the Convention which provides that enjoyment of Convention rights shall be secured without discrimination. In this respect it notes that one element of the applicants' complaint appears to be that they will receive less favourable treatment under the United Kingdom pension scheme than would other persons who have paid the same contributions but who have remained in the United Kingdom or emigrated to other countries. The Commission has therefore considered whether such differential treatment could amount to discrimination in the enjoyment of their rights under Article 1 of the Protocol contrary to Article 14. The Commission notes that it is a common feature of international life that social security agreements are entered into between different countries for the purpose of regulating the rights of persons moving from one country to another under the social security systems of each country. Such agreements commonly provide for the substitution, to a greater or lesser degree, of benefits under one system for those due under another. Under the Agreement between the United Kingdom and Australia the applicants' rights under the United Kingdom social security scheme are to some extent restricted and replaced by certain rights under the Australian scheme. The applicants, in their particular circumstances, will apparently be less well off than they would have been if they had remained in the United Kingdom or if they had gone to certain other countries. However it is almost inevitable that where a person in effect changes over from one social security system to another, he may find that his entitlements differ from those of persons in other countries. Depending on the circumstances such differences may or may not favour the individual. Furthermore the Commission notes that the applicants will only lose the benefit of future increases in their pensions, whose purpose broadly speaking is to compensate for rises in the cost of living in the United Kingdom. Given that they will not be living in the United Kingdom it appears reasonable that this element in their pension rights in particular should be replaced by the possibility of benefitting under the system of the country they are moving to.'

[42] There is no longer a social security agreement between Australia and the United Kingdom, and there has never been an agreement with South Africa. However, I do not read the Commission's decision as depending on the existence of such an agreement. That this interpretation of the decision is correct is confirmed by the next decision of the Commission to which I must refer.

[43] Two years after its decision in *JW*'s case, the Commission considered another complaint as to the government's failure to pay uprated pensions, this time by an applicant who had emigrated to South Africa. In *Corner v UK* App no 11271/84 (17 May 1985, unreported), the Commission rejected as manifestly ill-founded the complaint that the failure to pay uprating infringed art 1 of the First Protocol and art 14. (There was also a complaint of breach of art 2 of the Fourth Protocol, but this was rejected because the United Kingdom had not ratified that Protocol.) The Commission stated:

'The Commission recalls that it has previously held that, although art 1 of the First Protocol does not, as such, guarantee a right to a pension, the right to benefit from a social security system to which a person has contributed may, in some circumstances, be a property right protected by it ... However, the Commission has also held that art 1 does not guarantee a right to a pension of a particular amount, but that the right safeguarded by art 1 consists, at most, "in being entitled as a beneficiary of the social insurance scheme to any payments made by the fund" (see *Müller v Austria* (1975) 3 DR 25 at 31) in accordance with domestic legal requirements (see *X v Italy* (1977) 11 DR 114). Further, the Commission has held that the "freezing" of a pension at a particular level when a person leaves the United Kingdom does not amount to a deprivation of possessions infringing art 1 of the First Protocol (see *JW v UK* (1983) 34 DR 153). Moreover, the different treatment of persons entitled to pensions who remain in the country of payment compared with those who emigrate is justified on the grounds that the applicant will only lose the benefit of future increases in the pension, whose purpose broadly speaking is to compensate for rises in the cost of living in the United Kingdom and which the applicant will not have to endure (see *JW's* case). The Commission also considers that the economic state of third countries is not a matter which domestic pension authorities should be obliged to consider.'

[44] It is difficult to distinguish the present case from *Corner's* case, which if correct is fatal to the claimant's case. Moreover, *Corner's* case, unlike *JW's* case, cannot be explained on the basis of the reciprocal agreement between the United Kingdom and Australia. However, it and other pre-1996 decisions must be reconsidered in the light of the judgment of the European Court of Human Rights in *Gaygusuz v Austria* (1996) 23 EHRR 365. The applicant was a Turkish national resident in Austria. The Austrian government had refused to pay him emergency assistance, a social security benefit, entitlement to which depended on the payment of contributions into the state unemployment insurance fund. Austrian law confined entitlement to emergency assistance to Austrian nationals. Since the applicant had no right to benefit under Austrian law, the Austrian government contended that he had no right within the scope of art 14. The court held that the Austrian government had acted in breach of art 14 taken in conjunction with art 1 of the First Protocol. It said (at 380–382):

'41. The Court considers that the right to emergency assistance—in so far as provided for in the applicable legislation—is a pecuniary right for the purposes of Article 1 of Protocol No. 1. That provision is therefore applicable without it being necessary to rely solely on the link between entitlement to emergency assistance and the obligation to pay "taxes or other contributions". Accordingly, as the applicant was denied emergency assistance on a ground of distinction covered by Article 14, namely his nationality, that provision is also applicable. (See, among other authorities, *mutatis mutandis, Inze v. Austria* ((1988) 10 EHRR 394 at 405 (para 40)) and *Darby v. Sweden* ((1990) 13 EHRR 774 at 781 (para 30)).)

B. *Compliance with Article 14 of the Convention taken in conjunction with Article 1 of Protocol No. 1*

42. According to the Court's case law, a difference of treatment is discriminatory for the purposes of Article 14, if it "has no objective and reasonable justification", that is if it does not pursue a "legitimate aim" or if there is not a "reasonable relationship of proportionality between the means employed and the aim sought to be realised". Moreover the Contracting

States enjoy a certain margin of appreciation in assessing whether and to what extent differences in otherwise similar situations justify a different treatment. However, very weighty reasons would have to be put forward before the Court could regard a difference of treatment based exclusively on the ground of nationality as compatible with the Convention ...

45. The Austrian Government submitted that the statutory provision in question was not discriminatory. They argued that the difference in treatment was based on the idea that the State has special responsibility for its own nationals and must take care of them and provide for their essential needs. Moreover, sections 33 and 34 of the Unemployment Insurance Act [1977] laid down certain exceptions to the nationality condition. Lastly, at the material time, Austria was not bound by any contractual obligation to grant emergency assistance to Turkish nationals.

46. The Court notes in the first place that [Mr Gaygusuz] was legally resident in Austria and worked there at certain times, (See para. 10 above.) paying contributions to the unemployment insurance fund in the same capacity and on the same basis as Austrian nationals ...

50. The Court ... finds the arguments put forward by the Austrian Government unpersuasive. It considers, like the Commission, that the difference in treatment between Austrians and non-Austrians as regards entitlement to emergency assistance, of which [Mr Gaygusuz] was a victim, is not based on any "objective and reasonable justification".

51. Even though, at the material time, Austria was not bound by reciprocal agreements with Turkey, it undertook, when ratifying the Convention, to secure "to everyone within [its] jurisdiction" the rights and freedoms defined in section 1 of the Convention.

52. There has accordingly been a breach of Article 14 of the Convention, taken in conjunction with Article 1 of Protocol No. 1.'

[45] The fact that the court did not find a breach of art 1 of the First Protocol taken alone supports the view that a pecuniary right that may qualify as a possession for the purposes of that provision is defined by domestic law, in that case the law of Austria. A person who does not qualify for that right under domestic law is not 'deprived' of it for the purposes of that article. However, Gaygusuz's case establishes that a domestic law that disqualifies an individual from enjoyment of a pecuniary right of a kind protected by art 1 of the First Protocol on grounds prohibited by art 14 without objective and reasonable justification infringes art 14.

[46] The second sentence of para 41 of the court's judgment is framed in not untypical Delphic terms. It is unnecessary for me to decide what the court intended to lay down, but I read it as holding that a state benefit may be a pecuniary right protected by art 1 of the First Protocol even if it is not a contributory benefit entitlement to which is conditional on compulsory payment of a tax or other contribution. This is logical. There would be some logic in restricting art 1 to pecuniary rights derived from a defined investment funded by individual contributions. In such a case the right is a true right of property. Where, however, the payment of contributions is no more than a condition for entitlement to a benefit (as I assume was the position in Gaygusuz's case), it is difficult to see why entitlement to a benefit resulting from satisfaction of that condition should create a pecuniary right protected by art 1, when entitlement to benefit resulting from satisfaction of some other condition should not. In a case such as the present, the payment of benefit does not create a right of property in

any real sense. The earlier decisions of the court following *Gaygusuz's* case
indicated that my reading was incorrect (see *Skorkiewicz v Poland* App no 39860/98
(1 June 1999, unreported), *Coke v UK* App no 38696/97 (9 September 1998,
unreported) and *Bellet v France* App no 23805/94 (4 December 1995, unreported)),
and Moses J and Wilson J similarly held that non-contributory benefits were
outside the scope of art 1 of the First Protocol in *R (on the application of Hooper) v*
Secretary of State for Work and Pensions [2002] All ER (D) 193 (Feb) and in *R (on*
the application of Reynolds) v Secretary of State for Work and Pensions [2002] All ER
(D) 64 (Mar). However, in *Walden v Liechtenstein* App no 33916/96 (16 March
2000, unreported) (a decision on admissibility only) the court held that a non-
contributory pension was protected by art 1 of the First Protocol. In *Shackell v UK*
App no 45851/99 (27 April 2000, unreported), the court rejected the applicant's
complaint as manifestly ill-founded, but in the course of doing so was prepared to
assume that a non-contributory social security benefit was a pecuniary right for
the purposes of art 1 of the First Protocol. In *Matthews v UK* App no 40302/98
(15 July, 2002, unreported) (also a decision on admissibility only), the court held
that an allegation of discrimination on grounds of gender in relation to a bus pass,
a non-contributory benefit, 'raises complex issues under art 14 of the convention
and art 1 of the First Protocol taken together'.

[47] However, I entirely agree with Moses J in *Hooper's* case [2002] All ER (D)
193 (Feb) at [50], that a pecuniary right protected by art 1 is defined by the
domestic legislation that created it. I refer in particular to the decision of the
court in *Bellet's* case, in which the court stated:

> '... while no right to the grant of a pension is, as such, guaranteed by the
> convention, compulsory contributions to a retirement fund may give rise, in
> certain cases, to a right of ownership over part of the funds ... However, it is
> still necessary, in order for such a right to accrue, that the persons concerned
> should fulfil the conditions laid down by national law.'

[48] In the present case, United Kingdom legislation has never conferred a
right on the claimant to the uprating of her pension while she lived in South
Africa. She does not satisfy and has never satisfied the conditions for payment of
an uprated pension. She has never had a right to an uprated pension. There can
therefore be no question of her having been deprived of any such right.

[49] In my judgment, therefore, there has been no infringement of art 1 of the
First Protocol. I add, however, that it does not follow that legislation that
removes a right protected under art 1 of the First Protocol cannot infringe that
provision. That case is not before me. I also do not have to consider Mr Eadie's
submission that the claim under art 1 of the First Protocol must fail because that
provision does not guarantee payment of a pension of any particular amount, and
the claimant has not been deprived of the substance of the right. I do not find the
distinction between loss of part of a sum payable by reason of a pecuniary right
and impairment of the substance or essence of the right (see *Jankovic v Croatia* App
no 43440/98 (12 October 2000, unreported)) an easy one.

[50] I therefore turn to consider the allegation of breach of art 14 read with art
1 of the First Protocol.

ARTICLE 14 READ WITH ART 1 OF THE FIRST PROTOCOL

The questions to be considered

[51] In *Wandsworth London BC v Michalak* [2002] EWCA Civ 271 at [20], [2002]
All ER (D) 56 (Mar) at [20], Brooke LJ said:

'It appears to me that it will usually be convenient for a court, when invited to consider an art 14 issue, to approach its task in a structured way. For this purpose I adopt the structure suggested by Stephen Grosz, Jack Beatson QC and the late Peter Duffy QC in their book *Human Rights: The 1998 Act and the European Convention* (2000). If a court follows this model it should ask itself the four questions I set out below. If the answer to any of the four questions is "no", then the claim is likely to fail, and it is in general unnecessary to proceed to the next question. These questions are: (i) Do the facts fall within the ambit of one or more of the substantive convention provisions ...? (ii) If so, was there different treatment as respects that right between the complainant on the one hand and the other persons put forward for comparison ("the chosen comparators")? (iii) Were the chosen comparators in an analogous situation to the complainant's situation? (iv) If so, did the difference in treatment have an objective and reasonable justification: in other words, did it pursue a legitimate aim and did the differential treatment bear a reasonable relationship of proportionality to the aims sought to be achieved?'

[52] As I indicated in [15], above, in my judgment, there is a fifth question to be considered, although it may well be that Brooke LJ intended it to be encapsulated in his question (iii). That question is: is the basis for the different treatment of the complainant as against that of the chosen comparators based on 'any ground such as sex, race, colour, language ... or other status' within the meaning of art 14? Differences in treatment based on other factors are not discriminatory for the purposes of art 14 (see, for example, the decision of the Commission in *P v UK* App no 14751/89 (12 December 1990, unreported)) and those referred to in [55], below.

(i) *Do the facts fall within the ambit of a substantive convention provision?*
[53] The answer is clearly Yes: the present claim falls within the ambit of art 1 of the First Protocol. The applicant in *Gaygusuz v Austria* (1996) 23 EHRR 365 succeeded although he had no right under art 1 of the First Protocol. It follows from the decision of the court in that case that art 14 read with art 1 of the First Protocol applies equally in the present case.

(ii) *Is there any different treatment as respects that right between the claimant and her chosen comparators?*
[54] Again, the answer clearly is in the affirmative.

(iii)(a) *Is the basis for the different treatment of the claimant and the chosen comparators a ground within the scope of art 14?*
[55] Mr Eadie initially submitted that differences in the countries where people live are not differences in status. Persons who are in different places may be treated differently, and the differences in treatment do not amount to discrimination. He relied on the decisions of the Commission in *N v UK* App no 11077/84 (13 October 1986, unreported), in which the different treatment of offenders in Scotland and England was held not to be discriminatory, and in *Murray v UK* (1996) 22 EHRR 29, in which different treatment of detained suspects in Northern Ireland and in England was held not to be discriminatory. However, these are very different cases from the present. Regional differences, resulting from different bodies having jurisdiction, cannot be discriminatory: it seems to me that

a discrimination does not arise where different regions apply different rules without discrimination to all those within the region.

[56] In the present case, there is only one set of rules, namely the United Kingdom pensions legislation, and it applies differently to persons depending on their residence and presence abroad. A person ordinarily resident in Great Britain is entitled to her uprated pension even if absent (by definition temporarily) from b this country. A person who is not ordinarily resident in Great Britain is not entitled to an uprated pension unless she is present in this country (see reg 5 of the Social Security Benefit (Persons Abroad) Regulations 1975, SI 1975/563, as applied by reg 3 of the Social Security Benefits Up-rating Regulations 2001, SI 2001/910, both of which are set out in Annex 1 to this judgment).

[57] Residence applied as a criterion for the differential treatment of citizens is c in my judgment a ground within the scope of art 14. Like domicile and nationality, it is an aspect of personal status. Indeed, having discovered the judgment of *Darby v Sweden* (1990) 13 EHRR 774, in which differential treatment on the ground of residence outside Sweden was held to infringe art 14, Mr Eadie conceded the applicability of art 14. Under United Kingdom legislation, a person d is not entitled to have his pension uprated if he is ordinarily resident elsewhere. Ordinary residence is a ground of the kind referred to in art 14.

[58] In these circumstances, I do not have to decide whether temporary presence in a location, by itself, not amounting to residence, is a ground of differential treatment that is within the scope of art 14.

e
(iii)(b) *Are the chosen comparators in an analogous situation to the claimant's?*

[59] Since we are concerned with social security benefits, the comparison must take into account the social and economic circumstances and needs of the chosen comparators.

[60] There are two comparators to consider: persons resident in the United f Kingdom and those resident in those countries whose United Kingdom pensioners receive uprated United Kingdom pensions.

[61] So far as the first class of comparators is concerned, persons who live in other countries have different costs of living from those in Great Britain, and live in economies that are subject to different rates of inflation. If a comparison were g appropriate, it would be justifiable to compare the cost of living in sterling terms of a foreign pensioner with that in the United Kingdom. A pensioner resident abroad may be better off, in real terms, than a pensioner living in Great Britain, because of different local costs of living which are not fully reflected in exchange rates.

h [62] While I have no evidence before me, it is notorious that the cost of living in this country is relatively high, and certainly higher than that in South Africa, partly as a result of the equally notorious depreciation of the rand as against, in particular, sterling. The depreciation of the rand has doubtless led to inflation in South Africa in terms of the local currency, and the claimant's evidence refers to the facts that inflation and interest rates are higher there than here. However, the j purchasing power of her fixed United Kingdom pension is not fixed: it depends on the rate of inflation in South Africa and changes in the sterling/rand exchange rate. Importantly, the claimant does not state that the purchasing power in South Africa of her fixed sterling pension has declined because it has not been uprated; and as mentioned above the uprating so far refused to the claimant personally is a relatively small sum. Perhaps more fundamentally, she has not compared the

cost of living in South Africa with that in the United Kingdom. Lastly, she
obviously cannot provide a prediction as to whether her cost of living in South
Africa will increase in sterling terms.

[63] Similar comments apply to the comparison between the claimant and
those living in other countries.

[64] There are other differences between the circumstances of those resident
here and those resident abroad, of which the most obvious in the present context
are differences in local social security provision and in local taxation. The
claimant is unfortunate in that South Africa has limited social security provision,
or at least did so at the time of the Social Security Committee Report. The
position of pensioners in Australia is different: some of them benefit from
Australian social security provision, at significant cost to the Australian exchequer.
Of the (about) 220,000 United Kingdom pensioners in Australia, 158,000 qualify
for an Australian pension, which is payable to those who have been resident in
Australia for at least ten years and have reached retirement age, and have less
than a specified income. The position of pensioners in New Zealand, as described
in the 1996 DSS Memorandum, is different again: under the reciprocal agreement
between the United Kingdom and New Zealand, periods of residence in the
United Kingdom are treated as periods of residence in New Zealand. As a
result, United Kingdom pensioners living in New Zealand qualify for New
Zealand pensions (called superannuation), less the amount of their United
Kingdom pensions, by reason of their residence here or there. Increases in their
United Kingdom pensions would result in an equivalent reduction in their New
Zealand pensions.

[65] It seems to me that the comparison between the positions of persons
living in different countries, in different social and economic circumstances, and
under different tax and social security regimes, is complex, and cannot simply be
restricted to a comparison of the sterling amounts of their United Kingdom
pensions.

[66] The differences between the situation of United Kingdom pensioners
living abroad and those here led to the decisions of the Commission in *JW v UK*
(1983) 34 DR 153 and *Corner v UK* App no 11271/84 (17 May 1985, unreported).
The hope that *Gaygusuz v Austria* (1996) 23 EHRR 365 transformed the legal
position of persons in the position of the claimant would have been disappointed
by the decision of the Commission in *Havard v UK* App no 38882/97 (22 October 1998,
unreported) rejecting the complaint as inadmissible. The written decision of the
Commission does not disclose anything meaningful about Mr Havard's complaint
or the reasons for its being declared inadmissible, but it is common ground that
Mr Havard is a United Kingdom state pensioner living in Australia, was president
of the British Australia Pensioner Association, gave evidence to the House of
Commons Social Committee (referred to at paras 14 (p x) and 33 (p xvi) of their
report), and that his complaint to the Commission was that the United Kingdom
government had failed to pay him an uprated pension. The Commission found:

'... in so far as the matters complained of are within its competence, the
Committee (of the Commission) finds that they do not disclose any
appearance of a violation of the rights and freedoms set out in the
convention or its Protocols.'

The lack of any specific reasons is tantalising, and has left me to consider the
question of breach of art 14 without the benefit of the recent thinking of the

Commission. I should very much have liked to see the report and information referred to in the decision. I should like to think that the reasons of the Commission were similar to those set out above. As appears from what I have stated above, in my judgment the failure of the applications in *JW*'s case and *Havard*'s case did not depend on the existence of the then bilateral agreement between Australia and the United Kingdom, but on a more fundamental obstacle to their success, as the decision in *Corner*'s case indicates. In neither of the earlier cases was the position of the applicant compared with that of pensioners in countries where uprating is paid. For reasons I have given, I do not think that this makes their conclusions unreliable.

[67] It follows that the claimants' claim fails. In case I am wrong on this issue, however, I shall address the question of justification.

(iv) Is there an objective and reasonable justification?

[68] On this issue, it is important to take into account that the court is concerned with two areas of government in which it is clear that the judicial arm must give the greatest deference to the legislature and to the elected executive. The first concerns the allocation of resources: how much is to be raised by the government, by taxation or otherwise, and how the moneys available for expenditure by the government are to be spent. Those matters are not justiciable. In a different context, in *R v DPP, ex p Kebeline, R v DPP, ex p Rechachi* [1999] 4 All ER 801 at 844, [2000] 2 AC 326 at 381, Lord Hope of Craighead said:

'In this area difficult choices may have to be made by the executive or the legislature between the rights of the individual and the needs of society. In some circumstances it will be appropriate for the courts to recognise that there is an area of judgment within which the judiciary will defer, on democratic grounds, to the considered opinion of the elected body or person whose act or decision is said to be incompatible with the convention.'

These words were applied to the distribution of state benefit by Laws LJ (with whom the other members of the Court of Appeal agreed) in *R (on the application of Waite) v Hammersmith and Fulham London BC* [2002] EWCA Civ 482 at [36], [37]. Laws LJ said (at [37]): '... the distribution of state benefit lies peculiarly within the constitutional responsibility of elected government.' In *Steele Ford & Newton (a firm) v CPS* [1993] 2 All ER 769 at 774, [1994] 1 AC 22 at 33, Lord Bridge of Harwich referred to—

'... the special constitutional convention which jealously safeguards the exclusive control exercised by Parliament over both the levying and the expenditure of the public revenue.'

[69] I should also refer to the Social Security Committee Report (p xviii (para 39)):

'The allocation of scarce resources and the language of priorities are what politics and government are all about. It is not a question of first reaching a moral judgement about the rights and wrongs of the expatriates' case, and then deciding whether or not this country can afford to do anything about it. The decision about whether public expenditure on state retirement pensions should be increased in future by paying uprating increases which are not required by law at the moment is a political question which includes, but is not distinct from, the moral question. Ultimately, it must be for the House to decide, and that is our concluding recommendation: **That there should** be a free vote at prime time to allow Members to express their opinion on the principle of whether the Government should pay upratings to some or all of those pensioners living in countries where upratings are not paid at present.'

[70] The second area is that of foreign relations. Where uprated pensions are paid to expatriate pensioners, at present that is done either by virtue of the obligations imposed on members of the EU or pursuant to bilateral agreements between HM government and the government of the country in which the expatriates in question live. The court will not embark on questions whether it is or is not in the public interest for such agreements to be entered into (see *Blackburn v A-G* [1971] 2 All ER 1380, [1971] 1 WLR 1037; the International Tin Council litigation, culminating in *Maclaine Watson & Co Ltd v Dept of Trade and Industry, Maclaine Watson & Co Ltd v International Tin Council* [1989] 3 All ER 523, [1990] 2 AC 418; *Duke of Brunswick v King of Hanover* (1844) 6 Beav 1). Such questions are, in English law, the paradigm of questions that are non-justiciable. Although the payment of uprated pensions to expatriates does not require any agreement with their country of residence, relations with those countries are clearly involved, as the intervention of Australia in the present case demonstrates.

[71] European jurisprudence does not differ from English authority on the deference to be given to the democratically-elected organs of government in the field of social policy and public expenditure (see *Mellacher v Austria* (1989) 12 EHRR 391 at 408–409, 411–412 (paras 45 and 54), helpfully cited by Moses J in *R (on the application of Hooper) v Secretary of State for Work and Pensions* [2002] All ER (D) 193 (Feb) at [102]).

[72] The fundamental question is whether the United Kingdom government may lawfully restrict uprating of pensions to pensioners within Great Britain. It seems to me that the discussion of this question is illogically affected by the incorrect perception that a pension is the fruit of the investment by a pensioner of National Insurance contributions. If it were, the claimant would have a right protected by art 1 of the First Protocol; but I have held that she has no such right. What I am concerned with, therefore, is the scope of entitlement to a form of state benefit.

[73] The government has decided that uprated pensions are to be confined to those living in this country or living in certain other countries. It seems to me that a government may lawfully decide to restrict the payment of benefits of any kind to those who are within its territorial jurisdiction, leaving the care and support of those who live elsewhere to the governments of the countries in which they live. Such a restriction may be based wholly or partly on considerations of cost, but having regard to the wide margin of discretion that must be accorded to the government, I do not think it one that a court may say is unreasonable or lacking in objective justification. The lack of consistency in state practice indicates that there is no single right decision to be made as to the payment of pensions to those who go to live abroad. It is also difficult to criticise the position of the government if the limitation on the benefit has been published for some time, so that those who have gone to live abroad did know, or could easily have ascertained it, before deciding to live abroad. That is the case in relation to pensions.

[74] Similarly, I think that the government is entitled to consider the payment of uprated pensions to those living abroad on a country-by-country basis, taking into account the interests of this country in each case. I do not think that payment of uprated pensions to pensioners in any one foreign country (or several) is

a converted, by art 14, into an obligation to pay uprated pensions to all pensioners living abroad: yet this is the effect of the claimant's submissions. It would be curious indeed if art 14 were to compel the government to pay uprated pensions to those living abroad irrespective of any countervailing benefit offered by their countries of residence, yet again that would be the effect of the claimant's case. The accepted illogicality of the present position is the result of agreements

b providing for payment of uprated pensions having been entered into with some countries, but not others, at a time when governmental policy was different from the present policy. The Social Security Committee Report states at para 25 (p xiii) how this change of policy excluded pensioners in Canada from uprating:

c 'An opportunity was missed in 1972 to reach agreement with Canada which would have provided for upratings to be paid. The UK's proposal of a comprehensive agreement foundered because of difficulties on the part of Canada. By the time these were sorted out, the UK's position had moved on and uprating was no longer on offer.'

This emphasises both the political nature of the decisions involved and the

d relative complexity of the issues, and shows how the illogicality has arisen.

[75] Mr Drabble stated that there is no record of a policy decision underlying the present scheme, and no record of a reasoned debate. The matter has certainly been before Parliament (see para 12 of the DSS Memorandum cited above). There is a record of the policy for the refusal to extend payment of uprated pensions (see [33], [34], above). Lastly the reason for the payment of uprated retirement

e pensions to the residents of some foreign countries only is historical: changed political policies, different results.

CONCLUSIONS

[76] In my judgment, the remedy of the expatriate United Kingdom

f pensioners who do not receive uprated pensions is political, not judicial. The decision to pay them uprated pensions must be made by Parliament.

[77] For the reasons set out above, this claim for judicial review will be dismissed.

Application dismissed. Permission to appeal granted.

Martyn Gurr   Barrister.

Annex 1

THE UNITED KINGDOM LEGISLATION

(a) *Basic provisions*

1. State retirement pensions are made up of two components, either or both of which may be payable: the basic state pension (dependent on the number of qualifying years a person has in her working life) and an additional pension (dependent on a person's earnings since April 1978).

2. State retirement pensions are categorised in the Social Security Contributions and Benefits Act 1992 (SSCBA) into Categories A, B, C and D. Categories C and D are non-contributory and are not relevant. Categories A and B are contributory (see s 20(1)(f)). As contributory benefits, Category A and B pensions are dealt with under Pt II of the SSCBA. Category B pensions are payable on the basis of the contribution record of a spouse (see s 20(1)(f)(ii)); and, as such, are not relevant in this case. The claimant receives a Category A pension.

3. A Category A pension is payable on the basis of a person's own contribution record (s 20(1)(f)(i)). It consists of (a) a basic pension payable at a weekly rate and (b) an additional SERPS pension where the individual has not contracted out of that scheme (s 44(3)). Either or both may be payable.

4. Section 21 provides:

'(1) Entitlement to any of the benefits specified in section 20(1) above ... depends on contribution conditions being satisfied ...
(2) The class or classes of contribution which, for the purposes of subsection (1) above, are relevant in relation to each of those benefits are as follows ...
Category A retirement pension   Class 1, 2 or 3'

5. Section 44 of the SSCBA lays down the conditions under which a Category A retirement pension arises:

'(1) A person shall be entitled to a Category A retirement pension if—(a) he is over pensionable age; and (b) he satisfies the contribution conditions for a Category A retirement pension specified in Schedule 3, Part I, paragraph 5; and, subject to the provisions of this Act, he shall become so entitled on the day on which he attains pensionable age and his entitlement shall continue throughout his life ...
(3) A Category A retirement pension shall consist of—(a) a basic pension payable at a weekly rate; and (b) an additional pension payable where there are one or more surpluses in the pensioner's earnings factors for the relevant years.
(4) The weekly rate of the basic pension shall be [£72·50] ...'

The sum of £72·50 was substituted for the previous figure by the Social Security Benefits Up-rating (No 2) Order 2000, SI 2001/207, with effect from 9 April 2001.

6. The result of the applicable provisions is that a person is entitled to the basic element of a Category A pension if (a) she is of pensionable age and (b) she satisfies the contribution conditions for a Category A pension set out in s 21(1) and (2) and Sch 3, Pt I, para 5 (see s 44(1)). There are two such contribution conditions. First, the person must have achieved an earnings factor derived from a specified amount of National Insurance contributions actually paid. Secondly,

a the person must have achieved a minimum number of qualifying years during her working life: a qualifying year being linked to qualifying earnings in the tax year in question. If more than a quarter but less than the full number of qualifying years have been achieved, a reduced rate basic pension is payable. A person resident and working abroad can make voluntary contributions from abroad in order to protect her position and ensure that the requisite number of *b* qualifying years are achieved to qualify for the full basic element of the Category A pension. This is what the claimant did.

7. A person is entitled to the additional element of a Category A pension if (a) she has reached pensionable age; (b) had earnings between the lower earnings limit and upper earnings limit for National Insurance from 6 April 1978 until the end of the last complete tax year before she reached pensionable age and (c) had *c* not contracted out of SERPS (ss 44(3) and 45). SERPS is a scheme for those who are not contracted-out into an occupational or personal pension. It is earnings-related and payable to employees who have paid a specified level of Class 1 National Insurance contributions since April 1978. The amount of SERPS payable is quantified in accordance with a formula the complexity of which is not important.

d 8. Graduated retirement benefit is based on the amount of graduated National Insurance contributions a person paid when the graduated retirement scheme existed between April 1961 and April 1975. It is payable to any person who is of pensionable age and has paid graduated contributions (see ss 36 and 37 of the National Insurance Act 1965, and the Social Security (Graduated Retirement Benefit) (No 2) Regulations 1978, SI 1978/393).

e 9. All contributory benefits are paid out of the National Insurance Fund. This is operated on a pay-as-you-go basis: current income set annually (mainly from employers, employees and the self-employed) funds current expenditure.

(b) Uprating

f 10. Section 150 of the Social Security Administration Act 1992 (the SSAA) requires the Secretary of State in each tax year to review the sums specified in, among others, s 44(4) of the SSCBA (ie the amount of the basic pension). Section 150(2) requires the Secretary of State to lay before Parliament the draft of an up-rating order 'Where it appears to the Secretary of State that the general level *g* of prices is greater at the end of the period under review than it was at the beginning of that period'. The order must provide for the increase of, among others, the sum specified in s 44(4) of the SSCBA by a percentage not less than the percentage by which the general level of prices is greater at the end of the period than it was at the beginning. Section 150(9) provides that if a draft order laid before Parliament in pursuance of s 150 is approved by resolution of each House, *h* the Secretary of State shall make the order in the form of the draft. The 2000 order, which as mentioned above increased the sum specified in s 44(4) to £72·50, was made under s 150 of the SSAA.

THE DISAPPLICATION OF UPRATING TO THE CLAIMANT'S PENSION

j 11. Section 113 of the SSCBA contains general provisions as to disqualification from receiving benefits and for suspending payments. Section 113(1) provides, so far as relevant:

'Except where regulations otherwise provide, a person shall be disqualified for receiving any benefit under Parts II to V of this Act ... for any period during which the person—(a) is absent from Great Britain; or (b) is undergoing imprisonment or detention in legal custody.'

Section 113(3) provides:

'Regulations may provide for a person who would be entitled to any such benefit but for the operation of any provision of this Act ... to be treated as if entitled to it for the purposes of any rights or obligations ... which depend on his entitlement, other than the right to payment of the benefit.'

12. By s 113(1)(a), a person is therefore disqualified from what would otherwise be their statutory entitlement to a Category A retirement pension for any period during which they are absent from Great Britain, 'Except where regulations otherwise provide'.

13. The general statutory disqualification from receiving Category A retirement pension by reason of being absent from Great Britain is disapplied by reg 4(1) of the Social Security Benefit (Persons Abroad) Regulations 1975, SI 1975/563, which modifies the Act in relation to, inter alia, retirement pensions. It provides, so far as relevant:

'Subject to the provisions of this regulation and of regulation 5 below, a person shall not be disqualified for receiving ... a retirement pension of any category ... by reason of being absent from Great Britain.'

14. Regulation 5 of the 1975 regulations, however, provides for the reapplication of the disqualification in regulations providing for the uprating of retirement pensions:

'(1) Where regulations made in consequence of an order under section 63 of the Social Security Act 1986 (up-rating of benefits ...) provide for the application of this regulation to any additional benefit becoming payable by virtue of that order, the following provisions of this regulation shall ... have effect in relation to the entitlement to that benefit of persons absent from Great Britain ...

(3) ... where a person is not ordinarily resident in Great Britain immediately before the appointed date the provisions of these regulations (except this regulation) shall not, unless and until he becomes ordinarily resident in Great Britain, affect his disqualification while he is absent from Great Britain for receiving ... (c) ... any additional retirement pension of any category ... if that person had ... become entitled to a retirement pension ... before the appointed date.'

15. For those territories where uprating is disapplied, reg 3 of the Social Security Benefits Up-rating Regulations 2001, SI 2001/910 provides for the application of the disqualification to the additional benefit otherwise payable by virtue of the 2000 order. This includes the uprating of the retirement pension introduced by art 4 of the 2000 order with effect from 9 April 2001:

'Regulation 5 of the Social Security Benefit (Persons Abroad) Regulations 1975 (application of disqualification in respect of up-rating of benefit) shall apply to any additional benefit payable by virtue of the Up-rating Order.'

The payment of uprated pensions to those in certain foreign countries

16. Section 179 of the SSAA 1992 provides for modification or adaption of the applicable legislation in cases in which an Order in Council is made for the purpose of giving effect to a reciprocal agreement with another country. Such agreements may contain provisions dealing with a range of matters including uprating. Thus, uprating may be paid to those receiving a United Kingdom pension who are resident in some countries where (a) there is such provision in the relevant reciprocal agreement and (b) there is an Order in Council applying the terms of such agreement in domestic law. There are such reciprocal agreements and Orders in Council in relation to the countries mentioned in the judgment at [4], above.

Annex 2

'*Examples of restrictions imposed by other countries on payment of pension abroad*

Country	Restriction imposed
France	Non-nationals who are not living in France cannot claim old-age or widowhood benefits from abroad …
Germany	Non-nationals who are not treated as Germans receive only 70 per cent of the pension …
Sweden	Non-nationals can neither retain basic pension if they are abroad for more than a year, nor claim it from abroad …
Australia	It is not normally possible to claim an Australian pension from abroad … [Age pension is payable outside Australia only if it was awarded before the pensioner left there, unless that pensioner lives in a country with which Australia has a reciprocal agreement providing for the pension to be claimed from the other country.]
New Zealand	50 per cent of pension payable if permanently resident abroad. Claim from abroad not permitted …
Canada	Old Age Security (OAS) Pension can be paid abroad indefinitely, and claimed from abroad, if the claimant has resided in Canada for a minimum of 20 years after the age of 18. If the claimant has over 10 years of residence but less than 20, OAS can be paid for the month of departure and the following six months only …
Canada	Pension Plan benefits can be paid abroad and claimed from abroad.
USA	Subject to certain exceptions, payment of pension abroad to non-nationals is limited to six months …'

De Beer v Kanaar & Co (a firm) and another

[2001] EWCA Civ 1318

COURT OF APPEAL, CIVIL DIVISION

JONATHAN PARKER LJ AND RIMER J

27 JULY, 9 AUGUST 2001

Costs – Security for costs – Claimant ordinarily resident out of the jurisdiction and out of the jurisdiction of a convention state – Whether court precluded from ordering security for costs against such a claimant if he had assets in a convention state – CPR 25.13(2)(a).

The claimant was resident in the United States, but had assets in Switzerland, a contracting state of the Lugano Convention on Jurisdiction and the Enforcement of Judgments in Civil and Commercial Matters 1988 (as set out in Sch 3C to the Civil Jurisdiction and Judgments Act 1982). He issued proceedings against his former solicitors who subsequently applied for an order requiring him to give security for their costs of the action. Under CPR 25.13(2)(a)[a], such an order could only be made against a claimant who was an individual if he were (i) ordinarily resident out of the jurisdiction, and (ii) not 'a person against whom a claim can be enforced' under the Lugano Convention or the Brussels Convention on Jurisdiction and the Enforcement of Judgments in Civil and Commercial Matters 1968 (as set out in Sch 1 to the 1982 Act). The deputy judge held that r 25.13(2)(a) precluded her from ordering security for costs against the claimant since he had assets in a convention state against which an order for the costs of the action could be enforced and was therefore a person against whom a claim could be enforced under the conventions. The solicitors appealed.

Held – On its true construction, CPR 25.13(2)(a) did not preclude the court from making an order for security for costs against an individual claimant who was not ordinarily resident in the jurisdiction or in that of a convention state, but had assets in such a state. That construction was consistent with the purpose of r 25.13(2)(a), namely the elimination of any covert discrimination against nationals of other convention states which would or might have existed if condition (a) had simply read 'the claimant is an individual who is ordinarily resident out of the jurisdiction'. Rule 25.13(2) was directed to the juridical characteristics of the individual claimant, irrespective of what assets he might currently own or where those assets might currently be situated. Condition (a) confined the jurisdiction to cases where a claimant was an individual who was not ordinarily resident in the jurisdiction or in that of a convention state. Such a claimant could not therefore deprive the court of jurisdiction merely by placing an asset in a convention state. It followed in the instant case that the court did have jurisdiction to order security for costs to be given by the claimant. Accordingly, the appeal would be allowed, and the claimant would be required to give security in the sum sought by the solicitors (see [56], [58], [63], [91], below).

---

a   Rule 25.13, so far as material, is set out at [11], below

a *White Sea & Onega Shipping Co v International Transport Workers Federation*
[2001] All ER (D) 447 (Mar) applied.
Nasser v United Bank of Kuwait [2002] 1 All ER 401 considered.

Cases referred to in judgment

Bunzl v Martin Bunzl International Ltd [2000] All ER (D) 911, (2000) Times,
b   19 September.
Chequepoint SARL v McClelland [1997] 2 All ER 384, [1997] QB 51, [1996] 3 WLR
341, CA.
Fitzgerald v Williams, O'Regan v Williams [1996] 2 All ER 171, [1996] QB 657, [1996]
2 WLR 447, CA.
Leyvand v Barasch [2000] All ER (D) 181, (2000) Times, 23 March.
c *Mund & Fester v Hatrex Internationaal Transport* Case C-398/92 [1994] ECR I-467.
Nasser v United Bank of Kuwait [2001] EWCA Civ 556, [2002] 1 All ER 401, [2002]
1 WLR 1868.
Thune v London Properties Ltd [1990] 1 All ER 972, [1990] 1 WLR 562, CA.
White Sea & Onega Shipping Co v International Transport Workers Federation [2001]
d   EWCA Civ 377, [2001] All ER (D) 447 (Mar).

Notes

For the conditions to be satisfied before the court can make an order for security
for costs, see 37 *Halsbury's Laws* (4th edn reissue) para 835.

e ### Appeal

The first defendant, Kanaar & Co (a firm), appealed with permission of Elizabeth
Gloster QC from her decision, sitting as a deputy judge of the High Court on
19 February 2001, dismissing its application for an order requiring the claimant,
Hans David de Beer, to give security for its costs of the action in the sum of
f £130,000. The second defendant, Richard Kendall-Bush, took no part in the
proceedings. The facts are set out in the judgment of the court.

Philip Marshall (instructed by *Reynolds Porter Chamberlain*) for Kanaar.
Pushpinder Saini (instructed by *Pritchard Englefield*) for Mr de Beer.

g   *Cur adv vult*

9 August 2001. The following judgment of the court was delivered.

JONATHAN PARKER LJ.

h *Introduction*

[1] This is an appeal by Kanaar & Co (Kanaar), the first defendant in the
action, against an order made by Elizabeth Gloster QC, sitting as a deputy High
Court judge in the Chancery Division, on 19 February 2001. By her order, the
judge dismissed Kanaar's application that the claimant in the action, Mr Hans
j David de Beer, give security for its costs of the action. The judge concluded that
on the true construction of the relevant provisions of the CPR the court had no
jurisdiction to make the order sought. In the light of that conclusion further
questions as to whether the discretion to order security for costs should be
exercised, and if so on what terms, did not arise.

[2] Notwithstanding that Mr de Beer is ordinarily resident in the United States
of America, the judge concluded that there was no jurisdiction to order security

for costs against him since he currently had assets in Holland and in Switzerland, which states are respectively parties to the Brussels Conventions (as defined in the Civil Jurisdiction and Judgments Act 1982) and the Lugano Convention on Jurisdiction and the Enforcement of Judgments in Civil and Commercial Matters 1988 (as set out in Sch 3C to the 1982 Act. There is no material difference for present purposes between the provisions of the Brussels Conventions and those of the Lugano Convention. For convenience we will refer hereafter to the Brussels Conventions and the Lugano Convention as 'the conventions', and to states parties to the conventions or either of them as 'convention states'. The judge held that the fact that Mr de Beer had assets in a convention state meant that the court had no jurisdiction to order him to give security for costs.

[3] The judge gave permission to appeal against her dismissal of the application for security for costs, but refused permission to appeal against her dismissal of two further applications made by Kanaar. Kanaar applied for permission to appeal against the dismissal of the other applications, but permission was refused by Jonathan Parker LJ on the papers on 23 May 2001 and the application for permission has not been renewed.

[4] Kanaar appears on this appeal by Mr Philip Marshall of counsel; Mr de Beer by Mr Pushpinder Saini of counsel. Both counsel appeared before the judge.

The background to the dispute

[5] Kanaar is a firm of solicitors. The principal of the firm is Mr Nicholas Kanaar. The second defendant in the action, Mr Richard Kendall-Bush, is a former solicitor who acted at the material time (1991) as consultant to Kanaar. On 9 December 1998 Mr Kendall-Bush was ordered to be struck off the roll of solicitors for serious misconduct arising out of the transactions which have given rise to the present dispute. Mr de Beer is a Dutch national who lives in Florida. He is a real estate dealer and managing director of a company which carries on business in real estate.

[6] In her judgment, the judge summarised the background to, and nature of, the dispute as follows:

'In July 1991, Mr de Beer and several other individuals, described in the statement of claim as "the associates", agreed to act together as brokers in seeking to introduce a buyer for letters of credit to the value of $US 300m which were purportedly being issued [by] a self-styled Polish bank, Banque pour le Développement du Commerce (Decobank). However, the genuineness of the letters of credit is in issue, and [Kanaar] allege that the whole transaction was a prime bank instrument fraud. Indeed, the Law Society disciplinary tribunal concluded that, on the face of it, the purported transaction bore every hallmark of a prime bank instrument fraud. I would agree with this view. As now accepted by [Mr de Beer] in his reply, Decobank was not registered with the Polish authorities as a banking institution and there is no reference to any such bank in leading bank directories. Mr de Beer's case is that, in about September 1991 it was agreed between the associates and [Kanaar] that [Kanaar] would act for the associates in the sale of letters of credit and would share any commission to be paid as a result of brokering the transaction. [Kanaar] sought various buyers of the letters of credit on behalf of the Associates and found a so-called 'Tunisian group' whose representative was a Mr Victor Cruz who was based in Tunis. Mr Kendall-Bush went with a Mr Henriod (both of whom, together with [Kanaar], were to share in the commission) to Tunis in September 1991 with the aim of executing the sale of the letters of credit to the Tunisian group. Mr de Beer alleges that Mr Kendall-Bush and [Kanaar] have misappropriated $US 250,000 belonging to him in the following circumstances. Mr de Beer claims that on 31 October 1991 he transferred the sum of 374,210 Swiss francs (equivalent to $US 250,000) to the credit of an account of Mr Kendall-Bush ... in Tunis. This transfer was made in response to a letter dated 18 October 1991 in which Mr Kendall-Bush requested the associates to remit to him in Tunisia the sum of $US 250,000. Mr de Beer alleges that in this letter and orally Mr Kendall-Bush and Mr Kanaar assured him that the money was in effect to indicate bona fides on the part of the seller and that it would be returned without use within a matter of days. Mr de Beer claims that, on the same day that he transferred his money to Mr Kendall-Bush, the latter transferred the sum of 291,600 Swiss francs (equivalent to $US 200,000) to Mr Cruz. Mr de Beer claims this transfer was pursuant to a declaration by Mr Kendall-Bush on 19 October 1991 to remit to Mr Cruz $US 200,000 by way of penalty for non-performance by Decobank. Mr de Beer claims that the remaining $US 50,000 was at a later date transferred to Mr Kendall-Bush and that none of the money has been returned to him; in other words, that Mr Kendall-Bush has misappropriated Mr de Beer's money. Mr de Beer further alleges that at all material times Mr Kendall-Bush acted with the authority of [Kanaar] and that [Kanaar] expressly authorised Mr Kendall-Bush to act on their behalf in relation to the letters of credit. Mr de Beer therefore claims to be entitled in restitution to the return of $US 250,000 by [Kanaar] and/or Mr Kendall-Bush as money had and received. [Kanaar] claims by way of defence that, in relation to the transaction involving $US 250,000, Mr Kendall-Bush acted on his own behalf and not on behalf of the firm. [Kanaar] maintains that the whole nature of the transaction had changed, and that a letter dated 18 October 1991, which was faxed to the associates, indicated that any ostensible authority which Mr Kendall-Bush had had from [Kanaar] was terminated. [Kanaar] further claim that Mr de Beer was involved in a fraudulent and unlawful design in that Mr de Beer and the associates sought to obtain substantial funds by selling the letters of credit, when he knew that Decobank was not bona fide and that the letters of credit were bogus and worthless. [Kanaar] further contends that Mr de Beer pressed on with what he must have appreciated was a fraudulent transaction in order to obtain very substantial funds on the basis of false instruments ... In short, [Kanaar] contends that [Mr de Beer] was an active participant in the fraudulent scheme to obtain funds by means of discounting false bank instruments and that the deposit of the sum for which he now makes a claim formed a step in an attempt to implement the fraud. The exact nature of Mr Kendall-Bush's defence is unclear from his pleaded defence. It appears that he also alleges that Mr de Beer was involved in a fraudulent scheme.'

[7] The writ was issued on 28 October 1997, shortly before the expiry of the limitation period. On 28 March 2000, following close of pleadings, Master Bowles gave directions for a case management conference. By an application notice dated 30 June 2000 Kanaar applied for an order that Mr de Beer give security for its costs. The sum sought by way of security was £130,000, representing Kanaar's estimated costs to the end of the trial. On 2 November 2000 Master Bowles

directed that Kanaar's application be listed with the case management conference. The case management conference was held before the judge, and led to the order dismissing the application against which Kanaar now appeals.

[8] In his evidence in opposition to the application Mr de Beer disclosed that he had a right to an interest in the estate of a deceased person which was in the course of being administered in Holland by executors appointed there, and that he currently owned cash and equities held by UBS Bank in Switzerland. The situs of Mr de Beer's interest in the unadministered estate in Holland may have been open to question, but the judge regarded this as immaterial in the light of evidence that his assets in Switzerland were worth about £177,000. The judge was accordingly content to proceed on the footing that the Swiss assets were of sufficient value to meet any order for costs which might be made in favour of Kanaar.

[9] In the course of the hearing of this appeal Mr Saini told us that the current net value of Mr de Beer's assets in Switzerland was only some $US 28,753. He based this assertion on a statement provided by UBS. However, in a note which he has sent to us since the hearing he informs us that the current value of the Swiss assets is of the order of £162,000. In his note Mr Saini explains the reason for the error, as follows:

'It has been revealed that the UBS statement failed to include a substantial asset valued at US$ 195,000, namely 13,000 shares in Apogee Technology Inc at US$ 15 per share ... and that the true value of his assets held by UBS in Switzerland is, therefore, in fact of the order of US$ 223,753, which at the current rate of exchange ... is equivalent to £162,022·45.'

[10] Annexed to Mr Saini's note is a copy of a fax dated 31 July 2001 from UBS to Mr Michael Cohn, Mr de Beer's solicitor. The fax reads as follows (so far as material):

'Enclosed you will find a copy of the delivery receipt ... referring to 13,000 shares [in] Apogee Technology Inc. and we confirm that we hold the certificate for these shares on behalf of Mr Hans David de Beer. We need the form called "Irrevocable Stock or Bond Power" signed by Mr Hans David de Beer to book this stock into the UBS Custody Account. Unfortunately this form has not been signed and returned by Mr Hans David de Beer and it is for this reason that the stock was not included in the statement of assets as per July 26, 2001. Please be informed that we hold the stocks in our file but will not be able to sell or even transfer them unless receipt of the form "Irrevocable Stock or Bond Power". Should the form not be signed at the time we will return the share certificate [to] the client's correspondence address. We are able to confirm that the market value of the above stock on July 27 was USD 15 per share and that the above stock was included in the amount of CHF 446,800.-in our letter to Mr Hans David de Beer dated October 31, 2000.'

The provisions of the CPR relating to security for costs

[11] The provisions of the CPR relating to security for costs are to be found in section II of CPR Pt 25, which comprises rr 25.12–25.15 inclusive. Rule 25.14 (security for costs other than from the claimant) and r 25.15 (security for costs of

a an appeal) are not material for present purposes. Rules 25.12 and 25.13 provide as follows (so far as material):

> '25.12 (1) A defendant to any claim may apply under this Section of this Part for security for his costs of the proceedings ...
>
> *b* (3) Where the court makes an order for security for costs, it will— (a) determine the amount of security; and (b) direct—(i) the manner in which; and (ii) the time within which the security must be given.
>
> 25.13 (1) The court may make an order for security for costs under rule 25.12 if—(a) it is satisfied, having regard to all the circumstances of the case, that it is just to make such an order; and (b)(i) one or more of the conditions in paragraph (2) applies, or (ii) ...
>
> *c* (2) The conditions are—(a) the claimant is an individual—(i) who is ordinarily resident out of the jurisdiction; and (ii) is not *a person against whom a claim can be enforced* under the Brussels Conventions or the Lugano Convention, as defined by section 1(1) of the Civil Jurisdiction and Judgments Act 1982 ... (f) the claimant is acting as a nominal claimant ... and there is *d* reason to believe that he will be unable to pay the defendant's costs if ordered to do so; (g) the claimant has taken steps in relation to his assets that would make it difficult to enforce an order for costs against him.' (My emphasis.)

The issues on this appeal

e [12] The primary issue on this appeal is as to the true meaning and effect of the words in italics in r 25.13(2)(a)(ii). More particularly, the primary issue is whether an individual claimant who currently has assets in a convention state is 'a person against whom a claim can be enforced' under the conventions, with the consequence that there is no jurisdiction under the CPR to make an order that he *f* give security for costs. We refer to this issue hereafter as 'the jurisdiction issue'.

[13] By a respondent's notice, Mr de Beer seeks to uphold the judge's order on the footing that, if (contrary to his primary submission) the judge had jurisdiction to order security, she ought as a matter of discretion to have declined to exercise that jurisdiction in the circumstances of the instant case. Thus, if the jurisdiction issue is resolved in favour of Kanaar, further issues arise as to whether, as a matter *g* of discretion, security should be ordered, and if so on what terms. We refer hereafter to these issues compendiously as 'the discretion issue'.

The judgment of Elizabeth Gloster QC

[14] Having set out the background to the matter in the passage which I have *h* quoted, the judge considered what approach she should adopt to the merits of the claim against Kanaar and of Kanaar's defence. She expressed her conclusion (at para 7) on that question as follows:

> 'In my judgment, and despite the persuasive attempts of Mr Marshall to persuade me to do so, it is not appropriate for me ... to make any prima facie *j* determination as to the underlying merits or otherwise of the claim or [of Kanaar's] defence. There are clearly real and substantial issues which have to be resolved at trial as to the respective knowledge and roles of both parties. I am not in a position, and it is not appropriate for me, to make any determination in relation to these matters, even on a provisional basis, at this stage, and I do not propose to do so.'

[15] The judge then turned to the application for security for costs, identifying
the first issue for decision as being whether the court had jurisdiction to make the
order sought, given that Mr de Beer currently had assets in a convention state
(ie the jurisdiction issue). She pointed out that, whether or not Mr de Beer's right
to an interest in the estate being administered in the Netherlands was properly to
be regarded as located in the Netherlands, the existence of assets in Switzerland
sufficed to raise the jurisdiction issue.

[16] After summarising each side's arguments on the jurisdiction issue, the
judge turned to the authorities as to security for costs as they stood prior to the
introduction of the CPR, under the former Rules of the Supreme Court (RSC).
She referred to a number of authorities, including the Court of Appeal decision in
Fitzgerald v Williams, O'Regan v Williams [1996] 2 All ER 171, [1996] QB 657. In that
case the question arose whether and in what circumstances the court should
order security for costs against plaintiffs who were ordinarily resident in Ireland.
The relevant provision of the RSC was Ord 23 r 1(1)(a), which provided as
follows:

> 'Where, on the application of a defendant to an action or other proceeding
> in the High Court, it appears to the Court—(a) that the plaintiff is ordinarily
> resident out of the jurisdiction ... then if, having regard to all the
> circumstances of the case, the Court thinks it just to do so, it may order the
> plaintiff to give such security for the defendant's costs of the action or other
> proceeding as it thinks just.'

[17] For the Irish plaintiffs it was contended that since the Republic of Ireland
was a state party to the Brussels Conventions, their right to protection against
discrimination on grounds of nationality conferred by arts 6 and 220 of the EC
Treaty (now arts 12 EC and 293 EC) required the court to disapply r 1(1)(a). The
judge at first instance concluded that r 1(1)(a) did not contravene art 6, and
ordered the Irish plaintiffs to give security. The Court of Appeal allowed their
appeal, holding that r 1(1)(a) was covertly discriminatory on the ground of
nationality. The leading judgment was given by Bingham MR, with whom Waite
and Otton LJJ agreed. In the course of his judgment Bingham MR referred to the
decision of the Court of Justice of the European Communities in *Mund & Fester v
Hatrex Internationaal Transport* Case C-398/92 [1994] ECR I-467. He said:

> '(iii) Is the rule discriminatory? The rule plainly empowers the court to
> make orders against plaintiffs ordinarily resident out of the jurisdiction
> which it could not make against plaintiffs ordinarily resident within it ... It
> therefore involves discrimination in the sense used by the Court of Justice in
> *Mund*, in that different plaintiffs are treated differently. (iv) Is that discrimination
> based on nationality? On its face, the discrimination for which the rule
> provides is based on ordinary residence, not nationality. A British national
> ordinarily resident abroad may be required to give security, a foreign
> national ordinarily resident within the jurisdiction may not. But there is a
> close analogy with *Mund*: just as most German judgments to be enforced
> outside Germany would not be against Germans, so most plaintiffs in
> England ordinarily resident outside the jurisdiction would not be British.
> Just as para 917(2) [of the German Code of Civil Procedure] was held to be
> covertly discriminatory on grounds of nationality, so must the same
> conclusion follow in relation to the rule.' (See [1996] 2 All ER 171 at 182–183,
> [1996] QB 657 at 674.)

a

[18] Later in his judgment, Bingham MR said:

> 'The answer compelled by *Mund* in my view is: the English court should never exercise its discretion under the rule to order security to be given by an individual plaintiff who is a national of and resident in another member state party to the [Brussels] convention, at any rate in the absence of very cogent evidence of substantial difficulty in enforcing a judgment in that other

b
> member state.' (See [1996] 2 All ER 171 at 183, [1996] QB 657 at 675.)

[19] The judge in the instant case went on to observe that by parity of reasoning the same constraint applied to claimants who were ordinarily resident in states party to the Lugano Convention, which contained a non-discrimination provision in similar terms.

c
[20] The judge then turned to the relevant provisions of the CPR, and in particular to r 25.13(2)(a)(ii), remarking that, apart from an obiter comment by Ian Hunter QC sitting as a deputy High Court judge in *Bunzl v Martin Bunzl International Ltd* [2000] All ER (D) 911, the instant case appeared to be the first case in which the proper construction of the rule had been considered.

d
[21] The judge continued as follows:

> '29. The language of sub-para (a)(ii) requires the court to identify whether the claimant against whom security is sought is a person of a particular type. If he is a person of a particular type, ie a person against whom a claim can be enforced under the Brussels Conventions or the Lugano Convention, then

e
> the condition in para (2)(a) is not satisfied and therefore security cannot be awarded on that ground.
>
> 30. The first point to make is that the language of the sub-para does not describe persons by reference to residence in a convention state, nor by reference to nationality of a convention state. If the draftsman had so

f
> intended, he clearly could have described a person by reference to his residence. Residence, or, rather, ordinary residence, is a concept invoked in sub-para (2)(a)(i). On the contrary, as I have said, the only requirement specified under sub-para (2)(a)(ii) which has the result that the condition in sub-para (2)(a)(ii) is not satisfied is that a claim can be enforced "against such a person" under the Brussels Conventions or the Lugano Convention.'

g
[22] The judge then turned to the meaning of the word 'claim', concluding (at para 32):

> '... the natural construction of the words taken in context is that "claim" is referring to an order for costs in the current proceedings against the claimant,

h
> rather than a hypothetical claim for an unascertained amount which can be enforced against a claimant, whether because he is ordinarily resident in a convention state or because he has assets in such state.'

[23] The judge acknowledged, however, that the alternative construction was feasible.

j
[24] Then, after recording that it was common ground (a) that, under the conventions, a judgment obtained in one convention state could be enforced in another convention state by means of execution against assets of the judgment debtor situated in the latter state, and (b) that, on the facts of the instant case, a judgment obtained in the United Kingdom could be enforced against assets of Mr de Beer which were situated in Switzerland, the judge identified the critical

issue as being whether such enforcement would constitute the enforcement of a claim against Mr de Beer within the meaning of r 25.13(2)(a)(ii).

[25] The judge concluded that it would do so, for five reasons. Her first reason was that in her judgment the language of the conventions themselves clearly envisages that the enforcement in a convention state of a judgment obtained in another convention state is enforcement of a judgment 'against' a person, albeit that person is not domiciled or ordinarily resident in the state in which enforcement is effected. Her second reason was that had the intention been to adopt a residence-based exclusion as opposed to an enforceability-based exclusion, the draftsman could easily have achieved that end by express language. Her third reason was that notwithstanding that the effect of her construction of the rule was that whereas jurisdiction to order security for costs would have existed had Mr de Beer's assets been situated in England, the fact that they were situated in another convention state served to exclude such jurisdiction, that 'quirk' did not prevent the court from giving effect to what she considered to be the plain language of the rule. Her fourth reason was that Kanaar's reliance on the fact that, on her construction of the rule, a claimant could always avoid having to give security by the simple expedient of placing an asset (e g a cash deposit refundable on demand) in a convention state, was misplaced in that—

> '[t]o suggest that such a person is not a person against whom a claim can be enforced under the conventions because of the undoubted ability to move assets at short notice would ... be to draw an unwarranted and discriminatory distinction between liquid assets in England and liquid assets in other convention states.'

[26] The judge further concluded that r 25.13(2)(g) provided a sufficient safeguard from the suggested abuse. As to that, she said:

> 'In my judgment, the other conditions set out in para (2) and in particular that set out in para (g), "the claimant has taken steps in relation to his assets that would make it difficult to enforce an order for costs against him", provide a sufficient safeguard from this type of abuse. If, for example, some two months after an unsuccessful security application a claimant were to refuse to confirm, pursuant to a request made by a defendant, that he continued to hold sufficient assets in a convention state, or refused to identify those assets, a court might well be entitled to infer that the claimant fell within condition [(2)(g)] and that, accordingly, a subsequent application for security would be successful.'

[27] As her fifth reason for reaching her conclusion as to the true construction of the rule, the judge considered that the obiter dictum of Ian Hunter QC in Bunzl's case, on which Mr Marshall had relied, was of no assistance in the instant case since the effect and ambit of the CPR was not in issue in Bunzl's case.

[28] The judge concluded her judgment on the application for security for costs by saying:

> '37. I conclude that, in the light of the acceptance by Mr Marshall that the claimant does indeed have assets in convention states against which an order for the costs of the action could be enforced, the claimant is indeed a person against whom a claim could be enforced under the conventions. Accordingly, in my judgment, no security for costs can be awarded against him under CPR 25.13 because the condition set out in para [(2)(a)] is not satisfied ...

38. I do not propose, in view of the length of this judgment, to indicate what order I would have made had I not reached the view which I have on the construction of the new rule. I do not consider it is appropriate in all the circumstances for me to do so.'

The arguments on the jurisdiction issue

[29] Mr Marshall submits that on its true construction r 25.13(2)(a) precludes an order for security for costs being made against a claimant who is ordinarily resident in a convention state, and that it does not preclude such an order being made against a claimant who is not so resident but who happens to have assets, or an asset, in a convention state. He submits, further, that that was the intended meaning of the new rule, in that the purpose of the new rule was to limit the court's discretion to order security so as to make it fully compatible with Community law by providing that no order can be made against a claimant who is ordinarily resident in a convention state, thereby avoiding the tension which existed under the old rules between the court's discretion and art 6 of the EC Treaty (see the judgment of Bingham MR in *Fitzgerald v Williams, O'Regan v Williams* [1996] 2 All ER 171, [1996] QB 657 and his later judgment in *Chequepoint SARL v McClelland* [1997] 2 All ER 384, [1997] QB 51).

[30] In support of this submission Mr Marshall also relies on a discussion paper circulated by the Lord Chancellor's Department in 1997, prior to the introduction of the CPR, entitled *Civil Procedure Rules—Security for Costs*. He also refers to a note to that effect in *Civil Procedure* (Autumn 2000) vol 1. However, the corresponding note in the *Civil Procedure* (Spring 2001) vol 1, p 451, para 25.13 is framed in more circumspect terms, acknowledging that the precise construction of the rule is not free from doubt.

[31] Mr Marshall relies on the observation of Ian Hunter QC in *Bunzl's* case that 'the court no longer has any jurisdiction to make an order for security for costs against a person resident in a state party to the Brussels Convention or the Lugano Convention.' He submits that that is the correct interpretation of the rule. He submits out that the rule is 'person-specific' not 'asset-specific'. The current location of a claimant's assets is, he submits, irrelevant to the question of jurisdiction.

[32] Mr Marshall further submits that the judge's construction leads to absurd results. By way of example, he contrasts the position where a United States resident has assets in England (in which case the English courts have jurisdiction to order security) with the position where his assets are in another convention state (in which case, if the judge is right, there is no such jurisdiction). Further, he points out that if the words 'can be enforced' in r 25.13(2)(a)(ii) envisage enforcement leading to full recovery (that being the basis on which the judge proceeded) then the court would be concerned to satisfy itself as a matter of jurisdiction (a) that, having regard to current values, the asset or assets in question would be of sufficient value to satisfy an order for costs, and (b) that the courts in the convention state or states in which the asset or assets were situated would enforce any order for costs against such asset or assets.

[33] Mr Marshall submits that the reference to 'a claim' in r 25.13(2)(a)(ii) is to be contrasted with the express references to the enforcement of orders for costs in r 25.13(2)(f) and (g). He submits further that, in context, the reference to the enforcement of 'a claim' includes any hypothetical claim for relief, not necessarily limited to a money claim. He submits that only if a person is ordinarily resident

in a convention state can it be said that any hypothetical claim for relief is capable of being enforced against him in that state. Such a construction would, he submits, be fully workable.

[34] Mr Marshall also relies on two authorities decided since the judge delivered her judgment, namely the decision of Brooke LJ in *White Sea & Onega Shipping Co v International Transport Workers Federation* [2001] EWCA Civ 377, [2001] All ER (D) 447 (Mar), and the decision of the Court of Appeal in *Nasser v United Bank of Kuwait* [2001] EWCA Civ 556, [2002] 1 All ER 401, [2002] 1 WLR 1868.

[35] In the *White Sea* case [2001] All ER (D) 447 (Mar) the defendant/respondent applied for security for its costs of an appeal by the claimant, a shipping company incorporated and based in Russia. The claimant resisted the application for security on the ground (among other things) that there was no jurisdiction to grant security since, as the judge put it, 'the odds are that there will be a vessel owned by [the claimant] within the jurisdiction of one or other of the Brussels Convention or Lugano Convention countries'. In his judgment Brooke LJ said:

> '[12] Although it would be wrong to interpret the new rules simply as altering some of the inconveniences of the old rules—the CPR are a brand new code—in my judgment, there is a good deal of force in [counsel for the defendant's] submission that the wording of the new rule [a reference to r 25.13] was introduced in order to abolish the objection or discriminatory effect of the language of the old rule as set out in the judgments of Lord Bingham CJ in *Chequepoint SARL v McClelland* [1997] 2 All ER 384 at 389, 390, [1997] QB 51 at 59, 60 following, as they did, his earlier judgment in *Fitzgerald v Williams, O'Regan v Williams* [1996] 2 All ER 171, [1996] QB 657.
>
> [13] In my judgment, as a matter of interpretation of the rule, [counsel for the defendant's] approach to interpretation should be preferred. He has reminded me that the old security for costs provision under RSC Ord 23, although not unlawful, was held to be discriminatory under art 6 of the Treaty if applied to nationals and residents of other convention countries. Against this background I would interpret the rule as being confined to persons who are nationals of or residents of other convention countries. This decision goes to jurisdiction, and there may be, when it comes to the exercise of discretion, formidable reasons for declining to order security if, on the facts before the court in any particular case, it is not just to make an order.'

[36] Brooke LJ went on to cite a passage from the judgment of Lightman J in *Leyvand v Barasch* [2000] All ER (D) 181 in which Lightman J, referring to the exercise of the court's discretion to order security for costs, said this:

> 'The commonsense principle applies that the existence of assets within the jurisdiction, their fixity and permanence, are among a number of potentially relevant factors, their importance depending on the particular facts of the case.'

[37] In *Nasser v United Bank of Kuwait* [2002] 1 All ER 401, [2002] 1 WLR 1868, the Court of Appeal considered the jurisdiction to order security for costs under the CPR in the light of arts 6 and 14 of the European Convention for the Protection of Human Rights and Fundamental Freedoms 1950 (as set out in Sch 1 to the Human Rights Act 1998), with particular reference to applications for

a
security for the costs of an appeal. The leading judgment was given by Mance LJ, with whom Simon Brown LJ agreed. In his judgment Mance LJ drew attention to an important change effected by the CPR in the practice of the Court of Appeal as regards security for the costs of appeals, in that whereas under the old rules the court had a discretion to order security 'in special circumstances', and it was settled practice that impecuniosity of itself constituted such a special circumstance,
b
under CPR r 25.13 the court could only order security if one or more of the conditions in r 25.13(2) applies.

[38] Mance LJ commented (at [35]) that the requirement of r 25.13(2)(a)(i) that the claimant should be ordinarily resident out of the jurisdiction mirrors a ground for ordering security for costs against a plaintiff under the old rules. He continued:
c

'In that connection there was clear authority, indicating that, although foreign residence was a precondition to the making of such an order, once that precondition was satisfied, the court could have regard not merely to matters related directly to the foreign residence, but also to matters intrinsic
d
to the plaintiff wherever he or she might be, such as impecuniosity ...'

[39] Mance LJ said (at [46]):

'What remains as one ground on which security may be ordered is foreign residence—except in cases involving the "single legal market" to which the Brussels Conventions and Lugano Convention ... aspire in matters of
e
enforcement and recognition. The rationale of the discretion to order security on that ground is that enforcement of an order for security for costs abroad may be more difficult or costly than elsewhere (cf Sir Jeffery Bowman's 1997 Review (paras 33–37)). The single legal market of the Brussels and Lugano Conventions means that "abroad" in this context now
f
means not merely outside England or the United Kingdom, but outside the jurisdictions of the states party to those conventions.'

[40] Mance LJ (at [57]) referred to the distinction drawn in the CPR between claimants resident within and outside convention states. He continued:

g
'This distinction serves simply to identify *when* a discretion exists to order security for a defendant's or respondent's costs. In that context, the distinction between residents within and outside Brussels and Lugano states cannot be regarded as unduly discriminatory, since, first, it can be said that the recognition of separate categories makes sense as a broad rule of thumb, defining when any question of discretion can arise (rather than how it will be
h
exercised); and, secondly and in any event, the distinction drawn is in that context reasonable and objectively justifiable. The single legal market of the Brussels and Lugano Conventions is a significant achievement on the road to the easy and automatic recognition and enforcement of judgments, as recognised by the decision in the *Mund* case.'

j
[41] Turning to the considerations relevant to the exercise of the discretion itself, Mance LJ observed (at [58]):

'The distinction in the rules based on considerations of enforcement cannot be used to discriminate against those whose national origin is outside any Brussels and Lugano state on grounds unrelated to enforcement.'

[42] Mance LJ said (at [61]):

'Returning to rr 25.15(1), 25.13(1), (2)(a) and (b), if the discretion to order security is to be exercised, it should therefore be on objectively justified grounds relating to obstacles to or the burden of enforcement in the context of the particular foreign claimant or country concerned.'

[43] Later, Mance LJ said (at [62]):

'The justification for the discretion under rr 25.13(2)(a) [and] (b) … in relation to individuals and companies ordinarily resident abroad is that in some, it may well be many, cases there are likely to be substantial obstacles to or a substantial extra burden (e g of costs or delay) in enforcing an English judgment, significantly greater than there would be as regards a party resident in England or in a Brussels or Lugano state. In so far as impecuniosity may have a continuing relevance, it is not on the ground that the claimant lacks apparent means to satisfy any judgment, but on the ground (where this applies) that the effect of the impecuniosity would be either (i) to preclude or hinder or add to the burden of enforcement abroad against such assets as *do* exist abroad, or (ii) as a practical matter, to make it more likely that the claimant would take advantage of any available opportunity to avoid or hinder such enforcement abroad.'

[44] Mance LJ noted (at [65]) that no evidence had been put before the court to suggest that the defendants would face any difficulty in enforcing an order for costs against the claimant in the United States, but he went on to infer (at [66]) that some extra costs would be involved. Accordingly at [67] he said:

'The risk against which the present defendants are entitled to protection is, thus, not that the claimant will not have the assets to pay the costs, and not that the law of her state of residence will not recognise and enforce any judgment against her for costs. It is that the steps taken to enforce any such judgment in the United States will involve an extra burden in terms of costs and delay, compared with any equivalent steps that could be taken here or in any other Brussels/Lugano state. Any order for security for costs in this case should be tailored in amount to reflect the nature and size of the risk against which it is designed to protect.'

[45] Mr Marshall relies on both these recent decisions as supporting the view that the purpose and effect of r 25.13(2)(a)(ii) is to exclude from the scope of the court's discretion claimants who are ordinarily resident in a convention state, and that the rationale of that rule is the aspirational 'single legal market' made up of convention states and the ease with which judgments obtained in one convention state may be enforced in another.

[46] Mr Marshall accordingly submits that, construing the rule in accordance with its purpose and its natural meaning and so as to avoid absurdity, it must mean that jurisdiction is excluded where the individual claimant is ordinarily resident in another convention state.

[47] In the alternative, if (contrary to his primary submissions) the word 'claim' in the new rule is to be treated as a reference to a specific prospective judgment or order for costs in these proceedings, Mr Marshall nevertheless repeats his submissions as to the meaning and effect of the words 'can be enforced'.

a [48] Mr Saini supports the reasoning and conclusion of the judge on the jurisdiction issue. He submits that the purpose of the condition in r 25.13(2)(a)(ii) is to prevent security being awarded against individual claimants who have assets in convention states which can be used for the purpose of enforcement of costs orders made in this jurisdiction. He submits that the condition is 'enforceability-based' as opposed to 'residence-based'. He further submits that the construction

b contended for by Kanaar wholly ignores the plain wording of the condition and requires, in effect, that the condition be substantially rewritten. He also relies on sub-para (g) of the condition as extending the jurisdiction to cover cases in which a claimant seeks to shelter his assets from an application for security for costs.

[49] Mr Saini submits that the relevant question for the court is whether the 'person' referred to in the rule is a person against whom a claim can be enforced

c under the conventions, wherever his residence may be, and that in deciding whether a 'claim' can be enforced the court has to consider (a) whether the claim is of a type which can be enforced under the conventions and (b) whether the claimant has assets in a convention state against which execution can issue.

[50] As to the two recent authorities relied on by Mr Marshall (*White Sea &*

d *Onega Shipping Co v International Transport Workers Federation* [2001] All ER (D) 447 (Mar) and *Nasser v United Bank of Kuwait* [2002] 1 All ER 401, [2002] 1 WLR 1868), Mr Saini points out that in the *White Sea* case Brooke LJ (at [13]) interprets the rule as being confined 'to persons who are nationals of or residents of other convention countries'. Mr Saini submits that since Mr de Beer is a Dutch national (albeit resident in the United States), it follows that on Brooke LJ's

e interpretation of the rule there is no jurisdiction to order for security for costs against him. As to *Nasser*'s case, Mr Saini points out that the Court of Appeal was not concerned in that case with the question of the true construction of r 25.13(2)(a)(ii), but rather with general considerations as to the jurisdiction of the court (and in particular of the Court of Appeal) to order security for costs. He

f submits that whilst it is correct to say that Mance LJ referred on a number of occasions in the course of his judgment to a distinction being drawn between 'residence' within and outside convention states, Mance LJ did not have to focus on, still less decide, the question of construction raised in the instant case.

[51] We should record that, although we raised the point in the course of argument, and despite the focus which the conventions place on domicile,

g neither side sought to put forward any argument based on domicile.

Conclusions on the jurisdiction issue

[52] The drafting of r 25.13(2)(a)(ii) is on any footing unsatisfactory, and its meaning is not entirely clear. This has enabled each side to say with force that

h had the draftsman intended to achieve the result contended for by the other he could easily have done so by the use of clear words.

[53] The particular words which give rise to difficulty are the words 'a person against whom a claim can be enforced'. The concept of a 'claim' being 'enforced' is not an altogether happy one, since one would normally speak of a claim being

j 'brought' and of a judgment or order being 'enforced'. So the question arises which construction takes precedence: that is to say, whether (as the judge concluded) 'a claim' is to be construed as meaning a judgment or order (ie in the context of security for costs, a judgment or order for costs), or whether 'enforced' is to be construed as meaning 'brought'. Taking the words in isolation and out of context, either construction could be the correct one. For that reason alone,

we regard the judge's reference (at para 36(3) of her judgment) to 'the plain
language of the provision' as somewhat misplaced.

[54] That being so, it becomes important to consider the relevant context; that
is to say the background against which the new rule came to be introduced. In
this connection, we consider that it is legitimate to have regard to the mischief
which was perceived to exist under the old rule.

[55] As noted earlier, *Mund & Fester v Hatrex Internationaal Transport* Case
C-398/92 [1994] ECR I-467 established that the jurisdiction under the old rule was
incompatible with Community law in so far as it discriminated covertly against
nationals of other convention states. This in turn led to the decision in *Fitzgerald v
Williams, O'Regan v Williams* [1996] 2 All ER 171, [1996] QB 657, to the effect that
although the jurisdiction existed it should not be exercised in a manner which was
contrary to Community law. In the circumstances it is in our judgment a
fair—indeed, we would say inevitable—inference that it was a primary aim of the
new rule to remove that anomaly by limiting the *jurisdiction* to order security for
costs so as to ensure that the discretion which it confers is not capable of being
exercised in a manner which conflicts with Community law. As Mance LJ put it
in *Nasser's* case [2002] 1 All ER 401 at [46] (in a passage quoted earlier): '... "abroad"
... now means not merely outside England or the United Kingdom, but outside
the jurisdictions of the states party to [the] conventions ...'

[56] If, therefore, we are entitled to give a purposive construction to the new
rule—and we consider that we are so entitled—we take the purpose of
sub-para (a)(ii) to be to eliminate any covert discrimination against nationals of
other convention states which would or might have existed had sub-para (a)(ii)
not been included as part of the condition—that is to say, had condition (a) read
simply 'the claimant is an individual who is ordinarily resident out of the
jurisdiction'.

[57] On that footing, we return to the wording of the subparagraph. In the
first place, it seems to us entirely legitimate, as well as being consistent with what
we have taken to be the purpose of the subparagraph, to construe the words 'a
claim' in a general sense; that is to say, as including any claim (whether or not a
money claim) and not limited to an order for costs. Such a construction is also
consistent with the other conditions in r 25.13(2), all of which are directed at
claimants of a particular kind, rather than at execution against assets. Even
para (g), which relates to the sheltering of assets, is expressed in terms of a
particular category of claimant rather than by reference to the assets themselves.

[58] In our judgment, r 25.13(2) is directed at what we may call the juridical
characteristics of the particular individual claimant, irrespective of what assets he
may currently own or where those assets may currently be situated. We further
conclude that condition (a), on its true construction, confines the jurisdiction to
order security for costs to cases where the claimant is an individual who is not
ordinarily resident either in this jurisdiction or in that of a convention state. It
follows that, in our judgment, such a claimant cannot deprive the court of
jurisdiction merely by placing an asset in a convention state.

[59] We take that to be the construction of the rule adopted by Brooke LJ
reached in the *White Sea* case [2001] All ER (D) 447 (Mar). Although Brooke LJ
referred (at [13]) to the rule being confined to 'nationals of *or* residents of other
convention countries', that sentence must be read in the light of the immediately
preceding sentence of his judgment, where he refers to 'nationals *and* residents
of other convention countries' (my emphasis). Moreover, to interpret Brooke LJ's

a reference to nationals of other convention countries in the manner contended for by Mr Saini would make little sense, given that Brooke LJ earlier refers to—

> 'the ... discriminatory effect of the language of the old rule as set out in judgments of Lord Bingham CJ in *Chequepoint SARL v McClelland* [1997] 2 All ER 384, [1997] QB 51 ... following, as they did, his earlier judgment in *Fitzgerald v Williams, O'Regan v Williams* [1996] 2 All ER 171, [1996] QB 65 ...'

b

We refer in particular to the passages from the judgment of Bingham MR in *Fitzgerald's* case quoted earlier in this judgment. Further, in our judgment, although it addressed a somewhat different issue, *Nasser's* case provides further support for our conclusion.

c [60] We are also fortified in our conclusion by a consideration of the implications of the construction of the rule favoured by the judge.

[61] In the first place, it seems to us that a jurisdiction which is based upon such ephemeral considerations as the values and the situs of a claimant's assets current at the date when an application for security is heard would pose very considerable practical difficulties both for litigants and for the court. If the *d* existence of the jurisdiction were to depend upon whether or not there was a reasonable prospect of full recovery of costs from the assets in question (that being the basis on which the judge proceeded) then the existence of the jurisdiction would appear to depend not only upon the values of the assets from time to time, but, one presumes, also the defendant's estimates of the amount of *e* the costs which the claimant might be ordered to pay. Both may be expected to vary from time to time. By way of example, had Mr Saini's initial information as to the current value of Mr de Beer's Swiss assets been correct an extraordinary position would have been reached, in that (on the judge's construction) there would currently be jurisdiction to order security whereas at the date of the hearing before the judge the value of the Swiss assets was sufficient to exclude *f* jurisdiction.

[62] We further agree with Mr Marshall that the judge's construction would produce the extraordinary result that whilst jurisdiction would exist to order security for costs against a United States resident with assets in this jurisdiction (but in no other convention state), no such jurisdiction would exist if he moved *g* those assets to another convention state.

[63] We accordingly conclude, in disagreement with the judge, that the court has jurisdiction under r 25.13(1) to order security for costs to be given by Mr de Beer by reason of the fact that he is an individual claimant who is (a) ordinarily resident out of the jurisdiction and (b) not ordinarily resident in a convention state. We accordingly allow the appeal.

h [64] It follows that we must now move on to consider whether the jurisdiction which we have held to exist should be exercised, and if so on what terms: that is to say, to address the discretion issue.

The discretion issue

j [65] Mr Marshall submits that in considering whether to exercise its discretion to order security it is material for the court to consider whether there is a want of probity on the part of Mr de Beer. In support of this submission Mr Marshall cites a passage from the judgment of Lightman J in *Leyvand v Barasch* [2000] All ER (D) 181, which follows the passage quoted by Brooke LJ in the *White Sea* case. In his judgment in *Leyvand's* case Lightman J said (at para 6):

'The court will not infer the existence of a real risk that assets in this country will be dissipated or shipped abroad to avoid their being available to satisfy a judgment for costs unless there is reason to question the probity of the claimant: there is no such reason in this case. If there is reason to question the claimant's probity, the character of his property within the jurisdiction is relevant in assessing the risk: the risk may be greater if the property is cash or immediately realisable or transportable, and less if fixed and permanent.'

[66] Mr Marshall goes on to submit that want of probity on the part of Mr de Beer is demonstrated in the instant case (a) by the fact that triable allegations of dishonesty are made against him and (b) by the fact that he has made grossly and demonstrably misleading statements in his witness statement concerning his assets in Florida.

[67] He further submits that, on the authority of Lightman J's observations in *Leyvand*'s case, the court should also have regard to the fact that the assets presently held by Mr de Beer in Switzerland are capable of being moved at the push of a button.

[68] Mr Marshall also relies on observations made by Bingham LJ in *Thune v London Properties Ltd* [1990] 1 All ER 972, [1990] 1 WLR 562. In that case the claimants were Norwegian trustees in bankruptcy, and although there was no question but that they would act with complete rectitude in relation to the enforcement of an order for costs against the bankrupt's estate, there was nevertheless a risk that the defendants would be unable to achieve full recovery since there might be other competing priority claims of unknown amount. Bingham LJ said:

'Thus the defendants are put to the very great cost of defending this expensive litigation with the risk, however small, that if they are ultimately successful they will be unable to recover their taxed costs despite the ease of procedural enforcement in Norway. I consider, in the exercise of my discretion, that this is a risk to which the defendants should not be put and that security should be given ...' (See [1990] 1 All ER 972 at 981, [1990] 1 WLR 562 at 574.)

[69] Mr Marshall submits that a similar risk exists in the instant case, and that accordingly security should be ordered.

[70] As to the enforceability in Florida of an order for costs made in this jurisdiction, Mr Marshall referred us to the witness statement of a Mr Litsky, an American lawyer and Kanaar's expert witness, to the effect that although a costs order made by the English court is a type of judgment which is prima facie capable of recognition in Florida pursuant to a Florida statute, nevertheless Mr de Beer could argue that the statute does not apply on the ground that the order was obtained by fraud, alternatively on grounds of non-reciprocity. Mr Litsky's opinion is that such challenges by Mr de Beer could involve a fully argued hearing, possibly involving disclosure and expert evidence on English law.

[71] As to Mr de Beer's Swiss assets, in a note sent to us after the hearing by way of response to Mr Saini's note (referred to earlier in this judgment), Mr Marshall submits that on the available documentary material there must be considerable doubt whether enforcement could be effected in Switzerland against the shares in Apogee Technology Inc since the situs of the shares would appear to be the United States. At all events, he points out, there is no evidence

a either that the company was incorporated in Switzerland or that it maintains a register of members there. Mr Marshall further submits that the share certificate could easily be moved, or the shares themselves disposed of. Finally in relation to the Swiss assets, Mr Marshall says that the court below was never informed that the Swiss assets included shares in an American company, and that in consequence it was (as he puts it) extremely doubtful that they would be capable

b of being realised by enforcement in Switzerland.

[72] Mr Marshall accordingly submits that security should be ordered in the sum of £130,000, on the footing that that is a reasonable estimate of the amount of Kanaar's costs up to the end of the trial.

[73] Mr Saini accepts that £130,000 is a reasonable estimate of Kanaar's costs up to the end of the trial, but he submits that in the circumstances it would not

c be just to order any security; alternatively he submits that if security is to be ordered at all it should be ordered in a much smaller sum, proportionate to the degree of risk which Kanaar faces. In this connection, Mr Saini relies on Mance LJ's reference in *Nasser's* case [2001] 1 All ER 401 at [67] to any order for security being 'tailored in amount to reflect the nature and size of the risk against which it is

d designed to protect'.

[74] Mr Saini submits that the mere fact that an allegation of dishonesty is made against Mr de Beer on the pleadings cannot justify the court in proceeding on the footing that there is any want of probity on Mr de Beer's part. As to Mr de Beer's witness statement, Mr Saini accepts that it contains a misleading statement as to his assets in Florida, but he submits that there is no reason to

e infer that the statement was deliberately misleading; in any event, he submits, the witness statement establishes that Mr de Beer has substantial assets in Florida.

[75] As to possible difficulties of enforcement, Mr Saini referred us to the witness statement of Mr Louis Stinson, Mr de Beer's expert witness as to American law. In a short witness statement, Mr Stinson confirms that an order

f for costs made by an English court would be capable of enforcement in Florida in accordance with the Florida statute. He further states that the costs of enforcement in Florida 'assuming no dispute as to recognition or enforceability of the judgment' would be relatively modest.

[76] Mr Saini submits that in the light of Mr Stinson's evidence the court

g should proceed on the footing that there is no significant risk that enforcement of an order for costs may prove more difficult, or materially more expensive, in Florida.

[77] As to enforcement of an order for costs against Mr de Beer's Swiss assets, Mr Saini relies on para 32 of the judgment of Mr Ian Hunter QC in *Bunzl v Martin*

h *Bunzl International Ltd* [2000] All ER (D) 911, which reads as follows:

> 'In my judgment the consideration which requires careful attention in the circumstances of the present case is whether, as Bingham MR put it in *Fitzgerald v Williams, O'Regan v Williams* [1996] 2 All ER 171, [1996] QB 657, there is "any cogent evidence of substantial difficulty in enforcing a
> *j*   judgment" in Switzerland, notwithstanding that Switzerland is a party to the Lugano Convention. It is a matter for consideration whether the court should ever accede to the contention that there is or may be substantial difficulty in enforcing a judgment in a member state party to the Brussels or Lugano Conventions. After all, the whole purpose of those two conventions is to greatly reduce the opportunity for contesting

the recognition or enforcement of judgments from other contracting states and to produce in effect a free market in Community judgments. Member states of the European Union and the EEA [European Economic Area] are expected to give "full faith and credit" to the judgments of courts in other contracting states and judicial comity demands that the courts of one such state should not readily accede to the proposition that in practice the conventions are not achieving their purpose. On the other hand, there may be cases where cogent evidence to that effect is forthcoming: and where that is the case, the court should not hesitate to recognise the fact.'

[78] Mr Saini submits that there is no basis in the instant case for any suggestion that Kanaar would have difficulty in enforcing an order for costs in Switzerland, and he points to the fact that on current values the Swiss assets (including the shares in Apogee Technology Inc) are worth some £162,000.

[79] We accept Mr Saini's submission that the mere fact that Kanaar made serious allegations of dishonesty against Mr de Beer does not justify this court in proceeding on the footing that he lacks probity. On the other hand, we take a serious view of the misleading statement in his witness statement to which Mr Marshall has drawn our attention.

[80] In para 44 of his witness statement, which is dated 27 October 2000, under the heading 'Personal Finances', Mr de Beer says this:

'I am a Dutch citizen but my place of ordinary residence is Miami, Florida, United States of America. I have lived in the United States since 1987 and I have substantial assets in Florida. These include the following: (i) I am the owner of a property at 1222 Seabreeze Boulevard, Fort Lauderdale, Florida. The value of this property is about $US 1·2m and it is subject to a mortgage of about $US 210,000. This produces for me a monthly income of $US 5,000 ...'

[81] In a witness statement dated 4 December 2000 Mr Julian Aylmer, Kanaar's solicitor, states that he caused an investigator to visit the property in question, and that the investigator confirmed that it was up for sale. This drew a response from Mr Cohn (Mr de Beer's solicitor). In para 3.4 of his witness statement dated 8 December 2000 Mr Cohn says this:

'[Mr de Beer] put the house on the market through a real estate agent ... some months ago at a price of $US 895,000, and he has received a number of offers. While none has reached $US 895,000, [Mr de Beer] tells me that he would not, in fact, accept less than $US 1·2m for the property, as he considers that figure to reflect its true worth.'

[82] Mr Cohn then exhibits a letter from the agent dated 6 December 2000, addressed to Mr de Beer, in which the agent confirms that the house has been on the market 'for some months' at a price of $US 895,000. In the final paragraph of his letter, the agent says:

'You have told me that you personally consider the property to be worth $1,200,000 ... I consider that figure to be somewhat ambitious, but I recognize that you have considerable experience of property values and that your view may be correct.'

a

[83] In our judgment, the evidence of Mr Cohn, coupled with the letter from the agent, establishes that Mr de Beer's evidence about the property in Fort Lauderdale is materially misleading in what it does not say. It does not say that the property had been placed on the market for sale. It does not say that it was being marketed at a price substantially less than $US 1·2m. It does not say that although offers have been received, none has matched the asking price. It does

b not say that the valuation of $US 1·2m represents Mr de Beer's personal opinion of the value of the property (still less that it is an opinion which does not appear to be shared by the market). Moreover, it is difficult to see how Mr de Beer's evidence in this respect could have been other than deliberately misleading. In the circumstances, we take the view that it places a serious question mark over the reliability of the remainder of his evidence.

c

[84] Moreover, it appears from the evidence of Mr Litsky (which is not directly challenged in this respect by Mr Stinson) that there is, to put it at its lowest, a risk that an order for costs in Kanaar's favour may be difficult or even impossible to enforce in Florida.

[85] As to enforcement against Mr de Beer's Swiss assets, we are concerned

d that the court below may not have been told that by far the most valuable of these assets is the shareholding in Apogee Technology Inc. Certainly no mention of this fact is made in Mr de Beer's witness statement dated 27 October 2000, where he merely says: 'I also have cash, securities and Swiss mutual funds [on] deposit at UBS in Zurich amounting to about $US 175,000.'

[86] It seems to us that if the court below was not told that the Swiss assets

e included the shares in Apogee Technology Inc it plainly should have been, if only because (to put it at its lowest) it is by no means self-evident that an order for costs could be enforced in Switzerland against shares in an American company. However, not having heard oral submissions on the question of possible non-disclosure, it would not be appropriate for us to form any view on that

f question.

[87] The terms of the fax from UBS dated 31 July 2001, a copy of which is annexed to Mr Saini's note and the material parts of which we have quoted earlier in this judgment, also appear to raise doubts as to whether an order for costs could be enforced against the shares in Switzerland. On the face of it, unless and until Mr de Beer signs the requisite form, UBS cannot part with the share

g certificate other than to Mr de Beer.

[88] Once again, however, we take the view that since we have not heard oral argument on this question it would not be appropriate for us to form any view about it. In the circumstances we propose to proceed on the basis, favourable to Mr de Beer, that so far as enforcement of a costs order in Switzerland

h is concerned, the shares stand on the same footing as the other assets held by UBS.

[89] However, whilst we are content to proceed on the footing that there is in principle no reason to suppose that an order for costs might not be fully enforceable in Switzerland, we must also take into account the ease with which the assets

j presently held there may be moved. This applies to the Apogee shares as it does to the other assets.

[90] In all the circumstances, we conclude that Kanaar is at risk of being unable to enforce an order for costs against Mr de Beer, whether in part or at all, due either to lack of available assets against which such an order could be enforced, or to the unenforceability of such an order in Florida, or both.

[91] We further conclude that it is just in all the circumstances that Kanaar should be protected against that risk by the making of an order that Mr de Beer give security for its costs of the action to the end of the trial. Bearing in mind the nature and potential size of the risk, and given that Mr Saini's accepts that the proposed figure of £130,000 represents a reasonable estimate of Kanaar's costs up to the end of the trial, we order that security be given in that sum.

[92] We will hear counsel further as to the precise form of the order, in the event that it cannot be agreed.

Appeal allowed.

Gillian Crew　Barrister.

Millar v Dickson (Procurator Fiscal, Elgin) and other appeals

[2001] UKPC D4

PRIVY COUNCIL

LORD BINGHAM OF CORNHILL, LORD NICHOLLS OF BIRKENHEAD, LORD HOPE OF
CRAIGHEAD, LORD CLYDE AND LORD SCOTT OF FOSCOTE

2–4, 24 JULY 2001

Human rights – Right to a fair hearing – Impartial and independent tribunal –
Criminal proceedings – Appellants being prosecuted before tribunals that were not
impartial and independent for purposes of convention right to fair hearing – Whether
such prosecutions compatible with right to fair hearing if proceedings fair overall –
Human Rights Act 1998, Sch 1, Pt I, art 6(1).

Each of the defendants had either pleaded guilty to, or been convicted of, criminal
charges in proceedings before temporary sheriffs in Scotland, and had been
sentenced by such sheriffs. There was nothing to suggest that the outcome of any
of the cases would have been different if the relevant stages of the prosecution
had been conducted before permanent rather than temporary sheriffs. After the
conclusion of the proceedings against the defendants, the High Court of Justiciary
held in another case that a temporary sheriff was not an independent and
impartial tribunal for the purposes of the right to a fair hearing under art 6(1)[a] of
the European Convention for the Protection of Human Rights and Fundamental
Freedoms 1950 (as set out in Sch 1 to the Human Rights Act 1998). Relying on
that decision (the temporary sheriff decision), the defendants contended in
conjoined appeals to the High Court that their prosecutions had been unlawful
since, under s 57(2) of the Scotland Act 1998, the Lord Advocate had no power to
do any act that was incompatible with a convention right. The High Court
dismissed the appeals, holding that the defendants' agents had, through failing to
take the point at trial, waived their clients' right to object to the hearing of their
cases by temporary sheriffs. The defendants appealed to the Privy Council,
challenging that conclusion. On the appeals, the prosecution accepted that the
temporary sheriff decision was correct. They nevertheless contended that
the defendants had in fact received fair trials and that, in those circumstances, the
acts of the Lord Advocate in prosecuting their cases before temporary sheriffs had
not been incompatible with the defendants' rights under art 6(1) of the convention
since the critical issue was the fairness of the proceedings as a whole.

Held – The right of an accused in criminal proceedings to be tried by an independent
and impartial tribunal was one that could not be compromised or eroded unless
validly waived by the accused. The conduct of trials at all stages by such a
tribunal was recognised, subject to waiver where that was permissible, as a
necessary safeguard of the citizen's right to a fair trial, and the appearance of
independence and impartiality was just as important as the question whether
those qualities existed in fact. The issue whether there had been a breach of the
convention right to an independent and impartial tribunal could not be tested

---

a   Article 6, so far as material, is set out at [8], below

after the event by asking if the proceedings overall had been fair. In the context of that right, 'waiver' meant a voluntary, informed and unequivocal election by a party not to claim a right or raise an objection which it was open to that party to claim or raise. In the instant case, the defendants' agents had made no such waiver on behalf of their clients. They could only have done so if they had appreciated, or had to be taken to have appreciated, the effect of the eventual temporary sheriff decision or the real possibility of a decision to that or similar effect. There was no evidence that would justify such a finding or inference. Accordingly, the appeals would be allowed (see [16], [26], [27], [31], [38]–[40], [52]–[54], [60], [63], [66], [67], [70], [77], [83], [86], [87], below).

Notes

For the right to a fair trial in general and for independent and impartial tribunal in particular, see 8(2) *Halsbury's Laws* (4th edn reissue) paras 134, 140.

For the Human Rights Act 1998, Sch 1, Pt I, art 6, see 7 *Halsbury's Statutes* (4th edn) (1999 reissue) 523.

Cases referred to in judgments

Bradford v McLeod 1986 SLT 244, HC of Just.
Brown v Stott (Procurator Fiscal, Dunfermline) [2001] 2 All ER 97, [2001] 2 WLR 817, PC.
Bulut v Austria (1996) 24 EHRR 84, [1996] ECHR 17358/90, ECt HR.
Caledonian Rly Co v Ramsay (1897) 24 R (J) 48.
Clancy v Caird 2000 SC 441, Ct of Sess.
De Cubber v Belgium (1984) 7 EHRR 236, [1984] ECHR 9186/80, ECt HR.
Delcourt v Belgium (1970) 1 EHRR 355, [1970] ECHR 2689/65, ECt HR.
Deweer v Belgium (1980) 2 EHRR 439, [1980] ECHR 6903/75, ECt HR.
Dimes v Proprietors of Grand Junction Canal (1852) 3 HL Cas 759, 10 ER 301.
Doherty v McGlennan 1997 SLT 444, HC of Just.
Evans v Bartlam [1937] 2 All ER 646, [1937] AC 473, HL.
Findlay v UK (1997) 24 EHRR 221, [1997] ECHR 22107/93, ECt HR.
H v Belgium (1987) 10 EHRR 339, [1987] ECHR 8950/80, ECt HR.
Håkansson v Sweden (1990) 13 EHRR 1, ECt HR.
Howdle v Beattie 1995 JC 64, HC of Just.
Jones v Randall (1774) 1 Cowp 37.
Law v Chartered Institute of Patent Agents [1919] 2 Ch 276, [1918–19] All ER Rep Ext 1237.
Locabail (UK) Ltd v Bayfield Properties Ltd, Locabail (UK) Ltd v Waldorf Investment Corp, Timmins v Gormley, Williams v HM Inspector of Taxes, R v Bristol Betting and Gaming Licensing Committee, ex p O'Callaghan [2000] 1 All ER 65, [2000] QB 451, [2000] 2 WLR 870, CA.
Martindale v Falkner (1846) 2 CB 706.
McGonnell v UK (2000) 8 BHRC 56, [2000] ECHR 28488/95, ECt HR.
Oberschlick v Austria (1995) 19 EHRR 389, [1991] ECHR 11662/85, ECt HR.
Pfeifer v Austria (1992) 14 EHRR 692, [1990] ECHR 11855/95, ECt HR.
R (on the application of Alconbury Developments Ltd) v Secretary of State for the Environment, Transport and the Regions [2001] UKHL 23, [2001] 2 All ER 929, [2001] 2 WLR 1389.
R v Bow Street Metropolitan Stipendiary Magistrate, ex p Pinochet Ugarte (No 2) [1999] 1 All ER 577, [2000] 1 AC 119, [1999] 2 WLR 272, HL.
R v Gough [1993] 2 All ER 724, [1993] AC 646, [1993] 2 WLR 883, HL.
Rimmer v HM Advocate (23 May 2001, unreported), HC of Just.

a   *Skeen v Fullarton* 1980 SLT (Notes) 46, HC of Just.
Starrs v Procurator Fiscal (Linlithgow), Procurator Fiscal (Linlithgow) v Starrs (1999)
      8 BHRC 1, HC of Just.
Werner v Austria, Szücs v Austria (1997) 26 EHRR 310, [1997] ECHR 21835/93,
      ECt HR.
Zumtobel v Austria (1993) 17 EHRR 116, [1993] ECHR 12235/86, ECt HR.

b
Appeals

The appellants, David Cameron Millar, Kerry Payne, Paul Stewart and Joseph
Tracey, appealed from the decision of the High Court of Justiciary (Lord Prosser,
Lord Johnston and Lord Cowie) on 3 August 2000 (2000 JC 648) that they had
waived their right to a trial before an independent and impartial tribunal in
c   criminal proceedings before temporary sheriffs. The facts are set out in the
judgment of Lord Bingham of Cornhill.

Aidan O'Neill QC and *Simon Di Rollo* (instructed by *Purdie & Co*, Edinburgh)
      for Mr Stewart.
d *Mungo Bovey QC* and *Chris Shead* (instructed by *Patrick Wheatley*, Edinburgh) for
      Mr Millar and (instructed by *Drummond Miller WS*, Edinburgh) for Ms Payne.
Mungo Bovey QC and *Simon Collins* (instructed by *Purdie & Co*, Edinburgh) for
      Mr Tracey.
The Solicitor General for Scotland (Neil Davidson QC) and the *Advocate Depute
      (Robert McCreadie)* (instructed by the *Crown Agent*, Edinburgh) for the prosecution.
e
The Board took time for consideration.

24 July 2001. The following judgments were delivered.

f **LORD BINGHAM OF CORNHILL.**
    [1] Each of these four appellants (the accused) was the subject of criminal
proceedings before a temporary sheriff between 20 May 1999 and 11 November
1999. Mr Millar was convicted on indictment of drug offences in the sheriff court
at Elgin on 27 August 1999 and was sentenced on the same day to a term of
      imprisonment. Ms Payne pleaded guilty to assault and other offences in the sheriff
g court at Dundee on 16 September 1999 and was sentenced to a term of imprisonment
on 12 October 1999. Mr Stewart was summarily convicted of driving offences in
the sheriff court at Dundee on 16 February 1999, but appeared in the sheriff court
again after 20 May 1999, on 28 June 1999, and was then sentenced to non-custodial
penalties. Mr Tracey was summarily convicted of offensive weapon and assault
h offences in the sheriff court at Dundee on 23 September 1999 and was sentenced
to a term of imprisonment on 8 November 1999. All the accused were represented
by solicitors.
    [2] It was on 20 May 1999 that s 44(1)(c) of the Scotland Act 1998 came into
force. The Lord Advocate thereupon became a member of the Scottish Executive.
j As such, by virtue of s 57(2) of the Act, he had no power to do any act
incompatible with any of the convention rights defined in s 1 of the Human
Rights Act 1998 (unless the act in question fell within s 57(3)).
    [3] It was on 11 November 1999 that the High Court (the Lord Justice-Clerk
(Cullen), Lord Prosser and Lord Reed) gave its decision in *Starrs v Procurator Fiscal
(Linlithgow), Procurator Fiscal (Linlithgow) v Starrs* (1999) 8 BHRC 1, holding that
temporary sheriffs were not an 'independent and impartial tribunal' within the

meaning of art 6(1) of the European Convention for the Protection of Human Rights
and Fundamental Freedoms 1950 (as set out in Sch 1 to the Human Rights Act).   *a*

[4] Before the High Court and again before the Board the accused made the
same very simple complaint: that the Lord Advocate (and thus the respondent
procurators fiscal who conducted the prosecutions) acted incompatibly with the
convention right of the accused under art 6(1) by prosecuting them before
temporary sheriffs who were not an independent and impartial tribunal; that   *b*
such proceedings were accordingly ultra vires and null; and that the convictions
and sentences of Millar, Payne and Tracey and the sentence of Stewart should
accordingly be quashed. These complaints were resisted by the Solicitor General
on behalf of the respondents, and were rejected by the High Court on 3 August 2000
(2000 JC 648).
                                                                                      c
[5] The issues raised by each of the accused before the High Court were
devolution issues within para 1(d) of Sch 6 to the Scotland Act, namely—

> 'a question whether a purported or proposed exercise of a function by a
> member of the Scottish Executive [the Lord Advocate] is, or would be,
> incompatible with any of the Convention rights.'   *d*

On 15 August 2000 the High Court gave leave to the accused to appeal against its
determination of those issues, and the accused come before the Board by virtue
of s 98 of and para 13(a) of Sch 6 to that Act. The appeals are of obvious practical
importance since these cases have been selected for decision out of a significant
number of other cases brought before temporary sheriffs between 20 May and   *e*
11 November 1999. The sentences imposed upon the accused have been suspended
pending final resolution of these issues.

The High Court's decision in Starrs' case

[6] Before the High Court (2000 JC 648 at 651 (para 4)) and again before the   *f*
Board the Solicitor General accepted the correctness of the decision in *Starrs'* case
and accordingly accepted, on the basis of that decision, that the temporary
sheriffs were not at the material time 'an independent and impartial tribunal'. It
follows that the correctness of that decision is not open to review before the
Board. It is none the less necessary to summarise its effect since the present   *g*
appeals are based upon it.

[7] The accused, Starrs and Chalmers, appeared before a temporary sheriff on
a summary complaint on 5 May 1999, when their trial began but was not
concluded. The trial diet was adjourned to 8 July 1999, and on that date was
further adjourned and leave was given to the accused to raise a devolution issue   *h*
whether the procurator fiscal acted compatibly with art 6 of the convention in
prosecuting them before a temporary sheriff. When the devolution issue came
before the temporary sheriff he decided it against them. The accused challenged
the temporary sheriff's decision in the High Court. The issue in that court was
described by the Lord Justice-Clerk in this way ((1999) 8 BHRC 1 at 8):
                                                                                      j
> 'I come then to the main issue which was debated at some length, namely
> whether a temporary sheriff such as Temporary Sheriff Crowe, was an
> "independent and impartial tribunal" in the sense of art 6(1) of the convention.
> I should, of course, make it clear that this point does not involve any
> reflection whatsoever on his conduct. The point is of general importance,
> not only for its potential effect in individual cases but also for any future

a consideration of the terms of the relevant legislation and any appointments made thereunder.'

[8] In the course of their judgments the Lord Justice-Clerk and Lord Reed reviewed the legislation governing the appointment of temporary sheriffs and also some additional information (not previously public knowledge (see 10)) concerning the recent practice of the Lord Advocate in making appointments of
b temporary sheriffs (see 8–14, 31–38). The Lord Justice-Clerk (at 9, 11, 13, 23) drew attention in particular to the fact that temporary sheriffs were appointed for one year only and were subject to recall during that period at the instance of the Lord Advocate, perhaps without the possibility of challenge. The Lord Justice-Clerk (at 14) quoted the material terms of art 6(1) of the convention:

c
'In the determination of his civil rights and obligations or of any criminal charge against him, everyone is entitled to a fair and public hearing within a reasonable time by an independent and impartial tribunal established by law ...'

He made extensive reference (at 14–23) to Strasbourg and other authority on the
d meaning of 'an independent and impartial tribunal'. He expressed a number of conclusions:

(1) 'Rather than a control over numbers, the use of the one-year term suggests a reservation of control over the tenure of office by the individual, enabling it to be brought to an end within a comparatively short period. This
e reinforces the impression that the tenure of office by the individual temporary sheriff is at the discretion of the Lord Advocate. It does not, at least prima facie, square with the appearance of independence' (see 24).

(2) 'There is no question whatever as to the integrity and fair-mindedness with which the Lord Advocate has acted. However, what I have to consider is whether the basis on which the temporary sheriff holds office is truly
f independent, that is independent of the Executive, whether it presents an appearance of such independence, and whether and to what extent the lack of the former gives rise to the appearance of lack of impartiality. I do not have difficulty with the fact that temporary sheriffs are appointed by the Executive, following upon their selection by the Lord Advocate. [Counsel]
g did not contend to the contrary. However, appointment by the Executive is consistent with independence only if it is supported by adequate guarantees that the appointed judge enjoys security of tenure. It is clear that temporary sheriffs are appointed in the expectation that they will hold office indefinitely, but the control which is exercised by means of the one-year
h limit and the discretion exercised by the Lord Advocate detract from independence' (see 25).

(3) 'This line of reasoning seems to me to be persuasive and to support the view that even when full allowance is made for the matters relied upon by the Solicitor General, the power of recall under s 11(4) is incompatible with the independence and appearance of independence of the temporary sheriff.
j For the reasons which I have already indicated, I regard the one-year limit to the appointment as being a further critical factor arriving at the same result ... I also accept that in this case there is a link between perceptions of independence and perceptions of impartiality, of the kind which has been categorised in Canada as institutional impartiality. I consider that there is a real risk that a well-informed observer would think that a temporary sheriff might be influenced by his hopes and fears as to his [prospective] advancement.

I have reached the view that a temporary sheriff, such as Temporary Sheriff Crowe, was not an "independent and impartial tribunal" within the meaning of art 6(1) of the convention' (see 26).

(4) 'In the whole circumstances therefore I am of opinion that in proceeding with the trial the Lord Advocate, as represented by the procurator fiscal, acted incompatibly with the right of the accused under art 6(1) to trial by "an independent and impartial tribunal"' (see 27).

[9] Lord Prosser was in complete agreement. His conclusions were expressed as follows:

(1) '... the answer to the question of whether a person has had a hearing "by an independent and impartial tribunal established by law" when the tribunal is a temporary sheriff holding office at the pleasure of the Lord Advocate, with no security of tenure, can in my opinion be answered in the negative without any deep or detailed consideration of the words "independent and impartial". Nothing in the statutory provisions regarding temporary sheriffs, and nothing in the account which we were given of how they are selected and appointed, or how they are used, or how they cease to be used or to hold office, appears to me to point to any other answer. Equally, nothing in the authorities to which we were referred appears to me to point to any other answer. The opinions of your Lordships appear to me to demonstrate with great clarity why no other answer is appropriate' (see 28).

(2) 'As regards the actual words "independent" and "impartial", the latter appears to me to be of the essence of the judicial process. I would regard the concept of a partial judge as a contradiction in terms. But I am inclined to see independence—the need for a judge not to be dependent on others—as an additional substantive requirement, rather than simply a means of achieving impartiality or a perception of impartiality. Independence will guarantee not only that the judge is disinterested in relation to the parties and the cause, but also that in fulfilling his judicial function, generally as well as in individual cases, he is and can be seen to be free of links with others (whether in the Executive, or indeed the judiciary, or in outside life) which might, or might be thought to, affect his assessment of the matters entrusted to him. The requirement of independence seems to me to have an importance which runs even wider than that of impartiality. The two concepts appear to me to be inextricably interlinked, and I do not myself find it useful to try to separate the one from the other' (see 28).

(3) 'Like your Lordships, I am not suggesting in any way that there has ever been any impropriety, either on the part of temporary sheriffs or on the part of any holder of any ministerial office, or of their officials. But I would add that if a judge is not independent, then however great his integrity, it may be very difficult for him to know whether his want of independence affects the way in which he carries out his judicial duties. And however determined a minister or public servant may be to carry out his functions in relation to the judiciary only on the basis of wholly appropriate considerations, it will be important for him to remember that his own confidence in his own integrity is not, and cannot be regarded as, a guarantee' (see 30).

[10] Lord Reed delivered a comprehensive judgment. It is necessary to cite the following extracts only:

a

(1) 'Given that temporary sheriffs are very often persons who are hoping for graduation to a permanent appointment, and at the least for the renewal of their temporary appointment, the system of short renewable appointments creates a situation in which the temporary sheriff is liable to have hopes and fears in respect of his treatment by the Executive when his appointment comes up for renewal: in short, a relationship of dependency. This is in my

b

opinion a factor pointing strongly away from "independence" within the meaning of art 6' (see 41).

(2) 'There can be no doubt as to the importance of security of tenure to judicial independence: it can reasonably be said to be one of the cornerstones of judicial independence. The critical importance of judicial security of

c

tenure has been recognised in Scots law since at least the declaration in art 13 of the Claim of Right 1689 (cap 28, APS IX 38) that "the changing nature of the judges' gifts ad vitam aut culpam into commissions durante beneplacito" is "contrary to law"' (see 42).

(3) 'There is however no objective guarantee of security of tenure, such as

d

can be found in s 12 of the [Sheriff Courts (Scotland) Act 1971]; and I regard the absence of such a guarantee as fatal to the compatibility of the present system with art 6. The Solicitor General emphasised that it is inconceivable that the Lord Advocate would interfere with the performance of judicial functions. I would readily accept that; but that is not the point. Judicial independence can be threatened not only be interference by the Executive,

e

but also by a judge's being influenced, consciously or unconsciously, by his hopes and fears as to his possible treatment by the Executive. It is for that reason that a judge must not be dependent on the Executive, however well the Executive may behave: "independence" connotes the absence of "dependence"' (see 45–46).

f

(4) 'Even if I were mistaken in my conclusion that the necessary objective guarantees of independence were lacking, it seems to me that the need for the temporary sheriff's appointment to be renewed annually at the discretion of the Executive, and his lack of security of tenure, are in any event factors which could give rise to a reasonable perception of dependence upon the Executive. The necessary appearance of independence is therefore in my

g

opinion absent' (see 50).

(5) 'Given my conclusion that trial before a temporary sheriff violates the right of the accused under art 6 to a trial before an independent and impartial tribunal, and the Solicitor General's concession that such a trial involves the doing of acts which must be taken to be acts of the Lord Advocate for the

h

purposes of s 57(2) of the Scotland Act, it follows that s 57(2), if it is applicable, renders those acts incompetent' (see 53).

(6) 'Before concluding this part of my opinion, I wish to make it plain that I am not suggesting that any temporary sheriff has ever allowed his judicial conduct to be influenced by any consideration of how he might best advance

j

his prospects of obtaining the renewal of his appointment, or his promotion to a permanent appointment. Nor am I suggesting that any official or minister has ever sought to interfere with the judicial conduct of a temporary sheriff or would ever be likely to do so. There is however no objective guarantee that something of that kind could never happen; and that is why these appeals must succeed' (see 55).

The High Court's decision in the instant cases

[11] In his leading judgment in these cases (2000 JC 648 at 651 (para 4)) Lord Prosser defined the main issues then before the High Court:

'In relation to these cases, the Solicitor-General on behalf of the respondents conceded that there was a relevant 'act' for the purposes of para 1(d) of sched 6 to the Scotland Act 1998. It was accepted, upon the basis of the decision in *Starrs,* that the temporary sheriffs were not an 'independent and impartial tribunal' within the meaning of art 6(1). The Crown's position was, however, that each of these complainers had tacitly waived the right to an independent and impartial tribunal. And regardless of the question of waiver, the Crown's position was that, notwithstanding the decision in *Starrs,* the acts of each of the temporary sheriffs, in convicting and/or sentencing the complainers prior to the date of that decision were those of a *de facto* judge, and should be treated as valid. Moreover, it was not suggested on behalf of any of these complainers that waiver of the entitlement to an independent and impartial tribunal under art 6(1) would be incompetent or otherwise impossible as a matter of law: the question was not whether that entitlement could be waived, but whether it had been in these cases. It is convenient to deal with the question of waiver first, before considering the contention that these decisions are valid as decisions of *de facto* judges. Upon both issues, it appeared to me that there was no substantial difference between the submissions advanced on behalf of the different complainers, and I have not found it necessary to deal with these submissions separately from one another.'

Most of Lord Prosser's judgment, with which Lord Cowie agreed, and most of the shorter judgment of Lord Johnston, were devoted to the waiver issue, which was resolved against the accused and in favour of the Crown. The issue concerning de facto judges was decided against the Crown: in his written case the Solicitor General sought to challenge that adverse ruling, but in oral argument before the Board he did not seek to pursue that submission and no further reference need be made to it.

[12] It is clear that in the High Court the accused, relying on s 57(2) of the Scotland Act, challenged the vires of the Lord Advocate to pursue prosecutions against them before temporary sheriffs after 20 May 1999, but this issue does not appear to have featured prominently in the argument and was disposed of in a single paragraph of Lord Prosser's judgment (at 664 (para 39)):

'I should mention briefly one further argument which was advanced on behalf of the complainers in these four bills, which was founded upon this same proposition, that in terms of sec 57(2) of the [Scotland Act], the Lord Advocate was acting *ultra vires* in continuing the prosecution. Viewing the matter as one of *vires,* it was submitted that a waiver could not overcome his lack of *vires.* But in my opinion this argument is misconceived. Section 57(2) means that the Lord Advocate has no power to do any act so far as that act is incompatible with "any of the Convention rights". In terms of sec 126(1), that expression has the same meaning as in the Human Rights Act 1998. In terms of sec 1(1) of that Act "the Convention rights" means the rights and fundamental freedoms set out in, *inter alia,* Article 6. But where such a right can competently be waived, and in particular circumstances has been waived, it has in my opinion ceased to be a right of any kind, in those a circumstances. I do not think that it was actually suggested by counsel for the complainers that once such a Convention right had been waived, so that it was no longer a right of the complainer in the circumstances, the Lord Advocate was nonetheless still obliged, in terms of sec 57(2), not to do an act which would have been incompatible with that right if it had still existed, and was incompatible only with the description of the right which had been

b waived. At all events, I would reject any such contention. I would accept that speaking generally, waiver cannot render *intra vires* an act which is inherently *ultra vires*. But the whole question of the Lord Advocate's powers is related to the complainers' rights under the Convention, and I am unable to see him as debarred from acting incompatibly with rights which in the circumstances they do not have.'

c

[13] In argument before the Board the balance of the argument very substantially altered. Counsel for the accused forcefully submitted, in reliance on *Starrs'* case, that the Lord Advocate had no power to continue to prosecute them before temporary sheriffs after 20 May 1999, although counsel continued to argue

d that the accused had not waived their entitlement under art 6 to trial before an independent and impartial tribunal. The Solicitor General for his part placed very muted reliance on the waiver submission which had prevailed below, but joined issue with the vires argument of the accused, which became the primary focus of the debate before the board. It is accordingly convenient first to address the vires issue arising under s 57(2) of the Scotland Act.

e

Section 57(2)

[14] It was common ground between the parties that the relevant acts of the respondent procurators fiscal were to be treated as acts of the Lord Advocate, that the conduct of the procurators fiscal in continuing to prosecute the accused

f before temporary sheriffs after 20 May 1999 were 'acts' within the meaning of s 57(2), and that temporary sheriffs were not at the material time an independent and impartial tribunal within the meaning of art 6(1) (see 2000 JC 648 at 651, quoted at [11], above). The argument for the accused on this point was in essence both short and simple: by virtue of s 57(2) the Lord Advocate as a member of the Scottish Executive had no power to do any act incompatible with any of the

g convention rights of the accused; art 6(1) of the convention entitled the accused to trial of the criminal charges against them by an independent and impartial tribunal; temporary sheriffs were not at the material time an independent and impartial tribunal because *Starrs'* case so decided; the Lord Advocate acted incompatibly with the convention rights of the accused under art 6(1) by

h prosecuting them before temporary sheriffs as, again, *Starrs'* case decided; acts done in relation to the prosecution of the accused after 20 May 1999 were accordingly ultra vires, null, void and without legal effect; and the convictions and sentences of Millar, Payne and Tracey and the sentence of Stewart should therefore be quashed.

j [15] The Solicitor General sought to rebut this argument by distinguishing *Starrs'* case, essentially on the ground that the challenge in that case had been raised at a relatively early stage of the proceedings, before the trial had been concluded. Thus the court had no public or other interest to balance against the defect in the qualification of the temporary sheriff before whom the trial was proceeding. The judgments in that case, he rightly submitted, did not attempt to weigh the interests of the public against the interests of the accused, doubtless because no

argument was directed to that issue. But it was plain that rights under art 6, save
for the right to a fair trial, were not absolute; it was proper to consider the right *a*
allegedly infringed in the context of all the facts and circumstances of the case as
a whole, and to weigh the alleged infringement against the general interest of the
public. The ultimate issue was one of overall fairness, viewing the proceedings as
a whole, which could be done in these cases but could not be done in *Starrs'* case
because of the early stage in the proceedings at which the devolution issue had *b*
there been raised and determined. In making the submissions the Solicitor General
relied on recent observations of the Board in *Brown v Stott (Procurator Fiscal,
Dunfermline)* [2001] 2 All ER 97 at 115, 116–117, 118–119, 123, 128, 129, 134, 137,
139, 142, [2001] 2 WLR 817 at 836, 837–838, 839–840, 844, 850, 851, 856, 859,
861–862, 864–865, and on the Strasbourg authority there referred to. Applying
these principles to the present cases it could be seen that the trials of the accused *c*
after 20 May 1999, albeit before temporary sheriffs, had been fair in all respects.
Millar had been convicted by a jury and no criticism was made of the summing up
by the temporary sheriff. Payne had pleaded guilty; it made no practical
difference that her plea was tendered to a temporary sheriff and there was
nothing to suggest her sentence was excessive. Stewart no longer complained of *d*
his conviction before 20 May 1999, and the non-custodial penalties imposed after
that date were moderate. Tracey had been convicted by a temporary sheriff on
a summary complaint after 20 May 1999, but had demonstrated no grounds to
impugn conviction or sentence. Whatever the theoretical defects to which the
appointments of the respective temporary sheriffs were subject, none of them
was said to have shown any lack of independence or impartiality and none of the *e*
accused could show that he or she had, in the event, suffered any injustice.

[16] With these last submissions of the Solicitor General I have much
sympathy. There is indeed nothing to suggest that the outcome of any of these
cases would have been different had the relevant stages of the prosecution been
conducted before permanent instead of temporary sheriffs. There is no reason to *f*
doubt that the conduct of all the temporary sheriffs involved was impeccable, and
no reason to suppose that any of the accused suffered any substantial injustice.
But I cannot accept that the outcome in *Starrs'* case would have been different
had the challenge been raised after the trial in that case was concluded, and it is
in my view clear from authority that the right of an accused in criminal
proceedings to be tried by an independent and impartial tribunal is one which, *g*
unless validly waived by the accused, cannot be compromised or eroded.

[17] In *Locabail (UK) Ltd v Bayfield Properties Ltd, Locabail (UK) Ltd v Waldorf
Investment Corp, Timmins v Gormley, Williams v HM Inspector of Taxes, R v Bristol
Betting and Gaming Licensing Committee, ex p O'Callaghan* [2000] 1 All ER 65 at
69–70, [2000] QB 451 at 471–472 the Court of Appeal of England and Wales (Lord *h*
Bingham of Cornhill CJ, Lord Woolf MR and Scott V-C) said:

> '2. In determination of their rights and liabilities, civil or criminal, everyone
> is entitled to a fair hearing by an impartial tribunal. That right, guaranteed
> by the [convention], is properly described as fundamental. The reason is *j*
> obvious. All legal arbiters are bound to apply the law as they understand it
> to the facts of individual cases as they find them. They must do so without
> fear or favour, affection or ill-will, that is without partiality or prejudice.
> Justice is portrayed as blind not because she ignores the facts and circumstances
> of individual cases but because she shuts her eyes to all considerations
> extraneous to the particular case.

a   3. Any judge (for convenience, we shall in this judgment use the term "judge" to embrace every judicial decision-maker, whether judge, lay justice or juror) who allows any judicial decision to be influenced by partiality or prejudice deprives the litigant of the important right to which we have referred and violates one of the most fundamental principles underlying the administration of justice. Where in any particular case the

b   existence of such partiality or prejudice is actually shown, the litigant has irresistible grounds for objecting to the trial of the case by that judge (if the objection is made before the hearing) or for applying to set aside any judgment given. Such objections and applications based on what, in the case law, is called "actual bias" are very rare, partly (as we trust) because the existence of actual bias is very rare, but partly for other reasons also. The

c   proof of actual bias is very difficult, because the law does not countenance the questioning of a judge about extraneous influences affecting his mind; and the policy of the common law is to protect litigants who can discharge the lesser burden of showing a real danger of bias without requiring them to show that such bias actually exists.'

d   [18] These observations, although directed to impartiality, would apply equally to independence. I do not understand them to be in any way inconsistent with Scots law on this subject, which attaches no less weight than the English common law to the integrity of a tribunal carrying out judicial functions, not least in the criminal field.

e   [19] The observations are also, as I think, fully supported by the jurisprudence of the European Court of Human Rights. In *De Cubber v Belgium* (1984) 7 EHRR 236 the complaint was made, in reliance on an express prohibition in the national judicial code and art 6(1) of the convention, that a judge had acted as a trial judge after conducting the preliminary investigation into the offences alleged against the complainant. Having found that there was no evidence of actual bias on the

f   part of the judge, the court summarised its general approach (at 244 (para 26)):

> 'However, it is not possible for the Court to confine itself to a purely subjective test; account must also be taken of considerations relating to the functions exercised and to internal organisation (the objective approach). In this regard, even appearances may be important; in the words of the English
>
> g   maxim quoted in, for example, [*Delcourt v Belgium* (1970) 1 EHRR 355], "justice must not only be done: it must also be seen to be done". As the Belgian Court of Cassation has observed, any judge in respect of whom there is a legitimate reason to fear a lack of impartiality must withdraw. What is at stake is the confidence which the courts in a democratic society must
>
> h   inspire in the public and above all, as far as criminal proceedings are concerned, in the accused.'

The court continued (at 246 (para 30)):

> 'In conclusion, the impartiality of the Oudenaarde court was capable of
>
> j   appearing to the applicant to be open to doubt. Although the Court itself has no reason to doubt the impartiality of the member of the judiciary who had conducted the preliminary investigation, it recognises, having regard to the various factors discussed above, that his presence on the bench provided grounds for some legitimate misgivings on the applicant's part. Without underestimating the force of the Government's arguments and without adopting a subjective approach, the Court recalls that a restrictive interpretation

of Article 6(1)—notably in regard to observance of the fundamental principle
of the impartiality of the courts—would not be consonant with the object
and purpose of the provision, bearing in mind the prominent place which the
right to a fair trial holds in a democratic society within the meaning of the
Convention.'

The court went on to hold (at 248 (para 32)) that a lack of independence and
impartiality in the trial court could not be excused because such qualities were
met by another court to which an appeal lay.

[20] It was held in *Håkansson v Sweden* (1990) 13 EHRR 1 at 16 (para 66) that 'a
waiver must be made in an unequivocal manner and must not run counter to any
important public interest.'

[21] *Oberschlick v Austria* (1995) 19 EHRR 389 involved a journalist against
whom a criminal prosecution for defamation was brought. The case against him
was dismissed by a lower court but reinstated by a court of appeal which remitted
the case to the lower court for trial. The journalist was convicted by the lower
court, which held itself bound by the opinion of the court of appeal on the earlier
occasion. The journalist's appeal against that decision came before a court of
appeal over which the same judge as on the earlier occasion presided. This was
contrary to the national code of criminal procedure. The journalist complained
that the court of appeal on the second occasion was not an independent and
impartial tribunal. The main argument in the case turned on waiver, which, it
was said (at 420 (para 51)), had to be established in an unequivocal manner. Such
waiver was not established. It therefore followed that there had been a violation
of art 6(1) because the tribunal was not impartial.

[22] The complaint in *Pfeifer v Austria* (1992) 14 EHRR 692 again was that, in
breach of the national code of criminal procedure, the judges who had acted as
investigating judges sat also as trial judges. The court reiterated its position (at
712–713):

'37. ... According to the Court's case law, the waiver of a right guaranteed
by the Convention—in so far as it is permissible—must be established in an
unequivocal manner. Moreover, the Court agrees with the Commission
that in the case of procedural rights a waiver, in order to be effective for
Convention purposes, requires minimum guarantees commensurate to its
importance ...

39. Thus even supposing that the rights in question can be waived by a
defendant, the circumstances surrounding the applicant's decision deprived
it of any validity from the point of view of the Convention.'

A violation of art 6(1) was accordingly found.

[23] In *Bulut v Austria* (1996) 24 EHRR 84 a trial judge had yet again, in breach
of the national code of criminal procedure, acted as an investigating judge at an
earlier stage of the proceedings. But on this occasion the lawyer representing the
accused had been expressly asked, in writing before the trial and orally at the trial,
whether he objected to the participation of the judge in the trial. On neither
occasion did he object. In holding that there was no violation of art 6(1) the court
referred to the very limited participation of the judge at the investigatory stage
and held (at 101 (para 34)):

'In this limited context, the applicant's fear that the Innsbruck Regional
Court lacked impartiality cannot be regarded as objectively justified. In any
event, it is not open to the applicant to complain that he had legitimate

a reasons to doubt the impartiality of the court which tried him, when he had the right to challenge its composition but refrained from doing so.'

[24] In contrast with the other cases so far cited, *Findlay v UK* (1997) 24 EHRR 221 concerned the independence as well as the impartiality of the tribunal. A serving soldier pleaded guilty to a number of offences at a court-martial. The

b Commission (at 239–240 (paras 106, 108)) considered the court-martial, because of the way in which it was composed and administered, to lack both independence and impartiality. The court shared this view (at 244–245):

'73. The Court recalls that in order to establish whether a tribunal can be considered as "independent", regard must be had *inter alia* to the manner of

c appointment of its members and their term of office, the existence of guarantees against outside pressures and the question whether the body presents an appearance of independence. As to the question of "impartiality", there are two aspects to this requirement. First, the tribunal must be subjectively free of personal prejudice or bias. Secondly, it must also be impartial from an objective viewpoint, that is, it must offer sufficient

d guarantees to exclude any legitimate doubt in this respect. The concepts of independence and objective impartiality are closely linked and the Court will consider them together as they relate to the present case ...

76. In order to maintain confidence in the independence and impartiality of the court, appearances may be of importance. Since all the members of

e the court-martial which decided Mr Findlay's case were subordinate in rank to the convening officer and fell within his chain of command, Mr Findlay's doubts about the tribunal's independence and impartiality could be objectively justified.'

A violation of art 6 was found. It was further held (at 246 (para 79)) that the

f defects in the trial tribunal could not be cured by any subsequent review proceedings. No significance was attached to the fact that Findlay had pleaded guilty. The lack of independence and objective impartiality was fatal.

[25] There was no accusation of actual bias or prejudice against the Bailiff of Guernsey whose role was reviewed in *McGonnell v UK* (2000) 8 BHRC 56 (see 66

g (para 50)). But his dual role was 'capable of casting doubt on his impartiality' and the applicant had 'legitimate grounds for fearing' that he might have been influenced by his earlier involvement in the planning process (see 67 (para 57)). It followed that there was a breach of art 6(1).

[26] In *Brown v Stott (Procurator Fiscal, Dunfermline)* [2001] 2 All ER 97 at 118,

h [2001] 2 WLR 817 at 840 Lord Steyn said:

'And it is a basic premise of the convention system that only an entirely neutral, impartial and independent judiciary can carry out the primary task of securing and enforcing convention rights.'

j There are few, if any, convention rights of more practical importance to the citizen than the right to a fair trial. The conduct of trials at all stages by an independent and impartial tribunal is in my view recognised by the convention and the authorities, subject to waiver where that is permissible, as a necessary although not a sufficient safeguard of the citizen's right to a fair trial. It is a safeguard which should not, least of all in the criminal field, be weakened or diluted, whatever the administrative consequences.

[27] I accept the argument for the accused on this point. The Lord Advocate *a* had no power to act in a way which infringed any convention right of the accused. By continuing to prosecute the accused before a tribunal which was not independent and impartial, he infringed the right of the accused to have the criminal charges against them determined by a tribunal which was independent and impartial. Unless the accused validly waived their entitlement to trial before an independent and impartial tribunal, he acted in a way which s 57(2) denied him *b* power to do. I think this is the view taken by the High Court.

[28] No distinction is to be drawn between the case of Ms Payne, who pleaded guilty, and the other accused who pleaded not guilty and were convicted. It cannot be said that on the occasion when she entered her plea there was then no determination of a criminal charge against her within the meaning of art 6. The role of a court before which an accused pleads guilty is not entirely passive: it has *c* a duty to ensure that the accused understands the charge (a duty of greater significance when the accused is unrepresented) and that the plea is not equivocal. It is noteworthy that in *Findlay's* case the European Court of Human Rights drew no distinction between his plea of guilty and his sentence.

d

Section 57(3)

[29] Before the Board, although not before the High Court, the Solicitor General sought to rely on s 57(3) of the Scotland Act, which provides:

'Subsection (2) does not apply to an act of the Lord Advocate—(a) in prosecuting any offence, or (b) in his capacity as head of the systems of *e* criminal prosecution and investigation of deaths in Scotland, which, because of subsection (2) of section 6 of the Human Rights Act 1998, is not unlawful under subsection (1) of that section.'

Section 6 of the Human Rights Act, so far as relevant, provides:

'(1) It is unlawful for a public authority to act in a way which is *f* incompatible with a Convention right.
(2) Subsection (1) does not apply to an act if—(a) as the result of one or more provisions of primary legislation, the authority could not have acted differently; or (b) in the case of one or more provisions of, or made under, primary legislation which cannot be read or given effect in a way which is *g* compatible with the Convention rights, the authority was acting so as to give effect to or enforce those provisions.'

Relying on s 6(2)(b), the Solicitor General submitted that s 11 of the 1971 Act could not be read or given effect in a way compatible with the convention rights and that the prosecutors were acting to give effect to or enforce those provisions. *h*

[30] I cannot accept this argument. The appointment of temporary sheriffs under s 11 of the 1971 Act was one thing. The prosecution of offenders was quite another. In appointing temporary sheriffs under s 11 the Lord Advocate was giving effect to that section. In prosecuting the accused before temporary sheriffs so appointed the Lord Advocate (through the respective procurators fiscal) was *j* performing a distinct and different function, which did not give effect to or enforce s 11. Section 57(3) gives the Solicitor General no help in these cases.

Waiver

[31] In most litigious situations the expression 'waiver' is used to describe a voluntary, informed and unequivocal election by a party not to claim a right or

a raise an objection which it is open to that party to claim or raise. In the context of entitlement to a fair hearing by an independent and impartial tribunal, such is in my opinion the meaning to be given to the expression. That the waiver must be voluntary is shown by *Deweer v Belgium* (1980) 2 EHRR 439 at 465 (para 54), where the applicant's failure to insist on his right to a fair trial was held not to amount to a valid waiver because it was tainted by constraint. In *Pfeifer v Austria*

b (1992) 14 EHRR 692 at 713 (para 38) there was held to be no waiver where a layman had not been in a position to appreciate completely the implication of a question he had been asked. In any event, it cannot meaningfully be said that a party has voluntarily elected not to claim a right or raise an objection if he is unaware that it is open to him to make the claim or raise the objection. It is apparent from passages already cited from cases decided by the European Court

c of Human Rights that a waiver, to be effective, must be unequivocal, which I take to mean clear and unqualified. I infer that the High Court was of this opinion (see 2000 JC 648 at 654–655 (paras 12, 13)).

[32] Did the accused, then, make a voluntary, informed and unequivocal election not to claim their right to be tried by an independent and impartial

d tribunal or to raise no objection to the temporary sheriffs before whom they appeared as a tribunal which was not independent and impartial? There is no suggestion that any reference was made at any stage in these cases before sentence to the standing or qualification of the respective temporary sheriffs. Thus any election, if made, must have been tacit. It was on the grounds of tacit waiver that the High Court resolved this issue against the accused. The High

e Court recorded (at 655 (para 16)) that the parties were not really at issue as to the tests to be applied but as to application of those tests to the circumstances of the present cases.

[33] The High Court made its finding of tacit waiver in reliance on a series of very carefully formulated propositions. (1) If an accused or his agent wishes to

f take any point on the qualification of the trial court it should be taken timeously as a plea in bar of trial. If such a point is not taken, the omission to do so will be taken to show an intention to abandon or waive the point unless circumstances show that it was not intended to abandon or waive it or that the omission resulted from ignorance or misapprehension which provided a reasonable explanation of the failure to take it (see 656 (para 17)). (2) If knowledge of some material matter

g is absent, even an express intention to waive a right may readily be recognised as insufficient to constitute a binding abandonment of the right (see 656 (para 18)). (3) In general, regardless of the knowledge or ignorance or misapprehension of an accused or his agent as to the law, knowledge of the law will be imputed to him (see 656–657 (para 20)). (4) An authoritative decision of the courts operates

h retrospectively, stating not only what the law is at the date of the decision but what it has always been (see 657 (para 21)). (5) In judging whether a right has been waived, it may be seen as reasonable for a party to have proceeded upon the law as it appeared to be at the relevant time (see 657 (para 22)). (6) If the law is reasonably regarded as settled, that may afford a reasonable ground for not

j taking a point, even if the law is later changed, but it may be otherwise if the law is unsettled (see 657–658 (para 23)). (7) In the present case there was no settled view of what the law was at the crucial time, and the accused and their agents were not subject to misapprehension attributable to some established view of what the law was (see 658–659 (paras 24, 25)). (8) The accused and their agents must be deemed to have known that the enactment of s 57(2) of the Scotland Act had radically altered the rights of accused persons and that art 6(1) of the convention gave accused persons a right to an independent and impartial tribunal. Once the Scotland Act came into force the accused and their agents could not reasonably say how or why they took a view of the law which only the decision in *Starrs v Procurator Fiscal (Linlithgow), Procurator Fiscal (Linlithgow) v Starrs* (1999) 8 BHRC 1 revealed to be a misapprehension. Without deeming that they knew the law as declared in *Starrs'* case, they must be deemed to have known that the statute had changed the law and that new rights were in issue (see 658–659 (para 25)). (9) The same deemed knowledge must be attributed to the temporary sheriffs and the prosecutors, but they were under no obligation to inform the accused of these known changes (see 659 (para 26)). (10) It was of no real importance whether the accused's agents specifically knew that proceedings before temporary sheriffs were open to challenge, this being widely known in the legal profession (see 653, 659 (paras 10, 11, 27)). (11) The agents' deemed knowledge of the new legislation precluded any contention that the law could be assumed to be unchanged. It was for the agents to decide whether the new law created a new right or the possibility of asserting a new right. There was nothing which made it reasonable not to take the point (see 659–660 (para 28)). (12) The agents were not to be criticised for not taking the point, since waiver could well have been seen as the best course to follow in the interests of the accused (see 660 (para 29)).

[34] Proposition (1) may, as I respectfully think, be accepted as generally true and as providing the correct starting point. I would also accept proposition (2). But I cannot accept proposition (3). In *Martindale v Falkner* (1846) 2 CB 706 at 719 Maule J said, as I think correctly: 'There is no presumption in this country that every person knows the law; it would be contrary to common sense and reason if it were so.' In *Jones v Randall* (1774) 1 Cowp 37, where Mr Dunning had argued that 'all the judges know the laws', Lord Mansfield differed (at 40):

> 'As to the certainty of the law mentioned by Mr. Dunning, it would be very hard upon the profession, if the law was so certain, that every body knew it: the misfortune is that it is so uncertain, that it costs much money to know what it is, even in the last resort.'

More recently, in *Evans v Bartlam* [1937] 2 All ER 646 at 649, [1937] AC 473 at 479 Lord Atkin laid down what I take to be the true principle:

> 'For my part, I am not prepared to accept the view that there is in law any presumption that any one, even a judge, knows all the rules and orders of the Supreme Court. The fact is that there is not, and never has been, a presumption that every one knows the law. There is the rule that ignorance of the law does not excuse, a maxim of very different scope and application.'

Thus ignorance of the law will not excuse unlawful conduct; but it cannot suffice to found a plea of waiver.

[35] As to propositions (4) and (5), I cannot accept a declaratory theory of law, which depends upon a fiction, as apposite in the very practical field of waiver. That there is no waiver where a party relies on what is reasonably understood to be the law at the relevant time is not because such conduct is reasonable (although it plainly is), but because the party lacks the knowledge necessary to make an informed choice. As to proposition (6), I consider the true rule to be this: the more obvious and notorious it is that a point is available to be taken, the more readily may it be inferred that failure to take it represented a deliberate intention not to take it. The contrary is also true.

a [36] I can readily accept that the agents for the accused in Elgin and Dundee knew of the enactment of the Scotland Act, knew that the legal landscape had altered, knew that members of the Scottish Executive (including the Lord Advocate) were bound by the convention, knew at least in general terms of the fair trial guarantee in art 6(1) and knew that the powers of the Lord Advocate as a member of the Scottish Executive were subject to the convention (proposition (8)).

b Plainly, the standing of temporary sheriffs had been a subject of continuing discussion, both before the Scotland Act (see, for example, Willock 'Temporary Sheriffs' 1993 SLT (News) 352–354) and, with greater intensity, afterwards. I would readily accept the informed observations of the Court of Session in *Clancy v Caird* 2000 SC 441 at 453, 470 as to the state of professional belief (proposition (10)) and that the law was known to be in a state of flux. But it is in my opinion

c impossible to accept that the qualification of temporary sheriffs was generally known to be open to serious question and that the agents were subject to no misapprehension attributable to some established view of what the law was (proposition (7)). I doubt very much if the outcome of *Starrs'* case was widely foreseen. I cannot accept proposition (9) and, since waiver depends on the

d making of an informed choice, I cannot accept the opening part of proposition (10).

[37] Section 11(4) of the Sheriff Courts (Scotland) Act 1971, which provided in effect that temporary sheriffs held office at pleasure (see *Starrs'* case (1999) 8 BHRC 1 at 32 per Lord Reed), had stood unamended for nearly 30 years. No attempt had been made, in anticipation of the coming into force of the Scotland Act, to amend it or to provide for the appointment of temporary sheriffs for fixed

e terms longer than a year, no doubt because the qualification of temporary sheriffs was not recognised to be vulnerable. Had that vulnerability been recognised, the Lord Advocate would, one assumes, have taken before 20 May 1999 the steps he took after 11 November 1999, and would not have resisted the challenge to the standing of temporary sheriffs which was made in *Starrs'* case. Had the respective

f procurators fiscal apprehended that their conduct as prosecutors of the accused on behalf of the Lord Advocate was or might be ultra vires they would doubtless have raised the issue at the hearings and sought the consent of the accused or made other arrangements. Had the respective temporary sheriffs apprehended that they were or might not have been an independent and impartial tribunal, they would doubtless have acted in the same way. Both the procurators fiscal and

g the temporary sheriffs would have been under the clearest obligation, if they entertained any doubt about the temporary sheriffs' compliance with art 6, to share their doubts with the defence (see *Locabail (UK) Ltd v Bayfield Properties Ltd, Locabail (UK) Ltd v Waldorf Investment Corp, Timmins v Gormley, Williams v HM Inspector of Taxes, R v Bristol Betting and Gaming Licensing Committee, ex p O'Callaghan*

h [2000] 1 All ER 65 at 76, [2000] QB 451 at 478–479 (para 21), which I do not understand to be inconsistent with the law applicable in Scotland. I do not doubt that, if they had entertained any doubt, they would have acted in this way, and their failure to do so points towards an absence of doubt. The inescapable fact is that, until *Starrs'* case, no challenge was successfully made to the qualification

j of temporary sheriffs, despite their employment in greatly increased numbers over the years. It has not been suggested that their reputation was other than high. And to this day no accusation of actual bias has been made against them.

[38] It was of course for the agents of the accused to decide what points to make on behalf of their clients (proposition (11)) and they could have seen advantages in proceeding before temporary sheriffs (proposition (12)). But the point is whether the agents, on behalf of the accused, made a voluntary, informed

and unequivocal election not to claim trial before an independent and impartial tribunal and not to object to the respective temporary sheriffs as a tribunal not meeting the requirements of art 6(1). They could only have done this if they appreciated, or must be taken to have appreciated, the effect of the eventual decision in *Starrs'* case or the real possibility of a decision to that or similar effect. In my regretful conclusion there is no evidence, and nothing in the judicial decisions before the Board, which would entitle us to find that the accused or their agents appreciated this, nor is the Board entitled to infer that they must have done. A finding or inference to the opposite effect is in my view very much more compelling. I conclude, without enthusiasm, that the finding of tacit waiver cannot be supported.

[39] For these reasons, and those given by my noble and learned friends Lord Hope of Craighead and Lord Clyde, I am of opinion that these appeals should be allowed. All four cases will be remitted to the High Court for that court to consider what orders should now be made. The accused must have their costs against the respective procurators fiscal before the Board.

LORD NICHOLLS OF BIRKENHEAD.

[40] I agree that for the reasons given by my noble and learned friends Lord Bingham of Cornhill, Lord Hope of Craighead and Lord Clyde, these appeals should be allowed.

LORD HOPE OF CRAIGHEAD.

[41] Central to the rule of law in a modern democratic society is the principle that the judiciary must be, and must be seen to be, independent of the executive. Writing on the independence of the judiciary in the title on constitutional law in the *Stair Memorial Encyclopaedia* (1987) vol 5, pp 350–351, paras 663–667, Lord Fraser of Tullybelton identified security of tenure and immunity from suit as the two most important ways of ensuring that judges perform their duties impartially and without fear of the consequences. Of these, security of tenure is the more vulnerable to erosion at the hands of the executive.

[42] The appointment of temporary sheriffs to assist in the disposal of business in the sheriff courts was provided for by s 11 of the Sheriff Courts (Scotland) Act 1971. At first the use which was made of this additional judicial resource was modest and unremarkable. But as growth in the volume of business in the sheriff courts was matched by a tightening of controls over growth in public expenditure, the executive became increasing attracted to it. Preference was given to increasing the number of temporary sheriffs as a means of meeting the demand for more judges on the shrieval bench. Some doubted the wisdom of this policy. Professor ID Willock in his article 'Temporary Sheriffs' 1993 SLT (News) 352, observed that temporary sheriffs appeared to lack the independence which was attached to the permanent sheriffs. But there was no evidence that this was having any influence on the way in which the temporary sheriffs were in practice discharging their responsibilities. Furthermore, the Lord Advocate made it his business during this period to consult regularly with the Lord President and the Sheriffs Principal before making or terminating appointments to this branch of the judiciary.

[43] It was not until the coming into force of s 57(2) of the Scotland Act 1998 on 20 May 1999 that an opportunity arose for a challenge to be made to this system in the courts. It was not long in coming. On 30 July 1999 Temporary

a Sheriff Crowe resumed consideration of a case which had come before him for trial on summary complaint in Linlithgow sheriff court on 5 May 1999 and had been continued to a date after 20 May 1999 for the completion of the evidence. Minutes had been lodged under r 40.5 of the Act of Adjournal (Criminal Procedure Rules) 1996, SI 1996/513 as amended by the Act of Adjournal (Devolution Issues Rules) 1999, SI 1999/1346 raising a devolution issue as to

b whether, by continuing with their prosecution before a temporary sheriff, the Lord Advocate had acted in a way which was incompatible with the accused's convention right to a fair trial by an independent and impartial tribunal. Temporary Sheriff Crowe rejected this challenge to his presiding at the trial. But on 11 November 1999 it was upheld on appeal by the High Court of Justiciary in *Starrs v Procurator Fiscal (Linlithgow), Procurator Fiscal (Linlithgow) v Starrs* (1999)

c 8 BHRC 1, the effect of which has been summarised so helpfully by my noble and learned friend Lord Bingham of Cornhill. The Lord Advocate decided not to seek leave to appeal against that decision to the Judicial Committee. Instead the use of temporary sheriffs for whatever purpose in both civil and criminal cases, which had continued without interruption since 20 May 1999, was instantly terminated.

d [44] Legislation has been passed by the Scottish Parliament which provides for the creation of a new category of part-time sheriffs (see ss 11A–11D of the Sheriff Courts (Scotland) Act 1971, inserted by the Bail, Judicial Appointments, etc (Scotland) Act 2000, s 7). The appointment and removal from office of part-time sheriffs is the subject of new provisions which have been designed to be compatible with the convention rights. But the Scottish legal system now faces

e the not inconsiderable problem of dealing with objections which have been taken under the devolution legislation since *Starrs'* case to the disposal by temporary sheriffs of criminal cases under both solemn and summary procedure between 20 May 1999, when s 57(2) of the Scotland Act came into force, and 11 November 1999, when their use was terminated by the Scottish Executive.

f [45] The four cases which are now before your Lordships in this appeal were selected by the law officers to test the various factual situations that have arisen. David Millar was convicted after trial and sentenced by Temporary Sheriff Sinclair in solemn proceedings in Elgin on 27 August 1999. Kerry Payne, having pled guilty before Temporary Sheriff McSherry in summary proceedings in

g Dundee on 16 September 1999, was sentenced by Temporary Sheriff Eccles on 12 October 1999. Paul Stewart, who had been convicted after trial in summary proceedings in Dundee on 16 February 1999, was sentenced by Temporary Sheriff Pender on 28 June 1999. Joseph Tracey was convicted after trial in summary proceedings in Dundee on 23 September 1999 and sentenced by Temporary Sheriff Kelly on 8 November 1999. In the event no relevant point of

h distinction has emerged between them. They all stand or fall together on the same point, which is whether the continuation of the prosecutions before a temporary sheriff was an act by the prosecutor which was incompatible with the appellants' convention rights.

j *The issues*

[46] In the High Court of Justiciary (2000 JC 648) the Solicitor General conceded that there was a relevant act in each case for the purposes of para 1(d) of Sch 6 to the Scotland Act. He also accepted, in the light of *Starrs'* case, that the temporary sheriff before whom each case was conducted was not an 'independent and impartial tribunal' within the meaning of art 6(1) of the

European Convention for the Protection of Human Rights and Fundamental
Freedoms 1950 (as set out in Sch 1 to the Human Rights Act 1998). His argument
was that, as they did not take the objection at the appropriate time, the appellants
had each waived their convention right to object to the presiding judge on this
ground. He also argued that, regardless of the question of waiver, the acts of the
temporary sheriff were those of a de facto judge and should be treated as valid
notwithstanding the decision in *Starrs'* case. The High Court of Justiciary (Lords
Prosser, Johnston and Cowie) held that the appellants had waived their right to
object to the hearing of their cases by a temporary sheriff and that the Lord
Advocate was not obliged by s 57(2) to comply with a convention right which no
longer existed. The appellants sought and were granted leave to appeal against
this decision to the Judicial Committee. The High Court rejected the alternative
argument that the proceedings were valid as having taken place before a de facto
judge. The Crown did not seek leave to appeal against this decision. In my
opinion the application of the doctrine which gives validity to the acts of de facto
judges does not raise a devolution issue within the meaning of para 1 of Sch 6 to
the Scotland Act.

[47] The appellants have identified the issue in this appeal as being whether in
the proceedings before the temporary sheriffs their agents effectively waived, on
their behalf, their right to object to the presiding judge. As put, the question of
waiver might be thought in itself not to raise a devolution issue as defined in
para 1 of Sch 6 to the Scotland Act. But the point which the appellants wish to
raise can be put in a way which does bring the question within the jurisdiction of
the Judicial Committee under that Schedule. As Mr O'Neill QC for the appellant
Paul Stewart said, the point on waiver bears directly on the issue whether the
Lord Advocate was acting compatibly with the appellants' convention rights.
Falling within that broad issue there are a series of closely related issues which
may be raised by way of a preliminary objection. For example, a person cannot
bring proceedings under the Act on the ground that an act is incompatible with
the convention rights unless he would be a victim for the purposes of art 34 of the
convention if proceedings in respect of the right were brought in the European
Court of Human Rights (s 100(1)). So too the question may be raised whether the
person has waived his right to object to the act which is alleged to be
incompatible. In my opinion preliminary objections of that kind fall within the
scope of the questions which have been identified in para 1 of Sch 6 as devolution
issues.

[48] As the argument developed however the Solicitor General sought to raise
a new and more fundamental question in answer to the appellants' devolution
issue. This was whether, as the facts have turned out, there was truly an
incompatibility with the appellants' convention rights. He accepted the decision
in *Starrs'* case and did not seek to attack its analysis. But he maintained that an
infringement of the right to an independent and impartial tribunal in art 6(1) did
not necessarily mean that the act of continuing with the prosecution in these
cases was unlawful as being incompatible with that right. The question that had
now to be asked was whether in the light of all the facts and circumstances they
had had a fair trial. It had not been alleged that the temporary sheriffs were
affected by an actual lack of independence or impartiality, and it had not been
demonstrated that any of the appellants would benefit from being retried or
sentenced again by a permanent sheriff. There had been an irregularity, but no
more than that. So the acts of the Lord Advocate in continuing to prosecute these

cases before the temporary sheriffs were not made unlawful by s 57(2) of the Scotland Act.

[49] The statutory regime which sets the context for an examination of these questions is simple and uncompromising. Section 57(2) of the Scotland Act provides that a member of the Scottish Executive has no power to do any act which is incompatible with any of the convention rights. An act which he has no power to do is an unlawful act: see the corresponding provision in s 6(1) of the Human Rights Act. Two questions must therefore be addressed. The first is, what is the act which the Lord Advocate is said to have had no power to do? The issue of waiver belongs to that question. The second is, if he had no power to do that act, what are the consequences? To this question there belongs the Solicitor General's argument that the act was not unlawful as the appellants are unable to say that they did not have a fair trial.

The 'act'

[50] The act of the Lord Advocate which is in issue in these cases can best be described as conducting a prosecution in proceedings before a temporary sheriff. It is for the prosecutor to determine whether or not a case is to be called (see Renton and Brown *Criminal Procedure* (6th edn, 1972) p 448, para 20.02; *Howdle v Beattie* 1995 JC 64. He is the master of the instance, and no proceedings can take place in his absence. He is entitled to withdraw the indictment or complaint at any time (see *Skeen v Fullarton* 1980 SLT (Notes) 46 at 47. If a conviction results it is for him to lay any information before the court which the sheriff needs to have in order to pass sentence. From start to finish the procedure which takes place in the court is on his initiative. Had it not been for his participation in the proceedings the temporary sheriff would not have been able to determine the issues which were before the court.

[51] In each of the cases which are before us therefore, the determination of the criminal charges by the temporary sheriff was the result of an act by the prosecutor. Mr O'Neill said that, by having the case called in a court which was presided over by a temporary sheriff, the prosecutor was acting incompatibly with the appellants' convention right. But the prosecutor's act in conducting the prosecution did not end with the calling of the case. By maintaining the prosecution up to and including the moment when sentence was passed he was also performing an 'act' within the meaning of s 57(2) of the Scotland Act. It is for this reason that I do not see any grounds for distinguishing those cases where all the temporary sheriff was required to do after the case was called was to pass sentence from those where the case had to proceed to trial.

Waiver

[52] The right which a person has under art 6(1) of the convention to a hearing by an independent and impartial tribunal is fundamental to his right to a fair trial. Just as the right to a fair trial is incapable of being modified or restricted in the public interest, so too the right to an independent and impartial tribunal is an absolute right. The independence and impartiality of the tribunal is an essential element if the trial is to satisfy the overriding requirement of fairness. The remedy of appeal to a higher court is an imperfect safeguard. Many aspects of a decision taken at first instance, such as decisions on the credibility of witnesses or the exercise of judgment in matters which are at the discretion of the presiding judge, are incapable of being reviewed effectively on appeal. As Lord Steyn said

in *Brown v Stott (Procurator Fiscal, Dunfermline)* [2001] 2 All ER 97 at 118, [2001] 2 WLR 817 at 840, it is a basic premise of the convention system that only an entirely neutral, impartial and independent judiciary can carry out the primary task of securing and enforcing convention rights.

[53] Mr O'Neill said that there was no example in the case law of the Strasbourg court of a case in which a tribunal was held to be defective on this ground but that the right to object to it had been waived. But the court's jurisprudence shows that this element of the right to a fair trial, like the right to a public hearing, is not so fundamental that it is incapable of being waived if all the circumstances which give rise to the objection are known to the applicant and the waiver is unequivocal. In practice waiver of the right is not uncommon, as in the case where the parties agree to the resolution of their dispute by private arbitration or the payment of a fixed penalty is tendered in composition of a criminal charge. The legal system would be unduly hampered if the right to a public hearing by an independent and impartial tribunal were to be incapable in any case of being waived.

[54] In *Håkansson v Sweden* (1990) 13 EHRR 1 at 16 (para 66) the court said that, while the public character of court hearings constitutes a fundamental principle enshrined in art 6(1), neither the letter nor the spirit of this provision prevents a person from waiving of his own free will, either expressly or tacitly, the entitlement to have his case heard in public so long as this is made in an unequivocal manner and is not counter to any important public interest. The rule that, according to the court's case law, waiver of a right guaranteed by the convention, in so far as it is permissible, must be established in an unequivocal manner was emphasised in *Oberschlick v Austria* (1995) 19 EHRR 389 and *Pfeifer v Austria* (1992) 14 EHRR 692, in the context of a discussion in each case as to whether there had been a waiver of the right to an independent and impartial tribunal. The rigorous nature of the requirement that the waiver be unequivocal is illustrated by the grounds on which the argument on waiver was rejected.

[55] In *Oberschlick's* case (1995) 19 EHRR 389 at 420 (para 51) the court observed that neither the applicant not his counsel were aware until well after the hearing of all the circumstances which provided grounds for objecting to the tribunal on the ground of a lack of impartiality. In *Pfeifer's* case (1992) 14 EHRR 692 waiver was rejected because of the circumstances surrounding the decision not to object to the composition of the tribunal. The court observed (at 713 (para 38)) that the judge had approached Mr Pfeifer in the absence of his lawyer and put a question to him whose implication, as it was essentially a question of law, he was not in a position to understand completely. Similarly, in *Werner v Austria, Szücs v Austria* (1997) 26 EHRR 310, where it was contended that the applicant had waived his right to a public hearing because he did not ask for one, the court said (at 349 (para 48)) that the applicant could not be blamed for not having made an application for a public hearing of his case which had no prospects of success as the relevant provisions of Austrian legislation made no provision for such a hearing in his case.

[56] In *Bulut v Austria* (1996) 24 EHRR 84 at 101 (para 34) the court held that the applicant's fear that the tribunal lacked impartiality could not be regarded as objectively justified in view of the limited role that the judge whose impartiality was questioned had played in the questioning of witnesses during the preliminary investigation of the case. It also made this observation:

a 'In any event, it is not open to the applicant to complain that he had
legitimate reasons to doubt the impartiality of the court which tried him,
when he had the right to challenge its composition but refrained from
doing so.'

But that was a case where the facts were made known to the applicant's lawyer
before the trial began and they were mentioned again by the presiding judge before
b the court began to hear evidence. In *McGonnell v UK* (2000) 8 BHRC 56 the court
rejected the argument that the applicant, who was legally represented and did not
raise an objection to the fact that the bailiff was presiding over the Royal Court
when it was open to him to do so, had tacitly waived his right to an independent
and impartial tribunal. One of the reasons given for this decision (at 65 (para 44))
c was that the Court of Appeal had held that there was no structural conflict
between the bailiff's duties in the Royal Court and in the States of Deliberation.
It appears that this too was a case where, in the light of authority which was
binding on the Royal Court, the objection would have had no prospects of
success.

[57] In none of the cases which are before us was there an express waiver of
d the right to an independent and impartial tribunal. The High Court held that
waiver was to be implied from the fact that the appellants' agents remained silent.
As Lord Prosser put it (2000 JC 648 at 656), their failure to take a plea in bar of trial
was to be construed as a waiver of all rights which require to be asserted by such
a plea unless it appeared that there was some ignorance or misapprehension
e which could be regarded as a reasonable explanation for not taking the point.
Acknowledging that knowledge was at the heart of the matter, he said (at 656)
that the court was not concerned in this case with ignorance of facts but with an
alleged ignorance or misapprehension as to the law. He said (at 658–659) that the
appellants' agents must be deemed to have known that the effect of s 57(2) of the
Scotland Act was to introduce new provisions giving accused persons a right to
f an independent and impartial tribunal which could not be assumed to be of
no significance and that there were new, unsettled issues to be resolved.

[58] But it is one thing to know that the effect of s 57(2) was to introduce new
provisions giving accused persons a remedy in domestic law against acts of the
prosecutor which were incompatible with their art 6 convention rights. It is quite
g another to be in possession of all the information that was needed to appreciate
fully that the acts in question were incompatible. The Strasbourg jurisprudence
shows that, unless the person is in full possession of all the facts, an alleged waiver
of the right to an independent and impartial tribunal must be rejected as not being
unequivocal. It was not suggested that in any of the four cases which are before
us the appellants' agents were not aware that the sheriff before whom the case
h had called was a temporary sheriff or of the statutory provisions under which
they had been appointed. But no evidence has been produced by the prosecutor,
on whom the onus lies, to show that they were aware of the system which had
been developed by the executive for making and not renewing these appointments.
A full description of this system was given to the court in *Starrs v Procurator Fiscal
j (Linlithgow), Procurator Fiscal (Linlithgow) v Starrs* (1999) 8 BHRC 1 at 10–13. But,
as the Lord Justice-Clerk (Cullen) said (at 10), the content of that description was
not a matter of general public knowledge.

[59] There are other reasons for not regarding any waiver that might be
implied from the absence of a plea in bar of trial based on the convention right as
unequivocal. The circumstances in which the point was not taken are also

relevant to this issue. There is no suggestion that, if it had been taken, the *a*
prosecutor would have refrained from calling the case or that he would have
conceded the point after calling and sought an adjournment so that the case could
be called before a permanent sheriff. This is not one of those cases, of which
Oberschlick's and *Pfeifer's* cases provide examples, where there was an undoubted
right to object and a clear remedy in the event of doing so. Lord Prosser made it
clear (2000 JC 648 at 659) that he was not suggesting that the appellants' agents *b*
must be deemed to have known just how the unsettled issues in the new legal
landscape would be resolved. I agree that there is no basis for making that
assumption. But in my opinion the fact that there is no basis for it strengthens the
argument that it would not be reasonable to infer waiver in any of these cases.
The appellants were not, through their agents, in a position to make an informed
choice as to what to do, as they were in a situation where the law was unsettled *c*
and the consequences of that choice were not predictable.

[60] The Solicitor General, in a notable change of position from that which he
had adopted in the High Court, said that the issue of waiver was not central to
these appeals. He maintained that the decisive factor was the issue whether or
not the appellants had a fair trial, bearing in mind the lack of evidence as to any *d*
real difference in the result which was to have been expected if the cases had been
heard by a permanent sheriff. He did not seek to develop a sustained argument
in support of the reasons for holding waiver established which were given by the
High Court. In my opinion the High Court were in error on this point, as the
appellants' agents were not in a position to make a fully informed choice. I would
hold that sufficient grounds for holding that there was an unequivocal waiver of *e*
the convention right have not been made out and that, subject to the argument
to which I now turn, the appellants must succeed in these appeals.

The consequences

[61] The Solicitor General said that the facts and circumstances did not *f*
disclose any infringement of the appellants' right to an independent and impartial
tribunal amounting to an incompatibility with art 6(1) of the convention. In the
absence of such an incompatibility there was no 'act' of the Lord Advocate which
he had no power to do in terms of s 57(2) of the Scotland Act. Even if there was
such an incompatibility, there was nevertheless no unlawful act. He maintained *g*
that s 57(2) was disapplied by s 57(3) in this case, as he was giving effect to the
primary legislation under which the temporary sheriffs had been appointed and
were authorised to sit in the sheriff court.

[62] The essential point on which he based his main argument was that the
question as to whether the Lord Advocate's act was unlawful had to be tested at *h*
the date when the challenge was made. This had to be done in the light of all the
facts and circumstances which were known to exist at that time. All there was in
this case was a perception that the temporary sheriffs lacked independence. But
the reality was that they did not lack independence in fact. Their judgment was
unaffected, and there were no grounds for saying that the verdicts of guilty were
unsafe or the sentences imposed were excessive. The appellants were unable to *j*
show that they would derive any real benefit from being retried or sentenced
again. He invited us to hold that the decisive factor in these cases was not that
the right to an independent and impartial judge had been waived because no plea
in bar of trial had been taken at the outset, but that the use of temporary sheriffs
in these cases made no difference in fact to the result.

a [**63**] In my opinion this argument overlooks the fundamental importance of the convention right to an independent and impartial tribunal. These two concepts are closely linked, and the appearance of independence and impartiality is just as important as the question whether these qualities exist in fact. Justice must not only be done, it must be seen to be done. The function of the convention right is not only to secure that the tribunal is free from any actual **b** personal bias or prejudice. It requires this matter to be viewed objectively. The aim is to exclude any legitimate doubt as to the tribunal's independence and impartiality (see *McGonnell v UK* (2000) 8 BHRC 56 at 66 (para 48) quoting *Findlay v UK* (1997) 24 EHRR 221 at 244–245 (para 73)). As Lord Clarke said in *Rimmer v HM Advocate* (23 May 2001, unreported), the question of impartiality, actual or perceived, has to be judged from the very moment when the judge or tribunal **c** becomes first seised of the case. It is a question which, at least in a case of perceived impartiality, stands apart from any questions that may be raised about the character, quality or effect of any decisions which he takes or acts which he performs in the proceedings.

[**64**] There is ample authority in our domestic law to support these **d** propositions. In *Bradford v McLeod* 1986 SLT 244, the convictions and sentences were suspended on the ground of a suspicion that the sheriff was biased even although, as the Lord Justice-Clerk (Ross) said (at 248), there was no reason to think that the complainers did not in fact receive fair trials. Lord Dunpark said (at 249) that the question was not whether the complainers received fair trials but whether what the sheriff said was enough to create a suspicion that he might not **e** be impartial. The same result followed in *Doherty v McGlennan* 1997 SLT 444 where there was a suspicion about the sheriff's impartiality. These decisions were based on the rule which Eve J described in *Law v Chartered Institute of Patent Agents* [1919] 2 Ch 276 at 289, [1918–19] All ER Rep Ext 1237 at 1244 that, if circumstances exist which give rise to a suspicion about the judge's impartiality, **f** those circumstances are themselves sufficient to disqualify although in fact no bias exists. It is also worth noting that the same rule was applied in *R v Bow Street Metropolitan Stipendiary Magistrate, ex p Pinochet Ugarte (No 2)* [1999] 1 All ER 577 at 583, 589, [2000] 1 AC 119 at 129, 135 where, as Lord Browne-Wilkinson made clear, the result was in no way dependent on the judge personally holding any view or having any objective regarding the question whether Senator Pinochet **g** should be extradited. The fairness of the proceedings was not in question, but that was not the issue which the House had to decide.

[**65**] The principle of the common law on which these cases depend is the need to preserve public confidence in the administration of justice (see *Dimes v Proprietors of Grand Junction Canal* (1852) 3 HL Cas 759, 10 ER 301; *R v Gough* [1993] **h** 2 All ER 724 at 729–730, [1993] AC 646 at 661 per Lord Goff of Chieveley. It is no answer for the judge to say that he is in fact impartial, that he abided by his judicial oath and there was a fair trial. The administration of justice must be preserved from any suspicion that a judge lacks independence or that he is not impartial. If there are grounds which would be sufficient to create in the mind of **j** a reasonable man a doubt about the judge's impartiality, the inevitable result is that the judge is disqualified from taking any further part in the case. No further investigation is necessary, and any decisions he may have made cannot stand. The Solicitor General's submission that the matter, if raised after the event, should be considered in the light of all the facts bearing on the question whether there was a fair trial is contradicted by this line of authority.

[66] There is no reason to believe that the position is any different in the jurisprudence of the Strasbourg court. The Solicitor General said that he had not found any case where that court, having held that a tribunal was not an independent and impartial tribunal within the meaning of art 6(1) of the convention and that there had been no waiver of that convention right, nevertheless held that there had in the event been no breach of art 6(1). In *McGonnell v UK* (2000) 8 BHRC 56 at 67 (para 57) the court said that the applicant had legitimate grounds for fearing that the bailiff had been influenced by his prior participation in the adoption of the development plan which was in issue in the case, and that the doubt which this raised, however slight its justification, was sufficient in itself to vitiate the impartiality of the Royal Court. It is plain from this decision that there is no room for the argument that the question whether there was a breach of this convention right can be tested after the event by asking whether the proceedings overall were fair.

[67] The decision in *Starrs v Procurator Fiscal (Linlithgow), Procurator Fiscal (Linlithgow) v Starrs* (1999) 8 BHRC 1 leads therefore to this result. Temporary sheriffs, viewed objectively, lacked the quality of independence and impartiality to which all accused persons are entitled under art 6(1) of the convention. This lack of independence and impartiality, however slight, was sufficient to disqualify temporary sheriffs from taking any part in the determination of criminal charges at the instance of prosecutors acting under the authority of the Lord Advocate. It also made it unlawful for prosecutors to conduct proceedings in the sheriff court under the authority of the Lord Advocate with a view to the determination of criminal charges by temporary sheriffs in that court. The Lord Advocate had no power to conduct those proceedings before them in that court, as this was incompatible with the accused's convention right (see s 57(2) of the Scotland Act). The proceedings were thus vitiated from the moment when they were brought before the temporary sheriffs for their determination. The convention right and the statutory fetter which the Human Rights Act has imposed on the powers of the Lord Advocate thus march hand in hand. Under the devolved system the disqualification of a tribunal whose objective independence or impartiality is vitiated gives rise, at once and at the same time, to a lack of competence on the part of the Lord Advocate.

[68] As for the argument that s 57(2) was disapplied in regard to proceedings before temporary sheriffs by s 57(3), I think that this question is sufficiently closely linked to the question whether the Lord Advocate's exercise of his functions as prosecutor was incompatible with the appellants' convention rights to come within the scope of the devolution issue. But I do not think that there is anything in the argument.

[69] In *Starrs'* case (1999) 8 BHRC 1 at 27, 54 (per the Lord Justice-Clerk (Cullen) and Lord Reed respectively) the High Court rejected a submission which was made under reference to s 6(2)(a) of the Human Rights Act that the Lord Advocate could not have acted differently. The Solicitor General sought in this case to rely instead on s 6(2)(b), but in my opinion this submission too is unsound. The Lord Advocate was not giving effect to s 11 of the 1971 Act within the meaning of s 6(2)(b) of the Human Rights Act when these proceedings were being conducted before the temporary sheriffs by the procurator fiscal acting on his authority. Section 11 of the 1971 Act dealt with the appointment of temporary sheriffs. It did not define the circumstances in which they were to be used. Their appointment was not in itself incompatible with any of the convention rights.

a   Everything depended upon the use that was made of them as to whether there was an incompatibility. But no rules for their use were laid down by the statute, so it cannot be said that there was anything in s 11 to which effect was being given by the prosecutor.

Conclusion

b   [70] For these reasons, and those given by my noble and learned friend Lord Bingham of Cornhill, with which I agree, I would allow these appeals. I would leave it to the High Court to make such orders as fall to be made in consequence of this judgment in order to dispose of the various bills of advocation and suspension which the appellants presented to that court (see r 40.11 of the Act of *c*   Adjournal (Criminal Procedure Rules) 1996, SI 1996/513, as amended).

LORD CLYDE.

[71] On 20 May 1999 the holder of the office of Lord Advocate in Scotland became a member of the new Scottish Executive by virtue of the arrangements *d*   for devolution introduced by the Scotland Act 1998. On 11 November 1999 judgment was given by the High Court of Justiciary in *Starrs v Procurator Fiscal (Linlithgow), Procurator Fiscal (Linlithgow) v Starrs* (1999) 8 BHRC 1. In that case it was held that the continuation of a trial which was in course before a temporary sheriff constituted a violation of the right of the accused under art 6(1) of the European Convention for the Protection of Human Rights and Fundamental *e*   Freedoms 1950 (as set out in Sch 1 to the Human Rights Act 1998) to a trial before an 'independent and impartial tribunal'. Section 11 of the Sheriff Courts (Scotland) Act 1971 empowers the Secretary of State to appoint a temporary sheriff to act in a sheriffdom in certain circumstances. While the appointments were made by the Secretary of State, the Lord Advocate had in recent years come *f*   to play an important part in the finding of candidates for the office, in considering applications, in consulting and obtaining opinions on the suitability of candidates, and eventually forwarding a finalised list to the Scottish Courts Administration for the appointments to be made. Appointments were in practice made for a period of one year only and the Lord Advocate also played a significant part in the re-appointments of current temporary sheriffs. By s 11(4) of the 1971 Act the *g*   office of temporary sheriff was open to recall. That factor together with the one year limit were the two critical considerations which led the court in *Starrs'* case to hold that the temporary sheriff in that case did not possess and did not appear to possess the independence required by art 6(1). The lack of a security of tenure of the office was seen to be fatal to his independence.

h   [72] The appellants in three of the four appeals before us have been convicted and sentenced by temporary sheriffs during the period between 20 May 1999 and 11 November 1999. In the fourth case (*Stewart*) the proceedings began and the conviction occurred before 20 May 1999 but the proceedings continued after that date and the sentence was imposed on 28 June 1999. In one case (*Millar*) the proceedings *j*   were on indictment, while the other three cases were summary proceedings. In *Payne* the accused pleaded guilty and was subsequently sentenced. In *Tracey* the accused was found guilty after trial and subsequently sentenced. The four cases represent different situations but all give rise to the same problem. Following on the ruling in *Starrs'* case the appellants sought to have the effect of that decision applied to their own cases. They raised their appeals by way of bills of suspension, or in the case of Millar, a bill of advocation. The High Court of Justiciary refused the bills, principally on grounds of waiver.

[73] It was common ground between the parties before us that the appeals raised a 'devolution issue' within the meaning of para 1(d) of Pt I of Sch 6 to the Scotland Act. It is accepted that although it was the procurator fiscal who was purportedly exercising the function it was still to be treated as an exercise by the Lord Advocate. There was some discussion about the precise identity of the function in issue. 'Functions' is defined in s 126(1) as including powers and duties. In s 57(2) it is provided that a member of the Scottish Executive has no power to do any act so far as it is incompatible with any of the convention rights. But it was not suggested that there was any distinction to be made for the purpose of these provisions between the purported exercise of a function by the Lord Advocate and an act by him.

[74] For present purposes it is useful to identify what was the purported function or the act. The suggestion was made that it might be the calling of the case before the temporary sheriff, but even although the prosecutor may take an initiative in that matter, that approach seems to me to be too narrow. In my view in the circumstances of the present appeals this is not a matter to be analysed into a detailed study of every step which he took. The function which he was purporting to exercise in each case was that of conducting a prosecution. That was the act which he was doing on every occasion when the case came before the temporary sheriff. The question then is whether in conducting and continuing to conduct these cases before a temporary sheriff, his acts were incompatible with the appellants' convention rights.

[75] It was not submitted that the decision in *Starrs'* case was wrong. We were not invited to overrule it. The Solicitor General sought to distinguish it on the basis that the challenge was raised in *Starrs'* case while the proceedings were still current, while in the present cases the point has been raised by way of appeal some time after the dates of the conclusion of the cases. This difference enabled him to argue that in the present cases the whole circumstances could be viewed in the round in a way which was not possible and was not attempted in *Starrs'* case, and in a way which would accord with the global approach generally taken by the European Court of Human Rights. But while it is possible in that way to view the present cases in light of the whole course which they have taken, one is still faced with the decision in *Starrs'* case that a temporary sheriff is not an independent tribunal. What the Solicitor General sought to do was to argue that on the global view available in the present cases it can be held that the appellants have in the totality of the circumstances, and notwithstanding the lack of independence of the tribunal, nevertheless had a fair trial.

[76] This was a somewhat different argument from the one which was advanced before the High Court and accepted by them. No longer was the Solicitor General basing his case on waiver. He accepted that the focus of the argument had changed. The appellants had put at the forefront of their case a submission that the acts of the procurator fiscal were, in light of s 57(2), ultra vires and accordingly that they were null and void. It was in response to this argument that the Solicitor General submitted that on a global view of the whole facts and circumstances in each of the four cases it could still be held that they had each enjoyed a fair trial and that there was nothing in the acting of the procurator fiscal which ran counter to art 6(1). Thus as the case developed before us it became

evident that the battle was now joined on a quite different field than that on which the parties had been engaged before.

[77] Before leaving the former scene of combat I should say that I find it difficult to accept the argument on waiver on which the High Court proceeded. There is a question, to which I shall return later, whether in the context of criminal proceedings the right to an independent and impartial tribunal can always be waived, but, even assuming that it can be, I have not been persuaded that a case of waiver has been established in the present cases. No doubt the accused, or at least their legal advisers, will have known of the opportunity afforded by the Scotland Act to challenge acts by the Lord Advocate which were incompatible with a convention right. No doubt they will have been aware that under the convention their clients were entitled to trial before an independent and impartial tribunal. They may well have known that the sheriff before whom the case was being conducted was a temporary sheriff. But it has not been shown that they knew of the lack of security of tenure of the temporary sheriffs in general nor of the involvement of the Lord Advocate in their appointment. The way in which they were appointed and used, at least since May 1997, was, as the Lord Justice-Clerk (Cullen) observed in *Starrs'* case (1999) 8 BHRC 1 at 10, not a matter of general public knowledge. Without knowing the factual background to the appointment of temporary sheriffs and the close participation of the Lord Advocate in that process it would not be possible to make any waiver of the objection to the case proceeding before such a tribunal. Waiver must essentially depend upon a knowledge of the relevant facts on which the right to object is based. In the present cases there is no evidence to support the proposition that the accused, or their representatives, knew or even suspected that there might be grounds for objection. Without evidence to demonstrate such knowledge I do not consider that a case of waiver can be established. The Solicitor General made some submissions on the matter of waiver but his principal concern was to treat the possibility of waiver as an ingredient in the global view which he sought to promote and the submissions which he made in regard to waiver were to an extent at least directed to the significance of that possibility in the context of an overall view.

[78] The new approach to the case requires some consideration of art 6(1) and I now turn to that article. It is critical for the respondent's argument that the requirement for an independent and impartial tribunal should be seen as simply an aspect of the governing requirement for fairness, so that it would be possible to sustain the validity of a criminal conviction on grounds of fairness even although the tribunal lacked independence and impartiality. The approach which he advocates makes fairness the ultimate test, so that if on a review of the whole circumstances the trial can be found to be fair, the lack of an independent and impartial tribunal can be held not to be fatal.

[79] I would accept that on a broad view of art 6 the ultimate essential is that a fair trial should be secured. In *Deweer v Belgium* (1980) 2 EHRR 439 at 460 (para 49) it was recognised that the 'right to a court' is a constituent element of the right to a fair trial. But how the goal of a fair trial is achieved is a matter of the particular circumstances of each case so that general propositions cannot always be usefully or safely prescribed. The hearing to which everyone is entitled in terms of art 6(1) is a hearing which is fair, which is public, which is held within a reasonable time, and which is held by an independent and impartial tribunal established by law. The concept of fairness may, as was recognised in *Brown v*

Stott (Procurator Fiscal, Dunfermline) [2001] 2 All ER 97 at 136, [2001] 2 WLR 817 at 859, be in itself an absolute, but what is comprised in the concept is a matter of the circumstances of the particular case. In *Brown's* case the implied right not to incriminate oneself was seen as subsumed under the governing requirement for fairness. But that case was not concerned with the issue of an independent and impartial tribunal. The requirement that the hearing be in public is expressly qualified in the article itself, so it is not a universal necessity and it can be waived (eg *Zumtobel v Austria* (1993) 17 EHRR 116 at 133 (para 34), *Håkansson v Sweden* (1990) 13 EHRR 1 at 16 (paras 66, 67); *H v Belgium* (1987) 10 EHRR 339). The hearing must be within a reasonable time. But while that may in itself be categorised as an absolute requirement, the application of the concept, like the concept of fairness, is matter of consideration in light of the facts and circumstances of the particular case. No doubt the particular rights set out in art 6(2) and (3) are all aspects of the general requirement of fairness.

[80] There remains the requirement that the tribunal be independent and impartial and established by law. Freedom from bias may be analysed into distinct considerations of structural independence and objective impartiality, but the two concepts are closely linked and it may be sufficient to speak simply of independence. Judicial independence is of fundamental constitutional importance. It is an indispensable condition for the preservation of the rule of law. It is a principle which has been stoutly protected by the Scottish judges for centuries (Mitchell *Constitutional Law* (2nd edn, 1968) p 261). We are fortunate in this country that for a very considerable length of time this principle has never been lost, although through the annals of history there may have been times when its light burned less brightly. But the complaisance which such a situation can inspire should never allow it to be forgotten that the principle is not so robust that it can always withstand the pressures which some forms of government may impose upon it. In my view the requirement that a tribunal be independent and impartial is of such fundamental importance that it should not lightly be subordinated to other considerations of fairness.

[81] As matter of generality a lack of independence in the tribunal may not necessarily be fatal to the validity of a hearing. The recent decision of the House of Lords in *R (on the application of Alconbury Developments Ltd) v Secretary of State for the Environment, Transport and the Regions* [2001] UKHL 23, [2001] 2 All ER 929, [2001] 2 WLR 1389 provides one example where in the particular context of town and country planning an overall fairness in the process may be achieved despite a lack of independence in one of the stages. In such cases the global view of the whole proceedings may make it possible to conclude that overall there was a fair trial. But it is important to notice that the impartiality of the tribunal in criminal cases is not a matter which can be cured by the existence of a right of appeal to a court which itself satisfies the requirements of art 6(1) (see *De Cubber v Belgium* (1984) 7 EHRR 236). In *Findlay v UK* (1997) 24 EHRR 221 the court held that the lack of independence of the tribunal in court-martial proceedings was not remedied by the presence of safeguards, which included an oath taken by the court-martial board, and stated (at 246 (para 79)):

'Nor could the defects ... be corrected by any subsequent review proceedings. Since the applicant's hearing was concerned with serious charges classified as "criminal" under both domestic and Convention law, he was entitled to a first instance tribunal which fully met the requirements of Article 6(1).'

a It is clear that as matter of generality it is possible to waive a convention right. It has been repeatedly affirmed that to be effective a waiver must be established in an unequivocal manner and there must be 'minimum guarantees commensurate to its importance' (see *Pfeifer v Austria* (1992) 14 EHRR 692 at 712 (para 37)). But the critical question here is whether a waiver is possible where the matter is one of a lack of independence and the case is a criminal one. I have not been

b persuaded from the material put before us that an objection to the lack of independence and impartiality 'such as the one presented by the appellants here' has been recognised by the European Court of Human Rights as one which can be waived. In *Deweer v Belgium* (1980) 2 EHRR 439 at 460–461 (para 49) the court recognised that waivers could be made in civil matters in the form of arbitration clauses and in criminal cases in the form of fines paid by way of composition. The

c court stated: 'The waiver, which has undeniable advantages for the individual concerned as well as for the administration of justice, does not in principle offend against the convention.' But that is a very different kind of situation from that which is before us in the present cases. In *Pfeifer v Austria* (1992) 14 EHRR 692 at 713 (para 39) the court held that the decision in question was invalid 'even supposing

d that the rights in question can be waived by a defendant'. In *Bulut v Austria* (1996) 24 EHRR 84 two opportunities were given to the accused's lawyer to challenge one of the judges on the ground of his previous involvement in the case. On the first occasion the lawyer did not reply to the note asking whether he wished to make a challenge. On the second occasion, at the outset of the trial, the record of the court was to the effect that the parties had waived the right to raise the

e point. The European Court of Human Rights held that the fear of impartiality lacked objective justification, adding (at 101 (para 34)) that in any event—

> 'it is not open to the applicant to complain that he had legitimate reasons to doubt the impartiality of the court which tried him, when he had the right to challenge its composition but refrained from doing so.'

f The court did not decide whether a waiver could be made. Judge Morenilla, in his partly dissenting opinion (at 117–118 (para 5)), thought the right to an impartial tribunal was an absolute right which could not be waived and he pointed out that the court had had an opportunity to decide the issue but had not considered it

g appropriate to do so. I note that in Scotland it has even been doubted whether a declinature by a judge who was a shareholder in one of the parties to a criminal proceeding could be waived by consent of the parties (see *Caledonian Rly Co v Ramsay* (1897) 24 R (J) 48).

[82] In light of this consideration of the fundamental importance of the right to an independent tribunal in criminal cases I turn to consider the Solicitor General's

h proposition that, if a global view is taken of the whole proceedings in each of these four cases, it should be held that in each case there has been a fair trial. The Solicitor General listed several factors which he argued supported the fairness of the proceedings. All the appellants had been found or had pleaded guilty. There was nothing to show that the verdicts were unsafe or that a full-time sheriff

j would have done anything different from what was done, so that there was no real purpose to be served by requiring the appellants to undergo a second trial. The appellants had not made any challenge to the proceedings until after the proceedings were concluded. No criticism was made that the particular sheriffs in fact lacked independence or impartiality. Nor was it said that the system by which they had been appointed in fact lacked independence.

[83] But even if one was to adopt the global approach put forward by the
Solicitor General and test the matter by the criterion of fairness, it seems to me
that there are other considerations to be taken into account. What is required
here is a consideration of all the circumstances and forming a view in the light of
all of them. The decision in *Starrs v Procurator Fiscal (Linlithgow), Procurator Fiscal
(Linlithgow) v Starrs* (1999) 8 BHRC 1 was pronounced as one of general application
to temporary sheriffs. The Lord Justice-Clerk (Cullen) stated (at 8):

> 'The point is of general importance, not only for its potential effect in
> individual cases but also for any future consideration of the terms of the
> relevant legislation and any appointments made thereunder.'

So one has the situation of the appellants having been tried, convicted and
sentenced by a tribunal which was not independent. In the absence of any
defence of waiver it seems to me far from fair to them that they should not have
the benefit of a decision which plainly would have been applicable to their cases.
The appearance that justice is being done is as important as the actual doing of
justice. The independence of the judiciary is not an empty principle which can be
forgotten simply because one thinks that a correct conclusion has been reached.
Rightly or wrongly there is always room for an uneasy fear that there might have
been some improper influence affecting the mind of the judge where he lacks
independence. The principle is far too important to allow it to be passed over in
the way which the respondent suggested.

[84] The Solicitor General's final argument was that even if the actings in
question were incompatible with art 6(1) nevertheless they should not be held to
be outside his powers in terms of s 57(2) because they fell within the scope of
s 57(3). That section provides that sub-s (2) is not to apply to an act of the Lord
Advocate in prosecuting any offence which, because of s 6(2) of the Human
Rights Act, is not unlawful under s 6(1). Section 6(2) excepts the unlawfulness of
an act incompatible with the convention in two circumstances. The first is where
because of some provision of primary legislation he could not have acted
differently. That does not apply here and it was on the second that the
Solicitor General sought to found his argument. It provides:

> '(b) in the case of one or more provisions of ... primary legislation which
> cannot be read or given effect in a way which is compatible with Convention
> rights, the authority was acting so as to give effect to or enforce those
> provisions.'

The argument then is that s 11 of the 1971 Act is incompatible with the
convention and the procurator fiscal in conducting the prosecution was 'giving
effect' to that provision. In my view it is too strained a construction of s 57(3) to
say that proceeding with a case before a temporary sheriff is giving effect to the
power to appoint temporary sheriffs.

[85] It should not need to be said that these cases cast no reflection at all on
the character or conduct of the temporary sheriffs engaged on them, nor indeed
on any other of the temporary sheriffs. Their personal integrity and independence
of mind are not in doubt and it is not suggested that there was any conscious or
unconscious bias or any subjective partiality felt or displayed in their work. But
it is as important that the appearance of justice be safeguarded as well as the
actual doing of justice and it is on that account that I am driven to the conclusion
that the convictions in these four cases cannot be held to be fair. Now that it has

a been held that temporary sheriffs lack independence, a decision which has not
been questioned in these appeals, and in the absence of an effective plea of
waiver, I see no alternative to a finding that the acts of the prosecutors in each of
these four cases were unlawful for the same reasons as those which applied in
Starrs' case. The principle of independence and impartiality of the tribunal
'particularly in criminal cases' is too precious to be put at any risk. I should be
b sorry if in a case like the present we were to allow any derogation from that
principle, even if the consequences of holding to it involve the invalidation of
convictions which from every other angle were safe and unimpeachable.

[86] I would accordingly allow these appeals.

LORD SCOTT OF FOSCOTE.

c [87] I agree that for the reasons given by my noble and learned friends, Lord
Bingham of Cornhill, Lord Hope of Craighead and Lord Clyde, these appeals
should be allowed.

Appeals allowed.

Celia Fox   Barrister.

R v Spear and another
R v Boyd
R v Saunby and other appeals
[2002] UKHL 31

HOUSE OF LORDS

LORD BINGHAM OF CORNHILL, LORD STEYN, LORD HUTTON, LORD SCOTT OF FOSCOTE
AND LORD RODGER OF EARLSFERRY

11–13 JUNE, 18 JULY 2002

Court-martial – Permanent president of court-martial – Civil offence – Fair hearing –
Whether role of permanent president precluding court-martial from being independent
and impartial tribunal – Whether trial of civil offence by court-martial in United
Kingdom incompatible with right to fair hearing – Human Rights Act 1998, Sch 1, Pt I,
art 6.

In the first of two groups of conjoined appeals, the issue was whether, because of
the part played in the district courts-martial which had convicted the defendants
by the permanent president of the court-martial, those courts-martial had lacked
the qualities of independence and impartiality required of a tribunal by art 6(1)[a]
of the European Convention for the Protection of Human Rights and Fundamental
Freedoms 1950 (as set out in Sch 1 to the Human Rights Act 1998). The role of
the permanent president, who was an officer appointed to that post in the closing
years of his service career, was similar to that of a juror, except that, during the
period of his appointment, his full-time professional occupation was to sit in
courts-martial; he had administrative responsibilities in relation to the staging of
the court-martial; and it was his responsibility to see that the hearing was
conducted in accordance with service tradition. The Courts Martial Appeal
Court decided the issue against the defendants, and they appealed to the House
of Lords.

The second group of appeals against conviction, which had all been dismissed
by the Courts Martial Appeal Court, raised the issue whether a trial by
court-martial in the United Kingdom of an offence against the ordinary criminal
law of the land was compatible with art 6(1) of the convention, either generally
or in cases where the offence had been committed within the United Kingdom.
On their appeals to the House of Lords, the defendants raised no objection to the
trial by court-martial of purely military offences charged against servicemen,
wherever committed, and they accepted that civil offences charged against
servicemen abroad, in places where the local administration of justice had broken
down or was of unacceptable quality, could properly be tried by court-martial.
They nevertheless contended that, in relation to the trial of civil offences in the
United Kingdom, courts-martial lacked the independence and impartiality
required by art 6. In particular, they challenged the independence and impartiality of
junior officers who served on courts-martial, and further contended that the
whole culture and ethos of the services was such as to incline those who took part

---

a   Article 6, so far as material, is set out at [20], below *a* in courts-martial to attach excessive weight to the values of discipline and morale, to the point of rendering the trial of the accused unfair.

Held – (1) The part played by permanent presidents in courts-martial did not preclude such courts from having the independence and impartiality required of a judicial tribunal by art 6 of the convention. Permanent presidents had no
b effective hope of promotion and no effective fear of removal. While no doubt they were, as officers, answerable for any extra-judicial delinquency, as any judge might be, they were answerable to no one for the discharge of their decision-making function (see [10], [17]–[19], [58], [64], below); *Morris v UK* (2002) 34 EHRR 1253 adopted in part.

(2) A trial of a civil offence by court-martial in the United Kingdom was
c compatible with art 6(1) of the convention. The rules governing the role of junior officers as members of courts-martial were in practice such as effectively to protect the accused against the risk that they might be subject to external army influence. Moreover, whilst it was true that officers serving on courts-martial would disapprove of those found to have acted in breach of the law governing
d their respective service, judges and jurors in the Crown Court would similarly disapprove of those found to have infringed the ordinary criminal law. There was no reason to think that in the former case, any more than in the latter, such disapproval would infect the tribunals' approach to deciding whether the particular accused had broken the law in the manner charged. Further, a court-martial either was or was not an independent and impartial tribunal. Since
e courts-martial were to be regarded as independent and impartial tribunals for the trial of military offences and civil offences committed abroad in the conditions noted, it followed that they were also independent and impartial tribunals for the trial of civil offences committed in the United Kingdom. Accordingly, the appeals would be dismissed (see [12], [14]–[19], [44], [83], [91], [92], [101], below); *Morris v*
f *UK* (2002) 34 EHRR 1253 not adopted in part.

Notes
For independent and impartial tribunal, see 8(2) *Halsbury's Laws* (4th edn reissue) para 140.
For the Human Rights Act 1998, Sch 1, Pt I, art 6, see 7 *Halsbury's Statutes*
g (4th edn) (1999 reissue) 523.

Cases referred to in opinions
Boucher v R (1954) 110 Can CC 263, Can SC.
Brown v Stott (Procurator Fiscal, Dunfermline) [2001] 2 All ER 97, [2001] 2 WLR 817, PC.
h *Brumarescu v Romania* (1999) 33 EHRR 862, ECt HR.
Committee for Justice and Liberty v National Energy Board (1976) 68 DLR (3d) 716, Can SC.
Cox v Army Council [1962] 1 All ER 880, [1963] AC 48, [1962] 2 WLR 950, HL.
Engel v The Netherlands (No 1) (1976) 1 EHRR 647, ECt HR.
j *Findlay v UK* (1997) 24 EHRR 221, ECt HR.
Golder v UK (1975) 1 EHRR 524, ECt HR.
Grant v Gould (1792) 2 Hy Bl 69, [1775–1802] All ER Rep 182, 126 ER 434, CP.
Gregory v UK (1997) 25 EHRR 577, ECt HR.
MacKay v R (1980) 114 DLR (3d) 393, Can SC.
Millar v Dickson (Procurator Fiscal, Elgin) [2001] UKPC D4, [2002] 3 All ER 1041, [2002] 1 WLR 1615.

Montgomery v HM Advocate, Coulter v HM Advocate [2001] 2 WLR 779, PC.
Morris v UK (2002) 34 EHRR 1253, ECt HR.
Porter v Magill [2001] UKHL 67, [2002] 1 All ER 465, [2002] 2 WLR 37.
Pullar v UK (1996) 22 EHRR 391, ECt HR.
R v Généreux (1992) 88 DLR (4th) 110, Can SC.
R v McKendry (6 March 2000, unreported).
Randall v R [2002] UKPC 19, [2002] 1 WLR 2237.
Tracey, Re, ex p Ryan (1989) 166 CLR 518, Aust HC.

Appeals against conviction

R v Spear and anor

The appellants, John Spear and Philip David Hastie, appealed with leave of the
Appeal Committee of the House of Lords given on 20 June 2001 from the order
of the Courts Martial Appeal Court (Laws LJ, Holman and Goldring JJ) on 15 January
2001 ([2001] EWCA Crim 3, [2001] QB 804, [2001] 2 WLR 1692) dismissing their
appeals against their conviction by a district court-martial held at Osnabrück,
Germany, on 1 February 2000 of an offence of assault occasioning actual bodily
harm. The Appeal Court certified that a point of law of general public importance,
set out at [22], below, was involved in its decision. The facts, so far as material,
are set out in the opinion of Lord Rodger of Earlsferry.

R v Boyd

The appellant, David Morton Boyd, appealed with leave of the Appeal
Committee of the House of Lords given on 12 March 2002 from the order of the
Courts Martial Appeal Court (Laws LJ, Holman and Goldring JJ) on 15 January
2001 ([2001] EWCA Crim 3, [2001] QB 804, [2001] 2 WLR 1692) dismissing his
appeal against his conviction by a district court-martial held at RAF Akrotiri,
Cyprus, on 17 December 1999 of an offence of assault occasioning actual bodily
harm. The Appeal Court certified that a point of law of general public
importance, set out at [22], below, was involved in its decision. The facts, so far
as material, are set out in the opinion of Lord Rodger of Earlsferry.

R v Saunby

The appellant, David Saunby, appealed with leave of the Appeal Committee of
the House of Lords given on 4 March 2002 from the order of the Courts Martial
Appeal Court (Laws LJ, Turner and McCombe JJ) on 30 July 2001 ([2001] EWCA
Crim 2311, [2001] All ER (D) 425 (Jul)) dismissing his appeal against his conviction
by a district court-martial at Aldershot on 16 December 1999 of an offence of
doing an act tending and intending to pervert the course of public justice. The
Appeal Court certified that a point of law of general public importance, set out at
[22], below, was involved in its decision. The Secretary of State for Defence
participated in the proceedings as an interested party. The facts, so far as material,
are set out in the opinion of Lord Rodger of Earlsferry.

R v Clarkson and anor

The appellants, Lee Martin Clarkson and Paul Anthony English, appealed with
leave of the Appeal Committee of the House of Lords given on 4 March 2002
from the order of the Courts Martial Appeal Court (Laws LJ, Turner and
McCombe JJ) on 30 July 2001 ([2001] EWCA Crim 2311, [2001] All ER (D) 425
(Jul)) dismissing their appeals against their conviction by a district court-martial

a   at Colchester on 8 March 2000 of an offence of assault occasioning actual bodily
harm. The Appeal Court certified that a point of law of general public importance,
set out at [22], below, was involved in its decision. The Secretary of State for
Defence participated in the proceedings as an interested party. The facts, so far
as material, are set out in the opinion of Lord Rodger of Earlsferry.

b   *R v Williams*
The appellant, David Omar Williams, appealed with leave of the Appeal
Committee of the House of Lords given on 4 March 2002 from the order of the
Courts Martial Appeal Court (Laws LJ, Turner and McCombe JJ) on 30 July 2001
([2001] EWCA Crim 2311, [2001] All ER (D) 425 (Jul)) dismissing his appeal
against his conviction by a general court-martial at RAF St Mawgan on 5 April
c   2000 of an offence of common assault. The Appeal Court certified that a point of
law of general public importance, set out at [22], below, was involved in its
decision. The Secretary of State for Defence participated in the proceedings as an
interested party. The facts, so far as material, are set out in the opinion of Lord
Rodger of Earlsferry.

d   *R v Dodds*
The appellant, Andrew Alistair Dodds, appealed with leave of the Appeal
Committee of the House of Lords given on 4 March 2002 from the order of the
Courts Martial Appeal Court (Laws LJ, Turner and McCombe JJ) on 30 July 2001
([2001] EWCA Crim 2311, [2001] All ER (D) 425 (Jul)) dismissing his appeal
e   against his conviction by a district court-martial at RAF Cosford on 13 June 2000
of an offence of battery. The Appeal Court certified that a point of law of general
public importance, set out at [22], below, was involved in its decision. The
Secretary of State for Defence participated in the proceedings as an interested
party. The facts, so far as material, are set out in the opinion of Lord Rodger of
f   Earlsferry.

                                       R v Leese
The appellant, Henry Leese, appealed with leave of the Appeal Committee of the
House of Lords given on 4 March 2002 from the order of the Courts Martial
Appeal Court (Laws LJ, Turner and McCombe JJ) on 30 July 2001 ([2001] EWCA
g   Crim 2311, [2001] All ER (D) 425 (Jul)) dismissing his appeal against his conviction
by a district court-martial at RAF Lossiemouth on 20 October 2000 of an offence
of furnishing false information. The Appeal Court certified that a point of law of
general public importance, set out at [22], below, was involved in its decision.
The Secretary of State for Defence participated in the proceedings as an interested
h   party. The facts, so far as material, are set out in the opinion of Lord Rodger of
Earlsferry.

                                       R v Marsh
The appellant, Peter James Marsh, appealed with leave of the Appeal Committee
j   of the House of Lords given on 4 March 2002 from the order of the Courts Martial
Appeal Court (Laws LJ, Turner and McCombe JJ) on 30 July 2001 ([2001] EWCA
Crim 2311, [2001] All ER (D) 425 (Jul)) dismissing his appeal against his conviction
by a district court-martial at RAF Lossiemouth on 8 November 2000 of an offence
of furnishing false information. The Appeal Court certified that a point of law of
general public importance, set out at [22], below, was involved in its decision.
The Secretary of State for Defence participated in the proceedings as an interested

party. The facts, so far as material, are set out in the opinion of Lord Rodger of
Earlsferry.

R v Cormack

The appellant, James Albert Cormack Webb, appealed with leave of the Appeal
Committee of the House of Lords given on 4 March 2002 from the order of the
Courts Martial Appeal Court (Laws LJ, Turner and McCombe JJ) on 30 July 2001
([2001] EWCA Crim 2311, [2001] All ER (D) 425 (Jul)) dismissing his appeal against
his conviction by a district court-martial at RAF Lossiemouth on 24 November
2000 of an offence of furnishing false information. The Appeal Court certified that
a point of law of general public importance, set out at [22], below, was involved
in its decision. The Secretary of State for Defence participated in the proceedings
as an interested party. The facts, so far as material, are set out in the opinion of
Lord Rodger of Earlsferry.

R v Ashby

The appellant, Mark William Ashby, appealed with leave of the Appeal
Committee of the House of Lords given on 4 March 2002 from the order of the
Courts Martial Appeal Court (Laws LJ, Turner and McCombe JJ) on 30 July 2001
([2001] EWCA Crim 2311, [2001] All ER (D) 425 (Jul)) dismissing his appeal
against his conviction by a district court-martial at RAF Stafford on 18 December
2000 of an offence of false accounting. The Appeal Court certified that a point of
law of general public importance, set out at [22], below, was involved in its
decision. The Secretary of State for Defence participated in the proceedings as an
interested party. The facts, so far as material, are set out in the opinion of Lord
Rodger of Earlsferry.

Lord Thomas of Gresford QC (instructed by *Wilkin Chapman Epton Blades*, Lincoln)
and *Gilbert Blades* of that firm for the appellants.
Philip Havers QC, Dingle Clark and *Paul Rogers* (instructed by the *Army Prosecuting
Authority*, Uxbridge and the *Royal Air Force Prosecuting Authority*, Gloucester)
for the Crown.
Philip Havers QC and *Hugo Keith* (instructed by the *Treasury Solicitor*) for the
Secretary of State.

Their Lordships took time for consideration.

18 July 2002. The following opinions were delivered.

LORD BINGHAM OF CORNHILL.

[1] My Lords, the conjoined appeals before the House fall into two groups.
The first group comprises the three cases of Aircraftman Boyd and Messrs Spear
and Hastie. These three appellants were all non-commissioned officers, Boyd in
the Royal Air Force, Spear and Hastie in the army. All three were charged (Spear
and Hastie jointly) with assault occasioning actual bodily harm to another
member of their respective services. All three were tried by district court-martial,
pleaded not guilty, were convicted and were sentenced. At both the courts-martial
a permanent president of courts-martial (or PPCM, Wing Commander Chambers
in the first case, Lieutenant Colonel Stone in the second) presided. The sole
issue in the appeal before the House in these cases is whether, because of the part
played by the PPCM, the courts-martial lacked the qualities of independence and

a impartiality which art 6(1) of the European Convention for the Protection of Human Rights and Fundamental Freedoms 1950 (as set out in Sch 1 to the Human Rights Act 1998) requires of any judicial tribunal. The Courts Martial Appeal Court (Laws LJ, Holman and Goldring JJ) decided this issue against the accused (see [2001] EWCA Crim 3, [2001] QB 804, [2001] 2 WLR 1692).

[2] The second group of appeals comprises the cases of Mr Saunby, Sapper
b Clarkson, Lance Corporal English, Flying Officer Williams, Senior Aircraftman Dodds, Messrs Leese, Marsh and Webb and Aircraftman Ashby. They were charged with a variety of different offences (Clarkson and English jointly). All appeared before district courts-martial (DCMs) except Williams (who, as a commissioned officer, appeared before a general court-martial, or GCM). All pleaded not guilty but were convicted, save for Ashby who pleaded guilty. A variety of different
c sentences were passed, ranging from 84 days' imprisonment and dismissal (Saunby, Webb) to forfeiture of three years' seniority (Williams). Petitions for review were rejected in all cases save in that of Dodds, whose sentence of 112 days' detention was reduced to 28 days. The Courts Martial Appeal Court (Laws LJ, Turner and McCombe JJ) dismissed appeals by all appellants save in the
d case of Marsh, whose sentence of 56 days' imprisonment was reduced to 42 days' detention, a reduction which greatly mitigated the financial loss suffered by him on leaving the service (see [2001] EWCA Crim 2311, [2001] All ER (D) 425 (Jul)). All the offences of which these appellants were convicted were offences under the ordinary law applicable in the United Kingdom. All the offences (with two exceptions) were committed within the United Kingdom. The issue which arises
e in all these appeals is whether a trial by court-martial in the United Kingdom of an offence against the ordinary criminal law of the land is compatible with art 6(1) of the convention, either generally or in cases where the offence in question had been committed within the United Kingdom.

[3] Since the dawning of the modern age the defence of the state against the
f threats and depredations of external enemies has been recognised as one of the cardinal functions of government. To this end most countries have over time established regular armed forces, in this country a navy, then an army, and then in due course an air force. The effectiveness of such forces has been recognised to depend on their being disciplined forces: that is, forces in which lawful orders will be obeyed, the law will be observed and appropriate standards of self-control
g and conduct will be shown.

[4] While disciplinary rules and procedures will inevitably vary from state to state, three principles would now, I think, command acceptance in any liberal democracy governed by the rule of law. (In stating these principles I draw no distinction between different services, although the issues in these appeals do not
h concern the Royal Navy. Nor do I distinguish between regular and reserve or volunteer forces, or between men and women. It is convenient for purposes of exposition to speak of soldiers and of the army. Since the Army Act 1955 and the Air Force Act 1955 are, in the respects relevant to these appeals, indistinguishable, I shall refer only to the former and to the Courts-Martial (Army) Rules 1997,
j SI 1997/169). First, a man does not by becoming a soldier cease to be a citizen. On becoming a soldier he subjects himself to duties and exposes himself to the risk of penalties to which a civilian is not subject or exposed. But he remains subject to almost every law, including the criminal law, which binds other citizens and continues to enjoy almost all the same rights, including the right (if a charge of serious misconduct is made against him) to a fair trial before an independent and impartial tribunal. Secondly, the maintenance of the discipline

essential to the effectiveness of a fighting force is as necessary in peacetime as in wartime: a force which cannot display the qualities mentioned above in time of peace cannot hope to withstand the much more testing strains and temptations of war. Thirdly, and whatever the practice in former times, a modern code of military discipline cannot depend on arbitrary decision-making or the infliction of savage punishments, nor can it depend on inherited habits of deference or gradations of class distinction. Such a code must of course reflect the hierarchical structure of any army and respect the power of command. But an effective code of military discipline will buttress not only the respect owed to their leaders by those who are led but also, and perhaps even more importantly, the respect owed by leaders to those whom they lead and which all members of a fighting force owe to each other.

[5] The dual status of the soldier, as both soldier and citizen, raises no issue where he is said to have committed a purely military offence, that is, an offence which could not be committed by anyone who was not a soldier. Some such offences are potentially very serious: mutiny, desertion, absence without leave, striking a superior officer are examples. Since these are offences which cannot be committed by those not subject to military discipline, it is unsurprising that they cannot be tried in the ordinary courts of the land and can only be tried in a military tribunal. But the effect of s 70 of the 1955 Act (as my noble and learned friend Lord Rodger of Earlsferry, whose citation of the relevant legislation and authority I gratefully adopt and need not repeat, has pointed out) is to expose the soldier accused of an offence against the ordinary criminal law of the land to prosecution either in the ordinary courts or in a military tribunal. Since he cannot be tried in either tribunal if he has already been tried in the other for substantially the same offence (see s 133 of the 1955 Act, and the ordinary common law rules of autrefois convict and acquit), a question may arise whether he should face trial in a civil court or in a military tribunal. As my noble and learned friend has shown, no hard and fast rules have been laid down to resolve this problem where it arises. Instead, a pragmatic solution has been adopted, largely dependent on identification of the public interest which the soldier's allegedly criminal conduct has infringed. If it appears to be the general public interest which has been injured (as where a civilian has been injured or non-military property damaged or stolen) a civil court is ordinarily regarded as the more appropriate forum, since the defendant's status as a soldier is essentially irrelevant to his criminal conduct. If, however, the public interest which the soldier's allegedly criminal conduct has infringed is primarily a service interest (as where another soldier has been injured or military property has been damaged or stolen) the charge is ordinarily considered appropriate for trial by a military tribunal: the general public interest is much less directly engaged, and an internal offence of this kind may well have a direct effect on the morale and discipline of the unit involved.

[6] The practice of other states is not dissimilar to our own. So much appears from such decisions as *MacKay v R* (1980) 114 DLR (3d) 393 at 413–414, 416–418, 419–421, 423–426, *Re Tracey, ex p Ryan* (1989) 166 CLR 518 at 543–544, *R v Généreux* (1992) 88 DLR (4th) 110 at 135–136, 156–157. That there is a rational basis for the practice is made plain in those decisions, and in the statement of Air Chief Marshal Sir Anthony Bagnall, the vice-chief of the defence staff which is before the House. In *Findlay v UK* (1997) 24 EHRR 221 the defendant was charged with a number of offences of which the more serious were offences against the ordinary criminal law. The European Court of Human Rights (the European Court) found serious breaches of art 6(1) of the convention in the structure and

a procedure under which courts-martial were then conducted, and a number of changes were made in the Armed Forces Act 1996. The effect of these changes was well summarised by Laws LJ in the first of the judgments under appeal (see *R v Spear, R v Boyd* [2001] QB 804 at [18]). There is, however, nothing in the judgment of the European Court in *Findlay v UK*, or in the earlier case of *Engel v The Netherlands* (*No 1*) (1976) 1 EHRR 647 or in the more recent case of *Morris v UK*

b (2002) 34 EHRR 1253, to suggest that trial by court-martial, whether of civil or purely military offences, necessarily involves a violation of rights protected by art 6(1).

[7] Lord Thomas of Gresford QC directed his initial challenge on behalf of the second group of appellants to the terms of s 70 of the 1955 Act, which he criticised as incompatible with art 6(1). The short answer to this point is that given by

c Mr Havers QC, that this section does not engage art 6(1) at all. While the section provides that persons subject to military law who commit civil offences shall (save in the case of certain offences) be guilty of offences against the section, it makes no provision governing the constitution of the tribunal by which such persons shall be tried nor the procedure to be followed. Recognising this, Lord

d Thomas concentrated the weight of his argument on criticism of the independence and impartiality of courts-martial as a tribunal for the trial of civil offences committed by servicemen. In these appeals the House is concerned with GCMs and DCMs. It is unnecessary to consider field general courts-martial, which are governed by different provisions (see ss 103A(1) and (2) and 103B of the 1955 Act), nor is it necessary to explore the differences between GCMs and DCMs. A

e court-martial of either type has no exact equivalent elsewhere in the British legal system but has features closely reflecting those of well-established judicial models: (1) Central to the conduct of a court-martial is the judge-advocate, whose role is essentially that of the judge at a criminal trial on indictment in the Crown Court. He is a trained lawyer of standing and experience. He is responsible for

f ensuring the fair and regular conduct of the trial. He controls the course of evidence. He rules on legal objections. He gives all appropriate directions to the members of the court-martial on both the facts and the law. He elucidates issues on which the members seek further guidance. He plays no part in reaching a decision on guilt but (if the defendant is convicted) he guides the members on the question of sentence and casts a vote on that issue (see ss 84B(2) and (3), 94(6),

g 96(1A) of the 1955 Act and rr 31, 32(1), 39, 69, 70(1) and (2), 79, 80(2) of the 1997 rules, and see also Judge JW Rant QC *Courts-Martial Handbook* (1998) pp 10, 146). (2) The role of the members of the courts-martial is closely analogous to that of jurors. They come to the case with no legal training (see r 17(b)) and no knowledge of the facts or issues (see s 84C). At the outset of the hearing, the

h names of the members of the tribunal (and also of the judge-advocate and of any interpreter) are read out, as is the practice with jurors, and the accused has the right to object to any of them (see s 92 (as amended) and r 40). The members are bound to give effect to the legal directions given by the judge-advocate and will heed the guidance which he gives (see s 84B(4)). But they alone are the

j judges of fact, they alone must resolve issues of credibility and they alone decide whether the charge is proved or not (see s 94(6)). (3) The role of the PPCM (such as served in the first group of cases under appeal and in the military cases in the second group) is similar to that of a juror in all the respects just noted. But his role differs from that of a juror, and from that of the other military members of the court-martial: during the period of his appointment his full-time professional occupation is to sit in courts-martial; he has administrative responsibilities in relation to the staging of the court-martial; it is his responsibility to see that the hearing is conducted in accordance with service tradition (see r 33(1)); and during the deliberations of the tribunal he will no doubt chair the members' discussion in the manner of a good chairman. The PPCM is in practice more than a permanent foreman of the jury, because he performs the functions already noted and because he has a casting vote on sentence (see s 96(5)). Participating in a number of trials, he no doubt acquires a reasonable working knowledge of law and practice, such as a busy and experienced lay magistrate might acquire.

[8] The European Court has defined with great clarity and consistency the meaning of the art 6(1) requirement that a tribunal be independent and impartial. It is enough to quote the court's judgment in *Findlay v UK* (1997) 24 EHRR 221 at 244–245 (para 73):

'The Court recalls that in order to establish whether a tribunal can be considered as "independent", regard must be had *inter alia* to the manner of appointment of its members and their term of office, the existence of guarantees against outside pressures and the question whether the body presents an appearance of independence. As to the question of "impartiality", there are two aspects to this requirement. First, the tribunal must be subjectively free of personal prejudice or bias. Secondly, it must also be impartial from an objective viewpoint, that is, it must offer sufficient guarantees to exclude any legitimate doubt in this respect. The concepts of independence and objective impartiality are closely linked and the Court will consider them together as they relate to the present case.'

It should also be remembered, as the court pointed out (at 245 (para 76)) that in order to maintain confidence in the independence and impartiality of the tribunal appearances may be of importance. Relying on these statements of principle, Lord Thomas submitted that courts-martial, in relation to the trial of civil offences committed in England, despite the changes made by the 1996 Act, lack the independence and impartiality required of any judicial tribunal by art 6 of the convention. This radical challenge, rejected by the Court of Appeal, plainly calls for very careful consideration.

[9] Lord Thomas did not pursue in argument any challenge to the independence or impartiality of the Judge-Advocate General. Given the key role played by the Judge-Advocate General in the conduct of courts-martial, this is a very significant omission.

[10] Lord Thomas did challenge the independence and impartiality of the PPCM, and this challenge founded the first group of appeals. He naturally relied on the conclusion of Assistant Judge-Advocate General Pearson given at the court-martial of Lance Corporal McKendry held at Aldershot on 6 March 2000 that 'the appointments of permanent presidents do not give rise to an impartial and independent tribunal'. But Lord Thomas faced the difficulty that the European Court in *Morris v UK* (2002) 34 EHRR 1253 at 1276–1278 (paras 68–71), after and with full knowledge of the decisions both in *R v McKendry* (6 March 2000, unreported) and (by the Courts Martial Appeal Court) in the first group of appeals, reached the opposite conclusion. I do not for my part doubt that the Courts Martial Appeal Court and the European Court were correct. PPCMs are appointed to that office in the closing years of their service careers, whether in the army or the Royal Air Force. They are officers who have no effective hope of promotion and no effective fear of removal. While no doubt they are, as officers, answerable for any extra-judicial delinquency, as any judge might be, they are

a answerable to no one for the discharge of their decision-making function. The only factual matters on which Lord Thomas could rely were the reports written on Wing Commander Chambers who presided at the court-martial of Aircraftman Boyd (there being no report on any army PPCM). It would in my opinion be preferable if no annual report were written on officers serving as PPCMs, but those on Wing Commander Chambers gave no support in substance

b to Lord Thomas' argument. While praising the wing commander's efficiency and effectiveness as a PPCM, they made no allusion at all to the quality or outcome of any of his judicial decisions, but instead made express reference to the isolated, unsupervised and independent nature of his role. There is no substance in this challenge.

c [11] Lord Thomas also challenged the independence and impartiality of the junior officers who serve on courts-martial, and in this respect was able to rely on a finding of the European Court in Morris v UK (2002) 34 EHRR 1253 at 1278, 1279 (paras 72, 76) that such officers lacked the necessary qualities of independence and that the applicant's misgivings about the independence of the court-martial were objectively justified. In the first of these paragraphs the court said:

d 'However, the Court considers that the presence of these safeguards was insufficient to exclude the risk of outside pressure being brought to bear on the two relatively junior serving officers who sat on the applicant's court martial. In particular, it notes that those officers had no legal training, that they remained subject to army discipline and reports, and that there was no

e statutory or other bar to their being made subject to external army influence when sitting on the case. This is a matter of particular concern in a case such as the present where the offence charged directly involves a breach of military discipline. In this respect, the position of the military members of the court martial cannot generally be compared with that of a member of a

f civilian jury who is not open to the risk of such pressures.'

[12] It goes without saying that any judgment of the European Court commands great respect, and s 2(1) of the Human Rights Act 1998 requires the House to take any such judgment into account, as it routinely does. There were, however, a large number of points in issue in Morris v UK, and it seems clear that on this

g particular aspect the European Court did not receive all the help which was needed to form a conclusion. It is true that the junior officers who sit on courts-martial have very little legal training, but that is also true of the PPCM whose presence was accepted (at 1278 (para 71)) as a guarantee of the rights of the accused. It is also true that junior officers sitting on courts-martial remain subject to army discipline and reports. But there is nothing to suggest that any report

h ever is or ever has been made on any junior officer's decision-making as a member of a court-martial, and it is hard to see how any such report could be made given the prohibition on disclosure of the deliberations of the tribunal in the oath taken by the members. There is nothing to suggest that they remain subject to service discipline in relation to their judicial decision-making, and again

j it is hard to see how they could. It is true that there is no statutory bar on an officer being made subject to external army influence when sitting on the case. Any person seeking to influence the decision of a sitting member of a court-martial otherwise than at the hearing would, however, be at risk of prosecution either for perverting or attempting to pervert the course of justice or under s 69 of the 1955 Act. The officer members are drawn from a different command from the accused. Briefing notes sent to officer members of courts-martial before they sit enjoin them not to 'speak to any unit personnel and certainly not to any unit officer who may be attending the trial in an official capacity or as a spectator'. They are instructed in writing not to talk to anyone about the case (other than the other members of the court-martial, when all are together) for as long as the trial continues, and this instruction is routinely emphasised by the judge-advocate. The officers do not occupy accommodation at the unit of the accused and are told to be seen to avoid 'local unit influences'. They are instructed 'not to associate with Formation or Unit personnel either professionally or socially until the trial is over'. At the outset of the hearing the officers take an oath in terms quoted by the European Court in *Morris v UK* (2002) 34 EHRR 1253 at 1265 (para 27), swearing to try the accused 'according to the evidence' and to 'administer justice according to the Army Act 1955 without partiality, favour or affection'. In considering the independence and impartiality of the PPCM both the Court of Appeal in its judgment in *R v Spear, R v Boyd* [2001] QB 804 at [33], [35], [2001] 2 WLR 1692 and the European Court in *Morris v UK* (2002) 34 EHRR 1253 at 1276–1277 (paras 68–69) attached weight to established convention and practice. In my opinion the rules governing the role of junior officers as members of courts-martial are in practice such as effectively to protect the accused against the risk that they might be subject to 'external army influence', as I feel sure the European Court would have appreciated had the position been more fully explained.

[13] In its judgment in *Morris v UK* the European Court (at 1278–1279 (paras 73–75)) criticised the role of the reviewing authority established under s 113 of the 1955 Act. Lord Rodger has outlined the role of the reviewing authority and I need not repeat his account. Its role can certainly be seen as anomalous, since ordinarily a binding decision of any court cannot be disturbed otherwise than (exceptionally) by itself or by a superior appellate court. It is however to be noted that the review of conviction and sentence carried out by the reviewing authority, whether the accused seeks such review or not (see s 113(3) of both Acts), cannot work otherwise than to the advantage of the accused. The reviewing authority cannot substitute conviction of a more serious offence, nor can it substitute a sentence which is in its opinion more severe (see s 113AA(4)). This subsection does not confer a discretion, but calls for an exercise of judgment. It is essentially the same exercise of judgment as is required of the Court of Appeal under ss 4(3) and 11(3) of the Criminal Appeal Act 1968, which has not given rise to difficulty in practice. If the reviewing authority were to substitute a sentence which the accused considered to be more severe than that imposed by the court-martial, it would be open to the accused to challenge the substituted sentence on appeal to the Courts Martial Appeal Court, and it is important to note that the intervention of the reviewing authority in no way diminishes the rights of the accused on appeal. It is difficult to see any analogy with the situation which the European Court considered in *Brumarescu v Romania* (1999) 33 EHRR 862 where the applicant, with a final and irreversible judgment of a court in his favour, was deprived of the benefit of that judgment by a later decision in proceedings initiated by a party not involved in the earlier case. If a court-martial is not an independent and impartial tribunal for the trial of civil offences committed by service personnel in England and Wales, the reviewing authority could not be relied on to save it. But if it is, I find it difficult to understand how the role of the reviewing authority can undermine or reduce its independence and impartiality. Lord Thomas recognised the difficulty of this

argument and did not seek to sustain the judgment of the European Court on the point. For similar reasons I find it unnecessary to consider the role of the prosecuting authority, of which Lord Thomas made certain (to my mind unpersuasive) criticisms.

[14] Lord Thomas also advanced a more general criticism of trial by court-martial. The whole culture and ethos of the services, he submitted, is such as to incline those who take part in courts-martial to attach excessive weight to the values of discipline and morale, to the point of rendering the trial of the accused unfair. He complained of the ritual which has accompanied the conduct of courts-martial, at any rate in the past, as being oppressive and intimidatory. I would for my part have no hesitation in agreeing that a court-martial is a court of law, not a parade, and its procedures (while properly involving some formality) should be those appropriate to a court of law and not the parade ground. I would also accept that officers serving on courts-martial will disapprove of those found to have acted in breach of the law governing their respective service. But judges and jurors in the Crown Court will similarly disapprove of those found to have infringed the ordinary criminal law. There is no reason to think that in the former case any more than in the latter such disapproval will infect the tribunal's approach to deciding whether the particular accused has broken the law in the manner charged. Officers will appreciate, better than anyone, that to convict and punish those not shown to be guilty is not to promote the interests of good discipline and high morale but to sow the seeds of disaffection and perhaps even mutiny. In the absence of any evidence at all to support it, I could not accept the suggestion that any modern officer would, despite the oath he has taken, exercise his judgment otherwise than independently and impartially or be thought by any reasonable and informed observer to be at risk of doing so.

[15] In truth, as was pointed out in argument, Lord Thomas' submission was vitiated by a contradiction lying at its heart. For he raised no objection to the trial by court-martial of purely military offences charged against servicemen, wherever committed, and he accepted that civil offences charged against servicemen abroad, in places where the local administration of justice had broken down or was of unacceptable quality, could properly be tried by court-martial. But a court-martial either is or is not an independent and impartial tribunal. If it is, it can properly try civil as well as purely military offences. If it is not, it cannot, compatibly with art 6(1), try military offences, which may carry a severe sentence of imprisonment or detention. Nor, leaving aside issues concerning the territorial reach of the convention, and leaving aside also the special conditions in which a field general court-martial may be held, can it be compatible with the standard required by art 6(1) to subject service personnel accused of civil offences committed abroad to trial by court-martial if such is not an independent and impartial tribunal. Lord Thomas is not to be criticised for limiting his argument as he has, no doubt wisely, chosen to do. But if courts-martial are to be regarded, as in my opinion they are, as independent and impartial tribunals for the trial of military offences and civil offences committed abroad in the conditions noted, it must follow that they are also independent and impartial tribunals for the trial of civil offences committed in the United Kingdom.

[16] For these reasons, and those more fully given by Lord Rodger with which I am in full agreement, I would dismiss both groups of appeals.

LORD STEYN.

[17] My Lords, I have read the opinions of Lord Bingham of Cornhill and Lord Rodger of Earlsferry. For the reasons they give I would also dismiss the appeals.

LORD HUTTON.

[18] My Lords, I have had the advantage of reading in draft the speeches of my noble and learned friends Lord Bingham of Cornhill and Lord Rodger of Earlsferry. I agree with them, and for the reasons they give I would also dismiss the appeals.

LORD SCOTT OF FOSCOTE.

[19] My Lords, I have had the advantage of reading in draft the speeches of my noble and learned friends, Lord Bingham of Cornhill and Lord Rodger of Earlsferry. I agree with them and for the reasons they give I too would dismiss the appeals.

LORD RODGER OF EARLSFERRY.

[20] My Lords, the appeals before the House challenge the compatibility of the appellants' trials by court-martial with art 6 of the European Convention for the Protection of Human Rights and Fundamental Freedoms 1950 (as set out in Sch 1 to the Human Rights Act 1998). In particular on behalf of the appellants Lord Thomas of Gresford QC based his challenge on their right to the determination of the charges against them by 'an independent and impartial tribunal' in terms of the first sentence of art 6(1):

'In the determination of his civil rights and obligations or of any criminal charge against him, everyone is entitled to a fair and public hearing within a reasonable time by an independent and impartial tribunal established by law.'

[21] There are in total 12 appeals against decisions of the Courts Martial Appeal Court (the appeal court). In a judgment dated 15 January 2001 the appeal court, comprising Laws LJ, Holman and Goldring JJ, refused the appeals of John Spear and Philip Hastie along with the separate appeal of David Morton Boyd (see R v Spear, R v Boyd [2001] EWCA Crim 3, [2001] QB 804, [2001] 2 WLR 1692). I refer to the three appeals by that name. The appeal court (Laws LJ, Turner and McCombe JJ) subsequently refused the other nine appeals, along with an appeal by John Scofield, in an unreported judgment dated 30 July 2001 (see R v Williams [2001] EWCA Crim 2311, [2001] All ER (D) 425 (Jul)). In the documentation of these appeals before the House the appeal of David Saunby appeared first and it is therefore convenient to refer to them collectively under his name (R v Saunby).

[22] In R v Spear, R v Boyd the appeal court certified that the following question of law of general public importance was involved:

'Whether proceedings by way of courts-martial regularly constituted and conducted in accordance with a procedure prescribed by Parliament may nevertheless be incompatible with the provisions of art 6 of the convention when those proceedings are chaired by (a) a permanent president of the courts-martial and (b) a deputy judge-advocate.'

Before the House, Lord Thomas accepted that no issue arose as to the role of the deputy judge-advocate and he therefore concentrated on the role of the permanent president. In *R v Saunby* the appeal court certified that the nine appeals involved this point of law of general public importance:

> 'Is a trial by court-martial in the United Kingdom of a civilian criminal offence, that is to say, an offence falling under s 70 of the Air Force Act 1955 or s 70 of the Army Act 1955, compatible with art 6(1) of the convention (a) generally, or (b) at least in regard to cases where the offence in question is said to have been committed in the United Kingdom?'

At the hearing of the appeals there were accordingly two certified questions in play but both counsel treated the more particular question in *R v Spear, R v Boyd*, relating to the role of the permanent president, as one aspect of the wider challenge to the compatibility with art 6 of trial by courts-martial of what the certified question in *R v Saunby* calls 'civilian criminal offences'. The submissions of counsel in relation to this wider challenge were advanced in respect of all the appeals, while the submissions on the position of the permanent president were advanced in respect of all the appeals where the court-martial had been chaired by a permanent president.

[23] Since various other, discrete, issues were canvassed in the proceedings before the appeal court, it was necessary for that court to examine the circumstances of the individual cases in some detail. In the proceedings before the House, on the other hand, the debate was conducted without reference to the particular circumstances of the individual cases. For present purposes therefore I need not narrate those circumstances and I can simply, and gratefully, refer to the full accounts given by the appeal court in both their judgments. Some of the appellants were serving in the army and the others in the Royal Air Force. They were, accordingly, all persons to whom military law applied by virtue of s 205 of the Army Act 1955 or s 205 of the Air Force Act 1955.

[24] The military law set out in the 1955 Acts contains many offences which are peculiar to the forces, e g mutiny (see s 31), being absent without leave (see s 38) and spreading reports that are likely to create despondency or unnecessary alarm (see s 63A). In addition, however, s 70 provides, inter alia:

> '(1) Any person subject to military law who commits a civil offence, whether in the United Kingdom or elsewhere, shall be guilty of an offence against this section.
>
> (2) In this Act the expression "civil offence" means any act or omission punishable by the law of England or which, if committed in England, would be punishable by that law; and in this Act the expression "the corresponding civil offence" means the civil offence the commission of which constitutes the offence against this section ...
>
> (3) Subject to section 71A below, a person convicted by court-martial of an offence against this section shall—(a) if the corresponding civil offence is treason ... be liable to suffer death; (aa) if the corresponding civil offence is one for which the sentence is fixed by law as life imprisonment, be sentenced to imprisonment for life ... (b) in any other case, be liable to suffer any punishment or punishments which a civil court could award for the corresponding civil offence, if committed in England, being a punishment or punishments provided by this Act, or such punishment, less than the maximum punishment which a civil court could so award, as is so provided ...

(4) A person shall not be charged with an offence against this section committed in the United Kingdom if the corresponding civil offence is *a* treason, murder, manslaughter, treason-felony or rape ...

(6) A person subject to military law may be charged with an offence against this section notwithstanding that he could on the same facts be charged with an offence against any other provision of this Part of this Act.'

b The effect of sub-ss (1) and (2) is, first, that where anyone who is subject to military law is guilty of an act or omission in England that would be punishable by the law of England, he is also guilty of an offence under s 70. Similarly, anyone who is guilty of an act or omission that would be punishable by the law of England if committed in England is guilty of an offence under s 70 wherever he commits it, whether in some other part of the United Kingdom or elsewhere in *c* the world (see *Cox v Army Council* [1962] 1 All ER 880, [1963] AC 48). So, for instance, a soldier or airman who possesses cocaine in England is guilty not only of an offence under s 5(1) of the Misuse of Drugs Act 1971 but also of an offence against s 70 of the Army Act 1955 or the Air Force Act 1955, as the case may be, although he can, of course, be prosecuted for only one of them. If he possesses cocaine while on duty in Afghanistan, on the other hand, he does not commit an *d* offence under s 5(1) of the 1971 Act since the legislation does not apply there, but he is guilty of an offence under s 70 of the relevant 1955 Act, because he would have been guilty of a contravention of s 5(1) if he had been in possession of the drug in England. Offences of this kind, which mirror offences under English criminal law, are referred to as 'civil' offences (see s 70(2)). As s 70(3) makes clear, *e* these civil offences are triable by court-martial. All of the appellants were convicted of civil offences of this kind after trial by court-martial. The question of law certified by the appeal court in *R v Saunby* relates only to the trial by court-martial of such civil offences. Put shortly and subject to what I say later, Lord Thomas' contention was that, if committed in the United Kingdom or in a country with an acceptable criminal justice system, civil offences should be tried *f* by the ordinary criminal courts rather than by court-martial and that the appellants' art 6 right to a fair trial of the charges against them had been infringed by their being subjected to trial by court-martial.

[25] All the appellants were tried by a district court-martial comprising, in accordance with the minimum statutory requirement, a judge-advocate, a *g* president and two other officers (see s 84D(2)). In *R v Spear, R v Boyd* and in the cases of David Saunby, Lee Martin Clarkson and Paul Anthony English the president was a 'permanent president', ie an officer towards the end of his career whose only service function was to act as the president of courts-martial. In the other appeals the president, like the other members, was appointed ad hoc. The *h* powers of general and district courts-martial are set out in s 85:

'(1) A general court-martial shall have power to try any person subject to military law for any offence which under this Act is triable by court-martial, and ... to award for any such offence any punishment authorised by this Act for that offence. *j*

(2) A district court-martial shall have the powers of a general court-martial except that it shall not try an officer or sentence a warrant officer to imprisonment, discharge with ignominy, dismissal or detention, and shall not award the punishment of death or of imprisonment for a term exceeding two years or make an order committing a person to be detained under section 71AA of this Act for a period exceeding two years.'

The district courts-martial therefore had the appropriate powers of punishment from among those listed in s 71(1):

'(a) death, (b) imprisonment, (bb) detention by virtue of a custodial order made under section 71AA of this Act [dealing with young service offenders] ... (c) dismissal with disgrace from Her Majesty's service, (d) dismissal from Her Majesty's service, (e) detention for a term not exceeding two years, (f) forfeiture of seniority for a specified term or otherwise, (g) reduction to the ranks or any less reduction in rank, (h) fine, (i) severe reprimand, (j) reprimand, (k) in the case of an offence which has occasioned any expense, personal injury loss or damage, stoppages, and (l) such minor punishments as may from time to time be authorised by the Defence Council.'

Subsection (1) goes on to provide that:

'For the purposes of this Part of this Act a punishment specified in any of the above paragraphs shall be treated as less than the punishments specified in the paragraphs preceding that paragraph and greater than those specified in the paragraphs following it: Provided that [detention] shall not be treated as a less punishment than [imprisonment] if the term of detention is longer than the term of imprisonment ...'

[26] After the appellants had been convicted and sentenced by their respective district courts-martial, their conviction and sentence were subject to review by the reviewing authority under s 113. The reviewing authority reviews both conviction and sentence in all cases, whether or not the convicted person petitions for a review (see s 113(2)). For these purposes the reviewing authority is the Defence Council or any officer to whom all or any of the powers of the Defence Council as reviewing authority have been delegated (see s 113(5)(b)). In practice such reviews are carried out by an officer who gives the person affected the reasons for his decision (see r 83 of the Courts-Martial (Army) Rules 1997, SI 1997/169 and of the Courts-Martial (Royal Air Force) Rules, SI 1997/171 (the rules)). Conviction and sentence are also reviewed by the Judge-Advocate General who will advise the reviewing authority if he thinks that either the conviction or the sentence should be altered in the convicted person's favour. The advice is disclosed to the convicted person. The reviewing authority may quash a finding of guilt and quash the related sentence or substitute a finding of guilt if it is one that the court-martial could have validly made and the reviewing authority is of the opinion that the court-martial must have been satisfied of facts which would justify the making of that finding (see s 113AA(2)). Where the reviewing authority substitutes a finding in exercise of that power, it may—

'pass any such sentence (not being, in the opinion of the authority, more severe than the sentence originally passed) open to a court-martial on making such a finding as appears proper.'

Similarly, when reviewing sentence the authority may quash the original sentence or substitute a sentence which was open to the court-martial, 'not being, in the opinion of the authority, more severe than the sentence originally passed ...' (see s 113AA(4)).

[27] Two important points to notice about the powers of the reviewing authority are that they are confined by the terms of the original charge against the convicted person and that the reviewing authority cannot pass any sentence that

is, in its opinion, more severe than the sentence originally passed. The system is therefore intended to operate solely to the advantage of persons convicted and sentenced by court-martial. The House was supplied with figures showing that in the year 2000, in prosecutions under the Army Act 1955, 455 cases were reviewed, 107 after petition, the remaining 348 without any petition by the convicted person. In the petition cases 19 sentences were mitigated and three quashed, while in the non-petition cases five sentences were mitigated and three quashed. In fact, however, in none of the cases which form the subject of these appeals, except that of Andrew Alistair Dodds ([2001] All ER (D) 425 (Jul)), did the reviewing authority touch either the conviction or the sentence. The court-martial sentenced Dodds to 112 days' detention but on review this was reduced to 28 days.

[28] Even after a case has been reviewed by the reviewing authority, the convicted person may appeal to the appeal court against his conviction or sentence, with leave of that court, under s 8(1) of the Courts-Martial (Appeals) Act 1968. The appeal court must allow an appeal against conviction and quash the conviction if they think that it is unsafe (see s 12). Where a conviction is quashed on appeal, the person is not liable to be tried again for that offence by a court-martial or any other court (see s 18), unless the appeal court authorise a retrial by court-martial in the interests of justice (see s 19(1)). The appeal court have power to quash any sentence if they consider that it is not appropriate for the case and in that event they may pass a sentence that is not of greater severity than the one for which it is substituted (see s 16A). In addition the appeal court have, of course, a range of ancillary powers, eg to order the production of documents, to order that witnesses should be examined and to receive fresh evidence (see s 28(1)). It is unnecessary to explore these powers since there was no suggestion that the appeal court who heard the appeals in these cases lacked the powers necessary to provide an effective remedy.

[29] The present appeals are by no means an isolated phenomenon. They are the latest in a series of challenges to the system of trial by court-martial under United Kingdom law which has been going on for a number of years. These challenges have borne fruit in the shape of substantial reforms to the court-martial system. Particularly important was the judgment of the European Court of Human Rights (the European Court) in *Findlay v UK* (1997) 24 EHRR 221 which criticised the system as it stood before the Armed Forces Act 1996 introduced a number of very significant changes, in particular the abolition of the institutions of 'the convening officer' and 'the confirming officer'. The changes were designed to ensure the independence of the prosecuting authority and of its decision-making and also to make the courts-martial themselves independent of both the prosecuting authority and the wider service command structure. The effects of the reforms were accurately summarised by the appeal court in *R v Spear, R v Boyd* [2001] QB 804 at [18], [2001] 2 WLR 1692. In *Morris v UK* (2002) 34 EHRR 1253 at 1275 (para 61) the European Court noted that these reforms had gone a long way to meeting its concerns in *Findlay v UK*. All the appeals before the House arise from cases conducted in accordance with the reformed procedures. Despite the reforms, challenges to the system continue to come before the European Court. It was indeed only after leave to appeal to this House had been granted in the present cases that the European Court gave judgment in *Morris v UK*. Your Lordships were told that there were other cases in the pipeline. In *Morris v UK* the Third Chamber of the European Court rejected a challenge based on the role of the permanent president but upheld the contention that

a there were no adequate safeguards of the independence of the other two officers. The court also held that the role of the reviewing authority was incompatible with a court-martial being an independent 'tribunal' in terms of art 6(1). The government did not request that the case should be referred to the Grand Chamber. In these circumstances Lord Thomas placed considerable weight on the decision in *Morris v UK* as to the position of the officers other than the

b permanent president. For the respondents Mr Havers QC founded on the part of the decision where the European Court rejected the challenge to the role of the permanent president. He also indicated that, in cases still to be heard by the European Court, the government would argue that the decision in *Morris v UK* on the role of the other officers and of the reviewing authority had proceeded on a view of the factual position that was incomplete. While the decision in *Morris v UK*

c is not binding on the House, it is, of course, a matter which the House must take into account (see s 2(1)(a) of the Human Rights Act 1998) and which demands careful attention, not least because it is a recent expression of the European Court's view on these matters.

[30] In presenting the appeal, Lord Thomas made a number of separate

d criticisms of the system of trial by court-martial, his purpose being to show that, taken overall, the system as operated in the appellants' cases had infringed their right to a fair trial under art 6. In order to evaluate those criticisms, I must look in more detail at how the system actually works.

[31] When a possible offence is reported, it is necessary to decide whether it should be prosecuted and, if so, whether it should be prosecuted in the civil

e courts or dealt with by the service authorities, in particular by prosecution before a court-martial. The guiding principles, which have been agreed with the relevant civil authorities, are set out in Queen's Regulations. Where the offence is against military law only, jurisdiction will be with the service authorities (see para J7.002a(1)). Where, as in these appeals, the offence is a civil offence, in the United Kingdom

f jurisdiction lies with both the service authorities and the civil authorities except in a number of particularly serious offences, such as treason, murder, manslaughter and rape, when jurisdiction lies wholly with the civil authorities (see para J7.002a(2) and (3)). When the offence is committed abroad, jurisdiction lies wholly with the civil authorities if the offence is an offence only under the local law (see para J7.002b(2)). When the offence committed abroad is an offence against military law only, then,

g subject to the local law of the country concerned or the terms of any relevant agreement or treaty, jurisdiction is wholly with the service authorities (see para J7.002b(1)). When the offence is one against both military law and local law then, again subject to the law of the country concerned or the terms of any relevant treaty or agreement, jurisdiction lies with both the service authorities

h and the civil authorities (see para J7.002b(3)).

[32] The precise way in which a case involving an alleged civil offence is handled will depend, to some extent, on the way the alleged offence comes to light. For instance, an offence allegedly committed on service property is more likely to come initially to the notice of the service authorities, while the

j equivalent offence committed elsewhere may well first come to the notice of the civil police. In minor cases—and there are, of course, more minor than major cases—the commanding officer may feel able to handle the matter within the service disciplinary structure but, where it is necessary to involve the civil authorities, the matter will be reported to the chief police officer for the area. The relevant paragraph (J7.004A) makes it clear that, as well as cases of murder, manslaughter or rape, the commanding officer must report 'Any other case

where civilians are involved and Ministry of Defence Police are not in situ or
readily available'. In addition to certain road traffic offences, he must report any
other offence which may require to be dealt with by the civil authorities, for
example, because it is one of a category of offences of importance to the
community either locally or nationally.

[33] Where jurisdiction lies with either the service or the civil authorities,
para J7.005 provides that in cases reported to the police it is for the chief officer of
police to decide, normally after consultation with the commanding officer, whether
the alleged offender is to be tried by the civil court or is to be dealt with by the
service authorities. Counsel informed the House, however, that the decision is
nowadays one for the Crown Prosecution Service, just as, in Scotland, it is one
for the local procurator fiscal under the direction of the Lord Advocate (see
para J7.012a). Again, para J7.007 provides that certain qualifications have to be
taken into account, including:

> 'b. If the alleged offender was on duty at the time and the offence
> constituted a breach of that duty, the police will normally hand him over to
> the Service authorities even though the offence may affect the property of a
> civilian. This would not apply to a charge such as dangerous driving which
> involves risk to the general public.
> c. The Service authorities will generally deal with an offence committed
> by a member of the forces on Service premises, if it can be dealt with
> summarily, and was either a minor assault on a civilian or a minor offence
> against the property of a civilian.'

In Scotland these particular qualifications do not apply (see para J7.012a).

[34] Paragraph J7.013 deals with jurisdiction in Commonwealth and foreign
countries and provides inter alia:

> 'a. When United Kingdom forces are stationed in Commonwealth or
> foreign countries, or members of those forces are serving on loan or
> otherwise with the forces of such countries, it is the policy of Her Majesty's
> Government to secure arrangements which protect members of the United
> Kingdom forces, the civilian component, and their dependants from the
> jurisdiction of local military law and from the criminal jurisdiction of local
> courts. In some cases exclusive jurisdiction for the United Kingdom Service
> authorities is sought; elsewhere it is sought in respect of offences committed
> on duty and in certain other circumstances. Such arrangements are usually
> made by provisions included in Defence Agreements, Status of Forces, Loan
> or Training Team Agreements, or local Visiting Forces Acts.'

It is apparent, therefore, that the policy behind Queen's Regulations is very
different from the thinking behind the submission advanced by Lord Thomas.
Whereas he contended that the general rule should be that, wherever possible,
alleged acts which would constitute offences under both local and military law
should be tried by the local criminal courts, the policy of Queen's Regulations has
been to 'protect' members of the armed forces, the civilian component and their
dependants from local courts. Lord Thomas sees the court-martial system as
something from which service offenders should be shielded, whereas the
regulations see the availability of trial by court-martial as a boon to them.

[35] In a case of overlapping service and civil jurisdiction, it is ultimately the
civil authorities who decide whether an offender is to be dealt with under the civil
system or under military law. Lord Thomas stressed that in fact the majority of

a civil offences which go to trial are tried by the civil courts. So, he said, if the House were to hold that trial of civil offences by court-martial was incompatible with art 6, with the result that all such offences had to be tried by the civil courts, this would be neither a breakthrough in principle nor any very radical step in practice. He was merely arguing for a return to the position as understood by Lord Loughborough LC who held in *Grant v Gould* (1792) 2 Hy Bl 69 at 99–100,
b [1775–1802] All ER Rep 182 at 183 that—

> 'In this country, all the delinquencies of soldiers are not triable, as in most countries in *Europe*, by martial law; but where they are ordinary offences against the civil peace, they are tried by the common law courts.'

c That had indeed remained the position until the enactment of s 45 of the Naval Discipline Act 1866, in the case of the navy, and the enactment of s 41 of the Army Discipline and Regulation Act 1879. While returning to the original position would involve some increase in the workload of the civil prosecuting and judicial authorities, the increase would, said Lord Thomas, be relatively slight and could be accommodated.

d [36] Under the existing system, an allegation that a person subject to military law has committed an offence must be reported to his commanding officer in the form of a charge and the commanding officer must investigate the charge (see s 76(1) and (2) of the 1955 Acts). After investigation, the commanding officer may decide to refer the charge to higher authority under s 76(5)(b) and, if he does so, then the higher authority must usually refer the case to the prosecuting authority
e (see s 76A(1)). For these purposes 'the prosecuting authority' is an officer, appointed by Her Majesty, who has been legally qualified for at least ten years (see s 83A). If the prosecuting authority considers that court-martial proceedings should be instituted, he must determine any charge to be preferred and whether it is to be tried by general or district court-martial, and he must also prefer the
f charge (see s 83B(4)). The prosecuting authority must notify the accused's commanding officer and a court administration officer (see s 83B(6)). The prosecuting authority has the conduct of any subsequent court-martial proceedings against the accused and has power to make all the decisions relating to the prosecution (see s 83B(7) and (8)). The prosecuting authority may delegate any of his functions to officers whom he appoints as prosecuting officers, but they too must
g be legally qualified (see s 83C).

[37] When the prosecuting authority notifies a court administration officer of a prospective court-martial, that officer must by order convene a court-martial of the required description (see s 84C(1)). The order will specify which officers are to be members of the court-martial and which officer is to be president. It will
h also state that a judge-advocate appointed by or on behalf of the Judge-Advocate General is to be a member of the court-martial. The legislation prevents various people from sitting on the court-martial because their previous involvement might prejudice their independence or impartiality (see s 84C(4)).

[38] The composition of both a general and a district court-martial must
j include a judge-advocate in addition to the prescribed number of officers (see s 84D(1) and (2)). The judge-advocate to sit on a particular court-martial is appointed by the Judge-Advocate General under s 84B(1). No one can be appointed as a judge-advocate unless he has had rights of audience in the higher courts of the United Kingdom for at least five years (see s 84B(2)). At the court-martial the judge-advocate is robed and sits in the centre with the president of the court-martial and one of the officers to his left and with the other officer to

his right. All rulings and directions on questions of law (including questions of procedure and practice) are given by the judge-advocate and are binding on the court (see s 84B(3) and (4)). In these respects the judge-advocate's relationship with the other members of the court is similar to the relationship between a Crown Court judge and the members of the jury. Indeed counsel explained that the judge-advocates have available to them the same model directions prepared by the Judicial Studies Board as are available to Crown Court judges and that, when the members of a court-martial are to consider their verdict, the judge-advocate directs them in just the same way as a Crown Court judge would direct the members of a jury.

[39] At the start of the proceedings the accused has the right to object, on any reasonable grounds, to any member of the court (see s 92(1)). The officers sitting on the court-martial who are to try the case take an oath, recorded in the judgment in *Morris v UK* (2002) 34 EHRR 1253 at 1265 (para 27):

> 'I swear by almighty God that I will well and truly try the accused before the court according to the evidence, and that I will duly administer justice according to the Army Act 1955 without partiality, favour or affection, and I do further swear that I will not on any account at any time whatsoever disclose or discover the vote or opinion of the president or any member of this court martial, unless thereunto required in the due course of law.'

The decision of a district court-martial on the accused's guilt or innocence is taken by the president and the two other officers applying the directions on law which the judge-advocate has given them. They deliberate in private, without the judge-advocate (see s 94(6)). They reach their verdict by a vote and, unlike the position in a jury trial in England and Wales but like the position in Scotland, the accused may be convicted by a simple majority (see s 96). In terms of their oath, the members of the court-martial are forbidden to reveal the vote or opinion of any member.

[40] The decision on sentence is reached by vote of all the members of the court-martial, including the judge-advocate who may, in addition, give the other members guidance on the appropriate sentence to be imposed. Moreover, in terms of r 80(2) of the rules the reasons for the sentence must be given by the judge-advocate.

[41] Lord Thomas' submission that the appellants' rights under art 6(1) had been infringed did not depend on any specific circumstances relating to their trials or to the individuals who had made up the courts-martial: rather, his was a general challenge to the system of trial of civil offences allegedly committed in the United Kingdom by courts-martial duly set up in accordance with the legislation. In such cases courts-martial did not constitute an independent and impartial tribunal. In support, Lord Thomas cited the dissenting opinion of Laskin CJC in *MacKay v R* (1980) 114 DLR (3d) 393 at 401–402 where he was considering the case of a serviceman who had been tried by court-martial for various drugs offences under the Narcotic Control Act 1970. Laskin CJC said:

> 'In the present case, the charges against the accused were laid by the accused's commanding officer. The Standing Court Martial was ordered by a senior commander and a member of the armed forces, a lieutenant-colonel, was appointed from an approved list as the Standing Court Martial pursuant to s. 154 [of the National Defence Act 1970]. Both the officer constituting the Standing Court Martial and the prosecutor were part of the office of the

a   Judge Advocate-General. In short, the accused, who was tried on charges under a general federal statute, [the Narcotic Control Act 1970], was in the hands of his military superiors in respect of the charges, the prosecution and the tribunal by which he was tried. It is true that the Court Martial Appeal Court, consisting under s. 201 … of the *National Defence Act*, of Judges of the Federal Court of Canada and additional superior Court Judges appointed by

b   the Governor in Council, exhibits independence and the appearance of independence in its composition but the same cannot be said of the constitution of a Standing Court Martial when trying an accused for breach of the ordinary criminal law. Needless to say, there is no impugning of the integrity of the presiding officer; it is just that he is not suited, by virtue of his close involvement with the prosecution and with the entire military

c   establishment, to conduct a trial on charges of a breach of the ordinary criminal law. It would be different if he were concerned with a charge of breach of military discipline, something that was particularly associated with an accused's membership in the armed forces. The fact that "service offences" are so broadly defined as to include breaches of the ordinary law

d   does not, in my opinion, make a Standing Court Martial the equivalent of an independently appointed judicial officer or other than an *ad hoc* appointee, having no tenure and coming from the very special society of which both the accused, his prosecutor and his "Judge" are members: cf. *Committee for Justice and Liberty et al. v. National Energy Board et al.* ((1976) 68 DLR (3d) 716). In my opinion, it is fundamental that when a person, any person, whatever his or

e   her status or occupation, is charged with an offence under the ordinary criminal law and is to be tried under that law and in accordance with its prescriptions, he or she is entitled to be tried before a Court of Justice, separate from the prosecution and free from any suspicion of influence of or dependency on others. There is nothing in such a case, where the person charged is in the armed forces, that calls for any special knowledge or special

f   skill of a superior officer, as would be the case if a strictly service or discipline offence, relating to military activity, was involved.'

Laskin CJC went on to conclude that the trial of the appellant for a contravention of s 3 of the Narcotic Control Act 1970 offended s 2(f) of the

g   Canadian Bill of Rights 1960 in that he was not tried by an independent and impartial tribunal.

[42] Lord Thomas also referred to the opinion of Lamer CJC in the later case of *R v Généreux* (1992) 88 DLR (4th) 110 at 136 where he accepted that a military code of discipline would be less effective if the military did not have its own

h   courts to enforce its terms, but continued:

'However, I share the concerns expressed by Laskin C.J.C. and McIntyre J. in [*MacKay v R* (1980) 114 DLR (3d) 393] with the problems of independence and impartiality which are inherent in the very nature of military tribunals. In my opinion, the necessary association between the military hierarchy and military tribunals—the fact that members of the military serve on the

j   tribunals—detracts from the absolute independence and impartiality of such tribunals. As I shall elaborate in greater detail below, the members of a court martial, who are the triers of fact, and the judge advocate, who presides over the proceedings much like a judge, are chosen from the ranks of the military. The members of the court martial will also be at or higher in rank than captain. Their training is designed to insure that they are sensitive

to the need for discipline, obedience and duty on the part of the members of
the military and also to the requirement for military efficiency. Inevitably, *a*
the court martial represents to an extent the concerns of those persons who
are responsible for the discipline and morale of the military. In my opinion,
a reasonable person might well consider that the military status of a court
martial's members would affect its approach to the matters that come before
it for decision.' *b*

Lamer CJC went on (at 141–147) to identify and analyse a number of aspects of
the Canadian system of courts-martial at the time which, in his view, gave rise to
concern as to their independence. Some of these related to the position of the
judge-advocate, about which there is no issue in the present appeals. Others
arose out of the possibility that the performance of the officer members of *c*
courts-martial would be taken into account in determining their pay—not, as
such, a possibility raised in the present cases. Lamer CJC also criticised the role
of the convening officer who not only convened the court-martial and decided
who would sit, but also, with the consent of the judge-advocate, appointed the
prosecutor. It would thus be fair to say that some, at least, of the features of the *d*
system described and criticised by the two Chief Justices in *MacKay v R* and *R v
Généreux* resemble features of the British system of courts-martial as it was in
Findlay v UK (1997) 24 EHRR 221 before the reforms introduced by the 1996 Act.

[43] In both these passages on which Lord Thomas relied, a distinction is
drawn between courts-martial trying military offences and courts-martial trying
civil offences. Lord Thomas adopted the same distinction, limiting his challenge *e*
to trial of civil offences by court-martial in this country.

[44] Despite the apparent support for it in the passages which I have quoted
from the Canadian cases, I am unable to accept such a distinction. In principle,
either a tribunal is independent and impartial or it is not. If it is, then it is
independent and impartial whatever the offence it is trying, wherever the offence *f*
may have been committed and wherever the tribunal may be sitting; equally, if
it is not, then it is not independent or impartial whatever the offence it is trying,
wherever the offence may have been committed and wherever the tribunal may
be sitting. So far as military offences are concerned, members of courts-martial
may have a particular familiarity with the issues and values that underlie them.
That familiarity cannot, however, justify the members in reaching a decision on *g*
conviction or sentence that is anything other than the decision of an independent
and impartial tribunal. The art 6 guarantee applies in the trial of such purely
military offences, just as it does in the trial of civil offences. And this is indeed
plain from the decision of the European Court in *Morris v UK* where art 6 was held
to apply in the case of an applicant who had pled guilty to the military offence of *h*
being absent without leave. Indeed it would be astonishing if the standards of
independence and impartiality required of a court-martial trying, for instance, the
purely military offence of mutiny, which may attract the most severe punishment,
were one whit less strict than those required of a court-martial trying the civil
offence of assault. *j*

[45] So far as courts-martial held abroad for offences committed abroad are
concerned, as McIntyre J pointed out in a passage in his judgment in *MacKay v R*
(1980) 114 DLR (3d) 393 at 421 which I quote in [52], below, the character of the
members of the court-martial for independence and impartiality can hardly vary,
depending on where they happen to be called on to sit. Lord Thomas eventually
contended, however, under reference to *Golder v UK* (1975) 1 EHRR 524, that art 6

a might be subject to an inherent limitation that would make it inapplicable to overseas courts-martial. I did not find the submission compelling. But, even if any such limitation could apply, it could do so only in the most extreme circumstances, such perhaps as required the convening of a field general court-martial; it could certainly not apply in the case of a court-martial held in peacetime in a country such as Germany with a sophisticated local criminal

b justice system. Indeed Lord Thomas himself really accepted this since he was representing the appellants in *R v Spear, R v Boyd* [2001] QB 804, [2001] 2 WLR 1692 whose contention is that their art 6(1) rights were infringed in the case of a court-martial held in Osnabrück in Lower Saxony in respect of an assault in army barracks in Münster in Westphalia.

c [46] For these reasons, while the certified question in *R v Saunby* concerns only courts-martial trying civil offences, in my view the issue of principle is whether, in any case where it is permitted, trial by court-martial infringes the accused's art 6 rights. Indeed the only justiciable issue for your Lordships' House is whether the appellants' art 6 rights have been infringed by reason of their trial by court-martial. Even though the logic of his position was that most of the

d appellants should have been tried by jury, Lord Thomas, of course, acknowledged that art 6 conferred on them no right to jury trial. Hence they could not base their case against trial by court-martial on the simple fact that it was not trial by jury. Nor, in its judicial capacity, is this House concerned with whether, as a matter of policy, trial of civil offences by the civil courts might be preferable to trial by court-martial. But certain of the submissions advanced by Lord Thomas

e verged at least on policy arguments in favour of reforming the present system. For instance, he argued that the continued existence of a parallel system of trial by court-martial of civil offences ran counter to general developments over the last 40 years. Courts-martial were redolent of out-of-date attitudes of deference to rank. The formality of the proceedings, with the accused being marched into

f court under escort and with special rules, for instance, about wearing and removing head-dress, made them intimidating to both the accused and witnesses. All these undesirable features could be remedied by trying civil offences in civil courts. Lord Thomas had to accept, of course, that in certain respects trial in a civil court might even seem to be more intimidating: for instance, in a civil court the accused would sit in the dock, while in a court-martial he sits beside his

g defending counsel. Mr Havers indicated that the formality of court-martial proceedings had been considerably relaxed in recent years. The briefing notes provided to members of courts-martial certainly envisage that there can be some reduction of formality at times. The members are told that, if a plea of guilty is tendered, the accused and escort can be instructed to sit and the accused can be

h told to remove his head-dress. They are also told that, if the accused is unrepresented and has to be asked questions by the judge-advocate, to make sure, in terms of r 46(1) of the rules, that he understands the nature of the charges and the general effect of his plea, there is no reason why the accused and his escort should not sit for that part of the proceedings. There may indeed be some

j further room for relaxation and, doubtless, those who are familiar with service life and with the conduct of courts-martial today will continue to keep the remaining formalities under review.

[47] None of these matters highlighted by Lord Thomas is for the judgment of the House except in so far as it might have a bearing on whether trial by court-martial infringes the accused's art 6 rights. In the end Lord Thomas did not contend that they were, whether individually or cumulatively, of critical

significance for that core issue. When the core issue before the House is
formulated in this way, then at one level the answer is straightforward. The case
law of the European Court shows that, in principle, trial by court-martial does not
infringe an accused's right to a fair trial under art 6.

[48] In *Engel v The Netherlands (No 1)* (1976) 1 EHRR 647 five members of the
Netherlands armed forces were punished by their commanding officers for
offences against military discipline. They appealed to the Supreme Military Court
which confirmed their commanding officers' decisions. The applicants brought
proceedings in Strasbourg alleging breach of their rights under various articles of
the convention, including art 6. In this connection the European Court (at
657–658 (para 30)) considered the composition of the Supreme Military Court. It
comprised six members: two civilian jurists, one acting as the court's president,
and four military officers. The civilian jurists had to be justices of the Dutch
Supreme Court or Judges of the Court of Appeal and they were appointed by the
Crown on the joint advice of the ministers of justice and defence for a term of
office that was similar to their judicial term. The military members were also
appointed by the Crown on the recommendation of the ministers of justice and
of defence but they could be dismissed by the Crown on the recommendation of
the same ministers. The military members could therefore, in theory, be
removed without observance of the strict requirements and legal safeguards that
applied to the civilian members. On the other hand, their appointment as military
members of the court was normally the last in their service career and, in their
functions as judges on the court, they were not under the command of any higher
authority and they were not under a duty to account for their acts to the service
establishment. On assuming office, all members of the court swore an oath to be
just, honest and impartial.

[49] The European Court held (at 679–680 (para 85)) that in the case of three
of the applicants the charges against them fell within the criminal sphere and that
the convention therefore obliged the authorities to afford them the guarantees
under art 6. The court went on to hold (at 680 (para 89)) that the Supreme
Military Court constituted an independent and impartial tribunal established by
law and that there was nothing to indicate that it had failed to give the three
applicants a fair hearing. There was therefore no breach of art 6 in this respect,
although the European Court did go on to find, (at 681 (para 89)) that the
applicants' rights under art 6(1) had been infringed because the proceedings in the
Supreme Military Court had taken place in camera.

[50] In *Morris v UK* (2002) 34 EHRR 1253 at 1274 (para 59) the European Court
said:

'The Court notes that the practice of using courts staffed in whole or in part
by the military to try members of the armed forces is deeply entrenched in
the legal systems of many Member States. It recalls its own case law which
illustrates that a military court can, in principle, constitute an "independent
and impartial tribunal" for the purposes of Article 6(1) of the Convention.
For example, in the above-mentioned ... case [*Engel v The Netherlands (No 1)*
(1976) 1 EHRR 647], the Court found that the Dutch Supreme Military
Court, composed of two civilian Justices of the Supreme Court and four
military officers, was such a tribunal. However, the Convention will only
tolerate such courts as long as sufficient safeguards are in place to guarantee
their independence and impartiality.'

a While it is perhaps possible to detect some lack of enthusiasm in the use of the term 'tolerate', the passage shows clearly that, in principle, a military court can constitute an independent and impartial tribunal in terms of art 6(1). What is required is that there should be sufficient safeguards of the independence and impartiality of its members. Applying that approach, I would reject Lord Thomas' submission that, of its very nature, trial of civil offences by court-martial is

b incompatible with art 6(1). In principle such a trial can fully satisfy the requirements of art 6 that the tribunal should be independent and impartial and that the accused should have a fair trial.

[51] That being so, it is not necessary to 'justify' trial by court-martial, whether by reference to the history of the system here and in many other countries or by reference to the situation of the services today. Lord Thomas

c suggested that the government and the armed forces wished to retain courts-martial for civil offences for no other reason than that the system exists and the staff are there to run it. I should therefore not wish to leave unmentioned the substantial arguments that can be advanced in favour of a system of trial by court-martial that covers both military and civil offences. The case is put

d forcefully in the witness statement dated 12 July 2001 of Air Chief Marshal Sir Anthony Bagnall, the vice-chief of the defence staff. Before making the statement Sir Anthony had consulted senior members of all three services. Describing what he regarded as the special circumstances underpinning s 70 of the 1955 Acts and s 42 of the Naval Discipline Act 1957, he said inter alia:

e   '4. First and foremost of the special circumstances of the armed forces is that the willingness and readiness of every member and unit of the armed forces to act with the greatest possible speed and efficiency is essential for the defence of the realm from outside attack, for acting in operations outside the United Kingdom and sometimes for acting in aid of the civil power (as in Northern Ireland). It is essential that this readiness be maintained at all

f   times, not only in times when a threat is immediate. It applies with equal importance wherever a unit is based. The Royal Air Force, for example, must be ready to act anywhere from its bases within the United Kingdom. Success in operations depends on the ability of all members of a unit to act together as a single fighting force, in other words on operational efficiency.

g   5. Second, the requirements of service discipline reflect the fact that their fundamental purpose is essentially to fight. The services are armed organisations, required to train and fight in circumstances of extreme hardship, as has most recently been demonstrated in Northern Ireland, the Gulf, Kosovo and Sierra Leone.

h   6. The performance of their functions involves, not merely working together, but living together, often in conditions—whether in Northern Ireland, the Falkland Islands or Kosovo—of hardship, stress and danger. Yet, in carrying out these functions it is of the greatest importance that they retain respect for the civilians among whom they operate, civilians who, whether

j   in Northern Ireland or abroad, may be unsympathetic or even hostile. The fundamental purpose of a military justice system is to foster and promote the discipline and self-control required for the maintenance of the capability to act as an efficient fighting force, that is to say, operational effectiveness.

       7. It is the combination of the need for utmost readiness, unit solidarity and deeply imbued self-control over long periods and often in most difficult situations which necessitate a comprehensive system of command and

discipline, and require that this system should be capable of dealing fairly and, where possible, promptly with misconduct involving a criminal offence.

8. These factors make service life unique, but, while they are all important, I should make a further point about one of them. Members of the regular armed forces do not simply do a job. They are at all times members of the armed forces, very often sharing accommodation, whether barracks or temporary accommodation, even in peacetime.

9. The special status of members of the armed forces means that an act which may be a criminal offence under civilian criminal law also has a disciplinary aspect when committed in a service environment. The commanding officer (CO) is at the centre of the system of discipline. He is responsible for the behaviour of those under his command, both among themselves and in relation to the local community. As a result of the circumstances I have already referred to, the CO's powers of discipline are necessarily wide. He is able to deal summarily with a wide range of misconduct, including both criminal and purely service offences. His powers include limited powers of detention (basically a maximum of 28 days but up to 60 days with the permission of higher authority). A CO may typically deal with cases of minor theft or assault. These cases are often none the less of importance to discipline and morale. A minor theft, which might be insignificant in some civilian contexts, can erode trust between members of a unit and undermine the effectiveness of what should be a close-knit team. More serious cases are likely to go [to] court-martial. The CO and the service courts are uniquely placed to understand the circumstances of service life and the significance of misconduct by service personnel, especially where misconduct occurs in a service context.

10. A requirement for all criminal offences in the United Kingdom to be dealt with by civilian courts would seriously undermine the CO's authority. Moreover it seems to me that the exclusion of courts-martial from dealing with criminal cases in the United Kingdom would inevitably bring with it the exclusion of the COs from dealing with such criminal offences on a summary basis.

11. Subject to a point which I shall deal with at para 18 and following below [as to the exclusion of certain serious offences], s 70 broadly makes no distinction between criminal offences committed in the United Kingdom and those committed abroad. The fundamental reasons for this are the circumstances of service life which, as explained above, require a distinct system of command and discipline. Moreover the circumstances of service life, and service needs, would render artificial an exclusion of service courts for crimes in the United Kingdom. If, for example, a serviceman stole from another serviceman abroad, he could be dealt with by service discipline; but, if the theft occurred in England and the thief was identified only after the unit had gone abroad, the case could only be dealt with by a court in the United Kingdom. If s 70 did not apply to an offence committed in England, no disciplinary action could be taken against the guilty person; nor could the service police arrest him. He would not have committed a disciplinary offence.

12. A distinction between criminal and service offences is also in my view artificial. The same facts may amount both to a criminal and a purely service offence. A theft may sometimes be looting; the circumstances of an assault may amount to mutiny. It would be anomalous if criminal misconduct

a   could be dealt with, but only where the circumstances also amounted to a service offence. Nor is there a simple distinction in terms of seriousness. Looting, mutiny and desertion may be as serious as theft or even murder.'

[52] This authoritative and up-to-date statement of the reasons why the armed forces wish to maintain the jurisdiction of courts-martial in civil offences complements passages in certain of the authorities where judges have recognised b   that a distinct system of justice for the armed forces can be justified by their peculiar position. For instance, in *MacKay v R* (1980) 114 DLR (3d) 393 at 426 McIntyre J would have confined the jurisdiction of courts-martial to civil offences connected with the accused's military service and therefore found that there had been a breach of the guarantee of equality before the law under ss 1(b) and 2 of c   the Canadian Bill of Rights. None the less he was clear that trial by court-martial did not infringe the serviceman's, separate, right to a fair hearing by an independent and impartial tribunal under s 2(f) of the Bill of Rights. He said (at 420–421):

d   'With the greatest deference for those who hold opposing views, I am unable to conclude that a trial by court martial under the provisions of the *National Defence Act* of criminal offences, which are also offences at civil law, deprives the defendant of a fair hearing by an independent tribunal. From the earliest times, officers of the armed forces in this and, I suggest, all civilized countries have had this judicial function. It arose from practical e   necessity and, in my view, must continue for the same reason. It is said that by the nature of his close association with the military community and his identification with the military society, the officer is unsuited to exercise this judicial office. It would be impossible to deny that an officer is to some extent the representative of the class in the military hierarchy from which he comes; he would be less than human if he were not. But the same argument, f   with equal fairness, can be raised against those who are appointed to judicial office in the civilian society. We are all products of our separate backgrounds and we must all in the exercise of the judicial office ensure that no injustice results from that fact. I am unable to say that service officers, trained in the ways of service life and concerned to maintain the required standards of g   efficiency and discipline—which includes the welfare of their men—are less able to adjust their attitudes to meet the duty of impartiality required of them in this task than are others. Furthermore, the problems and the needs of the armed services, being in many respects special to the military, may well from time to time require the special knowledge possessed by officers of experience who, in this respect, may be better suited for the exercise of h   judicial duty in military courts than their civilian counterparts. It has been recognized that wide powers of discipline may be safely accorded in professional associations to senior members of such professions. The controlling bodies of most professions such as those of law, medicine, accountancy, engineering, among others, are given this power. I am unable j   to say that the close identification of such disciplinary bodies with the profession concerned, taken with the seniority enjoyed by such officers within their professional group, has ever been recognised as a disqualifying factor on grounds of bias or otherwise. Rather it seems that the need for special knowledge and experience in professional matters has been recognized as a reason for the creation of disciplinary tribunals within the separate professions. It must also be remembered that while this appeal

concerned only the armed services serving in Canada, the position of forces
serving abroad not being in issue, it must be recognized that in service
abroad the officers must assume the judicial role by reason of the absence of
any civil legal processes. The character of the officer for independence and
impartiality will surely not vary because he is serving overseas. The practical
necessities of the service require the performance of this function by officers
of the service and I find no offence to the Canadian Bill of Rights in this
respect. I would add that there now exists a Court Martial Appeal Court, a
professional Court of Appeal with a general appellate jurisdiction over the
courts martial. This is, in my view, a significant safeguard and its creation is
a realistic and practical step toward the provision of that protection which is
required in the circumstances.'

I refer also to the dissenting opinion of L'Heureux-Dubé J in *R v Généreux* (1992)
88 DLR (4th) 110 at 156–157.

[53] Lord Thomas put at the forefront of his submissions a general argument
that, because trial by court-martial infringed art 6 of the convention, s 70 of the
1955 Acts should be declared to be incompatible with that article. Counsel for the
respondents argued that this submission was totally misconceived since s 70 was
a section which created an offence rather than one which conferred jurisdiction
on courts-martial. In their judgment in *R v Saunby*, the appeal court accepted that
argument and I would do so too. But even supposing that Lord Thomas could
have founded such an argument on the reference in sub-s (3) to 'a person convicted
by court-martial', the argument would necessarily have failed since, as the
decision in *Morris v UK* (2002) 34 EHRR 1253 shows, it is impossible to say that in
their very nature all trials by court-martial involve an infringement of the
accused's art 6 rights.

[54] Since trial by court-martial does not necessarily involve an infringement
of the accused's rights under art 6, the decision as to whether the court is to be
regarded as an independent and impartial tribunal depends on the safeguards
which are in place. It follows that the decision in these appeals depends on
whether the safeguards of the independence and impartiality of the members of
the courts-martial in these cases can be regarded as satisfactory.

[55] In *Findlay v UK* (1997) 24 EHRR 221 at 244–245 (para 73) the European
Court recalled that—

> 'in order to establish whether a tribunal can be considered as
> "independent", regard must be had *inter alia* to the manner of appointment
> of its members and their term of office, the existence of guarantees against
> outside pressures and the question whether the body presents an appearance
> of independence. As to the question of "impartiality", there are two aspects
> to this requirement. First, the tribunal must be subjectively free of personal
> prejudice or bias. Secondly, it must also be impartial from an objective
> viewpoint, that is, it must offer sufficient guarantees to exclude any
> legitimate doubt in this respect.'

In *Porter v Magill* [2001] UKHL 67 at [103], [2002] 1 All ER 465 at [103], [2002]
2 WLR 37 Lord Hope of Craighead, with whom the other members of the House
agreed, having surveyed the European Court, United Kingdom and Commonwealth
case law on this point, concluded:

a
'The question is whether the fair-minded and informed observer, having considered the facts, would conclude that there was a real possibility that the tribunal was biased.'

[56] Lord Thomas did not suggest that the members of the courts-martial in these cases had been subjectively biased. He argued, however, that the fair-minded and informed observer would conclude that the safeguards were

b
inadequate to guarantee the independence and impartiality of the members of the courts-martial, especially having regard to the lack of security of tenure for permanent presidents and the ad hoc appointments of the other officers. Given their position as serving officers in the armed forces, the fair-minded observer would see it as possible that they would give undue weight to the need to

c
maintain service morale and discipline and that, as officers, they would be unable fairly to judge cases involving lower ranks, especially if, say, convicting an officer or acquitting a private meant disbelieving an officer or non-commissioned officer. Courts-martial could not, therefore, be regarded as objectively impartial in terms of art 6.

d
[57] A submission of this kind requires one, as a starting-point, to consider what is meant by the requirement that a tribunal should be independent and impartial. As the European Court noted in *Morris v UK* (2002) 34 EHRR 1253 at 1274 (para 58) the concepts of independence and objective impartiality are closely linked. In the present cases, in substance, the court-martial must be guarded from the risk of influence by the prosecution and guarded from the risk of influence by

e
the relevant service authorities, especially superior officers who might wish to secure some particular result, supposedly in the interests of the morale or discipline of the service or of some particular unit. As a result of the abolition of the role of the convening officer by the 1996 Act, no issue was raised in these cases as to the independence of the members of the tribunal from the prosecution. On the other hand, art 6 does not require that the members of the tribunal should not

f
share the values of the military community to which they belong any more than it requires that the judge or members of the jury in a civil court should be divorced from the values of the wider community of which they form part. What matters is that, while sharing the values of the service community, the members of the court-martial should put aside any prejudices which they may have and

g
act—and be seen to act—independently and impartially in deciding the issues in the case before them.

[58] Lord Thomas dealt first with the position of permanent president. In *R v Spear, R v Boyd* [2001] QB 804, [2001] 2 WLR 1692, in the trial involving Spear and Hastie, the president of the court-martial was a permanent president, Lieutenant Colonel Stone. In the trial of Boyd the president of the court-martial was again a

h
permanent president, Wing Commander Chambers. In the trial of Saunby also the president was a permanent president, Lieutenant Colonel de Lisle. Another permanent president, Lieutenant Colonel Hall, sat in the trial of Clarkson and English. In challenging the role of the permanent presidents in these cases Lord Thomas had, of course, to take account of the judgment of the European Court

j
on this point in *Morris v UK* (2002) 34 EHRR 1253 at 1276–1277:

'68 ... The Court notes that the Permanent President in the applicant's case was appointed to his post in January 1997 and was due to remain in post for four years, eight months until his retirement in September 2001. He also worked outside the chain of command. The Court considers that, in these respects, his position was similar to that of the military members of the

Dutch Supreme Military Court in the above-mentioned ... case [*Engel v The Netherlands (No 1)* (1976) 1 EHRR 647]. In that case, in declaring the military court "independen[t] and impartial", the Court drew attention to the fact that the appointment of the military members was usually the last of their careers and that they were not, in their functions as judges, under the command of any higher authority or under a duty to account for their acts to the service establishment. The Court recalls that, although irremovability of judges during their terms of office must in general be considered as a corollary of their independence, the absence of a formal recognition of such irremovability in the law does not in itself imply a lack of independence, provided that it is recognised in fact and that other necessary guarantees are present. It notes also that, as highlighted by the Court Martial Appeal Court in the above-mentioned cases of [*R v Spear, R v Boyd* [2001] QB 804, [2001] 2 WLR 1692], although there is no "written guarantee" against premature removal of Permanent Presidents, there is no record of a Permanent President ever having been removed from office.

69 The applicant argues that the independence of the Permanent President at the applicant's court martial could have been reinforced by formal security of tenure and by embodiment of his appointment in a legal instrument of some kind. However, the Court finds that the presence of the Permanent President did not call into question the independence of the court martial. Rather, his term of office and *de facto* security of tenure, the fact that he had no apparent concerns as to future army promotion and advancement and was no longer subject to army reports, and his relative separation from the army command structure, meant that he was a significant guarantee of independence on an otherwise ad hoc tribunal.'

[59] About two years before this judgment of the European Court, apparently giving a clean bill of convention health to permanent presidents, in *R v McKendry* (6 March 2000, unreported) Judge-Advocate Pearson had held that the president of that particular district court-martial should stand down because he could not be regarded as independent and impartial for purposes of art 6(1). Although the judge-advocate purported to limit his ruling to the particular case, the result of it was that the use of permanent presidents was forthwith abandoned. Officers who had been serving as permanent presidents found themselves without a role. It appears that, pending the outcome of these appeals, the use of permanent presidents has not been resumed.

[60] In *R v Spear, R v Boyd* [2001] QB 804, [2001] 2 WLR 1692 the appeal court summarised the information given to them about the two permanent presidents, Lieutenant Colonel Stone and Wing Commander Chambers, in this way:

'[22] ... Lt-Col Stone was appointed PPCM in January 1998. His appointment was specified to run until February 2002. It was always plain that this was to be his last posting; but in fact he was deployed in a staff job within First UK Armoured Division after and because of the abolition of the PPCM regime in May 2000 following *R v McKendry*, since at that date he still had some time to serve before retirement. He had no prospects of further promotion. He had no intention of seeking employment after his retirement within the Ministry of Defence as a retired officer. No reports were made upon him in his office as PPCM; indeed there have in the Army been no reports upon any PPCM since April 1997 when the 1996 Act came into force. Lt-Col Stone worked outside any regimental or other chain of command, *a* from his married quarters home, and eschewed the officers' mess because "to do otherwise could have compromised my position as a PPCM".

[23] There is also a statement from Group Captain Trace, who is deputy director within the Personnel Management Agency responsible for the career management of all officers of the General Duties and Operations Support Branches up to and including the rank of Wing Commander. He

b has perused the personal file of Wing Commander Chambers, who sat as PPCM in Boyd's case. Wing Commander Chambers was appointed PPCM in June 1998 initially for some two years, but he accepted a two-year extension. This was his last posting. He had no prospects of promotion. He worked from home, and his only contacts of any substance with the Service were for purposes of administration and welfare. No reports were made

c upon him in respect of his decision-making functions as PPCM. We should add that when Boyd's applications were renewed to this court, his solicitor Mr Blades noted on the renewal form: "Since this case was heard the president has been suspended. The Royal Air Force do not appear to believe that the president is independent." There was also a suggestion that Wing

d Commander Chambers had at some stage been disciplined or reprimanded. This is not supported by any material of any substance which we have seen. There is no reference to any such matter in the documents emanating from the Royal Air Force. It was not pressed with any force by Mr Blades, and is not within the purview of Boyd's leave to appeal granted by us. There may be scope for some confusion since it appears from Group Captain Trace's

e letter that Wing Commander Chambers held office as PPCM "until the *post* was suspended on 16 February 2000" (our emphasis).'

In *R v Saunby* no particular points were made about Lieutenant Colonel de Lisle or about Lieutenant Colonel Hall.

f [61] So far as Lieutenant Colonel Stone is concerned, Lord Thomas accepted that the position was as outlined by the appeal court. In particular he accepted that, since 1997, in the army there had been no reports on permanent presidents. That being so, in the appeals of Spear and Hastie Lord Thomas was not able to distinguish *Morris v UK*. Since he did not argue that, on its facts, this aspect of the decision in *Morris v UK* had been wrong, Lord Thomas' submissions on behalf

g of these appellants were really of a more general nature, dealing with the perceived weaknesses in the role of any officer as a member of a court-martial.

[62] In the case of the appellant Boyd, however, Lord Thomas argued that the position was not so straightforward as the account given by the appeal court would suggest. Unlike the army permanent presidents, in particular the

h permanent president in *Morris v UK*, Royal Air Force permanent presidents, such as Wing Commander Chambers, remained subject to reports. Mr Havers accepted that, for some reason that he could not explain, the air force had indeed continued the practice of preparing reports on officers who were serving as permanent presidents. In my view that practice is undesirable and, as the army experience shows, unnecessary. It would be better if it were discontinued. Lord

j Thomas went on to submit that, contrary to the conclusion of the appeal court, an examination of the reports on Wing Commander Chambers written in August 1999 and August 2000 suggested that the practice of reporting had indeed jeopardised his independence. He pointed out that in one report the permanent president's function was said to be one on which 'the service's disciplinary ethos is based' and comments were then made as to the enthusiasm which Wing

Commander Chambers brought to his role—for example, it was said that he
'relishes the challenge each court brings'. In 1999 the Air Secretary noted that he
was well suited to continue to his retirement in 2000 'when consideration could
again be given as to whether the post should be held by a recently retired officer ...'
In fact, Wing Commander Chambers' retirement date was extended for two
years from December 2000 and so that particular issue did not arise, but it might
be thought, said Lord Thomas, that an assessment of his performance as a
permanent president would have been relevant to the decision as to whether or
not his period of service should be extended. Thus the reporting process, with its
possible consequences for his future, could have affected his independence and
impartiality.

[63] As Mr Havers pointed out, however, while the reports make various
comments on the way that Wing Commander Chambers tackled his role as a
permanent president, these are better seen as referring to the administrative
aspects of the job, such as checking the trial facilities and briefing the other
participants. Crucially, there was not the slightest indication that the reports bore
on his actual decisions when sitting as president of a court. On the contrary the
reports recognise that that role is one in which the permanent president is
'isolated and unsupervised' and which requires independence which the Air
Secretary 'honour[s] and respect[s]', there being only an administrative and
welfare linkage. The reporting officer recognises the limitation on his role since
he is not—

> 'allowed any direct insight into the way [Wing Commander Chambers]
> has discharged his duties. Indeed a key ingredient is the ability to work
> without supervision.'

In these circumstances I readily conclude that neither the fact that Wing
Commander Chambers was subject to reports of this nature, nor the actual
reports themselves that were made on him, give the slightest reason for
considering that his independence or impartiality as a member of the appellant
Boyd's court-martial was compromised. On the contrary, all involved in making
these reports were well aware of the need not to intrude upon the decisions
reached by him when sitting as president. Even had anyone wished to intrude,
the oath of secrecy taken by the members of courts-martial would have made it
impossible to investigate those decisions.

[64] That being so, there is nothing in the particular circumstances of the cases
of Spear and Hastie or of Boyd which would be a reason to reach a different result
from the European Court in *Morris v UK* on the issue of the independence and
impartiality of the officers acting as president of their courts-martial. I
respectfully agree with and adopt the reasoning of the European Court on this
point. I would accordingly reject Lord Thomas' argument that these appellants'
rights under art 6(1) were infringed because the presidents of their courts-martial
were permanent presidents.

[65] When he turned to the position of the other officers on the
courts-martial, Lord Thomas was able to claim support for his argument from the
relevant aspect of the decision of the European Court in *Morris v UK* (2002) 34
EHRR 1253 at 1277–1278:

> '70 In contrast to the Permanent President, the two serving officers who
> sat on the applicant's court martial were not appointed for any fixed period
> of time. Rather, they were appointed on a purely ad hoc basis, in the

a knowledge that they would return to their ordinary military duties at the end of the proceedings. Although the Court does not consider that the ad hoc nature of their appointment was sufficient in itself to render the make-up of the court martial incompatible with the independence requirements of Article 6(1), it made the need for the presence of safeguards against outside pressures all the more important in this case.

b 71 The Court recognises that certain safeguards were in place in the present case. For example, the presence of the legally qualified, civilian judge advocate in his enhanced role under the 1996 Act was an important guarantee, just as the presence of two civilian judges in the Dutch Supreme Military court was found to be in the above-mentioned ... case [*Engel v The*

c *Netherlands (No 1)* (1976) 1 EHRR 647]. This was particularly so since the applicant's guilt, upon which the judge advocate would have had no vote, was not at issue before the court martial. As indicated at paragraph 69 above, the presence of the Permanent President provided another guarantee. The Court notes also the protection offered by the statutory and other rules about eligibility for selection to a court martial and the oath taken by its

d members.

72 However, the Court considers that the presence of these safeguards was insufficient to exclude the risk of outside pressure being brought to bear on the two relatively junior serving officers who sat on the applicant's court martial. In particular, it notes that those officers had no legal training, that they remained subject to army discipline and reports, and that there was no

e statutory or other bar to their being made subject to external army influence when sitting on the case. This is a matter of particular concern in a case such as the present where the offence charged directly involves a breach of military discipline. In this respect, the position of the military members of the court martial cannot generally be compared with that of a member of a

f civilian jury who is not open to the risk of such pressures.'

Lord Thomas submitted that the House should follow this part of the decision of the European Court in *Morris v UK* and that, indeed, it would be unprecedented for a court not to do so where the decision of the European Court was so recent.

g [66] In reaching its decisions the European Court always pays careful attention to the facts of the case as explained to it. In the jargon of the subject, its decisions are said to be 'fact-sensitive'. As can be seen from the passage in question, the decision in *Morris v UK* is no exception. For whatever reason, however, the European Court was given rather less information than the House about the safeguards relating to the officers serving on courts-martial. And, like

h the European Court, the House must have regard to all the relevant factual information presented to it when deciding whether the safeguards of the independence and impartiality of the members of the courts-martial were adequate.

[67] It is true that, apart from any permanent president, the officers selected

j to serve on courts-martial are appointed only ad hoc. As the European Court points out, that is not in itself sufficient to make the court incompatible with the independence requirements of art 6(1). Indeed, in performing the role only occasionally, the members of a court-martial resemble jurors and should bring to the task the freshness of approach which is one of the benefits of the jury system. Of course, as individuals and as officers in the armed forces, those asked to sit on a court-martial may well have certain prejudices. Jurors too have prejudices and, as McIntyre J rightly pointed out in *MacKay v R* (1980) 114 DLR (3d) 393 at 420–421 (see [52], above) the same can be said of those appointed to judicial office in civilian society. In the light of their experience of jury trial, however, courts in countries which operate with juries have concluded that the safeguards of the oath and the judge's directions are generally sufficient to ensure that jurors put aside their prejudices and reach a just verdict on the evidence. Indeed, as Lord Hope observed in *Montgomery v HM Advocate, Coulter v HM Advocate* [2001] 2 WLR 779 at 810, the entire system of trial by jury is based on the assumption that the jury will follow the instructions which they receive from the trial judge and that they will return a true verdict according to the evidence. The European Court too has recognised that the jurors' oath, to faithfully try the case and to give a true verdict according to the evidence, and their obligation to have regard to the directions given by the presiding judge will generally be sufficient to safeguard their independence and impartiality. This is so even in cases where there is reason to believe that one or more members of the jury may actually be prejudiced against the accused. I refer to the well-known decisions in *Pullar v UK* (1996) 22 EHRR 391 at 405 (para 40) and *Gregory v UK* (1997) 25 EHRR 577 at 593–595 (paras 43–48).

[68] In the cases under appeal these particular safeguards were present. The oath taken by the members of the court required them to well and truly try the accused 'according to the evidence' and to do justice according to the relevant 1955 Act 'without partiality, favour or affection'. In addition the judge-advocate gave the other members of the court-martial directions of the same kind as would have been given to a jury if the case had been tried in a civil court. There is no reason to suppose that the members of the court-martial would be any less faithful to their oath or any less diligent in applying the directions given by the judge-advocate than would the members of a jury. Indeed it is at the very least arguable that the officers on a court-martial, as members of the armed forces for whom trust and obedience to commands are particularly important, would be even more likely than civilian jurors to be true to their oath and to follow the directions given to them.

[69] In any event, the steps taken to ensure that the members of a court-martial act independently and impartially are, on one view, even more strict than with a jury. Although these additional steps were not fully explained to the European Court, they are in my view important and must be recorded at some length, even at the risk of repeating some of what has been said already about the procedure to be followed.

[70] In the first place, the officers to serve on any court-martial are always taken from another unit, the aim being to ensure that they do not know the people involved or anything about the case. When they have been nominated and the court-martial has been convened, the prospective members are sent briefing notes along with a list of the witnesses for the prosecution. The members are told to examine the list and to tell the administration office if any of the witnesses is known to them. They are told that, if they subsequently discover that they do know someone, they should discreetly advise the judge-advocate.

[71] The briefing notes, which in certain respects reflect the provisions in Pts V and VI of the rules, give an outline of the procedure that will be followed. Paragraph 2 emphasises the central role of the judge-advocate by telling the members:

'The main thing to remember is that the Judge Advocate conducts the court-martial ... He will therefore decide all questions of law, practice and procedure ... He is a member of the court and his rulings and directions are binding on the other members of the court and, of course, the parties to the proceedings. Subject to the Judge Advocate's conduct of the trial, it will be the President's duty to ensure that the trial befits the traditions and standards of the Service; and, in particular, that officers and other persons under instruction do not interfere in the trial ...'

[72] The notes go on to warn the members:

'3. When you arrive at the Courts-Martial Centre, do not speak to any unit personnel and certainly not to any unit officer who may be attending the trial in an official capacity or as a spectator. If you disregard this direction you may find yourself inadvertently talking to, for example, a witness or a lawyer involved in the case, which in turn might result in your being debarred from the trial or, indeed, the trial being prejudiced. If someone has spoken to you and you have any doubts about your position in this respect, you must tell the Judge Advocate privately before the trial commences. Any queries you may have should be addressed to the Clerk of the Court who will advise you.

4. Mention has been made above of the President's duties. Apart from that, the principal function of the President and the members is to decide, on the evidence, whether the accused is guilty or not guilty; and if guilty, then to decide, together with the Judge Advocate, the sentence to be imposed. The Judge Advocate will tell you all you need to know about the law and procedure in order to discharge those functions.'

[73] Paragraph 6 tells the members:

'You are exempted from occupying public accommodation at the accused's unit. Justice must manifestly be seen to be done and this aim is assisted by your being seen to avoid local unit influences.'

Paragraph 8 then advises them that:

'Save for resolving any queries members may have about court etiquette (eg. putting on and removal of head-dress etc.) under no circumstances must the President purport to carry out any form of briefing with other members of the court in the absence of the Judge Advocate.'

This, again, is obviously designed to support the pivotal role of the judge-advocate, while minimising any risk that the president may seek to influence the other members of the court.

[74] Paragraph 9 is to this effect:

'It is the C[ourt] A[dministration] O[fficer]'s duty to ensure that the officer members of the Court are qualified to act as members, ie. that they have the requisite number of years commissioned service and that they have not sat as members of a court-martial which has tried the accused before, or been involved in any investigation or inquiry into matters relating to the subject matter of the charge against the accused ... However if, before the date of trial, you think you may be ineligible ... or not qualified to sit, or know something about the accused which could prejudice your impartiality, or know someone who might be a witness in the case (you will receive prior notice from the CAO of persons who may be called as prosecution witnesses) you must not mention the matter to any other member but should tell the CAO who will, if necessary, arrange for your place on the court to be taken by someone else. If your concern about any of the above matters does not arise until you get to court, you must not talk about it to anyone else but should ask to see the Judge Advocate privately and tell him. Likewise, if during the trial you realise that you know a witness, you should tell the Judge Advocate privately without mentioning it to anyone else.'

[75] In para 20 the members are told that when the opening formalities are complete—

'The Judge Advocate may then publicly warn the court not to talk to anyone else about the case for as long as it continues. That includes family, friends, work associates, the prosecutor, defence counsel and, most importantly, the accused and anyone who may be a witness. To that end, other than when the Judge Advocate is sitting alone, members are not to leave the court room during the trial except to go to the lavatory, and for any overnight or luncheon adjournment; and are not to associate with Formation or Unit personnel either professionally or socially until the trial is over. Refreshments will be brought into the court room as required.

21. The President and members must not at any time, including when sitting alongside the Judge Advocate, look at papers lying on the desks of the judge advocate, prosecutor or defence counsel. Such papers might include information which the court must not see under any circumstances.'

[76] Although it appeared to be doubtful from counsel's submissions whether the practice was uniform, para 30 of the briefing notes, reflecting r 62(2), envisages that the president and members of the court may only put questions to a witness through the judge-advocate. If at the end of the witness' evidence the member feels that he must know the answer to a particular question in order to decide the guilt or innocence of the accused, then he should pass it in writing to the judge-advocate who can put it to the witness in the correct way. In para 33 the members are told that they must never take it upon themselves to visit the scene of the alleged crime before or during the trial. If there is a need for such a visit the whole court, counsel and the accused will go to see the scene.

[77] In para 35 (drawing on r 69) the members are told that, following the addresses by counsel, the judge-advocate will sum up the evidence and direct the other members of the court on the law relating to the case. He will also summarise the main points of the evidence (para 29). The members are not to ask the judge-advocate any questions during his summing up, but they can ask in writing for further directions which the judge-advocate must give in open court.

[78] Paragraph 36 (reflecting r 70) deals with the members' deliberations on their verdict:

'While the court is deliberating on the findings, no-one is to be present except the President, members and officers under instruction. The President and members are not to separate until the finding has been reached, unless the Judge Advocate directs that in the interests of justice they may separate ... If any person has to leave the court room for personal reasons he must be told by the President not to speak to any person on any account ie on the telephone, by letter or any other means. If the court wish to hear again

a   evidence recorded by the VCR, the Judge Advocate must be told and, on his
      direction, the court must be re-opened and the passage read in open court.'

Further guidance is given in para 39:

b   'The President will normally initiate the discussion on the issue of guilt or
      innocence. The President should ensure that every court member present
      gives his opinion as to the finding on each charge separately, in ascending
      order of seniority commencing with the junior member. A unanimous
      decision is preferable, but a majority of votes will decide the issue, and the
      finding of the majority will be recorded as the finding of the court. The
      President should write down the finding(s) on the record of findings sheet
      and sign it. Prior to re-opening the court, the President should remind any
c   members overruled by the majority that they must now adopt the finding of
      the court. This is important if it becomes necessary to consider the sentence,
      as their personal feelings regarding guilt or innocence should not influence
      their decisions.'

d   [79] Paragraph 40 explains that, when the court is reopened and the judge-
      advocate returns, he looks at the record to check that the findings are not
      contrary to law. If he is so satisfied, the findings are announced. If he is not so
      satisfied, then he gives the members further directions in open court. The court
      will then be closed once more and the members of the court will have to
      reconsider its findings in the light of his directions (see r 72(3) and (4)).

e   [80] Paragraph 25 explains what is to happen when sentence is being
      considered, either after a guilty plea or following conviction:

      'The court will close to deliberate on sentence. No-one will be present
      save for the members (including, of course, the Judge Advocate) and any
      person under instruction. The Judge Advocate will initiate discussion on the
f   sentence and will inform the members about maximum punishments and
      the principles to be observed. Sentence will be determined by a majority of
      votes if necessary and the opinions of the officer members will be given
      orally in ascending order of seniority, commencing with the junior member.
      The Judge Advocate will decide where he votes in the order. In the case of
      an equality of votes, the President has a second or casting vote which is
g   exercisable once, i.e. he has a final, determining vote. When sentence has
      been decided, it is entered on the record of sentence which the Judge
      Advocate holds. The President and Judge Advocate will sign that record.'

      [81] Once the trial has been completed, whether with an acquittal or with
h   conviction and sentence, the president announces that the trial is concluded and
      the judge-advocate dissolves the court (para 42). Thereafter the court orderly is
      to be instructed to burn or shred all scrap paper (para 45).

      [82] The various provisions which I have quoted from the briefing notes for
      the members of courts-martial reinforce significantly the message, proclaimed in
      any event by the oath and the directions of the judge-advocate, that the members
j   are to act independently and impartially. In order to be seen to avoid local unit
      influences, the members are not to stay in public accommodation at the accused's
      unit. They are not to speak to unit personnel and especially not to any officer
      who may be attending the trial—at the risk of being debarred from the trial or
      indeed of the trial being prejudiced. They are not to associate either professionally
      or socially with such personnel until the trial is over. There is a veto on the

president briefing the other members of the court in the absence of the judge-advocate. The members are to tell the court administration officer if they *a* know something about the accused which could prejudice their impartiality or if they know someone who might be a witness in the case. The members are warned not to talk to anyone else about the case as long as it continues. They are not to look at any papers which are before the judge-advocate, prosecutor or defence counsel, for fear of seeing something which they ought not to. When *b* they deliberate on conviction or sentence, the most junior member is to give his opinion orally first—again, obviously, with the aim of ensuring that the junior members express their own personal view, uninfluenced by the more senior members. In terms of the members' oath their deliberations are to be kept secret and this secrecy is further ensured by the instruction to the court orderly at the end of the proceedings to burn or shred all scrap paper. Again, the object is to *c* prevent the members feeling, or coming under, any outside pressure during or after the trial by reason of their participation in the decision in the case.

[83] Lord Thomas did not suggest that these were other than genuine instructions to the members which they were intended to observe. Nor was it suggested that the instructions were in practice ignored or that they had been *d* ignored in these particular cases. But if they are indeed observed, I find it hard, if not impossible, to see how anyone either in the court or, more particularly, outside the court could improperly influence the members' decision either on conviction or on sentence. Certainly, it is hard to see what more could be done to ensure that, while sitting in the court-martial, the officers act not as officers *e* subject to command but as independent and impartial members of the court, reaching the verdict and determining the sentence according to law but according also to their own individual conscience.

[84] Of course, the members of a court-martial are not just an ordinary jury. The difference shows itself in at least two different respects.

[85] First, the routines, the periods of boredom and the pleasures, pains and *f* pressures of service life would be unknown to most jurors today, although they would have been familiar to many of their fathers and grandfathers. By contrast, members of a court-martial know all about them and about the society in which the accused lives and works. Lord Thomas suggested that officers on a court-martial, imbued by their training with notions of rank and discipline, would always tend *g* to believe the evidence of a fellow officer or a non-commissioned officer rather than the evidence of a private. By contrast, he said, members of a jury, who carried no such burden of preconceptions, would be able to see more clearly and judge purely on the evidence before them. Of course, this submission was really just a matter of assertion. There was, and could be, no evidence to back it up. *h* Indeed, it was somewhat undermined by the conviction of the appellants, Lance Sergeant Spear and Lance Sergeant Hastie in *R v Spear, R v Boyd* [2001] QB 804, [2001] 2 WLR 1692. Their conviction was based on the evidence of Guardsman Lane and Guardsman Bright. In accepting the guardsmen's evidence, the court-martial must have disbelieved the evidence of their superiors in rank, the *j* two sergeants. In any event, it is possible to fashion an argument—equally a matter of assertion—that officers who are familiar with service life and who are in close contact with service personnel of all ranks may well be less impressed by mere rank and better able to gauge the underlying realities than jurors confronted for the first time with officers or non-commissioned officers telling an apparently plausible tale. Viewed in this light, the specialised knowledge and experience of

a the members of a court-martial could be seen as a positive advantage rather than as a disadvantage. However that may be, I see no reason to think that, when duly directed by the judge-advocate, officers on a court-martial cannot properly assess the evidence and return a true verdict based on it. I therefore reject the appellants' argument on this point.

[86] The members of a court-martial perform a role in deciding sentence
b which is no part of a jury's function in the United Kingdom. I accept that, in determining sentence, the members will indeed have regard to such issues as the impact of the offence on service morale and discipline. They will, inevitably, be more aware of these effects than a civil judge would be. Therefore, while the safeguards of the independence and impartiality of the members should mean that they approach their verdict in much the same way as jurors in a civil trial, it
c cannot be assumed that, when passing sentence, the court-martial will necessarily give exactly the same weight to these service factors as would a Crown Court judge. The sentences which a court-martial passes may therefore not coincide exactly with the sentences which a civil judge would pass on the same facts. In my view that does not call the decisions of the courts-martial into question, either
d generally or in terms of art 6. Any difference in sentencing does not mean that the members are not independent or impartial, but merely that, though both independent and impartial, they may assess the various factors differently. Even in the civil system it is recognised that judges or magistrates may use their knowledge of local conditions, such as the prevalence of a particular crime in a
e given area, in determining sentence. Similarly, in the sphere of professional discipline the courts acknowledge that a tribunal made up of senior members of the profession will have advantages in determining the appropriate penalty. It could not be suggested that, for this reason alone, in these cases the judge, magistrates or tribunal members are lacking in independence or impartiality. There is no more reason to accept such a suggestion in the case of the members
f of courts-martial. There are, besides, two additional points to bear in mind. The first is that the judge-advocate advises the other members on sentence and also has a vote on sentence. He will be able to bring to bear his informed view as a lawyer on what sentence would be suitable. The second safeguard is that any sentence imposed by the court-martial is subject not only to review by the
g reviewing authority but also to appeal, on the ground that it is not appropriate, with the leave of the appeal court. The members of the appeal court are civil judges and are in a position to correct any inappropriate punishment that the court-martial may impose by reason of the members' military background.

[87] All these matters must be kept in mind when considering the particular characteristics of the members of the court-martial to which the European Court
h attached importance in *Morris v UK* (2002) 34 EHRR 1253.

[88] The first was that the officer members had no legal training. That applies also in the present cases and indeed must apply in virtually all cases. As the briefing notes show, officers who may be called upon to sit on courts-martial are given some training by being allowed to sit and observe proceedings, including
j the members' deliberations. This should mean that, when they are eventually asked to sit, they should not find the procedures wholly unknown or strange, but it goes no further than that. While in *Morris v UK* the Third Chamber seem to have regarded the lack of formal legal training as a significant defect, as I have already noted, in *Engel v The Netherlands (No 1)* (1976) 1 EHRR 647 the European Court held that the Dutch Supreme Military Court was an independent and

impartial tribunal, even though four of the six members were military officers *a* with no legal training. Given the other safeguards which were in place in the present cases, I see no reason to conclude that the absence of legal training undermined the members' independence and impartiality.

[89] The European Court attached importance to the fact that the officers, other than the permanent president, remained subject to army discipline and reports. In so far as the members of the courts-martial in the present cases also *b* remained subject to service discipline, they simply shared the characteristic of all serving members of the armed forces. It must have been equally true of the military members of the Dutch Supreme Military Court in *Engel v The Netherlands*. Moreover, the fuller information available to the House about the safeguards in place to protect the independence of the members of courts-martial shows *c* clearly, in my view, that, just like the Dutch officers in *Engel v The Netherlands*, the officers in these cases would not have been under the command of any higher authority in their function as members of the courts-martial. Indeed, as Mr Havers pointed out, contrary to the assumption of the European Court, there was even a formal legal bar to any superior officer trying to influence their decision, since *d* this would have constituted the criminal offence of attempting to pervert the course of justice.

[90] It is true, of course, that, as in *Morris v UK*, so also in these cases, leaving aside the permanent presidents, the officers sitting on the courts-martial would have remained subject to reports. Lord Thomas indeed drew attention to a number of such reports where mention is made of the fact that, during the year *e* in question, the officer concerned had sat as a member of a court-martial. In itself that must be unobjectionable since the information that the particular officer has had this experience may be relevant at some future date if, for instance, consideration is being given to appointing a permanent president. What would be objectionable would be any report which made reference, whether favourable or unfavourable, to an officer's decisions when sitting on a court-martial. But *f* Lord Thomas could point to no report where this had been done. The only report which referred to an officer's performance in relation to a court-martial was one relating to Flight Lieutenant Hudson: 'Her foray into the court-martial arena has brought particular accolades for her thoughtful and incisive contribution to the legal process.' The report showed that Flight Lieutenant Hudson had acted not *g* only as junior member on several courts-martial but also as assistant defending officer to an airman tried by a general court-martial. It appears that the comment may well have related to this second role. In any event the report makes no comment on any decision reached by Flight Lieutenant Hudson when sitting as a member of a court-martial. Indeed counsel for the respondents showed the *h* House a number of statements from officers concerned with personnel matters who had read thousands of annual reports and had never seen mention of such a thing. That being so, again with the benefit of this more detailed information, I would not share the view of the European Court in *Morris v UK* that the independence and impartiality of officers sitting on courts-martial are compromised by the fact that they remain subject to the system of annual reports. *j*

[91] For all these reasons I consider that those charged with administering the system of courts-martial have been at pains to put in place a series of practical safeguards which are designed to secure the independence and impartiality of those sitting on these courts. Nor is this surprising. There is not a little force in the point made by the appeal court in *R v Saunby* that, if service factors are to be

a seen as an aspect or function of the public interest, they will themselves require that the court-martial process should be, and should be seen to be, fair and impartial and, so far as possible, to achieve accurate results. Otherwise both servicemen and the public would lose confidence in it, with consequential effects on good order and discipline.

b [92] Having regard in particular to the additional information which was not before the European Court, I would therefore hold that the safeguards built into the system are indeed such that no fair-minded and informed observer who had considered them would conclude that there was a real possibility that the courts-martial in these cases lacked independence or impartiality in this respect. In other words they were, objectively, independent and impartial. I would accordingly reject the art 6 challenge based on the role of the officer members.

c [93] In *Morris v UK* (2002) 34 EHRR 1253 at 1278–1279 the European Court went further, however, and held that the role played by the reviewing authority was in itself a reason for saying that the court-martial in that case had not been an independent and impartial tribunal:

d   '73 In relation to the applicant's complaints about the role played by the "reviewing authority", the Court recalls that the power to give a binding decision which may not be altered by a non-judicial authority is inherent in the very notion of "tribunal". The principle can also be seen as a component of the "independence" required by Article 6(1). In [*Findlay v UK* (1997) 24 EHRR 221], the role played by the "confirming officer" under the pre-1996 e   Act court martial system was found to be contrary to this well-established principle.

      74 In the present case, the applicant's sentence and conviction were subject, under changes introduced by the 1996 Act, to automatic review by the "reviewing authority". The Court notes that the authority was empowered to quash the applicant's conviction and the sentence imposed by f   the court martial. More importantly, it had powers to reach any finding of guilt which could have been reached by the court martial and to substitute any sentence which would have been open to the court martial, not being in the authority's opinion more serious than that originally passed. Any substituted verdict or sentence was treated as if it had been reached or g   imposed by the court martial itself.

      75 The Court considers that the very fact that the review was conducted by such a non-judicial authority as the "reviewing authority" is contrary to the principle cited at paragraph 73 above. The Court is particularly concerned by the fact that the decision whether any substituted sentence was h   more or less severe than that imposed by the court martial would have been left to the discretion of that authority. The Court's concerns are not answered by the Government's argument that the existence of the review serves the interests of convicted soldiers such as the applicant, nor by the essentially fair procedure followed by the authority when conducting its review.

j   76 The Court is of the view that the fundamental flaws which it has identified were not corrected by the applicant's subsequent appeal to the Courts Martial Appeal Court, since that appeal did not involve any rehearing of the applicant's case but rather determined, in the form of a decision which ran effectively to two sentences, that leave to appeal against conviction and sentence should be refused.

77 For all these reasons, the Court considers that the applicant's misgivings about the independence of the court martial and its status as a "tribunal" were objectively justified.'

Although Lord Thomas referred the House to this aspect of the court's decision in *Morris v UK* and submitted that it, too, would constitute a basis for allowing the appeal, he said, frankly, that he had difficulty in supporting the reasoning.

[94] The reviewing authority is, admittedly, an unusual institution. It does not operate like an ordinary court and, at a certain level of abstract theory, its existence could seem to be inconsistent with the charge against an accused being determined by only a system of 'tribunals'. That appears to be the way in which the European Court has treated it. But if, as the court indicates, the issue can also be characterised as relating to the independence of the court-martial, I find it difficult to see how the existence of this body affects that independence. It might, of course, be different if there were any suggestion that the decisions of the courts-martial were influenced by the existence of the reviewing authority, for example, because they tended to convict more readily or to impose heavier sentences in the knowledge that the reviewing authority could always quash them. But Lord Thomas made no such submission and there is nothing whatever in the information before the House that would support it. On the contrary, Lord Thomas accepted that the provision for review could only be to the benefit, and not to the detriment, of someone who had been convicted. In particular, it could provide a quick and simple means of correcting a mistaken decision by a court-martial.

[95] The reviewing authority is a creation of the 1996 Act to replace the role of the confirming officer and of the reviewing authorities to whom a convicted person could formerly present a petition. The procedure adopted by the new reviewing authority is more transparent: the convicted person is informed of the advice of the judge-advocate and is given not only the decision of the reviewing authority but the reasons for it (see r 83). Moreover, the powers of review are particularised in the statute and, unlike the position before 1997, the convicted person can appeal against sentence. Formerly, he could appeal only against conviction, with the result that the final say on sentence lay with a non-judicial body which did not give reasons for its decisions.

[96] In reaching its conclusion on this point the European Court was particularly concerned by the fact that the decision as to whether any substituted sentence was more or less severe than that imposed by the court-martial would have been left to the discretion of the reviewing authority. When making this observation the court does not appear to have been referred to, or to have had in mind, the coda to s 71(1) of the 1955 Acts which establishes, as a matter of law, the relative positions of particular punishments in the hierarchy of punishments set out in the subsection and which deals specifically with how detention and imprisonment are to relate to one another. Particularly when these provisions are taken into account, it is hard to see how, in reality, there is likely to be any scope for the reviewing authority to exercise the kind of discretion that appears to have troubled the European Court. In truth, counsel could refer to no case where any problem as to the relative severity of two punishments had arisen. If, by chance, however, the reviewing authority were to go wrong on the point, the person affected could ask the appeal court for leave to appeal.

[97] In all the cases under appeal except that of Dodds, the reviewing authority did not intervene, but the appellants were granted leave to appeal to the

a appeal court. Where they had other arguable grounds of appeal relating to conviction or sentence, the appeal court dealt with them, as well as with the art 6 grounds, in their reasoned judgments. In these circumstances I am, with due respect to the decision of the European Court in *Morris v UK*, unable to see why the mere existence of the reviewing authority, or the reduction of Dodds' period of detention, should lead to the conclusion that the determination of the charges
b against the appellants was not reached by a 'tribunal' that was 'independent and impartial' for the purposes of art 6. I would therefore reject the appellants' art 6 argument based on the role of the reviewing authority.

[98] Lord Thomas originally presented a separate argument to the effect that the decisions of the prosecuting authority to prosecute the appellants before a court-martial were themselves an infringement of the appellants' art 6 rights. In
c their judgment in *R v Saunby*, the appeal court rejected that argument and accepted the respondents' opposing argument that such decisions by a prosecutor lie outside the scope of art 6(1). Before the House Lord Thomas modified the appellants' contention and argued that the infringement of art 6 arose out of the congruence of unfair factors influencing the decision to prosecute and unfair
d factors influencing the court-martial's decisions on conviction and sentence. He therefore accepted that he could not succeed on the prosecution point unless he succeeded in persuading the House that the courts-martial had not themselves been independent and impartial—in which event, of course, on his own submission, the appeals would have to be allowed anyway. On that approach any
e point relating to the decision to prosecute was subsumed in the issue relating to the fairness of the court-martial proceedings. That being so, since I have found that the court-martial proceedings did not infringe the appellants' art 6 rights, I would also reject the appellants' art 6 argument relating to the decisions to prosecute them.

[99] In these circumstances it is unnecessary to consider in these appeals to
f what extent art 6 applies to the decision to prosecute. In this connection Mr Havers drew the attention of the House to certain passages in the opinions in *Montgomery v HM Advocate, Coulter v HM Advocate* [2001] 2 WLR 779, but any consideration of the point would need to take account also of what was said in *Brown v Stott (Procurator Fiscal, Dunfermline)* [2001] 2 All ER 97, [2001] 2 WLR 817
g and *Millar v Dickson (Procurator Fiscal, Elgin)* [2001] UKPC D4, [2002] 3 All ER 1041, [2002] 1 WLR 1615. I would wish to reserve my opinion on the point. Certain remarks of the appeal court in *R v Saunby*, when dealing with it in their judgment, might be open to the interpretation that fairness, independence and impartiality were more readily to be expected of courts than of prosecutors for
h whom the sufficiency of the evidence and the public interest would be the guiding values. An unduly narrow approach of that kind to what is expected of a prosecutor would not, however, sit easily with the familiar requirement that he should act fairly and as 'a minister of justice' (see *Randall v R* [2002] UKPC 19 at [10], [2002] 1 WLR 2237 per Lord Bingham of Cornhill citing *Boucher v R* (1954) 110 Can CC 263 at 270 per Rand J). In reserving my opinion on the merits of the
j argument as to the scope of art 6, I would therefore not wish to be thought to have silently endorsed the observations of the appeal court in this regard.

[100] For the respondents Mr Havers submitted that, even if the House had come to the conclusion that the members of the courts-martial had not been, objectively, independent or impartial, it would not necessarily have followed that the appeals should be allowed and the appellants' convictions quashed. The

appeals against conviction might still have been refused if the evidence against
the appellants had been sufficiently powerful. Had it been necessary to decide the
point, I would have rejected this submission. The Crown, which always acts in
the public interest, has no interest in maintaining a conviction flowing from the
decision of a court which is not seen to be independent and impartial. Such a
conviction should be quashed (see *Millar v Dickson (Procurator Fiscal, Elgin)* [2002]
3 All ER 1041 at [16], [65], [83]–[88] per Lord Bingham, Lord Hope and Lord
Clyde respectively). Depending on the circumstances, the appropriate course
may be to grant an order under s 19(1) of the Courts-Martial (Appeals) Act 1968
authorising a retrial.

[101] For these reasons, as well as for those given by my noble and learned
friend Lord Bingham, I would refuse the appeals.

Appeals dismissed.

Kate O'Hanlon   Barrister.

a
Shalson v Keepers and Governors of the Free Grammar School of John Lyon

[2002] EWCA Civ 538

COURT OF APPEAL, CIVIL DIVISION

b THORPE, BUXTON LJJ AND MOSES J

15 APRIL 2002

Landlord and tenant – Leasehold enfranchisement – Valuation – Improvement –
Former lessee converting property from single house into flats – Current lessee
converting property back into single house and thereby increasing value of property –
c *Whether lessee's works an 'improvement' for purposes of leasehold valuation if merely*
reversing work done by previous lessee that had depressed value of property – Leasehold
Reform Act 1967, s 9(1A)(d).

The respondent was the freehold owner of a residential property let under a lease
d granted in 1947. The house had originally been let in 1843 as a single house, but
following the grant of the 1947 lease it had been converted into five flats at the expense
of the then lessee. In 1991 the lease was acquired by the current lessee who, at his own
expense, converted the property into a single family house. In subsequent leasehold
valuation proceedings under the Leasehold Reform Act 1967, the valuation view was
that the property arranged in a number of flats would have been less valuable on a sale
e than the property taken as a whole. For that reason, the lessee contended that the
conversion of the property into a single family house had constituted an
'improvement carried out by the tenant or his predecessors in title at their own
expense' within the meaning of s 9(1A)(d)[a] of the 1967 Act, and that accordingly it was
an expense that went to the diminution of the price to be paid for the freehold. That
f contention was rejected by the Lands Tribunal, and the lessee appealed.

Held – Where the alleged works of improvement consisted only of reversing
work done by a predecessor in title (or even, remarkably, by the current tenant)
that had depressed the value of the property, they could not be said to be an
'improvement' within the meaning of s 9(1A)(d) of the 1967 Act. The Act treated
g the activities of 'the tenant or his predecessors in title' as a single whole, and it
could not be an improvement by that body simply to put right what that body
had earlier done wrong. The proper question to ask was whether the alleged
works of improvement were in fact doing no more than altering existing works
which, in the market at the valuation date (ie the time when the tenant gave
notice of his desire to have the freehold), would have had a depressive effect on
h the value of the property. It followed in the instant case that the alleged works of
improvement did not fall within s 9(1A)(d), and accordingly the appeal would be
dismissed (see [9], [10], [14], [16]–[19], below).

Notes

j For leasehold valuation, see 27(2) *Halsbury's Laws* (4th edn reissue) para 1297.
    For the Leasehold Reform Act 1967, s 9, see 23 *Halsbury's Statutes* (4th edn)
(1997 reissue) 224.

Case cited or referred to in skeleton arguments

King (decd), Re, Robinson v Gray [1963] 1 All ER 781, [1963] Ch 459, CA.

_____

a   Section 9, so far as material, is set out at [8], below

Appeal

Peter Shalson, the lessee of a property known as 98 Hamilton Terrace, St John's   *a*
Wood, London NW8, appealed with permission of the Court of Appeal
(Schiemann and Mance LJJ) granted on 19 July 2001 from the decision of the
Lands Tribunal (Mr Rose FRICS) on 19 April 2001 dismissing his appeal from the
decision of the Leasehold Valuation Tribunal that certain works carried out by
the lessee did not constitute an 'improvement' to the property for the purposes   *b*
of s 9(1A)(d) of the Leasehold Reform Act 1967 and were therefore not to be
disregarded in determining the price to be paid for the freehold by the lessee to
the respondent lessor, the Keepers and Governors of the Free Grammar School
of John Lyon. The facts are set out in the judgment of Buxton LJ.

Edwin Johnson (instructed by *David Conway & Co*) for the lessee.   *c*
Kenneth Munro (instructed by *Pemberton Greenish*) for the lessor.

BUXTON LJ (giving the first judgment at the invitation of Thorpe LJ).

[1] This is an appeal from a decision of the member of the Lands Tribunal,
Mr Rose FRICS, made in leasehold valuation proceedings on appeal from the
London Leasehold Valuation Tribunal.   *d*

[2] The question before Mr Rose was as to the proper valuation of the price to be
paid by the lessee, under leasehold valuation proceedings, of a property in Hamilton
Terrace, London NW8. The property is in a substantial and well-known road in St
John's Wood. It was described as being a detached period house, arranged on various
floors, with a garage and other desirable amenities. It was built under an agreement *e*
for lease that was dated 1840 and the first lease was granted in 1843. Subsequent leases
followed, and the present term was a term of 99 years, granted in March 1947.

[3] It was agreed for the purposes of this appeal that all of these leases could
be considered together under s 3(3) of the Leasehold Reform Act 1967. I should
however emphasise that the s 3(3) point has not been argued before us, and we   *f*
make no concluded decision on it.

[4] The short point that gives rise to this appeal is as follows. Following the grant
of the 1947 lease, the premises were converted into five flats and subsequently altered
by various assignees, in each case at the then lessee's own expense. The result was
that by 1991, when the appellant lessee acquired the lease, the accommodation had
been rearranged to provide two units only, a self-contained basement flat and the *g*
remainder of the house. The conversion to a single family house, as the property now
is, was completed in 1993 by the now lessee at his own expense.

[5] The question for the member was whether the work that had been done
to transform the premises from a building arranged in five flats to a single family
house was an improvement under the terms of s 9(1A)(d) of the 1967 Act, and *h*
therefore an expense that went to the diminution of a price to be paid.

[6] The arguments on each side were simple, though some of the background
arguments and the way in which they were deployed was not so straightforward.
The simple cases were this. The lessee said that the wording of s 9(1A)(d) was
clear. The value of the house and premises had been increased by an improvement
to it: that is to say, to convert it from a building in flats to a single property. The *j*
contention against that, which prevailed with the member, was that all that the
work had done was effectively to reverse a conversion of the property into the
five flats, which latter arrangement would, if left in place, have diminished its
total value at the valuation date in 1997.

[7] The case is a good example, as Mr Johnson in his careful submissions for
the lessee pointed out, of the way in which fashion, or need, in the occupation

and arrangement of property can vary over the years, and the way in which arrangements of property and their value can be affected by that. In 1947 it is probably the case (although I think that no one had confirmed that point) that the property as converted into five flats would have had a total value greater than when it was in single occupation. It was, however, the valuation view in 1996 that the property arranged in a number of flats would have been less valuable on a sale than the property taken as a whole, as it now is. It was for that reason, of course, that the lessee said that converting it to a single family house had indeed been a relevant improvement.

[8] Despite the detailed argument that we have heard, both orally and on paper, I consider that, certainly on the facts of this particular case, the point is a short one. The question concerns, under s 9(1A)(d) 'the extent to which the value of the house and premises has been increased by any improvement carried out by the tenant or his predecessors in title at their own expense'.

[9] That expression has to be construed as a whole. Speaking for myself, I simply do not see how it can be said to be such an improvement by the tenant or his predecessors in title, increasing the value of the house and premises, if the works relied on consist, as they consist in this case, only of reversing work done by a predecessor in title (or even, remarkably, by the instant tenant) that depressed the value of the house and premises; which, as at the valuation date, the conversion into five flats indeed would have so done.

[10] The reason for my saying that is that the Act treats the activities of 'the tenant or his predecessors in title' as a single whole, and it cannot, in my view, be an improvement by that body simply to put right what that body had earlier done wrong. In the present case, it may appear to be paradoxical that when the premises were converted into five flats, the landlord agreed to that being done and that all concerned thought at that time that would improve the value of the property. But the short point is that the valuation has to take place on the valuation date, at the time when the tenant chooses to give notice of his desire to have the freehold, and it is within the market conditions of that date that questions of 'improvement' to increase value have to be determined.

[11] There are other grounds for thinking that is the correct approach. Firstly, as the member accepted in para 42 of his determination, the construction contended for by the lessee could produce surprising results. If, for instance, for eccentric reasons peculiar to a particular tenant or to the way in which he wished to use the property, a property had been gutted or significantly altered in arrangement so that it pleased a tenant better but materially reduced the market value of the premises, on the construction contended for by the lessee in this case, putting that right even by that tenant himself (let alone by a successor tenant), would count as an improvement of which he should have the benefit. I cannot think that that is a sensible outcome.

[12] Further, the tenant, the person who applies for the freehold, obtains the benefit of what are in fact improvements created by his predecessors. In the present case the property had been improved (by the creation of a mansard roof and in other ways) by predecessors of the present tenant before 1947 and he rightly, under the statute, obtained credit for those improvements in the valuation. If the present tenant obtains the benefit of the acts of his predecessor, in my judgment it is not inequitable, and likely to be what Parliament intended, that he should bear the burden if he has chosen to put right, for reasons best known to himself, what are now seen to be errors committed by his predecessor.

[13] Mr Johnson said that such considerations were not dispositive, and that indeed there were aspects of the statute which should lead us not to be surprised

that such outcomes could arise from the construction that he urged. He *a* particularly drew attention to s 9(1A)(c), which requires the valuation to be made on the assumption that the tenant has no repair or maintenance liability under Pt I of the Landlord and Tenant Act 1954. Therefore, he said, the tenant could allow the property to fall into disrepair, probably the landlord could do nothing about it, and the tenant would, as it were, gain the benefit of that by a reduction of the open market price rather than by way of improvement. That I see, and to *b* some extent that outcome might be thought surprising. But it is what Parliament has chosen to provide. It is not a reason for giving the concept of 'improvement carried out by the tenant or his predecessors in title' a meaning that will produce, in my judgment, further and even more surprising outcomes.

[14] I therefore would determine this appeal on that short point: that on the facts of this case, looking at what are alleged to be the improvements, they cannot *c* be said to come under s 9(1A)(d) of the 1967 Act.

[15] I would sound a word of caution about the more expansive way in which the member expressed himself, largely adopting the contentions of Mr Munro on behalf of the respondent lessor. He appeared to accept that one should start from the property as it was at the original date of the lease—that is to say, in this case, *d* in 1843—and see whether the value has been increased or decreased by works carried on by the tenant and his predecessors thereafter. To the extent that that was suggested as the right approach in every case, I would be cautious about it because, as Mr Johnson pointed out, in many cases it is going to be impossible to perform that exercise. In many cases one simply will not know, by reason of the *e* history, what the position was at the very start of a lease as long as this one.

[16] But that, of course, is not a reason for adopting the construction of the section that Mr Johnson urges. The exercise that was carried out in this case would not, as a matter of fact, be possible unless there was a reliable history, as there is in this case, of why the works relied upon by the lessee were undertaken at all. The proper question to ask—and this is the question I ask myself in this *f* case—is whether the alleged works of improvement are doing no more than altering previous works to the property that, in the market as it existed at the valuation date, would have been a depressing rather than an increasing factor in the market price. The original condition of the property at the start of the lease is, of course, an important background to that inquiry, but where facts are available such *g* as those in the present case it is not necessary notionally to go back to the start of the lease, or to think that in every case it is going be necessary to know everything about the detailed history of the property; so long as it can be properly said that the works that are claimed are not an improvement at all, but simply a return of the property to a condition of equilibrium in which it existed before 1947.

[17] For those reasons, therefore, I would consider that the member came to *h* the correct conclusion in this case and I would dismiss this appeal.

MOSES J.

[18] I agree.

j

THORPE LJ.

[19] I also agree.

Appeal dismissed. Permission to appeal refused.

James Brooks   Barrister.

a # R (on the application of Giles) v Parole Board and another

[2002] EWCA Civ 951

b COURT OF APPEAL, CIVIL DIVISION

KENNEDY, MAY AND TUCKEY LJJ

21 MAY, 4 JULY 2002

Sentence – Custodial sentence – Custodial sentence longer than that commensurate
c *with seriousness of offence – Lawfulness of detention – Whether convention right*
requiring periodic review of lawfulness of continued detention of offender who had
served commensurate element of sentence – Criminal Justice Act 1991, s 2(2)(b) –
Powers of Criminal Courts (Sentencing) Act 2000, s 80(2)(b) – Human Rights Act 1998,
Sch 1, Pt I, art 5(4).

d
The claimant was sentenced to consecutive terms of imprisonment of four years'
for unlawful wounding and three years for assault occasioning actual bodily
harm. When imposing sentence, the judge made it clear that he was invoking
s 2(2)(b)[a] of the Criminal Justice Act 1991, subsequently re-enacted in identical
e terms in s 80(2)(b) of the Powers of Criminal Courts (Sentencing) Act 2000.
Under those provisions, which applied where the court was passing a custodial
sentence, not fixed by law, for a violent or sexual offence, the sentence was to be
for such longer term than that commensurate with the seriousness of the offence
(but not exceeding the permitted maximum) as was necessary in the opinion of
the court to protect the public from serious harm from the offender. The
f claimant was refused leave to appeal against the sentence, but subsequently
brought judicial review proceedings against the Secretary of State. He relied on
art 5(4)[b] of the European Convention for the Protection of Human Rights and
Fundamental Freedoms 1950 (as set out in Sch 1 to the Human Rights Act 1998),
which provided that everyone who was deprived of his liberty by detention was
g entitled to take proceedings by which the lawfulness of his detention would be
decided speedily by a court. The claimant contended that, when an offender had
served the commensurate sentence, he became entitled to benefit from art 5(4),
and that the requirements of that provision were not satisfied by the original
decision of the sentencing judge because the latter might, in the event, be
h mistaken in his assessment of when the offender would cease to be dangerous.
That contention was accepted by the judge. Accordingly, he granted a declaration
that, once a person was detained in circumstances where he would have been
released but for the imposition of the additional element of the sentence imposed
by virtue of s 80(2)(b) of the 2000 Act, his continuing period of detention should
j be subject to art 5(4) of the convention, such that it would need to be reviewed
periodically at reasonable intervals by a procedure compliant with art 5(4) in
order to determine whether the continued detention remained necessary to
protect the public from serious harm. The Secretary of State appealed.

---

a Section 2 is set out at [4], below
b Article 5(4) is set out at [2], below

Held – Where a judge had imposed a sentence under s 80(2)(b) of the 2000 Act, the supervision required by art 5(4) of the convention was incorporated in the decision, and accordingly there was no requirement for a periodic review of the lawfulness of the continued detention of an offender who had served the commensurate element of the sentence. The increased sentence under s 80(2)(b) was no more than the usual exercise by the sentencing court of its ordinary sentencing powers, even if the increase had a statutory basis. The decision to impose the longer term was plainly a judicial decision, every aspect of which was subject to appeal. The sentence was not indeterminate. It could not exceed the statutory maximum for the index offence, and it did not hand over to the executive the decision as to when the offender should be released. That was in contrast with the position in relation to many discretionary life sentences where the sentencing court concluded that the offender would remain a danger for an uncertain period of time. In cases such as the instant one, a period of time was fixed precisely because the sentencing judge considered that he was in a position to fix it even though it was clear that in many cases the risk presented to the public by the offender was capable of fluctuating with the passage of time. Accordingly, the appeal would be allowed and the declaration set aside (see [17]–[19], below).

Notes

For the right to take proceedings to determine the lawfulness of detention and for criteria for determining the length of custodial sentences, see respectively 8(2) *Halsbury's Laws* (4th edn reissue) para 127 and Supp to 11(2) *Halsbury's Laws* (4th edn reissue) para 1202A.

For the Criminal Justice Act 1991, s 2, see 12 *Halsbury's Statutes* (4th edn) (1997 reissue) 1287. Section 2 was replaced by s 80(2) of the Powers of Criminal Courts (Sentencing) Act 2000 with effect from 25 August 2000.

For the Human Rights Act 1998, Sch 1, Pt I, art 5, see 7 *Halsbury's Statutes* (4th edn) (1999 reissue) 522.

Cases referred to in judgments

De Wilde v Belgium (No 1) (1971) 1 EHRR 373, ECt HR.
E v Norway (1990) 17 EHRR 30, E Com HR.
Hussain v UK (1996) 22 EHRR 1, ECt HR.
Mansell v UK App No 32072/96 (2 July 1997, unreported), E Com HR.
R v Billam [1986] 1 All ER 985, [1986] 1 WLR 349, CA.
R v Chapman (2000) 1 Cr App R 77, CA.
R v Crow, R v Pennington (1994) 16 Cr App R (S) 409, CA.
R v Hodgson (1967) 52 Cr App R 113, CA.
R v Mansell (1994) 15 Cr App R (S) 771, CA.
R v Smith (2001) 2 Cr App R (S) 160, CA.
R v Wilson [2000] Crim LR 503, CA.
Silva Rocha v Portugal (1996) 32 EHRR 333, ECt HR.
Stafford v UK App No 46295/99 (28 May 2002, unreported), ECt HR.
Thynne, Wilson and Gunnell v UK (1990) 13 EHRR 666, ECt HR.
Van Droogenbroeck v Belgium (1982) 4 EHRR 443, ECt HR.
Weeks v UK (1987) 10 EHRR 293, ECt HR.
Wynne v UK (1994) 19 EHRR 333, ECt HR.

Cases also cited or referred to in skeleton arguments

R (Anderson) v Secretary of State for the Home Dept, R (Taylor) v Secretary of State for the Home Dept [2001] EWCA Civ 1698, [2002] 2 WLR 1143.

a R (on the application of Alconbury Developments Ltd) v Secretary of State for the
   Environment, Transport and the Regions [2001] UKHL 23, [2001] 2 All ER 929,
   [2001] 2 WLR 1389.
   R v Coull [1993] Crim LR 978.
   R v Parole Board, ex p Bradley [1990] 3 All ER 828, [1991] 1 WLR 134, DC.
   R v Secretary of State for the Home Dept, ex p Benson (1988) Times, 21 November, DC.
b R v Secretary of State for the Home Dept, ex p Handscomb (1987) 86 Cr App R 59, DC.
   R v Secretary of State for the Home Dept, ex p Stafford [1998] 4 All ER 7, [1999] 2 AC 38, HL.
   T v UK (1999) 7 BHRC 659, ECt HR.
   X v UK (1981) 4 EHRR 188, ECt HR.

c **Appeal**
   The appellant, the Secretary of State for the Home Department, appealed with
   permission of Elias J from his order of 5 October 2001 ([2001] EWHC Admin 834,
   [2002] 1 WLR 654) granting the declaration, set out at [1], below, in proceedings for
   judicial review brought by the respondent, Terry Giles, against the appellant and
d the Parole Board. The facts are set out in the judgment of Kennedy LJ.

   David Pannick QC and *Eleanor Grey* (instructed by the *Treasury Solicitor*) for the
      appellant.
   Edward Fitzgerald QC and *Phillippa Kaufmann* (instructed by *Irwin Mitchell*, Sheffield)
      for the respondent.
e
                                                              Cur adv vult

   4 July 2002. The following judgments were delivered.

f **KENNEDY LJ.**
      [1] This is an appeal by the Secretary of State from a decision of Elias J, sitting
   in the Administrative Court ([2001] EWHC Admin 834, [2002] 1 WLR 654), who
   on 5 October 2001 granted a declaration to the claimant in these terms:

         'Where a person has been sentenced pursuant to s 80(2)(b) of the Powers
g   of Criminal Courts (Sentencing) Act 2000 (or its statutory predecessor), once
      he is detained in circumstances where he would have been released but for
      the imposition of the additional element of the sentence imposed by virtue
      of that subsection, his continuing period of detention shall be subject to
      art 5(4) of [the European Convention for the Protection of Human Rights
      and Fundamental Freedoms 1950 (as set out in Sch 1 to the Human
h   Rights Act 1998)] such that it will need to be reviewed periodically at
      reasonable intervals by a procedure compliant with art 5(4) to determine
      whether the continued detention remains necessary to protect the public
      from serious harm.'

j *Article 5 and this case*
      [2] Article 5 of the convention, so far as material, reads as follows:

         '(1) Everyone has the right to liberty and security of person. No one shall
      be deprived of his liberty save in the following cases and in accordance with
      a procedure prescribed by law: (a) the lawful detention of a person after
      conviction by a competent court ...

(4) Everyone who is deprived of his liberty by arrest or detention shall be entitled to take proceedings by which the lawfulness of his detention shall be decided speedily by a court and his release ordered if the detention is not lawful.'

[3] It has long been established that where a criminal is convicted or pleads guilty to an offence, and is sentenced to a period of imprisonment which the court considers commensurate with the gravity of his offence, the decision of the sentencing court constitutes the necessary compliance with art 5(4)—see *De Wilde v Belgium (No 1)* (1971) 1 EHRR 373. However, the position is different where the detention, in a hospital or in a prison, is not to punish but to protect the public from harm that may be caused by the person detained. In such a case art 5(4) applies. In *Thynne, Wilson and Gunnell v UK* (1990) 13 EHRR 666 the applicants had all been sentenced to life imprisonment in the United Kingdom for offences for which such a sentence was not mandatory. The European Court of Human Rights held (at 694 (para 76)) that art 5(4) applied 'after the expiry of the punitive periods of their sentences'. In order to meet the requirements of art 5(4) sentencing judges now specify the tariff period or minimum term (ie the punitive period allowing for remission) after which the offender's case will be considered at intervals by the Parole Board, which operates in such a way as to comply with art 5(4). The same procedure is operated in relation to young offenders ordered to be detained for an indefinite period. The issue which arises in this case is whether that procedure should also have been adopted when a sentencing judge invoked the powers given to him by s 2(2)(b) of the Criminal Justice Act 1991, now re-enacted in identical terms in s 80(2)(b) of the Powers of Criminal Courts (Sentencing) Act 2000. As this case is concerned with a sentence passed in 1997 I will refer hereafter only to the provisions of the earlier Act.

The 1991 Act
[4] The 1991 Act was preceded by a White Paper *Crime, Justice and Protecting the Public* (1990) (Cm 965) (the White Paper) which proposed—

'a coherent legislative framework for sentencing, with the severity of the punishment matching the seriousness of the crime and a sharper distinction in the way the courts deal with violent and non-violent crimes.'

It also proposed 'new powers for the Crown Court to impose longer sentences for violent and sexual offences, if this is necessary to protect the public from serious harm'. That latter proposal was amplified in paras 3.12 and 3.13 which, so far as material, read:

'3.12 ... The Court of Appeal has indicated that sentences should be longer if the victims of violent crimes are very young or very old and so especially vulnerable.
3.13 The Government proposes to take this approach further by giving the Crown Court power to give custodial sentences longer than would be justified by the seriousness of the offence to persistent violent and sexual offenders, if this is necessary to protect the public from serious harm. There are a small number of offenders who become progressively more dangerous and who are a real risk to public safety. Some will be mentally disordered and can be detained under mental health legislation. For those convicted of the most serious crimes, a sentence of life imprisonment may be justified ... Some offenders will be convicted of less serious offences but the Crown

a Court will recognise that they are a serious risk to the public. In these circumstances, the Government considers that an exception should be made to the principle that the length of the individual sentence should be justified by the seriousness of the offence. The Crown Court would be able to give a longer sentence within the maximum penalty for the offence for which the offender has been convicted. For example, an assault causing actual bodily

b harm might be serious enough to justify a sentence of twelve months, but the Crown Court could give a longer sentence, up to the maximum penalty of five years, if it considered this necessary to protect the public from the risk of serious harm from the offender. The Court would, of course, have to state in open court why it was giving a longer sentence and it would be open to the defendant to appeal against his sentence.'

c That is the background to s 2 of the 1991 Act, which reads:

'(1) This section applies where a court passes a custodial sentence other than one fixed by law.

d (2) The custodial sentence shall be—(a) for such term (not exceeding the permitted maximum) as in the opinion of the court is commensurate with the seriousness of the offence, or the combination of the offence and one or more offences associated with it; or (b) where the offence is a violent or sexual offence, for such longer term (not exceeding that maximum) as in the opinion of the court is necessary to protect the public from serious harm

e from the offender.

(3) Where the court passes a custodial sentence for a term longer than is commensurate with the seriousness of the offence, or the combination of the offence and one or more offences associated with it, the court shall—(a) state in open court that it is of the opinion that subsection (2)(b) above applies and why it is of that opinion; and (b) explain to the offender in open court and in

f ordinary language why the sentence is for such a term.

(4) A custodial sentence for an indeterminate period shall be regarded for the purposes of subsections (2) and (3) above as a custodial sentence for a term longer than any actual term.'

g Part II of the 1991 Act deals with early release of prisoners, and provides that as soon as a short-term prisoner (ie one serving less than four years' imprisonment) has served half of his sentence he must be released (see s 33(1)). Others must be released after serving two-thirds of their sentences (see s 33(2)), and after a long-term prisoner has served half of his sentence the Secretary of State will release him on licence if required to do so by the Parole Board. That is the effect

h of s 35(1) read together with the regulations made under the 1991 Act.

Section 2(2)(b): operation and limitations

[5] Before turning to the facts of the present case it is worth pausing to consider the wording of s 2(2) of the 1991 Act. The first thing to be noticed is that

j where the offence is of a violent or sexual nature the court has to form an opinion as to whether a sentence longer than that commensurate with the seriousness of the offence is necessary to protect the public from serious harm from the offender, and if so, secondly, what is the length of sentence required for that purpose. However, thirdly, the sentence cannot exceed the permitted maximum for the offence which has brought the defendant before the court. Fourthly, any sentence passed under s 2(2)(b) is in substitution for the sentence which would otherwise be passed under s 2(2)(a). It is not additional to it, as can be seen from the use of the word 'or' at the end of s 2(2)(a).

Extent of relationship to offending

[6] Clearly therefore when the powers under s 2(2)(b) are exercised there remains a close link between the offence which has brought the offender before the court and the sentence imposed, illustrated by the fact that only one sentence is imposed, which the statute does not require the sentencing judge to divide into two parts, and by the fact that the sentence cannot be for any longer term than the statutory maximum for the relevant offence.

[7] Over the years since 1991 there has been a certain lack of consistency in judicial pronouncements as to the nature of the relationship between the index offence and the sentence imposed under s 2(2)(b), and in particular as to whether the sentence imposed when s 2(2)(b) is relied upon must be not only less than the maximum for the index offence but also in some way proportionate to it. In *R v Mansell* (1994) 15 Cr App R (S) 771 at 775 Lord Taylor of Gosforth CJ said that the judge—

'in each individual case has to try to balance the need to protect the public on the one hand with the need to look at the totality of the sentence and to see that it is not out of all proportion to the nature of the offending.'

In that case the trial judge indicated that under s 2(2)(a) he would have imposed a sentence of two-and-a-half years' imprisonment, and that was approved by the Court of Appeal, as was his conclusion that in order to protect the public from serious harm a total sentence of five years' imprisonment was required.

[8] In *R v Crow, R v Pennington* (1994) 16 Cr App R (S) 409 at 412 Lord Taylor CJ said:

'... we consider that even where section 2(2)(b) is applied, the sentence should, whilst long enough to give necessary protection to the public for an extended period, still bear a reasonable relationship to the offence for which it is being imposed.'

It does, however, have to be said that there is nothing in the statutory wording, or in the White Paper, other than the reference to the maximum sentence which can be imposed, which indicates that Parliament intended to establish such a relationship, and in *R v Chapman* (2000) 1 Cr App R 77 at 85 Lord Bingham of Cornhill CJ accepted counsel's submission (at 84) that 'there is no necessary ratio between the part of the sentence intended to punish and the part of the sentence intended to protect'. In that case the appellant had pleaded guilty to arson and had been sentenced to life imprisonment. On appeal that sentence was varied to one of ten years of imprisonment, three years being said to be the appropriate determinate term for the offence and seven years being added 'for purposes of public protection under section 2(2)(b)' (see 86). The earlier decisions were not referred to in the judgment, but it is clear from the report, and from what we have been told by Mr Fitzgerald QC who appeared in *R v Chapman*, that in that case *R v Mansell* was referred to in argument. *R v Chapman* was followed in *R v Wilson* [2000] Crim LR 503 and in *R v Smith* (2001) 2 Cr App R (S) 160 and, despite submissions made by Mr Pannick QC for the appellant to the contrary, I am satisfied that what was said in *R v Chapman* does represent the law, subject to any qualification that has to be made in the light of the implementation of the Human Rights Act 1998.

Facts of this case

a   [9] The respondent pleaded guilty to unlawful wounding and to assault occasioning actual bodily harm, and on 10 January 1997 he was sentenced to four years' imprisonment for the wounding and three years consecutive for the assault, a total of seven years. When imposing sentence the trial judge made it clear that he was invoking s 2(2)(b) of the 1991 Act, but he did not indicate what

b   sentence he would otherwise have imposed. Leave to appeal against sentence was refused, and the respondent was released on 17 May 2001, but the present action has been allowed to continue because the point which it raises is an important one in relation to which the decision of this court is required.

c   *The argument*

[10] The case for the respondent, which found favour in the court below, can be summarised thus—as interpreted by the European Court of Human Rights, art 5(4) of the convention requires an investigation of the nature and rationale of the sentence. When the only reason for continued detention is danger to the

d   public or rehabilitation of the offender, something which can change with the passage of time, then there must be provision for periodic review of the lawfulness of detention, because otherwise the detainee has no chance to show that the danger, which constitutes the sole justification for his continued detention, no longer exists. Mr Fitzgerald submits that part of any sentence imposed under s 2(2)(b) of the 1991 Act, whether determinate or indeterminate, is a sentence for

e   which the only justification is that in the opinion of the sentencing court, at the time of sentence, that part of the sentence was necessary to protect the public from serious harm from the offender, otherwise there would only be a commensurate sentence under s 2(2)(a). He further submits that when the offender has served the commensurate sentence (which in practice should always be identified by the sentencer) he becomes entitled to benefit from art 5(4), the

f   requirements of which are not satisfied by the original decision of the sentencing judge because he may, in the event, be mistaken in his assessment of when the offender will cease to be dangerous.

[11] For the appellant Mr Pannick contends that in relation to art 5(4) there is a distinction to be drawn between determinate and indeterminate sentences

g   passed pursuant to s 2(2)(b). Determinate sentences should be reasonably related to the gravity of the offending which has brought the offender before the court (whether or not the sentencer specifies what he considers a commensurate sentence would have been) and such sentences cannot exceed the statutory maximum for the index offence, so the whole sentence is pervaded by a punitive

h   element and is justified for the purposes of art 5(4) by the decision of the sentencing judge. As Mr Pannick points out, many sentences imposed without resort to s 2(2)(b) do contain a preventive element, and he further emphasises that as long as the sentence remains a determinate sentence, whether or not s 2(2)(b) is invoked, the court does not hand over to the executive the decision as

j   to when the offender should be released.

European authorities

[11] The starting point of a consideration of the European jurisprudence is bound to be the decision in *De Wilde v Belgium (No 1)* (1971) 1 EHRR 373 to which I have already referred. The European Court of Human Rights said (at 407 (para 76)):

'Where the decision depriving a person of his liberty is one taken by an *a* administrative body, there is no doubt that Article 5(4) obliges the Contracting States to make available to the person detained a right of recourse to a court; but there is nothing to indicate that the same applies when the decision is made by a court at the close of judicial proceedings. In the latter case, the supervision required by Article 5(4) is incorporated in the decision ...'

In *Van Droogenbroeck v Belgium* (1982) 4 EHRR 443 the applicant was sentenced to *b* two years' imprisonment for theft and attempted theft, and ordered to be 'placed at the Government's disposal' for ten years under the Social Protection in respect of Mental Defectives and Habitual Offenders Act of 1 July 1964, as a persistent offender. That Act conferred on the Minister of Justice a wide measure of discretion as to how the penalty should be implemented, ranging from detention *c* to probation, with powers of revocation. The European Court of Human Rights said (at 457 (para 40)):

'At the time of its decision, the court can, in the nature of things, do no more than estimate how the individual will develop in the future. The Minister of Justice, for his part, is able, through and with the assistance of his *d* officials, to monitor that development more closely and at frequent intervals but this very fact means that with the passage of time the link between his decisions not to release or to re-detain and the initial judgment gradually becomes less strong. The link might eventually be broken if a position were reached in which those decisions were based on grounds that had no *e* connection with the objectives of the legislature and the court or on an assessment that was unreasonable in terms of those objectives. In those circumstances, a detention that was lawful at the outset would be transformed into a deprivation of liberty that was arbitrary and, hence, incompatible with Article 5.'

The court said (at 460 (para 47)): *f*

'... in this context the nature and purpose of a given type of "detention" are of more importance than is the place which it occupies in the structure of the Convention. The system of placing recidivists and habitual offenders at the Government's disposal was established with specific objectives in mind. The *g* position taken by the Court of Cassation is that the measure in question, although assimilated to a penalty, is designed not only to protect society but also to provide the executive with an opportunity of endeavouring to reform the individuals concerned.'

The court went on to describe the disposal order as one which— *h*

'is striking for its relatively indeterminate character and will vary, in principle, according to the treatment required by the offender and the demands of the protection of society.'

The court said (at 462 (para 49)): *j*

'In the instant case, the Convention required an appropriate procedure allowing a court to determine "speedily", on application by Mr. van Droogenbroeck, whether the Minister of Justice was entitled to hold that detention was still consistent with the object and purpose of the 1964 Act. For the purposes of Article 5(4), this was not simply a question of expediency a   but one that bore on the very "lawfulness" of the deprivation of liberty at issue.'

[12] In *Weeks v UK* (1987) 10 EHRR 293 the offences were not particularly serious, and punishment was not a significant element in the sentence, but the offender was regarded as a dangerous young man, and the sentencing court accepted its inability to forecast for how long his instability and personality disorders would endure. He therefore received an indeterminate sentence. The European Court of Human Rights regarded his situation as analogous to that of the offender in *Van Droogenbroeck v Belgium*.

[13] In *E v Norway* (1990) 17 EHRR 30 the applicant was a Norwegian citizen with a record of offences of violence who complained to the European Court of Human Rights in relation to the adequacy, for the purposes of art 5(4), of judicial review proceedings in Norway. He was detained under art 39 of the Norwegian Penal Code, which gave the Ministry of Justice a wide discretion as to which security measure was to be imposed, and for how long. The European Court of Human Rights noted the similarity with the Belgian system which was at issue in *Van Droogenbroeck v Belgium* and continued (at 51 (para 52)): 'Under such systems the courts cannot at the time of their decisions do more than assess how the person concerned will develop in the future.' The court said (at 52 (para 53)):

'... the Convention required an appropriate procedure allowing a court to determine, on an application by Mr. E., whether the Ministry of Justice was entitled to hold that detention remained consistent with the object and purpose of Article 39(1) of the Penal Code. For the purposes of Article 5(4) of the Convention this was not simply a question of expediency but one that was essential for the lawfulness of the deprivation of liberty at issue.'

In *Thynne, Wilson and Gunnell v UK* (1990) 13 EHRR 666 all three appellants had been separately convicted of serious offences, and had been sentenced as a matter of discretion to life imprisonment. They contended that in English law a discretionary sentence of life imprisonment had a punitive element and a protective element (although at that time those elements were not usually expressly divided) and that after serving the punitive element they should, pursuant to art 5(4), have been entitled to take proceedings to determine the lawfulness of their continued detention. The European Court of Human Rights referred to *De Wilde*'s case and continued (at 691 (para 68)):

'In subsequent cases the Court made it clear that this finding related only to "the initial decision depriving a person of his liberty" and did not purport "to deal with an ensuing period of detention in which new issues affecting the lawfulness of the detention might arise."'

One of the 'subsequent cases' which the court had in mind was, it seems, *Weeks v UK* (see [12], above). In *Thynne's* case the United Kingdom government had argued that it was impossible to disentangle the punitive and security components of a discretionary life sentence (foreshadowing, Mr Fitzgerald submits, part of the case for the appellant before us) but the European Court of Human Rights rejected that argument, saying (at 693 (para 73)) that discretionary life sentences—

'are composed of a punitive element and subsequently of a security element designed to confer on the Secretary of State the responsibility for determining when the public interest permits the prisoner's release.'

Even though the offenders had committed grave crimes meriting lengthy
sentences of imprisonment the court was satisfied that in each case the punitive
element of the discretionary life sentences had expired, and (at 694 (para 76)) that
after the expiry of the punitive periods of their sentences their detention was
comparable with that at issue in *Van Droogenbroeck v Belgium* and *Weeks v UK*, from
which it followed that—

> 'at this phase in the execution of their sentences, the applicants are entitled
> under Article 5(4) to take proceedings to have the lawfulness of their
> continued detention decided by a court at reasonable intervals and to have
> the lawfulness of any re-detention determined by a court.'

That decision led to changes in English law which required sentencing judges to
specify the punitive element of discretionary life sentences, and required the
Secretary of State to accept recommendations of the Parole Board. In *Wynne v UK*
(1994) 19 EHRR 333 an unsuccessful attempt was made to extend the *Thynne*
approach to a mandatory life sentence. The European Court of Human Rights
(at 346 (para 33)) said of its own earlier jurisprudence:

> 'A clear distinction was drawn between the discretionary life sentence
> which was considered to have a protective purpose and a mandatory life
> sentence which was viewed as essentially punitive in nature.'

However in *Hussain v UK* (1996) 22 EHRR 1 the European Court of Human
Rights did extend the *Thynne* approach to a young applicant convicted of murder
who had been ordered to be detained during Her Majesty's pleasure, saying (at
24 (para 53)):

> '... an indeterminate term of detention for a convicted young person,
> which may be as long as that person's life, can only be justified by considerations
> based on the need to protect the public.'

The court then referred to 'the changes that inevitably occur with maturation'
and concluded (at 25 (para 54)):

> '... the applicant's sentence, after the expiration of his tariff, is more
> comparable to a discretionary life sentence ... The decisive ground for the
> applicant's continued detention was and continues to be his dangerousness
> to society, a characteristic susceptible to change with the passage of time.
> Accordingly, new issues of lawfulness may arise in the course of detention
> and the applicant is entitled under Article 5(4) to take proceedings to have
> these issues decided by a court at reasonable intervals.'

A decision on which Mr Pannick now places considerable reliance is *Silva Rocha v
Portugal* (1996) 32 EHRR 333 which was not cited in the court below. In July 1989
the applicant was arrested and remanded in custody in connection with a
neighbour's death. In July 1990, when brought before a criminal court on charges
of aggravated homicide and illegal possession of weapons, he was in a mentally
disturbed state and was found to be criminally irresponsible and dangerous. He
was ordered to be detained in a psychiatric asylum for a minimum of three years
in accordance with art 91(2) of the Portuguese Criminal Code. His detention was
deemed to have begun when he was remanded in custody, so his case was
reviewed in June 1992, and periodically thereafter until September 1993 when
there was psychiatric evidence to suggest that he was no longer dangerous, so the
court ordered his discharge. He contended that, as he was found not to be

a criminally responsible, the only reason for his detention was that he represented a danger to society, which could evolve with the passing of time, and that art 5(4) required judicial review to be available at reasonable intervals, but he could not be discharged until after three years, even if it was established before the expiration of that period that he was no longer dangerous. The European Court of Human Rights said (at 344):

b '28 The case involved a homicide committed by a person who could not be held responsible for his actions and who was at the same time dangerous. The seriousness of the offences together with the risk that he represented for himself as well as for others could reasonably justify his being removed from society for at least three years.

c 29 For that period the review required by Article 5(4) of the Convention was incorporated in the detention decision taken in this instance by the Oporto Criminal Court.

30 It was therefore not until those three years had elapsed that the applicant's right to "take proceedings by which the lawfulness of his detention shall be decided … by a court" at reasonable intervals took effect.'

d

Mr Pannick submits that the decision in *Silva Rocha v Portugal* shows that when an applicant is detained by reason of a factor which may change no right to a subsequent judicial review arises if the original sentence has been imposed by a court for a determinate period which must elapse before there can be any review, *e* and if that period is reasonable in the light of the conduct committed and in the light of the risk which the individual poses to himself and to society. For the respondent Mr Fitzgerald contends that in *Silva Rocha v Portugal* the court was really only concerned with the question for how long it was reasonable to postpone the first judicial review.

f [14] I next refer to the admissibility decision of the European Commission in *Mansell v UK* App No 32072/96 (2 July 1997, unreported), in respect of the conviction referred to earlier in this judgment. In that case the sentencing judge indicated that although a sentence of two-and-a-half years would be commensurate, pursuant to s 2(2)(a) of the 1991 Act, a longer than normal sentence was necessary to protect the public from serious harm from the offender, so a sentence of five *g* years' imprisonment was imposed pursuant to s 2(2)(b). Before the Commission the applicant contended that as soon as he had served the period he would have served if sentenced under s 2(2)(a) he should have been entitled to review by the Parole Board as though he was serving a discretionary sentence of life imprisonment. The Commission unanimously rejected that contention, saying:

h 'The sentence imposed on the applicant was a fixed term sentence of five years. There is no question of the sentence being imposed because of the presence of factors which "were susceptible to change with the passage of time, namely mental instability and dangerousness" (see *Thynne, Wilson and Gunnell v UK* (1990) 13 EHRR 666 (para 70)). Rather, there was an element *j* of "simple" punishment as well as an element of deterrence. It is true that the latter part of the sentence was imposed pursuant to s 2 of the Criminal Justice Act 1991, which provides for sentences in the case of violent or sexual offences to be longer than "normal" in order to protect the public from serious harm. Such an "increased" sentence is, however, no more than the usual exercise by the sentencing court of its ordinary sentencing powers, even if the "increase" has a statutory basis. In particular nothing in the sentencing procedure indicates that the fixed term sentence of five years' imprisonment was anything other than a sentence which was imposed as punishment for the offences committed.'

[15] Mr Fitzgerald submits that the decision of the Commission in *Mansell v UK* was wrong. It betrays a misunderstanding of the true distinction between s 2(2)(a) and s 2(2)(b) of the 1991 Act, and should not be followed. Mr Pannick submits that the Commission did not misunderstand anything, and that the approach adopted is the one which we should follow in the present case.

[16] After the conclusion of argument in the present case the European Court of Human Rights on 28 May 2002 gave judgment in *Stafford v UK* App No 46295/99 (unreported). The case concerned the power of the Secretary of State not to accept a recommendation of the Parole Board to release on licence an offender subject to a mandatory life sentence, whose previous licence had been revoked. What is of some significance for present purposes is that the court found that—

'there is no distinction between mandatory life prisoners, discretionary life prisoners and juvenile murderers as regards the nature of tariff-fixing. It is a sentencing exercise.'

The court went on to find that—

'the finding in *Wynne v UK* that the mandatory life sentence constituted punishment for life can no longer be regarded as reflecting the real position in the domestic criminal justice system of the mandatory life prisoner.'

From that it followed that—

'once the punishment element of the sentence (as reflected in the tariff) has been satisfied, the grounds for the continued detention, as in discretionary life and juvenile murderer cases, must be considerations of risk and dangerousness.'

Because those elements may change with the course of time—

'it can no longer be maintained that the original trial and appeal proceedings satisfied, once and for all, issues of compatibility of subsequent detention of mandatory life prisoners with the provisions of art 5(1) of the convention.'

Conclusion

[17] I confess that I have difficulty in following some of the reasoning of the Commission in *Mansell v UK*. It said that—

'there is no question of the sentence being imposed because of the presence of factors which were susceptible to change with the passage of time, namely mental instability and dangerousness.'

That was true of the commensurate element of the sentence, but the only justification for the extra two-and-a-half years was that in the opinion of the court it was necessary to protect the public from serious harm from the offender. In other words he was considered to be dangerous. Similarly in relation to the observation that there was an element of simple punishment as well as an element of deterrence. That would be true of any commensurate sentence. But the key to the Commission's decision in *Mansell v UK* does seem to be in the observation that the increased sentence (under s 2(2)(b) of the 1991 Act) is no more than the usual exercise by the sentencing court of its ordinary sentencing *a* powers, even if the increase has a statutory basis, and that I am prepared to accept. Often it is possible for a court to impose a sentence which is commensurate with the seriousness of the offence without regard to the question whether there is a need to protect the public from serious harm from the offender, or perhaps more accurately upon the basis that no such danger exists. For example, a young man with no previous convictions found guilty of raping a woman of similar age may *b* be sentenced to five years' imprisonment, but if he can be shown to have carried out a campaign of rape the court may conclude that he represents a more than ordinary danger and a sentence of 15 years or more may be appropriate (see *R v Billam* [1986] 1 All ER 985, [1986] 1 WLR 349) even though from the point of view of the individual victim the offending may be precisely the same. It is certainly possible to argue that for the purposes of s 2(2)(a) of the 1991 Act the 'seriousness *c* of the offence' includes a consideration of other offences committed by the offender, but equally it is clear that the longer determinate term is imposed, at least in part, because in the opinion of the court it is necessary to protect the public from serious harm from the offender. The decision to impose the longer term is plainly a judicial decision, every aspect of which is subject to appeal, and *d* so, as it seems to me, in the words used by the European Court of Human Rights in *De Wilde v Belgium (No 1)* (1971) 1 EHRR 373 at 407 (para 76) 'the supervision required by Article 5(4) is incorporated in the decision'. If that is right in relation to rape, why should the position be any different in relation to any of the other offences within the ambit of s 2(2)(b)? The sentence is not indeterminate. It cannot exceed the statutory maximum for the index offence, and it does not hand *e* over to the executive the decision as to when the offender should be released, which can be contrasted with the position in relation to many discretionary life sentences where the sentencing court concludes that the offender will remain a potential danger for an uncertain period of time (see *R v Hodgson* (1967) 52 Cr App R 113). In the type of case with which we are concerned a period of time is fixed *f* precisely because the sentencing judge considers that he or she is in a position to fix it even though it is clear that in many cases the risk which an offender will present to the public is capable of fluctuating with the passage of time. I would therefore allow this appeal, and set aside the declaration granted by the court below.

g **MAY LJ.**

[18] I agree that this appeal should be allowed for the reasons given by Kennedy LJ, whose account of the facts and circumstances of this case I gratefully adopt. The principal reasons which lead me to this conclusion are: (a) A sentence under s 2(2)(b) of the Criminal Justice Act 1991—now s 80(2)(b) of the Powers of *h* Criminal Courts (Sentencing) Act 2000—is a single determinate sentence, the product of a judicial decision. (b) Although the sentence is longer than it otherwise would have been because the sentencing judge is of the opinion that it is necessary to protect the public from serious harm from the offender, (i) the length of the sentence is, and is intended to be, determined by the judge at the *j* time of sentence; (ii) it is not intended to be reviewed, other than on appeal; and (iii) in particular, it is not intended to confer on the executive the responsibility for determining when the public interest permits the prisoner's release—see the European Court of Human Rights' judgment in *Thynne, Wilson and Gunnell v UK* (1990) 13 EHRR 666 at 693 (para 73), to which Kennedy LJ refers in his judgment (at [13], above). (c) All the European authorities to which Kennedy LJ has referred, which conclude that art 5(4) of the European Convention for the

Protection of Human Rights and Fundamental Freedoms 1950 (as set out in Sch 1
to the Human Rights Act 1998) requires an appropriate procedure allowing a
court to determine the continued lawfulness of detention, concern sentences which
were indeterminate *and* where otherwise the decision whether to release the
prisoner lay with the executive. Neither applies to sentences under s 2(2)(b) of
the 1991 Act. (d) Section 2(2)(b) applies to violent or sexual offences where the
court is of the opinion that it is necessary to protect the public from serious harm
from the offender. In some such combined circumstances, an indeterminate
sentence may be an available alternative. Even if that is not so, and although the
sentence requires an element of judicial prediction, the choice of sentence is a
judicial decision that a longer term necessary to protect the public should be
determined at the time of sentence.

TUCKEY LJ.
[19] I agree with both judgments.

Appeal allowed. Permission to appeal granted.

Dilys Tausz   Barrister.

End of Volume 3